COLLINS

SCOTLAND
ATLAS AND
GAZETTEER

CONTENTS

HarperCollinsPublishers

Key to Road Map Pages

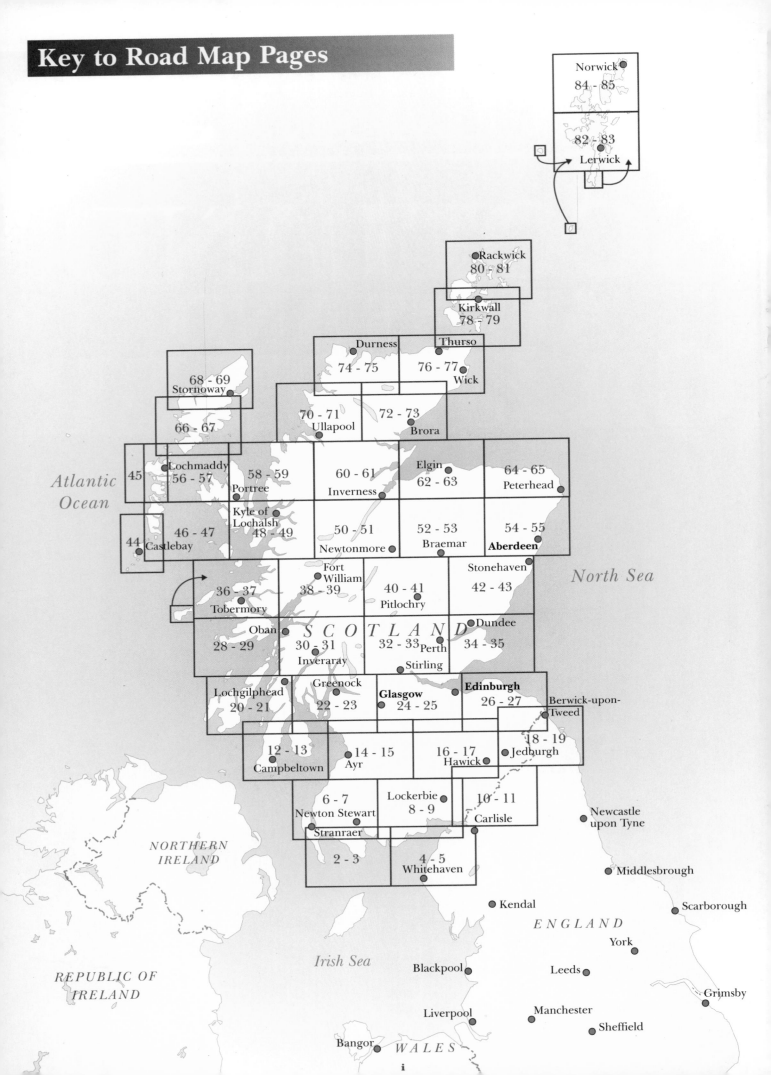

Norwick
84 - 85

82 - 83
Lerwick

Rackwick
80 - 81

Kirkwall
78 - 79

Durness
Thurso
74 - 75   **76 - 77**
Wick

68 - 69
Stornoway

66 - 67

70 - 71
Ullapool

72 - 73
Brora

Atlantic Ocean

45

Lochmaddy
56 - 57

58 - 59
Portree

60 - 61
Inverness

Elgin
62 - 63

64 - 65
Peterhead

Kyle of Lochalsh
48 - 49

44 Castlebay

46 - 47

50 - 51
Newtonmore

52 - 53
Braemar

54 - 55
Aberdeen

Fort William
38 - 39

Stonehaven
42 - 43

North Sea

36 - 37
Tobermory

40 - 41
Pitlochry

S C O T L A N D

Oban
28 - 29

30 - 31
Inveraray

32 - 33 Perth

Dundee
34 - 35

Stirling

Lochgilphead
20 - 21

Greenock
22 - 23

Glasgow
24 - 25

Edinburgh
26 - 27

Berwick-upon-Tweed

18 - 19
Jedburgh

12 - 13
Campbeltown

14 - 15
Ayr

16 - 17
Hawick

6 - 7
Newton Stewart

Lockerbie
8 - 9

10 - 11
Carlisle

Newcastle upon Tyne

NORTHERN IRELAND

Stranraer

2 - 3

4 - 5
Whitehaven

Middlesbrough

Kendal

Scarborough

E N G L A N D

Irish Sea

York

REPUBLIC OF IRELAND

Blackpool

Leeds

Grimsby

Liverpool

Manchester

Sheffield

Bangor   *W A L E S*

Key to Road Map Symbols

ROAD INFORMATION

M8	Motorway
20—**19**	Motorway junction with full / limited access
Kinross / Harthill Bothwell	Motorway service areas (off road, full & limited access)
	Projected or under construction motorway
A82	Primary route number
	Primary route dual carriageway
	Primary route single carriageway
	Primary route with passing places
A975	'A' Road number
	'A' Road dual carriageway
	'A' Road single carriageway
	'A' Road with passing places
	Projected or under construction 'A' Road
B6362	'B' Road number
	'B' Road dual carriageway
	'B' Road single carriageway
	'B' Road with passing places
	Projected or under construction 'B' Road
	Minor road
	Restricted access due to road condition or private ownership
⊗	Multi-level junction
	Roundabout
10	Road distances in miles
	Road tunnel
→	Steep hill (arrows point downhill)
×	Level crossing
Toll	Toll

OTHER TRANSPORT INFORMATION

Aberdeen 8 hrs	Car ferry route with journey times in hours
	Railway line and station
	Railway tunnel
✈	Airport with scheduled services
Ⓗ	Heliport

CITIES, TOWNS & VILLAGES

	Built up area
□ □ ▫	Towns, villages and other settlements
ABERDEEN	Primary route destination

TOURIST INFORMATION

A selection of tourist detail is shown. It is advisable to check with the local tourist information office regarding opening times and facilities available. The classification of tourist features specific to the Gazetteer is given, where appropriate, in italics.

i i	Tourist information office (all year / seasonal)
	Preserved railway *(other feature of interest)*
⚔ 1738	Battle site
m	Ancient monument *(historic / prehistoric site)*
✝	Ecclesiastical building
🏰	Castle
	Historic house (with or without garden)
✿	Garden
🏛	Museum / Art gallery *(leisure / recreation)*
	Theme park *(leisure / recreation)*
	Major sports venue *(leisure / recreation)*
⚑	Motor racing circuit
🏇	Racecourse
	Country park *(leisure / recreation)*
🦆	Nature reserve
🐘	Wildlife park or Zoo *(leisure / recreation)*
★	Other feature of interest
★ ⌛	Proposed millennium site; (relevant symbol shown)
⚐	Golf course
(NTS) (NT)	National Trust property; Scotland & England

OTHER FEATURES

	National boundary
	County / Council boundary
	National / Regional park boundary
	Forest park boundary
Danger Zone	Military range
	Woodland
468 ▲941	Spot height / Summit height in metres
	Beach
	Lake / Loch, dam and river
	Canal / Dry canal / Canal tunnel
▲**55**	Adjoining page indicator

water	land below	0	165	490	985	1640	2295	2950	ft
	sea level	0	50	150	300	500	700	900	m

Scale 1 : 202,752 (3.2 miles to 1 inch)

0	2	4	6	8 miles

0	2	4	6	8	10 kilometres

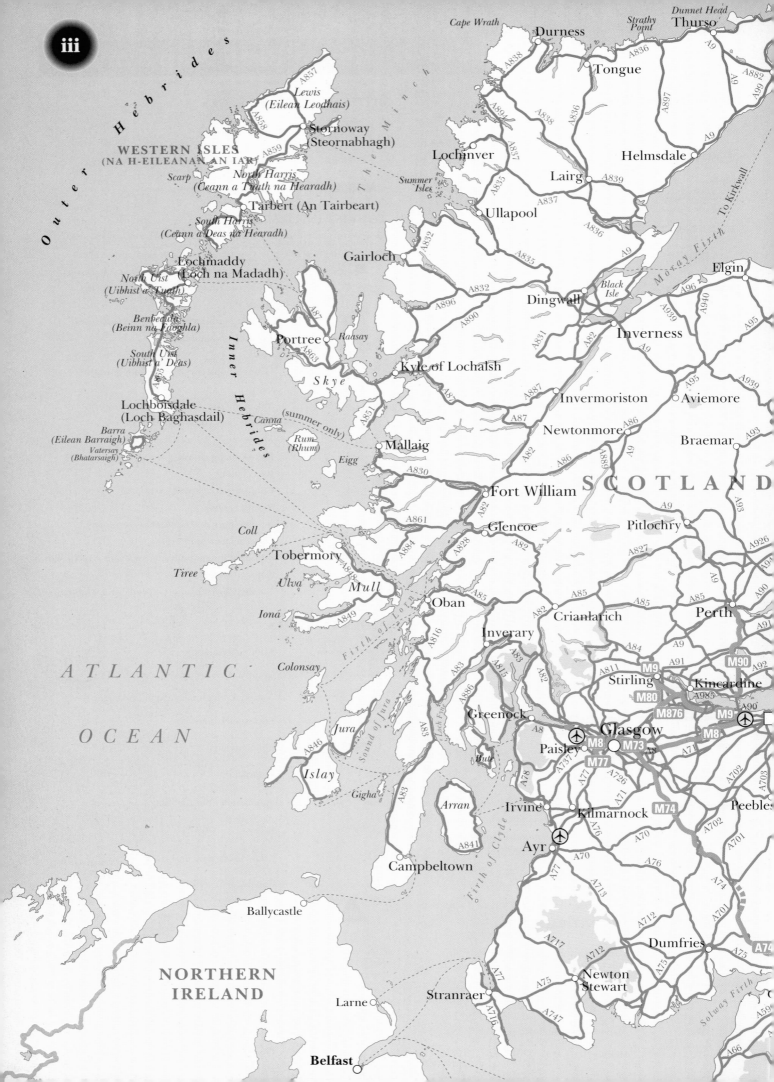

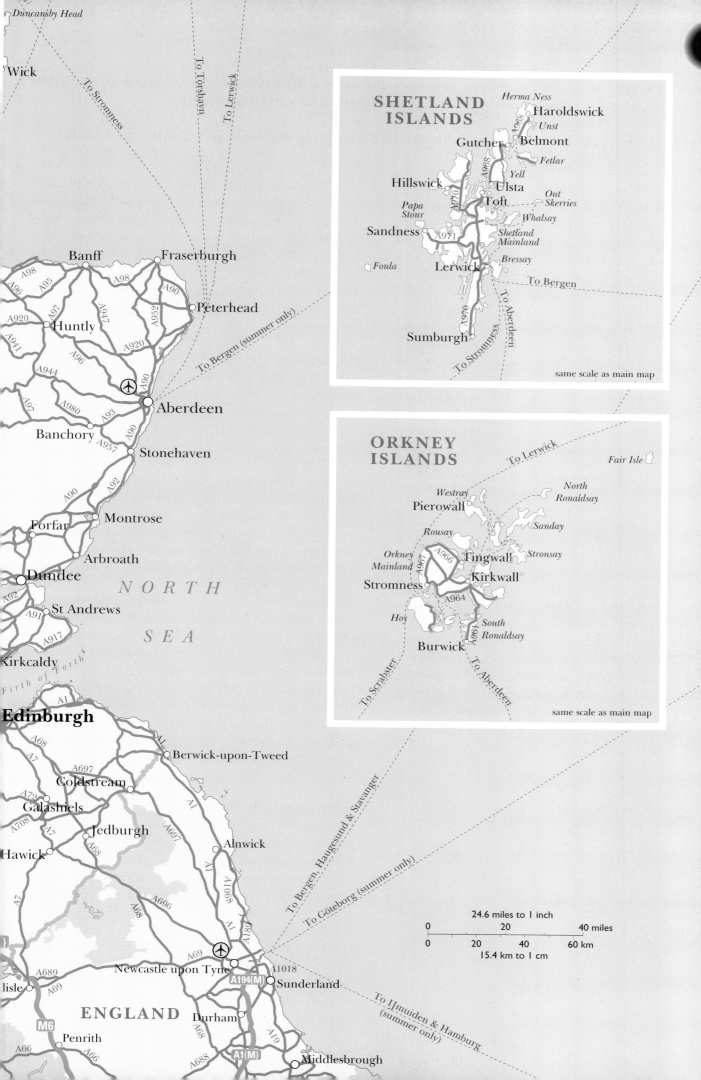

Duncansby Head

Wick

To Stromness

To Tórshavn

To Lerwick

SHETLAND ISLANDS

Herma Ness

Haroldswick

A968

Unst

Gutcher

Belmont

A968

Fetlar

Hillswick

A970

Yell

Ulsta

Toft

Out Skerries

Papa Stour

Whalsay

Sandness

A971

Shetland Mainland

Foula

Bressay

Lerwick

To Bergen

To Aberdeen

A970

To Stromness

Sumburgh

To Bergen (summer only)

same scale as main map

Banff

Fraserburgh

A98

A95

A98

A90

A96

A947

A952

Peterhead

A920

Huntly

A90

A920

A941

A96

A944

A980

A90

A93

Aberdeen

A97

Banchory

A957

A90

Stonehaven

A92

Montrose

Forfar

Arbroath

Dundee

A92

St Andrews

A91

A917

Kirkcaldy

Firth of Forth

Edinburgh

A1

A68

A7

Berwick-upon-Tweed

A697

Coldstream

A79

Galashiels

A1

A708

A7

Jedburgh

A697

Alnwick

Hawick

A68

A68

A1068

A1

ORKNEY ISLANDS

To Lerwick

Fair Isle

Westray

North Ronaldsay

Pierowall

Rousay

Sanday

Orkney Mainland

A966

Tingwall

Stronsay

A967

Stromness

A964

Kirkwall

Hoy

South Ronaldsay

A961

Burwick

To Scrabster

To Aberdeen

same scale as main map

To Bergen, Haugesund & Stavanger

To Göteborg (summer only)

N O R T H

S E A

A696

A69

A689

A69

Newcastle upon Tyne

A194(M)

A1018

Sunderland

isle

ENGLAND

M6

Durham

A68

Penrith

A1(M)

A19

A66

A688

Middlesbrough

To IJmuiden & Hamburg (summer only)

24.6 miles to 1 inch

0   20   40 miles

0   20   40   60 km

15.4 km to 1 cm

Introduction

This brand new atlas and gazetteer provides the user with information covering over 17,500 settlements, natural features and places of interest located within Scotland.

The places listed are referenced to fully-detailed mapping at a scale of 3.2 miles to 1 inch.

Each entry has a brief description of what type of feature it is, a reference for its location, a population figure where appropriate and many other interesting facts. The entries have been written in a structured and concise style. The name of the feature comes first and is in **blue** type, then the administrative area in *italics*, followed by the population figure if applicable. The entries have been categorized into broad feature types, such as village, hamlet, mountain etc, these are shown in ***bold italics***. A full list and explanation of all the different feature types can be found on page 86. Following this is a description of the place, then the height if applicable, the map reference and the National Grid Reference. For example:

Ben Cleuch *Clack.* ***Mountain***, summit of Ochil Hills, 3m/4km NW of Tillicoultry. Height 2362 feet or 720 metres. **33 D4** NN9000.

The Collins Scotland Atlas and Gazetteer also includes a full-colour map section at 3.2 miles to 1 inch. Most of the gazetteer entries are clearly referenced in **bold** to the appropriate grid square on the map. For entries depicted by a point symbol, such as man-made settlements, named summits and tourist detail, the reference indicates the grid square in which the symbol falls. Entries which relate to either a linear of area feature, such as rivers, sea features and mountain ranges, are referenced to the grid square in which the name begins. Where no such grid reference is given, then that feature, although it exists, is not shown on the map.

For example:

Achranich *High.* ***Locality***, in Lochaber district, near mouth of Rannoch River at head of Loch Aline. NM7047.

The above entry is not named on the map.

Cruden Bay *Aber.* Population: 1708. ***Village***, near mouth of Water of Cruden, 7m/11km S of Peterhead, with Port Erroll adjoining to SE. **55 F1** NK0936.

This entry is named on the road maps on page 55 in square F1.

The Gazetteer is listed alphabetically on a word by word basis whereby Far Out Head will come before Fara. Places such as East Tarbet and Upper Sanday have been listed under E and U, and places such as The Chancellor and Isle of Lewis have been listed under T and I respectively. All place names incorporating the word 'Saint' have been abbreviated to 'St.' but are listed as if they were given in full.

All distances are measured 'as the crow flies' and are shown in both miles and kilometres. Cardinal directions are abbreviated and include the eight compass points: N, NE, E, SE, S, SW, W and NW. In most cases heights are shown in feet as well as metres.

Human settlements are described as cities, towns, suburbs, villages, hamlets, settlements, or localities. The criteria dividing these are not definitive, with one category tending to merge into another, but a description has been included in the feature type listing, on page 86 which is as accurate as possible.

All places are given with the administrative area in which they fall. Exceptions to this are large or linear features such as mountain ranges or rivers which fall on, or cross boundaries. The administrative areas are shown in the map on pages (xi) to (xii) and include all the latest changes. In the main gazetteer listing, these have been abbreviated and are shown in *italics*. Full names and descriptions can be found in the administrative area lists which start on page 87.

The Scottish Parliament

On pages vii to ix, information on the devolved power and structure of the new Scottish Parliament has been included. Details on the background to the devolution, the composition, and responsibilities of the MSPs, have been outlined.

In addition to this, on page x, a large scale map of central Edinburgh shows the relevant locations, such as the site of the Scottish Parliament building, designed by Enric Miralles, adjacent to the Palace of Holyroodhouse.

The National Grid System

All main entries have a national grid reference: the reference given for rivers is that of its mouth or confluence with a river of a different name; mountains are referenced to their summits; and large features generally to a notional centre point.

The National Grid System was devised by the Ordnance Survey and consists of a series of letters and numbers, each representing progressively smaller squares. The first letter H, N, S or T represent 500km squares. These are then broken down into twenty-five 100km squares designated by the second letter in the reference. Within the 100km squares each smaller grid of 10km, 1km or 100m is numbered, firstly by the distance of its lower left-hand corner eastwards (eastings) and secondly northwards (northings). In the gazetteer the references are taken down to the 1km level with a four-figure reference, for example TQ2356.

Alternative Names and Cross References

Where possible, the most commonly used name has been used as the main entry. Where there are alternative names these have been added in brackets after the main entry name. A separate entry is also included for the alternative name which cross-references the main entry, and is shown in *italics*, for example:

Ben Armine (Gaelic form: Beinn an Armuinn). *High.* **Mountain**, in Sutherland district, 5m/8km SE of Loch Choire. Height 2309 feet or 704 metres. **72 B2** NC6924.

The above is the main entry.

Beinn an Armuinn *High. Gaelic form of Ben Armine, qv.*

This is the cross reference entry.

Some entries may also refer specifically to another, related, main entry at the end of their descriptive text, for example:

Lord Macdonald's Table *High.* **Island**, one of a group of islets 3m/5km NW of Rubha Hunish at N tip of Skye. See also Gaeilavore Island, and Gearran Island. NG3679.

Population figures

Population figures have been derived from '1991 Census: Key Statistics for Localities in Scotland', HMSO, 1995. Localities are generally defined as continuous built-up areas with a population of over 500.

Throughout this book, great care has been taken to be accurate, but if you have any suggestions or comments that you feel might help us to improve it still further, please contact us at:

Collins Gazetteer Check
HarperCollinsPublishers
4 Manchester Park
Tewkesbury Road
Cheltenham
GL51 9EJ

email: gazcheck@harpercollins.co.uk

Background

For most of its history, Scotland has had its own Parliament, then, in 1707, the Union of the Scottish and English Parliaments created a Parliament of Great Britain which was based in London.

Under the terms of the Union, Scotland retained its own legal system and various other aspects of public life, the most notable of which was its education system, but all major government decisions were taken by the Parliament in Westminster.

The UK Government department responsible for Scottish affairs was The Scottish Office which came under the control of the Secretary of State for Scotland. Despite being based in Edinburgh since 1939, The Scottish Office, like the rest of the UK Government, remained accountable to the Parliament in Westminster.

In the 1970s the Labour Party attempted to establish a Scottish Assembly. The Scotland Bill received Royal Assent on 31st July 1978 but failed to achieve the required 40% in favour vote from the referendum held on 1st March 1979. The Assembly was never established.

The Labour Party, elected on 1st May 1997, had a mandate to modernise the way in which Britain was governed. They proposed the devolution of power from Westminster to give those living in Scotland greater control of their own affairs particularly with regard to law-making and tax-raising.

A Government White Paper, published in July 1997, set out the broad framework for the operation of this new, devolved, Scottish Parliament and the proposals contained in this White Paper were convincingly endorsed by a referendum on 11th September 1997.

Following this referendum the Government introduced the Scotland Bill which received Royal Assent and became The Scotland Act 1998 on the 19th November 1998. This Act provides for the establishment of a Scottish Parliament along with administration and other changes to the government of Scotland, effective from 1st July 1999. The act also stipulates that the proceedings of the Scottish Parliament will be regulated by Standing Orders which will be written in plain English, thus ensuring wide understanding of the Parliament's procedures.

Powers

Although the Scottish Parliament has wide ranging powers to institute primary legislation through 'Acts of the Scottish Parliament' the Westminster Parliament remains the Sovereign Parliament of the United Kingdom and retains the power to legislate about any matter, including devolved matters, in Scotland. In particular the Westminster Parliament retains control of all 'reserved matters' such as: the constitution, foreign affairs, defence, the civil service, financial and economic matters, national security, immigration and nationality, misuse of drugs, trade and industry (e.g. competition, consumer protection), electricity (coal, gas and nuclear energy), some aspects of transport (eg. railways), social security, employment, abortion, genetics, surrogacy, medicines, broadcasting and equal opportunities.

Laws

Any laws created through 'Acts of the Scottish Parliament' must comply with rights under the European Convention on Human Rights, which will be given effect by the Human Rights Bill, and with European Community Law.

Elections

The poll for ordinary general elections will be held on the first Thursday in May every fourth calendar year.

Finance

The budget assigned to the Scottish Parliament is allocated by the Westminster Parliament and known as the 'Scottish Block'. In addition to this the Scottish Parliament has the power to raise or lower the Scottish basic rate of income tax by up to three pence in the pound with the proceeds either adding to, or reducing the Scottish Parliament's spending power.

The Scottish Executive is able to allocate the available budget as it sees fit, subject to approval by the Scottish Parliament.

Composition of the Scottish Parliament

The Scottish Parliament comprises of 129 members, 73 of these are elected under the 'first past the post' system. The constituencies are the same as the UK Parliamentary constituencies in Scotland but with Orkney and Shetland having separate representation. The remaining 56 members are selected on a proportional basis from party lists drawn up for each of the current eight European Parliamentary constituencies.

Each elector is able to cast two votes: one for a constituency MSP (Member of the Scottish Parliament) and one for the party of their choice under the list system.

The Presiding Officer

The Scottish Parliament is kept in order by a Presiding Officer and two deputies who are MSPs elected to the post by the Members.

Those elected as Presiding Officer and/or Deputy Presiding Officer hold the post throughout the life of that Parliament unless they die, resign or for one reason or another cease to be a Member of the Scottish Parliament.

Like the Speaker of the House of Commons the Presiding Officer is politically impartial. He or she presides over the Scottish Parliament taking the interests of all members equally.

The main duties of the Presiding Officer are:

1. To apply and give rulings on the Standing Orders
2. To chair the Business Committee which organises the business of the Parliament
3. To take decisions regarding the legislative competence of draft Bills and to determine functions associated with the legislative process
4. To represent the Scottish Parliament in interactions with the Scottish Administration, the devolved Assemblies in Northern Ireland and Wales and the United Kingdom Parliament

The Scottish Executive

The Scottish Executive whose members are collectively referred to as 'The Scottish Ministers' form the Scottish Government.

The members of the executive are:

1. The First Minister
2. The Lord Advocate and the Solicitor General for Scotland (known as the Law Officers)
3. Other Ministers appointed by the First Minister

The First Minister

Any members of the Scottish Parliament, provided they are supported by a proposer and seconder, may stand for nomination for First Minister. The names of the candidates are first submitted to the Presiding Officer, following which a series of elections take place.

Candidates are progressively eliminated by means of a roll-call vote of members until just one candidate, who has the support of a simple majority, remains. The required quorum for voting is 25% of the total number of seats. The successful candidate is then recommended by the Presiding Officer to Her Majesty The Queen for appointment to the post of First Minister.

Lord Advocate and Solicitor General

The Scotland Act provides that the First Minister, with parliamentary approval, may recommend to Her Majesty the appointment or removal of persons as Lord Advocate or Solicitor General. These two appointees, known collectively as the Scottish Law Officers, are members of the Scottish Executive and as such participate fully in all Parliamentary proceedings.

The persons appointed to these positions, however, need not be Members of Parliament but, either way, are fully accountable to the Parliament for their actions. If he or she is not a Member of Parliament then they are not eligible to vote.

Ministers

Once the First Minister has been appointed he or she appoints the other Scottish Ministers; this can only be done with the agreement of the Scottish Parliament, initially, and then with The Queen's approval.

The First Minister also has the power to appoint junior ministers who, although not members of the Executive, are appointed to assist the Scottish Ministers.

The current post of Secretary of State for Scotland remains within the UK Government but is not part of the Scottish Executive.

Members

Members of the Scottish Parliament are elected by the voters and serve for the life of the Parliament.

Under Section 39 of the Scotland Act provision is made for the registration and declaration of interests of all Members of the Scottish Parliament. There are restrictions upon the participation of members in the proceedings of the Parliament in any situations where they may have an interest to which the proceedings relate. The standard code of conduct for Members of the Scottish Parliament follows nine key principles which are broadly the same as the code of conduct for Westminster MPs; these are:

1. *Public Duty*
   Members have a duty to uphold the law and to act in accordance with the public trust placed in

them. They also have a duty to act in the interests of the Scottish Parliament as a whole and the public it serves.

2. *Duty to Constituents*

Members have a duty to be accessible to their constituents, they should consider carefully the views and wishes of their constituents and where appropriate help to ensure that their constituents are able to pursue their concerns.

3. *Selflessness*

Members should take decisions solely in terms of the public interest. They should not do so in order to gain financial or other material benefits for themselves, their family or their friends.

4. *Integrity*

Members should not place themselves under any financial or other obligation to any individual or organisation that might influence them in the performance of their duties.

5. *Honesty*

Members have a duty to declare any private interests relating to their public duties and to take steps to resolve any conflicts arising in any way that protects the public interest.

6. *Openness*

Members should be as open as possible about all the decisions and actions they take. They should give reasons for their decisions and restrict information only when the wider public interest clearly demands this course of action.

Where a member has received information in confidence, or where disclosure of information might breach an individual's privacy, that confidence or privacy should be respected, unless there are overwhelming reasons in the wider public interest for disclosure to be made.

7. *Responsibility for Decisions*

Members remain responsible for any decision they take. In carrying out public business, Members should consider issues on their merits taking account of the views of others.

8. *Accountability*

Members are accountable for their decisions and actions to the Scottish people and should submit themselves to whatever scrutiny is appropriate to their office.

9. *Leadership*

Members should promote and support these principles by leadership and example, to maintain and strengthen the public's trust and confidence in the integrity of members in conducting public business.

Under the provisions of the Scotland Act, Members of the Scottish Parliament are required to take the oath of allegiance provided by the Promissory Oaths Act 1868, or to make the corresponding affirmation.

It is possible for an individual to hold a 'dual mandate' as a member of both the UK and the Scottish Parliaments.

Section 14 of the Scotland Act provides that a Member of the Scottish Parliament may at any time resign his or her seat by giving notice in writing to the Presiding Officer.

Scottish Parliamentary Corporate Body

Section 21 of the Scotland Act states that there shall be a Scottish Parliamentary Corporate Body (SPCB). This body is responsible for the administration of the Parliament and comprises of the Presiding Officer and four members of the Parliament appointed in accordance with parliamentary standing orders.

New appointments to the SPCB take place after each General Election to the Parliament, though members of the SPCB are free to resign at any time.

The Scottish Parliament Building

The permanent home of the Scottish Parliament will be a custom designed building occupying a four acre site on the Royal Mile adjacent to the Palace of Holyroodhouse and Holyrood Park.

The site, at the end of the Royal Mile, is bounded by Holyrood Road and Cannongate and was the former Scottish and Newcastle Plc. building.

The architect responsible for the new Parliament Building is Enric Miralles of Barcelona who, in collaboration with RMJM (Scotland) Ltd, secured the contract with a dramatic design based upon a theme of upturned fishing boats. As the new Scottish Parliament building will not be ready for occupation until autumn 2001, from May 1999, the Parliament will operate from various locations within central Edinburgh.

The First Minister and several other Scottish Ministers will have their offices in St. Andrews House. In addition Members of the Scottish Parliament, including the Ministers will have office accommodation in the former City of Edinburgh Council building on George IV Bridge. The Parliament 'Debating Chamber' will be housed in the Church of Scotland Assembly Hall in Lawnmarket.

Scottish Parliament Buildings

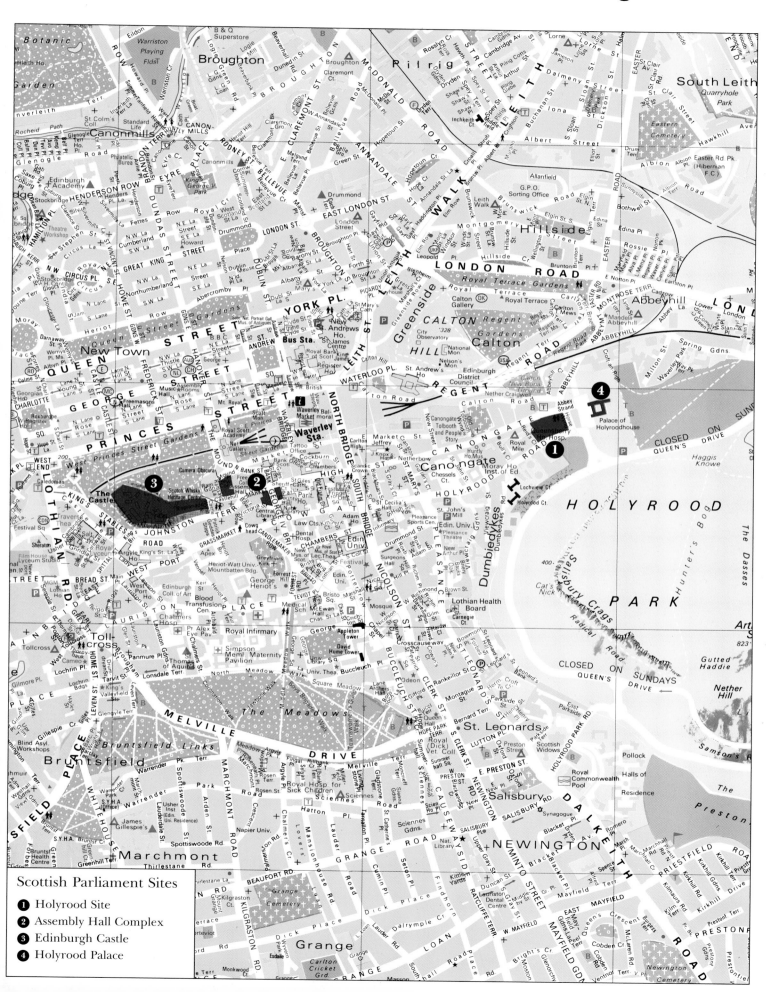

Scottish Parliament Sites

1. Holyrood Site
2. Assembly Hall Complex
3. Edinburgh Castle
4. Holyrood Palace

Scale 1:1,488,095

0   10   20   30   40 kilometres

0   10   20   30 miles

SCOTLAND COUNCILS

	ABERDEEN
	ABERDEENSHIRE
	ANGUS
	ARGYLL AND BUTE
1	CLACKMANNANSHIRE
	DUMFRIES AND GALLOWAY
	DUNDEE
	EAST AYRSHIRE
2	EAST DUNBARTONSHIRE
	EAST LOTHIAN
3	EAST RENFREWSHIRE
4	EDINBURGH
5	FALKIRK
	FIFE
6	GLASGOW
	HIGHLAND
7	INVERCLYDE
	MIDLOTHIAN
	MORAY
	NORTH AYRSHIRE
8	NORTH LANARKSHIRE
	ORKNEY
	PERTH AND KINROSS
9	RENFREWSHIRE
	SCOTTISH BORDERS
	SHETLAND
	SOUTH AYRSHIRE
	SOUTH LANARKSHIRE
	STIRLING
10	WEST DUNBARTONSHIRE
	WEST LOTHIAN
	WESTERN ISLES (NA H-EILEANAN AN IAR)

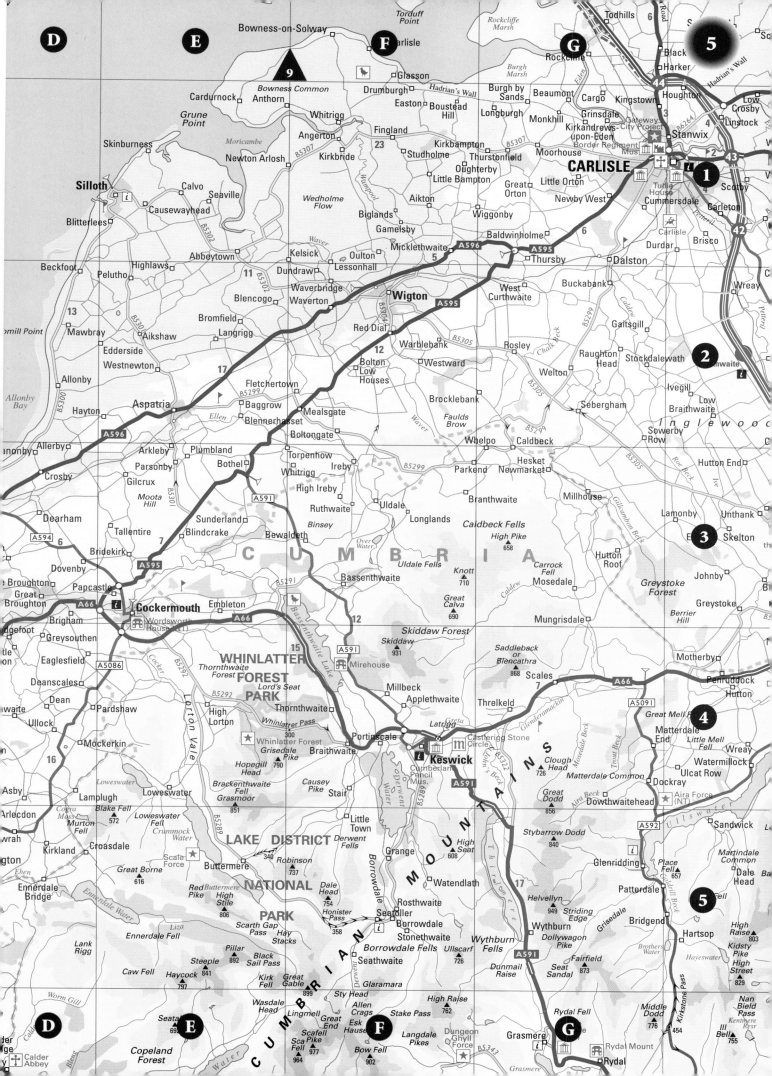

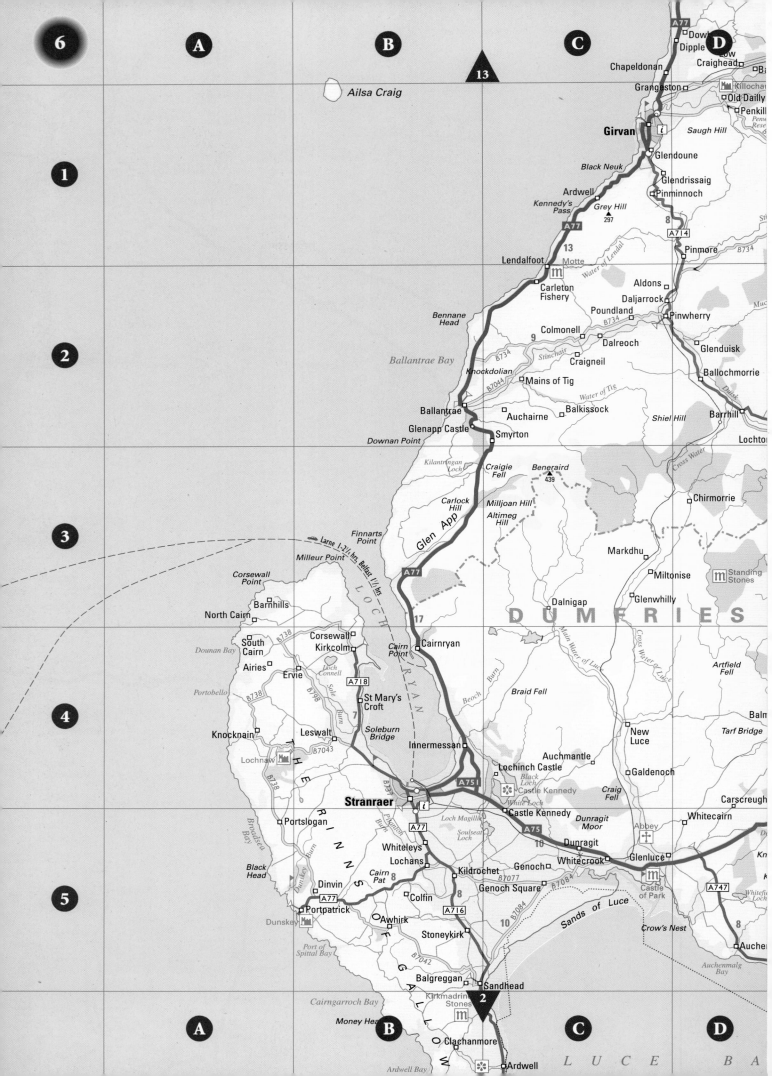

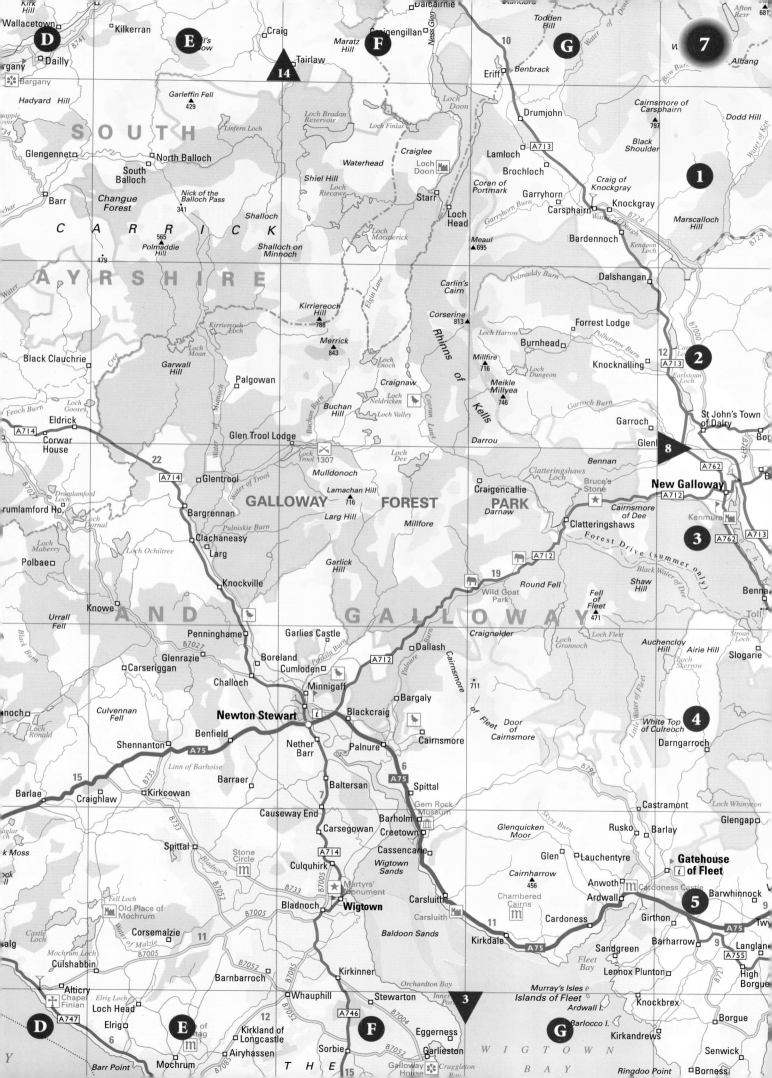

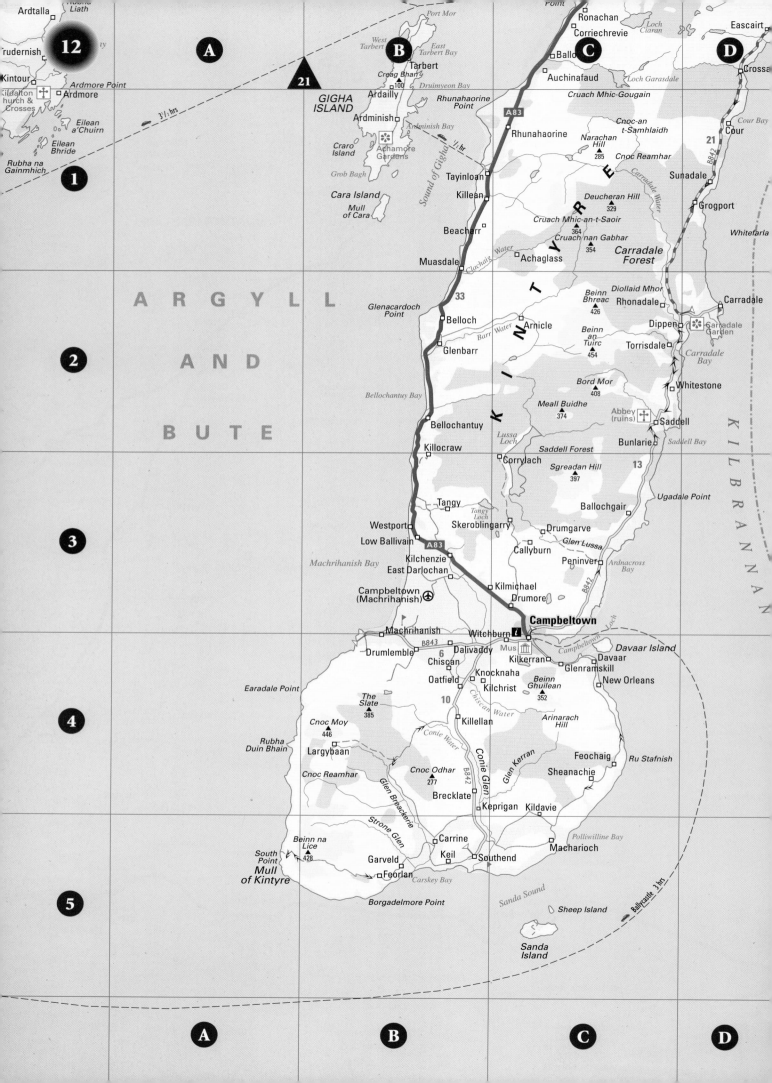

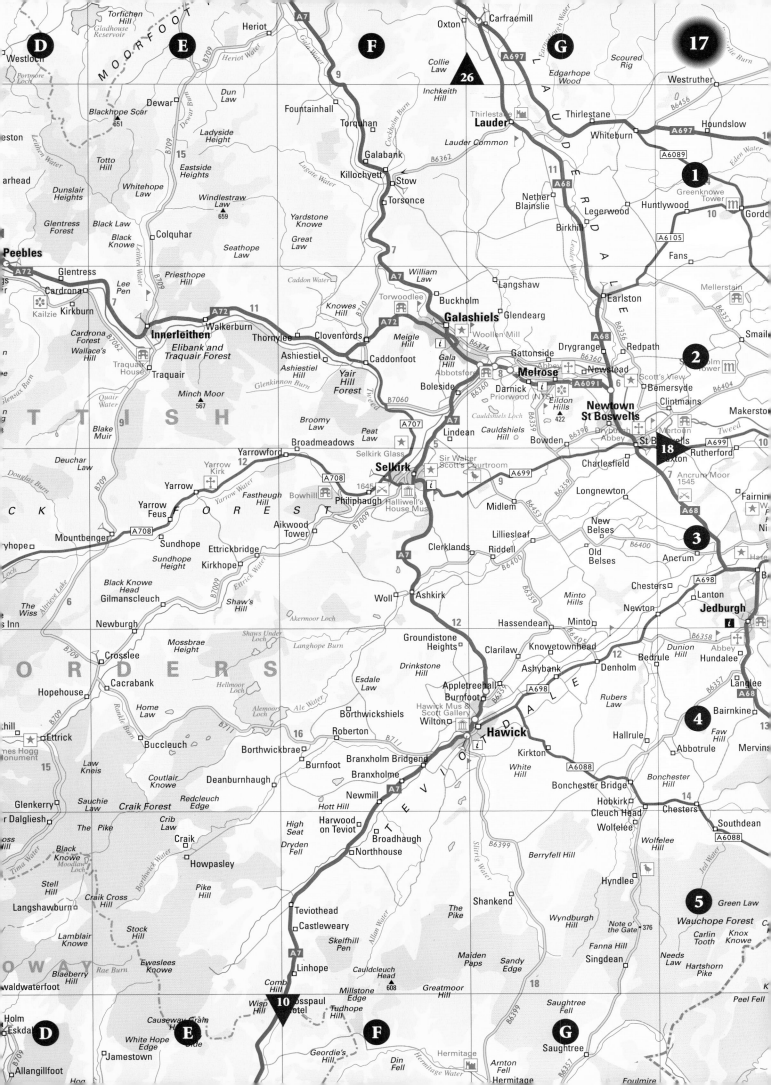

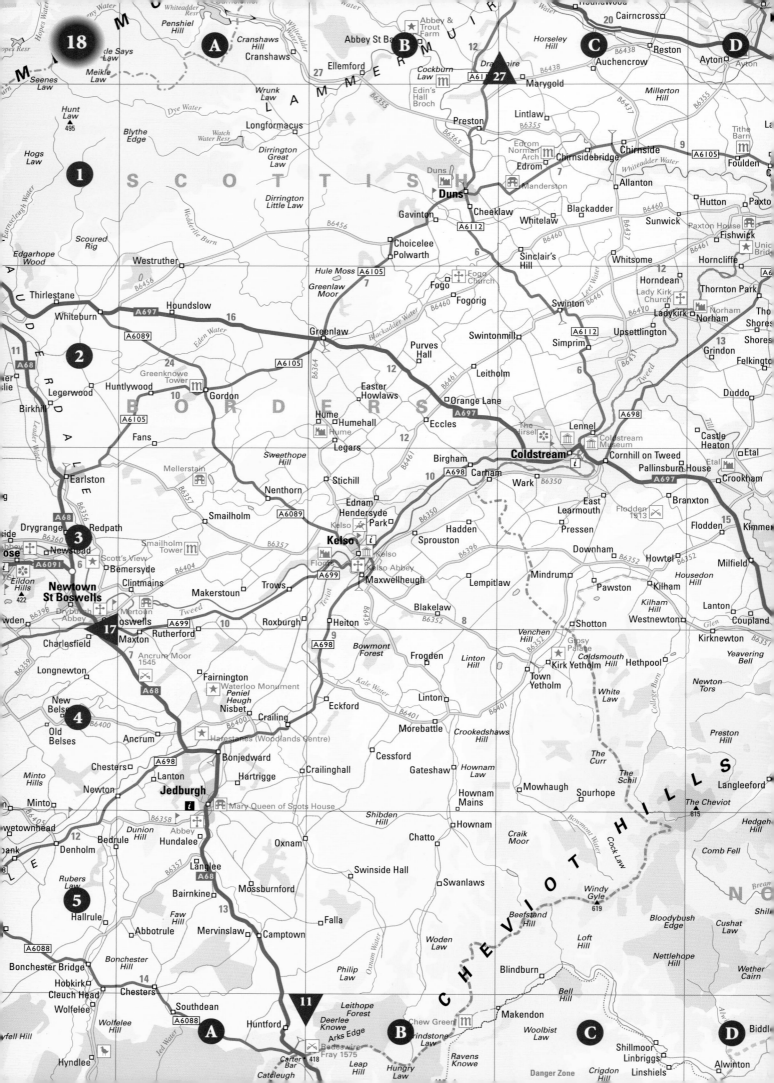

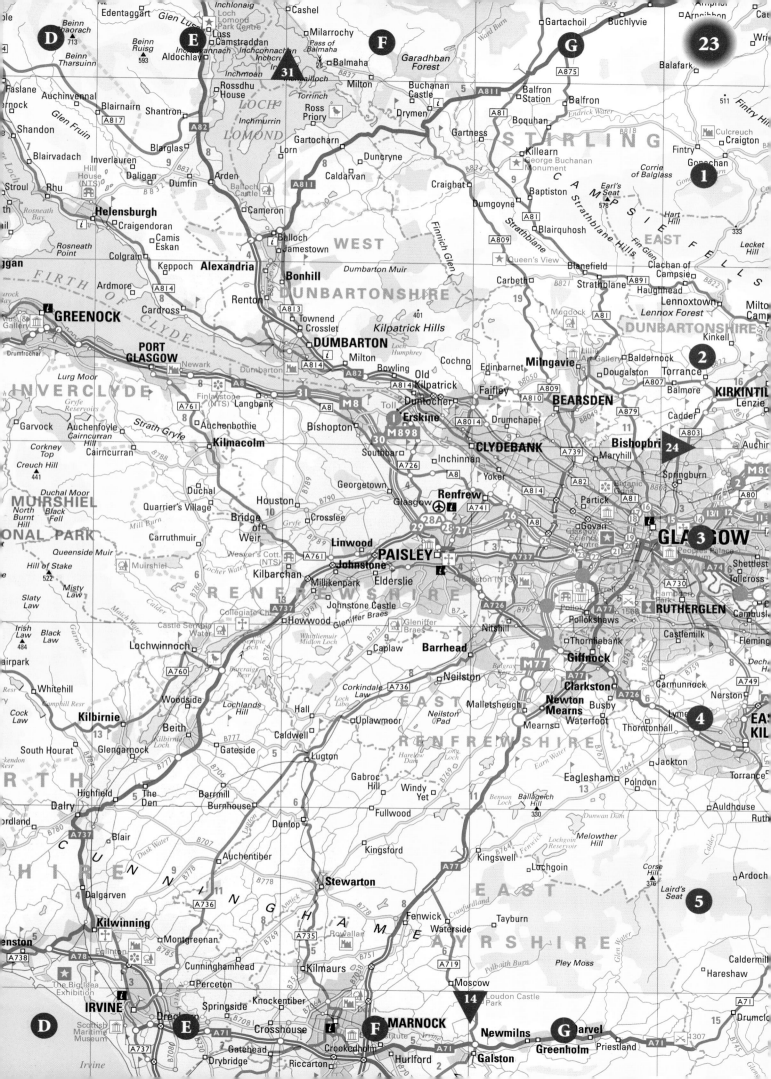

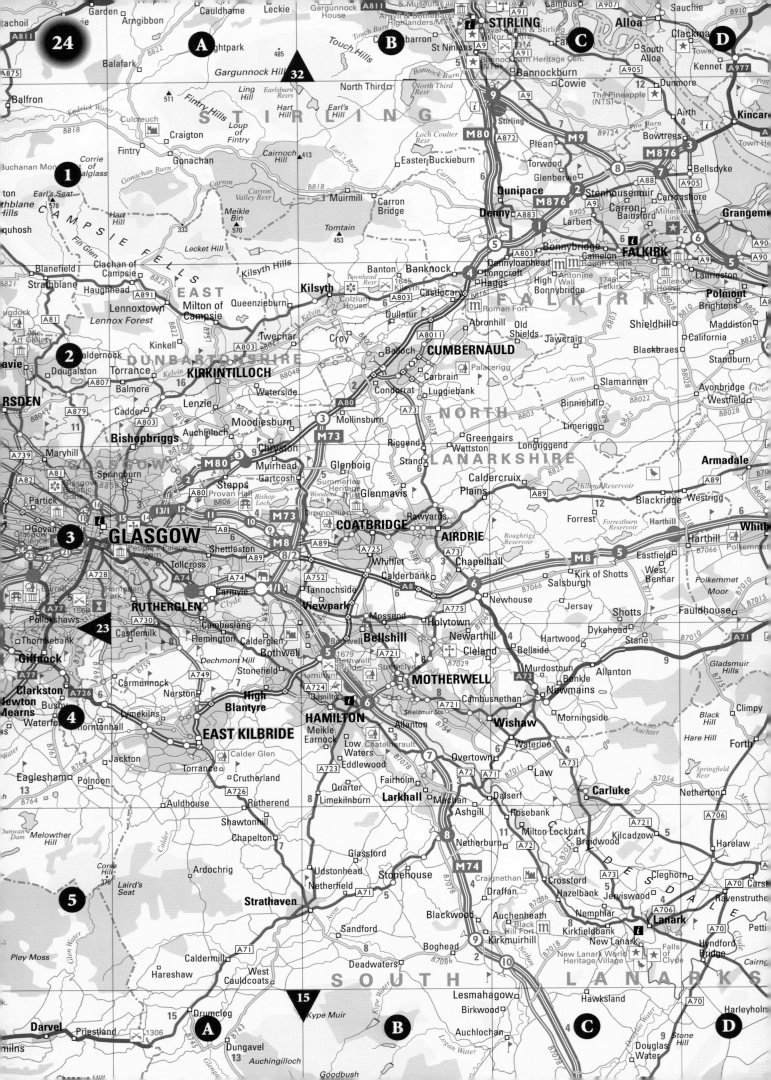

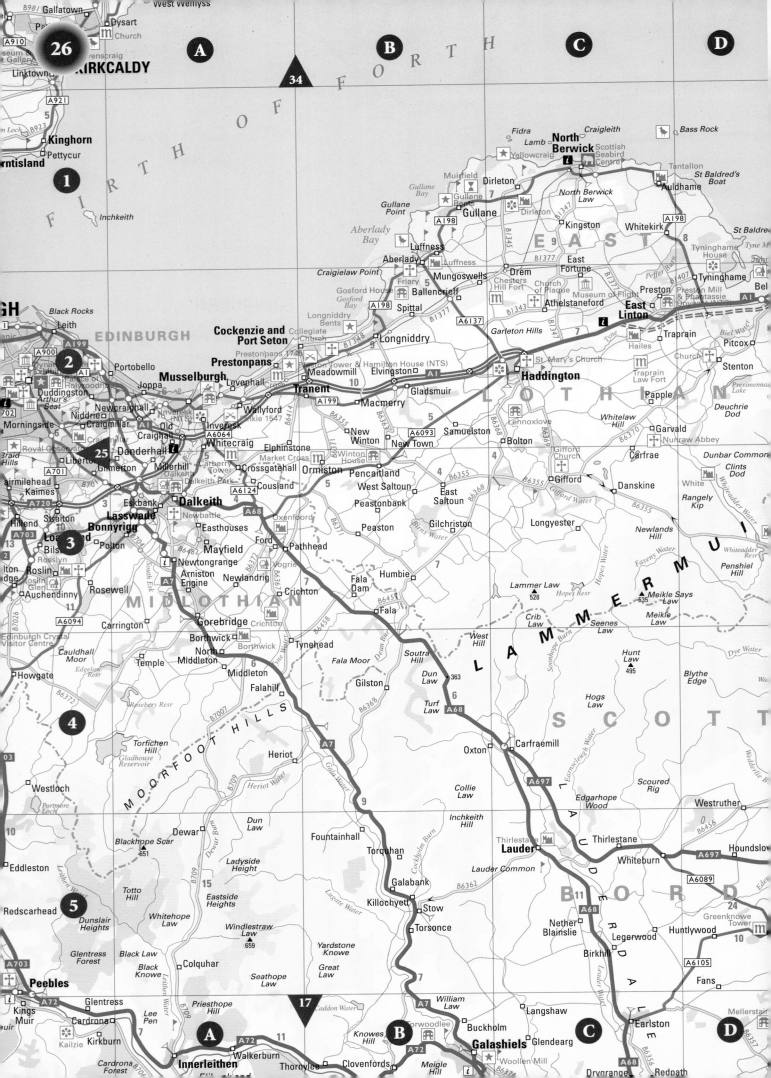

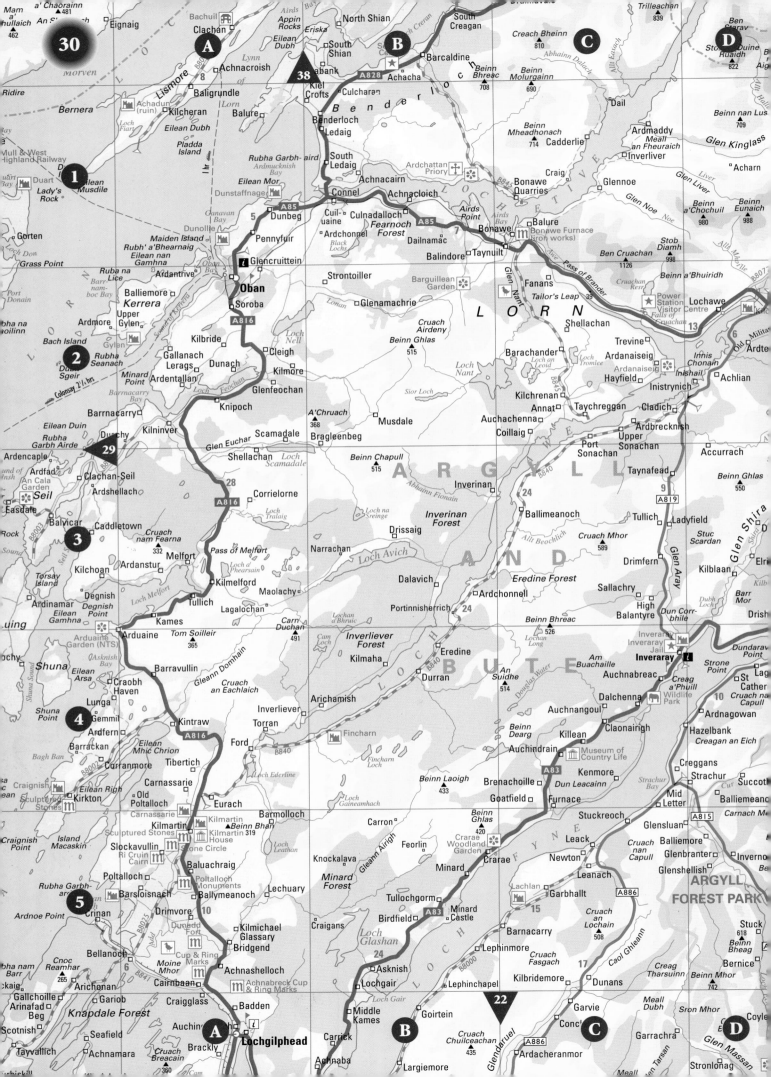

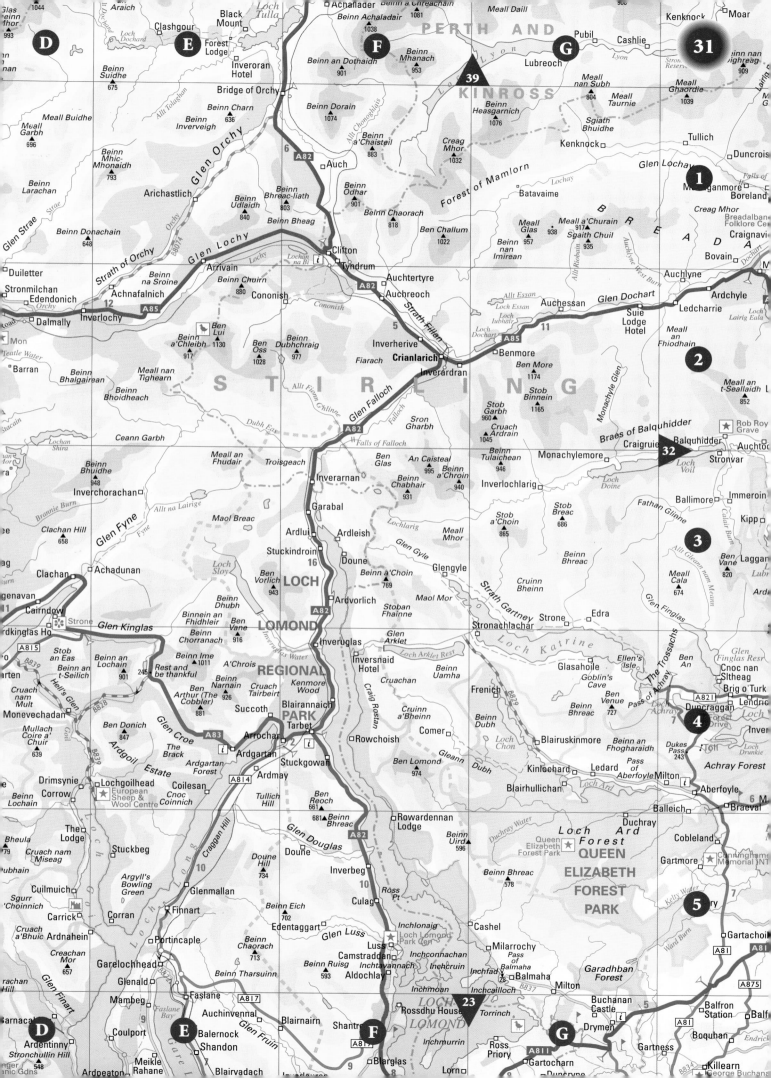

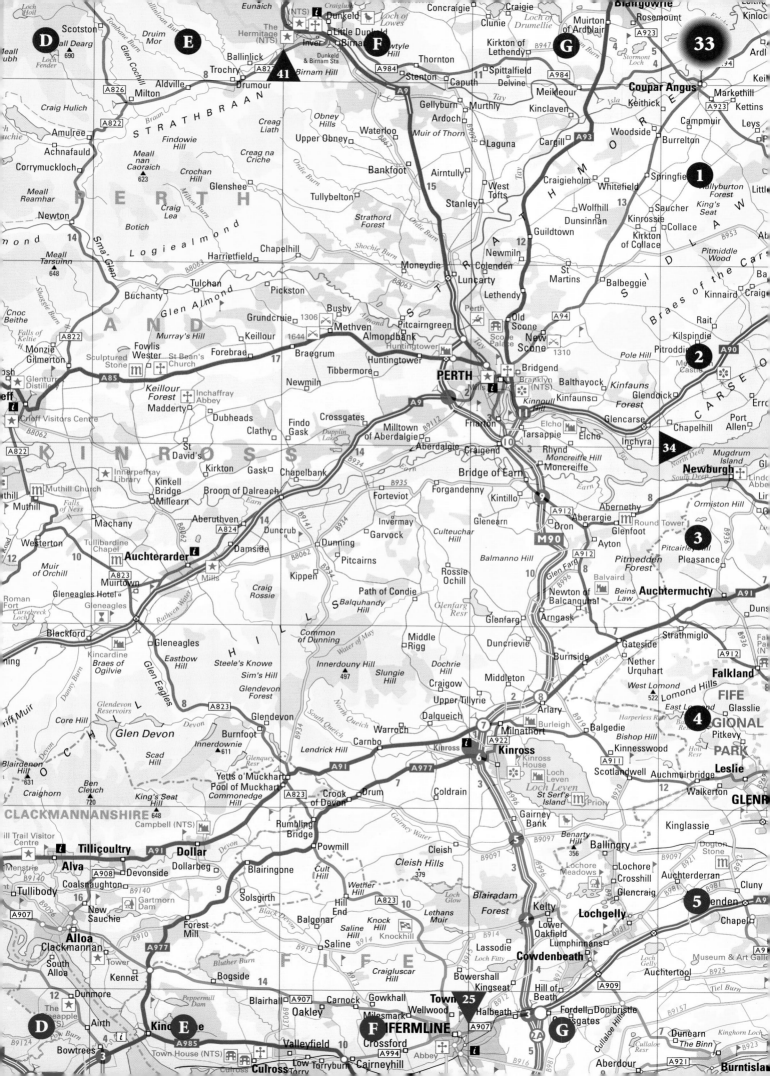

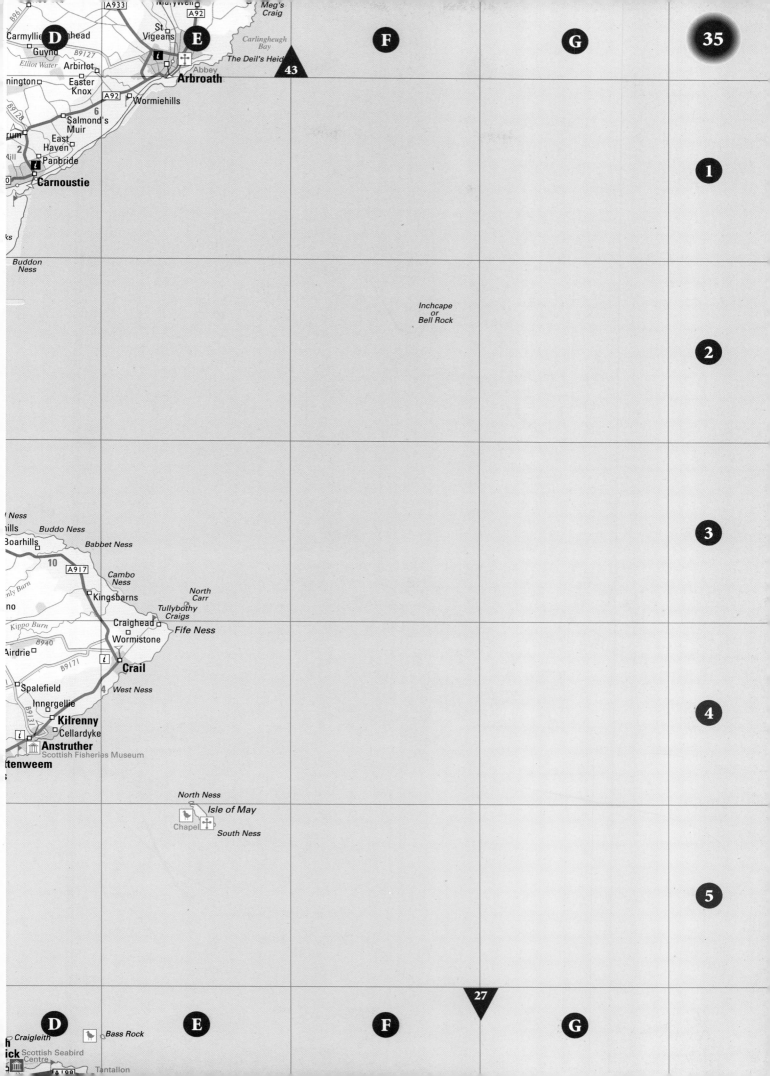

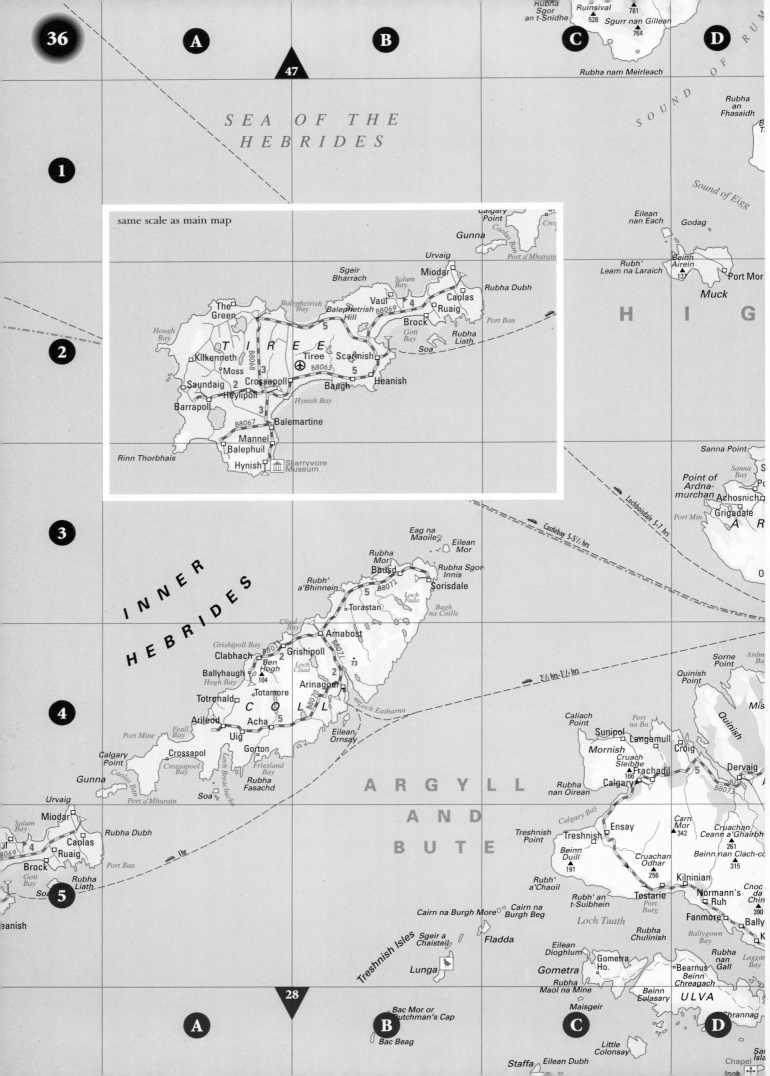

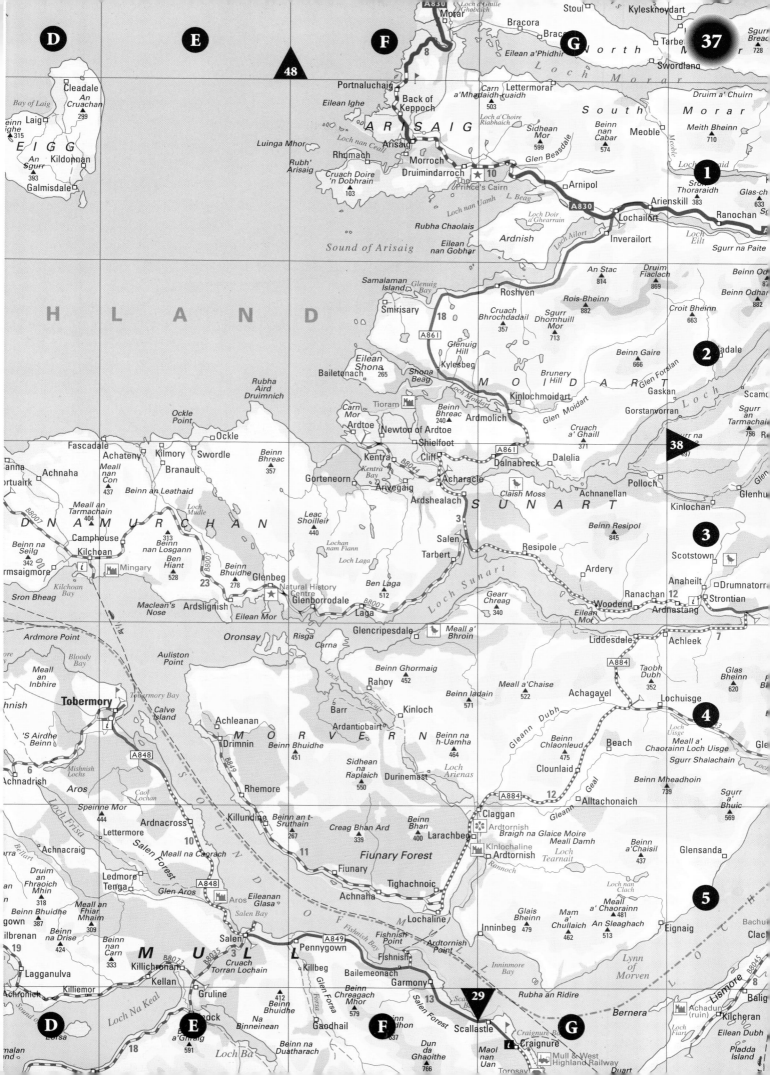

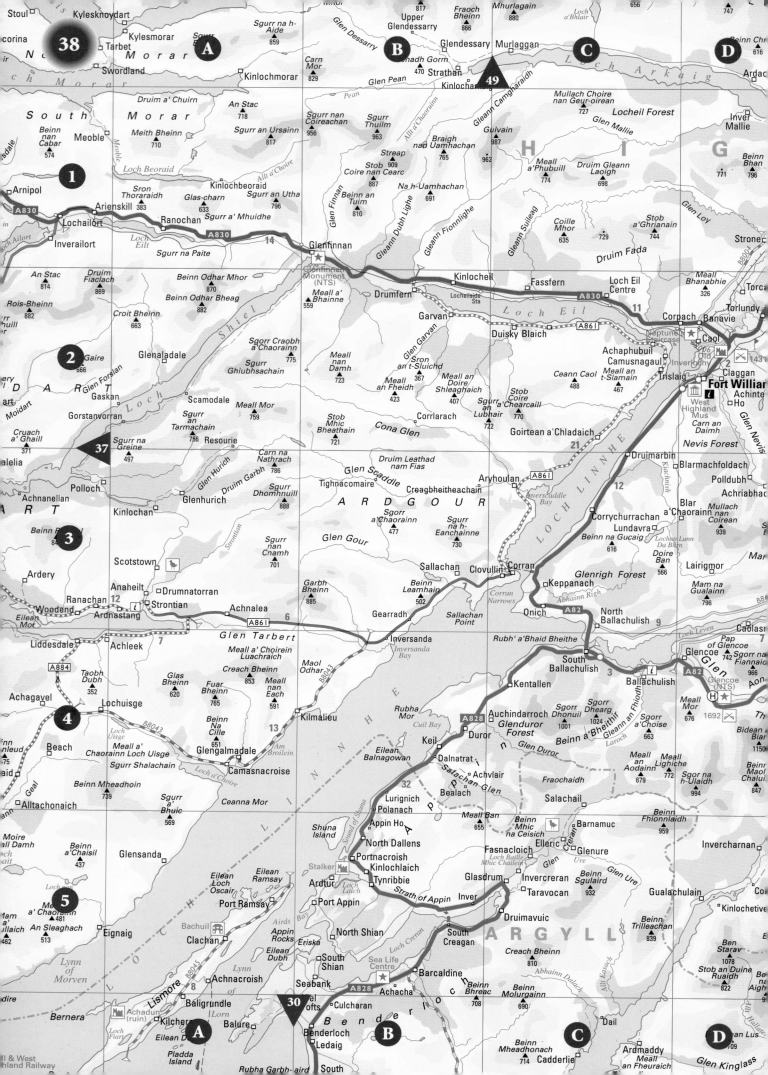

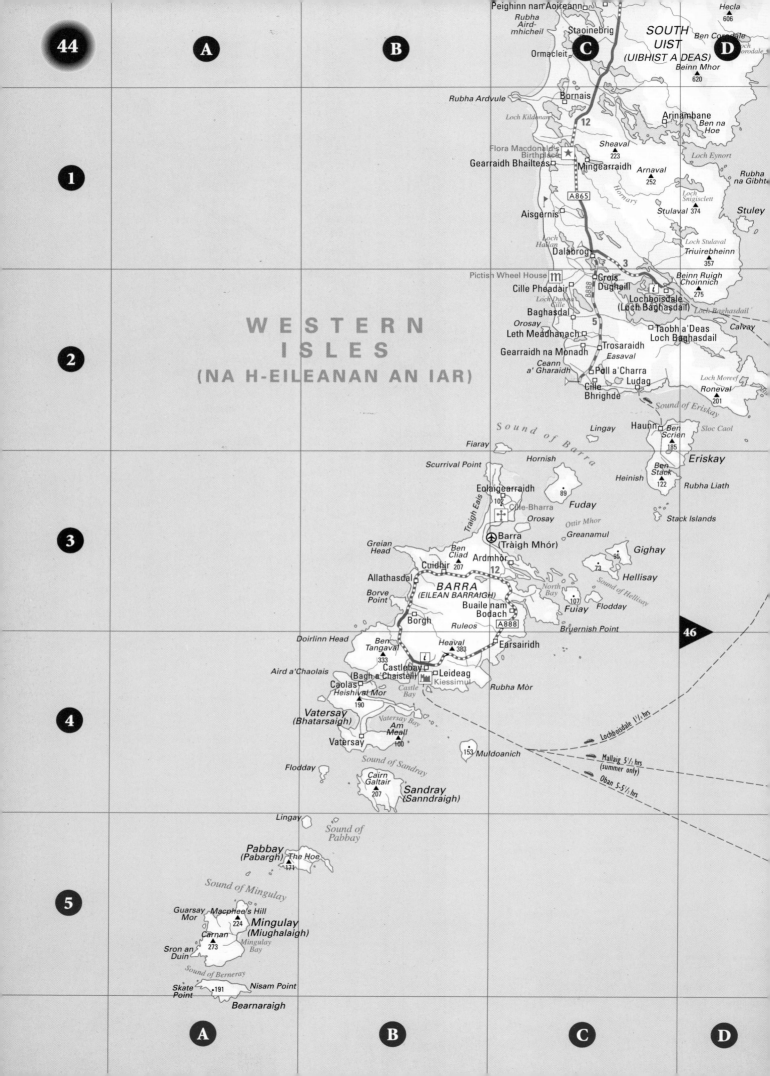

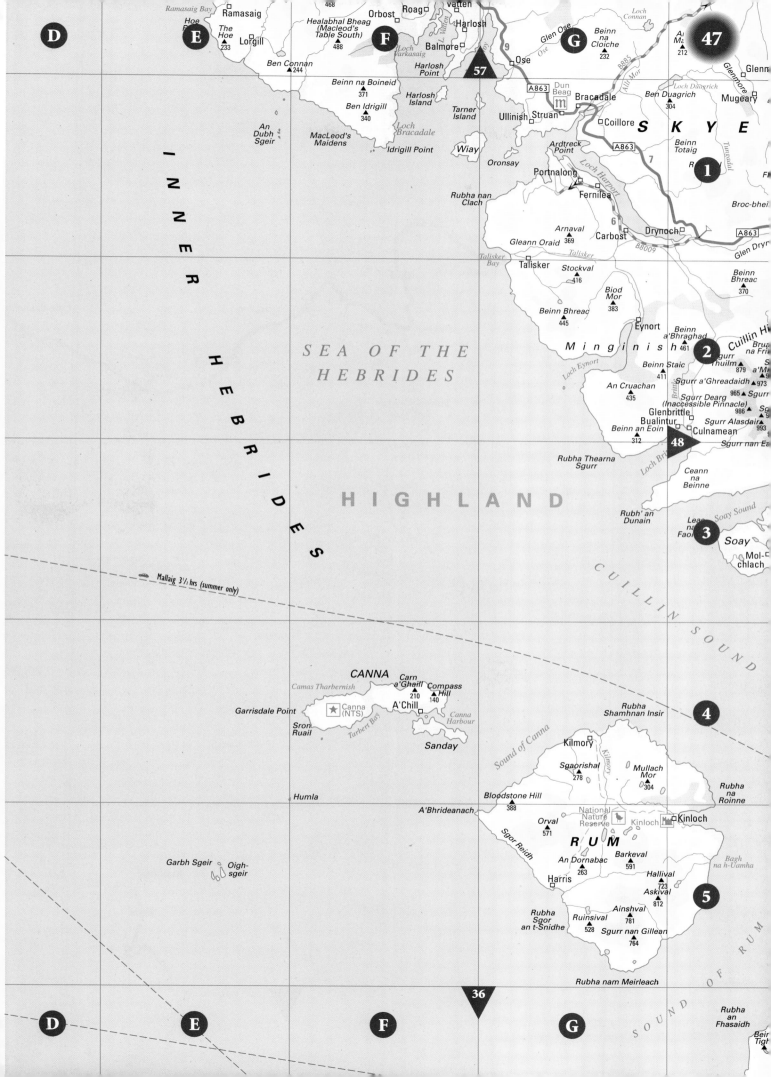

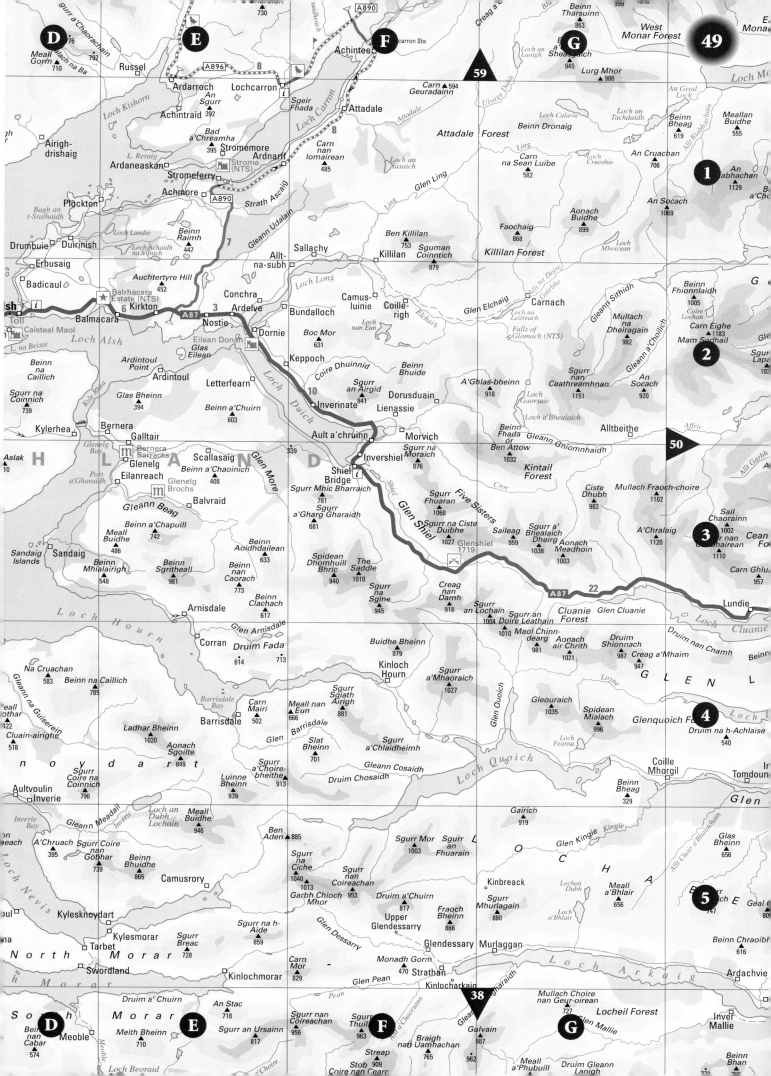

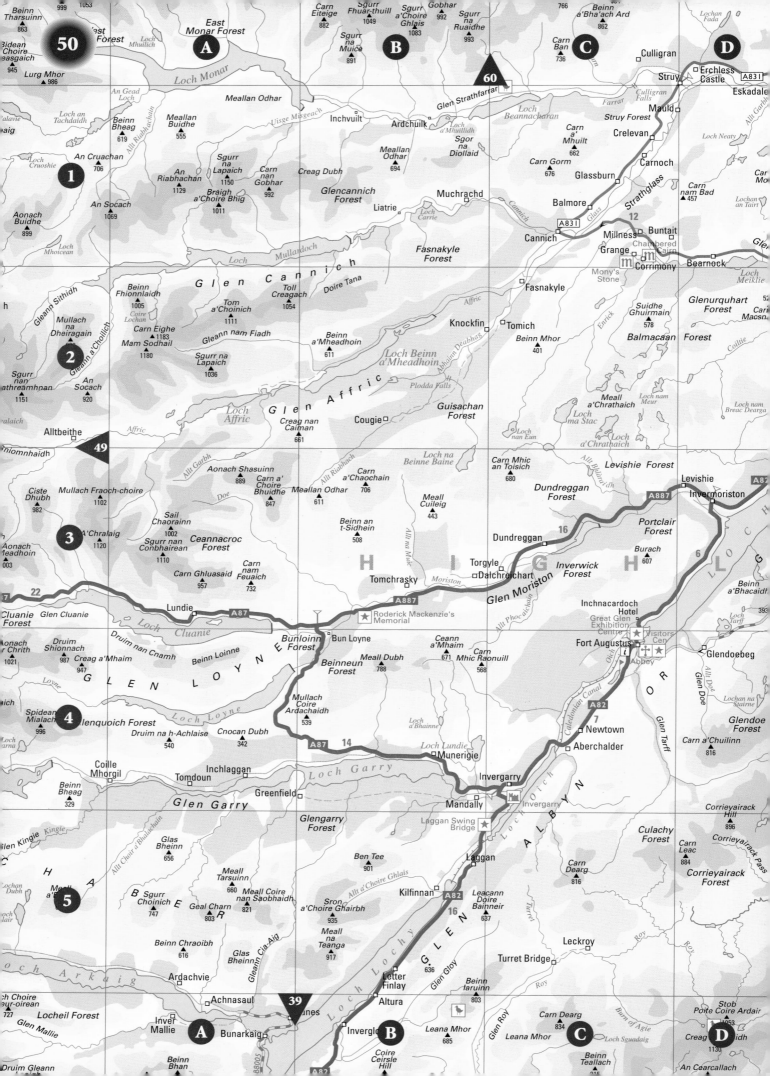

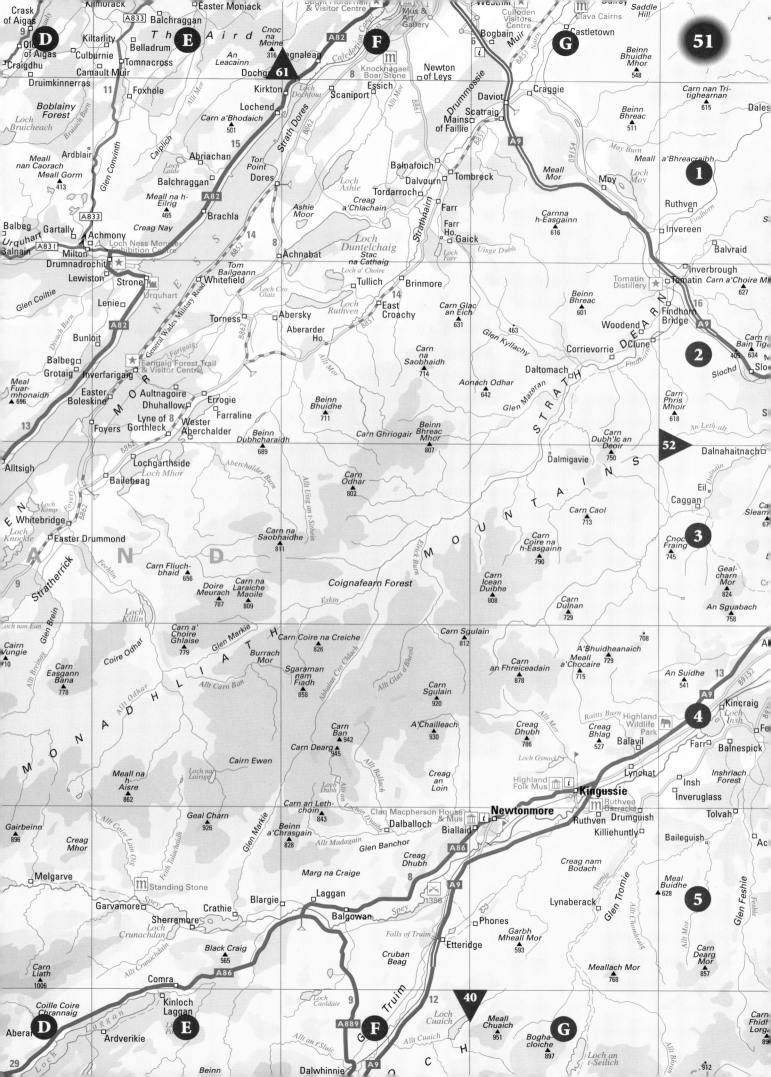

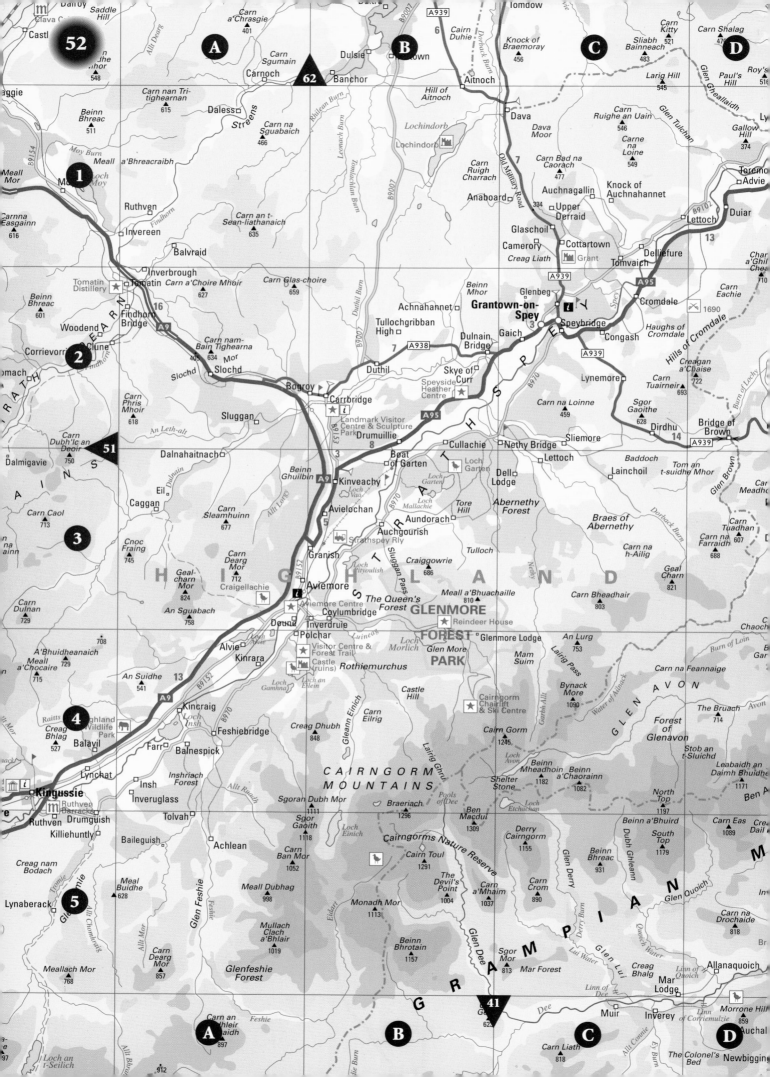

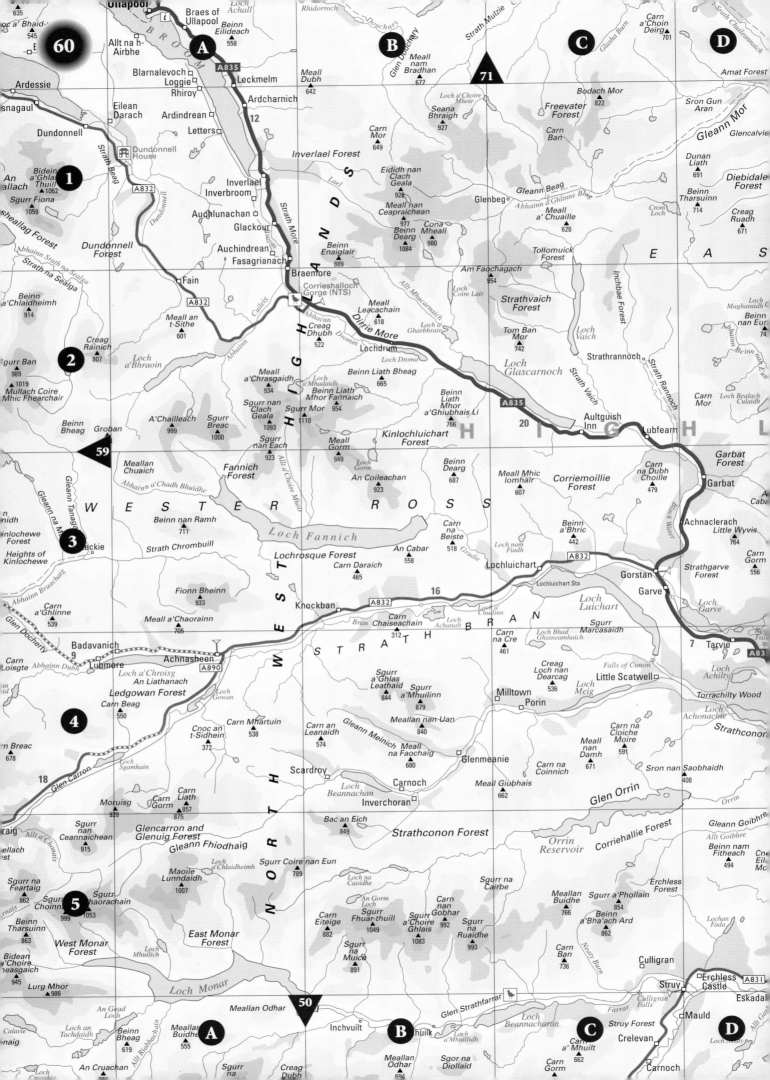

68

A   B   C   D

1

2

WESTERN
ISLES
(NA H-EILEANAN AN IAR)

3

Rubh'
an Dunair

Bagh
Dail Beag

Dail
Beag

Aird
Mhòr
Gearrannan   Dail Mòr   20

Mullach
Charlabhaigh

Craigeam   Borghastan   Carloway
Loch Carlabhagh   Cirbhig   (Carlabhagh)

Little
Bernera   Creag Mhòr   Carloway Broch

Gallan
Head   West Loch Roag

Pabaidh
Mòr   Tobson   Tolastadh a'Chaolais

Geodha
Nasavig   Aird
Uige   Bhaltos   Camas
Sandig   Great   East Loch Roag
Breacleit

Forsnaval   Nisa
205   Mhòr   Vacsay   Breacleit   Breascleit

Fiavig Bagh   Bernera

4

Aird Mhòr
Mangurstadh   Cradhlastadh   Timsgearraidh   Uigen   Vuia
Mòr   Barraglom   Kirkibost

Camas
Uig   Miabhig   Tacleit   Crulabhig   Eilean
Kearstay   Callanish

Mangurstadh   Loch
Sgaslabhal   Eadar dha
Fhadhail   Floday   Ben
Drovinish   Callanish   Gallanish
Cairisiadar   Standing   (Calanais)
Stones   Loch Cean
Thulabhig   Ga

Suainaval   Geisiadar   Linsiadar   3
429

Aird
Fenish   Loch
Suainaval   Loch Croistean   Teahaval   Griomarstaidh
256

Islibhig   Einacleit   Loch
Tungavat   Loch Cl
Steirmer

Aird
Breanais   Mealisval   Loch
Raonasgail   Tahaval   16   Scealascro   B8011
574   515

Breanais   Little Loch Roag   Loch an
Fhir Mhaoil

5

Cracaval   Loch
514   Grunavat   Giosla   Calltraiseal   Beinn Mohal
Bheag   207   Loch Airigh
226   na h-Airde

Mealasta   Tamanaisval   Loch Dibadale   Skeun   Coduinn   Roineval
467   Beinn   265   241   Calltraiseal   281
Mheadhonach   Mhòr
397   Loch Morsgail   228

Maghannan   Loch
Coirigerod

Mealasta Island   Loch na
Craobhaig   Sleiteachal
Mhòr   Stranda
248

Griomaval   Scalaval   Aird an
Troim

Liongan   66   Aird Bheag   Morsgail Fore   Loch
Loch Thealasbhaidh   Loch   Loch   Langavat
Gob na   Bodavat   Benisval
h-Airde Moire   Aird Mhòr   Loch Resort

A   B   Beinn   C   D
a'Bhoth
308

Sgeir   Sron
Moil   Romul   Kearnaval
Duinn   308   Mas

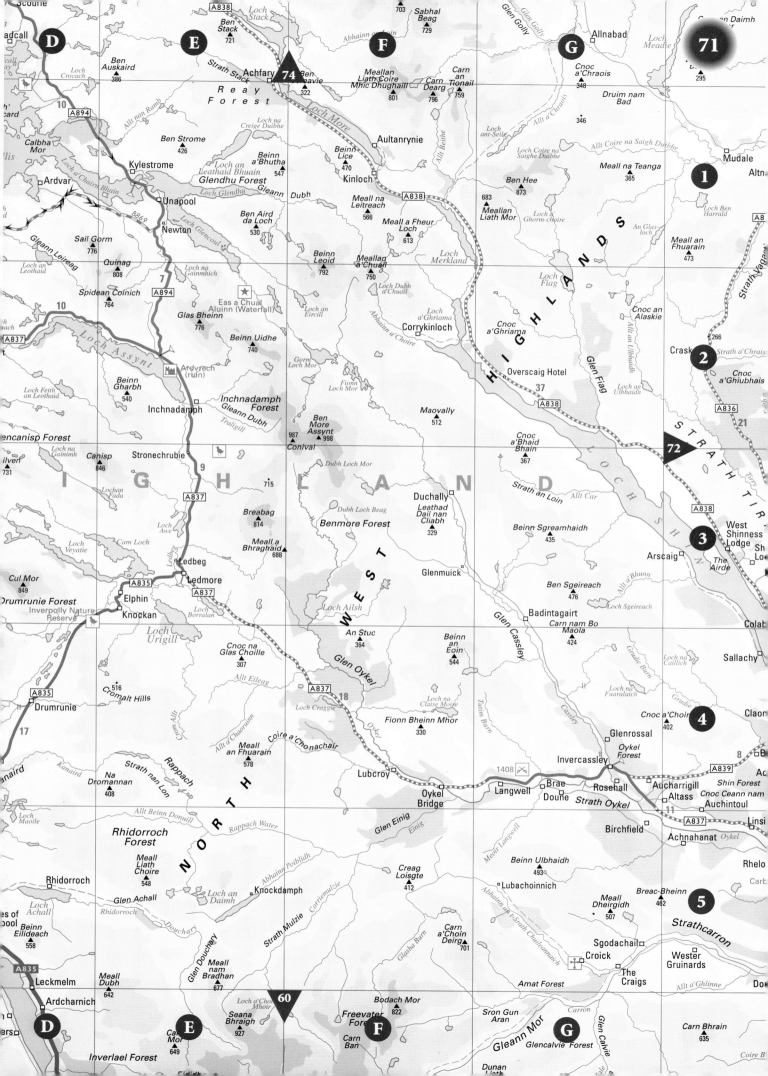

D · A897

Forsinard

Cnoc nan Gall
275

E

Meall a'
Bhealaich

F

Loch
a'Mhuilinn

Steach Water

Thur

G · havanich

Loch
Stemster

Stemster H
248

145

Loch
Ruard

Loch
Rangag

Rost

r Camst
annaiche

Rumsdale Water

76 · Dalganachan

Cnoc Cromuillt
365

Coire
na Beinne
226

A9

Crofts of
Benachielt

Sheppardstown

ntoul Forest

ch an
thair

Lochside

Meall a'
Bhealaich

Knockfin Heights
438

Ben Alisky
349

Cnocan
Conachreag
269

Ben-
a-chielt

Rumster
Forest

Upper
Lybste

A9

Achentoul

Cnoc
Coire
na
Fearna
437

Cnoc na
Saobhaidhe
290

Houstry

Reisgill
Spiney

1

Lybster

brace

Burnfoot

Glutt Water

Achnaclyth

Dunbeath Water

Nottingl

Gillivoan

Forse

Burnfoot

A897

Feith Gaineimh Mhor

Gobernuisgeach

Braemore

Smerral

Badnagie

Latheron

17

Suisgill Burn

Cnoc an Eireannaich
517

Morven
706

Maiden Pap
484

Berriedale Water

Achorn

Lhaidhay
Croft
Museum

Knockally

Dunbeath

Heritage Centre

Toremore

Latheronwheel

Strath of Kildonan

Helmsdale
Frithe

Kinbrace Burn

Loch
Scalabsdale

Creag
Scalabsdale
555

Garvery
Hill
333

Wag

Langwell Forest

Scaraben
626

Meall
na
Caorach

Inver

Dunbeath
Bay

Craggie

Cnoc Salislade
483

Aultibea

Ramscraigs

Kildonan Lodge

Beinn Dubhain
414

Mid
Hill
312

330

Blar
a'Ghille
Dhomhnaich

Braigh na
h-Eaglaise
422

Langwell Water

Langwell
House

Borgue

A9

Newport
Ceann
Leathad nam Bo

20

2

Craggie

Duible

Torrish Burn

Berriedale

Craggie Water

A897

Kilphedir

Creag Thoraraidh

Badbea

Ousdale

N

D

The Craggan
482

Ben
Uarie

Torrish

Caen

Eldrable Hill

Ord of
Caithness

A9

Glen Sletdale

Beinn Dhorain
628

Marrel

Navidale

East Helmsdale

3

nach

Meallan
Liath
Beag

Allt Smeorail

Glen Loth

Beinn
Mhealaich
592

Helmsdale

i

West Helmsdale

Gartymore

Col-
bheinn
538

Creag
a'Chrionaich
394

Lothmore

Portgower

Culgower

Lothbeg

A9

11

Kilmote

Brora

Gordonbush

Lothbeg Point

Killin

Kintradwell

Achrimsdale

West Clyne

Greenhill

Dalchalm

n Rock

aig

Clynelish

East
Brora

4

Doll

Brora

bin
e

A9

Dunrobin Castle

F I R T H

D

Port Mor

E · rbat
ss
aven

F

G

62

Innis Mhor

Hilton
Bindal

Portmahomack

5

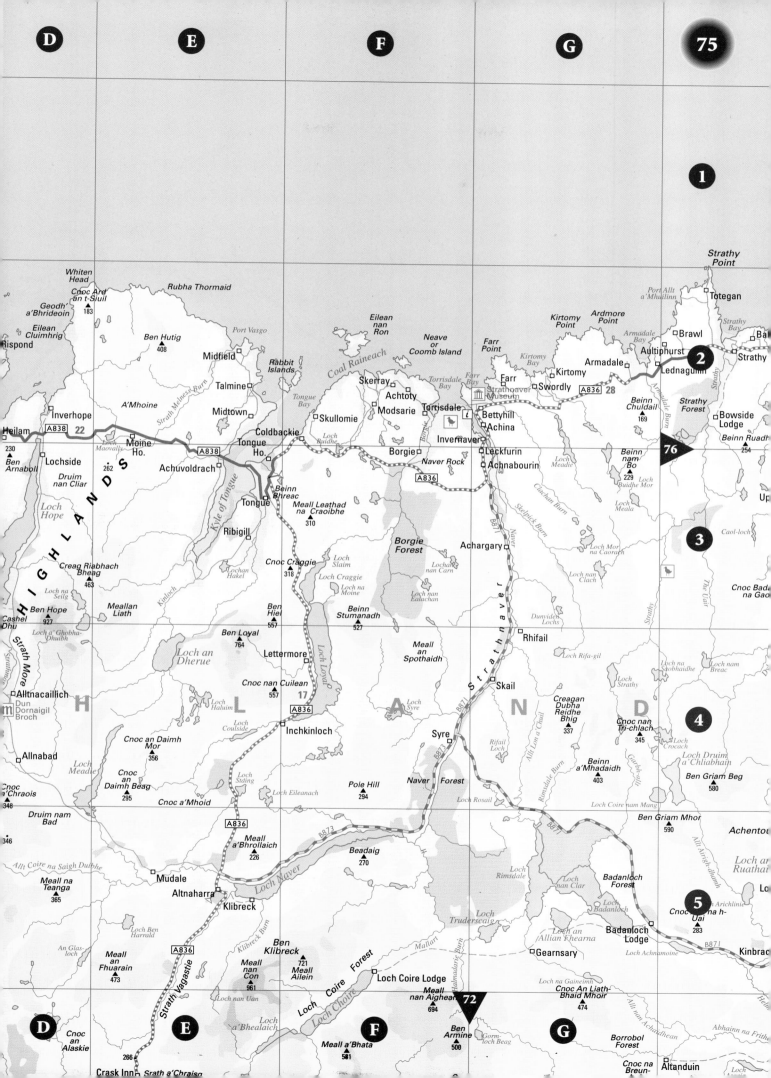

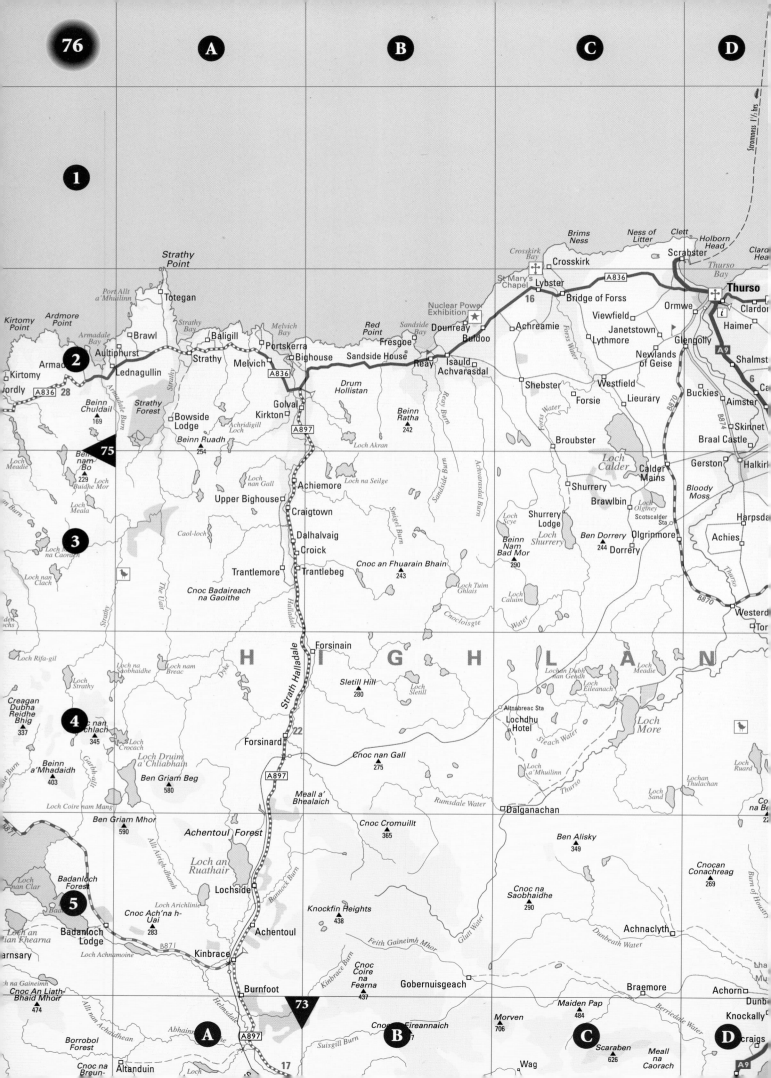

1

North Ronaldsay
Point of Sinsoss
Tor Ness
North
Ronaldsay
Linklet Bay
Hollandstoun
Bride's
Ness
South
Bay
Strom Ness

North Ronaldsay Firth

2

Tafts Ness

Holms of Ire
Whitemill
Point
Scar
Sandquoy
North Loch
Burness
Scuthvie
Bay
THE NORTH SOUND
North Bay
Otters Wick
Bay of
Lopness
Start
Point
4
7
Newark
Red
Head
Grey
Head
Broughtown
Sanday
Roadside
Cata
Sand
Sanday
Calf of Eday
Overbister
Bay of
Newark

3

uoy
Cairn
Calfsound
B9070
Kettletoft
Sty Wick
Quoy Ness
Stone of
Setter
4
Backaskail
Bay
Els
Ness
Quoyness
Chambered
Cairn
Tres
Ness
uith
Millbounds
Braeswick
Stove
6
SANDAY
SOUND
Eday
Loth
Spur Ness
B9063

Holm
of Huip
Huip Sound
Huip Ness
Papa
Stronsay
aland
Links Ness
Stronsay
Odie
Veness
3
Whitehall
Linga
Holm
B9062
B9060
War Ness
Mill Bay
Odness

4

ess
St
Catherine's
Bay
Aith
Stronsay
Odin
Bay
STRONSAY
Bay of
Bomasty
Everbay
Kirbister
ess of
ork
Rothiesholm
Grobister
B9061
B9060
2
Dishes
Burgh Head
FIRTH
Holland
one
Rothiesholm
Head
Greenli
Ness
Tor Ness
Bay of
Houseby
Lamb Head

Ingale
Skerry

5

nsay
Auskerry Sound
Foot
s
Auskerry

Invergorden 9 hrs
ick
d
ea
ng

Sound
Scarva Taing
Mull Head

The Gloup
Skaill
Roana Bay
B9050

82

A   **B**   ▲84   **C**   **D**

1
ST MAGNUS BAY

Ve Skerries

2

3

4

5

SHETLAND

Isle of Nibon
Taing
Sullom
Sullom Voe
Graven
B9076
Mangaster
Trondavoe
Islesburgh
Brae
Collafirth
Mavis Grind
Busta
Burravoe
Cunnigill Hill
Erne Stack
Busta Voe
Button Hills
Strom Ness
Roesound
Wethersta
A970
A968
Muckle Roe
Olna Firth
Hillside
Laxo
Linga
Voe
Papa Stour
Fogla Skerry
Biggings
Papa Stour
Gonfirth
West Kame
A970
Vementry
Papa Little
Swarbacks Minn
The Rona
11
Mid Kame
14
No Ness
Melby
Quilva Taing
Sandness
Garth
West Burrafirth
Brindister
Noonsbrough
Clousta
East Burrafirth
Scalla Field 281
East Kame
Aith
Sandness Hill 249
A971
Sulma Water
Unifirth
Aithsting
Setter
Catfirth
12
Burga Water
Sand Water
Bay of Deepdale
Twatt
Bixter
Westerfield
Heglibister
Mu Ness
Voe of Dale
Dale of Walls
Stourbrough Hill
Bridge of Walls
Effirth
A971
Tresta
15
Huxter
Girlsta
Wats Ness
Skarpigarth
A971
Browland
Stanydale
Semblister
Sound
Hellister
Walls
6
Gruting
Staneydale Temple
Sandsound
A971
Whiteness
Laxfir
Braga Ness
9
Garderhouse
Sand
Tingwall
Gott
Vaila
Culswick
Gossa Water
B9071
Whiteness Voe
Veensgarth
Strom Ness
Easter Skeld
Reawick
North Havra
South View
4
Ho
Wester Skeld
White Ness
A970
Cli
Westerwick
Silwick
Roe Ness
Burwick
Loch of Tingwall
Wester Wick
The Deeps
Hildasay
Skelda Ness
Scalloway
Cheynies
Papa
Cutts
Uradale
Oxna
Trondra
Easter Quarff
Br
Hamnavoe
B9074
5
West Quarff
Bridge End
East Burra
Muskna Field 292
Fladd
West Burra
Okraq
Ukna Skerry
Cliff Sound
Cliff Hills
16
Fugla Stack
Royl Field 293
Starkigarth
Kettla Ness
Houss Ness
Ward of Veester 257
Mail
South Havra
West Voe
Lamba
Maywick
A970
Leebo
Hoswick
Griskerry
Ireland
Channerwick
Sandwick
St Ninian's Isle
Bigton
Northpunds
St Ninian's Isle Church
Levenwick
Colsay
B9122
4
Blovid
Fora
ousburgh
Ness
Skelberry
Boddam

Fair Isle

Dronger
Skroo
Ward Hill 217
Breiti Stack
Bu Ness
Fair Isle
Bird Observatory
Stonybreck
Malcolm's Head
Sheep Rock
Swartz Geo
South Harbour

same scale as main map

Foula

East Hoevdi
Strem Ness
The Kame
The Sneug 418
Wester Hoevdi
Ham
Wick of Mucklabrek
Foula
Hellabrick's Wick
South Ness

same scale as main map

A   **B**   **C**   **D**

A   B   C   D

1

2

3

4

5

A   B   C   D

Ramna Stacks

Gruney

Garmus
Taing   Point of Fethaland

Uyea   Whale Geo

Hellir

South
Wick   Isbister

A970

Hevdadale Head   North Roe

Burra Voe

North   Muckle Holm
Roe   The
Roer Water   Castle

9

The Faither   Housetter   Head
Muckle Ossa   Neap of   of
Ronas   Colla Firth   Skea   Brough
Hill
450   Collafirth

A970   Quey Firth   Brother   Ness
The   Isle   of Sou
The Giants   Clifts   Voe   Lamba
Stones   Ollaberry   Uynarey

Head of Stanshi   Hamnavoe   Heylor   Little
Esha Ness   Ure   Scarff   Roe
Braehoulland   Eela Water   5   Gluss
10 Burnside   B9079   Isle   Brough
B9078   Urafirth   Bardister
Stenness   Tangwick   Hillswick   4   Gluss   Toft
Brue Wick   Sullom Voe
Ura Firth   Burraland   Oil Terminal
Baa   Firth
Taing   A970
Isle of   8   A9
Nibon   Sullom
Graven
A970

9   A968
Mangaster

Trondavoe

82

ST   Islesburgh   Brae   Button
MAGNUS BAY   Mavis Grind   Hills
Erne Stack   Busta   Burravoe
Strom   Busta   A970
Ness   Roesound   Voe   5

SHETL

YELL SOUND

We
Sandwic

Head
of
Brough

Geo of

Orka Voe

Dales Voe

Colla F

nigill
Hill

Feature Types

All the entries in the Gazetteer have been classified into broad feature types and are shown in **bold italics** in the listings. In many cases there is a degree of overlap, but an attempt has been made to use the one most appropriate. For example, a cave on the coast would be classified as a cave rather than a coastal feature as this is a more specific description. The feature types used are broken down into three main areas as follows:

Settlements and Localities

These categories are primarily man-made and have been divided into the following feature types:

City
Designated as a city by Royal Charter, they generally have a cathedral and are often large in size.

Town
Settlements with a definite central business district and urban character. They are administered as towns.

Small town
Administered as towns but are small and often have the character of a village.

Suburb
Primarily a residential locality linked to, or within a town or city.

Village
Settlements with a definite nucleus, possibly with a small number of facilities such as a post office, public house and village green.

Hamlet
Small collection of residential buildings, generally clustered together.

Settlement
Scattered buildings with no definite nucleus, or possibly, consisting of only one or two buildings.

Locality
This is a "catch all" category. It includes settlements that do not fall easily into any of the other categories. It may include industrial estates, areas within villages or several settlements with a collective name. It may also be a geographic region.

Physical Features

These feature types are essentially natural rather than man-made. The dividing lines between them are not always clear cut, but a best attempt has been made to choose the most applicable category.

Bay
These are water features and range from small coves to large bays such as Ayr Bay.

Cave
These include coastal and inland caves, and although this is generally a physical feature may also include caves modified and enlarged by man.

Coastal feature
These include only 'land' features such as headlands and cliffs and do not include 'sea' features such as straits, sounds and bays.

Forest/woodland
This is an area which is predominantly afforested.

Hill
For the purposes of the gazetteer these have been classified as being under 1000 feet or 305 metres in height.

Mountain
These are taken as being 1000 feet or 305 metres and over. A subdivision of this feature type is Munro, these are over 3000 feet or 914 metres and have been designated by the Scottish Mountaineering Club.

Inland physical feature
These include features which do not fit comfortably into any of the more specific categories and may include corries, ridges, swallow holes etc.

Island
Includes island rocks and groups of offshore rocks as well as the more traditional islands. Stacks adjacent to the shore are not included as these would be categorised as coastal features.

Lake/loch
These include all natural lakes, lochs, tarns and lochans but exclude sea lochs which would be considered to be sea features.

Large natural feature
Includes mountain ranges and plains.

Marsh/bog
This is an open space, with marshes generally considered to be coastal and bogs taken as being inland features.

Open space
Includes moorlands, hillslopes and areas with no specific defining features.

River
These range from small streams to large rivers.

Sea feature
These are 'water' features such as sea lochs, inlets, estuaries and straits.

Valley
These are commonly called vales, straths and glens and may be created by river or glacier.

Waterfall
This category also includes rapids as well as waterfalls.

Other Features

In many cases, the remaining feature types are self explanatory, or are clarified in the description that follows in the gazetteer listing.

The balance of the features type categories are listed below:

Airport/airfield, Battle site, Bridge, Canal, Castle, Ecclesiastical building, Educational establishment, Garden, Historic house, Historic/prehistoric site, Leisure/recreation, Military establishment, Motor racing circuit, Nature reserve, Other building, Other feature of interest, Other water feature, Racecourse and Reservoir.

Notes: Listed below are the administrative areas for Scotland used in this Gazetteer. Where an area is dual language, the English form is given first, followed by the alternative in parenthesis. Each entry includes its standard abbreviation in *italics* which will appear in the main listings. Population figures are derived from 1991 Census information, or mid Census estimates, with modifications to allow for the newly created unitary authorities. A brief description of the area then follows, which includes: adjoining administrative areas; main centres (based on descending order of population); historical, physical and economic characteristics. A selection of the most visited tourist attractions follows under the heading, **Places of interest**.

Aberdeen *Aberdeen* Population: 219,120.
Unitary authority surrounding Aberdeen, Scotland's third largest city, on the NE coast and neighbouring Aberdeenshire. Aberdeen is the major commercial and administrative centre for N Scotland. It is the second largest fishing port in Scotland, with docks at the mouth of the River Dee, and is the oil and gas capital of Europe.
Places of interest: Aberdeen Art Gallery; Aberdeen Exhibition and Conference Centre; Duthie Park & Winter Gardens; Provost Skene's House.

Aberdeenshire *Aber.* Population: 226,530.
Unitary authority on the NE coast of Scotland neighbouring Aberdeen, Angus, Highland, Moray and Perth & Kinross. Main centres are Peterhead, Fraserburgh, Inverurie, Stonehaven, Ellon, Banchory, Portlethen and Huntly. Aberdeenshire is split geographically into two main areas. The W is dominated by the Grampian Mountains and is largely unpopulated. The undulating lowlands of the E are mainly rural and are populated by farming and fishing communities. The major rivers are the Dee, which flows through Royal Deeside, and the Don.
Places of interest: Aden Country Park, Mintlaw; Balmedie Country Park; Balmoral Castle, Crathie; Crathes Castle (NTS); Haddo House Country Park (NTS); Storybook Glen, Maryculter.

Angus *Angus* Population: 111,329.
Unitary authority on the E coast of Scotland neighbouring Aberdeenshire, Dundee and Perth & Kinross. The chief centres are Arbroath, Forfar, Montrose, Carnoustie, the ancient cathedral city of Brechin, Kirriemuir and Monifieth. Angus occupies an area of 2200 square km and is an important agricultural area. It combines ancient relics and castles with highland terrain and market towns. Rivers include the North Esk, Isla and Prosen Water.
Places of interest: Glamis Castle; Monikie Country Park.

Argyll & Bute *Arg. & B.* Population: 90,550.
Unitary authority on the W coast of Scotland combining mainland and island life and neighbouring Highland, Inverclyde, North Ayrshire, Perth & Kinross, Stirling and West Dunbartonshire. The main towns are Helensburgh, Dunoon, Oban, Campbeltown, Rothesay and Lochgilphead. It includes the former districts of Argyll and Bute as well as the islands of Islay, Jura, Colonsay and Mull. The main industries are fishing, agriculture, whisky production and tourism.
Places of interest: Inveraray Castle; Inveraray Jail; Iona Abbey; Loch Lomond Park Centre, Luss.

Clackmannanshire *Clack.* Population: 47,679.
Unitary authority in central Scotland neighbouring Fife, Perth & Kinross and Stirling. The N includes the Ochil Hills, while the lowland surrounding the Forth estuary contains the chief towns which are Alloa, Tullibody, Tillicoultry and Alva. Clackmannanshire has over 50 sites of nature conservation and five historic castles and

towers. The main rivers are the Devon and the Forth.
Places of interest: Gartmorn Dam Country Park, Coalsnaughton; Mill Trail Visitor Centre, Alva.

Dumfries & Galloway *D. & G.* Population: 147,900.
Unitary authority in SW Scotland neighbouring East Ayrshire, Scottish Borders, South Ayrshire, South Lanarkshire, the English county of Cumbria and the sea. It comprises the former counties of Dumfries, Kirkcudbright, and Wigtown. Chief towns are Dumfries, Stranraer, Annan, Dalbeattie, Lockerbie, Castle Douglas, Newton Stewart and Kirkcudbright. The hilly area to the N is largely given over to sheep-grazing and afforestation, while farther S there is some good-quality arable farmland. At the extreme W of the area is the peninsula known as the Rinns of Galloway, and the port of Stranraer, which provides passenger and car ferry services to Larne in Northern Ireland. Main rivers are the Esk, Annan, Nith, Dee and Cree which descend S to the Solway Firth from the Tweedsmuir Hills, Lowther Hills and the Rhinns of Kells in the N.
Places of interest: Blacksmith's Shop, Gretna Green; Threave Gardens (NTS), Castle Douglas.

Dundee *Dundee* Population: 155,000.
Unitary authority on the E coast of Scotland surrounding the city of Dundee and neighbouring Angus and Perth & Kinross. Dundee is Scotland's fourth largest city and is a centre of excellence in a variety of areas from telecommunications to medical research. The Firth of Tay borders Dundee to the S.
Places of interest: Discovery Point & R.R.S. Discovery; McManus Galleries.

East Ayrshire *E.Ayr.* Population: 124,000.
Unitary authority in SW Scotland bounded by Dumfries & Galloway, East Renfrewshire, North Ayrshire, South Ayrshire and South Lanarkshire. The principal towns are Kilmarnock, Cumnock, Stewarton, Galston and Auchinleck. Traditional industries centred on textiles and lace in the Irvine valley, coal mining and engineering. Dairy farming is also an important industry, particularly beef and sheep production. The area is a popular tourist destination, with several castles, battle sites and associations with Robert Burns and Keir Hardie. Rivers include the Irvine, Annick and Cessnock.
Places of interest: Blackshaw Farm Park Ltd., Kilmarnock; Loudon Castle Park, Galston.

East Dunbartonshire *E.Dun.* Population: 110,220.
Unitary authority in central Scotland bounded by Glasgow, North Lanarkshire, Stirling and West Dunbartonshire. The chief centres are Bearsden, Bishopbriggs, Kirkintilloch and Milngavie. Much of the urban and industrial development occurs on the N periphery of Greater Glasgow. The Campsie Fells lie in the N of the area.
Places of interest: Lillie Art Gallery.

East Lothian *E.Loth.* Population: 85,500.

Unitary authority in central Scotland neighbouring Edinburgh, Midlothian, Scottish Borders and the North Sea. The main towns are Musselburgh, Haddington, Tranent, Prestonpans, Dunbar, North Berwick and Cockenzie and Port Seton. There are 43m of varied coastline and the topography includes the Lammermuir Hills in the S, and the ancient volcanoes at North Berwick and Traprain. Much of the urban and industrial development is in the NW and N of the area. Rivers include Whitehead Water, the Tyne, Peffer Burn and Gifford Water.

Places of interest: Gullane Bents; John Muir Country Park; Longniddry Bents; Yellowcraig, Dirleton.

East Renfrewshire *E.Renf.* Population: 86,780.

Unitary authority in SW Scotland bounded by East Ayrshire, Glasgow, Inverclyde, North Ayrshire, Renfrewshire and South Lanarkshire. The principal centres are Newton Mearns, Clarkston, Barrhead and Giffnock, which lie on the S periphery of Greater Glasgow. Over two-thirds of East Renfrewshire is farmland; the rest being mostly residential, with some light industry.

Edinburgh *Edin.* Population: 447,550.

Unitary authority on the E coast of central Scotland surrounding the city of Edinburgh and neighbouring East Lothian, Midlothian, West Lothian and the sea at the Firth of Forth. Edinburgh as the capital of Scotland, is a major administrative, cultural, commercial and tourist centre. It contains most of Scotland's national and cultural institutions. Its historic core is centred around Edinburgh Castle and the Royal Mile, attracting much tourism. The city is also a centre for education and scientific research; other important industries are electronics and food and drink production. The river Water of Leith runs through the city to the docks at Leith.

Places of interest: City Art Centre; Edinburgh Castle; Edinburgh Zoo; Gorgie City Farm; Museum of Antiquities; Museum of Childhood; National Gallery of Scotland; Palace of Holyroodhouse; People's Story Museum; Queen's Hall; Royal Botanic Garden; Royal Highland Centre; Royal Museum of Scotland; St. Giles Cathedral; Scotch Whisky Heritage Centre; Scottish National Gallery of Modern Art; Scottish National Portrait Gallery; Scottish United Services Museum, Edinburgh Castle; The Royal Scots Regimental Museum; Tron Kirk; Usher Hall.

Falkirk *Falk.* Population: 142,530.

Unitary authority in central Scotland surrounding Falkirk and neighbouring Clackmannanshire, Fife, North Lanarkshire, Stirling and West Lothian. Main towns are Falkirk, Grangemouth, Polmont, Stenhousemuir and Bo'ness. Petrochemical and chemical industries are important to the local economy, as well as bus manufacturing, toffees and paper-making. The Firth of Forth borders Falkirk to the N. Other rivers include the Carron and Pow Burn.

Places of interest: Blackness Castle, Linlithgow; Bo'ness & Kinneil Railway.

Fife *Fife* Population: 351,200.

Unitary authority in E Scotland neighbouring Clackmannanshire and Perth & Kinross, and lying between the Firth of Tay and Firth of Forth. Main towns are Dunfermline, Kirkcaldy, Glenrothes, Buckhaven, Cowdenbeath and St. Andrews. Fife comprises the former county of the same name, known since ancient times as the Kingdom of Fife, and is noted for its fine coastline with many distinctive small towns and fishing ports. The historic town of St. Andrews, on the coast between the two firths, is a university town, and the home of the world's premier golf club. Inland, the area is outstandingly fertile, with agriculture being an important industry. The SW of the area is a former coal-mining area.

Places of interest: Craigtoun Country Park, near St. Andrews; Deep Sea World, North Queensferry; Lochore Meadows Country Park, Crosshill; Sea Life Centre, St. Andrews.

Glasgow *Glas.* Population: 618,430.

Unitary authority in SW Scotland surrounding Glasgow and bounded by East Dunbartonshire, East Renfrewshire, North Lanarkshire, Renfrewshire, South Lanarkshire and West Dunbartonshire. Glasgow is Scotland's largest city and its principal industrial and shopping centre. The city developed significantly due to heavy industry, notably shipbuilding, being centred on the Clyde. While such industry has declined, Glasgow has emerged as a major cultural centre of Europe, due to its impressive arts and cultural scene. The River Clyde runs through the city.

Places of interest: Burrell Collection; Gallery of Modern Art; Glasgow Botanic Garden; Glasgow Cathedral; Hunterian Museum & Art Gallery; Kelvingrove Art Gallery & Museum; McLellan Galleries; Museum of Transport, Kelvin Hall; People's Palace Museum; Royal Concert Hall; St. Mungo's Museum; Scottish Exhibition & Conference Centre (S.E.C.C.).

Highland *High.* Population: 207,500.

Unitary authority covering a large part of N Scotland and neighbouring Aberdeenshire, Argyll & Bute, Moray and Perth & Kinross. It contains a mixture of mainland and island life, comprising the former districts of Badenoch and Strathspey, Caithness, Inverness, Lochaber, Nairn, Ross and Cromarty, Skye and Lochalsh and Sutherland. Main towns are Inverness, Fort William, Thurso, Nairn, Wick, Alness and Dingwall. Overall, Highland is very sparsely inhabited, being wild and remote in character. It is scenically outstanding, containing as it does part of the Cairngorm Mountains, Ben Nevis, and the North West Highlands. Many of the finest sea and inland lochs in Scotland are also here, such as Loch Ness, Loch Linnhe, Loch Torridon and Loch Broom. The discovery of North Sea oil has made an impact on the towns and villages around the Moray Firth. Elsewhere, tourism, crofting, fishing and skiing are important locally.

Places of interest: Aonach Mhor Mountain Gondola Lift & Nevis Range Ski Centre, Fort William; Ben Nevis, Fort William; Bught Floral Hall and Visitor Centre, Inverness; Culloden Visitor Centre, near Inverness; Dunvegan Castle; Fort Augustus Abbey Visitor Centre; Glencoe Visitor Centre (NTS); Inverewe Gardens (NTS), Londubh; Loch Ness Monster Exhibition Centre, Drumnadrochit; Rothiemurchus Visitor Centre & Forest Trail; Shin Falls; Speyside Heather Centre, Dulnain Bridge; Urquhart Castle, Drumnadrochit.

Inverclyde *Inclyde* Population: 89,990.

Unitary authority on the W coast of central Scotland, on the S bank of the River Clyde. It is bordered by North Ayrshire, Renfrewshire and the Firth of Clyde. The chief towns are Greenock, Port Glasgow, Gourock and Kilmacolm.

Places of interest: Lunderston Bay, Gourock; McLean Museum & Art Gallery, Greenock.

Midlothian *Midloth.* Population: 79,901.

Unitary authority in central Scotland neighbouring East Lothian, Edinburgh and Scottish Borders. Main towns are Penicuik, Bonnyrigg, Dalkeith, Gorebridge and

Loanhead. The area is mostly rural, including the rolling moorland of the Pentland Hills and Moorfoot Hills in the S. To the N, the urban area is comprised of satellite towns to the SE of Edinburgh. Rivers include Tyne Water and South Esk.
Places of interest: Edinburgh Crystal Visitor Centre, Penicuik; Vogrie Country Park, near Ford.

Moray *Moray* Population: 85,000.
Unitary authority in N Scotland neighboured by Aberdeenshire, Highland and the sea. Main towns are Elgin, Forres, Buckie, Lossiemouth and Keith. The area is mainly mountainous, including part of the Cairngorm Mountains in the S. It is dissected by many deep river valleys, most notably that of the River Spey. Along with the local grain and peat, the abundant waters provide the raw materials for half of Scotland's malt whisky distilleries, leading to the Whisky Trail and much tourism through Speyside.
Places of interest: Baxters Visitor Centre, Fochabers; Glenfiddich Distillery, Dufftown; Johnstons Cashmere Visitor Centre, Elgin.

North Ayrshire *N.Ayr.* Population: 139,175.
Unitary authority in central Scotland including the islands of Arran, Great Cumbrae and Little Cumbrae. It is bounded by East Ayrshire, East Renfrewshire, Inverclyde, Renfrewshire, South Ayrshire and the sea. The principal towns are Irvine, Kilwinning, Saltcoats, Largs, Ardrossan, Stevenston and Kirbirnie. The area includes mountains and part of Clyde Muirshiel Regional Park in the N, and the lower lands of Cunninghame in the S. There is a maritime heritage to the area; ferry routes operate from Largs and Ardrossan. Rivers include the Garnock, Dusk Water and Noddsdale Water.
Places of interest: Brodick Castle (NTS); Kelburn Country Centre, near Largs.

North Lanarkshire *N.Lan.* Population: 326,750.
Unitary authority in central Scotland neighbouring East Dunbartonshire, Falkirk, Glasgow, South Lanarkshire, Stirling and West Lothian. The chief centres are Cumbernauld, Coatbridge, Airdrie, Motherwell, Wishaw and Bellshill. North Lanarkshsire contains a mixture of urban and rural areas, and formerly depended heavily upon the coal, engineering and steel industries. Regeneration and diversification have occurred in recent years.
Places of interest: Drumpellier Country Park, Coatbridge; Palacerigg Country Park, Cumbernauld; Strathclyde Country Park, Motherwell; Summerlee Heritage Trust, Coatbridge.

Orkney *Ork.* Population: 19,900.
Group of some fifteen main islands and numerous smaller islands, islets and rocks. Designated an Islands Area for administrative purposes, and lying N of the NE end of the Scottish mainland across the Pentland Firth. Kirkwall is the capital, situated on the island Mainland, 24m/38km N of Duncansby Head. Stromness is the only other town. About twenty of the islands are inhabited. In general the islands are low-lying but have steep, high cliffs on W side. The climate is generally mild for the latitude but storms are frequent. Fishing and farming (mainly cattle-rearing) are the chief industries. The oil industry is also represented, with an oil terminal on the island of Flotta, and oil service bases at Car Ness and Stromness, Mainland and at Lyness, Hoy. Lesser industries include whisky distilling, knitwear and tourism. The islands are noted for their unique prehistoric and archaeological remains. The main airport is at Grimsetter, near Kirkwall, with most of the populated islands being served by airstrips. Ferries also operate from the Scottish mainland, and between islands in the group.
Places of interest: Italian Chapel, Lambholm; Skara Brae.

Perth & Kinross *P. & K.* Population: 131,780.
Unitary authority in Scotland bounded by Aberdeenshire, Angus, Argyll & Bute, Clackmannanshire, Fife, Highland and Stirling. Chief centres are the city of Perth, Blairgowrie, Crieff, Kinross, Auchterarder and Pitlochry. The area is mountainous, containing large areas of remote open moorland, especially in the N and W; the vast upland expanses of Breadalbane, Rannoch and Atholl, form the S edge of the Grampian Mountains. The lower land of the S and E is more heavily populated and is dominated by the ancient city of Perth. The area is rich in history as it links the Highlands to the N with the central belt and lowlands to the S via important mountain passes, most notably the Pass of Dromochter. The area has many castles, and Scottish Kings were traditionally enthroned at Scone Abbey, to the N of Perth. There are many lochs, including Loch Rannoch and Loch Tay. Main industries are tourism and whisky production. The world famous Gleneagles golf course is in the S of the area. Rivers include the Tay, Almond and Earn.
Places of interest: Blair Castle, Blair Atholl; Crieff Visitor Centre; Edradour Distillery, Pitlochry; Glenturret Distillery, Hosh; Hydro-Electrical Visitor Centre & Fish Ladder, Pitlochry; Queen's View Centre, Loch Tummel; Scone Palace, Perth.

Renfrewshire *Renf.* Population: 176,970.
Unitary authority in central Scotland bordering East Renfrewshire, Glasgow, Inverclyde, North Ayrshire, West Dunbartonshire and the Firth of Clyde. Main centres are Paisley, Renfrew, Johnstone, Erskine and Linwood. The area emerges W from the Greater Glasgow periphery into a contrasting countryside of highlands, lochs and glens. Industry is centred on the urban area and includes electronics, engineering, food and drink production and service sectors; in rural areas to the W, agriculture is still important. The W part of the area includes some of Clyde Muirshiels Regional Park; Glasgow Airport is in the E.
Places of interest: Castle Semple Country Park; Gleniffer Braes Country Park, Paisley.

Scottish Borders *Sc.Bord.* Population: 105,300.
Administrative region of SE Scotland bordering Dumfries & Galloway, East Lothian, Midlothian, South Lanarkshire, West Lothian, the English counties of Cumbria and Northumberland and the North Sea. It comprises the former counties of Berwick, Peebles, Roxburgh and Selkirk. Main towns are Hawick, Galashiels, Peebles, Kelso, Selkirk and Jedburgh. It extends from the Tweedsmuir Hills in the W to the North Sea on either side of St. Abb's Head in the E, and from the Pentland, Moorfoot and Lammermuir Hills in the N to the Cheviot Hills and the English border in the S. The fertile area of rich farmland between the hills to N and S is known as The Merse. The area around Peebles and Galashiels is noted for woollen manufacture. Elsewhere, the electronics industry is of growing importance. The River Tweed rises in the extreme W and flows between Kelso and Coldstream, finally passing into England, 4m/6km W of Berwick-upon-Tweed.
Places of interest: Abbotsford House, Melrose; St. Abb's Head.

Shetland *Shet.* Population: 22,522.
Group of over 100 islands, lying beyond Orkney to the NE of the Scottish mainland; Sumburgh Head being about 100m/160km from Duncansby Head. Designated an Islands Area for administrative purposes, the chief islands are Mainland, on which the capital and chief port of Lerwick is situated, Unst and Yell. Some twenty of the islands are inhabited. The islands are mainly low-lying, the highest point being Ronas Hill, on Mainland. The oil industry has made an impact on Shetland, with oil service bases at Lerwick and Sandwick, and a large terminal at Sullom Voe. Other industries include cattle and sheep-rearing, knitwear and fishing. The climate is mild, considering the latitude, but severe storms are frequent. The islands are famous for the small Shetland breed of pony, which is renowned for its strength and hardiness. There is an airport at Sumburgh, on S part of Mainland.
Places of interest: Jarlshof, Sumburgh; Shetland Museum, Lerwick.

South Ayrshire *S.Ayr.* Population: 114,000.
Unitary authority in SW Scotland bounded by Dumfries & Galloway, East Ayrshire, North Ayrshire and the sea. The chief towns are Ayr, Troon, Prestwick, Girvan and Maybole. The area consists of a long coastline, with lowlands surrounding Ayr Bay and higher ground to the S. Agriculture is a major economic activity on the uplands. To the N, aerospace and hi-tech industries are located near Prestwick International Airport and Ayr, the main retail centre. Notable sporting venues include a race course at Ayr and open championship golf courses at Troon and Turnberry. Tourism is a major feature of the local economy. The area was the birthplace of Robert the Bruce and Robert Burns; it contains Scotland's first country park at Culzean Castle; and it has a holiday camp on the coast near Ayr. Rivers include the Ayr, Water of Girvan and Stinchar.
Places of interest: Butlin's Wonderwest World, Ayr; Culzean Castle (NTS); Culzean Country Park (NTS); Tam o'Shanter Experience, Alloway.

South Lanarkshire *S.Lan.* Population: 307,400.
Unitary authority in central Scotland bordering Dumfries & Galloway, East Ayrshire, East Renfrewshire, Glasgow, North Lanarkshire, Scottish Borders and West Lothian. The main towns are East Kilbride, Hamilton, Blantyre, Larkhall, Carluke, Lanark and Bothwell. Urban development is mainly in the N, merging with the SE periphery of Greater Glasgow. The S part is mostly farmland and not highly populated. Tourism is mainly centred on the picturesque valley of the upper Clyde; there is a race course at Hamilton. The area has associations with the industrial philanthropist, Robert Owen, who built a model village at New Lanark. Rivers include the Clyde, Avon and Dippool Water.
Places of interest: Calder Glen Country Park, East Kilbride; Chatelherault Country Park, Hamilton; New Lanark World Heritage Village.

Stirling *Stir.* Population: 82,000.
Unitary authority in central Scotland neighbouring Argyll & Bute, Clackmannanshire, East Dunbartonshire, Falkirk, North Lanarkshire, Perth & Kinross and West Dunbartonshire. The chief centres are Stirling, the ancient cathedral city of Dunblane, Bannockburn, Bridge of Allan and Callander. The fertile agricultural lands of the Forth valley are in the centre of the area, bounded by mountains: The Trossachs and the mountain peaks of Ben Lomond, Ben More and Ben Lui in the N, while in the S are the Campsie Fells. Tourism is an important industry with Stirling including many sites of historical significance to Scotland, particularly during the struggle to retain independence. There are associations with Rob Roy, and the battle site of Bannockburn. Other features include The Trossachs, part of the Loch Lomond Regional Park and the Queen Elizabeth Forest Park. There are several lochs, including Loch Lomond, which forms part of the W border, and Loch Katrine. Scotland's only lake named as such, Lake of Menteith, is also in Stirling. The main river is the Forth.
Places of interest: Argyll & Sutherland Highlanders Museum; Bannockburn Heritage Centre; Blair Drummond Safari Park; Breadalbane Folklore Centre, Killin; Mugdock Country Park, Milngavie; Queen Elizabeth Forest Park, Aberfoyle; Rob Roy & Trossachs Visitor Centre, Callander; Royal Burgh of Stirling Visitor Centre; Stirling Castle; Wallace Monument, Causewayhead.

West Dunbartonshire *W.Dun.* Population: 97,790.
Unitary authority in central Scotland bordered by Argyll & Bute, East Dunbartonshire, Glasgow, Inverclyde, Renfrewshire and Stirling. The chief towns are Clydebank, Dumbarton, Alexandria and Bonhill. The area is mountainous, containing the Kilpatrick Hills, and is bounded by Loch Lomond in the N and the Firth of Clyde in the S. The urban SE area of West Dunbartonshire forms part of the NW periphery of Greater Glasgow. There is a broad base of light manufacturing and service sector industries. Tourism and leisure are a feature, with the SE tip of Loch Lomond Regional Park and the whole of Balloch Castle Country Park falling within the area. West Dunbartonshire includes the Erskine Bridge which spans the River Clyde, other rivers include the Leven.
Places of interest: Balloch Castle Country Park; Dumbarton Castle.

West Lothian *W.Loth.* Population: 147,870.
Unitary authority in central Scotland neighbouring Edinburgh, Falkirk, Midlothian, North Lanarkshire, Scottish Borders and South Lanarkshire. The chief towns are Livingston, Bathgate, Linlithgow, Broxburn, Whitburn and Armadale. The area undulates to the S of the Firth of Forth, and rises to moorland at the foot of the Pentland Hills in the S. The main urban areas are situated along commuter corridors between Glasgow, Edinburgh and Falkirk; elsewhere the area is mostly rural. Hi-tech and computing industries are in evidence.
Places of interest: Almondell & Calderwood Country Park, East Calder; Beecraigs Country Park, Linlithgow; Muiravonside Country Park, Linlithgow; Polkemmet Country Park, Whitburn.

Western Isles (Na h-Eileanan an Iar. Also known as Outer Hebrides.) *W.Isles* Population: 27,815.
String of islands off the W coast of Scotland and separated from Skye and the mainland by The Minch. They extend for some 130m/209km from Butt of Lewis in the N, to Barra Head in the S. Stornoway, situated on the Isle of Lewis, is the main town; elsewhere, there are mainly scattered coastal villages and settlements. The chief islands are Isle of Lewis, North Uist, Benbecula, South Uist and Barra. North Harris and South Harris form significant areas in the S part of the Isle of Lewis. The topography of the islands consists of undulating moorland, mountains and lochs. The main industries are fishing, grazing and, on the Isle of Lewis, tweed manufacture. There are airfields with scheduled passenger flights on the Isle of Lewis, Benbecula and Barra.
Places of interest: An Lanntair Gallery, Stornoway; Calanais

A' Bheinn Bhan *High.* ***Mountain***, 4m/7km NW of Sallachan Point, Lochaber district. Height 1565 feet or 477 metres. **38 B3** NM9466.
A' Bhrideanach *High.* ***Coastal feature***, headland on westernmost point of Rum. **47 F5** NM2999.
A' Bhuidheanach *High.* ***Mountain***, in Badenoch and Strathspey district 3m/5km W of head of Loch Laggan. Height 3172 feet or 967 metres. NN4890.
A' Bhuidheanach *High.* ***Mountain***, in Badenoch and Strathspey district, close to border with Perth & Kinross, 4m/6km S of Dalwhinnie. Height 2867 feet or 874 metres. NN6579.
A' Bhuidheanach Bheag ***Mountain***, on border of Highland and Perth & Kinross, 1m/2km S of A' Bhuidheanach. Munro: height 3070 feet or 936 metres. **40 B2** NN6677.
A' Bhuidheanaich *High.* ***Mountain***, in Badenoch and Strathspey district, 5m/8km NE of Kingussie. Height 2391 feet or 729 metres. **51 G4** NH7708.
A' Chailleach *High.* ***Mountain***, in Ross and Cromarty district 2m/3km S of Loch a' Bhraoin. Munro: height 3277 feet or 999 metres. **60 A2** NH1371.
A' Chailleach *High.* ***Mountain***, in Monadhliath range, in Badenoch and Strathspey district, 5m/8km NW of Kingussie. Munro: height 3050 feet or 930 metres. **51 F4** NH6804.
A' Chearc *W.Isles Gaelic form of Chicken Rock, qv.*
A' Chill *High.* ***Settlement***, on S coast of Canna, to W of Canna harbour opposite Sanday. **47 F4** NG2605.
A' Chleit *High.* ***Island***, rocky islet 2m/3km off Kirkaig Point on W coast of Sutherland district near Lochinver. **70 C2** NC0320.
A' Chràlaig (Anglicised form: Cralic. Also known as Garbh Leac). *High.* ***Mountain***, on border of Inverness and Skye and Lochalsh districts, 3m/5km NE of head of Loch Cluanie. Munro: height 3674 feet or 1120 metres. **49 G3** NH0914.
A' Chrannag *Arg. & B.* ***Hill***, on Ulva, 1m/2km W of easternmost point of island. Height 387 feet or 118 metres. **28 D1** NM4338.
A' Chrois *Arg. & B.* ***Mountain***, in Argyll 2m/3km N of head of Loch Long. Height 2785 feet or 849 metres. **31 E4** NN2807.
A' Chruach ***Inland physical feature***, ridge on border of Perth & Kinross and Highland between Blackwater Reservoir and Loch Laidon. Summit is Stob na Cruaiche, 2420 feet or 738 metres. **39 F4** NN3657.
A' Chruach *Arg. & B.* ***Mountain***, 5m/8km E of Kilninver. Height 1207 feet or 368 metres. **30 B2** NM9021.
A' Chruach *High.* ***Mountain***, 1m/2km S of Inverie, Lochaber district. Height 1296 feet or 395 metres. **49 D5** NM7797.
A' Chruach *N.Ayr.* ***Mountain***, on Arran, 3m/5km SW of Brodick. Height 1679 feet or 512 metres. **13 E2** NR9633.
A' Chùli *Arg. & B.* ***Island***, one of the Garvellachs group of islands in Firth of Lorn. Lies between Eileach an Naoimh and Garbh Eileach. **29 F3** NM6511.
A' Ghairbhe *High.* ***River***, flowing NE out of Loch Clair through Kinlochewe, just N of which it joins Abhainn Bruachaig to form Kinlochewe River. **59 G4** NH0362.
A' Ghlas-bheinn *High.* ***Mountain***, 4m/7km E of head of Loch Duich in Skye and Lochalsh district. Munro: height 3011 feet or 918 metres. **49 G2** NH0023.
A' Ghoil *High.* ***Island***, on W side of mouth of Kyle of Durness. **74 C1** NC3472.
A' Mhaighdean (Anglicised form: The Maiden.) *High.* ***Mountain***, summit in S part of Fisherfield Forest, Ross and Cromarty district. Munro: height 3172 feet or 967 metres. **59 G2** NH0074.
A' Mharconaich *High.* ***Mountain***, in Dalnaspidal Forest, 5m/8km SW of Dalwhinnie. Munro: height 3198 feet or 975 metres. **40 B2** NN6076.
A' Mhòine *High.* ***Locality***, on borders of Caithness and Sutherland districts, between Kyle of Tongue and Loch Eriboll, consisting of upland tract. **75 E2** NC5361.
Abbey and Trout Farm *Sc.Bord.* ***Other feature of interest***, at Abbey St. Bathans, 4m/6km SW of Grantshouse. **27 E3** NT7562.
Abbey Green *S.Lan. Alternative name for Lesmahagow, qv.*
Abbey Head *D. & G.* ***Coastal feature***, headland 3m/4km S of Dundrennan. **4 A2** NX7343.
Abbey St. Bathans *Sc.Bord.* ***Village***, on River Whiteadder, 5m/8km N of Duns. Church incorporates fragments of 13c nunnery. **27 E3** NT7562.
Abbeyhill *Edin.* ***Suburb***, 1m/2km E of Edinburgh city centre. NT2774.
Abbotrule *Sc.Bord.* ***Hamlet***, 2m/3km NE of Bonchester Bridge. **18 A5** NT6012.
Abbotsford House *Sc.Bord.* ***Historic house***, mansion erected by Sir Walter Scott on S bank of River Tweed, 2m/4km W of Melrose. Scott lived and died here. **17 G2** NT5034.
Abbotsinch Airport *Renf. Former name of Glasgow Airport, qv.*
Aberarder *High.* ***Settlement***, on NW side of Loch Laggan, 4m/6km W of Kinloch Laggan. **39 G1** NN4787.
Aberarder House *High.* ***Settlement***, 6m/9km SE of Dores. **51 F2** NH6225.
Aberargie *P. & K.* ***Village***, 2m/3km W of Abernethy. **33 G3** NO1615.
Aberchalder *High.* ***Settlement***, at NE end of Loch Oich, 5m/7km SW of Fort Augustus. **50 C4** NH3403.
Aberchalder Burn *High.* ***River***, formed by tributaries on slopes of Carn na Saobhaidhe and flowing NW into Loch Mhòr at Wester Aberchalder. **51 E3** NH5420.
Aberchirder *Aber.* Population: 1097. ***Village***, 8m/13km SW of Banff. **64 B4** NJ6252.
Abercorn *W.Loth.* ***Settlement***, on S side of Firth of Forth, 3m/5km W of Forth Road Bridge. **25 E2** NT0878.
Abercorn Church *W.Loth.* ***Ecclesiastical building***, to NW of Abercorn Deer Park, 3m/4km W of Queensferry. Present building dates from 12c; built on site of 7c monastery. **25 E2** NT0879.
Abercrombie *Fife* ***Settlement***, 1m/2km NW of St. Monans. **34 D4** NO5102.
Aberdalgie *P. & K.* ***Settlement***, 3m/5km SW of Perth. **33 F2** NO0720.
Aberdeen *Aberdeen* Population: 189,707. ***City***, cathedral and university city and commercial centre on E coast 57m/92km NE of Dundee. Known as 'The Granite City', local stone having been used in many of its buildings. By 13c, Aberdeen had become an important centre for trade and fishing and remains a major port and commercial base. In 19c ship building brought great prosperity to the city. These industries had receded by mid 20c but the city's prospects were transformed when North Sea oil was discovered in 1970, turning it into a city of great wealth. St. Machar's Cathedral at Old Aberdeen. Many museums and art galleries. Extensive flower gardens. Airport at Dyce, 6m/9km NW of Aberdeen. **55 E4** NJ9406.
Aberdeen Airport (Formerly known as Dyce Airport.) *Aberdeen* ***Airport/airfield***, international airport on S side of River Don, 6m/9km NW of Aberdeen. **55 D3** NJ8712.
Aberdeen Art Gallery *Aberdeen* ***Other feature of interest***, art gallery in Schoolhill, Aberdeen, with English and French paintings and a Henry Moore sculpture. British artists represented include Spencer, Nash and Bacon. **55 E4** NJ9307.
Aberdeen Maritime Museum *Aberdeen* ***Other feature of interest***, museum in Shiprow, Aberdeen, commemorating sea-faring history of Aberdeen, from harbour and port to offshore oil industry base. Exhibition features 8.5 metre high model of oil platform. Building includes Provost Ross's House. **55 E4** NJ9306.
Aberdour *Fife* Population: 1524. ***Small town***, resort on N shore of Firth of Forth, 3m/4km W of Burntisland. Remains of 14c castle (Historic Scotland). 12c St. Colomba's Abbey is sited on Inchcolm Island, just off shore. **25 F1** NT1985.
Aberdour Bay *Aber.* ***Bay***, on N coast of Buchan district, N of New Aberdour. **65 D3** NJ8965.
Aberdour Castle *Fife* ***Castle***, 14c castle (Historic Scotland) with 16c-17c additions in Aberdour, on N shore of Firth of Forth. Former home of Earl of Moray, then Douglas family. Circular dovecote. **25 F1** NT1985.
Aberfeldy *P. & K.* Population: 1748. ***Small town***, astride Urlar Burn near its confluence with River Tay, 8m/13km SW of Pitlochry. Distillery. St. Mary's Church (Historic Scotland), 3m/4km NE, is 16c parish church with finely painted wooden ceiling. **41 D5** NN8549.
Aberfoyle *Stir.* ***Village***, 8m/13km SW of Callander. Situated on River Forth between Achray and Loch Ard Forests and below SW end of Menteith Hills. **32 A4** NN5201.
Abergeldie Castle *Aber.* ***Castle***, 16c castle with 19c additions, on S bank of River Dee, 2m/3km E of Balmoral Castle. NO2895.
Aberlady *E.Loth.* ***Village***, on Aberlady Bay, 6m/10km SW of North Berwick. **26 B1** NT4679.
Aberlady Bay *E.Loth.* ***Nature reserve***, on Firth of Forth 6m/10km SW of North Berwick. **26 B1** NT4679.
Aberlemno *Angus* ***Village***, 5m/8km NE of Forfar. Aberlemno Sculptured Stones (Historic Scotland) in churchyard. **42 D4** NO5255.
Aberlemno Sculptured Stones *Angus* ***Historic/prehistoric site***, upright cross slab (Historic Scotland) with Pictish symbols and combat relief in churchyard at Aberlemno, 2m/3km SE of Finavon. Three other stones by B9134 road nearby. **42 D4** NO5255.
Aberlour *Moray Alternative name for Charlestown of Aberlour, qv.*
Abernethy *P. & K.* ***Village***, 3m/5km W of Newburgh. Round tower (Historic Scotland). Remains of Roman fortress and naval base to NE in grounds of Carpow, near S bank of River Tay. **33 G3** NO1916.
Abernethy Forest *High.* ***Forest/woodland***, coniferous forest 6m/10km S of Grantown-on-Spey in Badenoch and Strathspey district. **52 B3** NJ9917.
Abernethy Round Tower *P. & K.* ***Historic/prehistoric site***, tower (Historic Scotland) with lower part dating from 9c and upper part from late 11c, at SE side of Abernethy; height 74 feet or nearly 23 metres. **33 G3** NO1916.
Abernyte *P. & K.* ***Village***, 9m/14km W of Dundee. **34 A1** NO2531.
Aberscross *High.* ***Locality***, 1m/2km NW of head of Loch Fleet. **72 C4** NC7600.
Abersky *High.* ***Settlement***, 5m/8km S of Dores. **51 E2** NH5926.
Aberuthven *P. & K.* ***Village***, on Ruthven Water, 3m/4km NE of Auchterader. **33 E3** NN9715.
Abhainn a' Chadh' Bhuidhe *High.* ***River***, rising between Meallan Chuaich and Groban, flowing S, then E into NW part of Loch Fannich. **60 A3** NH1567.
Abhainn a' Choire *High.* ***River***, rising below Meallan a' Chuail, flowing through Loch Dubh a' Chuail, then flowing SE into Loch Shin. **71 F2** NC3625.
Abhainn a' Ghiubhais Li *High.* ***River***, flowing E from N slopes of Meall Gorm to confluence with Allt an Loch Sgeirich, forming Abhainn an Torrain Duibh. NH2672.
Abhainn a' Ghlinne Bhig *High.* ***River***, in Lochaber district running W into Sound of Sleat, 1m/2km SW of Glenelg. NG8018.
Abhainn a' Ghlinne Bhig *High.* ***River***, forming border between Ross and Cromarty and Sutherland districts. Formed from streams flowing down N slopes of Beinn Dearg massif and running E into Abhainn a' Ghlinne Mhòir just N of Meall a' Chaorainn. **60 C1** NH3684.
Abhainn a' Ghlinne Ghil *High.* ***River***, in Lochaber district, running W to River Aline 4m/6km N of Lochaline. NM6950.
Abhainn a' Ghlinne Mhòir *High.* ***River***, fed by Abhainn a' Ghlinne Bhig and flowing NE along Gleann Mòr to confluence with Alladale River, 3m/4km SW of The Craigs, Sutherland district. NH4489.
Abhainn an Fhasaigh *High.* ***River***, flowing SW from SE end of Lochan Fada, down Gleann Bianasdail, and into SE end of Loch Maree. **59 G3** NH0165.
Abhainn an Lòin *High.* ***River***, flowing W into Loch Stack, Sutherland district. **74 C4** NC3042.
Abhainn an t-Srath Chuileannaich *High.* ***River***, in Sutherland district, running SE along Strath Cuileannaich before becoming Black Water, S of Croick and flowing into Strathcarron 8m/13km W of Bonar Bridge. **71 G5** NH4393.
Abhainn an t-Srathain *High.* ***River***, in Sutherland district running NW to confluence with Lón Mòr at head of Strath Shinary. **74 B2** NC2363.
Abhainn an t-Stratha Charnaig *High.* ***River***, issuing from Loch Buidhe in Sutherland district, and flowing E along Srath Carnaig, passing over Torboll Falls, to confluence with River Fleet, 1m/2km NW of head of Loch Fleet. NH7598.
Abhainn Beinn nan Eun *High.* ***River***, rising in Kildermorie Forest, Ross and Cromarty district, and flowing S, then E, to enter W end of Loch Glass. **60 D2** NH4873.
Abhainn Bhearnais *High.* ***River***, flowing SW into Loch an Laoigh and forming boundary between Ross and Cromarty and Skye and Lochalsh districts. **59 G5** NH0343.
Abhainn Bhuidheach *High.* ***River***, flowing S into head of Loch Carron. **59 F5** NG9242.
Abhainn Bruachaig *High.* ***River***, in Ross and Cromarty district, flowing from Heights of Kinlochewe SW to Kinlochewe, where it joins with A' Ghairbhe to form Kinlochewe River. **59 G3** NH0362.
Abhainn Chuaig *High.* ***River***, flowing NW to W coast of Ross and Cromarty district, 2m/3km SW of Rubha na Fearn and entrance to Loch Torridon. **58 D4** NG7058.
Abhainn Chuil (Anglicised form: Coll.) *W.Isles* ***River***, on Isle of Lewis flowing SE into Loch a' Tuath between Col and Col Uarach. NB4639.
Abhainn Crò Chlach *High.* ***River***, running NE from N slopes of Carn Bàn into River Findhorn, 9m/15km NW of Kingussie. **51 F4** NH6512.
Abhainn Cuileig *High.* ***River***, flowing NE from Loch a' Bhraoin into River Broom, 1km NW of Corrieshalloch Gorge. **60 A2** NH1979.
Abhainn Dalach ***River***, running SE into Loch Etive, Argyll, 5m/8km NE of narrows at Bonawe. **38 C5** NN0538.
Abhainn Deabhag *High.* ***River***, formed at confluence of Féith na Leitreach and Allt Riabhach, and flowing NE to confluence with River Affric to form River Glass. **50 B2** NH3022.
Abhainn Dearg *High.* ***River***, flowing into S end of Loch Damh, Ross and Cromarty district. **59 E5** NG8647.
Abhainn Droma *High.* ***River***, rising in Loch Droma and flowing NW through Dirrie More to its confluence with Abhainn Cuileig to form River Broom. **60 B2** NH1979.
Abhainn Dubh *High.* ***River***, rising on mountains S of Loch Lundie and flowing N through loch into Loch Shieldaig, 7m/11km W of Torridon, Ross and Cromarty district. **59 D4** NG7854.

Abhainn Dubh *High.* ***River***, flowing E from Loch an Fhiarlaid into W end of Loch a' Chroisg, 4m/6km W of Achnasheen. **59 G4** NH0957.
Abhainn Duibhe ***River***, running NE down Gleann Duibhe to River Gaur below Loch Eigheach. **39 G5** NN4656.
Abhainn Fionain *Arg. & B.* ***River***, flowing E into Loch Awe, 3m/5km NE of Dalavich. **30 B3** NN0017.
Abhainn Gaoire *P. & K. Gaelic form of (River) Gaur, qv.*
Abhainn Ghriais *W.Isles Gaelic form of Gress (river), qv.*
Abhainn Ghuilbinn *High.* ***River***, running from Loch Ghuilbinn and flowing into Loch Laggan Reservoir 5m/8km E of Tulloch Station. **39 G2** NN4282.
Abhainn Glac an t-Seilich *High.* ***River***, rising N of Garbhan Mòr and flowing SW into Black Water at head of Strath Rusdale. **61 E1** NH5678.
Abhainn Inbhir Ghuiserein *High. See Gleann na Guiserein.*
Abhainn Mhòr Ceann Resort *W.Isles* ***River***, rising in Forest of Harris and flowing N through two adjoining lochs into head of Loch Resort. NB1017.
Abhainn Mòr *Arg. & B.* ***River***, in Knapdale, flowing SW into Loch Caolisport 1m/2km NE of Knapdale Head. **21 F2** NR7275.
Abhainn na Coinnich *High.* ***River***, in Lochaber district running SE from Loch Uisge to Loch a' Choire. NM8452.
Abhainn na Frithe *High.* ***River***, in Sutherland district, flowing E and joining River Helmsdale 2m/3km S of Burnfoot. **72 D2** NC8726.
Abhainn na Glasa *High.* ***River***, rising on E slopes of Beinn a' Chaisteil and flowing circuitously, but generally E then SE through Gleann Mhuire and into Loch Morie. **61 D1** NH5177.
Abhainn Poiblidh *High.* ***River***, flowing NE from Loch an Daimh into Rappach Water. **71 E5** NH3197.
Abhainn Rath *High.* ***River***, in Lochaber district running E to head of Loch Treig. **39 E3** NN3168.
Abhainn Righ *High.* ***River***, in Lochaber district running W down Glen Righ to Loch Linnhe, 1m/2km NW of Onich. Series of waterfalls nearly 1m/2km above mouth. **38 C3** NN0162.
Abhainn Sgeamhaidh *High.* ***River***, flowing SW to join River Tirry SW of Rhian, Sutherland district. **72 A3** NC5516.
Abhainn Strath na Sealga *High.* ***River***, running NW down Strath na Sealga into head of Loch na Sealga in W part of Ross and Cromarty district. **59 G1** NH0680.
Abhainnsuidhe (Also known as Amhuinnsuidhe.) *W.Isles* ***Locality***, on coast of North Harris, on N side of West Loch Tarbert, 2m/3km E of Gobhaig. **66 C3** NB0408.
Abington *S.Lan.* ***Village***, on River Clyde, 11m/18km SW of Biggar. **16 A3** NS9323.
Abington Services *S.Lan.* ***Other building***, motorway service station on M74, to N of Abington. **16 A3** NS9225.
Aboyne *Aber.* Population: 2067. ***Village***, on N bank of River Dee, 10m/16km E of Ballater, with Loch of Aboyne 1m/2km to NE. **54 A5** NO5298.
Abriachan *High.* ***Settlement***, on W side of Loch Ness, Inverness district, 3m/5km from NE end of loch. **51 E1** NH5535.
Abronhill *N.Lan.* ***Suburb***, 1m/2km NE of Cumbernauld town centre. **24 B2** NS7875.
Abune-the-Hill *Ork.* ***Settlement***, 1km S of N coast of Mainland. **80 A4** HY2828.
Accurrach *Arg. & B.* ***Settlement***, 8m/12km N of Inveraray. **30 D3** NN1120.
Acha *Arg. & B.* ***Settlement***, on Coll, 3m/5km SW of Arinagour. **36 A4** NM1854.
Achacha *Arg. & B.* ***Settlement***, 1km SW of Barcaldine. **38 B5** NM9440.
Achadacaie *Arg. & B.* ***Settlement***, on SE side of West Loch Tarbert, 4m/6km SW of Tarbert. **21 G3** NR8363.
Achadh-chaorrunn *Arg. & B.* ***Settlement***, on NW side of West Loch Tarbert, 9m/14km SW of Tarbert. **21 F4** NR7559.
Achadh Mòr (Anglicised form: Achmore.) *W.Isles* ***Village***, on Isle of Lewis, 8m/12km W of Stornoway. **69 E5** NB3029.
Achadophris *High.* ***Locality***, on E side of Loch Shin in Sutherland district, 4m/6km N of Lairg. NC5611.
Achadun Bay *Arg. & B.* ***Bay***, small bay on N coast of Lismore, in Loch Linnhe, 3m/5km W of Achnacroish. NM8039.
Achadun Castle *Arg. & B.* ***Castle***, remains of castle on N coast of Lismore in Loch Linnhe, 3m/5km W of Achnacroish. **30 A1** NM8039.
Achadunan *Arg. & B.* ***Settlement***, at SW end of Glen Fyne, 2m/3km NE of Cairndow. **31 D3** NN1913.
Achagavel *High.* ***Settlement***, near head of Gleann Dubh, 3m/4km SW of Liddesdale, Lochaber district. **37 G4** NM7656.
Achaglachgach Forest *Arg. & B.* ***Forest/woodland***, on Knapdale, on NW side of West Loch Tarbert. **21 F3** NR7861.
Achaglass *Arg. & B.* ***Settlement***, on Kintyre, 3m/5km S of Tayinloan. **21 F5** NR7041.
Achahoish *Arg. & B.* ***Village***, in Knapdale, Argyll, at head of Loch Caolisport and 7m/11km SW of Ardrishaig. **21 F2** NR7877.
Achairn Burn *High.* ***River***, in Caithness district, rising on Hill of Toftgun and flowing N, then E, briefly disappearing underground before flowing N to join Wick River, 3m/4km W of Wick. **77 E4** ND3252.
Achalader *P. & K.* ***Settlement***, 3m/5km W of Blairgowrie. **41 G5** NO1245.
Achaleven *Arg. & B.* ***Settlement***, on S shore of Loch Etive, Argyll, 1km E of Connel. NM9234.
Achallader *Arg. & B.* ***Settlement***, 3m/5km NE of Bridge of Orchy. **39 F5** NN3244.
Achallader Castle *Arg. & B.* ***Castle***, ruined castle in Argyll, 1m/2km E of NE corner of Loch Tulla. Ancient stronghold of Fletchers and later of Campbells; here massacre of Glencoe is said to have been planned. NN3244.
Achamore *Arg. & B.* ***Locality***, on E coast of Jura, 3m/5km NE of Ardfernal. **21 D2** NR5876.
Achamore Gardens *Arg. & B.* ***Garden***, on Gigha Island, developed over last 40 years, containing rhododendrons, camellias and many subtropical plants. **21 E5** NR6447.
Achanalt *High.* ***Locality***, in Ross and Cromarty district, 4m/6km W of head of Loch Luichart. NH2561.
Achandunie *High.* ***Settlement***, 1m/2km N of Alness. **61 F2** NH6472.
Achany *High.* ***Settlement***, to W of River Shin, 3m/5km S of Lairg. **72 A4** NC5601.
Achany Glen *High.* ***Valley***, carrying River Shin S from Loch Shin into Kyle of Sutherland. **72 A4** NC5703.
Achaphubuil *High.* ***Settlement***, 2m/3km NW of Fort William across head of Loch Awe. **38 C2** NN0876.
Acharacle *High.* ***Village***, in Lochaber district, 2m/4km N of Salen. **37 F3** NM6767.
Achargary *High.* ***Settlement***, on River Naver, 4m/7km S of Bettyhill, Caithness district. **75 G3** NC7154.
Acharn *Arg. & B.* ***Settlement***, in Glen Kinglass, 6m/10km NW of Dalmally. **30 D1** NN1235.
Acharn *P. & K.* ***Village***, on S shore of Loch Tay at foot of Acharn Burn, 2m/3km SW of Kenmore. **40 C5** NN7543.
Acharn Burn *P. & K.* ***River***, flowing into Loch Tay 2m/3km SW of Kenmore. Falls of Acharn, cascade nearly 1km S. **32 C1** NN7543.
Acharosson *Arg. & B.* ***Settlement***, 4m/6km NW of Tighnabruaich. **22 A2** NR9377.
Achateny *High.* ***Locality***, near N coast of Ardnamurchan peninsula, in Lochaber district, 7m/12km E of Point of Ardnamurchan. **37 E3** NM5270.
Achath *Aber.* ***Settlement***, 2m/3km NW of Dunecht. **54 C3** NJ7310.
Achavanich *High.* ***Locality***, in Caithness district, 6m/10km NW of Lybster. **77 D4** ND1742.
Achdalieu Lodge *High. See Loch Eil Centre.*
Achduart *High.* ***Settlement***, 1km E of Rubha Dubh Ard, Ross and Cromarty district. **70 C4** NC0403.
Achentoul *High.* ***Settlement***, in Sutherland district, 1m/2km N of Kinbrace. **76 A5** NC8733.
Achentoul Forest *High.* ***Forest/woodland***, tract in Sutherland district to N of Kinbrace. **76 A5** NC8638.
Achfary *High.* ***Settlement***, in Sutherland district, at lower end of Loch More. **74 B4** NC2939.
Achgarve *High.* ***Settlement***, 1m/2km NW of Laide, Ross and Cromarty district. **70 A5** NG8893.
Achiemore *High.* ***Settlement***, on W side of Kyle of Durness where it opens out to include Balnakeil Bay. **74 C2** NC3567.
Achiemore *High.* ***Settlement***, on E bank of Halladale River, 4m/6km S of Melvich. **76 A3** NC8958.
Achies *High.* ***Settlement***, 3m/4km S of Halkirk. **76 D3** ND1355.
Achiltibuie *High.* ***Village***, on NW coast of Ross and Cromarty district, 10m/16km NW of Ullapool. Location of The Hydroponicum. **70 C4** NC0208.
Achina *High.* ***Settlement***, near N coast of Caithness district, 1km S of Bettyhill. **75 G2** NC7060.
Achindown *High.* ***Settlement***, 1m/2km S of Cawdor. **62 A5** NH8348.
Achinduich *High.* ***Settlement***, 4m/6km S of Lairg, on E side of Achany Glen. **72 A4** NC5800.
Achingills *High.* ***Locality***, 3m/4km NE of Halkirk. Includes a number of scattered dwellings. **77 D2** ND1663.
Achinhoan Head *Arg. & B.* ***Coastal feature***, headland on E coast of Kintyre 4m/6km SE of Campbeltown. NR7617.
Achintee *High.* ***Settlement***, in Ross and Cromarty district, at head of Loch Carron. **59 F5** NG9441.
Achintee House *High.* ***Settlement***, in valley of River Nevis, 1m/2km SE of Fort William. **38 D2** NN1272.
Achintraid *High.* ***Locality***, at head of Loch Kishorn, Ross and Cromarty district. **49 E1** NG8438.
Achlean *High.* ***Settlement***, 6m/10km SE of Kingussie. **52 A5** NN8597.
Achleanan *High.* ***Settlement***, in Lochaber district, 1km SE of Drimnin. **37 E4** NM5654.
Achleek *High.* ***Settlement***, on S shore of Loch Sunart, 2m/3km SW of Strontian across loch. **37 G4** NM7959.
Achlian *Arg. & B.* ***Settlement***, near N end of Loch Awe, 3m/5km SW of Dalmally. **30 D2** NN1224.
Achluachrach *High.* ***Locality***, in Glen Spean, Lochaber district, 2m/4km E of Roybridge. NN3081.
Achlyness *High.* ***Settlement***, 1km NW of Rhiconich, at head of Loch Inchard, W coast of Sutherland district. **74 B3** NC2452.
Achmelvich *High.* ***Locality***, on W coast of Sutherland district, 2m/4km NW of Lochinver. **70 C2** NC0624.
Achmelvich Bay *High.* ***Bay***, NW of Achmelvich, 3m/5km NW of Lochinver. **70 C2** NC0525.
Achmony *High.* ***Settlement***, 1km NW of Drumnadrochit. **51 D1** NH5030.
Achmore *High.* ***Hamlet***, in Skye and Lochalsh district, 1m/2km SW of Stromeferry. **49 E1** NG8533.
Achmore *High.* ***Settlement***, on SW side of Annat Bay, 6m/10km NW of Ullapool. Access via ferry from Badluarach on S shore of Little Loch Broom, followed by overland tracks. **70 C5** NH0296.
Achmore *Stir.* ***Settlement***, 1km E of Killin across River Dochart. **32 A1** NN5832.
Achmore *W.Isles Anglicised form of Achadh Mòr, qv.*
Achnaba *Arg. & B.* ***Settlement***, on NW shore of Loch Fyne, 3m/4km SE of Lochgilphead. **22 A1** NR9085.
Achnabat *High.* ***Settlement***, 3m/5km S of Dores. **51 E1** NH5930.
Achnabourin *High.* ***Settlement***, 2m/3km S of Bettyhill, Caithness district. **75 G3** NC7058.
Achnabreck Cup and Ring Marks *Arg. & B.* ***Historic/prehistoric site***, Britain's largest site for rock carvings with 135 well-preserved Bronze Age cup and ring marks (Historic Scotland), 1m/2km N of Lochgilphead. Great range of techniques from rudimentary to skilled work. **30 A5** NR8590.
Achnacairn *Arg. & B.* ***Settlement***, on N shore of Loch Etive, 1m/2km NE of North Connel. **30 B1** NM9235.
Achnacarnin *High.* ***Settlement***, 3m/4km SE of Point of Stoer, W coast of Sutherland district. **70 C1** NC0431.
Achnacarry *High.* ***Settlement***, in Lochaber district, between Loch Lochy and foot of Loch Arkaig. Home of Camerons of Lochiel. NN1787.
Achnaclerach *High.* ***Settlement***, in valley of Black Water, 3m/4km N of Garve. **60 D3** NH4065.
Achnacloich *Arg. & B.* ***Settlement***, 3m/4km E of Connel. **30 B1** NM9533.
Achnacloich *High.* ***Settlement***, near W coast of Sleat peninsula, Skye, 1km S of Tarskavaig. **48 B4** NG5908.
Achnaclyth *High.* ***Settlement***, to N of Dunbeath Water, 5m/8km NW of Dunbeath. **76 C5** ND0933.
Achnacraig *Arg. & B.* ***Settlement***, on NE bank of River Bellart, 4m/6km NE of Fanmore, Mull. **37 D5** NM4747.
Achnacroish *Arg. & B.* ***Village***, with landing stage, halfway along E coast of Lismore in Loch Linnhe. **38 A5** NM8540.
Achnadrish *Arg. & B.* ***Settlement***, on Mull, 1m/2km E of Dervaig. **37 D4** NM4551.
Achnafalnich *Arg. & B.* ***Settlement***, in Glen Orchy, 4m/6km NE of Dalmally. **31 E2** NN2129.
Achnafauld *P. & K.* ***Settlement***, 9m/14km N of Crieff. **33 D1** NN8736.
Achnafree Craig *P. & K.* ***Mountain***, rising to over 720 metres, 9m/14km NE of Comrie. **32 C1** NN8034.
Achnagairn *High.* ***Settlement***, 2m/3km SE of Beauly. **61 E5** NH5544.
Achnagarron *High.* ***Locality***, in Ross and Cromarty district, 2m/3km NW of Invergordon. **61 F2** NH6870.
Achnaha *High.* ***Settlement***, on Ardnamurchan peninsula, 3m/5km NW of Kilchoan. **37 D3** NM4668.
Achnaha *High.* ***Settlement***, 2m/3km W of Lochaline, Lochaber district. **37 F5** NM6445.
Achnahaird Bay *High.* ***Sea feature***, inlet in Enard Bay, NW coast of Ross and Cromarty district, 4m/6km SE of Rubha Coigeach. NC0114.
Achnahanat *High.* ***Settlement***, in Sutherland district, 7m/12km NW of Bonar Bridge. **72 A5** NH5198.
Achnahannet *High.* ***Settlement***, 2m/3km NW of Dulnain Bridge. **52 B2** NH9727.
Achnairn *High.* ***Settlement***, on E side of Loch Shin in Sutherland district, 4m/7km N of Lairg. NC5512.
Achnalea *High.* ***Settlement***, 2m/3km E of Strontian, Lochaber district. **38 A3** NM8586.
Achnamara *Arg. & B.* ***Settlement***, on inlet on E side of Loch Sween in Knapdale, Argyll, 5m/7km S of Crinan. **21 F1** NR7787.
Achnanellan *High.* ***Settlement***, on S shore of Loch Shiel, 4m/7km NE of Salen. **37 G3** NM7467.
Achnasaul *High.* ***Settlement***, on N side of E end of Loch Arkaig, 1m/2km NW of Achnacarry across loch. **39 D1** NN1589.
Achnasheen *High.* ***Village***, at head of Strath Bran in Ross and Cromarty district. **60 A4** NH1658.
Achnashellach *High.* ***Settlement***, with lodge and railway station, in Glen Carron, Ross and Cromarty district, at NE end of Loch Dùghaill. **59 G5** NH0048.
Achnashellach Forest *High.* ***Open space***, deer forest astride Glen Carron. **59 G5** NH0048.
Achnashelloch *Arg. & B.* ***Settlement***, 3m/4km NW of Lochgilphead. **30 A5** NR8591.
Achnastank *Moray* ***Settlement***, 5m/8km SW of Dufftown. **53 E1** NJ2733.

Achorn *High.* ***Settlement***, 2m/3km W of Dunbeath. **76 D5** ND1330.
Achosnich *High.* ***Settlement***, 5m/8km NW of Dornoch. **72 C5** NH7293.
Achosnich *High.* ***Settlement***, on Ardnamurchan peninsula, 3m/5km NW of Kilchoan. **36 D3** NM4467.
Achranich *High.* ***Locality***, in Lochaber district, near mouth of Rannoch River at head of Loch Aline. NM7047.
Achray Forest *Stir.* ***Forest/woodland***, surrounding Loch Achray, W of Loch Venachar. Forms part of Queen Elizabeth Forest Park. **32 A4** NN5104.
Achray Forest Drive *Stir.* ***Other feature of interest***, scenic woodland drive on Forest Enterprise roads, in The Trossachs, 3m/4km N of Aberfoyle. **32 A4** NN5205.
Achreamie *High.* ***Settlement***, near N coast of Caithness district, 2m/3km E of Dounreay Atomic Energy Establishment. **76 C2** ND0166.
Achriabhach *High.* ***Settlement***, in Glen Nevis, 5m/8km NW of Kinlochleven. **38 D3** NN1468.
Achridigill Loch *High.* ***Lake/loch***, small loch 3m/4km SW of Melvich, Caithness district. **76 A2** NC8561.
Achriesgill *High.* ***Settlement***, 1m/2km N of Rhiconich, at head of Loch Inchard, W coast of Sutherland district. **74 B3** NC2554.
Achrimsdale *High.* ***Settlement***, 2m/3km N of Brora, Sutherland district. **73 E4** NC9006.
Achronich *Arg. & B.* ***Settlement***, on Mull, 5m/8km W of Gruline. **29 D1** NM4639.
Achterneed *High.* ***Locality***, in Ross and Cromarty district, 1m/2km N of Strathpeffer. NH4859.
Achtoty *High.* ***Settlement***, near N coast of Caithness district, 2m/4km W of Bettyhill across Torrisdale Bay. **75 F2** NC6762.
Achuvoldrach *High.* ***Settlement***, near causeway on W side of Kyle of Tongue. **75 E3** NC5658.
Achvaich *High.* ***Settlement***, in valley of River Evelix, 6m/10km NW of Dornoch. **72 C5** NH7194.
Achvarasdal *High.* ***Settlement***, in Caithness district, 1m/2km E of Reay. **76 B2** NC9864.
Achvarasdal Burn *High.* ***River***, flowing into E side of Sandside Bay, on N coast of Caithness district. **76 B3** NC9665.
Achvlair *High.* ***Settlement***, in Salachan Glen, 2m/3km S of Duror. **38 B4** NM9952.
Achvraie *High.* ***Settlement***, on Allt Ach' a' Bhraighe, 1km from W coast, Ross and Cromarty district. **70 C4** NC0406.
Ackergill *High.* ***Settlement***, in Caithness district, 1m/2km N of Wick. Airport to E. **77 F3** ND3553.
Ackergill Tower *High.* ***Historic/prehistoric site***, dates from 14c-15c, on S side of Sinclair's Bay. **77 F3** ND3554.
Acreknowe Reservoir *Sc.Bord.* ***Reservoir***, small reservoir 2m/3km S of Hawick. NT4910.
Adabrock *W.Isles* ***Settlement***, near N end of Isle of Lewis, 1m/2km S of Port Nis. NB5362.
Adamhill *S.Ayr.* ***Settlement***, 2m/3km N of Tarbolton. **14 C2** NS4330.
Add *Arg. & B.* ***River***, in Argyll rising 4m/7km NW of Furnace on W shore of Loch Fyne and flowing SW to Crinan Loch, Sound of Jura. **30 A5** NR7994.
Addie Hill *Moray* ***Hill***, 4m/6km SE of Buckie. Height 892 feet or 272 metres. **63 G4** NJ4459.
Addiewell *W.Loth.* Population: 1338. ***Village***, 4m/7km S of Bathgate. **25 D3** NS9862.
Aden Country Park *Aber.* ***Leisure/recreation***, country park covering 230 acres on estate dating from 18c, 1km NE of Old Deer. Ruined mansion, farm museum and woodland walks. **65 E5** NJ9848.
Advie *High.* ***Settlement***, in Badenoch and Strathspey district, 7m/12km NE of Grantown-on-Spey. **52 D1** NJ1234.
Adziel *Aber.* ***Settlement***, 1m/2km S of Strichen. NJ9453.
Ae Village (Village of Ae). *D. & G.* ***Village***, 8m/13km N of Dumfries, on S side of Forest of Ae. **9 D2** NX9889.
Affleck *Aber.* ***Settlement***, 1km E of Whiterashes. **55 D2** NJ8623.
Affleck *Angus* ***Settlement***, adjoining Monikie, 5m/8km NW of Carnoustie. **34 C1** NO4838.
Affleck Castle *Angus* ***Castle***, well-preserved 15c tower house (Historic Scotland), 7m/12km NE of Dundee. **34 C1** NO4938.
Affric *High.* ***River***, formed in Inverness district by streams of Allt Cam-bàn and Allt a Chòmhlain at their confluence just N of Ciste Dhubh. From there it flows NE through Glenaffric Forest, then E via Loch Affric and Loch Beinn a' Mheadhoin to River Glass at Fasnakyle. **50 B2** NH3028.
Affric Forest *High.* ***Forest/woodland***, surrounding and below Loch Beinn a' Mheadhoin, in lower part of Glen Affric, Inverness district. NH2828.
Afton Bridgend *E.Ayr.* ***Locality***, opposite New Cumnock, near mouth of Afton Water. **15 E4** NS6213.
Afton Reservoir *E.Ayr.* ***Reservoir***, in course of Afton Water, 6m/10km S of New Cumnock. **15 E5** NS6304.
Afton Water ***River***, rising on NW slopes of Alhang, 1m/2km S of Afton Reservoir and flowing N through reservoir to River Nith at New Cumnock. **15 E5** NS6214.
Aigas Forest *High.* ***Forest/woodland***, around Crask of Aigas. Contains dam and hydro-electric power station. NH4642.
Aignis (Anglicised form: Aignish.) *W.Isles* ***Hamlet***, on Eye Peninsula, Isle of Lewis, 2m/3km W of Garrabost. **69 F4** NB4832.
Aignish *W.Isles Anglicised form of Aignis, qv.*
Aiker Ness *Ork.* ***Coastal feature***, headland on NE coast of Mainland, 2m/3km N of Woodwick. Site of Broch of Gurness (Historic Scotland). **80 B4** HY3826.
Aiker Ness *Ork.* ***Coastal feature***, headland on E side of Aikerness peninsula on Westray. HY4552.
Aikerness *Ork.* ***Locality***, on N peninsula of Westray, running out to Bow Head. **80 C1** HY4552.
Aikers *Ork.* ***Settlement***, 2m/3km S of St. Margaret's Hope, South Ronaldsay. **79 D3** ND4590.
Aikwood Tower *Sc.Bord.* ***Historic house***, 3m/5km SW of Selkirk. 16c tower house restored in 1990s by Steel family. Exhibition of life and work of James Hogg, the 'Ettrick Shepherd' (1770-1835). **17 F3** NT4126.
Ailnack Water *See Water of Ailnack.*
Ailsa Craig *S.Ayr.* ***Island***, bleak granite island and prominent seamark in the Firth of Clyde, some 2m/3km in circumference, lying 10m/17km W of Girvan. 1114 feet or 340 metres high. Haunt of sea birds. Lighthouse on E side. Rock itself was used to make some of the finest curling stones. **6 B1** NX0199.
Aimster *High.* ***Settlement***, 1km E of Buckies and 3m/4km S of Thurso. **76 D2** ND1163.
Ainshval *High.* ***Mountain***, 2m/3km N of Rubha nam Meirleach, Rum. Height 2562 feet or 781 metres. **47 G5** NM3794.
Aird *W.Isles* ***Settlement***, on NW coast of Benbecula. **45 F4** NF7654.
Aird *W.Isles* ***Village***, on Eye Peninsula, Isle of Lewis, 1m/2km SW of Tiumpan Head. NB5536.
Aird a' Chaolais *W.Isles* ***Coastal feature***, headland on NW coast of Vatersay. **44 A4** NL6197.
Aird a' Mhachair (Anglicised form: Ardivachar.) *W.Isles* ***Settlement***, S of Ardivachar Point, at NW corner of South Uist. **45 F5** NF7445.
Aird a' Mhulaidh (Anglicised form: Ardvourlie.) *W.Isles* ***Settlement***, on W shore of Loch Seaforth, North Harris, opposite Seaforth Island. **67 D2** NB1810.
Aird an Rùnair *W.Isles* ***Coastal feature***, headland at westernmost point of North Uist. **45 E2** NF6870.
Aird an Troim *W.Isles* ***Locality***, 4m/6km SE of Baile Ailein on W shore of Loch Seaforth, Isle of Lewis. **67 E2** NB2206.
Aird Asaig (Anglicised form: Ardhasaig.) *W.Isles* ***Settlement***, on North Harris, 2m/4km NW of Tarbert. **66 D3** NB1202.
Aird Barvas *W.Isles* ***Coastal feature***, headland on NW coast of Isle of Lewis, 2m/4km N of Barvas. NB3553.
Aird Bheag *W.Isles* ***Coastal feature***, peninsula on W coast of Isle of Lewis to S of Loch Tamanavay. **66 C2** NB0219.
Aird Breanais (Anglicised form: Aird Brenish.) *W.Isles* ***Coastal feature***, headland on W coast of Isle of Lewis, 1m/2km NW of Breanais. **68 A5** NA9226.
Aird Brenish *W.Isles Anglicised form of Aird Breanais, qv.*
Aird Castle *Arg. & B. See Carradale.*
Aird Dell *W.Isles Anglicised form of Aird Dhail, qv.*
Aird Dhail (Anglicised form: Aird Dell.) *W.Isles* ***Settlement***, near NW coast of Isle of Lewis, 4m/6km SW of Butt of Lewis. **69 F1** NB4761.
Aird Fada *Arg. & B.* ***Coastal feature***, headland on S side of Loch Scridain, 5m/7km E of Bunessan on Mull. NM4424.
Aird Fenish *W.Isles* ***Coastal feature***, headland on W coast of Isle of Lewis, 7m/12km SW of Gallan Head. **68 A5** NA9929.
Aird Kilfinichen *Arg. & B.* ***Coastal feature***, low-lying headland on E side of Kilfinichen Bay on Loch Scridain, Mull. NM4927.
Aird Laimishader *W.Isles* ***Coastal feature***, headland with lighthouse on W coast of Isle of Lewis, 2m/4km W of Carloway. NB1742.
Aird Leimhe (Anglicised form: Ardslave.) *W.Isles* ***Settlement***, on SE coast of South Harris, 3m/5km SW of Greosabhagh. **66 D5** NG1189.
Aird Linn *D. & G.* ***Waterfall***, in course of Shinnel Water, 1km below Tynron. NX8192.
Aird Mhànais *W.Isles Gaelic form of Ard Manish, qv.*
Aird Mhige (Anglicised form: Ardvey.) *W.Isles* ***Settlement***, at head of Loch Stockinish, on E coast of South Harris. **66 D4** NG1292.
Aird Mhighe (Anglicised form: Ardvey.) *W.Isles* ***Settlement***, on S coast of South Harris, 3m/5km NE of Rodel. **66 C5** NG0787.
Aird Mhòr *W.Isles* ***Coastal feature***, peninsula on W coast of Isle of Lewis to N of entrance to Loch Resort. **66 C2** NB0217.
Aird Mhòr *W.Isles* ***Coastal feature***, promontory on NW coast of Isle of Lewis, 2m/3km NW of Carloway. **68 C3** NB1945.
Aird Mhòr Bragair *W.Isles* ***Coastal feature***, headland on NW coast of Isle of Lewis, 1m/2km N of Bragar. **69 D2** NB2850.
Aird Mhòr Mangurstadh (Anglicised form: Ard More Mangersta.) *W.Isles* ***Coastal feature***, headland on W coast of Isle of Lewis, 4m/6km W of Timsgearraidh. **68 A4** NA9932.
Aird Mòr *Arg. & B.* ***Hill***, on SW coast of Ross of Mull, 3m/4km NW of Rubh' Ardalanish. Height 292 feet or 89 metres. **28 C3** NM3217.
Aird na h-Iolaire *Arg. & B.* ***Coastal feature***, headland on W coast of Ardmeanach, Mull. **28 C2** NM4028.
Aird of Coigach *High.* ***Locality***, with notable viewpoint, to N of Loch Bad a' Ghaill. **70 C3** NC0611.
Aird of Kinloch *Arg. & B.* ***Coastal feature***, low-lying promontory almost enclosing Loch Beg, at head of Loch Scridain, Mull. **29 E2** NM5228.
Aird of Kinuachdrach *Arg. & B.* ***Coastal feature***, headland on NE coast of Jura, 2m/3km from N point of island. NR7098.
Aird of Sleat *High.* ***Village***, at S end of Sleat peninsula, Skye, 2m/4km E of Point of Sleat. **48 B4** NG5900.
Aird Point *High.* ***Coastal feature***, headland on Loch Snizort Beag on Skye, on E side of entrance to Loch Treaslane. NG4052.
Aird Thormaid *W.Isles* ***Coastal feature***, headland on NE coast of North Uist, 2m/3km E of Beinn Mhòr. **56 C2** NF9276.
Aird Thunga *W.Isles* ***Coastal feature***, headland on E coast of Isle of Lewis, 4m/6km NE of Stornoway across Melbost Sands. **69 F4** NB4636.
Aird Uige *W.Isles* ***Settlement***, 1km S of Gallan Head, Isle of Lewis. **68 B4** NB0437.
Aird Vanish *W.Isles* ***Coastal feature***, headland to W of Taransay. **66 B4** NF9999.
Airdrie *Fife* ***Settlement***, 3m/5km W of Crail. **35 D4** NO5608.
Airdrie *N.Lan.* Population: 36,998. ***Town***, 11m/17km E of Glasgow. **24 B3** NS7665.
Airdriehead *N.Lan.* ***Settlement***, 1m/2km NW of Cumbernauld town centre. NS7475.
Airds Bay *Arg. & B.* ***Bay***, on N side of entrance to Loch Creran, Argyll, just SW of Port Appin. **38 A5** NM9044.
Airds Bay *Arg. & B.* ***Bay***, 1m/2km SE of Airds Point in Loch Etive and 1km N of Taynuilt. **30 C1** NM9834.
Airds Moss *E.Ayr.* ***Open space***, desolate moorland area NE of Cumnock. Scene of skirmish in 1680 between Royalists and Covenanters. **15 D3** NS5924.
Airds Point *Arg. & B.* ***Coastal feature***, headland on S side of Loch Etive, Argyll, 2m/4km NW of Taynuilt. **30 B1** NM9834.
Airidh a' Bhruaich (Anglicised form: Aribruach.) *W.Isles* ***Village***, on Isle of Lewis at N end of Loch Seaforth, 4m/6km SW of Baile Ailein. **67 E2** NB2417.
Airie Hill *D. & G.* ***Hill***, 6m/9km S of New Galloway. Height 954 feet or 291 metres. **8 A4** NX6268.
Airieland *D. & G.* ***Settlement***, 3m/5km S of Castle Douglas. **8 B5** NX7557.
Airies *D. & G.* ***Locality***, comprising Mains of Airies and Little Airies, 7m/11km NW of Stranraer. **6 A4** NW9767.
Airigh-drishaig *High.* ***Settlement***, on coast of Ross and Cromarty district, 3m/5km NW of Plockton across entrance to Loch Carron. **49 D1** NG7636.
Airigh na Glaice *W.Isles* ***Locality***, 1km N of Ben Dell, Isle of Lewis. **69 F2** NB4957.
Airighean Beinn nan Caorach *W.Isles* ***Locality***, 3m/5km W of Cellar Head, Isle of Lewis. **69 G2** NB5156.
Airighean Loch Breihavat *W.Isles* ***Locality***, 5m/8km W of Cellar Head, Isle of Lewis. **69 F2** NB4854.
Airlie Castle *Angus* ***Castle***, remains of historic Ogilvy residence, sacked by Campbells in 1640, 3m/5km NE of Alyth. NO2952.
Airntully *P. & K.* ***Village***, 2m/3km N of Stanley. **33 F1** NO0935.
Airor *High.* ***Locality***, with jetty, on coast of Knoydart, Lochaber district, 4m/7km E of Kilbeg, Skye across Sound of Sleat. **48 D4** NG7105.
Airor Island *High.* ***Island***, in Sound of Sleat off coast of Knoydart. NG7105.
Airth *Falk.* ***Village***, 5m/7km N of Falkirk. **24 C1** NS8987.
Airth Castle *Falk.* ***Historic house***, modernised 16c mansion to S of Airth. NS8987.
Airthrey Castle *Stir.* ***Castle***, with estate on SE side of Bridge of Allan. Site of University of Stirling. Castle now houses CELT (Centre for English Language Training). NS8196.
Airyhassen *D. & G.* ***Settlement***, 4m/6km N of Monreith. **3 D2** NX3746.
Aisgernis *W.Isles* ***Locality***, near W coast of South Uist, 4m/6km S of Rubha Ardvule. **44 C1** NF7424.
Aith *Ork.* ***Locality***, at centre of Stronsay. **81 E4** HY6425.
Aith *Ork.* ***Settlement***, on SE shore of Loch of Skaill, Mainland. **80 A5** HY2417.
Aith *Shet.* ***Settlement***, near S coast of Fetlar. **85 F3** HU6390.
Aith *Shet.* ***Village***, on Mainland at head of Aith Voe. **82 C2** HU3455.
Aith Ness *Shet.* ***Coastal feature***, headland on Mainland on W side of entrance to Aith Voe. HU3359.
Aith Ness *Shet.* ***Coastal feature***, headland at N end of Bressay, S of Score Head. **83 E3** HU5144.

Aith Ness *Shet.* ***Coastal feature***, headland on coast of Fetlar to S of Aith, on N shore of Wick of Tresta. HU6390.
Aith Voe *Shet.* ***Sea feature***, large inlet S of Papa Little. **82 C2** HU3455.
Aith Voe *Shet.* ***Sea feature***, large inlet on N coast of Bressay. HU5043.
Aithsetter *Shet.* ***Settlement***, on Mainland, 1m/2km S of Fladdabister. HU4430.
Aithsting *Shet.* ***Locality***, SW of Aith Voe, Mainland. **82 C2** HU3355.
Aithsting and Sandsting *Shet.* ***Locality***, district of Mainland lying between Aith Voe and Bixter Voe. HU3254.
Aitnoch *Moray* ***Settlement***, 4m/6km SE of Ferness. **52 B1** NH9839.
Akermoor Loch *Sc.Bord.* ***Lake/loch***, small loch 4m/7km W of Ashkirk. **17 F3** NT4021.
Alcaig *High.* ***Village***, in Ross and Cromarty district, 1m/2km SE of Dingwall across head of Cromarty Firth. **61 E4** NH5657.
Aldclune *P. & K.* ***Settlement***, 2m/3km SE of Blair Atholl. **41 E3** NN9063.
Alder Bay *P. & K.* ***Bay***, indentation on W shore of Loch Ericht, 3m/5km N of dam at S end. NN4967.
Alder Burn ***River***, forming border of Perth & Kinross with Highland, and flowing SE into Alder Bay. NN4967.
Aldie *Aber.* ***Settlement***, 3m/4km NW of Cruden Bay. **55 F1** NK0639.
Aldie *High.* ***Settlement***, 1km SE of Tain. **61 G1** NH7880.
Aldie Water *High.* ***River***, stream in Ross and Cromarty district running E from Cnoc an Duin into River Tain, 2m/3km S of Tain. NH7679.
Aldinna Loch *S.Ayr.* ***Lake/loch***, small loch 3m/5km NW of Shalloch on Minnoch. NX3693.
Aldivalloch *Moray* ***Settlement***, 2m/3km W of Cabrach. **53 F2** NJ3626.
Aldochlay *Arg. & B.* ***Settlement***, on W shore of Loch Lomond, 1m/2km S of Luss. **31 F5** NS3591.
Aldons *S.Ayr.* ***Settlement***, in Stinchar valley, 5m/8km S of Girvan. **6 C2** NX1989.
Aldourie Castle *High.* ***Castle***, early 17c tower house near NE end of Loch Ness, 2m/3km N of Dores in Inverness district. NH6037.
Aldunie *Moray* ***Settlement***, 1m/2km W of Cabrach. **53 F2** NJ3626.
Aldville *P. & K.* ***Settlement***, 6m/10km SW of Dunkeld. **33 E1** NN9439.
Ale Water *Sc.Bord.* ***River***, running NE through Alemoor Loch to Ashkirk and Lilliesleaf. River then flows E to Ancrum, where it turns briefly S to run into River Teviot. **17 F4** NT6223.
Alemoor Loch *Sc.Bord.* ***Lake/loch***, and reservoir 7m/11km W of Hawick. **17 E4** NT3914.
Alexandria *W.Dun.* Population: 14,150. ***Town***, on River Leven, 3m/5km N of Dumbarton. **23 E2** NS3979.
Alford *Aber.* Population: 1394. ***Small town***, 23m/37km W of Aberdeen. Site of defeat of Covenanters by Montrose in 1645. Grampian Transport Museum. **54 A3** NJ5715.
Alhang ***Mountain***, rising to over 640 metres, on border of Dumfries & Galloway and East Ayrshire, 8m/13km S of New Cumnock. Source of Afton Water on NW slopes. **15 E5** NS6401.
Aline *High.* ***River***, in Lochaber district running S to head of Loch Aline. NM6947.
Alladale *High.* ***River***, rising on N slope of An Socach, flowing E then NE, via confluence with Water of Glencalvie, into River Carron. NH4791.
Allan Water ***River***, rising near Blackford and running SW down Strathallan to Dunblane, then continuing S to River Forth 2m/3km N of Stirling. **32 C4** NS7896.
Allan Water *Sc.Bord.* ***River***, running N to River Teviot at Newmill, 4m/7km SW of Hawick. **17 F5** NT4510.
Allanaquoich *Aber.* ***Settlement***, on N bank of Quoich Water, 2m/3km W of Braemar. **52 D5** NO1191.
Allancreich *Aber.* ***Settlement***, 1km NW of Marywell. **54 A5** NO5796.
Allandale *Falk.* ***Hamlet***, on SW side of Bonnybridge. NS7978.
Allanfearn *High.* ***Settlement***, in Inverness district, 4m/6km E of Inverness. NH7147.
Allangillfoot *D. & G.* ***Settlement***, on E bank of White Esk River, 5m/8km NW of Bentpath. **9 G1** NY2595.
Allanton *D. & G.* ***Settlement***, 3m/5km E of Dunscore. **8 D2** NX9184.
Allanton *E.Ayr.* ***Settlement***, 3m/4km E of Darvel. Site of Roman fort. NS6037.
Allanton *N.Lan.* Population: 1186. ***Village***, 4m/6km NE of Wishaw. **24 C4** NS8557.
Allanton *Sc.Bord.* ***Village***, 1m/2km S of Chirnside, at confluence of Blackadder Water and Whiteadder Water. **27 F4** NT8654.
Allanton *S.Lan.* ***Hamlet***, 2m/4km SE of Hamilton. **24 B4** NS7454.
Allardice *Aber.* ***Locality***, comprises Mains of Allardice, Mill of Allardice and Castle of Allardice, 1m/2km NW of Inverbervie. **43 G2** NO8174.
Allasdale *W.Isles* *Anglicised form of Allathasdal, qv.*
Allathasdal (Anglicised form: Allasdale.) *W.Isles* ***Settlement***, on W coast of Barra, 3m/5km N of Castlebay. **44 B3** NF6603.
Allean Forest *P. & K.* ***Forest/woodland***, on N side of Loch Tummel, 3m/4km S of Blair Atholl. NN8561.
Alligin *High.* *See Inveralligin.*
Alligin Shuas *High.* ***Settlement***, on N shore of Upper Loch Torridon, 4m/7km W of Torridon, Ross and Cromarty district. **59 E4** NG8358.
Allnabad *High.* ***Settlement***, 2m/3km NE of Loch Meadie. **75 D4** NC4641.
Alloa *Clack.* Population: 18,842. ***Town***, former coal port on N side of River Forth, 6m/9km E of Stirling. Small harbour. Alloa Tower (National Trust for Scotland), ancestral home of Earls of Mar, dates from 1497. **33 D5** NS8892.
Alloway *S.Ayr.* ***Village***, 2m/4km S of Ayr. Birthplace of Robert Burns, 1759; cottage is Burns museum. Auld Brig o'Doon, with Burns associations, spans River Doon to S. **14 B4** NS3318.
Alloway Kirk *S.Ayr.* ***Ecclesiastical building***, ancient church in Alloway, suburb to S of Ayr, where Robert Burns' father is buried. Described by Burns as 'auld haunted kirk' in poem, Tam o' Shanter. **14 B4** NS3218.
Allt a' Bhunn *High.* ***River***, rising from Loch Sgeireach and flowing E into Loch Shin. **71 G3** NC5112.
Allt a' Chaoil Reidhe *High.* ***River***, in Ben Alder Forest, flowing NE into Loch Pattack, 8m/12km SW of Dalwhinnie. **40 A2** NN5378.
Allt a' Chaoruinn *High.* ***River***, rising on NE slopes of Meall a' Bhùirich Rapaig and flowing N to join Allt nan Clach Aoil to form Allt Eilean. **71 E4** NC2806.
Allt a' Chaoruinn *High.* ***River***, in Lochaber district, flowing NE into River Pean 1m/2km W of head of Loch Arkaig. **38 B1** NM9690.
Allt a' Chireachain *P. & K.* ***River***, flowing SW into River Garry, 4m/6km NE of Trinafour. **40 C2** NN7569.
Allt a' Choire *High.* ***River***, flowing W into Loch Beoraid, Lochaber district. **38 A1** NM8584.
Allt a' Choire Ghlais *High.* ***River***, flowing NE from Sròn a' Choire Ghiarbh into Kilfinnan Burn, 1m/2km W of Laggan. **50 B5** NN2796.
Allt a' Choire Mhòir *High.* ***River***, flowing S from slopes of Sgurr nan Clach Geala into Loch Fannich. **60 A3** NH2066.
Allt a' Chonais *High.* ***River***, flowing N from slopes of Sgurr Choinnich, then NW to join River Carron, 3m/5km E of Achnashellach Station. **59 G5** NH0449.
Allt a' Chràisg *High.* ***River***, in Caithness district running NE down Strath Vagastie to become River Vagastie and flowing into head of Loch Naver. NC5327.
Allt a' Chuil *P. & K.* ***River***, flowing W into Bruar Water, 9m/14km N of Calvine. **40 D1** NN8180.
Allt a' Gheallaidh ***River***, running SE down Glen Gheallaidh and through Scootmore Forest to River Spey, nearly 1km N of confluence of River Spey and River Avon. The border of Highland and Moray follows this river to within 1m/2km of its confluence with River Spey. NJ1737.
Allt a' Ghlinne *High.* ***River***, rising on N slopes of Cnoc nan Sac and flowing NE into River Carron, 4m/6km W of Bonar Bridge. **72 A5** NH5491.
Allt a' Mhuilinn *High.* ***River***, flowing S and joining Allt Ach' a' Bhàthàich 1km N of confluence with River Brora, 2m/3km NW of Gordonbush. **72 D3** NC8211.
Allt Ach' a' Bhàthàich *High.* ***River***, flowing S and joining Allt a' Mhuilinn 1km N of confluence with River Brora, 2m/3km NW of Gordonbush. **72 D3** NC8211.
Allt Airigh-dhamh *High.* ***River***, in Sutherland district, flowing SE and joining Eileag Burn before flowing into Loch Arichlinie. **76 A5** NC8237.
Allt an Dùin *High.* ***River***, in Sutherland district, flowing N and joining Abhainn na Frithe at Altanduin. **72 D2** NC8126.
Allt an Ealaidh *High.* ***River***, in Sutherland district rising to N of Ben Armine and flowing SE to become River Skinsdale. **72 C2** NC7426.
Allt an Lochan Dhuibh *High.* ***River***, flowing out of Loch Dubh into River Calder, 3m/5km W of Newtonmore. **51 F4** NN6598.
Allt an Loin *High.* ***River***, flowing E through Leanachan Forest to its confluence with Allt Coire an Eòin, 2m/3km SE of Spean Bridge. **39 E2** NN2379.
Allt an Stacain *Arg. & B.* ***River***, flowing generally W into Cladich River, 1m/2km SE of Cladich. **30 D2** NN1120.
Allt an Tiaghaich *High.* ***River***, rising in Loch a' Ghlinnein and flowing NW into Lochan an Iasgaich. NC1524.
Allt an t'Sluic *High.* ***River***, flowing SE into River Truim, just N of Dalwhinnie. **40 B1** NN6485.
Allt an Ulbhaidh *High.* ***River***, rising SW of Meall an Fhuarain and flowing S through Loch an Ulbhaidh, to join River Tirry. **71 G2** NC5120.
Allt Arder *Moray* ***River***, rising on Carn Shalag and flowing E into River Spey 1km S of Upper Knockando. **63 D5** NJ1841.
Allt Bail a' Mhuilinn *P. & K.* ***River***, stream running N into River Lyon at Milton Eonan. **40 A5** NN5746.
Allt Ballach *High.* ***River***, rising on slopes of Carn Bàn and flowing S into River Calder, 3m/5km W of Newtonmore. **51 F4** NN6598.
Allt Beinn Donuill *High.* ***River***, small stream in Rhidorroch Forest, flowing E and, with other tributaries, forming Rappach Water. **71 E5** NH2399.
Allt Beithe *High.* ***River***, in Sutherland district, rising from Lochan a' Bhealaich between Carn Dearg and Carn an Tionail, and flowing S through Loch Ulbhach Coire before joining Allt na Glaise and Allt Coir' a' Chruiteir to form Allt nan Albannach. **74 C5** NC3833.
Allt Beochlich *Arg. & B.* ***River***, running W into Loch Awe, 3m/4km NE of Dalavich across loch. **30 C3** NN0115.
Allt Bhlàraidh *High.* ***River***, rising in Loch Liath and flowing SE into River Moriston 3m/4km W of Invermoriston. **50 C3** NH3816.
Allt Bhran *High.* ***River***, running NE into River Tromie, 6m/10km S of Kingussie. **40 D1** NN7590.
Allt Breinag *High.* ***River***, in Inverness district rising on Glendoe Forest and running N down Glen Brein to River Feehlin at Whitebridge, 3m/5km S of Foyers. **51 D4** NH4815.
Allt Cam *High.* ***River***, flowing N, then E into Abhainn Ghuilbinn, 3m/4km SW of Loch Laggan. **39 G2** NN4279.
Allt Cam *High.* ***River***, running NE by An Lairing, then ultimately SE into Loch Pattack, 7m/11km SW of Dalwhinnie. **40 A2** NN5379.
Allt Cam Ban *High.* ***River***, rising on W slopes of Sgaraman nam Fiadh and flowing W into Glen Markie, 10m/17km E of Fort Augustus. **51 E4** NH5407.
Allt Camghouran *P. & K.* ***River***, running NE into Loch Rannoch, 7m/11km W of Kinloch Rannoch. **40 A4** NN5456.
Allt Car *High.* ***River***, rising on E slopes of Cnoc Glas na Crìonaiche and flowing E along Strath an Lòin into Loch Shin. **71 G3** NC4716.
Allt Chaiseagail *High.* ***River***, flowing W into River Tirry, 2m/4km N of Lairg. **72 A3** NC5710.
Allt Choir a' Bhalachain *High.* ***River***, running NE from source, 2m/3km N of Loch Arkaig, into River Garry, 2m/3km W of head of Loch Garry. **50 A5** NH1301.
Allt Chomhraig *High.* ***River***, rising near Meallach Mhòr and flowing NE down Gleann Chomhraig, into River Feshie, 6m/9km E of Kingussie. **51 G5** NH8400.
Allt Chomraidh *P. & K.* ***River***, running NE down Gleann Chomraidh to River Gaur above Loch Rannoch. NN5056.
Allt Chonoghlais *Arg. & B.* ***River***, in Argyll rising on S side of Beinn a' Dothaidh and running in a wide loop round Beinn Dòrain to River Orchy, 1km S of Bridge of Orchy. **31 F1** NN2938.
Allt Coire a' Chaolain *High.* ***River***, rising on N slopes of Stob Gabhar, and flowing NE into River Etive 8m/12km SE of Glencoe village. **39 E5** NN1951.
Allt Coire an Eòin *High.* ***River***, flowing N through Killiechonate Forest to its confluence with Allt na Loin, 2m/3km SE of Spean Bridge. **39 E2** NN2379.
Allt Coire Lain Oig *High.* ***River***, running S through Sherramore Forest and entering River Spey 6m/9km W of Laggan. **51 E5** NN5294.
Allt Coire na Saighe Duibhe *High.* ***River***, rising from Loch Coire na Saighe Duibhe and flowing E, where it joins Allt an t-Strath a Dhuibh to form River Mudale. **75 D5** NC5135.
Allt Con *P. & K.* ***River***, flowing SE from Loch Con into Loch Errochty, 2m/3km NW of Trinafour. NN7066.
Allt Conait *P. & K.* ***River***, flowing generally SE from Loch an Daimh into River Lyon, 3m/5km SW of Bridge of Balgie. **40 A5** NN5344.
Allt Connie *Aber.* ***River***, stream running NE, which joins with other streams to flow into River Dee at Inverey. **41 F1** NO0786.
Allt Crunachdain *High.* ***River***, running NE down Glen Shirra, entering Loch Crunachdan 4m/7km SW of Laggan. **51 E5** NN5492.
Allt Cuaich *High.* ***River***, flowing W then NW into River Truim, 2m/3km NE of Dalwhinnie. **40 B1** NN6587.
Allt Darrarie *Aber.* ***River***, stream running N to River Muick nearly 1km N of Spittal of Glenmuick. **42 B1** NO3085.
Allt Dearg *High.* ***River***, rising on slopes of Cnoc nan Each Mòr and flowing into River Peffery just E of Strathpeffer. **61 D3** NH4958.
Allt Dearg *High.* ***River***, rising on NE slopes of Meall a' Bhreacain and flowing SE, then S into Loch Sheilah and into Balnagown River, 5m/8km NE of Alness. **61 F1** NH6777.
Allt Dearg *High.* ***River***, rising on N slopes of Carn nan Tri-tighearnan and flowing N to Dalcharn, then NE through Cawdor into River Nairn, 4m/6km SW of Nairn. Waterfalls in upper course. **62 A5** NH8451.
Allt Dearg *P. & K.* ***River***, stream in Dalnamein Forest, flowing S into Allt Glas Choire, 9m/15km SE of Dalwhinnie. **40 C2** NN7474.

Allt Dearg Mòr *High.* ***River***, rising on Cuillin Hills, Skye, and running NE to join River Sligachan about 1km above head of Loch Sligachan. **48 A2** NG4829.
Allt Dochard *Arg. & B.* ***River***, flowing S into Loch Dochard, 6m/9km NW of Bridge of Orchy. **39 E5** NN2142.
Allt Doe *High.* ***River***, rising in Glendoe Forest and flowing N through steep-sided Glen Doe into SE side of Loch Ness, 1m/2km E of Fort Augustus. **50 D4** NH4010.
Allt Easach ***River***, running S into Loch Etive, Argyll, 5m/7km from head of loch. **38 C5** NN0639.
Allt Eigheach ***River***, running S into Loch Eigheach. **39 G3** NN4457.
Allt Eileag *High.* ***River***, formed by confluence of Allt nan Clach Aoil and Allt a' Chaoruinn, flowing E to form River Oykel. **71 E4** NC3207.
Allt Essan *Stir.* ***River***, flowing E from Loch Essan, then S into River Dochart, 4m/6km NE of Crianlarich. **31 G2** NN4428.
Allt Fearnach *P. & K.* ***River***, running S down Gleann Fearnach to join Brerachan Water and form River Ardle, 3m/5km NW of Kirkmichael. NO0463.
Allt Fionn Ghlinne *Stir.* ***River***, running SE into River Falloch, 3m/5km NE of Ardlui, at head of Loch Lomond. **31 F2** NN3320.
Allt Garbh *High.* ***River***, rising on N slopes of Carn a' Choire Gairbh and flowing NE through Loch an Sgùid into E end of Loch Affric at Affric Lodge. **50 A3** NH1822.
Allt Garbh *High.* ***River***, rising on Eskdale Moor and flowing NE into River Beauly, 3m/4km E of Erchless Castle. **50 D1** NH4540.
Allt Garbh Buidhe *P. & K.* ***River***, flowing SW into River Tilt, 11m/18km NE of Blair Atholl. **41 E1** NN9879.
Allt Gharbh Ghaig *High.* ***River***, stream in Gaick Forest, flowing NW into Loch an t-Seilich, 8m/12km E of Dalwhinnie. **40 C1** NN7585.
Allt Ghlas *P. & K.* ***River***, flowing SW from Talla Bheith Forest into River Ericht at S end of Loch Ericht. **40 A3** NN5365.
Allt Girnaig *P. & K.* ***River***, running SW down Glen Girnaig to River Garry at Killiecrankie. NN9162.
Allt Glas a' Bheoil *High.* ***River***, rising on N slopes of Meall a' Bhothian and flowing NE into Elrick Burn, 8m/12km N of Newtonmore. **51 F4** NH6811.
Allt Glas Choire *P. & K.* ***River***, flowing S into River Garry, 12m/19km SE of Dalwhinnie. **40 C2** NN7569.
Allt Gleann Da-Eig *P. & K.* ***River***, running N into River Lyon 2m/4km E of Bridge of Balgie. Waterfalls 1km from mouth. **40 A5** NN6147.
Allt Gleann nam Meann *Stir.* ***River***, running S into Glen Finglas Reservoir, 6m/10km N of Aberfoyle. **32 A3** NN5210.
Allt Gobhlach *High.* ***River***, flowing S and joining An Crom-allt, 5m/8km S of W end of Loch Choire, to form River Brora. **72 B2** NC6218.
Allt Goibhre *High.* ***River***, running E into River Orrin 3m/5km W of Muir of Ord, Ross and Cromarty district. NH4751.
Allt Laire *High.* ***River***, in Lochaber district, flowing NE into River Spean, 5m/7km E of Roybridge. **39 F2** NN3479.
Allt Leachdach *High.* ***River***, flowing N into River Spean, 2m/3km SE of Spean Bridge. **39 E2** NN2580.
Allt Lon a' Chuil *High.* ***River***, rises on W slopes of Creagan Dubha Réidhe Bhig and flowing S into Loch Rimsdale, Caithness district. **75 G4** NC7339.
Allt Lorgy *High.* ***River***, rising on N slopes of Carn Dearg Mòr, and flowing NE into River Dulnain at Ellan. **52 A3** NH8922.
Allt Madagain *High.* ***River***, flowing E into River Calder, 3m/5km W of Newtonmore. **51 F5** NN6598.
Allt Menach *P. & K.* ***River***, stream rising in mountains to W of Glen Shee and flowing S to River Ardle, 1m/2km S of Kirkmichael. **41 F3** NO0858.
Allt Mheuran *High.* ***River***, in Lochaber district, rising between Stob Coir' an Albannaich and Glas Beinn Mhòr and running NW to River Etive 1m/2km E of Loch Etive. Eas nam Meirleach, or The Robbers' Waterfall, 1m/2km upstream from its confluence with River Etive. NN1346.
Allt Mhoille *Arg. & B.* ***River***, rising to NE of Ben Cruachan and flowing SE into River Strae, 2m/3km NW of Dalmally. **30 D1** NN1328.
Allt Mhucarnaich *High.* ***River***, rising between Beinn Dearg and Beinn Enaiglair, and flowing SE into Allt a' Gharbhrain. **60 B2** NH2678.
Allt Mòr *High.* ***River***, flowing SW into Loch Beag, near Bracadale, Skye. **47 G1** NG3638.
Allt Mòr *High.* ***River***, flowing NE through locality of Caiplich into Moniack Burn, 3m/5km SE of Beauly. **51 E1** NH5538.
Allt Mòr *High.* ***River***, formed from tributaries rising on N slopes of Carn Ghriogair and flowing NW into River Nairn, 6m/10km SE of Dores. **51 F2** NH6224.
Allt Mòr *High.* ***River***, flowing N from Loch Ashie into Big Burn, 3m/5km S of Inverness. **51 F1** NH6538.
Allt Mòr *High.* ***River***, rising on slopes of Meall na Gearra and flowing SE, then S, through Kingussie and into River Spey, 1km S of town. **51 G4** NH7500.
Allt Mòr *High.* ***River***, rising on Cairngorm Mountains and running N, then W, to head of Loch Morlich in Glenmore Forest Park, Badenoch and Strathspey district. NH9709.
Allt Mòr *High.* ***River***, flowing NE into Allt Chomhraig, 4m/7km SE of Kingussie. **52 A5** NN8298.
Allt Mòr *P. & K.* ***River***, flowing E, below S slopes of Schiehallion, into Keltney Burn 5m/8km S of Tummel Bridge. **40 C4** NN7652.
Allt na Caillich *High.* ***River***, in Sutherland district rising on S side of Ben Hope and running SW to Strathmore River, 3m/5km S of Loch Hope. High waterfall in course of stream at top of steep descent to mouth. NC4545.
Allt na Caim *High.* ***River***, flowing S into E end of Blackwater Reservoir. **39 F3** NN3761.
Allt na Doire Gairbhe *High.* ***River***, stream rising in Loch Mhoicean and flowing SW into Loch na Leitreach at Carnach, 6m/10km NE of head of Loch Duich. **49 G2** NH0228.
Allt na h-Airbhe *High.* ***Locality***, on W shore of Loch Broom, Ross and Cromarty district, opposite Ullapool. Ferry for pedestrians. **70 D5** NH1193.
Allt na h-Eirigh *High.* ***River***, flowing NW to W coast of Ross and Cromarty district, 1m/2km S of Rubha Chuaig. **58 D4** NG6956.
Allt na Lairige *Arg. & B.* ***River***, flowing W into River Fyne, 4m/6km NE of head of Loch Fyne. **31 E3** NN2316.
Allt na Lairige *High.* ***River***, in Lochaber district running S to head of Loch Treig. **39 E2** NN3069.
Allt na Lùibe *High.* ***River***, flowing SE and becoming Lettie River before joining River Fleet 7m/11km E of Lairg. NC6706.
Allt na Muic *High.* ***River***, flowing S from E slopes of Carn a' Chaochain into Glen Moriston, 1m/2km W of Dalchreichart. **50 B3** NH2613.
Allt-na-subh *High.* ***Settlement***, on N shore of Loch Long, 3m/4km NE of Dornie, Skye and Lochalsh district. **49 F2** NG9029.
Allt nan Achaidhean *High.* ***River***, rising on E slope of Cnoc an Liath-bhaid Mhòir, and flowing SE to join Abhainn na Frithe, 1m/2km NE of Altanduin. **72 B2** NC8127.
Allt nan Caorach *High.* ***River***, rising on Ben Wyvis, and flowing E into River Glass, 3m/4km NW of Evanton. **61 E3** NH5667.
Allt nan Ramh *High.* ***River***, rising in Reay Forest and flowing SW into Loch Allt nan Ramh. **74 B5** NC2036.
Allt Odhar *High.* ***River***, formed from tributaries on slopes of Meall Caca, and flowing NE into River Killin. **51 E4** NH5307.
Allt Phocaichain *High.* ***River***, formed from tributaries on slopes of Carn Mhic Raonuill and flowing N into River Moriston opposite Dundreggan. **50 C3** NH3214.
Allt Riabhach *High.* ***River***, flowing NE along NW slope of Meallan Odhar to form Abhainn Deabhag at Coudie. **50 B3** NH2421.
Allt Riabhachain *High.* ***River***, flowing N down slopes between Beinn Bheag and An Riabhachan into Loch Monar. **50 A1** NH1239.
Allt Riobain *Stir.* ***River***, flowing S into River Dochart, 9m/13km SW of Killin. **31 G2** NN4527.
Allt Ruadh *High.* ***River***, rising on NW slopes of Carn Bàn Mòr and flowing NW into River Feshie, 5m/9km E of Kingussie. **52 A4** NH8401.
Allt Ruighe nan Saorach *P. & K.* ***River***, flowing NE into Loch Errochty, 3m/5km N of Kinloch Rannoch. **40 B3** NN6664.
Allt Saigh *High.* ***River***, rising on E slopes of Carn a' Mheallain Odhair and flowing E to enter Loch Ness at Alltsigh, 3m/4km NE of Invermoriston. NH4519.
Allt Shallainn *P. & K.* ***River***, flowing E into S end of Loch Garry, 6m/10km NW of Kinloch Rannoch. **40 A3** NN5867.
Allt Sleibh *P. & K.* ***River***, flowing E into NW side of Loch Errochty, 4m/7km N of Kinloch Rannoch. **40 B3** NN6665.
Allt Srath a' Ghlinne *P. & K.* ***River***, flowing SE in Glen Artney and joining Water of Ruchill 8m/10km NE of Callander. **32 B3** NN6915.
Allt Tolaghan *Arg. & B.* ***River***, in Argyll running NE to join Linne nam Beathach at W end of Loch Tulla. **31 E1** NN2742.
Allt Uisg an t-Sithein *High.* ***River***, rising on slopes of Carn Mhic Iamhair and flowing N into River Farigaig, 3m/4km E of Errogie. **51 F3** NH6019.
Alltachonaich *High.* ***Settlement***, 7m/11km N of Rubha an Ridire, Lochaber district. **37 G4** NM7450.
Alltan Dubh *High.* ***Settlement***, on NW coast of Ross and Cromarty district, 4m/6km S of Rubha Coigeach. **70 B3** NB9812.
Alltbeithe *High.* ***Settlement***, with youth hostel, 4m/6km W of W end of Glen Affric. Not accessible by road. **49 G2** NH0820.
Alltcailleach Forest *Aber.* ***Forest/woodland***, 3m/5km SW of Ballater. NO3392.
Alltnacaillich *High.* ***Settlement***, on E side of Strath More, 3m/5km S of Loch Hope. **75 D4** NC4545.
Alltsigh *High.* ***Settlement***, on NW shore of Loch Ness, 3m/4km NE of Invermoriston. **51 D3** NH4519.
Almond *Edin.* ***River***, rising W of Whitburn and flowing NE to enter Firth of Forth, 1m/2km NE of Cramond Bridge. **25 F2** NT1877.
Almond *P. & K.* ***River***, rising 1km E of Loch Tay, and flows E through Glen Almond to join River Tay on N side of Perth. **33 F2** NO1026.
Almond Valley Heritage Centre (Also known as Livingston Mill Farm.) *W.Loth.* ***Other feature of interest***, museum of history and environment of West Lothian, on S bank of River Almond to W of Livingston Village. 20 acre site includes shale oil museum, activity centre and farmyard animals. **25 E3** NT0366.
Almondbank *P. & K.* Population: 1198. ***Village***, on River Almond, 4m/6km NW of Perth. **33 F2** NO0626.
Almondell and Calderwood Country Park *W.Loth.* ***Leisure/recreation***, in wooded River Almond valley, 1km N of East Calder. Over 200 acres of woods and riverside walks. Visitor centre holds local and natural history exhibitions and contains an aquarium. **25 E3** NT0868.
Almorness Point *D. & G.* ***Coastal feature***, headland at S end of peninsula, 6m/9km S of Dalbeattie. **8 C5** NX8451.
Alness *High. Alternative name for (River) Averon, qv.*
Alness *High.* Population: 5696. ***Small town***, on N side of Cromarty Firth, Ross and Cromarty district, 3m/5km W of Invergordon. Expansion in connection with North Sea oil developments. **61 F3** NH6569.
Alness Bay *High.* ***Bay***, on Cromarty Firth, 2m/3km SW of Alness. **61 F3** NH6367.
Alrick *Angus* ***Settlement***, 1km NW of Brewlands Bridge. **41 G3** NO1961.
Altanduin *High.* ***Settlement***, in Sutherland district, 4m/6km S of Loch Achnamoine. **72 D2** NC8026.
Altass *High.* ***Settlement***, in Sutherland district on edge of Oykel Forest, 7m/11km SW of Lairg. **72 A4** NC4900.
Altens *Aberdeen* ***Locality***, industrial area on coast, 2m/3km S of Aberdeen harbour. **55 E4** NJ9402.
Alterwall *High.* ***Settlement***, 1m/2km NE of Lyth. **77 E2** ND2865.
Altgaltraig *Arg. & B.* ***Locality***, comprising Upper Altgaltraig and Lower Altgaltraig in Argyll on E shore of Kyles of Bute, 1m/2km SE of Colintraive. NS0473.
Alticry *D. & G.* ***Settlement***, 7m/11km SE of Glenluce. **7 D5** NX2849.
Altimeg Hill *S.Ayr.* ***Open space***, hillslope rising to 340 metres on W side of Deer's How, 4m/7km SE of Ballantrae. **6 C3** NX1076.
Altnabreac *High.* ***Locality***, with railway station, in Caithness district, 12m/19km SW of Halkirk. **76 C4** ND0045.
Altnafeadh *High.* ***Settlement***, on approach to Pass of Glencoe, 4m/6km SE of Kinlochleven. **39 E4** NN2256.
Altnaharra *High.* ***Village***, in Caithness district at W end of Loch Naver, 13m/22km S of Tongue. **75 E5** NC5635.
Altonhill *E.Ayr.* ***Suburb***, N district of Kilmarnock. NS4239.
Altonside *Moray* ***Settlement***, on Red Burn, 5m/8km N of Rothes. **63 E4** NJ2957.
Altura *High.* ***Settlement***, on SE side of Loch Lochy, 5m/8km NE of Spean Bridge. **39 E1** NN2489.
Alturlie Bay *High.* ***Bay***, E of Alturlie Point, 4m/6km NE of Inverness. NH7149.
Alturlie Point *High.* ***Coastal feature***, headland in Inverness district on S side of Inner Moray Firth or Inverness Firth, 4m/7km NE of Inverness. **61 G5** NH7149.
Altyre Woods *Moray* ***Forest/woodland***, on E side of River Findhorn, 4m/6km S of Forres. **62 C4** NJ0253.
Alva *Clack.* Population: 5201. ***Small town***, 3m/4km N of Alloa. **33 D5** NS8896.
Alva Glen *Clack.* ***Valley***, steep and narrow valley carrying Alva Burn S from Ochil Hills to Alva. Waterfalls along course. NS8896.
Alves *Moray* ***Settlement***, 5m/9km W of Elgin. **62 D3** NJ1362.
Alvie *High.* ***Settlement***, in Badenoch and Strathspey district, on shore of Loch Alvie, 3m/4km SW of Aviemore. **52 A4** NH8609.
Alwhat *E.Ayr.* ***Mountain***, on border with Dumfries & Galloway, 1m/2km S of Afton Reservoir. Height 2063 feet or 629 metres. NS6402.
Alyth *P. & K.* Population: 2383. ***Small town***, market town, 5m/8km NE of Blairgowrie. Former cloth-manufacturing town. **42 A5** NO2448.
Alyth Burn *P. & K.* ***River***, rising in Forest of Alyth and flowing SE, by Alyth, to join River Isla 2m/3km E of Alyth. **41 G4** NO2749.
Am Balg *High.* ***Island***, group of islets 1m/2km NW of Rubh' a Bhuachaille headland, on NW coast of Sutherland district. **74 A2** NC1866.
Am Basteir *High.* ***Mountain***, in Cuillin Hills, Skye, 3m/4km N of head of Loch Coruisk. Munro: height 3067 feet or 935 metres. **48 A2** NG4625.
Am Bodach *High.* ***Mountain***, on Mamore Forest in Lochaber district, 2m/3km N of Kinlochleven. Munro: height 3392 feet or 1034 metres. **39 D3** NN1765.

Am Broilein *High.* ***Bay***, small bay on NW shore of Loch Linnhe, 1m/2km NE of Rubha na h-Airde Uinnsinn. **38 A4** NM8853.
Am Buachaille *Arg. & B.* ***Mountain***, in Argyll, 3m/4km W of Inveraray. Height 1059 feet or 323 metres. **30 C4** NN0507.
Am Buachaille *High.* ***Coastal feature***, headland 7m/11km SW of Cape Wrath, Sutherland district. **74 A2** NC2065.
Am Faochagach *High.* ***Mountain***, in Ross and Cromarty district 3m/5km W of head of Loch Vaich. Munro: height 3129 feet or 954 metres. **60 C2** NH3079.
Am Fiar Loch *High.* ***Lake/loch***, small loch in course of River Orrin, Ross and Cromarty district 5m/8km W of head of Orrin Reservoir. NH2446.
Am Fraoch Eilean *Arg. & B.* ***Island***, at S end of Jura, at entrance to Sound of Islay. **20 C3** NR4662.
Am Maol *High.* ***Hill***, 1m/2km N of Loch Duagrich, Skye. Height 695 feet or 212 metres. **58 A5** NG4041.
Am Meall *W.Isles* ***Hill***, at SE corner of Vatersay. Height 328 feet or 100 metres. **44 B4** NL6594.
Am Plastair *W.Isles* ***Island***, islet (National Trust for Scotland) off N coast of Soay and 1m/2km NW of St. Kilda. NA0502.
Amat Forest *High.* ***Open space***, deer forest at head of Strathcarron 8m/13km W of Bonar Bridge Woods on left bank of River Carron above its confluence with Abhainn an t-Srath Chuileannaich. **71 G5** NH4690.
Ambrismore *Arg. & B.* ***Settlement***, on Bute, 1km NE of Scalpsie Bay. **22 B4** NS0658.
Amhuinnsuidhe *W.Isles Alternative name for Abhainnsuidhe, qv.*
Amisfield Tower *D. & G.* ***Castle***, well-preserved stronghold of c. 1600, 1m/2km NW of Amisfield. NX9983.
Amisfield Town *D. & G.* ***Village***, 5m/7km NE of Dumfries. **9 E2** NY0082.
Ample Burn *Stir. Alternative name for Burn of Ample, qv.*
Amulree *P. & K.* ***Village***, on River Quaich, 9m/14km SW of Dunkeld. **33 D1** NN9036.
An Cabar *High.* ***Mountain***, in Ross and Cromarty district on SE side of Loch Fannich, 7m/11km NE of Achnasheen. Height 1830 feet or 558 metres. **60 B3** NH2564.
An Cabar *High.* ***Mountain***, summit to SW of Ben Wyvis, 5m/7km NE of Garve. Height 3116 feet or 950 metres. **60 D3** NH4566.
An Caisteal *High.* ***Mountain***, summit of Ben Loyal, Caithness district. Height 2506 feet or 764 metres. NC5748.
An Caisteal *Stir.* ***Mountain***, 4m/6km S of Crianlarich. Munro: height 3264 feet or 995 metres. **31 F3** NN3719.
An Cala Garden *Arg. & B.* ***Garden***, S of Seil, 1km E of Easdale and 6m/10km SW of Oban. Notable plants include rhododendron, rhabdotum, acer, hydrangea and camellia. **29 G3** NM7517.
An Cearcall *P. & K.* ***Open space***, steep slope to NE of Loch Garry, 9m/14km S of Dalwhinnie. **40 B2** NN6169.
An Cearcallach *High.* ***Mountain***, in Moy Forest, 2m/3km NW of SW end of Loch Laggan. Height 3257 feet or 993 metres. **39 G1** NN4285.
An Coileach *W.Isles* ***Mountain***, 1km E of Heileasbhal Mòr, South Harris. Height 1266 feet or 386 metres. **66 C4** NG0892.
An Coileachan *High.* ***Mountain***, in Ross and Cromarty district, 2m/3km NW of lower end of Loch Fannich. Munro: height 3027 feet or 923 metres. **60 B3** NH2468.
An Crom-allt *High.* ***River***, flowing SW and joining Allt Gobhlach, 5m/8km S of W end of Loch Craggie to form River Brora. **72 B2** NC6318.
An Cruachan *High.* ***Hill***, 1km SE of Cleadale, Eigg. Height 981 feet or 299 metres. **37 D1** NM4887.
An Cruachan *High.* ***Mountain***, 2m/3km NW of head of Loch Brittle, Skye. Height 1427 feet or 435 metres. **47 G2** NG3822.
An Cruachan *High.* ***Mountain***, in Skye and Lochalsh district, 4m/6km N of W end of Loch Mullardoch. Height 2316 feet or 706 metres. **49 G1** NH0935.
An Cuaidh *High.* ***Hill***, 1m/2km SE of Rubha Réidh, in Ross and Cromarty district. Radio mast. Height 971 feet or 296 metres. **59 D1** NG7689.
An Dornabac *High.* ***Hill***, 3m/4km N of Rubha Sgorr an t-Snidhe, Rum. Height 863 feet or 263 metres. **47 G5** NM3597.
An Dubh-sgeir *Arg. & B.* ***Island***, group of rocks nearly 1km N of Gigha. NR6655.
An Dubh-sgeir *High.* ***Island***, rock island on E side of Eilean Hoan at mouth of Loch Eriboll, N coast of Sutherland district. NC4568.
An Dubh Sgeir *High.* ***Island***, islet 4m/6km W of Idrigill Point, Skye. **47 E1** NG1936.
An Dubh-sgeir *High.* ***Island***, rock island nearly 1km off SW coast of Skye at S side of entrance to Loch Eynort. NG3422.
An Dùn *High.* ***Mountain***, 6m/10km SE of Dalwhinnie. Height 2706 feet or 825 metres. NN7180.
An Dùnan *Arg. & B.* ***Historic/prehistoric site***, fort on small headland on E coast of Jura, 1m/2km NE of Ardfernal across Lowlandman's Bay. **21 D2** NR5773.
An Fùr *High.* ***Mountain***, in Ross and Cromarty district, 6m/10km SW of Torridon. Height 1269 feet or 387 metres. **59 E4** NG8051.
An Garbh-eilean (Anglicised form: Garve Island.) *High.* ***Island***, islet lying off Cléit Dhubh headland on N coast of Sutherland district, 4m/7km E of Cape Wrath. **74 C1** NC3373.
An Garbh-mheall *High.* ***Mountain***, 5m/8km S of Rubha na Fearn, Ross and Cromarty district. Height 1617 feet or 493 metres. **58 D4** NG7252.
An Garbhanach *High.* ***Mountain***, peak along ridge to S of An Gearanach, 3m/5km N of Kinlochmore. Height 3198 feet or 975 metres. NN1866.
An Gead Loch *High.* ***Lake/loch***, 2m/3km S of W end of Loch Monar. **50 A1** NH1038.
An Gearanach *High.* ***Mountain***, in Lochaber district, on Mamore Forest 3m/5km N of Kinlochleven. Munro: height 3231 feet or 985 metres. **39 D3** NN1866.
An Glas-loch *High.* ***Lake/loch***, small loch 3m/5km NE of Loch Fiag, Sutherland district. **75 D5** NC4931.
An Gorm-loch *High.* ***Lake/loch***, in East Monar Forest, Ross and Cromarty district. **60 B5** NH2244.
An Grianan *High.* ***Mountain***, 5m/8km NE of Kinlochbervie, Sutherland district. Height 1532 feet or 467 metres. **74 B2** NC2662.
An Lairig *High.* ***Open space***, valley side comprising N slopes of Carn Dearg and Aonach Beag. **39 G2** NN4876.
An Leacainn *High.* ***Mountain***, in Inverness district, 5m/8km W of Inverness. Height 1358 feet or 414 metres. **61 E5** NH5741.
An Lean-charn *High.* ***Mountain***, situated between S ends of Loch Eriboll and Loch Hope. Height 1709 feet or 521 metres. **74 D3** NC4152.
An Leth-allt *High.* ***River***, rising on slopes below Carn Coire na Caorach and flowing E into River Dulnain, 4m/6km W of Carrbridge. **52 A2** NH8621.
An Liathanach *High.* ***Mountain***, in Ross and Cromarty district, consisting of twin peaks at 1666 feet or 508 metres and 1588 feet or 484 metres in height, on S shore of Loch a' Chroisg 2m/3km SW of Achnasheen. **60 A4** NH1057.
An Lurg *High.* ***Mountain***, 4m/7km E of Loch Morlich. Height 2470 feet or 753 metres. **52 C4** NJ0409.
An Riabhachan *High.* ***Mountain***, in Skye and Lochalsh district rising to N of Loch Mullardoch. Munro: height 3703 feet or 1129 metres. **50 A1** NH1334.
An Ruadh-mheallan *High.* ***Mountain***, 2m/3km W of Beinn Alligin, Ross and Cromarty district. Height 2204 feet or 672 metres. **59 E3** NG8361.
An Ruadh-stac *High.* ***Mountain***, peak on Ben-damph forest, Ross and Cromarty district, 4m/6km N of head of Loch Carron. Height 2926 feet or 892 metres. **59 F5** NG9248.
An Rubha *Arg. & B.* ***Coastal feature***, headland on W coast of Colonsay, 3m/4km W of Scalasaig. NR3595.
An Rubha *W.Isles Gaelic form of Eye Peninsula, qv.*
An Sgarsoch ***Mountain***, 12m/19km N of Blair Atholl, on border of Aberdeenshire and Perth & Kinross. Munro: height 3300 feet or 1006 metres. **41 E1** NN9383.
An Sguabach *High.* ***Mountain***, in Badenoch and Strathspey district, 4m/6km SW of Aviemore. Height 2486 feet or 758 metres. **52 A3** NH8310.
An Sgurr *High.* ***Mountain***, 3m/4km W of Lochcarron, Ross and Cromarty district. Height 1286 feet or 392 metres. **49 E1** NG8538.
An Sgurr (Also known as Scuir of Eigg or Sgurr of Eigg.) *High.* ***Mountain***, basaltic peak on Eigg, highest point on island. Height 1289 feet or 393 metres. **37 D1** NM4684.
An Sidhean *High.* ***Mountain***, on East Monar Forest, Ross and Cromarty district. Height 2670 feet or 814 metres. NH1745.
An Sleaghach *High.* ***Mountain***, 3m/5km NE of Rubha an Ridire, Lochaber district. Height 1683 feet or 513 metres. **37 G5** NM7643.
An Sligearnach *P. & K.* ***Mountain***, on NW side of Glen Tilt, 9m/15km NE of Blair Atholl. Height 2578 feet or 786 metres. **41 E2** NN9578.
An Socach *Aber.* ***Inland physical feature***, mountain ridge, 6m/9km S of Inverey. W summit is a Munro at height of 3097 feet or 944 metres. **41 F1** NO0879.
An Socach *High.* ***Mountain***, 3m/4km NE of Kinlochbervie, Sutherland district. Height 1174 feet or 358 metres. **74 B3** NC2658.
An Socach *High.* ***Mountain***, on border between Inverness and Skye and Lochalsh districts, 4m/6km S of W end of Loch Mullardoch. Munro: height 3018 feet or 920 metres. **49 G2** NH0822.
An Socach *High.* ***Mountain***, in Skye and Lochalsh district, 2m/3km N of W end of Loch Mullardoch. Munro: height 3506 feet or 1069 metres. **49 G1** NH0933.
An Stac *High.* ***Mountain***, 2m/3km S of Lochailort, Lochaber district. Height 2670 feet or 814 metres. **37 G2** NM7679.
An Stac *High.* ***Mountain***, peak in Lochaber district 1km S of head of Loch Morar. Height 2355 feet or 718 metres. **38 A1** NM8688.
An Staonach *High.* ***Mountain***, in Ross and Cromarty district, 4m/6km N of head of Loch Kishorn. Height 1683 feet or 513 metres. **59 E5** NG8348.
An Stuc *High.* ***Mountain***, rising above Glen Oykel, 3m/4km SE of Loch Ailsh. Height 1194 feet or 364 metres. **71 F4** NC3409.
An Stuc *P. & K.* ***Mountain***, in Ben Lawers group, 1m/2km N of Ben Lawers and 7m/12km NE of Killin. Munro: height 3667 feet or 1118 metres. NN6343.
An Suidhe *Arg. & B.* ***Mountain***, in Eredine Forest, 5m/9km W of Inveraray. Height 1686 feet or 514 metres. **30 C4** NN0007.
An Suidhe *High.* ***Mountain***, in Badenoch and Strathspey district, 5m/8km NE of Kingussie. Height 1774 feet or 541 metres. **52 A4** NH8107.
An t-Eilean Meadhoin *High.* ***Island***, wooded islet in Loch Morar, Lochaber district, 1m/2km E of dam at W end of loch. NM7092.
An T-ób *W.Isles Gaelic form of Leverburgh, qv.*
An t-Sàil *High.* ***Mountain***, midway between Loch Lurgainn and W coast of Ross and Cromarty district. Height 1607 feet or 490 metres. **70 C4** NC0607.
An Tairbeart *W.Isles Gaelic form of Tarbert, qv.*
An Teallach *High.* ***Mountain***, in W part of Ross and Cromarty district 3m/4km SW of Little Loch Broom. Summit is Bidein a' Ghlas Thuill, a Munro at height of 3483 feet or 1062 metres. **59 G1** NH0684.
An Torc (Also known as Boar of Badenoch.) ***Mountain***, on border of Perth & Kinross and Highland, on W side of Pass of Drumochter and 6m/9km S of Dalwhinnie. Height 2424 feet or 739 metres. **40 B2** NN6276.
An Tunna *N.Ayr.* ***Mountain***, on Arran, 3m/5km W of Brodick. Height 1184 feet or 361 metres. **13 E2** NR9736.
An Uidh *High.* ***River***, rising on slopes of Sròn Ach' a' Bhacaidh and flowing SE into Loch an Lagain, 3m/5km NE of Bonar Bridge. **72 B5** NH6297.
Anaboard *High.* ***Settlement***, 3m/4km E of S end of Lochindorb, and 3m/5km S of Dava. **52 C1** NJ0033.
Anaheilt *High.* ***Settlement***, adjoining to N of Strontian, Lochaber district. **38 A3** NM8162.
Ancient Yew Tree (Also known as Fortingall Yew.) *P. & K.* ***Other feature of interest***, yew tree in Fortingall churchyard, reputedly more than 3000 years old and possibly the oldest tree in Europe. **40 C5** NN7347.
Ancrum *Sc.Bord.* ***Village***, 3m/5km NW of Jedburgh. **18 A4** NT6224.
Angus Folk Museum *Angus* ***Other feature of interest***, National Trust for Scotland property in Glamis, 4m/7km S of Kirriemuir; collection of 19c domestic memorabilia and furniture. **42 B5** NO3846.
Anie *Stir.* ***Settlement***, 3m/5km NW of Callander. **32 A3** NN5810.
Ankerville *High.* ***Settlement***, in Ross and Cromarty district, 3m/5km W of Balintore on E coast. **62 A2** NH8174.
Ankerville Corner *High.* ***Locality***, adjoins to NE of Ankerville. NH8174.
Annan *D. & G.* ***River***, rising on Devil's Beeftub, N of Moffat, and flowing S past Moffat, Lochmaben and Annan to Solway Firth 1m/2km S of Annan. **9 F3** NY1963.
Annan *D. & G.* Population: 8930. ***Small town***, near mouth of River Annan, 15m/24km E of Dumfries and same distance NW of Carlisle across Solway Firth. Market. **9 F4** NY1966.
Annandale *D. & G.* ***Valley***, carrying River Annan from Ericstane in N to Moffat in S. **16 B5** NT0903.
Annandale Water Services *D. & G.* ***Other building***, motorway service station on A74(M) to E of Johnstonebridge and 7m/11km N of Lockerbie. **9 F1** NY1092.
Annat *Arg. & B.* ***Settlement***, on N side of Loch Awe, 1km S of Kilchrenan. **30 C2** NN0322.
Annat *High.* ***Locality***, at head of Loch Linnhe, 2m/4km NW of Fort William across head of loch. NN0877.
Annat *High.* ***Settlement***, at head of Upper Loch Torridon, Ross and Cromarty district, 1m/2km S of Torridon. **59 E4** NG8954.
Annat Bay *High.* ***Bay***, gently curving bay on SW side of entrance to Loch Broom, on W coast of Ross and Cromarty district. **70 C5** NH0496.
Annathill *N.Lan.* ***Settlement***, 3m/5km N of Coatbridge. NS7271.
Annbank *S.Ayr.* ***Village***, 5m/7km E of Ayr. **14 C3** NS4023.
Annet Burn *Stir.* ***River***, flowing S into River Teith, 5m/8km SE of Callander. **32 B4** NN7002.
Annick Water ***River***, running SW past Stewarton to join River Irvine on S side of town of Irvine. **23 F5** NS3237.
Anniesland *Glas.* ***Suburb***, 4m/6km NW of Glasgow city centre. NS5468.
Anstruther *Fife* Population: 3154. ***Small town***, resort and fishing port on Firth of Forth, 9m/14km SE of St. Andrews. Formerly port for herring fishing industry. Scottish Fisheries museum. **35 D4** NO5603.
Anstruther Easter *Fife* ***Locality***, adjoins to E of Anstruther, on N coast of Firth of Forth. NO5703.
Anstruther Wester *Fife* ***Locality***, adjoins to W of Anstruther, on N coast of Firth of Forth. NO5603.

Antermony Loch *E.Dun.* ***Lake/loch***, small loch 2m/3km NE of Kirkintilloch. NS6676.

Antonine Wall ***Historic/prehistoric site***, Roman fortification (Historic Scotland) dating from 1c, now only intermittently visible, extending 37m/60km from Old Kilpatrick on N bank of River Clyde to Carriden, E of Bo'ness on S bank of River Forth. **24 C2** NS7677.

Anwoth *D. & G.* ***Village***, 1m/2km W of Gatehouse of Fleet. 8c cross in churchyard of former, ruined, church. **7 G5** NX5856.

Aonach air Chrith *High.* ***Mountain***, peak to E of Maol Chinn-dearg and summit of ridge on border of Lochaber and Skye and Lochalsh districts. Munro: height 3349 feet or 1021 metres. **49 G4** NH0508.

Aonach Beag *High.* ***Mountain***, in Lochaber district 2m/3km E of Ben Nevis. Munro: height 4054 feet or 1236 metres. **39 D2** NN1971.

Aonach Beag *High.* ***Mountain***, in Badenoch and Strathspey district 2m/3km W of Loch an Sgòir. Munro: height 3654 feet or 1114 metres. **39 G2** NN4574.

Aonach Buidhe *High.* ***Mountain***, on Killilan Forest, Skye and Lochalsh district. Height 2949 feet or 899 metres. **49 G1** NH0532.

Aonach Dubh *High. See The Three Sisters.*

Aonach Eagach *High.* ***Inland physical feature***, mountain ridge on N side of Glen Coe. Summit is Sgorr nam Fiannaidh at W end of ridge; Munro at height 3172 feet or 967 metres. **38 D4** NN1458.

Aonach Meadhoin *High.* ***Mountain***, in Lochaber district on N side of Glen Shiel, 2m/4km W of Loch Cluanie. Munro: height 3290 feet or 1003 metres. **49 G3** NH0413.

Aonach Mhòr Gondola and Nevis Range Ski Centre *High.* ***Leisure/recreation***, 7m/11km NE of Fort William. Cable car runs for 1m/2km in ski area, rising to 2000 feet or 610 metres. **39 D2** NN1876.

Aonach Mòr *High.* ***Inland physical feature***, mountain ridge rising to summit of 2837 feet or 865 metres in Lochaber district, to W of Clach Leathad. **39 E5** NN2247.

Aonach Mòr *High.* ***Mountain***, E of Ben Nevis, 1m/2km along ridge to N of Aonach Beag. Munro: height 3998 feet or 1219 metres. **39 D2** NN1972.

Aonach Odhar *High.* ***Mountain***, in Inverness district, 15m/24km N of Newtonmore. Height 2106 feet or 642 metres. **51 G2** NH7022.

Aonach Sgoilte *High.* ***Inland physical feature***, mountain ridge in Knoydart, 1m/2km NE of Loch an Dubh-Lochain. **49 E4** NG8302.

Aonach Shasuinn *High.* ***Mountain***, in Inverness district 5m/8km N of dam of Loch Cluanie. Height 2916 feet or 889 metres. **50 A3** NH1718.

Aoradh *Arg. & B.* ***Settlement***, on Islay, 5m/8km NW of Bridgend. **20 A3** NR2767.

Appin ***Large natural feature***, mountainous area bounded by E shore of Loch Linnhe, Glen Creran and Glen Coe. Strath of Appin runs across SW part, forming a natural pass between Loch Linnhe and Loch Creran. NN0051.

Appin House *Arg. & B.* ***Settlement***, 3m/5km NE of Port Appin. **38 B5** NM9349.

Appin of Dull *P. & K. Alternative name for Strath of Appin, qv.*

Appin Rocks *Arg. & B.* ***Coastal feature***, 1km SW of Port Appin at NW entrance to Airds Bay. **38 A5** NM8944.

Applecross *High.* ***River***, runs SW into Applecross Bay on W coast of Ross and Cromarty district. **58 D5** NG7144.

Applecross *High.* ***Village***, at S end of Applecross Bay on W coast of Ross and Cromarty district, opposite Raasay across Inner Sound. **58 D5** NG7144.

Applecross Bay *High.* ***Bay***, on W coast of Ross and Cromarty district, N of Applecross, opposite Raasay across Inner Sound. NG7145.

Applecross Forest *High.* ***Open space***, deer forest to E of Applecross. **58 D5** NG7144.

Applegarth Town *D. & G.* ***Locality***, 3m/4km NW of Lockerbie. NY1084.

Appletreehall *Sc.Bord.* ***Settlement***, 2m/4km NE of Hawick. **17 G4** NT5117.

Aquhythie *Aber.* ***Locality***, 2m/3km N of Kemnay. NJ7418.

Arabella *High.* ***Locality***, in Ross and Cromarty district, 4m/7km S of Tain. NH8075.

Aray *Arg. & B.* ***River***, in Argyll running S down Glen Aray to Loch Fyne at Inveraray. NN0909.

Arbeadie *Aber.* ***Suburb***, NE district of Banchory. NO7096.

Arbigland *D. & G.* ***Garden***, on Solway Firth, 1m/2km SE of Kirkbean, which includes water gardens, woodland and a bay. Birthplace of John Paul, later known as Paul Jones, 1747-92, founder of the American navy, whose father was gardener here. **9 D5** NX9857.

Arbirlot *Angus* ***Village***, 3m/4km W of Arbroath. To SE is Kellie Castle, 16c and earlier, former seat of the Auchterlonies. **43 D5** NO6040.

Arbory Hill *S.Lan.* ***Mountain***, with hillfort at summit, 1m/2km E of Abington. Height 1407 feet or 429 metres. **16 A3** NS9423.

Arbroath *Angus* Population: 23,474. ***Town***, industrial town, port with small harbour, and resort, 15m/25km NE of Dundee. Substantial remains of Arbroath Abbey (Historic Scotland). Famed for local delicacy of traditionally smoked haddock, or smokies. **43 E5** NO6440.

Arbroath Abbey *Angus* ***Ecclesiastical building***, substantial remains of Tironensian monastery (Historic Scotland) in centre of Arbroath. Founded in 1178 by William the Lion, King of Scots, it is linked with Scottish nationalism. Declaration of Arbroath, asserting Scotland's independence from England was signed here in 1320, and Stone of Destiny was found here in 1951, having been taken from Westminster Abbey. Notable remains include good example of an abbot's residence. **43 E5** NO6441.

Arbuthnot Museum *Aber.* ***Other feature of interest***, museum of local fishing industry history and art gallery in St. Peter Street, Peterhead. Includes large coin collection. **65 G5** NK1247.

Arbuthnott *Aber.* ***Village***, 2m/4km NW of Inverbervie. **43 G2** NO8074.

Arbuthnott Church *Aber.* ***Ecclesiastical building***, 1km SE of Arbuthnott, on N bank of Bervie Water. Mainly 16c, but chancel dates from 1242. **43 G2** NO8074.

Arbuthnott House *Aber.* ***Historic house***, on N side of Bervie Water, 3m/4km NE of Inverbervie. 13c home of Arbuthnott family, featuring 17c walled garden. **43 F2** NO7975.

Archiestown *Moray* ***Village***, 4m/6km W of Craigellachie. **63 E5** NJ2344.

Arcuil *High. Gaelic form of Arkle, qv.*

Ard a' Chapuill (Anglicised form: Ardachuple). *Arg. & B.* ***Settlement***, lodge and farm dwellings, 1m/2km S of Auchenbreck. **22 B2** NS0279.

Ard a' Mhòrain *W.Isles* ***Coastal feature***, promontory on N coast of North Uist reaching to within 1m/2km of Boreray. NF8379.

Ard Bheinn *N.Ayr.* ***Mountain***, on Arran, 4m/6km NE of Blackwaterfoot. Height 1679 feet or 512 metres. **13 E2** NR9432.

Ard Ghunel *High.* ***Coastal feature***, headland on E coast of Sleat peninsula, Skye, 1km SE of Eilean Iarmain. NG7011.

Ard Manish (Gaelic form: Aird Mhànais.) *W.Isles* ***Island***, small island off SE coast of South Harris, 1km S of Aird Leimhe. **66 D5** NG1188.

Àrd Mhòr *W.Isles* ***Coastal feature***, peninsula on NE coast of Barra. NF7103.

Ard More Mangersta. *W.Isles Anglicised form of Aird Mhòr Mangurstadh, qv.*

Ard nam Madadh *W.Isles* ***Coastal feature***, headland on S side of entrance to Loch na Madadh, E coast of North Uist. Junction of land and submarine cables. NF9467.

Ard Neackie *High.* ***Coastal feature***, promontory on E bank of Loch Eriboll, Sutherland district, 4m/7km from head of loch. NC4459.

Ard Thurinish *High.* ***Coastal feature***, headland at S end of Sleat peninsula, Skye, 2m/4km E of Point of Sleat. **48 C5** NM5999.

Ard Veenish *W.Isles* ***Coastal feature***, peninsula at head of North Bay, Barra. NF7103.

Arda Beaga *W.Isles* ***Coastal feature***, promontory on W coast of North Harris, 1m/2km SE of Huisinis. **66 C2** NA9909.

Ardachadail *High.* ***Locality***, on NE shore of Loch Broom, 3m/5km NW of Ullapool. NH0997.

Ardacheranbeg *Arg. & B.* ***Settlement***, 1m/2km N of Clachan of Glendaruel. Standing stone to NE. **22 B1** NS0085.

Ardacheranmor *Arg. & B.* ***Settlement***, 3m/4km NE of Clachan of Glendaruel. **22 B1** NS0087.

Ardachoil *Arg. & B.* ***Settlement***, 3m/4km W of Grass Point, to N of Loch Spelve, Mull. **29 G1** NM7030.

Ardachuple *Arg. & B. Anglicised form of Ard a' Chapuill, qv.*

Ardachvie *High.* ***Settlement***, on NE side of Loch Arkaig, 4m/7km NW of Gairlochy. **50 A5** NN1390.

Ardailly *Arg. & B.* ***Settlement***, on N part of Gigha, just N of Mill Loch. **21 E4** NR6450.

Ardalanish *Arg. & B.* ***Settlement***, on Ross of Mull, 2m/3km S of Bunessan, a short distance inland from Ardalanish Bay on S coast. **28 C3** NM3719.

Ardalanish Bay *Arg. & B.* ***Bay***, on S coast on Ross of Mull. NM3718.

Ardalanish Point *Arg. & B. Anglicised form of Rubh' Ardalanish, qv.*

Ardallie *Aber.* ***Settlement***, 3m/5km NW of Hatton. **55 F1** NK0039.

Ardanaiseig *Arg. & B.* ***Settlement***, 3m/4km SW of Lochawe across NW arm of Loch Awe. **30 C2** NN0824.

Ardanaiseig Gardens *Arg. & B.* ***Garden***, mainly woodland gardens with a variety of trees, rhododendrons and flowering shrubs. Magnificent views across Loch Awe. 3m/4km SW of Lochawe across NW arm of Loch Awe. **30 C2** NN0824.

Ardaneaskan *High.* ***Settlement***, in Ross and Cromarty district, on N shore of Loch Carron, 2m/3km NE of Plockton across loch. **49 E1** NG8335.

Ardanstur *Arg. & B.* ***Settlement***, on N shore of Loch Melfort, on W side of Fearnach Bay. **30 A3** NM8213.

Ardantiobairt *High.* ***Settlement***, at head of Loch Teacuis, Lochaber district. **37 F4** NM6454.

Ardantrive *Arg. & B.* ***Settlement***, on Kerrera, 1km S of Rubh' a' Bhearnaig. **30 A2** NM8429.

Ardarroch *High.* ***Settlement***, in Ross and Cromarty district, at head of Loch Kishorn. **49 E1** NG8339.

Ardbeg *Arg. & B.* ***Hamlet***, S of Ardbeg Point, forming part of Port Bannatyne, large village and resort extending along coast on both sides of headland. **22 B3** NS0867.

Ardbeg *Arg. & B.* ***Settlement***, in Argyll, at head of Holy Loch. **22 C1** NS1583.

Ardbeg *Arg. & B.* ***Village***, small fishing village on S coast of Islay, 3m/5km E of Port Ellen. **20 C5** NR4146.

Ardbeg Point *Arg. & B.* ***Coastal feature***, headland on E coast of Bute between Kames Bay to N and Rothesay Bay to S. **22 B3** NS0867.

Ardblair *High.* ***Settlement***, 5m/7km N of Drumnadrochit. **51 D1** NH5036.

Ardbrecknish *Arg. & B.* ***Settlement***, on S side of Loch Awe, 1m/2km E of Portsonachan. **30 C2** NN0721.

Ardcharnich *High.* ***Settlement***, in Ross and Cromarty district, on E side of Loch Broom, 5m/7km SE of Ullapool. **60 A1** NH1788.

Ardchattan Gardens *Arg. & B.* ***Garden***, 4m/6km E of North Connel, to N of Loch Etive. 3 acres of wild and formal gardens, with good varieties of shrubs and roses. **30 B1** NM9734.

Ardchattan Priory *Arg. & B.* ***Ecclesiastical building***, 13c ruin (Historic Scotland) of Valliscaulian Priory on N side of Loch Etive, Argyll, opposite Airds Point. Meeting place of one of Robert the Bruce's parliaments in 1308; burned by English in 1654. **30 B1** NM9835.

Ardchiavaig *Arg. & B.* ***Settlement***, on S coast of Ross of Mull, 2m/3km S of Bunessan. **28 C3** NM3918.

Ardchonnel *Arg. & B.* ***Settlement***, 1m/2km S of Connel. **30 B1** NM9031.

Ardchonnell *Arg. & B.* ***Settlement***, on SE shore of Loch Awe, 1km E of Dalavich across loch. **30 B3** NM9812.

Ardchonnell Castle *Arg. & B. See Innis Chonnell.*

Ardchrishnish *Arg. & B.* ***Settlement***, near N coast of Ross of Mull, 3m/4km NE of Bunessan. **28 D2** NM4224.

Ardchronie *High.* ***Settlement***, on shore at NW end of Dornoch Firth, 2m/3km S of Bonar Bridge. **61 F1** NH6188.

Ardchuilk *High.* ***Settlement***, in Glen Strathfarrar, 11m/18km NW of Cannich. **50 B1** NH2638.

Ardchullarie More *Stir.* ***Settlement***, on E side of Loch Lubnaig, 4m/7km NW of Callander. **32 A3** NN5813.

Ardchyle *Stir.* ***Locality***, in Glen Dochart, 4m/7km SW of Killin. **32 A2** NN5229.

Ardclach Bell Tower *High.* ***Historic/prehistoric site***, fortified 17c belfry (Historic Scotland) above River Findhorn, 8m/13km SE of Nairn. **62 B5** NH9545.

Ardeer *N.Ayr.* ***Settlement***, adjoining to SE of Stevenston. NS2740.

Ardelve *High.* ***Settlement***, on N side of Loch Alsh, Skye and Lochalsh district, 1km W of Dornie across entrance to Loch Long. **49 E2** NG8726.

Ardelve Point *High.* ***Coastal feature***, promontory at entrance to Loch Long opposite Dornie, Skye and Lochalsh district. NG8726.

Arden *Arg. & B.* ***Hamlet***, on SW shore of Loch Lomond, 3m/4km NW of Balloch. **23 E1** NS3684.

Ardencaple *Arg. & B.* ***Settlement***, on Seil, 1m/2km W of Clachan Bridge. **29 G3** NM7619.

Ardencraig Gardens *Arg. & B.* ***Garden***, on Bute, 1km E of Rothesay. Rare plants, ornamental ponds and aviaries. **22 C3** NS1064.

Ardentallan *Arg. & B.* ***Settlement***, on N shore of Loch Feochan, 1m/2km NE of Kilninver across loch. **30 A2** NM8323.

Ardentinny *Arg. & B.* ***Village***, on W shore of Loch Long, 4m/7km N of Strone Point. **22 C1** NS1887.

Ardeonaig *Stir.* ***Village***, on S side of Loch Tay, 6m/10km NE of Killin. **32 B1** NN6635.

Ardersier (Formerly known as Campbelltown.) *High.* Population: 1055. ***Village***, in Inverness district, on E shore of Inner Moray Firth or Inverness Firth, 2m/3km SE of Fort George. **61 G4** NH7855.

Ardery *High.* ***Settlement***, in Sunart, Lochaber district, 4m/6km W of Strontian. **37 G3** NM7562.

Ardessie *High.* ***Settlement***, in Ross and Cromarty district, on S shore of Little Loch Broom, 5m/8km SE of Badluchrach. **59 G1** NH0589.

Ardessie Falls *High.* ***Waterfall***, high waterfall in course of Allt Airdeasaidh to S of Ardessie. NH0589.

Ardestie *Angus* ***Locality***, 1m/2km N of Monifieth, including ancient souterrain or earth-house (Historic Scotland). NO5034.

Ardfad *Arg. & B.* ***Settlement***, on Seil, 1m/2km N of Balvicar. **29 G3** NM7619.

Ardfern *Arg. & B.* ***Settlement***, on W side of Loch Craignish, in Argyll, 1m/2km SW of head of loch. **30 A4** NM8004.

Ardfin *Arg. & B.* ***Locality***, on Jura, 4m/6km SW of Craighouse. **20 C3** NR4863.

Ardgartan *Arg. & B.* ***Locality***, on W shore of Loch Long, at foot of Glen Croe, in Argyll. **31 E4** NN2702.

Ardgartan Forest *Arg. & B.* ***Forest/woodland***, to N and S along side of Loch Long, forming part of Argyll Forest Park. **31 E4** NN2702.
Ardgay *High.* ***Village***, in Sutherland district, 1m/2km SW of Bonar Bridge. Location of Bonar Bridge railway station. **72 A5** NH5990.
Ardgenavan *Arg. & B.* ***Settlement***, on N shore of NE arm of Loch Fyne, 5m/8km NE of Inveraray. **31 D3** NN1711.
Ardgoil Estate *Arg. & B.* ***Open space***, mountainous area between Loch Long and Loch Goil, forming part of Argyll Forest Park. **31 E4** NN2200.
Ardgoil Forest *Arg. & B.* ***Forest/woodland***, running along E side of Loch Goil in Argyll Forest Park. NS2198.
Ardgour *High.* ***Locality***, mountainous area of Lochaber district, to E of Sunart and bounded by Lochs Shiel, Eil and Linnhe. Mountains are noted for craggy rock faces and signs of glacial weathering. They rise above deeply incised valleys of Glen Cona, Glen Scaddle and Glen Gour which all run E to Loch Linnhe. **38 B3** NM9570.
Ardgowan *Inclyde* ***Settlement***, 1km N of Inverkip. **22 D2** NS2073.
Ardgowse *Aber.* ***Settlement***, on NW side of Corrennie Moor, 3m/5km SE of Alford. **54 B3** NJ6011.
Ardgye *Moray* ***Settlement***, 4m/6km W of Elgin. **62 D3** NJ1563.
Ardhallow *Arg. & B.* ***Settlement***, on Firth of Clyde, 3m/4km SW of Dunoon. **22 C2** NS1673.
Ardhasaig *W.Isles* *Anglicised form of Aird Asaig, qv.*
Ardheslaig *High.* ***Locality***, on SW side of Loch Torridon, Ross and Cromarty district, 3m/4km NW of Shieldaig. **59 D4** NG7856.
Ardiecow *Moray* ***Settlement***, on N side of Hill of Summertown, 1m/2km E of Kirktown of Deskford. **64 A3** NJ5361.
Ardinamar *Arg. & B.* ***Settlement***, on E coast of Luing, opposite Torsa. **29 G3** NM7511.
Ardindrean *High.* ***Settlement***, on W shore of Loch Broom, Ross and Cromarty district, 2m/4km from head of loch. **60 A1** NH1588.
Ardintigh Bay *High.* ***Bay***, small bay on W side of Ardintigh Point. NM7793.
Ardintigh Point *High.* ***Coastal feature***, promontory on S shore of Loch Nevis, Lochaber district, 1m/2km NW of Tarbet. NM7793.
Ardintoul *High.* ***Settlement***, on S shore of Loch Alsh, 2m/3km SE of Balmacara across loch. **49 E2** NG8324.
Ardintoul Point *High.* ***Coastal feature***, promontory on S shore of Loch Alsh, Skye and Lochalsh district, 2m/3km E of entrance to Kyle Rhea. **49 E2** NG8324.
Ardivachar *W.Isles* *Anglicised form of Aird a' Mhachair, qv.*
Ardivachar Point *W.Isles* ***Coastal feature***, headland at NW corner of South Uist. **45 F5** NF7445.
Ardjachie Point *High.* ***Coastal feature***, promontory on S shore of Dornoch Firth, 2m/4km NW of Tain. **61 G1** NH7585.
Ardkinglas House *Arg. & B.* ***Other building***, on S shore of NE arm of Loch Fyne, 5m/8km NE of Inveraray across loch. **31 D3** NN1710.
Ardkinglas Woodland Garden *Arg. & B.* ***Garden***, surrounding Strone House in valley of Kinglas Water, 6m/9km N of Lochgoilhead. Woodland section dominated by collection of giant conifers, with formal gardens containing rhododendrons and azaleas. **31 D3** NN1810.
Ardlair *Aber.* ***Settlement***, 1m/2km SE of Kennethmont and 2m/3km S of Knockandy Hill. **54 A2** NJ5528.
Ardlamont *Arg. & B.* ***Settlement***, on SE tip of Cowal peninsula, 4m/7km S of Tighnabruaich. **22 A3** NR9865.
Ardlamont Bay *Arg. & B.* ***Bay***, 1m/2km NW of Ardlamont Point, 6m/10km W of Rothesay across Kyles of Bute. **22 A3** NR9663.
Ardlamont Point *Arg. & B.* ***Coastal feature***, headland in Argyll on N side of Sound of Bute, at junction of Kyles of Bute and Loch Fyne. **22 A3** NR9963.
Ardle *P. & K.* ***River***, running SE down Strathardle to join Black Water below Bridge of Cally and form River Ericht. **41 G4** NO1451.
Ardleish *Arg. & B.* ***Settlement***, at N end of Loch Lomond, 1km E of Ardlui across loch. **31 F3** NN3215.
Ardler *P. & K.* ***Village***, 3m/5km E of Coupar Angus. **42 A5** NO2641.
Ardlui *Arg. & B.* ***Settlement***, at head of Loch Lomond, on W shore. **31 F3** NN3115.
Ardlussa *Arg. & B.* ***Settlement***, on E coast of Jura, nearly 1m/2km NE of Inverlussa, at mouth of Lussa River. Small bay and landing stage. **21 E1** NR6487.
Ardmaddy *Arg. & B.* ***Locality***, consisting of settlement and bay on E side of Loch Etive, Argyll, 5m/9km from head of loch. **30 C1** NN0737.
Ardmaddy Bay *Arg. & B.* ***Bay***, in Seil Sound, 4m/7km SW of Kilninver in Argyll. NM7816.
Ardmaddy Castle *Arg. & B.* ***Castle***, ancient seat of Marquess of Breadalbane, on Ardmaddy Bay in Seil Sound, 4m/7km SW of Kilninver in Argyll. NM7816.
Ardmair *High.* ***Locality***, on W coast of Ross and Cromarty district, 3m/5km NW of Ullapool. **70 D5** NH1198.
Ardmaleish *Arg. & B.* ***Settlement***, on E coast of Bute, 1km S of Ardmaleish Point. **22 B3** NS0768.
Ardmaleish Point *Arg. & B.* ***Coastal feature***, headland on Bute at entrance to E arm of Kyles of Bute. **22 B3** NS0769.
Ardmay *Arg. & B.* ***Settlement***, on NE shore of Loch Long, at its N end, 1m/2km SW of Arrochar. **31 E4** NN2802.
Ardmeanach *Arg. & B.* ***Locality***, district on W coast of Mull, N of Loch Scridain. At its SW corner lies Burg, an area of National Trust for Scotland property. **28 D2** NM4428.
Ardmenish *Arg. & B.* ***Settlement***, 2m/3km NE of Ardfernal across Lowlandman's Bay, Jura. **21 D2** NR5774.
Ardmhòr *W.Isles* ***Settlement***, on peninsula of Àrd Mhòr, NE coast of Barra. **44 C3** NF7103.
Ardmillan Castle *S.Ayr.* ***Historic house***, mansion dating from 16c and 18c, near coast 2m/4km S of Girvan. NX1694.
Ardminish *Arg. & B.* ***Village***, with jetty on Ardminish bay on E side of Gigha. **21 E5** NR6448.
Ardminish Bay *Arg. & B.* ***Bay***, on E side of Gigha. **21 E5** NR6448.
Ardminish Point *Arg. & B.* ***Coastal feature***, headland 1m/2km NE of Ardminish, on Gigha. NR6650.
Ardmolich *High.* ***Settlement***, at head of Loch Moidart. **37 G2** NM7172.
Ardmore *Arg. & B.* ***Settlement***, on Kerrera, 1km E of Rubha na Feundain. **29 G2** NM7927.
Ardmore *Arg. & B.* ***Settlement***, 7m/11km NE of Port Ellen, Islay. **20 C5** NR4650.
Ardmore *Arg. & B.* ***Settlement***, on peninsula, 2m/3km NW of Cardross. **23 E2** NS3178.
Ardmore *High.* ***Settlement***, on S shore of Dornoch Firth, 6m/9km NW of Tain, Ross and Cromarty district. **61 G1** NH7086.
Ardmore Bay *Arg. & B.* ***Bay***, on N coast of Mull, 3m/5km NW of Tobermory. **36 D4** NM4759.
Ardmore Bay *High.* ***Bay***, small bay on Skye, 4m/7km S of Vaternish Point. **57 F3** NG2260.
Ardmore Point *Arg. & B.* ***Coastal feature***, headland at E end of Ardmore Bay on N coast of Mull, 3m/5km NW of Tobermory. **37 D4** NM4759.
Ardmore Point *Arg. & B.* ***Coastal feature***, headland on SE coast of Islay, 5m/8km NE of Ardbeg. **20 C4** NR4750.
Ardmore Point *High.* ***Coastal feature***, headland on W coast of Sutherland district on E side of entrance to Loch Laxford. **74 A3** NC1851.
Ardmore Point *High.* ***Coastal feature***, headland on N coast of Caithness district, 2m/3km NW of Armadale. **75 G2** NC7666.
Ardmore Point *High.* ***Coastal feature***, headland on NW coast of Skye, 5m/8km S of Vaternish Point. **57 E4** NG2159.
Ardmore Point *High.* ***Coastal feature***, low-lying promontory to N of Ardmore, protruding into Dornoch Firth. NH7087.
Ardmucknish Bay *Arg. & B.* ***Bay***, on S side of Benderloch, between Rubha Garbh-àird and Ledaig Point, Argyll. **30 A1** NM8937.
Ardnackaig *Arg. & B.* ***Settlement***, 2m/3km N of Tayvallich. **29 G5** NR7490.
Ardnacross *Arg. & B.* ***Settlement***, on Mull, 4m/7km SE of Tobermory. **37 E5** NM5449.
Ardnacross Bay *Arg. & B.* ***Bay***, on E coast of Kintyre, 4m/7km NE of Campbeltown. **12 C3** NR7625.
Ardnadam *Arg. & B.* ***Village***, on S side of Holy Loch in Argyll, 2m/4km N of Dunoon. **22 C2** NS1780.
Ardnadrochet *Arg. & B.* ***Settlement***, on Mull, 1m/2km NW of Grass Point. **29 G1** NM7331.
Ardnagoine *High.* ***Settlement***, on Tanera Mòr, largest of Summer Isles group, off W coast of Ross and Cromarty district. **70 B4** NB9908.
Ardnagowan *Arg. & B.* ***Settlement***, on E shore of Loch Fyne, 3m/4km S of Inveraray across loch. **30 D4** NN1005.
Ardnagrask *High.* ***Settlement***, in Ross and Cromarty district, 1m/2km SW of Muir of Ord. **61 E5** NH5149.
Ardnahein *Arg. & B.* ***Settlement***, on W shore of Loch Goil, 1m/2km SE of Carrick. **31 E5** NS1993.
Ardnahoe *Arg. & B.* ***Settlement***, on shore of Ardnahoe Loch, on E coast of Islay, 1m/2km N of Port Askaig. **20 C2** NR4271.
Ardnahoe Loch (Loch Ardnahoe). *Arg. & B.* ***Lake/loch***, small loch 1m/2km N of Port Askaig, Islay. NR4271.
Ardnameacan *High.* ***Coastal feature***, headland on SE coast of Skye on E side of entrance to Loch na Dal. **48 D3** NG7114.
Ardnamurchan *High.* ***Locality***, large upland peninsula on W coast in Lochaber district, running W from Salen to Point of Ardnamurchan. **36 D3** NM5766.
Ardnandave Hill *Stir.* ***Mountain***, on W side of Loch Lubnaig, 5m/8km NW of Callander. Height 2345 feet or 715 metres. **32 A3** NN5612.
Ardnarff *High.* ***Locality***, on SE shore of Loch Carron, Skye and Lochalsh district. **49 E1** NG8935.
Ardnastang *High.* ***Settlement***, on N side of Loch Sunart, in Lochaber district, 1m/2km of W of Strontian. **38 A3** NM8161.
Ardnave *Arg. & B.* ***Settlement***, on N of Islay, 1m/2km SW of Ardnave Point. **20 A2** NR2873.
Ardnave Loch *Arg. & B.* ***Lake/loch***, on N coast of Islay, 1m/2km S of Ardnave Point. **20 A2** NR2872.
Ardnave Point *Arg. & B.* ***Coastal feature***, headland on N coast of Islay, on W side of entrance to Loch Gruinart. **20 A2** NR2975.
Ardneil Bay *N.Ayr.* ***Bay***, on Firth of Clyde, on E side of Farland Head, 1m/2km W of West Kilbride. **22 C5** NS1848.
Ardnish *High.* ***Coastal feature***, peninsula on coast of Lochaber district between Loch Ailort and Loch nan Uamh, the S and N arms respectively of Sound of Arisaig. **37 G1** NM7281.
Ardno *Arg. & B.* ***Settlement***, on S shore of NE arm of Loch Fyne, 3m/5km E of Inveraray across loch. **31 D4** NN1408.
Ardnoe Point *Arg. & B.* ***Coastal feature***, S side of mouth of Loch Crinan, 1m/2km W of Crinan. **29 G5** NR7794.
Ardo *Aber.* ***Locality***, comprises many dispersed settlements, 1m/2km N of Methlick and 4m/7km SW of New Deer. **55 D1** NJ8539.
Ardoch *D. & G.* ***Settlement***, above River Nith, 4m/7km SE of Sanquhar. **15 G5** NS8305.
Ardoch *Moray* ***Settlement***, 1km S of Dallas. **62 D4** NJ1251.
Ardoch *P. & K.* ***Settlement***, 1km S of Murthly. **33 F1** NO0937.
Ardoch Burn *Stir.* ***River***, running SE then S from Loch Mahaick to River Teith on S side of Doune. **32 C4** NN7300.
Ardoch Roman Camp *P. & K.* ***Historic/prehistoric site***, 4m/7km SW of Muthill. Well preserved site, but lacking visible stonework. Permanent camp for legions, dating from 1c-3c. Blackhall Roman Camps (Historic Scotland) to N. **33 D3** NN8309.
Ardochrig *S.Lan.* ***Settlement***, 4m/7km NW of Strathaven. **24 A5** NS6346.
Ardochu *High.* ***Settlement***, in Sutherland district, 6m/10km E of Lairg. **72 B4** NC6703.
Ardoyne *Aber.* ***Settlement***, 1m/2km NW of Oyne. **54 B2** NJ6527.
Ardpatrick *Arg. & B.* ***Settlement***, on NW coast of Kintyre, at seaward end of West Loch Tarbert, 9m/15km SW of Tarbert. **21 F3** NR7559.
Ardpatrick Point *Arg. & B.* ***Coastal feature***, headland at S end of Knapdale, Argyll, at entrance to West Loch Tarbert. **21 F4** NR7357.
Ardpeaton *Arg. & B.* ***Hamlet***, on E shore of Loch Long, 2m/3km N of Cove. **22 D1** NS2285.
Ardradnaig *P. & K.* ***Settlement***, on SE side of Loch Tay, 4m/7km SW of Kenmore. **40 C5** NN7142.
Ardrishaig *Arg. & B.* Population: 1315. ***Small town***, in Argyll on W shore of Loch Gilp, 2m/3km S of Lochgilphead. Television and radio transmitting station. SE terminus of Crinan Canal. **21 G1** NR8585.
Ardroe *High.* ***Settlement***, 2m/3km NW of Lochinver, Sutherland district. **70 C2** NC0623.
Ardroil *W.Isles* *Anglicised form of Eadar dha Fhadhail, qv.*
Ardross *High.* ***Settlement***, in Ross and Cromarty district, 4m/6km NW of Alness. NH6174.
Ardross Castle *Fife* ***Castle***, ruined 14c castle on N coast of Firth of Forth, between Elie and St. Monans. NO5000.
Ardross Castle *High.* ***Historic house***, mansion 1km SW of Ardross. NH6174.
Ardross Forest *High.* ***Forest/woodland***, to N of Ardross. NH6473.
Ardrossan *N.Ayr.* Population: 10,750. ***Town***, port on Firth of Clyde, 12m/20km W of Kilmarnock. Passenger boat services to Arran. **22 D5** NS2342.
Ardrossan Castle *N.Ayr.* ***Castle***, of mid 12c, situated on a hill overlooking Ardrossan Bay. Was destroyed by Cromwell and only the north tower and two arched cellars remain. **22 D5** NS2244.
Ardscalpsie *Arg. & B.* ***Settlement***, on Bute, above W side of Scalpsie Bay. **22 B4** NS0558.
Ardscalpsie Point *Arg. & B.* ***Coastal feature***, headland on W coast of Bute, on W side of Scalpsie Bay. NS0457.
Ardshave *High.* ***Settlement***, 4m/7km NW of Dornoch. **72 C5** NH7695.
Ardshealach *High.* ***Settlement***, 1km SE of Acharacle. **37 F3** NM6867.
Ardshellach *Arg. & B.* ***Settlement***, 3m/5km SW of Kilninver. **29 G3** NM7818.
Ardslave *W.Isles* *Anglicised form of Aird Leimhe, qv.*
Ardslignish *High.* ***Locality***, on S side of Ardnamurchan peninsula, in Lochaber district, 8m/13km W of Salen. **37 E3** NM5661.
Ardtalla *Arg. & B.* ***Settlement***, on E coast of Islay, 9m/14km NE of Port Ellen. **20 C4** NR4654.
Ardtalnaig *P. & K.* ***Village***, on S side of Loch Tay, 6m/10km SW of Kenmore. Old copper and lead mines in vicinity. **32 B1** NN7039.
Ardtarig *Arg. & B.* ***Settlement***, 1km S of head of Loch Striven on E shore, 8m/12km NW of Dunoon. **22 B1** NS0582.
Ardteatle *Arg. & B.* ***Locality***, 2m/3km SW of Dalmally. **30 D2** NN1325.

Ardtoe *High.* ***Settlement***, in Lochaber district, on N side of entrance to Kentra Bay, 3m/5km NW of Acharacle. **37 F2** NM6270.
Ardtornish *High.* ***Garden***, 24 acres of gardens surrounding Ardtornish House, at head of Loch Aline, Lochaber district. **37 G5** NM7047.
Ardtornish *High.* ***Settlement***, at head of Loch Aline, 3m/4km NE of Lochaline, Lochaber district. **37 G5** NM7047.
Ardtornish Bay *High.* ***Bay***, on E side of Ardtornish Point, on Sound of Mull. NM6942.
Ardtornish Point *High.* ***Coastal feature***, headland on Sound of Mull 1m/2km SE of entrance to Loch Aline, Lochaber district. Ruins of 14c castle, stronghold of the Lords of the Isles. **37 F5** NM6942.
Ardtreck Point *High.* ***Coastal feature***, headland in Loch Bracadale, Skye, at entrance to Loch Harport. **47 G1** NG3336.
Ardtrostan *P. & K.* ***Settlement***, on S side of Loch Earn, 1m/2km SW of St. Fillans. **32 B2** NN6723.
Ardtun *Arg. & B.* ***Settlement***, scattered locality on Ross of Mull, to NE of Bunessan. **28 C2** NM3923.
Ardtur *Arg. & B.* ***Settlement***, 1km NE of Port Appin. **38 B5** NM9146.
Arduaine *Arg. & B.* ***Locality***, on Asknish Bay, on coast of Argyll, 4m/6km SW of Kilmelford. **30 A4** NM8010.
Arduaine Garden *Arg. & B.* ***Garden***, to W of Arduaine, and inland from Arduaine Point. Woodland and gardens (National Trust for Scotland) with coastal viewpoint, including rhododendrons, azaleas and perennial borders. **29 G3** NM7910.
Ardullie *High.* ***Settlement***, 2m/3km SW of Evanton. **61 E3** NH5863.
Ardura *Arg. & B.* ***Settlement***, to S of Lussa River, near head of Loch Spelve, 4m/6km W of Grass Point, Mull. **29 F1** NM6830.
Ardvar *High.* ***Settlement***, on W side of Loch Ardvar, Sutherland district. **74 A5** NC1734.
Ardvasar *High.* ***Village***, on E coast of Sleat peninsula, Skye, 5m/8km NE of Point of Sleat. **48 C4** NG6303.
Ardveenish *W.Isles* ***Settlement***, on peninsula of Ard Veenish, at head of North Bay, Barra. NF7103.
Ardveich *Stir.* ***Settlement***, on N side of Loch Earn, 1m/2km E of Lochearnhead. **32 B2** NN6224.
Ardverikie *High.* ***Settlement***, on S shore of Loch Laggan, 3m/4km SW of Kinloch Laggan. **40 A1** NN5087.
Ardverikie Forest *High.* ***Open space***, deer forest in Badenoch and Strathspey district, S of Lochan na h-Earba. **39 G2** NN5081.
Ardvey *W.Isles Anglicised form of Aird Mhighe, qv.*
Ardvey *W.Isles Anglicised form of Aird Mhige, qv.*
Ardvorlich *Arg. & B.* ***Settlement***, on W side of N end of Loch Lomond, 2m/3km S of Ardlui. **31 F3** NN3211.
Ardvorlich *P. & K.* ***Settlement***, on S side of Loch Earn, 3m/4km SE of Lochearnhead. **32 B2** NN6322.
Ardvourlie *W.Isles Anglicised form of Aird a' Mhulaidh, qv.*
Ardvreck Castle *High.* ***Castle***, situated on promontory on N side of Loch Assynt. Ruined 16c tower where Montrose was handed over to Parliament in 1650. **71 E2** NC2323.
Ardwall *D. & G.* ***Settlement***, on N shore of Fleet Bay, 1m/2km SW of Gatehouse of Fleet. **7 G5** NX5854.
Ardwall Island *D. & G.* ***Island***, one of the Islands of Fleet, off E shore of Wigtown Bay. Foundations of several early Christian churches have been uncovered. **3 F2** NX5749.
Ardwell *D. & G.* ***Village***, on E coast of Rinns of Galloway, 3m/5km S of Sandhead. **2 B2** NX1045.
Ardwell *Moray* ***Settlement***, near confluence of Black Water and River Deveron, 2m/3km N of Cabrach. **53 F1** NJ3730.
Ardwell *S.Ayr.* ***Settlement***, on coast, 3m/4km S of Girvan. **6 C1** NX1694.
Ardwell Bay *D. & G.* ***Bay***, on W coast of Rinns of Galloway, 2m/4km W of Ardwell. **2 A2** NX1045.
Ardwell House *D. & G.* ***Garden***, woodland garden and pond walk with sea views, 1km from Ardwell on W side of Luce Bay. Displays of daffodils and rhododendrons. **2 A2** NX1045.
Ardwell Point *D. & G.* ***Coastal feature***, headland on S side of Ardwell Bay. NX0644.
Ardyne Burn *Arg. & B.* ***River***, running S down Glen Fyne to Firth of Clyde 2m/4km W of Toward Point. **22 C2** NS1068.
Ardyne Point *Arg. & B.* ***Coastal feature***, headland in Argyll, 3m/4km W of Toward Point. **22 B3** NS0968.
Arecleoch Forest *S.Ayr.* ***Forest/woodland***, 4m/6km SW of Barrhill. NX1879.
Argaty *Stir.* ***Settlement***, 1m/2km NE of Doune. **32 C4** NN7303.
Argrennan House *D. & G.* ***Settlement***, in Dee Valley, 4m/7km N of Kirkcudbright. **8 B5** NX7158.
Argyll and Sutherland Highlanders Museum *Stir.* ***Other feature of interest***, in Stirling Castle, with displays on regiment and a medal collection. **32 C5** NS7893.
Argyll Forest Park *Arg. & B.* ***Forest/woodland***, forest and mountain area in Argyll between Loch Long and Loch Fyne, occupying much of N part of Cowal peninsula. **30 D5** NS1396.
Argyll Wildlife Park *Arg. & B.* ***Leisure/recreation***, large collection of indigenous wildlife, waterfowl and owls, 2m/3km SW of Inveraray. **30 C4** NN0805.
Argyll's Bowling Green *Arg. & B.* ***Large natural feature***, mountainous area in Argyll between Loch Goil and Loch Long. **31 E5** NS2298.
Aribruach *W.Isles Anglicised form of Airidh a' Bhruaich, qv.*
Arichamish *Arg. & B.* ***Settlement***, on N shore of Loch Awe, 3m/4km NE of Ford. **30 B4** NM9005.
Arichastlich *Arg. & B.* ***Settlement***, in Glen Orchy, 5m/8km NW of Tyndrum. **31 E1** NN2534.
Arichonan *Arg. & B.* ***Settlement***, in Knapdale, 5m/7km W of Cairnbaan. **29 G5** NR7790.
Aridhglas *Arg. & B.* ***Settlement***, on Mull, 1m/2km S of Rubha nan Cearc. **28 C2** NM3123.
Arienskill *High.* ***Settlement***, 1m/2km E of Lochailort, Lochaber district. **37 G1** NM7883.
Arileod *Arg. & B.* ***Settlement***, on Coll, 4m/7km SW of Arinagour. **36 A4** NM1654.
Arinacrinachd *High.* ***Locality***, in Ross and Cromarty district, on SW coast of Loch Torridon, 6m/9km NW of Shieldaig. **58 D4** NG7458.
Arinafad Beg *Arg. & B.* ***Settlement***, on NW coast of Caol Scotnish, 3m/5km SW of Crinan. **21 F1** NR7689.
Arinagour *Arg. & B.* ***Village***, sole village and port of Coll, situated on SE coast 5m/8km from NE end, at head of Loch Eatharna. **36 B4** NM2256.
Arinambane *W.Isles* ***Settlement***, on South Uist, 3m/5km NE of Mingearraidh. **44 C1** NF7928.
Arinarach Hill *Arg. & B.* ***Mountain***, on Kintyre, 3m/4km SE of Campeltown. Height 1030 feet or 314 metres. **12 C4** NR7316.
Aris Dale *Shet.* ***Valley***, carrying Burn of Arisdale and running SE into Hamna Voe in S part of Yell. HU4882.
Arisaig *High.* ***Locality***, area in Lochaber district surrounding hinterland of village of Arisaig. It rises from coastal flats to mountains between South Morar and Moidart. **37 F1** NM6687.
Arisaig *High.* ***Village***, within surrounding area of Arisaig on W coast of Lochaber district. Village is 7m/11km S of Mallaig, at head of Loch nan Ceall. **37 F1** NM6586.
Arivegaig *High.* ***Settlement***, 1m/2km W of Acharacle, Lochaber district. **37 F3** NM6568.
Ark Hill *Angus* ***Mountain***, 3m/5km SW of Glamis. Height 1115 feet or 340 metres. **42 B5** NO3542.
Arkle (Gaelic form: Arcuil.) *High.* ***Mountain***, rising to ridge along summit in Sutherland district, 5m/8km SE of Rhiconich. Height 2581 feet or 787 metres. **74 C4** NC3046.
Arkleton *D. & G.* ***Settlement***, in valley of Ewes Water, 4m/7km N of Langholm. **10 B2** NY3791.
Arkleton Hill *D. & G.* ***Mountain***, steep-sided mountain, with rounded summit, 6m/9km NE of Langholm. Height 1709 feet or 521 metres. **10 C2** NY4092.
Arks Edge *Sc.Bord.* ***Inland physical feature***, mountain ridge E of Carter Bar in Cheviot Hills, 447 metres at highest point. **11 F1** NT7107.
Arlary *P. & K.* ***Settlement***, 1m/2km NE of Milnathort. **33 G4** NO1305.
Arlick *P. & K.* ***Mountain***, 1m/2km NW of Butterstone. Height 1046 feet or 319 metres. **41 F5** NO0746.
Armadale *High.* ***Locality***, 1km NE of Ardvasar, on E coast of Sleat peninsula on Skye. Includes Armadale Bay and pier, and Armadale Castle. **48 C4** NG6304.
Armadale *High.* ***Village***, near N coast of Caithness district, 6m/10km W of Melvich. **75 G2** NC7864.
Armadale *W.Loth.* Population: 8958. ***Small town***, 7m/11km SW of Linlithgow. **24 D3** NS9368.
Armadale Bay *High.* ***Bay***, to E of Armadale, on N coast of Caithness district. **75 G2** NC7965.
Armadale Bay *High.* ***Bay***, with pier, 1km NE of Ardvasar, on E coast of Sleat peninsula on Skye. **48 C4** NG6303.
Armadale Burn *High.* ***River***, stream running N into Armadale Bay. **75 G2** NC7864.
Armadale Castle *High.* ***Castle***, 1km N of Armadale Bay, estate and site of former castle of the Lords Macdonald, Barons of Sleat. NG6304.
Arnabost *Arg. & B.* ***Settlement***, 2m/3km NW of Arinagour, Coll. **36 B4** NM2060.
Arnaval *High.* ***Mountain***, 3m/5km N of Beinn Bhreac, Skye. Height 1210 feet or 369 metres. **47 G1** NG3431.
Arnaval *W.Isles* ***Hill***, 5m/8km SE of Rubha Ardvule, South Uist. Height 827 feet or 252 metres. **44 C1** NF7825.
Arncroach *Fife* ***Village***, 2m/4km N of St. Monans. **34 D4** NO5105.
Arngask *P. & K.* ***Hamlet***, to E of Glenfarg, 5m/8km N of Kinross. **33 G3** NO1510.
Arngibbon *Stir.* ***Settlement***, 2m/3km E of Buchlyvie. Ancient earthworks in wooded glen to W. **32 B5** NS6094.
Arngomery *Stir.* ***Settlement***, 1m/2km W of Kippen. **32 B5** NS6394.
Arnhall *Aber.* ***Hamlet***, 1km E of Edzell across River North Esk. **43 E3** NO6169.
Arnicle *Arg. & B.* ***Settlement***, on Kintyre, 3m/4km NE of Glenbarr. **12 C2** NR7138.
Arnipol *High.* ***Settlement***, 2m/3km NW of Lochailort, Lochaber district. **37 G1** NM7483.
Arnisdale *High.* ***Village***, in Lochaber district on N shore of Loch Hourn, some 5m/8km E of entrance to loch from Sound of Sleat. Also river running W down Glen Arnisdale to Loch Hourn, 1m/2km SE of village. **49 E3** NG8410.
Arnish *High.* ***Settlement***, on Raasay, 3m/5km from N end of island. **58 C5** NG5948.
Arnish Moor *W.Isles* ***Open space***, 3m/4km SE of Stornoway, Isle of Lewis, consisting of numerous small lochs and rocky outcrops. **69 E5** NB3929.
Arnish Point *W.Isles* ***Coastal feature***, headland with lighthouse on W side of entrance to Stornoway Harbour, Isle of Lewis. **69 F4** NB4330.
Arniston Engine *Midloth.* ***Suburb***, NW district of Gorebridge, 3m/5km S of Dalkeith. **26 A3** NT3462.
Arnol *W.Isles* ***River***, rising on Isle of Lewis among lochs to S of Arnol and flowing N between Arnol and Bragar into Loch Arnol and then into bay of Port Arnol. NB3048.
Arnol *W.Isles* ***Village***, near NW coast of Isle of Lewis, 3m/5km W of Barvas. Black House (Historic Scotland) to N. **69 E3** NB3148.
Arnot Reservoir *P. & K.* ***Reservoir***, small reservoir 3m/4km W of Leslie. NO2002.
Arnprior *Stir.* ***Village***, 12m/19km W of Stirling. **32 B5** NS6194.
Arnton Fell *Sc.Bord.* ***Mountain***, wooded on E side, 5m/8km NE of Castleton. Height 1328 feet or 405 metres. **10 D2** NY5294.
Aros *Arg. & B.* ***Locality***, on Mull, to S of Tobermory. **37 D4** NM5150.
Aros *Arg. & B.* ***River***, runs E down Glen Aros to Sound of Mull, 1m/2km N of Salen. NM5544.
Aros Bay *Arg. & B.* ***Bay***, small bay on E coast of Islay, 1m/2km N of Ardmore Point. NR4652.
Aros Bay *High.* ***Bay***, small bay on E coast of Vaternish peninsula, 5m/8km SE of Vaternish Point, Skye. **57 F3** NG2760.
Aros Castle *Arg. & B.* ***Castle***, formerly stronghold of the Lords of the Isles, at mouth of Aros River. **37 E5** NM5051.
Arradoul *Moray* ***Locality***, 1m/2km S of Buckie. **63 G3** NJ4263.
Arran *N.Ayr.* ***Island***, mountainous island, with mild though wet climate and fertile valleys, on W side of Firth of Clyde and separated from Kintyre by Kilbrannan Sound. Measures 20m/32km N to S and about 9m/15km E to W; area 166 square miles or 430 square km. Industries are tourism, sheep and cattle grazing and fishing. Highest point is Goat Fell, 2866 feet or 874 metres. Brodick, on E coast, is chief town. **13 E2** NR9536.
Arrat *Angus* ***Settlement***, 2m/3km SE of Brechin. **43 E4** NO6358.
Arrivain *Arg. & B.* ***Settlement***, in Glen Lochy, 4m/6km W of Tyndrum. **31 E1** NN2630.
Arrochar *Arg. & B.* ***Village***, at head of Loch Long on E side of loch, 1m/2km W of Tarbet on Loch Lomond and 13m/21km N of Helensburgh. **31 F4** NN2904.
Arscaig *High.* ***Settlement***, on W side of Loch Shin, 6m/10km NW of Lairg. **72 A3** NC5014.
Artfield Fell *D. & G.* ***Large natural feature***, 6m/10km N of Glenluce. Rising to height of 800 feet or 244 metres at Green Top. **6 D4** NX2267.
Arthrath *Aber.* ***Settlement***, 4m/6km N of Ellon. **55 E1** NJ9636.
Arthur's Point *Moray* ***Coastal feature***, headland on N coast at W end of Buckie. NJ4065.
Arthur's Seat *Edin.* ***Hill***, of volcanic origin, 1m/2km SE of Edinburgh city centre. Height 823 feet or 251 metres. **25 G2** NT2772.
Arthurstone *P. & K.* ***Settlement***, 1km N of Ardler. **42 A5** NO2542.
Artrochie *Aber.* ***Settlement***, 3m/4km NE of Ellon. **55 F1** NK0031.
Aruadh *Arg. & B.* ***Settlement***, 4m/6km NE of Kilchiaran. **20 A3** NR2464.
Aryhoulan *High.* ***Settlement***, in valley of River Scaddle, 5m/8km SW of Fort William across Loch Linnhe. **38 C3** NN0168.
Ascog *Arg. & B.* ***Village***, on E coast of Bute, 1m/2km SE of Rothesay, extending N and S of Ascog Point. **22 C3** NS1063.
Ascog Bay *Arg. & B.* ***Bay***, small bay on N side of Ascog Point, on E coast of Bute. NS1063.
Ascog Point *Arg. & B.* ***Coastal feature***, headland on E coast of Bute, 2m/3km SE of Rothesay. NS1063.
Ascreavie *Angus* ***Settlement***, 4m/6km NW of Kirriemuir. **42 B4** NO3357.
Ascrib Islands *High.* ***Island***, group of small uninhabited islands at entrance to Loch Snizort, Skye. Named islands, from N to S, are Eilean Iosal, Eilean Creagach, Sgeir na Capaill, Eilean Garave and South Ascrib. **57 G3** NG3064.
Asgog Bay *Arg. & B.* ***Bay***, on E side of Loch Fyne, Argyll, 4m/6km NW of Ardlamont Point. **22 A3** NR9367.
Asgog Loch *Arg. & B.* ***Lake/loch***, small loch 2m/3km N of Asgog Bay. **22 A3** NR9367.

Asgog Loch Castle *Arg. & B.* ***Castle***, on shore of Loch Asgog, 3m/4km SW of Tighnabruaich. **22 A2** NR9470.
Ashens *Arg. & B.* ***Settlement***, in Knapdale, 2m/3km N of Tarbert. **21 G2** NR8571.
Ashfield *Arg. & B.* ***Settlement***, in Knapdale, 5m/8km W of Ardrishaig. **21 F1** NR7685.
Ashfield *Stir.* ***Hamlet***, 2m/3km N of Dunblane. **32 C4** NN7803.
Ashgill *S.Lan.* Population: 1067. ***Village***, 2m/3km SE of Larkhall. **24 B4** NS7850.
Ashgrove *Moray* ***Suburb***, SE district of Elgin. NJ2262.
Ashie Moor *High.* ***Open space***, moorland 2m/3km S of Dores. **51 F1** NH6032.
Ashiestiel *Sc.Bord.* ***Settlement***, in River Tweed valley, 1m/2km W of Caddonfoot. **17 F2** NT4234.
Ashiestiel Hill *Sc.Bord.* ***Mountain***, 3m/4km SW of Clovenfords. Height 1315 feet or 401 metres. **17 F2** NT4134.
Ashkirk *Sc.Bord.* ***Village***, on Ale Water, 4m/6km S of Selkirk. **17 F3** NT4722.
Ashmore *P. & K.* ***Settlement***, 1m/2km N of Bridge of Cally. **41 G4** NO1453.
Ashton *Inclyde* ***Suburb***, SW district of Gourock. NS2377.
Ashybank *Sc.Bord.* ***Settlement***, 3m/5km NE of Hawick. **17 G4** NT5417.
Askival *High.* ***Mountain***, highest point on Rum, 3m/5km S of Kinloch. Height 2663 feet or 812 metres. **47 G5** NM3995.
Asknish *Arg. & B.* ***Historic house***, on Loch Gair in Argyll, on W side of Loch Fyne. **30 B5** NR9391.
Asknish Bay *Arg. & B.* ***Bay***, small bay on coast of Argyll, 4m/6km SW of Kilmelford. **29 G4** NM7910.
Asknish Forest *Arg. & B.* ***Forest/woodland***, on W side of Loch Fyne, to NW and SW of Asknish. NR9391.
Asloun *Aber.* ***Locality***, comprises Castleton of Asloun and Mains of Asloun surrounding Asloun Castle, 2m/3km SW of Alford. **54 A3** NJ5414.
Assich Forest *High.* ***Forest/woodland***, in Nairn district, to S and SW of Cawdor. **62 A5** NH8146.
Athelstaneford *E.Loth.* ***Village***, 3m/4km NE of Haddington. **26 C2** NT5377.
Athelstaneford Church *E.Loth.* *Alternative name for Church of Plaque, qv.*
Athlinne *W.Isles* ***Settlement***, on NW shore of Loch Seaforth, opposite Seaforth Island. **67 D2** NB1911.
Atholl *P. & K.* ***Locality***, area of some 450 square miles or 1200 square km at S end of Grampian Mountains, including Forest of Atholl. **40 C2** NN7671.
Atholl Sow *P. & K.* *Alternative name for The Sow of Atholl, qv.*
Attadale *High.* ***River***, flowing NW into Loch Carron at settlement of Attadale, Ross and Cromarty district. **49 F1** NG9138.
Attadale *High.* ***Settlement***, 2m/3km S of head of Loch Carron. **49 F1** NG9238.
Attadale Forest *High.* ***Open space***, deer forest on borders of Ross and Cromarty and Skye and Lochalsh districts SE of head of Loch Carron. **49 F1** NG9935.
Auch *Arg. & B.* ***Settlement***, 3m/4km SE of Bridge of Orchy. **31 F1** NN3235.
Aucha Lochy *Arg. & B.* ***Lake/loch***, small loch in Kintyre 1m/2km N of Campbeltown. NR7222.
Auchachenna *Arg. & B.* ***Settlement***, on NW shore of Loch Awe, 1m/2km SW of Kilchrenan. **30 C2** NN0221.
Auchagallon *N.Ayr.* ***Historic/prehistoric site***, stone circle (Historic Scotland) on W coast of Arran, 4m/7km N of Blackwaterfoot. **13 E2** NR8934.
Auchairne *S.Ayr.* ***Settlement***, 2m/3km E of Ballantrae. **6 C2** NX1081.
Auchalick *Arg. & B.* ***River***, in Argyll running SW to Auchalick Bay on E side of Loch Fyne, 3m/5km S of Kilfinan. NR9174.
Auchalick Bay *Arg. & B.* ***Bay***, on E side of Loch Fyne, 3m/5km S of Kilfinan. **21 G2** NR9174.
Auchallater *Aber.* ***Settlement***, 2m/3km S of Braemar. **41 G1** NO1588.
Auchameanach *Arg. & B.* ***Settlement***, on Kintyre, 1m/2km E of Claonaig. **21 G4** NR8956.
Auchamore (Also known as South Thundergay.) *N.Ayr.* ***Settlement***, on NW coast of Arran, 1m/2km N of Pirnmill. NR8745.
Aucharnie *Aber.* ***Settlement***, 4m/6km S of Inverkeithny. **64 B5** NJ6340.
Aucharrigill *High.* ***Settlement***, 1m/2km E of Invercassley. **71 G4** NC4901.
Auchattie *Aber.* ***Hamlet***, 1km S of Banchory. **54 B5** NO6994.
Auchavan *Angus* ***Settlement***, in Glen Isla, 5m/8km E of Spittal of Glenshee. **41 G3** NO1969.
Auchbraad *Arg. & B.* ***Settlement***, 3m/4km SW of Ardrishaig. **21 G1** NR8381.
Auchbreck *Moray* ***Settlement***, at road junction, 2m/3km N of Tomnavoulin. **53 E2** NJ2028.
Auchenback *E.Renf.* ***Suburb***, in SE part of Barrhead. NS5058.
Auchenblae *Aber.* ***Village***, 8m/12km NW of Inverbervie. **43 F2** NO7278.
Auchenbothie *Inclyde* ***Settlement***, 1km NW of Kilmacolm. **23 E2** NS3571.
Auchenbrack *D. & G.* ***Settlement***, 4m/6km N of Moniaive. **8 B1** NX7696.
Auchenbreck *Arg. & B.* ***Settlement***, to E of confluence of Auchenbreck Burn and River Ruel, 3m/4km SE of Clachan of Glendaruel. **22 B1** NS0281.
Auchencairn *D. & G.* ***Village***, 7m/11km S of Dalbeattie. **8 C5** NX7951.
Auchencairn Bay *D. & G.* ***Bay***, inlet on Solway Firth, to E of Auchencairn. **8 C5** NX7951.
Auchencloy Hill *D. & G.* ***Hill***, 1km N of Loch Skerrow, 8m/13km N of Gatehouse of Fleet. Height 686 feet or 209 metres. **7 G4** NX6069.
Auchencorth Moss *Midloth.* ***Large natural feature***, upland plateau on border with Scottish Borders, about 3m/5km SW of Penicuik. **25 F4** NT2055.
Auchencrow *Sc.Bord.* ***Village***, 3m/5km N of Chirnside. **27 F3** NT8560.
Auchendinny *Midloth.* ***Village***, 2m/3km NE of Penicuik. **25 G3** NT2562.
Auchendolly *D. & G.* ***Settlement***, 4m/6km N of Castle Douglas. **8 B4** NX7668.
Auchendores Reservoir *Inclyde* ***Reservoir***, small reservoir on border with Renfrewshire, 1m/2km N of Kilmacolm. NS3572.
Auchenfoyle *Inclyde* ***Settlement***, 3m/4km W of Kilmacolm. **23 E2** NS3170.
Auchengillan *Stir.* ***Settlement***, 3m/5km W of Strathblane. NS5180.
Auchengray *S.Lan.* ***Village***, 5m/8km N of Carnwath. **25 D4** NS9954.
Auchenhalrig *Moray* ***Settlement***, near N coast, 4m/6km SW of Buckie. **63 F3** NJ3761.
Auchenheath *S.Lan.* ***Hamlet***, 1m/2km E of Blackwood across River Nethan. **24 C5** NS8043.
Auchenhessnane *D. & G.* ***Settlement***, 5m/8km W of Thornhill. **8 C1** NX8096.
Auchenlochan *Arg. & B.* ***Hamlet***, in Argyll, on W shore of Kyles of Bute, 1km S of Tighnabruaich. **22 A2** NR9772.
Auchenmalg *D. & G.* ***Settlement***, adjacent to E of Glen of Luce, 4m/6km SE of Glenluce. **6 D5** NX2352.
Auchenmalg Bay *D. & G.* ***Bay***, S facing bay on E side of Luce Bay, 4m/7km SE of Glenluce. **6 D5** NX2351.
Auchenreoch Loch *D. & G.* ***Lake/loch***, 1m/2km SW of Crocketford. **8 C3** NX8171.
Auchenrivock *D. & G.* ***Settlement***, on W side of River Esk, 3m/4km S of Langholm. **10 B3** NY3780.
Auchenroddan Forest *D. & G.* ***Forest/woodland***, 4m/7km N of Lockerbie. NY1289.
Auchentiber *N.Ayr.* ***Hamlet***, 4m/6km W of Stewarton. **23 E5** NS3647.
Auchessan *Stir.* ***Settlement***, in Glen Dochart, 9m/13km SW of Killin. **31 G2** NN4427.
Auchgourish *High.* ***Settlement***, 2m/3km S of Boat of Garten. **52 B3** NH9315.
Auchinafaud *Arg. & B.* ***Settlement***, on W coast of Kintyre, 4m/6km NE of Tayinloan. **21 F4** NR7251.
Auchinairn *E.Dun.* ***Suburb***, 1km SE of Bishopbriggs. NS6169.
Auchinbee *N.Lan.* ***Settlement***, 2m/3km W of Cumbernauld town centre. NS7375.
Auchincruive *S.Ayr.* ***Educational establishment***, agricultural college 3m/5km E of Ayr. **14 B3** NS3823.
Auchindarrach *Arg. & B.* ***Hamlet***, just NW of Lochgilphead. **21 G1** NR8688.
Auchindarroch *High.* ***Settlement***, in Appin, 4m/6km SW of South Ballachulish. **38 C4** NN0055.
Auchindoun Castle *Moray* ***Castle***, ruined 16c fortress (Historic Scotland) built over ancient earthworks, 2m/3km SE of Dufftown. **53 F1** NJ3437.
Auchindrain *Arg. & B.* ***Settlement***, 2m/3km N of Furnace. An original West Highland township which has survived much in its original form, with buildings restored and equipped to demonstrate life of Highlanders in past centuries. **30 C4** NN0203.
Auchindrain Township Open Air Museum *Arg. & B.* ***Other feature of interest***, museum of original West Highland township, 5m/8km SW of Inveraray, showing Highland life through displays and exhibitions. **30 C4** NN0303.
Auchindrean *High.* ***Settlement***, in valley of River Broom, 10m/15km SE of Ullapool. **60 A1** NH1980.
Auchingilloch *S.Lan.* ***Mountain***, 6m/9km S of Strathaven. Height 1515 feet or 462 metres. **15 E2** NS7035.
Auchininna *Aber.* ***Settlement***, above S side of River Deveron, 4m/6km SE of Aberchirder. **64 B5** NJ6446.
Auchinleck *E.Ayr.* Population: 4116. ***Small town***, 1m/2km NW of Cumnock. **15 D3** NS5521.
Auchinloch *N.Lan.* ***Hamlet***, 2m/3km S of Kirkintilloch. **24 A2** NS6670.
Auchinner *P. & K.* ***Settlement***, in Glen Artney, 6m/10km NE of Callander. **32 B3** NN6915.
Auchinroath *Moray* ***Settlement***, 1m/2km N of Rothes. **63 E4** NJ2651.
Auchintaple Loch *Angus* ***Lake/loch***, small loch 3m/5km N of Kirkton of Glenisla. NO1964.
Auchintore *High.* ***Locality***, on E shore of Loch Linnhe, 1m/2km SW of Fort William. NN0972.
Auchintoul *Aber.* ***Locality***, comprises Auchintoul Moss and settlements of Newtown of Auchintoul and Home Farm Auchintoul, 1km NW of Aberchirder. **64 B4** NJ6152.
Auchintoul *Aber.* ***Settlement***, on S side of River Don, 3m/4km W of Alford. **54 A3** NJ5316.
Auchintoul *High.* ***Settlement***, in Sutherland district, 3m/4km W of Linsidemore. **72 A4** NH5299.
Auchinvennal *Arg. & B.* ***Settlement***, on N side of Glen Fruin, 4m/6km N of Helensburgh. **23 D1** NS2888.
Auchiries *Aber.* ***Settlement***, 1m/2km NW of Cruden Bay. **55 F1** NK0837.
Auchleven *Aber.* ***Village***, 3m/4km S of Insch. **54 B2** NJ6224.
Auchlochan *S.Lan.* ***Settlement***, on S bank of River Nethan, 2m/3km S of Lesmahagow. **15 G2** NS8037.
Auchlunachan *High.* ***Settlement***, in valley of River Broom, 1m/2km S of head of Loch Broom. **60 A1** NH1783.
Auchlunies *Aber.* ***Settlement***, 3m/5km NW of Portlethen. **55 D5** NO8899.
Auchlunkart *Moray* ***Settlement***, 4m/6km E of Rothes. **63 F5** NJ3449.
Auchlyne *Stir.* ***Settlement***, in Glen Dochart, 4m/7km SW of Killin. **32 A2** NN5129.
Auchlyne West Burn *Stir.* ***River***, running SE, then S into River Dochart, 5m/7km SW of Killin. **31 G1** NN5028.
Auchmacoy *Aber.* ***Locality***, and estate, 2m/4km E of Ellon. **55 E1** NJ9930.
Auchmair *Moray* ***Settlement***, on E side of River Deveron, 1km N of Cabrach. **53 F2** NJ3828.
Auchmannoch Muir *E.Ayr.* ***Open space***, moorland 2m/4km NW below Wedder Hill. **14 D2** NS5632.
Auchmantle *D. & G.* ***Settlement***, 2m/3km SW of New Luce. **6 C4** NX1562.
Auchmithie *Angus* ***Village***, with harbour, 3m/5km NE of Arbroath. **43 E5** NO6844.
Auchmuirbridge *Fife* ***Locality***, 2m/3km W of Leslie. **34 A4** NO2101.
Auchmull *Angus* ***Hamlet***, 4m/6km NW of Edzell. **43 D2** NO5874.
Auchmuty *Fife* ***Suburb***, central district of Glenrothes. NO2700.
Auchnabony *D. & G.* ***Settlement***, 4m/6km E of Kirkcudbright. **4 A2** NX7448.
Auchnabreac *Arg. & B.* ***Settlement***, on NW side of Loch Fyne, 1m/2km SW of Inveraray. **30 C4** NN0806.
Auchnacloich *P. & K.* ***Settlement***, in Glen Quaich, 10m/16km N of Crieff. **32 D1** NN8439.
Auchnacraig *Arg. & B.* ***Settlement***, on Mull, 1m/2km SW of Grass Point. **29 G2** NM7330.
Auchnacree *Angus* ***Hamlet***, 1m/2km E of Glenogil. **42 C3** NO4663.
Auchnafree *P. & K.* ***Settlement***, in Glen Almond, 8m/12km NW of Crieff. **32 D1** NN8133.
Auchnafree Hill *P. & K.* ***Mountain***, 2m/4km E of Ben Chonzie, S of Glen Almond. Height 2565 feet or 782 metres. **32 D1** NN8030.
Auchnagallin *High.* ***Settlement***, 4m/6km N of Grantown-on-Spey. **52 C1** NJ0533.
Auchnagatt *Aber.* ***Village***, 4m/6km S of Maud. **65 E5** NJ9341.
Auchnaha *Arg. & B.* ***Settlement***, on Cowal peninsula, 6m/10km NW of Tighnabruaich. **22 A1** NR9381.
Auchnangoul *Arg. & B.* ***Settlement***, 3m/5km SW of Inveraray. **30 C4** NN0505.
Aucholzie *Aber.* ***Settlement***, next to River Muick, 4m/6km SW of Ballater. **53 F5** NO3490.
Auchorrie *Aber.* ***Settlement***, 4m/7km W of Echt. **54 B4** NJ6605.
Auchrannie *Angus* ***Hamlet***, 3m/5km NE of Alyth. NO2852.
Auchraw *Stir.* ***Settlement***, to E of Lochearnhead. **32 A2** NN5923.
Auchreoch *Stir.* ***Settlement***, in Strath Fillan, 3m/4km NW of Crianlarich. **31 F2** NN3528.
Auchronie *Angus* ***Settlement***, 1m/2km E of Loch Lee. **42 C1** NO4480.
Auchtascailt *High.* ***Locality***, in Ross and Cromarty district, at head of Little Loch Broom on W coast. NH0987.
Auchter *N.Lan.* ***River***, rising on NW slopes of Black Law in Kingshill Plantation, and flowing E, then N to join South Calder Water to NE at Newmains. **24 C4** NS8356.
Auchterarder *P. & K.* Population: 3549. ***Small town***, former wool and linen-weaving town, 8m/12km SE of Crieff. Gleneagles golf courses nearby. Ardunie Roman Signal Station (Historic Scotland) at Trinity Gask, 4m/6km N. **33 E3** NN9412.
Auchtercairn *High.* ***Settlement***, adjoining to S of Gairloch, Ross and Cromarty district. **59 E2** NG8076.
Auchterderran *Fife* ***Village***, 4m/7km NE of Cowdenbeath. **34 A5** NT2196.
Auchterhouse *Angus* ***Settlement***, nearly 1m/2km W of Kirkton of Auchterhouse. **34 B1** NO3337.
Auchterhouse Hill *Angus* ***Mountain***, with ancient fort on Sidlaw Hills, 1m/2km W of Craigowl Hill and 6m/10km NW of Dundee. Height 1397 feet or 426 metres. **42 B5** NO3539.
Auchterless *Aber.* *Alternative name for Kirktown of Auchterless, qv.*
Auchtermuchty *Fife* Population: 1932. ***Small town***, 4m/7km S of Newburgh. Site of Roman camp on E side of town. **34 A3** NO2311.

Auchterneed *High.* ***Settlement***, 1km N of Strathpeffer. **61 D3** NH4859.
Auchtertool *Fife* ***Village***, 4m/6km W of Kirkcaldy. **34 A5** NT2190.
Auchtertyre *Angus* ***Settlement***, 1km W of Newtyle. **42 A5** NO2841.
Auchtertyre *High.* ***Settlement***, in Skye and Lochalsh district, 3m/4km W of Dornie. NG8427.
Auchtertyre *Moray* ***Settlement***, 3m/5km SW of Elgin. **63 D4** NJ1858.
Auchtertyre *Stir.* ***Settlement***, in Strath Fillan, 3m/5km NW of Crianlarich. **31 F2** NN3529.
Auchtertyre Hill *High.* ***Mountain***, in Skye and Lochalsh district, 1m/2km NW of Auchtertyre. Height 1483 feet or 452 metres. **49 E2** NG8328.
Auchtoo *Stir.* ***Settlement***, 1m/2km E of Balquidder. **32 A2** NN5520.
Auckengill *High.* ***Settlement***, near E coast of Caithness district, 6m/9km S of John o' Groats. **77 F2** ND3664.
Auds *Aber.* ***Settlement***, 2m/3km W of Banff. **64 B3** NJ6564.
Auld Brig o'Doon *S.Ayr.* *See Alloway.*
Auld Darkney *Angus* ***Mountain***, 1m/2km NE of Glenmoy. Height 1788 feet or 545 metres. **42 C3** NO4266.
Auld Kirk *S.Ayr.* ***Ecclesiastical building***, built 1654 in centre of Ayr. Robert Burns baptised here. **14 B3** NS3422.
Auld Wives' Lifts *E.Dun.* *See Craigmaddie Muir.*
Auldearn *High.* ***Village***, in Nairn district, 2m/4km E of Nairn. Site of battle in 1645 in which Montrose defeated Covenanters under General Hurry. **62 B4** NH9155.
Auldgirth *D. & G.* ***Village***, on E bank of River Nith, 7m/12km NW of Dumfries. NX9186.
Auldhame *E.Loth.* ***Hamlet***, 2m/3km N of Whitekirk. **26 C1** NT5984.
Auldhouse *S.Lan.* ***Settlement***, 3m/4km S of East Kilbride. **24 A4** NS6250.
Auldton Fell *D. & G.* ***Mountain***, 3m/4km NE of Moffat. Height 1643 feet or 501 metres. **16 C5** NT1108.
Aulich *P. & K.* ***Settlement***, on N shore of Loch Rannoch, 3m/5km W of Kinloch Rannoch. **40 B4** NN6059.
Aulich Burn *P. & K.* ***River***, flowing SE into Loch Rannoch, 3m/5km W of Kinloch Rannoch. **40 A3** NN6058.
Auliston Point *High.* ***Coastal feature***, headland to S of entrance into Loch Sunart, 3m/5km NE of Tobermory across Sound of Mull. **37 E4** NM5458.
Ault a' chruinn *High.* ***Settlement***, at head of Loch Duich, 1m/2km NE of Shiel Bridge. **49 F2** NG9420.
Aultanrynie *High.* ***Settlement***, on N side of Loch More, Sutherland district. **74 C5** NC3436.
Aultbea *High.* ***Village***, on E shore of Loch Ewe, W coast of Ross and Cromarty district, 5m/8km N of Poolewe. **59 E1** NG8789.
Aultgrishan *High.* ***Village***, on W coast of Ross and Cromarty district, 4m/6km S of Rubha Réidh. **58 D1** NG7485.
Aultguish Inn *High.* ***Settlement***, at SE end of Loch Glascarnoch, 5m/8km NW of Gorstan. **60 C2** NH3570.
Aultibea *High.* ***Settlement***, on N bank of River Langwell Water, 5m/8km W of Berriedale. **73 F2** ND0423.
Aultiphurst *High.* ***Settlement***, 3m/5km SW of Strathy Point, Caithness district. **76 A2** NC8065.
Aultmore *Moray* ***Forest/woodland***, wooded region 6m/9km NE of Keith. **63 G4** NJ4657.
Aultmore *Moray* ***Locality***, 2m/4km NW of Keith. Also wooded tract to NE, from which Burn of Aultmore runs S to River Isla. **63 G4** NJ4053.
Aultnagoire *High.* ***Settlement***, 3m/5km NE of Foyers. **51 E2** NH5423.
Aultnamain Inn *High.* ***Settlement***, 8m/12km SE of Bonar Bridge. **61 F1** NH6681.
Aultnapaddock *Aber.* ***Settlement***, 5m/8km E of Dufftown. **63 F5** NJ3941.
Aulton *Aber.* ***Settlement***, 2m/3km W of Insch. **54 B2** NJ6028.
Aultvaich *High.* ***Settlement***, in Ross and Cromarty district, 1m/2km SW of Muir of Ord. NH5148.
Aultvoulin *High.* ***Settlement***, adjoining to W of Inverie, on Inverie Bay, Lochaber district. **49 D4** NG7600.
Aundorach *High.* ***Settlement***, 3m/5km SW of Nethy Bridge. **52 B3** NH9816.
Auquhorthies *Aber.* ***Settlement***, 2m/3km NE of Oldmeldrum. **54 D2** NJ8329.
Auskerry *Ork.* ***Island***, uninhabited island 1m/2km N to S and 1km E to W, situated 2m/4km S of Stronsay across Auskerry Sound. Lighthouse at S end. **81 E5** HY6716.
Auskerry Sound *Ork.* ***Sea feature***, stretch of sea separating Auskerry and Stronsay islands. **81 E5** HY6716.
Averon (Also known as Alness (River)). *High.* ***River***, running from NW through Alness to Cromarty Firth. **61 F2** NH6569.
Avich *Arg. & B.* ***River***, in Argyll running from Loch Avich to Loch Awe. NM9713.
Avielochan *High.* ***Settlement***, 2m/3km N of Aviemore. **52 B3** NH9016.
Aviemore *High.* Population: 2214. ***Village***, and skiing centre on River Spey, in Badenoch and Strathspey district, 11m/18 km NE of Kingussie. **52 A3** NH8912.
Aviemore Centre *High.* ***Other feature of interest***, leisure, sport and conference centre in Aviemore, with particular emphasis on winter sports. **52 A3** NH8911.
Avoch *High.* Population: 1010. ***Village***, in Ross and Cromarty district, on W shore of Inner Moray Firth or Inverness Firth, 2m/3km SW of Fortrose. **61 F4** NH7055.
Avoch Bay *High.* ***Bay***, small bay at Avoch on Moray Firth, on S coast of Black Isle. **61 G4** NH6954.
Avon ***River***, rising on Cairngorm Mountains and running E through Loch Avon and down Glen Avon, then N to Tomintoul and down Strath Avon to River Spey just below Ballindalloch Castle, 7m/11km SW of Charlestown of Aberlour. **53 D3** NJ1737.
Avon ***River***, rising 2m/3km NW of Caldercruix and flowing N and NE before turning E below Fannyside Lochs, flowing to Avonbridge, NE to Linlithgow, NW towards Grangemouth, and finally NE to Firth of Forth between Grangemouth and Bo'ness. NS9882.
Avon Water ***River***, rising 6m/10km SE of Galston and flowing NE past Strathaven to Larkhall, then N to River Clyde 1m/2km E of Hamilton. **24 B5** NS7356.
Avonbridge *Falk.* ***Village***, 5m/8km S of Falkirk. **24 D2** NS9172.
Awe *Arg. & B.* ***River***, running from Loch Awe through Pass of Brander to Loch Etive at Bonawe. **30 C1** NN0132.
Awhirk *D. & G.* ***Settlement***, 3m/5km E of Portpatrick. **6 B5** NX0553.
Ay Wick *Shet.* ***Bay***, on Yell, to E of Aywick. HU5386.
Ayr *E.Ayr.* ***River***, rising E of Muirkirk and flowing W through Sorn and Catrine to Firth of Clyde. **14 C3** NS3321.
Ayr *S.Ayr.* Population: 47,962. ***Town***, resort on Firth of Clyde at mouth of River Ayr, 12m/19km SW of Kilmarnock. Commercial and administrative centre. Racecourse. **14 B3** NS3321.
Ayr Bay *S.Ayr.* ***Bay***, wide, W facing bay between Troon and Heads of Ayr. Town of Ayr is situated at centre of bay. **14 B3** NS3222.
Ayr Racecourse *S.Ayr.* ***Racecourse***, to NE of Ayr town centre across Water of Girvan. Stages Scottish Grand National. One mixed, sixteen flat and fourteen National Hunt race days each year. **14 B3** NS3522.
Ayton *P. & K.* ***Settlement***, 1m/2km SW of Abernethy. **33 G3** NO1615.
Ayton *Sc.Bord.* ***Village***, on Eye Water, 3m/4km SW of Eyemouth. **27 G3** NT9261.
Ayton Castle *Sc.Bord.* ***Castle***, on NW side of Ayton, 7m/11km N of Berwick-upon-Tweed. Mid 19c sandstone castle designed by James Gillespie Graham, and now fully restored. **27 G3** NT9261.
Ayton Hill *Sc.Bord.* ***Hill***, with mast, 2m/3km SE of Ayton. Height 653 feet or 199 metres. **27 G4** NT9459.
Aywick *Shet.* ***Locality***, on Yell, 1m/2km NE of Otterswick, comprising North Aywick and South Aywick. **85 E4** HU5386.

B

Bà *Arg. & B.* ***River***, on Mull running N from Loch Bà to head of Loch na Keal. NM5341.
Bà *High.* ***River***, in Lochaber district rising S of Clach Leathad and running E through Loch Buidhe, Lochan na Stainge and Loch Bà, to head of Loch Laidon. **39 E5** NN3551.
Baa Taing *Shet.* ***Coastal feature***, headland, with lighthouse, on S coast of Ness of Hillswick, Mainland. **84 B5** HU2774.
Babbet Ness *Fife* ***Coastal feature***, headland at SE end of St. Andrews Bay, 1m/2km N of Kingsbarn. **35 D3** NO5914.
Baby's Hill *Moray* ***Settlement***, on N flank of Ben Rinnes, 5m/8km W of Dufftown. **53 E1** NJ2437.
Bac (Anglicised form: Back.) *W.Isles* ***Village***, near E coast of Isle of Lewis, 6m/10km NE of Stornoway. **69 F3** NB4840.
Bac an Eich *High.* ***Mountain***, on Strathconon Forest, Ross and Cromarty district. Height 2785 feet or 849 metres. **60 B5** NH2248.
Bac Beag *Arg. & B.* ***Island***, at SW end of Treshnish Isles group, with larger island of Bac Mòr to N. **28 B1** NM2337.
Bac Mòr (Also known as Dutchman's Cap.) *Arg. & B.* ***Island***, towards SW end of Treshnish Isles group. Bac Beag, its neighbour to S, is at extreme SW of group. **28 B1** NM2438.
Baca Ruadh *High.* ***Mountain***, 3m/4km NW of The Storr, Skye. Height 2089 feet or 637 metres. **58 A4** NG4757.
Bach Island *Arg. & B.* ***Island***, small island in Firth of Lorn, off Rubha na Feundain at SW end of Kerrera. **29 G2** NM7726.
Bachelors' Club *S.Ayr.* ***Historic house***, thatched house (National Trust for Scotland) in Tarbolton where Burns and associates formed a literary debating society in 1780. Contains period furnishings. **14 C3** NS4327.
Bachuil *Arg. & B.* ***Historic house***, on Lismore, near Clachan. **38 A5** NM8543.
Back *W.Isles* *Anglicised form of Bac, qv.*
Back Bar *Aber.* ***Coastal feature***, sand dunes between Strathbeg Bay and Loch of Strathbeg on NE coast, 7m/11km SE of Fraserburgh. NK0759.
Back of Keppoch *High.* ***Settlement***, 1km NW of Arisaig, Lochaber district. **37 F1** NM6587.
Backaland *Ork.* ***Locality***, near S end of Eday. To E is Bay of Backaland. **81 D3** HY5730.
Backaskail Bay *Ork.* ***Bay***, wide bay on S coast of Sanday, 4m/6km W of Tres Ness. **81 E3** HY6438.
Backaskaill *Ork.* ***Settlement***, on W coast of Papa Westray. **80 C1** HY4850.
Backburn *Aber.* ***Settlement***, on NW side of Gartly Moor, 3m/5km S of Huntly. **54 A1** NJ5334.
Backfolds *Aber.* ***Settlement***, 3m/5km N of Mintlaw. **65 F4** NK0252.
Backhill *Aberdeen* ***Suburb***, 3m/5km W of Aberdeen city centre. NJ8905.
Backhill *Aber.* ***Locality***, 2m/3km NE of Fyvie. **54 C1** NJ7939.
Backhill of Clackriach *Aber.* ***Locality***, 1m/2km S of Maud. **65 E5** NJ9246.
Backhill of Trustach *Aber.* ***Settlement***, 4m/6km W of Banchory. **54 B5** NO6397.
Backies *High.* ***Settlement***, 1m/2km N of Golspie, Sutherland district. **72 D4** NC8302.
Backies *Moray* ***Settlement***, 6m/10km SE of Buckie. **63 G4** NJ4958.
Backlass *High.* ***Settlement***, 2m/3km W of Watten. **77 E3** ND2053.
Backmuir of New Gilston *Fife* ***Village***, 3m/5km N of Largo. **34 C4** NO4308.
Backside *Aber.* ***Settlement***, 6m/9km SE of Dufftown. **53 G1** NJ4136.
Backwater Reservoir *Angus* ***Reservoir***, nearly 4m/6km long N to S, in Glenisla Forest 7m/11km N of Alyth. **42 A3** NO2559.
Bad a' Chreamha *High.* ***Mountain***, in Ross and Cromarty district, 1m/2km N of Stromeferry across Loch Carron. Height 1296 feet or 395 metres. **49 E1** NG8536.
Bad an Fhithich *W.Isles* ***Coastal feature***, on NW coast of Isle of Lewis, 1m/2km SW of Butt of Lewis. **69 F1** NB5064.
Badachro *High.* ***River***, running N into Gair Loch at Badachro village. NG7873.
Badachro *High.* ***Village***, on S shore of Gair Loch, W coast of Ross and Cromarty district. **59 D2** NG7873.
Badandun Hill *Angus* ***Mountain***, 4m/7km NW from N end of Backwater Reservoir. Height 2427 feet or 740 metres. **41 G3** NO2067.
Badanloch Forest *High.* ***Open space***, deer forest in Sutherland district to NW of Kinbrace. **75 G5** NC8035.
Badanloch Lodge *High.* ***Settlement***, at W end of Loch Badanloch, Sutherland district. **75 G5** NC7933.
Badavanich *High.* ***Settlement***, on N shore of Loch a' Chroisg, 3m/5km W of Achnasheen. **60 A4** NH1058.
Badbea *High.* ***Other feature of interest***, ruined crofters' village on coast, 3m/5km SW of Berriedale. **73 F3** ND0819.
Badcall *High.* ***Locality***, comprising Upper Badcall and Lower Badcall, on N side of Badcall Bay, W coast of Sutherland district, 2m/3km S of Scourie. **74 A4** NC1541.
Badcall *High.* ***Settlement***, on N side of Loch Inchard, 1m/2km E of Kinlochbervie, near W coast of Sutherland district. **74 B3** NC2455.
Badcall Bay *High.* ***Bay***, on W coast of Sutherland district, 2m/3km S of Scourie. **74 A4** NC1541.
Badcaul *High.* ***Village***, on SW side of Little Loch Broom, W coast of Ross and Cromarty district. **70 C5** NH0191.
Badden *Arg. & B.* ***Settlement***, 1km N of Lochgilphead. **21 G1** NR8589.
Baddidarach *High.* ***Hamlet***, on N side of Loch Inver, Sutherland district, 1km SW of Lochinver. **70 C2** NC0823.
Baddinsgill Reservoir *Sc.Bord.* ***Reservoir***, on Pentland Hills 3m/4km NW of West Linton. **25 F4** NT1255.
Baddoch *High.* ***Mountain***, with twin summits, the S one being higher, 5m/8km E of Nethy Bridge. Height 1863 feet or 568 metres. **52 C3** NJ0719.
Baddoch Burn *Aber.* ***River***, stream running NE to join Clunie Water, 5m/8km S of Braemar. **41 G1** NO1383.
Baden Bay *High.* *Alternative name for Badentarbat Bay, qv.*
Badenoch *High.* ***Locality***, S part of Badenoch and Strathspey district round about Kingussie, traversed by River Spey, between Monadhliath Mountains and central Grampian Mountains, S of Cairngorm Mountains. **40 A1** NN6592.
Badenscoth *Aber.* ***Settlement***, 2m/3km NW of Rothienorman. **54 B1** NJ7038.

Badentarbat Bay (Also known as Baden Bay.) *High.* ***Bay***, on NW coast of Ross and Cromarty district, between Scottish mainland and Tanera Mòr, to W of Achiltibuie. **70 B4** NC0108.

Badenyon *Aber.* ***Settlement***, to N of Ladylea Hill, 4m/6km N of Strathdon. **53 F3** NJ3419.

Badernonach Hill *Aber.* ***Mountain***, 4m/6km NW of Tarland. Height 1558 feet or 475 metres. **53 G4** NJ4308.

Badicaul *High.* ***Settlement***, in Skye and Lochalsh district, on coast 1m/2km N of Kyle of Lochalsh. **49 D2** NG7529.

Badintagairt *High.* ***Settlement***, to E of River Cassley, 2m/3km NW of Glencassley Castle. **71 G3** NC4210.

Badlipster *High.* ***Settlement***, 3m/5km S of Watten. **77 E4** ND2449.

Badluarach *High.* ***Village***, on W side of Little Loch Broom, W coast of Ross and Cromarty district, nearly 2m/3km SE of Stattic Point. **70 B5** NG9994.

Badnaban *High.* ***Hamlet***, on S side of Loch Inver, Sutherland district, 2m/3km SW of Lochinver. **70 C2** NC0721.

Badnabay *High.* ***Settlement***, 1km SW of head of Loch Laxford. **74 B4** NC2146.

Badnafrave *Moray* ***Settlement***, 3m/5km SE of Tomintoul. **53 E3** NJ2015.

Badnagie *High.* ***Settlement***, 1km NW of Dunbeath. **77 D5** ND1531.

Badnambiast *P. & K.* ***Settlement***, 8m/12km SE of Dalwhinnie. **40 C2** NN7173.

Badninish *High.* ***Settlement***, 6m/10km NW of Dornoch. **72 C5** NH7693.

Badrallach *High.* ***Settlement***, on NE side of Little Loch Broom, on W coast of Ross and Cromarty district, 3m/5km from head of loch. **70 C5** NH0691.

Badyo *P. & K.* ***Settlement***, 4m/7km NE of Pitlochry. **41 E3** NN9861.

Bagh a' Chaisteil *W.Isles Gaelic form of Castlebay, qv.*

Bagh an t-Srathaidh *High.* ***Bay***, small bay on coast of Skye and Lochalsh district, 1m/2km SW of Plockton. **49 D1** NG7832.

Bàgh an Trailleich *Arg. & B.* ***Bay***, on NW coast of Coll, 3m/5km N of Arinagour. NM2161.

Bàgh Bàn *Arg. & B.* ***Bay***, small bay 3m/4km SW of Ardfern. **29 G4** NM7703.

Bagh Dail Beag (Anglicised form: Dalbeg Bay.) *W.Isles* ***Bay***, on NW coast of Isle of Lewis, 2m/4km NE of Carloway. **68 D3** NB2246.

Bàgh Gleann a' Mhaoil *Arg. & B.* ***Bay***, on SE coast of Scarba, 1km NE of Rubha Righinn. **29 G4** NM7103.

Bagh Gleann nam Muc *Arg. & B.* ***Bay***, 1km SW of N point of Jura. NM6800.

Bàgh Gleann Speireig *Arg. & B.* ***Bay***, on NW coast of Jura, 1km SW of Glengarrisdale Bay. **29 F5** NR6396.

Bàgh Hirivagh *W.Isles See Northbay.*

Bàgh Huisinis *W.Isles Gaelic form of Hushinish Bay, qv.*

Bàgh Loch an Ròin *High.* ***Bay***, on W coast of Sutherland district, 2m/3km SW of Kinlochbervie. **74 A3** NC1854.

Bagh na Coille *Arg. & B.* ***Bay***, on NE coast of Coll, 4m/7km NE of Arinagour. **36 B3** NM2762.

Bagh na h-Uamha *High.* ***Bay***, small bay on E coast of Rum, 2m/3km SE of Kinloch. **48 A5** NM4297.

Bagh nam Faoileann *W.Isles* ***Sea feature***, stretch of sea containing numerous islets between Benbecula and South Uist on E side. **45 G5** NF8444.

Bagh Phabail (Anglicised form: Bayble Bay.) *W.Isles* ***Bay***, consisting of two small bays, Bagh Phabail Uarach (Upper Bayble Bay) and Bagh Phabail Iarach (Lower Bayble Bay) to N and S respectively on SE coast of Eye Peninsula, Isle of Lewis. **69 G4** NB5230.

Bagh Phort Bholair *W.Isles Gaelic form of Portvoller Bay, qv.*

Bàgh Sheisiadar (Anglicised form: Sheshader Bay.) *W.Isles* ***Bay***, on E coast of Eye Peninsula, Isle of Lewis, to E of Seisiadar. NB5534.

Baghasdal (Anglicised form: North Boisdale.) *W.Isles* ***Village***, on South Uist, 2m/3km S of Dalabrog. **44 C2** NF7417.

Bail Hill *D. & G.* ***Mountain***, 4m/7km NW of Moniaive. Height 1692 feet or 516 metres. **8 B1** NX7295.

Baile a' Mhanaich *W.Isles Gaelic form of Balivanich, qv.*

Baile Ailein (Anglicised form: Balallan.) *W.Isles* ***Village***, on N side of Loch Erisort, E coast of Isle of Lewis, near head of loch. **69 D5** NB2920.

Baile an Truiseil (Anglicised form: Ballantrushal.) *W.Isles* ***Village***, near NW coast of Isle of Lewis, 3m/4km N of Barvas. **69 E2** NB3753.

Baile Boidheach *Arg. & B.* ***Settlement***, on SW side of Loch Caolisport, 3m/5km SW of Achahoish. **21 F2** NR7473.

Baile Gharbhaidh (Anglicised form: Balgarva.) *W.Isles* ***Settlement***, on N part of South Uist, 1m/2km E of Ardivachar Point. **45 F5** NF7646.

Baile Glas (Anglicised form: Ballaglasa.) *W.Isles* ***Settlement***, on Grimsay, between North Uist and Benbecula. **45 G4** NF8457.

Baile Mhartainn *W.Isles Gaelic form of Balmartin, qv.*

Baile Mhic Phail (Anglicised form: Newton.) *W.Isles* ***Settlement***, on North Uist, 1m/2km S of Port nan Long. **45 G2** NF8976.

Baile Mòr *Arg. & B.* ***Village***, on E coast of Iona. Site of 6c monastery; 13c remains. 15c Maclean's Cross (Historic Scotland). Cathedral to N. Ferry to Fionnphort on Mull across Sound of Iona. NM2824.

Baile Mòr (Anglicised form: Balemore.) *W.Isles* ***Settlement***, on North Uist, 4m/6km SE of Aird an Rùnair. **45 F3** NF7367.

Baile nan Cailleach (Anglicised form: Nunton.) *W.Isles* ***Locality***, on W coast of Benbecula. **45 F4** NF7653.

Baile Raghaill (Anglicised form: Balranald.) *W.Isles* ***Settlement***, on North Uist, 2m/3km E of Aird an Rùnair. Nature reserve to W. **45 F3** NF7269.

Bailebeag *High.* ***Settlement***, 2m/3km SE of Foyers. **51 E3** NH5018.

Baileguish *High.* ***Settlement***, 4m/7km SE of Kingussie. **52 A5** NN8298.

Bailemeonach *Arg. & B.* ***Settlement***, on Mull, 3m/4km S of Lochaline across Sound of Mull. **37 F5** NM6541.

Bailenacille *W.Isles* ***Settlement***, on S part of Pabbay. **45 G1** NF8886.

Bailetonach *High.* ***Settlement***, on Eilean Shona, Lochaber district. **37 F2** NM6373.

Baillieston *Glas.* ***Suburb***, 5m/9km E of Glasgow city centre. NS6763.

Bailliesward *Aber.* ***Settlement***, 3m/5km SE of Haugh of Glass. **53 G1** NJ4737.

Bainsford *Falk.* ***Suburb***, adjoining to N of Falkirk, on S bank of River Carron. **24 C1** NS8881.

Bainshole *Aber.* ***Settlement***, on N side of Glen Water in Glens of Foudland, 6m/9km SE of Huntly. **54 B1** NJ6035.

Baird's Monument *P. & K.* ***Other feature of interest***, monument on hill above N bank of River Earn, 3m/4km W of Crieff. Commemorates Sir David Baird, 1757-1829. NN8221.

Bairnkine *Sc.Bord.* ***Hamlet***, 2m/3km NW of Camptown. **18 A5** NT6415.

Bakebare *Moray* ***Settlement***, below N slopes of Hill of Mackalea, 3m/4km E of Dufftown. **53 F1** NJ3639.

Balachuirn *High.* ***Settlement***, near W coast of Raasay, 3m/4km N of Clachan. **58 B5** NG5540.

Balado *P. & K.* ***Settlement***, 2m/3km W of Kinross. NO0802.

Balafark *Stir.* ***Settlement***, 3m/4km N of Fintry. **32 B5** NS6190.

Balaldie *High.* ***Settlement***, 3m/5km N of Balintore. **62 A2** NH8779.

Balallan *W.Isles Anglicised form of Baile Ailein, qv.*

Balavil *High.* ***Settlement***, in Badenoch and Strathspey district, 2m/4km NE of Kingussie. **51 G4** NH7802.

Balbeg *High.* ***Settlement***, 4m/6km W of Drumnadrochit. **51 D1** NH4531.

Balbeg *High.* ***Settlement***, 4m/6km SW of Drumnadrochit. **51 D2** NH4924.

Balbeggie *P. & K.* ***Village***, 5m/8km NE of Perth. **33 G2** NO1629.

Balbegno Castle *Aber.* ***Castle***, 16c and later, built on an L-plan, 1km SW of Fettercairn. NO6473.

Balbirnie *Fife* ***Locality***, to NW of Glenrothes, comprising Balbirnie Burns and Balburnie House. **34 A4** NO2802.

Balbithan *Aber.* ***Garden***, surrounding late 17c tower house. Attractive old-world garden, 3m/5km SE of Inverurie. **54 D3** NJ8118.

Balbithan *Aber.* ***Settlement***, on E side of River Don, 1km E of Kintore. **54 C3** NJ7917.

Balblair *High.* ***Settlement***, in Inverness district, 1m/2km SW of Beauly. NH5045.

Balblair *High.* ***Settlement***, 2m/3km NW of Bonar Bridge. **72 A5** NH5894.

Balblair *High.* ***Settlement***, on W side of Edderton, in Ross and Cromarty district. NH7084.

Balblair *High.* ***Village***, on S side of Cromarty Firth, Ross and Cromarty district, opposite Invergordon. **61 G3** NH7066.

Balblair Forest *High.* ***Forest/woodland***, astride Kyle of Sutherland, NW of Bonar Bridge, Sutherland district. NH5895.

Balcary Bay *D. & G.* ***Bay***, 2m/3km SE of Auchencairn. NX8249.

Balcary Point *D. & G.* ***Coastal feature***, headland on SE side of Balcary Bay. **4 B2** NX8249.

Balcharn *High.* ***Settlement***, 1m/2km E of Lairg, Sutherland district. **72 A4** NC5906.

Balcherry *High.* ***Locality***, consisting of dispersed settlements, 2m/4km E of Tain. **62 A1** NH8183.

Balchers *Aber.* ***Settlement***, on SW side of Wood of Balchers, 4m/7km S of Macduff. **64 C4** NJ7158.

Balchladich *High.* ***Settlement***, on W coast of Sutherland district, 3m/5km S of Point of Stoer. **70 C1** NC0330.

Balchraggan *High.* ***Settlement***, 2m/3km SE of Beauly. **61 E5** NH5343.

Balchraggan *High.* ***Settlement***, 5m/7km NE of Drumnadrochit. **51 E1** NH5634.

Balchrick *High.* ***Village***, near W coast of Sutherland district, 3m/5km NW of Kinlochbervie. **74 A2** NC1959.

Balconie Point *High.* ***Coastal feature***, shingle point on Cromarty Firth, 1m/2km SE of Evanton. **61 F3** NH6265.

Balcurvie *Fife* ***Village***, adjoining to N of Windygates. **34 B4** NO3400.

Baldernock *E.Dun.* ***Settlement***, 1m/2km E of Milngavie. **23 G2** NS5775.

Baldinnie *Fife* ***Hamlet***, 4m/6km SE of Cupar. **34 C3** NO4211.

Baldoon Sands *D. & G.* ***Coastal feature***, area of mud and sand 2m/3km SE of Wigtown. **7 F5** NX4553.

Baldovan *Dundee* ***Suburb***, 3m/4km N of Dundee city centre. NO3834.

Baldovie *Angus* ***Settlement***, 1m/2km SW of Kirkton of Kingoldrum. **42 B4** NO3254.

Baldovie *Dundee* ***Settlement***, 4m/6km NE of Dundee city centre, to N of Dighty Water. **34 C1** NO4532.

Balduff Hill *P. & K.* ***Mountain***, 3m/5km NW of Alyth. Height 1394 feet or 425 metres. **42 A4** NO2253.

Balelone *W.Isles* ***Settlement***, on North Uist, 2m/3km S of Griminis Point. **45 F2** NF7273.

Balemartine *Arg. & B.* ***Village***, on Hynish Bay, Tiree, 4m/7km SW of Scarinish across the bay. **36 A2** NL9841.

Balemore *W.Isles Anglicised form of Baile Mòr, qv.*

Balendoch *P. & K.* ***Settlement***, 2m/3km N of Meigle. **42 A5** NO2847.

Balephetrish Bay *Arg. & B.* ***Bay***, wide bay on N coast of Tiree, 3m/5km NW of Scarinish. **36 A2** NM0047.

Balephetrish Hill *Arg. & B.* ***Hill***, rising to over 20 metres near N coast of Tiree, overlooking Balephetrish Bay. **36 B2** NM0147.

Balephuil *Arg. & B.* ***Settlement***, on E side of Balephuil Bay, Tiree. **36 A2** NL9540.

Balephuil Bay *Arg. & B.* ***Bay***, wide bay at SW end of Tiree. NL9440.

Balerno *Edin.* ***Village***, 7m/12km SW of Edinburgh. 17c Malleny House; garden (National Trust for Scotland). **25 F3** NT1666.

Balernock *Arg. & B.* ***Locality***, comprises High and Laigh Balernock, 2m/3km SE of Garelochhead. **23 D1** NS2588.

Baleromindubh *Arg. & B.* ***Settlement***, on S part of Colonsay, 1m/2km S of Scalasaig. **28 C5** NR3892.

Balerominmore *Arg. & B.* ***Settlement***, on S of Colonsay, 2m/3km S of Scalasaig. **28 C5** NR3891.

Baleshare *W.Isles* ***Island***, low-lying island off W coast of North Uist to W of Cairinis. **45 F4** NF7861.

Balevulin *Arg. & B.* ***Settlement***, on Mull, 4m/6km SE of Balnahard. **29 D2** NM4829.

Balfield *Angus* ***Settlement***, 1km E of Bridgend, in valley of West Water. **42 D3** NO5468.

Balfour *Aber.* ***Settlement***, 2m/3km SE of Aboyne. **54 A5** NO5596.

Balfour *Ork.* ***Hamlet***, and small harbour, on S coast of Shapinsay, near its western end. **80 C5** HY4716.

Balfour Castle *Angus See Kirkton of Kingoldrum.*

Balfour Castle *Ork.* ***Historic house***, baronial-style Victorian mansion to W of Balfour on S coast of Shapinsay. **80 C5** HY4716.

Balfron *Stir.* Population: 1397. ***Village***, 6m/9km N of Strathblane. **23 G1** NS5488.

Balfron Station *Stir.* ***Settlement***, at site of former railway station, 2m/3km W of Balfron. **23 G1** NS5289.

Balgarva *W.Isles Anglicised form of Baile Gharbhaidh, qv.*

Balgavies *Angus* ***Hamlet***, 2m/3km N of Letham. **42 D4** NO5351.

Balgavies Loch *Angus* ***Lake/loch***, small loch, 5m/8km E of Forfar. Wildlife Reserve. NO5350.

Balgedie *P. & K.* ***Locality***, comprises two villages of Wester Balgedie and Easter Balgedie, to NE of Loch Leven. **33 G4** NO1604.

Balgillie Reservoir *Fife* ***Reservoir***, small reservoir 1m/2km N of Leslie. NO2303.

Balgonar *Fife* ***Settlement***, 1m/2km N of Saline. **33 F5** NT0193.

Balgonie Castle *Fife* ***Castle***, 14c with later courtyard, on W side of Milton of Balgonie across River Leven. Garrisoned by Rob Roy MacGregor with 200 clansmen in 1716. NO3100.

Balgove *Aber.* ***Settlement***, 1km S of Barthol Chapel and 4m/7km SE of Fyvie. **54 D1** NJ8133.

Balgowan *D. & G.* ***Settlement***, on W coast of Luce Bay, 1m/2km S of Ardwell. **2 B2** NX1143.

Balgowan *High.* ***Settlement***, in Badenoch and Strathspey district, 1m/2km E of Laggan Bridge. **51 F5** NN6394.

Balgown *High.* ***Settlement***, 4m/6km N of Uig, Skye. **57 G3** NG3868.

Balgray *Angus* ***Village***, 5m/8km N of Dundee. **34 C1** NO4038.

Balgray Reservoir *E.Renf.* ***Reservoir***, 1m/2km SE of Barrhead. **23 G4** NS5157.

Balgreen *Aber.* ***Settlement***, 4m/7km SE of Macduff. **64 C4** NJ7458.

Balgreggan *D. & G.* ***Settlement***, 1km W of Sandhead, at W end of Sands of Luce. **6 B5** NX0950.

Balgy *High.* ***Settlement***, near S shore of Upper Loch Torridon, 3m/5km SW of Torridon. **59 E4** NG8454.

Balhaldie *Stir.* ***Settlement***, in Strathallan, 3m/4km NE of Dunblane. **32 D4** NN8105.

Balhalgardy *Aber.* ***Hamlet***, 2m/3km NW of Inverurie. **54 C2** NJ7623.

Balhary *P. & K.* ***Settlement***, 2m/3km SE of Alyth. **42 A5** NO2646.

Balhelvie *Fife* ***Hamlet***, 5m/8km NE of Newburgh. **34 B2** NO3021.
Balhinny *Moray Alternative name for Belhinnie, qv.*
Balhousie *Fife* ***Settlement***, 3m/4km N of Lower Largo. **34 C4** NO4206.
Baliasta *Shet.* ***Settlement***, on Unst, 1m/2km W of Baltasound. **85 F2** HP6009.
Baligill *High.* ***Settlement***, on N coast of Caithness district, 3m/5km SE of Strathy Point. **76 A2** NC8566.
Baligrundle *Arg. & B.* ***Settlement***, on Lismore, 4m/6km SW of Port Ramsay. **30 A1** NM8340.
Balindore *Arg. & B.* ***Settlement***, 1m/2km W of Taynuilt. **30 B1** NM9830.
Balintore *Angus* ***Hamlet***, and castle, 7m/11km NW of Kirriemuir. NO2859.
Balintore *High.* Population: 1181. ***Village***, on E coast of Ross and Cromarty district, 7m/11km SE of Tain. **62 A2** NH8675.
Balintraid *High.* ***Settlement***, on Cromarty Firth, Ross and Cromarty district, 2m/4km NE of Invergordon. Developed due to North Sea oil industry. **61 G2** NH7370.
Balintyre *P. & K.* ***Settlement***, 3m/5km W of Fortingall. **40 B5** NN6847.
Balivanich (Gaelic form: Baile a' Mhanaich.) *W.Isles* ***Village***, on NW coast of Benbecula. Benbecula (Baile a' Mhanaich) Aerodrome on low promontory to N. **45 F4** NF7855.
Balkeerie *Angus* ***Settlement***, 3m/5km NE of Newtyle. **42 B5** NO3244.
Balkissock *S.Ayr.* ***Settlement***, 3m/5km E of Ballantrae. **6 C2** NX1382.
Balla *W.Isles* ***Village***, at NW end of Eriskay. NF7811.
Ballachulish (Formerly known as East Laroch and West Laroch.) *High.* ***Settlement***, in Lochaber district on S shore of Loch Leven at mouth of River Laroch. Disused slate quarries. **38 C4** NN0858.
Ballageich Hill *E.Renf.* ***Mountain***, 3m/5km SW of Eaglesham. Height 1082 feet or 330 metres. **23 G4** NS5350.
Ballaglasa *W.Isles Anglicised form of Baile Glas, qv.*
Ballantrae *S.Ayr.* ***Small town***, small fishing port on Ballantrae Bay 12m/19km SW of Girvan. Not scene of Robert Louis Stevenson's Master of Ballantrae (for reference to this, see Borgue). **6 B2** NX0882.
Ballantrae Bay *S.Ayr.* ***Bay***, 12m/19km SW of Girvan. **6 B2** NX0882.
Ballantrushal *W.Isles Anglicised form of Baile an Truiseil, qv.*
Ballater *Aber.* Population: 1362. ***Village***, resort on River Dee, 14m/22km E of Braemar and 17m/28km W of Aberdeen. **53 F5** NO3695.
Ballaterach *Aber.* ***Settlement***, 3m/5km E of Ballater. **53 G5** NO4196.
Ballchraggan *High.* ***Village***, in Ross and Cromarty district, 5m/7km S of Tain. NH7675.
Ballechin *P. & K.* ***Settlement***, 3m/5km S of Pitlochry across River Tummel. **41 E4** NN9353.
Balleich *Stir.* ***Settlement***, on N edge of Loch Ard Forest, 1km SW of Aberfoyle. **32 A4** NN5100.
Ballencleuch Law *S.Lan.* ***Mountain***, in Lowther Hills, 8m/12km S of Elvanfoot. Height 2266 feet or 691 metres. **16 A5** NS9304.
Ballencrieff *E.Loth.* ***Village***, 3m/5km NW of Haddington. **26 B2** NT4878.
Ballharn Hill *High.* ***Hill***, 2m/3km N of Cnoc an Earrannaiche. Height 476 feet or 145 metres. **77 E4** ND2444.
Balliekine *N.Ayr.* ***Settlement***, on NW coast of Arran, 3m/4km S of Pirnmill. **13 D2** NR8739.
Balliemeanoch *Arg. & B.* ***Settlement***, on N side of Glenbranter Forest, 1km SE of Strachur. **30 D4** NN1000.
Balliemore *Arg. & B.* ***Settlement***, on Kerrera, 2m/3km SW of Rubh' a' Bhearnaig. **30 A2** NM8228.
Balliemore *Arg. & B.* ***Settlement***, 2m/3km S of Strachur. **30 D5** NS1099.
Balliemore *P. & K.* ***Settlement***, on N side of Dunalastair Water, 3m/4km E of Kinloch Rannoch. **40 C4** NN7059.
Ballimeanoch *Arg. & B.* ***Settlement***, on E shore of Loch Awe, 4m/6km NE of Dalavich. **30 C3** NN0116.
Ballimore *Arg. & B.* ***Settlement***, on Cowal peninsula, 5m/8km SE of Lochgilphead across Loch Fyne. **22 A1** NR9283.
Ballimore *Stir.* ***Settlement***, on W side of Glen Buckie, 2m/3km S of Balquhidder. **32 A3** NN5317.
Ballinaby *Arg. & B.* ***Settlement***, on NW of Islay, 1km NW of Loch Gorm. **20 A3** NR2267.
Ballindalloch Castle *Moray* ***Castle***, baronial castle, with modern additions and alterations, on E bank of River Avon near its confluence with River Spey 7m/11km SW of Charlestown of Aberlour. **53 D1** NJ1736.
Ballindean *P. & K.* ***Hamlet***, at foot of Braes of the Carse, 3m/5km W of Longforgan. **34 A2** NO2529.
Ballingry *Fife* Population: 6393. ***Small town***, 3m/4km N of Cowdenbeath. **33 G5** NT1797.
Ballinlick *P. & K.* ***Settlement***, in Strathbraan, 3m/5km SW of Dunkeld. **41 E5** NN9840.
Ballinloan Burn *P. & K.* ***River***, flowing SE into River Braan, 3m/5km SW of Dunkeld. **41 E5** NN9740.
Ballinluig *P. & K.* ***Settlement***, in Strathardle, 1m/2km S of Kirkmichael. **41 F4** NO0957.
Ballinluig *P. & K.* ***Village***, on River Tummel, 4m/7km SE of Pitlochry. **41 E4** NN9752.
Ballintuim *P. & K.* ***Village***, in Strathardle, 3m/5km NW of Bridge of Cally. **41 G4** NO1054.
Ballo Reservoir *Fife* ***Reservoir***, largest of a series of four small reservoirs in Lomond Hills, 2m/3km NW of Leslie. **34 A4** NO2106.
Balloch *Angus* ***Hamlet***, 3m/5km NW of Kirriemuir. **42 B4** NO3557.
Balloch *High.* Population: 1121. ***Hamlet***, in Inverness district, 4m/7km E of Inverness. **61 G5** NH7347.
Balloch *N.Lan.* ***Suburb***, 1m/2km W of Cumbernauld town centre. **24 B2** NS7374.
Balloch *P. & K.* ***Settlement***, 2m/3km SW of Crieff. **32 D3** NN8419.
Balloch *W.Dun.* ***Locality***, at S end of Loch Lomond, adjoining Alexandria to N. **23 E1** NS3981.
Balloch Castle Country Park *W.Dun.* ***Leisure/recreation***, 200 acre country park 1m/2km N of Balloch on S shore of Loch Lomond. Early 19c mansion of Balloch Castle is now visitor centre for park. Site of old castle is marked by a moated mound. **23 E1** NS3882.
Balloch Wood ***Forest/woodland***, on border of Aberdeenshire and Moray, 3m/5km E of Keith. **63 G5** NJ4748.
Ballochan *Aber.* ***Settlement***, in Forest of Birse, near head of Water of Feugh, 5m/8km S of Aboyne. **54 A5** NO5290.
Ballochandrain *Arg. & B.* ***Settlement***, 6m/9km N of Tighnabruaich. **22 A1** NR9983.
Ballochbuie Forest *Aber.* ***Forest/woodland***, forest on S side of River Dee 3m/5km E of Braemar. **41 G1** NO1990.
Ballochford *Moray* ***Settlement***, on W slopes of Garbet Hill, 4m/7km SE of Dufftown. **53 F1** NJ3633.
Ballochgair *Arg. & B.* ***Settlement***, on E coast of Kintyre, 2m/3km NW of Peninver. **12 C3** NR7727.
Ballochling Loch *E.Ayr.* ***Lake/loch***, small loch 2m/3km NW of S end of Loch Doon. NX4594.
Ballochmartin *N.Ayr.* ***Settlement***, on Great Cumbrae, 2m/3km NE of Millport. **22 C4** NS1757.
Ballochmorrie *S.Ayr.* ***Settlement***, on W bank of Duisk River, 2m/3km NW of Barrhill. **6 D2** NX2184.
Ballochmyle *E.Ayr.* ***Other building***, hospital complex halfway between Mauchline and Catrine. **14 D3** NS5216.
Ballochmyle House *E.Ayr. See Catrine.*
Ballochroy *Arg. & B.* ***Settlement***, on NW coast of Kintyre, 4m/7km NE of Tayinloan. **21 F4** NR7252.
Ballochyle Hill *Arg. & B.* ***Mountain***, above W bank of River Eachaig, 1m/2km W of Orchard. Height 1253 feet or 382 metres. **22 C1** NS1382.
Ballogie *Aber.* ***Locality***, and estate, 4m/6km SE of Aboyne. **54 A5** NO5795.
Ballyaurgan *Arg. & B.* ***Settlement***, on SE side of Loch Caolisport, 1m/2km SW of Clachbreck. **21 F2** NR7574.
Ballygown *Arg. & B.* ***Settlement***, on Ballygown Bay, on N side of Loch Tuath, Mull. Ruined broch. **36 D5** NM4343.
Ballygown Bay *Arg. & B.* ***Bay***, on N side of Loch Tuath, Mull. **36 D5** NM4343.
Ballygrant *Arg. & B.* ***Village***, on Islay, 3m/5km SW of Port Askaig. Loch Ballygrant, is small loch to E. **20 B3** NR3966.
Ballyhaugh *Arg. & B.* ***Settlement***, 3m/5km W of Arinagour, Coll. **36 A4** NM1757.
Ballymeanoch *Arg. & B.* ***Settlement***, 5m/8km N of Lochgilphead. **30 A5** NR8396.
Ballymichael *N.Ayr.* ***Settlement***, on Arran, 3m/4km NE of Blackwaterfoot. **13 E2** NR9231.
Balmacaan Forest *High.* ***Open space***, deer forest in Inverness district SW of Drumnadrochit. **50 C2** NH4125.
Balmacara *High.* ***Locality***, in Skye and Lochalsh district, 3m/5km E of Kyle of Lochalsh. Balmacara Estate (National Trust for Scotland) to N. **49 E2** NG8127.
Balmacara Bay *High.* ***Bay***, small bay on Loch Alsh, 3m/4km E of Kyle of Lochalsh. NG8027.
Balmacara Estate *High.* ***Open space***, National Trust for Scotland property to N of Balmacara on N shore of Loch Alsh, 4m/6km E of Kyle of Lochalsh. **49 E2** NG7828.
Balmaclellan *D. & G.* ***Village***, 1m/2km NE of New Galloway. **8 A3** NX6579.
Balmacneil *P. & K.* ***Settlement***, on W side of Strath Tay, 5m/8km SE of Pitlochry. **41 E4** NN9750.
Balmadies *Angus* ***Hamlet***, 1m/2km NE of Letham. **42 D5** NO5549.
Balmae *D. & G.* ***Settlement***, 4m/6km S of Kirkcudbright. **3 G2** NX6845.
Balmaha *Stir.* ***Village***, on E shore of Loch Lomond, 3m/5km W of Drymen. **31 G5** NS4290.
Balmalcolm *Fife* ***Hamlet***, 3m/4km NE of Freuchie. **34 B4** NO3108.
Balmanno Castle *P. & K.* ***Historic house***, restored 16c mansion at Dron, 5m/8km S of Perth. NO1415.
Balmanno Hill *P. & K.* ***Hill***, on N edge of Ochil Hills, 3m/4km N of Glenfarg. Height 751 feet or 229 metres. **33 G3** NO1414.
Balmaqueen *High.* ***Settlement***, near N end of Skye, 1m/2km S of Rubha na h-Aiseig. NG4474.
Balmartin (Gaelic form: Baile Mhartainn.) *W.Isles* ***Settlement***, near NW coast of North Uist, 2m/3km S of Griminis Point. **45 F2** NF7273.
Balmeanach *Arg. & B.* ***Settlement***, 1km S of Balnahard, Mull. **29 D1** NM4433.
Balmeanach Bay *High.* ***Bay***, on E coast of Skye, opposite S end of Raasay. NG5334.
Balmedie *Aber.* Population: 1260. ***Village***, 7m/12km N of Aberdeen. **55 E3** NJ9617.
Balmedie Country Park *Aber.* ***Leisure/recreation***, country park with over 150 acres of grassland and beach situated between Balmedie and Balmedie Beach. Attracts variety of seabirds. **55 E3** NJ9717.
Balmerino *Fife* ***Village***, on Firth of Tay, 5m/7km SW of Newport-on-Tay. Ruins of 13c abbey (National Trust for Scotland). **34 B2** NO3524.
Balmerino Abbey *Fife* ***Ecclesiastical building***, Cistercian abbey (National Trust for Scotland) in Balmerino, 5m/8km SW of Newport-on-Tay. Founded in 1229 and ruined during Reformation. **34 B2** NO3524.
Balminnoch *D. & G.* ***Settlement***, 1km W of Black Loch, 7m/11km NE of Glenluce. **7 D4** NX2765.
Balmoral Castle *Aber.* ***Historic house***, royal residence since 1852. New castle on site of earlier castle was completed in 1855 and was designed by Prince Albert and William Smith. Situated on S bank of River Dee, 7m/11km E of Braemar. **53 E5** NO2595.
Balmoral Forest *Aber.* ***Open space***, deer forest to S of Balmoral Castle. **42 A1** NO2595.
Balmore *E.Dun.* ***Village***, 3m/5km E of Milngavie. **24 A2** NS6073.
Balmore *High.* ***Settlement***, on Skye, 1m/2km NE of Harlosh Point. **57 F5** NG2941.
Balmore *High.* ***Settlement***, in Strathglass, 2m/3km NE of Cannich. **50 C1** NH3533.
Balmore *High.* ***Settlement***, 7m/11km S of Nairn. **62 A5** NH8845.
Balmullo *Fife* Population: 1108. ***Village***, 2m/3km W of Leuchars. **34 C2** NO4220.
Balmungie *High.* ***Settlement***, 1m/2km N of Rosemarkie. **61 G4** NH7459.
Balmyle *P. & K.* ***Hamlet***, 4m/6km NW of Bridge of Cally. **41 F4** NO1055.
Balnabodach *W.Isles Anglicised form of Buaile nam Bodach, qv.*
Balnaboth *Angus* ***Settlement***, 9m/15km NW of Kirriemuir. **42 B3** NO3166.
Balnabruaich *High.* ***Settlement***, 1m/2km N of Cromarty across mouth of Cromarty Firth. **61 G2** NH7969.
Balnacra *High.* ***Settlement***, in Glen Carron, Ross and Cromarty district, at SW end of Loch Dùghaill or Doule. **59 F5** NG9746.
Balnafoich *High.* ***Settlement***, in Inverness district, 7m/11km S of Inverness. **51 F1** NH6835.
Balnagall *High.* ***Settlement***, 3m/5km E of Tain. **62 A1** NH8381.
Balnagown *High.* ***River***, running into Nigg Bay on N side of Cromarty Firth, Ross and Cromarty district, 5m/9km NE of Invergordon. NH7873.
Balnagown Castle *High.* ***Castle***, 15c tower castle with modifications, 2m/3km NW of Invergordon, on S bank of River Balnagown. **61 G2** NH7575.
Balnaguard *P. & K.* ***Village***, in Strath Tay, 2m/3km W of confluence of Rivers Tay and Tummel. **41 E4** NN9451.
Balnaguard Burn *P. & K.* ***River***, rising on Grandtully Hill and flowing NE to Balnaguard and then into River Tay. Course includes Falls of Balnaguard, 1km upstream of Balnaguard. **41 E5** NN9551.
Balnaguisich *High.* ***Settlement***, 1m/2km NE of Alness. **61 F2** NH6771.
Balnahard *Arg. & B.* ***Locality***, on W coast of Mull, 1m/2km S of entrance to Loch na Keal. **29 D1** NM4534.
Balnahard *Arg. & B.* ***Settlement***, on NE corner of Colonsay, 4m/6km NE of Scalasaig. **28 D5** NR4199.
Balnahard Bay *Arg. & B.* ***Bay***, small E facing bay to N of Rubh' a' Geodha at NE tip of Colonsay. **28 D4** NM4300.
Balnain *High.* ***Settlement***, in Glen Urquhart, 4m/6km W of Drumnadrochit. **50 D1** NH4430.
Balnakailly Bay *Arg. & B.* ***Bay***, on N coast of Bute, 1km E of Buttock Point. NS0274.
Balnakeil *High.* ***Settlement***, on Balnakeil Bay, on N coast of Sutherland district, 1m/2km NW of Durness. **74 C2** NC3968.
Balnakeil Bay *High.* ***Bay***, on N coast of Sutherland district, 1m/2km NW of Durness. **74 C1** NC3968.
Balnakeil Craft Village *High.* ***Other feature of interest***, to S of Balnakeil and W of Durness. Consists of painters, potters, candle-makers and many other workshops. **74 C2** NC3968.
Balnaknock *High.* ***Settlement***, 1m/2km E of Uig, Skye. **58 A3** NG4162.
Balnamoon *Angus* ***Hamlet***, 4m/6km NW of Brechin. **42 D3** NO5563.
Balnapaling *High.* ***Settlement***, N of Cromarty, 1m/2km across mouth of Cromarty Firth. **61 G3** NH7969.

B

Balnespick *High.* ***Settlement***, 5m/8km E of Kingussie. **52 A4** NH8303.
Balornock *Glas.* ***Suburb***, 2m/3km NE of Glasgow city centre. NS6168.
Balquhandy Hill *P. & K.* ***Mountain***, 2m/3km S of Dunning. Height 1168 feet or 356 metres. **33 F3** NO0311.
Balquhidder *Stir.* ***Village***, at foot of Loch Voil, 4m/6km SW of Lochearnhead. Burial place of outlaw Rob Roy, d. 1734. **32 A2** NN5320.
Balranald *W.Isles Anglicised form of Baile Raghaill, qv.*
Balta *Shet.* ***Island***, uninhabited island 1m/2km N to S at entrance to Balta Sound, E coast of Unst. **85 F2** HP6608.
Balta Sound *Shet.* ***Sea feature***, large inlet between E coast of Unst and Balta. HP6208.
Baltasound *Shet.* ***Village***, at head of inlet of Balta Sound on E coast of Unst. To S lies Baltasound airstrip. **85 F2** HP6208.
Baltersan *D. & G.* ***Settlement***, 3m/4km S of Newton Stewart. **7 F4** NX4261.
Balthangie *Aber.* ***Settlement***, 2m/4km NE of Cuminestown. **64 D4** NJ8351.
Balthayock *P. & K.* ***Locality***, 4m/6km E of Perth. **33 G2** NO1723.
Baluachraig *Arg. & B.* ***Settlement***, 6m/9km N of Lochgilphead. Bronze Age marks on rocks at Baluachraig Cup and Ring (Historic Scotland) at Kilmartin Glen, 1m/2km SE of Kilmartin. **30 A5** NR8397.
Balulive *Arg. & B.* ***Settlement***, 1m/2km W of Port Askaig, on NE of Islay. **20 C3** NR4069.
Balure *Arg. & B.* ***Settlement***, 2m/3km W of Benderloch across Ardmucknish Bay. **30 A1** NM8738.
Balure *Arg. & B.* ***Settlement***, on S coast of Loch Etive, 1km NE of Taynuilt. **30 C1** NN0132.
Balvaird *High.* ***Settlement***, scattered settlement, 1km NE of Muir of Ord. **61 E4** NH5351.
Balvaird Castle *P. & K.* ***Castle***, remains of late 15c tower on an L-plan (Historic Scotland), 2m/4km E of Glenfarg. Extended in 1581 by addition of walled courtyard and gatehouse. **33 G3** NO1611.
Balvarran *P. & K.* ***Settlement***, 1m/2km N of Kirkmichael. **41 F3** NO0762.
Balvenie *Moray* ***Locality***, 1m/2km N of Dufftown. Includes remains of 13c moated Balvenie Castle (Historic Scotland). NJ3242.
Balvenie Castle *Moray* ***Castle***, ruin of 13c castle (Historic Scotland) on N side of Dufftown, with 15c-16c additions, dry moat and high stone walls. Visited by Mary, Queen of Scots in 1562. Jacobite troops stayed here after Battle of Killiecrankie in 1689. **63 F5** NJ3240.
Balvicar *Arg. & B.* ***Village***, on Balvicar Bay, E coast of Seil, 2m/4km S of Clachan Bridge. **29 G3** NM7616.
Balvicar Bay *Arg. & B.* ***Bay***, on E coast of Seil, 2m/4km S of Clachan Bridge. NM7617.
Balvraid *High.* ***Settlement***, in Gleann Beag, Skye and Lochalsh district, 3m/4km SE of Glenelg. **49 E3** NG8416.
Balvraid *High.* ***Settlement***, 5m/7km SE of Moy. **52 A1** NH8231.
Bamff *P. & K.* ***Settlement***, 3m/4km NW of Alyth. **42 A4** NO2251.
Banavie *High.* ***Hamlet***, adjacent to Lower Banavie, in Lochaber district, beside Caledonian Canal, 2m/3km N of Fort William. Series of locks on canal. **38 D2** NN1177.
Banchor *High.* ***Settlement***, 5m/7km SW of Ferness. **62 B5** NH9140.
Banchory *Aber.* Population: 6230. ***Small town***, on River Dee at its confluence with Water of Feugh, 11m/18km NW of Stonehaven. 1m/2km S is Bridge of Feugh, with salmon leap observation platform. **54 C5** NO6995.
Banchory-Devenick *Aber.* ***Locality***, 3m/5km SW of Aberdeen city centre across River Dee. **55 E4** NJ9102.
Bandon *Fife* ***Settlement***, 2m/3km N of Glenrothes. **34 A4** NO2704.
Banff *Aber.* Population: 4110. ***Small town***, on N coast, on W side of Banff Bay. Industrial estate adjoining town centre. To S is Duff House (Historic Scotland), in Georgian baroque style by William Adam. **64 B3** NJ6863.
Banff Bay *Aber.* ***Bay***, on N coast of Banff and Buchan district, between Banff and Macduff. **64 B3** NJ6863.
Bankend *D. & G.* ***Village***, on Lochar Water, 6m/10km SE of Dumfries. **9 E4** NY0268.
Bankend *S.Lan.* ***Locality***, comprises South and North Bankend, 2m/3km SW and 2m/3km W of Coalburn respectively. **15 G2** NS8033.
Bankfoot *P. & K.* Population: 1009. ***Village***, 5m/8km SE of Dunkeld. **33 F1** NO0635.
Bankglen *E.Ayr.* ***Hamlet***, 1m/2km SW of New Cumnock. NS5912.
Bankhead *Aberdeen* ***Suburb***, to NW of Aberdeen city centre. **55 D4** NJ8910.
Bankhead *Aber.* ***Settlement***, on E bank of River Don, 3m/5km NE of Alford. **54 B3** NJ6117.
Bankhead *Aber.* ***Settlement***, 3m/5km SW of Sauchen. **54 B4** NJ6507.
Bankhead *D. & G.* ***Settlement***, 1km NE of Dundreddan. **4 A2** NX7648.
Banknock *Falk.* Population: 2675. ***Village***, 4m/6km E of Kilsyth. **24 B2** NS7779.
Bankshill *D. & G.* ***Settlement***, 4m/6km E of Lockerbie. **9 F2** NY1981.
Bannock Burn *High.* ***River***, in Sutherland district, running S from Loch an Ruathair to River Helmsdale 1m/2km SW of Kinbrace. **76 A5** NC8530.
Bannock Burn *Stir.* ***River***, rising on E slopes of Earl's Hill, 6m/9km SW of Stirling, passing through North Third Reservoir and running E to Bannockburn, then NE to River Forth 2m/4km E of Stirling. **32 C5** NS8393.
Bannockburn *Stir.* Population: 5799. ***Small town***, 2m/4km SE of Stirling. Nearby is site of battle of 1314 in which Scots under Robert the Bruce routed English under Edward II. **32 D5** NS8393.
Bannockburn Monument and Heritage Centre *Stir.* ***Other feature of interest***, monument and heritage centre (National Trust for Scotland) at Borestone Brae, 1m/2km S of Stirling, commemorating Battle of Bannockburn 1314. Includes rotunda and equestrian statue of Robert the Bruce. **32 C5** NS7990.
Banton *N.Lan.* ***Village***, 2m/4km E of Kilsyth. **24 B2** NS7479.
Banvie Burn *P. & K.* ***River***, stream running SE down Glen Banvie, through grounds of Blair Castle, to River Garry on W side of Blair Atholl. NN8665.
Baosbheinn *High.* ***Mountain***, in W part of Ross and Cromarty district 5m/8km N of Upper Loch Torridon. Height 2870 feet or 875 metres. **59 E3** NG8665.
Baptiston *Stir.* ***Settlement***, 4m/6km NW of Strathblane. **23 G1** NS5283.
Barabhas *W.Isles Gaelic form of Barvas, qv.*
Barachander *Arg. & B.* ***Settlement***, 4m/6km SE of Taynuilt. **30 C2** NN0325.
Barassie *S.Ayr.* ***Locality***, on Firth of Clyde, adjoining to N of Troon. **14 B2** NS3232.
Baravaig *High.* ***Locality***, on Camas Baravaig, bay on E coast of Sleat peninsula, Skye, 2m/3km S of Eilean Iarmain. Loch Baravaig is small loch to W. NG6909.
Barbaraville *High.* ***Village***, on Nigg Bay, Cromarty Firth, 4m/6km NE of Invergordon, Ross and Cromarty district. **61 G2** NH7472.
Barbreck *Arg. & B.* ***River***, in Argyll running SW down Gleann Domhain to head of Loch Craignish. NM8205.
Barcaldine *Arg. & B.* ***Settlement***, on Dearg Abhainn, on S side of Loch Creran, Argyll. **38 B5** NM9641.
Barcaldine Forest *Arg. & B.* ***Forest/woodland***, to S and E of Barcaldine. NM9741.
Barcaple *D. & G.* ***Settlement***, 4m/6km N of Kirkcudbright. **8 A5** NX6757.
Barcraigs Reservoir *N.Ayr.* ***Reservoir***, western part of reservoir 2m/3km S of Howwood. Eastern part known as Rowbank Reservoir. **23 E4** NS3857.
Bard Head *Shet.* ***Coastal feature***, southernmost point of Bressay. **83 E4** HU5135.
Bardennoch *D. & G.* ***Settlement***, 1m/2km SE of Carsphairn. **7 G1** NX5791.
Bardister *Shet.* ***Settlement***, on Mainland, at head of Gluss Voe, 2m/3km S of Ollaberry. **84 C5** HU3577.
Bardon *Moray* ***Settlement***, 1m/2km NE of Glenlatterach Reservoir, 6m/9km S of Elgin. **63 E4** NJ2054.
Bardowie *E.Dun.* ***Hamlet***, 2m/3km SE of Milngavie, on E side of Bardowie Loch. NS5873.
Bardowie Castle *E.Dun.* ***Castle***, 16c castle on N shore of Bardowie Loch. NS5773.
Bardowie Loch *E.Dun.* ***Lake/loch***, 2m/3km SE of Milngavie. NS5773.
Bardrainney *Inclyde* ***Suburb***, 1m/2km SE of Port Glasgow. NS3372.
Barfad *Arg. & B.* ***Settlement***, in Knapdale, 1km N of Tarbert. **21 G3** NR8669.
Bargaly *D. & G.* ***Settlement***, in Bargaly Glen, 3m/5km E of Newton Stewart. **7 F4** NX4666.
Bargaly Glen *D. & G.* ***Valley***, carrying Palnure Burn and running S from Dallash to Palnure, 4m/6km E of Newton Stewart. NX4667.
Bargany *S.Ayr.* ***Settlement***, 2m/3km W of Dailly. Bargany House and estate to S across Water of Girvan. **14 A5** NS2400.
Bargany Gardens *S.Ayr.* ***Garden***, 4m/6km E of Girvan. Woodland walks with spring flowers and display of rhododendrons around lily pond in May and June. **7 D1** NX2400.
Bargatton Loch *D. & G.* ***Lake/loch***, small loch 2m/3km S of Laurieston. NX6961.
Bargeddie *N.Lan.* ***Small town***, 2m/3km W of Coatbridge. NS7064.
Bargrennan *D. & G.* ***Locality***, on river Cree, 8m/12km NW of Newton Stewart. **7 E3** NX3576.
Barguillean Garden *Arg. & B.* ***Garden***, natural garden with bulbs, azaleas and rhododendrons, 3m/4km SW of Taynuilt. **30 B2** NM9828.
Barhapple Loch *D. & G.* ***Lake/loch***, small loch 4m/7km E of Glenluce. NX2659.
Barharrow *D. & G.* ***Settlement***, 3m/4km S of Gatehouse of Fleet. **8 A5** NX6152.
Barholm *D. & G.* ***Settlement***, adjoining to NW of Creetown, 6m/9km SE of Newton Stewart. **7 F5** NX4759.
Barholm Castle *D. & G.* ***Castle***, ruined 16c-17c stronghold of the McCullochs, 5m/7km SE of Creetown. NX5253.
Barkeval *High.* ***Mountain***, 2m/3km SW of Kinloch, Rum. Height 1938 feet or 591 metres. **47 G5** NM3797.
Barkin Isles *W.Isles* ***Island***, group of islets at entrance to Loch Leurbost, E coast of Isle of Lewis. NB3923.
Barlae *D. & G.* ***Settlement***, 3m/5km W of Kirkcowan. **7 D4** NX2760.
Barlay *D. & G.* ***Settlement***, on E bank of Water of Fleet, 1m/2km N of Gatehouse of Fleet. **7 G5** NX5958.
Barlinnie *Glas.* ***Other building***, HM prison in Riddrie district, 3m/5km NE of Glasgow city centre. NS6366.
Barlocco Bay *D. & G.* ***Bay***, small bay 3m/4km E of Dundrennan. **4 A2** NX7946.
Barlocco Isle *D. & G.* ***Island***, southernmost of the Islands of Fleet, group of small islands near E side of Wigtown Bay. **3 F2** NX5748.
Barmekin Hill *Aber.* ***Hill***, 1m/2km NW of Echt. Height 899 feet or 274 metres. **54 C4** NJ7207.
Barmolloch *Arg. & B.* ***Settlement***, 8m/12km N of Lochgilphead. **30 A5** NR8799.
Barmore Island *Arg. & B.* ***Coastal feature***, peninsula on W side of Loch Fyne, Argyll, 2m/3km N of Tarbert. **21 G2** NR8771.
Barnacabber *Arg. & B.* ***Settlement***, 1m/2km NW of Ardentinny. **22 C1** NS1788.
Barnacarry *Arg. & B.* ***Settlement***, on S shore Loch Fyne, 2m/3km SW of Garbhallt. **30 C5** NS0094.
Barnamuc *Arg. & B.* ***Settlement***, in Glen Creran, 4m/7km NE of head of Loch Creran. **38 C5** NN0449.
Barnbarroch *D. & G.* ***Settlement***, 3m/5km SW of Wigtown. **7 E5** NX3951.
Barnbarroch *D. & G.* ***Settlement***, 3m/4km S of Dalbeattie. **8 C5** NX8456.
Barndennoch *D. & G.* ***Settlement***, 3m/5km NE of Dunscore. **8 C2** NX8988.
Barnhead *Angus* ***Settlement***, 3m/5km W of Montrose across Montrose Basin. **43 E4** NO6657.
Barnhill *Dundee* ***Suburb***, 1m/2km E of Broughty Ferry. NO4831.
Barnhill *Moray* ***Settlement***, 6m/9km SW of Elgin. 13c Pluscarden Priory to NE. **62 D4** NJ1457.
Barnhill Bay *Fife* ***Bay***, small shingle bay on N side of Firth of Forth, 1km SW of Aberdour. **25 F1** NT1884.
Barnhills *D. & G.* ***Settlement***, 1km SE of Corsewall Point. **6 A3** NW9871.
Barnhourie Sands *D. & G.* ***Coastal feature***, sandbank in Solway Firth, 1km S of Mersehead Sands. **8 D5** NX9150.
Barns Ness *E.Loth.* ***Coastal feature***, headland with lighthouse, 3m/5km E of Dunbar. **27 E2** NT7277.
Barnton *Edin.* ***Suburb***, 4m/7km NW of Edinburgh city centre. NT1975.
Barochan Cross *Renf.* ***Historic/prehistoric site***, weathered Celtic cross (Historic Scotland) in Paisley Abbey; formerly stood on hillock, 1m/2km N of Houston. NS4069.
Barons Point *Arg. & B.* ***Coastal feature***, headland on E side of entrance to Loch Long, between Cove and Kilcreggan. NS2280.
Barr *Arg. & B.* ***Settlement***, on Islay, 4m/7km E of Bowmore. **20 B3** NR3960.
Barr *High.* ***Settlement***, in Morvern, Lochaber district, 4m/7km W of Drimnin. **37 F4** NM6155.
Barr *S.Ayr.* ***Village***, on River Stinchar 6m/10km SE of Girvan. **7 D1** NX2794.
Barr Castle *Renf.* ***Castle***, with 16c tower, to NW of Barr Loch. NS3458.
Barr Loch *Renf.* ***Lake/loch***, with bird sanctuary on S side of Lochwinnoch. NS3557.
Barr Mòr *Arg. & B.* ***Hill***, on E side of Glen Shira, 3m/5km NE of Inveraray. Height 836 feet or 255 metres. **30 D3** NN1312.
Barr-nam-boc Bay *Arg. & B.* ***Bay***, on W coast of Kerrera, 4m/7km W of Oban across Sound of Kerrera. **29 G2** NM7928.
Barr Point *D. & G.* ***Coastal feature***, headland 2m/3km NW of Port William. **2 D2** NX3145.
Barr Water *Arg. & B.* ***River***, in Kintyre, running SW to Glenbarr and into Atlantic Ocean 1km SW of village. **12 B2** NR6635.
Barra (Gaelic form: Eilean Barraigh.) *W.Isles* ***Island***, about 20 square miles or 52 square km lying S of South Uist across Sound of Barra, shortest distance being 5m/7km (Scurrival Point to Cille Bhrighde). Island is hilly, rising to 1260 feet or 384 metres at Heaval. Silver sands on much indented coastline. Airfield (Northbay) on Tràigh Mhòr. Fishing and crofting are important. **44 B3** NF6801.
Barra (Tràigh Mhòr) Airport *W.Isles* ***Airport/airfield***, on Barra, located on Tràigh Mhòr strand 1m/2km SW of Eoligarry. **44 C3** NF7005.
Barra Head *W.Isles* ***Coastal feature***, headland on S coast of Bearnaraigh and most southerly point of Western Isles or Outer Hebrides. NL5579.
Barrachan *D. & G.* ***Hamlet***, 4m/6km NE of Port William. NX3649.
Barrackan *Arg. & B.* ***Settlement***, 2m/3km SW of Ardfern. **29 G4** NM7803.
Barraer *D. & G.* ***Settlement***, 3m/4km SW of Newton Stewart. **7 E4** NX3861.

Barraglom *W.Isles* ***Locality***, at S end of Great Bernera, W coast of Isle of Lewis, just E of road bridge connecting Great Bernera to main island. **68 C4** NB1634.
Barrahormid *Arg. & B.* ***Settlement***, 3m/4km SW of Tayvallich. **21 F1** NR7183.
Barran *Arg. & B.* ***Settlement***, 1m/2km S of Dalmally. No access by road. **31 D2** NN1624.
Barrapol *Arg. & B.* ***Settlement***, near W end of Tiree, 3m/4km SE of Rubha Chràiginis. **36 A2** NL9542.
Barravullin *Arg. & B.* ***Settlement***, 1m/2km N of head of Loch Craignish. **30 A4** NM8107.
Barrel of Butter *Ork.* ***Island***, rock with beacon in Scapa Flow, 2m/3km E of lighthouse at N end of Cava. **78 C2** HY3500.
Barrhead *E.Renf.* Population: 17,251. ***Town***, former textile town, 4m/6km S of Paisley. **23 G4** NS4958.
Barrhill *S.Ayr.* ***Village***, on Duisk River 10m/16km S of Girvan. **6 D2** NX2382.
Barrie's House *Angus* ***Historic house***, Kirriemuir birthplace of Sir J.M. Barrie (National Trust for Scotland), famous as creator of Peter Pan. Includes exhibition. **42 B4** NO3854.
Barrisdale *High.* ***Locality***, in Lochaber district, at head of Barrisdale Bay, on S side of Loch Hourn. **49 E4** NG8704.
Barrisdale *High.* ***River***, running W down Glen Barrisdale, then N into Barrisdale Bay. NG8604.
Barrisdale Bay *High.* ***Bay***, on S side of Loch Hourn. **49 E4** NG8704.
Barrmill *N.Ayr.* ***Village***, 2m/3km SE of Beith. **23 E4** NS3651.
Barrnacarry *Arg. & B.* ***Settlement***, 1m/2km NW of Kilninver. **30 A2** NM8122.
Barrnacarry Bay *Arg. & B.* ***Bay***, N facing bay on S side of entrance to Loch Feochan, in Argyll, 1m/2km NW of Kilninver. **29 G2** NM8122.
Barrock *High.* ***Settlement***, near N coast of Caithness district, 2m/4km E of Dunnet. **77 E1** ND2571.
Barry *Angus* ***Village***, 2m/3km W of Carnoustie. **34 D1** NO5334.
Barry Buddon Camp *Angus* ***Military establishment***, 1m/2km E of Monifieth. **34 D1** NO5132.
Barry Hill *P. & K.* ***Hill***, 2m/3km NE of Alyth, with Iron Age Fort at summit. Height 682 feet or 208 metres. NO2650.
Barry Links *Angus* ***Coastal feature***, large area of flat land forming headland between N bank of Firth of Tay and North Sea coast to S of Carnoustie. Buddon Ness is at S tip. **34 D1** NO5332.
Barry Mill *Angus* ***Other feature of interest***, 18c mill (National Trust for Scotland), 2m/3km W of Carnoustie. Displays and demonstrations. **34 D1** NO5335.
Barry Sands *Angus* ***Coastal feature***, extending W and N of Buddon Ness. NO5231.
Barsalloch Fort *D. & G.* ***Historic/prehistoric site***, Iron Age fort (Historic Scotland), on Barsalloch Point headland, 1m/2km S of Port William. **3 D2** NX3441.
Barsalloch Point *D. & G.* ***Coastal feature***, headland on E side of Luce Bay, 2m/3km S of Port William. **2 D2** NX3441.
Barscobe Castle *D. & G.* ***Castle***, remains of old castle, 2m/4km E of St. John's Town of Dalry. NX6680.
Barscobe Hill *D. & G.* ***Hill***, to E of Barscobe Castle. Height 823 feet or 251 metres. NX6780.
Barscobe Loch *D. & G.* ***Lake/loch***, to NE of Barscobe Castle. NX6681.
Barskimming *E.Ayr.* ***Settlement***, on N bank of River Ayr, 2m/3km SW of Mauchline. Old Barskimming to S of river across bridge. **14 C3** NS4825.
Barsloisnach *Arg. & B.* ***Settlement***, 2m/3km NE of Crinan across Loch Crinan. **30 A5** NR8195.
Barth Head *Ork.* ***Coastal feature***, headland on W coast of S part of South Ronaldsay. **78 D4** ND4285.
Barthol Chapel *Aber.* ***Village***, 4m/6km SE of Fyvie. **54 D1** NJ8134.
Barvas *W.Isles* ***River***, rising among lochs some 6m/10km S of Barvas village, Isle of Lewis, and flowing N down Gleann Mòr Bharabhais to Loch Mòr Barabhais and then into Atlantic Ocean 2m/3km SW of Aird Barvas. NB3450.
Barvas (Gaelic form: Barabhas.) *W.Isles* ***Village***, near NW coast of Isle of Lewis, 11m/18km NW of Stornoway. **69 E2** NB3649.
Barvick Burn *P. & K.* ***River***, flowing SE into Turret Burn, 1m/2km NW of Crieff. **32 D2** NN8524.
Barwhinnock *D. & G.* ***Settlement***, 1km NW of Twynholm, 3m/5km NW of Kirkcudbright. **8 A5** NX6554.
Barwinnock *D. & G.* ***Settlement***, 2m/4km NE of Monreith. **3 D2** NX3843.
Bass Rock *E.Loth.* ***Island***, small island of basalt rock in Firth of Forth 1m/2km N of Tantallon Castle. Height 350 feet or 107 metres. Haunt of sea birds, especially gannets. Lighthouse. **26 D1** NT6087.
Basta *Shet.* ***Settlement***, on Yell, on W side of Basta Voe. **85 E3** HU5294.
Basta Ness *Shet.* ***Coastal feature***, headland on E coast of Yell, 1m/2km SE of Basta. HU5393.
Basta Voe *Shet.* ***Sea feature***, long inlet on E coast of Yell, running up to Dalsetter. **85 E3** HU5296.
Batavaime *Stir.* ***Settlement***, at W end of Glen Lochy, 6m/10km NE of Crianlarich. **31 G1** NN4234.
Bathgate *W.Loth.* Population: 13,819. ***Town***, 5m/9km S of Linlithgow. Industrial town, previously important to weaving and coalmining. **25 D3** NS9768.
Battle of Airds Moss 1680 *E.Ayr.* ***Battle site***, scene of skirmish in 1680 between Royalists and Covenanters on Airds Moss, 3m/4km NE of Cumnock. **15 D3** NS5923.
Battle of Alford 1645 *Aber.* ***Battle site***, 1m/2km W of Alford. Site of battle where Montrose defeated Covenanters. **54 A3** NJ5616.
Battle of Ancrum Moor 1545 *Sc.Bord.* ***Battle site***, to N of Ancrum, 5m/8km NW of Jedburgh. Site of battle of 1545 in which Scots repelled English raiders after a dispute following death of James V over betrothal of infant Mary, Queen of Scots to Henry VIII's son, Edward. **18 A4** NT6127.
Battle of Auldearn 1645 *High.* ***Battle site***, to S of Auldearn, where Earl of Montrose defeated Covenanters. **62 B4** NH9155.
Battle of Bannockburn 1314 *Stir.* ***Battle site***, 2m/3km SE of Stirling and 1m/2km N of Bannockburn, where Scots under Robert the Bruce defeated English under Edward II, gaining independence and national identity. Battle is commemorated at Bannockburn Heritage Centre, 1m/2km SW. **32 D5** NS8191.
Battle of Barra Hill 1308 *Aber.* ***Battle site***, 1m/2km S of Oldmeldrum on Barra Hill. Battle where Robert the Bruce decisively defeated John Comyn on Christmas Eve. **54 C2** NJ8025.
Battle of Bothwell Bridge 1679 *S.Lan.* ***Battle site***, to SE of Bothwell, where Covenanters were heavily defeated by Monmouth and Claverhouse. **24 B4** NS7157.
Battle of Carbisdale 1650 *High.* ***Battle site***, 3m/5km NW of Bonar Bridge, where Montrose was defeated by Earl of Sutherland. Main battle fought on craggy hill to N, Creag a' Choineachan, with name derived from Craigcaoineadhain, meaning Rock of Lamentation. **72 A5** NH5694.
Battle of Corrichie 1562 *Aber.* ***Battle site***, 3m/5km N of Banchorry, where Earl of Huntly was defeated by followers of Mary, Queen of Scots, led by Moray. **54 B4** NJ6902.
Battle of Culloden 1746 *High.* ***Battle site***, on Culloden Muir, 5m/8km E of Inverness, where Jacobean cause led by Prince Charles Edward Stuart was finally defeated by Duke of Cumberland on 16th April 1746. Visitor Centre on battlefield site. **61 G5** NH7445.
Battle of Dunbar 1296 *E.Loth.* ***Battle site***, 2m/3km S of Dunbar, site of defeat of John Balliol by Edward I. **27 D2** NT6776.
Battle of Dunbar 1650 *E.Loth.* ***Battle site***, 2m/3km SE of Dunbar, where Cromwell defeated Charles, Prince of Wales, and his Scottish army under Leslie, hampering Royalists' campaign in N. **27 D2** NT6976.
Battle of Falkirk 1746 *Falk.* ***Battle site***, 1m/2km SW of Falkirk across Union Canal, where a Jacobite army of Highlanders defeated a Hanoverian army. **24 C2** NS8779.
Battle of Glen Trool 1307 *D. & G.* ***Battle site***, at E end of Glen Trool. Bruce's Stone marks the site of rout of English by Robert the Bruce's men in 1307. **7 F3** NX4279.
Battle of Glenshiel 1719 *High.* ***Battle site***, in Glen Shiel, 4m/7km SE of Shiel Bridge where Jacobites, backed by Spain, were defeated by George I's army. **49 F3** NG9913.
Battle of Harlaw 1411 *Aber.* ***Battle site***, 2m/4km NW of Inverurie, where Donald, Lord of the Isles, tried to claim Earldom of Ross and was defeated by Earl of Mar. **54 C2** NJ7524.
Battle of Haughs of Cromdale 1690 *High.* ***Battle site***, in Haughs of Cromdale, 4m/7km E of Grantown-on-Spey, where government forces defeated Jacobites in 1690. **52 D2** NJ1027.
Battle of Inveresk 1547 *E.Loth.* *Alternative name for Battle of Pinkie 1547, qv.*
Battle of Inverlochy 1429, 1431 and 1645 *High.* ***Battle site***, at Inverlochy Castle, built in 13c and scene of battles in 1429, 1431 and 1645. In last and most important battle, Covenanters led by Argyll were defeated by Montrose. This led to Charles I breaking off negotiations with Parliament and ultimately to his defeat. **38 D2** NN1375.
Battle of Invernahavon 1370 or 1386 *High.* ***Battle site***, at confluence of Rivers Spey and Truim, 4m/6km SW of Newtonmore. Battle of uncertain date between Clan Cameron and rival Clan Mackintosh, supported by Davidsons and Macphersons. Mackintoshes and followers suffered heavy losses, although battle ended with Camerons in flight. **51 F5** NN6895.
Battle of Keppoch 1688 *High.* ***Battle site***, at Keppoch, to SW of Roybridge across River Roy. Site of Scotland's last real clan battle, caused by territorial dispute between MacDonalds and Mackintoshes. **39 E2** NN2679.
Battle of Killiecrankie 1689 *P. & K.* ***Battle site***, where Government troops were defeated by Jacobites in 1689, 4m/6km N of Pitlochry. **41 E3** NN9162.
Battle of Kilsyth 1645 *N.Lan.* ***Battle site***, 1m/2km to E of Kilsyth. Battle site, now covered by Townhead Reservoir, where Montrose defeated Covenanters, killing some 6000 of enemy with loss of only ten men. **24 B2** NS7478.
Battle of Langside 1568 *Glas.* ***Battle site***, 3m/4km S of Glasgow city centre. Site where Mary, Queen of Scots' forces were defeated by Moray after her escape from Loch Leven. **23 G3** NS5861.
Battle of Loudoun Hill 1307 *E.Ayr.* ***Battle site***, to S of Loudoun Hill, 3m/5km E of Darvel, where Robert the Bruce defeated Earl of Pembroke. **15 E2** NS6037.
Battle of Mauchline 1648 *E.Ayr.* ***Battle site***, to SW of Mauchline, where there was a skirmish between Covenanters and English troops, the outcome of which is uncertain. **14 C3** NS4926.
Battle of Methven 1306 *P. & K.* ***Battle site***, to N of Methven, where Robert the Bruce was defeated by Earl of Pembroke. **33 F2** NO0226.
Battle of Musselburgh 1547 *E.Loth.* *Alternative name for Battle of Pinkie 1547, qv.*
Battle of Nechtanesmere 685 *Angus* ***Battle site***, 1km W of Letham, on Dunnichen Hill, where Egfrith of Northumbria was killed by Picts, ending Anglian incursions into this area. **42 D5** NO5148.
Battle of Philiphaugh 1645 *Sc.Bord.* ***Battle site***, on private land in grounds of Philiphaugh House, 1m/2km SW of Selkirk across Ettrick Water. Here, after defeating English, Scottish leader Sir David Leslie took prisoners to Newark Castle and murdered them in cold blood. **17 F3** NT4528.
Battle of Pinkie 1547 (Also known as Battle of Inveresk or Musselburgh.) *E.Loth.* ***Battle site***, 1km S of Pinkie Braes and 1m/2km SE of Musselburgh. Duke of Somerset, regent to Edward VI, sought to impose betrothal treaty between English and Scottish monarchs, leading to battle in 1547. Although English were victorious, they failed in their objective as Mary, Queen of Scots was sent to France to marry the Dauphin. **26 A2** NT3671.
Battle of Prestonpans 1745 *E.Loth.* ***Battle site***, 1m/2km W of Prestonpans, where English defeated Jacobites. **26 B2** NT4074.
Battle of Redeswire Fray 1575 *Sc.Bord.* ***Battle site***, just NE of Carter Bar summit. Site of last significant Borders skirmish between English and Scots, marked by stone. **11 F1** NT7007.
Battle of Rullion Green 1666 *Midloth.* ***Battle site***, in Pentland Hills 2m/3km NW of Penicuik, where 1000 Covenanters were defeated by superior Crown forces under General Dalziel. **25 G3** NT2162.
Battle of Scone 1310 *P. & K.* ***Battle site***, to SE of New Scone, 2m/3km NE of Perth. **33 G2** NO1425.
Battle of Sherrifmuir 1715 *Stir.* ***Battle site***, on Sherrif Muir, 3m/4km S of Greenloaning, where a Jacobite army fought army of George I. **32 D4** NN8202.
Battle of Stirling Bridge 1297 *Stir.* ***Battle site***, to NE of Stirling, at site of former bridge over River Forth, where Scots under Wallace routed English under Warenne. **32 D5** NS8094.
Battle of Strath Oykel 1369 or 1406 *High.* ***Battle site***, in Strath Oykel, to E of Langwell and 3m/4km E of Oykel Bridge. Bloody battle of uncertain date between Clan Mackay and rival Clan Macleod, which ended with heavy losses for Macleods. Conflict gave name of Tuiteam Tarvach, meaning plentiful fall or great slaughter, to vicinity. **71 G4** NC4202.
Battle of Strathpeffer 1411 *High.* ***Battle site***, on edge of Strathpeffer. Site of affray between Munros and Macdonalds and commemorated by Eagle Stone. **61 D4** NH4856.
Battle of Tibbermore 1644 *P. & K.* ***Battle site***, 1m/2km E of Tibbermore and 2m/3km SE of Methven. Site of first battle between Montrose and Covenanters, in which Montrose was victorious, gaining control of Perth. **33 F2** NO0623.
Battle of Tuiteam Tarvach 1369 or 1406 *See Battle of Strath Oykel 1369 or 1406.*
Battle of Turiff 1639 *Aber.* ***Battle site***, adjacent to NE of Turriff. Site of first skirmish in Civil War, known as 'Trot of Turriff', where Royalist Gordons defeated the Covenanters. **64 C4** NJ7350.
Battlefield *Glas.* ***Suburb***, 3m/5km S of Glasgow city centre. NS5861.
Bauds of Cullen *Moray* ***Locality***, between Bin of Cullen and Portnockie, 3m/5km E of Buckie. **63 G3** NJ4767.
Baugh *Arg. & B.* ***Settlement***, on S coast of Tiree, 1m/2km SW of Scarinish. **36 B2** NM0243.
Baulds *Aber.* ***Settlement***, 6m/9km SW of Banchory. **54 B5** NO6093.
Baxter's Visitor Centre *Moray* ***Other feature of interest***, museum and visitor centre at Baxter's food factory, on W side of River Spey at Fochabers. Includes factory tour and Baxter's family history since 1868. **63 F3** NJ3359.
Bay *High.* ***River***, running N into Loch Bay, NW coast of Skye. NG2654.
Bay of Backaland *Ork.* ***Bay***, on Eday, to E of Backaland. Includes landing stage. HY5730.
Bay of Bomasty *Ork.* ***Bay***, on W coast of Rothiesholm, Stronsay. **81 E4** HY6123.
Bay of Carness *Ork.* ***Bay***, on Mainland, to E of Car Ness. HY4613.
Bay of Cruden *Aber.* ***Bay***, extends S from Cruden Bay to headland opposite The Skares. Firm sands backed by sand dunes. **55 F1** NK0935.
Bay of Deepdale *Shet.* ***Bay***, on W coast of Mainland. Caves to N of bay. **82 A2** HU1754.

Bay of Firth *Ork.* ***Bay***, on coast of Mainland, facing NE towards Shapinsay. Village of Finstown at head of bay. **80 B5** HY3814.
Bay of Fladdabister *Shet.* ***Bay***, small bay on E coast of Mainland. HU4332.
Bay of Furrowend *Ork.* ***Bay***, large wide bay on W coast of Shapinsay. **80 C5** HY4718.
Bay of Heogan *Shet.* ***Bay***, small bay on NW coast of Bressay. HU4743.
Bay of Holland *Ork.* ***Bay***, large bay on S coast of Stronsay, between Greenli Ness and Tor Ness. **81 E4** HY6422.
Bay of Houseby *Ork.* ***Bay***, on S coast of Stronsay. **81 E4** HY6721.
Bay of Houton *Ork.* ***Bay***, small bay on S coast of Mainland, to E of Houton Head, 2m/4km NE of coast of Hoy across Bring Deeps. HY3103.
Bay of Ireland *Ork.* ***Bay***, on coast of Mainland, 2m/3km E of Stromness. HY2809.
Bay of Isbister *Ork.* ***Bay***, an inlet of Wide Firth, 5m/8km NW of Kirkwall across firth. **80 C5** HY3918.
Bay of Keisgaig *High.* ***Bay***, small bay on NW coast of Sutherland district, 4m/6km S of Cape Wrath. **74 B2** NC2469.
Bay of Kirkwall *Ork.* ***Bay***, on N side of Kirkwall. Contains harbour and opens out into Wide Firth. **80 C5** HY4411.
Bay of Laig *High.* ***Bay***, on W coast of Eigg. **37 D1** NM4688.
Bay of Linton *Ork.* ***Bay***, small bay on E coast of Shapinsay. **80 D5** HY5318.
Bay of Lopness *Ork.* ***Bay***, on Sanday, extending W from headland of Lop Ness to Long Taing of Newark. **81 F2** HY7443.
Bay of Meil *Ork.* ***Bay***, on coast of Mainland, between Head of Work and Head of Holland, 2m/3km E of Kirkwall. HY4812.
Bay of Newark *Ork.* ***Bay***, on SE coast of Sanday, to S of Newark. **81 F3** HY7242.
Bay of Pierowall *Ork.* ***Bay***, on E coast of Westray. HY4348.
Bay of Quendale *Shet.* ***Bay***, wide bay on S coast of Mainland, 4m/6km NW of Sumburgh Head. **83 F5** HU3713.
Bay of Sandoyne *Ork.* ***Bay***, on SW coast of Mainland, 1km NW of St. Mary's. **79 D2** HY4601.
Bay of Sandquoy *Ork.* ***Bay***, on N coast of Sanday, with Sandquoy to N end. HY7445.
Bay of Sannick *High.* ***Bay***, to W of Duncansby Head, 1km NE of John o' Groats. **77 F1** ND3973.
Bay of Scousburgh *Shet.* ***Bay***, rounded bay to NW of Scousburgh, Mainland. HU3718.
Bay of Skaill *Ork.* ***Bay***, small bay on W coast of Mainland, 4m/6km W of Dounby. On S side is Skara Brae, remains of Neolithic settlement. **80 A5** HY2319.
Bay of Stoer *High.* ***Bay***, small bay on W coast of Sutherland district, 4m/7km S of Point of Stoer and 5m/8km NW of Lochinver. **70 C2** NC0328.
Bay of Tuquoy *Ork.* ***Bay***, large bay on S coast of Westray. **80 C2** HY4644.
Bay of Work *Ork.* ***Bay***, small bay on Mainland on S side of Head of Work, opposite Shapinsay and 3m/5km NE of Kirkwall. HY4813.
Bayble Bay *W.Isles Anglicised form of Bagh Phabail, qv.*
Bayhead *W.Isles Anglicised form of Ceann a' Bhàigh, qv.*
Bayherivagh *W.Isles Alternative name for Northbay, qv.*
Bays Loch *W.Isles* ***Bay***, on SE coast of Berneray, 1km NE of Borve. **66 B5** NF9281.
Bea Ness *Ork.* ***Coastal feature***, headland on S coast of Sanday between Backaskail and Kettletoft Bays. HY6538.
Beach *High.* ***Settlement***, 6m/9km NE of Ardtornish, Lochaber district. **37 G4** NM7653.
Beacharr *Arg. & B.* ***Settlement***, on W coast of Kintyre, 2m/3km S of Tayinloan. **21 E5** NR6943.
Beacravik *W.Isles* ***Settlement***, on SE coast of South Harris, 1m/2km NE of Manais. NG1190.
Beadaig *High.* ***Hill***, S of Loch Naver and 5m/8km E of Altnaharra. Height 886 feet or 270 metres. **75 F5** NC6437.
Bealach *High.* ***Settlement***, in Salachan Glen, 1m/2km SE of Dalnatrat. **38 B4** NM9851.
Bealach a' Mhàim *High.* ***Other feature of interest***, mountain pass on N side of Cuillin Hills, Skye, between Glen Sligachan and Glen Brittle. NG4426.
Bealach na Bà *High.* ***Other feature of interest***, mountain pass between Meall Gorm and Sgurr a' Chaorachain in Ross and Cromarty district. Rises to 2053 feet or 626 metres, carrying highest road in Scotland, with steep gradients and sharp hairpin bends. Viewpoints across Loch Kishorn at S end, and to Raasay and Skye at N end. **59 D5** NG7742.
Beannan Mòr *W.Isles* ***Hill***, 1km SW of head of Loch Shell, Isle of Lewis. Height 794 feet or 242 metres. **67 E2** NB2810.
Beansburn *E.Ayr.* ***Suburb***, to N of Kilmarnock. NS4339.
Beaquoy *Ork.* ***Settlement***, to E of Loch of Sabiston, Mainland. **80 B4** HY3022.
Bearasay *W.Isles* ***Island***, small uninhabited island off W coast of Isle of Lewis, 2m/3km NW of Great Bernera. NB1242.
Bearnaraigh (Anglicised form: Berneray.) *W.Isles* ***Island***, of about 450 acres or 180 hectares nearly 1km S of Mingulay. High cliffs, with lighthouse, at W end of island. Grazing for sheep. The most southerly island of Western Isles or Outer Hebrides. **44 A5** NL5580.
Bearnie *Aber.* ***Settlement***, 3m/4km N of Ellon. **55 E1** NJ9634.
Bearnock *High.* ***Settlement***, in Glen Urquhart, 6m/9km W of Drumnadrochit. **50 D1** NH4130.
Bearnus *Arg. & B.* ***Settlement***, on Ulva, 1m/2km NW of Beinn Chreagach. **36 D5** NM3941.
Bearraich *Arg. & B.* ***Mountain***, near SW coast of Ardmeanach, Mull. Height 1417 feet or 432 metres. **28 D2** NM4127.
Bearreraig Bay *High.* ***Bay***, small bay on E coast of Skye, 1m/2km E of The Storr. **58 B4** NG5153.
Bearsden *E.Dun.* Population: 27,806. ***Town***, largely residential town on line of Antonine Wall 5m/8km NW of Glasgow. Bearsden Bathhouse (Historic Scotland) contains well-preserved 2c remains of bathhouse and latrine. **23 G2** NS5472.
Beasdale Burn *High.* ***River***, in Lochaber district running W down Glen Beasdale into Loch nan Uamh, 3m/4km SE of Arisaig. NM6984.
Beath Bleachfield *Fife* ***Suburb***, SW district of Cowdenbeath. NT1590.
Beatshach *Moray* ***Open space***, lower NE slopes of Ben Rinnes, 4m/6km S of Charlestown of Aberlour. **53 E1** NJ2537.
Beattock *D. & G.* ***Village***, 2m/3km S of Moffat. Site of Roman camp 1m/2km SE. **16 B5** NT0702.
Beattock Summit *S.Lan.* ***Other feature of interest***, highest point on London to Glasgow main railway line, 10m/16km NW of Beattock; height 1029 feet or 314 metres. **16 A4** NT0702.
Beauly *High.* ***River***, formed by confluence of Rivers Farrar and Glass, flowing NE past town of Beauly and into head of Beauly Firth. **61 D5** NH5246.
Beauly *High.* Population: 1354. ***Small town***, on River Beauly in Inverness district. Ruins of 13c priory (Historic Scotland). **61 E5** NH5246.
Beauly Firth *High.* ***Sea feature***, wide inlet at mouth of River Beauly, extends out to Inner Moray Firth or Inverness Firth. **61 E5** NH5246.
Beauly Priory *High.* ***Ecclesiastical building***, ruins of Valliscaulian Priory (Historic Scotland) founded in 13c at Beauly, on banks of River Beauly. **61 E5** NH5246.
Beauty Hill *Aber.* ***Hill***, 2m/3km NE of Newmachar. Height 548 feet or 167 metres. **55 D3** NJ9020.
Bedrule *Sc.Bord.* ***Village***, on Rule Water, 4m/6km SW of Jedburgh. **17 G4** NT6018.
Beech Hedge *P. & K. See Meikleour.*
Beecraigs Country Park *W.Loth.* ***Leisure/recreation***, 500 acre country park 2m/3km S of Linlithgow featuring rock climbing, water sports, deer park and trout farm. **25 D2** NT0074.
Beefstand Hill *Sc.Bord.* ***Mountain***, 3m/4km NW of Blindburn. Height 1840 feet or 561 metres. **18 C5** NT8214.
Beesdale *W.Isles* ***Valley***, hollowed-out valley near N coast of South Harris, 3m/4km W of Tarbert. NB1100.
Beeswing *D. & G.* ***Village***, 7m/11km SW of Dumfries. **8 C4** NX8969.
Beggshill *Aber.* ***Settlement***, 4m/6km E of Huntly. **54 A1** NJ5938.
Beich Burn ***River***, on border of Stirling and Perth & Kinross, running S down Glen Beich to Loch Earn, 2m/3km E of Lochearnhead. **32 B2** NN6124.
Beinn a' Bha'ach Ard *High.* ***Mountain***, in Inverness district 3m/5km NW of Struy Bridge. Height 2827 feet or 862 metres. **60 C5** NH3643.
Beinn a' Bhacaidh *High.* ***Mountain***, in Inverness district, on SE shore of Loch Ness, 4m/6km NE of Fort Augustus. Height 1820 feet or 555 metres. **50 D3** NH4311.
Beinn a' Bhainne *Arg. & B.* ***Mountain***, in Laggan Deer Forest, 2m/3km SE of Lochbuie, Mull. Height 1237 feet or 377 metres. **29 F2** NM6222.
Beinn a' Bheithir (Anglicised form: Ben Vair.) *High.* ***Inland physical feature***, horseshoe shaped ridge in Lochaber district S of Ballachulish. Summit is Sgorr Dhearg, a Munro at height of 3359 feet or 1024 metres. **38 C4** NN0555.
Beinn a' Bhoth *W.Isles* ***Mountain***, 2m/3km N of Rapaire. Height 1010 feet or 308 metres. **66 D2** NB1316.
Beinn a' Bhragaidh *High.* ***Mountain***, 1m/2km NW of Golspie, Sutherland district. Height 1292 feet or 394 metres. **72 D4** NC8100.
Beinn a' Bhràghad *High.* ***Mountain***, 2m/3km E of head of Loch Eynort, Skye. Height 1512 feet or 461 metres. **48 A2** NG4125.
Beinn a' Bhric *High.* ***Mountain***, in Ross and Cromarty district, 3m/5km NW of Gorstan. Height 1450 feet or 442 metres. **60 C3** NH3465.
Beinn a' Bhric *High.* ***Mountain***, in Lochaber district 3m/5km S of head of Loch Treig. Height 2873 feet or 876 metres. NN3164.
Beinn a' Bhuic ***Mountain***, on border of Perth & Kinross and Stirling, 4m/6km NW of Killin. Height 2667 feet or 813 metres. NN5639.
Beinn a' Bhùird *Aber.* ***Mountain***, fifth in height in Cairngorm Mountains, and with twin summits running N and S about 6m/10km NW of Braemar. North Top, a Munro on border with Moray, is higher at 3926 feet or 1197 metres, 5m/8km E of Loch Avon. South Top, almost 2m/3km distant, is 3861 feet or 1177 metres in height. E face of mass has many corries with craggy cliffs. **52 C5** NJ0900.
Beinn a' Bhùiridh *Arg. & B.* ***Mountain***, peak 2m/3km SE of summit of Ben Cruachan in Argyll. Height 2939 feet or 896 metres. **30 C2** NN0928.
Beinn a' Bhuna *W.Isles* ***Hill***, 2m/3km NE of Achadh Mòr, Isle of Lewis. Height 489 feet or 149 metres. **69 E4** NB3330.
Beinn a' Bhutha *High.* ***Mountain***, 2m/3km S of Loch More. Height 1794 feet or 547 metres. **74 B5** NC2934.
Beinn a' Chàisgein Beag *High.* ***Mountain***, in W part of Ross and Cromarty district, 3m/4km N of Beinn a' Chàisgein Mòr. Height 2230 feet or 680 metres. **59 F1** NG9682.
Beinn a' Chàisgein Mòr *High.* ***Mountain***, in W part of Ross and Cromarty district, 2m/3km N of head of Fionn Loch. Height 2811 feet or 857 metres. **59 F2** NG9878.
Beinn a' Chaisil *High.* ***Mountain***, 5m/8km E of Ardtornish. Height 1433 feet or 437 metres. **37 G5** NM7847.
Beinn a' Chaisteil ***Mountain***, on border of Argyll & Bute and Perth & Kinross, 4m/7km N of Tyndrum. Height 2906 feet or 886 metres. **31 F1** NN3436.
Beinn a' Chait *P. & K.* ***Mountain***, on Forest of Atholl 6m/10km N of Blair Atholl. Height 2949 feet or 899 metres. **41 D2** NN8674.
Beinn a' Chaoinich *High.* ***Mountain***, 3m/4km E of Glenelg, Skye and Lochalsh district. Height 1338 feet or 408 metres. **49 E3** NG8518.
Beinn a' Chaolais *Arg. & B.* ***Mountain***, westernmost and third in height of Paps of Jura. Height 2408 feet or 734 metres. **20 C2** NR4873.
Beinn a' Chaolais *W.Isles* ***Mountain***, 3m/5km E of Tarbert, North Harris. Height 1053 feet or 321 metres. **67 D3** NB2000.
Beinn a' Chaorainn *Aber.* ***Mountain***, in Cairngorm Mountains 4m/6km NE of Ben Macdui. Munro: height 3549 feet or 1082 metres. **52 C4** NJ0401.
Beinn a' Chaorainn *High.* ***Mountain***, in Lochaber district 3m/4km NE of W end of Loch Moy. Munro: height 3444 feet or 1050 metres. **39 F1** NN3884.
Beinn a' Chapuill *High.* ***Mountain***, in Lochaber district 3m/4km SE of Glenelg. Height 2434 feet or 742 metres. **49 E3** NG8215.
Beinn a' Charnain *W.Isles* ***Hill***, in NW Ronay; highest point of island. Height 377 feet or 115 metres. **45 G4** NF8856.
Beinn a' Charnain *W.Isles* ***Hill***, highest point on Pabbay. Height 643 feet or 196 metres. **45 G1** NF8988.
Beinn a' Chearcaill *High.* ***Mountain***, in Ross and Cromarty district, 6m/10km W of Kinlochewe. Height 2378 feet or 725 metres. **59 F3** NG9363.
Beinn a' Chlachair *High.* ***Mountain***, in Badenoch and Strathspey district, 2m/3km S of SW end of Lochan na h-Earba. Munro: height 3565 feet or 1087 metres. **39 G2** NN4778.
Beinn a' Chlaidheimh *High.* ***Mountain***, in Ross and Cromarty district, 10m/16km N of Kinlochewe. Munro: height 3000 feet or 914 metres. **59 G2** NH0677.
Beinn a' Chleibh ***Mountain***, peak on border of Argyll & Bute and Stirling, 1m/2km SW of summit of Ben Lui. Munro: height 3008 feet or 917 metres. **31 E2** NN2525.
Beinn a' Chochuill *Arg. & B.* ***Mountain***, in Lorn, 6m/10km E of Taynuilt. Munro: height 3214 feet or 980 metres. **30 D1** NN1032.
Beinn a' Choin *Stir.* ***Mountain***, on E side of Loch Lomond, 3m/4km SE of Ardlui across the loch. Height 2522 feet or 769 metres. **31 F3** NN3513.
Beinn a' Chonnaich *P. & K. Gaelic form of Ben Chonzie, qv.*
Beinn a' Chraisg *High.* ***Hill***, 2m/3km NE of Kinlochbervie, Sutherland district. Height 843 feet or 257 metres. **74 B3** NC2359.
Beinn a' Chràsgain *High.* ***Mountain***, in Badenoch and Strathspey district, 6m/10km W of Newtonmore. Height 2716 feet or 828 metres. **51 F5** NN6098.
Beinn a' Chreachain *P. & K.* ***Mountain***, 3m/5km N of head of Loch Lyon. Munro: height 3546 feet or 1081 metres. **39 F5** NN3744.
Beinn a' Chroin *Stir.* ***Mountain***, 4m/7km S of Crianlarich. Munro: height 3083 feet or 940 metres. **31 F3** NN3918.
Beinn a' Chruinnich *Moray* ***Mountain***, 5m/9km SE of Tomintoul. Height 2545 feet or 776 metres. **53 E3** NJ2313.
Beinn a' Chrùlaiste *High.* ***Mountain***, in Lochaber district, 5m/8km SE of Kinlochleven. Height 2811 feet or 857 metres. **39 E4** NN2456.
Beinn a' Chuallaich *P. & K.* ***Mountain***, 2m/4km NE of Kinloch Rannoch. Height 2922 feet or 891 metres. **40 B3** NN6861.

Beinn a' Chùirn *Arg. & B.* ***Mountain***, on border of Argyll & Bute and Perth & Kinross, 4m/6km E of Bridge of Orchy. Height 3027 feet or 923 metres. NN3640.
Beinn a' Chuirn *High.* ***Mountain***, mass in Skye and Lochalsh district, 3m/5km NE of Glenelg. Height 1978 feet or 603 metres. **49 E2** NG8621.
Beinn a' Chumhainn ***Mountain***, on border of Highland and Perth & Kinross, 2m/3km W of Ben Alder. Height 2959 feet or 902 metres. **39 G2** NN4671.
Beinn a' Ghlinne Bhig *High.* ***Hill***, 5m/8km W of Portree, Skye. Height 682 feet or 208 metres. **57 G5** NG3945.
Beinn a' Ghlo (Also known as Ben-y-Gloe.) *P. & K.* ***Mountain***, massif 8m/12km NE of Blair Atholl. Summit is Carn nan Gabha, a Munro at height 3674 feet or 1120 metres. **41 E2** NN9773.
Beinn a' Ghràig *Arg. & B.* ***Mountain***, on Mull, 2m/3km S of Gruline. Height 1938 feet or 591 metres. **29 E1** NM5436.
Beinn a' Mhadaidh *High.* ***Mountain***, 3m/4km W of Loch Druim a' Chliabhain, Caithness district. Height 1322 feet or 403 metres. **75 G4** NC7641.
Beinn a' Mhanaich *Arg. & B.* ***Mountain***, 3m/5km NE of Garelochhead. Height 2326 feet or 709 metres. NS2694.
Beinn a' Mheadhoin *High.* ***Mountain***, in Inverness district, on N side of Loch Beinn a' Mheadhoin. Height 2004 feet or 611 metres. **50 B2** NH2125.
Beinn a' Mhuil *W.Isles* ***Mountain***, 3m/4km E of head of Loch Langavat. Height 1214 feet or 370 metres. **67 D2** NB1913.
Beinn a' Mhùinidh *High.* ***Mountain***, summit in W area of Kinlochewe Forest, Ross and Cromarty district, 2m/4km N of Kinlochewe. Height 2270 feet or 692 metres. **59 G3** NH0366.
Beinn a' Sgà *High.* ***Mountain***, 6m/9km SE of Uig, Skye. Height 1483 feet or 452 metres. **58 A4** NG4356.
Beinn Achaladair ***Mountain***, on border of Argyll & Bute and Perth & Kinross, 2m/4km E of Loch Tulla. Munro: height 3405 feet or 1038 metres. **39 F5** NN3443.
Beinn Airein *High.* ***Hill***, highest point on Muck, 1m/2km W of Port Mòr. Height 449 feet or 137 metres. **36 D2** NM4079.
Beinn Airigh Chárr *High.* ***Mountain***, in Ross and Cromarty district, between Loch Maree and Fionn Loch, 4m/6km N of Talladale across Loch Maree. Height 2594 feet or 791 metres. **59 F2** NG9376.
Beinn Alligin *High.* ***Mountain***, in Ross and Cromarty district 2m/4km N of Upper Loch Torridon. The two peaks of Sgurr Mhòr, a Munro, and Tom na Gruagaich are respectively 3231 feet or 985 metres and 3018 feet or 920 metres in height. **59 E3** NG8660.
Beinn an Amair *High.* ***Hill***, to W of Kyle of Durness. Height 912 feet or 278 metres. **74 C2** NC3665.
Beinn an Armuinn *High.* *Gaelic form of Ben Armine, qv.*
Beinn an Dòthaidh *Arg. & B.* ***Mountain***, in Argyll, 2m/3km E of Bridge of Orchy. Munro: height 3293 feet or 1004 metres. **39 F5** NN3240.
Beinn an Eòin *High.* ***Mountain***, 1m/2km S of Loch Lurgainn. Height 2027 feet or 618 metres. **70 D4** NC1006.
Beinn an Eòin *High.* ***Mountain***, 4m/7km N of Oykel Bridge. Height 1784 feet or 544 metres. **71 F4** NC3808.
Beinn an Eòin *High.* ***Mountain***, 1m/2km W of head of Loch Brittle, Skye. Height 1046 feet or 319 metres. **47 G2** NG3820.
Beinn an Eòin *High.* ***Mountain***, in Ross and Cromarty district 5m/8km N of head of Upper Loch Torridon. Height 2804 feet or 855 metres. **59 F3** NG9064.
Beinn an Fhogharaidh *Stir.* ***Mountain***, on N side of Loch Ard, 4m/6km NW of Aberfoyle. Height 2020 feet or 616 metres. **31 G4** NN4703.
Beinn an Leathaid *High.* ***Mountain***, on Ardnamurchan peninsula, 3m/5km NE of Kilchoan. Height 1315 feet or 401 metres. **37 E3** NM5167.
Beinn an Lochain *Arg. & B.* ***Mountain***, in Argyll 4m/7km N of Lochgoilhead. Height 2955 feet or 901 metres. **31 E4** NN2107.
Beinn an Oir *Arg. & B.* ***Mountain***, highest of Paps of Jura. Height 2575 feet or 785 metres. **20 D2** NR4975.
Beinn an t-Seilich *Arg. & B.* ***Mountain***, in Argyll 4m/7km N of Lochgoilhead. Height 2358 feet or 719 metres. **31 D4** NN2007.
Beinn an t-Sìdhein *High.* ***Mountain***, rounded summit in Inverness district, 4m/7km NW of Dalchreichart. Height 1666 feet or 508 metres. **50 B3** NH2315.
Beinn an t-Sruthain *High.* ***Hill***, 5m/8km NW of Lochaline, Lochaber district. Height 876 feet or 267 metres. **37 F5** NM6048.
Beinn an Tuim *High.* ***Mountain***, 3m/4km NE of Glenfinnan, Lochaber district. Height 2657 feet or 810 metres. **38 B1** NM9283.
Beinn an Tuirc *Arg. & B.* ***Mountain***, on Kintyre, 4m/6km SW of Carradale. Height 1489 feet or 454 metres. **12 C2** NR7536.
Beinn Aoidhdailean *High.* ***Mountain***, 1m/2km NE of Beinn nan Caorach. Height 2076 feet or 633 metres. **49 E3** NG8813.
Beinn Bhalgairean *Arg. & B.* ***Mountain***, 3m/5km SE of Dalmally. Height 2086 feet or 636 metres. **31 D2** NN2024.
Beinn Bhàn *Arg. & B.* ***Mountain***, on Islay, 8m/11km NE of Port Ellen. Height 1545 feet or 471 metres. **20 C4** NR3956.
Beinn Bhan *Arg. & B.* ***Mountain***, 8m/12km N of Lochgilphead. Height 1046 feet or 319 metres. **30 A5** NR8599.
Beinn Bhàn *High.* ***Mountain***, mass in Ross and Cromarty district 6m/9km S of Shieldaig. Height 2939 feet or 896 metres. **59 E5** NG8045.
Beinn Bhàn *High.* ***Mountain***, rising to over 400 metres in Morvern, Lochaber district, 3m/4km N of Lochaline. **37 F5** NM6648.
Beinn Bhàn *High.* ***Mountain***, in Lochaber district 3m/4km W of SW end of Loch Lochy. Height 2611 feet or 796 metres. **38 D1** NN1385.
Beinn Bharrain (Anglicised form: Ben Varren.) *N.Ayr.* ***Mountain***, on Arran 2m/3km SE of Pirnmill. Height 2365 feet or 721 metres. **21 G5** NR9042.
Beinn Bheag ***Mountain***, on border of Argyll & Bute and Stirling, 2m/3km NW of Tyndrum. Height 2148 feet or 655 metres. **31 E1** NN3132.
Beinn Bheag *Arg. & B.* ***Mountain***, on Knapdale, 3m/4km SW of Ardrishaig. Height 1086 feet or 331 metres. **21 G1** NR8184.
Beinn Bheag *Arg. & B.* ***Mountain***, with craggy E face in Argyll Forest Park, rising above W shore of Loch Eck. Height 2027 feet or 618 metres. **30 D5** NS1293.
Beinn Bheag *High.* ***Mountain***, in Lochaber district, at E end of Loch Quoich. Height 1115 feet or 340 metres. **49 G4** NH0700.
Beinn Bheag *High.* ***Mountain***, with twin summits at 2191 feet or 668 metres and 2017 feet or 615 metres in height, in Ross and Cromarty district, 7m/11km NE of Kinlochewe. **59 G2** NH0771.
Beinn Bheag *High.* ***Mountain***, rounded summit in Skye and Lochalsh district, 2m/4km S of W end of Loch Monar. Height 2030 feet or 619 metres. **50 A1** NH1037.
Beinn Bheag *High.* ***Mountain***, 3m/5km SE of Kinlochleven. Height 2001 feet or 610 metres. **39 E4** NN2257.
Beinn Bheigeir *Arg. & B.* ***Mountain***, highest point on Islay, 3m/5km SW of McArthur's Head. Height 1610 feet or 491 metres. **20 C4** NR4256.
Beinn Bheòil *High.* ***Mountain***, in Badenoch and Strathspey district between Loch Ericht and Loch a' Bhealaich Bheithe. Munro: height 3342 feet or 1019 metres. **40 A2** NN5171.
Beinn Bheula *Arg. & B.* ***Mountain***, in Argyll, 4m/6km SW of Lochgoilhead. Height 2555 feet or 779 metres. **31 D5** NS1598.
Beinn Bhòidheach *Arg. & B.* ***Mountain***, in Argyll, 3m/5km SE of Dalmally. Height 1932 feet or 589 metres. **31 E2** NN1922.
Beinn Bhreac *Aber.* ***Mountain***, in Grampian Mountains, 5m/8km NW of Inverey. Munro: height 3054 feet or 931 metres. **52 C5** NO0597.
Beinn Bhreac *Arg. & B.* ***Hill***, on N part of Islay, 4m/7km NW of Ballygrant. Height 938 feet or 286 metres. **20 B2** NR3571.
Beinn Bhreac *Arg. & B.* ***Mountain***, 2m/3km SE of Barcaldine. Height 2322 feet or 708 metres. **30 B1** NM9940.
Beinn Bhreac *Arg. & B.* ***Mountain***, in Argyll, 4m/6km SE of Dalavich across Loch Awe. Height 1725 feet or 526 metres. **30 C3** NN0210.
Beinn Bhreac *Arg. & B.* ***Mountain***, 3m/5km S of Tarbet on W shore of Loch Lomond. Height 2234 feet or 681 metres. **31 F5** NN3200.
Beinn Bhreac *Arg. & B.* ***Mountain***, on Jura in N part of Jura Forest, 7m/11km N of Craighouse. Height 1440 feet or 439 metres. **20 D2** NR5377.
Beinn Bhreac *Arg. & B.* ***Mountain***, in N part of Jura, 4m/6km NW of Lussagiven. Height 1532 feet or 467 metres. **29 E5** NR5990.
Beinn Bhreac *Arg. & B.* ***Mountain***, on Kintyre, 4m/6km W of Carradale. Height 1397 feet or 426 metres. **12 C2** NR7538.
Beinn Bhreac *Arg. & B.* ***Mountain***, on Cowal peninsula, 3m/4km N of Tighnabruaich. Height 1489 feet or 454 metres. **22 A2** NR9877.
Beinn Bhreac *Arg. & B.* ***Mountain***, on tongue of land between Loch Riddon and Loch Striver. Height 1663 feet or 507 metres. **22 B2** NS0576.
Beinn Bhreac *High.* ***Hill***, highest point on Soay, off S coast of Skye. Height 462 feet or 141 metres. **48 A3** NG4615.
Beinn Bhreac *High.* ***Hill***, 3m/4km N of Acharacle, Lochaber district. Height 787 feet or 240 metres. **37 F2** NM6871.
Beinn Bhreac *High.* ***Mountain***, rising to over 310 metres, 1m/2km E of Tongue, Caithness district. **75 E3** NC6056.
Beinn Bhreac *High.* ***Mountain***, 3m/5km N of Dunvegan, Skye. Height 1073 feet or 327 metres. **57 F4** NG2553.
Beinn Bhreac *High.* ***Mountain***, 3m/4km W of head of Loch Eynort, Skye. Height 1460 feet or 445 metres. **47 G2** NG3426.
Beinn Bhreac *High.* ***Mountain***, 3m/4km SE of head of Loch Harport, Skye. Height 1214 feet or 370 metres. **48 A2** NG4328.
Beinn Bhreac *High.* ***Mountain***, on Skye, 3m/5km E of head of Loch Eishort. Height 1430 feet or 436 metres. **48 D3** NG7116.
Beinn Bhreac *High.* ***Mountain***, 3m/4km NW of Beinn Alligin, Ross and Cromarty district. Height 2047 feet or 624 metres. **59 E3** NG8363.
Beinn Bhreac *High.* ***Mountain***, in Inverness district, 3m/5km W of Tomatin. Height 1971 feet or 601 metres. **51 G2** NH7527.
Beinn Bhreac *High.* ***Mountain***, in Inverness district, 4m/6km E of Daviot. Height 1676 feet or 511 metres. **51 G1** NH7837.
Beinn Bhreac *High.* ***Mountain***, on Ardnamurchan peninsula, 3m/4km S of Rubha Aird Druimnich. Height 1171 feet or 357 metres. **37 E3** NM5968.
Beinn Bhreac (Anglicised form: Ben Vrackie.) *N.Ayr.* ***Mountain***, on Arran 2m/4km E of Pirnmill. Height 2332 feet or 711 metres. **22 A5** NR9044.
Beinn Bhreac *N.Ayr.* ***Mountain***, on N part of Arran, 3m/5km S of Lochranza. Height 1879 feet or 573 metres. **22 A5** NR9445.
Beinn Bhreac *N.Ayr.* ***Mountain***, on Arran, 5m/7km NE of Blackwaterfoot. Height 1650 feet or 503 metres. **13 E2** NR9531.
Beinn Bhreac *P. & K.* *Gaelic form of Ben Vrackie, qv.*
Beinn Bhreac *P. & K.* ***Mountain***, 2m/3km E of Ardtalnaig. Height 2348 feet or 716 metres. **40 C5** NN7340.
Beinn Bhreac *P. & K.* ***Mountain***, 10m/17km N of Blair Atholl. Height 2991 feet or 912 metres. **41 D1** NN8682.
Beinn Bhreac *Stir.* ***Inland physical feature***, mountain ridge rising to 2253 feet or 687 metres, 6m/9km SW of Strathyre. **31 G3** NN4714.
Beinn Bhreac *Stir.* ***Mountain***, 6m/9km NW of Aberfoyle. Height 2296 feet or 700 metres. **31 G4** NN4505.
Beinn Bhreac *Stir.* ***Mountain***, 4m/7km W of Killin. Height 2608 feet or 795 metres. NN5032.
Beinn Bhreac *Stir.* ***Mountain***, rising above E shore of Loch Lomond, 4m/6km N of Balmaha. Height 1893 feet or 577 metres. **31 G5** NS4296.
Beinn Bhreac-liath *Arg. & B.* ***Mountain***, in Argyll 3m/5km NW of Tyndrum. Height 2634 feet or 803 metres. **31 F1** NN3033.
Beinn Bhreac Mhòr *High.* ***Mountain***, in Inverness district 5m/8km S of East Croachy. Height 2647 feet or 807 metres. **51 F2** NH6719.
Beinn Bhrotain (Anglicised form: Ben Vrottan.) *Aber.* ***Mountain***, at S end of Cairngorm Mountains. Munro: height 3795 feet or 1157 metres. **52 B5** NN9592.
Beinn Bhuide *High.* ***Mountain***, in Skye and Lochalsh district, 3m/5km NE of Shiel Bridge. Height 2303 feet or 702 metres. **49 F2** NG9523.
Beinn Bhuidhe *Arg. & B.* ***Mountain***, 3m/4km E of Fanmore, Mull. Height 1269 feet or 387 metres. **37 D5** NM4644.
Beinn Bhuidhe *Arg. & B.* ***Mountain***, 3m/4km SE of Salen, Mull. Height 1351 feet or 412 metres. **29 E1** NM5939.
Beinn Bhuidhe *Arg. & B.* ***Mountain***, in Argyll 4m/7km N of head of Loch Fyne. Munro: height 3109 feet or 948 metres. **31 E3** NN2018.
Beinn Bhuidhe *High.* ***Hill***, 2m/3km NE of Rubha Suisnish, Skye. Height 909 feet or 277 metres. **48 C3** NG6017.
Beinn Bhuidhe *High.* ***Hill***, on Ardnamurchan peninsula, 1m/2km N of Rubha Aird Shlignich. Height 912 feet or 278 metres. **37 E3** NM5662.
Beinn Bhuidhe *High.* ***Mountain***, in Inverness district, 8m/13km E of Foyers. Height 2332 feet or 711 metres. **51 F2** NH6221.
Beinn Bhuidhe *High.* ***Mountain***, in Morvern, Lochaber district, 3m/5km E of Drimnin. Height 1479 feet or 451 metres. **37 F4** NM6052.
Beinn Bhuidhe *High.* ***Mountain***, in Knoydart, in Lochaber district, 2m/3km NE of Kylesknoydart on Loch Nevis. Height 2804 feet or 855 metres. **49 E5** NM8296.
Beinn Bhuidhe Mhòr *High.* ***Mountain***, in Inverness district, 4m/7km E of Daviot. Height 1797 feet or 548 metres. **61 G5** NH7840.
Beinn Bragar *W.Isles* ***Hill***, 3m/5km E of Carloway, Isle of Lewis. Height 856 feet or 261 metres. **69 D3** NB2643.
Beinn Capuill *Arg. & B.* ***Mountain***, on E side of Cowal peninsula, 1m/2km N of Tighnabruaich. Height 1437 feet or 438 metres. **22 A2** NR9775.
Beinn Ceannabeinne *High.* ***Mountain***, 3m/4km SE of Durness, Sutherland district. Height 1256 feet or 383 metres. **74 D2** NC4264.
Beinn Ceitlein *High.* ***Mountain***, in Argyll to E of Glen Etive, 5m/8km NE of head of Loch Etive. Height 2729 feet or 832 metres. **39 D5** NN1749.
Beinn Chabhair *Stir.* ***Mountain***, 5m/8km S of Crianlarich. Munro: height 3054 feet or 931 metres. **31 F3** NN3617.
Beinn Chàisgidle *Arg. & B.* ***Mountain***, 5m/8km N of Lochbuie, Mull. Height 1653 feet or 504 metres. **29 F1** NM6033.

Beinn Chaorach *Arg. & B.* ***Mountain***, 3m/5km E of Garelochhead. Height 2339 feet or 713 metres. **31 E5** NS2892.
Beinn Chaorach *High.* ***Mountain***, 1m/2km W of Loch Bà and 7m/11km SE of Kinlochleven. Height 1558 feet or 475 metres. **39 E4** NN2950.
Beinn Chaorach *Stir.* ***Mountain***, 2m/4km NE of Tyndrum. Height 2683 feet or 818 metres. **31 F1** NN3532.
Beinn Chapull *Arg. & B.* ***Mountain***, 2m/3km E of head of Loch Scammadale. Height 1689 feet or 515 metres. **30 B3** NM9319.
Beinn Cheathaich *Stir.* ***Mountain***, 8m/13km W of Killin. Height 3073 feet or 937 metres. NN4432.
Beinn Chladan *Arg. & B.* ***Hill***, 1km E of Aridhglas, Mull. Height 266 feet or 81 metres. **28 C2** NM3223.
Beinn Chlaonleud *High.* ***Mountain***, in Morvern, Lochaber district, 5m/8km NE of Ardtornish. Height 1568 feet or 478 metres. **37 G4** NM7452.
Beinn Chlianaig *High.* ***Mountain***, in Lochaber district, on S side of Glen Spean, 2m/3km SE of Roybridge. Height 2365 feet or 721 metres. **39 E2** NN2978.
Beinn Choinnich *W.Isles* ***Hill***, 4m/7km E of Carloway, Isle of Lewis. Height 689 feet or 210 metres. **69 D3** NB2843.
Beinn Chorranach *Arg. & B.* ***Mountain***, in Argyll 4m/7km NW of Arrochar. Height 2903 feet or 885 metres. **31 E4** NN2509.
Beinn Chraoibh *High.* ***Mountain***, in Lochaber district, on N side of Loch Arkaig, 6m/9km NW of Gairlochy. Height 2020 feet or 616 metres. **50 A5** NN1492.
Beinn Chreagach *Arg. & B.* ***Mountain***, highest point on Ulva, 1m/2km S of northernmost point of island. Height 1027 feet or 313 metres. **36 D5** NM4040.
Beinn Chreagach *Arg. & B.* ***Mountain***, 3m/5km S of Pennyghael, Mull. Height 1233 feet or 376 metres. **29 E2** NM5121.
Beinn Chreagach *High.* ***Mountain***, 4m/6km NE of Dunvegan, Skye. Height 1069 feet or 326 metres. **57 F4** NG2853.
Beinn Chreagach Mhòr *Arg. & B.* ***Mountain***, 4m/7km SE of Salen, Mull. Height 1899 feet or 579 metres. **29 F1** NM6339.
Beinn Chuirn ***Mountain***, on border of Argyll & Bute and Stirling, 3m/5km W of Tyndrum. Height 2886 feet or 880 metres. **31 E2** NN2829.
Beinn Chuldail *High.* ***Hill***, 1m/2km S of Armadale, near N coast of Caithness district. Height 554 feet or 169 metres. **75 G2** NC7961.
Beinn Clach an Fheadain *High.* ***Mountain***, in Ross and Cromarty district, 6m/9km SE of Bonar Bridge. Height 1565 feet or 477 metres. **61 F1** NH6383.
Beinn Clachach *High.* ***Mountain***, 2m/3km E of Arnisdale. Height 2027 feet or 618 metres. **49 E3** NG8710.
Beinn Cleith Bric *High. Gaelic form of Ben Klibreck, qv.*
Beinn Damh (Anglicised form: Ben Damph.) *High.* ***Mountain***, in Ross and Cromarty district 2km E of Loch Damh and 3m/5km S of head of Upper Loch Torridon. Height 2959 feet or 902 metres. **59 E4** NG8950.
Beinn Dearg *Arg. & B.* ***Mountain***, in Argyll, 3m/5km N of Furnace. Height 1581 feet or 482 metres. **30 C4** NN0204.
Beinn Dearg *High.* ***Inland physical feature***, mountain ridge on Skye, 2m/3km W of head of Loch Ainort. **48 B2** NG5027.
Beinn Dearg *High.* ***Mountain***, 6m/9km S of Cape Wrath. Height 1387 feet or 423 metres. **74 B2** NC2765.
Beinn Dearg *High.* ***Mountain***, in Ross and Cromarty district, 3m/5km N of head of Upper Loch Torridon. Height 2998 feet or 914 metres. **59 E3** NG8960.
Beinn Dearg *High.* ***Mountain***, in Ross and Cromarty district, 6m/9km SE of head of Loch Broom. Munro: height 3556 feet or 1084 metres. **60 B1** NH2581.
Beinn Dearg *High.* ***Mountain***, in Kinlochluichart Forest, Ross and Cromarty, 8m/13km NW of Garve. Height 2253 feet or 687 metres. **60 B3** NH2868.
Beinn Dearg *P. & K.* ***Mountain***, 2m/3km NE of Innerwick in Glen Lyon. Height 2703 feet or 824 metres. **40 B4** NN6049.
Beinn Dearg *P. & K.* ***Mountain***, on Forest of Atholl, 8m/12km N of Blair Atholl. Munro: height 3306 feet or 1008 metres. **41 D2** NN8577.
Beinn Dearg *Stir.* ***Mountain***, 4m/6km SW of Callander. Height 1397 feet or 426 metres. **32 A4** NN5803.
Beinn Dearg Mhòr *High.* ***Mountain***, 3m/5km W of Broadford, Skye. Height 2326 feet or 709 metres. **48 B2** NG5822.
Beinn Dearg Mòr *High.* ***Mountain***, in Fisherfield Forest, Ross and Cromarty district, 4m/6km SW of An Teallach. Height 2978 feet or 908 metres. **59 G1** NH0379.
Beinn Dhorain *High.* ***Mountain***, in Sutherland district, 3m/5km N of Lothbeg. Height 2060 feet or 628 metres. **73 E3** NC9215.
Beinn Dhubh *W.Isles* ***Mountain***, near N coast of South Harris. Height 1660 feet or 506 metres. **66 C3** NB0800.
Beinn Domhnaill *High.* ***Mountain***, in Sutherland district, 5m/8km NE of Bonar Bridge. Height 1145 feet or 349 metres. **72 B5** NH6796.
Beinn Donachain *Arg. & B.* ***Mountain***, in Lorn, 4m/6km NE of Dalmally. Height 2125 feet or 648 metres. **31 D1** NN1931.
Beinn Dòrain (Anglicised form: Ben Douran.) *Arg. & B.* ***Mountain***, in Argyll, 2m/3km SE of Bridge of Orchy. Munro: height 3523 feet or 1074 metres. **31 F1** NN3237.
Beinn Dronaig *High.* ***Mountain***, in Skye and Lochalsh district on SW side of Loch Calavie. Height 2611 feet or 796 metres. **49 G1** NH0338.
Beinn Dubh *Arg. & B.* ***Hill***, on E coast of Islay, 3m/5km S of Port Askaig. Height 876 feet or 267 metres. **20 C3** NR4263.
Beinn Dubh *Arg. & B.* ***Mountain***, on W side of Loch Sloy, 3m/5km NW of Inveruglas on W shore of Loch Lomond. Height 2535 feet or 773 metres. **31 E3** NN2711.
Beinn Dubh *Stir.* ***Mountain***, on NE side of Gleann Dubh, 3m/5km S of Stronachlachar. Height 1666 feet or 508 metres. **31 G4** NN4004.
Beinn Dubhain *Arg. & B.* ***Mountain***, rising above E shore of Loch Eck, 2m/3km E of Glenbranter. Height 2129 feet or 649 metres. **30 D5** NS1497.
Beinn Dubhain *High.* ***Mountain***, in Sutherland district, 2m/3km SE of Kildonan Lodge. Height 1358 feet or 414 metres. **73 E2** NC9320.
Beinn Dubhcharaidh *High.* ***Mountain***, rising above S side of Loch Conagleann, 6m/10km E of Foyers. Height 2260 feet or 689 metres. **51 E3** NH5819.
Beinn Dubhchraig *Stir.* ***Mountain***, 5m/8km W of Crianlarich. Munro: height 3205 feet or 977 metres. **31 F2** NN3025.
Beinn Duill *Arg. & B.* ***Hill***, on NW Mull, 4m/6km W of Kilninian. Height 626 feet or 191 metres. **36 C5** NM3447.
Beinn Eagagach *P. & K.* ***Mountain***, 5m/8km W of Pitlochry. Height 2260 feet or 689 metres. **41 D4** NN8556.
Beinn Edra *High.* ***Mountain***, 4m/7km W of Rubha nam Brathairean, Skye. Height 2004 feet or 611 metres. **58 A3** NG4562.
Beinn Eibhinn *High.* ***Mountain***, on border of Lochaber and Badenoch and Strathspey districts 2m/3km E of Loch Ghuilbinn. Munro: height 3611 feet or 1101 metres. **39 G2** NN4473.
Beinn Eich *Arg. & B.* ***Mountain***, 4m/6km W of Luss. Height 2303 feet or 702 metres. **31 F5** NS3094.
Beinn Eighe (Anglicised form: Ben Eay.) *High.* ***Mountain***, mass and national nature reserve in Ross and Cromarty district to W of Kinlochewe. Highest peak is Ruadh-stac Mòr, a Munro at 3312 feet or 1010 metres. Nature reserve is good example of old pine forest. **59 F3** NG9561.
Beinn Eilde *High.* ***Mountain***, in Badenoch and Strathspey district, 4m/7km W of Dalwhinnie. Height 2211 feet or 674 metres. **40 A1** NN5685.
Beinn Eilideach *High.* ***Mountain***, in Ross and Cromarty district, on N slope of Loch Broom, 3m/5km SE of Ullapool. Height 1830 feet or 558 metres. **71 D5** NH1692.
Beinn Enaiglair *High.* ***Mountain***, in Ross and Cromarty district, 2m/3km NE of Corrieshalloch Gorge. Height 2916 feet or 889 metres. **60 B1** NH2280.
Beinn Eolasary *Arg. & B.* ***Mountain***, 1m/2km E of W point of Ulva. Height 1004 feet or 306 metres. **28 C1** NM3840.
Beinn Eunaich *Arg. & B.* ***Mountain***, in Argyll 4m/6km NW of Dalmally. Munro: height 3241 feet or 988 metres. **30 D1** NN1332.
Beinn Fhada *Arg. & B.* ***Inland physical feature***, mountain ridge rising to 2303 feet or 702 metres in SE, 1m/2km N of Ben More, Mull. **29 E1** NM5335.
Beinn Fhada *Arg. & B.* ***Mountain***, 3m/5km NW of Lochbuie, Mull. Height 1643 feet or 501 metres. **29 F2** NM6329.
Beinn Fhada *High. See The Three Sisters.*
Beinn Fhada *High.* ***Inland physical feature***, mountain ridge rising to 3041 feet or 927 metres and running NE to SW on S side of Glen Coe, 5m/8km SE of Glencoe village. **39 D4** NN1553.
Beinn Fhada (Also known as Ben Attow.) *High.* ***Mountain***, on Kintail Forest (National Trust for Scotland), in Skye and Lochalsh district, 5m/8km E of Shiel Bridge. Munro: height 3385 feet or 1032 metres. **49 G3** NH0119.
Beinn Fhionnlaidh *Arg. & B.* ***Mountain***, in Argyll, 3m/5km N of head of Loch Etive. Munro: height 3146 feet or 959 metres. **38 C5** NN0949.
Beinn Fhionnlaidh *High.* ***Mountain***, on S side of Loch Mullardoch, Skye and Lochalsh district. Munro: height 3296 feet or 1005 metres. **50 A2** NH1128.
Beinn Gàire *High.* ***Mountain***, 5m/8km NE of Ardmolich, Lochaber district. Height 2184 feet or 666 metres. **37 G2** NM7874.
Beinn Gharbh *High.* ***Mountain***, with summit 1km S of Loch Assynt. Height 1771 feet or 540 metres. **71 E2** NC2122.
Beinn Ghlas *Arg. & B.* ***Mountain***, 5m/8km E of Kilmore. Height 1689 feet or 515 metres. **30 B2** NM9525.
Beinn Ghlas *Arg. & B.* ***Mountain***, in Argyll, 6m/10km NE of Inveraray. Height 1804 feet or 550 metres. **30 D3** NN1318.
Beinn Ghlas *Arg. & B.* ***Mountain***, 10m/16km NE of Lochgilphead. Height 1378 feet or 420 metres. **30 B5** NR9899.
Beinn Ghlas *P. & K.* ***Mountain***, SW shoulder (National Trust for Scotland) of Ben Lawers. Slopes noted for alpine plants. Munro: height 3618 feet or 1103 metres. **40 B5** NN6240.
Beinn Ghobhlach *High.* ***Mountain***, in Ross and Cromarty district, 5m/8km W of Ullapool across Loch Broom. Height 2083 feet or 635 metres. **70 C5** NH0594.
Beinn Ghormaig *High.* ***Mountain***, 2m/3km E of entrance to Loch Teacuis. Height 1483 feet or 452 metres. **37 F4** NM6557.
Beinn Ghuilbin *High.* ***Mountain***, in Badenoch and Strathspey district, 3m/4km N of Aviemore. Height 1896 feet or 578 metres. **52 A3** NH8917.
Beinn Ghuilean *Arg. & B.* ***Mountain***, on Kintyre, 2m/3km SE of Campbeltown. Height 1155 feet or 352 metres. **12 C4** NR7217.
Beinn Heasgarnich *P. & K.* ***Mountain***, 2m/3km S of Loch Lyon. Munro: height 3529 feet or 1076 metres. **31 G1** NN4138.
Beinn Iaruinn *High.* ***Mountain***, in Lochaber district 4m/7km S of head of Loch Lochy. Height 2634 feet or 803 metres. **50 B5** NN2990.
Beinn Ime (Anglicised form: Ben Ime.) *Arg. & B.* ***Mountain***, in Argyll 4m/6km NW of Arrochar. Munro: height 3316 feet or 1011 metres. **31 E4** NN2508.
Beinn Inverveigh *Arg. & B.* ***Mountain***, 2m/3km SE of Bridge of Orchy. Height 2096 feet or 639 metres. **31 E1** NN2738.
Beinn Iutharn Bheag ***Mountain***, on border of Aberdeenshire and Perth & Kinross, 1m/2km E of Beinn Iutharn Mhòr. Height 3126 feet or 953 metres. **41 F2** NO0679.
Beinn Iutharn Mhòr ***Mountain***, on border of Aberdeenshire and Perth & Kinross, 10m/16km SW of Braemar. Munro: height 3428 feet or 1045 metres. **41 F2** NO0479.
Beinn Iadain *High.* ***Mountain***, 7m/11km N of Lochaline, Lochaber district. Height 1873 feet or 571 metres. **37 F4** NM6955.
Beinn Làir *High.* ***Mountain***, in Letterewe Forest, Ross and Cromarty district, 1m/2km W of head of Lochan Fada. Height 2821 feet or 860 metres. **59 F2** NG9873.
Beinn Laoghal *High. Gaelic form of Ben Loyal, qv.*
Beinn Laoigh *Arg. & B.* ***Mountain***, 3m/5km N of Minard. Height 1420 feet or 433 metres. **30 B4** NM9601.
Beinn Laoigh *Stir. Gaelic form of Ben Lui, qv.*
Beinn Larachan *Arg. & B.* ***Mountain***, in Lorn, 5m/7km N of Dalmally. Height 2345 feet or 715 metres. **31 D1** NN1633.
Beinn Leabhain *Stir.* ***Mountain***, on NE side of Glen Ogle, 3m/4km S of Killin. Height 2312 feet or 705 metres. **32 A2** NN5728.
Beinn Leamhain *High.* ***Mountain***, 2m/3km W of Sallachan Point, Lochaber district. Height 1647 feet or 502 metres. **38 B3** NM9662.
Beinn Leòid (Also spelled Ben Leoid.) *High.* ***Mountain***, in Sutherland district 6m/10km NE of Inchnadamph. Height 2598 feet or 792 metres. **71 F2** NC3229.
Beinn Liath Bheag *High.* ***Mountain***, in Ross and Cromarty district, 4m/6km SE of Corrieshalloch Gorge. Height 2181 feet or 665 metres. **60 B2** NH2473.
Beinn Liath Mhòr *High.* ***Mountain***, in Ross and Cromarty district, 3m/5km NW of Achnashellach Lodge. Munro: height 3034 feet or 925 metres. **59 F4** NG9651.
Beinn Liath Mhòr a' Ghiubhais Li *High.* ***Mountain***, in Ross and Cromarty district, to SW of Loch Glascarnoch, 9m/15km NW of Garve. Height 2512 feet or 766 metres. **60 B2** NH2871.
Beinn Liath Mhòr Fannaich *High.* ***Mountain***, in Ross and Cromarty district, 4m/6km S of Corrieshalloch Gorge. Munro: height 3129 feet or 954 metres. **60 B2** NH2172.
Beinn Lice *High.* ***Mountain***, 1km S of Loch More. Height 1542 feet or 470 metres. **74 C5** NC3335.
Beinn Lochain *Arg. & B.* ***Mountain***, in Argyll 3m/4km W of Lochgoilhead. Height 2306 feet or 703 metres. **31 D4** NN1600.
Beinn Loinne *High.* ***Mountain***, in Inverness district on S side of Loch Cluanie. Height 2542 feet or 775 metres. **50 A4** NH1507.
Beinn Luibhean *Arg. & B.* ***Mountain***, in Argyll 4m/7km NW of Arrochar. Height 2811 feet or 857 metres. NN2407.
Beinn Lunndaidh *High.* ***Mountain***, 1km N of Loch Lunndaith, Sutherland district. Height 1463 feet or 446 metres. **72 C4** NC7902.
Beinn Lurachan *Arg. & B.* ***Mountain***, in Argyll 4m/7km N of Dalmally. Height 2345 feet or 715 metres. NN1633.
Beinn Maol Chaluim *High.* ***Inland physical feature***, mountain ridge rising to 2778 feet or 847 metres, above Glen Coe and Glen Etive, 5m/8km SE of Glencoe village. **38 D4** NN1451.

Beinn Mhanach (Anglicised form: Ben Vannoch.) *P. & K.* ***Mountain***, 1m/2km N of head of Loch Lyon. Munro: height 3126 feet or 953 metres. **39 F5** NN3741.

Beinn Mheadhoin *High.* ***Mountain***, 6m/10km S of Strontian, Lochaber district. Height 2424 feet or 739 metres. **37 G4** NM7951.

Beinn Mheadhoin *Moray* ***Mountain***, in Cairngorm Mountains, 3m/5km NE of Ben Macdui. Munro: height 3877 feet or 1182 metres. **52 C4** NJ0201.

Beinn Mheadhon *Arg. & B.* ***Mountain***, 4m/7km W of Craignure, Mull. Height 2089 feet or 637 metres. **29 F1** NM6537.

Beinn Mheadhonach *Arg. & B.* ***Mountain***, 4m/6km N of Taynuilt. Height 2342 feet or 714 metres. **30 C1** NN0136.

Beinn Mheadhonach *W.Isles* ***Mountain***, 4m/6km N of head of Loch Resort and 1m/2km S of Loch Grunavat, Isle of Lewis. Height 1302 feet or 397 metres. **68 B5** NB0923.

Beinn Mhealaich *High.* ***Mountain***, 4m/7km W of Helmsdale, Sutherland district. Height 1942 feet or 592 metres. **73 E3** NC9614.

Beinn Mhialairigh *High.* ***Mountain***, in Skye and Lochalsh district, 4m/6km S of Glenelg. Height 1797 feet or 548 metres. **49 E3** NG8012.

Beinn Mhic Chasgaig *High.* ***Mountain***, on E side of Glen Etive in Lochaber district, 1m/2km W of Clach Leathad. Height 2827 feet or 862 metres. **39 E4** NN2250.

Beinn Mhic-Mhonaidh *Arg. & B.* ***Mountain***, in Argyll 6m/10km NE of Dalmally. Height 2601 feet or 793 metres. **31 E1** NN2035.

Beinn Mhic na Ceisich *Arg. & B.* ***Mountain***, in Argyll, 15m/25km NE of Oban. Height 2093 feet or 638 metres. **38 C5** NN0149.

Beinn Mholach *P. & K.* ***Mountain***, 3m/5km SW of S end of Loch Garry. Height 2758 feet or 841 metres. **40 A3** NN5865.

Beinn Mholach *W.Isles* ***Hill***, 5m/8km NW of Stornoway, Isle of Lewis. Height 958 feet or 292 metres. **69 E4** NB3538.

Beinn Mhòr *Arg. & B.* ***Mountain***, in Argyll, 2m/3km W of Loch Eck. Height 2430 feet or 741 metres. **30 D5** NS1090.

Beinn Mhòr *High.* ***Mountain***, rounded summit, 4m/6km S of Cannich. Height 1315 feet or 401 metres. **50 C2** NH3225.

Beinn Mhòr *High.* ***Mountain***, in Badenoch and Strathspey district, 2m/3km N of Dulnain Bridge. Height 1545 feet or 471 metres. **52 B2** NH9828.

Beinn Mhòr *W.Isles* ***Hill***, on North Uist, 3m/5km NE of Maari. Height 623 feet or 190 metres. **45 G2** NF8976.

Beinn Mhòr *W.Isles* ***Mountain***, on Isle of Lewis, 2m/3km N of head of Loch Claidh. Height 1876 feet or 572 metres. **67 E3** NB2509.

Beinn Mhòr *W.Isles* ***Mountain***, on South Uist, 2m/4km N of Loch Eynort. Height 2034 feet or 620 metres. **46 B1** NF8031.

Beinn Mohal (Anglicised form: Ben Mohal.) *W.Isles* ***Hill***, 3m/4km E of head of Little Loch Roag, Isle of Lewis. Height 679 feet or 207 metres. **68 C5** NB1723.

Beinn Molurgainn *Arg. & B.* ***Mountain***, 5m/9km N of Taynuilt. Height 2263 feet or 690 metres. **30 C1** NN0140.

Beinn Muic Duibhe *Moray Gaelic form of Ben Macdui, qv.*

Beinn na Boineid *High.* ***Mountain***, 1km N of Ben Idrigill, Skye. Height 1217 feet or 371 metres. **47 F1** NG2339.

Beinn na Caillich *Arg. & B.* ***Mountain***, near E coast of Islay, 10m/16km NE of Port Ellen. Height 1105 feet or 337 metres. **20 C4** NR4559.

Beinn na Caillich *High.* ***Mountain***, 3m/4km W of Broadford, Skye. Height 2401 feet or 732 metres. **48 C2** NG6023.

Beinn na Caillich *High.* ***Mountain***, 2m/4km SE of Kyleakin near E end of Skye. Height 2394 feet or 730 metres. **49 D2** NG7722.

Beinn na Caillich *High.* ***Mountain***, in Knoydart, in Lochaber district, 3m/4km NW of Ladhar Bheinn. Height 2575 feet or 785 metres. **49 D4** NG7906.

Beinn na Caillich *High.* ***Mountain***, on N side of Loch Leven in Lochaber district, 3m/5km W of Kinlochleven. Height 2506 feet or 764 metres. NN1462.

Beinn na Cille *High.* ***Mountain***, in Lochaber district, 1m/2km N of Loch a' Choire. Height 2135 feet or 651 metres. **38 A4** NM8554.

Beinn na Cloiche *High.* ***Hill***, 2m/3km N of Bracadale, Skye. Height 761 feet or 232 metres. **57 G5** NG3641.

Beinn na Creiche *High.* ***Hill***, 3m/5km W of Dunvegan, Skye. Height 859 feet or 262 metres. **57 E5** NG2048.

Beinn na Croise *Arg. & B.* ***Mountain***, on Mull 3m/4km NE of Carsaig. Source of Leidle River. Height 1650 feet or 503 metres. **29 E2** NM5625.

Beinn na Drise *Arg. & B.* ***Mountain***, 6m/10km W of Salen, Mull. Height 1391 feet or 424 metres. **37 D5** NM4742.

Beinn na Duatharach *Arg. & B.* ***Mountain***, 1m/2km E of head of Loch Bà, Mull. Height 1492 feet or 455 metres. **29 E1** NM6036.

Beinn na Faoghla *W.Isles Gaelic form of Benbecula, qv.*

Beinn na Gainimh *P. & K.* ***Mountain***, 4m/7km W of Amulree. Height 2394 feet or 730 metres. NN8334.

Beinn na Greine *High.* ***Mountain***, 1m/2km SW of Portree, Skye. Height 1368 feet or 417 metres. **58 A5** NG4541.

Beinn na Gucaig *High.* ***Mountain***, in Lochaber district, 6m/9km SW of Fort William. Height 2020 feet or 616 metres. **38 C3** NN0665.

Beinn na h-Eaglaise *High.* ***Mountain***, on Ben-damph Forest, Ross and Cromarty district, 2m/3km S of head of Loch Torridon. Height 2417 feet or 737 metres. **59 F4** NG9052.

Beinn na h-Iolaire *High.* ***Hill***, 1km N of Torran, Raasay. Height 833 feet or 254 metres. **58 C4** NG6050.

Beinn na h-Uamha *High.* ***Mountain***, 6m/9km N of Lochaline, Lochaber district. Height 1522 feet or 464 metres. **37 F4** NM6853.

Beinn na h-Uamha *W.Isles* ***Mountain***, on North Harris, 1km NE of Muaithabhal. Height 1276 feet or 389 metres. **67 E2** NB2611.

Beinn na Lap *High.* ***Mountain***, in Lochaber district, 1m/2km N of Loch Ossian. Munro: height 3073 feet or 937 metres. **39 F3** NN3769.

Beinn na' Leac *High.* ***Mountain***, near E coast of Raasay, 2m/3km N of Eyre Point. Height 1046 feet or 319 metres. **48 B1** NG5937.

Beinn na Lice *Arg. & B.* ***Mountain***, at S end of Kintyre, 5m/8km W of Southend. Height 1404 feet or 428 metres. **12 B5** NR6008.

Beinn na Seamraig *High.* ***Mountain***, on Skye, 3m/4km S of Glen Arroch. Height 1840 feet or 561 metres. **48 D3** NG7217.

Beinn na Seilg *High.* ***Mountain***, 2m/3km W of Kilchoan. Height 1122 feet or 342 metres. **37 D3** NM4564.

Beinn na Sreine *Arg. & B.* ***Mountain***, 3m/4km S of Balnahard, Mull. Height 1702 feet or 519 metres. **29 D2** NM4530.

Beinn na Sroine *Arg. & B.* ***Mountain***, 4m/7km E of Dalmally. Height 2086 feet or 636 metres. **31 E2** NN2328.

Beinn nam Bad Mòr *High.* ***Hill***, rising above Loch Scye. Height 951 feet or 290 metres. **76 C3** NC9955.

Beinn nam Bò *High.* ***Hill***, 1m/2km W of Strathy Forest, Caithness district. Height 751 feet or 229 metres. **75 G3** NC7858.

Beinn nam Fitheach *High.* ***Mountain***, rounded summit in Inverness district, 7m/11km W of Beauly. Height 1620 feet or 494 metres. **60 D5** NH4146.

Beinn nam Fuaran *Arg. & B.* ***Mountain***, 4m/7km E of Bridge of Orchy. Height 2631 feet or 802 metres. NN3638.

Beinn nan Aighenan *Arg. & B.* ***Mountain***, in Argyll 4m/6km SE of head of Loch Etive. Munro: height 3139 feet or 957 metres. **38 D5** NN1440.

Beinn nan Cabar *High.* ***Mountain***, in South Morar, Lochaber district, 3m/4km N of Lochailort. Height 1883 feet or 574 metres. **37 G1** NM7686.

Beinn nan Caorach *High.* ***Mountain***, in Lochaber district 2m/3km NE of Arnisdale on Loch Hourn. Height 2535 feet or 773 metres. **49 E3** NG8712.

Beinn nan Capull *Arg. & B.* ***Hill***, on N coast of Jura, 8m/12km N of Ardlussa. Height 827 feet or 252 metres. **29 F5** NR6899.

Beinn nan Carn *Arg. & B.* ***Mountain***, 3m/5km NW of Gruline, Mull. Height 1092 feet or 333 metres. **37 E5** NM5042.

Beinn nan Càrn *High.* ***Hill***, 1km NW of Heast, Skye. Height 987 feet or 301 metres. **48 C3** NG6318.

Beinn nan Clach-corra *Arg. & B.* ***Mountain***, on Mull, 2m/3km N of Fanmore. Height 1033 feet or 315 metres. **36 D5** NM4247.

Beinn nan Eun *High.* ***Mountain***, in Ross and Cromarty district, 10m/15km NE of Gorstan. Height 2434 feet or 742 metres. **60 D2** NH4476.

Beinn nan Imirean *Stir.* ***Mountain***, 4m/7km NE of Crianlarich. Height 2768 feet or 844 metres. **31 G1** NN4130.

Beinn nan Losgann *High.* ***Mountain***, 1km W of head of Loch Mudle. Height 1027 feet or 313 metres. **37 E3** NM5364.

Beinn nan Lus *Arg. & B.* ***Mountain***, in Argyll on N side of Glen Kinglass. Height 2326 feet or 709 metres. **30 D1** NN1337.

Beinn nan Oighreag ***Mountain***, on border of Perth & Kinross and Stirling, 6m/10km W of Ben Lawers. Height 2982 feet or 909 metres. **40 A5** NN5441.

Beinn nan Ramh *High.* ***Mountain***, in Ross and Cromarty district, 8m/12km NE of Kinlochewe. Height 2332 feet or 711 metres. **60 A3** NH1366.

Beinn nan Surrag *W.Isles* ***Hill***, 4m/7km NW of Liurbost, Isle of Lewis. Height 656 feet or 200 metres. **69 E4** NB3131.

Beinn Narnain *Arg. & B.* ***Mountain***, in Argyll 2m/3km NW of head of Loch Long. Munro: height 3037 feet or 926 metres. **31 E4** NN2706.

Beinn Nuis *N.Ayr.* ***Mountain***, on Arran 2m/4km SW of Goat Fell. Height 2598 feet or 792 metres. **13 E2** NR9539.

Beinn Odhar ***Mountain***, on border of Argyll & Bute and Stirling, 2m/4km N of Tyndrum. Height 2955 feet or 901 metres. **31 F1** NN3333.

Beinn Odhar ***Mountain***, on border of Perth & Kinross and Stirling, 6m/10km NE of Callander. Height 2073 feet or 632 metres. **32 C3** NN7112.

Beinn Odhar Bheag *High.* ***Mountain***, nearly 1m/2km S of Beinn Odhar Mhòr. Height 2893 feet or 882 metres. **38 A2** NM8579.

Beinn Odhar Mhòr *High.* ***Mountain***, in Moidart, Lochaber district, 4m/6km W of Glenfinnan. Height 2854 feet or 870 metres. **38 A2** NM8579.

Beinn Pharlagain *P. & K.* ***Mountain***, on Rannoch Forest, 4m/6km N of Loch Eigheach. Height 2647 feet or 807 metres. **39 G3** NN4464.

Beinn Rahacleit *W.Isles* ***Hill***, 3m/5km E of Carloway, Isle of Lewis. Height 813 feet or 248 metres. **69 D3** NB2642.

Beinn Raimh *High.* ***Mountain***, in Skye and Lochalsh district, 3m/4km SW of Stromeferry. Height 1466 feet or 447 metres. **49 E1** NG8430.

Beinn Ràtha *High.* ***Hill***, in Caithness district, 2m/3km S of Reay. Height 794 feet or 242 metres. **76 B2** NC9561.

Beinn Reithe *Arg. & B.* ***Mountain***, in Argyll, 3m/4km SE of Lochgoilhead. Height 2142 feet or 653 metres. NS2298.

Beinn Resipol *High.* ***Mountain***, in Sunart, Lochaber district, 4m/6km W of Scotstown. Height 2772 feet or 845 metres. **37 G3** NM7665.

Beinn Rodagrich *W.Isles* ***Hill***, in S part of Ronay. Height 325 feet or 99 metres. **45 G4** NF8954.

Beinn Ruadh *Arg. & B.* ***Mountain***, 4m/6km SW of Dunoon. Height 1059 feet or 323 metres. **22 C2** NS1371.

Beinn Ruadh *High.* ***Hill***, 4m/6km S of Strathy, Caithness district. Height 833 feet or 254 metres. **76 A2** NC8459.

Beinn Ruigh Choinnich *W.Isles* ***Hill***, on South Uist, 1m/2km E of Lochboisdale. Height 902 feet or 275 metres. **46 B3** NF8019.

Beinn Ruisg *Arg. & B.* ***Mountain***, overlooking Loch Lomond, 2m/4km SW of Luss. Height 1945 feet or 593 metres. **31 F5** NS3291.

Beinn Sgaillinish *Arg. & B.* ***Hill***, on E coast of Jura, 2m/3km SW of Lussagiven. Height 623 feet or 190 metres. **21 E1** NR6184.

Beinn Sgreamhaidh *High.* ***Mountain***, 1m/2km S of Strath an Lòin. Height 1427 feet or 435 metres. **71 G3** NC4415.

Beinn Sgritheall (Also known as Ben Screel.) *High.* ***Mountain***, on Loch Hourn in Lochaber district, 1m/2km N of Arnisdale. Munro: height 3195 feet or 974 metres. **49 E3** NG8312.

Beinn Sgulaird *Arg. & B.* ***Mountain***, 3m/5km E of head of Loch Creran, Argyll. Munro: height 3073 feet or 937 metres. **38 C5** NN0546.

Beinn Shiantaidh *Arg. & B.* ***Mountain***, easternmost and second highest of Paps of Jura. Height 2476 feet or 755 metres. **20 D2** NR5174.

Beinn Sholum *Arg. & B.* ***Mountain***, on Islay, 4m/6km NE of Port Ellen. Height 1138 feet or 347 metres. **20 C5** NR3949.

Beinn Spionnaidh *High.* ***Mountain***, in Sutherland district 3m/4km NW of head of Loch Eriboll. Height 2532 feet or 772 metres. **74 C3** NC3657.

Beinn Staic *High.* ***Mountain***, 1m/2km NE of An Cruachan, Skye. Height 1348 feet or 411 metres. **47 G2** NG3923.

Beinn Stumanadh *High.* ***Mountain***, 1m/2km E of Loch Loyal. Height 1729 feet or 527 metres. **75 F3** NC6449.

Beinn Suidhe *Arg. & B.* ***Mountain***, in Argyll 6m/9km W of Bridge of Orchy. Height 2214 feet or 675 metres. **39 E5** NN2140.

Beinn Talaidh *Arg. & B.* ***Mountain***, 6m/10km N of Lochbuie, Mull. Height 2496 feet or 761 metres. **29 F1** NM6234.

Beinn Tarsuinn *Arg. & B.* ***Mountain***, with craggy slopes, 6m/10km N of Craighouse on Jura. Height 1364 feet or 416 metres. **21 D2** NR5476.

Beinn Tarsuinn *High.* ***Mountain***, in Ross and Cromarty district, 7m/11km N of Kinlochewe, on N side of Lochan Fada. Munro: height 3070 feet or 936 metres. **59 G2** NH0372.

Beinn Tarsuinn *N.Ayr.* ***Mountain***, on Arran, 4m/6km S of Lochranza. Comprises two distinct peaks at 1817 feet or 554 metres and 1715 feet or 523 metres. **22 A5** NR9244.

Beinn Tarsuinn *N.Ayr.* ***Mountain***, on Arran, 5m/8km NW of Brodick. Height 2706 feet or 825 metres. **22 A5** NR9540.

Beinn Tart a' Mhill *Arg. & B.* ***Hill***, on Rinns of Islay, 4m/6km NE of Portnahaven. Height 761 feet or 232 metres. **20 A4** NR2156.

Beinn Teallach *High.* ***Mountain***, in Lochaber district 3m/5km N of W end of Loch Moy. Munro: height 3001 feet or 915 metres. **39 F1** NN3685.

Beinn Tharsuinn *Arg. & B.* ***Mountain***, 3m/5km E of Garelochhead. Height 2152 feet or 656 metres. **31 E5** NS2891.

Beinn Tharsuinn *High.* ***Mountain***, on West Monar Forest on border of Ross and Cromarty and Skye and Lochalsh districts. Height 2831 feet or 863 metres. **59 G5** NH0543.

Beinn Tharsuinn *High.* ***Mountain***, in Sutherland district, 13m/22km N of Garve. Height 2342 feet or 714 metres. **60 D1** NH4183.

Beinn Tharsuinn *High.* ***Mountain***, in Ross and Cromarty district, 8m/12km S of Bonar Bridge. Height 2270 feet or 692 metres. **61 F2** NH6079.

Beinn Tighe *High.* ***Mountain***, 1km SE of Rubha an Fhasaidh, Eigg. Height 1033 feet or 315 metres. **37 D1** NM4486.

Beinn Toaig ***Mountain***, on border of Argyll & Bute and Highland, on SE side of Stob a' Choire Odhair and 2m/3km E of Stob Ghabhar. Height 2736 feet or 834 metres. NN2645.

Beinn Totaig *High.* ***Mountain***, rising to over 340 metres, 4m/6km SE of Bracadale, Skye. **48 A1** NG4036.

Beinn Trilleachan *Arg. & B.* ***Mountain***, 2m/3km SW of head of Loch Etive, on border with Highland. Height 2752 feet or 839 metres. **38 C5** NN0843.

Beinn Tulaichean *Stir.* ***Mountain***, 4m/6km SE of Crianlarich. Munro: height 3100 feet or 945 metres. **31 G3** NN4119.

Beinn Uamha *Stir.* ***Mountain***, 1m/2km S of Loch Arklet and 4m/7km NE of Tarbet across Loch Lomond. Height 1961 feet or 598 metres. **31 F4** NN3806.

Beinn Udlaidh *Arg. & B.* ***Mountain***, in Argyll 4m/6km NW of Tyndrum. Height 2755 feet or 840 metres. **31 E1** NN2833.

Beinn Udlamain *P. & K.* ***Mountain***, in Dalnaspidal Forest to E of Loch Ericht. Munro: height 3313 feet or 1010 metres. **40 A2** NN5773.

Beinn Uidhe *High.* ***Mountain***, 3m/4km NE of S end of Loch Assynt. Height 2427 feet or 740 metres. **71 E2** NC2825.

Beinn Uird *Stir.* ***Mountain***, overlooking E shore of Loch Lomond, 3m/4km E of Rowardennan Lodge. Height 1955 feet or 596 metres. **31 F5** NS3998.

Beinn Ulbhaidh *High.* ***Mountain***, rounded mountain with three summits, in Sutherland district, 4m/6km SW of Invercassley. Height 1617 feet or 493 metres. **71 G5** NH4396.

Beinn Uraraidh *Arg. & B.* ***Mountain***, rocky summit on Islay, 6m/10km NE of Port Ellen. Height 1489 feet or 454 metres. **20 C4** NR4153.

Beinneun Forest *High.* ***Open space***, deer forest on border of Inverness and Lochaber districts E of Loch Loyne. **50 B4** NH2208.

Beins Law *P. & K.* ***Hill***, in Ochil Hills, 3m/4km S of Abernethy. Height 879 feet or 268 metres. **33 G3** NO1812.

Beith *N.Ayr.* Population: 6358. ***Small town***, 10m/16km SW of Paisley. **23 E4** NS3453.

Beldorney Castle *Aber.* ***Castle***, 16c Z-plan tower on W side of River Deveron, 6m/10km E of Dufftown. **53 G1** NJ4137.

Belhaven *E.Loth.* ***Suburb***, W area of Dunbar. **27 D2** NT6678.

Belhaven Bay *E.Loth.* ***Bay***, on W side of Dunbar. **27 D2** NT6578.

Belhelvie *Aber.* ***Hamlet***, 7m/12km N of Aberdeen. **55 E3** NJ9417.

Belhinnie (Also known as Balhinny.) *Moray* ***Settlement***, 2m/4km W of Rhynie. **53 G2** NJ4627.

Belig *High.* ***Mountain***, on Skye, 1km NE of Garbh-bheinn. Height 2303 feet or 702 metres. **48 B2** NG5424.

Bell Craig *D. & G.* ***Mountain***, 3m/5km NW of Bodesbeck. Height 2047 feet or 624 metres. **16 C4** NT1812.

Bell Rock *Angus Alternative name for Inchcape Rock, qv.*

Bellabeg *Aber.* ***Settlement***, near bridge over River Don, at NE side of Strathdon. **53 F3** NJ3513.

Belladrum *High.* ***Settlement***, 3m/5km S of Beauly. **61 E5** NH5241.

Bellahouston *Glas.* ***Suburb***, 2m/4km SW of Glasgow city centre. NS5564.

Bellanoch *Arg. & B.* ***Hamlet***, in Argyll, on SW side of Crinan Canal, 2m/3km from Crinan village. Road bridge across canal and River Add. **30 A5** NR8092.

Bellart *Arg. & B.* ***River***, on Mull running NW to Loch na Cuilce, 5m/8km W of Tobermory. **37 D5** NM4351.

Bellaty *Angus* ***Settlement***, in valley of River Isla, 3m/5km N of Bridge of Craigisla. **42 A4** NO2359.

Bellehiglash *Moray* ***Settlement***, 4m/6km S of Upper Knockando. **53 D1** NJ1837.

Belliehill *Angus* ***Settlement***, 3m/5km NW of Brechin. **43 D3** NO5663.

Bellister *Shet.* ***Hamlet***, on S side of Dury Voe on Mainland, 1km NE of Laxfirth. HU4860.

Belloch *Arg. & B.* ***Settlement***, on W side of Kintyre, 1m/2km N of Glenbarr. **12 B2** NR6737.

Bellochantuy *Arg. & B.* ***Village***, on Bellochantuy Bay, on W coast of Kintyre. **12 B2** NR6632.

Bellochantuy Bay *Arg. & B.* ***Bay***, on W coast of Kintyre, 9m/15km NW of Campbeltown. **12 B2** NR6532.

Bellow Water *E.Ayr.* ***River***, running SW to join Glenmuir Water and form Lugar Water, 1km E of Lugar. NS5921.

Bellsdyke *Falk.* ***Settlement***, 3m/5km N of Falkirk. **24 D1** NS9085.

Bellshill *N.Lan.* Population: 21,624. ***Suburb***, 3m/4km NW of Motherwell. **24 B4** NS7360.

Bellside *N.Lan.* ***Hamlet***, 2m/3km NW of Newmains. **24 C4** NS8158.

Bellsquarry *W.Loth.* ***Suburb***, 2m/3km SW of Livingston town centre. **25 E3** NT0465.

Belmaduthy *High.* ***Settlement***, on Black Isle, 1m/2km N of Munlochy. **61 F4** NH6456.

Belmont *Shet.* ***Settlement***, at SW end of Unst near Wick of Belmont. **85 E2** HP5601.

Belmont *S.Ayr.* ***Suburb***, to S of Ayr. NS3420.

Belmont Castle *P. & K.* ***Historic house***, on S side of Meigle, former home of Sir H. Campbell-Bannerman, 1836-1908, prime minister. NO2843.

Belnahua *Arg. & B.* ***Island***, 1m/2km W of NW coast of Luing. **29 G3** NM7112.

Belston *S.Ayr.* ***Settlement***, 3m/4km E of Ayr. **14 B3** NS3820.

Belsyde *W.Loth.* ***Settlement***, 2m/3km SW of Linlithgow. **25 D2** NS9775.

Beltie Burn *Aber.* ***River***, rising on Corrennie Moor and flowing S, then SE, to Torphins and Glassel, where it becomes Burn of Canny and eventually joins River Dee, 2m/3km W of Banchory. **54 B4** NO6599.

Bemersyde *Sc.Bord.* ***Hamlet***, 4m/6km S of Earlston. **17 G2** NT5933.

Bemersyde House *Sc.Bord.* ***Historic house***, seat of Haigs since 1162 to SW of Bemersyde, 3m/5km E of Melrose across River Tweed. Present house includes 16c tower. Field-Marshal Lord Haig, d. 1928, is buried at Dryburgh Abbey 1m/2km S. NT5933.

Ben-a-chielt *High.* ***Hill***, 3m/4km N of Latheron. Height 941 feet or 287 metres. **77 D5** ND1937.

Ben A'an *Stir. Alternative name for Stob Binnein, qv.*

Ben Aden *High.* ***Mountain***, peak in Lochaber district 2m/3km W of head of Loch Quoich. Height 2903 feet or 885 metres. **49 F5** NM8998.

Ben Aigan *Moray* ***Mountain***, 2m/3km E of Rothes. Height 1545 feet or 471 metres. **63 F5** NJ3148.

Ben Aird da Loch *High.* ***Mountain***, 1km N of Loch Glencoul. Height 1738 feet or 530 metres. **74 B5** NC2831.

Ben Aketil *High.* ***Hill***, 4m/7km E of Dunvegan, Skye. Height 872 feet or 266 metres. **57 G5** NG3246.

Ben Alder *High.* ***Mountain***, in Badenoch and Strathspey district to W of Loch a' Bhealaich Bheithe. Munro: height 3765 feet or 1148 metres. **39 G2** NN4971.

Ben Alder Cottage *P. & K.* ***Settlement***, on E side of Loch Ericht, 8m/12km N of Bridge of Gaur. **39 G3** NN4968.

Ben Alder Forest *High.* ***Large natural feature***, mountain area extending NE of Ben Alder, on NW side of Loch Ericht. **40 A2** NN5275.

Ben Alder Lodge *High.* ***Settlement***, on NW shore of Loch Ericht, 5m/8km SW of Dalwhinnie. **40 A2** NN5778.

Ben Alisky *High.* ***Mountain***, 4m/6km SW of Loch More. Height 1141 feet or 348 metres. **76 C5** ND0438.

Ben An *Stir.* ***Mountain***, in The Trossachs, 4m/7km N of Aberfoyle. Height 1512 feet or 461 metres. **32 A4** NN5008.

Ben Armine (Gaelic form: Beinn an Armuinn.) *High.* ***Mountain***, in Sutherland district, 5m/8km SE of Loch Choire. Height 2309 feet or 704 metres. **72 B2** NC6924.

Ben Armine Forest *High.* ***Open space***, deer forest surrounding Ben Armine in Sutherland district. **72 B2** NC6621.

Ben Arnaboll *High.* ***Hill***, situated between Loch Eriboll and Loch Hope. Height 754 feet or 230 metres. **75 D3** NC4559.

Ben Arthur (Also known as The Cobbler.) *Arg. & B.* ***Mountain***, in Argyll 3m/4km W of Arrochar. Height 2890 feet or 881 metres. **31 E4** NN2505.

Ben Aslak *High.* ***Mountain***, on Skye, 4m/7km S of Kyleakin. Height 2001 feet or 610 metres. **49 D3** NG7518.

Ben Attow *High. Alternative name for Beinn Fhada, qv.*

Ben Auskaird *High.* ***Mountain***, 4m/7km SE of Scourie, Sutherland district. Height 1266 feet or 386 metres. **74 B4** NC2040.

Ben Avon *Aber.* ***Large natural feature***, massif 7m/11km N of Braemar. For individual peaks see Mullach Lochan nan Gabhar, Stob Bac an Fhurain, and the summit and Munro, Leabaidh an Daimh Bhuidhe. **52 D4** NJ1301.

Ben Buie *Arg. & B.* ***Mountain***, on Mull 1m/2km N of Lochbuie. Height 2352 feet or 717 metres. **29 F2** NM6027.

Ben Challum *Stir.* ***Mountain***, 4m/6km E of Tyndrum. Munro: height 3352 feet or 1022 metres. **31 F1** NN3832.

Ben Chonzie (Gaelic form: Beinn a' Chonnaich.) *P. & K.* ***Mountain***, 6m/9km N of Comrie. Munro: height 3054 feet or 931 metres. **32 C1** NN7730.

Ben Clach *P. & K.* ***Mountain***, 4m/7km SW of Comrie. Height 1748 feet or 533 metres. **32 C3** NN7515.

Ben Cleuch *Clack.* ***Mountain***, summit of Ochil Hills, 3m/4km NW of Tillicoultry. Height 2362 feet or 720 metres. **33 D4** NN9000.

Ben Cliad *W.Isles* ***Hill***, on Barra, 2m/3km W of Ardmhòr. Height 679 feet or 207 metres. **44 B3** NF6704.

Ben Connan *High.* ***Hill***, 4m/6km NW of Idrigill Point, Skye. Height 800 feet or 244 metres. **57 E5** NG1940.

Ben Corkeval *High.* ***Mountain***, rising to over 350 metres on Skye, 1m/2km E of Ramasaig. **57 E5** NG1844.

Ben Corodale *W.Isles* ***Mountain***, 1m/2km NE of Beinn Mhòr, South Uist. Height 1729 feet or 527 metres. **46 B1** NF8225.

Ben Creach *Arg. & B. Anglicised form of Creach Beinn, qv.*

Ben Cruachan *Arg. & B.* ***Mountain***, in Argyll 4m/6km E of Bonawe. Munro: height 3693 feet or 1126 metres. Hydro-electricity generating station within mountain pumps water from Loch Awe to Cruachan Reservoir. **30 C1** NN0630.

Ben Damph *High. Anglicised form of Beinn Damh, qv.*

Ben-damph Forest *High.* ***Open space***, deer forest in Ross and Cromarty district to S of Upper Loch Torridon. **59 E4** NG8852.

Ben Dearg *High.* ***Mountain***, 4m/6km N of Portree, Skye. Height 1811 feet or 552 metres. **58 A4** NG4750.

Ben Dell *W.Isles* ***Locality***, 4m/7km W of Cellar Head, Isle of Lewis. **69 F2** NB4956.

Ben Diubaig *High.* ***Hill***, 3m/5km NW of head of Loch Greshornish, Skye. Height 708 feet or 216 metres. **57 G4** NG3155.

Ben Donich *Arg. & B.* ***Mountain***, in Argyll 2m/4km N of Lochgoilhead. Height 2778 feet or 847 metres. **31 E4** NN2104.

Ben Dorrery *High.* ***Hill***, summit lies 1km to E of Loch Shurrery. Height 800 feet or 244 metres. **76 C3** ND0655.

Ben Douran *Arg. & B. Anglicised form of Beinn Dorain, qv.*

Ben Drovinish *W.Isles* ***Hill***, 3m/4km SW of Earshader, Isle of Lewis. Height 607 feet or 185 metres. **68 C4** NB1531.

Ben Duagrich *High.* ***Hill***, to S of Loch Duagrich, Skye. Height 997 feet or 304 metres. **48 A1** NG3938.

Ben Earb *P. & K.* ***Mountain***, 2m/3km SW of Spittal of Glenshee. Height 2627 feet or 801 metres. **41 F3** NO0769.

Ben Eay *High. Anglicised form of Beinn Eighe, qv.*

Ben Garrisdale *Arg. & B.* ***Mountain***, in N part of Jura, 5m/7km NW of Ardlussa. Height 1197 feet or 365 metres. **29 F5** NR6394.

Ben Geary *High.* ***Hill***, 4m/6km S of Vaternish Point, Skye. Height 932 feet or 284 metres. **57 F3** NG2561.

Ben Glas *Stir.* ***Mountain***, craggy area rising to over 610 metres, 3m/4km NE of Ardlui. **31 F3** NN3418.

Ben Gorm *High.* ***Mountain***, 3m/4km E of Uig, Skye. Height 1053 feet or 321 metres. **58 A3** NG4364.

Ben Griam Beg *High.* ***Mountain***, 1m/2km E of Loch Druim a' Chliabhain, Caithness district. Height 1902 feet or 580 metres. **76 A4** NC8341.

Ben Griam Mhòr *High.* ***Mountain***, 1km S of Loch Druim a' Chliabhain and 3m/5km NE of Loch nan Clàr, Sutherland district. Height 1935 feet or 590 metres. **76 A5** NC8038.

Ben Gulabin *P. & K.* ***Mountain***, 1m/2km N of Spittal of Glenshee. Height 2644 feet or 806 metres. **41 F2** NO1072.

Ben Halton *P. & K.* ***Mountain***, to N of Glen Artney, 4m/6km W of Dalginross. Height 2034 feet or 620 metres. **32 C2** NN7220.

Ben Hee *High.* ***Mountain***, in Sutherland district 9m/14km W of Altnaharra. Height 2863 feet or 873 metres. **74 D5** NC4233.

Ben Hiant *High.* ***Mountain***, near S coast of Ardnamurchan peninsula in Lochaber district 3m/5km E of Kilchoan. Height 1732 feet or 528 metres. **37 E3** NM5363.

Ben Hiel *High.* ***Mountain***, 2m/3km NW of Lettermore, Caithness district. Height 1752 feet or 534 metres. **75 E3** NC5950.

Ben Hogh *Arg. & B.* ***Hill***, 3m/4km NW of Arinagour, Coll. Height 341 feet or 104 metres. **36 A4** NM1858.

Ben Hope *High.* ***Mountain***, in Sutherland district 1m/2km E of head of Loch Hope. Munro: height 3041 feet or 927 metres. **75 D3** NC4750.

Ben Horn *High.* ***Mountain***, 1km E of Loch Horn, 4m/7km NW of Golspie. Height 1709 feet or 521 metres. **72 D4** NC8006.

Ben Horneval *High.* ***Hill***, 2m/4km NE of Dunvegan, Skye. Height 866 feet or 264 metres. **57 F5** NG2849.

Ben Hutig *High.* ***Mountain***, 3m/5km NW of Talmine, Caithness district. Height 1338 feet or 408 metres. **75 E2** NC5365.

Ben Idrigill *High.* ***Mountain***, rising to over 340 metres on Skye, 1m/2km NW of Idrigill Point. **47 F1** NG2338.

Ben Ime *Arg. & B. Anglicised form of Beinn Ime, qv.*

Ben Killilan *High.* ***Mountain***, in Skye and Lochalsh district 2km NE of Killilan and 2m/3km NE of head of Loch Long. Height 2470 feet or 753 metres. **49 F1** NG9631.

Ben Klibreck (Gaelic form: Beinn Cleith Bric.) *High.* ***Mountain***, in Caithness district 4m/6km S of Altnaharra. Summit of Meall nan Con is a Munro. Height 3152 feet or 961 metres. **75 E5** NC5829.
Ben Laga *High.* ***Mountain***, 3m/4km E of Glenborrodale, Lochaber district. Height 1679 feet or 512 metres. **37 F3** NM6462.
Ben Làir *High.* ***Mountain***, in Letterewe Forest, Ross and Cromarty district, 2m/4km NE of Letterewe on NE shore of Loch Maree. Height 2821 feet or 860 metres. NG9873.
Ben Lawers *P. & K.* ***Mountain***, 3m/5km NW of Lawers on Loch Tay. The peak and S slopes are National Trust for Scotland property. It commands views extending from Atlantic Ocean to North Sea. Munro: height 3982 feet or 1214 metres. Known as 'the echoing mountain'. **40 B5** NN6341.
Ben Lawers Visitor Centre *P. & K.* ***Other feature of interest***, visitor centre (National Trust for Scotland) 3m/5km SW of summit of Ben Lawers. Displays of mountain geology and natural history. **32 B1** NN6037.
Ben Ledi *Stir.* ***Mountain***, 4m/7km NW of Callander. Height 2883 feet or 879 metres. **32 A4** NN5609.
Ben Lee *High.* ***Mountain***, 1m/2km W of Peinchorran, Skye. Height 1460 feet or 445 metres. **48 B1** NG5033.
Ben Leoid *High. Alternative spelling of Beinn Leòid, qv.*
Ben Lomond *Stir.* ***Mountain***, 3m/5km N of Rowardennan on E shore of Loch Lomond. Munro: height 3195 feet or 974 metres. **31 F4** NN3602.
Ben Loyal (Gaelic form: Beinn Laoghal.) *High.* ***Mountain***, in Caithness district 5m/8km S of Tongue. Height 2506 feet or 764 metres. **75 E4** NC5748.
Ben Lui (Gaelic form: Beinn Laoigh.) *Stir.* ***Mountain***, 7m/11km E of Dalmally. Munro: height 3706 feet or 1130 metres. **31 E2** NN2626.
Ben Macdui (Gaelic form: Beinn Muic Duibhe.) *Moray* ***Mountain***, in Cairngorm Mountains 9m/15km SE of Aviemore. Highest mountain in Britain after Ben Nevis. Munro: height 4294 feet or 1309 metres. **52 B5** NN9898.
Ben Meabost *High.* ***Mountain***, 2m/3km NE of Elgol, Skye. Height 1135 feet or 346 metres. **48 B3** NG5315.
Ben Mohal *W.Isles Anglicised form of Beinn Mohal, qv.*
Ben Mòr Coigach *High.* ***Mountain***, 2m/3km E of Culnacraig. Height 2437 feet or 743 metres. **70 C4** NC0904.
Ben More *Arg. & B.* ***Mountain***, highest point on Mull, 3m/4km NW of head of Loch Scridain. Munro: height 3168 feet or 966 metres. **29 E1** NM5233.
Ben More *Stir.* ***Mountain***, 3m/5km E of Crianlarich. Munro: height 3851 feet or 1174 metres. **31 G2** NN4324.
Ben More Assynt *High.* ***Mountain***, in Sutherland district 5m/7km E of Inchnadamph at head of Loch Assynt. Munro: height 3273 feet or 998 metres. **71 F2** NC3120.
Ben na Hoe *W.Isles* ***Hill***, 7m/11km E of Rubha Ardvule, on South Uist. Height 843 feet or 257 metres. **46 B2** NF8128.
Ben Nevis *High.* ***Mountain***, in Lochaber district 4m/7km E of Fort William. Highest mountain in Britain. Munro: height 4408 feet or 1344 metres. **39 D2** NN1671.
Ben Oss *Stir.* ***Mountain***, 4m/7km SW of Tyndrum. Munro: height 3372 feet or 1028 metres. **31 E2** NN2825.
Ben Raah *W.Isles* ***Hill***, highest point on Tarasaigh, off the coast of South Harris. Height 876 feet or 267 metres. **66 C3** NB0301.
Ben Reoch *Arg. & B.* ***Mountain***, on W side of Loch Lomond, 2m/3km SW of Tarbet. Height 2168 feet or 661 metres. **31 F4** NN3002.
Ben Rinnes *Moray* ***Mountain***, 5m/8km SW of Dufftown. Height 2755 feet or 840 metres. Distillery to N at foot of mountain. **53 E1** NJ2535.
Ben Sca *High.* ***Hill***, 1km NE of Ben Aketil, Skye. Height 938 feet or 286 metres. **57 G5** NG3347.
Ben Scoravick *W.Isles* ***Hill***, highest point of Scalpay, 1km NE of Kennavay. Height 341 feet or 104 metres. **67 E4** NG2395.
Ben Screavie *High.* ***Mountain***, at N end of Loch More. Height 1089 feet or 332 metres. **74 C5** NC3039.
Ben Screel *High. Alternative name for Beinn Sgritheall, qv.*
Ben Scrien *W.Isles* ***Hill***, highest point on Eriskay, 1km SE of Haunn. Height 607 feet or 185 metres. **44 C2** NF7911.
Ben Sgeireach *High.* ***Mountain***, 2m/3km NE of Badintagairt, Glen Cassley. Height 1561 feet or 476 metres. **71 G3** NC4511.
Ben Shieldaig *High.* ***Inland physical feature***, mountain ridge in Ross and Cromarty district, rising to 1692 feet or 516 metres, 1m/2km S of Shieldaig and 5m/8km SW of Torridon. **59 E4** NG8353.
Ben Skriaig *High.* ***Mountain***, on Skye, 2m/3km S of Dunvegan Head. Height 1007 feet or 307 metres. **57 E4** NG1653.
Ben Stack *High.* ***Mountain***, rising steeply from SW shore of Loch Stack, Sutherland district. Height 2365 feet or 721 metres. **74 B4** NC2642.
Ben Stack *W.Isles* ***Hill***, on Eriskay, 2m/3km S of Haunn. Height 400 feet or 122 metres. **44 C3** NF7909.
Ben Starav *High.* ***Mountain***, 2m/3km S of foot of Glen Etive, on border of Argyll and Lochaber districts. Munro: height 3536 feet or 1078 metres. **38 D5** NN1242.
Ben Strome *High.* ***Mountain***, with summit 1m/2km NE of Kylestrome. Height 1397 feet or 426 metres. **74 B5** NC2436.
Ben Suardal *High.* ***Hill***, 2m/3km S of Broadford, Skye. Height 928 feet or 283 metres. **48 C2** NG6320.
Ben Tangaval *W.Isles* ***Mountain***, in SW part of Barra 2m/3km W of Castlebay. Height 1092 feet or 333 metres. **44 B4** NL6399.
Ben Tarbert *W.Isles* ***Hill***, 5m/9km SE of Hornish Point, South Uist. Height 551 feet or 168 metres. **46 B1** NF8039.
Ben Tee *High.* ***Mountain***, on Glengarry Forest, Lochaber district, 5m/8km SW of Invergarry. Height 2955 feet or 901 metres. **50 B5** NN2497.
Ben Tianavaig *High.* ***Mountain***, 3m/4km SE of Portree, Skye. Height 1355 feet or 413 metres. **58 B5** NG5140.
Ben Tirran *Angus* ***Mountain***, 3m/5km E of Clova. Height 2939 feet or 896 metres. **42 B2** NO3774.
Ben Uarie *High.* ***Mountain***, in Sutherland district, 4m/6km N of Lothbeg. Height 2043 feet or 623 metres. **73 E3** NC9216.
Ben Uigshader *High.* ***Hill***, 5m/8km S of Lyndale Point, Skye. Height 807 feet or 246 metres. **57 G5** NG3649.
Ben Vair *High. Anglicised form of Beinn a' Bheithir, qv.*
Ben Vane *Arg. & B.* ***Mountain***, 4m/6km NW of Arrochar. Munro: height 3004 feet or 916 metres. **31 E4** NN2709.
Ben Vannoch *P. & K. Anglicised form of Beinn Mhanach, qv.*
Ben Varren *N.Ayr. Anglicised form of Beinn Bharrain, qv.*
Ben Venue *Stir.* ***Mountain***, 4m/7km NW of Aberfoyle. Height 2385 feet or 727 metres. **31 G4** NN4706.
Ben Vorlich *Arg. & B.* ***Mountain***, 3m/4km SW of Ardlui at head of Loch Lomond. Munro: height 3093 feet or 943 metres. **31 E3** NN2912.
Ben Vorlich *P. & K.* ***Mountain***, 4m/6km SE of Lochearnhead. Munro: height 3231 feet or 985 metres. **32 B3** NN6218.
Ben Vrackie *N.Ayr. Anglicised form of Beinn Bhreac, qv.*
Ben Vrackie (Gaelic form: Beinn Bhreac.) *P. & K.* ***Mountain***, 3m/5km N of Pitlochry. Height 2758 feet or 841 metres. **41 E3** NN9563.
Ben Vrottan *Aber. Anglicised form of Beinn Bhrotain, qv.*
Ben Vuirich *P. & K.* ***Mountain***, 8m/13km NE of Blair Atholl. Height 2959 feet or 902 metres. NN9970.
Ben Wyvis *High.* ***Mountain***, in Ross and Cromarty district 8m/13km NW of Dingwall. Summit is Glas Leathad Mòr. Height 3431 feet or 1046 metres. **60 D3** NH4668.
Ben-y-Gloe *P. & K. Alternative name for Beinn a' Ghlo, qv.*
Benachally *P. & K.* ***Mountain***, to SW of Loch Benachally, in Forest of Clunie. Height 1594 feet or 486 metres. **41 F5** NO0648.
Benanchie *Aber. See Bennachie.*
Benaquhallie *Aber.* ***Mountain***, on Corrennie Moor, 3m/5km NE of Lumphanan. Height 1620 feet or 494 metres. **54 B4** NJ6008.
Benarty Hill *Fife* ***Mountain***, to S of Loch Leven, 1m/2km W of Benarty. Height 1168 feet or 356 metres. **33 G5** NT1597.
Benbecula (Gaelic form: Beinn na Faoghla.) *W.Isles* ***Island***, low-lying island, 6m/10km by 5m/8km in size, between North and South Uist, containing innumerable lochs. Sand dunes on W coast; many islets off E coast. Airfield to N of Balivanich at NW corner of island. Road causeways to both North and South Uist. **45 G4** NF8050.
Benbecula (Baile a' Mhanaich) Aerodrome *W.Isles* ***Airport/airfield***, local airport NE of Balivanich, at N end of Benbecula. **45 F4** NF7956.
Benbeoch *E.Ayr.* ***Mountain***, 2m/3km NW of Dalmellington. Height 1522 feet or 464 metres. **14 C5** NS4908.
Benbrack *E.Ayr.* ***Mountain***, 4m/7km SE of Dalmellington to E of Carsphain Forest. Height 1469 feet or 448 metres. **14 D5** NS5201.
Benbuie *D. & G.* ***Settlement***, 6m/9km NW of Moniaive. **8 B1** NX7196.
Bendcallt *High.* ***Mountain***, in Ross and Cromarty district, 5m/7km NW of Evanton. Height 1850 feet or 564 metres. **61 E2** NH5570.
Benderloch *Arg. & B.* ***Locality***, in Argyll, lying between Loch Creran and Loch Etive. **30 B1** NM9338.
Benderloch *Arg. & B.* ***Village***, on Ardmucknish Bay, Benderloch peninsula, 3m/4km N of Connel, Argyll. **30 B1** NM9038.
Beneraird ***Mountain***, to W of Arecleoch Forest, on border of Ayrshire and Dumfries & Galloway, 4m/6km SE of Ballantrae. Height 1440 feet or 439 metres. **6 C3** NX1378.
Benfield *D. & G.* ***Settlement***, 2m/4km SW of Newton Stewart. **7 E4** NX3763.
Bengairn *D. & G.* ***Mountain***, 5m/8km S of Castle Douglas. Height 1282 feet or 391 metres. **8 B5** NX7754.
Benholm *Aber.* ***Hamlet***, near E coast, 3m/4km SE of Inverbervie. **43 G3** NO8069.
Benholm Castle *Aber.* ***Castle***, 1km N of Benholm, early 15c tower of Earls Marischal. NO8070.
Beninner Gairy *D. & G.* ***Mountain***, 3m/5km NE of Carsphairn. Height 2329 feet or 710 metres. NX6097.
Benlister Burn *N.Ayr.* ***River***, on Arran, running E down Benlister Glen to Lamlash Bay on S side of Lamlash. NS0230.
Benlister Glen *N.Ayr.* ***Valley***, on Arran, carrying Benlister Burn. **13 E2** NS0230.
Benmore *Arg. & B.* ***Settlement***, at confluence of Rivers Massan and Eachaig, 2m/3km NW of Orchard. **22 C1** NS1385.
Benmore *Stir.* ***Settlement***, on W side of Ben More, 2m/3km E of Crianlarich. **31 G2** NN4125.
Benmore Forest *Arg. & B.* ***Forest/woodland***, on W side of Loch Eck in Argyll, in Argyll Forest Park. NS1391.
Benmore Forest *High.* ***Open space***, deer forest in Sutherland district to S of Ben More Assynt. **71 F3** NC3115.
Bennachie (Benanchie). *Aber.* ***Large natural feature***, upland area surrounded by Bennachie Forest, 7m/11km W of Inverurie. **54 B2** NJ6622.
Bennan *D. & G.* ***Mountain***, 1m/2km NE of Clatteringshaws Loch and 4m/7km W of New Galloway. Height 1250 feet or 381 metres. **7 G3** NX5679.
Bennan *D. & G.* ***Mountain***, rising to over 350 metres, 3m/4km N of Moniaive. **8 B1** NX7994.
Bennan *D. & G.* ***Settlement***, on W side of Loch Ken, 4m/6km SE of New Galloway. **8 A3** NX6571.
Bennan Head *N.Ayr.* ***Coastal feature***, headland on S coast of Arran, 7m/11km S of Lamlash. **13 E4** NR9920.
Bennan Loch *E.Renf.* ***Lake/loch***, and reservoir 4m/6km W of Eaglesham. **23 G4** NS5250.
Bennane Head *S.Ayr.* ***Coastal feature***, headland at N end of Ballantrae Bay. **6 B2** NX0986.
Benscravie *Angus* ***Mountain***, 2m/3km NE of Dykehead. Height 1404 feet or 428 metres. **42 B3** NO4062.
Benston *Shet.* ***Hamlet***, in South Nesting, Mainland, 2m/3km W of Moul of Eswick. HU4653.
Benthoul *Aberdeen* ***Settlement***, 3m/5km NW of Peterculter. **54 D4** NJ8003.
Bentpath *D. & G.* ***Village***, on River Esk, 5m/8km NW of Langholm. **10 B2** NY3190.
Benvane *Stir.* ***Mountain***, 4m/7km S of Balquhidder. Height 2690 feet or 820 metres. **32 A3** NN5313.
Benvie *Dundee* ***Hamlet***, 2m/3km NE of Longforgan. **34 B1** NO3231.
Benyellary *D. & G.* ***Mountain***, 2m/4km N of Loch Trool in Glentrool Forest Park. Height 2358 feet or 719 metres. NX4183.
Beoch Burn *D. & G.* ***River***, rising on E slopes of Beoch Hill and running SW into Loch Ryan near Leffnoll Point, 3m/4km NE of Stranraer. **6 B4** NX0764.
Beoraidbeg *High.* ***Hamlet***, in Lochaber district, 2m/3km S of Mallaig. NM6793.
Bernera *Arg. & B.* ***Island***, off W coast of Lismore, in Loch Linnhe. **29 G1** NM7939.
Bernera *High.* ***Settlement***, in Skye and Lochalsh district, 1km N of Glenelg. **49 E2** NG8020.
Bernera Barracks *High.* ***Other feature of interest***, ruins of 18c English garrison to N of Glenelg. **49 E3** NG8119.
Bernera Bay *Arg. & B.* ***Bay***, S facing bay formed by two islands of Bernera and Lismore. NM7939.
Berneray *W.Isles Anglicised form of Bearnaraigh, qv.*
Berneray (Gaelic form: Eilean Bhearnaraigh.) *W.Isles* ***Island***, on W side of Sound of Harris, lying off N end of North Uist. Nearly 4m/6km NE to SW and 2m/3km across at widest point. **45 G1** NF9181.
Bernice *Arg. & B.* ***Settlement***, at foot of Bernice Glen on W shore of Loch Eck, 4m/6km S of Invernoaden. **30 D5** NS1391.
Bernisdale *High.* ***Village***, on W side of head of Loch Snizort Beag, Skye, 7m/11km NW of Portree. **58 A4** NG4050.
Berriedale *High.* ***Village***, near E coast of Caithness district, 8m/12km NE of Helmsdale. Situated at confluence of Langwell Water and Berriedale Water. **73 G2** ND1122.
Berriedale Water *High.* ***River***, rising on Knockfin Heights and flowing E, S, then SE to join Langwell Water at Berriedale before combined river flows out to North Sea. **73 F2** ND1122.
Berry Top *Aber.* ***Hill***, 4m/6km W of Portlethen. Height 558 feet or 170 metres. **55 D5** NO8696.
Berryfell Hill *Sc.Bord.* ***Mountain***, 5m/8km SE of Hawick. Height 1289 feet or 393 metres. **17 G5** NT5307.
Berryhillock *Moray* ***Hamlet***, near N coast, 4m/6km S of Cullen. **64 A3** NJ5060.
Berst Ness *Ork.* ***Coastal feature***, headland on S coast of Westray. **80 C2** HY4441.
Berstane *Ork.* ***Settlement***, on Mainland, SE of Kirkwall and close to Bay of Berstane. **80 C5** HY4610.
Bervie Bay *Aber.* ***Bay***, on E side of Inverbervie. **43 G2** NO8372.
Bervie Water *Aber.* ***River***, rising in Drumtochty Forest and running SE to E coast at Bervie Bay, on E side of Inverbervie. **43 F2** NO8372.

Bettyhill *High.* ***Village***, near N coast of Caithness district, 9m/15km SW of Strathy Point. **75 G2** NC7061.

Beul an Toim *W.Isles* ***Sea feature***, channel between Baleshare and N coast of Benbecula. NF7857.

Bhalamus *W.Isles* ***Settlement***, on S coast of Isle of Lewis, 6m/9km S of head of Loch Shell. **67 E3** NB2901.

Bhaltos (Anglicised form: Valtos.) *W.Isles* ***Village***, on W shore of West Loch Roag, 3m/5km SE of Gallan Head. **68 B4** NB0936.

Bhatarsaidh *W.Isles Gaelic form of Vatarsay, qv.*

Bhatarsaigh *W.Isles Gaelic form of Vatersay (island), qv.*

Bhatarsaigh *W.Isles Gaelic form of Vatersay (settlement), qv.*

Bhatarsaigh Bay *W.Isles Gaelic form of Vatersay Bay, qv.*

Bhatasgeir *W.Isles Gaelic form of Vatisker, qv.*

Biallaid *High.* ***Settlement***, adjoining to W of Newtonmore across River Calder. **51 G5** NN7098.

Bidean an Eòin Deirg *High.* ***Mountain***, in Ross and Cromarty district 2m/3km NE of head of Loch Monar. Height 3431 feet or 1046 metres. NH1044.

Bidean nam Bian *High.* ***Mountain***, in Lochaber district, S of Glen Coe. Munro: height 3772 feet or 1150 metres. **38 D4** NN1454.

Bidein a' Choire Sheasgaich *High.* ***Mountain***, peak on West Monar Forest on border of Ross and Cromarty and Skye and Lochalsh districts, 2m/3km W of W end of Loch Monar. Munro: height 3100 feet or 945 metres. **59 G5** NH0441.

Bidein a' Ghlas Thuill *High.* ***Mountain***, summit of An Teallach in Ross and Cromarty district, 7m/11km SW of Ullapool across Loch Broom. Munro: height 3483 feet or 1062 metres. **59 G1** NH0684.

Bidhein Bad na h-Iolaire *High.* ***Mountain***, rising to over 520 metres, 2m/3km SE of Fort William. **38 D2** NN1070.

Biel Water *E.Loth.* ***River***, rising in Lammermuir Hills and flowing NW to North Sea at Belhaven Bay, 1m/2km W of Dunbar. **26 D2** NT6578.

Bieldside *Aberdeen* ***Suburb***, 4m/7km SW of Aberdeen city centre. **55 D4** NJ8802.

Big Balcraig *D. & G.* ***Historic/prehistoric site***, site of cup and ring marked rocks, 2m/4km E of Port William. NX3744.

Big Garvoun *Moray* ***Mountain***, 6m/10km S of Tomintoul. Height 2430 feet or 741 metres. **52 D4** NJ1408.

Big Sand *High.* ***Settlement***, on W coast of Ross and Cromarty district, 3m/5km NW of Gairloch. **59 D2** NG7578.

Bigga *Shet.* ***Island***, uninhabited island of about 235 acres or 95 hectares midway between Mainland and Yell at SE end of Yell Sound. **84 D5** HU4479.

Biggar *S.Lan.* Population: 1994. ***Small town***, 13m/21km W of Peebles. Slight remains of Boghall Castle on S side. **16 B2** NT0437.

Biggar Road *N.Lan.* ***Suburb***, adjoining to NE of Newarthill, 3m/5km NE of Hamilton. NS7860.

Biggings *Shet.* ***Settlement***, on Papa Stour, off Mainland. **82 A1** HU1760.

Bigholms *D. & G.* ***Settlement***, 4m/6km SW of Langholm. **10 B3** NY3181.

Bighouse *High.* ***Settlement***, at mouth of Halladale River, 1km E of Melvich. **76 A2** NC8964.

Bight of Bellister *Shet.* ***Bay***, on Mainland, to E of Bellister. HU4860.

Bight of Haggrister *Shet.* ***Bay***, on Sullom Voe, to S of Haggrister, Mainland. HU3470.

Bigton *Shet.* ***Village***, on bay of Bigton Wick, on W coast of Mainland, 9m/14km N of Sumburgh Head. **82 C5** HU3722.

Bigton Wick *Shet.* ***Bay***, forming N side of narrow isthmus between St. Ninian's Isle and W coast of Mainland. HU3721.

Bilbster *High.* ***Settlement***, 3m/4km SE of Watten. **77 E3** ND2852.

Billholm *D. & G.* ***Settlement***, in loop of River Esk, 3m/4km NW of Bentpath. **9 G1** NY2792.

Bilsdean *E.Loth.* ***Hamlet***, near coast, 6m/10km SE of Dunbar. **27 E2** NT7672.

Bilsdean Creek *E.Loth.* ***Coastal feature***, to E of Bilsdean. Site of Dunglass Castle above creek. NT7772.

Bilston *Midloth.* Population: 1648. ***Village***, 1m/2km SW of Loanhead. **25 G3** NT2664.

Bilston Glen *Midloth.* ***Locality***, to E of Bilston. NT2764.

Bimbister *Ork.* ***Settlement***, on Mainland, 3m/4km NW of Finstown. **80 B5** HY3216.

Bin of Cullen *Moray* ***Mountain***, 3m/5km SW of Cullen, commanding wide views. Height 1050 feet or 320 metres. **63 G3** NJ4764.

Bindal *High.* ***Settlement***, 1km E of Portmahomack. **62 B1** NH9284.

Bindalein Island *W.Isles* ***Island***, rock on S side of entrance to Loch Carlabhagh on W coast of Isle of Lewis, 2m/3km W of Carloway village. NB1741.

Binnein an Fhidhleir *Arg. & B.* ***Mountain***, on N side of Glen Kinglas, 8m/12km E of Inveraray. Height 2660 feet or 811 metres. **31 E3** NN2110.

Binnein Beag *High.* ***Mountain***, peak 1m/2km NE of Binnein Mòr. Munro: height 3083 feet or 940 metres. **39 E3** NN2267.

Binnein Mòr *High.* ***Mountain***, on Mamore Forest in Lochaber district 3m/5km NE of Kinlochleven. Munro: height 3700 feet or 1128 metres. **39 E3** NN2166.

Binnein Shuas *High.* ***Mountain***, between Loch Laggan and Lochan na h-Earba, 6m/10km SW of Kinloch Laggan. Height 2447 feet or 746 metres. **39 G1** NN4682.

Binniehill *Falk.* ***Settlement***, 1km S of Slamannan. **24 C2** NS8572.

Biod Mòr *High.* ***Mountain***, 1km NW of head of Loch Eynort, Skye. Height 1256 feet or 383 metres. **47 G2** NG3727.

Biod nan Laogh *High.* ***Coastal feature***, headland on E coast of Vaternish peninsula, 7m/11km SE of Vaternish Point, Skye. **57 G4** NG2958.

Biod Ruadh *High.* ***Coastal feature***, headland on W coast of Skye, 4m/7km SW of Carbost. NG3128.

Bioda Buidhe *High.* ***Mountain***, 3m/5km NE of Uig, Skye. Height 1528 feet or 466 metres. **58 A3** NG4366.

Birchfield *High.* ***Settlement***, 7m/11km SW of Lairg. **71 G5** NH4999.

Birdfield *Arg. & B.* ***Settlement***, on NW side of Loch Fyne, 2m/3km SE of Minard. **30 B5** NR9694.

Birdston *E.Dun.* ***Hamlet***, 1m/2km N of Kirkintilloch. NS6575.

Birgham *Sc.Bord.* ***Village***, 3m/5km W of Coldstream. **18 B3** NT7939.

Birichen *High.* ***Settlement***, in Sutherland district, 3m/5km NW of Dornoch. **72 C5** NH7592.

Birkenburn Reservoir *N.Lan.* ***Reservoir***, 3m/5km NE of Lennoxtown. NS6780.

Birkenhills *Aber.* ***Settlement***, 3m/5km SE of Turriff. **64 C5** NJ7445.

Birkhall *Aber.* ***Settlement***, 2m/3km SW of Ballater. **53 F5** NO3493.

Birkhill *Angus* Population: 920. ***Hamlet***, 4m/6km NW of Dundee. **34 B1** NO3534.

Birkhill *D. & G.* ***Settlement***, 4m/6km SW of St. Mary's Loch. **16 D4** NT2015.

Birkhill *Sc.Bord.* ***Settlement***, 4m/6km SE of Lauder. **26 C5** NT5642.

Birkshaw Forest *D. & G.* ***Forest/woodland***, 3m/4km S of Lockerbie, between River Annan and Water of Milk. NY1177.

Birkwood *S.Lan.* ***Locality***, adjoining to SW of Lesmahagow. Location of Birkwood Hospital **15 G2** NS8039.

Birnam *P. & K.* ***Village***, on S side of River Tay, 1km SE of Dunkeld. **41 F5** NO0341.

Birnam Hill *P. & K.* ***Mountain***, partly wooded summit of King's Seat, 1m/2km S of Dunkeld. Height 1312 feet or 400 metres. **41 F5** NO0340.

Birnam Wood *P. & K.* ***Forest/woodland***, famous from Shakespeare's Macbeth, 2m/3km SE of Birnam. NO0439.

Birnie *Moray* ***Locality***, comprising settlement of Nether Birnie and 12c church, 3m/4km S of Elgin. NJ2058.

Birnie Church *Moray* ***Ecclesiastical building***, 12c church to E of Paddockhaugh, 2m/4km S of Elgin. Small Norman church preceded by a prehistoric ritual site and, in c. AD 500, by a Celtic church. **63 E4** NJ2058.

Birnock Water *D. & G.* ***River***, rising on Swatte Fell and flowing SW to join River Annan at Moffat. **16 C5** NT0804.

Birns Water *E.Loth.* ***River***, rising on Lammermuir Hills and flowing NW, then N into River Tyne 4m/6km SE of Tranent. **26 B3** NT4568.

Birrenswark *D. & G. Alternative name for Burnswark, qv.*

Birrier *Shet.* ***Coastal feature***, small rocky promontory on E coast of Yell, 1m/2km NE of Aywick. **85 E4** HU5488.

Birsay *Ork.* ***Locality***, near NW end of Mainland, 1m/2km E of Brough Head. Earl's Palace, ruined 16c palace of Earls of Orkney. **80 A4** HY2825.

Birsay Bay *Ork.* ***Bay***, in NW Mainland, bounded by Brough Head to N. **80 A4** HY2427.

Birse *Aber.* ***Hamlet***, on N edge of Forest of Birse, 2m/3km SE of Aboyne. **54 A5** NO5597.

Birsemore *Aber.* ***Hamlet***, 1km S of Aboyne across River Dee. **54 A5** NO5297.

Biruaslum *W.Isles* ***Island***, uninhabited island off W coast of Vatersay. NL6096.

Bis Geos *Ork.* ***Coastal feature***, small indentations of W coast of Westray. **80 C2** HY4147.

Bishop Burn *D. & G.* ***River***, rising to SW of Newton Stewart and flowing SE, then NE into River Cree, opposite Creetown. NX4558.

Bishop Hill *P. & K.* ***Mountain***, rising to over 460 metres, 4m/7km E of Milnathort. Noted for gliding. **33 G4** NO1804.

Bishop Loch *Glas.* ***Lake/loch***, small loch 6m/10km E of Glasgow city centre. **24 A3** NS6866.

Bishopbriggs *E.Dun.* Population: 23,825. ***Suburb***, 3m/5km N of Glasgow. **24 A3** NS6070.

Bishopmill *Moray* ***Suburb***, N district of Elgin. **63 E3** NJ2665.

Bishopric *P. & K.* ***Open space***, upland area on W side of Tay valley, 5m/8km NW of Dunkeld. **41 E4** NN9548.

Bishop's and Earl's Palaces *Ork.* ***Historic/prehistoric site***, at Kirkwall, on Mainland. Earl Patrick's palace, built in 1607, is excellent example of Renaissance architecture. Nearby 13c Bishop's Palace has 16c round tower. **80 C5** HY4410.

Bishop's Seat *Arg. & B.* ***Mountain***, rising from upland plateau, 3m/4km W of Dunoon. Height 1653 feet or 504 metres. **22 C2** NS1377.

Bishopton *Renf.* Population: 5394. ***Village***, 6m/9km NW of Paisley. **23 F2** NS4371.

Bixter *Shet.* ***Settlement***, on Mainland, on E side of Bixter Voe, 6m/10km E of Walls. **82 C2** HU3352.

Bixter Voe *Shet.* ***Bay***, 6m/10km E of Walls, on Mainland. HU3252.

Bla Bheinn (Also known as Blaven.) *High.* ***Mountain***, 2m/4km W of head of Loch Slapin, Skye. Munro: height 3044 feet or 928 metres. **48 B2** NG5221.

Black Burn *D. & G.* ***River***, rising S of Barrhill near Eldrig Loch and running W into River Bladnoch, 3m/5km N of Kirkcowan. **7 D4** NX3365.

Black Burn *Moray* ***River***, rising on Romach Hill and flowing NE through Miltonduff to join River Lossie, 1m/2km W of Elgin. **62 D4** NJ1862.

Black Cart Water *Renf.* ***River***, running NE from Castle Semple Loch to join White Cart Water 3m/4km N of Paisley, flowing into River Clyde 1km further N. NS4968.

Black Clauchrie *S.Ayr.* ***Settlement***, 4m/7km E of Barrhill. **7 D2** NX2984.

Black Corries *High.* ***Inland physical feature***, corries on N slopes of A' Chruach, 2m/3km S of E end of Blackwater Reservoir. **39 F4** NN3757.

Black Corries Lodge *High.* ***Settlement***, on NW side of Rannoch Moor, 10m/16km N of Bridge of Orchy. **39 E4** NN2956.

Black Craig *Aber.* ***Mountain***, 3m/5km SW of Oldhall. Height 1735 feet or 529 metres. **53 G5** NO4394.

Black Craig *Arg. & B.* ***Mountain***, between Inverchaolain Glen and Glen Fyne. Height 1712 feet or 522 metres. **22 C2** NS1176.

Black Craig *High.* ***Mountain***, on NE side of Strath Mashie, 10m/15km SW of Newtonmore. Height 1853 feet or 565 metres. **51 E5** NN5791.

Black Crofts *Arg. & B.* ***Hamlet***, on N shore of Loch Etive, Argyll, 1m/2km E of Ledaig Point. NM9234.

Black Devon ***River***, rising as Nettly Burn, Saline Burn and Roughcleugh Burn and running W to Clackmannan, then SW into River Forth at Clackmannan Pow, 1m/2km below Alloa. **33 E5** NS8990.

Black Dod ***Mountain***, on border of South Lanarkshire and Scottish Borders, 5m/8km E of Elvanfoot. Height 1794 feet or 547 metres. NT0319.

Black Edge ***Open space***, on border of Dumfries & Galloway and Scottish Borders, on S side of Cooms Fell, 5m/8km NE of Langholm. **10 C3** NY4388.

Black Esk *D. & G.* ***River***, running S through Black Esk Reservoir and Castle O'er Forest to join River White Esk and form River Esk, 8m/13km NW of Langholm. **9 G1** NY2590.

Black Esk Reservoir *D. & G.* ***Reservoir***, 9m/14km to SE of Moffat, in Castle O'er Forest. **9 G1** NY2096.

Black Fell *N.Ayr.* ***Open space***, hillslope on E edge of North Burnt Hill, 6m/10km S of Greenock. **23 D3** NS2666.

Black Head *D. & G.* ***Coastal feature***, headland with lighthouse at S end of small Killantringan Bay on coast of Rinns of Galloway, 2m/3km NW of Portpatrick. Lighthouse is known as Killantringan Lighthouse. **6 A5** NW9856.

Black Hill ***Mountain***, on border of Aberdeenshire and Moray, 3m/4km E of Bridgend. Height 1656 feet or 505 metres. **53 G1** NJ4030.

Black Hill *Aber.* ***Hill***, 2m/3km S of Monymusk. Height 607 feet or 185 metres. **54 B3** NJ6711.

Black Hill *Aber.* ***Mountain***, on N side of River Don, 4m/6km S of Insch. Height 1410 feet or 430 metres. **54 B2** NJ6321.

Black Hill *D. & G.* ***Mountain***, in Lowther Hills, 1m/2km N of Durisdeer. Height 1742 feet or 531 metres. NS8905.

Black Hill *D. & G.* ***Mountain***, 4m/6km NW of Black Esk Reservoir. Height 1555 feet or 474 metres. **16 C5** NT1500.

Black Hill *E.Ayr.* ***Mountain***, 1m/2km N of Muirkirk. Height 1161 feet or 354 metres. **15 F3** NS7029.

Black Hill *Midloth.* ***Mountain***, in Pentland Hills Regional Park, 3m/4km SE of Balerno. Height 1637 feet or 499 metres. **25 F3** NT1863.

Black Hill *Moray* ***Hill***, 4m/6km SE of Buckie. Height 836 feet or 255 metres. **63 G3** NJ4660.

Black Hill *Moray* ***Hill***, with wooded summit, 5m/8km NE of Keith. Height 859 feet or 262 metres. **63 G4** NJ4757.

Black Hill *S.Lan.* ***Hill***, on border with West Lothian, rising to over 280 metres, 2m/3km NW of Forth. **24 D4** NS9155.

Black Hill of Mark ***Mountain***, 3m/4km S of Spittal of Glenmuick. Summit on border of Aberdeenshire and Angus. Height 2539 feet or 774 metres. **42 B1** NO3281.

Black Hillfort *S.Lan.* ***Historic/prehistoric site***, Iron Age hillfort (National Trust for Scotland) and settlement on Black Hill, 2m/4km E of Blackwood, with outlook point over River Clyde valley. **24 C5** NS8343.
Black Holm *Ork.* ***Island***, small islet 1km NW of Copinsay and 1m/2km S of Point of Ayre at E end of Mainland. HY5902.
Black House *W.Isles* ***Other feature of interest***, former dwelling house (Historic Scotland), now museum and national monument, to N of Arnol, near NW coast of Isle of Lewis. **69 E3** NB3149.
Black Isle *High.* ***Large natural feature***, peninsula in Ross and Cromarty district, between Cromarty Firth and Moray Firth, running out to Cromarty and South Sutor. **61 F4** NH6557.
Black Knowe ***Mountain***, on border of Dumfries & Galloway and Scottish Borders, 4m/7km S of Ettrick. Height 1479 feet or 451 metres. **17 D5** NT2807.
Black Knowe *Sc.Bord.* ***Mountain***, 4m/6km SW of Ettrick. Height 1771 feet or 540 metres. **16 D4** NT2210.
Black Knowe *Sc.Bord.* ***Mountain***, 4m/7km E of Peebles. Height 1709 feet or 521 metres. **26 A5** NT3140.
Black Knowe *Sc.Bord.* ***Mountain***, in Newcastleton Forest, 4m/6km E of Newcastleton. Height 1240 feet or 378 metres. **10 D3** NY5484.
Black Knowe Head *Sc.Bord.* ***Mountain***, 1m/2km NW of Gilmanscleuch. Height 1804 feet or 550 metres. **17 E3** NT3122.
Black Law *N.Ayr.* ***Mountain***, 4m/7km E of Largs. Height 1528 feet or 466 metres. **23 D4** NS2759.
Black Law *Sc.Bord.* ***Mountain***, on Ettrick Forest, 3m/5km NW of St. Mary's Loch. Height 2283 feet or 696 metres. **16 D3** NT2127.
Black Law *Sc.Bord.* ***Mountain***, 4m/6km NE of Peebles. Height 1765 feet or 538 metres. **26 A5** NT3042.
Black Linn Reservoir *W.Dun.* ***Reservoir***, 3m/5km NE of Dumbarton. NS4477.
Black Loch *D. & G.* ***Lake/loch***, within Lochinch Castle grounds, to E of White Loch and 4m/6km E of Stranraer. **6 C4** NX1161.
Black Loch *D. & G.* ***Lake/loch***, 1m/2km NE of Loch Ronald and 4m/7km NW of Kirkcowan. NX2865.
Black Loch *D. & G.* ***Lake/loch***, small and narrow loch to N end of Loch Ochiltree, 7m/11km SE of Barrhill. NX3175.
Black Loch *Falk.* ***Lake/loch***, on border with North Lanarkshire, 2m/3km S of Slamannan. NS8670.
Black Lochs *Arg. & B.* ***Lake/loch***, series of lochs, 2m/3km SE of Connel. **30 B1** NM9231.
Black Lochs of Kilquhockadale *D. & G.* ***Lake/loch***, two small lochs or tarns 6m/10km NW of Kirkcowan. NX2769.
Black Meldon *Sc.Bord.* ***Mountain***, 3m/5km NW of Peebles. Hillfort near summit. Height 1335 feet or 407 metres. **25 F5** NT2042.
Black Mill Bay *Arg. & B.* ***Bay***, on W coast of Luing, 1m/2km W of Toberonochy. **29 G4** NM7308.
Black Mount *Arg. & B.* ***Settlement***, on N side of Loch Tulla, 2m/3km NW of Bridge of Orchy. **39 E5** NN2842.
Black Mount *High.* ***Large natural feature***, moorland area on border of Lochaber district with Argyll, containing several small lochs and traversed by road running N from Bridge of Orchy towards Glen Coe. River Bà flows through centre of area from W to E. **39 E5** NN2747.
Black Mount *S.Lan.* ***Mountain***, above South Medwin valley, 1m/2km S of Dunsyre. Height 1692 feet or 516 metres. **25 E5** NT0746.
Black Neuk *S.Ayr.* ***Coastal feature***, headland 2m/3km SW of Girvan. **6 C1** NX1695.
Black Rock Gorge *High.* ***Inland physical feature***, rocky gorge in course of River Glass, 1m/2km long and 1m/2km W of Evanton. **61 E3** NH5866.
Black Rocks *Edin.* ***Coastal feature***, series of rocks on Firth of Forth coast, 1km NW of Leith. **25 G2** NT2777.
Black Shoulder *D. & G.* ***Mountain***, 4m/6km NE of Carsphairn. Height 2257 feet or 688 metres. **7 G1** NX5996.
Black Spout *P. & K.* ***Waterfall***, in wooded section of Edradour Burn, 1km SE of Pitlochry. NN9557.
Black Watch Memorial *P. & K.* ***Other feature of interest***, statue of kilted soldier, placed on large cairn, near to Wade's Bridge in Aberfeldy. **40 D4** NN8450.
Black Water *D. & G.* ***River***, issuing from Troston Loch and flowing W into Water of Ken, 5m/8km N of St. John's Town of Dalry. NX6188.
Black Water *High.* *Anglicised form of Uisge Dubh, qv.*
Black Water *High.* ***River***, in Sutherland district, running SE from Ben Armine Forest to River Brora 8m/12km NW of Brora village. **72 C3** NC8011.
Black Water *High.* ***River***, in Ross and Cromarty district running S down Strath Garve to Loch Garve, then SE through Contin to River Conon, 2m/3km S of Strathpeffer. **60 C3** NH4754.
Black Water *High.* ***River***, flowing from confluence of two tributaries at head of Strath Rusdale into River Averon, 5m/7km NW of Alness. **61 E2** NH5974.
Black Water *High.* ***River***, in Lochaber district running W to head of Blackwater Reservoir. **39 F3** NN3760.
Black Water *Moray* ***River***, rising 5m/7km SW of Cabrach and running NE to River Deveron, 3m/4km N of village. **53 F2** NJ3830.
Black Water *P. & K.* ***River***, originating in Shee Water and running S down Glen Shee to join River Ardle, forming River Ericht nearly 1km E of Bridge of Cally. NO1451.
Black Water *Stir.* ***River***, running from Loch Achray to Loch Venachar, W of Callander. NN5405.
Black Water of Dee *D. & G.* ***River***, issuing from Loch Dee and flowing through Clatteringshaws Loch, then W into Loch Ken. Stretch below Loch Ken is known as River Dee. **7 G3** NX6870.
Black Wood of Rannoch *P. & K.* ***Forest/woodland***, ancient firs on S side of Loch Rannoch, part of Tay Forest Park, 6m/10km W of Kinloch Rannoch. NN5656.
Blackacre *D. & G.* ***Settlement***, 3m/4km NE of Parkgate. **9 E1** NY0490.
Blackadder *Sc.Bord.* ***Hamlet***, 4m/6km SE of Duns. **27 F4** NT8452.
Blackadder Water *Sc.Bord.* ***River***, rising on Lammermuir and running SE to Greenlaw, then NE to Whiteadder Water at Allanton. **27 E5** NT8654.
Blackbraes *Aber.* ***Settlement***, 1km SE of Newmachar. **55 D3** NJ8918.
Blackbraes *Falk.* ***Settlement***, 1m/2km SE of Shieldhill. **24 D2** NS9075.
Blackburn *Aber.* Population: 1130. ***Village***, 8m/13km NW of Aberdeen. **54 D3** NJ8212.
Blackburn *W.Loth.* Population: 5014. ***Small town***, 2m/3km S of Bathgate. Former coalmining town. **25 D3** NS9865.
Blackburn Rig *Sc.Bord.* ***Open space***, steep NE facing hill, 1m/2km NW of Grantshouse. **27 E3** NT7966.
Blackcastle *High.* ***Settlement***, 4m/5km SW of Nairn. **62 A4** NH8254.
Blackchambers *Aber.* ***Settlement***, 3m/5km NW of Westhill. **54 C3** NJ7911.
Blackcraig *D. & G.* ***Locality***, 3m/4km E of Newton Stewart. **7 F4** NX4464.
Blackcraig *D. & G.* ***Settlement***, 6m/9km E of St. John's Town of Dalry. **8 B2** NX7180.
Blackcraig Castle *P. & K.* ***Historic house***, beside River Ardle, at N end of Blackcraig Forest. NO1053.
Blackcraig Forest *P. & K.* ***Forest/woodland***, on W side of Strathardle and Bridge of Cally. **41 G4** NO1051.
Blackcraig Hill *D. & G.* ***Mountain***, 5m/8km E of St. John's Town of Dalry. Height 1332 feet or 406 metres. **8 A2** NX7082.
Blackcraig Hill *E.Ayr.* ***Mountain***, 5m/8km S of New Cumnock. Height 2296 feet or 700 metres. **15 E5** NS6406.
Blackcraig Hill *P. & K.* ***Mountain***, in Blackcraig Forest, 3m/5km NW of Bridge of Cally. Height 1571 feet or 479 metres. **41 F4** NO0952.
Blackdog *Aber.* ***Settlement***, 1km inland from coast and 3m/4km S of Balmedie. **55 E3** NJ9514.
Blackdog Rock *Aber.* ***Coastal feature***, small rock on sands, 3m/4km S of Balmedie. **55 E3** NJ9613.
Blackford *Aber.* ***Settlement***, 1m/2km W of Rothienorman. **54 B1** NJ7035.
Blackford *P. & K.* ***Village***, 4m/6km SW of Auchterarder. **33 D4** NN8909.
Blackford Hill *Edin.* ***Hill***, 2m/3km S of Edinburgh city centre. Royal Observatory. Fort at summit. Height 538 feet or 164 metres. NT2570.
Blackhall *Edin.* ***Suburb***, 2m/4km W of Edinburgh city centre. **25 G2** NT2174.
Blackhall *Renf.* ***Suburb***, SE district of Paisley. NS4963.
Blackhall Forest *Aber.* ***Forest/woodland***, afforested estate to W of Banchory across River Dee. **54 B5** NO6795.
Blackhammer *Ork.* ***Historic/prehistoric site***, prehistoric cairn (Historic Scotland) on Rousay, 1m/2km W of Brinyan. HY4127.
Blackhaugh *Sc.Bord.* ***Settlement***, on Caddon Water, 2m/3km NW of Clovenfords. NT4238.
Blackhill *Aber.* ***Locality***, 2m/3km E of Crimond and 2m/3km S of Loch of Strathbeg. **65 F4** NK0755.
Blackhill *Aber.* ***Settlement***, 3m/5km W of Boddam. **65 F5** NK0843.
Blackhill *Glas.* ***Suburb***, 2m/4km E of Glasgow city centre. NS6266.
Blackhill *S.Lan.* ***Hill***, with viewpoint (National Trust for Scotland) and ancient hillfort, 3m/5km W of Lanark. Height 951 feet or 290 metres. NS8343.
Blackhillock *Moray* ***Locality***, 2m/3km S of Keith. **63 G5** NJ4348.
Blackhills *Aber.* ***Locality***, near E coast, 1km W of Murdoch Head and 3m/4km NE of Cruden Bay. NK1139.
Blackhills *Moray* ***Locality***, 4m/7km SE of Elgin. **63 E4** NJ2758.
Blackhope Scar *Sc.Bord.* ***Mountain***, highest in Moorfoot range, 6m/10km NE of Peebles. Height 2135 feet or 651 metres. **26 A5** NT3148.
Blackhouse Heights *Sc.Bord.* ***Mountain***, 4m/7km NW of St. Mary's Loch. Height 2214 feet or 675 metres. **16 D3** NT2229.
Blacklaw Hill *Dundee* ***Hill***, in Sidlaw Hills, 3m/5km NW of Longforgan. Height 932 feet or 284 metres. **34 A1** NO2834.
Blacklorg Hill *E.Ayr.* ***Mountain***, on border with Dumfries & Galloway, 6m/10km SE of New Cumnock. Height 2234 feet or 681 metres. **15 E5** NS6504.
Blacklunans *P. & K.* ***Village***, on Black Water, 9m/15km N of Blairgowrie. **41 G3** NO1460.
Blackness *Aber.* ***Settlement***, 2m/3km S of Banchory. **54 B5** NO6992.
Blackness *Dundee* ***Suburb***, 2m/3km W of Dundee city centre. NO3730.
Blackness *Falk.* ***Village***, on Blackness Bay, on S side of Firth of Forth, 4m/6km E of Bo'ness. **25 E2** NT0579.
Blackness *High.* ***Settlement***, 1km SE of Mid Clyth. **77 E5** ND2937.
Blackness Bay *Falk.* ***Bay***, on S side of Firth of Forth, 4m/6km E of Bo'ness. NT0580.
Blackness Castle *Falk.* ***Castle***, 3m/4km NE of Linlithgow. 14c-16c artillery fortress (Historic Scotland) with barracks added in 18c. Restored in 1920s. **25 E1** NT0580.
Blackridge *W.Loth.* Population: 1560. ***Village***, 3m/5km W of Armadale. **24 C3** NS8967.
Blackrock *Arg. & B.* ***Settlement***, at head of Loch Indaal, 2m/3km W of Bridgend, Islay. **20 B3** NR3064.
Black's Memorial Lighthouse *Arg. & B.* ***Other building***, lighthouse on E coast of Mull 1km S of Duart Point, built in memory of William Black, 19c novelist. NM7534.
Blackshaw *D. & G.* ***Settlement***, near shore of Solway Firth, 8m/13km S of Dumfries. **9 E4** NY0465.
Blackshaw Bank *D. & G.* ***Coastal feature***, sandbank to S of Blackshaw. **9 E4** NY0462.
Blackside *E.Ayr.* ***Inland physical feature***, mountain ridge, aligned NE to SW on border with South Lanarkshire, 3m/5km NE of Sorn, culminating in Wedder Hill (434 metres). NS5930.
Blacksmith's Shop *D. & G.* ***Other feature of interest***, at Gretna Green, one of first places in Scotland where young runaway lovers could be married without parental consent, 1km N of Gretna. **10 B5** NY3268.
Blacktop *Aberdeen* ***Hamlet***, 5m/8km W of Aberdeen. **55 D4** NJ8604.
Blackwater Forest *Moray* ***Forest/woodland***, astride upper reaches of Black Water, 8m/13km S of Dufftown. Contains deer. **53 E2** NJ3126.
Blackwater Reservoir *High.* ***Reservoir***, in Lochaber district, 8m/12km long E to W. Dam is 4m/6km E of Kinlochleven. **39 E3** NN3059.
Blackwaterfoot *N.Ayr.* ***Village***, on Drumadoon Bay, W coast of Arran, at mouth of Black Water, 9m/14km SW of Brodick. Machrie Moor Stone Circles and Moss Farm Road Stone Circle (both Historic Scotland) 3m/5km N. **13 E3** NR8928.
Blackwood *D. & G.* ***Settlement***, 1km NW of Auldgirth, 3m/5km NE of Dunscore. **8 D2** NX9087.
Blackwood *S.Lan.* Population: 1900. ***Village***, 6m/9km W of Lanark and adjoining to N of Kirkmuirhill. **24 B5** NS7943.
Bladnoch *D. & G.* ***River***, issuing from Loch Maberry and flowing generally SE to Glassoch, then S past Kirkcowan, and finally E through Bladnoch and into Wigtown Bay. **7 E5** NX4655.
Bladnoch *D. & G.* ***Village***, on N bank of River Bladnoch, 1m/2km SW of Wigtown. River issues from Loch Maberry and flows SE to Wigtown Bay on S side of Wigtown. **7 F5** NX4254.
Blaeberry Hill *D. & G.* ***Mountain***, on Eskdalemuir Forest, 3m/5km NE of Eskdalemuir. Height 1374 feet or 419 metres. **17 D5** NT2801.
Blaich *High.* ***Village***, in Lochaber district on S side of Loch Eil. **38 C2** NN0376.
Blainslie *Sc.Bord.* ***Locality***, 3m/4km S of Lauder. NT5443.
Blair Atholl *P. & K.* ***Village***, at confluence of River Tilt and River Garry, 6m/10km NW of Pitlochry. **41 D3** NN8765.
Blair Castle *N.Ayr.* ***Castle***, mainly of 17c, with later additions, 1m/2km SE of Dalry. **23 E5** NS3048.
Blair Castle *P. & K.* ***Castle***, to NW of Blair Atholl. White turreted in Scottish baronial style dating in part from 13c, seat of Dukes and Earls of Atholl. The present Duke maintains the only private army in Europe, The Atholl Highlanders. **41 D3** NN8765.
Blair Drummond *Stir.* ***Leisure/recreation***, estate with safari and leisure park on S bank of River Teith, 5m/8km NW of Stirling. **32 C5** NS7398.
Blairadam Forest *Fife* ***Forest/woodland***, partly in Perth & Kinross on W side of Kelty. **33 G5** NT1195.
Blairannaich *Arg. & B.* ***Settlement***, on W side of Loch Lomond, 1m/2km NE of Tarbet. **31 F4** NN3206.
Blairbuie *Arg. & B.* ***Settlement***, in Glen Fyne, 3m/4km NE of Knockdow. **22 C2** NS1174.
Blairdenon Hill *Clack.* ***Mountain***, 4m/7km SW of Blackford. Height 2070 feet or 631 metres. **33 D4** NN8601.
Blairdrummond Moss *Stir.* ***Open space***, low-lying area to N of River Forth and SW of Blair Drummond. NS7197.
Blairgowrie *P. & K.* Population: 8001. ***Small town***, on River Ericht, 17m/27km NW of Dundee. **41 G5** NO1745.
Blairhall *Fife* ***Village***, 6m/9km W of Dunfermline. **25 E1** NT0089.

Blairhoyle *Stir.* ***Settlement***, 2m/3km E of Port of Menteith. **32 B4** NN6101.
Blairhullichan *Stir.* ***Settlement***, on W shore of Loch Ard, 1km SW of Kinlochard. **31 G4** NN4401.
Blairingone *P. & K.* ***Village***, 4m/6km NW of Saline. **33 E5** NS9896.
Blairkip *E.Ayr.* ***Settlement***, 2m/4km NW of Sorn. **14 D2** NS5430.
Blairlinn *N.Lan.* ***Locality***, industrial area 1m/2km S of Cumbernauld town centre. NS7572.
Blairlogie *Stir.* ***Village***, 3m/5km NE of Stirling. **32 D5** NS8296.
Blairmore *Arg. & B.* ***Village***, resort in Argyll 1m/2km N of Strone Point at entrance to Loch Long. **22 C1** NS1981.
Blairmore *High.* ***Settlement***, near W coast of Sutherland district, 3m/4km NW of Kinlochbervie. **74 A2** NC1959.
Blairmore *High.* ***Settlement***, 1km E of Little Rogart, Sutherland district. **72 C4** NC7404.
Blairnairn *Arg. & B.* ***Settlement***, in Glen Fruin, 4m/6km N of Helensburgh. **23 E1** NS2988.
Blairnamarrow *Moray* ***Settlement***, 3m/5km SE of Tomintoul. **53 E3** NJ2115.
Blairpark *N.Ayr.* ***Settlement***, 3m/5km SE of Largs. **22 D4** NS2457.
Blairquhan *S.Ayr.* ***Settlement***, 1m/2km NW of Straiton. **14 B5** NS3605.
Blairquhosh *Stir.* ***Settlement***, 3m/4km NW of Strathblane. **23 G1** NS5282.
Blairs College *Aber.* ***Educational establishment***, Roman Catholic seminary founded in 1827, 5m/8km SW of Aberdeen. Present building dates from 1908. NJ8800.
Blair's Ferry *Arg. & B.* ***Settlement***, on W shore of Kyles of Bute, 2m/3km S of Tighnabruaich. **22 A3** NR9869.
Blairshinnoch *Aber.* ***Settlement***, 3m/5km SW of Banff. **64 B3** NJ6462.
Blairuskinmore *Stir.* ***Settlement***, at S end of Loch Chon, 6m/10km W of Aberfoyle. **31 G4** NN4303.
Blairvadach *Arg. & B.* ***Settlement***, above E shore of Gare Loch, 1m/2km NW of Rhu. **23 D1** NS2685.
Blairydryne *Aber.* ***Hamlet***, 4m/6km SE of Banchory. **54 C5** NO7492.
Blairythan *Aber.* ***Settlement***, 4m/6km N of Balmedie. **55 E2** NJ9723.
Blake Muir *Sc.Bord.* ***Mountain***, on Southern Upland Way, 4m/7km SW of Innerleithen. Height 1532 feet or 467 metres. **17 E2** NT3030.
Blakehope Head *Sc.Bord.* ***Mountain***, 4m/6km N of Tweedsmuir. Height 1781 feet or 543 metres. **16 B2** NT1030.
Blakelaw *Sc.Bord.* ***Settlement***, 4m/6km SE of Kelso. **18 B3** NT7630.
Blane Water *Stir.* ***River***, rising on Earl's Seat on Campsie Fells and flowing S before turning NW, then running down Strathblane to Endrick Water, 1m/2km W of Killearn. NS5085.
Blanefield *Stir.* ***Village***, 1km NW of Strathblane. **23 G2** NS5579.
Blanerne *Sc.Bord.* ***Settlement***, on Whiteadder Water, 4m/6km NE of Duns. NT8356.
Blantyre *S.Lan.* ***Town***, former cotton town, adjoining to NW of Hamilton. Birthplace of David Livingstone, 19c explorer. NS6857.
Blar a' Chaorainn *High.* ***Settlement***, 5m/8km NW of North Ballachulish. **38 D3** NN1066.
Blàr a' Ghille Dhomhnaich *High.* ***Mountain***, 7m/11km W of Berriedale. Height 1082 feet or 330 metres. **73 F2** ND0022.
Blargie *High.* ***Settlement***, in valley of River Spey, 8m/12km SW of Newtonmore. **51 F5** NN6094.
Blarglas *Arg. & B.* ***Settlement***, 4m/6km NE of Helensburgh. **23 E1** NS3486.
Blarmachfoldach *High.* ***Hamlet***, in Lochaber district, 3m/5km S of Fort William. **38 C3** NN0969.
Blarnalevoch *High.* ***Settlement***, 1m/2km W of Leckmelm across Loch Broom. **70 D5** NH1490.
Blashaval *W.Isles Anglicised form of Blathaisbhal, qv.*
Blathaisbhal (Anglicised form: Blashaval.) *W.Isles* ***Settlement***, on E coast North Uist, 2m/3km NW of Lochmaddy. **45 G2** NF8970.
Blatobulgium Roman Fort *D. & G.* ***Historic/prehistoric site***, 2m/3km E of Ecclefechan. Roman station occupied from AD 80 to AD 180. Visible remains date from AD 152, following construction of Antonine Wall. **9 G3** NY2175.
Blaven *High. Alternative name for Bla Bheinn, qv.*
Bleak Law *S.Lan.* ***Mountain***, in Pentland Hills, 2m/3km N of Dunsyre. Height 1460 feet or 445 metres. **25 E4** NT0651.
Bleaval *W.Isles* ***Mountain***, on South Harris, 3m/5km N of Leverburgh. Height 1305 feet or 398 metres. **66 C4** NG0391.
Blebocraigs *Fife* ***Village***, 5m/8km W of St. Andrews. **34 C3** NO4315.
Blervie Castle *Moray* ***Settlement***, 3m/4km SE of Forres. Standing stones and castle ruins nearby. **62 C4** NJ0757.
Blindburn *Aber.* ***Settlement***, 4m/6km N of Ellon. **55 E1** NJ9435.
Blindman's Bay *Arg. & B.* ***Bay***, on W side of Kyles of Bute, 1m/2km N of Ardlamont Point, Argyll. **22 A3** NR9965.
Blinkbonny Height *Sc.Bord.* ***Hill***, on NE side of Kershope Forest, 2m/3km SE of Newcastleton. Height 866 feet or 264 metres. **10 C3** NY4984.
Bloodstone Hill *High.* ***Mountain***, near NW coast of Rum, 1m/2km NE of A' Bhrìdeanach, westernmost point of island. Height 1273 feet or 388 metres. **47 G4** NG3100.
Bloody Bay *Arg. & B.* ***Bay***, on N coast of Mull, 2m/3km NW of Tobermory. **37 D4** NM4857.
Bloody Moss *High.* ***Open space***, moorland 1m/2km SW of Halkirk, to W of River Thurso. **76 D3** ND1157.
Blotchnie Fiold *Ork.* ***Hill***, situated to SE of Muckle Water. Height 820 feet or 250 metres. **80 C4** HY4128.
Blovid *Shet.* ***Coastal feature***, promontory on E coast of Mainland, 1m/2km SE of Levenwick. **83 G4** HU4119.
Blowup Nose *Aber.* ***Coastal feature***, headland on E coast between Hare Ness and Findon Ness, 5m/8km S of Aberdeen. NO9498.
Blue Head *High.* ***Coastal feature***, headland on Black Isle, 1m/2km E of Cromarty. **62 A3** NH8166.
Blue Mull *Shet.* ***Coastal feature***, headland on W coast of Unst, at N end of Bluemull Sound. HP5504.
Bluemull Sound *Shet.* ***Sea feature***, strait separating Unst and Yell. **85 E2** HP5503.
Bluther Burn ***River***, stream rising near Craigluscar Hill, flowing W before turning SE into Torry Bay on N side of Firth of Forth, to W of Torryburn. **33 E5** NT0186.
Blyth Bridge *Sc.Bord.* ***Village***, 6m/10km N of Broughton. **25 F5** NT1345.
Blythe Edge *Sc.Bord.* ***Inland physical feature***, mountain escarpment 1476 feet or 450 metres high and facing SW, 3m/5km W of Watch Water Reservoir. **26 D4** NT6056.
Boar of Badenoch *High. Alternative name for An Torc, qv.*
Boarhills *Fife* ***Village***, 4m/7km SE of St. Andrews. **35 D3** NO5714.
Boar's Head Rock *Moray* ***Island***, islet in Spey Bay, 4m/6km SE of Lossiemouth. **63 E3** NJ2867.
Boars of Duncansby *High.* ***Sea feature***, sea passage between Island of Stroma and Ness of Duncansby on N coast of Caithness district. **77 F1** ND3775.
Boat o' Brig *Moray* ***Settlement***, in River Spey valley, where road and railway cross river, 3m/5km NE of Rothes. **63 F4** NJ3151.
Boat of Garten *High.* ***Village***, on River Spey in Badenoch and Strathspey district, 5m/8km NE of Aviemore. **52 B3** NH9418.
Boath *High.* ***Locality***, 5m/8km NW of Alness. **61 E2** NH5774.
Boath Doocot *High. Alternative spelling of Boath Dovecot, qv.*
Boath Dovecot (Boath Doocot). *High.* ***Other feature of interest***, 17c dovecot, 2m/3km SE of Nairn, built on site of castle where Earl of Montrose raised standard of Charles I after defeating Covenanters in 1645. **62 B4** NH9155.
Boath of Toft *Shet. Alternative name for Toft, qv.*
Boblainy Forest *High.* ***Forest/woodland***, in Inverness district 6m/10km S of Beauly. Includes deer. **51 D1** NH4837.
Boc Mòr *High.* ***Mountain***, in Skye and Lochalsh district, 2m/3km E of Dornie. Height 2070 feet or 631 metres. **49 F2** NG9125.
Bochastle *Stir.* ***Settlement***, 1m/2km W of Callander. **32 B4** NN6007.
Bodach Mòr *High.* ***Mountain***, in Freevater Forest, Sutherland district, 7m/11km W of head of Strathcarron. Height 2696 feet or 822 metres. **60 C1** NH3689.
Boddam *Aber.* Population: 1435. ***Village***, fishing village on E coast, 2m/4km S of Peterhead. **65 G5** NK1342.
Boddam *Shet.* ***Settlement***, at head of inlet on E coast of Mainland, 5m/8km N of Sumburgh Head. **83 G4** HU3915.
Boddam Castle *Aber.* ***Castle***, ruin to S of Boddam, 3m/4km S of Peterhead. NK1341.
Boddin Point *Angus* ***Coastal feature***, headland on E coast at N end of Lunan Bay, 3m/5km S of Montrose. **43 F4** NO7153.
Bodendun Hill *Angus* ***Mountain***, to E of Glen Isla, 5m/8km N of Kirkton of Glenisla. Height 2427 feet or 740 metres. NO2067.
Bodesbeck *D. & G.* ***Settlement***, in Moffat Water valley, 6m/9km NW of Moffat. **16 C5** NT1509.
Bodesbeck Law *D. & G.* ***Mountain***, 1m/2km NE of Bodesbeck. Height 2171 feet or 662 metres. **16 C4** NT1610.
Bogallan *High.* ***Settlement***, on Black Isle, 2m/3km SW of Munlochy. **61 F4** NH6350.
Bogany Point *Arg. & B.* ***Coastal feature***, headland on E coast of Bute, at E end of Rothesay Bay. **22 C3** NS1065.
Bogbain *High.* ***Settlement***, 2m/3km NW of Daviot. **61 G5** NH7041.
Bogbrae *Aber.* ***Settlement***, 2m/3km SW of Hatton. **55 F1** NK0334.
Bogbuie *High.* ***Settlement***, 3m/4km E of Conon Bridge. **61 E4** NH5855.
Bogend *S.Ayr.* ***Settlement***, 1m/2km NE of Symington. **14 B2** NS3932.
Bogfern *Aber.* ***Settlement***, 3m/5km NE of Tarland. **54 A4** NJ5207.
Bogfields *Aber.* ***Settlement***, 4m/6km NE of Tarland. **54 A4** NJ5208.
Bogfold *Aber.* ***Settlement***, on E side of Bracklamore Hill, 3m/4km NW of New Pitsligo. **64 D4** NJ8558.
Bogha-cloiche *High.* ***Mountain***, on Gaick Forest, in Badenoch and Strathspey district, 7m/11km E of Dalwhinnie. Height 2942 feet or 897 metres. **40 C1** NN7486.
Boghall *W.Loth.* ***Village***, 1m/2km E of Bathgate. NS9968.
Boghall Castle *S.Lan. See Biggar.*
Boghead *Aber.* ***Settlement***, 3m/4km E of Aberchirder. **64 B4** NJ6553.
Boghead *E.Ayr.* ***Settlement***, 5m/8km NE of Cumnock. **15 E3** NS6324.
Boghead *S.Lan.* ***Village***, 1m/2km SW of Kirkmuirhill. **24 B5** NS7741.
Boghole Farm *High.* ***Settlement***, 5m/8km E of Nairn. **62 B4** NH9655.
Bogie *Aber.* ***River***, rising on E side of The Buck and running NE to Rhynie, then N to River Deveron 1m/2km NE of Huntly. Upper course is known as Water of Bogie. **54 A1** NJ5341.
Bogmoor *Moray* ***Settlement***, 3m/5km N of Fochabers. **63 F3** NJ3562.
Bogniebrae *Aber.* ***Settlement***, on E side of Fourman Hill, 4m/7km S of Aberchirder. **64 A5** NJ5945.
Bograxie *Aber.* ***Settlement***, 3m/4km NW of Kemnay. **54 C3** NJ7019.
Bogrie Hill *D. & G.* ***Mountain***, 3m/5km S of Moniaive. Height 1417 feet or 432 metres. **8 B2** NX7885.
Bogroy *High.* ***Settlement***, adjoining to N of Carrbridge. **52 B2** NH9023.
Bogside *Fife* ***Settlement***, 4m/6km SE of Clackmannan. **33 E5** NS9690.
Bogston *Aber.* ***Settlement***, 4m/6km SE of Strathdon. **53 F4** NJ3909.
Bogton *Aber.* ***Settlement***, 3m/5km W of Turriff. **64 B4** NJ6751.
Bogton Loch *E.Ayr.* ***Lake/loch***, in course of River Doon, 1m/2km W of Dalmellington. **14 C5** NS4605.
Bogue *D. & G.* ***Settlement***, 2m/3km E of St. John's Town of Dalry. **8 A2** NX6481.
Bohenie *High.* ***Settlement***, at S end of Glen Roy, 2m/3km NE of Roybridge. **39 E1** NN2982.
Bohuntine *High.* ***Settlement***, in Lochaber district, 2m/3km NE of Roybridge. **39 E1** NN2883.
Bohuntine Hill *High.* ***Mountain***, in Lochaber district, on W side of Glen Roy, 3m/4km NE of Roybridge. Summit is Beinn a' Mhonicag. Height 1860 feet or 567 metres. **39 E1** NN2885.
Boirseam (Anglicised form: Borsham.) *W.Isles* ***Settlement***, on S coast of South Harris, 3m/4km NE of Rodel. **66 C5** NG0785.
Boleside *Sc.Bord.* ***Settlement***, in Tweed valley, 2m/3km S of Galashiels. **17 F2** NT4933.
Bolfracks *P. & K.* ***Settlement***, 2m/3km W of Aberfeldy. **40 D5** NN8248.
Bolshan *Angus* ***Settlement***, 2m/3km NE of Friockheim. **43 E4** NO6152.
Bolton *E.Loth.* ***Village***, 3m/4km S of Haddington. **26 C2** NT5070.
Bombie *D. & G.* ***Settlement***, 2m/3km E of Kirkcudbright. **8 B5** NX7150.
Bonahaven *Arg. & B. Anglicised form of Bunnahabhainn, qv.*
Bonaly Country Park *Edin.* ***Leisure/recreation***, country park at foot of Pentland Hills 1m/2km SW of suburb of Bonaly and 6m/9km SW of Edinburgh city centre. Park features undeveloped countryside with woodland, open moorland, gorges, burns and reservoirs. Spectacular views across Edinburgh to Fife. **25 G3** NT2066.
Bonaly Reservoir *Edin.* ***Reservoir***, 6m/9km SW of Edinburgh city centre. NT2066.
Bonar Bridge *High.* ***Village***, in Sutherland district at head of Dornoch Firth, 14m/23km W of Dornoch. Railway station at Ardgay, 1m/2km SW. **72 B5** NH6191.
Bonawe *Arg. & B.* ***Locality***, in Argyll, on N side of Loch Etive, 1m/2km N of Taynuilt. **30 C1** NN0033.
Bonawe Furnace *Arg. & B.* ***Historic/prehistoric site***, restored charcoal-fuelled iron works (Historic Scotland) on S side of Loch Etive, 1km NE of Taynuilt. Furnace operated from 1753 to 1874, producing canon and shot for navy. **30 C1** NN0131.
Bonawe Quarries *Arg. & B.* ***Settlement***, on N coast of Loch Etive, 1m/2km N of Taynuilt across loch. **30 C1** NN0133.
Bonchester Bridge *Sc.Bord.* ***Village***, on Rule Water, 6m/9km E of Hawick. **17 G4** NT5812.
Bonchester Hill *Sc.Bord.* ***Mountain***, rising to over 320 metres, to E of Bonchester. Surmounted by ancient earthworks. **17 G4** NT5911.
Bo'ness (Name contracted from Borrowstounness.) *Falk.* Population: 14,595. ***Town***, industrial town on S side of Firth of Forth, 17m/27km W of Edinburgh. Kinneil House, 1m/2km SW, is 16c-17c mansion. Vintage train centre. **25 D1** NS9981.

Bo'ness and Kinneil Railway *Falk.* ***Other feature of interest***, tourist steam railway running from Bo'ness docks to Birkhill Clay Mine, 3m/4km SW of Bo'ness, crossing line of Antonine Wall. Examples of locomotives, carriages and wagons. Exhibition tells story of movement of goods and people before motorway travel. **25 D1** NS9781.
Bonhill *W.Dun.* Population: 10,094. ***Town***, on E bank of River Leven 3m/5km N of Dumbarton. **23 E2** NS3979.
Bonjedward *Sc.Bord.* ***Hamlet***, 2m/3km N of Jedburgh. **18 A4** NT6523.
Bonkle *N.Lan.* ***Village***, 3m/5km NE of Wishaw. **24 C4** NS8356.
Bonnington *Angus* ***Settlement***, 3m/5km N of Carnoustie. **35 D1** NO5739.
Bonnington *Edin.* ***Hamlet***, 1m/2km SW of Ratho. NT1269.
Bonnington Linn *S.Lan.* ***Waterfall***, on River Clyde 2m/3km S of Lanark. **24 C5** NS8840.
Bonny Water ***River***, running E through Bonnybridge to River Carron, 3m/5km W of Falkirk. NS8481.
Bonnybank *Fife* ***Settlement***, 1m/2km NE of Kennoway. **34 B4** NO3503.
Bonnybridge *Falk.* Population: 6017. ***Village***, on Bonny Water, 4m/6km W of Falkirk. To E is well-preserved section of Antonine Wall, with Roman fort of Rough Castle (Historic Scotland). Seabegs Wood (Historic Scotland) is a stretch of rampart and ditch. **24 C1** NS8280.
Bonnykelly *Aber.* ***Locality***, 2m/3km SW of New Pitsligo. **65 D4** NJ8553.
Bonnyrigg *Midloth.* Population: 13,696. ***Town***, 2m/3km SW of Dalkeith. **26 A3** NT3065.
Bonnyton *Aber.* ***Settlement***, 3m/4km SE of Kirkton of Culsalmond. **54 B1** NJ6730.
Bonnyton *Angus* ***Hamlet***, 3m/5km SE of Newtyle. **34 B1** NO3338.
Bonnyton *Angus* ***Hamlet***, 4m/6km SW of Montrose. **43 E4** NO6655.
Bonnyton *E.Ayr.* ***Suburb***, to W of Kilmarnock. NS4138.
Boondreigh Water *Sc.Bord.* ***River***, formed by confluence of Blyth Water and Brunta Burn, 3m/5km E of Lauder, and flowing SW to join Leader Water, 2m/3km SE of Lauder. NT5545.
Boor *High.* ***Settlement***, near head of Loch Ewe, 1km NW of Poolewe. **59 E1** NG8481.
Boquhan *Stir.* ***Settlement***, 1m/2km SW of Balfron. **23 G1** NS5387.
Boquhan Burn *Stir.* ***River***, rising on Fintry Hills and running N via waterfall, Spout of Ballochleam, at edge of hills, then continuing N into River Forth, 1m/2km NE of Kippen. NS6696.
Bord Mòr *Arg. & B.* ***Mountain***, on Kintyre, 5m/8km SW of Carradale. Height 1338 feet or 408 metres. **12 C2** NR7533.
Border Forest Park ***Leisure/recreation***, large area of hills and conifer forests crossing border of England and Scotland, running from Wooler in NE to Bewcastle Fells in SW. NY7090.
Bore Stane *Midloth.* ***Other feature of interest***, outcrop of rocks in Pentland Hills, 3m/4km NW of Carlops. **25 F3** NT1459.
Boreland *D. & G.* ***Settlement***, 2m/3km N of Newton Stewart. **7 E4** NX3967.
Boreland *D. & G.* ***Village***, 6m/10km N of Lockerbie. **9 F1** NY1791.
Boreland *Stir.* ***Settlement***, 1m/2km NW of Killin. **32 A1** NN5534.
Boreraig *High.* ***Locality***, on N shore of Loch Eishort, Skye, 2m/3km E of Rubha Suisnish. NG6116.
Boreraig *High.* ***Settlement***, on W shore of Loch Dunvegan, Skye, 2m/3km S of Dunvegan Head. **57 E4** NG1853.
Boreray *W.Isles* ***Island***, rocky island (National Trust for Scotland) with steep cliffs, in St. Kilda group about 52m/83km W of North Harris. Area about 190 acres or 77 hectares. Haunt of sea birds. NA1505.
Boreray *W.Isles* ***Island***, uninhabited island off N coast of North Uist, measuring 1m/2km by 1km. **45 G1** NF8581.
Borgadelmore Point *Arg. & B.* ***Coastal feature***, headland on S coast of Kintyre, 2m/3km E of Mull of Kintyre. **12 B5** NR6305.
Borgh (Anglicised form: Borve.) *W.Isles* ***Village***, on Barra, 2m/3km N of Castlebay. Ancient burial ground between village and Borve Point. Chambered cairn 1m/2km E. **44 B3** NF6501.
Borgh (Anglicised form: Borve.) *W.Isles* ***Village***, on SE coast of Berneray, in Sound of Harris. **66 B5** NF9281.
Borghastan (Anglicised form: Borrowston.) *W.Isles* ***Settlement***, on N shore of Loch Carlabhagh, Isle of Lewis. **68 C3** NB1942.
Borgie *High.* ***River***, in Caithness district, running NE through Lochs Loyal and Craggie to Torrisdale Bay on N coast. **75 F2** NC6862.
Borgie *High.* ***Settlement***, 2m/4km SW of Bettyhill. **75 F3** NC6759.
Borgie Bridge *High.* ***Bridge***, carries A836 road over River Borgie at N end of Borgie Forest. NC6658.
Borgie Forest *High.* ***Forest/woodland***, afforested area astride River Borgie 3m/5km S of Torrisdale Bay, N coast of Caithness district. **75 F3** NC6653.
Borgue *D. & G.* ***Village***, 4m/6km SW of Kirkcudbright. Scene of Robert Louis Stevenson's Master of Ballantrae. **3 G2** NX6348.
Borgue *High.* ***Settlement***, near E coast of Caithness district, 3m/5km SW of Dunbeath. **73 G2** ND1325.
Bornais (Anglicised form: Bornish.) *W.Isles* ***Settlement***, on South Uist, on N side of Loch Bornish, 1m/2km E of Rubha Ardvule. **44 C1** NF7329.
Bornaskitaig *High.* ***Settlement***, on N coast of Skye, inland from Ru Bornaskitaig and 5m/8km N of Uig. NG3771.
Borness *D. & G.* ***Settlement***, 5m/8km SW of Kirkcudbright. **3 G2** NX6145.
Bornish *W.Isles Anglicised form of Bornais, qv.*
Borrobol Forest *High.* ***Open space***, deer forest in Sutherland district to SW of Kinbrace. **72 C2** NC7726.
Borrodale Burn *High.* ***River***, flowing SW and joining Beasdale Burn at Druimindarroch, Lochaber district. NM6984.
Borron Point *D. & G.* ***Coastal feature***, headland on Solway Firth, 3m/4km NE of Southerness. **9 E5** NX9958.
Borrowfield *Aber.* ***Settlement***, 1m/2km W of Netherley. **54 D5** NO8393.
Borrowston *W.Isles Anglicised form of Borghastan, qv.*
Borrowstounness *Falk. Full name of Bo'ness, qv.*
Borsham *W.Isles Anglicised form of Boirseam, qv.*
Borthwick *Midloth.* ***Hamlet***, 2m/3km SE of Gorebridge. **26 A4** NT3659.
Borthwick Castle *Midloth.* ***Castle***, massive 15c tower house 12m/20km SE of Edinburgh. **26 A4** NT3759.
Borthwick Water *Sc.Bord.* ***River***, running NE along SE side of Craik Forest to Roberton, then E to River Teviot 2m/3km SW of Hawick. **17 E5** NT4713.
Borthwickbrae *Sc.Bord.* ***Settlement***, with adjacent pastureland, to NE of Burnfoot. **17 F4** NT4113.
Borthwickshiels *Sc.Bord.* ***Settlement***, 4m/7km W of Hawick. **17 F4** NT4315.
Borve *High.* ***Village***, 4m/6km W of Portree, Skye. **58 A5** NG4448.
Borve *W.Isles Anglicised form of Borgh (Barra), qv.*
Borve *W.Isles Anglicised form of Borgh (Berneray), qv.*
Borve *W.Isles* ***River***, in N part of Isle of Lewis, running NW into Atlantic Ocean 1km N of High Borve. NB4057.
Borve Hill *W.Isles* ***Hill***, to NW of Borve on Berneray. Height 279 feet or 85 metres. **66 B5** NF9181.
Borve Point *W.Isles* ***Coastal feature***, headland 1m/2km W of Borgh. Ancient burial ground between headland and Borgh. **44 B3** NF6402.
Borvemore *W.Isles Anglicised form of Buirgh, qv.*
Botarua *W.Isles* ***Settlement***, on N coast of North Uist, at S end of Vallay Strand. **45 F2** NF7873.
Bothwell *S.Lan.* Population: 6542. ***Small town***, 2m/3km NW of Hamilton across River Clyde. Developed around coal, iron and steel industries. To SE, site of Battle of Bothwell Bridge 1679. **24 B4** NS7058.
Bothwell Castle *S.Lan.* ***Castle***, ruined 13c castle (Historic Scotland) standing in woods above River Clyde, 1m/2km NW of Bothwell. **24 A4** NS6859.
Bothwell Services *S.Lan.* ***Other building***, motorway service station on southbound carriageway of M74, 1km NE of Bothwell. **24 B4** NS7059.
Bothwell Water *Sc.Bord.* ***River***, rising in Lammermuir Hills and flowing S to join Whiteadder Water, 1km NW of Cranshaws. **27 D3** NT6863.
Botich *P. & K.* ***Mountain***, 7m/11km NW of Crieff. Height 1758 feet or 536 metres. **33 E1** NN9231.
Bottacks *High.* ***Settlement***, 1m/2km N of Strathpeffer. **61 D3** NH4860.
Bottle Island *High.* ***Island***, small island in Summer Isles group. Lies 1m/2km SW of Eilean Dubh. **70 B4** NB9501.
Bottomcraig *Fife* ***Hamlet***, 1km NW of Gauldry. **34 B2** NO3624.
Boultenstone *Aber.* ***Settlement***, with hotel, at bridge over Deskry Water, 4m/6km E of Strathdon. **53 G3** NJ4110.
Bound Skerry *Shet. See Out Skerries.*
Bousd *Arg. & B.* ***Settlement***, in N part of Coll, 4m/7km NE of Arinagour. **36 B3** NM2563.
Bovain *Stir.* ***Settlement***, at NE end of Glen Dochart, 3m/4km SW of Killin. **32 A1** NN5430.
Bow *Ork.* ***Settlement***, on Flotta, 1km SW of Pan. **78 C3** ND3693.
Bow Burn *D. & G.* ***River***, rising to W of Moorbrock Hill and flowing NW, then SW to join Water of Deugh, 2m/4km N of Carsphairn. **15 E5** NX5597.
Bow Head *Ork.* ***Coastal feature***, headland at N end of Westray. **80 C1** HY4553.
Bow of Fife *Fife* ***Locality***, 4m/6km W of Cupar. **34 B3** NO3213.
Bowbeat Hill ***Mountain***, in Moorfoot range on border of Midlothian and Scottish Borders, 3m/5km E of Eddleston. Height 2053 feet or 626 metres. NT2846.
Bowden *Sc.Bord.* ***Village***, 2m/4km S of Melrose beyond Eildon Hills. **17 G2** NT5530.
Bowdun Head *Aber.* ***Coastal feature***, headland on E coast, 1m/2km SE of Stonehaven, at N end of Castle Haven. NO8884.
Bowermadden *High.* ***Settlement***, in Caithness district, 4m/6km SE of Castletown. **77 E2** ND2364.
Bowershall *Fife* ***Hamlet***, 2m/3km N of Dunfermline. **33 F5** NT0991.
Bowertower *High.* ***Settlement***, 4m/6km SE of Castletown. **77 E2** ND2362.
Bowhill *Sc.Bord.* ***Historic house***, house and estate 3m/5km W of Selkirk. Excellent collections of art and French furniture. Home of Dukes of Buccleuch. **17 F3** NT4227.
Bowhousebog (Also known as Liquo.) *N.Lan.* ***Settlement***, 2m/3km SW of Shotts, on banks of South Calder Water. NS8558.
Bowland *Sc.Bord.* ***Settlement***, on Gala Water, 3m/5km NW of Galashiels. NT4540.
Bowling *W.Dun.* ***Village***, on N bank of River Clyde, 3m/5km E of Dumbarton. Developed via shipbuilding and distilling industries. W terminus of Forth and Clyde Canal (disused). **23 F2** NS4474.
Bowmont Forest *Sc.Bord.* ***Forest/woodland***, 3m/5km S of Kelso. **18 B4** NT7328.
Bowmont Water ***River***, rising in Cheviot Hills, on slopes of Cock Law, and flowing N across border of Scotland and England via Mowhaugh, Town Yetholm and Pawston, then W to join with College Burn to become River Glen, NE of Westnewton. **18 C5** NT9030.
Bowmore *Arg. & B.* ***Village***, fishing port on E side of Loch Indaal, Islay, 4m/6km NE of Laggan Point. **20 B4** NR3159.
Bowside Lodge *High.* ***Settlement***, on E side of River Strathy, 3m/5km S of Strathy Bay. **76 A2** NC8261.
Bowtrees *Falk.* ***Settlement***, 1m/2km S of Airth. **24 D1** NS9086.
Boydston *S.Ayr.* ***Settlement***, 1m/2km S of Crossroads. **14 C2** NS4632.
Boyndie *Aber.* ***Village***, 3m/5km W of Banff. **64 B3** NJ6463.
Boyndie Bay *Aber.* ***Bay***, sandy bay extending W from Banff to Knock Head, on N coast of Banff and Buchan district. **64 B3** NJ6463.
Boyndlie *Aber.* ***Locality***, comprising Upper and Nether Boyndlie near N coast, 5m/9km SW of Fraserburgh. NJ9062.
Boyne Bay *Aber.* ***Bay***, on N coast of Banff and Buchan district, 2m/3km E of Portsoy. Burn of Boyne runs N into bay. **64 B3** NJ6166.
Boyne Castle *Aber.* ***Castle***, remains located on Burn of Boyne nearly 1km from Boyne Bay. **64 B3** NJ6166.
Boysack *Angus* ***Hamlet***, 2m/3km E of Friockheim, on S bank of Lunan Water. **43 E5** NO6249.
Braal Castle (Also spelled Brawl Castle.) *High.* ***Castle***, ancient castle on W bank of River Thurso on NE side of Halkirk, Caithness district. **76 D2** ND1360.
Braan *P. & K.* ***River***, running NE down Strath Braan to River Tay at Dunkeld. **33 E1** NO0242.
Brabster *High.* ***Locality***, in Caithness district, 4m/6km S of St. John's Point on Pentland Firth. **77 F2** ND3269.
Bracadale *High.* ***Village***, near SW coast of Skye, 10m/16km NW of Sligachan. Loch Bracadale is large inlet to W. **47 G1** NG3438.
Bracadale Point *High.* ***Coastal feature***, headland 1m/2km SW of Bracadale, Skye. NG3337.
Brachla *High.* ***Settlement***, on W shore of Loch Ness, 4m/7km NE of Drumnadrochit. **51 E1** NH5633.
Bracken Bay *S.Ayr.* ***Bay***, on W side of Heads of Ayr, at S end of Firth of Clyde. NS2718.
Brackens *Aber.* ***Settlement***, on W side of Hill of Brackans, 3m/5km NE of Fyvie. **64 C4** NJ7553.
Brackla *High.* ***Locality***, in Nairn district, 4m/6km SW of Nairn. Includes distillery which produces Royal Brackla whisky. NH8651.
Bracklach *Moray* ***Settlement***, 1m/2km S of Cabrach. **53 F2** NJ3824.
Bracklamore *Aber.* ***Settlement***, on SE side of Bracklamore Hill, 3m/4km NW of New Pitsligo. **64 D4** NJ8458.
Bracklamore Hill *Aber.* ***Hill***, 4m/7km SE of Gardenstown. Height 722 feet or 220 metres. **64 D4** NJ8358.
Brackletter *High.* ***Settlement***, 3m/4km NW of Spean Bridge. **39 D1** NN1882.
Brackley *High.* ***Settlement***, 3m/5km SE of Ardersier. **62 A4** NH8052.
Bracklinn Falls (Falls of Bracklinn). *Stir.* ***Waterfall***, in course of Keltie Water 1m/2km E of Callander. **32 B4** NN6408.
Brackly *Arg. & B.* ***Settlement***, 1m/2km SW of Lochgilphead across Crinan Canal. **21 G1** NR8587.
Braco *P. & K.* ***Village***, on River Knaik, 6m/10km NE of Dunblane. In grounds of Ardoch House to N is well-preserved site of Roman fort; site of Blackhall Roman camps (Historic Scotland) 1km N of fort. **32 D4** NN8309.
Braco Castle *P. & K.* ***Castle***, 16c tower house, with L-shaped plan added in 18c, 1m/2km NW of Braco. NN8211.
Bracobrae *Moray* ***Locality***, on W side of Sillyearn Wood, 4m/6km NW of Milltown of Rothiemay. **64 A4** NJ5053.

Bracora *High.* ***Settlement***, on N shore of Loch Morar, in Lochaber district, 4m/6km SE of Mallaig. **48 D5** NM7192.
Bracorina *High.* ***Settlement***, in Lochaber district, 1km E of Bracora. **48 D5** NM7292.
Brae *D. & G.* ***Settlement***, 7m/11km NE of Dumfries. **8 C3** NX8674.
Brae *High.* ***Settlement***, on S side of River Oykel, at confluence with Meoir Langwell, 1km NW of Doune. **71 G4** NC4301.
Brae *Shet.* ***Village***, on Mainland at head of Busta Voe. To W is the narrow neck of land separating Busta Voe from Sullom Voe. **82 C1** HU3567.
Brae of Achnahaird *High.* ***Settlement***, near NW coast of Ross and Cromarty district, 3m/5km SE of Rubha Coigeach. NC0013.
Brae of Glenbervie *Aber.* ***Inland physical feature***, hillside to S of Fetteresso Forest, 2m/4km N of Glenbervie. **43 F1** NO7684.
Brae Wick *Shet.* ***Bay***, on N shore of St. Magnus Bay, 1m/2km E of Esha Ness, Mainland. Locality of Braewick at head of bay. **84 B5** HU2478.
Braeantra *High.* ***Settlement***, at head of Strath Rusdale, 8m/12km NW of Alness. **61 E2** NH5678.
Braedownie *Angus* ***Settlement***, at head of Glen Clova, 3m/5km NW of Clova. **42 A2** NO2875.
Braefoot *Aber.* ***Settlement***, 3m/4km SW of Turriff. **64 C5** NJ7146.
Braegrum *P. & K.* ***Settlement***, 1m/2km SW of Methven. **33 F2** NO0025.
Braehead *Angus* ***Settlement***, 3m/5km SW of Montrose. **43 E4** NO6853.
Braehead *D. & G.* ***Hamlet***, 1km N of Kirkinner, to S of Wigtown. NX4252.
Braehead *Moray* ***Settlement***, 4m/7km NE of Dufftown. **63 F5** NJ3843.
Braehead *Ork.* ***Hamlet***, on Westray, 1km SE of Pierowall. **80 C2** HY4447.
Braehead *Ork.* ***Settlement***, in S part of Mainland, 1km N of Cornquoy. **79 E2** HY5101.
Braehead *S.Ayr.* ***Suburb***, N district of Ayr. NS3422.
Braehead *S.Lan.* ***Hamlet***, adjoining to E of Coalburn. **15 G2** NS8134.
Braehead *S.Lan.* ***Village***, 3m/5km NW of Carnwath. **25 D4** NS9550.
Braehoulland *Shet.* ***Settlement***, S of Hamna Voe, on neck of Esha Ness, Mainland. **84 B5** HU2479.
Braeleny *Stir.* ***Settlement***, 2m/3km N of Callander. **32 B3** NN6310.
Braemar *Aber.* ***Village***, in district of same name, on Clunie Water near its confluence with River Dee. Tourist centre. Braemar Gathering (Highland Games) held in September. Castle dates from 17c. **53 D5** NO1591.
Braemar Castle *Aber.* ***Castle***, 1km NE of Braemar, in River Dee valley. 17c stronghold of Earl of Mar. Rebuilt in 18c and lived in today. **53 D5** NO1592.
Braemore *High.* ***Settlement***, 3m/4km SW of Lairg. **72 A4** NC5503.
Braemore *High.* ***Settlement***, in Caithness district, 5m/8km W of Dunbeath. **76 C5** ND0730.
Braemore *High.* ***Settlement***, in valley of River Broom, 1m/2km NW of Corrieshalloch Gorge. **60 A2** NH1979.
Braemore Forest *High.* ***Open space***, deer forest astride head of Strath More, S of Loch Broom in Ross and Cromarty district. NH1876.
Braenaloin *Aber.* ***Settlement***, 3m/5km NE of Bush Crathie. **53 E5** NO2799.
Braeriach (Gaelic form: Braigh Riabhach.) ***Mountain***, in Cairngorm Mountains on border of Aberdeenshire and Highland, 4m/7km SW of Cairn Gorm and 18m/28km SE of Aviemore. Munro: height 4251 feet or 1296 metres. **52 B4** NN9599.
Braeroddach Loch *Aber.* ***Lake/loch***, lochan or tarn 3m/4km NW of Aboyne. NJ4800.
Braes o' Lochaber *High.* ***Large natural feature***, part of Glen Spean, in Lochaber district, between Roybridge and confluence of Rivers Spean and Treig. **39 F1** NN3280.
Braes of Abernethy *High.* ***Open space***, upland area E of Abernethy Forest in Badenoch and Strathspey district. **52 C3** NJ0615.
Braes of Balquhidder *Stir.* ***Large natural feature***, upland area W of Balquhidder and N of Loch Doine and Loch Voil. **31 G2** NN4921.
Braes of Doune *Stir.* ***Large natural feature***, upland area, 3m/5km NW of Doune. **32 B4** NN6905.
Braes of Enzie *Moray* ***Settlement***, 3m/4km S of Portgordon. **63 F4** NJ3959.
Braes of Foss *P. & K.* ***Settlement***, 3m/4km SW of Tummel Bridge. **40 C4** NN7555.
Braes of Glenlivet *Moray* ***Large natural feature***, upland area, S of Glenlivet, 5m/8km E of Tomintoul. **53 E2** NJ2421.
Braes of Ogilvie *P. & K.* ***Locality***, in Strathallan, 1km S of Blackford. **33 E4** NN8907.
Braes of the Carse *P. & K.* ***Large natural feature***, foothills of Sidlaw Hills, above Carse of Gowrie, between Perth and Dundee. **33 G2** NO2530.
Braes of Ullapool *High.* ***Settlement***, on E shore of Loch Broom, Ross and Cromarty district, 1m/2km SE of Ullapool. **70 D5** NH1493.
Braes Wick *Ork.* ***Bay***, small bay on W coast of Sanday, 2m/4km N of Spur Ness. HY6137.
Braeside *Inclyde* ***Suburb***, 1m/2km S of Gourock. NS2375.
Braeswick *Ork.* ***Settlement***, on small bay of Braes Wick, on W coast of Sanday, 2m/4km N of Spur Ness. **81 E3** HY6137.
Braeval *Stir.* ***Settlement***, 1km SE of Aberfoyle. **32 A4** NN5300.
Braewick *Shet.* ***Settlement***, at head of Brae Wick bay, on Mainland. HU2478.
Braga Ness *Shet.* ***Coastal feature***, headland on W coast of Mainland, 2m/3km SE of Wats Ness. **82 A3** HU1948.
Bragar *W.Isles* ***Village***, near NW coast of Isle of Lewis, 5m/7km W of Barvas. **69 D3** NB2947.
Bragleenbeg *Arg. & B.* ***Settlement***, 1km E of Loch Scammadale. **30 B2** NM9020.
Brahan Castle *High.* ***Castle***, ruin in Ross and Cromarty district 4m/6km SW of Dingwall. Formerly stronghold of Earls of Seaforth, chiefs of Clan Mackenzie. NH5154.
Braid *Edin.* ***Suburb***, 2m/4km S of Edinburgh city centre. NT2470.
Braid Cairn ***Mountain***, on border of Aberdeenshire and Angus, 6m/10km SE of Ballater. Height 2909 feet or 887 metres. **42 C1** NO4287.
Braid Fell *D. & G.* ***Hill***, 3m/5km SE of Cairnryan, on E side of Loch Ryan. Height 771 feet or 235 metres. **6 C4** NX1166.
Braid Hills *Edin.* ***Hill***, rising to over 210 metres, to SE of Braid. **25 G3** NT2569.
Braidford *Glas.* ***Suburb***, 3m/5km SE of Glasgow city centre. NS6363.
Braidon Bay *Aber.* ***Bay***, small bay, 4m/6km NE of Inverbervie. **43 G2** NO8677.
Braidwood *S.Lan.* ***Village***, 2m/3km S of Carluke. **24 C5** NS8447.
Bràigh a' Choire Bhig *High.* ***Inland physical feature***, mountain ridge in Ross and Cromarty district, 1m/2km S of summit of Sgurr na Lapaich. **50 A1** NH1533.
Bràigh Coire Chruinn-bhalgain *P. & K.* ***Mountain***, to W of Beinn a' Ghlo massif, 6m/10km NE of Blair Atholl. Munro: height 3510 feet or 1070 metres. **41 E2** NN9472.
Bràigh Mòr *W.Isles* ***Sea feature***, stretch of sea separating South Harris from Scalpay. NG1994.
Bràigh na Glaice Mòire *High.* ***Open space***, upland moor 1m/2km NE of Ardtornish, Lochaber district. **37 G5** NM7248.
Braigh na h-Aoidh *W.Isles Gaelic form of Branahuie Banks, qv.*
Braigh na h-Eaglaise *High.* ***Mountain***, 4m/6km W of Berriedale. Height 1384 feet or 422 metres. **73 F2** ND0622.
Bràigh-nam-bàgh *W.Isles* ***Locality***, on South Harris to W of Loch Langavat, comprising numerous small lochs. **66 C5** NG0789.
Bràigh nan Uamhachan *High.* ***Mountain***, 6m/9km NE of Glenfinnan. Height 2509 feet or 765 metres. **38 B1** NM9786.
Braigh Riabhach *Gaelic form of Braeriach, qv.*
Bràigh Sròn Ghorm *P. & K.* ***Mountain***, 3m/5km E of Beinn Dearg, N of Blair Atholl. Height 2883 feet or 879 metres. **41 E2** NN9078.
Braigo *Arg. & B.* ***Settlement***, on NW of Islay, 8m/12km NW of Bridgend. **20 A3** NR2369.
Bran *High.* ***River***, in Ross and Cromarty district, running E from Achnasheen down Strath Bran to Loch Luichart. NH3162.
Branahuie *W.Isles* ***Settlement***, adjoining Melbost, 2m/4km E of Stornoway, Isle of Lewis. NB4632.
Branahuie Banks (Gaelic form: Braigh na h-Aoidh.) *W.Isles* ***Bay***, to S of Branahuie, Isle of Lewis. **69 F4** NB4632.
Branault *High.* ***Settlement***, on Ardnamurchan peninsula, 4m/7km NE of Kilchoan. **37 E3** NM5269.
Branchill *Moray* ***Settlement***, 5m/8km SE of Forres. **62 C4** NJ0852.
Branderburgh *Moray* ***Town***, on N coast adjoining, and forming, N part of, Lossiemouth. **63 E2** NJ2371.
Brandsbutt *Aber.* ***Locality***, in NW part of Inverurie, 15m/23km NW of Aberdeen. NJ7622.
Brandsbutt Stone *Aber.* ***Historic/prehistoric site***, located at Brandsbutt in Inverurie. Stone (Historic Scotland) has 8c Pictish symbols and oghamic inscriptions. NJ7522.
Branklyn Garden *P. & K.* ***Garden***, collection of rare plants (National Trust for Scotland), in Perth, including Himalayan blue poppy, golden Cedrus, rhododendrons and alpines. **33 G2** NO1222.
Brannie Burn *Arg. & B.* ***River***, flowing generally W from slopes of Beinn Bhuidhe into River Shira, 6m/10km NE of Inveraray. **31 D3** NN1416.
Bransly Hill *E.Loth.* ***Mountain***, 4m/6km S of Spott. Height 1302 feet or 397 metres. **27 D2** NT6770.
Branxholm Bridgend *Sc.Bord.* ***Settlement***, 1m/2km NE of Branxholme, on River Teviot. **17 F4** NT4712.
Branxholme *Sc.Bord.* ***Settlement***, with castle, in Teviotdale, 3m/5km SW of Hawick. Old castle blown up in 1570; present house dates in part from 1571-6. **17 F4** NT4611.
Branxholme Easter Loch *Sc.Bord.* ***Lake/loch***, 2m/3km W of Branxholme. NT4311.
Branxholme Wester Loch *Sc.Bord.* ***Lake/loch***, 3m/4km W of Branxholme. NT4211.
Brat Bheinn *Arg. & B.* ***Mountain***, on Jura, 2m/3km W of Craighouse. Height 1122 feet or 342 metres. **20 C3** NR4966.
Brathens *Aber.* ***Locality***, 2m/4km NW of Banchory. **54 B5** NO6798.
Brawl *High.* ***Settlement***, 3m/4km SW of Strathy Point, Caithness district. **76 A2** NC8066.
Brawl Castle *High. Alternative spelling of Braal Castle, qv.*
Brawlbin *High.* ***Locality***, in Caithness district, 1m/2km S of Loch Calder. **76 C3** ND0757.
Breabag *High.* ***Mountain***, 4m/6km SE of Loch Assynt. Height 2355 feet or 718 metres. **71 E3** NC2917.
Breac-Bheinn *High.* ***Mountain***, on N side of Strathcarron, in Sutherland district, 8m/12km NW of Bonar Bridge. Height 1515 feet or 462 metres. **71 G5** NH4995.
Breac Leathad *Moray* ***Open space***, 3m/5km E of Tomintoul. **53 E3** NJ2118.
Breachacha Castle *Arg. & B.* ***Castle***, 14c stronghold of the Macleans at head of Loch Breachacha on S coast of Coll, 5m/7km SW of Arinagour. 18c mansion that succeeded it is nearby. NM1553.
Breackerie Water *Arg. & B.* ***River***, in Kintyre running S down Glen Breackerie to join Strone Water as it enters Carskey Bay on S coast of peninsula. NR6507.
Breacleit (Anglicised form: Breaclete.) *W.Isles* ***Village***, at centre of Great Bernera, off W coast of Isle of Lewis. **68 C4** NB1536.
Breaclete *W.Isles Anglicised form of Breacleit, qv.*
Breadalbane ***Large natural feature***, area of Grampian Mountains between Glen Lyon and Strathearn, and between Bridge of Orchy and Dunkeld. **31 G1** NN4735.
Breadalbane Folklore Centre *Stir.* ***Other feature of interest***, centre at Killin, with tourist information centre, waterwheel, story of Breadalbane and history of local clans. Also includes sacred healing stones of Celtic monk St. Fillan, an early Christian missionary who settled in Glen Dochart. **32 A1** NN5732.
Breagach Hill *Aber.* ***Mountain***, 1m/2km NW of Strathdon. Height 1824 feet or 556 metres. **53 F3** NJ3313.
Breakish (Also known as Upper Breakish.) *High.* ***Settlement***, 2m/3km E of Broadford, Skye. **48 C2** NG6823.
Breakon *Shet.* ***Settlement***, on N coast of Yell. **85 E2** HP5204.
Breanais (Anglicised form: Brenish.) *W.Isles* ***Village***, near W coast of Isle of Lewis, 6m/10km SW of Timsgearraidh. **68 A5** NA9926.
Breascleit (Anglicised form: Breasclete.) *W.Isles* ***Village***, on East Loch Roag, W coast of Isle of Lewis, 13m/21km W of Stornoway. **68 D4** NB2135.
Breasclete *W.Isles Anglicised form of Breascleit, qv.*
Breawick *Shet.* ***Settlement***, on Mainland, on W side of Aith Voe, 1m/2km N of Aith. HU3357.
Brechin *Angus* Population: 7655. ***City***, ancient cathedral city on River South Esk, 7m/12km W of Montrose. Remains of 13c cathedral with 11c round tower attached. Iron Age hill forts of White Caterthun and Brown Caterthun (both Historic Scotland) 5m/8km NW. Maison Dieu Chapel (Historic Scotland) is part of medieval hospital founded in 1260; S wall has finely-detailed doors and windows. **43 E3** NO5960.
Brechin Cathedral *Angus* ***Ecclesiastical building***, built in 13c on site of previous foundation in centre of Brechin. Brechin Round Tower (Historic Scotland) is attached. **43 D4** NO5960.
Brechin Round Tower *Angus* ***Historic/prehistoric site***, Irish-type round tower dating from 11c (Historic Scotland), attached to Brechin Cathedral in centre of city. One of two such towers remaining on Scottish mainland. **43 D4** NO5960.
Breck Ness *Ork.* ***Coastal feature***, headland on W coast of Mainland, 2m/3km W of Stromness. **78 B2** HY2209.
Brecklate *Arg. & B.* ***Settlement***, at S end of Kintyre, 2m/3km N of Southend. **12 B4** NR6912.
Breckonside *D. & G.* ***Settlement***, 6m/9km SE of Sanquhar. **15 G5** NS8302.
Brei Wick *Shet.* ***Bay***, bounded by Lerwick, Mainland, to N and Ness of Sound to S. **83 D4** HU4740.
Breibhig (Anglicised form: Breivig.) *W.Isles* ***Settlement***, near E coast of Isle of Lewis, 1km S of Bac. **69 F4** NB4839.
Breich *W.Loth.* ***Settlement***, 3m/5km S of Whitburn. **25 D3** NS9660.
Breich Water *W.Loth.* ***River***, running NE to River Almond 5m/7km NE of Breich. **25 D3** NS9660.
Breiti Stack *Shet.* ***Coastal feature***, stack off W coast of Fair Isle. **82 A5** HZ2072.
Breivig *W.Isles Anglicised form of Breibhig, qv.*
Brenachoille *Arg. & B.* ***Settlement***, 1m/2km N of Furnace. **30 C4** NN0102.
Brenfield Point *Arg. & B.* ***Coastal feature***, headland on W side of Loch Fyne, 2m/3km S of Ardrishaig, Argyll. NR8582.
Brenish *W.Isles Anglicised form of Breanais, qv.*

Breoch *D. & G.* ***Settlement***, 2m/3km SE of Castle Douglas. **8 B5** NX7859.

Brerachan Water *P. & K.* ***River***, running E down Glen Brerachan to join Allt Fearnach and form River Ardle, 3m/5km NW of Kirkmichael. NO0463.

Bressay *Shet.* ***Island***, 11 square miles or 28 square km off E coast of Mainland, from which it is separated by Bressay Sound. Island attains height of 741 feet or 226 metres, with Ward of Bressay being the highest point. **83 E3** HU4453.

Bressay Sound *Shet.* ***Sea feature***, channel separating Mainland from Bressay. The sound affords protection to shipping and the harbour of Lerwick. HU4841.

Bretabister (Also spelled Brettabister.) *Shet.* ***Settlement***, on South Nesting Bay, Mainland, 2m/3km NE of Skellister. **83 D2** HU4857.

Brettabister *Shet. Alternative spelling of Bretabister, qv.*

Brevig *W.Isles* ***Settlement***, on Brevig Bay, on Barra, 2m/3km E of Castlebay. NL6998.

Brevig Bay *W.Isles* ***Bay***, on Barra, 2m/3km E of Castlebay. NL6998.

Briach *Moray* ***Settlement***, 4m/7km SE of Forres. **62 C4** NJ0954.

Bride's Ness *Ork.* ***Coastal feature***, rocky headland on SE coast of North Ronaldsay. **81 F1** HY7752.

Brideswell *Aber.* ***Settlement***, 3m/5km E of Huntly. **54 A1** NJ5739.

Bridge End *Shet.* ***Hamlet***, on West Burra, at road bridge connection with East Burra. **82 C4** HU3733.

Bridge of Alford *Aber.* ***Hamlet***, at road bridge across River Don, 1m/2km NW of Alford. **54 A3** NJ5617.

Bridge of Allan *Stir.* Population: 4864. ***Small town***, former Victorian spa town, 3m/4km N of Stirling. **32 C5** NS7997.

Bridge of Avon *Moray* ***Bridge***, road bridge over River Avon 1km above Ballindalloch Castle, 7m/11km SW of Charlestown of Aberlour. **53 D1** NJ1835.

Bridge of Balgie *P. & K.* ***Locality***, in Glen Lyon, 10m/16km W of Fortingall. **40 A5** NN5746.

Bridge of Bogendreip *Aber.* ***Settlement***, beside Water of Dye, 4m/6km SW of Banchory. **54 B5** NO6691.

Bridge of Brewlands *Angus* ***Settlement***, with road bridge across River Isla, 2m/3km NW of Kirkton of Glenisla. **41 G3** NO1961.

Bridge of Brown *High.* ***Settlement***, on border with Moray, 3m/5km NW of Tomintoul. **52 D2** NJ1220.

Bridge of Cally *P. & K.* ***Village***, at road crossing of River Ardle, 5m/7km NW of Blairgowrie. **41 G4** NO1451.

Bridge of Canny *Aber.* ***Village***, and road bridge over Burn of Canny, 3m/5km W of Banchory. **54 B5** NO6597.

Bridge of Coe *High.* ***Bridge***, road bridge across River Coe at foot of Glen Coe, Lochaber district. NN1058.

Bridge of Craigisla *Angus* ***Locality***, on River Isla, 4m/6km N of Alyth. Reekie Linn waterfall to SE. **42 A4** NO2553.

Bridge of Dee *Aberdeen* ***Bridge***, 16c bridge, with seven arches, spanning River Dee on S approach to Aberdeen. **55 E4** NJ9203.

Bridge of Dee *Aber.* ***Locality***, at S side of Banchory, next to road crossing of River Dee. **54 B5** NO6995.

Bridge of Dee *Aber.* ***Settlement***, where A93 road crosses River Dee, 3m/4km E of Braemar. **53 D5** NO1891.

Bridge of Dee *D. & G.* ***Village***, settlement and road bridge across River Dee, 3m/4km SW of Castle Douglas. **8 B4** NX7360.

Bridge of Don *Aberdeen* ***Village***, on N bank of River Don, 2m/4km N of centre of Aberdeen. Road bridge spans river. **55 E4** NJ9409.

Bridge of Dun *Angus* ***Hamlet***, with railway station on Brechin to Bridge of Dun Railway, on N side of River South Esk, 3m/5km W of Montrose. **43 E4** NO6658.

Bridge of Dye *Aber.* ***Locality***, in Glen Dye, 4m/6km S of Strachan. **43 E1** NO6586.

Bridge of Earn *P. & K.* Population: 2386. ***Village***, on River Earn, 4m/6km S of Perth. **33 G3** NO1318.

Bridge of Ericht *P. & K.* ***Settlement***, and road bridge near mouth of River Ericht, on N side of Loch Rannoch. **40 A4** NN5258.

Bridge of Ess *Aber.* ***Settlement***, 1m/2km SW of Aboyne, on Water of Tanar. **54 A5** NO5097.

Bridge of Feugh *Aber.* ***Bridge***, road bridge over Water of Feugh, 1km S of Banchory. Incorporates platform for observing salmon-leap. **54 B5** NO7095.

Bridge of Forss *High.* ***Settlement***, and bridge in Caithness district, carrying A836 road over Forss Water, 5m/8km W of Thurso. **76 C2** ND0368.

Bridge of Gairn *Aber.* ***Hamlet***, 1m/2km NW of Ballater, where A93 road crosses River Gairn. **53 F5** NO3497.

Bridge of Gaur *P. & K.* ***Settlement***, at W end of Loch Rannoch. 18c house The Barracks sited on S bank of River Gaur. **40 A4** NN5056.

Bridge of Muchalls *Aber.* ***Hamlet***, 1km SW of Muchalls. **55 D5** NO8991.

Bridge of Oich *High.* ***Bridge***, splendid suspension bridge (Historic Scotland) in Glen Mòr crossing Caledonian Canal and River Oich at NE end of Loch Oich, 4m/7km SW of Fort Augustus. Designed by James Dredge in 1854, with double cantilevered chains and massive granite pylon arches at each end. NH3303.

Bridge of Orchy *Arg. & B.* ***Village***, on River Orchy, 2m/3km S of Loch Tulla, Argyll. **31 F1** NN2939.

Bridge of Tilt *P. & K.* ***Settlement***, adjoining to N of Blair Atholl. **41 D3** NN8765.

Bridge of Tynet *Moray* ***Settlement***, at bridge over Burn of Tynet, 3m/5km SW of Buckie. **63 F3** NJ3861.

Bridge of Walls *Shet.* ***Settlement***, on Mainland, at head of Gruting Voe. **82 B2** HU2651.

Bridge of Weir *Renf.* Population: 5151. ***Small town***, on River Gryfe, 6m/10km W of Paisley. **23 E3** NS3865.

Bridgend *Aber.* ***Settlement***, on N bank of Priest's Water, 3m/5km S of Huntly. **54 A1** NJ5136.

Bridgend *Aber.* ***Settlement***, on S side of Turriff across Burn of Turriff. NJ7249.

Bridgend *Aber.* ***Settlement***, 1km S of Ballater. **53 F5** NO3694.

Bridgend *Angus* ***Settlement***, on West Water, 4m/6km W of Edzell. **42 D3** NO5368.

Bridgend *Arg. & B.* ***Village***, on Islay, at NE end of Loch Indaal. **20 B3** NR3362.

Bridgend *Arg. & B.* ***Village***, 3m/4km N of Lochgilphead, in valley of River Add. **30 A5** NR8592.

Bridgend *Fife* ***Village***, 2m/3km SE of Cupar. **34 B3** NO3911.

Bridgend *Moray* ***Locality***, 6m/10km SE of Dufftown. **53 F1** NJ3731.

Bridgend *P. & K.* ***Suburb***, to E of Perth across River Tay. **33 G2** NO1223.

Bridgend *W.Loth.* ***Village***, 3m/5km E of Linlithgow. **25 E2** NT0475.

Bridgend of Lintrathen *Angus* ***Village***, on E side of Loch of Lintrathen. **42 A4** NO2854.

Bridgeness *Falk.* ***Suburb***, on S side of Firth of Forth, adjoining to E of Bo'ness. NT0181.

Bridgeton *Aber.* ***Settlement***, 3m/4km SW of Alford. **54 A3** NJ5512.

Bridgeton *Glas.* ***Suburb***, 1m/2km SE of Glasgow city centre. NS6164.

Brig o'Turk *Stir.* ***Village***, 6m/10km W of Callander. **32 A4** NN5306.

Brigehaugh *Moray* ***Settlement***, at bridge over River Fiddich, 3m/4km SE of Dufftown. **53 F1** NJ3435.

Brighouse Bay *D. & G.* ***Sea feature***, inlet on E side of Wigtown Bay, 2m/3km S of Borgue. NX6345.

Brightons *Falk.* ***Village***, 3m/5km SE of Falkirk. **24 D2** NS9277.

Brimmond Hill *Aberdeen* ***Hill***, with panoramic viewpoint, 5m/8km W of Aberdeen. Height 869 feet or 265 metres. **55 D4** NJ8509.

Brims *Ork.* ***Settlement***, at S end of Hoy, 1m/2km SE of Melsetter. ND2888.

Brims Ness *High.* ***Coastal feature***, headland on N coast of Caithness district, 5m/8km W of Thurso. **76 C1** ND0471.

Brims Ness *Ork.* ***Coastal feature***, headland on Hoy to E of Brims. **78 B4** ND2888.

Brinacory *High.* ***Settlement***, on N shore of Loch Morar, in Lochaber district, 4m/7km E of foot of loch. NM7591.

Brinacory Island *High.* ***Island***, islet in Loch Morar, to S of Brinacory. NM7590.

Brindister *Shet.* ***Settlement***, on Mainland, on W shore of Brindister Voe. **82 B2** HU2857.

Brindister *Shet.* ***Settlement***, on Mainland, 1m/2km N of Easter Quarff. **82 D4** HU4336.

Brindister Voe *Shet.* ***Sea feature***, narrow inlet on Mainland off St. Magnus Bay, S of Vementry. HU2857.

Bring Deeps *Ork.* ***Sea feature***, sea passage between Bring Head on Hoy and Houton Head on Mainland. **78 B2** HY2902.

Bring Head *Ork.* ***Coastal feature***, headland at N end of Hoy, 3m/4km E of Ward Hill. HY2702.

Bring Head *Ork.* ***Coastal feature***, headland on NW coast of Rousay. **80 B3** HY3633.

Brinmore *High.* ***Settlement***, 10m/16km S of Inverness. **51 F2** NH6628.

Brinyan *Ork.* ***Locality***, with pier or landing stage, at SE end of Rousay. **80 C4** HY4327.

British Golf Museum *Fife* ***Other feature of interest***, at N side of St. Andrews. Displays on championships and famous players, as well as history of golf. Exhibitions of evolution of golf equipment and fun features of game. **34 D3** NO5017.

Brittle *High.* ***River***, in S part of Skye, rising in Cuillin Hills and running down to head of Loch Brittle. **48 A2** NG4020.

Broad Bay *W.Isles Alternative name for Loch a' Tuath, qv.*

Broad Cairn ***Mountain***, on border of Aberdeenshire and Angus, 2m/3km W of head of Loch Muick. Munro: height 3273 feet or 998 metres. **42 A1** NO2481.

Broad Head *D. & G.* ***Mountain***, on uplands to S of Craik Forest, 6m/10km N of Langholm. Height 1614 feet or 492 metres. **10 B2** NY3494.

Broad Hill *S.Lan.* ***Mountain***, 2m/3km SE of Lamington. Height 1522 feet or 464 metres. **16 A3** NT0029.

Broad Law *Sc.Bord.* ***Mountain***, 3m/5km E of Tweedsmuir. Height 2755 feet or 840 metres. **16 C3** NT1423.

Broad Taing *Ork.* ***Coastal feature***, headland to E of Bay of Isbister, Mainland. **80 C5** HY4117.

Broadfield *Inclyde* ***Suburb***, 1m/2km SE of Port Glasgow. NS3473.

Broadford *High.* ***Village***, on Broadford Bay, Skye, 7m/11km SW of Kyleakin. **48 C2** NG6423.

Broadford Airport *High.* ***Airport/airfield***, 3m/5km E of Broadford, Skye. **48 C2** NG6924.

Broadford Bay *High.* ***Bay***, on Skye, 7m/11km SW of Kyleakin. **48 C2** NG6423.

Broadhaugh *Sc.Bord.* ***Settlement***, 2m/3km SW of Branxholme. **17 F5** NT4409.

Broadhaven *High.* ***Settlement***, to E of Wick, on small bay of Broad Haven, on E coast of Caithness district. ND3751.

Broadley *Moray* ***Settlement***, near N coast, 3m/5km SW of Buckie. **63 F3** NJ3961.

Broadmeadows *Sc.Bord.* ***Hamlet***, 4m/6km NW of Selkirk. **17 F3** NT4130.

Broadrashes *Moray* ***Settlement***, 3m/4km N of Keith. **63 G4** NJ4354.

Broadsea *Aber.* ***Suburb***, to NW of Fraserburgh. **65 E3** NJ9967.

Broadsea Bay *D. & G.* ***Bay***, 4m/6km N of Portpatrick. **6 A5** NW9759.

Broc-bheinn *High.* ***Mountain***, rising to over 1083 feet or 330 metres, 3m/4km NE of head of Loch Harport, Skye. **48 A1** NG4333.

Brocair *W.Isles Gaelic form of Broker, qv.*

Broch of Burland *Shet.* ***Historic/prehistoric site***, fortified Iron Age homestead situated on headland, 1m/2km NE of Easter Quarff, Mainland. **82 D4** HU4436.

Broch of Gurness *Ork.* ***Historic/prehistoric site***, prehistoric castle and domestic settlement (Historic Scotland) on headland of Aiker Ness, Mainland. **80 B4** HY3826.

Broch of Mousa *Shet.* ***Historic/prehistoric site***, fine Iron Age broch tower (Historic Scotland) on W coast of Mousa. It is 45 feet or 14 metres high and thought to be nearly 2000 years old. Stairs can be climbed to parapet. **83 D5** HU4523.

Brochel *High.* ***Locality***, near E coast of Raasay, 5m/7km from N end of Skye. Ruined castle of Macleods of Raasay. **58 B5** NG5846.

Brochloch *D. & G.* ***Settlement***, 2m/4km NW of Carsphairn. **7 G1** NX5395.

Brock *Arg. & B.* ***Settlement***, on E shore of Gott Bay, Tiree, immediately S of Ruaig. **36 B2** NM0647.

Brodick (Formerly known as Invercloy.) *N.Ayr.* ***Small town***, port and resort on Brodick Bay on E coast of Arran. Passenger ferry to Ardrossan on mainland. **13 F2** NS0136.

Brodick Bay *N.Ayr.* ***Bay***, on E coast of Arran. **13 F2** NS0136.

Brodick Castle *N.Ayr.* ***Castle***, on Arran, with country park (National Trust for Scotland) 2m/3km N of Brodick. Mainly Victorian but original parts date from 13c. Famous rhododendron collection and one of Europe's best woodland gardens. **13 F2** NS0136.

Brodie Castle *Moray* ***Castle***, seat of Brodie of Brodie (National Trust for Scotland), 4m/6km W of Forres. Oldest parts date from 16c, with 17c and 19c additions. Park contains notable Pictish stone and impressive daffodil collection. **62 B4** NH9757.

Broker (Gaelic form: Brocair.) *W.Isles* ***Settlement***, on Eye Peninsula, Isle of Lewis, 1m/2km SW of Tiumpan Head. NB5536.

Brolass *Arg. & B.* ***Forest/woodland***, tract on Ross of Mull between Pennyghael to N and Malcolm's Point to S. **29 D2** NM5022.

Bronie Burn *Aber.* ***River***, rising on Burreldale Moss and flowing NE, past Pitmedden, to merge with Yowlie Burn before joining River Ythan 2m/3km W of Ellon. **55 E2** NJ9230.

Brookfield *Renf.* ***Hamlet***, 1m/2km NW of Johnstone. NS4164.

Brooklands *D. & G.* ***Settlement***, 4m/6km SE of Corsock. **8 C3** NX8173.

Broom *Fife* ***Suburb***, to NW of Leven. NO3701.

Broom *High.* ***River***, running N down Strath More to head of Loch Broom, Ross and Cromarty district. **60 A1** NH1785.

Broom Hill *Aber.* ***Mountain***, 3m/5km N of Tarland. Height 1883 feet or 574 metres. **53 G4** NJ4609.

Broom of Dalreach *P. & K.* ***Hamlet***, 2m/3km NW of Dunning. **33 F3** NO0017.

Broomfield *Aber.* ***Settlement***, 1m/2km N of Ellon. **55 E1** NJ9532.

Broomhead *Aber.* ***Settlement***, 2m/3km S of Fraserburgh. **65 E3** NJ9863.

Broomhill *Glas.* ***Suburb***, 3m/4km NW of Glasgow city centre in Partick district. NS5467.

Broomhouse *Edin.* ***Suburb***, 4m/6km SW of Edinburgh city centre. NT2071.

Broomy Law *Sc.Bord.* ***Mountain***, 2m/3km N of Broadmeadows. Height 1519 feet or 463 metres. **17 F2** NT4131.

Brora *High.* ***River***, rising on Ben Armine Forest and flowing SE down Strath Brora, through Loch Brora to E coast at Brora. **73 D4** NC9103.

Brora *High.* Population: 1687. ***Village***, on E coast of Sutherland district at mouth of River Brora, 10m/17km SW of Helmsdale. **73 E4** NC9004.

Brosdale Island *Arg. & B.* ***Island***, off S coast of Jura, 4m/6km SW of Craighouse. **20 D3** NR4962.
Brother Isle *Shet.* ***Island***, uninhabited island off Mainland in Yell Sound, 1m/2km N of Mio Ness. **84 D4** HU4281.
Brother Loch *E.Renf.* ***Lake/loch***, small loch 4m/6km S of Barrhead. NS5052.
Brotherton *W.Loth.* ***Locality***, 3m/4km SW of Livingston. NT0365.
Broubster *High.* ***Settlement***, 3m/4km N of Loch Shurrery. **76 C2** ND0360.
Brough *High.* ***Hamlet***, 2m/4km SE of Easter Head, N coast of Caithness district. **77 E1** ND2273.
Brough *Ork.* ***Settlement***, on Mainland, 2m/3km SE of Dounby. **80 B5** HY3118.
Brough *Shet.* ***Settlement***, on NE coast of Mainland, opposite SW end of Yell. **84 D5** HU4377.
Brough *Shet.* ***Settlement***, near E coast of Mainland, 2m/3km W of Moul of Eswick. HU4754.
Brough *Shet.* ***Settlement***, 1km SE of Setter, Bressay. **83 E3** HU5141.
Brough *Shet.* ***Settlement***, on W side of Burravoe, Yell. **85 E5** HU5179.
Brough *Shet.* ***Village***, near N coast of Whalsay. **83 E1** HU5565.
Brough Head *High.* ***Coastal feature***, headland on E coast of Caithness district, 6m/10km S of John o' Groats. **77 F2** ND3763.
Brough Head *Ork.* ***Coastal feature***, headland with beacon at W end of islet of Brough of Birsay, off NW coast of Mainland, accessible on foot at low tide. St. Peter's Chapel (Historic Scotland), at other end of islet. **80 A4** HY2328.
Brough Head *Shet.* ***Coastal feature***, headland on W coast of Whalsay, 1km W of Brough. HU5464.
Brough Lodge *Shet.* ***Settlement***, near to W coast of Fetlar, 3m/5km NW of Harbie. **85 E3** HU5892.
Brough Ness *Ork.* ***Coastal feature***, headland to S of Brough at S end of South Ronaldsay. **78 D4** ND4482.
Brough of Birsay *Ork.* ***Historic/prehistoric site***, remains of Romanesque church and Norse settlement (Historic Scotland) on Brough of Birsay islet, off NW coast of Mainland. **80 A4** HY2328.
Brough Taing *Shet.* ***Coastal feature***, rocky headland on E coast of Unst. **85 F2** HP6304.
Broughton *Ork.* ***Settlement***, on clifftop to S of Bay of Pierowall, Westray. **80 C2** HY4448.
Broughton *Sc.Bord.* ***Village***, 4m/7km E of Biggar. **16 C2** NT1136.
Broughton Heights *Sc.Bord.* ***Mountain***, 3m/5km NE of Skirling. Height 1873 feet or 571 metres. **25 F5** NT1141.
Broughton House *D. & G.* ***Historic house***, Georgian mansion (National Trust for Scotland) on River Dee in Kirkcudbright, containing art gallery and museum with extensive collection of rare Scottish books. Japanese-style garden. **8 A5** NX6851.
Broughtown *Ork.* ***Settlement***, on Sanday, 1km SW of head of Otters Wick bay. **81 E2** HY6641.
Broughty Castle *Dundee* ***Castle***, 15c castle (Historic Scotland), located at Broughty Ferry. **34 C1** NO4630.
Broughty Ferry *Dundee* ***Suburb***, 4m/6km E of Dundee city centre. **34 C1** NO4631.
Brow Well *D. & G.* ***Other feature of interest***, 3m/5km S of Carrutherstown. Ancient mineral well, visited by Robert Burns. **9 E4** NY0867.
Browland *Shet.* ***Settlement***, on Mainland, on E side of Voe of Browland. **82 B2** HU2651.
Brown Carrick Hill *S.Ayr.* ***Hill***, commanding wide views, 2m/3km E of Dunure. Height 941 feet or 287 metres. **14 A4** NS2815.
Brown Caterthun *Angus* ***Historic/prehistoric site***, Iron Age fort (Historic Scotland) with four concentric entrenchments, 5m/8km NW of Brechin. **43 D3** NO5566.
Brown Cow Hill *Aber.* ***Mountain***, 3m/4km E of Loch Builg and 9m/15km SE of Tomintoul. Height 2699 feet or 823 metres. **53 E4** NJ2204.
Brown Head *N.Ayr.* ***Coastal feature***, headland on SW coast of Arran, 2m/3km S of Blackwaterfoot. **13 D3** NR9025.
Brownhill *Aber.* ***Settlement***, 2m/3km N of Methlick. **65 D5** NJ8640.
Brownhills *Fife* ***Hamlet***, 1m/2km SE of St. Andrews. **34 D3** NO5315.
Broxburn *E.Loth.* ***Hamlet***, 1m/2km SE of Dunbar. **27 D2** NT6977.
Broxburn *W.Loth.* Population: 11,607. ***Town***, 11m/18km W of Edinburgh. **25 E2** NT0872.
Bru (Anglicised form: Brue.) *W.Isles* ***Village***, near NW coast of Isle of Lewis, 1m/2km W of Barvas across River Barvas. **69 E2** NB3449.
Bruach na Frithe *High.* ***Mountain***, peak of Cuillin Hills, Skye. Munro: height 3142 feet or 958 metres. **48 A2** NG4625.
Bruachmary *High.* ***Settlement***, 6m/10km S of Nairn. **62 A5** NH8846.
Bruan *High.* ***Settlement***, on E coast of Caithness district, 5m/8km NE of Lybster. **77 F5** ND3039.
Bruar Water *P. & K.* ***River***, running S down Glen Bruar to River Garry, 3m/5km W of Blair Atholl. Falls of the Bruar 1m/2km NE of Calvine. **40 D2** NN8265.
Brucefield *W.Loth.* ***Village***, 3m/4km SW of Livingston. NT0464.
Brucehill *W.Dun.* ***Suburb***, to W of Dumbarton town centre. NS3875.
Bruce's Cave *D. & G.* ***Cave***, man-made cave in cliff face in valley of Kirtle Water, 1km W of Kirkpatrick-Fleming. Here Robert the Bruce lay hidden for about three months in 1306. NY2670.
Bruce's Stone (The King's Stone). *D. & G.* ***Other feature of interest***, granite boulder on E shore of Clatteringshaws Loch, 5m/8km W of New Galloway. Marks site of battle of 1307 in which Robert the Bruce defeated English. **7 G3** NX5576.
Brucklay *Aber.* ***Locality***, comprising Brucklay Castle and Brucklay House, 3m/5km S of Strichen. NJ9150.
Brucklay Castle *Aber.* ***Castle***, ruined building 3m/4km NE of New Deer. NJ9150.
Brue *W.Isles Anglicised form of Bru, qv.*
Bruernish *W.Isles* ***Settlement***, on NE coast of Barra, 1km SE of Northbay. NF7202.
Bruernish Point *W.Isles* ***Coastal feature***, 1m/2km SE of Bruernish. **44 C3** NF7300.
Bruiach Burn *High.* ***River***, flowing E from Loch Bruicheach, then NE through Boblainy Forest and into River Beauly, 1m/2km N of Kiltarlity. **51 D1** NH5043.
Bruichladdich *Arg. & B.* ***Village***, on W side of Loch Indaal, Islay, 2m/3km N of Port Charlotte. **20 A3** NR2661.
Brunerican Bay *Arg. & B.* ***Bay***, on S coast of Kintyre, 1km S of Southend. NR6907.
Brunery Hill *High.* ***Mountain***, 2m/3km NE of Ardmolich, Lochaber district. Height 1548 feet or 472 metres. **37 G2** NM7373.
Brunt Hill *E.Loth.* ***Hill***, 3m/4km S of Dunbar. Height 738 feet or 225 metres. **27 D2** NT6774.
Bruntland *Aber.* ***Settlement***, 3m/4km W of Rhynie. **53 G2** NJ4528.
Brunton *Fife* ***Village***, 5m/8km NW of Cupar. **34 B2** NO3220.
Bruntsfield *Edin.* ***Suburb***, 1m/2km SW of Edinburgh city centre. NT2472.
Bruntshiel Hill *D. & G.* ***Hill***, rising to over 250 metres in Tinnisburn Forest, 3m/5km E of Langholm. **10 C3** NY4182.
Bruray *Shet.* ***Island***, second largest of Out Skerries group of islands, NE of Whalsay. Island is connected to Housay by a road bridge. **85 F5** HU6972.
Brux Hill *Aber.* ***Mountain***, 4m/6km S of Rhynie. Height 1558 feet or 475 metres. **54 A2** NJ5021.
Bruxie Hill *Aber.* ***Hill***, 3m/5km E of Glenbervie. Mast at summit. Height 708 feet or 216 metres. **43 G1** NO8280.
Brydekirk *D. & G.* ***Village***, 3m/4km N of Annan. **9 F3** NY1870.
Brylach Hill *Moray* ***Mountain***, 3m/5km NW of Rothes. Height 1066 feet or 325 metres. **63 E4** NJ2352.
Bu Ness *Shet.* ***Coastal feature***, promontory on E coast of Fair Isle, approximately 1km from N to S, connected to Mainland by narrow neck of land. **82 A5** HZ2272.
Buachaille Etive Beag *High.* ***Large natural feature***, ridge in Lochaber district, to S of Glen Coe and W of Buachaille Etive Mòr. Summit is Stob Dubh at SW end of ridge; Munro at height of 3142 feet or 958 metres. **39 D4** NN1753.
Buachaille Etive Mòr *High.* ***Large natural feature***, mountain mass (National Trust for Scotland) on Royal Forest, on N side of Glen Etive, Lochaber district. Summit is Stob Dearg, at NE end; Munro at height of 3352 feet or 1022 metres. **39 D4** NN2254.
Buaile an Ochd *W.Isles* ***Settlement***, on E coast of Isle of Lewis, on S side of Bac. NB4839.
Buaile nam Bodach (Anglicised form: Balnabodach.) *W.Isles* ***Settlement***, on E part of Barra, 4m/6km NE of Castlebay. **44 C3** NF7101.
Bualadubh *W.Isles* ***Settlement***, at N end of South Uist, 3m/5km E of Ardivachar Point. NF7846.
Bualintur *High.* ***Settlement***, in SW part of Skye, at head of Loch Brittle. **48 A2** NG4020.
Bualnaluib *High.* ***Settlement***, on E shore of Loch Ewe, Ross and Cromarty district, 1m/2km NW of Aultbea. **59 E1** NG8690.
Buccleuch *Sc.Bord.* ***Hamlet***, on Rankle Burn, 11m/18km W of Hawick. **17 E4** NT3214.
Buchan *Aber.* ***Locality***, stretch of country lying roughly NE of a line drawn from Banff, on N coast, to Newburgh, on E. **64 D4** NJ9549.
Buchan *D. & G.* ***Settlement***, on W bank of Carlingwark Loch, 1km S of Castle Douglas. **8 B4** NX7561.
Buchan Burn *D. & G.* ***River***, rising on S side of Mewick and flowing S, with waterfalls, to Loch Troon, 5m/8km NE of Bargrennan. **7 F2** NX4181.
Buchan Hill *D. & G.* ***Mountain***, 1m/2km N of Loch Trool, 6m/9km NE of Bangrennan. Height 1617 feet or 493 metres. **7 F2** NX4281.
Buchan Ness *Aber.* ***Coastal feature***, headland with lighthouse on E coast, 3m/4km S of Peterhead. **65 G5** NK1342.
Buchanan Castle *Stir.* ***Castle***, remains of former seat of Duke of Montrose, 1km W of Drymen. **23 F1** NS4688.
Buchanhaven *Aber.* ***Suburb***, N district of Peterhead. **65 G5** NK1247.
Buchanty *P. & K.* ***Settlement***, in Glen Almond, 6m/9km NE of Crieff. **33 E2** NN9328.
Buchlyvie *Stir.* ***Village***, 14m/22km W of Stirling. **32 A5** NS5793.
Bucinch *Stir.* ***Island***, wooded islet (National Trust for Scotland) in Loch Lomond, 2m/4km W of Balmaha. NS3891.
Buckhaven *Fife* Population: 17,069. ***Town***, and former fishing port on N coast of Firth of Forth, 7m/11km NE of Kirkcaldy. Formerly a joint burgh with Methil. **34 B5** NT3698.
Buckholm *Sc.Bord.* ***Hamlet***, 2m/3km NW of Galashiels. **17 F2** NT4838.
Buckie *Moray* Population: 8425. ***Small town***, fishing port and resort on Spey Bay, 13m/21km E of Elgin. **63 G3** NJ4265.
Buckie Drifter *Moray* ***Other feature of interest***, museum in Buckie, 5m/8km N of Keith, detailing lives of fishing communities and local importance of herring. Museum named after fishing vessel. **63 G3** NJ4265.
Buckies *High.* ***Hamlet***, 3m/4km NW of Halkirk. **76 D2** ND1063.
Bucklerheads *Angus* ***Hamlet***, 1km N of Kellas. **34 C1** NO4636.
Buckny Burn *P. & K.* ***River***, stream rising in mountains of Forest of Clunie, and flowing SE to join Lunan Burn, 4m/7km NE of Dunkeld. **41 F5** NO0845.
Buckpool *Moray* ***Suburb***, to W of Buckie, on N coast. NJ4165.
Buckquoy Point *Ork. See Point of Buckquoy.*
Bucksburn *Aberdeen* ***Suburb***, to NW of Aberdeen. **55 D4** NJ8909.
Buddo Ness *Fife* ***Coastal feature***, rocky headland on North Sea coast, 3m/5km SE of St. Andrews. **35 D3** NO5515.
Buddon Ness *Angus* ***Coastal feature***, low headland on N side of entrance to Firth of Tay, 3m/5km S of Carnoustie. **35 D2** NO5430.
Buidhe Bheinn *High.* ***Mountain***, in Lochaber district 1m/2km N of Kinloch Hourn. Height 2883 feet or 879 metres. **49 F4** NG9508.
Builg Burn *Moray* ***River***, issuing from Loch Builg and flowing N to join River Avon, 7m/11km S of Tomintoul. **53 D4** NJ1707.
Buirgh (Anglicised form: Borvemore.) *W.Isles* ***Locality***, on W coast of South Harris, 5m/7km N of Leverburgh. **66 C4** NG0294.
Bulabhall *W.Isles* ***Mountain***, 1m/2km N of Loch Langavat, South Harris. Height 1161 feet or 354 metres. **66 C4** NG0593.
Buldoo *High.* ***Settlement***, 2m/4km NE of Reay, Caithness district. Airfield to N. **76 B2** NC9966.
Bulg *Angus* ***Mountain***, 1m/2km S of Fernybank. Height 1991 feet or 607 metres. **42 D2** NO5476.
Bull Hole *Arg. & B.* ***Sea feature***, narrow strait in Sound of Iona separating Eilean nam Ban from Ross of Mull. NM3024.
Bullers of Buchan *Aber.* ***Coastal feature***, huge circular cavern on E coast, 2m/3km NE of Cruden Bay. Sea enters cavern at its base, top being open to sky. In stormy weather sea climbs to top of vertical walls of rock. **55 G1** NK1138.
Bullie Burn *P. & K.* ***River***, flowing E, then S through Braco and into River Allan at Greenloaning. **32 C4** NN8307.
Bullwood *Arg. & B.* ***Settlement***, on Firth of Clyde, 1m/2km SW of Dunoon. **22 C2** NS1674.
Bulwark *Aber.* ***Locality***, 1m/2km S of Maud. **65 E5** NJ9345.
Bun Abhainn Eadarra (Anglicised form: Bunavoneader.) *W.Isles* ***Hamlet***, on North Harris at head of Loch Bun Abhainn-eadar, inlet of West Loch Tarbert. **66 D3** NB1304.
Bun Loyne *High.* ***Settlement***, 2m/3km E of E end of Loch Cluanie. **50 B4** NH2109.
Bun Sruth *W.Isles* ***Sea feature***, inlet near SE extremity of South Uist, 4m/7km E of Ludag. **46 B3** NF8414.
Bunacaimb *High.* ***Settlement***, on W coast of Lochaber district, 1m/2km N of Arisaig. NM6588.
Bunarkaig *High.* ***Settlement***, in Lochaber district, on NW shore of Loch Lochy, 2m/3km N of S end of loch. **39 D1** NN1887.
Bunavoneader *W.Isles Anglicised form of Bun Abhainn Eadarra, qv.*
Bunchrew *High.* ***Locality***, in Inverness district, to S of Beauly Firth, 3m/5km W of Inverness. **61 F5** NH6145.
Bundalloch *High.* ***Settlement***, on shore of Loch Long, Skye and Lochalsh district, 1m/2km NE of Dornie. **49 E2** NG8927.
Buness *Shet.* ***Settlement***, with small jetty, to E of Baltasound, Unst. **85 F2** HP6208.
Bunessan *Arg. & B.* ***Village***, on Ross of Mull, at SE corner of Loch na Lathaich. **28 C2** NM3821.
Bunlarie *Arg. & B.* ***Settlement***, on Kintyre, 8m/12km NE of Campbeltown. **12 C2** NR7830.
Bunloinn Forest *High.* ***Open space***, deer forest in Inverness district between Lochs Cluanie and Loyne. **50 A4** NH1608.
Bunloit *High.* ***Settlement***, on NW side of Loch Ness, 3m/5km S of Drumnadrochit, Inverness district. **51 E2** NH5025.

Bunmhullin *W.Isles* ***Settlement***, on N coast of Eriskay. NF7912.

Bunnahabhainn (Anglicised form: Bonahaven.) *Arg. & B.* ***Village***, on bay of same name on NE coast of Islay, 3m/4km N of Port Askaig. **20 C2** NR4273.

Bunnahabhainn Bay *Arg. & B.* ***Bay***, small bay on E coast of Islay, to N of Bunnahabhain. **20 C2** NR4273.

Buntait *High.* ***Locality***, scattered settlement 4m/6km E of Cannich. **50 C1** NH3930.

Bunzeach Forest *Aber.* ***Open space***, deer forest 7m/11km N of Ballater. NJ3707.

Bur Wick *Shet.* ***Bay***, on coast of Mainland, 1km NW of Scalloway. HU3940.

Burach *High.* ***Mountain***, in Inverness district, 3m/4km SW of Invermoriston. Height 1991 feet or 607 metres. **50 C3** NH3814.

Burdiehouse *Edin.* ***Suburb***, 4m/7km S of Edinburgh city centre. NT2767.

Burg *Arg. & B.* ***Locality***, area on Mull (National Trust for Scotland), at SW end of Ardmeanach, rising steeply from Loch Scridain and culminating in mountain of Bearraich, 1416 feet or 432 metres. **28 D2** NM4226.

Burg *Arg. & B.* ***Settlement***, near W coast of Mull, 3m/5km E of Rubh' a' Chaoil. Dùn Bàn is 1c galleried fort to SE on coast. NM3845.

Burga Water *Shet.* ***Lake/loch***, on Mainland, L-shaped and 1km by 1km at its widest points. **82 B2** HU2353.

Burgh Head *Ork.* ***Coastal feature***, headland on E coast of Stronsay. **81 F4** HY6923.

Burghead *Moray* Population: 1495. ***Village***, large fishing village, 8m/12km NW of Elgin. Radio transmitting station. Well, or early Christian baptistry (Historic Scotland) in King Street, within remains of Iron Age fort. **62 D3** NJ1168.

Burghead Bay *Moray* ***Bay***, extends W from Burghead to mouth of River Findhorn. **62 C3** NJ0767.

Burghead Well *Moray* ***Other feature of interest***, spring-fed pool, formerly a water source for Burghead, situated in carved rock chamber (Historic Scotland). **62 D3** NJ1169.

Burleigh Castle *P. & K.* ***Castle***, ruined 15c-16c castle (Historic Scotland) on E side of Milnathort. **33 G4** NO1204.

Burn of Acharole *High.* ***River***, flowing NE to join Strath Burn 1km S of Watten. **77 D3** ND2150.

Burn of Agie *High.* ***River***, flowing N through Braeroy Forest into River Roy at upper reach of Glen Roy, 2m/3km E of Turret Bridge. **39 F1** NN3692.

Burn of Ample (Also known as Ample Burn.) *Stir.* ***River***, running N down Glen Ample to Loch Earn, 1m/2km E of Lochearnhead. Falls of Edinample on S side of loch. NN6023.

Burn of Arisdale *Shet.* ***River***, running S down Aris Dale valley to Hamna Voe. **85 D4** HU4882.

Burn of Aultmore *Moray* ***River***, rising on Hill of Clashmadin and flowing S to River Isla, 2m/3km E of Keith. **63 G4** NJ4551.

Burn of Boyne *Aber.* ***River***, rising on NE slopes of Knock Hill and flowing NE to enter sea at Boyne Bay, 2m/3km E of Portsoy. **64 A4** NJ6166.

Burn of Branny *Angus* ***River***, flowing S to Water of Mark, one of headwaters of River North Esk. **42 C1** NO4480.

Burn of Brown *See Glen Brown.*

Burn of Cairnie ***River***, on Aberdeenshire and Moray border, flowing E to Cairnie then NE by Ruthven to River Isla, 5m/8km N of Huntly. **63 G5** NJ5147.

Burn of Calletar *Angus* ***River***, stream flowing E of West Water, 1m/2km NW of Bridgend. **42 C3** NO5269.

Burn of Cambus *Stir.* ***Settlement***, 5m/8km SE of Callander. **32 C4** NN7003.

Burn of Canny *Aber.* ***River***, running S into River Dee 2m/3km W of Banchory. NO6796.

Burn of Cattie *Aber.* ***River***, stream rising in Forest of Birse, and flowing E to join River Dee 4m/7km W of Banchory. **54 A5** NO6295.

Burn of Corrichie *Aber.* ***River***, rising on Hill of Fare and flowing E, then S between Brown Hill and Meikle Tap, to merge with Bo Burn. **54 C4** NO7399.

Burn of Cowlatt *Moray* ***River***, issuing from Loch of the Cowlatt and flowing E to join Knockando Burn, 1m/2km N of Upper Knockando. **62 D5** NJ1744.

Burn of Craig *Aber.* ***River***, flowing E to join Burn of Glenny near Auchindoir, 2m/3km SW of Rhynie. **53 G2** NJ4724.

Burn of Durn *Aber.* ***River***, rising on W slopes of Hill of Summertown and flowing NE to sea at Links Bay, Portsoy. **64 A3** NJ5966.

Burn of Forgue *Aber.* ***River***, running N to River Deveron at Inverkeithny. NJ6247.

Burn of Hillside *Ork.* ***River***, flowing NW into Loch of Hundland, Mainland. **80 B4** HY2925.

Burn of Houstry *High.* ***River***, flowing S to join Dunbeath Water 1km NW of Dunbeath. **76 D5** ND1530.

Burn of Kergord *Shet.* *See Weisdale.*

Burn of Lochy (Lochy Burn). ***River***, continuance of Burn of Brown running NE down Glen Lochy to River Avon, 4m/7km N of Tomintoul. **52 D2** NJ1424.

Burn of Loin *Moray* ***River***, flowing E through Glen Loin, then S to join River Avon at E end of Glen Avon. **52 D4** NJ1506.

Burn of Lyth *High.* ***River***, in Caithness district, running SE from Loch Heilen to Sinclair's Bay, N of Wick. **77 E2** ND3357.

Burn of Maitland *Shet.* ***River***, on Unst running N through Loch of Cliff to head of Burra Firth. HP6114.

Burn of Ore *Ork.* ***River***, on Hoy, rising on Bakingstone Hill and flowing E into Ore Bay. **78 B3** ND2693.

Burn of Pettawater *Shet.* *See Sand Water.*

Burn of Rothes *Moray* ***River***, rising in wooded area between Carn na Cailliche and Green Hill, and flowing E to join River Spey on NE side of Rothes. **63 E5** NJ2850.

Burn of Sandwater *Shet.* ***River***, on Mainland, rising as Burn of Pettawater above small lake of Petta Water. Sand Water lake is in course of burn. HU4154.

Burn of Setter *Shet.* ***River***, on Yell, running N into Whale Firth. HU4891.

Burn of Sheeoch *Aber.* ***River***, running NE to River Dee, 5m/8km E of Banchory. **43 F1** NO7796.

Burn of Tennet *Angus* ***River***, stream which flows SW to join Water of Tarf, 1m/2km N of Tarfside. **42 D1** NO4981.

Burn of Tulchan (Also known as Tulchan.) *High.* ***River***, stream in Badenoch and Strathspey district running SE down Glen Tulchan to River Spey, 8m/12km NE of Grantown-on-Spey. NJ1235.

Burn of Turret *Angus* ***River***, stream which flows S to join River North Esk at Millden Lodge. **42 D1** NO5478.

Burn of Weisdale *Shet.* ***River***, flowing S through Weisdale, on Mainland, into head of Weisdale Voe. HU3952.

Burnbank *S.Lan.* ***Suburb***, to NW of Hamilton. NS7056.

Burnbrae *N.Lan.* ***Settlement***, 1km S of Shotts to W of Stane. NS8759.

Burnbrae Reservoir *W.Dun.* ***Reservoir***, small reservoir 3m/5km NW of Clydebank. NS4774.

Burncrooks Reservoir *Stir.* ***Reservoir***, on border with West Dunbartonshire, 5m/8km W of Strathblane. NS4879.

Burnend *Aber.* ***Locality***, in valley of Burn of Asleid, 5m/8km NE of Fyvie. **64 D5** NJ8441.

Burness *Ork.* ***Locality***, in NW part of Sanday. **81 E2** HY6644.

Burnfoot *High.* ***Settlement***, in Sutherland district, 1m/2km S of Kinbrace. **76 A5** NC8630.

Burnfoot *P. & K.* ***Settlement***, 4m/6km NE of Dollar. **33 E4** NN9804.

Burnfoot *Sc.Bord.* ***Hamlet***, 1m/2km SW of Roberton. **17 F4** NT4112.

Burnfoot *Sc.Bord.* ***Suburb***, adjoining to N of Hawick. **17 G4** NT5116.

Burnhaven *Aber.* ***Village***, 1m/2km S of Peterhead across Peterhead Bay. **65 G5** NK1244.

Burnhead *D. & G.* ***Settlement***, 6m/9km NW of St. John's Town of Dalry. **7 G2** NX5485.

Burnhead *D. & G.* ***Settlement***, 1km W of Thornhill. **8 C1** NX8695.

Burnhervie *Aber.* ***Hamlet***, on River Don, 3m/5km W of Inverurie. **54 C3** NJ7319.

Burnhouse *N.Ayr.* ***Hamlet***, 3m/5km SE of Beith. **23 E4** NS3850.

Burnmouth *Sc.Bord.* ***Village***, on coast, 2m/3km S of Eyemouth. **27 G3** NT9560.

Burnock Water ***River***, running N to Lugar Water at Ochiltree. NS5121.

Burns' Cottage *S.Ayr.* ***Historic house***, museum commemorating birthplace of Robert Burns in 1759. Located in Alloway, suburb to S of Ayr. **14 B4** NS3318.

Burnside *Aber.* ***Settlement***, 3m/5km SW of Kintore. **54 C3** NJ7712.

Burnside *Angus* ***Hamlet***, 3m/5km E of Forfar. **42 D4** NO5050.

Burnside *E.Ayr.* ***Hamlet***, 3m/4km SW of New Cumnock. **15 D4** NS5811.

Burnside *Fife* ***Hamlet***, 4m/6km SW of Strathmiglo. **33 G4** NO1608.

Burnside *Shet.* ***Settlement***, on Mainland, 1m/2km W of head of Ura Firth. **84 B5** HU2778.

Burnside *W.Loth.* ***Locality***, adjacent to E of Broxburn. **25 E2** NT0972.

Burnside of Duntrune *Angus* ***Hamlet***, on Fithie Burn, 4m/6km NE of Dundee. **34 C1** NO4334.

Burnswark (Also known as Birrenswark.) *D. & G.* ***Hill***, 3m/4km N of Ecclefechan. Earthworks of Roman and earlier settlements. Height 630 feet or 192 metres. NY1878.

Burnswark *D. & G.* ***Settlement***, 3m/4km N of Ecclefechan, below E slopes of Burnswark hill. **9 F3** NY1978.

Burnswark Hill Roman Camp *D. & G.* ***Historic/prehistoric site***, Iron Age hillfort on Burnswark, 3m/4km N of Ecclefechan, flanked by Roman artillery range and two practice seige works below hill. **9 F3** NY1878.

Burnt Islands *Arg. & B.* ***Island***, group of small islands in Kyles of Bute on E side of Buttock Point, at N end of Bute. NS0275.

Burntisland *Fife* Population: 5951. ***Small town***, resort on N bank of Firth of Forth, 4m/7km SW of Kirkcaldy. 17c Rossend Castle overlooks harbour. **25 G1** NT2385.

Burnton *E.Ayr.* ***Hamlet***, 1km N of Dalmellington. **14 C5** NS4706.

Burnton *E.Ayr.* ***Settlement***, 3m/5km E of Drongan. **14 C4** NS4917.

Burra Firth *Shet.* ***Sea feature***, deep inlet on N coast of Unst. **85 F1** HP6114.

Burra Ness *Shet.* ***Coastal feature***, headland on S coast of Yell, 1km SW of Burravoe. HU5178.

Burra Ness *Shet.* ***Coastal feature***, headland at easternmost point of Yell. **85 E3** HU5595.

Burra Sound *Ork.* ***Sea feature***, narrow sea channel between Graemsay and Hoy. HY2404.

Burra Voe *Shet.* ***Bay***, on NE coast of Mainland, on Yell Sound, 4m/6km S of Point of Fethaland. **84 C4** HU3689.

Burrach Mòr *High.* ***Mountain***, in Monadhliath range, 10m/16km NW of Newtonmore. Height 2716 feet or 828 metres. **51 E4** NH5808.

Burrafirth *Shet.* ***Locality***, at head of Burra Firth inlet. **85 F1** HP6114.

Burraland *Shet.* ***Settlement***, to N of, and overlooking, Loch of Burraland, Mainland. **84 C5** HU3475.

Burravoe *Shet.* ***Hamlet***, on Mainland, on E shore of Busta Voe. **82 C1** HU3667.

Burravoe *Shet.* ***Village***, on inlet of Burra Voe, at SE end of Yell. **85 E5** HU5179.

Burray *Ork.* ***Island***, inhabited island between South Ronaldsay and Mainland and linked to both by Churchill Barrier. Measures 4m/6km E to W and 2m/4km N to S. **79 D3** ND4796.

Burray Haas *Ork.* ***Coastal feature***, headland at NE end of Burray. ND4998.

Burray Ness *Ork.* ***Coastal feature***, headland at E end of Burray. ND5096.

Burrell Collection *Glas.* ***Other feature of interest***, art gallery set in Pollok Grounds, 3m/5km SW of Glasgow city centre. **23 G3** NS5562.

Burrelton *P. & K.* ***Village***, adjoining to S of Woodside, 2m/4km SW of Coupar Angus. **33 G1** NO2037.

Burrian Broch *Ork.* ***Historic/prehistoric site***, remains of Iron Age fortification or castle at S end of North Ronaldsay. HY7651.

Burrier Wick *Shet.* ***Sea feature***, sound between Uyea and Mainland. HU3192.

Burrigill *High.* ***Settlement***, near E coast of Caithness district, 1m/2km W of Lybster. ND2234.

Burrow Head *D. & G.* ***Coastal feature***, headland 2m/3km SW of Isle of Whithorn, at W end of Wigtown Bay. **3 E3** NX4534.

Burwick *Ork.* ***Settlement***, on S coast of South Ronaldsay. **78 D4** ND4384.

Burwick *Shet.* ***Settlement***, 1m/2km NW of Scalloway, Mainland. **82 C3** HU3940.

Burwick Holm *Shet.* ***Island***, tiny island at entrance to Bur Wick, Mainland. HU3840.

Busbie Muir Reservoir *N.Ayr.* ***Reservoir***, small reservoir 3m/4km N of Ardrossan. NS2446.

Busby *E.Renf.* Population: 1617. ***Suburb***, 6m/9km S of Glasgow. **23 G4** NS5756.

Busby *P. & K.* ***Settlement***, 1km NE of Methven. **33 F2** NO0326.

Bush Crathie *Aber.* ***Settlement***, 1m/2km NW of Crathie. **53 E5** NO2596.

Bush House *Midloth.* ***Educational establishment***, University of Edinburgh agricultural research station, 2m/4km N of Penicuik. NT2463.

Busta *Shet.* ***Settlement***, on W side of Busta Voe, Mainland, 1km N of Roesound. **82 C1** HU3466.

Busta Voe *Shet.* ***Sea feature***, inlet on W side of Mainland, E of Muckle Roe. **82 C1** HU3566.

Bute *Arg. & B.* ***Island***, in Firth of Clyde, separated from mainland of Argyll by narrow channel, the Kyles of Bute. E coast, S of Kyles of Bute, is about 5m/8km from Argyll mainland across Firth of Clyde, and SW coast about 6m/10km from Arran. Area nearly 50 square miles or 130 square km. Chief town and port is Rothesay. Mild climate. Industries include tourism and farming, especially dairy farming. Car ferry services from Colintraive and Wemyss Bay. **22 B2** NS0563.

Bute Museum *Arg. & B.* ***Other feature of interest***, on Bute, in Rothesay. Artefacts and exhibitions concerning natural history and the Isle of Bute. **22 B3** NS0964.

Buthill *Moray* ***Settlement***, 3m/4km SE of Burghead. **62 D3** NJ1365.

Butlins Wonderwest World Theme Park *S.Ayr.* ***Leisure/recreation***, holiday camp 3m/4km SW of Ayr. Includes funfair and birds of prey collection. **14 B4** NS3018.

Butsa *Shet.* ***Coastal feature***, headland at SE end of Fetlar, 1m/2km S of Funzie. HU6688.

Butt of Lewis (Gaelic form: Rubha Robhanais.) *W.Isles* ***Coastal feature***, headland with lighthouse at N end of Isle of Lewis. **69 F1** NB5166.

Butterstone *P. & K.* ***Village***, 3m/5km NE of Dunkeld. Loch of Butterstone is small loch to SW. **41 F5** NO0645.

Buttock Point *Arg. & B.* ***Coastal feature***, headland on Kyles of Bute at N end of Bute. **22 B2** NS0175.

Button Hills *Shet.* ***Large natural feature***, range of hills rising to 827 feet or 252 metres, to NE of Burravoe, Mainland. **82 C1** HU3868.

Bynack Burn *Aber.* ***River***, running NE to Geldie Burn, 5m/8km W of Inverey. NO0086.
Bynack More (Formerly known as Caiplich.) *High.* ***Mountain***, in Cairngorm Mountains, in Badenoch and Strathspey district, 3m/4km NE of Cairn Gorm. Munro: height 3575 feet or 1090 metres. **52 C4** NJ0406.
Byrehope Mount *Sc.Bord.* ***Mountain***, in Pentland Hills, 3m/5km NW of West Linton. Height 1752 feet or 534 metres. **25 E4** NT1055.

C

Caaf Reservoir *N.Ayr.* ***Reservoir***, small reservoir 2m/4km W of Dalry. **22 D4** NS2550.
Cabaan Forest *High.* ***Open space***, in Ross and Cromarty district N of Orrin Reservoir. NH3650.
Cabharstadh (Anglicised form: Caversta.) *W.Isles* ***Locality***, on S side of Loch Erisort, Isle of Lewis, 2m/4km SE of Lacasaigh. **69 E5** NB3620.
Cabrach *Arg. & B.* ***Settlement***, on Jura, 3m/5km SW of Craighouse. **20 C3** NR4964.
Cabrach *Moray* ***Village***, on River Deveron, 7m/11km W of Rhynie. **53 F2** NJ3826.
Cac Carn Beag *Aber.* ***Mountain***, summit of Lochnagar ridge. Munro: height 3788 feet or 1155 metres. **42 A1** NO2486.
Cac Carn Mòr *Aber. See Lochnagar.*
Cachlaidh Mhòr *Arg. & B.* ***Open space***, 3m/5km E of Bridgend, Islay. **20 B3** NR3961.
Cacra Hill *Sc.Bord.* ***Mountain***, on E side of Ettrick Water at its confluence with Rankle Burn, and 2m/3km N of Buccleuch. Height 1545 feet or 471 metres. NT3117.
Cacrabank *Sc.Bord.* ***Settlement***, 3m/4km NE of Ettrick. **17 E4** NT3017.
Cadboll *High.* ***Settlement***, 2m/3km NE of Balintore. **62 A2** NH8777.
Caddam Wood *Angus* ***Forest/woodland***, 1m/2km N of Kirriemuir. Location of most northerly known Roman road. NO3855.
Cadder *E.Dun.* ***Hamlet***, on W bank of Forth and Clyde Canal, 2m/3km N of Bishopbriggs. Roman fort to N. **24 A2** NS6172.
Cadderlie *Arg. & B.* ***Settlement***, 4m/7km NE of Taynuilt across Loch Etive. **30 C1** NN0436.
Caddletown *Arg. & B.* ***Settlement***, on Ardmaddy Bay, 4m/7km SW of Kilninver. **29 G3** NM7815.
Caddon Water *Sc.Bord.* ***River***, rising on N side of Windlestraw Law and flowing SE via Stantling Craig Reservoir to River Tweed at Caddonfoot, 3m/5km W of Galashiels. **17 F2** NT4434.
Caddonfoot *Sc.Bord.* ***Settlement***, at mouth of Caddon Water, 3m/5km W of Galashiels. **17 F2** NT4434.
Cademuir Hill *Sc.Bord.* ***Mountain***, two distinct summits at 1361 feet or 415 metres and 1335 feet or 407 metres, 2m/3km SW of Peebles. **16 D2** NT2237.
Cadham *Fife* ***Suburb***, NE district of Glenrothes. **34 A4** NO2702.
Cadzow *S.Lan.* ***Suburb***, S district of Hamilton. Cadzow Castle (Historic Scotland) to E. NS7153.
Cadzow Castle *S.Lan.* ***Castle***, remains of 13c royal residence (Historic Scotland) beside Avon Water in grounds of Chatelherault Country Park, to E of Cadzow. NS7353.
Caen *High.* ***Settlement***, 2m/3km NW of Helmsdale, to N of River Helmsdale. **73 F3** ND0117.
Caen Lochan Nature Reserve *Angus* ***Nature reserve***, in mountains, 4m/7km NW of Glendoll Lodge. **42 A2** NO2177.
Caenlochan Forest *Angus* ***Open space***, deer forest to S of Glas Maol. National Nature Reserve. **41 G2** NO1775.
Caerlaverock Castle *D. & G.* ***Castle***, ruined late 13c castle (Historic Scotland) near shore of Solway Firth, 7m/12km SE of Dumfries. **9 E4** NY0265.
Caerlaverock Wildfowl and Wetlands Trust *D. & G.* ***Nature reserve***, on E side of mouth of River Nith. One of Britain's largest unclaimed saltmarshes. Breeding ground for natterjack toad and winter feeding ground of barnacle geese. **9 E4** NY0365.
Cagar Feosaig *High.* ***Mountain***, 1m/2km N of Backries, Sutherland district. Height 1237 feet or 377 metres. **72 D4** NC8404.
Caggan *High.* ***Settlement***, in River Dulnain valley, 5m/8km NW of Aviemore. **52 A3** NH8216.
Cailiness Point *D. & G.* ***Coastal feature***, headland on E side of Rinns of Galloway, 3m/5km N of Mull of Galloway. **2 B3** NX1535.
Cailleach Head *High.* ***Coastal feature***, headland on NE side of entrance to Little Loch Broom, W coast of Ross and Cromarty district. **70 B5** NG9898.
Caiplich *High. Former name of Bynack More, qv.*
Caiplich *High.* ***Locality***, 5m/8km NE of Drumnadrochit. **51 E1** NH5437.
Caiplich Water *See Water of Ailnack.*
Cairinis (Anglicised form: Carinish.) *W.Isles* ***Village***, at S end of North Uist, 8m/13km SW of Lochmaddy. **45 G4** NF8159.
Cairisiadar (Anglicised form: Carishader.) *W.Isles* ***Village***, on Isle of Lewis, 1m/2km SE of Miabhig. **68 B4** NB0933.
Cairminis (Anglicised form: Carminish.) *W.Isles* ***Settlement***, on SW coast of South Harris, 1km SE of Leverburgh. **66 C5** NG0284.
Cairn Baddoch *Angus* ***Mountain***, 2m/3km N of Runtaleave, on W side of Glenclova Forest. Height 1932 feet or 589 metres. **42 A2** NO2770.
Cairn Bannoch ***Mountain***, 3m/5km W of Loch Muick, with summit on border of Angus and Aberdeenshire. Munro: height 3319 feet or 1012 metres. **42 A1** NO2282.
Cairn Cattoch *Moray* ***Mountain***, 3m/5km SW of Rothes. Height 1210 feet or 369 metres. **63 E5** NJ2346.
Cairn Daunie *Angus* ***Mountain***, 3m/5km W of Runtaleave. Height 2070 feet or 631 metres. **42 A3** NO2468.
Cairn Duhie *High.* ***Mountain***, 2m/3km SE of Ferness. Height 1023 feet or 312 metres. **62 B5** NH9842.
Cairn Edward Forest *D. & G.* ***Forest/woodland***, to S and SW of New Galloway, astride River Dee valley and enclosing Cairn Edward Hill. NX6173.
Cairn Edward Hill *D. & G.* ***Mountain***, within Cairn Edward Forest, 3m/4km S of New Galloway. Height 1066 feet or 325 metres. NX6273.
Cairn Ellick *Moray* ***Mountain***, 3m/5km NE of Tomintoul. Height 1735 feet or 529 metres. **53 D2** NJ1823.
Cairn Ewen *High.* ***Mountain***, on border of Inverness and Badenoch and Strathspey districts, 9m/12km NW of Newtonmore. Height 2870 feet or 875 metres. **51 E4** NH5802.
Cairn Galtar *W.Isles* ***Hill***, highest point on Sandray. Height 679 feet or 207 metres. **44 B4** NL6491.
Cairn Geldie *Aber.* ***Mountain***, 6m/10km S of Ben Macdui and 10m/15km W of Braemar. Height 2043 feet or 623 metres. **41 E1** NN9988.
Cairn Gibbs *Angus* ***Mountain***, 4m/6km W of Bellaty. Height 1706 feet or 520 metres. **41 G4** NO1859.
Cairn Gorm ***Mountain***, in Cairngorm Mountains on border of Highland and Moray, 8m/13km SE of Aviemore. Range named after peak although only fourth in altitude. Munro: height 4084 feet or 1245 metres. Ski slopes and chair lifts on NW side. **52 C4** NJ0004.
Cairn Gorm of Derry *Aber. Alternative name for Derry Cairngorm, qv.*
Cairn Leuchan *Aber.* ***Mountain***, 3m/5km S of Ballater. Height 2194 feet or 669 metres. **53 F5** NO3891.
Cairn Lochan ***Mountain***, SW peak of Cairn Gorm on border of Highland and Moray. Height 3985 feet or 1215 metres. NH9802.
Cairn-mon-earn *Aber.* ***Mountain***, 3m/5km NW of Rickarton, in Durris Forest. Masts at summit. Height 1240 feet or 378 metres. **54 C5** NO7891.
Cairn Mona Gowan *Aber.* ***Mountain***, 4m/7km S of Strathdon. Height 2457 feet or 749 metres. **53 F4** NJ3305.
Cairn Muir *Sc.Bord.* ***Open space***, mountainous moorland area in Pentland Hills, 4m/6km NW of West Linton, traversed N to S by Old Drove Road. **25 F4** NT1156.
Cairn Muldonich *Moray* ***Mountain***, 2m/3km E of Tomnavoulin. Height 1902 feet or 580 metres. **53 E2** NJ2427.
Cairn na Burgh Beg *Arg. & B.* ***Island***, at NE end of Treshnish Isles, with remains of an old fort. **36 C5** NM3044.
Cairn na Burgh More *Arg. & B.* ***Island***, at NE end of Treshnish Isles, with ruin of an ancient castle. **36 B5** NM3044.
Cairn of Barns *Angus* ***Mountain***, 1m/2km SW of Clova. Height 2135 feet or 651 metres. **42 B2** NO3271.
Cairn of Barpa Langass *W.Isles* ***Historic/prehistoric site***, ancient communal burial-chamber on North Uist, on N side of Loch Langass at head of Loch Euphoirt, 5m/9km W of Lochmaddy. NF8365.
Cairn of Claise ***Mountain***, on Aberdeenshire and Angus border, 7m/12km NE of Spittal of Glenshee. Munro: height 3490 feet or 1064 metres. **41 G2** NO1878.
Cairn of Get (Also known as Garrywhin.) *High.* ***Historic/prehistoric site***, prehistoric chambered tomb (Historic Scotland), 1km NW of Ulbster. **77 F4** ND3141.
Cairn o'Mount (Cairn o'Mounth). *Aber.* ***Mountain***, summit of lower Grampian Mountains, 5m/8km N of Fettercairn, along Old Military Road linking Fettercairn and Banchory. Height 1492 feet or 455 metres. **43 E1** NO6480.
Cairn o'Mounth *Aber. Alternative spelling of Cairn o'Mount, qv.*
Cairn Pat *D. & G.* ***Hill***, 3m/4km S of Stranraer. Mast and ancient fort at summit. Height 597 feet or 182 metres. **6 B5** NX0456.
Cairn Point *D. & G.* ***Coastal feature***, point with lighthouse on E side of Loch Ryan, 5m/8km N of Stranraer. **6 B4** NX0668.
Cairn Table *S.Lan.* ***Mountain***, 3m/5km SE of Muirkirk. Height 1945 feet or 593 metres. **15 F3** NS7224.
Cairn Taggart *Aber. Alternative name for Carn an t-Sagairt Mòr, qv.*
Cairn Toul *Aber.* ***Mountain***, in Cairngorm Mountains 2m/3km SW of Ben Macdui. Munro: height 4234 feet or 1291 metres. **52 B5** NN9697.
Cairn Uish *Moray* ***Mountain***, 3m/4km S of Kellas. Height 1197 feet or 365 metres. **63 D4** NJ1750.
Cairn Vachich *Aber.* ***Mountain***, 2m/3km N of Corgarff. Height 2135 feet or 651 metres. **53 E3** NJ2611.
Cairn Vungie *High.* ***Mountain***, in Inverness district, 5m/8km E of Fort Augustus. Height 2329 feet or 710 metres. **51 D4** NH4507.
Cairn Water *D. & G.* ***River***, flowing SE from near Moniaive to join Old Water and form Cluden Water, 6m/10km NW of Dumfries. NX8879.
Cairn William *Aber.* ***Mountain***, in Pitfichie Forest, 2m/3km NW of Monymusk. Height 1469 feet or 448 metres. **54 B3** NJ6516.
Cairnacay *Moray* ***Mountain***, 4m/7km N of Tomnavoulin. Height 1607 feet or 490 metres. **53 E1** NJ2032.
Cairnargat *Aber.* ***Settlement***, 2m/3km E of Haugh of Glass. **53 G1** NJ4539.
Cairnbaan *Arg. & B.* ***Village***, on Crinan Loch, in Argyll, 2m/4km NW of Lochgilphead. Cup and ring marked rocks (Historic Scotland); also at Achnabreck, 1m/2km E. **30 A5** NR8390.
Cairnbaan Cup and Ring Marks *Arg. & B.* ***Historic/prehistoric site***, adjacent to N of Cairnbaan, 3m/4km NW of Lochgilphead. Two cup and ring marked rocks (Historic Scotland); ringed carvings feature up to four rings. **30 A5** NR8391.
Cairnbeathie *Aber.* ***Settlement***, 1km S of Lumphanan. **54 A4** NJ5703.
Cairnbrallan *Moray* ***Mountain***, 4m/6km SW of Cabrach. Height 2027 feet or 618 metres. **53 F2** NJ3324.
Cairnbrogie *Aber.* ***Settlement***, 3m/4km E of Oldmeldrum. **55 D2** NJ8426.
Cairnbulg *Aber.* ***Locality***, on NE coast, adjoining to W of Inverallochy. **65 F3** NK0365.
Cairnbulg Castle *Aber.* ***Castle***, set in woodland 2m/3km SE of Fraserburgh. Mid-13c rectangular tower, with later additions, and home of Comyn family. Converted to a mansion late 19c. **65 F3** NK0163.
Cairnbulg Point *Aber.* ***Coastal feature***, headland to NW of Cairnbulg, at E end of Fraserburgh Bay. **65 F3** NK0366.
Cairncross *Sc.Bord.* ***Hamlet***, 2m/3km SW of Coldingham. **27 F3** NT8963.
Cairncurran *Inclyde* ***Settlement***, 3m/4km W of Kilmacolm. **23 E3** NS3169.
Cairncurran Hill *Inclyde* ***Hill***, 4m/6km W of Kilmacolm. Height 909 feet or 277 metres. **23 D2** NS2970.
Cairndoon *D. & G.* ***Settlement***, 2m/3km SE of Monreith. **3 D3** NX3838.
Cairndow *Arg. & B.* ***Village***, at mouth of Kinglas Water, on Loch Fyne in Argyll, near head of loch. **31 D3** NN1711.
Cairne *Aber.* ***Settlement***, 1m/2km SW of Westhill. **54 D4** NJ8005.
Cairness *Aber.* ***Settlement***, 5m/7km SE of Fraserburgh. **65 F3** NK0360.
Cairney Lodge *Fife* ***Hamlet***, 1m/2km N of Cupar. **34 B3** NO3717.
Cairneyhill *Fife* Population: 2092. ***Village***, 3m/5km W of Dunfermline. **25 E1** NT0486.
Cairngarroch Bay *D. & G.* ***Bay***, on coast of Rinns of Galloway, 4m/6km SE of Portpatrick. **2 A2** NX0449.
Cairngorm Chairlift and Ski Centre *High.* ***Other feature of interest***, two-stage chairlift, 9m/13km SE of Aviemore, serving Britain's most popular ski resort. Lift operates from Cairngorm Day Lodge (2150 feet or 655 metres) to Ptarmigan Café (3600 feet or 1097 metres), below summit of Cairn Gorm. **52 B4** NH9805.
Cairngorm Mountains ***Large natural feature***, granite mountain mass with rounded summits within Grampian Mountains on borders of Aberdeenshire, Highland and Moray between Aviemore and Braemar. Popular with walkers, climbers and skiers. Deep defile of Lairig Ghru divides range into E and W parts. Summit is Ben Macdui, 4296 feet or 1309 metres. **52 B4** NJ0103.
Cairngorms National Nature Reserve ***Nature reserve***, largest nature reserve in Britain, in S part of Cairngorm Mountains, about 12m/16km NW of Braemar. Notable for sub-arctic summit plateau with arctic-alpine animal and plant communities. Wildlife includes eagles, buzzards, mountain hare, wild cat and deer. **52 B5** NN9396.
Cairngryffe Hill *S.Lan.* ***Mountain***, rising to over 330 metres with quarried SE face, 4m/6km SE of Lanark. **24 D5** NS9441.
Cairnharrow *D. & G.* ***Mountain***, 4m/7km W of Gatehouse of Fleet. Height 1496 feet or 456 metres. **7 G5** NX5355.
Cairnhill *Aber.* ***Settlement***, 1m/2km E of Kirkton of Culsalmond. **54 B1** NJ6632.
Cairnhill *Aber.* ***Settlement***, 2m/3km S of Ellon. **55 E2** NJ9427.
Cairnholy *D. & G.* ***Historic/prehistoric site***, chambered cairns (Historic Scotland), 4m/6km SE of Creetown. **7 G5** NX5153.
Cairnie *Aber.* ***Hamlet***, on N side of Burn of Cairnie, 4m/7km NW of Huntly. **63 G5** NJ4844.
Cairnkinna Hill *D. & G.* ***Mountain***, 5m/8km S of Sanquhar. Height 1811 feet or 552 metres. **15 F5** NS7901.

Cairnoch Hill *Stir.* ***Mountain***, overlooking N shore of Carron Valley Reservoir, 5m/8km E of Fintry. Height 1355 feet or 413 metres. **24 B1** NS6985.

Cairnorrie *Aber.* ***Settlement***, 4m/6km S of New Deer. **65 D5** NJ8641.

Cairnpapple Hill *W.Loth.* ***Hill***, rising to over 300 metres, 1m/2km SE of Torphichen. Henge and cairn (Historic Scotland) at summit. **25 D2** NS9871.

Cairnryan *D. & G.* ***Small town***, port on E side of Loch Ryan. Car ferry service to Larne in Northern Ireland. **6 B4** NX0668.

Cairns of Coll *Arg. & B.* ***Island***, two island rocks lying nearly 2m/3km NE of Coll. NM2866.

Cairnsmore *D. & G.* ***Settlement***, 4m/6km E of Newton Stewart. **7 F4** NX4764.

Cairnsmore of Carsphairn (Also known as Cairnsmore of Deugh.) *D. & G.* ***Mountain***, 4m/6km NE of Carsphairn. Height 2614 feet or 797 metres. **7 G1** NX5998.

Cairnsmore of Dee *D. & G.* ***Mountain***, 3m/5km W of New Galloway. Height 1617 feet or 493 metres. **7 G3** NX5875.

Cairnsmore of Deugh *D. & G. Alternative name for Cairnsmore of Carsphairn, qv.*

Cairnsmore of Fleet *D. & G.* ***Mountain***, massif 6m/9km E of Newton Stewart. Height 2329 feet or 710 metres. **7 F4** NX5067.

Cairntrodlie *Aber.* ***Suburb***, W district of Peterhead. NK1246.

Cairnwell Pass *P. & K.* ***Other feature of interest***, mountain pass to E of The Cairnwell, carrying road from Braemar to Spittal of Glenshee, is highest main road pass in Britain (2199 feet or 670 metres). NO1477.

Cairnywhing *Aber.* ***Open space***, hillslope with settlement, 1m/2km NW of New Pitsligo. **65 D4** NJ8757.

Caisteal Abhail *N.Ayr.* ***Mountain***, on Arran, 6m/9km NW of Brodick. Height 2818 feet or 859 metres. **22 A5** NR9644.

Caisteal Dubh *P. & K. See Moulin.*

Caisteal Maol (Anglicised form: Castle Moil.) *High.* ***Castle***, remains of 14c keep on Skye, to E of Kyleakin. **49 D2** NG7526.

Caiteshal *W.Isles* ***Mountain***, rising steeply on E shore of Loch Seaforth, 2m/3km N of entrance to loch. Height 1473 feet or 449 metres. **67 E3** NB2404.

Caithness Glass *High.* ***Other feature of interest***, displays and demonstrations on the history of local glass production at Wick. **77 F3** ND3651.

Caiy Stane *Edin.* ***Historic/prehistoric site***, ancient standing stone, National Trust for Scotland property, 4m/6km S of Edinburgh city centre. 9 feet or 3 metres high, with traces of cup marks on E side. **25 G3** NT2468.

Calabrie Island (Gaelic form: Eilean Chalaibrigh.) *W.Isles* ***Island***, islet at entrance to Loch Erisort, E coast of Isle of Lewis. NB3822.

Calair Burn *Stir.* ***River***, flowing N into head of Loch Voil at Balquhidder. **32 A3** NN5320.

Calanais *W.Isles Gaelic form of Callanish, qv.*

Calbha Beag (Anglicised form: Calva Beg). *High.* ***Island***, one of two small uninhabited islands in Eddrachillis Bay, along with Calbha Mòr, 3m/5km S of Badcall, W coast of Sutherland district. **74 A5** NC1536.

Calbha Mòr (Anglicised form: Calva Mòr.) *High.* ***Island***, one of two small uninhabited islands in Eddrachillis Bay, along with Calbha Beag, 3m/5km S of Badcall, W coast of Sutherland district. **74 A5** NC1636.

Calbost *W.Isles* ***Settlement***, on E coast of Isle of Lewis, 2m/4km N of Kebock Head across mouth of Loch Odhairn. **67 G2** NB4117.

Caldarvan *W.Dun.* ***Settlement***, 3m/5km NE of Balloch. **23 F1** NS4384.

Caldarvan Loch *W.Dun.* ***Lake/loch***, small loch 3m/5km NE of Alexandria. NS4283.

Caldback *Shet.* ***Settlement***, situated in centre of Unst, with chambered cairn and Hill of Caldback to SE. **85 F2** HP6007.

Calder *High.* ***River***, in Badenoch and Strathspey district, running E to River Spey 1m/2km SW of Newtonmore. NN7097.

Calder *Renf.* ***River***, rising as Calder Water on slopes N of Burnt Hill and flowing E and SE before widening into River Calder below weir to W of Muirshiel Country Park. River continues SE to Castle Semple Loch, to SE of Lochwinnoch. **23 E3** NS3558.

Calder Burn *High.* ***River***, flowing N down Glen Buck from N slopes of Aberchalder Forest, then flowing NE to enter Loch Oich just S of Aberchalder. NH3303.

Calder Dam *Inclyde* ***Reservoir***, small reservoir on border with Renfrewshire, 5m/8km SW of Kilmacolm. NS2965.

Calder Glen Country Park *S.Lan.* ***Leisure/recreation***, country park centred around Torrance House on Calder Water, 1m/2km E of East Kilbride town centre. 300 acres of grounds including parkland, children's zoo and several waterfalls. **24 A4** NS6552.

Calder Mains *High.* ***Hamlet***, 1km E of Loch Calder. **76 C3** ND0959.

Calder Water ***River***, rising as Calder Burn and running E into Avon Water, 1km below Caldermill and 3m/5km SW of Strathaven. NS6741.

Calder Water (Also known as Rotten Calder.) ***River***, rising S of East Kilbride and running NE into River Clyde 4m/6km E of Rutherglen. NS6761.

Calderbank *N.Lan.* Population: 1709. ***Village***, 2m/3km S of Airdrie. **24 B3** NS7763.

Caldercruix *N.Lan.* Population: 2292. ***Village***, 4m/7km NE of Airdrie. **24 C3** NS8267.

Calderglen *S.Lan.* ***Settlement***, 3m/5km NW of Hamilton. **24 A4** NS6859.

Caldermill *S.Lan.* ***Hamlet***, on Calder Water, 3m/5km SW of Strathaven. **24 A5** NS6641.

Calderpark Zoological Gardens (Glasgow Zoo). *Glas.* ***Leisure/recreation***, 6m/10km SE of Glasgow city centre, by North Calder Water. Regular animal displays, including birds of prey and snake handling. **24 A3** NS6862.

Calderwood *S.Lan.* ***Suburb***, to N of East Kilbride town centre. NS6455.

Caldhame *Angus* ***Hamlet***, 2m/3km S of Forfar. **42 C5** NO4748.

Caldwell *E.Renf.* ***Settlement***, 1m/2km SW of Uplawmoor. **23 F4** NS4154.

Caledonian Canal *High.* ***Canal***, ship canal built by Thomas Telford, connecting Moray Firth at Inverness to Loch Linnhe, through Lochs Ness, Oich, Lochy and mouth of Loch Eil. Nowadays used by small cargo boats and pleasure craft. **61 F5** NH6446.

Caledonian Railway *Angus* ***Other feature of interest***, tourist railway which runs 4m/6km from Victorian terminus at Brechin down a 1 in 70 gradient to Bridge of Dun, a junction of former Strathmore main line. **43 E4** NO6658.

Calf of Eday *Ork.* ***Island***, uninhabited island of about 750 acres or 300 hectares lying off NE coast of Eday, separated from it by narrow strait of Calf Sound. **81 D3** HY5839.

Calf of Flotta *Ork.* ***Island***, small uninhabited island off NE end of Flotta across narrow strait of Calf Sound. **78 C3** ND3896.

Calf Sound *Ork.* ***Sea feature***, narrow strait separating Calf of Eday from Eday. HY5638.

Calfsound *Ork.* ***Settlement***, at NE end of Eday. Uninhabited island of Calf of Eday to N across Calf Sound. **81 D3** HY5738.

Calgary *Arg. & B.* ***Village***, near W coast of Mull, at Calgary Bay. Emigrants from here gave Calgary in Alberta its name, Canada. **36 C4** NM3751.

Calgary Bay *Arg. & B.* ***Bay***, on W coast of Mull. **36 C5** NM3751.

Calgary Point *Arg. & B.* ***Coastal feature***, headland at SW end of Coll. **36 A4** NM0152.

Caliach Point *Arg. & B.* ***Coastal feature***, headland on W coast of Mull, 10m/16km W of Tobermory. **36 C4** NM3454.

Califer *Moray* ***Settlement***, 3m/4km E of Forres. **62 C4** NJ0857.

California *Falk.* ***Village***, 3m/5km SE of Falkirk. **24 D2** NS9076.

Calkin Rig (Also spelled Cauldkine Rig.) *D. & G.* ***Mountain***, 5m/8km NW of Langholm. Height 1476 feet or 450 metres. **9 G2** NY2987.

Callander *Stir.* Population: 2622. ***Small town***, 14m/22km NW of Stirling. Tourist centre on edge of Trossachs. **32 B4** NN6207.

Callanish (Gaelic form: Calanais.) *W.Isles* ***Village***, on W coast of Isle of Lewis, 13m/21km W of Stornoway and 1m/2km S of Breascleit. Callanish Standing stones (Historic Scotland). **68 D4** NB2133.

Callanish Standing Stones *W.Isles* ***Historic/prehistoric site***, thirty-nine standing stones (Historic Scotland), are ancient gravestones of uncertain date, near coast of Isle of Lewis at entrance to Loch Cean Thulabhig, 1m/2km S of Breascleit. **68 D4** NB2133.

Callater Burn *Aber.* ***River***, running N through Loch Callater and down Glen Callater to join Clunie Water 2m/3km S of Braemar. NO1588.

Callender House *Falk.* ***Historic house***, set in parkland to SE of Falkirk town centre. Contains a working kitchen of 1825 and an exhibition charting its 900 year history. **24 C2** NS8979.

Calligarry *High.* ***Settlement***, 1km W of Ardvasar, on E side of Sleat peninsula, Skye. **48 C4** NG6203.

Callisterhall *D. & G.* ***Settlement***, at head of Pokeskine Sike, 4m/6km NE of Waterbeck. **9 G2** NY2881.

Callop *High.* ***River***, flowing NW into head of Loch Shiel, to E of Glenfinnan. NM9080.

Calltraiseal Bheag (Anglicised form: Caultrashal Beag.) *W.Isles* ***Hill***, 1km E of head of Little Loch Roag, Isle of Lewis. Height 741 feet or 226 metres. **68 C5** NB1424.

Calltraiseal Mhòr (Anglicised form: Caultrashal Mòr.) *W.Isles* ***Hill***, 1m/2km SE of head of Little Loch Roag, Isle of Lewis. Height 748 feet or 228 metres. **68 C5** NB1522.

Callyburn *Arg. & B.* ***Settlement***, on Kintyre, 3m/4km N of Campbeltown. **12 C3** NR7225.

Calpa Mòr *High.* ***Mountain***, on Coignafearn Forest in Inverness district, 15m/25km NW of Newtonmore. Height 2670 feet or 814 metres. NH6610.

Calrossie *High.* ***Settlement***, 3m/4km SE of Tain. **61 G2** NH8077.

Calternish *W.Isles* ***Locality***, on E coast of South Uist, 4m/6km E of Geirninis. NF8341.

Calton *Glas.* ***Suburb***, 1m/2km SE of Glasgow city centre. NS6064.

Calton Hill *Edin.* ***Hill***, to E of Edinburgh city centre. National Monument, Nelson's Monument, City Observatory located here. Height 328 feet or 100 metres. NT2674.

Calva Beg *High. Anglicised form of Calbha Beag, qv.*

Calva Mòr *High. Anglicised form of Calbha Mòr, qv.*

Calvay *W.Isles* ***Island***, islet in Sound of Eriskay, off NE point of Eriskay. NF8112.

Calvay *W.Isles* ***Island***, small island with lighthouse on S side of entrance to Loch Baghasdail, South Uist. **46 B3** NF8218.

Calve Island *Arg. & B.* ***Island***, uninhabited island at entrance to Tobermory Bay, Mull. **37 E4** NM5254.

Calvine *P. & K.* ***Village***, near confluence of Errochty Water and River Garry, 4m/7km W of Blair Atholl. **40 D3** NN8065.

Calzeat *Sc.Bord.* ***Locality***, part of Broughton village, 4m/7km E of Biggar. NT1135.

Cam Chreag *P. & K.* ***Mountain***, 3m/5km NW of Bridge of Balgie. Height 2821 feet or 860 metres. **40 A5** NN5949.

Cam Creag *Stir.* ***Mountain***, 4m/6km NE of Tyndrum. Height 2900 feet or 884 metres. NN3734.

Cam Loch *Arg. & B.* ***Lake/loch***, small loch in Inverliever Forest, 4m/7km SE of Kilmelford. **30 B4** NM9009.

Cam Loch *Arg. & B.* ***Lake/loch***, small loch 3m/4km SW of Lochgilphead. **21 G1** NR8287.

Cam Loch *High.* ***Lake/loch***, loch in Sutherland district 6m/9km S of Inchnadamph. **71 E3** NC2113.

Cama' Choire *P. & K.* ***Valley***, carrying Allt a' Chama' Choire, with waterfalls to W, 5m/8km SE of Dalwhinnie. **40 B2** NN6978.

Camas Baravaig *High. See Baravaig.*

Camas Coille *High.* ***Sea feature***, small inlet on NE coast of Rubha Mòr peninsula, Ross and Cromarty district. **70 C3** NC0016.

Camas Cuil an t-Saimh *Arg. & B.* ***Bay***, wide bay on W coast of Iona. NM2623.

Camas Eilean Ghlais *High.* ***Bay***, small bay on W coast of Ross and Cromarty district, 4m/6km NW of Polbain. **70 B3** NB9615.

Camas Fhionnairigh *High.* ***Sea feature***, inlet of Loch Scavaig on S coast of Skye, 3m/5km N of Elgol. **48 B3** NG5118.

Camas Luinge *High.* ***Bay***, small bay with landing stage on S side of Loch Morar, Lochaber district, at mouth of River Meoble. NM7889.

Camas Mòr *High.* ***Bay***, to N of the mouth of River Kanaird, 4m/7km NW of Ullapool. **70 C4** NC1000.

Camas Mòr *High.* ***Bay***, small bay on coast of Ross and Cromarty district, 1m/2km E of Rubha Rèidh and 10m/16km NW of Poolewe. **70 A5** NG7591.

Camas Mòr *High.* ***Sea feature***, small inlet on W coast of Trotternish peninsula, Skye, 4m/7km SW of Rubha Hunish. **57 G2** NG3470.

Camas na Ceardaich *Arg. & B.* ***Bay***, small, shallow bay on NE coast of Kintyre, 5m/8km SE of Tarbert. **22 A3** NR9162.

Camas na Fisteodh *High.* ***Bay***, small bay on E coast of Scalpay, Skye and Lochalsh district. **48 C2** NG6328.

Camas nan Gall *High.* ***Bay***, on S coast of Soay, island off S coast of Skye. **48 A3** NG4514.

Camas Sandig *W.Isles* ***Bay***, small bay on W coast of Great Bernera, off W coast of Isle of Lewis. **68 C4** NB1338.

Camas Sgiotaig *High.* ***Bay***, on W coast of Eigg, N of Bay of Laig. NM4689.

Camas Shallachain *High.* ***Bay***, on W side of Sallachan Point, Lochaber district, and on W shore of Loch Linnhe. NM9862.

Camas Tharbernish *High.* ***Bay***, small bay on N coast of Canna, 2m/3km E of Garrisdale Point. **47 F4** NG2306.

Camas Uig *W.Isles* ***Bay***, on W coast of Isle of Lewis, 2m/3km W of Timsgearraidh. **68 B4** NB0233.

Camascross *High.* ***Settlement***, on bay of same name, on E coast of Sleat peninsula, Skye, 1km S of Eilean Iarmain. **48 D3** NG6911.

Camasnacroise *High.* ***Settlement***, in Lochaber district, 1km W of Rubha na h-Airde Uinnsinn. **38 A4** NM8652.

Camastianavaig *High.* ***Settlement***, on E coast of Skye, 3m/5km SE of Loch Portree. **48 B1** NG5039.

Camasunary *High.* ***Settlement***, on S coast of Skye, 3m/5km N of Elgol. **48 B3** NG5118.

Camault Muir *High.* ***Settlement***, in Inverness district, 4m/7km S of Beauly. **61 E5** NH5040.

Camb *Shet.* ***Hamlet***, on Yell, on N side of Mid Yell Voe. **85 E3** HU5192.

Cambo Ness *Fife* ***Coastal feature***, rocky headland 2m/4km NW of Fife Moss. **35 E3** NO6011.

Cambus *Clack.* ***Village***, 2m/3km W of Alloa. **33 D5** NS8593.

Cambus o'May *Aber.* ***Settlement***, 3m/5km NE of Ballater, on N side of River Dee. **53 G5** NO4198.

Cambusbarron *Stir.* ***Suburb***, 1m/2km W of Stirling. **32 C5** NS7792.
Cambuscurrie Bay *High.* ***Bay***, on S side of Dornoch Firth and E side of Edderton, Ross and Cromarty district. **61 G1** NH7285.
Cambushinnie Hill *Stir.* ***Hill***, 5m/8km N of Dunblane. Height 876 feet or 267 metres. **32 C4** NN7809.
Cambuskenneth *Stir.* ***Hamlet***, with remains of medieval abbey (Historic Scotland), 1km NE of Stirling across River Forth (footbridge). **32 D5** NS8094.
Cambuskenneth Abbey *Stir.* ***Ecclesiastical building***, ruins of abbey with fine detached tower (Historic Scotland) founded in 1147 for Augustinian canons, 1km E of Stirling town centre across loop in River Forth. Location of Robert the Bruce's Parliament and burial place of James III. **32 D5** NS8094.
Cambuslang *S.Lan.* ***Town***, on S bank of River Clyde, 5m/8km SE of Glasgow. Previously known for iron and steel manufacturing. **24 A3** NS6460.
Cambusnethan *N.Lan.* ***Suburb***, adjoining to E of Wishaw. **24 C4** NS8155.
Camchuart *Arg. & B.* ***Settlement***, 7m/11km N of Tighnabruaich. **22 A1** NR9985.
Camelon *Falk.* ***Locality***, residential and industrial area to W of Falkirk. **24 C1** NS8680.
Cameron *W.Dun.* ***Locality***, on Loch Lomond, 1km N of foot of loch. **23 E1** NS3782.
Cameron Burn *Fife* ***River***, stream which flows E from Cameron Reservoir to join with Kinaldy Burn to form Kenly Water, 4m/6km SE of St. Andrews and 3m/5km from where Kenly Water flows into North Sea. **34 D3** NO5411.
Cameron Reservoir *Fife* ***Reservoir***, small reservoir, 4m/7km SW of St. Andrews. **34 C3** NO4611.
Camerory *High.* ***Settlement***, 3m/4km N of Grantown-on-Spey. **52 C1** NJ0231.
Camghouran *P. & K.* ***Settlement***, on S side of Loch Rannoch, 8m/12km W of Kinloch Rannoch. **40 A4** NN5556.
Camis Eskan *Arg. & B.* ***Settlement***, 1km E of Craigendoran. **23 E1** NS3381.
Camlachie *Glas.* ***Suburb***, 2m/3km E of Glasgow city centre. NS6164.
Cammachmore *Aber.* ***Village***, 7m/12km S of Aberdeen. **55 E5** NO9094.
Cammoch Hill *P. & K.* ***Mountain***, 3m/4km NW of Pitlochry. Height 1391 feet or 424 metres. **41 D4** NN8959.
Camore *High.* ***Hamlet***, in Sutherland district, 1m/2km W of Dornoch. **72 C5** NH7790.
Campay *W.Isles* ***Island***, small uninhabited island off W coast of Isle of Lewis, 1m/2km N of Great Bernera. NB1442.
Campbelltown *High. Former name of Ardersier, qv.*
Campbeltown *Arg. & B.* Population: 5722. ***Small town***, chief town and port of Kintyre, at head of Campbeltown Loch, 30m/48km S of Tarbert. **12 C4** NR7120.
Campbeltown (Machrihanish) Airport *Arg. & B.* ***Airport/airfield***, to NE of Machrihanish beyond Machrihanish Water, on Kintyre peninsula. **12 B3** NR6320.
Campbeltown Loch *Arg. & B.* ***Sea feature***, sea-loch on Kintyre, to E of Cambeltown. **12 C4** NR7120.
Campbeltown Museum and Library *Arg. & B.* ***Other feature of interest***, in Campbeltown, on Kintyre, 12m/20km SW of Carradale, with exhibits on local history. **12 C4** NR7220.
Camperdown Country Park *Dundee* ***Leisure/recreation***, country park containing 500 acres of gardens, parkland and woodland with many rare trees, 3m/4km NW of Dundee city centre. Also includes wildlife centre with Scottish and European wildlife, golf course, adventure playground and nature trails. **34 B1** NO3632.
Camphill Reservoir *N.Ayr.* ***Reservoir***, 3m/5km W of Kilbirnie. **23 D4** NS2755.
Camphouse *High.* ***Settlement***, on Ardnamurchan peninsula, 1m/2km E of Kilchoan. **37 E3** NM5164.
Cample Water *D. & G.* ***River***, rising on Lowther Hills and running S, then W to River Nith on S side of Thornhill. NX8693.
Campmuir *P. & K.* ***Hamlet***, 2m/3km S of Coupar Angus. Site of Roman camp to SE. **34 A1** NO2137.
Camps *W.Loth.* ***Village***, 1km N of Kirknewton. NT1068.
Camps Reservoir *S.Lan.* ***Reservoir***, 3m/5km E of Crawford. **16 B3** NT0022.
Camps Water *S.Lan.* ***River***, issuing from Camps reservoir and flowing W to join River Clyde to N of Crawford. **16 A3** NS9521.
Campsie *E.Dun. Alternative name for Clachan of Campsie, qv.*
Campsie Fells ***Large natural feature***, range of hills E of Killearn. Summit is Earl's Seat at 578m, with other notable summits: Garloch Hill at 1781 feet or 543 metres; Holehead at 1807 feet or 551 metres; Lecket Hill at 1791 feet or 546 metres and Cort-ma Law at 1742 feet or 531 metres. Source of River Carron is on slopes 3m/4km N of Lennoxtown. **23 G1** NS5783.
Camptown *Sc.Bord.* ***Settlement***, on Jed Water, 5m/8km S of Jedburgh. **18 A5** NT6713.
Camsail *Arg. & B.* ***Settlement***, 2m/3km NE of Kilcreggan. **23 D1** NS2581.
Camserney *P. & K.* ***Village***, 2m/4km W of Aberfeldy. **40 D5** NN8149.
Camster Burn *High.* ***River***, rising to NE of Upper Camster and flowing N by Lower Camster to Rowens where it becomes Rowens Burn. **77 E4** ND2248.
Camstraddan *Arg. & B.* ***Settlement***, on W shore of Loch Lomond, 1km S of Luss. **31 F5** NS3692.
Camus Castle *High. Alternative name for Knock Castle, qv.*
Camus Croise *High.* ***Settlement***, adjoining to S of Eilean Iarmain, Skye. **48 C3** NG6911.
Camus-luinie *High.* ***Settlement***, in Skye and Lochalsh district, 4m/6km NE of Dornie. **49 F2** NG9428.
Camusdarrach *High.* ***Locality***, on coast of Lochaber district, 3m/5km N of Arisaig. NM6691.
Camusnagaul *High.* ***Settlement***, on S shore of Little Loch Broom, Ross and Cromarty district, 2m/3km from head of loch. **59 G1** NH0689.
Camusnagaul *High.* ***Settlement***, 1km N of Fort William across Loch Linnhe. **38 C2** NN0975.
Camusrory *High.* ***Settlement***, on N shore and near head of Loch Nevis, 6m/10km SE of Inverie, Lochaber district. **49 E5** NM8595.
Camusteel *High.* ***Settlement***, on W coast of Ross and Cromarty district, 1m/2km S of Applecross. **58 D5** NG7042.
Camusterrach *High.* ***Hamlet***, on W coast of Ross and Cromarty district, 2m/3km S of Applecross. **58 D5** NG7141.
Camusurich *P. & K.* ***Settlement***, on S side of Loch Tay, 4m/6km NE of Killin. **32 B1** NN6334.
Camusvrachan *P. & K.* ***Settlement***, in Glen Lyon, 3m/5km E of Bridge of Balgie. **40 B5** NN6247.
Camy *Ork.* ***Coastal feature***, rocky foreshore 1m/2km SW of narrow isthmus joining Deerness to SE part of Mainland. **79 E2** HY5401.
Candacraig *Aber.* ***Settlement***, 3m/5km NW of Ballater. **53 F5** NO3399.
Candy Mill *S.Lan.* ***Hamlet***, on Candy Burn, 3m/5km NE of Biggar. **25 E5** NT0741.
Canisbay *High.* ***Village***, near N coast of Caithness district, 4m/6km W of Duncansby Head. **77 F1** ND3472.
Canisp *High.* ***Mountain***, in Sutherland district 4m/6km SW of Inchnadamph. Height 2775 feet or 846 metres. **71 E3** NC2018.
Canna *High.* ***Island***, property of National Trust for Scotland in Inner Hebrides, 4m/6km NW of Rum. Nearly 5m/8km E to W and up to 1m/2km N to S. Crofting, lobster fishing. Harbour at E end. **47 F4** NG2405.
Canna Harbour *High.* ***Sea feature***, inlet separating Sanday and Canna. **47 F4** NG2804.
Cannich *High.* ***River***, rising from E end of Loch Mullardoch and initially flowing NE through a series of small lochs, then E and finally SE to enter River Glass just E of Cannich. **50 C1** NH3431.
Cannich *High.* ***Village***, in Inverness district, at confluence of Rivers Cannich and Glass, 7m/11km SW of Struy Bridge. **50 C1** NH3431.
Canonbie *D. & G.* ***Village***, on River Esk, 6m/9km S of Langholm. **10 B4** NY3976.
Canterbury *Aber.* ***Settlement***, 1m/2km NW of Cornhill and 4m/7km S of Portsoy. **64 A4** NJ5659.
Cantick Head *Ork.* ***Coastal feature***, headland on Hoy at E end of South Walls peninsula. Lighthouse on S side and beacon on N. **78 C4** ND3489.
Cantick Sound *Ork.* ***Sea feature***, strait between Cantick Head on South Walls peninsula on Hoy and Switha. ND3590.
Cantray *High.* ***Locality***, 1m/2km S of Croy. **61 G5** NH7948.
Cantraydoune *High.* ***Settlement***, 2m/3km SW of Croy. **61 G5** NH7846.
Cantraywood *High.* ***Settlement***, 1m/2km SW of Croy. **61 G5** NH7848.
Caol *High.* ***Village***, at head of Loch Linnhe in Lochaber district, 1m/2km N of Fort William. **38 D2** NN1076.
Caol Fladda *High.* ***Sea feature***, narrow channel separating Eilean Fladday from Raasay. NG5950.
Caol Ghleann *Arg. & B.* ***Valley***, narrow steep sided valley carrying upper River Ruel, 5m/8km SW of Strachur. **30 C5** NS0693.
Caol Ila *Arg. & B.* ***Other feature of interest***, distillery at Ruadh-phort Mòr to N of Port Askaig, Islay. NR4269.
Caol-loch *High.* ***Lake/loch***, small narrow loch, 1m/2km E of S end of Strathy Forest. **76 A3** NC8455.
Caol Lochan *Arg. & B.* ***Lake/loch***, small loch 3m/4km S of Tobermory, Mull. **37 E4** NM5150.
Caol Mòr *High. Alternative name for Kyle More, qv.*
Caol Rona *High. Alternative name for Kyle Rona, qv.*
Caol Scotnish *Arg. & B.* ***Sea feature***, long narrow arm of Loch Sween in Knapdale, Argyll, at N end of loch. NR7689.
Caolard Rubha *Arg. & B.* ***Coastal feature***, headland on Loch Fyne, 3m/5km SE of Lochgilphead in Argyll. **21 G1** NR8783.
Caolas *Arg. & B.* ***Settlement***, near E end of Tiree, 1km W of Rubha Dubh. **36 B2** NM0848.
Caolas *W.Isles* ***Settlement***, on N coast of Vatersay. **44 B4** NL6397.
Caolas a' Mhòrain *W.Isles* ***Sea feature***, stretch of sea separating Boreray from North Uist. **45 G1** NF8480.
Caolas a' Tuath *W.Isles* ***Sea feature***, stretch of sea separating Isle of Lewis from Eilean Iubhard, 1km S of Leumrabhagh. **67 F2** NB3810.
Caolas an Eilein *Arg. & B.* ***Sea feature***, strait between S coast of Islay and Texa. **20 B5** NR3944.
Caolas an Eilein *W.Isles* ***Sea feature***, stretch of sea separating Mealasta Island from Isle of Lewis. **68 A5** NA9821.
Caolas an Scarp *W.Isles* ***Sea feature***, narrow strait between Scarp and W coast of North Harris. **66 B2** NA9913.
Caolas Bàn *Arg. & B.* ***Sea feature***, strait dividing Gunna from Coll. **36 A4** NM1052.
Caolas Mòr *Arg. & B.* ***Sea feature***, strait separating Oronsay from Eilean Ghaoideamal and rocks to SW thereof. **20 B1** NR3687.
Caolas Mòr *High.* ***Sea feature***, stretch of sea separating Crowlin Islands from Scottish mainland. **48 C1** NG7035.
Caolas Port na Lice *Arg. & B.* ***Sea feature***, strait between Eilean Craobhach and SE coast of Islay, to S of Ardmore Point. NR4649.
Caolas Scalpaigh (Anglicised form: Kyles Scalpay.) *W.Isles* ***Settlement***, on N coast of East Loch Tarbert, opposite Scalpay. **67 E4** NG2198.
Caolas Scalpay *High.* ***Sea feature***, stretch of sea separating Scalpay from Skye. **48 C2** NG6027.
Caolasnacon *High.* ***Settlement***, on S side of Loch Leven, 3m/5km W of Kinlochleven. **38 D3** NN1360.
Cape Law *Sc.Bord.* ***Mountain***, rising to over 710 metres, 1m/2km NE of Hart Fell and 2m/3km SE of Fruid Reservoir. **16 C4** NT1315.
Cape Wrath *High.* ***Coastal feature***, headland with lighthouse at NW point of Sutherland district. **74 B1** NC2574.
Capel Fell ***Mountain***, on border of Dumfries & Galloway and Scottish Borders, 5m/8km E of Moffat. Height 2224 feet or 678 metres. **16 C5** NT1606.
Capel Water *D. & G.* ***River***, rising on S slopes of Earncraig Hill as Capel Burn and running S to join Water of Ae in Forest of Ae, 3m/5km N of Ae village. NX9893.
Caplaw *E.Renf.* ***Settlement***, 4m/7km SW of Paisley. **23 F4** NS4458.
Caplaw Dam *E.Renf.* ***Reservoir***, small reservoir 4m/6km W of Barrhead. NS4358.
Cappercleuch *Sc.Bord.* ***Locality***, on W shore of St. Mary's Loch, in Ettrick Forest. **16 D3** NT2423.
Capplegill *D. & G.* ***Hamlet***, 5m/8km NE of Moffat. **16 C5** NT1409.
Caputh *P. & K.* ***Village***, 4m/7km E of Dunkeld. **41 F5** NO0840.
Car Ness *Ork.* ***Coastal feature***, headland on Mainland, 2m/4km NE of Kirkwall. Oil service base. **80 C5** HY4614.
Cara Island *Arg. & B.* ***Island***, 1km S of Gigha. **21 E5** NR6344.
Carbellow *E.Ayr.* ***Settlement***, 3m/5km NE of Cumnock. **15 E3** NS6122.
Carberry Tower *E.Loth.* ***Historic house***, enlarged 16c house, now a Church of Scotland training centre, 2m/4km SE of Musselburgh. **26 A2** NT3669.
Carbeth *Stir.* ***Locality***, scattered settlement 2m/4km W of Strathblane. **23 G2** NS5379.
Carbeth Loch *Stir.* ***Lake/loch***, small loch 1km E of Carbeth. NS5379.
Carbisdale Castle *High.* ***Other building***, youth hostel in Kyle of Sutherland 3m/5km NW of Bonar Bridge, Sutherland district. **72 A5** NH5795.
Carbost *High.* ***Settlement***, 5m/8km NW of Portree, Skye. **58 A5** NG4248.
Carbost *High.* ***Village***, on SW shore of Loch Harport, Skye, 10m/16km SW of Portree. **47 G1** NG3731.
Carbrain *N.Lan.* ***Suburb***, central district of Cumbernauld. **24 B2** NS7674.
Carcary *Angus* ***Hamlet***, 4m/6km SE of Brechin. **43 E4** NO6455.
Carco *D. & G.* ***Settlement***, 3m/4km N of Sanquhar. **15 F4** NS7813.
Cardenden *Fife* Population: 5390. ***Village***, 4m/7km NE of Cowdenbeath. **34 A5** NT2195.
Cardno *Aber.* ***Locality***, comprises Easter Cardno, Wester Cardno, Mains of Cardno and Ord of Cardno, 2m/3km SW of Fraserburgh. **65 E3** NJ9664.
Cardonald *Glas.* ***Suburb***, on S side of River Clyde, 4m/6km W of Glasgow city centre. NS5264.
Cardoness *D. & G.* ***Settlement***, on W shore of Fleet Bay, 3m/4km SW of Gatehouse of Fleet. **7 G5** NX5653.
Cardoness Castle *D. & G.* ***Castle***, ruined 15c tower of the McCullochs (Historic Scotland), 1m/2km SW of Gatehouse of Fleet. **7 G5** NX5955.
Cardow *Moray* ***Hamlet***, 6m/10km W of Craigellachie. **63 D5** NJ1942.
Cardrona *Sc.Bord.* ***Settlement***, 3m/4km NW of Innerleithen. **17 D2** NT2938.
Cardrona Forest *Sc.Bord.* ***Forest/woodland***, 2m/3km W of Innerleithen across River Tweed. Ruined tower of Cardrona on NE edge of forest. **17 D2** NT3036.

Cardross *Arg. & B.* Population: 1958. ***Village***, on N side of Firth of Clyde, 3m/5km NW of Dumbarton. Robert the Bruce died here from leprosy in 1329. 18c novelist Tobias Smollett born here. **23 E2** NS3477.
Careston *Angus* ***Settlement***, 4m/7km W of Brechin. **42 D3** NO5360.
Careston Castle *Angus* ***Castle***, mainly 15c, 4m/7km W of Brechin. NO5359.
Carfin *N.Lan.* ***Village***, 2m/3km NE of Motherwell. Contains Carfin Grotto. NS7758.
Carfin Grotto *N.Lan.* ***Ecclesiastical building***, within Carfin, 2m/3km NE of Motherwell. Replica of Grotto of Our Lady of Lourdes, created in 1920; a place of pilgrimage. **24 B4** NS7758.
Carfrae *E.Loth.* ***Hamlet***, 1m/2km N of Danskine. **26 C3** NT5769.
Carfraemill *Sc.Bord.* ***Settlement***, with hotel, 4m/6km NW of Lauder. **26 C4** NT5153.
Cargen *D. & G.* ***Settlement***, 2m/4km S of Dumfries. **9 D3** NX9672.
Cargen Water *D. & G.* ***River***, stream flowing E then SE to River Nith, 2m/4km S of Dumfries. NX9772.
Cargenbridge *D. & G.* ***Village***, on Cargen Water, 1m/2km SW of Dumfries. **9 D3** NX9574.
Cargill *P. & K.* ***Hamlet***, on River Tay, 5m/8km W of Coupar Angus. **33 G1** NO1536.
Carie *P. & K.* ***Settlement***, on S side of Loch Rannoch, 3m/4km SW of Kinloch Rannoch. **40 B4** NN6157.
Carie *P. & K.* ***Settlement***, just N of Loch Tay, 6m/9km NE of Killin. **32 B1** NN6437.
Carinish *W.Isles Anglicised form of Cairinis, qv.*
Carishader *W.Isles Anglicised form of Cairisiadar, qv.*
Carity Burn *Angus* ***River***, stream rising NE of Loch of Lintrathen and flowing E to River South Esk, 4m/6km NE of Kirriemuir. **42 B4** NO4257.
Carlabhagh *W.Isles Gaelic form of Carloway, qv.*
Carleton Castle *S.Ayr.* ***Castle***, ruined medieval castle on S side of Lendalfoot. NX1389.
Carleton Fishery *S.Ayr.* ***Settlement***, at end of Carleton Bay, 5m/8km NE of Ballantrae. **6 C2** NX1289.
Carlin Tooth *Sc.Bord.* ***Mountain***, in Cheviot Hills, 3m/4km E of Note o' the Gate. Height 1807 feet or 551 metres. **11 E1** NT6302.
Carlingheugh Bay *Angus* ***Bay***, small bay 2m/3km NE of Arbroath. **43 E5** NO6742.
Carlingwark Loch *D. & G.* ***Lake/loch***, loch on S side of Castle Douglas. Haunt of wildfowl. **8 B4** NX7661.
Carlin's Cairn *D. & G.* ***Mountain***, rising to over 800 metres, 9m/14km NW of St. John's Town of Dalry. **7 F2** NX4988.
Carlock Hill *S.Ayr.* ***Mountain***, 3m/5km S of Ballantrae. Height 1046 feet or 319 metres. **6 B3** NX0877.
Carlops *Sc.Bord.* ***Village***, on E side of Pentland Hills, 3m/5km N of West Linton. **25 F4** NT1655.
Carloway *W.Isles* ***River***, rising among lochs to S of Carloway and flowing into Loch Carlabhagh, on W coast of Isle of Lewis. NB2042.
Carloway (Gaelic form: Carlabhagh.) *W.Isles* ***Village***, near W coast of Isle of Lewis at head of estuary of Carloway River, which rises among lochs to S. **68 D3** NB2042.
Carluke *S.Lan.* Population: 12,921. ***Town***, 5m/8km NW of Lanark. **24 C4** NS8450.
Carlungie *Angus* ***Settlement***, 2m/4km N of Monifieth, including ancient souterrain or earth-house (Historic Scotland). NO5135.
Carlyle's Birthplace *D. & G.* ***Historic house***, at Ecclefechan. Known as The Arched House and birthplace of Thomas Carlyle, scholar and Victorian thinker, in 1795. Now a museum (National Trust for Scotland). **9 F3** NY1974.
Carmacoup *S.Lan.* ***Settlement***, 1m/2km SW of Glespin. **15 F3** NS7927.
Carman Reservoir *W.Dun.* ***Reservoir***, small reservoir 1km W of Renton, to NW of Dumbarton. NS3778.
Carmichael *S.Lan.* ***Settlement***, 3m/5km W of Thankerton. NS9339.
Carminish *W.Isles Anglicised form of Cairminis, qv.*
Carminish Islands *W.Isles* ***Island***, group of islets off S coast of South Harris about 3m/5km NW of Renish Point. **66 B5** NG0185.
Carmont *Aber.* ***Hamlet***, 4m/7km W of Stonehaven. **43 G1** NO8184.
Carmunnock *Glas.* ***Village***, 3m/5km NW of East Kilbride. **24 A4** NS5957.
Carmyle *Glas.* ***Suburb***, on N bank of River Clyde, 4m/7km SE of Glasgow. **24 A3** NS6561.
Carmyllie *Angus* ***Locality***, 6m/10km W of Arbroath. **42 D5** NO5442.
Carn *Arg. & B.* ***Settlement***, on SE coast of Rinns of Islay, 1m/2km SW of Port Charlotte. **20 A4** NR2457.
Carn a' Bhacain *Aber.* ***Mountain***, 7m/11km NW of Ballater. Height 2440 feet or 744 metres. **53 E4** NJ2904.
Carn a' Bhodaich *High.* ***Mountain***, in Inverness district, 6m/10km NE of Drumnadrochit. Height 1643 feet or 501 metres. **51 E1** NH5737.
Carn a' Bhodaich *Moray* ***Mountain***, 8m/13km W of Cabrach. Height 2148 feet or 655 metres. **53 E2** NJ2628.
Carn a' Chaochain *High.* ***Mountain***, in Inverness district, 5m/8km NW of Dalchreichart. Height 2316 feet or 706 metres. **50 B3** NH2318.
Carn a' Chlamain *P. & K.* ***Mountain***, in Forest of Atholl, 7m/11km NE of Blair Atholl. Munro: height 3159 feet or 963 metres. **41 E2** NN9175.
Carn a' Choin Deirg *High.* ***Mountain***, in Sutherland district, 6m/9km S of Oykel Bridge. Height 2299 feet or 701 metres. **71 F5** NH3992.
Carn a' Choire Bhuidhe *High.* ***Mountain***, in Inverness district 4m/7km N of dam of Loch Cluanie. Height 2778 feet or 847 metres. **50 A3** NH1817.
Carn a' Choire Ghairbh *High.* ***Mountain***, on Glenaffric Forest, Inverness district, 2m/3km S of head of Loch Affric. Height 2837 feet or 865 metres. NH1318.
Carn a' Choire Ghlaise *High.* ***Mountain***, in Inverness district 11m/17km E of Fort Augustus. Height 2555 feet or 779 metres. **51 E4** NH5408.
Carn a' Choire Mhòir *High.* ***Mountain***, in Inverness district, 3m/4km E of Tomatin. Height 2057 feet or 627 metres. **52 A2** NH8429.
Carn a' Chrasgie *High.* ***Mountain***, in Nairn district, 5m/7km S of Cawdor. Height 1315 feet or 401 metres. **62 A5** NH8643.
Carn a' Chuilinn *High.* ***Mountain***, on Glendoe Forest, Inverness district, 4m/6km SE of Fort Augustus. Height 2676 feet or 816 metres. **50 D4** NH4103.
Carn a' Coire Bhoidheach *Aber.* ***Mountain***, peak to NW of White Mounth, 3m/5km NW of Loch Muick. Munro: height 3641 feet or 1110 metres. **42 A1** NO2284.
Carn a' Ghaill *High.* ***Hill***, highest point of Canna, 1km N of A' Chill. Height 689 feet or 210 metres. **47 F4** NG2606.
Carn a' Gheoidh ***Mountain***, on border of Aberdeenshire and Perth & Kinross, 4m/7km N of Spittal of Glenshee. Munro: height 3198 feet or 975 metres. **41 G2** NO1076.
Carn a' Ghlinne *High.* ***Mountain***, rounded summit in Ross and Cromarty district, on NE side of Glen Docherty, 2m/4km E of Kinlochewe. Height 1768 feet or 539 metres. **59 G3** NH0660.
Carn a' Mhadaidh-ruaidh *High.* ***Mountain***, 3m/5km NE of Arisaig. Height 1650 feet or 503 metres. **37 G1** NM7088.
Carn a' Mhaim *Aber.* ***Mountain***, in Cairngorm Mountains 2m/4km S of Ben Macdui. Munro: height 3401 feet or 1037 metres. **52 B5** NN9995.
Carn a' Mhuilt *High.* ***Mountain***, rounded summit on NW side of Strathglass, 3m/5km N of Cannich. Height 2171 feet or 662 metres. **50 C1** NH3436.
Carn Ait *P. & K.* ***Mountain***, 3m/5km NE of Spittal of Glenshee. Height 2834 feet or 864 metres. **41 G2** NO1473.
Carn an Daimh *P. & K.* ***Mountain***, 2m/3km NE of Spittal of Glenshee. Height 2476 feet or 755 metres. **41 G2** NO1371.
Carn an Fhidhleir (Anglicised form: Carn Ealar.) ***Mountain***, on borders of Aberdeenshire, Highland and Perth & Kinross, 12m/19km N of Blair Atholl. Munro: height 3260 feet or 994 metres. **41 E1** NN9084.
Carn an Fhidhleir Lorgaidh *High.* ***Mountain***, on Glenfeshie Forest in Badenoch and Strathspey district, 10m/16km SE of Kingussie. Height 2785 feet or 849 metres. **41 D1** NN8587.
Carn an Fhreiceadain *High.* ***Mountain***, in Monadhliath range in Badenoch and Strathspey district, 5m/7km NW of Kingussie. Height 2880 feet or 878 metres. **51 G4** NH7207.
Carn an Leanaidh *High.* ***Mountain***, in Ross and Cromarty district, 4m/6km NW of Inverchoran. Height 1883 feet or 574 metres. **60 B4** NH2154.
Carn an Leth-choin *High.* ***Mountain***, in Badenoch and Strathspey district, 5m/8km W of Newtonmore. Height 2765 feet or 843 metres. **51 F5** NN6299.
Carn an Righ *P. & K.* ***Mountain***, 7m/11km NW of Spittal of Glenshee. Munro: height 3375 feet or 1029 metres. **41 F2** NO0277.
Carn an t-Sagairt Mòr (Also known as Cairn Taggart). *Aber.* ***Mountain***, 6m/9km SE of Braemar. Munro: height 3434 feet or 1047 metres. **42 A1** NO2084.
Carn an t-Sean-liathanaich *High.* ***Mountain***, on borders of Inverness and Nairn districts, 15m/24km S of Nairn. Height 2083 feet or 635 metres. **52 A1** NH8632.
Carn an t-Suidhe *Moray* ***Mountain***, 6m/10km SE of foot of Glenlivet. Height 2401 feet or 732 metres. **53 E2** NJ2626.
Carn an Tionail *High.* ***Mountain***, 1km E of Carn Dearg. Height 2490 feet or 759 metres. **74 C5** NC3939.
Carn an Tuirc *Aber.* ***Mountain***, 7m/11km S of Braemar. Munro: height 3342 feet or 1019 metres. **41 G1** NO1780.
Carn Aosda *Aber.* ***Mountain***, 8m/12km S of Braemar. Munro: height 3008 feet or 917 metres. **41 G2** NO1379.
Carn Bad na Caorach *High.* ***Mountain***, 4m/7km N of Grantown-on-Spey. Height 1565 feet or 477 metres. **52 C1** NJ0335.
Carn Bàn *Arg. & B.* ***Hill***, 1m/2km NW of Rubha na Faoilinn, Mull. Height 813 feet or 248 metres. **29 G2** NM7228.
Carn Bàn *High.* ***Mountain***, in Inverness district, 6m/10km N of Cannich. Height 2414 feet or 736 metres. **60 C5** NH3341.
Carn Bàn *High.* ***Mountain***, in Freevater Forest in Ross and Cromarty district, 5m/8km N of Loch Vaich. Height 2772 feet or 845 metres. **60 C1** NH3387.
Carn Bàn *High.* ***Mountain***, in Monadhliath range, on border of Inverness and Badenoch and Strathspey districts, 6m/9km NW of Newtonmore. Height 3090 feet or 942 metres. **51 F4** NH6303.
Carn Ban *N.Ayr.* ***Historic/prehistoric site***, long cairn (Historic Scotland) on Arran, 4m/6km W of Whiting Bay. NR9926.
Carn Bàn Mòr *High.* ***Mountain***, in Badenoch and Strathspey district in W part of Cairngorm Mountains, 7m/11km SE of Kincraig. Height 3451 feet or 1052 metres. **52 A5** NN8997.
Carn Beag *High.* ***Mountain***, in Ledgowan Forest, Ross and Cromarty district, 4m/6km SW of Achnasheen. Height 1804 feet or 550 metres. **60 A4** NH1055.
Carn Beag Dearg *High. See Carn Mòr Dearg.*
Carn Bhac ***Mountain***, on border of Aberdeenshire and Perth & Kinross, 5m/8km SW of Inverey. Munro: height 3018 feet or 920 metres. **41 F1** NO0482.
Carn Bheadhair *High.* ***Mountain***, 6m/10km SE of Nethy Bridge. Height 2634 feet or 803 metres. **52 C3** NJ0511.
Carn Bhrain *High.* ***Mountain***, in Sutherland district, 6m/9km SW of Bonar Bridge. Height 2083 feet or 635 metres. **61 E1** NH5287.
Carn Breac *High.* ***Mountain***, in Ross and Cromarty district, 4m/6km NE of Achnashellach Station. Height 2224 feet or 678 metres. **59 G4** NH0453.
Carn Caol *High.* ***Mountain***, on border of Inverness and Badenoch and Strathspey districts, 9m/15km N of Kingussie. Height 2339 feet or 713 metres. **51 G3** NH7616.
Carn Cas nan Gabhar *High.* ***Mountain***, in Ross and Cromarty district, 10m/16km NW of Alness. Height 1975 feet or 602 metres. **61 E1** NH5280.
Carn Chaiseachain *High.* ***Mountain***, low, rounded summit in Ross and Cromarty district on S side of Strath Bran, 5m/9km NE of Achnasheen. Height 1023 feet or 312 metres. **60 B3** NH2560.
Carn Chòis *P. & K.* ***Mountain***, on W side of Loch Turret Reservoir. Height 2578 feet or 786 metres. **32 C2** NN7927.
Carn Chrom *Moray* ***Mountain***, 4m/6km S of Dufftown. Height 1650 feet or 503 metres. **53 F1** NJ3333.
Carn Chuinneag *High.* ***Mountain***, in Diebidale Forest on border of Ross and Cromarty and Sutherland districts, 5m/7km NW of head of Loch Morie. Height 2749 feet or 838 metres. **61 D1** NH4883.
Carn Coire na Creiche *High.* ***Mountain***, in Inverness district, 9m/13km NW of Newtonmore. Height 2709 feet or 826 metres. **51 F4** NH6108.
Carn Coire na h-Easgainn *High.* ***Mountain***, in Monadhliath range, on border of Inverness and Badenoch and Strathspey districts, 8m/13km N of Kingussie. Height 2591 feet or 790 metres. **51 G3** NH7313.
Carn Crom *Aber.* ***Mountain***, in Grampian Mountains, 6m/9km NW of Inverey. Height 2919 feet or 890 metres. **52 C5** NO0295.
Carn Daimh *Moray* ***Mountain***, to E of Strath Avon and 2m/3km W of Tomnavoulin. Height 1837 feet or 560 metres. **53 D2** NJ1824.
Carn Daraich *High.* ***Mountain***, in Ross and Cromarty district, 5m/8km NE of Achnasheen. Height 1525 feet or 465 metres. **60 B3** NH2363.
Carn Dearg ***Mountain***, on border of Highland and Perth & Kinross, 3m/5km E of head of Loch Ossian. Munro: height 3086 feet or 941 metres. **39 G3** NN4166.
Carn Dearg *High.* ***Mountain***, 4m/6km N of Loch Merkland. Height 2611 feet or 796 metres. **74 C5** NC3738.
Carn Dearg *High.* ***Mountain***, summit of Monadhliath range, in Badenoch and Strathspey district, 8m/12km W of Kingussie. Munro: height 3100 feet or 945 metres. **51 F4** NH6302.
Carn Dearg *High.* ***Mountain***, NW and SW peaks of Ben Nevis, in Lochaber district. Height of NW peak 3975 feet or 1212 metres; height of SW peak 3347 feet or 1020 metres. **39 D2** NN1572.
Carn Dearg *High.* ***Mountain***, in Lochaber district 7m/11km NE of Roybridge. Height 2736 feet or 834 metres. **39 F1** NN3488.
Carn Dearg *High.* ***Mountain***, in Lochaber district 4m/6km E of NE end of Loch Lochy. Height 2673 feet or 815 metres. **50 C5** NN3496.
Carn Dearg *High.* ***Mountain***, rising E side of above Glen Turret, 4m/7km of NE end of Loch Lochy. Height 2519 feet or 768 metres. NN3594.
Carn Dearg *High.* ***Mountain***, in Badenoch and Strathspey district, 10m/16km SW of Dalwhinnie. Munro: height 3392 feet or 1034 metres. **40 A2** NN5076.
Carn Dearg *High.* ***Settlement***, 3m/4km W of Gairloch, in Ross and Cromarty district. **59 D2** NG7677.

Carn Dearg Mòr *High.* ***Mountain***, in Badenoch and Strathspey district, 2m/3km E of Aviemore. Height 2335 feet or 712 metres. **52 A3** NH8613.
Carn Dearg Mòr *High.* ***Mountain***, in Badenoch and Strathspey district, 7m/11km SE of Kingussie. Height 2811 feet or 857 metres. **52 A5** NN8291.
Carn Deas *High.* ***Island***, small island in Summer Isles group. Adjacent to and E of Carn Iar, Carn Deas lies less than 1km SW of Eilean Dubh. NB9602.
Carn Dubh'Ic an Deòir *High.* ***Mountain***, on border of Inverness and Badenoch and Strathspey districts, 9m/14km NW of Aviemore. Height 2460 feet or 750 metres. **51 G3** NH7719.
Carn Duchan *Arg. & B.* ***Mountain***, 3m/5km SE of Kilmelford. Height 1610 feet or 491 metres. **30 A4** NM8910.
Carn Dulnan *High.* ***Mountain***, rising to over 740 metres in Badenoch and Strathspey district, 6m/10km N of Kingussie. **51 G3** NH7510.
Carn Eachie *High.* ***Mountain***, on Hills of Cromdale, 5m/8km N of Bridge of Brown. Height 2296 feet or 700 metres. **52 D2** NJ1328.
Carn Ealar *Anglicised form of Carn an Fhidhleir, qv.*
Carn Ealasaid ***Mountain***, on border of Aberdeenshire and Moray, 6m/9km SE of Tomintoul. Height 2598 feet or 792 metres. **53 E3** NJ2211.
Carn Eas *Aber.* ***Mountain***, in Grampian Mountains, 5m/8km NW of Braemar. Height 3572 feet or 1089 metres. **52 D5** NO1299.
Carn Easgann Bàna *High.* ***Mountain***, in Inverness district, 7m/11km E of Fort Augustus. Height 2552 feet or 778 metres. **51 D4** NH4806.
Carn Eige *High.* ***Mountain***, on border of Inverness and Skye and Lochalsh districts, 3m/5km N of Loch Affric. Munro: height 3880 feet or 1183 metres. **50 A2** NH1226.
Carn Eilrig *High.* ***Mountain***, in Badenoch and Strathspey district, to S of Rothiemurchus and 5m/8km SE of Aviemore. Height 2434 feet or 742 metres. **52 B4** NH9305.
Carn Eiteige *High.* ***Mountain***, peak on East Monar Forest, Ross and Cromarty district, 2m/4km N of dam of Loch Monar. Height 2893 feet or 882 metres. **60 B5** NH2143.
Carn Fliuch-bhaid *High.* ***Mountain***, in Inverness district, 12m/20km SE of Foyers. Height 2152 feet or 656 metres. **51 E3** NH5512.
Carn Geuradainn *High.* ***Mountain***, in Attadale Forest, 4m/6km E of Attadale. Height 1948 feet or 594 metres. **49 F1** NG9839.
Carn Ghiubhais *Moray* ***Mountain***, 6m/10km NE of Dava. Height 1410 feet or 430 metres. **62 C5** NJ0845.
Carn Ghluasaid *High.* ***Mountain***, peak on border of Inverness and Skye and Lochalsh districts, 3m/5km NW of dam of Loch Cluanie. Munro: height 3139 feet or 957 metres. **50 A3** NH1412.
Carn Ghriogair *High.* ***Mountain***, in Inverness district, 15m/24km NW of Newtonmore. Height 2640 feet or 805 metres. **51 F2** NH6520.
Carn Glac an Eich *High.* ***Mountain***, in Inverness district, 16m/26km N of Newtonmore. Height 2070 feet or 631 metres. **51 F2** NH6926.
Carn Glas-choire *High.* ***Mountain***, on borders of Inverness, Nairn and Badenoch and Strathspey districts, 4m/6km N of Carrbridge. Height 2162 feet or 659 metres. **52 A2** NH8928.
Carn Gorm *High.* ***Mountain***, on Glencarron and Glenuig Forest, Ross and Cromarty district, 6m/9km S of Achnasheen. Height 2870 feet or 875 metres. **60 A4** NH1350.
Carn Gorm *High.* ***Mountain***, in Inverness district, 3m/4km N of Cannich. Height 2217 feet or 676 metres. **50 C1** NH3235.
Carn Gorm *High.* ***Mountain***, in Ross and Cromarty district, 4m/6km E of Gorstan. Height 1824 feet or 556 metres. **60 D3** NH4362.
Càrn Gorm *P. & K.* ***Mountain***, 6m/9km S of Kinloch Rannoch. Munro: height 3375 feet or 1029 metres. **40 B4** NN6350.
Carn Iar *High.* ***Island***, small island in Summer Isles group. Lies 1km SW of Eilean Dubh. NB9602.
Carn Icean Duibhe *High.* ***Mountain***, in Monadhliath range, on border of Inverness and Badenoch and Strathspey districts, 7m/12km NW of Kingussie. Height 2650 feet or 808 metres. **51 G3** NH7111.
Carn Kitty *Moray* ***Mountain***, 6m/9km NE of Dava. Height 1709 feet or 521 metres. **62 C5** NJ0842.
Carn Leac *High.* ***Mountain***, on borders of Inverness, Lochaber, and Badenoch and Strathspey districts, 7m/12km S of Fort Augustus. Height 2900 feet or 884 metres. **50 D5** NN4097.
Carn Leac Saighdeir *Aber.* ***Mountain***, 1m/2km S of Corgarff. Height 2293 feet or 699 metres. **53 E4** NJ2706.
Carn Liath *Aber.* ***Mountain***, on border of Aberdeenshire and Moray, 6m/10km W of Strathdon. Height 2598 feet or 792 metres. **53 E3** NJ2515.
Carn Liath *Aber.* ***Mountain***, 4m/6km SW of Inverey. Height 2683 feet or 818 metres. **41 F1** NO0386.
Carn Liath *Aber.* ***Mountain***, in Grampian Mountains, 4m/6km N of Braemar. Height 2827 feet or 862 metres. **53 D5** NO1697.
Carn Liath *High.* ***Historic/prehistoric site***, chambered cairn 1m/2km S of Eyre, Skye. **58 A4** NG4151.
Carn Liath *High.* ***Mountain***, in Ross and Cromarty district, forming twin summit with Carn Gorm in Glencarron and Glenuig Forest, 8m/12km W of Inverchoran. Height 2811 feet or 857 metres. **60 A4** NH1350.
Carn Liath *High.* ***Mountain***, in Badenoch and Strathspey district, 4m/6km W of head of Loch Laggan. Munro: height 3300 feet or 1006 metres. **51 D5** NN4790.
Carn Liath *Moray* ***Mountain***, to E of Strath Avon and 2m/3km W of Tomnavoulin. Height 1801 feet or 549 metres. **53 D2** NJ1726.
Carn Liath *P. & K.* ***Mountain***, SW shoulder of Beinn a' Ghlo, 7m/12km N of Pitlochry. Munro: height 3198 feet or 975 metres. **41 E3** NN9369.
Carn Loisgte *High.* ***Mountain***, rounded summit in Ross and Cromarty district, 8m/12km W of Achnasheen. Height 1463 feet or 446 metres. **59 G4** NH0357.
Carn Macsna *High.* ***Mountain***, in Inverness district, 4m/6km SW of Drumnadrochit. Height 1722 feet or 525 metres. **50 D2** NH4427.
Càrn Mairg *P. & K.* ***Mountain***, 5m/8km S of Kinloch Rannoch. Munro: height 3418 feet or 1042 metres. **40 B4** NN6851.
Carn Màiri *High.* ***Mountain***, 1km NE of mouth of River Barrisdale, near S shore of Loch Hourn. Height 1647 feet or 502 metres. **49 E4** NG8805.
Carn Meadhonach *Moray* ***Mountain***, 2m/3km W of Tomintoul. Height 1929 feet or 588 metres. **52 D3** NJ1317.
Carn Mhartuin *High.* ***Mountain***, rounded summit in Ross and Cromarty district, 5m/8km S of Achnasheen. Height 1765 feet or 538 metres. **60 A4** NH1754.
Carn Mhic an Toisich *High.* ***Mountain***, in Dundreggan Forest, Ross and Cromarty district, 3m/5km N of Dundreggan. Height 2230 feet or 680 metres. **50 C3** NH3118.
Carn Mhic Raonuill *High.* ***Mountain***, rounded summit in Inverness district, 5m/8km W of Fort Augustus. Height 1856 feet or 566 metres. **50 B4** NH2908.
Carn Mòr *Arg. & B.* ***Mountain***, on Mull, 2m/3km N of Kilninian. Height 1122 feet or 342 metres. **36 D5** NM3948.
Carn Mòr *High.* ***Hill***, 1km S of Farquhar's Point, Lochaber district. Height 400 feet or 122 metres. **37 F2** NM6271.
Carn Mòr *High.* ***Mountain***, in Ross and Cromarty district, 10m/14km SE of Ullapool. Height 2129 feet or 649 metres. **60 B1** NH2486.
Carn Mòr *High.* ***Mountain***, rounded summit in Ross and Cromarty district, 6m/10km NE of Gorstan. Height 2099 feet or 640 metres. **60 D2** NH4271.
Carn Mòr *High.* ***Mountain***, rocky summit in Inverness district, 5m/8km NW of Drumnadrochit. Height 1496 feet or 456 metres. **50 D1** NH4334.
Carn Mòr *High.* ***Mountain***, 3m/4km E of head of Loch Morar, Lochaber district. Height 2719 feet or 829 metres. **49 F5** NM9090.
Carn Mòr *Moray* ***Mountain***, highest point of Ladder Hills, 6m/10km E of Tomintoul. Height 2637 feet or 804 metres. **53 E3** NJ2618.
Carn Mòr Dearg *High.* ***Mountain***, in Lochaber district 1m/2km NE of Ben Nevis. Munro: height 4011 feet or 1223 metres. Carn Beag Dearg, 1m/2km along ridge to NW, 3264 feet or 995 metres. **39 D2** NN1772.
Carn na Béiste *High.* ***Hill***, 4m/6km S of entrance to Little Loch Broom, Ross and Cromarty district. Height 991 feet or 302 metres. **59 F1** NG9989.
Carn na Bèiste *High.* ***Mountain***, in Ross and Cromarty district, at E end of Loch Fannich and 2m/3km NE of Achanalt. Height 1699 feet or 518 metres. **60 B3** NH2864.
Carn na Cailliche *Moray* ***Mountain***, 3m/4km N of Upper Knockando. Height 1325 feet or 404 metres. **63 D5** NJ1847.
Carn na Caim ***Mountain***, on border of Highland and Perth & Kinross, 3m/5km SE of Dalwhinnie. Munro: height 3086 feet or 941 metres. **40 B1** NN6782.
Carn na Cloiche Mòire *High.* ***Mountain***, in Ross and Cromarty district, 10m/16km NW of Beauly. Height 1938 feet or 591 metres. **60 C4** NH3753.
Carn na Cóinnich *High.* ***Mountain***, in Ross and Cromarty district, 2m/3km N of W end of Orrin Reservoir. Height 2207 feet or 673 metres. **60 C4** NH3251.
Carn na Crè *High.* ***Mountain***, in Ross and Cromarty district, 2m/3km N of Milton. Height 1499 feet or 457 metres. **60 C4** NH3059.
Carn na Drochaide *Aber.* ***Mountain***, in Grampian Mountains, 3m/4km NW of Braemar. Height 2683 feet or 818 metres. **52 D5** NO1293.
Carn na Dubh Choille *High.* ***Mountain***, in Ross and Cromarty district, 3m/5km N of Gorstan. Height 1571 feet or 479 metres. **60 C3** NH3867.
Carn na Farraidh *High.* ***Mountain***, 4m/6km SW of Tomintoul. Height 2257 feet or 688 metres. **52 D3** NJ1114.
Carn na Feannaige *Moray* ***Mountain***, on N side of Glen Avon, 8m/12km SW of Tomintoul. Height 2394 feet or 730 metres. **52 C4** NJ1008.
Carn na h-Ailig *High.* ***Mountain***, 6m/9km SE of Nethy Bridge. Height 2089 feet or 637 metres. **52 C3** NJ0614.
Carn na h-Easgainn *High.* ***Mountain***, in Inverness district, 5m/8km SE of Daviot. Height 2020 feet or 616 metres. **51 G1** NH7432.
Carn na Làraiche Maoile *High.* ***Mountain***, in Monadhliath range, 9m/13km SE of Foyers. Height 2654 feet or 809 metres. **51 E3** NH5811.
Carn na Loinne *High.* ***Mountain***, 3m/4km NE of Nethy Bridge. Height 1506 feet or 459 metres. **52 C2** NJ0322.
Carn na Nathrach *High.* ***Mountain***, 4m/6km SE of Scamodale and 1m/2km SW of Lochan Dubh, Lochaber district. Height 2578 feet or 786 metres. **38 A3** NM8869.
Carn na Saobhaidh *High.* ***Mountain***, in Inverness district, 12m/20km S of Inverness. Height 2342 feet or 714 metres. **51 F2** NH6724.
Carn na Saobhaidhe *High.* ***Mountain***, in Inverness district, 9m/13km SE of Foyers. Height 2660 feet or 811 metres. **51 E3** NH5914.
Carn na Sean-lùibe *High.* ***Mountain***, in Killilan Forest, Skye and Lochalsh district. Height 1909 feet or 582 metres. **49 G1** NH0235.
Carn na Sguabaich *High.* ***Mountain***, in Nairn district, 12m/20km S of Nairn. Height 1528 feet or 466 metres. **52 A1** NH8737.
Carn nam Bad *High.* ***Mountain***, rocky summit in Inverness district, 4m/7km NE of Cannich. Height 1499 feet or 457 metres. **50 D1** NH4033.
Carn nam-Bain Tighearna *High.* ***Mountain***, on border of Inverness and Badenoch and Strathspey districts, 4m/6km SE of Tomatin. Height 2080 feet or 634 metres. **52 A2** NH8425.
Carn nam Bò Maola *High.* ***Mountain***, 1m/2km NE of Glencassley Castle, on E side of Glen Cassley. Height 1391 feet or 424 metres. **71 G4** NC4509.
Carn nam Buailtean *High.* ***Mountain***, in Ross and Cromarty district, 6m/9km W of head of Little Loch Broom. Height 1260 feet or 384 metres. **59 G1** NH0087.
Carn nam Feuaich *High.* ***Mountain***, in Inverness district, 1m/2km N of E end of Loch Cluanie. Height 2401 feet or 732 metres. **50 A3** NH1712.
Carn nan Coireachan Cruaidh *High.* ***Mountain***, in Inverness district 5m/8km N of dam of Loch Cluanie. Height 2827 feet or 862 metres. NH1818.
Carn nan Gabhar *P. & K.* ***Mountain***, summit of Beinn a' Ghlo, 8m/12km NE of Blair Atholl. Munro: height 3677 feet or 1121 metres. **41 E2** NN9773.
Carn nan Gobhar *High.* ***Mountain***, in Inverness district 3m/5km NW of dam of Loch Mullardoch. Munro: height 3254 feet or 992 metres. **50 A1** NH1834.
Carn nan Gobhar *High.* ***Mountain***, in Inverness district, 4m/6km S of Inverchoran. Munro: height 3254 feet or 992 metres. **60 B5** NH2743.
Carn nan Iomairean *High.* ***Mountain***, 3m/5km E of Stromeferry. Height 1594 feet or 486 metres. **49 F1** NG9135.
Càrn nan Sgeir *High.* ***Island***, 1m/2km SW of Horse Island, off W coast of Ross and Cromarty district. **70 C4** NC0101.
Carn nan Tri-tighearnan *High.* ***Mountain***, on border of Inverness and Nairn districts, 5m/7km NE of Moy. Height 2017 feet or 615 metres. **52 A1** NH8239.
Carn Odhar *High.* ***Mountain***, in Inverness district, 12m/20km NW of Newtonmore. Height 2631 feet or 802 metres. **51 F3** NH6317.
Carn Phris Mhòir *High.* ***Mountain***, on border of Inverness and Badenoch and Strathspey districts, 9m/13km NW of Aviemore. Height 2027 feet or 618 metres. **52 A2** NH8021.
Carn Ruigh Charrach *High.* ***Mountain***, 5m/8km NW of Grantown-on-Spey. Height 1588 feet or 484 metres. **52 B1** NH9834.
Carn Ruighe an Uain *High.* ***Mountain***, 4m/6km E of Dava. Height 1791 feet or 546 metres. **52 C1** NJ0637.
Carn Sgùlain *High.* ***Mountain***, in Monadhliath range on border of Inverness and Badenoch and Strathspey districts, 6m/9km NW of Kingussie. Munro: height 3018 feet or 920 metres. **51 F4** NH6805.
Carn Sgùlain *High.* ***Mountain***, on borders of Inverness and Badenoch and Strathspey districts, 6m/10km N of Newtonmore. Height 2663 feet or 812 metres. **51 F4** NH6909.
Carn Sgumain *High.* ***Mountain***, in Nairn district, 10m/16km S of Nairn. Height 1368 feet or 417 metres. **62 A5** NH8740.
Carn Shalag *Moray* ***Mountain***, with plateau 4m/7km W of Upper Knockando. Height 1542 feet or 470 metres. **62 D5** NJ1142.
Carn Sleamhuinn *High.* ***Mountain***, in Kinveachy Forest, Badenoch and Strathspey district, 3m/5km NW of Aviemore. Height 2221 feet or 677 metres. **52 A3** NH8516.
Carn Tuadhan *High.* ***Mountain***, 3m/5km S of Bridge of Brown. Height 1991 feet or 607 metres. **52 D3** NJ1215.
Carn Tuairneir *High.* ***Mountain***, on Hills of Cromdale, 2m/3km NW of Bridge of Brown. Height 2273 feet or 693 metres. **52 C2** NJ0923.

Carna *High.* ***Island***, at entrance to Loch Teacuis, Lochaber district. **37 F4** NM6158.
Carnach *High.* ***River***, in Lochaber district running SW to head of Loch Nevis. NM8696.
Carnach *High.* ***Settlement***, on N shore of Little Loch Broom, near mouth of loch. Virtually inaccessible by road, with main access being by ferry from Badluarach on S side of loch. **70 C5** NH0196.
Carnach *High.* ***Settlement***, 6m/10km NE of Morvich at head of Loch Duich. Accessible only by narrow track. **49 G2** NH0228.
Carnach Mòr *Arg. & B.* ***Mountain***, 2m/3km NE of Glenbranter. Height 2080 feet or 634 metres. **30 D5** NS1499.
Carnachie *Moray* ***Mountain***, in wooded area, 5m/8km NW of Knockando. Height 1178 feet or 359 metres. **62 D5** NJ1047.
Carnan *W.Isles* ***Hill***, highest point on Mingulay. Height 895 feet or 273 metres. **44 A5** NL5582.
Carnan Mòr *Arg. & B.* ***Hill***, near SW end of Tiree, to E of Balephuil Bay. Highest point of island. Height 462 feet or 141 metres. NL9640.
Carnassarie *Arg. & B.* ***Settlement***, 1m/2km N of Kilmartin. **30 A4** NM8301.
Carnassarie Castle *Arg. & B.* ***Castle***, 16c castle (Historic Scotland) in Argyll, 3m/5km S of head of Loch Craignish. **30 A4** NM8300.
Carnbane Castle *P. & K.* ***Castle***, ruined stronghold of the Macnaughtons in Glen Lyon, 1m/2km E of Invervar. NN6747.
Carnbee *Fife* ***Village***, 3m/5km NW of Anstruther. **34 D4** NO5306.
Carnbo *P. & K.* ***Village***, 4m/7km W of Kinross. **33 F4** NO0503.
Carndu *High.* ***Settlement***, in Skye and Lochalsh district, on shore of Loch Long, 1km NE of Dornie. NG8827.
Carnduncan *Arg. & B.* ***Settlement***, on N of Islay, 1km NE of Loch Gorm. **20 A3** NR2467.
Carne na Lòine *High.* ***Mountain***, 4m/7km E of Dava. Height 1801 feet or 549 metres. **52 C1** NJ0736.
Carnethy Hill *Midloth.* ***Mountain***, in Pentland Hills, with cairn at summit, 3m/4km NW of Penicuik. Height 1889 feet or 576 metres. **25 F3** NT2061.
Carnferg *Aber.* ***Mountain***, 3m/5km S of Aboyne. Height 1722 feet or 525 metres. **54 A5** NO5293.
Carnichal *Aber.* ***Settlement***, 3m/4km SW of Strichen. **65 E4** NJ9351.
Carnmore *Arg. & B.* ***Settlement***, 1km NW of Port Ellen. **20 B5** NR3545.
Carnoch *High.* ***River***, in Lochaber district, running W from top of Glen Tarbert to head of Loch Sunart. NM8360.
Carnoch *High.* ***Settlement***, in valley of River Meig, 8m/12km SE of Achnasheen. **60 B4** NH2551.
Carnoch *High.* ***Settlement***, in Strathglass, 4m/6km NE of Cannich. **50 C1** NH3836.
Carnoch *High.* ***Settlement***, 10m/16km S of Nairn. **62 A5** NH8740.
Carnock *Fife* ***Village***, 3m/5km W of Dunfermline. **25 E1** NT0489.
Carnousie *Aber.* ***Locality***, includes Auldtown of Carnousie and Newton of Carnousie, 4m/6km W of Turriff. **64 B4** NJ6650.
Carnoustie *Angus* Population: 10,673. ***Town***, and coastal resort, 6m/10km SW of Arbroath. Golf courses, including one of championship status. **35 D1** NO5634.
Carntyne *Glas.* ***Suburb***, 2m/4km E of Glasgow city centre. NS6365.
Carntyne Industrial Estate *Glas.* ***Locality***, to S of Carntyne, 3m/4km E of Glasgow city centre. NS6365.
Carnwadric *Glas.* ***Suburb***, 5m/7km SW of Glasgow city centre. NS5459.
Carnwath *S.Lan.* Population: 1353. ***Village***, 7m/11km E of Lanark. **25 D5** NS9846.
Caroy *High.* ***River***, flowing S into Loch Caroy, 4m/7km SE of Dunvegan, Skye. **57 G5** NG3043.
Carpow *P. & K.* *See Abernethy.*
Carradale *Arg. & B.* ***Village***, on E coast of Kintyre, 1m/2km E of Dippen. Ruins of Aird Castle on cliff to S of pier. **12 D2** NR8138.
Carradale Bay *Arg. & B.* ***Bay***, on E coast of Kintyre, 11m/18km NE of Campbeltown. **12 D2** NR8037.
Carradale Forest *Arg. & B.* ***Forest/woodland***, astride Carradale Water, Kintyre. **21 F5** NR7842.
Carradale Garden *Arg. & B.* ***Garden***, on Kintyre, 1km SW of Carradale overlooking Kilbrennan Sound, with flowering shrubs, mainly rhododendrons. **12 D2** NR8037.
Carradale Point *Arg. & B.* ***Coastal feature***, headland to S of Carradale, on E side of Carradale Bay, on E coast of Kintyre. Remains of ancient fort. NR8136.
Carradale Water *Arg. & B.* ***River***, running S into Carradale Bay. **21 F5** NR8037.
Carragrich *W.Isles* ***Settlement***, on N side of East Loch Tarbert, 3m/4km E of Tarbet, North Harris. **67 D4** NG1998.
Carraig Bhàn *Arg. & B.* ***Coastal feature***, rocky area on N coast of Islay, 9m/13km NW of Bridgend. **20 A2** NR2571.
Carraig Fhada *Arg. & B.* ***Coastal feature***, headland with lighthouse on E coast of The Oa, Islay, 1m/2km SW of Port Ellen across Kilnaughton Bay. NR3444.
Carraig Mhic Thòmais *Arg. & B.* ***Coastal feature***, rock below cliffs on SW coast of Ardmeanach, Mull. **28 D2** NM4026.
Carrbridge *High.* ***Village***, on River Dulnain, in Badenoch and Strathspey district, 7m/11km N of Aviemore. Landmark, a forest heritage park, has exhibition explaining history of local environment. **52 B2** NH9022.
Carrick *Arg. & B.* ***Settlement***, 3m/4km E of Lochgilphead. **22 A1** NR9087.
Carrick *Arg. & B.* ***Village***, on W shore of Loch Goil, 2m/3km NW of its junction with Loch Long. **31 D5** NS1994.
Carrick *Fife* ***Hamlet***, 1m/2km NW of Leuchars. **34 C2** NO4422.
Carrick *S.Ayr.* ***Locality***, extensive upland area lying S of River Doon, to S of Ayr. The Prince of Wales, as Steward of Scotland, bears title of Earl of Carrick. **7 D1** NX3095.
Carrick Castle *Arg. & B.* ***Castle***, in Carrick, on W shore of Loch Goil, consisting of keep dating mainly from 15c. **31 D5** NS1994.
Carrick Forest *S.Ayr.* ***Forest/woodland***, forming part of Glen Trool Forest Park, 5m/8km S of Straiton. NX4296.
Carrick Lane *E.Ayr.* ***River***, formed by confluence of Eglin Lane and Whitespout Lane and running E into Loch Doon. NX4794.
Carrickstone *N.Lan.* ***Suburb***, 1m/2km NW of Cumbernauld town centre. NS7675.
Carriden *Falk.* ***Village***, on S side of Firth of Forth, 1m/2km E of Bo'ness. Site of Roman fort, most easterly fort of Antonine Wall, 1km SE. **25 E1** NT0181.
Carrine *Arg. & B.* ***Settlement***, 7m/11km SW of Campbeltown. **12 B5** NR6708.
Carrington *Midloth.* ***Village***, 2m/3km W of Gorebridge across River South Esk. **26 A3** NT3160.
Carroch *D. & G.* ***Settlement***, 6m/10km W of Moniaive. **8 A1** NX6791.
Carroglen *P. & K.* ***Settlement***, in Glen Lednock, 3m/4km N of Comrie. **32 C2** NN7626.
Carrol *High.* ***Settlement***, to W of Loch Brora, 2m/3km S of Gordonbush, Sutherland district. **73 D4** NC8407.
Carrol Rock *High.* ***Hill***, with rock outcrops to E, on E side of Loch Brora, 1m/2km S of Gordonbush. Height 682 feet or 208 metres. **72 D4** NC8407.
Carron ***River***, rising on Campsie Fells and flowing E through Carron Valley Reservoir into Firth of Forth on N side of Grangemouth. **24 A1** NS9484.
Carron *Arg. & B.* ***Settlement***, 3m/5km NW of Minard. **30 B5** NR9499.
Carron *Falk.* Population: 3605. ***Locality***, adjoining to N of Falkirk. Iron works founded in 1760. Site of Roman temple. **24 C1** NS8882.
Carron *High.* ***River***, in Ross and Cromarty district, rising above Loch Sgamhain and running SW down Glen Carron to head of Loch Carron. NG9341.
Carron *High.* ***River***, in Sutherland district running E down Strathcarron to Kyle of Sutherland at Bonar Bridge. **61 D1** NH6091.
Carron *Moray* ***Settlement***, with distillery on W bank of River Spey, 5m/8km SW of Craigellachie. **63 E5** NJ2241.
Carron Bridge *Stir.* ***Settlement***, at crossing point of River Carron, 4m/6km NE of Kilsyth. **24 B1** NS7483.
Carron Valley Reservoir *Stir.* ***Reservoir***, on border with North Lanarkshire, 5m/8km NE of Lennoxtown, and almost surrounded by Carron Valley state forest. **24 A1** NS6983.
Carron Water *Aber.* ***River***, rising in hills N of Glenbervie and flowing E to enter North Sea at Stonehaven. **43 F1** NO8785.
Carron Water *D. & G.* ***River***, rising on Lowther Hills and running S to River Nith at Carronbridge, 2m/3km N of Thornhill. NX8697.
Carronbridge *D. & G.* ***Village***, at confluence of River Nith and Carron Water. Site of Roman fort. **8 C1** NX8698.
Carronshore *Falk.* ***Locality***, 2m/3km N of Falkirk. **24 C1** NS8983.
Carrot *Angus* ***Hamlet***, 3m/4km SE of Gateside, on N side of Carrot Hill. **42 C5** NO4641.
Carrot Hill *Angus* ***Hill***, 3m/4km SE of Gateside. Height 850 feet or 259 metres. **42 C5** NO4540.
Carrugh an t-Sruith *Arg. & B.* ***Coastal feature***, headland on W coast of Jura, 2m/3km N of Feolin Ferry. NR4371.
Carrutherstown *D. & G.* ***Village***, 7m/11km NW of Annan. **9 F3** NY1071.
Carruthmuir *Inclyde* ***Settlement***, 3m/5km S of Kilmacolm. **23 E3** NS3564.
Carry *Arg. & B.* ***Settlement***, at S end of Cowal peninsula, 4m/6km S of Tighnabruaich. **22 A3** NR9867.
Carsaig *Arg. & B.* ***Locality***, on Carsaig Bay, on S coast of Mull, 2m/3km W of entrance to Loch Buie. **29 E2** NM5321.
Carsaig Arches *Arg. & B.* ***Coastal feature***, large tunnels carved by sea out of rocks on S coast of Mull, 3m/5km SW of Carsaig. NM4918.
Carsaig Bay *Arg. & B.* ***Bay***, on S coast of Mull, 2m/3km W of entrance to Loch Buie. **29 E2** NM5321.
Carsaig Bay *Arg. & B.* ***Bay***, on W coast of Knapdale, 1km NW of Tayvallich in Argyll. **21 F1** NR7387.
Carsaig Island *Arg. & B.* ***Island***, small island on SE side of Sound of Jura, 1m/2km NW of Tayvallich. **21 F1** NR7389.
Carscreugh *D. & G.* ***Settlement***, 2m/3km NE of Glenluce. **6 D4** NX2259.
Carse *Arg. & B.* ***Locality***, on Kintyre, 9m/14km SW of Tarbert. **21 F3** NR7561.
Carse Bay *D. & G.* ***Bay***, at mouth of Kirkbean Burn, 4m/6km N of Southerness. **9 D4** NX9860.
Carse of Ardersier *High.* ***Settlement***, 2m/3km NE of Ardersier. **62 A4** NH8057.
Carse of Balloch *Aber.* ***Open space***, moorland 4m/7km NW of Cruden Bay. **65 F5** NK0441.
Carse of Gowrie *P. & K.* ***Open space***, fertile tract on N side of Firth of Tay, between Perth and Dundee. **34 A2** NO2524.
Carse of Stirling *Stir.* ***Valley***, wide, level, fertile area to W of Stirling, extending N and S of River Forth from foothills of Highlands to Gargunnock Hills. NS6597.
Carsebreck Loch *P. & K.* ***Lake/loch***, 5m/8km SW of Auchterarder. **33 D3** NN8609.
Carsebridge *Clack.* ***Locality***, 1m/2km NE of Alloa. NS8993.
Carsegowan *D. & G.* ***Settlement***, 2m/4km N of Wigtown. **7 F5** NX4258.
Carseriggan *D. & G.* ***Settlement***, 4m/7km N of Kirkcowan. **7 E4** NX3167.
Carsethorn *D. & G.* ***Village***, on Solway Firth at mouth of River Nith, 10m/16km S of Dumfries. **9 D5** NX9959.
Carsfad Loch *D. & G.* ***Lake/loch***, loch and reservoir in course of Water of Ken 3m/5km N of St. John's Town of Dalry. **8 A2** NX6086.
Carsgailoch Hill *E.Ayr.* ***Mountain***, 4m/6km SW of Cumnock. Height 1194 feet or 364 metres. **14 D4** NS5414.
Carsgoe *High.* ***Settlement***, 3m/4km N of Halkirk. **76 D2** ND1363.
Carsie *P. & K.* ***Locality***, 2m/3km S of Blairgowrie. NO1742.
Carskey Bay *Arg. & B.* ***Bay***, on S coast of Kintyre, 4m/7km E of Mull of Kintyre. **12 B5** NR6607.
Carsluith *D. & G.* ***Hamlet***, on E shore of Wigtown Bay, 2m/4km S of Creetown. **7 F5** NX4854.
Carsluith Castle *D. & G.* ***Castle***, remains of castle (Historic Scotland) with 16c tower house, 1km SE of Carsluith. **7 F5** NX4954.
Carsphairn *D. & G.* ***Village***, 9m/14km SE of Dalmellington. **7 G1** NX5693.
Carsphairn Forest *D. & G.* ***Forest/woodland***, on border with East Aryshire, to N of Carsphairn. NS5602.
Carsphairn Lane *D. & G.* ***River***, running SE into Water of Deugh 1km W of Carsphairn village. NX5593.
Carstairs *S.Lan.* ***Village***, 4m/6km E of Lanark. **24 D5** NS9346.
Carstairs Junction *S.Lan.* ***Village***, and railway junction, 1m/2km SE of Carstairs. **25 D5** NS9545.
Carter Bar ***Other feature of interest***, point in Cheviot Hills at which A68 road crosses border between England and Scotland. **11 E1** NT6906.
Carter Fell ***Inland physical feature***, mountain ridge running NE to SW, on border of Cumbria and Scottish Borders, 6m/10km NE of Kielder. Height 1824 feet or 556 metres. **11 E1** NT6603.
Carthagena Bank *P. & K.* ***Coastal feature***, large area of mud, covered at high water, on N side of Firth of Tay, 1m/2km E of Errol. **34 A2** NO2722.
Carthat Hill *D. & G.* ***Hill***, 3m/4km SW of Hightae. Height 794 feet or 242 metres. **9 E3** NY0677.
Cartland *S.Lan.* ***Hamlet***, 2m/3km NW of Lanark. NS8646.
Cashel *Stir.* ***Settlement***, on E shore of Loch Lomond, 3m/4km NW of Balmaha. **31 G5** NS3994.
Cashel Dhu *High.* ***Locality***, at the mouth of Strathmore River where it flows into Loch Hope. **75 D3** NC4550.
Cashlie *P. & K.* ***Settlement***, in Glen Lyon, 8m/12km NW of Killin. **39 G5** NN4842.
Caskieberran *Fife* ***Suburb***, W district of Glenrothes. NO2500.
Cassencarie *D. & G.* ***Settlement***, 1km S of Creetown. **7 F5** NX4757.
Cassley *High.* ***River***, in Sutherland district, running SE down Glen Cassley into River Oykel 8m/12km SW of Lairg. **71 G4** NC4700.
Castle Bay *W.Isles* ***Bay***, on S coast of Barra. **44 B4** NL6697.
Castle Campbell (Formerly known as Castle Gloom.) *Clack.* ***Castle***, dating from late 15c (Historic Scotland), in Dollar Glen (National Trust for Scotland) nearly 1m/2km N of Dollar. **33 E5** NS9699.
Castle Dhu *P. & K.* *See Moulin.*
Castle Douglas *D. & G.* Population: 3697. ***Small town***, at N end of Carlingwark Loch, 9m/14km NE of Kirkcudbright. **8 B4** NX7662.

Castle Fraser *Aber.* ***Castle***, baronial tower house (National Trust for Scotland) 6m/10km SW of Inverurie. Built 1575-1636, with notable Great Hall and walled garden. Said to be haunted. **54 C3** NJ7212.
Castle Gloom *Clack. Former name of Castle Campbell, qv.*
Castle Grant *High.* ***Castle***, former seat of the chiefs of Grant, Earls of Seafield, in Badenoch and Strathspey district 2m/3km N of Grantown-on-Spey. **52 C1** NJ0430.
Castle Haven *Aber.* ***Bay***, shingle and rocky bay between Bowdun Head to N and Dunnottar Castle to S, 1m/2km S of Stonehaven. **43 G1** NO8884.
Castle Hill *High.* ***Mountain***, in Badenoch and Strathspey district, 5m/9km SE of Aviemore. Height 2388 feet or 728 metres. **52 B4** NH9505.
Castle Huntly *Dundee* ***Castle***, dating from 15c, 1m/2km SW of Longforgan. NO3029.
Castle Island *N.Ayr.* ***Island***, small island off E coast of island of Little Cumbrae. Remains of medieval tower at N end. NS1551.
Castle Island *P. & K.* ***Island***, in Loch Leven, 1m/2km E of Kinross. Remains of 15c castle (Historic Scotland). NO1301.
Castle Kennedy *D. & G.* ***Village***, 3m/5km E of Stranraer. Ruins of late 16c castle destroyed by fire in 1715 to N, on isthmus between Black Loch and White Loch within grounds of Lochinch Castle. **6 C5** NX1059.
Castle Kennedy Gardens *D. & G.* ***Garden***, 75 acres of garden laid out by Field Marshall Lord Stair and troops in 18c on isthmus between White Loch and Black Loch, with ruins of Castle Kennedy and Lochinch Castle at either end, 3m/5km E of Stranraer. Contains original specimens from Sir Joseph Hooker's Himalayan expeditions. Famous for rhododendrons, azaleas, magnolias and embothriums. **6 C4** NX1161.
Castle Knowe *Sc.Bord. Alternative name for Fast Castle, qv.*
Castle Lachlan (Also known as Lachlan Castle.) *Arg. & B.* ***Historic house***, in Argyll near mouth of Strathlachlan River. Ruined 16c tower of Maclachlans on shore of Loch Fyne to W. **30 C5** NS0195.
Castle Leod *High.* ***Castle***, 12c tower house, re-modelled in 1606, 1km N of Strathpeffer. Seat of Earls of Cromartie. **61 D4** NH4859.
Castle Levan *Inclyde* ***Hamlet***, 2m/3km SW of Gourock. Castle. **22 D2** NS2176.
Castle Loch *D. & G.* ***Lake/loch***, loch 6m/10km E of Glenluce. Remains of castle on islet near E end of loch. **7 D5** NX2853.
Castle Loch *D. & G.* ***Lake/loch***, to S of Lochmaben. Remains of 14c castle on S shore. With Hightae Mill Loch, 1km further S, it forms nature reserve. **9 E2** NY0881.
Castle Menzies *P. & K.* ***Historic house***, 16c mansion 1m/2km W of Aberfeldy across River Tay. **40 D4** NN8349.
Castle Moil *High. Anglicised form of Caisteal Maol, qv.*
Castle Moy *Arg. & B.* ***Castle***, ruined keep at Lochbuie, Mull. Former stronghold of Maclaines of Loch Buie. NM6124.
Castle O'er *D. & G.* ***Historic/prehistoric site***, ancient earthwork surrounded by Castle O'er Forest, S of Eskdalemuir. **9 G1** NY2492.
Castle O'er Forest *D. & G.* ***Forest/woodland***, to S of Eskdalemuir. **9 G1** NY2393.
Castle of Cobbie Row *Ork. Alternative name for Cubbie Roo's Castle, qv.*
Castle of Dunnideer *Aber.* ***Historic/prehistoric site***, remains of ancient hillfort 1m/2km W of Insch. NJ6128.
Castle of Fiddes *Aber.* ***Castle***, tower of late 16c, restored 1965, 4m/7km SW of Stonehaven. NO8281.
Castle of Inverallochy *Aber.* ***Castle***, old stronghold of the Comyns, 1m/2km S of Inverallochy. NK0462.
Castle of Mey *High.* ***Castle***, to E of Harrow on N coast, 4m/7km NE of Dunnet. Built between 1566 and 1572 by George, Fourth Earl of Caithness. Additions and alterations between 17c and 20c. **77 E1** ND2873.
Castle of Old Wick (Also known as Old Man of Wick.) *High.* ***Castle***, ruined 12c-14c tower (Historic Scotland), on E coast of Caithness district, 1m/2km S of Wick. **77 F4** ND3648.
Castle of Park *D. & G.* ***Castle***, castellated late 16c tower house, 1km W of Glenluce across Water of Luce. **6 C5** NX1857.
Castle Rock of Muchalls *Aber.* ***Coastal feature***, on North Sea coast, 1m/2km S of Muchalls. **55 D5** NO9090.
Castle Semple Collegiate Church *Renf.* ***Ecclesiastical building***, remains of church (Historic Scotland), founded 1504, at NE end of Castle Semple Loch. **23 E3** NS3760.
Castle Semple Loch *Renf.* ***Lake/loch***, loch on E side of Lochwinnoch. **23 E4** NS3659.
Castle Semple Water Country Park *Renf.* ***Leisure/recreation***, water park and bird sanctuary, at Castle Semple Loch, E of Lochwinnoch. **23 E4** NS3659.
Castle Stalker *Arg. & B.* ***Castle***, on islet at entrance to Loch Laich, Argyll, S of Shuna Island. Originally built for James IV, late 15c. **38 B5** NM9247.
Castle Stuart *High.* ***Castle***, built in 1625 by James Stuart, 3rd Earl of Moray, 5m/8km E of Inverness. **61 G4** NH7449.
Castle Sween *Arg. & B.* ***Castle***, ruined castle (Historic Scotland) of the MacNeils, dating from 11c, on E side of Loch Sween in Argyll, opposite Danna Island. **21 F2** NR7178.
Castlebay (Gaelic form: Bagh a' Chaisteil.) *W.Isles* ***Small town***, at head of Castle Bay on S coast of Barra. Chief port and settlement of island, although airfield is at N end. **44 B4** NL6698.
Castlecary *N.Lan.* ***Hamlet***, 3m/5km SW of Bonnybridge. Site of Roman camp, traversed by railway. Tollpark and Garnhall (Historic Scotland), well-preserved section of ditch of Antonine Wall, to W. **24 B2** NS7878.
Castlecary Roman Fort *Falk.* ***Historic/prehistoric site***, to E of Castlecary. Remains (Historic Scotland) of one of line of forts along Antonine Wall; site of camp now traversed by railway. **24 B2** NS7977.
Castlecraig *High.* ***Settlement***, 2m/3km NE of Cromarty across mouth of Cromarty Firth. **62 A3** NH8269.
Castlecraig *Sc.Bord.* ***Settlement***, 1km S of Blyth Bridge. **25 F5** NT1344.
Castledykes *D. & G. Alternative name for Kirkcudbright, qv.*
Castlefairn *D. & G.* ***Settlement***, 8m/12km NE of St. John's Town of Dalry. **8 B2** NX7387.
Castlefairn Water *D. & G.* ***River***, running NE to join Dalwhat Water and form Cairn Water, 1km SE of Moniaive. NX7890.
Castlehead *Renf.* ***Suburb***, to SW of Paisley town centre. NS4763.
Castlehill *W.Dun.* ***Suburb***, NW district of Dumbarton. NS3876.
Castlehill Point *D. & G.* ***Coastal feature***, headland at E side of estuary of Urr Water, 6m/9km S of Dalbeattie. **8 C5** NX8552.
Castlehill Reservoir *P. & K.* ***Reservoir***, 1m/2km N of Yetts o'Muckhart. NN9903.
Castlelaw Fort *Midloth. See Glencorse.*
Castlelaw Hillfort *Midloth.* ***Historic/prehistoric site***, small Iron Age hillfort (Historic Scotland) consisting of three concentric ramparts and souterrain to SW of Castlelaw Hill, 2m/4km N of Penicuik. Occupied into Roman times. **25 G3** NT2263.
Castlemilk *D. & G.* ***Settlement***, on E side of Water of Milk, 3m/5km NW of Ecclefechan. **9 F3** NY1577.
Castlemilk *Glas.* ***Suburb***, 2m/3km SW of Rutherglen. **24 A4** NS6059.
Castlesea Bay *Angus* ***Bay***, small bay, 3m/5km NE of Arbroath. NO6843.
Castleton *Aber.* ***Settlement***, 4m/6km N of Turriff. **64 C4** NJ7256.
Castleton *Angus* ***Hamlet***, 3m/5km NE of Meigle. **42 B5** NO3346.
Castleton *Arg. & B.* ***Settlement***, 3m/4km SE of Lochgilphead. **21 G1** NR8884.
Castleton *Sc.Bord.* ***Locality***, in Liddesdale, 3m/4km NE of Newcastleton. **10 D2** NY5190.
Castletown *High.* ***Settlement***, 5m/8km SE of Inverness. **61 G5** NH7442.
Castletown *High.* Population: 1028. ***Village***, with small harbour on Dunnet Bay, N coast of Caithness district, 5m/8km E of Thurso. **77 D2** ND1968.
Castleweary *Sc.Bord.* ***Settlement***, 1m/2km S of Teviothead. **17 F5** NT4003.
Castlewigg *D. & G.* ***Settlement***, 4m/6km SW of Garlieston. **3 E2** NX4242.
Castramont *D. & G.* ***Settlement***, 3m/4km N of Gatehouse of Fleet. **7 G4** NX5960.
Cat Firth *Shet.* ***Sea feature***, inlet on Mainland, to N of Lambgarth Head on E coast. **82 D2** HU4453.
Cat Law *Angus* ***Mountain***, 6m/9km NW of Kirriemuir. Height 2224 feet or 678 metres. **42 B3** NO3161.
Cata Sand *Ork.* ***Coastal feature***, large area of sand with dunes on seaward side, on E coast of Sanday. Overbister lies to W. **81 E2** HY6940.
Catacol *N.Ayr.* ***Hamlet***, on N side of Catacol Bay, on NW coast of Arran. NR9149.
Catacol Bay *N.Ayr.* ***Bay***, on NW coast of Arran. **21 G5** NR9049.
Catcleugh Shin *Sc.Bord.* ***Mountain***, 1km W of Carter Bar in Cheviot Hills. Height 1742 feet or 531 metres. **11 E1** NT6806.
Caterthun *Angus* ***Locality***, includes sites of Brown Caterthun and White Caterthun Iron Age forts, 6m/9km NW of Brechin. NO5566.
Catfirth *Shet.* ***Settlement***, at head of Cat Firth inlet. **82 D2** HU4354.
Cathcart *Glas.* ***Suburb***, 4m/6km S of Glasgow city centre. NS5860.
Cathkin *S.Lan.* ***Suburb***, 3m/4km SE of Rutherglen and 3m/4km N of East Kilbride. NS6258.
Catlodge *High.* ***Settlement***, in Badenoch and Strathspey district, 5m/8km N of Dalwhinnie. NN6392.
Catrine *E.Ayr.* Population: 2327. ***Village***, on River Ayr, 2m/3km SE of Mauchline. Ballochmyle House, 1km NW, is subject of two songs by Burns. **14 D3** NS5225.
Catstone *Sc.Bord.* ***Mountain***, in Pentland Hills, 3m/5km W of West Linton. Height 1469 feet or 448 metres. **25 E4** NT0952.
Cattadale *Arg. & B.* ***Settlement***, on Islay, 4m/7km E of Bowmore. **20 B4** NR3860.
Catterline *Aber.* ***Village***, on E coast, 5m/8km S of Stonehaven. **43 G2** NO8678.
Cauldcleuch Head *Sc.Bord.* ***Mountain***, 5m/7km SE of Teviothead. Height 1994 feet or 608 metres. **17 F5** NT4600.
Cauldcots *Angus* ***Settlement***, 1m/2km SW of Inverkeilor. **43 E5** NO6547.
Cauldhall Moor *Midloth.* ***Open space***, moorland 2m/3km E of Howgate. **25 G4** NT2758.
Cauldhame *Stir.* ***Settlement***, 2m/3km E of Dunblane. **32 D4** NN8201.
Cauldhame *Stir.* ***Village***, adjoining to SW of Kippen, 9m/15km W of Stirling. **32 B5** NS6494.
Cauldkine Rig *D. & G. Alternative spelling of Calkin Rig, qv.*
Cauldshiels Hill *Sc.Bord.* ***Mountain***, 3m/4km SW of Melrose. Height 1076 feet or 328 metres. **17 G2** NT5131.
Cauldshiels Loch *Sc.Bord.* ***Lake/loch***, small loch 2m/4km SW of Melrose. **17 G2** NT5132.
Cauldside *D. & G.* ***Settlement***, 4m/7km NE of Canonbie. **10 C3** NY4381.
Caulkerbush *D. & G.* ***Settlement***, 7m/11km SE of Dalbeattie. **8 D5** NX9257.
Caultrashal Beag *W.Isles Anglicised form of Calltraiseal Bheag, qv.*
Caultrashal Mòr *W.Isles Anglicised form of Calltraiseal Mhòr, qv.*
Causamul *W.Isles* ***Island***, group of rocks nearly 2m/3km W of Aird an Rùnair, W coast of North Uist. **45 E2** NF6670.
Causeway End *D. & G.* ***Settlement***, 3m/5km N of Wigtown. **7 F4** NX4260.
Causeway Grain Head ***Mountain***, rising to over 490 metres, astride border of Dumfries & Galloway and Scottish Borders, on S edge of Craik Forest, 6m/9km NE of Bentpath. **10 B2** NY3598.
Causewayhead *Stir.* ***Suburb***, 1m/2km N of Stirling. **32 D5** NS8095.
Causeyend *Aber.* ***Settlement***, 2m/3km NW of Balmedie. **55 E3** NJ9419.
Cava *Ork.* ***Island***, uninhabited island of about 180 acres or 70 hectares lying 1m/2km off E coast of Hoy at SE end of Bring Deeps. Lighthouse at N end of island. **78 C3** ND3299.
Cavens *D. & G.* ***Settlement***, 3m/4km N of Southerness. **9 D5** NX9758.
Cavers *Sc.Bord.* ***Hamlet***, 2m/4km NE of Hawick. NT5315.
Caversta *W.Isles Anglicised form of Cabharstadh, qv.*
Cawdor *High.* ***Village***, in Nairn district, 5m/8km SW of Nairn. Castle dating from 15c and later. **62 A4** NH8449.
Cawdor Castle *High.* ***Castle***, on E bank of Allt Dearg across from Cawdor. Central tower built in 1342, fortified in 1454 and surrounded by 16c buildings. Associated with Shakespeare's Macbeth. Grounds contain notable gardens with herbaceous borders plus roses, shrubs, lilies, holly maze, thistle garden and white garden. **62 A4** NH8449.
Ceallan (Anglicised form: Kallin.) *W.Isles* ***Settlement***, on E coast of Grimsay, between North Uist and Benbecula. **45 G4** NF8755.
Ceann a' Bhàigh (Anglicised form: Lingarabay.) *W.Isles* ***Settlement***, on S coast of South Harris, 2m/3km NE of Rodel. **66 C5** NG0685.
Ceann a' Bhàigh (Anglicised form: Bayhead.) *W.Isles* ***Village***, near W coast of North Uist, 5m/9km S of Griminis Point. **45 F3** NF7468.
Ceann a Deas na Hearadh *W.Isles Gaelic form of South Harris, qv.*
Ceann a' Gharaidh *W.Isles* ***Coastal feature***, headland at SW point of South Uist. **44 C2** NF7315.
Ceann a' Mhàim *High.* ***Mountain***, in Inverness district on S side of Glen Moriston, 6m/10km W of Fort Augustus. Height 2201 feet or 671 metres. **50 B4** NH2708.
Ceann a Tuath na Hearadh *W.Isles Gaelic form of North Harris, qv.*
Ceann an t-Sàilein *Arg. & B.* ***Sea feature***, narrow inlet of Loch Sween, Argyll, running up to N end of Danna Island. NR7079.
Ceann Caol *High.* ***Inland physical feature***, mountain ridge on Ardgour rising to 1601 feet or 488 metres, forming NE part of Bràigh Bhlàich, 4m/6km W of Fort William across Loch Linnhe. **38 C2** NN0474.
Ceann Ear *W.Isles* ***Island***, one of Heisker Islands group. Sands between Ceann Ear and adjoining Ceann Iar to W are fordable at low tide. **45 E3** NF6462.
Ceann Garbh *Arg. & B.* ***Mountain***, peak in Argyll to NE of summit of Beinn Bhuidhe and 6m/9km SE of Dalmally. Height 2634 feet or 803 metres. **31 E2** NN2220.
Ceann Iar *W.Isles* ***Island***, one of Heisker Islands group to W of Ceann Ear. **45 E3** NF6162.
Ceann Leathad nam Bò *High.* ***Coastal feature***, headland 4m/6km SW of Dunbeath. **73 G2** ND1323.
Ceann Loch Shiphoirt (Anglicised form: Seaforth Head.) *W.Isles* ***Settlement***, at head of Loch Seaforth, Isle of Lewis, 3m/4km S of Baile Ailein across Loch Erisort. **67 E2** NB2916.

Ceann na Beinne *High.* ***Hill***, 3m/4km NE of Rubh' an Dùnain, Skye. Height 738 feet or 225 metres. **48 A3** NG4217.
Ceann na Circ (Anglicised form: Chicken Head.) *W.Isles* ***Coastal feature***, headland at S end of Eye Peninsula, Isle of Lewis. **69 F5** NB4929.
Ceann-na-Cleithe *W.Isles Gaelic form of Kennacley, qv.*
Ceann Reamhar *W.Isles* ***Mountain***, on South Harris, 2m/3km SW of Tarbert. Height 1532 feet or 467 metres. **66 D4** NG1199.
Ceanna Mòr *High.* ***Coastal feature***, headland on S side of entrance to Loch a' Choire, Lochaber district. **38 A4** NM8551.
Ceannacroc Forest *High.* ***Open space***, deer forest in Inverness district N of Loch Cluanie. Also forest in Glen Moriston to E. Power station for hydro-electricity scheme at Ceannacroc Bridge. **50 A3** NH1713.
Ceardach *Stir.* ***Island***, islet (National Trust for Scotland) in Loch Lomond, 2m/3km W of Balmaha. NS3991.
Cearsiadar (Anglicised form: Kershader.) *W.Isles* ***Village***, on S side of Loch Erisort, Isle of Lewis, opposite Lacasaigh. **69 E5** NB3420.
Ceathramh Garbh *High.* ***Locality***, area to N of Loch a' Chadh-Fi, Sutherland district. **74 B3** NC2252.
Ceathramh Meadhanach (Anglicised form: Middlequarter.) *W.Isles* ***Settlement***, on North Uist, 1km W of Solas. **45 F2** NF7974.
Cellar Head (Gaelic form: Rubha an t-Seileir.) *W.Isles* ***Coastal feature***, headland on NE coast of Isle of Lewis, 6m/9km N of Tolsta Head. **69 G2** NB5656.
Cellardyke *Fife* ***Suburb***, central district of Anstruther. **35 D4** NO5703.
Ceos (Anglicised form: Keose.) *W.Isles* ***Village***, near E coast of Isle of Lewis, 1m/2km of Lacasaigh. **69 E5** NB3521.
Ceres *Fife* ***Village***, 3m/4km SE of Cupar. **34 B3** NO4011.
Cessford *Sc.Bord.* ***Settlement***, 3m/4km W of Morebattle. **18 B4** NT7323.
Cessford Castle *Sc.Bord.* ***Castle***, ruined 14c stronghold of Kers, 11m/18km SE of Newtown St. Boswells. NT7323.
Cessnock Castle *E.Ayr.* ***Historic house***, early 15c tower, with 16c-17c house attached, 1m/2km SE of Galston. NS5135.
Cessnock Water ***River***, rising 3m/5km S of Darvel and running circuitously NW to River Irvine between Galston and Kilmarnock. **14 D2** NS4737.
Chaipaval *W.Isles* ***Mountain***, on South Harris, 2m/3km SE of Toe Head. Height 1197 feet or 365 metres. **66 B4** NF9792.
Challister *Shet.* ***Settlement***, on N coast of Whalsay, 1km E of Brough. HU5665.
Challister Ness *Shet.* ***Coastal feature***, headland on N coast of Whalsay, 1m/2km NE of Challister. **83 E1** HU5767.
Challoch *D. & G.* ***Settlement***, 2m/3km NW of Newton Stewart. **7 E4** NX3867.
Champany *Falk.* ***Settlement***, 2m/3km NE of Linlithgow. **25 E2** NT0278.
Changue Forest *S.Ayr.* ***Forest/woodland***, in Glentrool Forest Park, 2m/3km E of Barr. **7 E1** NX3193.
Changue Hill *E.Ayr.* ***Hill***, 2m/3km S of Darvel. Height 977 feet or 298 metres. **15 D2** NS5635.
Channer Wick *Shet.* ***Sea feature***, inlet on E coast of Mainland 12m/20km S of Lerwick. HU4023.
Channerwick *Shet.* ***Settlement***, at head of Channer Wick inlet on Mainland, 1km SW of Hoswick. **82 D5** HU4023.
Chanonry Point *High.* ***Coastal feature***, headland with lighthouse in Ross and Cromarty district at entrance to Inner Moray Firth or Inverness Firth opposite Fort George. **61 G4** NH7455.
Chaoruinn *High.* ***Mountain***, in Badenoch and Strathspey district, 5m/7km S of Dalwhinnie. Height 3004 feet or 916 metres. NN6477.
Chapel *Fife* ***Suburb***, NW district of Kirkcaldy. **34 A5** NT2593.
Chapel Finian *D. & G.* ***Historic/prehistoric site***, traces of 10c-11c chapel (Historic Scotland) on E shore of Luce Bay, 5m/8km NW of Port William. **2 C2** NX2748.
Chapel Hill *Aber.* ***Settlement***, near E coast, 2m/3km E of Cruden Bay. **55 F1** NK0635.
Chapel Ness *Fife* ***Coastal feature***, headland at W end of bay enclosing Elie harbour. **34 C5** NT4899.
Chapel of Garioch *Aber.* ***Village***, 4m/6km NW of Inverurie. 9c Maiden Stone (Historic Scotland) 1m/2km NW. **54 C2** NJ7124.
Chapel Rossan *D. & G.* ***Settlement***, on W coast of Luce Bay, adjoining to S of Ardwell. **2 B2** NX1145.
Chapelbank *P. & K.* ***Hamlet***, on N bank of River Earn, 3m/4km NW of Dunning. **33 F3** NO0017.
Chapelcross *D. & G.* ***Other building***, nuclear power station, first in Scotland, 3m/4km NE of Annan. NY2269.
Chapeldonan *S.Ayr.* ***Settlement***, 2m/3km NE of Girvan. **13 G5** NS1900.
Chapelgill Hill *Sc.Bord.* ***Mountain***, 5m/8km S of Biggar. Height 2283 feet or 696 metres. NT0630.
Chapelhall *N.Lan.* Population: 4405. ***Village***, 2m/3km SE of Airdrie. **24 B3** NS7862.
Chapelhill *High.* ***Settlement***, 3m/4km SW of Balintore. **62 A2** NH8273.
Chapelhill *P. & K.* ***Hamlet***, 3m/5km W of Errol. **34 A2** NO2021.
Chapelhill *P. & K.* ***Settlement***, 3m/4km N of Methven. **33 F1** NO0030.
Chapelknowe *D. & G.* ***Village***, 3m/5km NE of Kirkpatrick-Fleming. **10 B4** NY3173.
Chapelton *Aber.* ***Settlement***, 3m/5km SW of Stonehaven. **43 G1** NO8582.
Chapelton *Angus* ***Hamlet***, 3m/4km SE of Friockheim. **43 E5** NO6247.
Chapelton *High.* ***Locality***, in Badenoch and Strathspey district, 2m/3km W of Boat of Garten. NH9119.
Chapelton *S.Lan.* ***Village***, 3m/5km NW of Strathaven. **24 A5** NS6848.
Chapeltown *Moray* ***Settlement***, 5m/8km E of Tomintoul. **53 E2** NJ2421.
Charlesfield *Sc.Bord.* ***Settlement***, 1m/2km SE of Newtown St. Boswells. **17 G3** NT5829.
Charleston *Angus* ***Village***, 1km S of Glamis. **42 B5** NO3845.
Charleston *Renf.* ***Suburb***, 1m/2km S of Paisley town centre. NS4862.
Charlestown *Aberdeen* ***Hamlet***, 4m/6km S of Aberdeen. **55 E4** NJ9300.
Charlestown *Aber.* ***Locality***, on NE coast, at N end of St. Combs. **65 F3** NK0563.
Charlestown *Fife* ***Village***, small port on N side of Firth of Forth, 3m/5km SW of Dunfermline. **25 E1** NT0683.
Charlestown *High.* ***Hamlet***, in Ross and Cromarty district, on N shore of Beauly Firth, 1m/2km W of North Kessock. **61 F5** NH6448.
Charlestown *High.* ***Village***, at head of Gair Loch, W coast of Ross and Cromarty district, 1m/2km S of Gairloch village. **59 E2** NG8074.
Charlestown of Aberlour (Also known as Aberlour.) *Moray* ***Small town***, on S bank of River Spey, 4m/6km S of Rothes. Built in 19c by Charles Grant from whom name was taken. **63 E5** NJ2643.
Charn a' Ghille Chear ***Mountain***, one of Hills of Cromdale on border of Highland and Moray, 7m/11km E of Grantown-on-Spey. Height 2329 feet or 710 metres. **52 D2** NJ1329.
Charterhall *Sc.Bord.* ***Motor racing circuit***, 4m/6km E of Greenlaw. NT7646.
Chatelherault Country Park *S.Lan.* ***Leisure/recreation***, 500 acre country park on banks of Avon Water, 2m/3km SE of Hamilton. Encompasses Cadzow Castle (Historic Scotland) and Chatelherault Hunting Lodge. **24 B4** NS7353.
Chatto *Sc.Bord.* ***Settlement***, on Kale Water, 2m/3km SW of Hownam. **18 B5** NT7618.
Cheeklaw *Sc.Bord.* ***Suburb***, at S edge of Duns. **27 E4** NT7852.
Chesterhill *Midloth.* ***Village***, 3m/5km SE of Dalkeith. NT3765.
Chesters *E.Loth.* ***Historic/prehistoric site***, earthworks of ancient fort (Historic Scotland), 1km S of Drem. Similar site of same name 3m/5km S of Dunbar. **26 C2** NT5078.
Chesters *Sc.Bord.* ***Settlement***, 2m/3km SW of Ancrum. **18 A4** NT6022.
Chesters *Sc.Bord.* ***Village***, 5m/9km NW of Carter Bar. **18 A5** NT6210.
Cheviot Hills ***Large natural feature***, N end of The Pennines, extending along border of England and Scotland, highest part being The Cheviot at 2673 feet or 815 metres. Hills contain vast areas of moorland, forests and peat and provide pasturage for sheep, especially breed known as Cheviots. **11 E2** NT6804.
Cheynies *Shet.* ***Island***, uninhabited island of 24 acres or 10 hectares 4m/6km W of Scalloway, Mainland. **82 C4** HU3438.
Chicken Head *W.Isles Anglicised form of Ceann na Circ, qv.*
Chicken Rock (Gaelic form: A' Chearc.) *W.Isles* ***Island***, offshore from Ceann na Circ, Isle of Lewis, with beacon. NB4928.
Chirmorrie *S.Ayr.* ***Settlement***, 4m/6km S of Barrhill. **6 D3** NX2076.
Chirnside *Sc.Bord.* Population: 1253. ***Village***, 6m/9km E of Duns. **27 F4** NT8656.
Chirnsidebridge *Sc.Bord.* ***Village***, 1m/2km W of Chirnside on Whiteadder Water. **27 F4** NT8556.
Chiscan *Arg. & B.* ***Settlement***, on Kintyre, 2m/3km W of Campbeltown. **12 B4** NR6718.
Chiscan Water *Arg. & B.* ***River***, stream on Kintyre, running generally N into Machrihanish Water. **12 B4** NR6820.
Chno Dearg *High.* ***Mountain***, in Lochaber district 3m/5km SE of foot of Loch Treig. Munro: height 3434 feet or 1047 metres. **39 F2** NN3774.
Choicelee *Sc.Bord.* ***Hamlet***, 3m/5km SW of Duns. **27 E4** NT7451.
Choinneachain Hill *P. & K.* ***Mountain***, on E side of Loch Turret Reservoir. Height 2581 feet or 787 metres. NN8128.
Chorrie Island *High. Anglicised form of Eilean Choraidh, qv.*
Chrisswell *Inclyde* ***Settlement***, 3m/4km SW of Greenock. **22 D2** NS2274.
Christskirk *Aber.* ***Settlement***, with historic Christ's Kirk, 2m/3km SW of Insch. NJ6026.
Chrona Island *High. Anglicised form of Eilean Chrona, qv.*
Chryston *N.Lan.* Population: 3057. ***Village***, adjoining to N of Muirhead, 4m/7km NW of Coatbridge. **24 A2** NS6870.
Church of Plaque (Athelstaneford Church). *E.Loth.* ***Ecclesiastical building***, 3m/4km NE of Haddington. Plaque by church tells of origins of St. Andrew's Cross (the Saltire) first adopted as Scottish symbol here. Book of the Saltire on display in church. **26 C2** NT5377.
Church of St. Andrew and St. George *Edin.* ***Ecclesiastical building***, 18c oval-shaped church in St. Andrew Square, Edinburgh. Scene of 1843 Disruption which led to establishment of Free Church of Scotland. **25 G2** NT2574.
Church of St. Mary (St. Mary's Collegiate Church). *E.Loth.* ***Ecclesiastical building***, 14c medieval church on E side of Haddington, built on scale of cathedral. Burne Jones and Sax Shaw windows. **26 C2** NT5274.
Church of St. Mary *S.Lan.* ***Ecclesiastical building***, Collegiate church, built in 1546 at Biggar. **16 B2** NT0437.
Church of St. Monan *Fife* ***Ecclesiastical building***, Royal Votive Chapel, in St. Monans, 12m/20km S of St. Andrews. Possibly founded as early as AD 400, it became a parish church in 1646. **34 D4** NO5201.
Churchhill *Edin.* ***Suburb***, 1m/2km SW of Edinburgh city centre. NT2471.
Churchill Barrier *Ork.* ***Other feature of interest***, series of causeways carrying roads and linking islands of Mainland, Lamb Holm, Glimps Holm, Burray, and South Ronaldsay. Built in World War II to block eastern approaches to anchorage of Scapa Flow. ND4798.
Ciaran Water *High.* ***River***, flowing S from Loch Chiarain into Blackwater Reservoir. **39 F3** NN2860.
Cille-Bharra *W.Isles* ***Ecclesiastical building***, on Barra, 1m/2km SE of Scurrival Point on N of island. Ruined church of St. Barr and restored chapel of St. Mary formed part of medieval monastery. Replica of unique Celtic/Norse stone at the site. **44 C3** NF7007.
Cille Bhrighde (Anglicised form: Kilbride.) *W.Isles* ***Village***, at SW end of South Uist. **44 C2** NF7514.
Cille Pheadair (Anglicised form: Kilpheder.) *W.Isles* ***Settlement***, on South Uist, 1m/2km SW of Dalabrog. **44 C2** NF7419.
Cìoch Mhòr *High.* ***Mountain***, in Ross and Cromarty district, 8m/12km E of Gorstan. Height 1581 feet or 482 metres. **61 E3** NH5063.
Cioch-na-h-Oighe *N.Ayr.* ***Mountain***, on Arran, 6m/9km N of Brodick. Height 2168 feet or 661 metres. **22 A5** NR9943.
Cir Mhòr *N.Ayr.* ***Mountain***, National Trust for Scotland property on Arran, 3m/5km W of Corrie. Height 2617 feet or 798 metres. **22 A5** NR9743.
Cirbhig (Anglicised form: Kirivick.) *W.Isles* ***Settlement***, 1km SW of Carloway, Isle of Lewis. **68 C3** NB1941.
Cirean Geardail *High.* ***Coastal feature***, headland 1m/2km SW of Point of Stoer, Sutherland district. **70 B1** NC0034.
Ciste Dhubh *High.* ***Mountain***, on border of Inverness and Skye and Lochalsh districts, 3m/5km N of head of Loch Cluanie. Munro: height 3221 feet or 982 metres. **49 G3** NH0616.
Citadel *High.* ***Suburb***, to N of Inverness town centre. NH6646.
Clabhach *Arg. & B.* ***Settlement***, near NW coast of Coll, 3m/5km NW of Arinagour. **36 A4** NM1858.
Clach Bheinn *Arg. & B.* ***Mountain***, with craggy summit, in Argyll Forest Park, rising above W shore of Loch Eck. Height 2109 feet or 643 metres. **22 C1** NS1288.
Clach-bhreac *Arg. & B.* ***Settlement***, near head of Loch Caolisport, 8m/12km NW of Tarbert. **21 F2** NR7675.
Clach Dhian *Moray Gaelic form of Shelter Stone, qv.*
Clach Leathad (Also known as Clachlet). *High.* ***Mountain***, in Lochaber district, 7m/11km NW of Bridge of Orchy, with skiing facilities. Height 3601 feet or 1098 metres. **39 E5** NN2449.
Clachaig *Arg. & B.* ***River***, on Mull, running N to Loch Bà 1m/2km NW of head of loch. NM5737.
Clachaig *Arg. & B.* ***Settlement***, on Little Eachaig River in Argyll, 5m/8km NW of Dunoon. **22 C1** NS1181.
Clachaig Water *Arg. & B.* ***River***, on Kintyre, flowing W to enter sea at Muasdale, 4m/6km S of Tayinloan. **21 E5** NR6840.
Clachan *Arg. & B.* ***Locality***, with power station, at head of Loch Fyne, in Argyll. **31 D3** NN1812.
Clachan *Arg. & B.* ***Settlement***, on Lismore, 2m/3km SW of Port Ramsay. **38 A5** NM8643.
Clachan *Arg. & B.* ***Village***, in Kintyre, Argyll, 10m/16km SW of Tarbert. **21 F4** NR7656.
Clachan *High.* ***Hamlet***, on W coast of Raasay, 2m/3km NW of S end of island. **48 B1** NG5436.
Clachan *W.Isles* ***Settlement***, 2m/3km E of Ardivachar Point on South Uist. **45 F5** NF7746.
Clachan-a-Luib *W.Isles* ***Settlement***, near W coast of North Uist, 3m/5km N of Cairinis. NF8163.
Clachan Bridge (Commonly known as The Atlantic Bridge.) *Arg. & B.* ***Bridge***, hump-backed road bridge connecting Seil with mainland of Argyll. NM7819.

C

Clachan Burn *High.* ***River***, flowing NW into sea at Farr Bay, Caithness district. **75 G3** NC7162.
Clachan Hill *Arg. & B.* ***Mountain***, to N of Loch Fyne, 7m/11km NE of Inveraray. Height 2158 feet or 658 metres. **31 D3** NN1815.
Clachan Mòr *Arg. & B.* ***Settlement***, on N coast of Tiree, 5m/7km NW of Scarinish. NL9847.
Clachan of Campsie (Also known as Campsie.) *E.Dun.* ***Village***, 2m/3km NW of Lennoxtown. **24 A2** NS6179.
Clachan of Glendaruel *Arg. & B.* ***Village***, in Argyll, on River Ruel, 4m/6km N of head of Loch Riddon. Churchyard contains Kilmodan Sculptured Stones (Historic Scotland), a group of West Highland carved grave slabs. **22 B1** NR9984.
Clachan-Seil *Arg. & B.* ***Settlement***, on Seil, nearly 1m/2km S of Clachan Bridge. **29 G3** NM7819.
Clachan Yell *Aber.* ***Mountain***, 6m/10km SE of Ballater. Height 2053 feet or 626 metres. **53 G5** NO4491.
Clachandhu *Arg. & B.* ***Settlement***, 1km N of Balnahard, Mull. **29 D1** NM4535.
Clachaneasy *D. & G.* ***Settlement***, 7m/11km NW of Newton Stewart. **7 E3** NX3574.
Clachanmore *D. & G.* ***Settlement***, 7m/11km SE of Portpatrick. **2 A2** NX0846.
Clachanturn *Aber.* ***Settlement***, 1m/2km SE of Craithie, S of River Dee. **53 E5** NO2794.
Clachlet *High. Alternative name for Clach Leathad, qv.*
Clachnaben *Aber.* ***Mountain***, 2m/3km W of Bridge of Dye. Height 1932 feet or 589 metres. **43 E1** NO6186.
Clachnabrain *Angus* ***Settlement***, in Glen Clova, 2m/3km S of Rottal. **42 B3** NO3766.
Clachnaharry *High.* ***Suburb***, in Inverness district, at N terminus of Caledonian Canal, on NW side of Inverness. **61 F5** NH6446.
Clachtoll *High.* ***Hamlet***, on W coast of Sutherland district, 5m/8km S of Point of Stoer. **70 C2** NC0427.
Clackmannan *Clack.* Population: 3420. ***Small town***, former wool manufacturing town, 2m/3km E of Alloa. Remains of 14-15c tower. **33 E5** NS9191.
Clackmannan Pow *Clack.* ***Sea feature***, small harbour where mouth of Black Devon River joins River Forth, 1m/2km SW of Clackmannan. NS8990.
Clackmannan Tower *Clack.* ***Historic/prehistoric site***, tall 15c tower to W of Clackmannan. **33 E5** NS9092.
Clackmarras *Moray* ***Settlement***, 3m/5km SE of Elgin. NJ2458.
Clackriach *Aber.* ***Locality***, 1m/2km S of Maud with remains of castle. NJ9246.
Cladach a' Chaolais (Anglicised form: Claddach Kyles.) *W.Isles* ***Settlement***, on North Uist, 6m/9km SE of Aird an Rùnair. **45 F3** NF7666.
Cladach Chircebost (Anglicised form: Claddach Kirkibost.) *W.Isles* ***Settlement***, on North Uist, 6m/10km SE of Aird an Rùnair. **45 F3** NF7865.
Claddach Kirkibost *W.Isles Anglicised form of Cladach Chircebost, qv.*
Claddach Kyles *W.Isles Anglicised form of Cladach a' Chaolais, qv.*
Cladich *Arg. & B.* ***Settlement***, in Argyll, near E side of Loch Awe, 5m/9km SW of Dalmally. **30 C2** NN0921.
Claggain Bay *Arg. & B.* ***Bay***, on E coast of Islay, 4m/6km S of McArthur's Head. **20 C4** NR4653.
Claggan *High.* ***Locality***, in Lochaber district, 4m/6km N of Lochaline. **37 G5** NM6949.
Claggan *High.* ***Settlement***, adjoining to NE of Fort William. **38 D2** NN1274.
Claigan *High.* ***Settlement***, on Skye, 2m/3km SW of Rubha Maol. **57 F4** NG2353.
Clairinch *Stir.* ***Island***, wooded islet in Loch Lomond, 1km SW of Balmaha. Part of nature reserve also comprising Inchcailloch and Torrinch. NS4189.
Claish Moss *High.* ***Marsh/bog***, 2m/4km NE of Salen, Lochaber district. **37 G3** NM7167.
Clan Donald Centre *High.* ***Other feature of interest***, museum depicting history of Clan Donald as Lords of the Isles, set at Armadale Castle, to N of Armadale on SE coast of Sleat peninsula. **48 C4** NG6304.
Clan Macpherson House and Museum *High.* ***Other feature of interest***, exhibition relating to history of Clan Macpherson, in Newtonmore. **51 G5** NN7099.
Clanyard Bay *D. & G.* ***Bay***, on W coast of Rinns of Galloway, 2m/3km S of Port Logan. **2 A3** NX0938.
Claonaig *Arg. & B.* ***Settlement***, in Kintyre, Argyll, 2m/3km W of Skipness. **21 G4** NR8756.
Claonaig Bay *Arg. & B.* ***Bay***, in Kintyre, 8m/12km S of Tarbert. NR8756.
Claonaig Water *Arg. & B.* ***River***, running S through Claonaig to Claonaig Bay, Kintyre, 8m/12km S of Tarbert. NR8756.
Claonairigh *Arg. & B.* ***Settlement***, 3m/5km SW of Inveraray. **30 C4** NN0504.
Claonel *High.* ***Settlement***, 1m/2km SW of Lairg. **72 A4** NC5604.
Clappers *Sc.Bord.* ***Hamlet***, 1m/2km E of Foulden. **27 G4** NT9455.
Clardon *High.* ***Locality***, includes Clardon Hill and scattered settlements to E of Thurso. **76 D2** ND1368.
Clardon Head *High.* ***Coastal feature***, headland on N coast of Caithness district, 3m/4km NE of Thurso. **76 D1** ND1570.
Clarebrand *D. & G.* ***Settlement***, 2m/3km N of Castle Douglas. **8 B4** NX7665.
Clarencefield *D. & G.* ***Village***, 7m/11km W of Annan. **9 E4** NY0968.
Clarilaw *Sc.Bord.* ***Settlement***, 3m/5km NE of Hawick. **17 G4** NT5218.
Clarkston *E.Renf.* Population: 18,899. ***Suburb***, 5m/8km S of Glasgow. Includes Greenbank Garden (National Trust for Scotland), which surrounds elegant Georgian house and has wide range of plants, shrubs and trees, and contains fountain garden and woodland walks. **23 G4** NS5757.
Clashach Point *Moray* ***Coastal feature***, point on N coast 1km NE of Hopeman. Clashnach Cove is bay to E. **63 D2** NJ1570.
Clashban *High.* ***Settlement***, 3m/5km NE of Bonar Bridge. **72 B5** NH6496.
Clashcoig *High.* ***Settlement***, 3m/4km NE of Bonar Bridge. **72 B5** NH6393.
Clashdorran *High.* ***Settlement***, in Ross and Cromarty district, 1m/2km SW of Muir of Ord. NH5148.
Clashgour *Arg. & B.* ***Settlement***, 4m/7km NW of Bridge of Orchy. **39 E5** NN2342.
Clashindarroch *Aber.* ***Settlement***, on W side of Kirkney Water, 3m/4km W of Gartly. **53 G1** NJ4831.
Clashindarroch Forest *Aber.* ***Forest/woodland***, 6m/9km SW of Huntly. **53 G1** NJ4633.
Clashmach Hill *Aber.* ***Mountain***, 4m/7km E of Haugh of Glass. Height 1230 feet or 375 metres. **53 G1** NJ4938.
Clashmore *High.* ***Settlement***, 3m/5km S of Point of Stoer, W coast of Sutherland district. NC0331.
Clashmore *High.* ***Village***, in Sutherland district, 3m/5km W of Dornoch. **72 C5** NH7489.
Clashmore Wood *High.* ***Forest/woodland***, on slopes of Creagan Asdale, 3m/5km W of Dornoch. **72 C5** NH7490.
Clashnessie *High.* ***Hamlet***, on Clashnessie Bay, W coast of Sutherland district, 4m/6km SE of Point of Stoer. **70 C1** NC0530.
Clashnessie Bay *High.* ***Bay***, on W coast of Sutherland district, 4m/6km SE of Point of Stoer. **70 C1** NC0531.
Clashnoir *Moray* ***Locality***, 5m/7km NE of Tomintoul. **53 E2** NJ2222.
Clathy *P. & K.* ***Settlement***, 6m/9km NE of Auchterarder. **33 E2** NN9920.
Clatt (Also known as Kirktown of Clatt). *Aber.* ***Village***, 3m/5km E of Rhynie. **54 A2** NJ5325.
Clatterin Brig *Aber.* ***Settlement***, 3m/5km N of Fettercairn. **43 E2** NO6678.
Clatteringshaws *D. & G.* ***Settlement***, on E side of Clatteringshaws Loch, 6m/9km W of New Galloway. **7 G3** NX5576.
Clatteringshaws Loch *D. & G.* ***Lake/loch***, large loch and reservoir (Galloway Hydro-electricity Scheme) 5m/9km W of New Galloway. Bruce's Stone (National Trust for Scotland), granite boulder on E shore. Galloway Deer Museum on E shore 1km S of Bruce's Stone. **7 G3** NX5476.
Clatteringshaws Wild Goat Park *D. & G.* ***Leisure/recreation***, enclosure of feral goats, 3m/5km SW of Clatteringshaws Loch and 7m/11km NE of Newton Stewart, within Galloway Forest Park. **7 G3** NX4972.
Clatto Country Park *Dundee* ***Leisure/recreation***, 3m/4km N of Dundee city centre. Reservoir is focal point of this 35 acre country park. **34 B1** NO3634.
Clatto Hill *Fife* ***Hill***, 3m/4km N of Kennoway. Height 813 feet or 248 metres. **34 B4** NO3506.
Clatto Reservoir *Dundee* ***Reservoir***, small reservoir in NW part of Dundee. Country Park adjacent. NO3634.
Clauchan Water *N.Ayr.* ***River***, on Arran, rising near Cnoc a' Chapuill and flowing W to Drumadoon Bay. NR9230.
Clauchlands Point *N.Ayr.* ***Coastal feature***, headland on E coast of Arran, at N end of Lamlash Bay. **13 F2** NS0532.
Clauchrie Burn *D. & G.* ***River***, stream rising on Auchercairn Height and flowing S to join River Nith, 1km N of Auldgirth. **8 D2** NX9087.
Clava Cairns *High.* ***Historic/prehistoric site***, group of three Stone Age-Bronze Age burial cairns (Historic Scotland), 6m/9km E of Inverness beyond Culloden. **61 G5** NH7544.
Clawfin *E.Ayr.* ***Settlement***, 2m/3km NE of Dalmellington. **14 D5** NS5007.
Clay of Allan *High.* ***Settlement***, 4m/6km SE of Tain. **62 A2** NH8276.
Clayock *High.* ***Locality***, 1m/2km E of Georgemas Junction Station. **77 D3** ND1659.
Claypotts Castle *Dundee* ***Castle***, 16c castle (Historic Scotland), 1km NW of Broughty Ferry. **34 C1** NO4531.
Claythorn *Glas.* ***Suburb***, 3m/5km NW of Glasgow city centre. NS5468.
Cleadale *High.* ***Hamlet***, at NW end of Eigg. **37 D1** NM4788.
Cleat *Ork.* ***Settlement***, near S end of South Ronaldsay, 1m/2km NE of Brough Ness. **79 D4** ND4584.
Cleat *W.Isles* ***Settlement***, on N coast of Barra, 1m/2km E of Greian Head. NF6604.
Cleghorn *S.Lan.* ***Settlement***, 2m/3km NE of Lanark. **24 D5** NS8946.
Cleigh *Arg. & B.* ***Settlement***, in Argyll, 3m/5km S of Oban. **30 A2** NM8725.
Cleiseval *W.Isles* ***Mountain***, in Forest of Harris, 2m/3km SW of head of Loch Meavaig. Height 1676 feet or 511 metres. **66 C3** NB0708.
Cleish *P. & K.* ***Village***, 3m/5km SW of Kinross at foot of Cleish Hills. **33 F5** NT0998.
Cleish Castle *P. & K.* ***Castle***, restored 16c-17c castle to W of Cleish. NT0897.
Cleish Hills *P. & K.* ***Large natural feature***, hills extend from Saline in W to Kelty in E, SW of Loch Leven. **33 F5** NT0696.
Cléit Dhubh *High.* ***Coastal feature***, headland on N coast of Sutherland district, 4m/7km E of Cape Wrath. NC3273.
Cleland *N.Lan.* Population: 2945. ***Village***, 3m/5km E of Motherwell. **24 B4** NS7958.
Clephanton *High.* ***Settlement***, 5m/8km SW of Nairn. **62 A4** NH8150.
Clerklands *Sc.Bord.* ***Hamlet***, 3m/5km SE of Selkirk. **17 G3** NT5024.
Clermiston *Edin.* ***Suburb***, 4m/6km W of Edinburgh city centre. NT1974.
Clestrain *Ork.* ***Settlement***, in S part of Mainland, E of Skerries of Clestrain. **78 C2** HY3006.
Clestrain Sound *Ork.* ***Sea feature***, sea passage between islands of Mainland and Graemsay. Named after locality on Mainland to E. **78 B2** HY2706.
Clett *High.* ***Island***, islet on W side of Holborn Head, Caithness district, 2m/3km N of Thurso. **76 C1** ND1071.
Clett *High.* ***Island***, islet off NW coast of Skye, 1m/2km S of Ardmore Point. NG2258.
Clett Ard *W.Isles* ***Mountain***, with notable viewpoint, 2m/3km NW of Marvig, to W of Loch Seaforth, North Harris. Height 1076 feet or 328 metres. **67 D3** NB1808.
Clett Head *Shet.* ***Coastal feature***, headland at S end of Whalsay. **83 E1** HU5560.
Clett Nisabost *W.Isles* ***Hill***, near W coast of South Harris, 3m/4km N of Loch Langavat. Height 518 feet or 158 metres. **66 C4** NG0495.
Clettack Skerry *Ork.* ***Island***, one of Pentland Skerries, most easterly of group. ND4877.
Cleuch Head *Sc.Bord.* ***Hamlet***, 1m/2km SE of Bonchester Bridge. **17 G4** NT5910.
Cleuchbrae *D. & G.* ***Settlement***, 2m/3km N of Mouswald and 6m/10km W of Dumfries. **9 E3** NY0673.
Cliad Bay *Arg. & B.* ***Bay***, on NW coast of Coll, 3m/4km NW of Arinagour. **36 A3** NM1960.
Cliatasay *W.Isles* ***Island***, islet in Loch Roag, W coast of Isle of Lewis, opposite entrance to Little Loch Roag. NB1333.
Click Mill *Ork.* ***Historic/prehistoric site***, 2m/3km NE of Dounby. Only working specimen of traditional Orcadian horizontal water mill (Historic Scotland). **80 B4** HY3222.
Clickimin Broch *Shet.* ***Historic/prehistoric site***, broch or castle (Historic Scotland) at end of causeway running out into Loch of Clickimin on W side of Lerwick. **83 D3** HU4640.
Cliff *High.* ***Settlement***, on E bank of River Shiel, 1m/2km N of Acharacle, Lochaber district. **37 F3** NM6769.
Clift Hills *Shet.* ***Large natural feature***, line of hills running N and S on Mainland, on E side of Clift Sound. **82 C4** HU3931.
Clift Sound *Shet.* ***Sea feature***, sea channel S of Scalloway between Mainland and islands of Trondra and East Burra. **82 C4** HU3934.
Clifton *Stir.* ***Village***, on NW side of Tyndrum. **31 F1** NN3230.
Climpy *S.Lan.* ***Settlement***, 1m/2km NW of Forth. **24 D4** NS9255.
Clinterty *Aberdeen* ***Locality***, comprises Little Mill of Clinterty and Haughs of Clinterty, together with nearby Meikle Clinterty and Clinterty Home Farm, to SW of Kirkhill Forest, 3m/4km N of Westhill. **54 D3** NJ8310.
Clintmains *Sc.Bord.* ***Hamlet***, 2m/3km NE of St. Boswells, over River Tweed. **18 A3** NT6132.
Clints Dod *E.Loth.* ***Mountain***, in Lammermuir Hills, 3m/5km NW of Whiteadder Reservoir. Height 1309 feet or 399 metres. **26 D3** NT6268.
Clisham *W.Isles* ***Mountain***, in North Harris 5m/7km N of Tarbert. Highest point on Isle of Lewis. Height 2621 feet or 799 metres. **67 D3** NB1507.
Clivocast *Shet.* ***Settlement***, on S coast of Unst, 1km E of Uyeasound. **85 F2** HP6000.
Cloch Point *Inclyde* ***Coastal feature***, headland with lighthouse, on Firth of Clyde opposite Dunoon, 3m/4km SW of Gourock. **22 C2** NS2075.
Clochan *Moray* ***Village***, near N coast, 3m/5km S of Buckie. **63 G3** NJ4060.
Clochtow *Aber.* ***Settlement***, 1km W of Radel Haven, 4m/7km SW of Cruden Bay. **55 F1** NK0530.
Clockhill *Aber.* ***Settlement***, 3m/4km SW of Maud. **65 D5** NJ8945.
Cloddach *Moray* ***Settlement***, 3m/4km S of Elgin. **63 D4** NJ1958.
Cloichran *Stir.* ***Settlement***, 4m/6km SW of Ardeonaig on S bank of Loch Tay. **32 B1** NN6133.

Clola *Aber.* ***Village***, 8m/13km W of Peterhead. **65 F5** NK0043.
Clonrae *D. & G.* ***Settlement***, 6m/10km NE of Moniaive. **8 C1** NX8293.
Closeburn *D. & G.* ***Village***, 2m/4km SE of Thornhill. **8 C1** NX8992.
Closeburn Castle *D. & G.* ***Castle***, 14c tower house, to E of Closeburn, 3m/4km SE of Thornhill. NX9092.
Clothan *Shet.* ***Settlement***, on SW coast of Yell, 1km N of Ulsta. **85 D4** HU4581.
Cloud Hill *D. & G.* ***Mountain***, 3m/5km SW of Sanquhar. Height 1479 feet or 451 metres. **15 F5** NS7305.
Clounlaid *High.* ***Settlement***, 4m/7km NE of Ardtornish, Lochaber district. **37 G4** NM7552.
Clousta *Shet.* ***Hamlet***, on Mainland, at head of Voe of Clousta. **82 C2** HU3057.
Clouston *Ork.* ***Settlement***, in Stenness, Mainland, 1km S of Loch of Stenness. **80 B5** HY3011.
Clova *Aber.* ***Settlement***, to E of Clova Hill, 4m/6km SW of Rhynie. **53 G2** NJ4522.
Clova *Angus* ***Village***, in Glen Clova, 12m/19km N of Kirriemuir. **42 B2** NO3273.
Clova Castle *Angus* ***Castle***, fragment of castle overlooking Clova in Glen Clova, 12m/19km N of Kirriemuir. NO3273.
Clovenfords *Sc.Bord.* ***Village***, 3m/4km W of Galashiels. **17 F2** NT4436.
Clovenstone *Aber.* ***Locality***, 3m/4km S of Inverurie. **54 C3** NJ7717.
Cloverhill *Aberdeen* ***Settlement***, 1km inland from coast and 4m/6km N of Aberdeen harbour. **55 E3** NJ9412.
Cloves *Moray* ***Settlement***, 5m/8km W of Elgin. **62 D3** NJ1361.
Clovullin *High.* ***Hamlet***, on W shore of Loch Linnhe in Lochaber district, 1m/2km NE of Sallachan Point. **38 C3** NN0063.
Cloyntie *S.Ayr.* ***Settlement***, 3m/5km SE of Maybole. **14 B5** NS3305.
Cluanach *Arg. & B.* ***Settlement***, on Islay, 3m/5km E of Bowmore. **20 B4** NR3659.
Cluanie Deer Park Farm *High.* ***Leisure/recreation***, wildlife centre with red and fallow deer and birds of prey, 4m/6km SW of Beauly. **61 D5** NH4743.
Cluanie Forest *High.* ***Open space***, deer forest in Skye and Lochalsh district to S and W of head of Loch Cluanie. **49 G3** NH0409.
Cluas Deas *High.* ***Coastal feature***, small headland 3m/4km SW of Point of Stoer, Sutherland district. **70 B1** NC0032.
Clubbie Craig *Aber.* ***Coastal feature***, headland on N coast at Fraserburgh, 1km W of Kinnairds Head. NJ9967.
Clubbiedean Reservoir *Edin.* ***Reservoir***, small reservoir 2m/4km E of Balerno. Bonaly Country Park at E side. NT2066.
Cluden Water *D. & G.* ***River***, formed by confluence of Cairn Water and Old Water to S of Newtonairds, and running SE to River Nith, 1m/2km N of Dumfries. NX9677.
Cluer *W.Isles* ***Settlement***, on E coast of South Harris, 1m/2km S of Greosabhagh. **66 D4** NG1490.
Clugston Loch *D. & G.* ***Lake/loch***, small loch 3m/4km SE of Kirkcowan. NX3457.
Clunas *High.* ***Locality***, 3m/5km SE of Cawdor. **62 A5** NH8746.
Clunas Reservoir *High.* ***Reservoir***, 7m/11km S of Nairn. NH8545.
Clune *High.* ***Settlement***, in Strathdearn, 2m/3km S of Tomatin. **51 G2** NH7925.
Clune *Moray* ***Settlement***, 2m/3km S of Cullen. **64 A3** NJ5163.
Clunes *High.* ***Hamlet***, in Lochaber district on NW shore of Loch Lochy, 3m/5km NE of foot of loch. **39 D1** NN2088.
Clunes Forest *High.* ***Forest/woodland***, round NW shore of Loch Lochy. NN2189.
Clunie *Aber.* ***Locality***, comprises Clunie Hill, Backhill of Clunie and Home Farm of Clunie, 1m/2km SE of Aberchirder. **64 B4** NJ6350.
Clunie *P. & K.* ***Settlement***, on W shore of Loch of Clunie, 4m/7km W of Blairgowrie. **41 G5** NO1143.
Clunie Water *Aber.* ***River***, running N down Glen Clunie to River Dee on N side of Braemar. **41 G1** NO1492.
Cluny *Aber.* ***Locality***, and castle 3m/4km N of Banchory. NO6899.
Cluny *Fife* ***Settlement***, 3m/5km NW of Kirkcaldy. **34 A5** NT2495.
Cluny House Gardens *P. & K.* ***Garden***, wild woodland garden with wide range of Himalayan plants, 2m/3km NE of Aberfeldy. **41 D4** NN8751.
Clyde ***River***, rising S of Abington and W of Moffat and flowing NW through Glasgow to Firth of Clyde at Dumbarton. **24 A3** NS3974.
Clyde Law ***Mountain***, on border of Scottish Borders and South Lanarkshire, 5m/8km E of Elvanfoot. Height 1791 feet or 546 metres. **16 B4** NT0217.
Clydebank *W.Dun.* Population: 29,171. ***Town***, industrial town on N bank of River Clyde, 6m/10km NW of Glasgow. Formerly a shipbuilding town, the QEII was built here. **23 G3** NS5069.
Clydesdale ***Valley***, carrying mid section of River Clyde, stretching from confluence with Medwin Water at The Meetings, 1m/2km SE of Carstairs Junction, to urban development S of Motherwell. Valley is broad from The Meetings, before narrowing at Hyndford Bridge and becoming a gorge, with many waterfalls, notably Bonnington Linn and Corra Linn, and nature trails around Lanark. Beyond Crossford, valley broadens again, with steep parallel sides as river meanders NE. **24 C5** NS8249.
Clynder *Arg. & B.* ***Village***, on W shore of Gare Loch, 3m/4km N of Kilcreggan. **22 D1** NS2484.
Clynelish *High.* ***Settlement***, in Sutherland district, 1m/2km NW of Brora. **73 D4** NC8905.
Clyth *High.* ***Locality***, near E coast of Caithness district, 2m/3km E of Lybster, containing Upper and Mid Clyth. ND2736.
Clyth Ness *High.* ***Coastal feature***, headland with lighthouse on E coast of Caithness district, 3m/4km E of Lybster. ND2936.
Cnap Chaochan Aitinn *Moray* ***Mountain***, rising to N above Glen Loin, 6m/9km S of Tomintoul. Height 2342 feet or 714 metres. **52 D4** NJ1409.
Cnap Coire na Spreidhe *High.* ***Mountain***, NE peak of Cairn Gorm, in Badenoch and Strathspey district. Height 3775 feet or 1151 metres. NJ0104.
Cnoc (Anglicised form: Knock.) *W.Isles* ***Village***, on Eye Peninsula, Isle of Lewis, 4m/7km E of Stornoway. **69 F4** NB4931.
Cnoc a' Bhaid Bhàin *High.* ***Mountain***, rising to N of Strath an Lòin and E shore of Loch Shin. Height 1207 feet or 368 metres. **71 G3** NC4219.
Cnoc a' Bhaid-rallaich *High.* ***Mountain***, in Ross and Cromarty district, 4m/6km W of Ullapool across Loch Broom. Height 1788 feet or 545 metres. **70 C5** NH0693.
Cnoc a' Bhaile-shios *Arg. & B.* ***Mountain***, on Kintyre, 4m/6km S of Tarbert. Height 1384 feet or 422 metres. **21 G3** NR8662.
Cnoc a' Bharaille *Arg. & B.* ***Mountain***, on Knapdale, 5m/7km NW of Tarbert. Height 1545 feet or 471 metres. **21 F2** NR8072.
Cnoc a' Chapuill *N.Ayr.* ***Mountain***, on Arran, 4m/6km W of Lamlash. Height 1368 feet or 417 metres. **13 E3** NR9629.
Cnoc a' Choire *High.* ***Mountain***, to S of Strath Grudie, 3m/4km NE of Invercassley. Height 1319 feet or 402 metres. **72 A4** NC5004.
Cnoc a' Chraois *High.* ***Mountain***, situated to S of Strath More. Height 1141 feet or 348 metres. **75 D4** NC4540.
Cnoc a' Ghiubhais *High.* ***Hill***, 3m/5km S of Cape Wrath. Height 974 feet or 297 metres. **74 B1** NC2670.
Cnoc a' Ghiubhais *High.* ***Mountain***, S of Srath a' Chràisg, 7m/11km S of Altnaharra, Sutherland district. Height 1135 feet or 346 metres. **72 A2** NC5423.
Cnoc a' Ghriama *High.* ***Mountain***, in Sutherland district, rising to E of Loch a' Ghriama. Height 1220 feet or 372 metres. **71 G2** NC4026.
Cnoc a' Mhadaidh *Arg. & B.* ***Mountain***, in Argyll Forest Park, 1m/2km NE of Orchard. Height 1542 feet or 470 metres. **22 C1** NS1683.
Cnoc a' Mhoid *High.* ***Hill***, 4m/6km SW of S end of Loch Loyal, Caithness district. Height 830 feet or 253 metres. **75 E4** NC5740.
Cnoc Ach'na h-Uai *High.* ***Hill***, in Sutherland district, 1km N of Loch Achnamoine. Height 928 feet or 283 metres. **76 A5** NC8133.
Cnoc an Alaskie *High.* ***Mountain***, 3m/4km SE of S end of Loch Fiag, Sutherland district. Height 1023 feet or 312 metres. **71 G2** NC4926.
Cnoc an dà Chinn *Arg. & B.* ***Mountain***, 3m/4km E of Kilninian, Mull. Height 1282 feet or 391 metres. **36 D5** NM4444.
Cnoc an Daimh Beag *High.* ***Hill***, 1m/2km E of Loch Meadie. Height 968 feet or 295 metres. **75 E4** NC5240.
Cnoc an Daimh Mòr *High.* ***Mountain***, 3m/4km S of Loch an Dherue, Caithness district. Height 1168 feet or 356 metres. **75 E4** NC5342.
Cnoc an Earrannaiche *High.* ***Hill***, 4m/6km N of Lybster. Height 692 feet or 211 metres. **77 E4** ND2441.
Cnoc an Eireannaich *High.* ***Mountain***, on border of Sutherland and Caithness districts, 2m/3km SE of Cnoc Coire na Feàrna. Height 1696 feet or 517 metres. **73 E2** NC9527.
Cnoc an Fhuarain Bhàin *High.* ***Hill***, 4m/6km E of Trantlebeg. Height 797 feet or 243 metres. **76 B3** NC9553.
Cnoc an Liath-bhaid Mhòir *High.* ***Mountain***, 2m/4km S of Loch an Alltan Fheàrna, Sutherland district. Height 1424 feet or 434 metres. **72 C2** NC7529.
Cnoc an t-Sabhail *High.* ***Mountain***, with rounded summit in Ross and Cromarty district, 6m/10km NE of Alness. Height 1243 feet or 379 metres. **61 F2** NH6879.
Cnoc an t-Samhlaidh *Arg. & B.* ***Hill***, on Kintyre, 3m/5km NW of Grogport. Height 866 feet or 264 metres. **21 F5** NR7949.
Cnoc an t-Sìdhein *High.* ***Mountain***, rounded summit in Ross and Cromarty district, 3m/4km S of Achnasheen. Height 1220 feet or 372 metres. **60 A4** NH1553.
Cnoc an t-Soluis *W.Isles Gaelic form of Lighthill, qv.*
Cnoc Ard an t-Siùil *High.* ***Hill***, situated just S of Whiten Head. Height 600 feet or 183 metres. **75 D2** NC4967.
Cnoc Badaireach na Gaoithe *High.* ***Hill***, 2m/3km SE of S end of Strathy Forest. Height 699 feet or 213 metres. **76 A3** NC8451.
Cnoc Beithe *P. & K.* ***Mountain***, 3m/5km N of Crieff. Height 1460 feet or 445 metres. **33 D2** NN8626.
Cnoc Breac *High.* ***Hill***, 5m/8km SE of Rubha Réidh, Ross and Cromarty district. Height 961 feet or 293 metres. **59 D1** NG7884.
Cnoc Ceann nam Bad *High.* ***Hill***, 4m/7km S of Lairg, to W of Achany Glen. Height 879 feet or 268 metres. **72 A4** NC5500.
Cnoc Céislein *High.* ***Mountain***, in Ross and Cromarty district, 4m/6km W of Alness. Height 1715 feet or 523 metres. **61 E2** NH5870.
Cnoc Coinnich *Arg. & B.* ***Mountain***, in area of Argyll known as Argyll's Bowling Green, between Loch Goil and Loch Long. Height 2496 feet or 761 metres. **31 E4** NN2300.
Cnoc Coire na Feàrna *High.* ***Mountain***, on border of Sutherland and Caithness districts, 4m/7km E of Burnfoot. Height 1430 feet or 436 metres. **76 B5** NC9329.
Cnoc Corr Guinie *High.* ***Mountain***, rounded summit, in Ross and Cromarty district, 4m/6km NE of Alness. Height 1302 feet or 397 metres. **61 F2** NH6676.
Cnoc Craggie *High.* ***Mountain***, rising above W shore of Loch Craggie. Height 1046 feet or 319 metres. **75 F3** NC6052.
Cnoc Cromuillt *High.* ***Mountain***, on border of Sutherland and Caithness districts, 4m/7km SE of Forsinard. Height 1200 feet or 366 metres. **76 B5** NC9438.
Cnoc Eille Mòr *High.* ***Mountain***, in Inverness district, 5m/7km W of Beauly. Height 1322 feet or 403 metres. **60 D5** NH4548.
Cnoc Fraing *High.* ***Mountain***, in Badenoch and Strathspey district, 6m/9km NW of Aviemore. Height 2444 feet or 745 metres. **52 A3** NH8014.
Cnoc Freiceadain *High. See Reay.*
Cnoc Glac na Luachrach *High.* ***Hill***, rising to over 140 metres, 2m/3km S of Broadford Airport, Skye. **48 C2** NG6921.
Cnoc Leamhnachd *High.* ***Hill***, 1km E of Loch Beannach and 2m/4km N of Rhilochan. Height 961 feet or 293 metres. **72 C3** NC7511.
Cnoc Meadhonach *High.* ***Mountain***, in Sutherland district, 5m/8km N of Gordonbush. Height 1128 feet or 344 metres. **72 D3** NC8417.
Cnoc Moy *Arg. & B.* ***Mountain***, rounded summit on S part of Kintyre, 6m/10km NW of Southend. Height 1463 feet or 446 metres. **12 B4** NR6115.
Cnoc Muigh-bhlàraidh *High.* ***Mountain***, in Ross and Cromarty district, 6m/10km SE of Bonar Bridge. Height 1791 feet or 546 metres. **61 F1** NH6382.
Cnoc na Breun-choille *High.* ***Mountain***, 1m/2km SW of Altanduin, Sutherland district. Height 1197 feet or 365 metres. **72 C2** NC7824.
Cnoc na Carriage *Arg. & B.* ***Hill***, at SE end of Cowal peninsula, 3m/5km S of Tighnabruaich. Height 679 feet or 207 metres. **22 A3** NR9768.
Cnoc na Feannaig *High.* ***Mountain***, 2m/4km NW of Dalbreck, on NW side of Srath na Seilge. Height 1260 feet or 384 metres. **72 C3** NC7119.
Cnoc na Glas Choille *High.* ***Mountain***, summit lies 1m/2km SE of Loch Urigill. Height 1007 feet or 307 metres. **71 E4** NC2708.
Cnoc na h-Innse Mòire *High.* ***Mountain***, 3m/5km W of Craggie, Sutherland district. Height 1102 feet or 336 metres. **72 D3** NC8219.
Cnoc na Moine *High.* ***Mountain***, with forested summit in Inverness district, 5m/7km SW of Inverness. Height 1036 feet or 316 metres. **61 E5** NH5942.
Cnoc na Saobhaidhe *High.* ***Hill***, 3m/4km SW of Ben Alisky. Height 951 feet or 290 metres. **76 C5** ND0235.
Cnoc nan Cuilean *High.* ***Mountain***, 1m/2km SW of Lettermore, Caithness district. Height 1827 feet or 557 metres. **75 E4** NC5946.
Cnoc nan Gall *High.* ***Hill***, on border of Sutherland and Caithness districts, 3m/5km E of Forsinard. Height 902 feet or 275 metres. **76 B4** NC9442.
Cnoc nan Sltheag *Stir.* ***Open space***, partly wooded hillslope, 4m/6km N of Aberfoyle. **32 A4** NN5307.
Cnoc nan Tri-chlach *High.* ***Mountain***, rising above W shore of Loch Cròcach, Caithness district. Height 1132 feet or 345 metres. **75 G4** NC7943.
Cnoc Odhar *Arg. & B.* ***Hill***, on S part of Kintyre, 5m/8km SW of Campbeltown. Height 909 feet or 277 metres. **12 B4** NR6612.
Cnoc Reamhar *Arg. & B.* ***Hill***, on S part of Kintyre, 6m/9km NW of Southend. Height 895 feet or 273 metres. **12 B4** NR6013.
Cnoc Reamhar *Arg. & B.* ***Hill***, on Knapdale, 5m/7km W of Cairnbaan. Height 869 feet or 265 metres. **29 G5** NR7691.

C

Cnoc Reamhar *Arg. & B.* ***Hill***, on Kintyre, 2m/3km NW of Grogport. Height 666 feet or 203 metres. **21 F5** NR7746.
Cnoc Salislade *High.* ***Mountain***, 2m/4km NE of Kildonan Lodge, Sutherland district. Height 1584 feet or 483 metres. **73 E2** NC9423.
Cnoc Uaine *High. Gaelic form of Knock, qv.*
Cnocan Conachreag *High.* ***Hill***, 6m/9km NW of Dunbeath. Height 882 feet or 269 metres. **76 D5** ND1136.
Cnocan Dubh *High.* ***Mountain***, in Lochaber district, between Loch Loyne and Loch Garry. Height 1122 feet or 342 metres. **50 A4** NH1703.
Cnocloisgte Water *High.* ***River***, in Caithness district, running NE and joining Cnocglass Water just S of Loch Calium. **76 B3** ND0251.
Coachford *Aber.* ***Settlement***, 4m/6km SE of Keith. **63 G5** NJ4645.
Coalburn *S.Lan.* Population: 1169. ***Village***, 3m/5km S of Lesmahagow. **15 G2** NS8134.
Coalsnaughton *Clack.* ***Village***, 1km S of Tillicoultry across River Devon. **33 E5** NS9295.
Coaltown of Balgonie *Fife* ***Village***, 1m/2km S of Markinch. **34 B5** NT3099.
Coaltown of Wemyss *Fife* ***Village***, 1km N of West Wemyss and 4m/7km NE of Kirkcaldy. **34 B5** NT3295.
Coast *High.* ***Settlement***, 1km W of Second Coast and 1m/2km SE of Laide, in Ross and Cromarty district. **70 B5** NG9291.
Coatbridge *N.Lan.* Population: 43,617. ***Town***, 9m/14km E of Glasgow. Former steel town, with industrial museum. **24 B3** NS7265.
Cobairdy *Aber.* ***Settlement***, on S side of Fourman Hill, 4m/6km NE of Huntly. **64 A5** NJ5743.
Cobbinshaw Reservoir *W.Loth.* ***Reservoir***, 3m/5km S of West Calder. **25 E4** NT0158.
Cobleland *Stir.* ***Settlement***, on River Forth, 1m/2km NE of Gartmore. **32 A5** NS5398.
Coburty *Aber.* ***Locality***, 3m/4km S of Rosehearty. **65 E3** NJ9264.
Cochill Burn *P. & K.* ***River***, running S down Glen Cochill to join River Quaich and form River Braan 2m/3km NE of Amulree. NN9238.
Cochno *W.Dun.* ***Settlement***, 3m/4km N of Clydebank. **23 F2** NS4974.
Cochno Loch *Renf.* ***Lake/loch***, small loch on Kilpatrick Hills 4m/6km W of Milngavie. NS4976.
Cochrage Muir *P. & K.* ***Open space***, fairly flat area of hill and moorland, 4m/6km NW of Blairgowrie. **41 G5** NO1249.
Cochran *Aber.* ***Locality***, adjoining to SE of Kincardine O'Neil. NO5999.
Cock Bridge *Aber.* ***Settlement***, near road bridge over River Don 8m/12km SE of Tomintoul. 16c-17c Corgarff Castle (Historic Scotland) to SW. **53 E4** NJ2509.
Cock Cairn ***Mountain***, 4m/6km SW of Ballochan. Summit on border of Aberdeenshire and Angus. Height 2385 feet or 727 metres. **42 C1** NO4688.
Cock Hill *Aber.* ***Mountain***, 2m/3km SE of Ballochan. Height 1961 feet or 598 metres. **42 D1** NO5387.
Cock Law *N.Ayr.* ***Mountain***, to W of and overlooking Camphill Reservoir. Height 1174 feet or 358 metres. **23 D4** NS2555.
Cock Law *Sc.Bord.* ***Mountain***, rising to over 410 metres and aligned N to S, in Cheviot Hills to E of Kelsocleugh Burn. **18 C5** NT8518.
Cock of Arran *N.Ayr.* ***Coastal feature***, headland at N end of Arran. **22 A4** NR9552.
Cockburn Law *Sc.Bord.* ***Mountain***, with hillfort at summit, 2m/3km SE of Abbey St. Bathans. Height 1066 feet or 325 metres. **27 E3** NT7659.
Cockburnspath *Sc.Bord.* ***Village***, near coast, 8m/12km SE of Dunbar. **27 E2** NT7771.
Cockenzie and Port Seton *E.Loth.* Population: 4235. ***Small town***, on Firth of Forth, 4m/6km NE of Musselburgh. Power station to W. Seton Sands beach on coast to E. **26 B2** NT4075.
Cocker Hill *D. & G.* ***Mountain***, 3m/4km NE of Kirkconnel. Height 1650 feet or 503 metres. **15 F4** NS7515.
Cockholm Burn *Sc.Bord.* ***River***, small stream which rises in mountains 4m/7km NW of Lauder, and flows S to join Gala Water at Stow. **26 B5** NT4444.
Cocklaw Hill *E.Loth.* ***Mountain***, 1m/2km NW of Oldhamstocks. Height 1050 feet or 320 metres. **27 E2** NT7271.
Cockleroy *W.Loth.* ***Hill***, with fort and panoramic viewpoint, 2m/3km SW of Linlithgow. Height 912 feet or 278 metres. **25 D2** NS9874.
Cockmuir *Aber.* ***Settlement***, 3m/4km E of Strichen. NJ9855.
Cockpen *Midloth.* ***Settlement***, 2m/3km S of Dalkeith. NT3263.
Coduinn *W.Isles* ***Hill***, 1m/2km SW of head of Little Loch Roag, Isle of Lewis. Height 790 feet or 241 metres. **68 C5** NB1129.
Cóig Peighinnean (Anglicised form: Five Penny Ness.) *W.Isles* ***Village***, 1m/2km S of Butt of Lewis and 1m/2km NW of Port Nis. **69 G1** NB5264.
Cóig Peighinnean Bhuirgh (Anglicised form: Five Penny Borve.) *W.Isles* ***Village***, near NW coast of Isle of Lewis adjoining High Borve and 5m/8km NE of Barvas. **69 E2** NB4056.
Coigach *High.* ***Large natural feature***, upland area in Ross and Cromarty district, 6m/9km N of Ullapool and 6m/9km SE of Achiltibuie. **70 C4** NC1004.
Coignafearn Forest *High.* ***Open space***, deer forest on Monadhliath Mountains in Inverness district, astride upper reaches of River Findhorn. **51 F3** NH6412.
Coilantogle *Stir.* ***Settlement***, 2m/3km W of Callander. **32 A4** NN5906.
Coileitir *High.* ***Settlement***, in Glen Etive, 2m/3km NE of head of Loch Etive. **38 D5** NN1446.
Coilesan *Arg. & B.* ***Settlement***, on NE side, near N end of Loch Long, 3m/5km SW of Arrochar. **31 E4** NN2600.
Coiliochbhar Hill *Aber.* ***Mountain***, 4m/7km W of Alford. Height 1745 feet or 532 metres. **54 A3** NJ5015.
Coillaig *Arg. & B.* ***Settlement***, to N of Loch Awe, 2m/3km SW of Kilchrenan. **30 C2** NN0120.
Coille Coire Chrannaig *High.* ***Forest/woodland***, small wooded area to NW of Loch Laggan, 3m/5km W of Kinloch Laggan. **39 G1** NN4789.
Coille Mhòr *High.* ***Mountain***, W summit of Druim Fhada, 6m/10km NW of Fort William. Height 2083 feet or 635 metres. **38 C1** NN0382.
Coille Mhorgil *High.* ***Settlement***, 13m/21km W of Invergarry. **50 A4** NH1001.
Coille-righ *High.* ***Settlement***, in Glen Elchaig, 5m/8km E of Dornie, Skye and Lochalsh district. **49 F2** NG9627.
Coilleag a' Phrionnsa *W.Isles* ***Coastal feature***, 'The Prince's Beach' on W coast of Eriskay where Prince Charles Edward Stuart first landed on Scottish soil in 1744. NF7810.
Coillemore Point *N.Ayr.* ***Coastal feature***, headland at N end of Arran, on W side of entrance to Loch Ranza. NR9251.
Coillore *High.* ***Settlement***, 1km SE of Bracadale across Loch Beag, Skye. **47 G1** NG3537.
Coiltie *High.* ***River***, in Inverness district running NE to Urquhart Bay on NW side of Loch Ness. **50 D2** NH5229.
Coiltry *High.* ***Locality***, in Inverness district, 3m/4km SW of Fort Augustus. NH3506.
Coirc Bheinn *Arg. & B.* ***Mountain***, 3m/4km SE of Balnahard, Mull. Height 1840 feet or 561 metres. **29 D1** NM4832.
Coire a' Chonachair *High.* ***Open space***, hillslope to SW of Mullach Chonachair and 1m/2km W of Lubcroy. **71 E4** NC3302.
Coire Bog *High.* ***River***, rising on NE slope of Sròn na Saobhaidhe and flowing E into Wester Fearn Burn, 3m/5km SW of Kincardine. **61 E1** NH5885.
Coire Cas *High.* ***Inland physical feature***, corrie in Badenoch and Strathspey district. Main skiing area on NW slope of Cairn Gorm. NH9904.
Coire Ceirsle Hill *High.* ***Mountain***, in Lochaber district, 3m/5km NE of Spean Bridge. Height 2145 feet or 654 metres. **39 E1** NN2485.
Coire Dhuinnid *High.* ***Valley***, carrying An Leth-allt SW into Loch Duich, 3m/4km SE of Dornie. **49 F2** NG9224.
Coire Fhionn Lochan *N.Ayr.* ***Lake/loch***, tarn below N slope of Beinn Bhreac on Arran, 3m/5km SW of Lochranza. NR9045.
Coire Làgan *High.* ***Inland physical feature***, corrie and noted climbing area in Cuillin Hills to W of Sgurr Alasdair, Skye. NG4320.
Coire Lochan *High.* ***Lake/loch***, on N slope of Carn Eige and 1m/2km S of W part of Loch Mullardoch. **50 A2** NH1227.
Coire na Beinne *High.* ***Hill***, 6m/10km N of Dunbeath. Height 741 feet or 226 metres. **76 D4** ND1440.
Coire na Ciste *High.* ***Inland physical feature***, corrie in Badenoch and Strathspey district, below Cairn Gorm, 1m/2km N of summit. Used for skiing, it contains a chair lift and several ski tows. NJ0006.
Coire nan Capull *Arg. & B.* ***Mountain***, rounded summit on Kintyre, 3m/5km S of Tarbert. Height 1096 feet or 334 metres. **21 G3** NR8561.
Coire Nochd Mòr *P. & K.* ***Mountain***, 7m/11km NE of Callander. Height 1630 feet or 497 metres. **32 C3** NN7411.
Coire Odhar *High.* ***Inland physical feature***, corrie to W of Meall nan Ruadhag, 9m/14km SE of Fort Augustus. **51 E4** NH5006.
Coire Odhar *P. & K.* ***Locality***, SW slope (National Trust for Scotland) of Ben Lawers, headquarters of Scottish Ski club. NN6140.
Coirefrois Burn *High.* ***River***, flowing E and joining Black Water river to E of Dalbreck. **72 B3** NC7415.
Col (Anglicised form: Coll.) *W.Isles* Population: 1161. ***Village***, near E coast of Isle of Lewis, 5m/8km NE of Stornoway. **69 F3** NB4640.
Col-bheinn *High.* ***Mountain***, 4m/6km W of Lothbeg, Sutherland district. Height 1765 feet or 538 metres. **73 D3** NC8811.
Col Sands (Gaelic form: Tràigh Chuil.) *W.Isles* ***Coastal feature***, beach on E coast of Isle of Lewis, 4m/7km NE of Stornoway. **69 F4** NB4638.
Col Uarach (Anglicised form: Upper Coll.) *W.Isles* ***Village***, 1km SW of Col across Abhainn Chuil. NB4539.
Colaboll *High.* ***Settlement***, on NE shore of Loch Shin, 2m/4km NE of Lairg. **72 A3** NC5610.
Coladoir *Arg. & B.* ***River***, on Mull, running W down Glen More to head of Loch Scridain. NM5328.
Colbost *High.* ***Settlement***, on W coast of Loch Dunvegan, 3m/4km NW of Dunvegan, Skye. **57 F5** NG2148.
Colbost Croft Museum *High.* ***Other feature of interest***, in Colbost, 3m/4km NW of Dunvegan, Skye, with exhibits on 19c Scottish Highlands. **57 F5** NG2148.
Cold Chapel *S.Lan.* ***Settlement***, 1m/2km N of Abington. **16 A3** NS9324.
Coldbackie *High.* ***Village***, to S of Tongue Bay, N coast of Caithness district, 2m/4km NE of Tongue. **75 F2** NC6160.
Coldingham *Sc.Bord.* ***Village***, 3m/5km NW of Eyemouth. Ruins of 12c priory. **27 F3** NT9066.
Coldingham Bay *Sc.Bord.* ***Bay***, 1m/2km E of Coldingham. **27 G3** NT9066.
Coldingham Loch *Sc.Bord.* ***Lake/loch***, 1m/2km SW of St. Abb's Head. **27 F3** NT8968.
Coldingham Moor *Sc.Bord.* ***Open space***, moorland 2m/4km NW of Coldingham. **27 F3** NT8567.
Coldingham Priory *Sc.Bord.* ***Ecclesiastical building***, in Coldingham, 3m/5km NW of Eyemouth. 13c priory, largely demolished during Civil War, but some features survived and are incorporated into parish church. **27 G3** NT9065.
Coldrain *P. & K.* ***Settlement***, 3m/4km E of Crook of Devon. **33 F4** NO0800.
Coldstream *Sc.Bord.* Population: 1746. ***Small town***, on River Tweed 9m/14km NE of Kelso. Coldstream Guards raised here by General Monk, 1660. **18 C3** NT8439.
Coldwells *Aber.* ***Settlement***, near E coast, 1m/2km W of Murdoch Head. **65 G5** NK1040.
Coleburn *Moray* ***Settlement***, 4m/7km S of Elgin. NJ2455.
Colenden *P. & K.* ***Settlement***, 1km E of Luncarty across River Tay. **33 G2** NO1029.
Colfin *D. & G.* ***Settlement***, 4m/6km E of Portpatrick. **6 B5** NX0555.
Colgrain *Arg. & B.* ***Settlement***, 2m/4km NW of Cardross. **23 E1** NS3280.
Colgrave Sound *Shet.* ***Sea feature***, sea passage between Yell and Fetlar, S of Hascosay. **85 E4** HU5789.
Colinsburgh *Fife* ***Village***, built in 18c, 2m/4km NW of Elie. **34 C4** NO4703.
Colinton *Edin.* ***Suburb***, 4m/6km SW of Edinburgh city centre. **25 G3** NT2168.
Colintraive *Arg. & B.* ***Village***, in Argyll on E shore of Kyles of Bute, 2m/3km SE of entrance to Loch Riddon. Car and pedestrian ferry service to Rhubodach on Bute. **22 B2** NS0374.
Coll *Arg. & B.* ***Island***, sparsely populated island of Inner Hebrides, measuring 12m/20km NE to SW and nearly 4m/6km at greatest width. NE point is 9m/15km W of Ardnamurchan Point on mainland and SW point is 2m/3km NE of neighbouring island of Tiree. Coll is fairly low-lying, and somewhat bleak and windswept. Lochs noted for trout fishing. **36 A4** NM2058.
Coll *W.Isles Anglicised form of Col (village), qv.*
Coll *W.Isles Anglicised form of Abhainn Chuil (river), qv.*
Colla Firth *Shet.* ***Sea feature***, inlet of Yell Sound on NE coast of Mainland. **84 C4** HU3583.
Colla Firth *Shet.* ***Sea feature***, inlet on E coast of Mainland, 4m/6km N of Laxo and head of Dury Voe. **82 D1** HU4369.
Collace *P. & K.* ***Settlement***, 8m/12km NE of Perth. **34 A1** NO2032.
Collafirth *Shet.* ***Locality***, comprises settlements of North and South Collafirth at head of Colla Firth, 1m/2km SW of Housetter, Mainland. **84 C4** HU3583.
Collafirth *Shet.* ***Settlement***, at head of Colla Firth, on E coast of Mainland. **82 D1** HU4368.
College Milton *S.Lan.* ***Suburb***, and industrial estate, 1m/2km NW of East Kilbride town centre. NS6155.
Collessie *Fife* ***Village***, 6m/9km W of Cupar. **34 A3** NO2813.
Collie Head *Aber.* ***Coastal feature***, headland on N coast, 1km SW of Troup Head. NJ8167.
Collie Law *Sc.Bord.* ***Mountain***, 4m/6km NW of Lauder. Height 1250 feet or 381 metres. **26 B4** NT4850.
Collieston *Aber.* ***Village***, on E coast, 3m/5km NE of Newburgh across River Ythan and Sands of Forvie. **55 F2** NK0328.
Collin *D. & G.* ***Village***, 4m/6km E of Dumfries. **9 E3** NY0276.
Collin Hags *D. & G.* ***Hill***, 4m/6km NE of Waterbeck. Height 836 feet or 255 metres. **10 B3** NY2980.
Colliston *Angus* ***Village***, 4m/6km NW of Arbroath. 16c Colliston Castle, much altered in 17c, 1km NE. **43 E5** NO6045.
Collmuir *Aber.* ***Settlement***, 4m/6km NE of Tarland. **54 A4** NJ5306.
Collynie *Aber.* ***Settlement***, 5m/8km E of Fyvie. **54 D1** NJ8436.
Colmonell *S.Ayr.* ***Village***, in River Stinchar valley, 5m/7km NE of Ballantrae. **6 C2** NX1486.

Colnabaichin *Aber.* ***Settlement***, near crossing point of River Don, 1m/2km E of Corgarff. **53 E4** NJ2908.
Colonsay *Arg. & B.* ***Island***, 16 square miles or 40 square km lying 8m/13km NW of Jura in Inner Hebrides. Has rocky coastline interspersed with sandy beaches. Chief settlement is Scalasaig on E coast. Diverse wildlife includes seabirds, seal colonies, otters and wild goats. Joined to Oronsay to S at low tide. **28 C5** NR3793.
Colonsay House *Arg. & B.* ***Other building***, on Colonsay to NE of Kiloran. Woodland garden includes rhododendrons, mimosa, eucalyptus and palm trees. **28 C5** NR3793.
Colpy *Aber.* ***Settlement***, 9m/14km SE of Huntly. **54 B1** NJ6432.
Colquhar *Sc.Bord.* ***Settlement***, with remains of tower, 3m/5km N of Innerleithen. **26 A5** NT3341.
Colsay *Shet.* ***Island***, uninhabited island of 54 acres or 22 hectares lying off W coast of Mainland opposite Bay of Scousburgh. **83 F4** HU3618.
Colston *E.Dun.* ***Suburb***, 3m/4km N of Glasgow city centre. NS6069.
Colt Hill *D. & G.* ***Mountain***, 7m/11km NW of Moniaive. Height 1961 feet or 598 metres. **8 A1** NX6998.
Coltfield *Moray* ***Settlement***, 3m/5km S of Burghead. **62 D3** NJ1163.
Coltness *N.Lan.* ***Suburb***, 1m/2km N of Wishaw. NS7956.
Colvend *D. & G.* ***Locality***, at S end of White Loch, 5m/8km SE of Dalbeattie. **8 C5** NX8654.
Colvister *Shet.* ***Settlement***, on W side of Basta Voe, Yell. **85 E3** HU5196.
Colzium House *N.Lan.* ***Garden***, walled garden of rare shrubs and trees in grounds of Colzium House to NE of Kilsyth. House also contains Kilsyth Heritage Museum. **24 B2** NS7278.
Comb Hill *Sc.Bord.* ***Mountain***, 3m/5km S of Teviothead. Mast at summit. Height 1686 feet or 514 metres. **17 E5** NT3900.
Comb Law *S.Lan.* ***Mountain***, in Lowther Hills, 2m/3km NE of Ballencleuch Law. Height 2109 feet or 643 metres. **16 A5** NS9407.
Comely Bank *Edin.* ***Suburb***, 1m/2km NW of Edinburgh city centre. NT2374.
Comer *Stir.* ***Settlement***, at NW end of Gleann Dubh, 4m/6km SW of Stronachlachar. **31 F4** NN3804.
Comers *Aber.* ***Settlement***, 8m/12km N of Banchory. **54 B4** NJ6707.
Comiston *Edin.* ***Suburb***, 3m/5km S of Edinburgh city centre. NT2468.
Comlongon Castle *D. & G.* ***Castle***, 15c castle with dungeons and well-preserved Great Hall, 1km W of Clarencefield. **9 E4** NY0769.
Commando Memorial *High.* ***Other feature of interest***, sculpture erected in 1952, 1m/2km W of Spean Bridge and 9m/14km NE of Fort William, to commemorate World War II commandos who trained in this area. **39 E1** NN2082.
Common Law *Sc.Bord.* ***Mountain***, 3m/5km SW of Broughton. Height 1545 feet or 471 metres. **16 B2** NT0732.
Common of Dunning *P. & K.* ***Open space***, forested mountain area, 3m/5km S of Dunning. **33 F4** NO0109.
Commonedge Hill *Clack.* ***Mountain***, on Ochil Hills, 3m/4km NE of Dollar. Height 1538 feet or 469 metres. **33 E4** NN9801.
Compass Hill *High.* ***Hill***, near E end of Canna. Height 459 feet or 140 metres. **47 F4** NG2706.
Comra *High.* ***Settlement***, 1km E of Kinloch Laggan. **51 E5** NN5490.
Comrie *Fife* ***Village***, 5m/7km W of Dunfermline. NT0189.
Comrie *P. & K.* Population: 1439. ***Village***, at junction of Glen Artney, Glen Lednock, and Strathearn, 6m/10km W of Crieff. Drummond Trout Farm and Fishery. **32 C2** NN7722.
Cona *High.* ***River***, in Lochaber district, running E down Cona Glen to River Scaddle, 1m/2km W of Inverscaddle Bay. NN0169.
Cona Glen *High.* ***Valley***, carrying Cona River in Lochaber district, running E to River Scaddle, W of Loch Linnhe. **38 B2** NM9472.
Cona' Mheall *High.* ***Mountain***, rocky summit in Ross and Cromarty district, with scree-covered W slope, 1m/2km E of Beinn Dearg and 12m/20km SE of Ullapool. Munro: height 3214 feet or 980 metres. **60 B1** NH2781.
Conachair *W.Isles* ***Mountain***, summit of St. Kilda. Height 1410 feet or 430 metres. NA0900.
Conachcraig *Aber.* ***Mountain***, 2m/3km NW of Spittal of Glenmuick. Height 2827 feet or 862 metres. **42 A1** NO2887.
Conamheall *Clack.* *Gaelic form of Conival, qv.*
Conamheall *High.* ***Mountain***, with Strath Dionard and River Dionard to W and Loch Dionard to SW. Height 1581 feet or 482 metres. **74 C3** NC3651.
Conchra *Arg. & B.* ***Settlement***, 3m/5km NE of Clachan of Glendaruel. **22 B1** NS0288.
Conchra *High.* ***Settlement***, 1km N of Dornie across Loch Long, Skye and Lochalsh district. **49 E2** NG8827.
Concraigie *P. & K.* ***Hamlet***, 3m/4km SE of Butterstone. **41 G5** NO1044.
Condorrat *N.Lan.* ***Suburb***, 2m/3km SW of Cumbernauld town centre. **24 B2** NS7373.
Coney Island *High.* *Anglicised form of Eilean a' Chonnaidh, qv.*
Congash *High.* ***Settlement***, 1m/2km SE of Grantown-on-Spey. **52 C2** NJ0526.
Conglass Water *Moray* ***River***, flowing NW to join River Avon, 3m/5km NW of Tomintoul. **53 D3** NJ1422.
Conicavel *Moray* ***Settlement***, 4m/7km SW of Forres across River Findhorn. **62 B4** NH9953.
Conie Glen *Arg. & B.* ***Valley***, carrying Conieglen Water to Brunerican Bay on S coast of Kintyre peninsula. **12 B4** NR6907.
Conieglen Water *Arg. & B.* ***River***, on S part of Kintyre, rising on E slopes of The Slate and flowing E, then S through Conie Glen into sea at W end of Brunerican Bay. **12 B4** NR6907.
Conisby *Arg. & B.* ***Settlement***, on Islay, 1km N of Bruichladdich. **20 A3** NR2661.
Conival (Gaelic form: Conamheall.) *High.* ***Mountain***, in Sutherland district 4m/6km E of Inchnadamph. Munro: height 3237 feet or 987 metres. **71 F2** NC3019.
Conlach Mhòr *P. & K.* ***Mountain***, rising to over 860 metres, 8m/12km N of Blair Atholl. NN9376.
Conland *Aber.* ***Settlement***, 5m/8km NE of Huntly. **64 B5** NJ6043.
Connel *Arg. & B.* ***Village***, on S side of entrance to Loch Etive, Argyll. Cantilever bridge with span of some 500 feet or 150 metres carries road (formerly railway) across loch. Falls of Lora nearby. **30 B1** NM9134.
Connel Ferry Bridge *Arg. & B.* ***Bridge***, railway bridge across entrance to Loch Etive, built in 1901. Second largest cantilever bridge in Britain. NM9134.
Connel Park *E.Ayr.* ***Village***, 1m/2km SW of New Cumnock. **15 E4** NS6012.
Conon *High.* ***River***, on Skye running W into Uig Bay. NG3963.
Conon *High.* ***River***, in Ross and Cromarty district running E from Loch Luichart to head of Cromarty Firth. Falls of Conon below Loch Luichart. NH5658.
Conon Bridge *High.* Population: 2592. ***Village***, in Ross and Cromarty district on River Conon near head of Cromarty Firth. **61 E4** NH5455.
Cononish *Stir.* ***River***, rising on slopes of Ben Lui and running E to River Fillan, 1m/2km SE of Tyndrum. **31 F2** NN3328.
Cononish *Stir.* ***Settlement***, 6m/9km NW of Crianlarich. **31 F2** NN3028.
Cononsyth *Angus* ***Hamlet***, 3m/5km SE of Letham. **43 D5** NO5646.
Conostom *W.Isles* ***Hill***, 3m/4km S of Earshader, Isle of Lewis. Height 840 feet or 256 metres. NB1630.
Contin *High.* ***Village***, in Ross and Cromarty district, 2m/3km SW of Strathpeffer. **61 D4** NH4556.
Contlaw *Aberdeen* ***Locality***, comprises Nether Contlaw and Contlaw Mains, 1m/2km N of Peterculter. **54 D4** NJ8302.
Contullich *High.* ***Settlement***, 1km NW of Alness. **61 F2** NH6370.
Coodham *S.Ayr.* ***Settlement***, 1m/2km NE of Symington. **14 B2** NS3932.
Cookney *Aber.* ***Hamlet***, 3m/4km W of Newtonhill. **55 D5** NO8793.
Cook's Cairn *Moray* ***Mountain***, 5m/8km W of Cabrach. Height 2476 feet or 755 metres. **53 F2** NJ3027.
Cookston *Aber.* ***Settlement***, 2m/3km NW of Ellon. **55 E1** NJ9432.
Coom Burn *D. & G.* *See Garroch Burn.*
Coomb Dod ***Mountain***, on border of South Lanarkshire and Scottish Borders, 7m/11km S of Coulter. Height 2083 feet or 635 metres. **16 B3** NT0423.
Coomb Island *High.* *Alternative name for Neave Island, qv.*
Cooran Lane *D. & G.* ***River***, formed from various burns, flowing S in Silver Flowe valley to E of Craighaw and becoming Black Water of Dee, 1km E of Loch Dee. **7 F2** NX4880.
Copinsay *Ork.* ***Island***, uninhabited island of about 200 acres or 80 hectares 2m/3km SE of Point of Ayre, Mainland. Steep cliffs on E side, with lighthouse. Bird sanctuary. **79 F2** HY6101.
Copister *Shet.* ***Settlement***, at S end of Yell, to W of Hamna Voe. **85 D5** HU4879.
Coppay *W.Isles* ***Island***, small uninhabited island 1m/2km W of Toe Head, W coast of South Harris. NF9393.
Coralhill *Aber.* ***Settlement***, 1m/2km S of St. Combs. **65 F3** NK0561.
Coran of Portmark *D. & G.* ***Mountain***, 1m/2km E of Loch Doon. Height 2040 feet or 622 metres. **7 G1** NX5093.
Corbet Tower *Sc.Bord.* *See Morebattle.*
Corbie Head *Shet.* ***Coastal feature***, headland on W coast of Fetlar, 3m/4km W of Houbie. HU5891.
Corbiegoe *High.* ***Settlement***, 1km SE of Thrumster. **77 F4** ND3444.
Corby Loch *Aberdeen* ***Lake/loch***, small loch 5m/8km N of Aberdeen. **55 E3** NJ9214.
Cordach *Aber.* ***Settlement***, 1m/2km SE of Kincardine O'Neil. **54 B5** NO6097.
Cordon Hill *Sc.Bord.* ***Mountain***, 4m/7km S of Biggar. Height 2217 feet or 676 metres. NT0631.
Core Hill *Aber.* ***Hill***, 1km E of Cross of Jackston, and 3m/5km S of Fyvie. Height 804 feet or 245 metres. **54 C1** NJ7633.
Core Hill *P. & K.* ***Mountain***, in Ochil Hills, 8m/12km N of Alloa. Height 1781 feet or 543 metres. **33 D4** NN8804.
Corgarff *Aber.* ***Hamlet***, 1m/2km E of Cock Bridge. Corgarff Castle (Historic Scotland) to W across River Don. **53 E4** NJ2708.
Corgarff Castle *Aber.* ***Historic house***, derelict tower house (Historic Scotland) dating from 16c or early 17c, to W of Corgarff across River Don. **53 E4** NJ2508.
Corgrain Point *High.* ***Coastal feature***, headland in Ross and Cromarty district, on N shore of Beauly Firth 4m/6km W of North Kessock. NH5948.
Corkerhill *Glas.* ***Suburb***, on W side of Pollok Grounds, 4m/6km SW of Glasgow city centre. NS5462.
Corkindale Law *E.Renf.* ***Hill***, 4m/6km S of Johnstone. Height 850 feet or 259 metres. **23 F4** NS4456.
Corkney Top *Inclyde* ***Mountain***, 1m/2km NE of Creuch Hill. Height 1174 feet or 358 metres. **23 D3** NS2769.
Corlabhadh *W.Isles* ***Hill***, 1m/2km SE of head of Loch Shell, Isle of Lewis. Height 977 feet or 298 metres. **67 F3** NB3018.
Corlarach Forest *Arg. & B.* ***Forest/woodland***, in Argyll between Dunoon and Ardyne Point. NS1373.
Corlarach Hill *Arg. & B.* ***Mountain***, 3m/5km SW of Dunoon. Height 1374 feet or 419 metres. **22 C2** NS1373.
Cormiston *S.Lan.* ***Locality***, 2m/3km W of Biggar. NT0037.
Corn Holm *Ork.* ***Island***, small uninhabited island 1km W of Copinsay. **79 E2** HY5901.
Cornabus *Arg. & B.* ***Settlement***, 2m/3km NW of Port Ellen, Islay. **20 B5** NR3346.
Cornharrow Hill *D. & G.* ***Mountain***, rising to over 500 metres, 6m/9km W of Moniaive. **8 A1** NX6993.
Cornhill *Aber.* ***Village***, 5m/8km S of Portsoy. **64 A4** NJ5858.
Cornish Loch *S.Ayr.* ***Lake/loch***, small loch 9m/14km SW of Dalmellington. NX4094.
Cornquoy *Ork.* ***Settlement***, in far S of Mainland, 8m/13km SE of Kirkwall. **79 E2** HY5299.
Corntown *High.* ***Settlement***, 1km NE of Conon Bridge. **61 E4** NH5556.
Corodale Bay *W.Isles* ***Bay***, small bay on E coast of South Uist, 3m/4km N of Loch Eynort. To N lies 'Prince's Cave' where Charles Edward Stuart sought refuge after Battle of Culloden, 1746. NF8331.
Corpach *High.* ***Village***, in Lochaber district at entrance to Caledonian Canal, 2m/3km N of Fort William across head of Loch Linnhe. **38 D2** NN0976.
Corpach Bay *Arg. & B.* ***Bay***, on NW coast of Jura, 7m/11km NW of entrance to Loch Tarbert. **29 E5** NR5691.
Corr Eilean *Arg. & B.* ***Island***, in sound of Jura, at seaward end of Loch Sween. **21 E2** NR6775.
Corra-bheinn *Arg. & B.* ***Mountain***, 3m/5km E of Ben More, Mull. Height 2309 feet or 704 metres. **29 E1** NM5732.
Corra Linn *S.Lan.* ***Waterfall***, on River Clyde 1m/2km S of Lanark. NS8841.
Corrachree *Aber.* ***Settlement***, 1m/2km W of Tarland. Symbol Stone nearby. **53 G4** NJ4604.
Corran *Arg. & B.* ***River***, on Jura, rising on slopes of Paps of Jura and flowing E, then S to Loch na Mile on E side of Leargybreck. **20 D2** NR5471.
Corran *Arg. & B.* ***Settlement***, isolated settlement on E shore of Loch Goil, opposite Ardnahein. **31 E5** NS2193.
Corran *High.* ***Settlement***, in Lochaber district, on NE shore of Loch Hourn, 1m/2km SE of Arnisdale. **49 E4** NG8509.
Corran *High.* ***Settlement***, on W shore of Loch Linnhe, in Lochaber district. Vehicle ferry to opposite shore across Corran Narrows. **38 C3** NN0163.
Corran Narrows *High.* ***Sea feature***, narrow neck of Loch Linnhe by Corran. Vehicle ferry operates. **38 C3** NN0163.
Corran Seilebost *W.Isles* ***Coastal feature***, headland on W coast of South Harris, 1km N of Seilebost. **66 C4** NG0698.
Corranbuie *Arg. & B.* ***Settlement***, on SE shore of West Loch Tarbert, near head of loch, 2m/3km SW of Tarbert. **21 G3** NR8465.
Corranmore *Arg. & B.* ***Settlement***, on NW shore of Loch Craignish, 1km SW of Ardfern. **29 G4** NM7903.
Correen Hills *Aber.* ***Large natural feature***, small range of hills between Alford in SE and Rhynie in NW. **54 A2** NJ5122.
Correnie Forest *Aber.* ***Forest/woodland***, 6m/9km SE of Alford. **54 B4** NJ6410.
Correnie Moor *Aber.* ***Open space***, upland area to W of Correnie Forest, 4m/7km SE of Alford. **54 B3** NJ6109.
Corribeg *High.* ***Settlement***, in Lochaber district, on N shore of Loch Eil, 1m/2km E of Kinlocheil. NM9978.
Corrie *N.Ayr.* ***Village***, on E coast of Arran, 4m/7km N of Brodick. **22 B5** NS0243.
Corrie Common *D. & G.* ***Village***, 5m/9km NE of Lockerbie. **9 G2** NY2086.

Corrie na Urisgean *Stir. Gaelic form of Goblin's Cave, qv.*
Corrie of Balglass *Stir.* ***Inland physical feature***, N facing corrie, 1m/2km across at back wall, on N edge of Campsie Fells, 4m/6km SE of Balfron. **23 G1** NS5885.
Corrie Water *D. & G.* ***River***, flowing S from Little Whitriggs to join Water of Milk, 3m/5km E of Lockerbie. **9 G2** NY1882.
Corriechrevie *Arg. & B.* ***Settlement***, on Kintyre, 2m/3km SW of Clachan. **21 F4** NR7353.
Corriecravie *N.Ayr.* ***Settlement***, near SW coast of Arran, 3m/5km SE of Blackwaterfoot. Remains of Iron Age fort of Torr a' Chaisteil (Historic Scotland). **13 E3** NR9223.
Corriedoo *D. & G.* ***Settlement***, 4m/6km E of St. John's Town of Dalry. **8 A2** NX6782.
Corriehallie Forest *High.* ***Open space***, deer forest in Ross and Cromarty district S of Orrin Reservoir. **60 C5** NH3748.
Corrielorne *Arg. & B.* ***Settlement***, 3m/5km NE of Melfort. **30 A3** NM8717.
Corriemoillie Forest *High.* ***Open space***, deer forest in Ross and Cromarty district SE of Loch Glascarnoch. **60 C3** NH3567.
Corriemulzie *High.* ***River***, in Sutherland district, running NE down Strath Mulzie into River Einig 4m/6km SW of Oykel Bridge. **71 F5** NH3397.
Corriemulzie Burn *Aber.* ***River***, stream running N to River Dee, 3m/5km SW of Braemar. Cascades at Linn of Corriemulzie in wooded valley. NO1189.
Corrieshalloch Gorge *High.* ***Inland physical feature***, spectacular gorge (National Trust for Scotland) in Ross and Cromarty district, 5m/8km S of head of Loch Broom. Contains Falls of Measach (National Trust for Scotland). **60 A2** NH2077.
Corrievorrie *High.* ***Settlement***, in Strathdearn, 3m/5km SW of Tomatin. **51 G2** NH7724.
Corrieyairack Forest *High.* ***Open space***, deer forest in Badenoch and Strathspey district, running up to border with Inverness and Lochaber districts 7m/11km SE of Fort Augustus. **50 D5** NN4296.
Corrieyairack Hill *High.* ***Mountain***, peak in Corrieyairack Forest on border of Badenoch and Strathspey and Inverness districts. Height 2939 feet or 896 metres. **50 D5** NN4299.
Corrieyairack Pass *High.* ***Other feature of interest***, carries General Wade's Military Road over to Culachy Forest and Glen Tarff. **50 D5** NN4099.
Corrigall Farm Museum *Ork.* ***Other feature of interest***, restored mid-19c Orkney farmhouse in Corrigall, Mainland. **80 B5** HY3219.
Corrimony *High.* ***Hamlet***, in Inverness district, 8m/12km W of Drumnadrochit. Prehistoric chambered cairn (Historic Scotland) to E. **50 C1** NH3730.
Corrimony Chambered Cairn *High.* ***Historic/prehistoric site***, well-preserved, roughly circular passage grave (Historic Scotland) 60 feet in diameter and 8 feet high, in Glen Urquhart just E of Corrimony, 3m/4km E of Cannich. **50 C1** NH3830.
Corrlarach *High.* ***Settlement***, in Cona Glen, Lochaber district, 4m/7km S of head of Loch Eil. **38 B2** NM9671.
Corrour Forest *High.* ***Forest/woodland***, bordering Loch Ossian in Lochaber district. Also deer forest to SE of loch. **39 G3** NN4167.
Corrour Shooting Lodge *High.* ***Settlement***, at NE end of Loch Ossian, 4m/6km NE of Corrour Station. **39 G3** NN4169.
Corrour Station *High.* ***Other building***, railway station on West Highland line to Fort William, 1m/2km SW of head of Loch Ossian and 11m/17km E of Kinlochleven. **39 F3** NN3566.
Corrow *Arg. & B.* ***Settlement***, at N end of Loch Goil, 1m/2km SW of Lochgoilhead. **31 D4** NN1800.
Corry *High.* ***Settlement***, adjoining to N of Broadford, Skye. **48 C2** NG6424.
Corrychurrachan *High.* ***Settlement***, on E shore of Loch Linnhe, 6m/9km SW of Fort William. **38 C3** NN0466.
Corrygills Point *N.Ayr.* ***Coastal feature***, headland on E coast of Arran, 2m/3km SE of Brodick Bay. NS0435.
Corryhabbie Hill *Moray* ***Mountain***, 6m/10km E of foot of Glenlivet. Height 2562 feet or 781 metres. **53 E2** NJ2828.
Corrykinloch *High.* ***Settlement***, situated at NW end of Loch Shin, Sutherland district. **71 F2** NC3625.
Corrylach *Arg. & B.* ***Settlement***, on Kintyre, on W side of Loch Lussa, 6m/9km N of Campbeltown. **12 C3** NR7030.
Corrymuckloch *P. & K.* ***Settlement***, 1m/2km S of Amulree. **33 D1** NN8934.
Corsback *High.* ***Settlement***, 4m/7km E of Halkirk. **77 E2** ND2060.
Corsback *High.* ***Settlement***, near N coast of Caithness district, 1m/2km E of Dunnet. ND2372.
Corse *Aber.* ***Settlement***, 5m/7km E of Huntly. **64 B5** NJ6040.
Corse Castle *Aber.* ***Castle***, ruined castle, bearing date 1581, 3m/5km NW of Lumphanan. NJ5507.
Corse Hill *E.Renf.* ***Mountain***, 4m/6km SE of Eaglesham. Height 1233 feet or 376 metres. **23 G5** NS5946.
Corse of Kinnoir *Aber.* ***Settlement***, 3m/5km NE of Huntly. **64 A5** NJ5443.
Corsebank *D. & G.* ***Settlement***, 4m/7km NE of Sanquhar. **15 G4** NS8016.
Corsegight *Aber.* ***Settlement***, 3m/5km NW of New Deer. NJ8450.
Corsehill *D. & G.* ***Settlement***, 2m/3km SE of Boreland. **9 F2** NY1889.
Corsemalzie *D. & G.* ***Settlement***, 4m/7km SW of Wigtown. **7 E5** NX3753.
Corserine *D. & G.* ***Mountain***, summit of Rhinns of Kells, 4m/6km S of S end Loch Doon. Height 2670 feet or 814 metres. **7 F2** NX4987.
Corsewall *D. & G.* ***Settlement***, on W side of Loch Ryan, 6m/9km N of Stranraer. **6 B4** NX0369.
Corsewall Castle *D. & G.* ***Castle***, ruins of castle, 1m/2km SE of Corsewall Point. NW9971.
Corsewall Point *D. & G.* ***Coastal feature***, headland with lighthouse, 4m/6km NW of Kirkcolm. Ruins of Corsewall Castle 1m/2km SE. **6 A3** NW9872.
Corsindae *Aber.* ***Settlement***, 4m/6km NW of Echt. **54 B4** NJ6808.
Corsock *D. & G.* ***Village***, 8m/13km E of New Galloway. **8 B3** NX7576.
Corsock Loch *D. & G.* ***Lake/loch***, small loch 1km SW of Corsock. **8 B3** NX7575.
Corstorphine *Edin.* ***Suburb***, 4m/6km W of Edinburgh city centre. **25 F2** NT1972.
Corstorphine Dovecot *Edin.* ***Historic/prehistoric site***, well-preserved circular beehive dovecote (or doocot) on former estate of Corstorphine Castle, 4m/6km W of Edinburgh city centre. **25 F2** NT1972.
Corstorphine Hill *Edin.* ***Suburb***, to NE of Corstophine. NT2073.
Cortachy *Angus* ***Settlement***, and castle, near foot of Glen Clova, 4m/6km N of Kirriemuir. Noted for breeding of Aberdeen Angus cattle. **42 B4** NO3959.
Corúna (Anglicised form: Corunna.) *W.Isles* ***Settlement***, near W coast of North Uist, opposite Baleshare. **45 G3** NF8161.
Corunna *W.Isles Anglicised form of Corúna, qv.*
Corwar House *S.Ayr.* ***Settlement***, 3m/5km SE of Barrhill. **7 D2** NX2780.
Corwharn *Angus* ***Mountain***, 2m/3km SW of Balnaboth. Height 2004 feet or 611 metres. **42 A3** NO2865.
Coshieville *P. & K.* ***Settlement***, 3m/4km N of Kenmore. **40 C5** NN7749.
Costa *Ork.* ***Settlement***, at N end of Mainland, 1m/2km E of Loch of Swannay. **80 B4** HY3328.
Costa Head *Ork.* ***Coastal feature***, headland on N coast of Mainland. **80 B3** HY3130.
Cot-town *Aber.* ***Settlement***, 1km E of Rhynie. **54 A2** NJ5026.
Cot-town *Aber.* ***Settlement***, 4m/6km NE of Fyvie. **64 D5** NJ8240.
Cothall *Aber.* ***Settlement***, on N side of River Don, 3m/4km NW of Dyce. **55 D3** NJ8715.
Cottartown *High.* ***Settlement***, 2m/3km N of Grantown-on-Spey. **52 C1** NJ0331.
Cottown *Aber.* ***Settlement***, 1m/2km SW of Kintore. **54 C3** NJ7615.
Cougie *High.* ***Settlement***, 4m/6km SE of Affric Lodge. **50 B2** NH2421.
Coul Point *Arg. & B.* ***Coastal feature***, headland on W coast of Islay, 2m/3km W of Loch Gorm. **20 A3** NR1864.
Coulaghailtro *Arg. & B.* ***Settlement***, on W of Kintyre, 1m/2km N of Kilberry. **21 F3** NR7165.
Coulags *High.* ***Settlement***, 3m/5km NE of head of Loch Carron. **59 F5** NG9645.
Coulin *High.* ***River***, formed by confluence of Easan Dorcha and Allt Doire Bheithe, and flowing N into Loch Coulin. NH0255.
Coulin Forest *High.* ***Open space***, deer forest in Ross and Cromarty district SW of Kinlochewe beyond Loch Clair. **59 F4** NG9954.
Coull *Aber.* ***Settlement***, 3m/4km N of Aboyne. Site of medieval castle. **54 A4** NJ5102.
Coulport *Arg. & B.* ***Settlement***, on E shore of Loch Long, 4m/6km N of Cove. **22 D1** NS2087.
Coulregrain *W.Isles* ***Settlement***, on Isle of Lewis, adjoining to NE of Stornoway. NB4334.
Coulter *S.Lan.* ***Village***, 3m/4km S of Biggar. **16 B2** NT0233.
Coulter Motte Hill *S.Lan.* ***Historic/prehistoric site***, early medieval castle mound (Historic Scotland), originally moated, 2m/3km N of Coulter on River Clyde. **16 B2** NT0136.
Coultra *Fife* ***Settlement***, 1m/2km W of Gauldry. **34 B2** NO3523.
Countam *D. & G.* ***Mountain***, 6m/10km SW of Sanquhar. Height 1558 feet or 475 metres. **15 F5** NS7102.
Countam *D. & G.* ***Mountain***, 5m/8km N of Moniaive. Height 1640 feet or 500 metres. **8 B1** NX7698.
Coupall *High.* ***River***, rising between Buachaille Etive Mòr and Buachaille Etive Beag in Lochaber district and running NE, then E to River Etive at head of Glen Etive. **39 E4** NN2454.
Coupar Angus *P. & K.* Population: 2223. ***Small town***, 4m/7km SE of Blairgowrie. Fragment of 12c abbey. 18c tollbooth. **42 A5** NO2240.
Cour *Arg. & B.* ***Settlement***, on Kintyre, 3m/4km N of Grogport. **21 G5** NR8248.
Cour Bay *Arg. & B.* ***Bay***, on E coast of Kintyre, Argyll, 3m/5km N of Grogport. **21 G5** NR8248.
Courteachan *High.* ***Settlement***, in Lochaber district, to E of Mallaig across harbour. NM6897.
Cousland *Midloth.* ***Village***, 3m/5km E of Dalkeith. **26 A3** NT3768.
Coustonn *Arg. & B.* ***Settlement***, on W coast of Loch Striven, 2m/3km N of Strone Point. **22 B2** NS0774.
Coutlair Knowe *Sc.Bord.* ***Mountain***, in Craik Forest, 3m/4km NW of Craik. Height 1371 feet or 418 metres. **17 E4** NT3311.
Cove *Arg. & B.* ***Village***, on Cove Bay, on E shore of Loch Long, 1m/2km NW of Kilcreggan. **22 D1** NS2282.
Cove *High.* ***Village***, on W shore of Loch Ewe, Ross and Cromarty district, 7m/11km NW of Poolewe. **70 A5** NG8090.
Cove *Sc.Bord.* ***Settlement***, next to small bay on North Sea coast, 1km NE of Cockburnspath. **27 E2** NT7772.
Cove Bay *Aberdeen* Population: 4887. ***Village***, on E coast, 3m/5km S of Aberdeen. **55 E4** NJ9501.
Cove Bay *Arg. & B.* ***Bay***, on E shore of Loch Long, W of Cove and 1m/2km NW of Kilcreggan. NS2282.
Coves Reservoir *Inclyde* ***Reservoir***, small reservoir 1m/2km SE of Gourock. NS2476.
Covesea *Moray* ***Settlement***, near N coast of region, 3m/5km W of Lossiemouth. Lighthouse (Covesea Skerries) 1m/2km E. **63 D2** NJ1870.
Covesea Skerries *Moray* ***Island***, group of islands off N coast, 3m/4km W of Lossiemouth. **63 D2** NJ1971.
Covington *S.Lan.* ***Settlement***, 1m/2km N of Thankerton. **16 A2** NS9739.
Cow Castle and Settlement *S.Lan.* ***Historic/prehistoric site***, Iron Age hillfort and large D-shaped settlement, 1m/2km SE of Coulter. **16 B2** NT0433.
Cowal *Arg. & B.* ***Large natural feature***, tongue of land in Argyll, between Loch Fyne and Loch Long, 17m/28km SW of Crianlarich. Cowal Hydro-electricity Scheme at head of Loch Striven. NS1090.
Cowan Fell *D. & G.* ***Mountain***, 1km SW of Loch Fell and 4m/6km S of Bodesbeck. Height 1850 feet or 564 metres. **16 C5** NT1603.
Cowdenbeath *Fife* Population: 12,126. ***Town***, former coalmining town 5m/8km NE of Dunfermline. **33 G5** NT1691.
Cowdenburn *Sc.Bord.* ***Settlement***, 3m/4km SW of Leadburn. NT2052.
Cowdenknowes *Sc.Bord.* ***Other building***, 16c tower on E bank of Leader Water 1m/2km S of Earlston; formerly stronghold of Homes, now incorporated in modern house. NT5736.
Cowgill Lower *S.Lan.* ***Reservoir***, one of Cowgill Reservoirs, about 2m/4km SE of Lamington. NT0128.
Cowgill Reservoirs *S.Lan.* ***Reservoir***, two small reservoirs, Cowgill Upper and Cowgill Lower, about 2m/4km SE of Lamington. NT0028.
Cowgill Upper *S.Lan.* ***Reservoir***, one of Cowgill Reservoirs, about 2m/4km SE of Lamington. NT0029.
Cowglen *Glas.* ***Suburb***, 4m/6km SW of Glasgow city centre. NS5361.
Cowhythe Head *Aber.* ***Coastal feature***, headland on N coast, 2m/3km E of Portsoy. Boyne Bay to S and E. NJ6166.
Cowie *Aber.* ***Village***, adjoining to N of Stonehaven, at mouth of Cowie Water. **43 G1** NO8786.
Cowie *Stir.* Population: 2049. ***Village***, 4m/6km SE of Stirling. **24 C1** NS8489.
Cowie Water *Aber.* ***River***, rising on hills to W of Cowie and running E through Fetteresso Forest. Glenury Viaduct is 1km from mouth of river. **43 G1** NO8786.
Cowlairs *Glas.* ***Suburb***, 2m/3km NE of Glasgow city centre. NS6067.
Coylet *Arg. & B.* ***Settlement***, on E shore of Loch Eck, 4m/6km N of Orchard. **22 C1** NS1488.
Coylton *S.Ayr.* Population: 1907. ***Village***, 5m/8km E of Ayr. **14 C4** NS4119.
Coylumbridge *High.* ***Hamlet***, in Badenoch and Strathspey district, 2m/3km SE of Aviemore. **52 B3** NH9110.
Coynach *Aber.* ***Settlement***, 3m/4km W of Tarland. **53 G4** NJ4305.
Coynachie *Aber.* ***Settlement***, 6m/9km SE of Haugh of Glass. **53 G1** NJ4934.
Cracaval *W.Isles* ***Mountain***, near W coast of Isle of Lewis 1m/2km S of Mealisval. Height 1686 feet or 514 metres. **68 B5** NB0225.
Crackaig *Arg. & B.* ***Settlement***, on SE coast of Jura, 1km S of Craighouse. **20 D3** NR5265.
Cradhlastadh (Anglicised form: Crowlista.) *W.Isles* ***Settlement***, near W coast of Isle of Lewis, 1m/2km W of Timsgearraidh. **68 B4** NB0433.
Craggan *High.* ***Locality***, in Badenoch and Strathspey district, 1m/2km SW of Grantown-on-Spey, comprising Upper Craggan and Wester Craggan. NJ0126.
Craggan *Moray* ***Settlement***, 4m/6km N of Tomnavoulin. **53 D1** NJ1832.
Craggan *P. & K.* ***Settlement***, 4m/7km SE of Comrie. **32 D3** NN8117.
Craggan Hill *Arg. & B.* ***Hill***, elongated hill, aligned SW to NE above E shore of Loch Long and 4m/7km NE of Garelochhead. Height 958 feet or 292 metres. **31 E5** NS2698.

Craggan More *Moray* ***Mountain***, 9m/14km SW of Charlestown of Aberlour. Height 1558 feet or 475 metres. NJ1634.
Cragganruar *P. & K.* ***Settlement***, to N of Loch Tay, 10m/16km SW of Kenmore. **40 B5** NN6941.
Craggie *High.* ***Settlement***, 2m/4km SW of Kildonan Lodge, Sutherland district. **73 D2** NC8719.
Craggie *High.* ***Settlement***, 1km E of Daviot across River Nairn. **51 G1** NH7239.
Craggiemore *High.* ***Locality***, in Inverness district, 5m/9km SE of Inverness. NH7339.
Craibstone *Aberdeen* ***Settlement***, 6m/9km NW of Aberdeen. Site of agricultural college. **55 D3** NJ8712.
Craibstone *Moray* ***Settlement***, 6m/9km SE of Buckie. **63 G4** NJ4959.
Craichie *Angus* ***Hamlet***, 4m/6km SE of Forfar. **42 C5** NO5047.
Craig *Angus* ***Locality***, parish to S of Montrose, including village of Kirkton of Craig. NO7055.
Craig *Arg. & B.* ***Settlement***, on Mull, 3m/4km E of head of Loch Scridain. **29 E2** NM5829.
Craig *Arg. & B.* ***Settlement***, on N shore of Loch Etive, 3m/5km NE of Taynuilt across loch. **30 C1** NN0334.
Craig *D. & G.* ***Settlement***, 2m/4km W of Crossmichael. **8 A4** NX6967.
Craig *High.* ***River***, flowing W to NE shore of Loch Torridon, Ross and Cromarty district. **59 D3** NG7663.
Craig *High.* ***Settlement***, 4m/7km SE of Redpoint, on NE shore of Loch Torridon, Ross and Cromarty district. **59 D3** NG7763.
Craig *High.* ***Settlement***, 9m/15km SW of Achnasheen, Ross and Cromarty district. **59 G5** NH0349.
Craig *S.Ayr.* ***Settlement***, 2m/3km S of Straiton. **14 B5** NS3802.
Craig a Barns *P. & K.* ***Mountain***, 1m/2km NW of Dunkeld. Height 1105 feet or 337 metres. **41 F5** NO0143.
Craig Bhagailteach *P. & K.* ***Mountain***, in Atholl, 5m/7km NW of Blair Atholl. Height 1614 feet or 492 metres. **40 D3** NN8169.
Craig Castle *Aber.* ***Castle***, 16c castle with 18c portal and wing, overlooking wooded glen 2m/3km N of Lumsden. **53 G2** NJ4724.
Craig Castle *Angus* ***Castle***, to N of Kirkton of Craig. 15c tower with 17c house. NO7056.
Craig Ewen *Aber.* ***Coastal feature***, headland on N side of Peterhead. **65 G5** NK1247.
Craig Fell *D. & G.* ***Hill***, on E side of Glenwhan Moor and 2m/3km S of New Luce. Height 538 feet or 164 metres. **6 C4** NX1761.
Craig Head *Moray* ***Coastal feature***, headland on N coast to W of Findochty. NJ4667.
Craig Hill *P. & K.* ***Mountain***, 3m/5km SW of Aberfeldy. Height 1843 feet or 562 metres. **40 D5** NN8145.
Craig Hulich *P. & K.* ***Mountain***, 1km N of Amulree. Height 1811 feet or 552 metres. **33 D1** NN8937.
Craig Lea *P. & K.* ***Mountain***, rising to over 510 metres, 8m/13km NE of Crieff. **33 E1** NN9432.
Craig Mellon *Angus* ***Mountain***, 1m/2km NW of Glendoll Lodge. Height 2840 feet or 866 metres. **42 A2** NO2677.
Craig nan Caisean *P. & K.* ***Mountain***, in Tummel Forest, 1m/2km NE of Tummel Bridge. Height 1565 feet or 477 metres. **40 C3** NN7760.
Craig of Bunzeach *Aber.* ***Mountain***, 3m/4km SE of Strathdon. Height 1742 feet or 531 metres. **53 F4** NJ3609.
Craig of Dalfro *Aber.* ***Mountain***, 1m/2km S of Strachan. Height 1040 feet or 317 metres. **43 E1** NO6789.
Craig of Knockgray *D. & G.* ***Mountain***, 1km NE of Carsphairn. Height 1256 feet or 383 metres. **7 G1** NX5794.
Craig Rossie *P. & K.* ***Mountain***, on N edge of Ochil Hills, 3m/4km E of Auchterarder. Height 1345 feet or 410 metres. **33 E3** NN9811.
Craig Rostan *Stir.* ***Open space***, slopes of Creag a' Bhocain, above E shore of Loch Lomond opposite Tarbet. **31 F4** NN3404.
Craig Veann ***Mountain***, on border of Aberdeenshire and Moray, 5m/8km S of Tomintoul. Height 2332 feet or 711 metres. **53 D3** NJ1810.
Craigallian Loch *Stir.* ***Lake/loch***, small loch 3m/4km NW of Milngavie. NS5378.
Craigandaive *Arg. & B.* ***Settlement***, at head of Loch Striven on W shore, 1km NW of Ardtaraig. **22 B1** NS0583.
Craiganour Forest *P. & K.* ***Open space***, upland area and game forest in Atholl to N of Loch Rannoch, 6m/9km NW of Kinloch Rannoch. **40 A3** NN6064.
Craigans *Arg. & B.* ***Settlement***, 4m/7km NE of Lochgilphead. **30 B5** NR9094.
Craigbeg *High.* ***Settlement***, in Glen Spean, 11m/18km E of Spean Bridge. **39 G1** NN4081.
Craigcaffie Castle *D. & G.* ***Castle***, 16c keep near E side of Loch Ryan, 3m/4km NE of Stranraer across head of loch. NX0864.
Craigcleuch *D. & G.* ***Settlement***, 2m/3km NW of Langholm. **10 B3** NY3486.
Craigculter *Aber.* ***Settlement***, 2m/3km SE of New Pitsligo. **65 E4** NJ9054.
Craigdallie *P. & K.* ***Settlement***, at foot of Braes of the Carse, 4m/6km N of Errol. **34 A2** NO2428.
Craigdam *Aber.* ***Settlement***, 3m/5km NE of Oldmeldrum. **54 D1** NJ8430.
Craigdarroch *D. & G.* ***Settlement***, 2m/4km W of Moniaive. **8 B1** NX7490.
Craigdarroch *E.Ayr.* ***Settlement***, in Glen Afton, 4m/7km S of New Cumnock. **15 E5** NS6306.
Craigdhu *D. & G.* ***Settlement***, 3m/4km E of Monreith. **3 D2** NX3940.
Craigdhu *High.* ***Settlement***, 6m/10km SW of Beauly. **61 D5** NH4440.
Craigdow Loch *S.Ayr.* ***Lake/loch***, small loch 3m/5km SW of Maybole. NS2606.
Craigdullyeart Hill *E.Ayr.* ***Mountain***, rising to over 410 metres, 3m/5km NE of New Cumnock. **15 E4** NS6515.
Craigeam *W.Isles* ***Island***, rock island off W coast of Isle of Lewis, 2m/4km W of Carloway. **68 C3** NB1643.
Craigearn *Aber.* ***Hamlet***, 1m/2km SW of Kemnay. Lang Stane o'Craigearn is standing stone to N. **54 C3** NJ7214.
Craigellachie *Moray* ***Village***, at confluence of River Fiddich and River Spey, 3m/5km S of Rothes. **63 E5** NJ2845.
Craigellachie Nature Reserve *High.* ***Nature reserve***, on slopes to W of Aviemore. Noted for variety of habitats which encourage wildlife, especially birds: birchwood on lower slopes supports tree warblers, spotted flycatchers and willow warblers, moorland areas and woodland margins are home to red and black grouse respectively, while cliffs provide breeding sites for kestrels, jackdaws and peregrine falcons. **52 A3** NH8711.
Craigellie *Aber.* ***Settlement***, 3m/5km S of Inverallochy. **65 F3** NK0260.
Craigencallie *D. & G.* ***Settlement***, 2m/3km W of Clatteringshaws Loch. **7 G3** NX5077.
Craigend *Moray* ***Settlement***, on N bank of River Lossie, 1km E of Dallas. **62 D4** NJ1353.
Craigend *P. & K.* ***Settlement***, 2m/3km S of Perth. **33 G2** NO1220.
Craigendoran *Arg. & B.* ***Suburb***, at E end of Helensburgh. Terminus for passenger boat services. **23 E1** NS3081.
Craigendunton Reservoir *E.Ayr.* ***Reservoir***, 5m/8km SW of Eaglesham. NS5245.
Craigengar *W.Loth.* ***Mountain***, in Pentland Hills, 4m/7km NW of West Linton. Height 1699 feet or 518 metres. **25 E4** NT0955.
Craigengillan *E.Ayr.* ***Settlement***, 2m/3km S of Dalmellington. **14 C5** NS4702.
Craigenloch Hill ***Mountain***, on border of Angus and Perth & Kinross, 4m/6km E of Spittal of Glenshee. Height 2421 feet or 738 metres. NO1669.
Craigenputtock *D. & G.* ***Settlement***, 5m/9km S of Moniaive. **8 B2** NX7782.
Craigenreoch *S.Ayr.* ***Mountain***, in Glentrool Forest Park, 4m/7km SE of Barr. Height 1853 feet or 565 metres. NX3391.
Craigens *Arg. & B.* ***Settlement***, at head of Loch Gruinart, Islay, 4m/6km NW of Bridgend. **20 A3** NR2967.
Craigens *E.Ayr.* ***Village***, 1m/2km SE of Cumnock. NS5818.
Craiggiecat *Aber.* ***Hill***, 4m/6km W of Newtonhill. Height 649 feet or 198 metres. **54 D5** NO8492.
Craigglass *Arg. & B.* ***Settlement***, 1km SE of Cairnbaan. **21 G1** NR8490.
Craiggowrie *High.* ***Mountain***, in Badenoch and Strathspey district, 4m/6km E of Aviemore. Height 2250 feet or 686 metres. **52 B3** NH9613.
Craighall *Fife* ***Settlement***, on Craighall Burn, 3m/5km SE of Cupar. **34 C3** NO4010.
Craighat *Stir.* ***Settlement***, 3m/5km NW of Carbeth. **23 F1** NS4984.
Craighead *Fife* ***Hamlet***, on North Sea coast, next to Fife Ness. **35 E4** NO6309.
Craighead *High.* ***Settlement***, on Black Isle, 4m/6km SW of Cromarty. **61 G3** NH7561.
Craighlaw *D. & G.* ***Historic house***, 1m/2km W of Kirkcowan. **7 E4** NX3061.
Craighoar Hill *D. & G.* ***Mountain***, in Lowther Hills, 5m/8km SW of Moffat. Height 1761 feet or 537 metres. **16 B5** NT0002.
Craighorn *Clack.* ***Mountain***, 4m/7km N of Alloa. Height 2066 feet or 630 metres. **33 D4** NN8800.
Craighouse *Arg. & B.* ***Village***, and small port on E coast of Jura, 3m/5km N of S end of island. **20 D3** NR5267.
Craigie *Aber.* ***Settlement***, 2m/3km E of Newmachar. **55 E3** NJ9119.
Craigie *Dundee* ***Suburb***, 2m/3km NE of Dundee city centre. NO4231.
Craigie *P. & K.* ***Suburb***, SW district of Perth. NO1122.
Craigie *P. & K.* ***Village***, on SE side of Loch of Clunie, 4m/6km W of Blairgowrie. **41 G5** NO1143.
Craigie *S.Ayr.* ***Suburb***, E district of Ayr. NS3521.
Craigie *S.Ayr.* ***Village***, 4m/6km S of Kilmarnock. **14 C2** NS4232.
Craigie Brae *Aber.* ***Settlement***, to E of Upper Lake, 3m/4km NE of Tarves. **55 D1** NJ8834.
Craigie Fell *S.Ayr.* ***Open space***, hillslope of Auchencrosh Hill, 3m/5km SE of Ballantrae. **6 C3** NX1078.
Craigieburn *D. & G.* ***Settlement***, 1m/2km E of Moffat, on W bank of Moffat Water. **16 C5** NT1105.
Craigieholm *P. & K.* ***Settlement***, 3m/4km SW of Burrelton. **33 G1** NO1634.
Craigielaw *E.Loth.* ***Settlement***, 1km W of Aberlady. NT4579.
Craigielaw Point *E.Loth.* ***Coastal feature***, headland to W of Craigielaw, on Firth of Forth at SW end of Aberlady Bay. **26 B2** NT4480.
Craigievar Castle *Aber.* ***Castle***, turreted Baronial 17c castle (National Trust for Scotland) 4m/6km S of Alford. Castle is seven storeys high and surrounded by notable grounds. **54 A4** NJ5609.
Craiglee *E.Ayr.* ***Mountain***, 1m/2km W of Loch Doon. Height 1715 feet or 523 metres. **7 F1** NX4796.
Craigleith *E.Loth.* ***Island***, small island 1m/2km N of North Berwick. Haunt of puffins. **26 C1** NT5587.
Craigleith *Edin.* ***Suburb***, 2m/3km NW of Edinburgh city centre. NT2374.
Craiglich *Aber.* ***Mountain***, 3m/5km E of Tarland. Height 1561 feet or 476 metres. **54 A4** NJ5305.
Craiglockhart *Edin.* ***Suburb***, 3m/5km SW of Edinburgh city centre. **25 G2** NT2270.
Craiglug *Aber.* ***Settlement***, 3m/5km W of Kirkton of Maryculter. **54 D5** NO8197.
Craigluscar Hill *Fife* ***Hill***, 3m/4km SE of Saline. Height 745 feet or 227 metres. **33 F5** NT0690.
Craigluscar Reservoirs *Fife* ***Reservoir***, two small reservoirs below Craigluscar Hill 2m/4km NW of Dunfermline. NT0690.
Craigmaddie Castle *E.Dun.* ***Castle***, with moated tower, 1m/2km NE of Craigmaddie Reservoir. NS5776.
Craigmaddie Muir *E.Dun.* ***Open space***, moorland to E of Craigmaddie Reservoir. Includes boulders known as Auld Wives' Lifts. NS5876.
Craigmaddie Reservoir *E.Dun.* ***Reservoir***, small reservoir on NE side of Milngavie. NS5675.
Craigmahandle *Aber.* ***Mountain***, 2m/3km W of Ballochan. Height 1883 feet or 574 metres. **53 G5** NO4890.
Craigmaid *Sc.Bord.* ***Mountain***, summit lies 1m/2km S of Fruid Reservoir. Height 1814 feet or 553 metres. **16 B4** NT0717.
Craigmaud *Aber.* ***Settlement***, 2m/3km N of New Pitsligo. **65 D4** NJ8858.
Craigmillar *Edin.* ***Suburb***, 3m/4km SE of Edinburgh city centre. **25 G2** NT2871.
Craigmillar Castle *Edin.* ***Castle***, impressive, mainly medieval, ruined castle (Historic Scotland) to S of Craigmillar. **25 G2** NT2870.
Craigmore *Arg. & B.* ***Settlement***, on Bute, SE of Bogany Point, 1m/2km E of Rothesay. **22 C3** NS1065.
Craigmyle House *Aber.* ***Settlement***, 1km E of Torphins. **54 B4** NJ6301.
Craignafeich *Arg. & B.* ***Settlement***, on Cowal peninsula, 2m/3km SW of Tighnabruaich. **22 A2** NR9571.
Craignair *D. & G.* ***Locality***, 1km W of Dalbeattie. **8 C4** NX8260.
Craignavie *Stir.* ***Settlement***, 1km SW of Killin. **32 A1** NN5631.
Craignaw *D. & G.* ***Mountain***, 1m/2km SE of Loch Enoch. Height 2116 feet or 645 metres. **7 F2** NX4683.
Craigneil *S.Ayr.* ***Settlement***, 1km SW of Colmonell. **6 C2** NX1485.
Craigneil Castle *S.Ayr.* ***Castle***, 13c stronghold of Kennedys 1km from Craigneil, opposite Colmonell across River Stinchar. NX1485.
Craignelder *D. & G.* ***Mountain***, 2m/3km W of Loch Grannoch and 6m/10km NE of Newton Stewart. Height 1971 feet or 601 metres. **7 G4** NX5069.
Craignethan Castle *S.Lan.* ***Castle***, restored 15c tower house (Historic Scotland), 1km W of Crossford. **24 C5** NS8146.
Craigneuk *N.Lan.* ***Suburb***, 1m/2km E of Motherwell, adjoining to NW of Shieldmuir. NS7756.
Craignish *Arg. & B.* ***Locality***, peninsula parish on W coast of Argyll, including Craignish Castle. NM7701.
Craignish Castle *Arg. & B.* ***Castle***, dating from 16c, near S end of peninsula, W of Loch Craignish in Argyll. **29 G4** NM7701.
Craignish Point *Arg. & B.* ***Coastal feature***, headland at S end of Craignish peninsula and seaward end of Loch Craignish. **29 G5** NR7599.
Craignure *Arg. & B.* ***Hamlet***, on Craignure Bay, E coast of Mull, opposite entrance to Loch Linnhe. Car ferry to Oban. **29 G1** NM7137.
Craignure Bay *Arg. & B.* ***Bay***, on E coast of Mull, opposite entrance to Loch Linnhe. **29 G1** NM7137.
Craigo *Angus* ***Village***, on River North Esk, 5m/7km N of Montrose. **43 E3** NO6864.
Craigoch *S.Ayr.* ***Settlement***, 4m/6km S of Maybole. **14 B5** NS2904.
Craigow *P. & K.* ***Hamlet***, 2m/3km NW of Milnathort. **33 F4** NO0806.
Craigower *P. & K.* ***Mountain***, 1m/2km NW of Pitlochry, rising to over 400 metres. Viewpoint (National Trust for Scotland) looks W across Pass of Killiecrankie towards Loch Tummel. **41 E3** NN9260.

Craigowl Hill *Angus* ***Mountain***, summit of Sidlaw Hills, 6m/10km N of Dundee. Mast at summit. Height 1492 feet or 455 metres. **42 B5** NO3740.
Craigrothie *Fife* ***Village***, 2m/4km S of Cupar. **34 B3** NO3710.
Craigroy *Moray* ***Settlement***, 1m/2km S of Dallas. **62 D4** NJ1250.
Craigroy Farm *Moray* ***Settlement***, on W bank of River Avon, 6m/9km S of Upper Knockando. **53 D1** NJ1834.
Craigruie *Stir.* ***Settlement***, on N shore of Loch Voil, 3m/4km W of Balquhidder. **32 A2** NN4920.
Craigsanquhar *Fife* ***Settlement***, 3m/5km NE of Cupar. **34 B3** NO3919.
Craigshill *W.Loth.* ***Suburb***, central district of Livingston. NT0668.
Craigston Castle *Aber.* ***Castle***, 17c castle 4m/7km NE of Turriff. **64 C4** NJ7655.
Craigton *Aberdeen* ***Hamlet***, just NW of Peterculter. **54 D4** NJ8301.
Craigton *Angus* ***Village***, 4m/7km SW of Kirriemuir. **42 B4** NO3250.
Craigton *Angus* ***Village***, 4m/6km NW of Carnoustie. **34 D1** NO5138.
Craigton *Glas.* ***Suburb***, 3m/5km W of Glasgow city centre across River Clyde. NS5464.
Craigton *High.* ***Settlement***, in Ross and Cromarty district, at entrance to Beauly Firth, opposite Inverness. NH6648.
Craigton *Stir.* ***Settlement***, at foot of Fintry Hills, 1m/2km E of Fintry across Endrick Water. **24 A1** NS6286.
Craigton Point *High.* ***Coastal feature***, headland at entrance to Beauly Firth opposite Inverness, with beacon. **61 F5** NH6647.
Craigtoun Country Park *Fife* ***Leisure/recreation***, 50 acre country park 3m/4km SW of St. Andrews. Features range from landscaped gardens and ponds to extensive range of activities including trampolining, crazy golf and adventure playground. **34 C3** NO4714.
Craigtown *High.* ***Settlement***, on E bank of Halladale River, 2m/3km N of Croik. **76 A3** NC8956.
Craigvinean Forest *P. & K.* ***Forest/woodland***, on W side of Strath Tay above Dunkeld. **41 E5** NN9943.
Craik *Aber.* ***Settlement***, 3m/4km SW of Rhynie. **53 G2** NJ4625.
Craik *Sc.Bord.* ***Village***, to N of Borthwick Water, in Craik Forest area, 5m/8km SW of Burnfoot. **17 E5** NT3408.
Craik Cross Hill ***Mountain***, on border of Dumfries & Galloway and Scottish Borders, 5m/9km NE of Eskdalemuir. Site of Roman signal station. Height 1473 feet or 449 metres. **17 D5** NT3004.
Craik Forest *Sc.Bord.* ***Forest/woodland***, 10m/16km W of Hawick. Encloses Crib Law mountain. **17 E4** NT3309.
Craik Moor *Sc.Bord.* ***Open space***, moorland 2m/4km SW of Hownam. **18 C5** NT8018.
Crail *Fife* Population: 1449. ***Small town***, and resort, 2m/4km SW of Fife Ness. Specialises in crab and lobster fishing. 16c tolbooth. Several old houses restored by National Trust for Scotland. **35 E4** NO6107.
Crailing *Sc.Bord.* ***Village***, 4m/6km NE of Jedburgh. **18 A4** NT6824.
Crailinghall *Sc.Bord.* ***Hamlet***, 3m/5km NE of Jedburgh. **18 A4** NT6922.
Crailzie Hill *Sc.Bord.* ***Mountain***, 3m/4km SE of Romannobridge. Height 1561 feet or 476 metres. **25 F5** NT1945.
Cralic *High. Anglicised form of A' Chràlaig, qv.*
Crammag Head *D. & G.* ***Coastal feature***, headland with lighthouse on W coast of Rinns of Galloway, 5m/8km NW of Mull of Galloway. **2 A3** NX0834.
Cramond *Edin.* ***Suburb***, 5m/7km of Edinburgh city centre. Site of Roman fort to N. **25 F2** NT1976.
Cramond Bridge *Edin.* ***Suburb***, 5m/8km NW of Edinburgh city centre, at road crossing of River Almond. NT1775.
Cramond Island *Edin.* ***Island***, small island 1m/2km N of Cramond in Firth of Forth, accessible across sands at low tide. **25 F2** NT1978.
Cran Loch *High.* ***Lake/loch***, small loch in Nairn district 4m/7km E of Nairn. NH9459.
Cranna *Aber.* ***Locality***, comprises North Cranna, South Cranna and Mains of Cranna, 1m/2km NE of Aberchirder. **64 B4** NJ6353.
Crannach *Moray* ***Settlement***, 4m/7km NE of Keith. **63 G4** NJ4954.
Cranshaws *Sc.Bord.* ***Village***, on Whiteadder Water, 8m/12km NW of Duns. **27 D3** NT6961.
Cranshaws Hill *Sc.Bord.* ***Mountain***, 1m/2km W of Cranshaws. Height 1243 feet or 379 metres. **27 D3** NT6761.
Cransmill Hill *Aber.* ***Mountain***, rising to over 420 metres, 4m/6km W of Gartly. **53 G1** NJ4631.
Cranstackie *High.* ***Mountain***, in Sutherland district 3m/4km W of head of Loch Eriboll. Height 2624 feet or 800 metres. **74 C3** NC3555.
Craobh Haven *Arg. & B.* ***Settlement***, 2m/3km S of Arduaine. **29 G4** NM7907.
Crarae *Arg. & B.* ***Village***, on Loch Fyne, 2m/4km SW of Furnace, near Inveraray. **30 B5** NR9897.
Crarae Lodge *Arg. & B.* ***Garden***, overlooking Loch Fyne, 10m/16km NE of Lochgilphead. Noted for rhododendrons, conifers and ornamental shrubs. **30 B5** NR9897.
Craro Island *Arg. & B.* ***Island***, small island off W coast of Gigha, 1m/2km from S end. **21 E5** NR6247.
Crask Inn *High.* ***Settlement***, on N side of Srath a' Chràisg, Sutherland district. **72 A2** NC5224.
Crask of Aigas *High.* ***Settlement***, in wooded area beside River Beauly, 4m/7km SW of Beauly town, in Inverness district. **61 D5** NH4642.
Craskins *Aber.* ***Settlement***, 2m/3km NE of Tarland. **54 A4** NJ5106.
Crathes *Aber.* ***Village***, on N side of River Dee, 3m/5km E of Banchory. **54 C5** NO7596.
Crathes Castle *Aber.* ***Castle***, built in 16c with later additions (National Trust for Scotland), 1m/2km W of Crathes. Gardens include early 18c yew hedges. **54 C5** NO7396.
Crathie *Aber.* ***Village***, on River Dee, 1km E of Balmoral Castle. **53 E5** NO2695.
Crathie *High.* ***Settlement***, in valley of River Spey, 9m/13km SW of Newtonmore. **51 E5** NN5894.
Crathie Church *Aber.* ***Ecclesiastical building***, church in Craithie, 1km E of Balmoral Castle and 8m/12km W of Ballater. Used by Royal Family when in residence at Balmoral. **53 E5** NO2694.
Crathie Point *Aber.* ***Coastal feature***, headland on N coast, 2m/4km E of Cullen. NJ5467.
Craufurdland Water ***River***, running SW to confluence with Fenwick Water 1m/2km NE of Kilmarnock. Combined stream, known as Kilmarnock Water, flows through Kilmarnock to River Irvine on S side of town. **23 F5** NS4339.
Craw *N.Ayr.* ***Settlement***, on NW coast of Arran, 3m/4km NE of Pirnmill. **21 G5** NR8948.
Crawford *S.Lan.* ***Village***, on River Clyde, 2m/4km SE of Abington. Site of Roman fort and fragment of old castle to N across river. **16 A3** NS9520.
Crawfordjohn *S.Lan.* ***Village***, 3m/5km W of Abington. **15 G3** NS8823.
Crawfordton *D. & G.* ***Settlement***, 1m/2km E of Moniaive. **8 B1** NX7990.
Crawhin Reservoir *Inclyde* ***Reservoir***, small reservoir 4m/6km SW of Greenock. NS2470.
Crawick *D. & G.* ***Village***, 1m/2km NW of Sanquhar. **15 F4** NS7711.
Crawick Water *D. & G.* ***River***, running SW to River Nith, 1km to S of Crawick. **15 G4** NS7711.
Crawston Hill *D. & G.* ***Hill***, 1m/2km NE of Dunscore. Height 712 feet or 217 metres. **8 C2** NX8885.
Crawton *Aber.* ***Settlement***, on North Sea coast, 4m/6km S of Stonehaven Nature Reserve. Bay to S of settlement. **43 G2** NO8779.
Crawton Bay *Aber.* ***Bay***, small bay, 4m/6km S of Stonehaven. Nature Reserve around headland at E end of bay. **43 G2** NO8779.
Cray *P. & K.* ***Hamlet***, on Shee Water, in Glen Shee, 4m/7km SE of Spittal of Glenshee. **41 G3** NO1463.
Creach Beinn (Anglicised form: Ben Creach.) *Arg. & B.* ***Mountain***, on Mull 3m/4km NE of Lochbuie. Height 2289 feet or 698 metres. **29 F2** NM6427.
Creach Bheinn *Arg. & B.* ***Mountain***, on Ardmeanach peninsula, Mull, 1m/2km E of Aird na h-Iolaire. Height 1610 feet or 491 metres. **28 D2** NM4129.
Creach Bheinn *Arg. & B.* ***Mountain***, in Argyll, 2m/4km SE of Loch Creran. Height 2657 feet or 810 metres. **38 C5** NN0242.
Creach Bheinn *High.* ***Mountain***, in Lochaber district 3m/5km SE of head of Loch Sunart. Height 2798 feet or 853 metres. **38 A4** NM8757.
Creachan Mòr *Arg. & B.* ***Mountain***, 1km N of Malcolm's Point, Mull. Height 1082 feet or 330 metres. **29 D3** NM4919.
Creachan Mòr *Arg. & B.* ***Mountain***, in Argyll 2m/3km W of junction of Loch Goil with Loch Long. Height 2155 feet or 657 metres. **31 D5** NS1891.
Creag a' Chaorainn *High.* ***Inland physical feature***, mountain ridge 5m/8km E of head of Loch Carron. **59 F5** NH0043.
Creag a' Chlachain *High.* ***Mountain***, in Inverness district, 4m/6km SE of Dores. Height 1197 feet or 365 metres. **51 F1** NH6433.
Creag a' Chrionaich *High.* ***Mountain***, with rock outcrops to E, 1m/2km NW of Lothbeg, Sutherland district. Height 1292 feet or 394 metres. **73 E3** NC9211.
Creag a' Ghreusaiche *High.* ***Mountain***, in Badenoch and Strathspey district 3m/5km E of Aviemore. Mast at summit. Height 1427 feet or 435 metres. NH9412.
Creag a' Lain *High.* ***Mountain***, 3m/4km S of Beinn Edra, Skye. Height 1998 feet or 609 metres. **58 A4** NG4658.
Creag a' Mhadaidh *P. & K.* ***Mountain***, in Craiganour Forest, 4m/7km NW of Kinloch Rannoch. Height 2007 feet or 612 metres. **40 B3** NN6365.
Creag a' Mhaim *High.* ***Mountain***, rocky summit in Inverness district, 2m/4km S of W end of Loch Cluanie. Munro: height 3106 feet or 947 metres. **49 G4** NH0808.
Creag a' Phuill *Arg. & B.* ***Coastal feature***, headland on SE shore of Loch Fyne, 1m/2km S of Inveraray across loch. **30 C4** NN1005.
Creag an Dail Bheag *Aber.* ***Inland physical feature***, area of cliffs with scree below, above River Gain stream in Grampian Mountains, 4m/7km N of Braemar. **52 D5** NO1498.
Creag an Eunaich *P. & K.* ***Mountain***, 3m/5km NW of Dunkeld. Height 1506 feet or 459 metres. **41 E5** NN9743.
Creag an Fheadain *Stir.* ***Mountain***, peak 1m/2km SW of dam of Loch an Daimh. Height 2909 feet or 887 metres. NN4945.
Creag an Funan *Aber.* ***Mountain***, 5m/8km S of Cabrach. Height 2073 feet or 632 metres. **53 F3** NJ3819.
Creag an Loch *P. & K.* ***Mountain***, 3m/5km NW of Amulree, on S side of Loch Fender. Height 2175 feet or 663 metres. NN8740.
Creag an Lochain *P. & K.* ***Mountain***, on W side of Lochan na Lairige. Height 2762 feet or 842 metres. NN5940.
Creag an Lòin *High.* ***Mountain***, in Badenoch and Strathspey district, 1m/2km NW of Newtonmore. Height 1794 feet or 547 metres. **51 F4** NH6901.
Creag an Sgliata *P. & K.* ***Mountain***, 3m/4km S of Acharn. Height 2286 feet or 697 metres. **40 C5** NN7639.
Creag an-t Sithein *P. & K.* ***Mountain***, with crags on E side of summit, 1m/2km N of Glen Brerachan. Height 2083 feet or 635 metres. **41 F3** NO0166.
Creag an Tarmachain ***Mountain***, one of Hills of Cromdale, on border of Highland and Moray, 8m/12km N of Tomintoul. Height 2119 feet or 646 metres. **53 D1** NJ1531.
Creag Beinn nan Eun *P. & K.* ***Inland physical feature***, crag on SW side of Findhu Glen, 7m/11km NE of Callander. **32 C3** NN7213.
Creag Bhalg *Aber.* ***Mountain***, 1m/2km N of Inverey. Height 2191 feet or 668 metres. **52 C5** NO0991.
Creag Bhàn *Arg. & B.* ***Hill***, 1m/2km N of Ardminish, Gigha. Height 328 feet or 100 metres. **21 E4** NR6450.
Creag Bhàn Ard *High.* ***Mountain***, in Morvern, Lochaber district, 4m/6km NW of Lochaline. Height 1112 feet or 339 metres. **37 F5** NM6348.
Creag Bhlag *High.* ***Mountain***, in Badenoch and Strathspey district, 2m/3km NE of Kingussie. Height 1729 feet or 527 metres. **51 G4** NH7603.
Creag Dhubh *High.* ***Mountain***, in Ross and Cromarty district, 1m/2km SE of Corrieshalloch Gorge. Height 1712 feet or 522 metres. **60 B2** NH2176.
Creag Dhubh *High.* ***Mountain***, in Badenoch and Strathspey district, 3m/5km NE of Newtonmore. Height 2578 feet or 786 metres. **51 G4** NH7203.
Creag Dhubh *High.* ***Mountain***, in Badenoch and Strathspey district, 5m/9km S of Aviemore. Height 2781 feet or 848 metres. **52 B4** NH9004.
Creag Dhubh *High.* ***Mountain***, in Lochaber district, on N side of Glen Spean, 3m/5km NE of Roybridge. Height 2158 feet or 658 metres. **39 F1** NN3282.
Creag Dhubh *High.* ***Mountain***, rising to over 740 metres, 2m/3km SW of Newtonmore. **51 F5** NN6797.
Creag Dhubh *P. & K.* ***Inland physical feature***, steep SE flank of Blath Bhalg mountain, 1968 feet or 600 metres high. **41 F3** NO0160.
Creag Dionard *High.* ***Mountain***, to SW of Loch Dionard. Height 2552 feet or 778 metres. **74 C4** NC3348.
Creag Dubh *High.* ***Mountain***, peak in Inverness district 3m/4km NW of dam of Loch Mullardoch. Height 3103 feet or 946 metres. **50 B1** NH1935.
Creag Each *P. & K.* ***Hill***, with craggy summit, 2m/3km NE of Comrie. Height 991 feet or 302 metres. **32 C2** NN7924.
Creag Fhraoch *W.Isles* ***Coastal feature***, cliff 4m/7km SW of Tolsta Head, Isle of Lewis. **69 G3** NB5142.
Creag Gharbh *Stir.* ***Mountain***, on S side of Loch Tay, 6m/10km NE of Lochearnhead. Height 2089 feet or 637 metres. **32 B1** NN6333.
Creag Ghoraidh (Anglicised form: Creagorry.) *W.Isles* ***Settlement***, on S coast of Benbecula, 4m/7km S of Benbecula (Baile a' Mhanaich) Aerodrome. **45 G5** NF7948.
Creag Ghorm a' Bhealaich *High.* ***Mountain***, peak in Inverness district, 4m/6km NE of dam of Loch Monar, on E side of Sgurr Fhuar-thuill. Height 3378 feet or 1030 metres. NH2443.
Creag Island *Arg. & B.* ***Island***, islet off S coast of Lismore, nearly 1km S of Eilean Dubh and on W side of Pladda Island. NM8337.
Creag Leacach *Angus* ***Mountain***, 4m/6km NE of Spittal of Glenshee. Munro: height 3237 feet or 987 metres. **41 G2** NO1574.
Creag Liath *High.* ***Mountain***, 3m/4km NW of Grantown-on-Spey. Height 1476 feet or 450 metres. **52 C1** NJ0031.
Creag Liath *P. & K.* ***Mountain***, 3m/4km NW of Comrie. Height 1637 feet or 499 metres. **32 C2** NN7324.
Creag Liath *P. & K.* ***Mountain***, 4m/7km SW of Dunkeld. Height 1397 feet or 426 metres. **33 E1** NN9837.

Creag Loch nan Dearcag *High.* ***Mountain***, in Ross and Cromarty district on N slopes of River Meig valley, and 2m/3km NE of Milltown. Height 1758 feet or 536 metres. **60 C4** NH3356.
Creag Loisgte *High.* ***Mountain***, in Sutherland district, 4m/6km SW of Oykel Bridge. Height 1351 feet or 412 metres. **71 F5** NH3695.
Creag Meagaidh *High.* ***Mountain***, on border of Lochaber and Badenoch and Strathspey districts, 3m/5km N of E end of Loch Moy. Munro: height 3706 feet or 1130 metres. **39 G1** NN4187.
Creag-mheall Beag *High.* ***Mountain***, 6m/9km SE of Laide, Ross and Cromarty district. Height 1138 feet or 347 metres. **59 F1** NG9786.
Creag Mhòr ***Mountain***, on border of Perth & Kinross and Stirling, 5m/8km NE of Tyndrum. Munro: height 3434 feet or 1047 metres. **31 F1** NN3936.
Creag Mhòr *High.* ***Mountain***, 5m/8km SE of Loch Choire, Sutherland district. Height 2339 feet or 713 metres. **72 B2** NC6924.
Creag Mhòr *High.* ***Mountain***, in Sherramore Forest, 10m/16km SE of Fort Augustus. Height 2506 feet or 764 metres. **51 D5** NN4897.
Creag Mhòr *P. & K.* ***Mountain***, to N of Loch Tay, 6m/10km NW of Kenmore. Munro: height 3218 feet or 981 metres. **40 B5** NN6949.
Creag Mhòr *Stir.* ***Mountain***, 4m/6km W of Killin. Height 2358 feet or 719 metres. **32 A1** NN5134.
Creag Mhòr *W.Isles* ***Hill***, on coast, to S of entrance to Loch Carlabhagh, Isle of Lewis. Height 226 feet or 69 metres. **68 C3** NB1741.
Creag na Caillich *Stir.* ***Mountain***, 3m/5km N of Killin. Height 3004 feet or 916 metres. NN5637.
Creag na Criche *P. & K.* ***Mountain***, craggy summit, 6m/10km NW of Methven. Height 1492 feet or 455 metres. **33 E1** NN9835.
Creag na h-lolaire *Arg. & B.* ***Mountain***, 3m/4km N of Lochbuie, Mull. Height 1660 feet or 506 metres. **29 E2** NM6129.
Creag nam Bodach *High.* ***Mountain***, in Badenoch and Strathspey district, 3m/4km S of Dalwhinnie. Height 1574 feet or 480 metres. **51 G5** NN7596.
Creag nam Fìadh *High.* ***Mountain***, 2m/4km SW of Kinbrace, Sutherland district. Height 1269 feet or 387 metres. **72 D2** NC8423.
Creag Nam Fiadh Mòr *Arg. & B.* ***Hill***, on central Jura, 1m/2km SW of Tarbert. Height 859 feet or 262 metres. **21 D1** NR5981.
Creag nam Fitheach *Arg. & B.* ***Mountain***, on Mull, 3m/5km E of Lochbuie. Height 1030 feet or 314 metres. **29 F2** NM6624.
Creag nam Mial *P. & K.* ***Mountain***, 5m/8km E of Ballingluig. Height 1840 feet or 561 metres. **41 F4** NO0554.
Creag nan Caiman *High.* ***Mountain***, in Inverness district, 2m/3km SE of Affric Lodge. Height 2168 feet or 661 metres. **50 A2** NH1920.
Creag nan Damh *High.* ***Mountain***, peak on border of Lochaber and Skye and Lochalsh districts 4m/6km NE of Kinloch Hourn. Munro: height 3011 feet or 918 metres. **49 F3** NG9811.
Creag nan Gabhar *Aber.* ***Mountain***, 4m/7km S of Braemar. Height 2736 feet or 834 metres. **41 G1** NO1584.
Creag nan Gall *Aber.* ***Mountain***, 2m/3km S of Balmoral Castle, with large rock outcrop on NW side. Height 1971 feet or 601 metres. **53 E5** NO2691.
Creag Nay *High.* ***Mountain***, in Inverness district, 1m/2km NE of Drumnadrochit. Height 1240 feet or 378 metres. **51 E1** NH5230.
Creag Pitridh *High.* ***Mountain***, in Badenoch and Strathspey district, 1m/2km E of SW end of Lochan na h-Earba. Munro: height 3031 feet or 924 metres. **39 G1** NN4881.
Creag Rainich *High.* ***Mountain***, in Ross and Cromarty district, 8m/13km S of Dundonnell. Height 2647 feet or 807 metres. **59 G2** NH0975.
Creag Riabhach *High.* ***Mountain***, 7m/11km S of Cape Wrath. Height 1591 feet or 485 metres. **74 B2** NC2763.
Creag Riabhach Bheag *High.* ***Mountain***, 2m/3km NE of Ben Hope. Height 1519 feet or 463 metres. **75 D3** NC4952.
Creag Riabhach na Greighe *High.* ***Mountain***, 4m/6km S of W end of Loch Choire, Sutherland district. Height 1512 feet or 461 metres. **72 B2** NC6120.
Creag Ruadh *High.* ***Mountain***, with twin summits at 2201 feet or 671 metres and 2148 feet or 655 metres on borders of Sutherland and Ross and Cromarty districts, 12m/20km NE of Garve. **60 D1** NH4381.
Creag Scalabsdale *High.* ***Mountain***, on border of Sutherland and Caithness districts, to SE of Loch Scalabsdale. Height 1820 feet or 555 metres. **73 E2** NC9624.
Creag Tharsuinn *Arg. & B.* ***Mountain***, with craggy E face, rising to form W side of Garrachra Glen, 7m/11km S of Strachur. Height 2102 feet or 641 metres. **30 C5** NS0891.
Creag Thoraraidh *High.* ***Mountain***, 2m/3km NE of Helmsdale. Height 1322 feet or 403 metres. **73 F3** ND0318.
Creag Uchdag ***Mountain***, on border of Perth & Kinross and Stirling, 3m/5km SE of Ardeonaig on S shore of Loch Tay. Height 2883 feet or 879 metres. **32 C1** NN7032.
Creagan *Arg. & B.* ***Settlement***, on N shore of Loch Creran, Argyll, 3m/5km E of Portnacroish. NM9744.
Creagan a' Chaise *Moray* ***Mountain***, summit of Hills of Cromdale, 5m/8km SE of Grantown-on-Spey. Height 2368 feet or 722 metres. **52 D2** NJ1024.
Creagan an Eich *Arg. & B.* ***Mountain***, on E side of Loch Fyne, 3m/5km S of Inveraray across the loch. Height 1096 feet or 334 metres. **30 D4** NN1003.
Creagan Asdale *High.* ***Hill***, in Sutherland district, 5m/8km NW of Dornoch. Height 722 feet or 220 metres. **72 C5** NH7292.
Creagan Dubha Réidhe Bhig *High.* ***Mountain***, 4m/6km E of Syre, Caithness district. Height 1105 feet or 337 metres. **75 G4** NC7544.
Creagan Glas *High.* ***Mountain***, 2m/3km S of Muie, Sutherland district. Height 1027 feet or 313 metres. **72 B4** NC6701.
Creagan Mòr *High.* ***Mountain***, on SE side of Loch Ericht, 3m/4km SW of Dalwhinnie. Height 2539 feet or 774 metres. **40 B1** NN6180.
Creagan na Beinne *P. & K.* ***Mountain***, 3m/5km SW of Ardtalnaig. Height 2913 feet or 888 metres. **32 C1** NN7436.
Creagbheitheachain *High.* ***Settlement***, in Glen Scaddle, 4m/7km N of Sallachan Point, Lochaber district. **38 B3** NM9868.
Creagnaneun Forest *High.* ***Forest/woodland***, in Inverness district on NW shore of Loch Ness, NE of Invermoriston. NH4418.
Creagorry *W.Isles Anglicised form of Creag Ghoraidh, qv.*
Creca *D. & G.* ***Hamlet***, 3m/5km NE of Annan. **9 G3** NY2270.
Cree ***River***, whose headwaters are in Glentrool Forest Park. River then flows S to Newton Stewart and Wigtown Bay. **7 E2** NX4655.
Creebridge *D. & G.* ***Village***, opposite Newton Stewart across River Cree. NX4165.
Creed (Also known as Greeta River.) *W.Isles* ***River***, on Isle of Lewis rising among lochs some 6m/10km NW of Stornoway and flowing SE into Stornoway Harbour. NB4131.
Creetown *D. & G.* ***Village***, on E side of River Cree estuary at mouth of Moneypool Burn, 6m/10km SE of Newton Stewart. Granite quarries to S. **7 F5** NX4758.
Creggans *Arg. & B.* ***Settlement***, in Argyll, on E shore of Loch Fyne, 1m/2km NW of Strachur. **30 C4** NN0802.
Creich *Arg. & B.* ***Locality***, at NW end of Ross of Mull, 1m/2km NE of Fionnphort. NM3124.
Creich *Fife* ***Settlement***, 5m/8km NW of Cupar. **34 B2** NO3221.
Creigh Hill *Angus* ***Mountain***, comprises two distinct summits over 490 metres, with cairns, at SW end of Backwater Reservoir and 2m/3km NE of Dykend. **42 A4** NO2658.
Creinch *W.Dun.* ***Island***, in Loch Lomond, 2m/3km E of Rossdhu House. NS3988.
Creise *High.* ***Mountain***, peak to S of Stob a' Ghlais Choire, 7m/11km SE of Kinlochleven. Munro: height 3608 feet or 1100 metres. **39 E4** NN2350.
Crelevan *High.* ***Settlement***, in Strathglass, 5m/8km NE of Cannich. **50 C1** NH3837.
Creran ***River***, rising S of Sgor na h-Ulaidh and running W, then SW down Glen Creran to head of Loch Creran. NM9945.
Cretshengan *Arg. & B.* ***Settlement***, on W of Kintyre, 2m/3km N of Kilberry. **21 F3** NR7166.
Creuch Hill *Inclyde* ***Mountain***, on NW fringe of Duchal Moor. Height 1446 feet or 441 metres. **23 D3** NS2668.
Crianlarich *Stir.* ***Village***, on River Fillan, 12m/20km SW of Killin. Railway junction of Oban and Fort William lines. **31 F2** NN3825.
Crib Law *Sc.Bord.* ***Mountain***, with fire tower in Craik Forest, 1m/2km NW of Craik. Height 1387 feet or 423 metres. **17 E5** NT3309.
Crib Law *Sc.Bord.* ***Mountain***, in Lammermuir Hills, 2m/3km SW of Hopes Reservoir. Height 1670 feet or 509 metres. **26 C3** NT5260.
Crichie *Aber.* ***Locality***, comprises many dispersed settlements, 1m/2km SW of Stuartfield. **65 E5** NJ9544.
Crichope Linn *D. & G.* ***Waterfall***, in course of burn of Crichope Linn, 2m/3km E of Thornhill. NX9195.
Crichton *Midloth.* ***Hamlet***, 2m/3km S of Pathhead. **26 A3** NT3862.
Crichton Castle *Midloth.* ***Castle***, 14c and later, one of largest castles in Scotland (Historic Scotland), 6m/10km SE of Edinburgh. **26 A3** NT3861.
Crieff *P. & K.* Population: 6023. ***Small town***, above E bank of River Earn, 16m/25km W of Perth. Noted for local crafts. **33 D2** NN8621.
Crieff Visitors Centre *P. & K.* ***Other feature of interest***, craft centre in Crieff where visitors can view production process of traditional whisky flagons, tableware and glass paperweights. Plant centre with cacti from all over world. **33 D2** NN8621.
Criffell *D. & G.* ***Mountain***, prominent landmark commanding extensive views, 3m/4km S of New Abbey. Height 1866 feet or 569 metres. **9 D4** NX9561.
Crimond *Aber.* ***Village***, near NE coast, 8m/13km NW of Peterhead. **65 F4** NK0556.
Crimonmogate *Aber.* ***Settlement***, in woodland near small lake, 3m/5km S of St. Combs. **65 F4** NK0358.
Crinan *Arg. & B.* ***Village***, on Crinan Loch, in Argyll, 6m/10km NW of Lochgilphead. **29 G5** NR7894.
Crinan Canal *Arg. & B.* ***Canal***, connects Crinan Loch with Ardrishaig and Loch Fyne, running across N part of Kintyre peninsula. Lighthouse at Ardrishaig entrance to canal. NR8191.
Crinan Ferry *Arg. & B.* ***Settlement***, to E of Crinan across River Add; ferry for pedestrians across river. NR7993.
Crinan Loch (Also known as Loch Crinan.) *Arg. & B.* ***Sea feature***, sea-loch in Argyll, 6m/10km NW of Lochgilphead. **29 G5** NR7895.
Crindledyke *N.Lan.* ***Settlement***, 1m/2km E of Newmains. NS8356.
Cringletie *Sc.Bord.* ***Settlement***, 3m/4km N of Peebles. **25 G5** NT2344.
Crionaig *W.Isles* ***Locality***, upland area of S part of Isle of Lewis, rising to over 460 metres, 3m/5km S of head of Loch Shell. **67 E3** NB2906.
Croachy *High.* ***Locality***, comprising settlement of West Croachy and hamlet of East Croachy, in Inverness district, 5m/9km SE of Dores. NH6427.
Croalchapel *D. & G.* ***Settlement***, 3m/4km SE of Thornhill. **8 D1** NX9091.
Crochan Hill *P. & K.* ***Mountain***, on N side of Glen Almond, 9m/15km NE of Crieff. Height 1660 feet or 506 metres. **33 E1** NN9533.
Crock Ness *Ork.* ***Coastal feature***, headland on E coast of Hoy opposite Flotta. **78 C3** ND3293.
Crocketford (Also known as Nine Mile Bar.) *D. & G.* ***Village***, 7m/12km NE of Castle Douglas. **8 C3** NX8372.
Croe *High.* ***River***, running NW to head of Loch Duich in Skye and Lochalsh district. **49 G3** NG9521.
Croft Head *D. & G.* ***Mountain***, 4m/7km E of Moffat. Height 2086 feet or 636 metres. **16 C5** NT1505.
Croftamie *Stir.* ***Village***, on Catter Burn, 2m/3km S of Drymen. NS4786.
Croftfoot *Glas.* ***Suburb***, 3m/5km S of Glasgow city centre. NS6060.
Croftmoraig *P. & K.* ***Locality***, with triple stone circle on S side of River Tay near its confluence with River Lyon. NN7947.
Croftmore *P. & K.* ***Settlement***, in valley of River Tilt, 3m/4km N of Blair Atholl. **41 D3** NN8868.
Crofts *D. & G.* ***Settlement***, 3m/4km SE of Corsock. **8 B3** NX7974.
Crofts of Benachielt *High.* ***Settlement***, 3m/5km N of Latheron. **77 D5** ND1838.
Crofts of Buinach *Moray* ***Settlement***, 1m/2km NE of Kellas. **63 D4** NJ1855.
Crofts of Haddo *Aber.* ***Locality***, 4m/7km E of Fyvie. **54 D1** NJ8337.
Crogary Mòr *W.Isles* ***Hill***, on North Uist, 1km NE of Maari. Height 590 feet or 180 metres. **45 G2** NF8673.
Croggan *Arg. & B.* ***Village***, on S side of entrance to Loch Spelve, Mull. **29 G2** NM7027.
Croic-bheinn *High.* ***Mountain***, in Ross and Cromarty district, 3m/5km SW of Shieldaig. Height 1617 feet or 493 metres. **59 D4** NG7652.
Croick *High.* ***Locality***, in Sutherland district, at foot of Strath Chuilionaich, 10m/15km W of Bonar Bridge. **71 G5** NH4591.
Croick *High.* ***Settlement***, on E side of Halladale River, 1km N of Trantlebeg. **76 A3** NC8954.
Croick Church *High.* ***Ecclesiastical building***, 9m/14km W of Ardgay. One of 32 'parliamentary' churches built in the Highlands and Islands in the 1820s. Designed by Thomas Telford. **71 G5** NH4591.
Croig *Arg. & B.* ***Settlement***, on N coast of Mull, 3m/5km E of Caliach Point. **36 D4** NM4053.
Crois Dughaill (Anglicised form: Crossdougal.) *W.Isles* ***Settlement***, on South Uist, 1km S of Dalabrog. **44 C2** NF7520.
Croit Bheinn *High.* ***Mountain***, 4m/6km SE of Lochailort, Lochaber district. Height 2175 feet or 663 metres. **38 A2** NM8177.
Crom Allt *High.* ***River***, flows N into Loch Urigill, Ross and Cromarty district. **71 E4** NC2509.
Cròm Allt *High.* ***River***, rising on NW slopes of Carn na Crìche and flowing N into Allt Odhar, 10m/16km E of Fort Augustus. NH5306.
Crom Loch *High.* ***Lake/loch***, small loch on border of Sutherland and Ross and Cromarty districts, 13m/21km N of Garve. **60 C1** NH3983.
Cromalt Hills *High.* ***Large natural feature***, upland area on border of Ross and Cromarty and Sutherland districts, 4m/6km S of Elphin. **71 E4** NC2106.
Cromar *Aber.* ***Locality***, between Aboyne and Tarland. **53 G4** NJ4704.
Cromarty *High.* ***Small town***, with harbour in Ross and Cromarty district, on S side of entrance to Cromarty Firth, 15m/24km NE of Inverness. Hugh Miller's Cottage (National Trust for Scotland), birthplace of eminent geologist, dates from 1650; contains small museum. **61 G3** NH7867.

Cromarty Bay *High.* ***Bay***, on S side of Cromarty Firth, Ross and Cromarty district, between Balblair and Cromarty. **61 G3** NH7466.
Cromarty Court House *High.* ***Historic house***, in Cromarty, 15m/24km NE of Inverness. Built in 1773, containing reconstruction of trial, animated figures and history of Cromarty. **61 G3** NH7967.
Cromarty Firth *High.* ***Sea feature***, long inlet of Moray Firth extending past Nigg Bay and Invergordon to Dingwall, Ross and Cromarty district. **61 F3** NH6667.
Cromarty Firth Bridge *High.* ***Bridge***, road bridge carrying A9 across Cromarty Firth, 3m/5km E of Dingwall. NH5960.
Crombie *Fife* ***Village***, 3m/5km SW of Dunfermline. NT0485.
Crombie Castle *Aber.* ***Castle***, medieval castle 2m/4km W of Aberchirder. **64 A4** NJ5952.
Crombie Country Park *Angus* ***Leisure/recreation***, adjacent to Crombie Reservoir, 2m/3km NE of Monikie. 250 acre park surrounding Victorian reservoir styled to resemble natural loch. **42 D5** NO5240.
Crombie Mill *Angus* ***Settlement***, to SE of Crombie Reservoir, 2m/3km NE of Monikie. **42 D5** NO5340.
Crombie Reservoir *Angus* ***Reservoir***, small reservoir 4m/7km NW of Carnoustie. **42 D5** NO5240.
Cromblet *Aber.* ***Settlement***, 2m/3km SE of Fyvie. **54 C1** NJ7834.
Cromdale *High.* ***Village***, in Badenoch and Strathspey district, 3m/5km E of Grantown-on-Spey. **52 C2** NJ0728.
Cromlet *P. & K.* ***Mountain***, rounded summit, 7m/11km N of Dunblane. Height 1328 feet or 405 metres. **32 C3** NN7811.
Cromore *W.Isles Anglicised form of Gleann Ghrabhair, qv.*
Cronberry *E.Ayr.* ***Village***, 3m/5km NE of Cumnock. **15 E3** NS6022.
Crook of Devon *P. & K.* ***Village***, on bend of River Devon, 5m/9km W of Kinross. **33 F4** NO0300.
Crookedholm *E.Ayr.* ***Locality***, 2m/3km E of Kilmarnock town centre. **14 C2** NS4537.
Crookedshaws Hill *Sc.Bord.* ***Mountain***, 2m/3km E of Morebattle. Height 1010 feet or 308 metres. **18 B4** NT8024.
Crookston *Glas.* ***Suburb***, 2m/4km E of Paisley. NS5263.
Crookston Castle *Glas.* ***Castle***, early 15c castle (Historic Scotland) surrounded by 12c earthworks, 3m/4km SE of Paisley. **23 G3** NS5262.
Cros (Anglicised form: Cross.) *W.Isles* ***Village***, near N end of Isle of Lewis, 2m/4km SW of Port Nis. **69 F1** NB5062.
Crosbie *N.Ayr.* ***Locality***, 1m/2km NE of West Kilbride. Includes large caravan site and remains of Crosbie Tower. **22 D5** NS2150.
Crosbost (Anglicised form: Crossbost.) *W.Isles* ***Village***, on E coast of Isle of Lewis, on N side of entrance to Loch Leurbost. **69 E5** NB3924.
Cross *W.Isles Anglicised form of Cros, qv.*
Cross Hill *Sc.Bord.* ***Mountain***, 4m/7km SW of Ettrick. Height 1450 feet or 442 metres. **16 D5** NT2507.
Cross Kirk *Sc.Bord.* ***Ecclesiastical building***, remains of 13c Trinitarian Friary (Historic Scotland) on W side of Peebles, consisting of W tower and nave. **25 G5** NT2440.
Cross Law *Sc.Bord.* ***Hill***, 3m/4km NW of Coldingham. Height 745 feet or 227 metres. **27 F3** NT8768.
Cross of Jackston *Aber.* ***Settlement***, at road junction, 5m/8km NW of Oldmeldrum. **54 C1** NJ7432.
Cross Water *S.Ayr.* ***River***, rising in Arecleoch Forest and flowing NE to join Duisk River at Barrhill, 9m/15km E of Ballantrae. **6 D3** NX2382.
Cross Water of Luce ***River***, rising in vicinity of Arecleoch Forest, E of Ballantrae, and flowing S to join Main Water of Luce at New Luce, to form Water of Luce. **6 C4** NX1764.
Crossaig *Arg. & B.* ***Settlement***, on E coast of Kintyre, 5m/7km N of Grogport. **21 G4** NR8351.
Crossaig Glen *Arg. & B.* ***Valley***, running E into Port nan Gamhna on E coast of Kintyre, Argyll. NR8251.
Crossapol *Arg. & B.* ***Settlement***, in SW part of Coll, overlooking Crossapol Bay. **36 A4** NM1253.
Crossapol Bay *Arg. & B.* ***Bay***, wide bay on S coast of Coll, near SW end of island. **36 A4** NM1352.
Crossapoll *Arg. & B.* ***Settlement***, on S coast of Tiree, 3m/5km W of Scarinish. **36 A2** NL9943.
Crossapoll Point *Arg. & B.* ***Coastal feature***, headland to S of Crossapoll, Tiree. NL9942.
Crossbost *W.Isles Anglicised form of Crosbost, qv.*
Crossdougal *W.Isles Anglicised form of Crois Dughaill, qv.*
Crossford *D. & G.* ***Settlement***, 4m/6km E of Moniaive. **8 C2** NX8388.
Crossford *Fife* Population: 2756. ***Village***, 2m/3km W of Dunfermline. **25 E1** NT0686.
Crossford *S.Lan.* ***Village***, near confluence of Rivers Nethan and Clyde, 3m/4km SW of Carluke. **24 C5** NS8246.
Crossgatehall *E.Loth.* ***Hamlet***, 3m/4km NE of Dalkeith. **26 A3** NT3669.
Crossgates *Fife* Population: 1937. ***Village***, 2m/3km SW of Cowdenbeath. **25 F1** NT1488.
Crossgates *P. & K.* ***Settlement***, 4m/7km SW of Perth. **33 F2** NO0420.
Crosshands *E.Ayr.* ***Settlement***, at road junction, 2m/4km NW of Mauchline. **14 C2** NS4830.
Crosshill *Fife* ***Locality***, adjoining to S of Lochore. **33 G5** NT1796.
Crosshill *Glas.* ***Suburb***, 2m/4km S of Glasgow city centre, in Govanhill district. NS5862.
Crosshill *Glas.* ***Suburb***, 6m/9km E of Glasgow, in Baillieston district. NS6863.
Crosshill *S.Ayr.* ***Village***, 3m/5km SE of Maybole. **14 B5** NS3206.
Crosshouse *E.Ayr.* Population: 2670. ***Village***, 2m/3km W of Kilmarnock. **14 B2** NS3938.
Crosskirk *High.* ***Settlement***, near N coast of Caithness district, 5m/9km W of Thurso. Ruined chapel of St. Mary (Historic Scotland), probably 12c. **76 C1** ND0369.
Crosskirk Bay *High.* ***Bay***, small bay on N coast of Caithness district, to NW of Crosskirk. **76 C1** ND0270.
Crosslee *Renf.* ***Hamlet***, 2m/4km NW of Johnstone. **23 F3** NS4066.
Crosslee *Sc.Bord.* ***Hamlet***, 3m/5km NE of Ettrick. **17 E4** NT3018.
Crosslet *W.Dun.* ***Suburb***, NE district of Dumbarton. **23 F2** NS4076.
Crossmichael *D. & G.* ***Village***, 4m/6km NW of Castle Douglas. **8 B4** NX7366.
Crossmyloof *Glas.* ***Suburb***, 2m/4km S of Glasgow city centre. NS5762.
Crossraguel Abbey *S.Ayr.* ***Ecclesiastical building***, mainly 15c to 16c ruins of abbey founded in 1244 (Historic Scotland), 2m/3km SW of Maybole. **14 A5** NS2708.
Crossroads *Aber.* ***Settlement***, 3m/5km SE of Banchory. **54 C5** NO7594.
Crossroads *E.Ayr.* ***Settlement***, at road junction, 4m/6km SE of Kilmarnock. **14 C2** NS4733.
Crossroads *Fife* ***Suburb***, central district of Methil. NT3699.
Crosswood Reservoir *W.Loth.* ***Reservoir***, 4m/7km SE of West Calder. **25 E4** NT0557.
Crovie *Aber.* ***Village***, on E side of Gamrie Bay, 6m/10km E of Macduff. **64 D3** NJ8065.
Crovie Head *Aber.* ***Coastal feature***, headland to N of Crovie. **64 C3** NJ8066.
Crowlin Islands *High.* ***Island***, group of three islands lying close together 1m/2km off W coast of Ross and Cromarty district on N side of entrance to Loch Carron. Total area 420 acres or 170 hectares. Eilean Mòr is largest and nearest to mainland. Eilean Meadhonach lies to its W; Eilean Beag, smallest, is immediately N of Eilean Meadhonach. Beacon on Eilean Beag. **48 C1** NG6934.
Crowlista *W.Isles Anglicised form of Cradhlastadh, qv.*
Crow's Nest *D. & G.* ***Coastal feature***, headland to NW of Stairhaven, 3m/4km S of Glenluce. **6 C5** NX2053.
Croy *High.* ***Village***, in Inverness district close to border with Nairn district, 7m/11km SW of Nairn. **61 G5** NH7649.
Croy *N.Lan.* Population: 1148. ***Village***, 1m/2km SE of Kilsyth. Part of Antonine Wall ditch and two beacon platform on W side of Croy Hill (Historic Scotland) to E. **24 B2** NS7275.
Croy Brae *S.Ayr.* ***Open space***, hillslope near coast at N end of Culzean Bay, where by an optical illusion known as 'Electric Brae' a downward slope appears to go upward. **14 A4** NS2513.
Cruach *Arg. & B.* ***Settlement***, 1m/2km SE of Bowmore, Islay. **20 B4** NR3258.
Cruach a' Bhuic *Arg. & B.* ***Mountain***, partly in Argyll Forest Park, 2m/3km W of Carrick. Height 2083 feet or 635 metres. **31 D5** NS1693.
Cruach a' Ghaill *High.* ***Mountain***, in Moidart, Lochaber district, 3m/4km SE of Ardmolich. Height 1217 feet or 371 metres. **37 G2** NM7570.
Cruach a' Phubuill *Arg. & B.* ***Mountain***, on Knapdale, 5m/8km NW of Tarbert. Height 1565 feet or 477 metres. **21 G2** NR8276.
Cruach Airde *Arg. & B.* ***Hill***, on W of Kintyre, 1m/2km E of Kilberry. Height 699 feet or 213 metres. **21 F3** NR7363.
Cruach Airdeny *Arg. & B.* ***Mountain***, 2m/3km N of head of Loch Nant. Height 1299 feet or 396 metres. **30 B2** NM9927.
Cruach an Eachlaich *Arg. & B.* ***Mountain***, 2m/3km N of Ford. Height 1148 feet or 350 metres. **30 A4** NM8606.
Cruach an Lochain *Arg. & B.* ***Mountain***, 6m/9km SW of Strachur. Height 1666 feet or 508 metres. **30 C5** NS0493.
Cruach an t-Sithein *Arg. & B.* ***Mountain***, 4m/7km NE of Garelochhead. Height 2244 feet or 684 metres. NS2796.
Cruach an t-Sorchain *Arg. & B.* ***Mountain***, on Kintyre, 2m/3km S of Tarbert. Height 1125 feet or 343 metres. **21 G3** NR8765.
Cruach Ardrain *Stir.* ***Mountain***, 3m/5km SE of Crianlarich. Munro: height 3428 feet or 1045 metres. **31 G2** NN4021.
Cruach Ardura *Arg. & B.* ***Hill***, on Mull, 6m/9km NE of Lochbuie. Height 708 feet or 216 metres. **29 F2** NM6629.
Cruach Bhrochdadail *High.* ***Mountain***, in Moidart, 3m/4km E of Rois-bheinn. Height 1171 feet or 357 metres. **37 G2** NM7176.
Cruach Breacain *Arg. & B.* ***Mountain***, on Knapdale, 2m/3km W of Ardrishaig. Height 1181 feet or 360 metres. **21 G1** NR8286.
Cruach Choireadail *Arg. & B.* ***Mountain***, 4m/6km S of head of Loch Bà, Mull. Height 2027 feet or 618 metres. **29 E1** NM5930.
Cruach Chuilceachan *Arg. & B.* ***Mountain***, on Cowal peninsula, 9m/14km N of Tighnabruaich. Height 1427 feet or 435 metres. **22 A1** NR9887.
Cruach Doire Léithe *Arg. & B.* ***Mountain***, on Kintyre, 3m/5km S of Tarbert. Height 1237 feet or 377 metres. **21 G3** NR8763.
Cruach Doire 'n Dòbhrain *High.* ***Hill***, 3m/4km SW of Arisaig, Lochaber district. Height 338 feet or 103 metres. **37 F1** NM6384.
Cruach Fasgach *Arg. & B.* ***Mountain***, 2m/3km S of Garbhallt. Height 1096 feet or 334 metres. **30 C5** NS0293.
Cruach Ionnastail *Arg. & B.* ***Hill***, in N part of Jura, 3m/4km N of Ardlussa. Height 968 feet or 295 metres. **29 F5** NR6491.
Cruach Lusach *Arg. & B.* ***Mountain***, in Knapdale, 4m/7km SW of Ardrishaig. Height 1528 feet or 466 metres. **21 F1** NR7883.
Cruach Mhic-an-t-Saoir *Arg. & B.* ***Mountain***, on Kintyre, 4m/6km W of Grogport. Height 1194 feet or 364 metres. **21 F5** NR7442.
Cruach Mhic-Gougain *Arg. & B.* ***Hill***, on Kintyre, 5m/8km NW of Grogport. Height 813 feet or 248 metres. **21 F5** NR7550.
Cruach Mhòr *Arg. & B.* ***Mountain***, in Argyll, 4m/7km NW of Inveraray. Height 1932 feet or 589 metres. **30 C3** NN0514.
Cruach na Seilcheig *Arg. & B.* ***Hill***, on Jura, 2m/3km W of Aird of Kinuachdrachd and 7m/11km N of Ardlussa. Height 971 feet or 296 metres. **29 F5** NR6898.
Cruach nam Fearna *Arg. & B.* ***Mountain***, 1m/2km NW of Melfort. Height 1089 feet or 332 metres. **30 A3** NM8215.
Cruach nam Fiadh *Arg. & B.* ***Hill***, on Kintyre, 3m/5km W of Claonaig. Height 882 feet or 269 metres. **21 G4** NR8256.
Cruach nam Miseag *Arg. & B.* ***Mountain***, with craggy summit in Argyll Forest Park, rising above W shore of Loch Goil and 3m/4km SW of Lochgoilhead. Height 1988 feet or 606 metres. **31 D5** NS1898.
Cruach nam Mult *Arg. & B.* ***Mountain***, 4m/7km SE of Inveraray across Loch Fyne. Height 2004 feet or 611 metres. **31 D4** NN1605.
Cruach nan Caorach *Arg. & B.* ***Mountain***, on Cowal peninsula with craggy face, 5m/8km N of Tighnabruaich. Height 1502 feet or 458 metres. **22 A1** NR9980.
Cruach nan Capull *Arg. & B.* ***Mountain***, in Argyll, 4m/6km SE of Inveraray across Loch Fyne. Height 1853 feet or 565 metres. **30 D4** NN1405.
Cruach nan Capull *Arg. & B.* ***Mountain***, 3m/5km SW of Strachur. Height 1578 feet or 481 metres. **30 C5** NS0797.
Cruach nan Capull *Arg. & B.* ***Mountain***, overlooking Loch Striven, 5m/8km W of Dunoon. Height 2004 feet or 611 metres. **22 B2** NS0979.
Cruach nan Con *Arg. & B.* ***Mountain***, 4m/6km E of Pennyghael, Mull. Height 1627 feet or 496 metres. **29 E2** NM5726.
Cruach nan Cuilean *Arg. & B.* ***Mountain***, 1km NW of Loch Striven and 11m/17km SW of Strachur. Height 1417 feet or 432 metres. **22 B1** NS0484.
Cruach nan Gabhar *Arg. & B.* ***Mountain***, on Kintyre, 4m/6km SW of Grogport. Height 1161 feet or 354 metres. **21 F5** NR7541.
Cruach Neuran *Arg. & B.* ***Mountain***, rising above S shore of Loch Tarsan. Height 1991 feet or 607 metres. **22 B1** NS0881.
Cruach Scarba *Arg. & B.* ***Mountain***, highest point on Scarba, 1m/2km NW of Rubha Righinn. Height 1473 feet or 449 metres. **29 F4** NM6904.
Cruach Sganadail *Arg. & B.* ***Mountain***, in N part of Jura, 3m/4km W of Lussagiven. Height 1181 feet or 360 metres. **21 D1** NR5987.
Cruach Sléibhe *Arg. & B.* ***Hill***, 1km NW of Calgary, Mull. Height 544 feet or 166 metres. **36 C4** NM3752.
Cruach Tairbeirt *Arg. & B.* ***Mountain***, between N end of Loch Long and W side of Loch Lomond, 1km N of Tarbet. Height 1361 feet or 415 metres. **31 E4** NN3105.
Cruach Torran Lochain *Arg. & B.* ***Mountain***, 1m/2km E of Gruline, Mull. Height 1138 feet or 347 metres. **37 E5** NM5640.
Cruachan *Arg. & B.* ***Hill***, summit of Lunga, and highest point of Treshnish Isles. Height 338 feet or 103 metres. NM2741.
Cruachan *Stir.* ***Mountain***, on E side of Loch Lomond, 3m/5km NE of Tarbet across the loch. Height 1761 feet or 537 metres. **31 F4** NN3507.
Cruachan Beinn a' Chearcaill *High.* ***Hill***, 5m/8km N of Bracadale, Skye. Height 889 feet or 271 metres. **57 G5** NG3546.

Cruachan Ceann a' Ghairbh *Arg. & B.* ***Hill***, 3m/5km N of Fanmore, Mull. Height 856 feet or 261 metres. **36 D5** NM4248.
Cruachan Dearg *Arg. & B.* ***Mountain***, 3m/4km E of Ben More, Mull. Height 2309 feet or 704 metres. **29 E1** NM5633.
Cruachan Mìn *Arg. & B.* ***Mountain***, 3m/4km N of Rubha nam Bràithrean, Mull. Height 1233 feet or 376 metres. **28 D2** NM4421.
Cruachan Odhar *Arg. & B.* ***Hill***, 1m/2km NW of Kilninian, Mull. Height 840 feet or 256 metres. **36 C5** NM3846.
Cruachan Power Station Visitor Centre *Arg. & B.* ***Other feature of interest***, on shore of NW arm of Loch Awe, with exhibition and information on pumped storage scheme under Ben Cruachan. **30 C2** NN0726.
Cruachan Reservoir *Arg. & B.* ***Reservoir***, 1m/2km SE of Ben Cruachan, in Argyll, with hydro-electric power station. **30 C2** NN0828.
Cruban Beag *High.* ***Mountain***, in Badenoch and Strathspey district, 5m/8km SW of Newtonmore. Height 1935 feet or 590 metres. **51 F5** NN6692.
Cruchie *Aber.* ***Settlement***, 4m/6km NE of Huntly. **64 A5** NJ5842.
Crucifixion Cave *Arg. & B. See Davaar Island.*
Cruden Bay *Aber.* Population: 1708. ***Village***, near mouth of Water of Cruden, 7m/11km S of Peterhead, with Port Erroll adjoining to SE. **55 F1** NK0936.
Cruffell *D. & G.* ***Mountain***, 6m/9km SW of Kirkconnel. Polvaird Loch is small loch to S of summit. Height 1827 feet or 557 metres. **15 E5** NS6804.
Cruggleton *D. & G.* ***Locality***, and ruined castle of the Comyns on W side of Wigtown Bay, 3m/5km NE of Whithorn. NX4843.
Cruggleton Bay (Also known as Rigg Bay.) *D. & G.* ***Bay***, to N of Cruggleton, on W side of Wigtown Bay. **3 E2** NX4844.
Cruggleton Castle *D. & G.* ***Castle***, on coast near Cruggleton Point, 2m/3km S of Garlieston. 12c-13c ruins of castle which belonged to Lords of Galloway, who ruled Scotland at this time. **3 E2** NX4843.
Cruick Water *Angus* ***River***, rising in mountains N of Noranside, and flowing S before turning E to flow through a wide valley and entering West Water, 3m/4km SE of Edzell. **42 C3** NO6265.
Cruim Leacainn *High.* ***Hill***, 6m/9km NE of Fort William. Height 748 feet or 228 metres. **39 D1** NN1680.
Cruinn a' Bheinn *Stir.* ***Mountain***, peak between Ben Lomond and Loch Arklet. Height 2076 feet or 633 metres. **31 F4** NN3605.
Cruinn Bheinn *Stir.* ***Mountain***, on N side of Loch Katrine, 2m/3km NW of Stronachlachar across loch. Height 1788 feet or 545 metres. **31 G3** NN4312.
Cruivie Castle *Fife* ***Castle***, late 15c L-plan tower house, 2m/4km NW of Leuchars. **34 C2** NO4122.
Crùlabhig (Anglicised form: Crulivig.) *W.Isles* ***Settlement***, on W side of Isle of Lewis, 1km SE of bridge connecting Great Bernera with main island. **68 C4** NB1733.
Crulivig *W.Isles Anglicised form of Crùlabhig, qv.*
Crumpton Hill *D. & G.* ***Mountain***, 4m/7km N of Langholm. Height 1574 feet or 480 metres. **10 B2** NY3491.
Crutherland *S.Lan.* ***Settlement***, 2m/3km SE of East Kilbride. **24 A4** NS6651.
Cruys *Angus* ***Mountain***, 3m/4km S of Glenlee. Height 2430 feet or 741 metres. **42 C2** NO4275.
Cuaig *High.* ***Settlement***, near W coast of Ross and Cromarty district, 1m/2km S of Rubha Chuaig. **58 D4** NG7057.
Cuan Sound *Arg. & B.* ***Sea feature***, narrow stretch of sea separating Seil and Luing. **29 G3** NM7514.
Cubbie Roo's Castle (Also known as Castle of Cobbie Row.) *Ork.* ***Castle***, remains of 12c Norse castle (Historic Scotland) on Wyre. Cubbie Roo or Cobbie Row are corruptions of 'Kolbein Hruga', the name of chieftain who built it. **80 C4** HY4426.
Cuffhill Reservoir *N.Ayr.* ***Reservoir***, small reservoir 4m/6km E of Beith. NS3855.
Cuiashader *W.Isles Anglicised form of Cuidhaseadair, qv.*
Cuidhaseadair (Anglicised form: Cuiashader.) *W.Isles* ***Settlement***, near E coast of Isle of Lewis, 3m/5km NW of Cellar Head. **69 G2** NB5458.
Cuidhe Cròm *Aber. See Lochnagar.*
Cuidhir (Anglicised form: Cuier.) *W.Isles* ***Settlement***, on Barra, 2m/4km W of Ardmhòr. **44 B3** NF6703.
Cuidhtinis (Anglicised form: Quidnish.) *W.Isles* ***Settlement***, on SE coast of South Harris, 4m/6km NE of Rodel. **66 C5** NG0987.
Cuidrach *High.* ***Settlement***, on W coast of Trotternish peninsula, 3m/5km S of Uig, Skye. **57 G4** NG3759.
Cuier *W.Isles Anglicised form of Cuidhir, qv.*
Cuil Bay *High.* ***Bay***, on E side of Loch Linnhe, extending SE from Rubha Mòr. **38 B4** NM9754.
Cuil Hill *D. & G.* ***Mountain***, 5m/8km E of Dalbeattie. Height 1378 feet or 420 metres. **8 D4** NX9163.
Cuil-uaine *Arg. & B.* ***Settlement***, 1m/2km SE of Connel. **30 B1** NM9232.
Cuilags *Ork.* ***Mountain***, situated in NW section of Hoy. Height 1420 feet or 433 metres. **78 B2** HY2003.
Cuillin Hills *High.* ***Large natural feature***, group of gabbroic mountains with serrated peaks in S part of Skye, to E and NE of Loch Brittle in district known as Minginish. There are several peaks of over 3000 feet (914 metres), highest being Sgurr Alasdair, 3258 feet or 993 metres. Range is noted for rock climbing. **48 A2** NG4422.
Cuillin Sound *High.* ***Sea feature***, stretch of sea separating Rum, Canna and Sanday from Skye and Soay. **47 G3** NG3612.
Cuilmuich *Arg. & B.* ***Settlement***, on W shore of Loch Goil, to N of Carrick. **31 D5** NS1995.
Cùl a' Bhogha *High.* ***Coastal feature***, hillslope backing small bay, 2m/4km NW of Ullapool in Ross and Cromarty district. **70 C5** NH1098.
Cul Beag *High.* ***Mountain***, 2m/4km SW of Cul Mòr. Height 2522 feet or 769 metres. **70 D4** NC1408.
Cul Mòr *High.* ***Mountain***, in Ross and Cromarty district 8m/13km SW of Inchnadamph. Height 2785 feet or 849 metres. **71 D3** NC1611.
Culachy Forest *High.* ***Open space***, deer forest in Inverness district, 6m/10km S of Fort Augustus. **50 C5** NN3999.
Culag *Arg. & B.* ***Settlement***, on W shore of Loch Lomond, 2m/3km N of Luss. **31 F5** NS3595.
Culardoch *Aber.* ***Mountain***, in Grampian Mountains, 5m/8km N of Bridge of Dee. Height 2952 feet or 900 metres. **53 D5** NO1998.
Culbin Forest *Moray* ***Forest/woodland***, on coast extending W towards Nairn from Findhorn Bay. Planted on drifting sands which buried original farmland. **62 B3** NH9861.
Culblean Hill *Aber.* ***Mountain***, 4m/6km NE of Ballater. Height 1981 feet or 604 metres. **53 F4** NJ3901.
Culbo *High.* ***Settlement***, on N side of Black Isle, 5m/7km N of Munlochy. **61 F3** NH6360.
Culbokie *High.* ***Village***, on Black Isle, Ross and Cromarty district nearly 1m/2km from SE shore of Cromarty Firth and 7m/12km NE of Muir of Ord. **61 F4** NH6059.
Culburnie *High.* ***Settlement***, in Inverness district, 4m/6km SW of Beauly. **61 D5** NH4941.
Culcabock *High.* ***Suburb***, to E of Inverness. **61 F5** NH6844.
Culcharan *Arg. & B.* ***Settlement***, 1km NE of Benderloch. **30 B1** NM9139.
Culcharry *High.* ***Hamlet***, in Nairn district, 4m/7km S of Nairn. **62 A4** NH8650.
Culcreuch Castle *Stir.* ***Castle***, located at foot of Fintry Hills, 1km NE of Fintry. 16c tower house, part of a larger building. **24 A1** NS6287.
Culdrain *Aber.* ***Settlement***, on W bank of River Bogie, 4m/6km S of Huntly. **54 A1** NJ5233.
Culduie *High.* ***Settlement***, 1m/2km N of Toscaig, on W coast of Ross and Cromarty district. **58 D5** NG7140.
Culgower *High.* ***Settlement***, 2m/4km NE of Lothbeg, Sutherland district. **73 E3** NC9711.
Culindrach *Arg. & B.* ***Settlement***, on E coast of Kintyre, 3m/5km NE of Claonaig. **22 A4** NR9159.
Culkein *High.* ***Village***, 2m/3km SE of Point of Stoer, W coast of Sutherland district. **70 C1** NC0332.
Cullachie *High.* ***Settlement***, 2m/3km W of Nethy Bridge. **52 B2** NH9720.
Cullaloe Hills *Fife* ***Large natural feature***, partly wooded hills, 5m/8km E of Dunfermline and 1m/2km N of Dalgety Bay, on Firth of Forth. **25 F1** NT1787.
Cullaloe Reservoir *Fife* ***Reservoir***, small reservoir 1m/2km N of Aberdour. **25 F1** NT1985.
Cullen *Moray* Population: 1420. ***Village***, on Cullen Bay on N coast, 6m/10km E of Buckie. Bin of Cullen, hill 3m/5km SW, commands wide views. **64 A3** NJ5167.
Cullen Bay *Moray* ***Bay***, to N of Cullen, on N coast of Moray, 6m/10km E of Buckie. **64 A3** NJ5067.
Cullen House *Moray* ***Historic house***, partly 13c, 1km SW of Cullen. **64 A3** NJ5066.
Cullerlie Stone Circle (Also known as Garlogie Stone Circle.) *Aber.* ***Historic/prehistoric site***, Bronze Age circle (Historic Scotland) of eight boulders and 30 foot diameter, enclosing excavated burial chambers, nearly 1m/2km S of Garlogie. **54 C4** NJ7804.
Culli Voe *Shet.* ***Sea feature***, inlet on NE coast of Yell. HP5402.
Cullicudden *High.* ***Settlement***, scattered settlement on SE side of Cromarty Firth, Ross and Cromarty district, 3m/5km SW of Balblair. **61 F3** NH6564.
Culligran *High.* ***Other building***, hydro-electric power station on N side of River Farrar in Inverness district, 1m/2km W of Struy Bridge. **60 C5** NH3841.
Culligran Falls *High.* ***Waterfall***, in River Farrar 1km SW of Culligran. **60 C5** NH3740.
Cullipool *Arg. & B.* ***Village***, on NW coast of Luing. **29 G3** NM7313.
Cullivoe *Shet.* ***Village***, on NE coast of Yell, at head of inlet of Culli Voe. **85 E2** HP5402.
Culloch *P. & K.* ***Settlement***, 3m/5km S of Comrie. **32 C3** NN7817.
Culloden *High.* Population: 3669. ***Locality***, includes site of Battle of Culloden (1746), 5m/8km E of Inverness. **61 G5** NH7246.
Culloden Forest *High.* ***Forest/woodland***, to NE and to S of Culloden Muir. **61 G5** NH7647.
Culloden Muir *High.* ***Open space***, tract in Inverness district, 4m/7km E of Inverness. Site of battle in 1746 in which army of Prince Charles Edward Stuart was destroyed by Duke of Cumberland's forces. Various sites, museum, and visitor centre, all owned by National Trust for Scotland. **61 G5** NH7445.
Culloden Visitors' Centre *High.* ***Other feature of interest***, permanent exhibition (National Trust for Scotland) on Battle of Culloden (1746) and its aftermath, located on battlefield site, 5m/8km E of Inverness. **61 G5** NH7445.
Cullykhan Bay *Aber.* ***Bay***, 2km SE of Troup Head, 6m/9km W of Rosehearty. NJ8366.
Culmaily *High.* ***Settlement***, 1m/2km W of Golspie. **72 D5** NH8099.
Culnacraig *High.* ***Settlement***, 1m/2km E of Achduart, Ross and Cromarty district. **70 C4** NC0603.
Culnadalloch *Arg. & B.* ***Settlement***, 2m/3km E of Connel. **30 B1** NM9433.
Culnaknock *High.* ***Settlement***, near NE coast of Skye, 3m/5km S of Staffin. **58 B3** NG5162.
Culnamean *High.* ***Settlement***, at head of Loch Brittle, Skye. **48 A2** NG4120.
Culquhirk *D. & G.* ***Settlement***, 1km N of Wigtown. **7 F5** NX4256.
Culrain *High.* ***Hamlet***, in Sutherland district, 3m/5km NW of Bonar Bridge. **72 A5** NH5794.
Culross *Fife* ***Small town***, on N side of River Forth 7m/11km W of Dunfermline. Several National Trust for Scotland properties in town, which displays good examples of 16c and 17c Scottish domestic architecture. **25 D1** NS9885.
Culross Abbey *Fife* ***Ecclesiastical building***, remains of Cistercian monastery (Historic Scotland) founded in 1217, 7m/11km W of Dunfermline. Includes ruins of nave, cellars and domestic buildings. Part of Abbey Church now forms present parish church. NS9986.
Culross Palace *Fife* ***Historic house***, situated in Culross and built between 1597 to 1611 for local entrepreneur, Sir George Bruce. **25 D1** NS9885.
Culross Town House *Fife* ***Historic house***, National Trust for Scotland property in Culross, 7m/11km W of Dunfermline. Built in 1626 as a result of wealth generated by coal exports. **25 D1** NS9885.
Culroy *S.Ayr.* ***Settlement***, 3m/5km NE of Maybole. **14 B4** NS3114.
Culsalmond *Aber. Alternative name for Kirkton of Culsalmond, qv.*
Culsh *Aber.* ***Settlement***, 2m/3km NW of Ballater. **53 F5** NO3497.
Culsh Earth House *Aber.* ***Historic/prehistoric site***, site of prehistoric earth house or souterrain (Historic Scotland) at settlement of Culsh, 2m/3km E of Tarland. **54 A4** NJ5005.
Culshabbin *D. & G.* ***Settlement***, 5m/8km NW of Port William. **7 E5** NX3050.
Culswick *Shet.* ***Settlement***, on Mainland, 4m/6km W of Garderhouse. **82 B3** HU2745.
Cult Hill *Fife* ***Hill***, 1m/2km SE of Powmill. Height 866 feet or 264 metres. **33 F5** NT0296.
Culter Allers Farm *S.Lan.* ***Settlement***, 2m/3km S of Coulter, in Culter Water valley. **16 B2** NT0331.
Culter Cleuch Shank *S.Lan.* ***Mountain***, 4m/6km SW of Tweedsmuir. Height 1801 feet or 549 metres. **16 B3** NT0322.
Culter Fell ***Mountain***, on border of South Lanarkshire and Scottish Borders, 6m/9km S of Biggar. Height 2453 feet or 748 metres. **16 B3** NT0529.
Culter Water *S.Lan.* ***River***, rising in mountain S of Biggar on slopes of Gathersnow Hill, and flowing NW through Culter Waterhead Reservoir, N to Coulter, joining River Clyde 1km NW of Coulter. **16 B2** NT0135.
Culter Waterhead Reservoir *S.Lan.* ***Reservoir***, 4m/7km S of Coulter. **16 B3** NT0327.
Cultercullen *Aber.* ***Settlement***, 3m/5km SE of Pitmedden. **55 E2** NJ9224.
Culteuchar Hill *P. & K.* ***Mountain***, 2m/3km S of Forgandenny. Height 1027 feet or 313 metres. **33 F3** NO0915.
Cults *Aberdeen* ***Suburb***, 3m/5km SW of Aberdeen city centre. **55 D4** NJ8903.
Cults *Aber.* ***Locality***, to W of Knockandy Hill, 1m/2km SE of Gartly. **54 A1** NJ5330.
Cults *D. & G.* ***Settlement***, 2m/3km S of Garlieston. **3 E2** NX4643.
Cultybraggan Camp *P. & K.* ***Military establishment***, military training camp 1m/2km S of Comrie. **32 C3** NN7619.
Culvennan Fell *D. & G.* ***Hill***, 3m/4km N of Kirkcowan. Height 699 feet or 213 metres. **7 E4** NX3164.
Culvie *Aber.* ***Settlement***, 2m/3km W of Aberchirder. **64 A4** NJ5953.
Culwatty Bay *Arg. & B.* ***Bay***, on N side of Rosneath Point, near entrance to Gare Loch. NS2781.
Culzean Bay *S.Ayr.* ***Bay***, extends N from Culzean Castle towards Dunure. **14 A4** NS2310.
Culzean Castle *S.Ayr.* ***Historic house***, late 18c mansion (National Trust for Scotland) built around medieval tower of the Kennedys, on coast 4m/7km W of Maybole. Surrounding grounds became Scotland's first country park. **14 A5** NS2311.

C
D

Culzean Country Park *S.Ayr.* ***Leisure/recreation***, National Trust for Scotland property of 563 acres surrounding Culzean Castle, 4m/7km W of Maybole. First park in Scotland to become a Country Park. Includes wide variety of terrain, including gardens, woodland and shoreline. **14 A5** NS2309.
Cumberhead *S.Lan.* ***Settlement***, 4m/7km SW of Lesmahagow. **15 F2** NS7734.
Cumberland Stone *High.* ***Historic/prehistoric site***, huge stone (National Trust for Scotland) at road junction to SE of Culloden Muir, 3m/5km E of Inverness, from which Duke of Cumberland is said to have viewed battlefield of Culloden. **61 G5** NH7545.
Cumbernauld *N.Lan.* Population: 48,762. ***Town***, 12m/20km NE of Glasgow. New Town designated 1955. Original village of Cumbernauld 1m/2km N of town centre. **24 B2** NS7674.
Cuminestone *Aber. Alternative spelling of Cuminestown, qv.*
Cuminestown *Aber.* ***Village***, 5m/8km E of Turriff. Alternative spellings: Cuminestone, Cummestone, Cumminestown. **64 D4** NJ8050.
Cumlewick Ness *Shet.* ***Coastal feature***, headland on E coast of Mainland, 9m/14km N of Sumburgh Head. Situated on W side of entrance to bay of Sand Wick. HU4222.
Cumloden *D. & G.* ***Settlement***, 1m/2km N of Newton Stewart. **7 F4** NX4167.
Cummertrees *D. & G.* ***Village***, near shore of Solway Firth, 4m/6km W of Annan. **9 F4** NY1366.
Cummestone *Aber. Alternative spelling of Cuminestown, qv.*
Cumminestown *Aber. Alternative spelling of Cuminestown, qv.*
Cummingstown *Moray* ***Village***, on N coast 1m/2km E of Burghead. **62 D3** NJ1368.
Cumnock (Also known as Cumnock and Holmhead.) *E.Ayr.* Population: 9607. ***Small town***, on Lugar Water 14m/23km E of Ayr. **15 D3** NS5619.
Cumnock and Holmhead *E.Ayr. Alternative name for Cumnock, qv.*
Cumrue *D. & G.* ***Settlement***, 3m/4km N of Lochmaben. **9 E2** NY0786.
Cumstoun *D. & G.* ***Settlement***, 1m/2km N of Kirkcudbright. **8 A5** NX6853.
Cunndal *W.Isles* ***Bay***, small bay, 1km SW of Butt of Lewis. **69 F1** NB5165.
Cunnigill Hill *Shet.* ***Hill***, 1km S of Collafirth, Mainland. Height 577 feet or 176 metres. **82 D1** HU4367.
Cunning Park *S.Ayr.* ***Suburb***, S district of Ayr. NS3220.
Cunninghame ***Locality***, area of land between West Kilbride and Corse Hill, 5m/8km S of East Kilbride. **23 D5** NS4046.
Cunninghamhead *N.Ayr.* ***Hamlet***, 4m/6km NE of Irvine. **23 E5** NS3741.
Cunningsburgh *Shet.* ***Locality***, on E coast of Mainland, 8m/13km S of Lerwick. HU4329.
Cunnister *Shet.* ***Settlement***, on E side of Basta Voe, 1km SE of Sellafirth, Yell. **85 E3** HU5296.
Cunnoquhie *Fife* ***Settlement***, to W of Fernie. **34 B3** NO3115.
Cupar *Fife* Population: 7545. ***Small town***, royal burgh, with charter from 1363, on River Eden, 9m/14km S of Newport-on-Tay and 10m/16km NE of Glenrothes. Mainly Georgian architecture. **34 B3** NO3714.
Cupar Muir *Fife* ***Hamlet***, 1m/2km SW of Cupar. **34 B3** NO3513.
Cur *Arg. & B.* ***River***, flowing SW then, 1km S of Strachur, SE into head of Loch Eck. **30 D4** NS1296.
Currie *Edin.* ***Suburb***, on Water of Leith, 6m/9km SE of Edinburgh. Heriot-Watt University (Riccarton Campus) 1m/2km NW. **25 F3** NT1866.
Curriehill Station *Edin.* ***Other building***, railway station 1km NW of Currie. **25 F3** NT1768.
Cushnie *Aber.* ***Settlement***, 2m/3km S of Gardenstown. **64 C3** NJ7962.
Cutcloy *D. & G.* ***Settlement***, 1km N of Burrow Head and 3m/5km S of Whithorn. **3 E3** NX4535.
Cuthill *High.* ***Locality***, on N shore of Dornoch Firth, 3m/5km SW of Dornoch. **61 G1** NH7587.
Cutts *Shet.* ***Settlement***, on NE of Trondra. **82 D4** HU4038.
Cuttyhill *Aber.* ***Settlement***, 6m/10km NW of Peterhead. **65 F4** NK0450.
Cuween Hill *Ork.* ***Historic/prehistoric site***, site of communal burial cairn (Historic Scotland) of c. 1800 BC, 1km S of Finstown, Mainland. **80 B5** HY3612.

D

Daaey *Shet.* ***Island***, small island off N coast of Fetlar opposite Urie Ness. HU6095.
Dabton *D. & G.* ***Settlement***, 1km SE of Carronbridge, 1m/2km N of Thornhill. **8 C1** NX8796.
Daer Reservoir *S.Lan.* ***Reservoir***, in course of Daer Water. **16 A5** NS9513.
Daer Water *S.Lan.* ***River***, rising on Lowther Hills and flowing N through large Daer Reservoir to join Potrail Water and form River Clyde, 2m/3km S of Elvanfoot. NS9513.
Daff Reservoir *Inclyde* ***Reservoir***, 4m/7km SW of Greenock. NS2370.
Dail *Arg. & B.* ***Settlement***, on NE shore of Loch Etive, 6m/9km NE of Taynuilt across loch. **30 C1** NN0539.
Dail Beag (Anglicised form: Dalbeg.) *W.Isles* ***Settlement***, near NW coast of Isle of Lewis, 2m/3km NE of Carloway. **68 D3** NB2245.
Dail Bho Dheas (Anglicised form: South Dell.) *W.Isles* ***Village***, 4m/6km SW of Butt of Lewis. **69 F1** NB4861.
Dail Bho Thuath (Anglicised form: North Dell.) *W.Isles* ***Settlement***, between Dail Bho Dheas and Cros, 3m/5km S of Butt of Lewis. **69 F1** NB4961.
Dail Mòr (Anglicised form: Dalmore.) *W.Isles* ***Settlement***, near NW coast of Isle of Lewis, 2m/3km NE of Carloway. Dalmore Bay on coast to NW. **68 D3** NB2144.
Dail-na-mine Forest *P. & K.* ***Open space***, deer forest on Forest of Atholl 9m/15km NW of Blair Atholl. NN7777.
Dailly *S.Ayr.* Population: 1007. ***Village***, on S bank of Water of Girvan, 6m/9km E of Girvan. **14 A5** NS2701.
Dailnamac *Arg. & B.* ***Settlement***, 3m/4km NW of Taynuilt. **30 B1** NM9732.
Dairsie (Also known as Dairsiemuir or Osnaburgh). *Fife* ***Village***, 3m/5km NE of Cupar. Remains of medieval castle 1m/2km S, near 17c bridge over River Eden. **34 C3** NO4117.
Dairsiemuir *Fife Alternative name for Dairsie, qv.*
Dalabrog (Anglicised form: Daliburgh.) *W.Isles* ***Village***, near W coast of South Uist, 3m/5km NW of Lochboisdale. **44 C1** NF7521.
Dalavich *Arg. & B.* ***Settlement***, on W shore of Lock Awe, in Argyll, 1km S of mouth of River Avich. **30 B3** NM9612.
Dalballoch *High.* ***Settlement***, in Glen Banchor, 3m/5km W of Newtonmore. **51 F5** NN6598.
Dalbeattie *D. & G.* Population: 4421. ***Small town***, small granite town on Kirkgunzeon Lane, 13m/20km SW of Dumfries. **8 C4** NX8361.
Dalbeattie Forest *D. & G.* ***Forest/woodland***, to S of Dalbeattie. **8 C5** NX8361.
Dalbeg *W.Isles Anglicised form of Dail Beag, qv.*
Dalbeg Bay *W.Isles Anglicised form of Bagh Dail Beag, qv.*
Dalbeth *Glas.* ***Suburb***, on N bank of River Clyde, 3m/5km SE of Glasgow city centre, in Tollcross district. NS6362.
Dalblair *E.Ayr.* ***Settlement***, at confluence of Glenmuir Water and Guelt Water, 4m/7km E of Darvel. **15 E4** NS6419.
Dalbog *Angus* ***Hamlet***, 2m/3km NW of Edzell. **43 D2** NO5871.
Dalbreck *High.* ***Settlement***, at confluence of rivers Black Water and Coirefrois Burn, 5m/9km N of Rhilochan. **72 C3** NC7416.
Dalcairnie *E.Ayr.* ***Settlement***, 1m/2km SW of Dalmellington. **14 C5** NS4604.
Dalcairnie Linn *E.Ayr.* ***Waterfall***, in course of Dalcairnie Burn, 1m/2km SW of Dalmellington. NS4604.
Dalchalloch *P. & K.* ***Settlement***, in Glen Errochty, adjoining to Trinafour. **40 C3** NN7264.
Dalchalm *High.* ***Settlement***, on E coast of Sutherland district, 1m/2km N of Brora. **73 E4** NC9105.
Dalchenna *Arg. & B.* ***Settlement***, on NE shore of Loch Fyne, 2m/3km SW of Inveraray. **30 C4** NN0705.
Dalchirach *Moray* ***Settlement***, in Avon valley, 9m/14km SW of Dufftown. **53 D1** NJ1934.
Dalchork *High.* ***Settlement***, near mouth of River Tirry, NE of Loch Shin, 2m/4km N of Lairg. **72 A3** NC5710.
Dalchreichart *High.* ***Settlement***, in Glen Moriston, Inverness district, 6m/9km NW of Fort Augustus. **50 B3** NH2912.
Dalchruin *P. & K.* ***Settlement***, in Glen Artney, 8m/12km NE of Callander. **32 C3** NN7116.
Dalchuirn *High.* ***Locality***, in Ross and Cromarty district on NW shore of Loch Carron, adjoining Lochcarron. NG9039.
Dalcross *High.* ***Locality***, 1m/2km SW of Croy. **61 G5** NH7748.
Dalcross Airport *High. Former name of Inverness Airport, qv.*
Daldownie *Aber.* ***Settlement***, on S bank of River Gairn, 4m/6km NW of Craithie. **53 E4** NJ2400.
Dale of Walls *Shet.* ***Settlement***, adjacent to E of Voe of Dale, on W coast of Mainland. **82 A2** HU1852.
Dalelia *High.* ***Settlement***, with pier, on N shore of Loch Shiel, in Lochaber district, 3m/4km SE of Kinlochmoidart. **37 G3** NM7369.
Dales Farm *Aber. See Peterhead.*
Dales Voe *Shet.* ***Sea feature***, narrow inlet on NE coast of Mainland, 2m/4km SE of Scatsta. **84 D5** HU4270.
Dales Voe *Shet.* ***Sea feature***, inlet on E coast of Mainland, 3m/5km N of Lerwick. **83 D3** HU4546.
Daless *High.* ***Settlement***, in valley of River Findhorn, 6m/10km NE of Moy. **52 A1** NH8638.
Dalestie *Moray* ***Settlement***, on E bank of River Avon, 4m/7km S of Tomintoul. **53 D3** NJ1610.
Dalfad *Aber.* ***Settlement***, on N side of River Gairn, 4m/7km NW of Ballater. **53 F4** NJ3100.
Dalganachan *High.* ***Settlement***, situated just W of confluence of Rumsdale Water and Glutt Water, where they form River Thurso. **76 C4** ND0040.
Dalgarven *N.Ayr.* ***Settlement***, on River Garnock, 2m/3km N of Kilwinning. **23 D5** NS2945.
Dalgety Bay *Fife* Population: 7860. ***Small town***, housing development on bay of same name 3m/4km E of Inverkeithing. Donibristle Industrial Estate adjoins to NW. On shore of bay is ruined church of St. Bridget (Historic Scotland), dating from 1244. **25 F1** NT1683.
Dalgig *E.Ayr.* ***Settlement***, 4m/6km E of New Cumnock. **15 D4** NS5512.
Dalginross *P. & K.* ***Village***, on S side of River Earn opposite Comrie. Roman sites to S. **32 C2** NN7721.
Dalgonar *D. & G.* ***Settlement***, 6m/9km SW of Sanquhar. **15 F5** NS7003.
Dalguise *P. & K.* ***Settlement***, on W side of Strath Tay, 4m/6km NW of Dunkeld. **41 E5** NN9947.
Dalhalvaig *High.* ***Village***, in Strath Halladale, in Caithness district, 6m/10km S of Melvich. **76 A3** NC8954.
Dalhousie Castle *Midloth.* ***Castle***, dating from mid-15c, 1m/2km W of Newtongrange across River South Esk. Formerly seat of Ramsays. NT3263.
Daliburgh *W.Isles Anglicised form of Dalabrog, qv.*
Daligan *Arg. & B.* ***Settlement***, 2m/4km NE of Helensburgh. **23 E1** NS3284.
Dalinlongart *Arg. & B.* ***Settlement***, 4m/6km NW of Dunoon. **22 C1** NS1482.
Dalivaddy *Arg. & B.* ***Settlement***, on Kintyre, 3m/4km W of Campbeltown. **12 B4** NR6719.
Daljarrock *S.Ayr.* ***Other building***, hotel 1km N of Pinwherry. **6 C2** NX1988.
Dalkeith *Midloth.* Population: 11,567. ***Town***, market town astride Rivers North and South Esk, 6m/10km SE of Edinburgh. **26 A3** NT3367.
Dalkeith Country Park *Midloth.* ***Leisure/recreation***, 800 acre country park with nature trails, farm animals and 18c bridge. Situated to N of Dalkeith. Rivers North and South Esk flow through park. **26 A3** NT3367.
Dalkeith House *Midloth.* ***Historic house***, to N of Dalkeith, built c. 1700, formerly seat of Dukes of Buccleuch. **26 A3** NT3367.
Dall *P. & K.* ***Locality***, on S shore of Loch Rannoch, 5m/7km W of Kinloch Rannoch. House (1855) is part of Rannoch boys' public school. NN5956.
Dall Burn *P. & K.* ***River***, running generally NE through Rannoch Forest into Loch Rannoch, 4m/7km W of Kinloch Rannoch. NN5956.
Dallachoilish *Arg. & B.* ***Settlement***, on S side of the narrows of Loch Creran, Argyll. NM9744.
Dallas *Moray* ***Village***, on River Lossie, 9m/14km SW of Elgin. Ruins of Tor Castle to N. **62 D4** NJ1252.
Dallas Forest *Moray* ***Forest/woodland***, to N of Dallas. **62 D4** NJ1252.
Dallaschyle *High.* ***Settlement***, 2m/3km E of Croy. **62 A5** NH8149.
Dallash *D. & G.* ***Settlement***, on W bank of Palnure Burn, 4m/6km NE of Newton Stewart. **7 F4** NX4769.
Dalleagles *E.Ayr.* ***Settlement***, 4m/6km SW of New Cumnock. NS5710.
Dalmacallan Forest *D. & G.* ***Forest/woodland***, 2m/4km SE of Moniaive. NX8087.
Dalmadilly *Aber.* ***Settlement***, 1km N of Kemnay. **54 C3** NJ7317.
Dalmahoy *Edin.* ***Locality***, 1m/2km SE of Ratho. Golf course. NT1468.
Dalmally *Arg. & B.* ***Village***, on River Orchy in Argyll, 2m/3km E of NE end of Loch Awe. **31 D2** NN1627.
Dalmarnock *Glas.* ***Suburb***, on N bank of River Clyde, 2m/3km SE of Glasgow city centre. NS6163.
Dalmarnock *P. & K.* ***Settlement***, on W side of Strath Tay, 3m/4km NW of Dunkeld. **41 E5** NN9945.
Dalmary *Stir.* ***Settlement***, 1m/2km S of Gartmore. **32 A5** NS5095.
Dalmellington *E.Ayr.* Population: 1597. ***Small town***, on tributary of nearby River Doon, 13m/21km SE of Ayr. Site of 13c priory. **14 C5** NS4805.
Dalmeny *Edin.* ***Village***, 1m/2km E of South Queensferry. **25 F2** NT1477.
Dalmeny House *Edin.* ***Historic house***, 19c home of Earls of Rosebery to E of Dalmeny Park overlooking Firth of Forth, 2m/3km NE of Dalmeny. Scotland's first Gothic Revival house, designed by William Wilkins. Contains important collections of porcelain, paintings and furniture. **25 F2** NT1678.
Dalmichy *High.* ***Settlement***, on E bank of River Tirry, 4m/7km N of Lairg. **72 A3** NC5713.
Dalmigavie *High.* ***Settlement***, 12m/19km N of Kingussie. **51 G3** NH7419.
Dalmilling *S.Ayr.* ***Suburb***, E district of Ayr. NS3622.
Dalmore *High.* ***Locality***, on N shore of Cromarty Firth, Ross and Cromarty district, 1m/2km SE of Alness. **61 F3** NH6668.
Dalmore *W.Isles Anglicised form of Dail Mòr, qv.*
Dalmuir *W.Dun.* ***Suburb***, 1km NW of Clydebank town centre. NS4970.
Dalmunzie Hotel *P. & K.* ***Settlement***, 1m/2km NW of Spittal of Glenshee. **41 F2** NO0971.
Dalnabreck *High.* ***Settlement***, in Lochaber district, 3m/5km N of Salen across head of Loch Shiel. **37 G3** NM7069.
Dalnacardoch Forest *P. & K.* ***Open space***, deer forest to N of Dalnacardoch Lodge in Glen Garry. **40 B2** NN6875.

Dalnacarn *P. & K.* ***Settlement***, 6m/9km NE of Pitlochrie. **41 F3** NO0063.
Dalnaglar Castle *P. & K.* ***Hamlet***, in Glen Shee, 1km N of Cray. **41 G3** NO1464.
Dalnaha *Arg. & B.* ***Settlement***, on S shore of Loch Spelve, 5m/8km E of Lochbuie, Mull. **29 F2** NM6826.
Dalnahaitnach *High.* ***Settlement***, 4m/6km SW of Carrbridge. **52 A3** NH8519.
Dalnamain *High.* ***Settlement***, 8m/11km NW of Dornoch. **72 C5** NH7298.
Dalnamein Forest *P. & K.* ***Open space***, upland area in Forest of Atholl, 9m/14km SE of Dalwhinnie. **40 C2** NN7678.
Dalnaspidal Forest *P. & K.* ***Open space***, mountainous area NW of Loch Garry. Dalnaspidal Lodge and railway station near foot of Loch Garry to E. NN6074.
Dalnatrat *High.* ***Settlement***, on SE shore of Loch Linnhe, 1m/2km S of Rubha Mòr. **38 B4** NM9653.
Dalnavie *High.* ***Settlement***, 3m/4km N of Alness. **61 F2** NH6473.
Dalness *High.* ***Settlement***, in Glen Etive, Lochaber district, SW of Buachaille Etive Mòr. Series of waterfalls in River Etive. Mountainous area to N is property of National Trust for Scotland. **39 D4** NN1651.
Dalnessie *High.* ***Settlement*** on River Brora, 12m/20km NE of Lairg. **72 B3** NC6315.
Dalnigap *D. & G.* ***Settlement***, 8m/12km SE of Ballantrae. **6 C3** NX1371.
Dalqueich *P. & K.* ***Hamlet***, 3m/5km NW of Kinross. **33 F4** NO0704.
Dalquharran *S.Ayr.* ***Settlement***, with 15c castle beside Water of Girvan, situated to N of Dailly across river. NS2702.
Dalreoch *S.Ayr.* ***Settlement***, in Stinchar valley, 6m/9km NE of Ballantrae. **6 C2** NX1686.
Dalriech *P. & K.* ***Settlement***, in valley of River Almond, 7m/11km N of Comrie. **32 C1** NN7833.
Dalroy *High.* ***Settlement***, 8m/12km E of Inverness. **61 G5** NH7644.
Dalrulzian *P. & K.* ***Settlement***, at S end of Glen Shee, 5m/8km N of Bridge of Cally. **41 G4** NO1358.
Dalry *D. & G. Alternative name for St. John's Town of Dalry.*
Dalry *Edin.* ***Suburb***, 1m/2km SW of Edinburgh city centre. NT2372.
Dalry *N.Ayr.* Population: 5732. ***Small town***, former 18c weaving centre on River Garnock, 6m/10km NE of Ardrossan. **23 D5** NS2949.
Dalrymple *E.Ayr.* Population: 1297. ***Village***, 5m/8km S of Ayr. **14 B4** NS3514.
Dalserf *S.Lan.* ***Village***, 2m/4km E of Larkhall. **24 B4** NS8050.
Dalsetter *Shet.* ***Settlement***, on Yell, near head of Basta Voe. HU5099.
Dalshangan *D. & G.* ***Settlement***, 3m/5km SE of Carsphairn. **7 G2** NX5988.
Dalskairth *D. & G.* ***Settlement***, 3m/5km SW of Dumfries. **8 D3** NX9372.
Dalswinton *D. & G.* ***Village***, 6m/10km N of Dumfries. Site of Roman fort to SW beside railway. **8 D2** NX9385.
Dalswinton Common *D. & G.* ***Open space***, moorland 8m/13km N of Dumfries. **8 D2** NX9488.
Daltomach *High.* ***Settlement***, in Strathdearn, 6m/10km SW of Tomatin. **51 G2** NH7421.
Dalton *D. & G.* ***Village***, 7m/11km NW of Annan. **9 F3** NY1174.
Daltot *Arg. & B.* ***Settlement***, on SE side of Loch Sween, 3m/5km NE of Achnamara. **21 F1** NR7583.
Daltra *High.* ***Settlement***, 1m/2km SW of Ferness. **62 B5** NH9443.
Dalveen Pass *D. & G.* ***Other feature of interest***, pass carrying A702 road from Carronbridge to Elvanfoot through Lowther Hills. **15 G5** NS9007.
Dalveich *Stir.* ***Settlement***, on N side of Loch Earn, 2m/3km E of Lochearnhead. **32 B2** NN6124.
Dalvennan *E.Ayr.* ***Settlement***, 2m/3km W of Patna. **14 B4** NS3810.
Dalvourn *High.* ***Settlement***, 8m/12km S of Inverness. **51 F1** NH6834.
Dalwhat Water *D. & G.* ***River***, rising on S slopes of Black Hill and flowing SE to join Castlefairn Water and form Cairn Water, 1km SE of Moniaive. **8 B1** NX7890.
Dalwhinnie *High.* ***Village***, on River Truim, in Badenoch and Strathspey district, 12m/20km SW of Kingussie. **40 B1** NN6384.
Dalzell House *N.Lan.* ***Historic house***, with 15c tower in Dalzell Park, along with Lord Gavin's Temple, 1m/2km S of Motherwell. NS7655.
Dalziel *N.Lan.* ***Locality***, parish between Motherwell and Wishaw on N bank of River Clyde. Contains Dalzell House, with 15c tower. NS7654.
Damnaglaur *D. & G.* ***Settlement***, 1km SW of Drummore, on W side of Luce Bay. **2 B3** NX1235.
Damsay *Ork.* ***Island***, in Bay of Firth on E coast of Mainland. **80 B5** HY3914.
Damside *P. & K.* ***Settlement***, 2m/3km NE of Auchterarder. **33 E3** NN9614.
Dandaleith *Moray* ***Settlement***, on W bank of River Spey, 1km N of Craigellachie. **63 E5** NJ2845.
Danderhall *Midloth.* Population: 2599. ***Hamlet***, 2m/3km NW of Dalkeith. **26 A3** NT3069.
Dandeugh Forest *D. & G.* ***Forest/woodland***, to S of Carsphairn. NX5690.
Danestone *Aberdeen* ***Locality***, on N side of River Don, 2m/3km SE of Dyce. **55 E3** NJ9110.
Danna Island (Also known as Island of Danna.) *Arg. & B.* ***Coastal feature***, peninsula in Argyll, joined by an isthmus of a road's width to S end of peninsula between Loch Sween and Sound of Jura. **21 E2** NR6978.
Danny Burn *P. & K.* ***River***, stream flowing NE into Allan Water at Blackford. **33 D4** NN8805.
Danskine *E.Loth.* ***Settlement***, 3m/4km SE of Gifford. **26 C3** NT5667.
Danskine Loch *E.Loth.* ***Lake/loch***, small loch 2m/3km E of Gifford. NT5667.
Darnabo *Aber.* ***Settlement***, 3m/4km NE of Fyvie. **64 C5** NJ7841.
Darnaw *D. & G.* ***Mountain***, rising to over 470 metres, 2m/3km W of Clatteringshaws Loch. **7 G3** NX5176.
Darnaway Castle *Moray* ***Castle***, seat of Earl of Moray, 1m/2km SW of Forres. Dating from 15c, Great Hall has survived with 19c mansion in front of it. **62 B4** NH9955.
Darnaway Forest ***Forest/woodland***, afforested area on W side of River Findhorn and on border of Highland and Moray, 5m/8km SW of Forres. **62 B4** NH9851.
Darnconner *E.Ayr.* ***Settlement***, 2m/4km NE of Auchinleck. **15 D3** NS5723.
Darnford *Aber.* ***Settlement***, 3m/4km S of Crathes. **54 C5** NO7692.
Darngarroch *D. & G.* ***Settlement***, 4m/7km N of Gatehouse of Fleet. **8 A4** NX6263.
Darnick *Sc.Bord.* ***Village***, 1m/2km W of Melrose. 16c peel tower. **17 G2** NT5334.
Darra *Aber.* ***Settlement***, 2m/3km SE of Turriff. **64 C5** NJ7447.
Darrou *D. & G.* ***Mountain***, rising to over 470 metres, 2m/3km NW of Clatteringshaws Loch. **7 G2** NX5080.
Dartfield *Aber.* ***Settlement***, 2m/3km W of Crimond. **65 F4** NK0257.
Darvel *E.Ayr.* Population: 3759. ***Small town***, on River Irvine, 9m/14km E of Kilmarnock. Birthplace of Sir Alexander Fleming, 1881-1955, who discovered penicillin. **15 D2** NS5637.
Daugh of Cairnborrow *Aber.* ***Hill***, rising to over 290 metres on N side of River Deveron, 3m/4km NE of Haugh of Glass. **63 G5** NJ4541.
Daugh of Carron *Moray* ***Open space***, tract surrounding Burn of Carron, 4m/6km SW of Charlestown of Aberlour. **53 D1** NJ2139.
Daugh of Invermarkie *Aber.* ***Open space***, on N side of Hill of Talnamounth, 1m/2km NW of Haugh of Glass. **63 G5** NJ4341.
Daugh of Kinermony *Moray* ***Settlement***, 2m/3km SW of Charlestown of Aberlour. **63 E5** NJ2441.
Dava *High.* ***Settlement***, on border with Moray, 7m/11km NW of Grantown-on-Spey. **52 C1** NJ0038.
Dava Moor *High.* ***Open space***, moorland to SE of Dava. **52 C1** NJ0137.
Davaar *Arg. & B.* ***Settlement***, on S side of Kildalloig Bay, 2m/3km E of Campbeltown. **12 C4** NR7518.
Davaar Island *Arg. & B.* ***Island***, opposite entrance to Campbeltown Loch on E coast of Kintyre. Lighthouse at N point. On SE side is cave known as Crucifixion Cave. **12 C4** NR7520.
Davan *Aber.* ***Settlement***, to N of Loch Davan, 3m/5km SW of Tarland. **53 G4** NJ4401.
Davidson's Mains (Formerly known as Muttonhole.) *Edin.* ***Suburb***, 3m/5km NW of Edinburgh city centre. NT2075.
Davington *D. & G.* ***Hamlet***, in valley of River White Esk, 3m/5km NW of Eskdalemuir. **16 D5** NT2302.
Daviot *Aber.* ***Village***, 5m/7km NW of Inverurie. Loanhead Stone Circle (Historic Scotland) to N is 4000 to 4500 years old. **54 C2** NJ7528.
Daviot *High.* ***Settlement***, in Inverness district, 5m/8km SE of Inverness. **51 G1** NH7239.
Davoch of Grange *Moray* ***Settlement***, 3m/5km E of Keith. **63 G4** NJ4851.
Dawyck House *Sc.Bord.* ***Historic house***, house, park and gardens in River Tweed valley, 6m/10km SW of Peebles. **16 C2** NT1635.
Deadwaters *S.Lan.* ***Settlement***, 2m/4km W of Kirkmuirhill. **24 B5** NS7541.
Dean Burn *Midloth.* ***River***, small stream rising on Fala Moor and flowing N to join East Water 1km SE of Fala. One of numerous streams which join to flow into River Tyne. **26 B4** NT4458.
Dean Castle *E.Ayr.* ***Castle***, 14c stronghold, enlarged and embellished in 15c, with country park on hill overlooking confluence of Fenwick Water and Craufurdland Water, 1m/2km NE of Kilmarnock town centre. Once seat of the Boyds, Lords of Kilmarnock, last of whom lost his head after Battle of Culloden 1746. Collection of armour and medieval musical instruments. **14 C2** NS4339.
Dean Water ***River***, running W from Loch of Forfar, past Glamis Castle, to River Isla 3m/5km SE of Alyth. **42 B5** NO2845.
Deanburnhaugh *Sc.Bord.* ***Hamlet***, 3m/4km SW of Roberton, on Borthwick Water. **17 E4** NT3911.
Deans *W.Loth.* ***Suburb***, W district of Livingston. NT0269.
Deans Industrial Estate *W.Loth.* ***Locality***, in Deans suburb of Livingston. NT0269.
Deanston *Stir.* ***Village***, 1m/2km W of Doune across River Teith. **32 C4** NN7101.
Dearg Abhainn *Arg. & B.* ***River***, stream in Argyll, running NW down Gleann Salach to Loch Creran 2m/3km SW of Dallachoilish. NM9541.
Dearg Sgeir *Arg. & B.* ***Island***, islet midway between Mull and Torran Rocks group, 2m/3km S of Erraid. **28 B3** NM2915.
Deasker *W.Isles* ***Island***, islet 3m/5km SW of Aird an Rùnair on North Uist. **45 E3** NF6466.
Debate *D. & G.* ***Settlement***, 2m/3km SE of Paddockhole. **9 G2** NY2582.
Dechmont *W.Loth.* Population: 1134. ***Hamlet***, 1m/2km SW of Uphall. **25 E2** NT0470.
Dechmont Hill *S.Lan.* ***Hill***, 3m/5km N of East Kilbride, with remains of hillfort on S slopes. Height 600 feet or 183 metres. **24 A4** NS6558.
Dedda Skerry *Shet.* ***Coastal feature***, rocky headland on E coast of Mainland, S of Helli Ness. **83 D5** HU4627.
Dedridge *W.Loth.* ***Suburb***, 1m/2km S of Livingston town centre. NT0666.
Dee ***River***, major river of NE Scotland rising at Pools of Dee in Cairngorm Mountains and running E past Braemar, Balmoral, Ballater and Banchory for about 90m/145km to North Sea at Aberdeen. **54 D5** NJ9605.
Dee *D. & G.* ***River***, issuing from Loch Ken to flow S through Tongland Loch and past Kirkcudbright into Kirkcudbright Bay. Stretch above Loch Ken is known as Black Water of Dee or River Dee. **8 B4** NX6746.
Deecastle *Aber.* ***Hamlet***, 4m/7km E of Ballater. **53 G5** NO4396.
Deer Abbey *Aber.* ***Ecclesiastical building***, scant remains of 13c Cistercian monastery (Historic Scotland), on N bank of South Ugie Water, 1km W of Old Deer. **65 E5** NJ9648.
Deer Law *Sc.Bord.* ***Mountain***, 3m/4km NW of St. Mary's Loch. Height 2063 feet or 629 metres. **16 D3** NT2225.
Deer Sound *Ork.* ***Sea feature***, large inlet on N coast of Mainland, between Mull Head to E and Rerwick Head to W. **79 E2** HY5307.
Deerdykes *N.Lan.* ***Settlement***, 3m/5km SW of Cumbernauld town centre. NS7172.
Deerhill *Moray* ***Settlement***, on S side of Aultmore, 4m/6km NE of Keith. **63 G4** NJ4656.
Deerlee Knowe *Sc.Bord.* ***Open space***, steep forested hillside, between 300 and 350 metres, on W of Lamblain Edge in Cheviot Hills, 1m/2km NE of Carter Bar. **11 F1** NT7108.
Deerness *Ork.* ***Locality***, on peninsula at E end of Mainland, 8m/13km SE of Kirkwall beyond Deer Sound. HY5605.
Deer's Hill *Aber.* ***Hill***, 3m/5km S of Cuminestown. Height 584 feet or 178 metres. **64 D5** NJ8045.
Degnish *Arg. & B.* ***Settlement***, 1km NE of Degnish Point. **29 G3** NM7812.
Degnish Point *Arg. & B.* ***Coastal feature***, headland at N side of entrance to Loch Melfort. **29 G3** NM7712.
Deil's Caldron *P. & K.* ***Inland physical feature***, chasm containing Falls of Lednock, in course of River Lednock, 1m/2km N of Comrie. **32 C2** NN7623.
Deil's Craig Dam *Stir.* ***Reservoir***, small reservoir 1km S of Strathblane. NS5578.
Deil's Dyke *D. & G.* ***Historic/prehistoric site***, series of ancient earthworks of uncertain origin to S of Sanquhar. NS7708.
Deil's Elbow *S.Ayr.* ***Other feature of interest***, sharp bend on minor road, caused by narrow valley below steep SW slopes of Clauchrie Hill, 5m/7km E of Dailly. **14 B5** NS3401.
Delavorar *Moray* ***Settlement***, on W bank of River Avon, 2m/3km S of Tomintoul. **53 D3** NJ1615.
Delfrigs *Aber.* ***Settlement***, 2m/3km N of Balmedie. **55 E2** NJ9621.
Delgatie Castle (Also spelled Delgaty Castle.) *Aber.* ***Castle***, 11c tower house containing the widest turnpike stair in Scotland, 2m/3km E of Turriff. **64 C4** NJ7550.
Delgatie Forest *Aber. Alternative spelling of Delgaty Forest, qv.*
Delgaty Castle *Aber. Alternative spelling of Delgatie Castle, qv.*
Delgaty Forest (Also spelled Delgatie Forest.) *Aber.* ***Forest/woodland***, to SE of Delgatie Castle and to E of Turriff. **64 C5** NJ7550.
Dell *W.Isles* ***River***, in N part of Isle of Lewis running N into Atlantic Ocean, 1km N of Dail Bho Dheas and 3m/5km SW of Butt of Lewis. **69 G2** NB4862.
Dell Lodge *High.* ***Settlement***, 1km SE of Nethy Bridge. **52 C3** NJ0119.
Delliefure *High.* ***Settlement***, 3m/5km NE of Grantown-on-Spey. **52 C1** NJ0730.
Delnabo *Moray* ***Settlement***, 1m/2km SW of Tomintoul. **53 D3** NJ1617.

D

Delny *High.* ***Settlement***, in Ross and Cromarty district, 3m/5km NE of Invergordon. **61 G2** NH7372.
Delphorie *Aber.* ***Settlement***, on W bank of River Don at foot of Ardhuncart Hill, 6m/9km S of Rhynie. **53 G3** NJ4818.
Delting *Shet.* ***Locality***, of Mainland between Dales Voe and Olna Firth. HU4067.
Delvine *P. & K.* ***Settlement***, 2m/3km E of Caputh. **41 G5** NO1240.
Den of Ogil Reservoir *Angus* ***Reservoir***, small reservoir 3m/5km NW of Tannadice. NO4361.
Denbeath *Fife* ***Suburb***, N district of Buckhaven. NT3698.
Denend *Aber.* ***Settlement***, 4m/7km E of Huntly. **54 A1** NJ5937.
Denhead *Aber.* ***Settlement***, 1m/2km S of Kintore. **54 C3** NJ7914.
Denhead *Aber.* ***Settlement***, 1m/2km S of New Leeds. **65 E4** NJ9952.
Denhead *Angus* ***Settlement***, 2m/3km NW of Arbirlot. **43 D5** NO5742.
Denhead *Dundee* ***Settlement***, 3m/5km to NW of Dundee city centre. **34 B1** NO3431.
Denhead *Fife* ***Settlement***, 3m/5km SW of St. Andrews. **34 C3** NO4613.
Denholm *Sc.Bord.* ***Village***, 5m/8km NE of Hawick. **17 G4** NT5618.
Denmill *Aber.* ***Settlement***, 4m/6km W of Newmachar. **54 D3** NJ8218.
Denmoss *Aber.* ***Settlement***, 4m/6km SE of Inverkeithny. **64 B5** NJ6541.
Dennis Head *Ork.* ***Coastal feature***, headland at E extremity of North Ronaldsay, at NE end of Linklet Bay. HY7955.
Dennis Ness *Ork.* ***Coastal feature***, headland with lighthouse at NE end of North Ronaldsay. HY7855.
Dennistoun *Glas.* ***Suburb***, 1m/2km E of Glasgow city centre. NS6065.
Denny *Falk.* Population: 11,061. ***Town***, industrial town on River Carron, 5m/8km W Falkirk. Forms one town with Dunipace. **24 C1** NS8182.
Denny Reservoir *Falk.* ***Reservoir***, small reservoir 1m/2km SW of Denny. NS8081.
Dennyloanhead *Falk.* ***Village***, 2m/3km S of Denny. **24 C1** NS8080.
Denside *Aber.* ***Settlement***, 2m/3km E of Kirkton of Durris. **54 D5** NO8095.
Dererach *Arg. & B.* ***Settlement***, on N shore of Loch Scridain, Mull, 2m/3km N of Pennyghael across loch. **29 E2** NM5129.
Dernaglar Loch *D. & G.* ***Lake/loch***, small loch 4m/7km E of Glenluce. **7 D5** NX2658.
Derry *Stir.* ***Settlement***, on N side of Loch Earn, 3m/5km E of Lochearnhead. **32 B2** NN6424.
Derry Burn *Aber.* ***River***, rising in Cairngorm Mountains and flowing S through Glen Derry to join Lui Water at Derry Lodge, 4m/6km NW of Inverey. **52 C5** NO0493.
Derry Cairngorm (Also known as Cairn Gorm of Derry). *Aber.* ***Mountain***, in Cairngorm Mountains, 2m/3km E of Ben Macdui. Munro: height 3788 feet or 1155 metres. **52 C5** NO0198.
Dervaig *Arg. & B.* ***Village***, on Mull, 5m/8km W of Tobermory. Group of standing stones 1km E. **36 D4** NM4352.
Derybruich *Arg. & B.* ***Settlement***, 3m/5km SW of Tighnabruaich. **22 A2** NR9370.
Deskford Church *Moray* ***Ecclesiastical building***, ruin of small medieval church (Historic Scotland) on Burn of Deskford, 3m/5km S of Cullen. Contains carved sacrament house. **64 A3** NJ5161.
Deskry Water *Aber.* ***River***, rising to E of Mullachdubh and flowing NE before turning N, then W to join River Don 3m/4km E of Strathdon. **53 F4** NJ3812.
Dessarry *High.* ***River***, in Lochaber district running E down Glen Dessarry to join River Pean 1km above head of Loch Arkaig. NM9791.
Deuchar Hill *Angus* ***Hill***, 1km S of Auchnacree. Height 977 feet or 298 metres. **42 C3** NO4662.
Deuchar Law *Sc.Bord.* ***Mountain***, 4m/7km NE of St. Mary's Loch. Height 1778 feet or 542 metres. **17 D3** NT2829.
Deuchary Hill *P. & K.* ***Mountain***, 4m/6km N of Dunkeld. Height 1670 feet or 509 metres. **41 F5** NO0348.
Deucheran Hill *Arg. & B.* ***Mountain***, on Kintyre, 3m/5km W of Grogport. Height 1079 feet or 329 metres. **21 F5** NR7644.
Deuchrie Dod *E.Loth.* ***Hill***, 1m/2km S of Stenton. Height 974 feet or 297 metres. **26 D2** NT6272.
Deveron ***River***, rising S of Cabrach, and flowing NE by Huntly and Turriff to Banff Bay on E side of Banff. **64 B5** NJ6964.
Devilla Forest *Fife* ***Forest/woodland***, to E of Kincardine. NS9588.
Devil's Beef Tub *D. & G.* ***Large natural feature***, vast semicircular hollow in hills, 5m/8km N of Moffat. Source of River Annan. **16 B4** NT0613.
Devil's Bridge *D. & G.* ***Coastal feature***, stack at Burrow Head, 2m/3km SW of Isle of Whithorn. **3 E3** NX4634.
Devil's Elbow *P. & K.* ***Other feature of interest***, double hairpin bend, now bypassed, 1km S of Cairnwell Pass on road from Braemar to Spittal of Glenshee. **41 G2** NO1476.
Devil's Staircase *High.* ***Other feature of interest***, on Old Military Road, running down steep SE slope of Stob Mhic Mhartuin, 3m/5km SE of Kinlochleven. **39 E4** NN2157.
Devon ***River***, rising on Ochil Hills and flowing through Glendevon Reservoirs and E down Glen Devon to Glendevon, then SE to Crook of Devon, where it turns sharply to run almost due W to S side of Menstrie, then S to River Forth 2m/4km W of Alloa. **33 E5** NS8493.
Devonside *Clack.* ***Village***, on S bank of River Devon opposite Tillicoultry. **33 E5** NS9296.
Dewar *Sc.Bord.* ***Settlement***, 8m/12km N of Innerleithen. **26 A5** NT3448.
Dewar Burn *Sc.Bord.* ***River***, small stream which rises on Dewar Hill and flows N to become Heriot Water, 1m/2km NE of Dewar. **26 A5** NT3550.
Dhuhallow *High.* ***Settlement***, 3m/4km E of Inverfarigaig. **51 E2** NH5522.
Diabhal *W.Isles Gaelic form of Diaval, qv.*
Diaval (Gaelic form: Diabhal.) *W.Isles* ***Hill***, rising to over 150 metres, 7m/12km NW of Tolsta Head, Isle of Lewis. **69 F2** NB4552.
Dick Hatteraick's Cave *D. & G.* ***Cave***, on E shore of Wigtown Bay, on NW side of Ravenshall Point. Largest of several caves in the vicinity. NX5152.
Dick Institute *E.Ayr.* ***Other feature of interest***, museum and art gallery in Kilmarnock, with exhibits which include local and natural history, as well as engineering and geology displays. **14 C2** NS4337.
Diebidale *High.* ***River***, in Sutherland district running NE down Glen Diebidale to head of Glen Calvie. **60 D1** NH4686.
Diebidale Forest *High.* ***Open space***, deer forest extending E and W of river Diebidale. **60 D1** NH4686.
Digg *High.* ***Settlement***, on NE coast of Skye, W of Staffin Bay. **58 A3** NG4669.
Dighty Water *Dundee* ***River***, rising in Sidlaw Hills and flowing E by N side of Dundee city, entering Firth of Tay 1km W of Monifieth. **34 B1** NO4831.
Dildawn *D. & G.* ***Settlement***, 3m/5km SW of Castle Douglas. **8 B5** NX7259.
Din Fell *Sc.Bord.* ***Mountain***, 6m/9km N of Newcastleton. Height 1735 feet or 529 metres. **10 C2** NY4596.
Dingleton *Sc.Bord.* ***Suburb***, adjoining to S of Melrose. NT5433.
Dingwall *High.* Population: 5228. ***Small town***, chief town of Ross and Cromarty district at head of Cromarty Firth, 11m/18km NW of Inverness. **61 E4** NH5458.
Dingwall Town House *High.* ***Other feature of interest***, exhibits on local history in Dingwall. Features display of military career of Sir Hector MacDonald (1853-1903). **61 E4** NH5458.
Dinlabyre *Sc.Bord.* ***Settlement***, on E bank of Liddel Water, 4m/6km NE of Newcastleton. **10 D2** NY5291.
Dinnet *Aber.* ***Settlement***, on N side of River Dee, 6m/10km E of Ballater. Muir of Dinnet is flat area to W. **53 G5** NO4598.
Dinnings Hill *D. & G.* ***Mountain***, 2m/3km W of Eskdalemuir. Height 1089 feet or 332 metres. **9 G1** NY2197.
Dinvin *D. & G.* ***Settlement***, 1km NE of Portpatrick. **6 B5** NX0055.
Dinwoodie Mains *D. & G.* ***Settlement***, straddling railway, 6m/9km N of Lockerbie. **9 F1** NY1090.
Diollaid Mhòr *Arg. & B.* ***Mountain***, on Kintyre, 3m/4km NW of Carradale. Height 1187 feet or 362 metres. **12 C2** NR7739.
Dionard *High.* ***River***, in Sutherland district, rising on Reay Forest and running N down Strath Dionard into Kyle of Durness. **74 C3** NC3661.
Dippen *Arg. & B.* ***Village***, near E coast of Kintyre, 4m/6km N of Saddell. **12 C2** NR7937.
Dippen Bay *Arg. & B.* ***Bay***, to S of Dippen, on E coast of Kintyre. NR7937.
Dippin *N.Ayr.* ***Settlement***, on Arran, 1km W above Dippin Head. **13 F3** NS0422.
Dippin Head *N.Ayr.* ***Coastal feature***, headland at SE end of Arran 2m/4km S of Whiting Bay. **13 F3** NS0522.
Dipple *Moray* ***Settlement***, 1m/2km W of Fochabers. **63 F4** NJ3258.
Dipple *S.Ayr.* ***Locality***, on coast, 2m/3km S of Turnberry. **14 A5** NS2002.
Dippool Water *S.Lan.* ***River***, rising to W of Auchengray and flowing SW to join Mouse Water, 2m/3km N of Carstairs. **25 D5** NS9448.
Dirdhu *High.* ***Settlement***, 3m/4km W of Bridge of Brown. **52 C2** NJ0720.
Dirleton *E.Loth.* ***Village***, 2m/4km W of North Berwick. Massive ruins of 13c castle (Historic Scotland). **26 C1** NT5184.
Dirleton Castle *E.Loth.* ***Castle***, 3m/4km SW of North Berwick at Dirleton. 13c stone castle (Historic Scotland) built on earlier motte, with alterations in 14c-15c. Damaged on Robert the Bruce's orders in 13c and also during Civil War. 16c and Victorian gardens. **26 C1** NT5183.
Dirrie More *High.* ***Other feature of interest***, pass between Loch Glascarnoch and Strath More, Ross and Cromarty district, carrying road from Dingwall to Ullapool. Height 915 feet or 279 metres. **60 B2** NH2475.
Dirrington Great Law *Sc.Bord.* ***Mountain***, conical hill on Lammermuir, 2m/3km S of Longformacus. Height 1309 feet or 399 metres. **27 D4** NT6954.
Dirrington Little Law *Sc.Bord.* ***Mountain***, conical hill 1m/2km SW of Dirrington Great Law. Height 1191 feet or 363 metres. **27 D4** NT6954.
Discovery Point and RRS Discovery *Dundee* ***Other feature of interest***, in Dundee, near Tay Road Bridge, where Captain Scott kept his Antarctic ship. Exhibitions show story of ship, from expeditions up to Russian Revolution and World War I. **34 C2** NO4029.
Dishes *Ork.* ***Settlement***, on Stronsay, overlooking Bay of Holland. **81 E4** HY6623.
Dishig *Arg. & B.* ***Settlement***, 4m/7km SW of Gruline, Mull. **29 D1** NM4935.
Distinkhorn *E.Ayr.* ***Mountain***, 3m/5km SE of Darvel. Height 1260 feet or 384 metres. **15 D2** NS5833.
Divach Burn *High.* ***River***, formed by tributaries from slopes of Glas-bheinn Beag and flowing NE into River Coiltie, 2m/3km SW of Drumnadrochit. **51 D2** NH4927.
Divach Falls *High.* ***Waterfall***, in course of Divach Burn, Inverness district, 2m/3km SW of Drumnadrochit. NH4927.
Divie ***River***, rising on Carn Bad na Caorach and flowing N to join Dorback Burn and continue N to River Findhorn 6m/10km S of Forres. **62 C5** NJ0049.
Dochanassie *High.* ***Locality***, on SE shore of Loch Lochy in Lochaber district, opposite Bunarkaig across loch. NN2085.
Dochart *Stir.* ***River***, running NE down Glen Dochart to join River Lochay at head of Loch Tay. **32 A1** NN5733.
Dochgarroch *High.* ***Settlement***, on Caledonian Canal, 4m/7km SW of Inverness. **61 F5** NH6140.
Dochrie Hill *P. & K.* ***Mountain***, 4m/7km NW of Kinross. Height 1197 feet or 365 metres. **33 F4** NO0808.
Dodd Hill *D. & G.* ***Mountain***, 6m/10km NE of Carsphairn. Height 1633 feet or 498 metres. **8 A1** NX6498.
Doe *High.* ***River***, in Inverness district rising on Glenaffric Forest and running SE to Glen Moriston 3m/5km E of dam of Loch Cluanie. **50 A3** NH2211.
Dog Bank *P. & K.* ***Coastal feature***, large intertidal area of mud on N side of Firth of Tay, about 3m/4km S of Longforgan. **34 B2** NO3024.
Dog Fall *High.* ***Waterfall***, in Glen Affric 1m/2km E of Loch Beinn a' Mheadhoin, Inverness district. NH2828.
Dog Hillock *Angus* ***Mountain***, 3m/5km E of Rottal in Glen Clova. Height 2368 feet or 722 metres. **42 C3** NO4269.
Dogton Stone *Fife* ***Historic/prehistoric site***, ancient Celtic cross (Historic Scotland), 1m/2km S of Kinglassie, with traces of human and animal sculpture; now without top and arms. **34 A5** NT2397.
Doire Ban *High.* ***Mountain***, 3m/5km NE of North Ballachulish. Height 1856 feet or 566 metres. **38 C3** NN0964.
Doire Meurach *High.* ***Mountain***, in Monadhliath range, 9m/12km SE of Foyers. Height 2581 feet or 787 metres. **51 E3** NH5611.
Doire Tana *High.* ***Open space***, N facing hillslope in Fasnakyle Forest above E end of Loch Mullardoch. **50 B2** NH2128.
Doirlinn Head *W.Isles* ***Coastal feature***, headland on W coast of Barra, 3m/4km W of Castlebay. **44 A4** NL6299.
Doll *High.* ***Settlement***, 1m/2km W of Brora, on E coast of Sutherland district. **73 D4** NC8803.
Dollar *Clack.* Population: 2670. ***Small town***, at foot of Ochil Hills, 6m/10km NE of Alloa. Castle Campbell is late 15c. **33 E5** NS9697.
Dollar Law *Sc.Bord.* ***Mountain***, 5m/8km SE of Drumelzier. Height 2680 feet or 817 metres. **16 C3** NT1727.
Dollarbeg *Clack.* ***Settlement***, 1m/2km S of Dollar. **33 E5** NS9796.
Dolphinton *S.Lan.* ***Village***, 7m/11km NE of Biggar. **25 F5** NT1046.
Don ***River***, major river of NE Scotland which rises 7m/11km S of Tomintoul and flows E by Strathdon, Alford and Inverurie to North Sea at Bridge of Don on N side of Aberdeen. **54 B3** NJ9509.
Donibristle *Fife* ***Settlement***, 3m/4km NW of Aberdour. **25 F1** NT1688.
Donibristle Bay *Fife* ***Bay***, on S coast of Fife, 3m/4km SW of Aberdour. NT1682.
Donibristle Industrial Estate *Fife* ***Locality***, 2m/3km E of Inverkeithing and 1km N of Donibristle Bay. NT1583.
Donolly Reservoir *E.Loth.* ***Reservoir***, small reservoir 3m/4km E of Gifford. NT5768.
Doon ***River***, issuing from Loch Doon and flowing NW through Bogton Loch, Patna and Dalrymple to Firth of Clyde, at S end of Ayr. **14 C5** NS3219.

Doonfoot *S.Ayr.* ***Suburb***, to S of Ayr, on Firth of Clyde, at mouth of River Doon. NS3219.
Doonhill Homestead *E.Loth.* ***Other feature of interest***, site of 6c British chief's wooden hall (Historic Scotland), superseded by 7c Anglian chief's hall, 2m/3km S of Dunbar. **27 D2** NT6875.
Doonie Point *Aber.* ***Coastal feature***, rocky headland, 1km S of Muchalls. **55 E5** NO9090.
Door of Cairnsmore *D. & G.* ***Open space***, craggy hillslope on S side of Cairnsmore of Fleet, 6m/10km E of Newton Stewart. **7 G4** NX5164.
Dorback Burn ***River***, running N from Lochindorb to join River Divie and flowing into River Findhorn 6m/10km S of Forres. NJ0147.
Dorback Burn *High.* ***River***, in Badenoch and Strathspey district running NW to River Nethy, 1m/2km SE of Nethy Bridge. **52 C3** NJ0119.
Dorback Burn *Moray* ***River***, flowing NE from Lochindorb, then N to join River Findhorn 1km S of Logie. **62 B5** NJ0049.
Dore Holm *Shet.* ***Island***, small island off W coast of Mainland to SE of Stenness. HU2176.
Dores *High.* ***Village***, in Inverness district, on E side of Loch Ness, 2m/3km S of NE end of loch. **51 E1** NH5934.
Dorlin *High.* ***Locality***, on S side of Loch Moidart in Lochaber district, 5m/8km N of Salen. NM6672.
Dornell Loch *D. & G.* ***Lake/loch***, small loch 4m/7km NW of Castle Douglas. NX7065.
Dornie *High.* ***Village***, in Skye and Lochalsh district on E side of entrance to Loch Long, 8m/12km E of Kyle of Lochalsh. **49 E2** NG8826.
Dornoch *High.* Population: 1196. ***Small town***, in Sutherland district on N shore of Dornoch Firth 12m/19km E of Bonar Bridge. 13c cathedral, rebuilt 19c. **61 G1** NH7989.
Dornoch Cathedral *High.* ***Ecclesiastical building***, in centre of Dornoch, founded in 1224, restored in 17c and 20c, and containing some fine 13c stonework. **72 C5** NH7990.
Dornoch Craft Centre *High.* ***Other feature of interest***, in old jail at Dornoch, showing crafts and displays on 19c prison life. **61 G1** NH7989.
Dornoch Firth *High.* ***Sea feature***, marks border between Ross and Cromarty and Sutherland districts and runs 22m/36km from Bonar Bridge out to Tarbet Ness. **61 G1** NJ7989.
Dornoch Firth Bridge *High.* ***Bridge***, road bridge carrying A9 across Dornoch Firth, 4m/6km SW of Dornoch. NH7485.
Dornoch Point *High.* ***Coastal feature***, headland 1m/2km S of Dornoch. **62 A1** NH7989.
Dornoch Sands *High.* ***Coastal feature***, extensive sandy area on N coast of Dornoch Firth, 1m/2km SW of Dornoch. **61 G1** NH7788.
Dornock *D. & G.* ***Village***, 3m/4km E of Annan. **9 G4** NY2366.
Dorrery *High.* ***Settlement***, 1m/2km W of Scotscalder Station. **76 C3** ND0754.
Dorsell *Aber.* ***Settlement***, 2m/3km SW of Alford. **54 A3** NJ5414.
Dorusduain *High.* ***Settlement***, in Skye and Lochalsh district, 4m/6km NE of Shiel Bridge. **49 F2** NG9822.
Double Dykes *D. & G.* ***Historic/prehistoric site***, earthworks, supposedly Pictish defence works, on neck of land 1m/2km W of Mull of Galloway. NX1430.
Douchary *High.* ***River***, on borders of Ross and Cromarty and Sutherland districts, running N down Glen Douchary into Rhiddorach River above Loch Achall, E of Ullapool. **71 E5** NH2593.
Dougalston *E.Dun.* ***Hamlet***, 1km E of Milngavie. **23 G2** NS5673.
Dougarie *N.Ayr.* ***Settlement***, on NW coast of Arran, 8m/12km W of Brodick. **13 D2** NR8837.
Dougarie Point *N.Ayr.* ***Coastal feature***, headland on NW coast of Arran, 4m/6km S of Pirnmill. **13 D2** NR8738.
Douglas *S.Lan.* Population: 1616. ***Small town***, with industrial estate, 8m/13km S of Lanark. St. Bride's Church (Historic Scotland) is 12c chancel in churchyard. **15 G2** NS8330.
Douglas and Angus *Dundee* ***Suburb***, 3m/4km NE of Dundee city centre. **34 C1** NO4432.
Douglas Burn *Sc.Bord.* ***River***, rising in mountains of Ettrick Forest and flowing SE to join Yarrow Water, 1m/2km E of St. Mary's Loch. **17 D3** NT2924.
Douglas Castle *S.Lan.* ***Castle***, fragment of castle to NE of Douglas. NS8431.
Douglas Hall *D. & G.* ***Settlement***, 1m/2km E of Colvend and 2m/4km NE of Rockcliffe. **8 C5** NX8855.
Douglas Water *Arg. & B.* ***River***, in Argyll, running E to Loch Fyne 3m/5km S of Inveraray. **30 C4** NN0704.
Douglas Water *Arg. & B.* ***River***, rising on Tullich Hill and running E down Glen Douglas to Loch Lomond at Inverbeg. NS3498.
Douglas Water *S.Lan.* ***Hamlet***, to E of river of same name, 1m/2km N of Rigside. **15 G2** NS8736.
Douglas Water *S.Lan.* ***River***, rising 7m/11km SW of Douglas and flowing past town and past hamlet of Douglas Water, to River Clyde 3m/4km SE of Lanark. **15 G2** NS8330.
Douglastown *Angus* ***Village***, 3m/5km SW of Forfar. **42 C5** NO4147.
Dounan Bay *D. & G.* ***Bay***, 8m/12km NW of Stranraer. **6 A4** NW9668.
Dounby *Ork.* ***Village***, on Mainland, 6m/10km NW of Finstown. **80 A4** HY2920.
Doune *Arg. & B.* ***Settlement***, near N end of Loch Lomond, 1m/2km SE of Ardlui across loch. **31 F3** NN3314.
Doune *Arg. & B.* ***Settlement***, in Glen Douglas, 2m/3km W of Inverbeg. **31 F5** NS3198.
Doune *High.* ***Settlement***, 1km E of Brae, to S of River Oykel. **71 G4** NC4400.
Doune *High.* ***Settlement***, 1m/2km S of Aviemore. **52 A3** NH8910.
Doune *Stir.* Population: 1212. ***Village***, 4m/6km W of Dunblane. 14c Doune Castle (Historic Scotland) to S. **32 C4** NN7201.
Doune Castle *Stir.* ***Castle***, partially restored late 14c courtyard castle (Historic Scotland) built for Regent Albany, to S of Doune beside River Teith. **32 C4** NN7201.
Doune Hill *Arg. & B.* ***Mountain***, 5m/7km S of Arrochar. Height 2408 feet or 734 metres. **31 E5** NS2997.
Doune Motor Museum *Stir.* ***Other feature of interest***, vintage and post-vintage cars collected by Earl of Moray, 1km NE of Doune. **32 C4** NN7102.
Doune Park *Aber.* ***Settlement***, 1m/2km S of Macduff. **64 C3** NJ7162.
Dounepark *S.Ayr.* ***Suburb***, S district of Girvan. NX1897.
Douneside *Aber.* ***Settlement***, 1km N of Tarland. **53 G4** NJ4805.
Dounie *High.* ***Settlement***, 2m/3km W of Ardgay. **72 A5** NH5690.
Dounie *High.* ***Settlement***, 6m/9km NW of Tain. **61 F1** NH6986.
Dounreay *High.* ***Locality***, on N coast of Caithness district, 8m/13km W of Thurso. Site of Experimental Reactor Establishment of Atomic Energy Authority. **76 B2** NC9867.
Dounreay Nuclear Power Development Establishment *High.* ***Other feature of interest***, on N coast of Caithness district, 8m/13km W of Thurso, with exhibitions on nuclear processes. Site now decommissioned. **76 B2** NC9867.
Dowally *P. & K.* ***Hamlet***, in Strath Tay, 3m/5km S of Ballinluig. **41 F5** NO0048.
Dowanhill *Glas.* ***Suburb***, 2m/3km NW of Glasgow city centre. NS5667.
Dowhill *S.Ayr.* ***Settlement***, 2m/3km S of Turnberry. **14 A5** NS2002.
Downan Point *S.Ayr.* ***Coastal feature***, headland at S end of Ballantrae Bay. **6 B2** NX0680.
Downfield *Dundee* ***Suburb***, NW district of Dundee. **34 B1** NO3833.
Downie Point *Aber.* ***Coastal feature***, headland on E coast, 1km SE of Stonehaven, at N end of Strathlethan Bay. NO8885.
Downies *Aber.* ***Village***, on E coast, 7m/11km S of Aberdeen. **55 E5** NO9295.
Draffan *S.Lan.* ***Settlement***, 4m/6km SE of Larkhall. **24 B5** NS7945.
Dragon Ness *Shet.* ***Coastal feature***, headland on E coast of Mainland opposite West Linga. HU5164.
Drake Law *S.Lan.* ***Mountain***, with forested summit, 2m/3km SW of Abington. Height 1584 feet or 483 metres. **15 G3** NS9022.
Drakemire *Sc.Bord.* ***Locality***, 3m/4km S of Grantshouse. **27 E3** NT8061.
Drakemyre *N.Ayr.* ***Village***, 1km N of Dalry. NS2950.
Drambuie *D. & G.* ***Settlement***, 1m/2km SE of Kirkconnel, across River Nith and Kello Water. **15 F4** NS7410.
Dreghorn *N.Ayr.* Population: 3960. ***Village***, 3m/5km E of Irvine. **14 B2** NS3538.
Drem *E.Loth.* ***Village***, 4m/6km N of Haddington. **26 C2** NT5179.
Driesh *Angus* ***Mountain***, 4m/6km W of Clova. Munro: height 3106 feet or 947 metres. **42 A2** NO2773.
Drimfern *Arg. & B.* ***Settlement***, in Glen Aray, 4m/7km N of Inveraray. **30 C3** NN0814.
Drimlee *Arg. & B.* ***Settlement***, at head of Glen Shira, 6m/9km NE of Inveraray. **30 D3** NN1416.
Drimnin *High.* ***Village***, on E shore of Sound of Mull, 4m/6km E of Tobermory across sound. **37 E4** NM5554.
Drimore *W.Isles* ***Settlement***, on South Uist, 4m/7km S of Hornish Point. **46 A1** NF7640.
Drimsynie *Arg. & B.* ***Settlement***, at N end of Loch Goil, 1km W of Lochgoilhead. **31 D4** NN1901.
Drimvore *Arg. & B.* ***Settlement***, in valley of River Add, 5m/7km NW of Lochgilphead. **30 A5** NR8394.
Drinan *High.* ***Settlement***, 2m/3km NE of Elgol, Skye. **48 B3** NG5415.
Drinishader *W.Isles* ***Settlement***, on inlet of East Loch Tarbert, South Harris, 4m/6km SE of Tarbert. NG1794.
Drinkstone Hill *Sc.Bord.* ***Mountain***, 3m/5km NW of Hawick. Height 1043 feet or 318 metres. **17 F4** NT4818.
Drip Moss *Stir.* ***Open space***, low-lying area between Rivers Forth and Teith, 3m/5km NW of Stirling. **32 C5** NS7595.
Drishaig *Arg. & B.* ***Settlement***, on N shore of NE arm of Loch Fyne, 4m/7km NE of Inveraray. **31 D3** NN1510.
Drissaig *Arg. & B.* ***Settlement***, 3m/4km NW of Dalavich, to N of Loch Avich. **30 B3** NM9415.
Drochaid Mhòr *High.* ***Locality***, on River Dionard, 1m/2km S of head of Kyle of Durness. **74 C2** NC3460.
Dron *P. & K.* ***Village***, 5m/8km S of Perth. **33 G3** NO1415.
Drongan *E.Ayr.* Population: 2910. ***Village***, 7m/11km E of Ayr. **14 C4** NS4418.
Dronger *Shet.* ***Coastal feature***, rocky headland on NW of Fair Isle. **82 A5** HZ2074.
Dronley *Angus* ***Hamlet***, 1m/2km S of Kirkton of Auchterhouse. **34 B1** NO3435.
Druie *High.* ***River***, in Badenoch and Strathspey district running NW into River Spey at Aviemore. NH8911.
Druim a' Chùirn *High.* ***Large natural feature***, mountain ridge rising to 1916 feet of 584 metres, 2m/3km NE of Meoble, South Morar, Lochaber district. **38 A1** NM8189.
Druim a' Chuirn *High.* ***Mountain***, 3m/5km NW of Loch Arkaig, Lochaber district. Height 2696 feet or 822 metres. **49 F5** NM9695.
Druim an Fhraoich Mhin *Arg. & B.* ***Mountain***, 4m/7km E of Kilninian. Height 1043 feet or 318 metres. **37 D5** NM4645.
Druim Chòsaidh *High.* ***Inland physical feature***, mountain ridge in Lochaber district running E and W on N side of head of Loch Quoich, and attaining height of 2995 feet or 913 metres at Sgurr a' Choire-bheithe. **49 F4** NG9100.
Druim Dearg *Angus* ***Mountain***, 1m/2km W of Bellaty. Height 1486 feet or 453 metres. **42 A4** NO2158.
Druim Fada *Arg. & B.* ***Mountain***, in Laggan Deer Forest, Mull, 3m/4km SE of Lochbuie. Height 1328 feet or 405 metres. **29 F2** NM6422.
Druim Fada *High.* ***Inland physical feature***, mountain ridge in Lochaber district running E and W on N side of narrow part of Loch Hourn, SE of Arnisdale. Highest point 2327 feet or 709 metres. **49 E4** NG8908.
Druim Fada *High.* ***Inland physical feature***, mountain ridge on Locheil Forest, Lochaber district, 5m/8km N of Fort William. Summit, at E end of ridge, is Stob a' Ghrianain, 2440 feet or 744 metres. **38 C1** NN0882.
Druim Fiaclach *High.* ***Inland physical feature***, mountain ridge in Moidart, Lochaber district, 3m/4km SE of Lochailort. Attains height of 2850 feet or 869 metres. **37 G2** NM7979.
Druim Garbh *High.* ***Inland physical feature***, mountain ridge, 5m/8km NE of Strontian, Lochaber district. **38 A3** NM8668.
Druim Gleann Laoigh *High.* ***Mountain***, 8m/12km NW of Fort William. Height 2289 feet or 698 metres. **38 C1** NN0685.
Druim Hain *High.* ***Inland physical feature***, mountain ridge 1m/2km NE of Loch Coruisk, Skye. **48 A2** NG4922.
Druim Leathad nam Fias *High.* ***Inland physical feature***, mountain ridge and watershed between Cona Glen and Glen Scaddle in Lochaber district, 9m/15km W of Fort William. **38 B3** NM9670.
Druim Mòr *P. & K.* ***Inland physical feature***, mountain ridge rising to 1204 feet or 367 metres to W of Strath Tay, 5m/8km W of Dunkeld. **41 E5** NN9242.
Druim na Cluain-airighe *High.* ***Inland physical feature***, mountain ridge in Knoydart, Lochaber district, 2m/4km NW of Inverie. **49 D4** NG7503.
Druim na h-Achlaise *High.* ***Mountain***, in Skye and Lochalsh district, on S side of Loch Loyne. Height 1771 feet or 540 metres. **50 A4** NH1303.
Druim nam Bad *High.* ***Marsh/bog***, marshy area with number of small lochs. Beinn Direach and Ben Hee lie to W and SW respectively. **75 D5** NC4738.
Druim nan Cliar *High.* ***Locality***, includes a large number of lochs to E of Loch Hope. **75 D3** NC4957.
Druim nan Cnamh *High.* ***Inland physical feature***, mountain ridge on border of Inverness and Skye and Lochalsh districts, between Lochs Cluanie and Loyne. Summit 2555 feet or 779 metres. **50 A4** NH1307.
Druim Shionnach *High.* ***Mountain***, in Inverness district, forming part of Cluanie Forest, 1m/2km S of W end of Loch Cluanie. Munro: height 3237 feet or 987 metres. **49 G4** NH0708.
Druimarbin *High.* ***Settlement***, on E shore of Loch Linnhe, 2m/4km SW of Fort William. **38 C3** NN0771.
Druimavuic *Arg. & B.* ***Settlement***, at head of Loch Creran, 12m/21km NE of Oban. **38 C5** NN0044.

Druimdrishaig *Arg. & B.* ***Settlement***, on NW coast of Kintyre, 4m/6km N of Kilberry. **21 F2** NR7370.
Druimindarroch *High.* ***Locality***, on N side of Loch nan Uamh, 2m/3km SE of Arisaig, in Lochaber district. **37 F1** NM6884.
Druimkinnerras *High.* ***Settlement***, 6m/9km SW of Beauly. **61 D5** NH4639.
Druimyeon Bay *Arg. & B.* ***Bay***, on E side of Gigha, N of Ardminish Point. **21 E4** NR6550.
Drum *Arg. & B.* ***Settlement***, on Cowal peninsula, 4m/6km NW of Tighnabruaich. **22 A2** NR9376.
Drum *P. & K.* ***Village***, 5m/7km W of Kinross. **33 F4** NO0400.
Drum Castle *Aber.* ***Castle***, medieval castle tower (National Trust for Scotland) with Jacobean and Victorian extensions, 3m/5km W of Peterculter. Grounds contain 16c chapel and unique Garden of Historic Roses. **54 C4** NJ7900.
Drum Hollistan *High.* ***Open space***, hillslope below N slopes of Beinn Ruadh in Caithness district, 2m/3km W of Reay. **76 B2** NC9263.
Drum Mains *N.Lan.* ***Settlement***, 3m/5km W of Cumbernauld town centre. NS7173.
Drumachloy *Arg. & B.* ***Settlement***, on Bute, 1km N of Ettrick Bay. **22 B3** NS0367.
Drumadoon Bay *N.Ayr.* ***Bay***, on W coast of Arran, extending either side of Blackwaterfoot. **13 D3** NR8927.
Drumadoon Point *N.Ayr.* ***Coastal feature***, headland at NW end of Drumadoon Bay on Arran, 1m/2km NW of Blackwaterfoot. NR8828.
Drumbeg *High.* ***Village***, on S side of Eddrachillis Bay, W coast of Sutherland district. **74 A5** NC1232.
Drumblade *Aber.* ***Locality***, 4m/6km E of Huntly. **64 A5** NJ5840.
Drumblair *Aber.* ***Settlement***, 3m/4km S of Inverkeithny. **64 B5** NJ6343.
Drumbowie Reservoir *Falk.* ***Reservoir***, small reservoir 2m/3km SW of Denny. NS7881.
Drumbreddan Bay *D. & G.* ***Bay***, 9m/13km SE of Portpatrick. **2 A2** NX0743.
Drumbuie *High.* ***Settlement***, in Skye and Lochalsh district, 2m/4km NE of Kyle of Lochalsh. **49 D1** NG7731.
Drumchapel *Glas.* ***Suburb***, 5m/8km NW of Glasgow city centre. **23 G2** NS5270.
Drumchardine *High.* ***Settlement***, 3m/5km E of Beauly. **61 E5** NH5644.
Drumchork *High.* ***Settlement***, on E shore of Loch Ewe, 5m/8km N of Poolewe. **59 E1** NG8788.
Drumclog *S.Lan.* ***Village***, 5m/8km E of Darvel. Monument 1m/2km NW commemorates battle of 1679 in which Covenanters defeated Life Guards under Claverhouse, later Viscount Dundee, leading to confrontation at Battle of Bothwell Bridge 1679. **15 E2** NS6338.
Drumcoltran Tower *D. & G.* ***Historic/prehistoric site***, 16c tower (Historic Scotland) 1m/2km N of Kirkgunzeon and 5m/8km NE of Dalbeattie. **8 C4** NX8668.
Drumdelgie *Aber.* ***Settlement***, 6m/9km SE of Keith. **63 G5** NJ4842.
Drumderfit *High.* ***Settlement***, 1m/2km S of Munlochy. **61 F4** NH6551.
Drumderg *P. & K.* ***Mountain***, in Forest of Alyth, 3m/5km NE of Bridge of Cally. Height 1384 feet or 422 metres. **41 G4** NO1754.
Drumeldrie *Fife* ***Hamlet***, 2m/3km E of Lower Largo. **34 C4** NO4403.
Drumelzier *Sc.Bord.* ***Village***, on Drumelzier Burn near its confluence with River Tweed, 8m/13km SW of Peebles. Ruins of Tinnis Castle on hillside to NE. **16 C2** NT1334.
Drumelzier Burn *Sc.Bord.* ***River***, joining River Tweed to NW of Drumelzier, 8m/13km SW of Peebles. NT1334.
Drumelzier Castle *Sc.Bord.* ***Castle***, faint remains of castle beside River Tweed 1km SW of Drumelzier. NT1233.
Drumelzier Law *Sc.Bord.* ***Mountain***, 2m/3km SE of Drumelzier. Height 2191 feet or 668 metres. **16 C2** NT1431.
Drumfearn *High.* ***Settlement***, at head of Sleat peninsula, Skye, 3m/4km NW of Eilean Iarmain. **48 C3** NG6715.
Drumfern *High.* ***Settlement***, 1km W of head of Loch Eil, Lochaber district. **38 B2** NM9578.
Drumgarve *Arg. & B.* ***Settlement***, on Kintyre, 3m/5km N of Campbeltown. **12 C3** NR7226.
Drumgley *Angus* ***Hamlet***, 3m/4km W of Forfar. **42 C5** NO4150.
Drumguish *High.* ***Hamlet***, on S side of valley of River Spey, 2m/3km SE of Kingussie. **51 G5** NN7899.
Drumhead *Aber.* ***Settlement***, 6m/10km SW of Banchory. **54 B5** NO6092.
Drumin *Moray* ***Settlement***, 3m/5km NW of Tomnavoulin. **53 D1** NJ1830.
Drumine *High.* ***Settlement***, 6m/10km W of Nairn. **61 G4** NH7951.
Drumine Forest *Moray* ***Forest/woodland***, 5m/8km S of Forres. **62 C4** NJ0250.
Drumjohn *D. & G.* ***Settlement***, 6m/9km SE of Dalmellington. **7 G1** NX5297.
Drumlamford House *S.Ayr.* ***Settlement***, on W side of Loch Dornal, 5m/8km SE of Barrhill. **7 D3** NX2876.
Drumlamford Loch *S.Ayr.* ***Lake/loch***, small loch 4m/7km SE of Barrhill. **7 D3** NX2877.
Drumlanrig Castle *D. & G.* ***Castle***, seat of the Duke of Buccleuch, dating from late 17c, in Nithsdale 3m/5km NW of Thornhill. **8 C1** NX8599.
Drumlasie *Aber.* ***Settlement***, 3m/4km NE of Torphins. **54 B4** NJ6405.
Drumlemble *Arg. & B.* ***Village***, in Kintyre, 4m/6km W of Campbeltown. **12 B4** NR6619.
Drumlithie *Aber.* ***Village***, 6m/10km SW of Stonehaven. **43 F1** NO7880.
Drummoddie *D. & G.* ***Locality***, 4m/6km E of Port William. NX3945.
Drummond *High.* ***Settlement***, 1km S of Evanton across River Sgitheach, Ross and Cromarty district. **61 F3** NH6065.
Drummond *Stir.* ***Settlement***, 3m/4km SE of Callander. **32 B4** NN6706.
Drummond Castle *P. & K.* ***Castle***, founded in 15c, 3m/4km SW of Crieff. Much restored. Surrounded by formal garden, including topiary, terraces and Victorian parterre with fountains. **32 D3** NN8418.
Drummond Hill *P. & K.* ***Mountain***, elongated wooded mass to N of Kenmore, at foot at Loch Tay. Height 1502 feet or 458 metres. **40 C5** NN7646.
Drummore *D. & G.* ***Village***, on Drummore Bay on E coast of Rinns of Galloway, 4m/7km N of Mull of Galloway. **2 B3** NX1336.
Drummore Bay *D. & G.* ***Bay***, on E coast of Rinns of Galloway, 4m/7km N of Mull of Galloway. NX1336.
Drummossie Muir *High.* ***Large natural feature***, moorland tract in Inverness district, centred on S part of Culloden Forest, 3m/5km SE of Inverness. **51 F1** NH7343.
Drummuir Castle *Moray* ***Historic house***, Victorian castle and home of Duff family, with notable Lantern Tower, 4m/7km NE of Dufftown. **63 F5** NJ3744.
Drumnadrochit *High.* ***Village***, on River Enrick, 1m/2km W of Urquhart Bay on Loch Ness, Inverness district. **51 E1** NH5029.
Drumnagorrach *Moray* ***Settlement***, 3m/5km NW of Milltown of Rothiemay and 6m/9km E of Keith. **64 A4** NJ5252.
Drumnatorran *High.* ***Settlement***, 1km N of Strontian, Lochaber district. **38 A3** NM8262.
Drumoak *Aber.* ***Village***, 3m/5km W of Peterculter. **54 C5** NO7998.
Drumochter *See Pass of Drumochter.*
Drumore *Arg. & B.* ***Settlement***, on Kintyre, 1m/2km NW of Campbeltown. **12 C3** NR7022.
Drumour *P. & K.* ***Settlement***, 5m/8km SW of Dunkeld. **41 E5** NN9639.
Drumoyne *Glas.* ***Suburb***, 3m/4km W of Glasgow city centre, in Govan district. NS5465.
Drumpellier Country Park *N.Lan.* ***Leisure/recreation***, country park with lakeside walk and children's play area, 1m/2km NW of Coatbridge. Butterfly house, boating and train rides operate in summer. **24 B3** NS7165.
Drumrash *D. & G.* ***Settlement***, on E bank of Loch Ken, 4m/7km SE of New Galloway. **8 A3** NX6871.
Drumrunie *High.* ***Settlement***, on River Runie, 3m/4km NE of Strathkanaird. **71 D3** NC1605.
Drumrunie Forest *High.* ***Open space***, deer forest in Ross and Cromarty district around Cul Mòr, 10m/16km N of Ullapool. Part of Inverpolly National Nature Reserve. **71 E3** NC1810.
Drumry *Renf.* ***Suburb***, 1km N of Clydebank town centre. NS5070.
Drums *Aber.* ***Settlement***, 2m/3km SW of Newburgh. **55 E2** NJ9822.
Drumsturdy *Angus* ***Hamlet***, 2m/3km N of Monifieth. **34 C1** NO4835.
Drumtassie Burn *Falk.* ***River***, rising on Blawhorn Moss to NW of Blackridge, and flowing NE to join River Avon to W of Avonbridge. Forms part of border with West Lothian. **24 C3** NS9172.
Drumtochty Castle *Aber.* ***Castle***, in Glen of Drumtochty, 4m/7km W of Glenbervie. NO6980.
Drumtochty Forest *Aber.* ***Forest/woodland***, to N and S of Drumtochty Castle, 6m/10km N of Laurencekirk. **43 E2** NO6980.
Drumtroddan Standing Stones *D. & G.* ***Historic/prehistoric site***, site of two Bronze Age standing stones (Historic Scotland), with nearby cup and ring marks of similar age, on natural rock face just S of Drumtroddan, 8m/12km SW of Wigtown. **3 D2** NX3644.
Drumuie *High.* ***Settlement***, 3m/4km NW of Portree, Skye. **58 A5** NG4546.
Drumuillie *High.* ***Settlement***, in Badenoch and Strathspey district, 3m/4km NE of Boat of Garten. **52 B2** NH9420.
Drumvaich *Stir.* ***Settlement***, 3m/4km SE of Callander. **32 B4** NN6704.
Drumwhindle *Aber.* ***Locality***, 4m/7km NW of Ellon. **55 E1** NJ9236.
Drumwhirn *D. & G.* ***Settlement***, 7m/11km E of Galloway. **8 B2** NX7480.
Drunkendub *Angus* ***Settlement***, 2m/3km S of Inverkeilor. **43 E5** NO6646.
Dry Burn *E.Loth.* ***River***, rising in Lammermuir Hills, and flowing NE to North Sea, 4m/6km SE of Dunbar. **27 D2** NT7375.
Dry Harbour *High.* ***Settlement***, in centre of Rona. **58 C4** NG6258.
Drybridge *Moray* ***Settlement***, near N coast on Burn of Buckie, 2m/3km S of Buckie. **63 G3** NJ4362.
Drybridge *N.Ayr.* ***Hamlet***, with standing stone, 2m/3km SE of Irvine, on bend of River Irvine. **14 B2** NS3636.
Dryburgh *Sc.Bord.* ***Village***, 1km N of St. Boswells across River Tweed. Large statue of William Wallace, erected in 1814, to N of village. NT5932.
Dryburgh Abbey *Sc.Bord.* ***Historic/prehistoric site***, remains of abbey (Historic Scotland) founded in 1150, in loop of River Tweed, 1m/2km S of Bemersyde. Burial place of Sir Walter Scott, d. 1832, and of Field-Marshal Lord Haig, d. 1928. **17 G2** NT5931.
Dryden Fell *Sc.Bord.* ***Mountain***, 2m/3km N of Teviothead. Height 1151 feet or 351 metres. **17 F5** NT3908.
Dryfe Water *D. & G.* ***River***, rising on S side of Loch Fell and running S to River Annan, 2m/3km W of Lockerbie. **9 F1** NY1082.
Drygrange *Sc.Bord.* ***Settlement***, 2m/3km S of Earlston, next to W bank of Leader Water. **17 G2** NT5735.
Dryhope *Sc.Bord.* ***Hamlet***, at NE end of St. Mary's Loch, 2m/3km NE of Cappercleuch. **17 D3** NT2624.
Drylaw *Edin.* ***Suburb***, 2m/3km NW of Edinburgh city centre. NT2275.
Drymen *Stir.* ***Village***, 7m/11km NE of Balloch. To W is site of Buchanan Castle. **23 F1** NS4788.
Drymuir *Aber.* ***Locality***, 1m/2km SW of Maud. **65 E5** NJ9145.
Drynoch *High.* ***River***, on Skye, flowing W to head of Loch Harport, on S side of settlement of Drynoch. NG4031.
Drynoch *High.* ***Settlement***, at head of Loch Harport, Skye. **48 A1** NG4031.
Dryrigs Hill *S.Lan.* ***Mountain***, with forested summit, 4m/7km SE of Muirkirk. Height 1443 feet or 440 metres. **15 F3** NS7424.
Duachy *Arg. & B.* ***Settlement***, 1m/2km SW of Kilninver, on NW shore of Loch Seil. **30 A2** NM8020.
Duart Bay *Arg. & B.* ***Bay***, to W of Duart Point, on E coast of Mull. **29 G1** NM7435.
Duart Castle *Arg. & B.* ***Castle***, on Duart Point, Mull, seat of the chief of the Macleans. **29 G1** NM7435.
Duart Point *Arg. & B.* ***Coastal feature***, headland on E coast of Mull opposite entrance to Loch Linnhe. **29 G1** NM7435.
Dubford *Aber.* ***Settlement***, 1m/2km S of Gardenstown. **64 C3** NJ7963.
Dubh Artach *Arg. & B.* ***Island***, rock lying 16m/26km SW of Mull. NM1203.
Dubh Bheinn *Arg. & B.* ***Mountain***, on Jura, 3m/4km NW of Craighouse. Height 1738 feet or 530 metres. **20 C3** NR4868.
Dubh Bheinn *Arg. & B.* ***Mountain***, on N part of Jura, 4m/6km NW of Lussagiven. Height 1574 feet or 480 metres. **21 D1** NR5889.
Dubh Chreag *Arg. & B.* ***Mountain***, on Knapdale, 5m/7km NW of Tarbert. Height 1574 feet or 480 metres. **21 F3** NR7970.
Dubh Eas *Stir.* ***River***, flowing SE into River Falloch, 3m/4km N of Ardlui. **31 E2** NN3219.
Dubh Eilean *Arg. & B.* ***Island***, rocky island off W coast of Oronsay. **20 B1** NR3388.
Dubh Ghleann *Aber.* ***Valley***, narrow, steep-sided valley in Grampian Mountains to E of Beinn Bhreac, with a stream flowing in a N to S direction to Glen Quoich. **52 C5** NO0697.
Dubh Loch *Aber.* ***Lake/loch***, small loch 2m/3km W of Loch Muick and 7m/12km SE of Braemar. **42 A1** NO2382.
Dubh Loch *Arg. & B.* ***Lake/loch***, small loch in Argyll in course of River Shira, 2m/3km NE of Inveraray. **30 D3** NN1111.
Dubh Loch *High.* ***Lake/loch***, upper part of Loch Bad an Sgalaig, Ross and Cromarty district. **59 E3** NG8470.
Dubh Loch *High.* ***Lake/loch***, in W part of Ross and Cromarty district adjacent to head of Fionn Loch and 1m/2km S of Beinn a' Chàisgein Mòr. **59 F2** NG9876.
Dubh Loch Beag *High.* ***Lake/loch***, small round loch in Benmore Forest, 1km E of River Oykel. **71 F3** NC3216.
Dubh Loch Mòr *High.* ***Lake/loch***, small corrie loch with Ben More Assynt rising steeply to N. **71 F3** NC3119.
Dubh Lochain *High.* ***Lake/loch***, small loch in Lochaber district 3m/5km E of Arnisdale. NG8809.
Dubh Sgeir *Arg. & B.* ***Island***, rock island in Firth of Lorn, 1m/2km SW of Bach Island. **29 G2** NM7625.
Dubh Sgeirean *High.* ***Island***, group of island rocks 1m/2km off W coast of Sutherland district, 4m/6km SW of Kinlochbervie. NC1654.
Dubhchladach *Arg. & B.* ***Settlement***, at head of West Loch Tarbert, 1m/2km W of Tarbert. **21 G3** NR8468.

Dubheads *P. & K.* ***Settlement***, 6m/9km N of Auchterarder. **33 E2** NN9621.
Dubton *Angus* ***Hamlet***, 3m/4km NW of Friockheim. **43 D4** NO5652.
Duchal *Inclyde* ***Settlement***, 1m/2km S of Kilmacolm. **23 E3** NS3567.
Duchal Moor *Inclyde* ***Open space***, moorland to E and SE of North Burnt Hill and Creuch Hill respectively. **23 D3** NS2766.
Duchally *High.* ***Settlement***, on E side of Glen Cassley, 6m/9km W of Loch Shin. **71 F3** NC3817.
Duchray Castle *Stir.* ***Castle***, former stronghold of the Grahams, on S bank of Duchray Water in Loch Ard Forest, to W of Aberfoyle. **31 G5** NS4899.
Duchray Hill *P. & K. Alternative name for Mealna Letter, qv.*
Duchray Water *Stir.* ***River***, flows E through Loch Ard Forest to join River Forth 1m/2km W of Aberfoyle. **31 G5** NS4899.
Duchrie Burn *Aber.* ***River***, rising on N slopes of Culardoch and flowing SE, then NE, to join River Gairn 1km E of Daldownie. **53 E5** NJ2500.
Duddingston *Edin.* ***Suburb***, 3m/5km E of Edinburgh city centre. **25 G2** NT2972.
Duddingston Loch *Edin.* ***Nature reserve***, bird sanctuary 2m/3km SW of Edinburgh city centre. Known for wintering pochard. Hide gives good views over loch. NT2972.
Duff House *Aber.* ***Historic house***, on SW side of Banff. Fine example of Georgian baroque architecture (Historic Scotland), designed by William Adam for first Earl of Fife in 1735. Housed German prisoners in World War II. Houses fine National Galleries of Scotland collections of paintings, furniture, tapestries and artefacts. **64 B3** NJ6963.
Dufftown *Moray* Population: 1710. ***Small town***, at confluence of Dullan Water and River Fiddich 16m/26km SE of Elgin. Auchindown Castle (Historic Scotland), ruined 15c castle 2m/3km SE. **63 F5** NJ3239.
Dufftown Museum *Moray* ***Other feature of interest***, museum in Dufftown clock tower with exhibits on local history, distilling and a reconstructed laundry. **53 F1** NJ3239.
Duffus *Moray* ***Village***, near N coast, 5m/8km NW of Eligin. St. Peter's Kirk and shaft of 14c cross (Historic Scotland) on E side of village. **63 D3** NJ1768.
Duffus Castle *Moray* ***Castle***, ruined 14c castle (Historic Scotland) standing on earlier motte, 1m/2km SE of Duffus. **63 D3** NJ1768.
Duiar *High.* ***Settlement***, on E bank of River Spey, 7m/11km SW of Upper Knockando. **52 D1** NJ1233.
Duible *High.* ***Settlement***, 2m/3km SE of Kildonan Lodge, to N of River Helmsdale. **73 E2** NC9219.
Duich *Arg. & B.* ***River***, flowing W, then NW, into River Laggan at N end of Laggan Bay, Islay. **20 B4** NR3055.
Duiletter *Arg. & B.* ***Settlement***, 2m/3km N of Dalmally. **31 D2** NN1530.
Duinish *P. & K.* ***Settlement***, 6m/9km NW of Kinloch Rannoch. **40 B3** NN6167.
Duirinish *High.* ***Large natural feature***, mountainous peninsula, including Healabhal Mhòr and Healabhal Beag, in extreme W of Skye. N part separated from Vaternish peninsula by Loch Dunvegan to E, and S part bounded by Loch Bracadale to E. Fine cliff scenery. NG2045.
Duirinish *High.* ***Settlement***, in Skye and Lochalsh district, 3m/5km NE of Kyle of Lochalsh. **49 D1** NG7831.
Duisdalemore *High.* ***Settlement***, on E side of Sleat peninsula, Skye, 1km N of Eilean Iarmain. **48 D3** NG7013.
Duisk *S.Ayr.* ***River***, rising SE of Barrhill and running NW, past Barrhill, to join River Stinchar at Pinwherry. **6 D2** NX1986.
Duisky *High.* ***Settlement***, on S shore of Loch Eil, 6m/10km W of Fort William across Loch Linnhe. **38 C2** NN0076.
Dukes Pass *Stir.* ***Other feature of interest***, mountain pass at height of 797 feet or 243 metres in Achray Forest, between The Trossachs and Aberfoyle. **32 A4** NN5103.
Dulax *Aber.* ***Settlement***, 3m/5km N of Strathdon. **53 F3** NJ3518.
Dull *P. & K.* ***Village***, 3m/5km W of Aberfeldy. **40 D5** NN8049.
Dullan Water *Moray* ***River***, rising on NW side of Glenfiddich Forest and flowing NE down Glen Rinnes to River Fiddich at Dufftown. **53 E1** NJ3339.
Dullatur *N.Lan.* ***Village***, 2m/3km NW of Cumbernauld. Well-preserved section of Antonine Wall ditch (Historic Scotland) to E. **24 B2** NS7476.
Dulnain *High.* ***River***, in Badenoch and Strathspey district rising on Monadhliath Mountains and running NE to River Spey, 1m/2km SE of Dulnain Bridge. **52 A3** NJ0023.
Dulnain Bridge *High.* ***Village***, in Badenoch and Strathspey district, 3m/5km SW of Grantown-on-Spey. **52 B2** NH9924.
Dulsie *High.* ***Settlement***, 3m/4km SW of Ferness. **62 B5** NH9341.
Dumbarton *W.Dun.* Population: 21,962. ***Town***, situated at confluence of River Leven and River Clyde, 14m/22km NW of Glasgow. Previously an important engineering and shipbuilding town; the 'Cutty Sark' was built here in 1869. Ancient castle (Historic Scotland) on basalt rock prominence above River Clyde. **23 F2** NS3975.
Dumbarton Castle *W.Dun.* ***Castle***, ancient castle (Historic Scotland) built on site of Roman fort to S of Dumbarton, on basalt rock prominence overlooking N bank of River Clyde estuary. Castle was a royal seat for Mary, Queen of Scots. Since beginning of 17c has been used as a garrison and artillery fortress. **23 F2** NS4074.
Dumbarton Muir *W.Dun.* ***Open space***, moorland area to NE of Dumbarton. **23 F2** NS4579.
Dumbreck *Glas.* ***Suburb***, 2m/3km SW of Glasgow city centre. NS5663.
Dumbrock Loch *Stir.* ***Lake/loch***, small loch 1m/2km SW of Strathblane. NS5578.
Dumcrieff *D. & G.* ***Locality***, on Moffat Water, 1m/2km SE of Moffat. **16 C5** NT1003.
Dumeath *Aber.* ***Settlement***, on W side of River Deveron, 1m/2km S of Haugh of Glass. **53 G1** NJ4237.
Dumfin *Arg. & B.* ***Settlement***, 3m/5km NE of Helensburgh. **23 E1** NS3484.
Dumfries *D. & G.* Population: 32,136. ***Town***, on River Nith, 60m/97km SE of Glasgow and 29m/47km NW of Carlisle across head of Solway Firth. Known for cotton spinning and weaving. Burns lived in town from 1791 to his death in 1796, and town contains many related tourist attractions. **9 D3** NX9776.
Dumfries Museum and Camera Obscura *D. & G.* ***Other feature of interest***, contained in 18c windmill, 1km W of Dumfries town centre, with exhibits on local history. Camera Obscura gives table-top panorama of Dumfries and surrounding area. **9 D3** NX9876.
Dumgoyne *Stir.* ***Settlement***, 4m/6km NW of Strathblane. **23 G1** NS5283.
Dun *Angus* ***Settlement***, 3m/5km NW of Montrose. **43 E4** NO6659.
Dun *W.Isles* ***Island***, steep, rocky, uninhabited island (National Trust for Scotland) in St. Kilda group, about 54m/86km W of South Harris and 35m/56km W of North Uist, lying off SE end of St. Kilda itself. Narrow island nearly 1m/2km wide. Haunt of sea birds. NF1097.
Dùn Bàn *Arg. & B. See Burg.*
Dùn Beag Broch *High.* ***Historic/prehistoric site***, 1km W of Bracadale, Skye. Fine example of Hebridean broch (Historic Scotland), occupied until 18c. **47 G1** NG3438.
Dùn Borve Broch *W.Isles* ***Historic/prehistoric site***, on NW coast of Isle of Lewis, 8m/13km SW of Butt of Lewis. **69 F2** NB4158.
Dùn Caan *High.* ***Mountain***, highest point on Raasay, with caves on S side, 4m/6km from S end of island. Height 1453 feet or 443 metres. **48 B1** NG5739.
Dun Carloway *W.Isles* ***Settlement***, near W coast of Isle of Lewis, 1m/2km SW of Carloway village. Here is Iron Age broch or fort (Historic Scotland). **68 C3** NB1841.
Dùn Chonnuill (Also known as Eileach Chonail.) *Arg. & B.* ***Island***, most northerly of Garvellachs group of islands in Firth of Lorn. Ruins of 13c castle. NM6812.
Dun Corr-bhile *Arg. & B.* ***Mountain***, on W side of Loch Shira, 1m/2km NE of Inveraray. Height 1056 feet or 322 metres. **30 C3** NN1010.
Dun Creich *High.* ***Historic/prehistoric site***, ancient fort on N shore of Dornoch Firth 3m/5km SE of Bonar Bridge, in Sutherland district. NH6588.
Dùn da Ghaoithe *Arg. & B.* ***Mountain***, 3m/5km W of Craignure, Mull. Height 2512 feet or 766 metres. **29 F1** NM6736.
Dun Dornaigil Broch *High.* ***Historic/prehistoric site***, situated on E side of Strath More, 9m/14km NW of Altnaharra. Well-preserved Iron Age broch (Historic Scotland) standing to a height of 22 feet or 6 metres above entrance passage. **75 D4** NC4545.
Dun Hill *Arg. & B. Alternative name for Dun I, qv.*
Dun I (Also known as Dun Hill). *Arg. & B.* ***Hill***, summit of Iona, 1km N of Baile Mòr. Height 328 feet or 100 metres. **28 B2** NM2825.
Dun Law *Sc.Bord.* ***Mountain***, on NW flank of Mount Main, 2m/3km E of Dewar. Height 1542 feet or 470 metres. **26 A5** NT3748.
Dun Law *Sc.Bord.* ***Mountain***, 3m/4km SE of Fala. Height 1292 feet or 394 metres. **26 B4** NT4657.
Dun Law *S.Lan.* ***Mountain***, in Lowther Hills, 2m/4km SE of Leadhills. Height 2214 feet or 675 metres. NS9113.
Dun Leacainn *Arg. & B.* ***Mountain***, on N shore of Loch Fyne, 1m/2km NE of Furnace. Height 1178 feet or 359 metres. **30 C4** NN0301.
Dùn-Mòr *Arg. & B.* ***Hill***, rising to over 80 metres on W coast of Seil, to N of Ellanbeich. **29 G3** NM7417.
Dùn Mòr Vaul *Arg. & B.* ***Historic/prehistoric site***, excavated broch of 1c-3c, on N coast of Tiree to NW of Vaul. NM0449.
Dun Rig *E.Ayr.* ***Hill***, above Greenock Water on SW slopes of Meanlour Hill. Height 836 feet or 255 metres. **15 E3** NS6329.
Dun Rig *Sc.Bord.* ***Mountain***, 6m/9km S of Peebles. Height 2437 feet or 743 metres. **17 D2** NT2531.
Dunach *Arg. & B.* ***Settlement***, on N shore of Loch Feochan, 1m/2km SW of Kilmore. **30 A2** NM8624.
Dunadd *Arg. & B.* ***Historic/prehistoric site***, ancient fort (Historic Scotland) of 6c in Argyll 4m/6km N of Lochgilphead. **30 A5** NR8393.
Dunagoil *Arg. & B.* ***Historic/prehistoric site***, remains of Iron Age fort on SW coast of Bute, 1m/2km NW of Garroch Head. NS0853.
Dunagoil Bay *Arg. & B.* ***Bay***, on SW coast of Bute, to N of Dunagoil. **22 B4** NS0853.
Dunalastair *P. & K.* ***Settlement***, just E of Dunalastair Water, 3m/5km W of Tummel Bridge. **40 C4** NN7159.
Dunalastair Water *P. & K.* ***Reservoir***, in course of River Tummel below Kinloch Rannoch. **40 C4** NN6958.
Dunan *Arg. & B.* ***Locality***, in Argyll, on W shore of Firth of Clyde, adjoining to NE of Innellan. **22 C2** NS1570.
Dunan *High.* ***Settlement***, 1m/2km E of Luib, on W shore of Loch na Cairidh, opposite Scalpay. **48 B2** NG5827.
Dunan Liath *High.* ***Mountain***, in Sutherland district, 14m/23km N of Garve. Height 2266 feet or 691 metres. **60 D1** NH4184.
Dùnan Ruadh *W.Isles* ***Historic/prehistoric site***, site of ancient burial-chambers on W coast of Fuday, off Barra. NF7208.
Dunans *Arg. & B.* ***Settlement***, 6m/9km NE of Clachan of Glendaruel. **30 C5** NS0491.
Dunbar *E.Loth.* Population: 6518. ***Small town***, coastal resort with small harbour, 27m/43km E of Edinburgh. Scant remains of castle on headland. 2m/3km S is site of battle of 1296 in which English defeated Scots. 2m/3km SE is site of battle of 1650 in which Cromwell defeated supporters of Charles II under Leslie. **27 D2** NT6878.
Dunbar Common *E.Loth.* ***Open space***, moorland on N side of Lammermuir Hills, 3m/4km SE of Garvald. **26 D3** NT6369.
Dunbeath *High.* ***Village***, on E coast of Caithness district, 18m/29km SW of Wick, at mouth of Dunbeath Water. Clifftop castle 1m/2km S. **73 G2** ND1629.
Dunbeath Bay *High.* ***Bay***, on E coast of Caithness district, to SE of Dunbeath. **73 G2** ND1629.
Dunbeath Castle *High.* ***Castle***, in Dunbeath, 15c with 17c additions. **73 G2** ND1529.
Dunbeath Heritage Centre *High.* ***Other feature of interest***, on E coast, 1km NE of Dunbeath. Details the life of novelist, Neil Gunn, who was born in Dunbeath. **77 D5** ND1730.
Dunbeath Water *High.* ***River***, rising 11m/17km W of Dunbeath and flowing into sea on E coast of Caithness at Dunbeath. **76 C5** ND1629.
Dunbeg *Arg. & B.* ***Village***, on Dunstaffnage Bay, 2m/3km W of Connel, Argyll. **30 A1** NM8733.
Dunblane *Stir.* Population: 7368. ***City***, ancient cathedral city on Allan Water 5m/8km N of Stirling. 13c cathedral. Site of Roman camp to SW. **32 C4** NN7801.
Dunblane Cathedral *Stir.* ***Ecclesiastical building***, dating mainly from 13c, but incorporating 12c tower. In centre of Dunblane, 5m/8km N of Stirling. **32 C4** NN7701.
Dunbog *Fife* ***Village***, 3m/5km E of Newburgh. **34 A3** NO2818.
Duncangill Head *S.Lan.* ***Mountain***, one of three summits rising to over 560 metres on upland plateau, 5m/8km E of Abington. **16 B3** NT0025.
Duncansby *High.* ***Locality***, in NE corner of Caithness district. Duncansby Head is headland to NE, Stacks of Duncansby are group of rocks off coast to E and Ness of Duncansby is headland to N. ND3872.
Duncansby Head *High.* ***Coastal feature***, headland with lighthouse, nearly 2m/3km E of John o' Groats. **77 G1** ND3872.
Duncanston *Aber.* ***Village***, 4m/6km W of Insch. **54 A2** NJ5726.
Duncanston *High.* ***Settlement***, 2m/3km SW of Culbokie, on Black Isle, Ross and Cromarty district. **61 E4** NH5856.
Duncolm *W.Dun.* ***Mountain***, summit of Kilpatrick Hills, 5m/8km E of Dumbarton. Height 1315 feet or 401 metres. NS4777.
Duncow *D. & G.* ***Hamlet***, 3m/4km NW of Locharbriggs. **9 D2** NX9683.
Duncow Burn *D. & G.* ***River***, rising on White Hill and flowing generally S to join River Nith 1m/2km W of Locharbriggs. **9 D2** NX9680.
Duncraggan *Stir.* ***Settlement***, 3m/5km N of Aberfoyle. **32 A4** NN5306.
Duncraig Castle College *High.* ***Educational establishment***, school of domestic science in Skye and Lochalsh district, 1km E of Plockton across bay. NG8133.
Duncrievie *P. & K.* ***Village***, 3m/5km N of Milnathort. **33 G4** NO1309.

D

Duncroist *Stir.* ***Settlement***, in Glen Lochay, 3m/5km NW of Killin. **32 A1** NN5336.

Duncrub *P. & K.* ***Hamlet***, 1km NW of Dunning. **33 F3** NO0014.

Duncryne *W.Dun.* ***Locality***, comprises Duncryne Hill and High Duncryne settlement, 1km SE of Gartocharn. **23 F1** NS4385.

Dundarave Point *Arg. & B.* ***Coastal feature***, headland on N shore of Loch Fyne, 3m/5km NE of Inveraray. **30 D4** NN1308.

Dundarg Castle *Aber.* ***Castle***, ruined 13c castle on site of an Iron Age fort on Aberdour Bay. On N coast, 3m/5km SW of Rosehearty. NJ8964.

Dundas Castle *Edin.* ***Historic house***, large 19c mansion with 15c tower adjoining, 1km S of Forth Road Bridge. NT1176.

Dundee *Dundee* Population: 158,981. ***City***, Scotland's fourth largest city, commercial and industrial centre and port, 18m/29km E of Perth on N side of Firth of Tay, crossed here by a 1m/2km road bridge and a 2m/3km railway bridge. Robert the Bruce declared King of the Scots in Dundee in 1309. Sustained severe damage during Civil War and again prior to Jacobite uprising. City recovered in early 19c and became Britain's main processor of jute. One of largest employers in Dundee today is D.C. Thomson, publisher of The Beano and The Dandy. Many museums and art galleries. Cultural centre, occasionally playing host to overflow from Edinburgh Festival. Episcopal cathedral on site of former castle. Universities. Ship 'Discovery' in which Captain Cook travelled to Antarctic has returned to Victoria dock, where she was built. **34 C1** NO4030.

Dundee Airport *Dundee* ***Airport/airfield***, alongside Firth of Tay, 2m/3km W of Dundee city centre. **34 B2** NO3729.

Dundee Law *Dundee* ***Hill***, 1km NW of Dundee city centre. Bears war memorial. Height 571 feet or 174 metres. NO3931.

Dundonald *S.Ayr.* Population: 2403. ***Village***, 4m/6km NE of Troon. **14 B2** NS3634.

Dundonald Castle *S.Ayr.* ***Castle***, remains of castle (Historic Scotland), mainly 13c, built by Walter Stewart, 5m/8km SW of Kilmarnock. **14 B2** NS3634.

Dundonnell *High.* ***River***, in W part of Ross and Cromarty district, running N through Dundonnell Forest to head of Little Loch Broom. **60 A1** NH0888.

Dundonnell *High.* ***Settlement***, at head of Little Loch Broom, 4m/7km NE of Ullapool across Loch Broom. **59 G1** NH0887.

Dundonnell Forest *High.* ***Open space***, deer forest in W part of Ross and Cromarty district, between Strath na Sealga and Strath More, 8m/13km S of Ullapool. **59 G1** NH1181.

Dundonnell House *High.* ***Garden***, formal garden with aviary and fine collection of bonsai surrounding house by Dundonnell River, 2m/3km SE of Dundonnell. **60 A1** NH1086.

Dundreggan *High.* ***Settlement***, in Glen Moriston, Inverness district, 7m/11km W of Invermoriston. **50 C3** NH3114.

Dundreggan Forest *High.* ***Open space***, deer forest to NE of Dundreggan. **50 C3** NH3114.

Dundreich *Sc.Bord.* ***Mountain***, on Moorfoot range, 2m/4km NE of Eddleston. Height 2040 feet or 622 metres. NT2749.

Dundrennan *D. & G.* ***Village***, 5m/7km SE of Kirkcudbright. Ruined 12c abbey (Historic Scotland). **4 A2** NX7447.

Dundrennan Abbey *D. & G.* ***Ecclesiastical building***, substantial Cistercian ruin (Historic Scotland), founded by David I in 1142 at Dundrennan. Mary, Queen of Scots, spent her last night in Scotland here in 1568. **4 A2** NX7447.

Dunduff Castle *S.Ayr.* ***Castle***, ruins of old baronial fortress 1m/2km E of Dunure. **14 A4** NS2716.

Dunearn *Fife* ***Settlement***, 2m/3km NW of Burntisland. **25 G1** NT2187.

Duneaton Water *S.Lan.* ***River***, rising on slopes of Cairn Table and running E to River Clyde 2m/3km N of Abington. **15 G3** NS9326.

Dunecht *Aber.* ***Village***, 2m/4km N of Echt. **54 C4** NJ7509.

Dunfallandy Stone *P. & K.* ***Historic/prehistoric site***, Pictish sculptured stone (Historic Scotland) with a cross on one face and sculptured figures on both faces. Originally near Killiecrankie, it is now situated 1m/2km S of Pitlochry. **41 E4** NN9456.

Dunfermline *Fife* Population: 55,083. ***Town***, historic town 13m/20km NW of Edinburgh across Firth of Forth. Residence of Scottish kings; burial place of several, including Robert the Bruce. Scottish capital until 1603. Birthplace of Charles I in 1600. Birthplace of Andrew Carnegie, 1835. Abbey and palace (Historic Scotland). **25 E1** NT0987.

Dunfermline Abbey *Fife* ***Ecclesiastical building***, late 11c Benedictine abbey (Historic Scotland) founded by Queen Margaret at Dunfermline. Burial place of Robert the Bruce. **25 E1** NT0887.

Dungavel *S.Lan.* ***Other building***, HM prison 5m/8km SW of Strathaven. **15 E2** NS6537.

Dungavel Hill *S.Lan.* ***Mountain***, 1m/2km N of Roberton. Height 1673 feet or 510 metres. **16 A2** NS9430.

Dunglas *E.Loth.* ***Settlement***, near coast 7m/11km SE of Dunbar. Collegiate church (Historic Scotland), dating from 15c, has vaulted nave, choir and transepts, all with stone slab roofs. **27 E2** NT7671.

Dunglass *Stir.* ***Hill***, outcrop of volcanic rock, including columnar basalt, 1m/2km E of Strathblane. Height 502 feet or 153 metres. NS5778.

Dunglass Burn *River*, rising in Lammermuir Hills and flowing E to North Sea, 1m/2km N of Cockburnspath. Forms boundary between East Lothian and Scottish Borders. NT7772.

Dunglass Castle *E.Loth.* ***Castle***, 15c L-plan tower house on site of castle on coast, above Bilsdean Creek, 7m/11km SE of Dunbar. NT7671.

Dunglass Point *W.Dun.* ***Coastal feature***, headland on N bank of River Clyde at W end of Bowling and 3m/4km E of Dumbarton. Ruins of old castle. NS4373.

Dunino *Fife* ***Village***, 4m/6km SE of St. Andrews. Site of Roman camp 2km NE. **34 D3** NO5311.

Dunion Hill *Sc.Bord.* ***Mountain***, 1m/2km SW of Jedburgh. Height 1082 feet or 330 metres. **18 A5** NT6218.

Dunipace *Falk.* Population: 2420. ***Small town***, adjoining to NW of Denny across River Carron, 6m/9km W of Falkirk. **24 C1** NS8083.

Dunira *P. & K.* ***Settlement***, 3m/4km NW of Comrie. **32 C2** NN7323.

Dunkeld *P. & K.* ***City***, ancient cathedral city on River Tay, 10m/15km W of Blairgowrie. Dunkeld Cathedral, partly ruined, dates from 12c, though mainly from 14c-15c. Houses (National Trust for Scotland) near cathedral, late 17c, restored. Stanley Hill (National Trust for Scotland), wooded hill to W. **41 F5** NO0242.

Dunkeld and Birnam Station *P. & K.* ***Other building***, railway station at Birnam, S of River Tay from Dunkeld. **41 F5** NO0341.

Dunkeld Cathedral *P. & K.* ***Ecclesiastical building***, next to River Tay at Dunkeld, in particularly attractive setting. Part is ruined, but choir has been restored and is in use as parish church (Historic Scotland). Dates partly from 12c, but nave and NW tower are 15c. **41 F5** NO0242.

Dunlappie *Angus* ***Hamlet***, 1m/2km SW of Edzell. **43 D3** NO5867.

Dunlop *E.Ayr.* ***Village***, 2m/4km N of Stewarton. Gives name to local cheese. **23 F5** NS4049.

Dunloskin *Arg. & B.* ***Settlement***, 1m/2km NW of Dunoon. **22 C2** NS1678.

Dunman *D. & G.* ***Hill***, 3m/5km SW of Drummore. Fort on SW slope. Height 525 feet or 160 metres. **2 B3** NX1033.

Dunmore *Arg. & B.* ***Settlement***, on NW side of West Loch Tarbert, 6m/10km SW of Tarbert. **21 F3** NR7961.

Dunmore *Falk.* ***Settlement***, on W bank of River Forth, 1m/2km N of Airth. **24 C1** NS8989.

Dunn *High.* ***Settlement***, 3m/5km W of Watten. **77 D3** ND1955.

Dunnabie *D. & G.* ***Settlement***, 2m/3km SE of Paddockhole. **9 G2** NY2581.

Dunnet *High.* ***Village***, on Dunnet Bay, N coast of Caithness district, 7m/11km E of Thurso. **77 E1** ND2271.

Dunnet Bay *High.* ***Bay***, on N coast of Caithness district, 7m/11km E of Thurso. **77 D1** ND2271.

Dunnet Head *High.* ***Coastal feature***, promontory on N coast of Caithness district, to N of Dunnet, culminating in headland of Easter Head. **77 D1** ND2271.

Dunnet Hill *High.* ***Hill***, 2m/3km SW of Dunnet Head on N coast. Height 397 feet or 121 metres. **77 D1** ND1973.

Dunnichen *Angus* ***Village***, 4m/6km E of Forfar. To E, site of Battle of Dunnichen (or Nechtansmere), 685, in which Picts defeated Angles. **42 D5** NO5048.

Dunning *P. & K.* ***Village***, 5m/8km E of Auchterarder. St. Serf's Church (Historic Scotland) has square Romanesque tower and tower arch, with remainder of church dating from 1810. **33 F3** NO0114.

Dunnottar *Aber.* ***Locality***, 1m/2km S of Stonehaven. NO8783.

Dunnottar Castle *Aber.* ***Castle***, on rock on coast to E of Dunnottar, dating in part from late 14c. **43 G1** NO8783.

Dunollie Castle *Arg. & B.* ***Castle***, partly ruined 12c-15c castle on coast, 1m/2km N of Oban. Ancient stronghold of MacDougalls, it is owned by Chief of Clan MacDougall. **30 A1** NM8531.

Dunoon *Arg. & B.* Population: 9038. ***Small town***, and resort in Argyll, 4m/7km W of Gourock across Firth of Clyde. Ferry services for vehicles and pedestrians to Gourock and Wemyss Bay. Traces of medieval castle on conical rock above pier. **22 C2** NS1776.

Dunphail *Moray* ***Locality***, comprising house and castle on E bank of River Divie, 7m/11km S of Forres. NJ0047.

Dunragit *D. & G.* ***Village***, 3m/5km W of Glenluce. **6 C5** NX1557.

Dunragit Moor *D. & G.* ***Open space***, afforested area 1m/2km N of Dunragit and 6m/9km E of Stranraer. **6 C5** NX1559.

Dunrobin Castle *High.* ***Castle***, seat of Sutherland family on E coast of Sutherland district, 1m/2km NE of Golspie. **73 D4** NC8500.

Dunrobin Castle Station *High.* ***Other building***, private railway station for Dunrobin Castle, 2m/3km NE of Golspie. **72 D4** NC8401.

Dunrobin Glen *High.* ***Valley***, carrying Golspie Burn, 3m/5km NW of Golspie. **72 D4** NC8003.

Dunrossness *Shet.* ***Locality***, district on Mainland, in parish of same name, 5m/8km N of Sumburgh Head. HU3915.

Dunrostan *Arg. & B.* ***Settlement***, on SE side of Loch Sween, 5m/7km SW of Achnamara. **21 F1** NR7380.

Dunruchan Hill *P. & K.* ***Hill***, 4m/12km SE of Comrie. Height 997 feet or 304 metres. **32 C3** NN7916.

Duns *Sc.Bord.* Population: 2444. ***Small town***, market town, 13m/21km W of Berwick-upon-Tweed. Nearby Manderston House notable for azalea and rhododendron garden. **27 E4** NT7853.

Duns Castle *Sc.Bord.* ***Historic house***, 19c mansion to NW of Duns. **27 E4** NT7853.

Dun's Dish *Angus* ***Lake/loch***, small loch 3m/5km E of Brechin. **43 E3** NO6460.

Duns Law *Sc.Bord.* ***Hill***, to N of Duns, surmounted by earthworks of ancient fort and by Covenanters' Stone, which commemorates encampment of Covenanters' army here in 1639. Height 715 feet or 218 metres. NT7854.

Dunscaith Castle *High.* ***Castle***, ruined castle of the Barons of Sleat, on S side of entrance to Loch Eishort, Skye. **48 C3** NG5912.

Dunscore *D. & G.* ***Village***, 8m/13km NW of Dumfries. **8 C2** NX8684.

Dunshelt *Fife* ***Village***, 2m/3km N of Falkland. **34 A3** NO2410.

Dunshillock *Aber.* ***Locality***, 1m/2km W of Mintlaw. NJ9848.

Dunside Reservoirs *S.Lan.* ***Reservoir***, pair of small reservoirs 5m/7km SW of Lesmahagow. NS7437.

Dunsinane Hill *P. & K.* ***Hill***, rising to over 300 metres in Sidlaw range, 8m/12km NE of Perth. Surmounted by ancient fort identified by Shakespeare with castle of Macbeth. NO2131.

Dunsinnan *P. & K.* ***Settlement***, with adjoining parkland, 3m/5km SW of Burrelton. **33 G1** NO1632.

Dunskeig Bay *Arg. & B.* ***Bay***, on W coast of Kintyre, Argyll, 1m/2km W of Clachan. NR7556.

Dunskey Burn *D. & G.* ***River***, flowing SW into Port Kale, 1km NW of Portpatrick. **6 B5** NW9955.

Dunskey Castle *D. & G.* ***Castle***, ruined early 16c castle on coast of Rinns of Galloway, 1km S of Portpatrick. **6 B5** NX0053.

Dunslair Heights *Sc.Bord.* ***Mountain***, 3m/5km NE of Peebles. Height 1975 feet or 602 metres. **25 G5** NT2843.

Dunstaffnage Bay *Arg. & B.* ***Bay***, N facing bay, 2m/3km W of Connel, Argyll. NM8834.

Dunstaffnage Castle *Arg. & B.* ***Castle***, remains of 13c castle (Historic Scotland) on W side of Dunstaffnage Bay. Ruins of chapel (Historic Scotland) to SW. **30 A1** NM8834.

Dunsyre *S.Lan.* ***Village***, 6m/9km E of Carnwath. **25 E5** NT0748.

Duntarvie Castle *W.Loth.* ***Castle***, ruined castle 1m/2km N of Winchburgh. NT0976.

Duntocher *W.Dun.* Population: 7882. ***Small town***, on line of Antonine Wall, 2m/3km N of Clydebank. Site of Roman fort to E. **23 F2** NS4972.

Duntreath Castle *Stir.* ***Castle***, remains of castle, partly 15c, 2m/3km NW of Strathblane. NS5381.

Duntrune Castle *Arg. & B.* ***Castle***, modernised castle in Argyll on N shore of Crinan Loch. Formerly stronghold of the Campbells, dating from 13c. **29 G5** NR7995.

Duntulm *High.* ***Settlement***, near N coast of Skye, 7m/11km N of Uig. **58 A2** NG4174.

Duntulm Bay *High.* ***Bay***, to NW of Duntulm, Skye. **57 G2** NG4174.

Duntulm Castle *High.* ***Castle***, ancient castle restored 1911, a S end of Duntulm Bay, Skye. **58 A2** NG4174.

Dunure *S.Ayr.* ***Village***, on coast, 5m/8km NW of Maybole. Fragment of old castle. **14 A4** NS2515.

Dunure Castle *S.Ayr.* ***Castle***, on rocky cliff to W of Dunure. 13c tower castle with vaulted basement and 15c additions; now in ruins. **14 A4** NS2415.

Dunure Mains *S.Ayr.* ***Settlement***, 1km S of Dunure. **14 A4** NS2514.

Dunvegan *High.* ***Village***, at head of Loch Dunvegan on NW coast of Skye. **57 F5** NG2547.

Dunvegan Castle *High.* ***Castle***, ancient stronghold of the Macleods, 1m/2km N of Dunvegan, Skye. **57 F5** NG2547.

Dunvegan Head *High.* ***Coastal feature***, headland on W side of entrance to Loch Dunvegan, Skye. **57 E4** NG1756.

Dunviden Lochs *High.* ***Lake/loch***, two small lochs in course of Achanellan Burn, which flows into River Naver, Caithness district. **75 G3** NC7451.
Dunwan Dam *E.Renf.* ***Reservoir***, 2m/3km SW of Eaglesham. **23 G5** NS5549.
Dupplin Castle *P. & K.* ***Historic house***, mansion of 1832, 5m/7km SW of Perth. Stone cross to SW marks site of battle of 1332 in which Balliol defeated Mar. NO0519.
Dupplin Lake *P. & K.* ***Lake/loch***, small lake 2m/3km E of Findo Gask and 6m/9km W of Perth. **33 F2** NO0320.
Dura *Fife* ***Settlement***, on W side of Ceres Burn, 3m/4km E of Cupar. **34 C3** NO4114.
Durinemast *High.* ***Settlement***, in Morvern, Lochaber district, on N shore of Loch Arienas. **37 F4** NM6752.
Durisdeer *D. & G.* ***Village***, 5m/9km N of Thornhill. Sites of Roman camps to S. **15 G5** NS8903.
Durisdeermill *D. & G.* ***Settlement***, 1km W of Durisdeer. NS8804.
Durn Hill *Aber.* ***Hill***, 1km E of Fordyce, and 2m/3km SW of Portsoy. Height 653 feet or 199 metres. **64 A3** NJ5763.
Durnamuck *High.* ***Village***, on SW side of Little Loch Broom, W coast of Ross and Cromarty district. **70 C5** NH0192.
Durness *High.* ***Village***, near N coast of Sutherland district, 3m/4km S of Far Out Head. Smoo Cave 1m/2km SE. **74 C2** NC4067.
Durness Old Church *High.* ***Ecclesiastical building***, in Balnakeil, situated on S side of Balnakeil Bay. Attractive, but ruined site of church built in 1619. **74 C2** NC3968.
Durno *Aber.* ***Hamlet***, 6m/9km NW of Inverurie. **54 C2** NJ7128.
Duror ***River***, running W into Cuil Bay on E shore of Loch Linnhe. NM9754.
Duror *High.* ***Settlement***, on N bank of River Duror, 1km E of Cuil Bay. **38 B4** NM9854.
Durran *Arg. & B.* ***Settlement***, 3m/5km S of Dalavich, on SE shore of Loch Awe. **30 B4** NM9507.
Durran *High.* ***Locality***, 3m/4km S of Castletown. **77 D2** ND1964.
Durris Forest *Aber.* ***Forest/woodland***, 6m/9km E of Banchory across River Dee. Mast. **54 C5** NO7892.
Dury *Shet.* ***Settlement***, 1km W of Laxfirth, Mainland. **83 D1** HU4560.
Dury Voe *Shet.* ***Sea feature***, large inlet on E coast of Mainland opposite Whalsay. **83 D1** HU4762.
Dusk Water *N.Ayr.* ***River***, flowing SW from Lochlands Hill to join River Garnock 2m/3km N of Kilwinning. **23 E5** NS2946.
Duslic *High.* ***Island***, small rock island 1km NE of Cape Wrath. **74 B1** NC2675.
Dutchman's Cap *Arg. & B.* *Alternative name for Bac Mòr, qv.*
Duthie Park and Winter Gardens *Aberdeen* ***Garden***, 50-acre park with boating lake by River Dee, 1m/2km S of Aberdeen city centre. Park contains Winter Gardens covering 2 acres, with exotic plants and birds; also cactus house. **55 E4** NJ9304.
Duthil *High.* ***Village***, in Badenoch and Strathspey district, 2m/3km E of Carrbridge. **52 B2** NH9324.
Duthil Burn *High.* ***River***, flowing S from S slopes of Carn Allt Laoigh into River Dulnain, 1m/2km E of Carrbridge. **52 B2** NH9223.
Dwarfie Stane *Ork.* ***Historic/prehistoric site***, Neolithic communal burial-chamber (Historic Scotland) cut into huge block of sandstone on Hoy, 3m/5km E of Rackwick. **78 B2** HY2400.
Dwarwick Head *High.* ***Coastal feature***, headland on N side of Dunnet Bay. **77 D1** ND2071.
Dyce *Aberdeen* Population: 6359. ***Village***, 5m/9km NW of Aberdeen. Aberdeen (Dyce) Airport on W side of village. **55 D3** NJ8812.
Dyce Airport *Aberdeen* *Former name of Aberdeen Airport, qv.*
Dyce Symbol Stones *Aberdeen* ***Historic/prehistoric site***, two Pictish symbol stones (Historic Scotland) located in ruined Dyce Old Kirk, 2m/3km N of Dyce. **55 D3** NJ8715.
Dye Water ***River***, rising on Lammermuir Hills and running E to Whiteadder Water 2m/4km SE of Cranshaws. **26 D4** NT7159.
Dyke *High.* ***River***, running NE into River Halladale 8m/13km S of Melvich. **76 A4** NC8952.
Dyke *Moray* ***Village***, 6m/10km E of Nairn and 3m/5km W of Forres. **62 B4** NJ9858.
Dykehead *Angus* ***Village***, near foot of Glen Clova, 4m/6km N of Kirriemuir. **42 B3** NO3860.
Dykehead *N.Lan.* ***Locality***, 5m/9km NE of Wishaw. **24 C4** NS8759.
Dykehead *Stir.* ***Settlement***, 3m/4km S of Port of Menteith. **32 A5** NS5997.
Dykelands *Aber.* ***Hamlet***, 2m/3km NE of Marykirk. **43 F3** NO7068.
Dykends *Angus* ***Settlement***, 1m/2km SE of Bellaty. **42 A4** NO2557.
Dykeside *Aber.* ***Settlement***, 4m/6km S of Turriff. **64 C5** NJ7243.
Dysart *Fife* ***Locality***, on Firth of Forth, adjoining to NE of Kirkcaldy. **34 B5** NT3093.

E

Eabost *High.* ***Settlement***, on E side of Loch Bracadale, 2m/3km W of Bracadale, Skye. NG3139.
Eachaig *Arg. & B.* ***River***, in Argyll running S through Loch Eck to head of Holy Loch. NS1582.
Eachkamish (Gaelic form: Eachcamais.) *W.Isles* ***Coastal feature***, peninsula on S part of Baleshare, with sand dunes. **45 F3** NF7860.
Eadar dha Fhadhail (Anglicised form: Ardroil.) *W.Isles* ***Settlement***, at head of Camas Uig bay, 4m/7km S of Gallan Head, Isle of Lewis. **68 B4** NB0432.
Eag na Maoile *Arg. & B.* ***Island***, group of islets lying nearly 1m/2km off NE end of Coll. **36 B3** NM2765.
Eagle Rock (Hunters Craig). *Edin.* ***Historic/prehistoric site***, on S coast of Firth of Forth, 1m/2km NE of Cramond Bridge. Worn sculpture (Historic Scotland) once thought to have been an eagle, now thought to be a statue of Mercury. **25 F2** NT1877.
Eaglesfield *D. & G.* ***Village***, 3m/5km E of Ecclefechan. **9 G3** NY2374.
Eaglesham *E.Renf.* Population: 3382. ***Village***, 4m/7km SW of East Kilbride. **23 G4** NS5751.
Earadale Point *Arg. & B.* ***Coastal feature***, headland on W coast of Kintyre, 4m/6km SW of Machrihanish. **12 A4** NR5917.
Earlish *High.* ***Settlement***, 1m/2km S of Uig, Skye. **57 G3** NG3861.
Earl's Burn *Stir.* ***River***, rising on Gargunnock Hills and flowing SE through Earlsburn Reservoirs to join River Carron 1km W of Carron Bridge. **24 B1** NS7283.
Earl's Hill *Stir.* ***Mountain***, with mast at summit, 6m/9km SW of Stirling. Height 1446 feet or 441 metres. **24 B1** NS7188.
Earl's Palace *Ork.* ***Historic/prehistoric site***, impressive remains of 16c courtyard palace of Earls of Orkney (Historic Scotland) situated at Birsay on Brough Head, NW Mainland. **80 A4** HY2428.
Earl's Seat *E.Dun.* ***Mountain***, summit of Campsie Fells on border with Stirling, 3m/5km SE of Killearn. Height 1896 feet or 578 metres. **23 G1** NS5683.
Earlsburn Reservoirs *Stir.* ***Reservoir***, two small reservoirs 7m/11km SW of Stirling. **24 A1** NS7089.
Earlsferry *Fife* ***Town***, and resort on Firth of Forth, adjoining to W of Elie. **34 C4** NT4889.
Earlsford *Aber.* ***Settlement***, 5m/8km SE of Fyvie. **54 D1** NJ8334.
Earlshall Castle *Fife* ***Castle***, 16c Z-plan castle to E of Leuchars, restored by Sir Robert Lorimer. Grounds are noted for topiary. **34 C2** NO4621.
Earlston *Sc.Bord.* Population: 1629. ***Small town***, in Lauderdale 4m/6km NE of Melrose. **17 G2** NT5738.
Earlstoun Castle *D. & G.* ***Castle***, to E of head of Earstoun Loch, is ruined seat of the Gordons. NX6184.
Earlstoun Loch *D. & G.* ***Lake/loch***, loch and reservoir 1m/2km N of St. John's Town of Dalry. **8 A2** NX6183.
Earn *P. & K.* ***River***, flowing E from Loch Earn down Strath Earn to River Tay 6m/10km SE of Perth. **33 F3** NO1918.
Earn Water *E.Renf.* ***River***, flowing NE to join White Cart Water at Waterfoot, 2m/3km N of Eaglesham. **23 G4** NS5654.
Earncraig Hill *S.Lan.* ***Mountain***, in Lowther Hills on border with Dumfries & Galloway, 7m/11km W of Beattock. Height 2001 feet or 610 metres. **16 A5** NS9701.
Earnscleugh Water *Sc.Bord.* ***River***, rising in Lammermuir Hills and flowing SW to join Leader Water to NE of Lauder. **26 C4** NT5348.
Earnsheugh Bay *Aber.* ***Bay***, small bay 1m/2km NE of Portlethen. **55 E5** NO9498.
Earsairidh (Anglicised form: Ersary.) *W.Isles* ***Village***, on E coast of Barra, 3m/5km E of Castlebay. **44 C4** NL7099.
Earshader (Gaelic form: Iarsiadar.) *W.Isles* ***Settlement***, on W side of Isle of Lewis, on S side of bridge connecting Great Bernera with main island. NB1633.
Earshaw Hill *D. & G.* ***Open space***, hillslope 1m/2km SW of Langholm. **10 B3** NY3482.
Eas a' Chùal Aluinn (Also known as Eas Caul Aulin.) *High.* ***Waterfall***, 1m/2km SE of head of Loch Glencoul. Height 658 feet or 201 metres; highest in Britain. **71 E2** NC2827.
Eas Caul Aulin *High.* *Alternative name for Eas a' Chùal Aluinn, qv.*
Eas Daimh *P. & K.* ***River***, flowing E into Loch an Daimh, 8m/12km W of Bridge of Balgie. **39 G5** NN4546.
Eas Fors *Arg. & B.* ***Waterfall***, 1m/2km NW of Laggan Bay, in course of Allt an Eas Fors on N side of Loch Tuath, W coast of Mull. NM4442.
Eas Mòr *N.Ayr.* ***Waterfall***, on Arran, 1m/2km NW of Kildonan Castle. NS0222.
Eas nam Meirleach (Also known as The Robbers' Waterfall). *High.* ***Waterfall***, in course of Allt Mheuran, Lochaber district, 2m/3km E of head of Loch Etive. NN1444.
Easaval *W.Isles* ***Hill***, rising to over 240 metres, 1m/2km N of Ludag, near S coast of South Uist. **44 C2** NF7715.
Eascairt *Arg. & B.* ***Settlement***, on Kintyre, 3m/4km SW of Claonaig. **21 G4** NR8453.
Easdale *Arg. & B.* ***Island***, small island off W coast of Seil. Former slate quarries. Ferry to Seil across narrow Easdale Sound. **29 G3** NM7317.
Easdale *Arg. & B.* ***Settlement***, on W coast of Seil, opposite Easdale island. **29 G3** NM7417.
Easdale Folk Museum *Arg. & B.* ***Other feature of interest***, local history museum on Easdale, off W coast of Seil, displaying photographs and artefacts from local area, especially in relation to former quarrying industry. **29 G3** NM7316.
Easdale Sound *Arg. & B.* ***Sea feature***, narrow channel between Easdale and Seil. NM7317.
Eassie and Nevay *Angus* ***Village***, 4m/6km W of Glamis. **42 B5** NO3345.
Eassie Sculptured Stone *Angus* ***Historic/prehistoric site***, good example of elaborately carved early Christian monument (Historic Scotland) with Celtic cross on one side and Pictish symbols on reverse, 7m/11km W of Forfar. **42 B5** NO3447.
East Aquhorthies *Aber.* *Alternative name for Easter Aquhorthies, qv.*
East Auchronie *Aber.* ***Settlement***, 2m/3km N of Westhill. **54 D4** NJ8109.
East Brora *High.* ***Settlement***, 1km W of Brora, Sutherland district. **73 D4** NC8904.
East Burra *Shet.* ***Island***, one of two long, narrow, adjacent islands S of Scalloway, Mainland, to S of Trondra. Connected to West Burra by a road bridge. **82 C4** HU3832.
East Burra Firth *Shet.* ***Sea feature***, inlet on E side of Aith Voe, Mainland. HU3557.
East Burrafirth *Shet.* ***Settlement***, at head of East Burra Firth inlet, 4m/6km SW of Voe. **82 C2** HU3657.
East Cairn Hill *W.Loth.* ***Mountain***, in Pentland Hills, 3m/5km NW of Carlops. Height 1840 feet or 561 metres. **25 F4** NT1159.
East Cairnbeg *Aber.* ***Hamlet***, 2m/3km SW of Auchenblae. **43 F2** NO7076.
East Calder *W.Loth.* Population: 8692. ***Village***, 2m/3km E of Livingston. **25 E3** NT0867.
East Clyne *High.* ***Hamlet***, in Sutherland district, 1m/2km N of Brora. NC9006.
East Clyth *High.* ***Settlement***, 1m/2km NE of Mid Clyth. **77 E5** ND2939.
East Croachy *High.* ***Hamlet***, part of Croachy locality, in Inverness district, 5m/9km SE of Dores. **51 F2** NH6527.
East Darlochan *Arg. & B.* ***Settlement***, to N of airfield, 4m/6km NW of Campeltown. **12 B3** NR6723.
East Davoch *Aber.* ***Settlement***, 2m/3km NW of Tarland. **53 G4** NJ4607.
East Fortune *E.Loth.* ***Locality***, 4m/6km S of North Berwick. Former airfield now museum of flight. **26 C2** NT5579.
East Fortune Museum of Flight *E.Loth.* ***Other feature of interest***, 4m/6km S of North Berwick, exhibiting over 35 aircraft, including a Spitfire and oldest flying machine in Britain. **26 C2** NT5478.
East Gerinish *W.Isles* ***Locality***, 4m/6km E of Geirninis, South Uist. NF8339.
East Haven *Angus* ***Settlement***, on coast, 2m/3km NE of Carnoustie. **35 D1** NO5836.
East Helmsdale *High.* ***Settlement***, just N of Helmsdale. **73 F3** ND0316.
East Hoevdi *Shet.* ***Coastal feature***, headland on N coast of Foula. **82 B5** HT9541.
East Hogaland *Shet.* ***Settlement***, on Mainland, 1m/2km SW of Ollaberry. HU3579.
East Kame *Shet.* ***Hill***, 4m/6km SE of Voe, Mainland. Height 558 feet or 170 metres. **82 D2** HU4257.
East Kilbride *S.Lan.* Population: 70,422. ***Town***, 7m/11km S of Glasgow. New Town designated 1947. **24 A4** NS6354.
East Kip *Midloth.* ***Mountain***, rising to over 530 metres in Pentland Hills, 1km SW of summit of Scald Law and 3m/5km W of Penicuik. **25 F3** NT1860.
East Langwell *High.* ***Locality***, in Sutherland district, 8m/13km NW of Golspie. **72 C4** NC7206.
East Laroch *High.* *Former name of Ballachulish, qv.*
East Learney *Aber.* ***Settlement***, 1m/2km NE of Torphins. **54 B4** NJ6303.
East Linga *Shet.* ***Island***, small uninhabited island 2m/4km E of Whalsay, 3m/5km S of Skaw Taing. **83 F1** HU6162.
East Linton *E.Loth.* Population: 1422. ***Small town***, on River Tyne 6m/9km W of Dunbar. Nesting for several hundred birds at Phantassie Doocot (National Trust for Scotland), to S. 18c cornmill, in working order, to N at Preston. **26 C2** NT5977.
East Loch Ollay *W.Isles* *See Ollay Lochs.*
East Loch Roag *W.Isles* ***Sea feature***, large inlet on W coast of Isle of Lewis, on E side of Great Bernera. **68 C4** NB1837.
East Loch Tarbert *Arg. & B.* ***Sea feature***, inlet of Loch Fyne at N end of Kintyre, Argyll, running up to Tarbert, for which it provides a harbour. **21 G3** NR8769.

East Loch Tarbert *W.Isles* ***Sea feature***, large inlet between E coast of North and South Harris. Village and port of Tarbert on isthmus between this inlet and West Loch Tarbert. **67 D4** NG1896.

East Lomond *Fife* ***Mountain***, with viewpoint at summit, 4m/6km NW of Glenrothes. Height 1391 feet or 424 metres. **34 A4** NO2406.

East Lunna Voe *Shet.* ***Bay***, on Mainland, E of Lunna and 4m/6km SW of Lunna Ness. HU4868.

East Mains *Aber.* ***Settlement***, 2m/3km NW of Banchory. **54 B5** NO6797.

East March *Angus* ***Settlement***, 1m/2km NW of Kellas. **34 C1** NO4436.

East Mey *High.* ***Settlement***, 2m/3km NE of Mey. **77 F1** ND3073.

East Monar Forest *High.* ***Open space***, deer forest in Ross and Cromarty district N of lower part of Loch Monar. **60 A5** NH1042.

East Morriston *Sc.Bord.* ***Hamlet***, 3m/4km SW of Gordon. NT6041.

East Roisnish (Gaelic form: Roisnis an Ear.) *W.Isles* ***Coastal feature***, headland on NW coast of Eye Peninsula, Isle of Lewis. **69 F4** NB5034.

East Saltoun *E.Loth.* ***Village***, 5m/8km SE of Tranent. **26 B3** NT4767.

East Stocklett *W.Isles* ***Hill***, on South Harris 4m/6km SW of Tarbert. Height 574 feet or 175 metres. **66 D4** NG1195.

East Suisnish *High.* ***Settlement***, on S coast of Raasay, 1m/2km W of Eyre Point. **48 B1** NG5634.

East Tarbert Bay *Arg. & B.* ***Bay***, one of two bays on either side of Gigha, near N end of island. **21 E4** NR6552.

East Tarbet *D. & G.* ***Locality***, on Mull of Galloway, 3m/5km S of Cailiness Point on W side of Luce Bay. **2 B3** NX1431.

East Voe of Quarff *Shet.* ***Bay***, on E coast of Mainland, 1m/2km N of Fladdabister. HU4335.

East Wemyss *Fife* Population: 1762. ***Village***, on Firth of Forth, 5m/8km NE of Kirkcaldy. 14c ruin of Macduff's Castle to E. **34 B5** NT3396.

East Whitburn *W.Loth.* ***Hamlet***, adjoining to E of Whitburn. **25 D3** NS9665.

East Yell *Shet.* ***Locality***, 1km S of Otterswick, Yell. **85 E4** HU5284.

Eastbow Hill *P. & K.* ***Mountain***, 3m/5km S of Auchterarder. Height 1561 feet or 476 metres. **33 E4** NN9407.

Easter Aquhorthies (Also known as East Aquhorthies.) *Aber.* ***Historic/prehistoric site***, site of ancient stone circle (Historic Scotland), 3m/5km W of Inverurie. **54 C2** NJ7320.

Easter Ardross *High.* ***Settlement***, 2m/3km W of Ardross and 3m/5km N of Alness. **61 F2** NH6373.

Easter Balgedie *P. & K.* ***Village***, nearly 1km SE of Wester Balgedie and 3m/5km E of Milnathort. NO1703.

Easter Balloch *Angus* ***Mountain***, 4m/6km W of Glenlee. Height 2736 feet or 834 metres. **42 B1** NO3480.

Easter Balmoral *Aber.* ***Settlement***, on S bank of River Dee, 1m/2km SE of Balmoral Castle. **53 E5** NO2694.

Easter Boleskine *High.* ***Settlement***, 1m/2km NE of Foyers. **51 E2** NH5022.

Easter Borland *Stir.* ***Settlement***, 4m/7km E of Port of Menteith. **32 B4** NN6400.

Easter Brae *High.* ***Settlement***, on Black Isle, 8m/11km NE of Munlochy. **61 F3** NH6663.

Easter Buckieburn *Stir.* ***Settlement***, 6m/9km SW of Stirling. **24 B1** NS7585.

Easter Bush *Midloth.* ***Locality***, location of veterinary field station of Royal (Dick) School of Veterinary Studies, 6m/10km S of Edinburgh. NT2463.

Easter Drummond *High.* ***Settlement***, 4m/6km SE of Invermoriston across Loch Ness. **51 D3** NH4714.

Easter Dullater *Stir.* ***Settlement***, 2m/3km SW of Callander. **32 A4** NN6006.

Easter Elchies *Moray* ***Settlement***, with distillery, 1m/2km W of Craigellachie across River Spey. NJ2744.

Easter Ellister *Arg. & B.* ***Settlement***, on Rinns of Islay, 2m/3km NE of Portnahaven. **20 A4** NR2053.

Easter Fearn *High.* ***Settlement***, 4m/6km SE of Ardgay. **61 F1** NH6486.

Easter Fearn Burn *High.* ***River***, stream running NE into Dornoch Firth at Easter Fearn Point, Ross and Cromarty district. **61 F1** NH6487.

Easter Fearn Point *High.* ***Coastal feature***, low-lying promontory in Ross and Cromarty district, protruding into Dornoch Firth, 4m/6km SE of Ardgay. NH6487.

Easter Galcantray *High.* ***Settlement***, 3m/4km SW of Cawdor. **62 A5** NH8148.

Easter Head *High.* ***Coastal feature***, headland in Caithness district with lighthouse, at N end of Dunnet Head, 4m/6km N of Dunnet. Most northerly point of Scottish mainland. **77 D1** ND2076.

Easter Howgate *Midloth.* ***Settlement***, 3m/5km N of Penicuik. NT2464.

Easter Howlaws *Sc.Bord.* ***Settlement***, 3m/4km SE of Greenlaw. **27 E5** NT7242.

Easter Kinkell *High.* ***Hamlet***, on Black Isle, Ross and Cromarty district, 4m/7km NE of Muir of Ord. **61 E4** NH5755.

Easter Knox *Angus* ***Hamlet***, 3m/5km W of Arbroath. **43 D5** NO5839.

Easter Lednathie *Angus* ***Settlement***, in Glen Prosen, 6m/10km NW of Kirriemuir. **42 B3** NO3363.

Easter Moniack *High.* ***Settlement***, 3m/4km SE of Beauly. **61 E5** NH5544.

Easter Ord *Aber.* ***Settlement***, 1m/2km S of Westhill. **54 D4** NJ8304.

Easter Pencaitland *E.Loth.* ***Village***, to S of Tyne Water, 5m/8km SW of Haddington. NT4468.

Easter Poldar *Stir.* ***Settlement***, on N bank of River Forth, 2m/3km N of Kippen. **32 B5** NS6497.

Easter Quarff *Shet.* ***Village***, on E coast of Mainland at head of East Voe of Quarff Bay, 5m/8km SW of Lerwick. **82 D4** HU4235.

Easter Ross *High.* ***Locality***, large area, mainly upland, extending E from Loch Vaich to E coast between Dornoch Firth and Moray Firth, and making up E part of Ross and Cromarty district. **60 C1** NH4979.

Easter Skeld *Shet.* ***Village***, on Mainland, at head of Skelda Voe, to W of Reawick. **82 C3** HU3144.

Easter Slumbay *High.* ***Locality***, forms Slumbay along with adjoining locality Wester Slumbay, on NW of shore of Loch Carron to SW of Lochcarron, Ross and Cromarty district. NG8939.

Easter Suddie *High.* ***Settlement***, on Black Isle, 1m/2km NE of Munlochy. **61 F4** NH6655.

Easter Tulloch *Aber.* ***Hamlet***, 3m/5km E of Laurencekirk. **43 F2** NO7671.

Easter Whyntie *Aber.* ***Settlement***, 1km S of Boyne Bay, 3m/4km E of Portsoy. **64 B3** NJ6265.

Easterhouse *Glas.* ***Suburb***, 6m/10km E of Glasgow city centre. NS6865.

Eastfield *Fife* ***Locality***, on SE side of Glenrothes. NT2999.

Eastfield *N.Lan.* ***Suburb***, 1m/2km W of Cumbernauld town centre. NS7474.

Eastfield *N.Lan.* ***Village***, 3m/5km W of Whitburn. **24 C3** NS8964.

Easthouses *Midloth.* ***Village***, 1m/2km SE of Dalkeith. **26 A3** NT3465.

Eastriggs *D. & G.* Population: 1943. ***Village***, 3m/5km E of Annan. **9 G4** NY2466.

Eastside *Ork.* ***Settlement***, 2m/3km SE of St. Margaret's Hope, South Ronaldsay. **79 D3** ND4691.

Eastside Heights *Sc.Bord.* ***Mountain***, 3m/5km NE of Colquhar. Height 1945 feet or 593 metres. **26 A5** NT3545.

Eaval *W.Isles* ***Mountain***, at SE end of North Uist and highest point on the island. Height 1138 feet or 347 metres. **45 G3** NF8960.

Eaval *W.Isles* ***River***, in North Harris, rising in Forest of Harris and flowing S, through a succession of lochs, into West Loch Tarbert 1km SE of Abhainnsuidhe. NB0407.

Ecclaw *Sc.Bord.* ***Settlement***, 2m/3km SW of Cockburnspath. **27 E3** NT7568.

Ecclaw Hill *Sc.Bord.* ***Hill***, 1km S of Ecclaw and 3m/4km SW of Cockburnspath. Height 912 feet or 278 metres. **27 E3** NT7567.

Ecclefechan *D. & G.* ***Small town***, 5m/8km N of Annan. Birthplace of Thomas Carlyle, 1795-1881, in house (National Trust for Scotland) in main street. **9 F3** NY1974.

Eccles *Sc.Bord.* ***Village***, 5m/8km W of Coldstream. **27 E5** NT7641.

Ecclesgreig *Aber.* ***Settlement***, 1m/2km NW of St. Cyrus. **43 F3** NO7365.

Ecclesmachan *W.Loth.* ***Village***, 3m/5km N of Livingston. **25 E2** NT0568.

Echnaloch Bay *Ork.* ***Bay***, on NW side of Burray. **79 D3** ND4697.

Echoing Mountain *P. & K.* *See Ben Lawers.*

Echt *Aber.* ***Village***, 12m/20km W of Aberdeen. **54 C4** NJ7305.

Eckford *Sc.Bord.* ***Village***, 5m/8km NE of Jedburgh. **18 B4** NT7026.

Eday *Ork.* ***Island***, 8m/12km long N to S and from 2m/4km to under 1km wide, lying between islands of Stronsay and Westray. Peat is plentiful, and is used as fuel on this and other islands in group. **80 D3** HY5634.

Eday Airfield *Ork.* ***Airport/airfield***, in centre of Eday, between Ferness Bay and Bay of London. **81 D3** HY5634.

Eday Sound *Ork.* ***Sea feature***, strait between islands of Eday and Sanday, to E of Eday. **81 D3** HY5834.

Edderton *High.* ***Village***, on S side of Dornoch Firth, Ross and Cromarty district, 5m/8km W of Tain. **61 G1** NH7084.

Edderton Burn *High.* ***River***, flowing N from slopes of Cnoc an t-Sabhail into Dornoch Firth, 1km SE of Edderton. **61 G1** NH7181.

Eddleston *Sc.Bord.* ***Village***, 4m/7km N of Peebles. **25 G5** NT2447.

Eddleston Water *Sc.Bord.* ***River***, stream running S through Eddleston village to River Tweed at Peebles. **25 G5** NT2447.

Eddlewood *S.Lan.* ***Suburb***, S district of Hamilton. **24 B4** NS7153.

Eddrachillis Bay *High.* ***Bay***, on W coast of Sutherland district, extending NE from Point of Stoer to Badcall. **74 A5** NC1336.

Eden ***River***, rising N of Kinross and flowing E through Fife region to North Sea at St. Andrews Bay. **33 G4** NO4921.

Eden Castle *Aber.* ***Castle***, ruins of 16c tower house on E side of River Deveron, 4m/6km S of Banff. **64 B4** NJ6958.

Eden Mouth *Fife* ***Sea feature***, where River Eden enters North Sea between sandbanks at low water. **34 D2** NO5021.

Eden Water *Sc.Bord.* ***River***, rising in hills 4m/7km SE of Lauder, and flowing SE to join River Tweed, 3m/5km NE of Kelso. **26 D5** NT7637.

Edendonich *Arg. & B.* ***Settlement***, in Strath of Orchy, 1km N of Dalmally. **31 D2** NN1627.

Edentaggart *Arg. & B.* ***Settlement***, in Glen Luss, 2m/4km W of Luss. **31 F5** NS3293.

Edgarhope Wood *Sc.Bord.* ***Forest/woodland***, 2m/3km NW of Lauder. **26 C4** NT5450.

Edgehead *Midloth.* ***Hamlet***, 3m/5km SE of Dalkeith. NT3765.

Edgelaw Reservoir *Midloth.* ***Reservoir***, small reservoir 4m/6km SW of Gorebridge. **25 G4** NT3058.

Edinample *Stir.* ***Historic house***, old castellated house on S side of Loch Earn, 1m/2km SE of Lochearnhead across head of loch. **32 B2** NN6022.

Edinbain (Also spelled Edinbane.) *High.* ***Village***, at head of Loch Greshornish, on N coast of Skye. **57 G4** NG3450.

Edinbanchory *Aber.* ***Settlement***, 5m/8km S of Rhynie. **53 G3** NJ4819.

Edinbane *High.* *Alternative spelling of Edinbain, qv.*

Edinbarnet *W.Dun.* ***Settlement***, 3m/4km N of Clydebank. **23 G2** NS5074.

Edinburgh *Edin.* Population: 401,910. ***City***, historic city and capital of Scotland, built on a range of rocky crags and extinct volcanoes, on S side of Firth of Forth, 41m/66km E of Glasgow and 334m/537km NNW of London. Administrative, financial and legal centre of Scotland. Medieval castle (Historic Scotland) on rocky eminence overlooks central area and was one of main seats of Royal court since reign of King Malcolm Canmore in 11c, while Arthur's Seat (largest of the volcanoes) guards eastern approaches. Three universities. Port at Leith, where Royal Yacht Britannia is now docked and open to public. Important industries include brewing, distilling, food and electronics. Edinburgh is second most popular tourist destination in UK. Palace of Holyroodhouse (Historic Scotland) is chief royal residence of Scotland. Old Town typified by Gladstone's Land (Historic Scotland), 17c six-storey tenement with arcaded front, outside stair and stepped gables. Numerous literary associations including Sir Arthur Conan Doyle who was born here. Many galleries and museums including National Gallery of Scotland. Annual arts festival attracts over a million visitors each year and is largest such event in the world. **25 G2** NT2573.

Edinburgh (Turnhouse) Airport *Edin.* ***Airport/airfield***, 6m/10km W of city centre. **25 F2** NT1573.

Edinburgh Castle *Edin.* ***Castle***, standing on basalt crag, dominating Edinburgh city centre. Originated in 11c as a wooden fortress, later becoming a palace, treasury, refuge and prison. Existing castle (Historic Scotland) was mainly built after 17c. Houses Scottish crown jewels and 15c gun, Mons Meg. **25 G2** NT2573.

Edinburgh Crystal Visitor Centre *Midloth.* ***Other feature of interest***, in Penicuik, with glassmaking, factory tour and exhibitions. **25 G3** NT2360.

Edinburgh Racecourse *E.Loth.* ***Racecourse***, at Musselburgh, E of Edinburgh. Twelve flat and eight National Hunt race days a year. **26 A2** NT3573.

Edinburgh Zoo *Edin.* ***Leisure/recreation***, in Corstorphine, 3m/5km W of Edinburgh city centre. Established in 1913 in parkland now extending over 80 acres and with more than 1000 animals. Attractions include Darwin Maze and world's largest penguin enclosure. **25 G2** NT2073.

Edinchip *Stir.* ***Settlement***, 1m/2km SW of Lochearnhead. **32 A2** NN5722.

Edin's Hall Broch *Sc.Bord.* ***Historic/prehistoric site***, unusually large Iron Age broch (Historic Scotland), 2m/3km SE of Abbey St. Bathans. One of only ten known in lowland Scotland. Occupied in Roman times. **27 E3** NT7760.

Edintore *Moray* ***Settlement***, 3m/4km S of Keith. **63 G5** NJ4246.

Edinvale *Moray* ***Settlement***, 6m/10km E of Forres. **62 D4** NJ1153.

Edmonstone *Ork.* ***Settlement***, on NE peninsula of Shapinsay. **80 D4** HY5220.

Ednam *Sc.Bord.* ***Village***, 2m/3km N of Kelso. **18 B3** NT7337.

Edra *Stir.* ***Settlement***, on N shore of Loch Katrine, 8m/12km NW of Aberfoyle. **31 G3** NN4610.

Edradour *P. & K.* ***Locality***, 1m/2km E of Pitlochry. Edradour Distillery, smallest in Scotland. NN9558.

Edradour Distillery *P. & K.* ***Other feature of interest***, distillery at Edradour, 1m/2km E of Pitlochry. Established in 1825, it is smallest distillery in Scotland. **41 E4** NN9557.
Edradynate *P. & K.* ***Settlement***, in upper part of Tay valley, 5m/8km SW of Pitlochry. **41 D4** NN8852.
Edrom *Sc.Bord.* ***Village***, 3m/5km E of Duns. **27 F4** NT8255.
Edrom Norman Arch *Sc.Bord.* ***Historic/prehistoric site***, good example of Norman chancel arch (Historic Scotland) from church built c. 1105 by Thor Longus, 3m/4km W of Chirnside. **27 F4** NT8255.
Edzell *Angus* ***Village***, on River North Esk, 6m/9km N of Brechin. Remains of castle with 16c tower (Historic Scotland), 1m/2km W. **43 D3** NO6068.
Edzell Castle *Angus* ***Castle***, early 16c tower house (Historic Scotland), with 17c alterations and additions by Sir David Lindsay, 1m/2km W of Edzell and 6m/10km N of Brechin. Vandalised after second Jacobite uprising. Includes Lindsay's formal decorated garden, or Pleasaunce. **43 D3** NO5869.
Eela Water *Shet.* ***Lake/loch***, small but deep loch on Mainland 2m/4km SW of Ollaberry. **84 C5** HU3378.
Effirth *Shet.* ***Settlement***, on Mainland, near head of small inlet of Effirth Voe, W of Bixter. **82 C2** HU3152.
Effirth Voe *Shet.* ***Sea feature***, small inlet W of Bixter, Mainland. HU3152.
Eggerness *D. & G.* ***Settlement***, 1m/2km NE of Garlieston, on W side of Wigtown Bay. **3 E2** NX4947.
Eggerness Point *D. & G.* ***Coastal feature***, headland at E end of Garlieston Bay, on W side of Wigtown Bay. NX4946.
Egilsay *Ork.* ***Island***, sparsely populated island off E coast of Rousay, 3m/5km long N to S, 2km wide near N end, tapering to a point at S end. Remains of St. Magnus Church. **80 C4** HY4730.
Egilsay *Shet.* ***Island***, uninhabited island of 54 acres or 22 hectares off W coast of Mainland at entrance to Mangaster Voe. HU3169.
Eglin Lane *E.Ayr.* ***River***, running N from Loch Enoch and continuing N to join Whitespout Lane and form Carrick Lane. NX4693.
Eglinton *N.Ayr.* ***Suburb***, 2m/3km SE of Kilwinning, in N part of Irvine. NS3141.
Eglinton Castle *N.Ayr.* ***Castle***, remains of late 18c castle set in loop of River Lugton, 2m/3km SE of Kilwinning. Eglinton Park includes formal gardens, rock gardens and large rhododendrons. **23 E5** NS3242.
Egypt *Glas.* ***Suburb***, 3m/5km SE of Glasgow city centre, in Tollcross district. NS6463.
Eidart *High.* ***River***, flowing generally S through Glenfeshie Forest into River Feshie, 9m/13km SW of Beinn MacDuibh. **52 B5** NN9192.
Eididh nan Clach Geala *High.* ***Mountain***, in Ross and Cromarty district 2m/3km N of Beinn Dearg. Munro: height 3044 feet or 928 metres. **60 B1** NH2584.
Eigg *High.* ***Island***, in Inner Hebrides of about 9 square miles or 23 square km lying 4m/7km SE of Rum across Sound of Rum. Rises to 1291 feet or 393 metres (An Sgurr or Scuir of Eigg). Sound of Eigg is sea passage between Eigg and Muck. **37 D1** NM4687.
Eignaig *High.* ***Settlement***, on NW shore of Loch Linnhe, 4m/7km NE of Rubha an Ridire. **37 G5** NM7943.
Eigneig Bheag *W.Isles* ***Coastal feature***, headland on E coast of North Uist, 2m/3km E of Eaval. **56 C4** NF9260.
Eigneig Mhòr *W.Isles* ***Coastal feature***, headland on E coast of North Uist, 1km N of Eigneig Bheag. **56 C3** NF9361.
Eil *High.* ***Settlement***, in River Dulnain valley, 5m/8km NW of Aviemore. **52 A3** NH8217.
Eilanreach *High.* ***Settlement***, on coast of Skye and Lochalsh district, 1km S of Glenelg. **49 E3** NG8017.
Eildon *Sc.Bord.* ***Village***, on E side of Eildon Hills, 2m/3km SE of Melrose. NT5732.
Eildon Hills *Sc.Bord.* ***Mountain***, with three conspicuous peaks on S side of Melrose. Middle peak rises to 1384 feet or 422 metres; N peak, 1325 feet or 404 metres, shows traces of prehistoric settlement; S peak rises to 1217 feet or 371 metres. **17 G2** NT5432.
Eileach an Naoimh *Arg. & B.* ***Island***, narrow uninhabited island, 1m/2km long NE to SW, at SW end of Garvellachs group between Jura and Mull. Remains of Celtic monastery (Historic Scotland). Lighthouse at SW end. **29 F4** NM6409.
Eileach an Naoimh Monastery *Arg. & B.* ***Ecclesiastical building***, ruin of monastery (Historic Scotland) on Eileach an Naoimh, most southwesterly of Garvellachs group in Firth of Lorn. **29 F4** NM6409.
Eileach Chonail *Arg. & B.* *Alternative name for Dùn Chonnuill, qv.*
Eilean a' Bhreitheimh *High.* ***Island***, small island in Eddrachillis Bay, Sutherland district. **74 A5** NC1240.
Eilean a' Chalmain *Arg. & B.* ***Island***, small island off SW end of Mull, nearly 1m/2km S of Erraid. **28 B3** NM3017.
Eilean a' Chaoil *High.* ***Island***, islet at entrance to Tongue Bay, 1km E of Midfield, Caithness district. NC5965.
Eilean a' Chaolais *High.* ***Island***, islet off S side of Rubha Chaolais, 4m/7km SE of Arisaig across entrance to Loch nan Uamh. NM6980.
Eilean a' Chàr *High.* ***Island***, small island in Summer Isles group. Lies 1m/2km W of Tanera Mòr and nearly 4m/6km W of Achiltibuie on NW coast of Ross and Cromarty district. NB9608.
Eilean a' Chléirich *High.* *Alternative name for Priest Island, qv.*
Eilean a' Chonnaidh (Anglicised form: Coney Island.) *High.* ***Island***, small uninhabited island off W coast of Sutherland district, 1m/2km NW of Kinlochbervie. NC2057.
Eilean a' Chuirn *Arg. & B.* ***Island***, off SE coast of Islay, 1m/2km S of Ardmore Point. **20 C5** NR4749.
Eilean a' Ghobha *W.Isles* ***Island***, one of Flannan Isles group, lying 2m/3km W of main island, Eilean Mòr. NA6946.
Eilean a' Mhuineil *High.* ***Island***, islet in Loch Hourn at E end of Poll a' Mhuineil. NG8406.
Eilean a' Mhuneil *High.* *See Poll a' Mhuneil.*
Eilean a' Phidhir *High.* ***Island***, wooded island in Loch Morar, Lochaber district, 1m/2km E of dam. **48 D5** NH7092.
Eilean a' Phiobaire *High.* ***Island***, islet in Lochaber district off SW shore of Loch Hourn, 1m/2km SW of Corran across loch. NG8308.
Eilean an Eireannaich *High.* ***Island***, small uninhabited island at junction of Loch Laxford and Loch a' Chadh-Fi near W coast of Sutherland district. NC2050.
Eilean an Fhraoich *High.* ***Island***, islet in Kyle Rona, between Raasay and Rona. NG6153.
Eilean an Ròin Beag *High.* ***Island***, one of two uninhabited islands off W coast of Sutherland district, 3m/5km NW of Kinlochbervie. NC1758.
Eilean an Ròin Mòr *High.* ***Island***, one of two uninhabited islands off W coast of Sutherland district, 3m/5km NW of Kinlochbervie. **74 A3** NC1758.
Eilean an Rubha *Arg. & B.* ***Island***, forming E boundary of Lussa Bay on E coast of Jura. **21 E1** NR6486.
Eilean an Tighe *W.Isles* ***Island***, islet at head of East Loch Roag, W coast of Isle of Lewis. NB2230.
Eilean an Tighe *W.Isles* ***Island***, one of Shiant Islands group to S of Garbh Eilean, to which it is joined by an isthmus. **67 G4** NG4296.
Eilean Annraidh *Arg. & B.* ***Island***, islet off NE point of Iona. NM2926.
Eilean Ard *High.* ***Island***, small uninhabited island in Loch Laxford, on W coast of Sutherland district. NC1850.
Eilean Arsa *Arg. & B.* ***Island***, small island between Shuna and mainland of Argyll. **29 G4** NM7807.
Eilean Balnagowan *High.* ***Island***, nearly 1m/2km off E shore of Loch Linnhe at foot of Salachan Glen. **38 B4** NM9653.
Eilean Bàn *High.* ***Island***, wooded islet in Loch Morar, Lochaber district, 1km E of dam at W end of loch. NM6992.
Eilean Barraigh *W.Isles* *Gaelic form of Barra, qv.*
Eilean Beag *High.* ***Island***, smallest of Crowlin Islands group, 2m/3km off W coast of Ross and Cromarty district on N side of entrance to Loch Carron. Lighthouse. NG6835.
Eilean Beag a' Bhàigh *W.Isles* *See Eilean Mòr a' Bhàigh.*
Eilean Bhearnaraigh *W.Isles* *Gaelic form of Berneray, qv.*
Eilean Bhrìde *Arg. & B.* ***Island***, rocky islet off SE coast of Islay, 3m/4km NE of Ardbeg. **20 C5** NR4547.
Eilean Bhride *Arg. & B.* ***Island***, most northerly of Small Isles group off E coast of Jura. **21 D3** NR5569.
Eilean Chalaibrigh *W.Isles* *Gaelic form of Calabrie Island, qv.*
Eilean Chalbha *Arg. & B.* ***Island***, islet off N coast of Iona, 1m/2km W of Eilean Annraidh. **28 B2** NM2826.
Eilean Chaluim Chille *W.Isles* ***Island***, small uninhabited island at entrance to Loch Erisort, E coast of Isle of Lewis. Ruins of St. Columb's Church at S end. **69 E5** NB3821.
Eilean Chasgaidh *High.* *Alternative name for Eilean Chathastail, qv.*
Eilean Chathastail (Also known as Eilean Chasgaidh.) *High.* ***Island***, small uninhabited island off Galmisdale at SE end of Eigg, with lighthouse on E coast. NM4883.
Eilean Cheois *W.Isles* *Gaelic form of Keose Island, qv.*
Eilean Choraidh (Anglicised form: Chorrie Island.) *High.* ***Island***, nearly 1m/2km in length in Loch Eriboll, in Sutherland district, 2m/4km from head of loch. **74 D3** NC4258.
Eilean Chrona (Anglicised form: Chrona Island.) *High.* ***Island***, small uninhabited island 1m/2km W of Oldany Island, off W coast of Sutherland district. **70 C1** NC0633.
Eilean Clùimhrig *High.* ***Island***, islet at mouth of Loch Eriboll, N coast of Sutherland district, 1m/2km SE of Eilean Hoan. **75 D2** NC4665.
Eilean Coltair *Arg. & B.* ***Island***, islet near N shore of Loch Melfort, 3m/5km W of Kilmelford in Argyll. NM8012.
Eilean Craobhach *Arg. & B.* ***Island***, off SE coast of Islay, 1m/2km S of Ardmore Point. NR4649.
Eilean Creagach *Arg. & B.* ***Island***, small island between Shuna and mainland. NM7809.
Eilean Creagach *High.* ***Island***, one of Ascrib Islands group in Loch Snizort, 4m/6km E of Vaternish Point, Skye. NG2965.
Eilean Darach *High.* ***Settlement***, in Strath Beag, 1km E of Dundonnell. **60 A1** NH1088.
Eilean Dearg *Arg. & B.* ***Island***, islet in Loch Riddon, Argyll, with ruins of 17c fort. NS0077.
Eilean Dearg *High.* ***Island***, one of the group of islets off shore of Knoydart, Lochaber district, off W end of Sandaig Bay. NG7000.
Eilean Dioghlum *Arg. & B.* ***Island***, islet on S side of entrance to Loch Tuath, Mull, off NW coast of Gometra. **36 C5** NM3542.
Eilean Dìomhain *Arg. & B.* ***Island***, one of Small Isles group off E coast of Jura. NR5468.
Eilean Donan *High.* ***Island***, rocky islet at entrance to Loch Duich, S of Dornie, Skye and Lochalsh district, with restored castle of the Macraes. NG8825.
Eilean Donan Castle *High.* ***Castle***, former Jacobite stronghold of the Macraes on Eilean Donan at entrance to Loch Duich. Destroyed in 1719 and restored in 19c; now contains Jacobite relics. **49 E2** NG8825.
Eilean Dubh *Arg. & B.* ***Coastal feature***, rock at N point of Staffa. **28 C1** NM3236.
Eilean Dubh *Arg. & B.* ***Island***, small island off SW end of Mull between Eilean a' Chalmain and Erraid. Another small island of same name lies off W coast of Erraid. **28 B3** NM3018.
Eilean Dubh *Arg. & B.* ***Island***, islet off N point of Colonsay. **28 D4** NM4201.
Eilean Dubh *Arg. & B.* ***Island***, small island in Loch Craignish, 1m/2km E of Craignish Castle. NM7902.
Eilean Dubh *Arg. & B.* ***Island***, islet off S coast of Lismore, 2m/3km S of Achnacroish. Joined by causeway to Eilean na Cloiche. Other islets in same group are Eilean nan Gamhna, Creag Island and Pladda Island. **30 A1** NM8338.
Eilean Dubh *Arg. & B.* ***Island***, small island in Loch Linnhe between Lismore and mainland to E. **38 A5** NM8742.
Eilean Dubh *Arg. & B.* ***Island***, on SE side of Sound of Jura, 1m/2km E of Tayvallich. **21 F1** NR7187.
Eilean Dubh *Arg. & B.* ***Island***, small island on W side of entrance to Loch Riddon, Argyll. NS0075.
Eilean Dubh *High.* ***Island***, one of Summer Isles group. Lies 2m/3km S of Tanera Mòr. Area about 200 acres or 80 hectares. **70 B4** NB9703.
Eilean Dubh *High.* ***Island***, islet near S shore of Loch Eishort, Skye, 3m/5km NE of Tarskavaig. NG6114.
Eilean Dubh a' Bhàigh *W.Isles* *See Eilean Mòr a' Bhàigh.*
Eilean Dubh Mòr *Arg. & B.* ***Island***, uninhabited island of about 150 acres or 60 hectares, lying 2m/3km W of Luing. Smaller island, Eilean Dubh Beag, lies across narrow channel to N. **29 F4** NM6910.
Eilean Dùin *Arg. & B.* ***Island***, small island off coast of Argyll, 3m/4km W of Kilninver. **29 G2** NM7821.
Eilean Fada Mòr *High.* ***Island***, one of Summer Isles group, between Tanera Mòr and Tanera Beg. Area about 150 acres or 60 hectares. NB9707.
Eilean Fhianain *High.* ***Island***, islet in the narrows of Loch Shiel in Lochaber district. Ruined chapel of St. Finnan. NM7568.
Eilean Fladday (Also known as Fladday.) *High.* ***Island***, uninhabited island of about 360 acres or 145 hectares lying off W coast of Raasay midway between Manish Point and Eilean Tigh, and separated from Raasay by narrow channel of Caol Fladda. **58 B4** NG5851.
Eilean Flodaigh (Anglicised form: Flodda.) *W.Isles* ***Island***, small low-lying island off N coast of Benbecula 4m/6km E of Benbecula (Baile a' Mhanaich) Aerodrome. **45 G4** NF8455.
Eilean Flodigarry *High.* ***Island***, small uninhabited island 1km off NE coast of Skye, 2m/3km N of Staffin. **58 A2** NG4871.
Eilean Fraoch *Arg. & B.* ***Island***, islet in Loch Awe opposite entrance to arm of loch running NW to Pass of Brander in Argyll. Ruined castle of the Macnaughtons. NN1025.
Eilean Furadh Mòr (Also known as Foura.) *High.* ***Island***, islet off W coast of Ross and Cromarty district 4m/6km E of Rubha Réidh. **70 A5** NG7993.
Eilean Gaineamhach Boreraig *High.* ***Island***, islet off Skye in Loch Eishort, opposite Boreraig and 2m/4km E of Rubha Suisnish. NG6215.
Eilean Gamhna *Arg. & B.* ***Island***, islet at entrance to Loch Melfort, Argyll. **29 G3** NM7810.
Eilean Garave (Also known as Eilean Geary.) *High.* ***Island***, one of Ascrib Islands group in Loch Snizort, 4m/7km E of Vaternish Point, Skye. NG2964.
Eilean Garbh *Arg. & B.* ***Coastal feature***, promontory at N end of West Tarbert Bay, Gigha. NR6553.
Eilean Garbh *Arg. & B.* ***Island***, islet in Loch Tuath between Ulva and mainland of Mull. NM4440.
Eilean Garbh *High.* ***Island***, small uninhabited island off W coast of Rona. NG6056.
Eilean Geary *High.* *Alternative name for Eilean Garave, qv.*
Eilean Ghaoideamal *Arg. & B.* ***Island***, islet off SE coast of Oronsay across Caolas Mòr. **20 B1** NR3787.

E

Eilean Ghòmain *Arg. & B.* ***Island***, islet off NW end of Erraid at S end of Sound of Iona. NM2820.
Eilean Glas *W.Isles* ***Island***, islet at entrance to Loch Erisort, E coast of Isle of Lewis. NB3922.
Eilean Heast *High.* ***Island***, small uninhabited island near N shore of Loch Eishort 1km S of locality of Heast. **48 C3** NG6416.
Eilean Hoan *High.* ***Island***, small uninhabited island with rocky coast on W side of entrance to Loch Eriboll, N coast of Sutherland district. Island lies 2m/4km E of Durness and 1km from coast of mainland. **74 D2** NC4467.
Eilean Horrisdale *High.* ***Island***, small island in Gair Loch, W coast of Ross and Cromarty district, opposite Badachro. **59 D2** NG7874.
Eilean Iarmain (Also known as Isleornsay or Isle Ornsay.) *High.* ***Village***, on E coast of Sleat peninsula, Skye, 7m/11km SE of Broadford. Harbour formed by coast of Sleat and W coast of Isle Ornsay. **48 C3** NG7012.
Eilean Ighe *High.* ***Island***, small uninhabited island off coast of Lochaber district, 2m/3km W of Arisaig. **37 F1** NM6388.
Eilean Imersay *Arg. & B.* ***Island***, off S coast of Islay, 1km E of Ardbeg across Loch an t-Sàilein inlet. NR4246.
Eilean Iosal *High.* ***Island***, small uninhabited island off W coast of Eilean nan Ròn, off N coast of Caithness district. NC6365.
Eilean Iosal *High.* ***Island***, one of Ascrib Islands group in Loch Snizort, 4m/6km E of Vaternish Point, Skye. NG2865.
Eilean Iubhard *W.Isles* ***Island***, uninhabited island at mouth of Loch Shell, E coast of Isle of Lewis. **67 F3** NB3809.
Eilean Kearstay *W.Isles* ***Island***, small uninhabited island off W coast of Isle of Lewis opposite Callanish. **68 C4** NB1933.
Eilean Leodhais *W.Isles Gaelic form of Isle of Lewis, qv.*
Eilean Loain *Arg. & B.* ***Island***, near E shore of Loch Sween in Knapdale, Argyll, 1m/2km SE of Tayvallich across loch. **21 F1** NR7585.
Eilean Loch Oscair *Arg. & B.* ***Island***, small uninhabited island off NW coast of Lismore, 2m/3km W of Port Ramsay. **38 A5** NM8645.
Eilean Meadhonach *High.* ***Island***, second largest of Crowlin Islands group, in Inner Sound between Skye and Applecross peninsula, to W of Eilean Mòr. **48 C1** NG6834.
Eilean Mhic Chrion *Arg. & B.* ***Island***, narrow island 1m/2km long NE to SW, near W shore of Loch Craignish in Argyll, 1m/2km from head of loch. **30 A4** NM8003.
Eilean Mhic Coinnich *Arg. & B.* ***Island***, off S end of Rinns of Islay, 1km S of Rubha na Faing. NR1652.
Eilean Mhucaig *Arg. & B.* ***Island***, rocky islet to N of Oronsay. **20 B1** NR3589.
Eilean Mhuire *W.Isles* ***Island***, one of Shiant Islands group, 1km E of Garbh Eilean. **67 G4** NG4398.
Eilean Mòineseach *High.* ***Island***, islet in Enard Bay between Eilean Mòr and NW coast of Ross and Cromarty district. NC0617.
Eilean Molach *Stir. Gaelic form of Ellen's Isle, qv.*
Eilean Molach *W.Isles* ***Island***, islet off Aird Mhòr Mangurstadh, headland on W coast of Isle of Lewis 4m/6km W of Timsgearraidh. NA9932.
Eilean Mòr *Arg. & B.* ***Island***, small island, but largest of a group, lying 1km off NE end of Coll. **36 B3** NM2764.
Eilean Mòr *Arg. & B.* ***Island***, small island off S shore of Ross of Mull, 1m/2km W of Rubh' Ardalanish. **28 C3** NM3416.
Eilean Mòr *Arg. & B.* ***Island***, islet opposite Dunstaffnage Bay, 2m/3km W of Connel, Argyll. **30 A1** NM8834.
Eilean Mòr *Arg. & B.* ***Island***, off NW coast of Islay, 10m/15km NW of Bridgend. **20 A3** NR2169.
Eilean Mòr *Arg. & B.* ***Island***, in Sound of Jura lying 2m/3km SE of Danna Island, in Argyll. Remains of St. Cormac's Chapel (Historic Scotland), medieval chapel with upper chamber. **21 E2** NR6675.
Eilean Mòr *Arg. & B.* ***Island***, in Loch Fyne, 3m/5km SE of Lochgilphead, Argyll. **21 G1** NR8883.
Eilean Mòr *High.* ***Island***, small uninhabited island in Enard Bay 1km off NW coast of Ross and Cromarty district. **70 C3** NC0517.
Eilean Mòr *High.* ***Island***, in Inner Sound, between Skye and Applecross peninsula. Largest of Crowlin Islands group and nearest to Scottish mainland. **48 D1** NG6934.
Eilean Mòr *High.* ***Island***, small island opposite Oronsay in Loch Sunart, off S coast of Ardnamurchan peninsula. **37 E3** NM5861.
Eilean Mòr *High.* ***Island***, in Loch Sunart, 5m/8km SE of Salen. **37 G3** NM7560.
Eilean Mòr *W.Isles* ***Island***, largest of Flannan Isles, having an area of some 30 acres or 12 hectares. Lighthouse to N, and to S of this are ruins of small chapel dedicated to St. Flannan. NA7246.
Eilean Mòr a' Bhàigh *W.Isles* ***Island***, small uninhabited island off S coast of Isle of Lewis 1m/2km SE of entrance to Loch Seaforth. Islets of Eilean Dubh a' Bhàigh and Eilean Beag a' Bhàigh lie between island and coast of Isle of Lewis to N. **67 E3** NB2600.
Eilean Mòr Bayble *W.Isles Anglicised form of Eilean Mòr Phabail, qv.*
Eilean Mòr Chapel *Arg. & B.* ***Ecclesiastical building***, chapel and parts of two crosses on Eilean Mòr in Sound of Jura, off NW coast of Kintyre peninsula. **21 E2** NR6675.
Eilean Mòr Laxay *W.Isles* ***Island***, small uninhabited island near N shore of Loch Erisort, Isle of Lewis, S of Lacasaigh. NB3320.
Eilean Mòr Phabail (Anglicised form: Eilean Mòr Bayble.) *W.Isles* ***Island***, islet off Bagh Phabail Iarach, E coast of Eye Peninsula, Isle of Lewis. NB5330.
Eilean Mullagrach *High.* ***Island***, one of Summer Isles group, nearly 2m/3km off NW coast of Ross and Cromarty district near Alltan Dubh. Area about 180 acres or 75 hectares. **70 B3** NB9511.
Eilean Musdile *Arg. & B.* ***Island***, with lighthouse off SW end of Lismore, 2m/3km E of Duart Point on Mull. **29 G1** NM7735.
Eilean na Bà *High.* ***Island***, small uninhabited island off W coast of Ross and Cromarty district, 4m/7km S of Applecross. NG6938.
Eilean na Cloiche *Arg. & B.* ***Island***, islet off S coast of Lismore, 2m/3km SW of Achnacroish. Joined by causeway to Eilean Dubh to S. Other islets in same group are Eilean nan Gamhna, Creag Island and Pladda Island. NM8338.
Eilean na Gàmhna *High.* ***Island***, one of group of islets off shore of Knoydart, Lochaber district, off W end of Sandaig Bay. NG7001.
Eilean na h-Airde *High.* ***Island***, islet off S coast of Skye opposite Rubha na h-Easgainne and 2m/3km S of Elgol. NG5211.
Eilean na h-Aiteig *High.* ***Island***, islet off W coast of Sutherland district 2m/4km NW of Kinlochbervie. NC1958.
Eilean na h-Aon Chaorach *Arg. & B.* ***Island***, islet 1km off S coast of Iona. NM2520.
Eilean na Saille *High.* ***Island***, islet off W coast of Sutherland district 5m/8km W of Rhiconich. NC1753.
Eilean nam Ban *Arg. & B.* ***Island***, small island in Sound of Iona 1km N of Fionnphort. Separated from Ross of Mull by strait of Bull Hole. NM3024.
Eilean nam Breac *High.* ***Island***, wooded islet in Loch Morar, on S side of Eilean a' Phidhir. NM7091.
Eilean nam Feannag *W.Isles* ***Island***, islet in Loch Roag, W coast of Isle of Lewis, 1m/2km NE of entrance to Little Loch Roag. NB1433.
Eilean nam Muc *Arg. & B.* ***Island***, small island off W coast of Erraid at SW end of Mull. NM2819.
Eilean nan Coinein *Arg. & B.* ***Island***, one of Small Isles group off E coast of Jura. NR5468.
Eilean nan Each *High.* ***Island***, small uninhabited island off NW end of Muck, in Inner Hebrides. **36 C1** NM3981.
Eilean nan Gabhar *Arg. & B.* ***Island***, largest and most southerly of Small Isles group off E coast of Jura. **20 D3** NR5367.
Eilean nan Gamhna *Arg. & B.* ***Island***, islet off NW coast of Kerrera. **30 A1** NM8130.
Eilean nan Gamhna *Arg. & B.* ***Island***, islet off S coast of Lismore, 1km S of Kilcheran Loch. In same group of islets are Eilean na Cloiche, Eilean Dubh, Creag Island and Pladda Island. NM8338.
Eilean nan Gillean *High.* ***Island***, small uninhabited island (National Trust for Scotland) 1m/2km NW of Kyle of Lochalsh, Skye and Lochalsh district. NG7428.
Eilean nan Gobhar *High.* ***Island***, islet at entrance to Loch Ailort, Lochaber district. **37 F1** NM6979.
Eilean nan Ron *Arg. & B.* ***Island***, rocky island, just off S end of Oronsay. **20 B1** NR3386.
Eilean nan Ròn (Also known as Roan Island.) *High.* ***Island***, fertile island of about 300 acres or 120 hectares, with rocky coast, at entrance to Tongue Bay, N coast of Caithness district. **75 F2** NC6465.
Eilean Orasaigh *W.Isles Gaelic form of Orasay Island, qv.*
Eilean Orasaigh (Anglicised form: Orinsay Island.) *W.Isles* ***Island***, small uninhabited island off E coast of Isle of Lewis, on S side of entrance to Loch Erisort. **69 F5** NB4121.
Eilean Ornsay *Arg. & B.* ***Island***, small island lying off SE coast of Coll, on W side of entrance to Loch Eatharna. **36 B4** NM2255.
Eilean Ramsay *Arg. & B.* ***Island***, small uninhabited island off N coast of Lismore. **38 A5** NM8845.
Eilean Ràrsaidh *High.* ***Island***, islet off N shore of Loch Hourn in Lochaber district, 2m/3km W of Arnisdale. NG8111.
Eilean Righ *Arg. & B.* ***Island***, narrow island nearly 2m/3km long NE to SW near E shore of Loch Craignish in Argyll. **29 G4** NM8001.
Eilean Rosaidh *W.Isles Gaelic form of Rosay, qv.*
Eilean Ruairidh *High.* ***Island***, islet on S side of entrance to Loch Eishort, Skye. NG5912.
Eilean Ruairidh Mòr *High.* ***Island***, wooded island in Loch Maree, Ross and Cromarty district. **59 E2** NG8973.
Eilean Rubha an Ridire *High.* ***Island***, islet in Sound of Mull lying 1km NW of Rubha an Ridire, Lochaber district. NM7240.
Eilean Scalpaigh *W.Isles Gaelic form of Scalpay, qv.*
Eilean Sgorach *High.* ***Island***, islet off Skye, lying close to Point of Sleat on W side. NM5599.
Eilean Shamadalain *High.* ***Island***, islet off NW coast of Knoydart, Lochaber district, 1m/2km NE of Airor. NG7306.
Eilean Shona *High.* ***Island***, hilly and partly wooded island at entrance to Loch Moidart in Lochaber district. E part of island is known as Shona Beag, joined to rest of island by narrow neck of land. **37 F2** NM6573.
Eilean Sneth Dian *Arg. & B. Alternative name for Frank Lockwood's Island, qv.*
Eilean Sùbhainn *High.* ***Island***, in Loch Maree, Ross and Cromarty district, nearly 1m/2km NE of Talladale. **59 F2** NG9272.
Eilean Tigh *High.* ***Island***, uninhabited island off N end of Raasay. Area about 180 acres or 75 hectares. **58 B4** NG6053.
Eilean Tighe *W.Isles* ***Island***, second in size of the Flannan Isles, lying to S of the largest, Eilean Mòr. NA7246.
Eilean Tioram *High.* ***Island***, islet at head of Loch Alsh, Skye and Lochalsh district, opposite entrance to Loch Duich. NG8726.
Eilean Tràighe *Arg. & B.* ***Island***, at entrance to West Loch Tarbert, Argyll, between Knapdale and Kintyre. NR7457.
Eilean Trodday *High.* ***Island***, small uninhabited island 1m/2km N of Rubha na h-Aiseig, headland at N point of Skye. Used for sheep grazing. **58 A2** NG4478.
Eilean Vow (Also known as Island I Vow). *Arg. & B.* ***Island***, islet in Loch Lomond 2m/3km S of Ardlui. Ruined castle of the Macfarlanes. NN3312.
Eileanan Diraclett *W.Isles* ***Island***, group of islets in East Loch Tarbert, off South Harris coast, 1m/2km SE of Tarbert. NG1698.
Eileanan Glasa *Arg. & B.* ***Island***, group of islets in Sound of Mull 2m/3km NE of Salen. **37 E5** NM5945.
Eileanan Gleann Righ *Arg. & B.* ***Island***, group of islets in Loch Tarbert, Jura, 1m/2km SE of Rubh' an t-Sàilein. NR5182.
Eileanan Iasgaich *W.Isles* ***Island***, group of islets in Loch Baghasdail, South Uist. NF7818.
Eileanan nan Glas Leac (Also known as Na Glas Leacan.) *High.* ***Island***, group of islets off N coast of Sutherland district, 3m/5km W of Faraid Head (or Far Out Head) across entrance to Balnakeil Bay. NC3472.
Eileann Sionnach *High.* ***Island***, islet with lighthouse in Sound of Sleat, off SE coast of Isle Ornsay. NG7112.
Einacleit (Anglicised form: Enaclete.) *W.Isles* ***Settlement***, 1m/2km N of Giosla, Isle of Lewis. **68 C5** NB1228.
Einig *High.* ***River***, in Sutherland district, running E down Glen Einig into River Oykel 1km SE of Oykel Bridge. **71 F5** NC3900.
Eiriosgaigh *W.Isles Gaelic form of Eriskay, qv.*
Eisgean (Anglicised form: Eishken.) *W.Isles* ***Settlement***, on Isle of Lewis, on N side of Loch Shell, 4m/6km W of Leumrabhagh. **67 F2** NB3211.
Eishken *W.Isles Anglicised form of Eisgean, qv.*
Eitshal *W.Isles* ***Hill***, 4m/7km NW of Liurbost, Isle of Lewis. Mast at summit. Height 731 feet or 223 metres. **69 E4** NB3030.
Elchaig *High.* ***River***, in Skye and Lochalsh district, running NW to head of Loch Long. NG9330.
Elchies Forest *Moray* ***Open space***, moorland tract to W of Rothes. **63 D5** NJ2246.
Elcho *P. & K.* ***Hamlet***, with castle, on S bank of River Tay, 3m/4km NE of Bridge of Earn. **33 G2** NO1620.
Elcho Castle *P. & K.* ***Historic/prehistoric site***, 16c stronghold (Historic Scotland) of the Earls of Wemyss. **33 G2** NO1621.
Elderslie *Renf.* Population: 5286. ***Small town***, adjoining to E of Johnstone. Traditional birthplace of William Wallace. **23 F3** NS4462.
Eldrable Hill *High.* ***Mountain***, 2m/4km NW of Helmsdale, Sutherland district. Height 1368 feet or 417 metres. **73 E3** NC9816.
Eldrick *S.Ayr.* ***Settlement***, 3m/5km E of Barrhill. **7 D2** NX2881.
Eldrig Loch *D. & G.* ***Lake/loch***, small loch or tarn 7m/11km NW of Kirkcowan. NX2569.
Electric Brae *S.Ayr. See Croy Brae.*
Elgin *Moray* Population: 19,027. ***Town***, market town with cathedral on River Lossie, 5m/8km S of Lossiemouth and 36m/59km E of Inverness. Notable ruins of 13c cathedral (Historic Scotland), traces of ancient castle, 16c Bishop's House (Historic Scotland). Much of medieval street layout remains intact. Museum. **63 E3** NJ2162.
Elgin Cathedral *Moray* ***Ecclesiastical building***, remains of 13c cathedral (Historic Scotland) in centre of Elgin. Known as Lantern of the North, it once rivalled St. Andrews Cathedral. Founded in 1224 and rebuilt after fires in 1270 and 1390, it fell into disrepair during the Reformation. Notable features include octagonal chapter house and Pictish slab in the choir. **63 E3** NJ2263.

Elgin Lane *E.Ayr.* ***River***, issuing from Loch Enoch and flowing N to its confluence with Whitespout Lane to form Carrick Lane. **7 F2** NX4693.
Elgin Museum *Moray* ***Other feature of interest***, museum in Elgin with Pictish, geological and local history displays. Most notable are exotic anthropological exhibits, including a mummy from Peru. **63 E3** NJ2063.
Elgol *High.* ***Village***, on E side of Loch Scavaig, on S coast of Skye. **48 B3** NG5214.
Elibank *Sc.Bord.* ***Locality***, and ruined stronghold of Murrays, 4m/7km E of Innerleithen across River Tweed. NT3936.
Elibank and Traquair Forest *Sc.Bord.* ***Forest/woodland***, on S side of River Tweed, to E of Innerleithen. **17 E2** NT3635.
Eliburn *W.Loth.* ***Locality***, 2m/3km W of Livingston. NT0367.
Elie *Fife* ***Town***, resort on Firth of Forth, 5m/8km W of Anstruther. Merged with Earlsferry in 1929. Small harbour. **34 C4** NO4900.
Elie Ness *Fife* ***Coastal feature***, headland with lighthouse at E end of bay enclosing Elie harbour. NT4999.
Eliock *D. & G.* ***Locality***, straddling River Nith, 2m/3km SE of Sanquhar. **15 G5** NS8007.
Elishader *High.* ***Settlement***, near E coast of Skye, 3m/4km NW of Rubha nam Brathairean. **58 B3** NG5065.
Ellanbeich *Arg. & B.* ***Settlement***, adjoining Easdale, on W coast of Seil, in Argyll. NM7417.
Ellary *Arg. & B.* ***Settlement***, on NW side of Loch Caolisport, 2m/3km W of Clachbreck across loch. **21 F2** NR7475.
Ellemford *Sc.Bord.* ***Settlement***, 3m/4km SW of Abbey St. Bathans. **27 E3** NT7260.
Ellen's Isle (Gaelic name: Eilean Molach). *Stir.* ***Island***, islet at E end of Loch Katrine. **31 G4** NN4808.
Elleric *Arg. & B.* ***Settlement***, in Glen Creran, 3m/5km NE of head of Glen Creran. **38 C5** NN0348.
Elliot Water *Angus* ***River***, rising to W of Redford, and flowing SE by Arbirlot into North Sea, 2m/3km SW of Arbroath. **43 D5** NO6239.
Ellisland *D. & G.* ***Other feature of interest***, farm on W bank of River Nith, 6m/9km NW of Dumfries, once rented by Robert Burns. NX9283.
Ellon *Aber.* Population: 8627. ***Small town***, market town on River Ythan, 15m/24km N of Aberdeen. **55 E1** NJ9530.
Ellwick *Ork.* *Alternative spelling of Elwick, qv.*
Elphin *High.* ***Village***, in Sutherland district, 7m/11km S of Inchnadamph. **71 E3** NC2111.
Elphinstone *E.Loth.* ***Village***, 2m/3km S of Tranent. **26 A2** NT3970.
Elrick *Aber.* ***Locality***, 7m/12km W of Aberdeen. **54 D4** NJ8206.
Elrick *Moray* ***Settlement***, 2m/3km E of Cabrach. **53 G2** NJ4225.
Elrick Burn *High.* ***River***, rising on N slope of Meall nan Laogh and flowing N into River Findhorn, 10m/16km N of Newtonmore. **51 F3** NH6714.
Elrick More *P. & K.* ***Mountain***, on W side of Strath Tay, 4m/7km NW of Dunkeld. Height 1696 feet or 517 metres. **41 E5** NN9646.
Elrig *D. & G.* ***Village***, 3m/5km N of Port William. **2 D2** NX3247.
Elrig Loch *D. & G.* ***Lake/loch***, small loch 1km N of Elrig. **2 D2** NX3247.
Elrigbeag *Arg. & B.* ***Settlement***, in Glen Shira, 4m/7km NE of Inveraray. **30 D3** NN1314.
Els Ness *Ork.* ***Coastal feature***, peninsula on S coast of Sanday, 2m/4km W of Tres Ness. **81 E3** HY6737.
Elsrickle *S.Lan.* ***Village***, 3m/5km N of Biggar. **25 E5** NT0643.
Elvan Water *S.Lan.* ***River***, rising on Lowther Hills and flowing E to join River Clyde at Elvanfoot. **16 A4** NS9517.
Elvanfoot *S.Lan.* ***Village***, at confluence of Elvan Water and River Clyde, 4m/7km S of Abington. **16 A4** NS9517.
Elvingston *E.Loth.* ***Settlement***, 3m/5km W of Haddington. **26 B2** NT4674.
Elwick (Also spelled Ellwick.) *Ork.* ***Locality***, on E side of Elwick bay, S coast of Shapinsay. Balfour is situated on W side of bay. HY4816.
Embo *High.* ***Village***, on E coast of Sutherland district, 2m/3km N of Dornoch. **72 D5** NH8192.
Embo Street *High.* ***Settlement***, 1m/2km SW of Embo. **72 D5** NH8091.
Enaclete *W.Isles* *Anglicised form of Einacleit, qv.*
Enard Bay *High.* ***Bay***, on NW coast of Ross and Cromarty district, on E side of Rubha Coigeach, 5m/8km SW of Lochinver. **70 C3** NC0318.
Endrick Water ***River***, rising on Fintry Hills and flowing W past Fintry, Balfron and Drymen along an increasingly contorted and meandering course before flowing into Loch Lomond nearly 1m/2km S of Balmaha. **23 G1** NS4289.
Ennochdhu (Also spelled Enochdu.) *P. & K.* ***Hamlet***, in Strathardle, 2m/3km NW of Kirkmichael. Field study centre at Kindrogan, below Kindrogan Hill and across River Ardle. **41 F3** NO0662.
Enoch Hill *E.Ayr.* ***Mountain***, above N edge of Carsphairn Forest, 5m/8km E of Dalmellington. Height 1866 feet or 569 metres. **15 D5** NS5606.
Enochdu *P. & K.* *Alternative spelling of Ennochdhu, qv.*
Enrick *High.* ***River***, in Inverness district running E down Glen Urquhart to Urquhart Bay on NW side of Loch Ness. **50 C2** NH5229.
Ensay *Arg. & B.* ***Settlement***, on Mull, 3m/5km NW of Kilninian. **36 C5** NM3648.
Ensay *W.Isles* ***Island***, sparsely populated island in Sound of Harris, 2m/4km off W coast of Harris at Leverburgh. Measures nearly 2m/3km N to S and 1km E to W. **66 B5** NF9686.
Enterkin Burn *D. & G.* ***River***, joins River Nith at Enterkinfoot, 6m/9km N of Thornhill. **15 G5** NS8504.
Enterkinfoot *D. & G.* ***Locality***, at confluence of River Nith and Enterkin Burn. **15 G5** NS8504.
Eochar *W.Isles* *Anglicised form of Iochda, qv.*
Eolaigearraidh (Anglicised form: Eoligarry.) *W.Isles* ***Village***, on Barra, 1m/2km S of Scurrival Point. **44 C3** NF7007.
Eoligarry *W.Isles* *Anglicised form of Eolaigearraidh, qv.*
Eorabus *Arg. & B.* ***Settlement***, on Mull, 1m/2km N of Bunessan. **28 C2** NM3823.
Eorodal *W.Isles* ***Settlement***, 1km S of Port Nis, Isle of Lewis. **69 G1** NB5362.
Eoropaidh (Anglicised form: Eoropie.) *W.Isles* ***Village***, 1m/2km S of Butt of Lewis. **69 G1** NB5164.
Eoropie *W.Isles* *Anglicised form of Eoropaidh, qv.*
Eorsa *Arg. & B.* ***Island***, uninhabited island in Loch na Keal, W coast of Mull. Area about 250 acres or 100 hectares. Provides grazing for sheep. **29 D1** NM4837.
Erbusaig *High.* ***Settlement***, in Skye and Lochalsh district, on Erbusaig Bay. **49 D2** NG7629.
Erbusaig Bay *High.* ***Bay***, 1m/2km N of Kyle of Lochalsh. NG7529.
Erchless Castle *High.* ***Settlement***, site of 15c seat of The Chisholm, chief of clan owning Strathglass, located at foot of Strathglass and just N of confluence of Rivers Farrar and Glass. **60 D5** NH4040.
Erchless Forest *High.* ***Open space***, deer forest in Inverness district W of Beauly and S of Orrin Reservoir. **60 C5** NH4145.
Eredine *Arg. & B.* ***Historic house***, to S of Loch Awe, near N end of Eredine Forest. **30 B4** NM9609.
Eredine Forest *Arg. & B.* ***Forest/woodland***, on E side of Loch Awe in Argyll above Portinnisherrich. **30 C3** NM9609.
Eriboll *High.* ***Settlement***, on E side of Loch Eriboll, Sutherland district, 2m/4km NE of head of loch. **74 D3** NC4356.
Ericht *P. & K.* ***River***, issuing from Loch Ericht and flowing S to Loch Rannoch. **40 A3** NN5257.
Ericht *P. & K.* ***River***, formed by River Ardle and Black Water, and running S to Blairgowrie then SE to River Isla 2m/3km NE of Coupar Angus. **42 A5** NO2342.
Ericstane *D. & G.* ***Settlement***, 3m/5km N of Moffat. **16 B4** NT0711.
Eriff *E.Ayr.* ***Settlement***, on S shore of Loch Muck, 4m/6km SE of Dalmellington. **14 D5** NS5100.
Erines *Arg. & B.* ***Settlement***, in Knapdale, on W shore of Loch Fyne, 4m/6km N of Tarbert. **21 G2** NR8675.
Erisgeir *Arg. & B.* ***Island***, flat-topped rocky islet 2m/4km NW of Rubha nan Goirteanan on W coast of Mull and 3m/4km S of Little Colonsay. Provides occasional grazing for sheep. **28 C1** NM3832.
Eriska *Arg. & B.* ***Island***, at entrance to Loch Creran. Causeway to mainland on S side. **38 B5** NM9043.
Eriskay (Gaelic form: Eiriosgaigh.) *W.Isles* ***Island***, of about 3 square miles or 8 square km lying 1m/2km S of South Uist and 5m/8km E of N point of Barra. Small village at N end. Prince Charles Edward first landed on Scottish soil here in 1744 at Coilleag a' Phrionnsa. **46 B4** NF7910.
Ernan Water *Aber.* ***River***, flowing E, then SE down Glen Ernan to join River Don, 2m/3km SW of Strathdon. **53 F3** NJ3310.
Erne Stack *Shet.* ***Coastal feature***, rocky promontory on NW coast of Muckle Roe. **82 B1** HU3067.
Erradale *High.* ***River***, flowing NW to coast of Ross and Cromarty district, 1m/2km N of Redpoint. **59 D3** NG7371.
Erraid *Arg. & B.* ***Island***, sparsely populated island of 1 square mile or 3 square km, lying off W end of Ross of Mull across Erraid Sound. Described in unflattering terms by R.L. Stevenson in 'Kidnapped'. **28 B3** NM2919.
Erraid Sound *Arg. & B.* ***Sea feature***, channel between Erraid and W end of Ross of Mull. Channel is fordable at low tide. NM3020.
Errochty Water *P. & K.* ***River***, running E from Loch Errochty down Glen Errochty to River Garry near Calvine. **40 C3** NN8065.
Errogie *High.* ***Settlement***, near NE end of Loch Mhòr, in Inverness district, 3m/4km E of Inverfarigaig. **51 E2** NH5622.
Errol *P. & K.* Population: 1143. ***Village***, in Carse of Gowrie, 8m/13km E of Perth. **34 A2** NO2522.
Errollston *Aber.* ***Settlement***, 1km N of Cruden Bay. **55 F1** NK0837.
Ersary *W.Isles* *Anglicised form of Earsairidh, qv.*
Erskine *Renf.* Population: 13,186. ***Town***, on S side of River Clyde near Erskine Bridge, 4m/6km NW of Renfrew. **23 F2** NS4571.
Erskine Bridge *Renf.* ***Bridge***, road bridge across River Clyde from Erskine to Old Kirkpatrick, 3m/5km NW of Clydebank. NS4672.
Ervie *D. & G.* ***Locality***, 6m/9km NW of Stranraer. **6 B4** NW9967.
Es Wick *Shet.* ***Bay***, to N of Eswick, Mainland. HU4853.
Escart *Arg. & B.* ***Settlement***, 2m/3km SW of Tarbert. **21 G3** NR8466.
Esdale Law *Sc.Bord.* ***Mountain***, 4m/7km NW of Hawick. Height 1168 feet or 356 metres. **17 F4** NT4417.
Esha Ness *Shet.* ***Coastal feature***, peninsula on NW coast of Mainland, 5m/8km W of Hillswick Lighthouse. Skerry of Eshaness is small island to S. **84 A5** HU2178.
Esk ***River***, formed by confluence of North and South Esk Rivers, 1m/2km N of Dalkeith, and flowing N to enter Firth of Forth at Musselburgh. **26 A3** NT3474.
Esk ***River***, rising as Rivers Black Esk and White Esk and flowing SE to Langholm, then S to Canonbie. Continuing S, it passes into England and flows past Longtown to head of Solway Firth, its channel joining that of River Eden SE of Annan. **10 B3** NY2463.
Eskadale *High.* ***Settlement***, 6m/9km SW of Beauly. **50 D1** NH4439.
Eskbank *Midloth.* ***Suburb***, to SW of Dalkeith. **26 A3** NT3266.
Eskdalemuir *D. & G.* ***Settlement***, and church on River White Esk, 11m/17km NW of Langholm. Traces of Roman fort nearly 1m/2km N at Raeburnfoot. **9 G1** NY2597.
Eskdalemuir Observatory *D. & G.* ***Other building***, geomagnetic observatory 3m/5km N of Eskdalemuir. NT2302.
Eskielawn *Angus* ***Mountain***, 3m/4km W of Balnaboth. Height 1991 feet or 607 metres. **42 A3** NO2766.
Eskin *High.* ***River***, formed by several tributaries from E slopes of Carn na Làraiche Maoile and flowing E into River Findhorn, 9m/15km NW of Kingussie. **51 F3** NH6512.
Esknish *Arg. & B.* ***Settlement***, on Islay, 3m/4km NE of Bridgend. **20 B3** NR3664.
Esragan *Arg. & B.* ***River***, running S into Loch Etive, Argyll, opposite Airds Point. NM9934.
Ess of Glenlatterach *Moray* ***Waterfall***, in course of Leanoch Burn 1m/2km from its confluence with River Lossie and 6m/10km S of Elgin. NJ1953.
Essich *High.* ***Settlement***, in Inverness district, 4m/6km S of Inverness. **51 F1** NH6439.
Esslemont *Aber.* ***Locality***, comprises many dispersed settlements near Bronie Burn, 2m/3km SW of Ellon. **55 E2** NJ9228.
Eswick *Shet.* ***Settlement***, near E coast of Mainland, 1km W of headland Moul of Eswick. HU4853.
Ethie Mains *Angus* ***Hamlet***, 2m/3km SE of Inverkeilor. **43 E5** NO6948.
Etive *High.* ***River***, in Lochaber district, running SW down Glen Etive to head of Loch Etive. NN1145.
Etteridge *High.* ***Settlement***, 4m/7km SW of Newtonmore. **51 F5** NN6892.
Ettrick *Sc.Bord.* ***Village***, on Ettrick Water, 15m/24km W of Hawick. Birthplace of James Hogg, poet, 1770-1835. **17 D4** NT2714.
Ettrick Bay *Arg. & B.* ***Bay***, wide bay on W coast of Bute, 3m/5km W of Rothesay. **22 B3** NS0365.
Ettrick Forest *Sc.Bord.* ***Large natural feature***, large area of moorland to S of Peebles, much used for sheep grazing. **16 C3** NT4832.
Ettrick Pen ***Mountain***, on border of Dumfries & Galloway and Scottish Borders, with cairn at summit, 7m/12km E of Moffat. Height 2270 feet or 692 metres. **16 C5** NT1907.
Ettrick Water *Sc.Bord.* ***River***, rising 6m/9km E of Moffat and flowing NE through Ettrick Forest to River Tweed, 3m/4km NE of Selkirk. **17 E3** NT4832.
Ettrickbridge *Sc.Bord.* ***Village***, on Ettrick Water, 6m/9km SW of Selkirk. **17 E3** NT3824.
Ettrickhill *Sc.Bord.* ***Settlement***, 1km W of Ettrick. **17 D4** NT2614.
Euchan Water *D. & G.* ***River***, rising on mountains 9m/14km SW of Sanquhar and running NE to River Nith on S side of Sanquhar. **15 F5** NS7809.
Euchar *Arg. & B.* ***River***, in Argyll, running W from Loch Scamadale, down Glen Euchar to Loch Feochan, N of Kilninver. NM8222.
Eunay Mòr *W.Isles* ***Island***, islet in West Loch Roag, W coast of Isle of Lewis, close to W shore of Great Bernera. NB1336.
Eurach *Arg. & B.* ***Settlement***, 2m/3km SW of Ford. **30 A4** NM8401.
European Sheep and Wool Centre *Arg. & B.* ***Other feature of interest***, attraction with 19 different breeds of sheep, shearing demonstrations and sheepdog obedience trials. **31 E4** NN2000.
Evan Water *D. & G.* ***River***, rising on Lowther Hills and running S to River Annan 2m/3km S of Moffat. NT0902.
Evanton *High.* Population: 1225. ***Village***, near N shore of Cromarty Firth, Ross and Cromarty district, 6m/9km NE of Dingwall. **61 F3** NH6066.

Evelix *High.* ***River***, in Sutherland district running S into Dornoch Firth at Ferrytown, 5m/8km W of Dornoch. **72 C5** NH7286.
Evelix *High.* ***Settlement***, 2m/3km NW of Dornoch. **72 C5** NH7691.
Everbay *Ork.* ***Settlement***, on Stronsay, 1m/2km NE of Dishes. **81 E4** HY6724.
Everley *High.* ***Settlement***, 1km N of Freswick. **77 F2** ND3669.
Everton *Shet.* ***Locality***, on Mainland, 8m/13km N of Sumburgh Head. HU4121.
Evertown *D. & G.* ***Village***, 2m/3km W of Canonbie. **10 B4** NY3576.
Evie (Also known as Georth.) *Ork.* ***Settlement***, on Mainland, 2m/3km NW of Woodwick. **80 B4** HY3625.
Ewe Burn *High.* ***River***, stream flowing NE to join Halladale River 1km N of Forsinard, Caithness district. NC8945.
Ewe Hill *S.Lan.* ***Mountain***, 2m/3km NE of Biggar. Height 1178 feet or 359 metres. **25 E5** NT0540.
Ewes Water *D. & G.* ***River***, flowing S to River Esk at Langholm. **10 B2** NY3684.
Eweslees Knowe *D. & G.* ***Mountain***, 4m/7km SW of Craik. Height 1469 feet or 448 metres. **17 E5** NT3201.
Exnaboe *Shet.* ***Locality***, on Mainland, to N of Sumburgh Airport across Pool of Virkie. **83 G5** HU3911.
Ey Burn *Aber.* ***River***, running N down Glen Ey to River Dee at Inverey, 4m/7km W of Braemar. **41 F1** NO0889.
Eye Peninsula (Gaelic form: An Rubha. Also known as Point.) *W.Isles* ***Coastal feature***, peninsula on E side of Isle of Lewis, 4m/6km E of Stornoway, measuring 7m/11km NE to SW and up to 2m/4km NW to SE. Forms SE arm of Loch a' Tuath. **69 G4** NB5232.
Eye Water ***River***, rising on Lammermuir Hills, 2m/3km SW of Oldhamstocks, and running E by Grantshouse and Ayton to North Sea at Eyemouth. **27 F3** NT9464.
Eyebroughty *E.Loth.* ***Coastal feature***, offshore rock accessible at low water, 4m/6km W of North Berwick. Haunt of sea birds. NT4986.
Eyemouth *Sc.Bord.* Population: 3473. ***Small town***, and resort on coast, 8m/13km NW of Berwick-upon-Tweed. **27 G3** NT9464.
Eyemouth Museum *Sc.Bord.* ***Other feature of interest***, in Eyemouth town centre, dedicated to memory of 129 fishermen who died in 1881, and includes 15 foot Eyemouth tapestry and exhibits on local history. **27 G3** NT9464.
Eynhallow *Ork.* ***Island***, uninhabited island, 1km across, in Eynhallow Sound between islands of Mainland and Rousay. Faint remains of medieval monastery (Historic Scotland). **80 B4** HY3529.
Eynhallow Church *Ork.* ***Ecclesiastical building***, largely ruined 12c church on Eynhallow, 1km off NE coast of Mainland. **80 B4** HY3528.
Eynhallow Sound *Ork.* ***Sea feature***, between islands of Mainland and Rousay. **80 B4** HY3529.
Eynort *High.* ***River***, running S to head of Loch Eynort on SW coast of Skye. NG3826.
Eynort *High.* ***Settlement***, at head of Loch Eynort, Skye. **47 G2** NG3826.
Eyre *High.* ***Settlement***, on Skye, on E side of Loch Snizort Beag at entrance to Loch Eyre, 7m/11km S of Uig. **58 A4** NG4152.
Eyre Point *High.* ***Coastal feature***, headland with lighthouse at SE point of Raasay. NG5834.

F

Faebait *High.* ***Settlement***, 3m/5km W of Muir of Ord. **61 D4** NH4850.
Faifley *W.Dun.* Population: 6087. ***Small town***, 2m/3km N of Clydebank. **23 G2** NS5073.
Fail *S.Ayr.* ***Settlement***, 1m/2km NW of Tarbolton. **14 C3** NS4228.
Failford *S.Ayr.* ***Hamlet***, on N bank of meander of River Ayr, 3m/4km W of Mauchline. **14 C3** NS4526.
Fain *High.* ***Settlement***, 6m/9km SE of Dundonnell. **60 A2** NH1379.
Fair Bhuidhe *P. & K.* ***Mountain***, rounded summit 3m/4km NW of Blair Atholl. Height 1515 feet or 462 metres. **40 D3** NN8467.
Fair Isle *Shet.* ***Island***, sparsely inhabited island (National Trust for Scotland), about 3m/5km N to S and 1m/2km E to W, lying 24m/39km SW of Sumburgh Head. Harbour at S end of island. **82 A5** HZ2172.
Fair Isle Airstrip *Shet.* ***Airport/airfield***, 1km NE of Stonybreck. **82 A5** HZ2172.
Fairgirth *D. & G.* ***Settlement***, 1m/2km NW of Sandyhills Bay, 4m/6km SE of Dalbeattie. **8 C5** NX8756.
Fairhill *S.Lan.* ***Suburb***, S district of Hamilton. NS7154.
Fairholm *S.Lan.* ***Suburb***, adjoining to NW of Larkhall. **24 B4** NS7651.
Fairley *Aberdeen* ***Settlement***, 2m/3km E of Westhill. **55 D4** NJ8607.
Fairlie *N.Ayr.* Population: 1516. ***Small town***, resort on Firth of Clyde, 3m/5km S of Largs. Remains of 16c castle inland in Fairlie Glen. **22 D4** NS2055.
Fairlie Roads *N.Ayr.* ***Sea feature***, sea passage between mainland and the Cumbraes. **22 C4** NS2055.
Fairmilehead *Edin.* ***Suburb***, 4m/6km S of Edinburgh city centre. **25 G3** NT2468.
Fairnington *Sc.Bord.* ***Hamlet***, 3m/4km NE of Ancrum. **18 A4** NT6427.
Fala *Midloth.* ***Village***, to N of Fala Moor, 4m/6km SE of Pathhead. **26 B3** NT4360.
Fala Dam *Midloth.* ***Hamlet***, 1km NW of Fala. **26 B3** NT4261.
Fala Moor *Midloth.* ***Open space***, moorland 6m/9km SE of Gorebridge and 2m/3km SW of Fala. **26 B4** NT4360.
Falahill *Sc.Bord.* ***Hamlet***, on NE side of Moorfoot Hills, 4m/7km SE of Gorebridge. **26 A4** NT3956.
Falconer Museum *Moray* ***Other feature of interest***, in Forres, with local history exhibits and memorabilia on Hugh Falconer. **62 C4** NJ0459.
Falfield *Fife* ***Settlement***, 3m/5km SE of Ceres. **34 C4** NO4408.
Falkirk *Falk.* Population: 35,610. ***Town***, industrial town 23m/37km W of Edinburgh. Sections of Antonine Wall visible in town and vicinity, best section of which is ditch of Watling Lodge (Historic Scotland). Scene of battle in 1746 in which Prince Charles Edward defeated government forces. **24 C2** NS8880.
Falkirk Museum *Falk.* ***Other feature of interest***, museum in central Falkirk with displays on archaeology and history of district, especially local pottery and foundry products. **24 D1** NS8990.
Falkland *Fife* Population: 1197. ***Small town***, attractive historic town below NE slope of Lomond Hills, 4m/7km N of Glenrothes. Royal Palace (National Trust for Scotland), 16c. **34 A4** NO2507.
Falkland Palace *Fife* ***Historic house***, in Falkland, 11m/18km N of Kirkcaldy. Country hunting lodge of Stuart monarch from 16c (National Trust for Scotland). Good example of Renaissance style, with beautiful gardens and, reputedly, oldest tennis court in world. **34 A4** NO2507.
Fall of Warness *Ork.* ***Sea feature***, stretch of sea dividing Eday from Muckle Green Holm. **80 D4** HY5328.
Falla *Sc.Bord.* ***Hamlet***, 2m/3km E of Camptown. **18 B5** NT7013.
Fallin *Stir.* Population: 2479. ***Village***, 3m/4km SE of Stirling. **32 D5** NS8391.
Falloch ***River***, rising on W side of Beinn a' Chroin and flowing N, then SW down Glen Falloch and S to head of Loch Lomond. **31 F2** NN3115.
Falls of Acharn *P. & K.* ***Waterfall***, cascade along Acharn Burn, nearly 1km S of where river enters Loch Tay and 2m/3km SW of Kenmore. **40 C5** NN7543.
Falls of Balnaguard *P. & K.* *See Balnaguard Burn.*
Falls of Barvick *P. & K.* ***Waterfall***, in course of Barvick Burn 2m/3km NW of Crieff. **33 D2** NN8524.
Falls of Bracklinn *Stir.* *Alternative name for Bracklinn Falls, qv.*
Falls of Clyde *S.Lan.* ***Waterfall***, series of waterfalls in course of River Clyde in vicinity of Lanark. Former impressiveness modified by hydro-electricity schemes. **24 C5** NS8840.
Falls of Conon *High.* ***Waterfall***, series of cascades in course of River Conon below Loch Luichart, Ross and Cromarty district. **60 C4** NH3857.
Falls of Cruachan *Arg. & B.* ***Waterfall***, in course of stream in Argyll running from Cruachan Reservoir into Loch Awe. Diminished since construction of reservoir. **30 C2** NN0727.
Falls of Damff *Angus* ***Waterfall***, in course of Water of Unich, 1km SW of its confluence with Water of Lee. NO3879.
Falls of Drumly Harry *Angus* ***Waterfall***, in Noran Water, 3m/5km NW of Tannadice. **42 C3** NO4562.
Falls of Edinample *Stir.* ***Waterfall***, in Burn of Ample on S side of Loch Earn, 1m/2km SE of Lochearnhead. NN6022.
Falls of Falloch *Stir.* ***Waterfall***, in Glen Falloch, 4m/7km SW of Crianlarich. **31 F2** NN3320.
Falls of Fender *P. & K.* *See Fender Burn.*
Falls of Foyers *High.* ***Waterfall***, two waterfalls in course of Foyers River, supplying water for hydro-electricity scheme, augmented by pump-storage system from Loch Mhòr. NH4920.
Falls of Garbh Allt *Aber.* ***Waterfall***, in course of stream running N through Ballochbuie Forest to River Dee 3m/5km E of Braemar. **41 G1** NO1989.
Falls of Garry *High.* ***Waterfall***, in Lochaber district, below dam of Loch Garry. NH2701.
Falls of Glomach *High.* ***Waterfall***, National Trust for Scotland property in Allt a' Ghlomaich, Skye and Lochalsh district, 5m/9km SE of Killilan. Height 370 feet or 113 metres. **49 G2** NH0125.
Falls of Keltie *P. & K.* ***Waterfall***, in course of Keltie Burn 1m/2km W of Monzie. **33 D2** NN8625.
Falls of Keltney *P. & K.* *See Keltney Burn.*
Falls of Kirkaig *High.* ***Waterfall***, in course of River Kirkaig, 1km W of Fionn Loch. **70 D3** NC1118.
Falls of Lednock *P. & K.* ***Waterfall***, in course of River Lednock passing through chasm of Deil's Caldron, 1m/2km N of Comrie. NN7623.
Falls of Leny *Stir.* ***Waterfall***, in Pass of Leny, wooded defile below Loch Lubnaig, 2m/4km W of Callander. NN5908.
Falls of Lochay *Stir.* ***Waterfall***, in River Lochay 2m/4km NW of Killin. Hydro-electricity power station to E. **32 A1** NN5435.
Falls of Lora *Arg. & B.* ***Waterfall***, cataract at Connel on Loch Etive, Argyll, formed by reef of rocks stretching two-thirds of way across entrance to loch on E side of road bridge. NM9134.
Falls of Measach *High.* ***Waterfall***, in course of Abhainn Droma, headstream of River Broom, Ross and Cromarty district. Waterfall (National Trust for Scotland) occurs where river passes through Corrieshalloch Gorge. NH2077.
Falls of Moness *P. & K.* ***Waterfall***, series of three waterfalls in Urlar Burn 1m/2km S of Aberfeldy. **41 D5** NN8547.
Falls of Monzie *P. & K.* ***Waterfall***, in course of Shaggie Burn, 1m/2km N of Monzie village. NN8826.
Falls of Ness *P. & K.* ***Waterfall***, in course of Machany Water 1m/2km SE of Muthill. **33 D3** NN8815.
Falls of Orrin *High.* ***Waterfall***, in course of River Orrin, 4m/7km SW of Dingwall and 3m/5km SW from confluence of Rivers Orrin and Conon. **61 D4** NH4652.
Falls of Shin *High.* ***Waterfall***, in course of River Shin, 2m/3km above mouth. **72 A5** NH5799.
Falls of Tarf *P. & K.* ***Waterfall***, in course of Tarf Water, 11m/17km NE of Blair Atholl. **41 E1** NN9879.
Falls of the Bruar *P. & K.* ***Waterfall***, in fir plantation in course of Bruar Water, 1km from its outfall into River Garry E of Calvine. **40 D3** NN8166.
Falls of Truim *High.* ***Waterfall***, in Glen Truim, Badenoch and Strathspey district, 3m/5km above mouth of River Truim. **51 F5** NN6792.
Falls of Tummel *P. & K.* ***Waterfall***, in course of River Tummel, 2m/3km NW of Pitlochry. **41 D4** NN9059.
Falls of Turret *P. & K.* ***Waterfall***, in Glen Turret 3m/4km NW of Crieff. **32 D2** NN8324.
Falls of Unich *Angus* *See Water of Unich.*
Fallside *N.Lan.* ***Suburb***, 3m/5km S of Coatbridge. NS7160.
Fanagmore *High.* ***Settlement***, on S side of Loch Laxford, 4m/6km N of Scourie, in Sutherland district. **74 A3** NC1749.
Fanans *Arg. & B.* ***Settlement***, 2m/3km SE of Taynuilt. **30 C2** NN0329.
Fanellan *High.* ***Locality***, in Inverness district, 4m/6km SW of Beauly. NH4842.
Fankerton *Falk.* ***Village***, 1m/2km W of Denny. NS7883.
Fanmore *Arg. & B.* ***Settlement***, on Mull, on N side of Loch Tuath, 5m/8km S of Dervaig. **36 D5** NM4144.
Fanna Hill *Sc.Bord.* ***Mountain***, in Wauchope Forest area of Cheviot Hills, 1m/2km NW of Singdean. Height 1686 feet or 514 metres. **17 G5** NT5603.
Fannich Forest *High.* ***Open space***, deer forest in Ross and Cromarty district N of Loch Fannich. **60 A3** NH1969.
Fannyside Lochs *N.Lan.* ***Lake/loch***, two lochs, 2m/4km and 3m/5km E of Cumbernauld. NS8073.
Fans *Sc.Bord.* ***Settlement***, 2m/4km SW of Gordon. **26 D5** NT6240.
Faochaig *High.* ***Mountain***, in Killilan Forest, Skye and Lochalsh district. Height 2847 feet or 868 metres. **49 G1** NH0231.
Far Out Head *High.* *Alternative name for Faraid Head, qv.*
Fara *Ork.* *Alternative spelling of Faray, qv.*
Fara *Ork.* ***Island***, sparsely inhabited island of about 200 acres or 80 hectares between E coast of Hoy and Flotta. **78 C3** ND3295.
Faraclett Head *Ork.* ***Coastal feature***, headland at NE end of Rousay on E side of Saviskaill Bay. **80 C3** HY4433.
Faraid Head (Also known as Far Out Head.) *High.* ***Coastal feature***, headland on N coast of Sutherland district, 3m/4km N of Durness. **74 C1** NC3971.
Faray (Also spelled Fara or Pharay.) *Ork.* ***Island***, narrow uninhabited island less than 2m/3km long N to S, lying 1m/2km W of Eday across Sound of Faray. **80 D3** HY5336.
Farg *P. & K.* ***River***, running NE down Glen Farg to River Earn 5m/8km SE of Perth. NO1717.
Farigaig *High.* ***River***, running N then W into Loch Ness at Inverfarigaig, 2m/4km NE of Foyers, Inverness district. **51 E2** NH5223.
Farigaig Forest Trail and Visitor Centre *High.* ***Other feature of interest***, Forestry Commission interpretation centre for wildlife conservation, with bird and animal displays and local walks, 17m/27km SW of Inverness. **51 E2** NH5224.
Farland Head *N.Ayr.* ***Coastal feature***, headland on Firth of Clyde, 5m/8km NW of Ardrossan. **22 C5** NS1748.
Farlary *High.* ***Locality***, 6m/9km NW of Golspie, Sutherland district. **72 C4** NC7705.
Farmtown *Moray* ***Settlement***, at S end of Sillyearn Wood, 3m/5km NW of Milltown of Rothiemay. **64 A4** NJ5051.
Farnell *Angus* ***Village***, 3m/5km SE of Brechin. **43 E4** NO6255.

Farnell Castle *Angus* ***Castle***, in Farnell, 1m/2km SE of Brechin. Dates from 12c when it was built as palace for Bishops of Brechin; much altered and enlarged. NO6255.
Farquhar's Point *High.* ***Coastal feature***, headland on S side of entrance to Loch Moidart in Lochaber district, opposite W end of Eilean Shona. NM6272.
Farr *High.* ***Settlement***, in Inverness district, 8m/12km S of Inverness. Loch Farr is small loch to S. **51 F1** NH6833.
Farr *High.* ***Settlement***, 5m/8km NE of Kingussie. **52 A4** NH8203.
Farr *High.* ***Village***, near N coast of Caithness district, 1m/2km NE of Bettyhill. **75 G2** NC7263.
Farr Bay *High.* ***Bay***, on N coast of Caithness district, 1km W of Farr. **75 F2** NC7263.
Farr House *High.* ***Settlement***, 9m/14km S of Inverness. **51 F1** NH6831.
Farr Point *High.* ***Coastal feature***, headland on N coast of Caithness district, 1m/2km N of Farr. **75 G2** NC7263.
Farragon Hill *P. & K.* ***Mountain***, 4m/7km N of Aberfeldy. Height 2558 feet or 780 metres. **40 D4** NN8455.
Farraline *High.* ***Settlement***, at NE end of Loch Mhòr, 3m/5km SE of Inverfarigaig across loch. **51 E2** NH5621.
Farrar *High.* ***River***, running E from Loch Monar to join River Glass 1km below Struy Bridge in Inverness district. **50 C1** NH4039.
Farrmheall *High.* ***Mountain***, 5m/8km NE of Rhiconich. Height 1709 feet or 521 metres. **74 C3** NC3058.
Fasag *High.* ***Settlement***, adjoining to N of Torridon, Ross and Cromarty district. **59 E4** NG8956.
Fasagrianach *High.* ***Settlement***, in valley of River Broom, 1m/2km NW of Corrieshalloch Gorge. **60 A1** NH1980.
Fascadale *High.* ***Settlement***, on N coast of Ardnamurchan peninsula, 4m/7km N of Kilchoan. **37 E2** NM5070.
Faseny Water *E.Loth.* ***River***, rising on slopes of Meikle Says Law in Lammermuir Hills, and flowing E to Whiteadder Reservoir. **26 C3** NT6463.
Fasheilach ***Mountain***, 3m/4km S of Linn of Muick Cottage, with summit on border of Aberdeenshire and Angus. Height 2365 feet or 721 metres. **42 B1** NO3485.
Fashven *High.* ***Mountain***, 3m/5km W of Achiemore. Height 1499 feet or 457 metres. **74 C2** NC3167.
Faskadale *High.* ***Settlement***, on Faskadale Bay, 3m/5km W of Ockle Point, on N coast of Ardnamurchan peninsula, Lochaber district. NM5070.
Faslane *Arg. & B.* ***Locality***, 1m/2km SE of Garelochhead. **23 D1** NS2589.
Faslane Bay *Arg. & B.* ***Bay***, on E side of Gare Loch, 1m/2km S of Garelochhead. Nuclear submarine base. **22 D1** NS2489.
Fasnacloich *Arg. & B.* ***Settlement***, 2m/3km NE of head of Loch Creran. **38 C5** NN0247.
Fasnakyle *High.* ***Locality***, in Inverness district, where Glen Affric runs into Strathglass. Hydro-electricity power station. **50 C2** NH3128.
Fasnakyle Forest *High.* ***Open space***, deer forest to NW of Fasnakyle. **50 B1** NH3128.
Fasque House *Aber.* ***Historic house***, early 19c home of Gladstone family, 1m/2km N of Fettercairn. Little changed in furnishings and domestic items. **43 E2** NO6475.
Fassfern *High.* ***Settlement***, on N side of Loch Eil, in Lochaber district, 3m/5km E of Kinlocheil. **38 C2** NN0278.
Fast Castle (Also known as Castle Knowe.) *Sc.Bord.* ***Castle***, scant remains of 12c motte castle on cliff, 4m/6km NW of St. Abb's Head. **27 F2** NT8671.
Fastheugh Hill *Sc.Bord.* ***Mountain***, in Ettrick Forest, 5m/8km W of Selkirk. Height 1643 feet or 501 metres. **17 E3** NT3827.
Fathan Glinne *Stir.* ***Valley***, carrying Allt Fathan Glinne and running E then SE into valley of Calair Burn, 3m/4km SW of Balquhidder. **31 G3** NN4917.
Fattahead *Aber.* ***Settlement***, 4m/6km NE of Aberchirder. **64 B4** NJ6557.
Fauldhouse *W.Loth.* Population: 4690. ***Village***, 3m/4km S of Whitburn. **24 D3** NS9360.
Favillar *Moray* ***Settlement***, 5m/8km SW of Dufftown. **53 E1** NJ2734.
Faw Hill *Sc.Bord.* ***Mountain***, 3m/5km NE of Bonchester Bridge. Height 1086 feet or 331 metres. **18 A5** NT6213.
Faw Side *D. & G.* ***Mountain***, on uplands to S of Craik Forest, 5m/8km NE of Bentpath. Height 1722 feet or 525 metres. **10 B2** NY3596.
Fawsyde *Aber.* ***Hamlet***, adjacent to W of Roadside of Kinneff, 3m/5km N of Inverbervie. **43 G2** NO8477.
Feadda Ness *Shet.* ***Coastal feature***, southernmost headland on Isle of Noss. **83 E4** HU5438.
Feall Bay *Arg. & B.* ***Bay***, on NW coast of Coll, 2m/3km from SW end of island. **36 A4** NM1354.
Feardan Burn *Aber.* ***River***, small stream which rises in Grampian Mountains and flows SW, then SE, to join River Dee 1m/2km SW of Balmoral. **53 E5** NO2393.
Fearn *High.* ***Settlement***, near E coast of Ross and Cromarty district, 2m/3km NW of Balintore. **62 A2** NH8377.
Fearn Abbey *High.* ***Ecclesiastical building***, 2m/3km NW of Balintore. Originally founded in 13c and restored after roof fell down in 1742, killing 42 people. Still a parish church. **62 A2** NH8377.
Fearn Station *High.* ***Other building***, railway station on Inverness to Wick line, 3m/5km SE of Tain. **62 A2** NH8178.
Fearnach *Arg. & B.* ***Settlement***, above Bàgh Fearnoch, 3m/5km S of Auchenbreck. **22 B2** NS0276.
Fearnach Bay *Arg. & B.* ***Bay***, at head of Loch Melfort, 1m/2km W of Kilmelford in Argyll. NM8313.
Fearnan *P. & K.* ***Village***, on N shore of Loch Tay, 3m/5km W of Kenmore. **40 C5** NN7244.
Fearnbeg *High.* ***Locality***, in Ross and Cromarty district, on SW side of Loch Torridon, 1m/2km SE of Rubha na Fearn. **58 D4** NG7359.
Fearnmore *High.* ***Settlement***, on SW side of Loch Torridon, Ross and Cromarty district, 1km S of Rubha na Fearn. **58 D3** NG7260.
Fearnoch *Arg. & B.* ***Settlement***, on Cowal peninsula, 5m/8km NW of Tighnabruaich. **22 A2** NR9279.
Fearnoch Forest *Arg. & B.* ***Forest/woodland***, 2m/3km W of Taynuilt, Argyll. **30 B1** NM9631.
Feehlin *High.* ***River***, in Inverness district running N into River Foyers, 2m/3km S of Foyers on Loch Ness. **51 E3** NH4917.
Feinne-bheinn Mhòr *High.* ***Mountain***, 3m/5km SW of S end of Loch Hope. Height 1525 feet or 465 metres. **74 D4** NC4346.
Feirihisval *W.Isles* ***Mountain***, 3m/4km N of head of Loch Shell, Isle of Lewis. Height 1069 feet or 326 metres. **67 E2** NB3014.
Féith a' Chaoruinn *High.* ***River***, flowing SE to join Abhainn Sgeamhaidh 1m/2km E of Rhian. **72 A2** NC5717.
Féith Gaineimh Mhòr *High.* ***River***, in Caithness district, flowing E and joining Féith Chaorunn Mhòr to form Berriedale Water, 5m/8km W of Braemore. **76 B5** NC9831.
Feith-hill *Aber.* ***Settlement***, 3m/5km SE of Inverkeithny. Stone Circle nearby. **64 B5** NJ6643.
Féith Osdail *High.* ***River***, flowing W into River Tirry, 5m/8km N of Lairg. **72 B3** NC5713.
Féith Talachaidh *High.* ***River***, flowing generally SW into River Spey, 6m/9km W of Laggan. **51 E5** NN5396.
Fell Loch *D. & G.* ***Lake/loch***, small loch 7m/11km E of Glenluce. **7 E5** NX3155.
Fell of Carleton *D. & G.* ***Hill***, near coast 3m/5km SE of Monreith. Height 479 feet or 146 metres. **3 D3** NX4037.
Fell of Fleet *D. & G.* ***Mountain***, 6m/10km SW of New Galloway. Height 1542 feet or 470 metres. **7 G3** NX5670.
Fellonmore *Arg. & B.* ***Settlement***, on shore of Loch Spelve, 4m/7km NE of Lochbuie. **29 F2** NM6827.
Fence Bay *N.Ayr.* ***Bay***, on Fairlie Roads, Firth of Clyde, 1m/2km S of Fairlie. NS2053.
Fender Burn *P. & K.* ***River***, running SW down Glen Fender to River Tilt, 1m/2km N of Blair Atholl. Falls of Fender near junction with River Tilt. **41 E2** NN8766.
Fendoch *P. & K.* ***Historic/prehistoric site***, site of Roman station, 5m/9km NE of Crieff. NN9128.
Fenton Barns *E.Loth.* ***Hamlet***, 3m/5km SW of North Berwick. NT5181.
Fenton Tower *E.Loth.* ***Historic/prehistoric site***, ruined 16c stronghold at Kingston, 2m/3km S of North Berwick. NT5482.
Fenwick *E.Ayr.* Population: 1057. ***Village***, 4m/7km NE of Kilmarnock. **23 F5** NS4643.
Fenwick Water ***River***, running SW to confluence with Craufurdland Water 1m/2km NE of Kilmarnock. Combined stream, known as Kilmarnock Water, flows through Kilmarnock to River Irvine on S side of town. **23 G5** NS4339.
Feoch Burn *S.Ayr.* ***River***, rising in Loch Crongart and flowing SW to join Duisk River, 1m/2km SE of Barrhill. **7 D2** NX2581.
Feochag Bay *High.* ***Bay***, small bay on W coast of Ross and Cromarty district, 1km SW of Rubha Coigeach. **70 B3** NB9717.
Feochaig *Arg. & B.* ***Settlement***, on SE side of S end of Kintyre, 5m/8km SE of Campbeltown. **12 C4** NR7613.
Feolin *Arg. & B.* ***Settlement***, on SE coast of Jura, 1m/2km N of Craighouse. **20 D3** NR5369.
Feolin Ferry *Arg. & B.* ***Locality***, with pier, on W coast of Jura; ferry across Sound of Islay to Port Askaig, 1km W of Islay. **20 C3** NR4469.
Feorlan *Arg. & B.* ***Settlement***, at S end of Kintyre, 3m/5km W of Southend. **12 B5** NR6307.
Feorlin *Arg. & B.* ***Settlement***, 2m/3km NE of Minard. **30 B5** NR9597.
Ferguslie Park *Renf.* ***Suburb***, W district of Paisley. NS4664.
Ferindonald *High.* ***Settlement***, on E side of Sleat peninsula, Skye, 1m/2km SW of Teangue. NG6507.
Feriniquarrie *High.* ***Settlement***, near NW coast of Skye, 4m/7km S of Dunvegan Head. **57 E4** NG1750.
Fern *Angus* ***Settlement***, 2m/4km N of Tannadice. **42 C3** NO4861.
Ferness *High.* ***Settlement***, in Nairn district, 8m/13km SE of Nairn. **62 B5** NH9644.
Fernie *Fife* ***Hamlet***, 4m/6km W of Cupar. **34 B3** NO3114.
Ferniegair *S.Lan.* ***Hamlet***, 1m/2km SE of Hamilton. NS7354.
Ferniehill *Edin.* ***Suburb***, 4m/6km SE of Edinburgh city centre. NT2969.
Ferniehirst Castle *Sc.Bord.* ***Castle***, ancient stronghold of Kerrs, rebuilt in 1598, 1m/2km S of Jedburgh. Kerr Museum. NT6518.
Fernilea *High.* ***Settlement***, on W side of Loch Harport, Skye, 1m/2km NW of Carbost. **47 G1** NG3633.
Fernybank *Angus* ***Settlement***, 3m/5km SE of Tarfside, on N side of River North Esk. **42 D2** NO5378.
Ferry Point *High.* ***Coastal feature***, promontory on S side of Dornoch Firth and 4m/6km NW of Tain, Ross and Cromarty district. NH7385.
Ferryden *Angus* ***Village***, on S side of River South Esk, opposite Montrose. **43 F4** NO7156.
Ferryhill *Aberdeen* ***Suburb***, to S of Aberdeen city centre. NJ9305.
Ferrytown *High.* ***Locality***, at mouth of River Evelix on N shore of Dornoch Firth, 5m/8km W of Dornoch, Sutherland district. NH7287.
Fers Ness *Ork.* ***Coastal feature***, N facing headland on W coast of Eday, on W side of wide Fersness Bay. **80 D3** HY5334.
Fersit *High.* ***Settlement***, in valley of River Treig, 1m/2km S of Tulloch Station. **39 F2** NN3578.
Fersness Bay *Ork.* ***Bay***, wide bay on W coast of Eday. HY5434.
Feshie *High.* ***River***, in Badenoch and Strathspey district, rising on S side of Glenfeshie Forest and running N down Glen Feshie to River Spey 1km below Kincraig. **41 D1** NH8406.
Feshiebridge *High.* ***Locality***, in Badenoch and Strathspey district, 1m/2km SE of Kincraig. **52 A4** NH8504.
Fetlar *Shet.* ***Island***, large sparsely inhabited island of about 14 square miles or 36 square km S of Unst and E of Yell. Nature reserve. **85 F3** HU6391.
Fetterangus *Aber.* ***Village***, 2m/3km N of Mintlaw. **65 E4** NJ9850.
Fettercairn *Aber.* ***Village***, 11m/17km NW of Montrose. Contains shaft of town cross of Kincardine. **43 E2** NO6573.
Fetteresso Forest *Aber.* ***Forest/woodland***, 6m/10km W of Stonehaven. **43 F1** NO7787.
Fetternear House *Aber.* ***Settlement***, 1m/2km NW of Kemnay. Remains of Fetternear House and Bishops Palace. **54 C3** NJ7217.
Fettes College *Edin.* ***Educational establishment***, boys' public school in Edinburgh, 1m/2km NW of city centre. NT2375.
Feus of Caldhame *Aber.* ***Settlement***, 4m/6km SW of Lawrencekirk. **43 E3** NO6567.
Fiag *High.* ***River***, in Sutherland district, running S from Loch Fiag, along Glen Fiag, to Loch Shin. NC4620.
Fiarach *Stir.* ***Mountain***, 3m/4km NW of Crianlarich. Height 2139 feet or 652 metres. **31 F2** NN3425.
Fiaray *W.Isles* ***Island***, small uninhabited island off Scurrival Point at N end of Barra. **44 B2** NF7010.
Fiavig Bàgh *W.Isles* ***Bay***, on W coast of Isle of Lewis, 3m/4km SW of Gallan Head. **68 B4** NB0335.
Fibhig (Anglicised form: Fivig.) *W.Isles* ***Settlement***, near NW coast of Isle of Lewis, NE of North Shawbost. **69 D3** NB2648.
Fichlie *Aber.* ***Settlement***, on N side of River Don, 7m/11km E of Strathdon. **53 G3** NJ4513.
Fidden *Arg. & B.* ***Settlement***, on W coast of Ross of Mull, 1m/2km S of Fionnphort. **28 C2** NM3021.
Fiddich *Moray* ***River***, rising on Corryhabbie Hill, Glenfiddich Forest, and running NE down Glen Fiddich, then W to Dufftown, then NW to River Spey at Craigellachie. **53 F1** NJ2945.
Fidra *E.Loth.* ***Island***, small island off shore 3m/4km W of North Berwick. Haunt of sea birds. Lighthouse. **26 C1** NT5186.
Fife Folk Museum *Fife* ***Other feature of interest***, museum at Ceres, 3m/4km SE of Cupar, with displays on Fife's agricultural past, including farm and blacksmiths' implements and domestic material. **34 B3** NO4011.
Fife Keith *Moray* ***Locality***, adjoining to W of Keith, connected to it by early 17c bridge. **63 G4** NJ4250.
Fife Ness *Fife* ***Coastal feature***, headland at E extremity of Fife, 9m/15km SE of St. Andrews. **35 E4** NO6309.
Fife Regional Park *Fife* ***Large natural feature***, designated park around Lomond Hills, to NW of Glenrothes. **34 A4** NO2405.
Filla *Shet.* ***Island***, small round-shaped island in SW part of Out Skerries group of islands. **83 F1** HU6668.
Fin Glen *E.Dun.* ***Valley***, carrying Finglen Burn, stream rising on Campsie Fells and running SE to Glazert Water, 1m/2km NW of Lennoxtown. **23 G1** NS5980.

Finalty Hill *Angus* ***Mountain***, 4m/6km W of Glendoll Lodge. Height 2968 feet or 905 metres. **42 A2** NO2175.
Finart Bay *Arg. & B.* ***Bay***, small bay in Argyll on W side of Loch Long, on N side of Ardentinny. NS1887.
Finavon *Angus* ***Settlement***, on River South Esk, 5m/8km NE of Forfar. **42 C4** NO4957.
Finavon Castle *Angus* ***Castle***, ruined 16c stronghold of Earls of Crawford, 1km S of Finavon and 4m/6km SW of Brechin. **42 D4** NO4956.
Finavon Doocot *Angus* ***Other feature of interest***, 16c dovecot (National Trust for Scotland) at Milton of Finavon, to S of Finavon across River South Esk. Largest in Scotland with 2400 nesting boxes. **42 D4** NO4957.
Finbracks *Angus* ***Mountain***, 2m/3km E of Rottal. Height 2480 feet or 756 metres. **42 B2** NO4070.
Fincharn Castle *Arg. & B.* ***Castle***, remains of former stronghold of the Macdonalds on E shore of Loch Awe in Argyll, 2m/3km E of head of loch. **30 B4** NM8904.
Fincharn Loch *Arg. & B.* ***Lake/loch***, small loch 4m/6km E of Ford. **30 B4** NM9303.
Findhorn ***River***, formed from many tributaries on Monadhliath Mountains, and flowing from Coignafearn Forest NE through Strathdearn, then E from Drynachan Lodge to Dulsie, finally following an increasingly meandering course NE to enter W end of Burghead Bay at Findhorn. **51 G2** NJ0364.
Findhorn *Moray* ***Village***, fishing village on E side of sandy Findhorn Bay at mouth of River Findhorn, N of Forres. **62 C3** NJ0364.
Findhorn Bay *Moray* ***Bay***, sandy bay at mouth of River Findhorn, N of Forres. **62 C3** NJ0364.
Findhorn Bridge *High.* ***Settlement***, on River Findhorn, 1km S of Tomatin. **52 A2** NH8027.
Findhu Glen *P. & K.* ***Valley***, running NW into Glen Artney, 5m/8km SW of Dalginross. **32 C3** NN7314.
Findhuglen *P. & K.* ***Settlement***, 8m/12km NE of Callander. **32 C3** NN7215.
Findlater Castle *Aber.* ***Castle***, ruined castle on cliffs 2m/3km E of Cullen. **64 A3** NJ5467.
Findlay's Seat *Moray* ***Hill***, 3m/4km N of Rothes. Height 859 feet or 262 metres. **63 E4** NJ2853.
Findo Gask *P. & K.* ***Locality***, surrounded by Roman sites, 7m/12km W of Perth. **33 F2** NO0020.
Findochty *Moray* Population: 1092. ***Village***, fishing village and resort at E end of Spey Bay, 3m/5km NE of Buckie. **63 G3** NJ4667.
Findochty Castle *Moray* ***Castle***, ruins of 16c tower house, 1km SW of Findochty. NJ4567.
Findon (Also known as Finnan.) *Aber.* ***Village***, near E coast, 5m/9km S of Aberdeen. Finnan is name from which smoked haddock takes its name. **55 E5** NO9397.
Findon Forest *High.* ***Forest/woodland***, on Black Isle, Ross and Cromarty district, 5m/8km W of Fortrose. NH6458.
Findon Mains *High.* ***Settlement***, 5m/8km NE of Conon Bridge. **61 F3** NH6060.
Findon Ness *Aber.* ***Coastal feature***, headland on coast at Findon. **55 E5** NO9397.
Findowie Hill *P. & K.* ***Mountain***, 8m/12km NW of Methven. Height 1912 feet or 583 metres. **33 E1** NN9435.
Findrassie *Moray* ***Settlement***, 2m/3km NW of Elgin. **63 D3** NJ1965.
Findron *Moray* ***Settlement***, 1km E of Tomintoul. **53 D3** NJ1718.
Finegand *P. & K.* ***Settlement***, on Shee Water, 3m/5km SE of Spittal of Glenshee. **41 G3** NO1366.
Fingal's Cave *Arg. & B.* ***Cave***, large cave at S end of Staffa with pillars of basalt at entrance. Dimensions: height 66 feet or 20 metres; depth from entrance to back 227 feet or 69 metres; width of entrance 42 feet or 13 metres. **28 C1** NM3235.
Fingask *Aber.* ***Settlement***, 2m/3km W of Oldmeldrum. **54 C2** NJ7727.
Fingask Castle *P. & K.* ***Castle***, restored castle, 7m/12km E of Perth, dating from 16c. NO2227.
Fingask Loch *P. & K.* ***Lake/loch***, small loch 2m/3km SW of Blairgowrie. NO1642.
Fingland *D. & G.* ***Settlement***, 5m/8km NW of Sanquhar. **15 F4** NS7517.
Fingland *D. & G.* ***Settlement***, 1m/2km N of Davington. **16 D5** NT2304.
Fingland Fell *D. & G.* ***Mountain***, in woodland, 3m/5km NW of Boreland. Height 1273 feet or 388 metres. **9 F1** NY1495.
Finglas Water *Stir.* ***River***, running SE down Glen Finglas, through Glen Finglas Reservoir, to Black Water between Loch Achray and Loch Venachar, W of Callander. NN5306.
Finglen Burn ***River***, stream rising on Campsie Fells and running SE to Glazert Water, 1m/2km NW of Lennoxtown. NS6178.
Finglen Burn *Stir.* ***River***, flowing SW into Loch Tay, just N of Ardeonaig. **32 B1** NN6636.
Finlarig *Stir.* ***Settlement***, 1km N of Killin. **32 A1** NN5733.
Finlarig Castle *Stir.* ***Castle***, early 17c remains of former seat of Earls of Breadalbane in Killin, 10m/16km NW of Callender. **32 A1** NN5733.
Finlas Water *Arg. & B.* ***River***, running SE down Glen Finlas into Loch Lomond, 1m/2km S of Rossdhu House. Small reservoir at head of glen. NS3687.
Finlaystone House *Inclyde* ***Historic house***, home of Chief of Clan MacMillan, 3m/4km W of Port Glasgow. House contains doll collection and Celtic art displays and is surrounded by notable gardens. **23 E2** NS3673.
Finnan *Aber.* *Alternative name for Findon, qv.*
Finnan *High.* ***River***, in Lochaber district running S down Glen Finnan to head of Loch Shiel. NM9080.
Finnart *Arg. & B.* ***Locality***, site of former oil terminal in Argyll on E side of Loch Long, 3m/4km N of Garelochhead. **31 E5** NS2495.
Finnart *P. & K.* ***Settlement***, on S side of Loch Rannoch, 1km from head of loch. **40 A4** NN5157.
Finnarts Bay *S.Ayr.* ***Bay***, small bay near N end of Loch Ryan, at mouth of Water of App, 6m/10km S of Ballantrae. NX0572.
Finnarts Point *S.Ayr.* ***Coastal feature***, headland 1m/2km N of Finnarts Bay. **6 B3** NX0572.
Finnich Glen ***Valley***, on border of Stirling and West Dunbartonshire, carrying Burn Crooks NW from Burncrooks Reservoir. **23 F1** NS4780.
Finnieston *Glas.* ***Suburb***, 1m/2km W of Glasgow city centre. Scottish Exhibition and Conference Centre situated to W. NS5765.
Finnygaud *Aber.* ***Locality***, 2m/3km NW of Aberchirder. **64 B4** NJ6054.
Finsbay *W.Isles* ***Settlement***, on Loch Finsbay, on SE coast of South Harris, 2m/4km SW of Manais. NG0786.
Finstown *Ork.* ***Village***, on Mainland at head of Bay of Firth, 6m/10km W of Kirkwall. Tormiston Mill, 2m/4km W, is excellent example of 19c Scottish water mill and also reception centre for megalithic tomb of Maes Howe (both Historic Scotland). **80 B5** HY3513.
Fintry *Aber.* ***Settlement***, 4m/6km NE of Turriff. **64 C4** NJ7554.
Fintry *Stir.* ***Village***, on Endrick Water, 5m/7km E of Balfron. **24 A1** NS6186.
Fintry Hills *Stir.* ***Large natural feature***, small mountain range 2m/3km NE of Fintry, with highest summit Stronend (511 metres). **24 A1** NS6488.
Finzean *Aber.* ***Settlement***, 2m/3km SW of Marywell. **54 A5** NO5993.
Fiola Meadhonach *Arg. & B.* ***Island***, small island immediately N of Lunga. NM7109.
Fionn Bheinn (Anglicised form: Foinaven.) *High.* ***Mountain***, in Ross and Cromarty district 2m/4km N of Achnasheen. Munro: height 3060 feet or 933 metres. **60 A3** NH1462.
Fionn Bheinn Mhòr *High.* ***Mountain***, 2m/3km NW of Oykel Bridge. Height 1082 feet or 330 metres. **71 F4** NC3704.
Fionn Loch *High.* ***Lake/loch***, long narrow loch 1m/2km N of Loch Sionascaig and 3m/5km SE of Inverkirkaig. **70 D3** NC1218.
Fionn Loch *High.* ***Lake/loch***, near W coast of Ross and Cromarty district 5m/8km E of Poolewe. Length over 5m/8km NW to SE; width about 1km. **59 F1** NG9478.
Fionn Loch Mòr *High.* ***Lake/loch***, irregular-shaped loch fed by Fionn Allt, to SE of Gorm Loch Mòr, 5m/8km E of Inchnadamph. **71 F2** NC3324.
Fionnphort *Arg. & B.* ***Village***, on Sound of Iona, at W end of Ross of Mull. Ferry to Iona. **28 C2** NM3023.
Firrhill *Edin.* ***Suburb***, 3m/5km SW of Edinburgh city centre. NT2369.
Firth *Shet.* ***Settlement***, on NE coast of Mainland, 1m/2km S of Mossbank across Firths Voe inlet. Firth Ness is headland 1m/2km E. **84 D5** HU4473.
Firth Ness *Shet.* ***Coastal feature***, headland 1m/2km E of Firth, Mainland. HU4473.
Firth of Clyde ***Sea feature***, estuary of River Clyde running from Dumbarton past Gourock, then turning S and continuing between Strathclyde mainland to E and islands of Bute and Arran to W. **13 F5** NS1043.
Firth of Forth ***Sea feature***, estuary of River Forth, running E and widening out into North Sea between Fife Ness and North Berwick. At its narrowest point (1m/2km), between North and South Queensferry, firth is spanned by Forth road and railway bridges. **25 G1** NT2181.
Firth of Lorn *Arg. & B.* ***Sea feature***, sea passage between SE coast of Mull and Scottish mainland. **29 F3** NM7021.
Firth of Tay ***Sea feature***, estuary of River Tay extending E from confluence of Rivers Tay and Earn past Dundee to Buddon Ness. Length about 23m/37km; maximum width nearly 3m/5km at Invergowrie, although channel is comparatively narrow owing to presence of sandbanks. **34 B2** NO3737.
Firths Voe *Shet.* *See Firth.*
Fish Holm *Shet.* ***Island***, small island off NE coast of Mainland 2m/3km E of Mossbank. **85 D5** HU4774.
Fishcross *Clack.* ***Hamlet***, 2m/3km NE of Alloa. NS9095.
Fisherfield Forest *High.* ***Open space***, deer forest in Ross and Cromarty district, centre of which is about 8m/13km E of Poolewe. **59 F1** NG9980.
Fisherford *Aber.* ***Settlement***, 9m/15km E of Huntly. **54 B1** NJ6635.
Fisherrow *E.Loth.* ***Locality***, W part of Musselburgh. Small harbour. NT3373.
Fisherton *High.* ***Settlement***, in Inverness district, on E side of Inner Moray Firth, 1m/2km W of Dalcross Airport. **61 G4** NH7451.
Fisherton *S.Ayr.* ***Settlement***, 1km NE of Dunure. **14 A4** NS2616.
Fishnish *Arg. & B.* ***Locality***, on E coast of Mull; jetty for ferries from Lochaline on Scottish mainland. **37 F5** NM6641.
Fishnish Bay *Arg. & B.* ***Bay***, on Sound of Mull, 4m/7km E of Salen, Mull. **37 F5** NM6442.
Fishnish Point *Arg. & B.* ***Coastal feature***, headland on E side of Fishnish Bay, Mull. **37 F5** NM6442.
Fishtown of Usan (Also known as Usan.) *Angus* ***Village***, on E coast, 2m/3km S of Montrose. **43 F4** NO7254.
Fishwick *Sc.Bord.* ***Hamlet***, 2m/3km SW of Paxton. **27 G4** NT9151.
Fiskavaig *High.* ***Locality***, with small bay on W coast of Skye, on S shore of Loch Bracadale. NG3334.
Fitful Head *Shet.* ***Coastal feature***, headland on W coast of Mainland, 5m/8km NW of Sumburgh Head. The steep cliffs rise to 929 feet or 283 metres. **83 F4** HU3413.
Fiunary *High.* ***Settlement***, on SW coast of Morvern, Lochaber district, 4m/6km NW of Lochaline. **37 F5** NM6246.
Fiunary Forest *High.* ***Forest/woodland***, in Lochaber district to NW of Lochaline. **37 F5** NM6647.
Five Penny Borve *W.Isles* *Anglicised form of Còig Peighinnean Bhuirgh, qv.*
Five Penny Ness *W.Isles* *Anglicised form of Còig Peighinnean, qv.*
Five Sisters (Also known as Five Sisters of Kintail.) *High.* ***Large natural feature***, chain of peaks on Kintail Forest (National Trust for Scotland), Skye and Lochalsh district; from N to S, Sgurr na Moraich, Sgurr nan Saighead, Sgurr Fhuaran (or Scour Ouran), Sgurr na Carnach, and Sgurr na Ciste Duibhe. **49 F3** NG9717.
Five Sisters of Kintail *High.* *Alternative name for Five Sisters, qv.*
Fivig *W.Isles* *Anglicised form of Fibhig, qv.*
Fladda *Arg. & B.* ***Island***, one of larger islands of the Treshnish Isles, lying towards NE end of group. **36 C5** NM2943.
Fladda *Arg. & B.* ***Island***, islet with lighthouse 1m/2km off NW coast of Luing. NM7212.
Fladda-chuain *High.* ***Island***, narrow uninhabited island, nearly 1m/2km long NW to SE, 4m/6km NW of Rubha Hunish, Skye. **67 F5** NG3681.
Fladdabister *Shet.* ***Settlement***, on E coast of Mainland, 6m/10km S of Lerwick, near head of small Bay of Fladdabister. **82 D4** HU4332.
Fladday *High.* *Alternative name for Eilean Fladday, qv.*
Fladday *W.Isles* ***Island***, small uninhabited island off E coast of Scarp opposite entrance to Loch Resort, W coast of Isle of Lewis. NA9915.
Flanders Moss *Stir.* ***Marsh/bog***, boggy area between River Forth and Goodie Water, SW of Thornhill. **32 B5** NS6398.
Flannan Isles *W.Isles* ***Island***, group of small uninhabited islands about 21m/34km W of Gallan Head, Isle of Lewis. The main islands, in order of size, are: Eilean Mòr, Eilean Tighe, Eilean a' Ghobha, Soray, Roareim, Sgeir Toman, and Sgeir Righinn. There are several smaller islets and rocks. Larger islands are grass-covered and are used for grazing. Birds abound. NA7246.
Flashader *High.* ***Settlement***, on E side of Loch Greshornish, on N coast of Skye. **57 G4** NG3553.
Fleet *High.* ***River***, rising near Lairg in Sutherland district and flowing SE to Loch Fleet and coast, 4m/6km N of Dornoch. NH8195.
Fleet Bay *D. & G.* ***Sea feature***, inlet of Wigtown bay at mouth of Water of Fleet. **7 G5** NX5652.
Fleet Forest *D. & G.* ***Forest/woodland***, wooded area to S of Gatehouse of Fleet. NX6055.
Fleisirin *W.Isles* *Gaelic form of Flesherin, qv.*
Flemington *S.Lan.* ***Locality***, 3m/5km SE of Rutherglen. **24 A4** NS6659.
Flemington *S.Lan.* ***Suburb***, adjoining to NE of Strathaven. NS7044.
Fleoideabhagh (Anglicised form: Flodabay.) *W.Isles* ***Settlement***, on SE coast of South Harris, 4m/7km NE of Rodel. **66 C5** NG0988.
Flesherin (Gaelic form: Fleisirin.) *W.Isles* ***Settlement***, on Eye Peninsula, Isle of Lewis, 1km SW of Portnaguran. NB5536.
Fleuchats *Aber.* ***Settlement***, below N slopes of Meikle Charsk Hill, 3m/4km S of Strathdon. **53 F4** NJ3309.
Flodabay *W.Isles* *Anglicised form of Fleoideabhagh, qv.*
Floday *W.Isles* ***Island***, small uninhabited island in Loch Roag, W coast of Isle of Lewis, 1m/2km SE of Miabhig. **68 C4** NB1033.
Floday *W.Isles* ***Island***, small uninhabited island off W coast of Isle of Lewis, nearly 1m/2km NW of Great Bernera. NB1241.
Flodda *W.Isles* *Anglicised form of Eilean Flodaigh, qv.*

Flodday *W.Isles* ***Island***, small uninhabited island 3m/5km E of Northbay village, Barra. **44 C3** NF7502.
Flodday *W.Isles* ***Island***, uninhabited island in Loch na Madadh, E coast of North Uist, 1m/2km E of Lochmaddy. NF9469.
Flodday *W.Isles* ***Island***, small uninhabited island 1m/2km W of Sandray and 1m/2km SW of SW point of Vatersay. **44 A4** NL6192.
Floddaybeg *W.Isles* ***Island***, small uninhabited island just off SE tip of North Uist. **56 C4** NF9158.
Floddaymore *W.Isles* ***Island***, uninhabited island off SE coast of North Uist, E of Ronay across narrow strait. **56 C4** NF9157.
Flodigarry *High.* ***Settlement***, on NE coast of Skye, 5m/8km SE of Rubha Hunish. **58 A2** NG4672.
Floors *Moray* ***Settlement***, 4m/7km E of Keith. **63 G4** NJ4952.
Floors Castle *Sc.Bord.* ***Castle***, seat of Duke of Roxburghe, 1m/2km NW of Kelso. Built by William Adam in 1721, much altered and enlarged in mid 19c. Reputedly largest inhabited castle in Scotland. **18 B3** NT7134.
Flora Macdonald's Birthplace *W.Isles* ***Other feature of interest***, ruins of birthplace of Flora Macdonald, 2m/4km SE of Rubha Ardvule, South Uist. Cairn commemorates Flora, who famously helped Charles Edward Stuart (Bonnie Prince Charlie) escape from English troops. **44 C1** NF7426.
Flotta *Ork.* ***Island***, low-lying island of about 4 square miles or 10 square km lying between Hoy and South Ronaldsay. **78 C3** ND3593.
Flotta *Shet.* ***Island***, small island at entrance to Weisdale Voe, Mainland. HU3746.
Flotta Oil Terminal *Ork.* ***Other building***, large oil terminal on N coast of Flotta. **78 C3** ND3595.
Flowerdale Forest *High.* ***Open space***, deer forest in W part of Ross and Cromarty district about 8m/13km SE of Gairloch. NG8867.
Flushing *Aber.* ***Settlement***, 1km E of Longside and 4m/7km W of Peterhead. **65 F5** NK0546.
Fochabers *Moray* Population: 1534. ***Village***, on E bank of River Spey, 8m/13km E of Elgin. **63 F4** NJ3458.
Fochabers Folk Museum *Moray* ***Other feature of interest***, local museum housed in old church on NE side of Fochabers. Includes large collection of horse-drawn carts. **63 F4** NJ3458.
Fodderletter *Moray* ***Locality***, comprises Easter Fodderletter, Mid Fodderletter and Wester Fodderletter, 1m/2km E of Bridge of Brown. **52 D2** NJ1421.
Fodderty *High.* ***Village***, in Ross and Cromarty district, 2m/4km W of Dingwall. **61 E4** NH5159.
Foffarty *Angus* ***Hamlet***, 2m/3km SE of Glamis. **42 C5** NO4145.
Fogla Skerry *Shet.* ***Island***, small island off W coast of Papa Stour. **82 A1** HU1361.
Fogo *Sc.Bord.* ***Settlement***, 2m/3km S of Gavinton. **27 E5** NT7749.
Fogo Church *Sc.Bord.* ***Ecclesiastical building***, 3m/5km SW of Duns. Earliest parts of church date from 12c, but completely restored in 1755. **27 E5** NT7749.
Fogorig *Sc.Bord.* ***Settlement***, 4m/6km NE of Greenlaw. **27 E5** NT7748.
Foinaven *High.* *Anglicised form of Fionn Bheinn, qv.*
Foinaven *High.* ***Large natural feature***, mountain ridge running N to S, in Sutherland district, at N end of Reay Forest. Highest peak is Ganu Mòr. **74 C3** NC3150.
Foindle *High.* ***Locality***, on S side of Loch Laxford, near W coast of Sutherland district. **74 A4** NC1948.
Folda *Angus* ***Settlement***, in Glen Isla, 3m/5km NW of Kirkton of Glenisla. **41 G3** NO1864.
Folla Rule *Aber.* ***Settlement***, 3m/4km NE of Kirktown of Rayne. **54 C1** NJ7333.
Footdee *Aberdeen* ***Locality***, on N side of Aberdeen port at mouth of River Dee at Aberdeen. NJ9505.
Fora Ness *Shet.* ***Coastal feature***, headland on SW side of Mainland, extending out into Muckle Sound. **83 F4** HU3518.
Fora Ness *Shet.* ***Coastal feature***, long narrow peninsula on Mainland on W side of entrance to Sandsound Voe, 5m/8km NW of Scalloway. HU3546.
Fora Ness *Shet.* ***Coastal feature***, headland on NE coast of Mainland, almost an island, 1m/2km S of Firth. **84 D5** HU4571.
Forbestown *Aber.* ***Settlement***, on N bank of River Don, to E of Strathdon. **53 F3** NJ3612.
Ford *Arg. & B.* ***Settlement***, nearly 1km SW of head of Loch Awe, in Argyll. **30 A4** NM8603.
Ford *Midloth.* ***Settlement***, just W of Pathhead. **26 A3** NT3864.
Fordell *Fife* ***Village***, 3m/5km NW of Aberdour. **25 F1** NT1588.
Fordoun *Aber.* ***Village***, 2m/4km SE of Auchenblae. In churchyard (adjoining to S of Auchenblae) is fragment of St. Palladius' chapel, 'the mother church of the Mearns'. **43 F2** NO7278.
Fordyce *Aber.* ***Village***, near N coast, 3m/4km SW of Portsoy. **64 A3** NJ5563.
Fordyce Hill *Aber.* ***Hill***, between Burn of Fordyce and Burn of Durn, 1km SE of Fordyce and 3m/4km SW of Portsoy. Height 590 feet or 180 metres. **64 A3** NJ5662.
Forebrae *P. & K.* ***Settlement***, 3m/5km SW of Methven. **33 E2** NN9824.
Foreland *Arg. & B.* ***Settlement***, on Islay, 4m/7km W of Bridgend. **20 A3** NR2664.
Forest Lodge *Arg. & B.* ***Settlement***, 3m/4km NW Of Bridge of Orchy. **39 E5** NN2742.
Forest Lodge *P. & K.* ***Settlement***, in Glen Tilt, 6m/4km NE of Blair Atholl. **41 E2** NN9374.
Forest Mill *Clack.* ***Village***, 3m/5km NE of Clackmannan. **33 E5** NS9593.
Forest of Ae *D. & G.* ***Forest/woodland***, to N of Ae Village. **9 D1** NX9889.
Forest of Alyth *P. & K.* ***Open space***, moorland area NW of Alyth. **41 G4** NO1855.
Forest of Atholl *P. & K.* ***Open space***, deer and game forest to N of Glen Garry. **40 C2** NN7970.
Forest of Birse *Aber.* ***Open space***, deer forest 4m/7km S of Aboyne. **54 A5** NO5291.
Forest of Clunie *P. & K.* ***Open space***, moorland area W of Bridge of Cally. **41 F4** NO0850.
Forest of Deer *Aber.* ***Forest/woodland***, N of Old Deer. **65 E4** NJ9750.
Forest of Glenartney *P. & K.* ***Large natural feature***, mountain area on NW side of Glen Artney. **32 B3** NN6818.
Forest of Glenavon *Moray* ***Open space***, deer forest on E side of Cairngorm Mountains astride Glen Avon. **52 C4** NJ1005.
Forest of Glentanar *Aber.* ***Forest/woodland***, large area of forest SW of Aboyne, on either side of Glen Tanar. **53 G5** NO4593.
Forest of Harris *W.Isles* ***Large natural feature***, area of mountains, streams and lochs in North Harris, between Loch Resort and Loch Seaforth. **66 C3** NB0509.
Forest of Mamlorn *Stir.* ***Large natural feature***, mountainous area between head of Glen Lochay and that of Glen Lyon, 7m/11km NE of Crianlarich. **31 F1** NN4034.
Forfar *Angus* Population: 12,961. ***Town***, market town, 12m/20km N of Dundee. Former jute and linen-milling centre. Ruins of Restenneth Priory (Historic Scotland), with 11c tower, to N. **42 C4** NO4550.
Forgandenny *P. & K.* ***Village***, 4m/6km SW of Perth. **33 F3** NO0818.
Forgewood *N.Lan.* ***Suburb***, N district of Motherwell. NS7458.
Forgie *Moray* ***Locality***, 3m/5km NW of Keith. **63 F4** NJ3854.
Forglen *Aber.* ***Locality***, on W bank of River Deveron, 3m/4km NE of Turriff. NJ6951.
Forgue *Aber.* ***Hamlet***, 2m/3km SW of Inverkeithny and 6m/10km NE of Huntly. Glendronach Distillery is 1m/2km SE in Glen Dronach. NJ6045.
Formartine *Aber.* ***Locality***, large undulating area to N and NE of Oldmeldrum. **54 C2** NJ8628.
Forneth *P. & K.* ***Settlement***, 2m/3km E of Butterstone. **41 F5** NO0845.
Fornighty *High.* ***Settlement***, 5m/7km SE of Nairn. **62 B4** NH9351.
Forres *Moray* Population: 8531. ***Small town***, 4m/6km S of mouth of River Findhorn, and 12m/19km W of Elgin. On NE side of town is Sueno's Stone, ancient Celtic obelisk (Historic Scotland). 19c Dallas Dhu Distillery (Historic Scotland) 1m/2km S. **62 C4** NJ0358.
Forrest *N.Lan.* ***Settlement***, 1km S of Forrestfield. **24 C3** NS8566.
Forrest Lodge *D. & G.* ***Settlement***, 6m/9km NW of St. John's Town of Dalry. **7 G2** NX5586.
Forrestburn Reservoir *N.Lan.* ***Reservoir***, aligned SW to NE and about 1m/2km in length, 2m/4km W of Harthill. **24 C3** NS8664.
Forret Hill *Fife* ***Hill***, 4m/6km N of Cupar. Height 571 feet or 174 metres. **34 B2** NO3920.
Forsa *Arg. & B.* ***River***, on Mull, running N down Glen Forsa to Sound of Mull 2m/3km E of Salen. Small airfield at mouth of river on W side. **29 F1** NM5943.
Forse *High.* ***Settlement***, near E coast of Caithness district, 1m/2km E of Latheron. **77 E5** ND2134.
Forsie *High.* ***Settlement***, 4m/7km SW of Thurso. **76 C2** ND0463.
Forsinain *High.* ***Settlement***, situated in Strath Halladale, 3m/4km S of Trantlebeg. **76 B4** NC9148.
Forsinard *High.* ***Settlement***, with railway station, in Caithness district, 14m/22km S of Melvich. **76 A4** NC8943.
Forsnaval *W.Isles* ***Hill***, 2m/3km S of Gallan Head, Isle of Lewis. Height 672 feet or 205 metres. **68 B4** NB0635.
Forss Water *High.* ***River***, in Caithness district, running N from Loch Shurrey to N coast 6m/9km W of Thurso. **76 C2** ND0279.
Fort Augustus *High.* ***Village***, in Inverness district, at entrance to Caledonian Canal from SW end of Loch Ness; lighthouse marks canal entrance. Village grew up around fort built in 1730 by General Wade; fort later incorporated into 19c Benedictine monastery. **50 C4** NH3709.
Fort Augustus Abbey *High.* ***Ecclesiastical building***, 19c abbey, incorporating part of General Wade's 18c fort, located in Fort Augustus at SW end of Loch Ness. Visitor centre includes displays on Benedictine monks in residence at abbey, Loch Ness and Great Glen, Jacobite risings and history of Scottish Highlander. Clansman Centre depicts 17c life. **50 C4** NH3808.
Fort Charlotte *Shet.* ***Historic/prehistoric site***, 17c pentagonal artillery fort (Historic Scotland) in Lerwick. Burnt by Dutch in 1675 and rebuilt in 1781. **83 D3** HU4740.
Fort George *High.* ***Military establishment***, military depot (Historic Scotland) built after Jacobite rising of 1745, in Inverness district at entrance to Inner Moray Firth, or Inverness Firth, opposite Chanonry Point. Fort remains a garrison and is partly open to public with museum and Grand Magazine Collection. **61 G4** NH7656.
Fort William *High.* Population: 10,391. ***Town***, in Lochaber district on E side of Loch Linnhe near head of loch. Pulp mill at Annat. Tourist and mountaineering centre. West Highland Museum. **38 D2** NN1073.
Forter *Angus* ***Settlement***, in Glen Isla, 4m/6km NW of Kirkton of Glenisla. **41 G3** NO1864.
Forter Castle *Angus* ***Castle***, ruined castle, sacked and burnt in 1640, 10m/16km NE of Pitlochry. NO1864.
Forteviot *P. & K.* ***Village***, 6m/9km SW of Perth. Site of Roman camp to W. **33 F3** NO0517.
Forth ***River***, major river of central Scotland formed by two headstreams rising N of Ben Lomond and meeting 1m/2km W of Aberfoyle. It then flows E by Stirling and Alloa to Kincardine, where it widens into Firth of Forth. **32 B5** NS9287.
Forth *S.Lan.* Population: 2560. ***Village***, 7m/12km NE of Lanark. **24 D4** NS9453.
Forth and Clyde Canal ***Canal***, traversing Scotland from River Forth at Grangemouth to River Clyde. Completed in 1790; closed in 1962. NS9483.
Forth Bridge *Fife* ***Bridge***, railway bridge across Firth of Forth between Dalmeny Station on S side and North Queensferry. **25 F2** NT1379.
Forth Road Bridge *Fife* ***Bridge***, spanning 1m/2km across Firth of Forth from Queensferry on S bank to North Queensferry. **25 F2** NT1279.
Forthill *Dundee* ***Suburb***, to NE of Broughty Ferry. NO4631.
Forthside *Stir.* ***Locality***, industrial estate on S bank of River Forth to E of Stirling town centre. NS8093.
Fortingall *P. & K.* ***Village***, in Glen Lyon, 7m/12km W of Aberfeldy. Famed for ancient yew trees. **40 C5** NN7347.
Fortingall Yew *P. & K.* *Alternative name for Ancient Yew Tree, qv.*
Fortrie *Aber.* ***Settlement***, 3m/4km SE of Inverkeithny. **64 B5** NJ6645.
Fortrose *High.* Population: 758. ***Small town***, resort in Ross and Cromarty district on Inner Moray Firth 2m/3km W of Fort George across strait. Ruined 14c cathedral. **61 G4** NH7256.
Fortrose Cathedral *High.* ***Ecclesiastical building***, scant remains of 13c vaulted undercroft of chapter house and substantial remains of S aisle of nave of 14c cathedral (Historic Scotland) at Fortrose on S coast of Black Isle. **61 G4** NH7256.
Forvie Ness (Also known as Hackley Head.) *Aber.* ***Coastal feature***, headland N of mouth of River Ythan, on seaward side of Sands of Forvie and at S end of Hackley Bay. **55 F2** NK0226.
Foss *P. & K.* ***Locality***, on S side of Loch Tummel, 2m/3km SE of Tummel Bridge. **40 C4** NN7958.
Fothringham Hill *Angus* ***Hill***, forested hill, with mast at summit, 3m/5km S of Forfar. Height 820 feet or 250 metres. **42 C5** NO4645.
Foubister *Ork.* ***Settlement***, in S of Mainland, 1km S of Bay of Suckquoy. **79 E2** HY5103.
Foula *Shet.* ***Island***, sparsely inhabited island of about 6 square miles or 15 square km lying 26m/42km W of Scalloway, Mainland. Foula has high cliffs and is noted as haunt of sea birds. Chief human settlement is Ham, on Ham Voe, on E coast. **82 B5** HT9639.
Foula Airstrip *Shet.* ***Airport/airfield***, landing strip to S of Foula, just NE of Hametoun. **82 B5** HT9737.
Foulbog *D. & G.* ***Settlement***, 3m/5km N of Davington. **16 D5** NT2407.
Foulden *Sc.Bord.* ***Village***, 5m/8km W of Berwick-upon-Tweed. **27 G4** NT9255.
Foulden Tithe Barn *Sc.Bord.* ***Historic/prehistoric site***, attractive two-storey tithe barn (Historic Scotland) with external stairs and crow-stepped gables, at Foulden 3m/5km S of Ayton. **27 G4** NT9355.
Foulis Castle *High.* ***Castle***, residence of chiefs of Clan Munro, nearly 1m/2km NW of Foulis Point and 4m/7km NE of Dingwall. NH5864.
Foulis Point *High.* ***Coastal feature***, point on NW shore of Cromarty Firth, Ross and Cromarty district, 2m/3km SW of Evanton. NH5963.
Foulmire Heights *Sc.Bord.* ***Open space***, partly wooded moorland 2m/4km W of Kielder. **11 D2** NY5894.
Foulzie *Aber.* ***Settlement***, 3m/5km S of Macduff. **64 C3** NJ7159.

F G

Fountainhall *Sc.Bord.* ***Village***, on Gala Water, 3m/5km N of Stow. **26 B5** NT4349.

Foura *High.* *Alternative name for Eilean Furadh Mòr, qv.*

Fourman Hill *Aber.* ***Mountain***, on S side of River Deveron, 2m/3km SE of Milltown of Rothiemay. Height 1128 feet or 344 metres. **64 A5** NJ5745.

Fourpenny *High.* ***Settlement***, 3m/4km N of Dornoch. **72 C5** NH8094.

Foveran *Aber.* ***Settlement***, 1km SW of Newburgh. **55 E2** NJ9924.

Foveran Burn *Aber.* ***River***, flowing E to join River Ythan at Newburgh. **55 E2** NK0025.

Fowlis (Also known as Fowlis Easter.) *Angus* ***Village***, 6m/9km NW of Dundee. Early 17c castle. **34 B1** NO3233.

Fowlis Easter *Angus* *Alternative name for Fowlis, qv.*

Fowlis Wester *P. & K.* ***Village***, 4m/7km E of Crieff. 8c cross (Historic Scotland). **33 E2** NN9224.

Fowlis Wester Sculptured Stone *P. & K.* ***Historic/prehistoric site***, Pictish cross slab (Historic Scotland) at Fowlis Wester, with replica in village square. Also Neolithic stone circles, Bronze Age cairn and standing stones in locality. **33 E2** NN9224.

Foxhole *High.* ***Settlement***, 6m/9km N of Drumnadrochit. **51 E1** NH5238.

Foyers *High.* ***River***, formed by confluence of Allt Breineag and River Fechlin and flowing N, entering Loch Ness at Foyers. NH4920.

Foyers *High.* ***Village***, on SE side of Loch Ness in Inverness district, at mouth of River Foyers. **51 D2** NH4921.

Frachadil *Arg. & B.* ***Settlement***, 1km E of Calgary, Mull. **36 C4** NM3851.

Frank Lockwood's Island (Also known as Eilean Sneth Dian.) *Arg. & B.* ***Island***, islet off S coast of Mull, 2m/4km E of entrance to Loch Buie. **29 F3** NM6219.

Fraoch Bheinn *High.* ***Mountain***, in Lochaber district 2m/3km N of head of Loch Arkaig. Height 2814 feet or 858 metres. **49 F5** NM9894.

Fraoch Eilean *High.* *Alternative name for Fraochlan, qv.*

Fraochaidh *High.* ***Mountain***, in Appin, 5m/8km S of South Ballachulish. Height 2883 feet or 879 metres. **38 C4** NN0251.

Fraochlan (Also known as Fraoch Eilean.) *High.* ***Island***, islet in Enard Bay 1km off NW coast of Ross and Cromarty district. NC0518.

Fraserburgh *Aber.* Population: 12,843. ***Town***, fishing town and port at W end of Fraserburgh Bay, 15m/24km NW of Peterhead. Once a herring port, now a whitefish port. Kinnaird Head has 16c century castle and Scotland's oldest lighthouse. **65 E3** NJ9966.

Fraserburgh Bay *Aber.* ***Bay***, at NE tip of Buchan district, extending E of Fraserburgh to Cairnbulg Point. **65 F3** NJ9966.

Freester *Shet.* ***Settlement***, in South Nesting, Mainland, 1m/2km SW of Skellister. **83 D2** HU4553.

Freevater Forest *High.* ***Open space***, deer forest in Sutherland district E of Seana Bhraigh. **60 C1** NH3588.

Frenchman's Rocks *Arg. & B.* ***Coastal feature***, group of rocks off Rubha na Faing, W coast of Rinns of Islay. NR1553.

Frendraught *Aber.* ***Locality***, comprises Frendraught House and Mains of Frendraught, 3m/5km S of Inverkeithny. **64 B5** NJ6141.

Frenich *Stir.* ***Settlement***, at N end of Loch Chon, 3m/4km SE of Stronachlachar. **31 G4** NN4106.

Fresgoe *High.* ***Settlement***, with jetty, on W side of Sandside Bay, 10m/16km W of Thurso. **76 B2** NC9566.

Freswick *High.* ***Settlement***, at head of Freswick Bay, on E coast of Caithness district, 4m/6km S of Duncansby Head. **77 F2** ND3767.

Freswick Bay *High.* ***Bay***, on E coast of Caithness district. **77 F2** ND3767.

Freuchie *Fife* Population: 1033. ***Village***, 4m/6km N of Glenrothes. **34 A4** NO2806.

Friars Carse *D. & G.* ***Settlement***, 6m/10km NW of Dumfries. **8 D2** NX9284.

Friarton *P. & K.* ***Suburb***, S district of Perth. **33 G2** NO1121.

Friarton Island (Also known as Moncreiffe Island.) *P. & K.* ***Island***, in River Tay at Perth, to NE of Friarton. NO1121.

Friesland Bay *Arg. & B.* ***Bay***, on S coast of Coll, 3m/5km SW of Arinagour. **36 A4** NM1853.

Friockheim *Angus* ***Village***, 6m/10km NW of Arbroath. **43 D5** NO5949.

Frogden *Sc.Bord.* ***Settlement***, 2m/3km NW of Morebattle. **18 B4** NT7628.

Frosty Hill *Aber.* ***Mountain***, on S side of River Don, 4m/7km N of Tarland. Height 1351 feet or 412 metres. **53 G3** NJ4610.

Fruid Reservoir *Sc.Bord.* ***Reservoir***, in course of Fruid Water, 3m/4km S of Tweedsmuir. **16 B3** NT0820.

Fruid Water *Sc.Bord.* ***River***, running N through Fruid Reservoir to River Tweed, 1m/2km SW of Tweedsmuir. NT0823.

Fruin Water *Arg. & B.* ***River***, rising on W slopes of Maol on Fheidh and The Strone, and running SE down Glen Fruin, then E into Loch Lomond 2m/4km N of foot of loch. NS3685.

Fuam an Tolla *W.Isles* ***Island***, islet off North Harris in East Loch Tarbert to W of Scalpay. NG2096.

Fuar Bheinn *High.* ***Mountain***, in Lochaber district 2m/4km N of Loch a' Choire. Height 2509 feet or 765 metres. **38 A4** NM8556.

Fuar Loch Mòr *High.* ***Lake/loch***, small loch in Ross and Cromarty district, 6m/10km N of head of Loch Maree. **59 F2** NH0076.

Fuar Tholl *High.* ***Mountain***, in Ross and Cromarty district, 2m/3km W of Achnashellach Lodge. Height 2975 feet or 907 metres. **59 F5** NG9748.

Fuday *W.Isles* ***Island***, uninhabited island of about 500 acres or 200 hectares 2m/3km E of Scurrival Point, Barra. Ancient remains at Dùnan Ruadh. **44 C3** NF7308.

Fugla Stack *Shet.* ***Coastal feature***, rock adjacent to W coast of West Burra. **82 C4** HU3530.

Fuiay *W.Isles* ***Island***, uninhabited island off North Bay, Barra. **44 C3** NF7402.

Fullarton *Glas.* ***Suburb***, 4m/6km E of Glasgow. NS6462.

Fullarton *N.Ayr.* ***Suburb***, S district of Irvine. NS3238.

Fullwood *E.Ayr.* ***Settlement***, 3m/5km NE of Stewarton. **23 F5** NS4449.

Funlack Burn *High.* ***River***, in Inverness district, running SE from Loch Moy to River Findhorn 2m/4km N of Tomatin. NH8032.

Funzie *Shet.* ***Settlement***, on Fetlar, 3m/4km E of Houbie. Funzie Bay to SE. **85 F4** HU6690.

Funzie Bay *Shet.* ***Bay***, on Fetlar, to SE of Funzie. HU6689.

Funzie Ness *Shet.* ***Coastal feature***, peninsula at SE corner of Fetlar, to S of Funzie. HU6588.

Furnace *Arg. & B.* ***Village***, on W shore of Loch Fyne in Argyll, 7m/11km SW of Inveraray. **30 C4** NN0300.

Furnace *High.* ***Settlement***, on NE shore of Loch Maree, 1km SE of Letterewe. **59 F2** NG9670.

Furrah Head *Aber.* ***Coastal feature***, headland on E coast at S end of Sandford Bay, 1km N of Boddam. NK1243.

Fyn Loch *W.Dun.* ***Lake/loch***, small loch on Kilpatrick Hills 4m/7km E of Dumbarton. NS4577.

Fyne *Arg. & B.* ***River***, in Argyll running SW down Glen Fyne to head of Loch Fyne, 6m/10km NE of Inveraray. **31 E3** NN1810.

Fyvie *Aber.* ***Village***, on River Ythan, 8m/13km S of Turriff. **54 C1** NJ7637.

Fyvie Castle *Aber.* ***Castle***, fortress palace dating from 14c, with late 16c additions and a wheel staircase, 1m/2km N of Fyvie. **54 C1** NJ7637.

Fyvie Church *Aber.* ***Ecclesiastical building***, church 7m/11km NW of Oldmeldrum, noted for stained glass, 17c panelling and Celtic stones. **54 C1** NJ7737.

G

Gabhsunn Bho Dheas (Anglicised form: South Galson.) *W.Isles* ***Settlement***, adjacent to Gabhsunn Bho Thuath, near NW coast of Isle of Lewis, 7m/11km SW of Port Nis. **69 F2** NB4358.

Gabhsunn Bho Thuath (Anglicised form: North Galson.) *W.Isles* ***Settlement***, adjacent to Gabhsunn Bho Dheas, near NW coast of Isle of Lewis, 7m/11km SW of Port Nis. **69 F2** NB4459.

Gablon *High.* ***Settlement***, 6m/10km E of Bonar Bridge. **72 C5** NH7191.

Gabroc Hill *E.Ayr.* ***Settlement***, 4m/6km NE of Stewarton. **23 F4** NS4550.

Gadie Burn *Aber.* ***River***, rising to N of Correen Hills and flowing E, through Clatt and Auchleven, to join River Urie 1km E of Kirkton of Oyne. **54 A2** NJ6925.

Gaeilavore Island *High.* ***Island***, one of a group of islets 3m/5km NW of Rubha Hunish at N tip of Skye. See also Gearran Island & Lord Macdonald's Table. **57 G2** NG3679.

Gaich *High.* ***Settlement***, 2m/3km SW of Grantown-on-Spey. **52 C2** NJ0125.

Gaick *High.* ***Settlement***, 9m/14km S of Inverness. **51 F1** NH6831.

Gaick Forest *High.* ***Open space***, deer forest in Badenoch and Strathspey district, 7m/11km E of Dalwhinnie. **40 C1** NN7584.

Gaick Lodge *High.* ***Settlement***, in Gaick Forest, 8m/12km E of Dalwhinnie. **40 C1** NN7585.

Gailes *N.Ayr.* ***Settlement***, 3m/5km S of Irvine. NS3335.

Gair Loch *High.* ***Sea feature***, wide inlet on W coast of Ross and Cromarty district, 8m/13km S of Rubha Réidh. **58 D2** NG7775.

Gairbeinn *High.* ***Mountain***, on Corrieyairack Forest, in Badenoch and Strathspey district, 8m/13km SE of Fort Augustus. Height 2939 feet or 896 metres. **51 D5** NN4698.

Gairich *High.* ***Mountain***, in Lochaber district, 3m/5km SW of dam of Loch Quoich. Munro: height 3014 feet or 919 metres. **49 G5** NN0299.

Gairletter Point *Arg. & B.* ***Coastal feature***, headland in Argyll, on W side of Loch Long, 3m/4km N of Strone Point. **22 C1** NS1984.

Gairloch *High.* ***Village***, on W coast of Ross and Cromarty district, at head of Gair Loch. **59 E2** NG8076.

Gairloch Heritage Museum *High.* ***Other feature of interest***, museum in Gairloch, including reconstruction of Crofter's cottage, geological displays and archives of local history. **59 E2** NG8076.

Gairlochy *High.* ***Settlement***, on Caledonian Canal, at SW end of Loch Lochy, in Lochaber district. **39 D1** NN1784.

Gairn *Aber.* ***River***, rising on Invercauld Forest and running E to River Dee 1m/2km NW of Ballater. **53 E4** NO3596.

Gairney Bank *P. & K.* ***Settlement***, 2m/3km S of Kinross. **33 G5** NT1299.

Gairney Water *P. & K.* ***River***, rising near Drum and flowing E to enter Loch Leven 2m/3km SE of Kinross. **33 F5** NT1499.

Gairnshiel Lodge *Aber.* ***Settlement***, on E bank of River Gairn, 6m/9km NW of Ballater. **53 E4** NJ2900.

Gairsay *Ork.* ***Island***, sparsely populated island of about 500 acres or 200 hectares at N end of Wide Firth between Mainland and Shapinsay. **80 C4** HY4422.

Gairsay Sound *Ork.* ***Sea feature***, off E coast of Mainland between Wyre to N and Gairsay to S. **80 C4** HY4223.

Gaisgaer *W.Isles* *Gaelic form of Gasker, qv.*

Gala Hill *Sc.Bord.* ***Hill***, 1km S of Galashiels. Height 905 feet or 276 metres. **17 F2** NT4934.

Gala Lane *D. & G.* ***River***, rising 3m/4km E of Merrick, and running N into S end of Loch Doon. NX4892.

Gala Water *Sc.Bord.* ***River***, rising in Moorfoot Hills and flowing SE by Stow and Galashiels to enter River Tweed 2m/3km W of Melrose. **26 B4** NT5134.

Galabank *Sc.Bord.* ***Settlement***, in valley of Gala Water, 1m/2km NW of Stow. **26 B5** NT4445.

Galashiels *Sc.Bord.* Population: 13,753. ***Town***, on Gala Water, 14m/22km N of Hawick. Once known for its wool industry. **17 F2** NT4936.

Galdenoch *D. & G.* ***Settlement***, on E side of Water of Luce, 2m/3km S of New Luce. **6 C4** NX1761.

Gallachan Bay *Arg. & B.* ***Bay***, small bay on SW coast of Bute, between Scalpsie Bay and Stravanan Bay. NS0656.

Gallan Head *W.Isles* ***Coastal feature***, headland on W coast of Isle of Lewis on W side of entrance to West Loch Roag. **68 B4** NB0539.

Gallanach *Arg. & B.* ***Settlement***, 3m/5km SW of Oban. **30 A2** NM8225.

Gallatown *Fife* ***Locality***, adjoining to N of Kirkcaldy. **34 A5** NT2994.

Gallchoille *Arg. & B.* ***Settlement***, on NW coast of Caol Scotnish, 3m/4km SW of Crinan. **21 F1** NR7689.

Gallery *Angus* ***Settlement***, 1m/2km W of Marykirk across River North Esk. **43 E3** NO6765.

Gallow Hill *Aber.* ***Hill***, 1m/2km NE of Aberchirder. Height 741 feet or 226 metres. **64 B4** NJ6453.

Gallow Hill *Angus* ***Mountain***, 3m/5km S of Glamis. Height 1243 feet or 379 metres. **42 B5** NO3941.

Gallow Hill *D. & G.* ***Hill***, afforested hill rising to N of Moffat. Height 833 feet or 254 metres. **16 B5** NT0806.

Gallow Hill *High.* ***Mountain***, to S of Glen Gheallaidh, 5m/8km SW of Upper Knockando. Height 1227 feet or 374 metres. **52 D1** NJ1336.

Galloway Deer Museum *D. & G.* *See Clatteringshaws Loch.*

Galloway Forest Park *D. & G.* ***Leisure/recreation***, large area of mountains, lochs and forest to N of Newton Stewart. Coarse and game fishing, visitor centre, deer range and wild goat park. **7 E3** NX4083.

Galloway House Gardens *D. & G.* ***Garden***, laid out in 1740s, 1km S of Garlieston. **3 E2** NX4845.

Gallowfauld *Angus* ***Hamlet***, 4m/7km SE of Glamis. **42 C5** NO4442.

Gallowhill *Renf.* ***Suburb***, N district of Paisley. NS4965.

Galltair *High.* ***Settlement***, in Skye and Lochalsh district, 1km N of Glenelg. **49 E3** NG8119.

Galmisdale *High.* ***Locality***, on SE coast of Eigg. Landing stage. **37 D1** NM4883.

Galston *E.Ayr.* Population: 5154. ***Small town***, on River Irvine, 5m/8km E of Kilmarnock. Unusual Byzantine-style Roman Catholic church. **14 D2** NS5036.

Galta Mòr *High.* ***Island***, rock islet on NE coast of Skye, 4m/6km SE of Rubha Hunish. **58 A2** NG4673.

Galtrigill *High.* ***Settlement***, 2m/3km S of Dunvegan Head, Skye. **57 E4** NG1854.

Gamelshiel Castle *E.Loth.* ***Castle***, scant remains of castle 11m/17km NW of Duns. **26 D3** NT6464.

Gameshope Loch *Sc.Bord.* ***Lake/loch***, small loch 2m/3km SE of S end of Fruid Reservoir. **16 C4** NT1316.

Gamhna Gigha *Arg. & B.* ***Island***, group of rocks lying nearly 1m/2km E of Rubh' a' Chairn Bhàin near N end of Gigha. NR6854.

Gamhnach Mhòr *Arg. & B.* ***Island***, islet at entrance to Carsaig Bay on S coast of Mull. NM5420.

Gamla *Shet.* ***Coastal feature***, headland with lighthouse above cliffs on E coast of Yell, 3m/5km NE of Otterswick. HU5489.

Gamrie *Aber.* ***Locality***, near N coast, 5m/9km E of Macduff. **64 C3** NJ7962.

Gamrie Bay *Aber.* ***Bay***, 1m/2km N of Gamrie, between Crovie Head and More Head, 9m/13km W of Rosehearty. **64 C3** NJ7965.

Gana Hill *S.Lan.* ***Mountain***, in Lowther Hills, 3m/4km SE of Ballencleuch Law. Height 2191 feet or 668 metres. **16 A5** NS9501.
Ganavan Bay *Arg. & B.* ***Bay***, 2m/3km N of Oban, Argyll. **30 A1** NM8532.
Gannochy *Angus* ***Hamlet***, 1m/2km N of Edzell. **43 E2** NO5970.
Gannochy *P. & K.* ***Suburb***, NE district of Perth, on E side of River Tay. NO1224.
Ganu Mòr *High.* ***Mountain***, peak of Foinaven mountain ridge, in Sutherland district 5m/9km SW of head of Loch Eriboll. Height 2978 feet or 908 metres. NC3150.
Gaodhail *Arg. & B.* ***Settlement***, in Glen Forsa, Mull, 4m/7km SE of Salen. **29 F1** NM6138.
Gaor Bheinn *High. Gaelic form of Gulvain, qv.*
Garabal *Arg. & B.* ***Settlement***, 1m/2km N of Ardlui, at N end of Loch Lomond. **31 F3** NN3117.
Garadhban Forest *Stir.* ***Forest/woodland***, at S end of Loch Lomond, 2m/4km N of Drymen. **31 G5** NS4790.
Garadheancal *High.* ***Settlement***, on Tanera Mòr, largest of Summer Isles group, off W coast of Ross and Cromarty district. **70 B4** NB9907.
Garbat *High.* ***Settlement***, 4m/7km NE of Garve. **60 D3** NH4168.
Garbat Forest *High.* ***Open space***, deer forest in Ross and Cromarty district on W side of Ben Wyvis. **60 D3** NH4368.
Garbh Allt *High.* ***River***, headstream of River Nethy rising on E side of Cairn Gorm and flowing N into head of Strath Nethy. **52 C4** NJ0205.
Garbh-bheinn *High.* ***Mountain***, 2m/4km NW of head of Loch Slapin, Skye. Height 2644 feet or 806 metres. **48 B2** NG5323.
Garbh Bheinn *High.* ***Mountain***, 5m/8km E of Strontian, Lochaber district. Height 2903 feet or 885 metres. **38 B3** NM9062.
Garbh Bheinn (Anglicised form: Garven). *High.* ***Mountain***, in Lochaber district 1m/2km SW of Kinlochleven. Height 2844 feet or 867 metres. **39 D4** NN1760.
Garbh Bheinn *High.* ***Mountain***, in Lochaber district, on E side of Loch Treig, 6m/9km S of Tulloch Station. Height 2814 feet or 858 metres. **39 F2** NN3571.
Garbh Chioch Mhòr *High.* ***Mountain***, 3m/5km E of Camusrory, Lochaber district. Munro: height 3323 feet or 1013 metres. **49 F5** NM9195.
Garbh Eileach *Arg. & B.* ***Island***, largest of Garvellachs group of islands in Firth of Lorn. Lies between A' Chùli and Dùn Chonnuill. **29 F3** NM6812.
Garbh Eilean *High.* ***Island***, small uninhabited island off S end of Rona. NG6153.
Garbh Eilean *W.Isles* ***Island***, islet in Loch Erisort, Isle of Lewis, 1km SE of Ceos and 2m/3km E of Lacasaigh. NB3621.
Garbh Eilean *W.Isles* ***Island***, largest of Shiant Islands group, joined to Eilean an Tighe by a narrow neck of land. **67 G4** NG4198.
Garbh Ghaoir *P. & K.* ***River***, running 2m/3km from Loch Laidon to head of Loch Eigheach. NN4456.
Garbh Leac *High. Alternative name for A' Chràlaig, qv.*
Garbh Lochan *High.* ***Lake/loch***, to S of Blackwater Reservoir, 10m/16km E of Kinlochleven. **39 F4** NN3259.
Garbh Mheall Mòr *High.* ***Mountain***, in Badenoch and Strathspey district, 4m/6km S of Newtonmore. Height 1945 feet or 593 metres. **51 G5** NN7292.
Garbh Rèisa *Arg. & B.* ***Island***, small island nearly 1km S of Craignish Point at entrance to Loch Craignish in Argyll. NR7597.
Garbh Sgeir *High.* ***Island***, islet to W of Oigh-sgeir and 9m/14km W of Rum. **47 E5** NM1596.
Garbhallt *Arg. & B.* ***Settlement***, on N bank of Strathlachlan River, 5m/8km SW of Strachur. **30 C5** NS0295.
Garcrogo Forest *D. & G.* ***Forest/woodland***, 4m/7km E of Balmaclellan. **8 B3** NX7278.
Garden *Stir.* ***Settlement***, 2m/3km E of Buchlyvie. **32 A5** NS5994.
Gardenstown *Aber.* ***Village***, fishing village on Gamrie Bay on N coast, 6m/9km E of Macduff. **64 C3** NJ8064.
Garderhouse *Shet.* ***Settlement***, on Mainland, at head of Seli Voe, 7m/11km NW of Scalloway across entrance to Weisdale Voe. **82 C3** HU3347.
Gardyne Castle *Angus* ***Castle***, 16c castle, 1m/2km SW of Friockheim. NO5748.
Gare Loch *Arg. & B.* ***Sea feature***, inlet of River Clyde running S from Garelochhead to Helensburgh. **22 D1** NS2486.
Garelochhead *Arg. & B.* Population: 1298. ***Village***, and resort at head of Gare Loch, 7m/11km NW of Helensburgh. **31 E5** NS2391.
Garelochhead Forest *Arg. & B.* ***Forest/woodland***, to S of Garelochhead, on W side of Gare Loch. NS2391.
Garenin *W.Isles Anglicised form of Gearrannan, qv.*
Garf Water *S.Lan.* ***River***, rising to N of Robert Law and flowing E to join River Clyde, 2m/3km E of Wiston. **16 A2** NS9832.
Gargunnock *Stir.* ***Village***, 6m/9km W of Stirling. **32 C5** NS7094.
Gargunnock Hills *Stir.* ***Large natural feature***, range of hills to S and SW of Gargunnock. **32 B5** NS7094.
Gargunnock House *Stir.* ***Historic house***, ancestral 16c home of Stirling family, 1km E of Gargunnock. **32 C5** NS7194.
Gariob *Arg. & B.* ***Settlement***, 3m/4km S of Crinan. **21 F1** NR7889.
Garioch *Aber.* ***Locality***, large area to NE of Inverurie and S of River Urie and Gadie Burn. **54 B2** NJ6824.
Garleffin Fell *S.Ayr.* ***Mountain***, 10m/16km E of Girvan. Height 1407 feet or 429 metres. **7 E1** NX3598.
Garleton Hills *E.Loth.* ***Hill***, small group of hills 2m/3km N of Haddington, rising to over 180 metres. Observation towers. Monument commemorates Earl of Hopetoun, Peninsula War hero. **26 C2** NT5076.
Garlick Hill *D. & G.* ***Mountain***, 5m/8km N of Newton Stewart. Height 1460 feet or 445 metres. **7 F3** NX4372.
Garlies Castle *D. & G.* ***Castle***, scant remains of 16c castle 3m/4km N of Newton Stewart; visited by Mary, Queen of Scots in 1563. **7 F4** NX4269.
Garlieston *D. & G.* ***Village***, on Garlieston Bay, on W side of Wigtown Bay, 6m/10km SE of Wigtown. **3 E2** NX4746.
Garlieston Bay *D. & G.* ***Bay***, on W side of Wigtown Bay, 6m/10km SE of Wigtown. NX4846.
Garlogie *Aber.* ***Settlement***, 3m/5km E of Echt. Nearly 1m/2km S is Cullerlie Stone Circle (Historic Scotland). **54 C4** NJ7805.
Garlogie Stone Circle *Aber. Alternative name for Cullerlie Stone Circle, qv.*
Garmond *Aber.* ***Village***, 5m/9km E of Turriff. **64 D4** NJ8052.
Garmony *Arg. & B.* ***Locality***, on Mull, at W end of Sallastle Bay, on Sound of Mull, 7m/11km E of Salen. **37 F5** NM6740.
Garmony Point *Arg. & B.* ***Coastal feature***, headland on Mull, to E of Garmony and opposite Ardtornish Point across Sound of Mull. NM6740.
Garmouth *Moray* ***Village***, near mouth of River Spey, 8m/12km E of Elgin. **63 F3** NJ3364.
Garmus Taing *Shet.* ***Coastal feature***, headland on N coast of Mainland, 3m/5km N of North Roe. **84 C3** HU3694.
Garngad *Glas.* ***Suburb***, 1m/2km NE of Glasgow city centre. NS6066.
Garnock *N.Ayr.* ***River***, rising about 5m/8km E of Largs and flowing S through Kilbirnie and Dalry to River Irvine, close to Irvine Bay. **23 D4** NS3038.
Garpel Water *E.Ayr.* ***River***, rising on Stony Hill and running NW to River Ayr, 1m/2km SW of Muirkirk. NS6826.
Garrabost *W.Isles* ***Village***, on Eye Peninsula, Isle of Lewis, 4m/7km SW of Tiumpan Head. **69 G4** NB5133.
Garrachcroit Bàgh *Arg. & B.* ***Bay***, on E coast of Kintyre, Argyll, 4m/7km N of Carradale. NR8144.
Garrachra *Arg. & B.* ***Settlement***, to W of River Massan, 4m/6km NW of Benmore. **22 B1** NS0888.
Garralburn *Moray* ***Settlement***, 3m/5km NE of Keith. **63 G4** NJ4555.
Garraries Forest *D. & G.* ***Forest/woodland***, forming part of Glentrool Forest Park, to NW of Clatteringshaws Loch. NX4882.
Garrick *P. & K.* ***Settlement***, 3m/5km SW of Muthill. **32 D3** NN8412.
Garrisdale Point *High.* ***Coastal feature***, headland at westernmost point of Canna. **47 E4** NG2005.
Garrison of Inversnaid *Stir. See Inversnaid.*
Garroch *D. & G.* ***Settlement***, 1m/2km W of St. John's Town of Dalry. **7 G2** NX5981.
Garroch Burn *D. & G.* ***River***, stream rising on E side of Rig of Clenrie and flowing E to confluence with Glenlee Burn, thereafter continuing SE as Coom Burn for about 1km to its confluence with Water of Ken, 1km SW of St. John's Town of Dalry. **7 G2** NX6081.
Garroch Head *Arg. & B.* ***Coastal feature***, headland at S end of Bute. **22 C4** NS0951.
Garrochty *Arg. & B.* ***Settlement***, at S tip of Bute, 1km NW of Garroch Head. **22 B4** NS0952.
Garron Point *Aber.* ***Coastal feature***, headland on N coast at W end of Sandend Bay, 3m/4km E of Cullen. NJ5567.
Garron Point *Aber.* ***Coastal feature***, headland on E coast, 2m/3km NE of Stonehaven. **43 G1** NO8987.
Garros *High.* ***Settlement***, 3m/5km S of Staffin, Skye. **58 B3** NG4963.
Garrow *P. & K.* ***Settlement***, 5m/8km SW of Aberfeldy. **32 D1** NN8240.
Garry *High.* ***River***, formed at confluence of River Kingie and Gearr Garry, and flowing E into Loch Garry. NH1600.
Garry *P. & K.* ***River***, running SE from Loch Garry down Glen Garry to River Tummel 2m/3km NW of Pitlochry. **41 D3** NN9159.
Garry-a-siar *W.Isles* ***Coastal feature***, headland on W coast of Benbecula. **45 F4** NF7553.
Garryhorn *D. & G.* ***Settlement***, 1m/2km W of Carsphairn. **7 G1** NX5493.
Garryhorn Burn *D. & G.* ***River***, rising on N slopes of Meaul and flowing E to join Water of Deugh at Carsphairn, 8m/13km N of St. John's Town of Dalry. **7 G1** NX5592.
Garrynamonie *W.Isles Anglicised form of Gearraidh na Monadh, qv.*
Garrywhin *High. Alternative name for Cairn of Get, qv.*
Gars-bheinn *High.* ***Mountain***, one of the peaks of Cuillin Hills on Skye, at S end of range. Height 2936 feet or 895 metres. **48 A3** NG4618.
Garscadden *Glas.* ***Suburb***, 5m/8km NW of Glasgow city centre. NS5268.
Gartachoil *Stir.* ***Settlement***, 3m/5km N of Balfron. **32 A5** NS5393.
Gartally *High.* ***Locality***, comprises settlements of Upper and Lower Gartally, 2m/3km NW of Drumnadrochit. **51 D1** NH4831.
Gartavaich *Arg. & B.* ***Settlement***, on Kintyre, 2m/3km NW of Claonaig. **21 G4** NR8558.
Gartbreck *Arg. & B.* ***Settlement***, on E coast of Loch Indaal, 2m/3km E of Port Charlotte across loch. **20 A4** NR2858.
Gartcosh *N.Lan.* ***Village***, 3m/4km NW of Coatbridge. **24 A3** NS6968.
Garth *Shet.* ***Settlement***, 1km NE of Norby, Mainland. **82 B2** HU2157.
Garth *Shet.* ***Settlement***, in South Nesting, Mainland, 1km SE of Skellister. HU4754.
Garth Castle *P. & K.* ***Castle***, in side valley of Keltney Burn 6m/9km W of Aberfeldy. Built in 14c by the 'Wolf of Badenoch'. NN7650.
Garth Head *Ork.* ***Coastal feature***, headland on S coast of South Walls peninsula, Hoy. **78 C4** ND3188.
Garthamlock *Glas.* ***Suburb***, 4m/7km E of Glasgow city centre. NS6666.
Garthdee *Aberdeen* ***Suburb***, 2m/4km SW of Aberdeen city centre. NJ9103.
Garths Voe *Shet.* ***Bay***, on E side of Sullom Voe, 2m/3km W of Firths Voe on E coast of Mainland. HU4073.
Gartincaper *Stir.* ***Settlement***, 2m/3km SW of Doune. **32 B4** NN6900.
Gartly *Aber.* ***Hamlet***, 5m/8km S of Huntly. **54 A1** NJ5232.
Gartmore *Stir.* ***Village***, 3m/4km S of Aberfoyle. **32 A5** NS5297.
Gartmorn Dam *Clack.* ***Lake/loch***, with country park, 2m/3km NE of Alloa. **33 E5** NS9294.
Gartnagrenach *Arg. & B.* ***Settlement***, on Kintyre, 7m/11km SW of Tarbert. **21 F4** NR7959.
Gartnatra *Arg. & B.* ***Settlement***, 1m/2km E of Bowmore, Islay. **20 B4** NR3260.
Gartness *Stir.* ***Settlement***, on Endrick Water, 1m/2km W of Killearn. **23 G1** NS5086.
Gartocharn *W.Dun.* ***Village***, 4m/6km NE of Balloch. **23 F1** NS4286.
Gartymore *High.* ***Settlement***, in Sutherland district, 1m/2km SW of Helmsdale. **73 F3** ND0114.
Garvald *E.Loth.* ***Village***, 8m/12km SW of Dunbar. **26 C2** NT5870.
Garvamore *High.* ***Settlement***, in River Spey valley, 5m/8km W of Laggan. **51 E5** NN5294.
Garvan *High.* ***Settlement***, on S shore of Loch Eil, 1km S of Kinlocheil across loch. **38 B2** NM9777.
Garvard *Arg. & B.* ***Settlement***, at S end of Colonsay, 3m/4km SW of Scalasaig. **28 C5** NR3691.
Garvary Burn *High.* ***River***, rising to E of Creag Mhòr and flowing SE into River Skinsdale, 2m/4km N of Pollie. **72 C2** NC7519.
Garve *High.* ***Settlement***, in Ross and Cromarty district, 10m/15km W of Dingwall. Loch Garve is 1m/2km SE. **60 C3** NH3961.
Garve Island *High. Anglicised form of An Garbh-eilean, qv.*
Garveld *Arg. & B.* ***Settlement***, on S tip of Kintyre, 3m/4km W of Southend. **12 B5** NR6507.
Garvellachs (Also known as Isles of the Sea.) *Arg. & B.* ***Island***, chain of small uninhabited islands, comprising of A' Chùli, Dùn Chonnuill, Eileach an Naoimh and Garbh Eileach, at SW end of Firth of Lorn, 5m/8km W of Luing. **29 F3** NM6511.
Garvellan Rocks *D. & G.* ***Island***, group of offshore rocks on W side of entrance to Fleet Bay. NX5551.
Garven *High. Anglicised form of Garbh Bheinn, qv.*
Garvery Hill *High.* ***Mountain***, in Caithness district, 2m/4km S of Morven. Height 1092 feet or 333 metres. **73 E2** NC9924.
Garvie *Arg. & B.* ***Settlement***, 4m/7km NE of Clachan of Glendaruel. **22 B1** NS0390.
Garvock *Aber.* ***Settlement***, 2m/3km E of Laurencekirk. **43 F2** NO7470.
Garvock *Inclyde* ***Settlement***, on S shore of Loch Thorn, 4m/6km SW of Garvock. **23 D2** NS2571.
Garvock *P. & K.* ***Settlement***, 1m/2km E of Dunning. **33 F3** NO0314.
Garwald *D. & G.* ***Hamlet***, 3m/4km NW of Eskdalemuir. **16 D5** NT2200.
Garwald Water *D. & G.* ***River***, running SE to White Esk 2m/3km N of Eskdalemuir. NT2400.
Garwaldwaterfoot *D. & G.* ***Settlement***, situated where Garwaldwater joins River White Esk, 2m/3km N of Eskdalemuir. **16 D5** NT2400.

G

Garwall Hill *D. & G.* ***Mountain***, 7m/11km E of Barrhill. Height 1145 feet or 349 metres. **7 E2** NX3483.
Garynahine (Gaelic form: Gearraidh na h-Aibhne.) *W.Isles* ***Settlement***, near W coast of Isle of Lewis, 3m/5km SE of Breascleit. **68 D4** NB2331.
Garyvard *W.Isles Anglicised form of Gearraidh Bhaird, qv.*
Gas Terminal *Aber.* ***Other building***, North Sea gas terminal on E coast, 5m/8km NW of Peterhead, fed by Brent and Frigg fields. **65 G4** NK0953.
Gask *Aber.* ***Settlement***, on N side of Burn of Gask, 2m/3km S of Turriff. **64 C5** NJ7247.
Gask *Aber.* ***Settlement***, 3m/4km N of Cruden Bay. **65 F5** NK0840.
Gask *P. & K.* ***Locality***, 4m/7km NE of Auchterarder. **33 E3** NN9918.
Gaskan *High.* ***Settlement***, on N shore of Loch Shiel, 3m/4km N of Pollock, Lochaber district. **38 A2** NM8072.
Gasker (Gaelic form: Gaisgear.) *W.Isles* ***Island***, small uninhabited island 6m/10km W of Hushinish Point, W coast of North Harris. **66 A2** NA8711.
Gasker Beg *W.Isles* ***Island***, sea rock about 1km SE of Gasker. NA8810.
Gass *S.Ayr.* ***Settlement***, 2m/3km E of Straiton. **14 C5** NS4105.
Gass Water *E.Ayr.* ***River***, rising to S of Wardlaw Hill and flowing NW to become Bellow Water 4m/7km NE of Cumnock. **15 E3** NS6224.
Gasstown *D. & G.* ***Locality***, 2m/3km E of Dumfries. NX9976.
Gatehead *E.Ayr.* ***Hamlet***, 2m/4km SW of Kilmarnock. **14 B2** NS3936.
Gatehouse *Arg. & B.* ***Settlement***, on E side of Jura, 1m/2km SW of Lagg. **21 D2** NR5877.
Gatehouse *P. & K.* ***Settlement***, 2m/3km SE of Aberfeldy. **41 D5** NN8747.
Gatehouse of Fleet *D. & G.* ***Small town***, former cotton town, near mouth of Water of Fleet, 6m/10km NW of Kirkcudbright. **8 A5** NX6056.
Gatelawbridge *D. & G.* ***Locality***, 2m/3km E of Thornhill. **8 D1** NX9096.
Gateshaw *Sc.Bord.* ***Settlement***, 2m/3km S of Morebattle. **18 B4** NT7722.
Gateside *Aber.* ***Settlement***, 3m/4km E of Alford. **54 B3** NJ6116.
Gateside *Angus* ***Hamlet***, 4m/6km S of Forfar. **42 C5** NO4344.
Gateside *Fife* ***Village***, 2m/3km W of Strathmiglo. **33 G4** NO1809.
Gateside *N.Ayr.* ***Hamlet***, 1m/2km E of Beith. **23 E4** NS3653.
Gateslack *D. & G.* ***Settlement***, 3m/5km NE of Carronbridge. **15 G5** NS8902.
Gathersnow Hill ***Mountain***, on border of South Lanarkshire and Scottish Borders, 6m/9km S of Coulter. Height 2263 feet or 690 metres. **16 B3** NT0525.
Gattonside *Sc.Bord.* ***Hamlet***, with housing development on N side of River Tweed, opposite Melrose. Footbridge across river. **17 G2** NT5435.
Gauldry *Fife* ***Village***, 4m/6km SW of Newport-on-Tay. **34 B2** NO3723.
Gaur (Gaelic form: Abhainn Gaoire.) *P. & K.* ***River***, running E from Loch Eigheach to W end of Loch Rannoch. **39 G4** NN5056.
Gavinton *Sc.Bord.* ***Village***, 2m/3km SW of Duns. **27 E4** NT7652.
Geal Charn ***Mountain***, NE extension of Ladder Hills on border of Aberdeenshire and Moray, 6m/10km NW of Strathdon. Height 2240 feet or 683 metres. **53 F2** NJ3121.
Geal Charn *Aber.* ***Mountain***, 2m/3km N of Corgarff. Height 2207 feet or 673 metres. **53 E3** NJ2810.
Geal-charn *High.* ***Mountain***, at NW end of Cairngorm Mountains in Badenoch and Strathspey district, 7m/11km S of Aviemore. Height 3018 feet or 920 metres. NH8801.
Geal Charn *High.* ***Mountain***, in Badenoch and Strathspey district, 8m/12km SE of Nethy Bridge. Height 2693 feet or 821 metres. **52 C3** NJ0912.
Geal Charn *High.* ***Mountain***, in Lochaber district, 4m/7km NW of Achnacarry. Height 2637 feet or 804 metres. **50 A5** NN1594.
Geal Charn *High.* ***Mountain***, on Corrieyairack Forest on border of Inverness and Badenoch and Strathspey districts, 8m/12km SE of Fort Augustus. Height 2873 feet or 876 metres. NN4498.
Geal Charn *High.* ***Mountain***, 11m/17km SW of Kinloch Laggan. Munro: height 3713 feet or 1132 metres. **39 G2** NN4774.
Geal Charn *High.* ***Mountain***, on Ardverikie Forest in Badenoch and Strathspey district, 4m/6km E of SW end of Loch Laggan. Munro: height 3441 feet or 1049 metres. **40 A1** NN5081.
Geal Charn *High.* ***Mountain***, in Monadhliath range in Badenoch and Strathspey district, 4m/7km NW of Laggan Bridge. Munro: height 3037 feet or 926 metres. **51 E5** NN5698.
Geal-chàrn *High.* ***Mountain***, in Badenoch and Strathspey district, on E side of Loch Ericht and 5m/8km S of Dalwhinnie. Munro: height 3008 feet or 917 metres. **40 A2** NN5978.
Geal Chàrn *P. & K.* ***Mountain***, 3m/5km SE of Kinloch Rannoch. Height 2591 feet or 790 metres. **40 B4** NN6854.
Geal-charn Mòr *High.* ***Mountain***, in Badenoch and Strathspey district 4m/6km W of Aviemore. Height 2703 feet or 824 metres. **52 A3** NH8312.
Geal Loch *Arg. & B.* ***Lake/loch***, small loch on E side of River Falloch near head of Loch Lomond. NN3116.
Geallaig Hill *Aber.* ***Mountain***, 3m/5km NE of Crathie. Height 2437 feet or 743 metres. **53 E5** NO2998.
Geanies House *High.* ***Settlement***, 3m/5km NE of Balintore. **62 A2** NH8979.
Gearach *Arg. & B.* ***Settlement***, on Rinns of Islay, 1m/2km W of Port Charlotte. **20 A4** NR2358.
Gearnsary *High.* ***Settlement***, 1m/2km S of Loch Rimsdale, Sutherland district. **75 G5** NC7332.
Gearr Aonach *High. See The Three Sisters.*
Gearr Chreag *High.* ***Mountain***, 6m/10km E of Glenborrodale across Loch Sunart. Height 1115 feet or 340 metres. **37 G3** NM7061.
Gearr Garry *High.* ***River***, flowing SE out of E end of Loch Quoich into Glen Garry by Kingie Pool. NH0900.
Gearradh *High.* ***Settlement***, on NW shore of Loch Linnhe, 2m/3km W of Sallachan Point. **38 B3** NM9560.
Gearraidh Bhailteas (Anglicised form: Milton.) *W.Isles* ***Locality***, near W coast of South Uist 3m/4km S of Rubha Ardvule. Birthplace of Flora MacDonald. **44 C1** NF7326.
Gearraidh Bhaird (Anglicised form: Garyvard.) *W.Isles* ***Settlement***, on S side of Loch Erisort, Isle of Lewis, 2m/3km SE of Lacasaigh across loch. **69 E5** NB3620.
Gearraidh na h-Aibhne *W.Isles Gaelic form of Garynahine, qv.*
Gearraidh na Monadh (Anglicised form: Garrynamonie.) *W.Isles* ***Settlement***, near S end of South Uist, 1m/2km N of Cille Bhrighde. **44 C2** NF7516.
Gearran Island *High.* ***Island***, one of a group of islets 3m/5km NW of Rubha Hunish at N tip of Skye. See Gaeilavore Island; Lord Macdonald's Table. **57 G2** NG3679.
Gearrannan (Anglicised form: Garenin.) *W.Isles* ***Settlement***, 1m/2km NW of Carloway, Isle of Lewis. **68 C3** NB1944.
Geary *High.* ***Settlement***, on Skye, on W side of Loch Snizort, 4m/6km SE of Vaternish Point. **57 F3** NG2661.
Gedintailor *High.* ***Settlement***, on E coast of Skye, 5m/8km SE of Loch Portree. NG5235.
Geilston *Arg. & B.* ***Suburb***, adjoining to N of Cardross. NS3477.
Geirninis (Anglicised form: West Geirinish.) *W.Isles* ***Village***, towards N end of South Uist, on S side of Loch Bee. **45 F5** NF7741.
Geisiadar (Anglicised form: Geshader.) *W.Isles* ***Settlement***, in W part of Isle of Lewis, 3m/5km SE of Miabhig. **68 C4** NB1131.
Gelder Burn *Aber.* ***River***, running N down Glen Gelder to River Dee, 1m/2km SW of Balmoral Castle. NO2494.
Geldie Burn *Aber.* ***River***, running E to River Dee, 4m/6km W of Inverey. **41 E1** NO0288.
Gellyburn *P. & K.* ***Locality***, to NW of Murthly. **33 F1** NO0938.
Gelston *D. & G.* ***Village***, 2m/4km S of Castle Douglas. **8 B5** NX7758.
Gem Rock Museum *D. & G.* ***Other feature of interest***, museum at Creetown, 6m/10km SE of Newton Stewart, with large collection of gems, rocks and minerals with displays on cutting, shaping and polishing. **7 F5** NX4758.
Gemmil *Arg. & B.* ***Settlement***, 1m/2km NW of Ardfern. **29 G4** NM7805.
General Wade's Military Road *High.* ***Other feature of interest***, road built in 18c and traversing part of Highlands of Scotland via Glen Ore, Fort Augustus, and Corrieyairack Pass, with object of facilitating subjugation of Highlanders after Jacobite rising of 1715. **51 E2** NH5325.
Genoch *D. & G.* ***Locality***, including Genoch Mains and Little Genoch, 5m/8km SE of Stranraer. **6 C5** NX1356.
Genoch Square *D. & G.* ***Locality***, at road junction, 5m/8km SE of Stranraer. **6 C5** NX1355.
Gentlemen's Cave *Ork.* ***Coastal feature***, cave on W coast of Westray, 1m/2km SE of Noup Head. Formerly haunt of Jacobites. **80 B2** HY3948.
Geo Luon *Ork.* ***Coastal feature***, coastal gully on SW coast of Eday. **80 D4** HY5429.
Geo of Markamouth *Shet.* ***Coastal feature***, small indentation situated on W coast of Yell below Hill of Markamouth. **84 D2** HP4701.
Geo of Vigon *Shet.* ***Coastal feature***, small indentation on W coast of Yell at mouth of North Burn of Vigon. **85 D2** HP4704.
Geodh' a' Bhrideoin *High.* ***Coastal feature***, headland 3m/4km SW of Whiten Head. **75 D2** NC4866.
Geodha Mòr *High.* ***Coastal feature***, 1m/2km SE of Culnacraig, Ross and Cromarty district. **70 C4** NC0702.
Geodha Nasavig *W.Isles* ***Coastal feature***, on W coast of Isle of Lewis, 2m/3km SW of Gallan Head. **68 B4** NB0336.
Geodha Ruadh na Fola *High.* ***Coastal feature***, headland 3m/4km S of Cape Wrath. **74 B1** NC2471.
Geordie's Hill ***Mountain***, astride border of Dumfries & Galloway and Scottish Borders, 6m/10km NW of Newcastleton. Height 1522 feet or 464 metres. **10 C2** NY4396.
George Buchanan Monument *Stir.* ***Other feature of interest***, large obelisk in Killearn commemorating George Buchanan (1506-82), humanist, reformer, historian and tutor to Mary, Queen of Scots and her son James VI. **23 G1** NS5285.
Georgemas Junction Station *High.* ***Other building***, railway station 1m/2km E of Halkirk, where Thurso spur joins main line. **77 D3** ND1559.
Georgetown *Renf.* ***Settlement***, 3m/5km NW of Paisley. **23 F3** NS4567.
Georgian House *Edin.* ***Historic house***, New Town house, typical of late 18c to early 19c (National Trust for Scotland), designed by Robert Adam in Charlotte Square, Edinburgh, 1km W of city centre. Contains period furnishings. **25 G2** NT2473.
Georth *Ork. Alternative name for Evie, qv.*
Gerston *High.* ***Settlement***, on W bank of River Thurso, to W of Halkirk. **76 D3** ND1259.
Geshader *W.Isles Anglicised form of Geisiadar, qv.*
Geur Rubha *High.* ***Coastal feature***, headland on SW coast of Sleat peninsula, Skye, 1m/2km N of Point of Sleat. **48 B4** NG5501.
Ghlas-bheinn *High.* ***Mountain***, 1m/2km SW of head of Kyle of Durness. Height 1089 feet or 332 metres. **74 C2** NC3361.
Gib Bheinn *Arg. & B.* ***Inland physical feature***, craggy cliff face on Ardmeanach, Mull, 2m/3km N of Aird Fada across Loch Scridain. **28 D2** NM4428.
Gibbshill *D. & G.* ***Settlement***, 5m/8km E of New Galloway. **8 B3** NX7278.
Giffnock *E.Renf.* Population: 16,190. ***Suburb***, 5m/8km S of Glasgow. **23 G4** NS5659.
Gifford *E.Loth.* ***Village***, 4m/6km S of Hadington. 1m/2km SE is Yester House, 18c mansion, seat of Marquess of Tweeddale, beyond which are ruins of 13c Yester Castle. **26 C3** NT5368.
Gifford Church *E.Loth.* ***Ecclesiastical building***, Dutch style church of early 18c in Gifford, 4m/7km S of Haddington. Tablet nearby commemorates Reverend John Witherspoon, born at Gifford, only clergyman to sign American Declaration of Independence. **26 C3** NT5368.
Gifford Water *E.Loth.* ***River***, rising in Lammermuir Hills and flowing NW to become Colstoun Water, 1m/2km NW of Gifford. **26 C3** NT5269.
Giffordland *N.Ayr.* ***Settlement***, 1m/2km W of Dalry. **23 D5** NS2648.
Giffordtown *Fife* ***Hamlet***, 1m/2km NW of Ladybank. NO2811.
Gigha *Arg. & B.* ***Island***, narrow island of 9 square miles or 23 square km, 6m/10km long N to S, lying about 2m/3km off W coast of Kintyre, Argyll, opposite Rhunahaorine Point across Sound of Gigha. **21 E5** NR6449.
Gighay *W.Isles* ***Island***, uninhabited island at S end of Sound of Barra and 4m/6km E of Barra (Tràigh Mhòr) Airport. **44 C3** NF7604.
Gight Castle *Aber.* ***Castle***, ruined 16c tower house beside N bank of River Ythan, 4m/6km E of Fyvie; built by Gordon family. NJ8239.
Gigolum Island *Arg. & B.* ***Island***, small island lying to E of S end of Gigha. NR6445.
Gilchriston *E.Loth.* ***Settlement***, 2m/3km S of East Saltoun. **26 B3** NT4865.
Gill Burn *High.* ***River***, in NE corner of Caithness district rising near Brabster and running E into Freswick Bay 4m/6km S of John o' Groats. ND3767.
Gillen *High.* ***Settlement***, 5m/8km SE of Vaternish Point, Skye. **57 F3** NG2659.
Gillenbie *D. & G.* ***Settlement***, between Hope Burn and Corrie Water, 4m/6km S of Boreland. **9 F2** NY1785.
Gillfoot *D. & G.* ***Settlement***, 3m/4km N of New Abbey. **9 D3** NX9570.
Gillfoot Bay *D. & G.* ***Bay***, on Solway Firth, 6m/10km S of New Abbey. **9 D5** NX9755.
Gillivoan *High.* ***Settlement***, to N of Latheron. **77 D5** ND1934.
Gillock *High.* ***Settlement***, 5m/8km E of Halkirk. **77 E3** ND2059.
Gills *High.* ***Settlement***, near N coast of Caithness district, 2m/3km S of St. John's Point. **77 F1** ND3272.
Gills Bay *High.* ***Bay***, to NE of Gills, 3m/5km W of John o' Groats. **77 F1** ND3373.
Gilmanscleuch *Sc.Bord.* ***Hamlet***, 4m/6km SW of Ettrickbridge. **17 E3** NT3321.
Gilmerton *Edin.* ***Suburb***, 4m/7km SE of Edinburgh city centre. **25 G3** NT2968.
Gilmerton *P. & K.* ***Village***, 2m/3km NE of Crieff. **33 D2** NN8823.

Gilmilnscroft *E.Ayr.* ***Settlement***, 2m/4km N of Auchinleck. **15 D3** NS5525.
Gilsay *W.Isles* ***Island***, small uninhabited island in Sound of Harris, 2m/3km SW of Renish Point. **56 D2** NG0279.
Gilston *Sc.Bord.* ***Settlement***, 3m/4km S of Fala. **26 B4** NT4456.
Giosla (Anglicised form: Gisla.) *W.Isles* ***Settlement***, at mouth of Gisla River on W shore of Little Loch Roag, Isle of Lewis. **68 C5** NB1225.
Gipsy Palace *Sc.Bord.* ***Other feature of interest***, cottage at Kirk Yetholm, home of Esther Faa Blythe (d. 1883), last Queen of the Gipsies. **18 C4** NT8328.
Girdle Ness *Aberdeen* ***Coastal feature***, headland with lighthouse, 2m/3km E of Aberdeen city centre across River Dee. **55 E4** NJ9705.
Girdle Toll *N.Ayr.* ***Suburb***, to NE of Irvine town centre. NS3440.
Girlsta *Shet.* ***Settlement***, on E coast of Mainland, at S end of deep freshwater Loch of Girlsta, 6m/10km N of Lerwick. **82 D2** HU4350.
Girnigoe Castle *High.* ***Castle***, twin castle of adjacent Sinclair Castle, Caithness seat of chief of Clan Sinclair, on S coast of Sinclair's Bay, 1km W of Noss Head and 3m/4km NE of Wick. Second Earl of Caithness built Girnigoe Castle c. 1470; Sinclair Castle was built about 100 years later. **77 F3** ND3754.
Girnock Burn *Aber.* ***River***, running N down Glen Girnock to River Dee 3m/4km W of Ballater. **53 F5** NO3396.
Girthon *D. & G.* ***Settlement***, 2m/3km S of Gatehouse of Fleet. **8 A5** NX6053.
Girvan *S.Ayr.* Population: 7449. ***Small town***, fishing town and resort at mouth of Water of Girvan, 17m/28km SW of Ayr. **6 C1** NX1897.
Gisla *W.Isles Anglicised form of Giosla (settlement), qv.*
Gisla *W.Isles* ***River***, flowing E from Loch Grunavat, through Loch Coirgavat and into Little Loch Roag at Giosla, Isle of Lewis. NB1225.
Giùr-bheinn *Arg. & B.* ***Mountain***, on N of Islay, 4m/6km NW of Port Askaig. Height 1036 feet or 316 metres. **20 B2** NR3872.
Glack *Aber.* ***Settlement***, 1km W of Daviot. **54 C2** NJ7327.
Glackour *High.* ***Settlement***, in valley of River Broom, 9m/13km SE of Ullapool. **60 A1** NH1882.
Glacks of Balloch Pass *Moray* ***Other feature of interest***, road pass at 365 metres, between Meikle Balloch Hill and Little Balloch Hill, 4m/6km SE of Dufftown. **53 F1** NJ3534.
Gladhouse Reservoir *Midloth.* ***Reservoir***, large reservoir 5m/8km SE of Penicuik. **26 A4** NT2953.
Gladsmuir *E.Loth.* ***Village***, 4m/6km W of Haddington. **26 B2** NT4573.
Gladsmuir Hills *W.Loth.* ***Large natural feature***, small mountain range rising to height of 1168 feet or 365 metres at Leven Seat, 3m/4km N of Forth. Former mining area. **24 D4** NS9157.
Gladstone Court Museum *S.Lan.* ***Other feature of interest***, museum in late 19c coach house in Biggar. Authentic shops in rebuilt village street. **16 B2** NT0238.
Glaic *Arg. & B.* ***Settlement***, to W of Strone Point, 3m/5km N of Port Bannatyne. **22 B2** NS0771.
Glais Bheinn *High.* ***Mountain***, 2m/3km NE of Ardtornish Point, Lochaber district. Height 1571 feet or 479 metres. **37 G5** NM7243.
Glaister *N.Ayr.* ***Settlement***, on Arran, 5m/8km W of Brodick. **13 E2** NR9334.
Glaisters Burn *D. & G.* ***River***, stream rising on E slopes of Long Fell and flowing N to join Kirkgunzeon Lane, 1km N of Kirkgunzeon and 4m/6km NE of Dalbeattie. NX8767.
Glamaig *High.* ***Mountain***, 2m/3km E of Sligachan, Skye. Height 2542 feet or 775 metres. **48 B2** NG5130.
Glame *High.* ***Settlement***, on Raasay, 4m/6km S of Manish Point. **58 B5** NG5642.
Glamis *Angus* ***Village***, 10m/16km N of Dundee. Angus Folk Museum (National Trust for Scotland). **42 B5** NO3846.
Glamis Castle *Angus* ***Castle***, 1m/2km N of Glamis, mainly 17c but with parts of much earlier date; birthplace of Princess Margaret, 1930. **42 B5** NO3846.
Glanderston *Aber.* ***Settlement***, 3m/5km W of Insch. **54 A2** NJ5829.
Glas Bheinn *Arg. & B.* ***Mountain***, 4m/6km NE of Lochbuie, Mull. Height 1610 feet or 491 metres. **29 F2** NM6528.
Glas Bheinn *Arg. & B.* ***Mountain***, near E coast of Islay, 19m/30km NE of Port Ellen. Height 1545 feet or 471 metres. **20 C4** NR4259.
Glas Bheinn *Arg. & B.* ***Mountain***, on Jura, 3m/4km NW of Craighouse. Height 1840 feet or 561 metres. **20 D3** NR5069.
Glas Bheinn *High.* ***Mountain***, 3m/5km N of Inchnadamph. Height 2545 feet or 776 metres. **71 E2** NC2526.
Glas Bheinn *High.* ***Mountain***, in Skye and Lochalsh district, 2m/3km N of Glenelg. Height 1292 feet or 394 metres. **49 E2** NG8122.
Glas Bheinn *High.* ***Mountain***, 3m/5km SE of Strontian, Lochaber district. Height 2043 feet or 623 metres. **38 A4** NM8357.
Glas Bheinn *High.* ***Mountain***, in Lochaber district, 10m/14km NW of Gairlochy. Height 2152 feet or 656 metres. **50 A5** NN1397.
Glas Bheinn *High.* ***Mountain***, in Lochaber district, on N side of E end of Loch Arkaig, 3m/4km N of Achnacarry. Height 2401 feet or 732 metres. **50 A5** NN1791.
Glas Bheinn (Anglicised form: Glasven.) *High.* ***Mountain***, in Lochaber district 1m/2km E of Loch Eilde Mòr. Height 2588 feet or 789 metres. **39 E3** NN2564.
Glas Bheinn Mhòr ***Mountain***, on border of Argyll & Bute and Highland, 3m/5km SE of head of Loch Etive. Munro: height 3270 feet or 997 metres. **39 D5** NN1542.
Glas Bheinn Mhòr *High.* ***Mountain***, 1m/2km SE of head of Loch Ainort, Skye. Height 1870 feet or 570 metres. **48 B2** NG5525.
Glas-charn *High.* ***Mountain***, 1km S of head of Loch Beoraid, Lochaber district. Height 2076 feet or 633 metres. **38 A1** NM8483.
Glas Eilean *Arg. & B.* ***Island***, small uninhabited island off W coast of Luing. **29 G3** NM7311.
Glas Eilean *Arg. & B.* ***Island***, islet off SW shore of Jura 3m/4km S of Feolin Ferry. NR4465.
Glas Eilean *High.* ***Island***, islet at entrance to Loch Nevis, 1m/2km SW of Sandaig Bay, Knoydart, in Lochaber district. NG7000.
Glas Eilean *High.* ***Island***, islet in Loch Alsh, Skye and Lochalsh district, 2m/4km W of Dornie. **49 E2** NG8425.
Glas Eileanan *Arg. & B.* ***Island***, twin islets, the more easterly having a lighthouse, in Sound of Mull 2m/3km E of Scallastle Bay. NM7139.
Glas-leac Beag *High.* ***Island***, small uninhabited island, outlier of Summer Isles group, 6m/9km NE of Greenstone Point on W coast of Ross and Cromarty district. **70 B4** NB9205.
Glas-leac Mòr *High.* ***Island***, one of Summer Isles group. Lies nearly 2m/3km off NW coast of Ross and Cromarty district near Polbain. Area about 150 acres or 60 hectares. **70 B4** NB9509.
Glas Leathad Mòr *High.* ***Mountain***, summit of Ben Wyvis, 5m/8km NE of Garve. Munro: height 3431 feet or 1046 metres. **61 D3** NH4668.
Glas-loch Mòr *High.* ***Lake/loch***, small loch 1m/2km NE of Meallan Liath Mòr, in Ben Armine Forest, 10m/16km NE of Lairg. **72 B3** NC6719.
Glas Maol *Angus* ***Mountain***, 6m/9km NE of Spittal of Glenshee. Munro: height 3503 feet or 1068 metres. **41 G2** NO1676.
Glas Meall Bheag *P. & K.* ***Mountain***, 1m/2km SW of Glas Meall Mòr. Height 2890 feet or 881 metres. NN6775.
Glas Meall Mòr *P. & K.* ***Mountain***, 6m/9km SE of Dalwhinnie. Height 3044 feet or 928 metres. **40 B2** NN6876.
Glas Tulaichean *P. & K.* ***Mountain***, 5m/8km NW of Spittal of Glenshee. Munro: height 3447 feet or 1051 metres. **41 F2** NO0576.
Glasahoile *Stir.* ***Settlement***, on S shore of Loch Katrine, 6m/10km, NW of Aberfoyle. **31 G4** NN4608.
Glascarnoch *High.* ***River***, in Ross and Cromarty district, running E from Loch Glascarnoch to join Strath Rannoch at Inchbae Lodge. NH3969.
Glaschoil *High.* ***Settlement***, 3m/4km N of Grantown-on-Spey. **52 C1** NJ0232.
Glasclune Castle *P. & K.* ***Castle***, remains of former stronghold of Blairs, 2m/3km NW of Blairgowrie. NO1546.
Glascorrie *Aber.* ***Settlement***, 2m/3km NE of Ballater. **53 F5** NO3997.
Glasdrum *Arg. & B.* ***Settlement***, 1km NE of head of Loch Creran. **38 C5** NN0146.
Glasgow *Glas.* Population: 662,954. ***City***, largest city in Scotland. Port and commercial, industrial, cultural and entertainment centre on River Clyde, 41m/66km W of Edinburgh and 346m/557km NW of London. Major industrial port and important trading point with America until War of Independence. During industrial revolution, nearby coal seams boosted Glasgow's importance and its population increased ten-fold between 1800 and 1900. By beginning of 20c shipbuilding dominated the city, although industry went into decline in 1930's and is now a shadow of its former greatness. Glasgow is now seen to be a city of culture and progress. It has a strong performing arts tradition and many museums and galleries including Burrell Collection (set in Pollok Country Park). Cathedral is rare example of an almost complete 13c church. Early 19c Hutcheson's Hall (National Trust for Scotland) in Ingram Street is one of city's most elegant buildings; Tenement House (National Trust for Scotland) is late Victorian tenement flat retaining many original features. Three universities. Airport 7m/11km W. **23 G3** NS5965.
Glasgow Airport (Formerly known as Abbotsinch Airport.) *Renf.* ***Airport/airfield***, located on site of former locality, Abbotsinch, 2m/3km N of Paisley, to W of Renfrew. **23 F3** NS4766.
Glasgow Botanic Gardens *Glas.* ***Garden***, on S bank of River Kelvin, 2m/3km NW of Glasgow city centre in Kelvinside district. Contains Kibble's glass palace and houses National Begonia Collection. **23 G3** NS5767.
Glasgow Cathedral *Glas.* ***Ecclesiastical building***, impressive medieval cathedral (Historic Scotland), 1m/2km E of Glasgow city centre. The only intact surviving cathedral of Reformation on Scottish mainland, it contains intricate stone carvings, a vaulted crypt, and incomplete Blackadder aisle. **24 A3** NS6065.
Glasgow Zoo *Glas. See Calderpark Zoological Gardens.*
Glasha Burn *High.* ***River***, flowing from W slope of Bodach Mòr, then NE into Abhainn an t-Srath Chuileannaich, 5m/7km S of Oykel Bridge. **71 F5** NH3793.
Glashmore *Aber.* ***Settlement***, 2m/3km NW of Drumoak. **54 C4** NJ7600.
Glasnacardoch *High.* ***Locality***, on N side of Loch Ailort, on Ardnish peninsula in Lochaber district, 1m/2km E of Rubha Chaolais. NM7080.
Glasnacardoch *High.* ***Settlement***, on coast of Lochaber district, 1km S of Mallaig, on Glasnacardoch Bay. **48 C5** NM6795.
Glasnacardoch Bay *High.* ***Bay***, on coast of Lochaber district, 1km S of Mallaig. NM6795.
Glasnakille *High.* ***Settlement***, on E side of Strathaird Peninsula, Skye, 1m/2km N of Strathaird Point. Spar Cave on shore of Loch Slapin. **48 B3** NG5313.
Glass *High.* ***River***, in Inverness district, running NE down Strathglass to join River Farrar 1km SE of Struy Bridge. **50 C1** NH4039.
Glass *High.* ***River***, in Ross and Cromarty district, running SE from Loch Glass to Cromarty Firth E of Evanton. **61 E3** NH6265.
Glassaugh *Aber.* ***Settlement***, 3m/4km W of Portsoy. **64 A3** NJ5564.
Glassburn *High.* ***Settlement***, in Strathglass, 3m/4km NE of Cannich. **50 C1** NH3634.
Glassel *Aber.* ***Hamlet***, 1m/2km N of Bridge of Canny. **54 B5** NO6599.
Glasserton *D. & G.* ***Locality***, 2m/3km SW of Whithorn. **3 E3** NX4238.
Glassford *S.Lan.* ***Village***, 2m/4km NE of Strathaven. **24 B5** NS7247.
Glassingall *Stir.* ***Settlement***, in Strathallan, 2m/3km N of Dunblane. **32 C4** NN7904.
Glasslie *Fife* ***Locality***, comprises Wester Glasslie and Easter Glasslie, to NE of Ballo Reservoir. **34 A4** NO2305.
Glasterlaw *Angus* ***Settlement***, 1m/2km N of Friockheim. **43 D4** NO5951.
Glasven *High. Anglicised form of Glas Bheinn, qv.*
Gleann a' Chilleine *P. & K.* ***Valley***, carrying Allt a' Chilleine N towards Ardtalnaig, on SE side of Loch Tay. **32 C1** NN7238.
Gleann a' Choilich *High.* ***Valley***, running NE from Loch Coire nan Dearcag into W end of Loch Mullardoch. **49 G2** NH0723.
Gleann Airigh *Arg. & B.* ***Valley***, central valley of River Add before it reaches flood plain on Mòine Mhòr, 5m/8km NE of Lochgilphead. **30 B5** NR9296.
Gleann an Dubh-Lochain *High.* ***Valley***, upper valley of Inverie River in Knoydart, Lochaber district, containing Loch an Dubh-Lochain. NG8100.
Gleann an Fhiodh *High.* ***Valley***, carrying River Laroch N to S shore of Loch Leven at Ballachulish. **38 C4** NN0755.
Gleann Aoistail *Arg. & B.* ***Valley***, carrying Abhainn Ghleann Aoistail S into head of Loch Tarbert, Jura. **21 E1** NR5983.
Gleann Asdale *Arg. & B.* ***Valley***, on Jura, running W between Beinn Chaolais and Aonach-bheinn. **20 C2** NR4871.
Gleann Beag *Arg. & B. See Hell's Glen.*
Gleann Beag *High.* ***Valley***, of Abhainn a' Ghlinne Bhig in Lochaber district, running W into Sound of Sleat, 1m/2km SW of Glenelg. **49 E3** NG8018.
Gleann Beag *High.* ***Valley***, carrying Abhainn a' Ghlinne Bhig E from Glenbeg to its junction with Gleann Mòr, just N of Meall a' Chaorainn. **60 C1** NH3283.
Gleann Beag *P. & K.* ***Valley***, carrying Allt a' Ghlinne Bhig S to Glen Shee at Spittal of Glenshee. **41 G2** NO1172.
Gleann Bhruthadail *W.Isles* ***Valley***, 3m/5km SE of Bragar, Isle of Lewis. **69 E3** NB3244.
Gleann Bianasdail *High.* ***Valley***, carrying stream of Abhainn an Fhasaigh SW from S end of Lochan Fada into SE end of Loch Maree. **59 G3** NH0165.
Gleann Camgharaidh *High.* ***Valley***, carrying Allt Camgharaidh NE towards Loch Arkaig, 1m/2km S of head of loch, Lochaber district. **38 B1** NM9788.
Gleann Chomraidh *P. & K.* ***Valley***, carrying Allt Chomraidh and running NE to River Gaur above Loch Rannoch. NN4955.
Gleann Cia-Aig *High.* ***Valley***, carrying Abhainn Chia-aig S to E end of Lock Arkaig. **50 A5** NN1890.

G

Gleann Còsaidh *High.* ***Valley***, carrying Abhainn Chòsaidh in Barrisdale Forest, 1m/2km N of W end of Loch Quoich. **49 F4** NG9202.
Gleann Da-Eig *P. & K.* ***Valley***, carrying Allt Gleann Da-Eig, running N into River Lyon 2m/4km E of Bridge of Balgie. NN6045.
Gleann Dà-ghob *P. & K.* ***Valley***, carrying Allt Dà-ghob to N of Loch Tay, 5m/8km W of Kenmore. **40 B5** NN6744.
Gleann Domhain *Arg. & B.* ***Valley***, carrying Barbreck River in Argyll, running SW to head of Loch Craignish. **30 A4** NM8508.
Gleann Dorch *Arg. & B.* ***Valley***, on Jura, carrying Abhainn a' Ghleann Duirch SW into head of Loch Tarbert. **21 D1** NR5783.
Gleann Dubh *High.* ***Valley***, carrying River Traligill NW to Loch Assynt. River valley has extensive cave system 1m/2km SE of Inchnadamph. **71 E2** NC2621.
Gleann Dubh (Also known as Glen Dhu.) *High.* ***Valley***, steep-sided valley in Sutherland district running into head of Loch Glendhu, 4m/6km E of Kylesku Ferry. Situated in Glendhu Forest, westerly extension of Reay Forest. **74 B5** NC2833.
Gleann Dubh *High.* ***Valley***, in Morvern, carrying Black Water SW below Beinn Chlaonleud. **37 G4** NM7152.
Gleann Dubh *Stir.* ***Valley***, upper valley of Duchray Water, 4m/7km S of Stronachlachar. **31 F4** NN4003.
Gleann Dubh Lighe *High.* ***Valley***, carrying Dubh Lighe SW, 2m/3km E of Glenfinnan. **38 B1** NM9380.
Gleann Duibhe *P. & K.* ***Valley***, carrying Abhainn Duibhe, running NE to River Gaur below Loch Eigheach. **39 G4** NN4555.
Gleann Einich *High.* ***Valley***, carrying Am Beanaidh running N for 3m/4km from Loch Einich. **52 B4** NH9202.
Gleann Fearnach *P. & K.* ***Valley***, carrying Allt Fearnach, running S to head of Strathardle. **41 F3** NO0468.
Gleann Fhiodhaig *High.* ***Valley***, carrying River Meig E from N slopes of Maoile Lunndaidh to Loch Beannacharain, 2m/4km NW of Inverchoran. **60 A5** NH1247.
Gleann Fionnlighe *High.* ***Valley***, carrying Fionn Lighe SW towards Loch Eil, 4m/6km E of Glenfinnan, Lochaber district. **38 B1** NM9680.
Gleann Geal *High.* ***Valley***, carrying Abhainn a' Ghlinne Ghil in Lochaber district, running W to River Aline 4m/6km N of Lochaline. **37 G5** NM7250.
Gleann Ghrabhair (Anglicised form: Cromore.) *W.Isles* ***Village***, on S side of entrance to Loch Erisort, E coast of Isle of Lewis. Loch Cromore is small loch to S. **69 E5** NB4021.
Gleann Gniomhaidh *High.* ***Valley***, carrying stream Allt Gleann Gniomhaidh and running E from N slopes of Beinn Fhada to River Affric, 5m/7km W of Loch Affric. **49 G2** NH0320.
Gleann Goibhre *High.* ***Valley***, carrying Allt Goibhre, upper part marking boundary between districts of Inverness and Ross and Cromarty. **60 D5** NH4248.
Gleann Leireag (Anglicised form: Glen Leirg.) *High.* ***Valley***, running NW into Loch Nedd and Eddrachillis Bay, W coast of Sutherland district. **74 A5** NC1531.
Gleann Lichd *High.* ***Valley***, upper valley of River Croe in Kintail Forest, Skye and Lochalsh district. NG9818.
Gleann Meadail *High.* ***Valley***, carrying Allt Gleann Meadail W to Inverie River, 3m/5km W of Inverie, Lochaber district. **49 D5** NM8298.
Gleann Meadhonach *High.* ***Valley***, running W to W coast of Sleat peninsula, Skye, 3m/4km S of Tarskavaig Point. **48 B4** NG5905.
Gleann Meinich *High.* ***Valley***, running SE between Meallan nan Uan and Meall na Faochaig into River Meig at Glenmeanie. **60 B4** NH2553.
Gleann Mòr *High.* ***Valley***, carrying Abhainn a' Ghlinne Mhòir SE from just N of Meall a' Chaorainn to its convergence with valley of Alladale River. **60 D1** NH4086.
Gleann Mòr *P. & K.* *See Keltney Burn.*
Gleann Mòr *P. & K.* ***Valley***, narrow valley through which Allt a' Ghlinne Mhòir flows W and N to join numerous other streams to form headwaters of River Tilt, 1km SE of Falls of Tarf. **41 F2** NO0176.
Gleann Mòr Barvas *W.Isles* *Anglicised form of Gleann Mòr Bharabhais, qv.*
Gleann Mòr Bharabhais (Anglicised form: Gleann Mòr Barvas.) *W.Isles* ***Valley***, carrying River Barvas, near NW coast of Isle of Lewis, to S of Barvas. **69 E3** NB3548.
Gleann na Guiserein (Anglicised form: Glen Guseran.) *High.* ***Valley***, carrying Abhainn Inbhir Ghuiserein stream in Knoydart, Lochaber district, running NW to Sound of Sleat at Inverguseran. **49 D4** NG7703.
Gleann na Muice *High.* ***Valley***, in Ross and Cromarty district, running S from Loch Gleann na Muice at SE of Lochan Fada, and carrying Abhainn Gleann na Muice, which then forms part of Abhainn Bruachaig at Heights of Kinlochewe. **59 G3** NH0666.
Gleann nam Fiadh *High.* ***Valley***, carrying Abhainn Gleann nam Fiadh and running between Tom a' Chòinich and Am Meallan, then turning S to enter W end of Loch Beinn a' Mheadhoin. **50 A2** NH1425.
Gleann Oraid *High.* ***Valley***, carrying River Talisker, running down to Talisker Bay on W coast of Skye. **47 G1** NG3230.
Gleann Salach *Arg. & B.* ***Valley***, carrying Dearg Abhainn in Argyll, running NW to Loch Creran, 2m/3km SW of Dallachoilish. NM9739.
Gleann Sithidh *High.* ***Valley***, in Ross and Cromarty district, carrying Abhainn Sithidh N from N slopes of Sgurr nan Ceathreamhnan to a point 1m/2km W of Loch Mullardoch. **49 G2** NH0727.
Gleann Suileag *High.* ***Valley***, carrying An t-Suileag S into Loch Eil. **38 C1** NN0181.
Gleann Tanagaidh *High.* ***Valley***, running from S slopes of Beinn Bheag, continuing S and joining Strath Chrombuill 4m/6km NE of Kinlochewe. **59 G3** NH0768.
Gleann Tholastaidh (Anglicised form: Glen Tolsta.) *W.Isles* ***Locality***, near E coast of Isle of Lewis, on E side of valley of same name, 3m/4km SW of Tolsta Head. **69 G3** NB5244.
Gleann Udalain *High.* ***Valley***, carrying Allt Gleann Udalain, 3m/4km S of Stromeferry, Skye and Lochalsh district. **49 E1** NG8730.
Glecknabae *Arg. & B.* ***Settlement***, on NW coast of Bute, 6m/9km NW of Rothesay. **22 B3** NS0068.
Glen *D. & G.* ***Settlement***, 3m/5km W of Gatehouse of Fleet. **7 G5** NX5457.
Glen *D. & G.* ***Settlement***, to SW of Glenkiln Reservoir, 3m/4km W of Shawhead. **8 C3** NX8376.
Glen Achall *High.* ***Valley***, in Ross and Cromarty district, to E of Ullapool. **71 E5** NH1795.
Glen Affric *High.* ***Valley***, largely forested valley carrying River Affric NE through Loch Affric and Loch Beinn a' Mheadhoin to River Glass, Inverness district. **50 A2** NH1521.
Glen Albyn *High.* *See Glen Mòr.*
Glen Aldie *High.* ***Valley***, in Ross and Cromarty district, running down to S shore of Dornoch Firth on E side of Tain. **61 G1** NH7679.
Glen Almond *P. & K.* ***Valley***, to NW of Methven, carrying River Almond about 13m/20km E towards confluence with River Tay at Perth. **33 E2** NN9128.
Glen Ample *Stir.* ***Valley***, carrying Burn of Ample, running N to Loch Earn, 1m/2km E of Lochearnhead. **32 A3** NN5919.
Glen App *S.Ayr.* ***Valley***, carrying Water of App, running SW of Finnarts Bay near N end of Loch Ryan. **6 B3** NX0674.
Glen Aray *Arg. & B.* ***Valley***, carrying River Aray in Argyll, running S to Loch Fyne at Inveraray. **30 C3** NN0812.
Glen Arklet *Stir.* ***Valley***, containing Loch Arklet, located between Loch Lomond and Loch Katrine. **31 F4** NN3609.
Glen Arnisdale *High.* ***Valley***, carrying River Arnisdale, 1m/2km SE of Arnisdale. **49 E4** NG8709.
Glen Aros *Arg. & B.* ***Valley***, on Mull, carrying Aros River. **37 E5** NM5345.
Glen Arroch *High.* ***Valley***, on Skye, 3m/5km SW of Kyleakin. **48 D2** NG7321.
Glen Artney *P. & K.* ***Valley***, carrying Water of Ruchill, running NE to Strathearn at Comrie. **32 C3** NN7217.
Glen Ashdale *N.Ayr.* ***Valley***, on Arran, carrying Glenashdale Burn to Whiting Bay. **13 F3** NS0425.
Glen Avon *Moray* ***Valley***, steep-sided valley which runs NE, then E, on N side of Forest of Glenavon. **52 C4** NJ0906.
Glen Banchor *High.* ***Valley***, carrying River Calder NE to valley end, 1km NW of Newtonmore. **51 F5** NN6397.
Glen Banvie *P. & K.* ***Valley***, carrying Banvie Burn, running SE to River Garry on W side of Blair Atholl. **40 D3** NN8468.
Glen Barrisdale *High.* ***Valley***, carrying River Barrisdale in Lochaber district, to S of Loch Hourn. **49 E4** NG8704.
Glen Barry ***Valley***, between Knock Hill and Barry Hill on border of Aberdeenshire and Moray, 3m/5km SW of Cornhill. Contains settlement of Glenbarry. **64 A4** NJ5654.
Glen Bay *W.Isles* *Alternative name for Loch a' Ghlinne, qv.*
Glen Beasdale *High.* ***Valley***, steep-sided valley on South Morar carrying Beasdale Burn and running W to sea at Loch nan Uamh. **37 G1** NM7285.
Glen Beich *Stir.* ***Valley***, carrying Beich Burn and running S to Loch Earn, 2m/3km E of Lochearnhead. **32 B2** NN6328.
Glen Borrodale *High.* ***Valley***, on Ardnamurchan peninsula in Lochaber district, running S to Glenborrodale Bay. NM6062.
Glen Bragar *W.Isles* ***Valley***, carrying River Arnol, S of Bragar, Isle of Lewis. **69 E3** NB3042.
Glen Breackerie *Arg. & B.* ***Valley***, carrying Breackerie Water in Kintyre and running S to Carskey Bay, on S coast of peninsula. **12 B4** NR6510.
Glen Brein *High.* ***Valley***, carrying Allt Breinag in Inverness district and running N to River Feehlin at Whitebridge, 3m/5km S of Foyers. **51 D4** NH4809.
Glen Brerachan *P. & K.* ***Valley***, carrying Brerachan Water and running E to head of Strathardle. **41 F3** NO0263.
Glen Brittle *High.* ***Valley***, carrying River Brittle on Skye, below Glen Brittle Forest and W edge of Cuillin Hills. NG4023.
Glen Brittle Forest *High.* ***Forest/woodland***, upland tract and forest on Skye to W of River Brittle. NG4026.
Glen Brown ***Valley***, on border of Highland and Moray and carrying Burn of Brown, running N into head of Glen Lochy at Bridge of Brown, 3m/5km NW of Tomintoul, on border of Highland and Moray. **52 D3** NJ1219.
Glen Bruar *P. & K.* ***Valley***, carrying Bruar Water and running S to River Garry, 3m/5km W of Blair Atholl. Falls of the Bruar 1m/2km NE of Calvine. **40 D2** NN8272.
Glen Buchat *Aber.* ***Valley***, carrying Water of Buchat and running SE below Ladder Hills to River Don. NJ3616.
Glen Callater *Aber.* ***Valley***, carrying Callater Burn and running N to join Clunie Water, 2m/3km S of Braemar. **41 G1** NO1685.
Glen Calvie *High.* ***Valley***, carrying Water of Glencalvie in Sutherland district and running N into River Carron at Glencalvie Lodge on S side of Amat Forest. **61 D1** NH4687.
Glen Cannel *Arg. & B.* ***Valley***, carrying Glencannel River to head of Loch Bà, on Mull. NM5836.
Glen Cannich *High.* ***Valley***, in Inverness district, containing Loch Mullardoch and carrying River Cannich E to River Glass. **50 A2** NH1930.
Glen Carron *High.* ***Valley***, carrying River Carron, in Ross and Cromarty district, running down to Loch Carron from Loch Sgamhain. **59 G4** NH0852.
Glen Cassley *High.* ***Valley***, deep U-shaped valley carrying River Cassley, running SE, in Sutherland district. **71 G3** NC3913.
Glen Catacol *N.Ayr.* ***Valley***, running down to Catacol Bay on NW coast of Arran. **22 A5** NR9248.
Glen Chalmadale *N.Ayr.* ***Valley***, running NW to Loch Ranza on NW coast of Arran. **22 A5** NR9550.
Glen Clova *Angus* ***Valley***, steep sided glacial valley carrying River South Esk SE to confluence with Prosen Water and containing village of Clova. **42 A2** NO3570.
Glen Cluanie *High.* ***Valley***, section of Glen Shiel carrying River Cluanie, above head and to W of Loch Cluanie. **49 G3** NH0610.
Glen Clunie *Aber.* ***Valley***, narrow, steep-sided valley, with Clunie Water flowing N to River Dee at Braemar. **41 G1** NO1485.
Glen Cochill *P. & K.* ***Valley***, carrying Cochill Burn and running S to head of Strath Braan. **41 E5** NN9041.
Glen Coe *High.* ***Valley***, carrying River Coe in Lochaber district and running W to Loch Leven, 3m/5km E of Ballachulish. Scene of notorious massacre in 1692. Much of glen and country to S in care of National Trust for Scotland. Mountain peaks of The Three Sisters overlook glen to S. **38 D4** NN1557.
Glen Coiltie *High.* ***Valley***, carrying River Coiltie and running E from lower slopes of Carn a' Bhainne to Urquhart Bay on Loch Ness. **51 D2** NH4526.
Glen Convinth *High.* ***Valley***, carrying Allt Dearg N from NE of Meall Gorm to Kiltarlity. **51 E1** NH5035.
Glen Coul *High.* ***Valley***, steep-sided valley in Sutherland district, running into head of Loch Glencoul 4m/6km SE of Kylestrome. NC2730.
Glen Creran *Arg. & B.* ***Valley***, wooded valley carrying River Creran SW to head of Loch Creran, Argyll. **38 C5** NN0450.
Glen Croe *Arg. & B.* ***Valley***, carrying Croe Water SE to Loch Long, near head of loch on NE side. **31 E4** NN2504.
Glen Cross *W.Isles* ***Valley***, carrying Cross River, 4m/6km S of Butt of Lewis. **69 G1** NB5061.
Glen Dale *High.* ***Valley***, carrying Hamara River, 5m/8km S of Dunvegan Head, Skye. **57 F5** NG1848.
Glen Damff *Angus* ***Valley***, carrying Glendamff Burn S to Backwater Reservoir. **42 A3** NO2466.
Glen Dee *Aber.* ***Valley***, carrying upper River Dee, 10m/16km W of Braemar. **52 B5** NN9894.
Glen Derry *Aber.* ***Valley***, carrying Derry Burn and running in a N to S direction to Glen Lui. **52 C5** NO0396.
Glen Dessarry *High.* ***Valley***, carrying River Dessary in Lochaber district and running E to junction with Glen Pean, 1km above head of Loch Arkaig. **49 F5** NM9592.
Glen Devon *P. & K.* ***Valley***, carrying River Devon between Dollar and Auchterarder. **33 E4** NN9505.
Glen Dhu *High.* *Alternative name for Gleann Dubh, qv.*
Glen Diebidale *High.* ***Valley***, carrying River Diebidale, in Sutherland district. **60 D1** NH4583.
Glen Dochart *Stir.* ***Valley***, carrying River Dochart and running NE to join Glen Lochay at head of Loch Tay. **31 G2** NN4828.
Glen Docherty *High.* ***Valley***, in Ross and Cromarty district, running from a point 5m/9km W of Achnasheen NW to Kinlochewe. Excellent viewpoint, giving views NW to Loch Maree and surrounding mountains. **59 G3** NH0460.
Glen Doe *High.* ***Valley***, carrying Allt Doe in Inverness district and running N into Loch Ness, 1m/2km below head of loch. **50 D4** NH4108.

Glen Doll *Angus* ***Valley***, carrying White Water in Angus district and running SE to River South Esk at head of Glen Clova. **42 A2** NO2576.
Glen Douchary *High.* ***Valley***, with waterfalls, in Ross and Cromarty district, carrying River Douchary and running S between Glen Achall and Glean a' Chadha Dheirg. **71 E5** NH2593.
Glen Douglas *Arg. & B.* ***Valley***, carrying Douglas Water and running E to Loch Lomond at Inverbeg. **31 F5** NS3198.
Glen Dronach *Aber. See Forgue.*
Glen Drynoch *High.* ***Valley***, carrying River Drynoch and running W to head of Loch Harport, Skye. **48 A1** NG4330.
Glen Duror *High.* ***Valley***, carrying River Duror in Lochaber district and running W to Cuil Bay on E shore of Loch Linnhe. **38 C4** NN0154.
Glen Dye *Aber.* ***Valley***, carrying Water of Dye and running N to Water of Feugh on W side of Strachan. **43 E1** NO6484.
Glen Eagles *P. & K.* ***Valley***, carrying upper reaches of Ruthven Water, to S of Auchterarder. **33 E4** NN9308.
Glen Effock *Angus* ***Valley***, carrying Water of Effock and running NE to Glen Esk, 2m/3km W of Tarfside. **42 C2** NO4477.
Glen Einig *High.* ***Valley***, carrying River Einig and running N from N slopes of Mullach a' Chadha Bhuidhe, then NE into Strath Oykel just SE of Oykel Bridge. **71 F5** NH3498.
Glen Elchaig *High.* ***Valley***, carrying River Elchaig W below Sgùman Coinntich to head of Loch Long, Skye and Lochalsh district. **49 F2** NG9727.
Glen Ernan *Aber.* ***Valley***, carrying Ernan Water and running SE to River Don, 5m/8km E of Cock Bridge. **53 F3** NJ3310.
Glen Errochty *P. & K.* ***Valley***, carrying Errochty Water and running E from Loch Errochty to River Garry, near Calvine. **40 C3** NN7663.
Glen Esk *Angus* ***Valley***, carrying River North Esk in its upper reaches E between Auchronie and Fernybank. **42 C2** NO4678.
Glen Etive *High.* ***Valley***, carrying River Etive, Lochaber district, running SW to head of Loch Etive. **39 E4** NN1751.
Glen Euchar *Arg. & B.* ***Valley***, carrying River Euchar, in Argyll, running W and NW from Loch Scamadale to Loch Feochan. **30 A2** NM8319.
Glen Ey *Aber.* ***Valley***, carrying Ey Burn and running N to River Dee at Inverey, 4m/7km W of Braemar. **41 F1** NO0886.
Glen Ey Forest *Aber.* ***Open space***, deer forest astride Glen Ey. **41 F1** NO0886.
Glen Eynort *High.* ***Valley***, carrying River Eynort and running down to head of Loch Eynort, Skye. NG3828.
Glen Falloch *Stir.* ***Valley***, carrying River Falloch SW towards head of Loch Lomond. Falls of Falloch, 4m/7km SW of Crianlarich. **31 F2** NN3421.
Glen Farg *P. & K.* ***Valley***, carrying River Farg NE to River Earn, 5m/8km SE of Perth. **33 G3** NO1513.
Glen Fender *P. & K.* ***Valley***, carrying Fender Burn and running SW to River Tilt, 1m/2km N of Blair Atholl. NN9068.
Glen Fenzie *Aber.* ***Valley***, carrying Glenfenzie Burn SE between Clashanruich and Lary Hill, 5m/8km NW of Ballater. **53 F4** NJ3202.
Glen Feochan *Arg. & B.* ***Valley***, in Argyll, running W to head of Loch Feochan 4m/6km S of Oban. NM8924.
Glen Feshie *High.* ***Valley***, carrying River Feshie in Badenoch and Strathspey district, running N to River Spey 1km below Kincraig. **52 A5** NN8594.
Glen Fiag *High.* ***Valley***, carrying River Fiag S from Loch Fiag to Loch Shin. **71 G2** NC4526.
Glen Fiddich *Moray* ***Valley***, carrying River Fiddich NE to Dufftown. **53 F1** NJ3234.
Glen Finart *Arg. & B.* ***Valley***, carrying stream in Argyll SE to Loch Long at Finart Bay on N side of Ardentinny. **31 D5** NS1790.
Glen Finglas *Stir.* ***Valley***, carrying Finglas Water SE to Black Water between Loch Achray and Loch Venachar, to W of Callander. **31 G3** NN5209.
Glen Finglas Reservoir *Stir.* ***Reservoir***, in course of Finglas Water, within Glen Finglas. **32 A4** NN5209.
Glen Finlas *Arg. & B.* ***Valley***, carrying Finlas Water SE to Loch Lomond, 1m/2km S of Rossdhu House. Small reservoir near head of glen. NS3388.
Glen Finlet *Angus* ***Valley***, forested valley carrying Finlet Burn S to Newton Burn. **42 A3** NO2267.
Glen Finnan *High.* ***Valley***, carrying River Finnan, in Lochaber district, S to head of Loch Shiel. **38 B1** NM9083.
Glen Forsa *Arg. & B.* ***Valley***, on Mull, carrying River Forsa N to Sound of Mull, 2m/3km E of Salen. **37 F5** NM6039.
Glen Forslan *High.* ***Valley***, in Moidart, carrying Glenforslan River W to Glen Moidart, Lochaber district, 3m/5km S of Lochailort. **37 G2** NM7773.
Glen Fruin *Arg. & B.* ***Valley***, carrying Fruin Water SE to Loch Lomond, 2m/4km N of foot of loch. **23 D1** NS2987.
Glen Fyne *Arg. & B.* ***Valley***, carrying River Fyne SW to head of Loch Fyne, 6m/10km NE of Inveraray, Argyll. **31 E3** NN2215.
Glen Fyne *Arg. & B.* ***Valley***, carrying Ardyne Burn S to Firth of Clyde, 2m/4km W of Toward Point, Argyll. NS1172.
Glen Gairn *Aber.* ***Valley***, to NW of Ballater, carrying River Gairn. **53 F4** NJ3100.
Glen Garry *High.* ***Valley***, in Lochaber district, running E from Loch Quoich and containing Gearr Garry, Loch Garry and River Garry. **50 A4** NH1300.
Glen Garry *P. & K.* ***Valley***, carrying River Garry SE from Loch Garry to River Tummel, 2m/3km NW of Pitlochry. **40 C3** NN7569.
Glen Garvan *High.* ***Valley***, carrying North Garvan River NE towards Loch Eil, 2m/3km SW of Kinlocheil across Loch Eil. **38 B2** NM9574.
Glen Gelder *Aber.* ***Valley***, carrying Gelder Burn N to River Dee, 2m/3km SW of Balmoral Castle. NO2491.
Glen Gheallaidh ***Valley***, carrying Allt a' Gheallaidh and running E between steep hillsides, to NE of Grantown-on-Spey. Border of Highland and Moray follows river down valley. **62 D5** NJ1238.
Glen Girnaig *P. & K.* ***Valley***, carrying Allt Girnaig SW to River Garry at Killiecrankie. **41 E3** NN9466.
Glen Girnock *Aber.* ***Valley***, carrying Girnock Burn N to River Dee, 3m/4km W of Ballater. NO3396.
Glen Glass *High.* ***Valley***, carrying River Glass, Ross and Cromarty district, to W of Evanton. **61 E3** NH5667.
Glen Gloy *High.* ***Valley***, carrying River Gloy SW to Glenfintaig, 3m/4km N of Spean Bridge. **50 B5** NN2689.
Glen Golly *High.* ***River***, in Sutherland district rising on E side of Reay Forest and running SE down Glen Golly to head of Strath More. **74 D4** NC4442.
Glen Golly *High.* ***Valley***, steep-sided valley in Sutherland district, carrying Glen Golly River SE to head of Strath More. NC4243.
Glen Gour *High.* ***Valley***, carrying River Gour in Lochaber district and running E to Camas Shallachain, on W side of Sallachan Point on Loch Linnhe. **38 B3** NM9464.
Glen Grant and Caperdonich Distillery *Moray* ***Other feature of interest***, adjacent distilleries to N of Rothes. Glen Grant distillery was established in 1840 and its 'sister', Caperdonich, built in 1897 alongside it. Caperdonich closed in 1901, but was reopened and modernised in 1967. **63 E5** NJ2750.
Glen Guseran *High. Anglicised form of Gleann na Guiserein, qv.*
Glen Gyle *Stir.* ***Valley***, carrying Glengyle Water SE to head of Loch Katrine. **31 F3** NN3614.
Glen Hurich *High.* ***Valley***, carrying River Hurich in Lochaber district and running SW to Loch Doilet. **38 A3** NM8468.
Glen Iorsa *N.Ayr.* ***Valley***, carrying Iorsa Water, on Arran, SW into Kilbrannan Sound at N end of Machrie Bay. **13 E2** NR9239.
Glen Isla *Angus* ***Valley***, upper valley of River Isla, from source to Airlie Castle. **42 A3** NO2563.
Glen Kerran *Arg. & B.* ***Valley***, on S part of Kintyre, running SW into Conie Glen. **12 C4** NR7112.
Glen Kin *Arg. & B.* ***Valley***, running N to Little Eachaig River in Argyll, 2m/3km W of Holy Loch. NS1380.
Glen Kingie *High.* ***Valley***, carrying River Kingie in Lochaber district and running E into Glen Garry, 2m/3km SE of dam of Loch Quoich. **49 G5** NN0397.
Glen Kinglas *Arg. & B.* ***Valley***, carrying Kinglas Water in Argyll and running W to near head of Loch Fyne at Cairndow. **31 E3** NN2109.
Glen Kinglass *Arg. & B.* ***Valley***, carrying River Kinglass W into Loch Etive, Argyll, on S side of Ardmaddy Bay. **30 D1** NN1235.
Glen Kyllachy *High.* ***Valley***, running E from S slopes of Carn Eitidh into Strathdearn, 5m/7km SW of Tomatin. **51 G2** NH7424.
Glen Lean *Arg. & B.* ***Valley***, upper valley of Little Eachaig River, in Argyll. Chalybeate spring on roadside, 1m/2km above Clachaig. NS0982.
Glen Lednock *P. & K.* ***Valley***, carrying River Lednock SE to Strathearn at Comrie. Loch Lednock Reservoir near head of glen. **32 C2** NN7327.
Glen Lee *Angus* ***Valley***, carrying Water of Lee and running E to join Water of Mark at head of River North Esk, 3m/4km W of Tarfside. **42 B1** NO4079.
Glen Leidle *Arg. & B.* ***Valley***, on Mull, carrying Leidle River NW to Loch Scridain at Pennyghael. NM5224.
Glen Leirg *High. Anglicised form of Gleann Leireag, qv.*
Glen Liever *Arg. & B.* ***Valley***, carrying River Liever in Argyll S to Loch Awe, 1m/2km E of head of loch. NM8905.
Glen Ling *High.* ***Valley***, carrying River Ling SW into head of Loch Long, Skye and Lochalsh district. **49 F1** NG9432.
Glen Liver *Arg. & B.* ***Valley***, carrying River Liver W into Loch Etive, Argyll, 7m/11km from head of loch. **30 C1** NN0835.
Glen Loch *P. & K.* ***Valley***, in Forest of Atholl, to S of Loch Loch, 9m/13km NE of Blair Atholl. **41 E2** NN9874.
Glen Lochay *Stir.* ***Valley***, carrying River Lochay W to join Glen Dochart at head of Loch Tay. **31 G1** NN4836.
Glen Lochsie *P. & K.* ***Valley***, carrying Glen Lochsie Burn SE to head of Glen Shee at Spittal of Glenshee. **41 F2** NO0472.
Glen Lochsie Burn *P. & K.* ***River***, stream running SE to head of Glen Shee at Spittal of Glenshee. NO0871.
Glen Lochy *Arg. & B.* ***Valley***, carrying River Lochy W to Glen Orchy, 2m/3km E of Dalmally, Argyll. **31 E1** NN2428.
Glen Lochy *Moray* ***Valley***, carrying Burn of Lochy and running NE below Hills of Cromdale to River Avon, 4m/7km N of Tomintoul. NJ1323.
Glen Logie *Angus* ***Valley***, running S towards Glen Prosen at Balnaboth. **42 B3** NO3069.
Glen Loin *Arg. & B.* ***Valley***, carrying Loin Water S to head of Loch Long. NN3006.
Glen Lonan *Arg. & B.* ***Valley***, carrying River Lonan W to head of Loch Nell, 3m/5km E of Oban, Argyll. NM9427.
Glen Loth *High.* ***Valley***, in Sutherland district, running S towards coast at Lothbeg. **73 E3** NC9412.
Glen Loy *High.* ***Valley***, carrying River Loy in Lochaber district and running SE into River Lochy, 2m/4km SW of Gairlochy. **38 D1** NN1084.
Glen Loy Forest *High.* ***Forest/woodland***, astride River Loy. NN1084.
Glen Loyne *High.* ***Valley***, surrounding Loch Loyne, which lies between Loch Cluanie and Loch Garry. **49 G4** NH1006.
Glen Lui *Aber.* ***Valley***, carrying Lui Water SE to River Dee, 5m/8km W of Braemar. **52 C5** NO0592.
Glen Luss *Arg. & B.* ***Valley***, carrying Luss Water and running E to Loch Lomond at Luss village. **31 F5** NS3193.
Glen Lussa *Arg. & B.* ***Valley***, carrying Lussa Water on Kintyre into Ardnacross Bay, 4m/6km NE of Campbeltown. **12 C3** NR7325.
Glen Lyon *P. & K.* ***Valley***, carrying River Lyon E from Loch Lyon to River Tay, 4m/6km W of Aberfeldy. **40 A5** NN5646.
Glen Mallie *High.* ***Valley***, carrying River Mallie, in Lochaber district, E into S side of Loch Arkaig. **38 C1** NN0887.
Glen Mark *Angus* ***Valley***, carrying Water of Mark and running first NE then SE to head of River North Esk, 3m/4km W of Tarfside. **42 B1** NO4979.
Glen Markie *High.* ***Valley***, carry Glenmarkie Burn and running from W slopes of Burrach Mòr SW to River Killin, 10m/16km E of Fort Augustus. **51 E4** NH5507.
Glen Markie *High.* ***Valley***, carrying Markie Burn in Badenoch and Strathspey district and running S to River Spey 1m/2km W of Laggan Bridge. **51 E5** NN5893.
Glen Massan *Arg. & B.* ***Valley***, carrying River Massan in Argyll and running SE to River Eachaig, 2m/4km NW of head of Holy Loch. **22 C1** NS1286.
Glen Mazeran *High.* ***Valley***, running E, then NE, into Strathdearn, 5m/8km SW of Tomatin. **51 G2** NH7121.
Glen Moidart *High.* ***Valley***, carrying River Moidart SW towards Loch Moidart, Lochaber district. **37 G2** NM7572.
Glen Mòr (Great Glen). *High.* ***Valley***, large valley extending 60m/97km along Great Glen faultline from Loch Linnhe at Fort William to Moray Firth at Inverness. Contains Lochs Lochy, Oich, and Ness, and is traversed by Caledonian Canal. NE section of valley, which includes Loch Ness, is also known as Glen Albyn. **50 B5** NH3607.
Glen More *Arg. & B.* ***Valley***, on Mull, carrying two rivers: River Coladoir flows W towards Loch Schridain; River Lussa flows NE below Loch Squabain. **29 F1** NM6029.
Glen More *Arg. & B.* ***Valley***, carrying Glenmore Burn S to Ettrick Bay, Bute. NS0269.
Glen More *High.* ***Valley***, section of valley to E of Beinn a' Chaionich and 4m/6km E of Glenelg in Lochaber district, carrying River Glenmore E to Glenelg Bay. **49 E3** NG8818.
Glen More *High.* ***Valley***, carrying Allt Mòr in Glenmore Forest Park, Badenoch and Strathspey district, running N then W into head of Loch Morlich. **52 B4** NH9808.
Glen Moriston *High.* ***Valley***, carrying River Moriston, Inverness district, E from Loch Cluanie to Loch Ness. Power station for hydro-electricity scheme at Ceannacroc Bridge. **50 C3** NH4216.
Glen Muick *Aber.* ***Valley***, carrying River Muick NE from Loch Muick to River Dee, 1km S of Ballater. **42 B1** NO3187.
Glen Nant *Arg. & B.* ***Valley***, carrying River Nant S from Taynuilt to Loch Nant. **30 C2** NN0128.
Glen Nevis *High.* ***Valley***, carrying Water of Nevis, in Lochaber district, running down to Loch Linnhe at Fort William. **38 D2** NN1468.
Glen Noe *Arg. & B.* ***Valley***, carrying River Noe NW to Loch Etive, Argyll, 3m/4km E of Bonawe. **30 C1** NN0733.
Glen of Coachford *Aber.* ***Valley***, to S of The Balloch, 3m/5km SE of Keith. **63 G5** NJ4646.

Glen of Rothes *Moray* ***Valley***, traversed by A941 road and carrying Broad Burn SE to N of Rothes. **63 E4** NJ2552.
Glen Ogil *Angus* ***Valley***, carrying Noran Water, 4m/7km NW of Tannadice. **42 C3** NO4464.
Glen Ogilvy *Angus* ***Valley***, small, wide valley running in a NE direction and containing settlement of Milton of Ogilvie, 2m/3km S of Glamis. **42 B5** NO3743.
Glen Ogle *Stir.* ***Valley***, running SE down to head of Loch Earn at Lochearnhead. **32 A2** NN5726.
Glen Orchy *Arg. & B.* ***Valley***, carrying River Orchy SW to NE end of Loch Awe, Argyll. **31 E1** NN2433.
Glen Orrin *High.* ***Valley***, carrying River Orrin and running E from Am Fiar-Loch to N of Carn Doire Mhurchaidh. Contains Orrin Reservoir. **60 C4** NH3449.
Glen Ose *High.* ***Valley***, on Skye, carrying River Ose SW to Loch Bracadale. **57 G5** NG3241.
Glen Ouirn *W.Isles* ***River***, flowing W into Loch Sgibacleit, Isle of Lewis. **67 F2** NB3216.
Glen Oykel *High.* ***Valley***, carrying upper reaches of River Oykel, Sutherland district, 7m/11km SE of Elphin. **71 F4** NC3207.
Glen Pean *High.* ***Valley***, in Lochaber district, carrying River Pean E to junction with Glen Dessarry 1km above head of Loch Arkaig. **49 F5** NM9590.
Glen Prosen *Angus* ***Valley***, carrying Prosen Water and running SE of River South Esk at foot of Glen Clova, 3m/5km NE of Kirriemuir. **42 A3** NO2967.
Glen Quaich *P. & K.* ***Valley***, carrying River Quaich and running SE then E to head of Strath Braan. NN8638.
Glen Quoich *Aber.* ***Valley***, in Braemar Forest, and through which flows Quoich Water in a SE direction to River Dee valley, 2m/3km W of Braemar. **52 C5** NO0893.
Glen Quoich *High.* ***Valley***, in Lochaber district, carrying River Quoich S into Loch Quoich. **49 G4** NH0107.
Glen Righ *High.* ***Valley***, carrying Abhainn Righ, in Lochaber district, W to Loch Linnhe 1m/2km NW of Onich. NN0563.
Glen Rinnes *Moray* ***Valley***, carrying Dullan Water and running down to River Fiddich at Dufftown. **53 E1** NJ3339.
Glen Rock *High.* ***Hill***, with rock outcrops on N and E sides, 3m/5km NW of Golspie, on SW side of Dunrobin Glen. Height 886 feet or 270 metres. **72 C4** NC8003.
Glen Rosa *N.Ayr.* ***Valley***, on Arran, carrying Glenrosa Water to Brodick Bay. **22 A5** NS0136.
Glen Roy *High.* ***Valley***, in Lochaber district, carrying River Roy and running down to River Spean at Roybridge. On sides of valley are Parallel Roads of Glen Roy, shelves or terraces marking successive levels of lake dammed by glaciers during Ice Age. **39 F1** NN2780.
Glen Sannox *N.Ayr.* ***Valley***, on Arran running NE from Cir Mhòr to E coast at Sannox Bay. **22 A5** NR9944.
Glen Scaddle *High.* ***Valley***, carrying River Scaddle in Lochaber district and running E to Inverscaddle Bay on Loch Linnhe. **38 B3** NM9668.
Glen Scorrodale *N.Ayr.* ***Valley***, carrying Sliddery Water SW from S of The Ross Valley to 1km E of Sliddery. **13 E3** NR9523.
Glen Shader *W.Isles* ***Valley***, carrying Shader River SE from NW coast of Isle of Lewis at Siadar Uarach. **69 F2** NB3953.
Glen Shee *P. & K.* ***Valley***, deep valley carrying Shee Water S from Spittal of Glenshee towards Bridge of Cally. Below Blacklunans, river becomes Black Water and valley narrows to the confluence with River Ericht. **41 G3** NO1462.
Glen Shiel *High.* ***Valley***, carrying River Shiel, Skye and Lochalsh district, running NW to Shiel Bridge and head of Loch Duich. 5m/8km SE of Shiel Bridge is site of skirmish in course of Jacobite rising, 1719. **49 F3** NG9614.
Glen Shira *Arg. & B.* ***Valley***, carrying River Shira SW into N end of Loch Fyne, 1m/2km NE of Inveraray. **30 D3** NN1112.
Glen Sletdale *High.* ***Valley***, in Sutherland district, running SE then E into Glen Loth, 2m/3km N of Lothbeg. **73 E3** NC9312.
Glen Sligachan *High.* ***Valley***, carrying River Sligachan to head of Loch Sligachan on E coast of Skye. **48 A2** NG4927.
Glen Spean *High.* ***Valley***, carrying River Spean in Lochaber district and running W through Loch Moy to Spean Bridge and River Lochy below Loch Lochy. **39 F1** NN3479.
Glen Strae *Arg. & B.* ***Valley***, carrying River Strae in Argyll and running SW to River Orchy, 2m/3km W of Dalmally. **31 D1** NN1531.
Glen Strathfarrar *High.* ***Valley***, carrying River Farrar and running E from 1m/2km E of E end of Loch Monar to its convergence with Strathglass by Erchless Castle. **50 B1** NH2638.
Glen Suie *Moray* ***Valley***, carrying Black Burn through Blackwater Forest, at S end of which it meets River Livet. **53 E2** NJ2826.
Glen Tanar *Aber.* ***Valley***, to SW of Aboyne, carrying Water of Tanar. **53 G5** NO4795.
Glen Tarbert *High.* ***Valley***, steep-sided valley in Lochaber district, between Loch Linnhe and head of Loch Sunart. From summit of glen, Carnoch River runs W to Loch Sunart, while River Tarbert runs E to Loch Linnhe. **38 A4** NM8960.
Glen Tarff *High.* ***Valley***, carrying River Tarff in Inverness district and running generally NW to Fort Augustus at head of Loch Ness. **50 C4** NH3902.
Glen Tarken *P. & K.* ***Valley***, running S to N edge of Loch Earn, 2m/3km NW of St. Fillans. **32 B2** NN6626.
Glen Tarsan *Arg. & B.* ***Valley***, in Argyll, running S to head of Loch Tarsan. **22 B1** NS0785.
Glen Tennet *Angus* ***Valley***, small, narrow, steep-sided valley through which Burn of Tennet flows in a SW direction to Water of Tarf. **42 D1** NO5183.
Glen Tilt *P. & K.* ***Valley***, carrying River Tilt SW to River Garry at Blair Atholl. **41 E2** NN8870.
Glen Tolsta *W.Isles Anglicised form of Gleann Tholastaidh, qv.*
Glen Torridon *High.* ***Valley***, carrying River Torridon W below Liathach peaks to head of Upper Loch Torridon. **59 F4** NG9356.
Glen Tromie *High.* ***Valley***, carrying River Tromie in Badenoch and Strathspey district and running N to River Spey, 1m/2km E of Kingussie. **51 G5** NN7694.
Glen Trool *D. & G.* ***Valley***, carrying Water of Trool SW and containing Loch Trool, 9m/15km N of Newton Stewart. NX4180.
Glen Trool Lodge *D. & G.* ***Settlement***, on N side of Loch Trool, 4m/7km NE of Bargrennan. **7 F2** NX4080.
Glen Truim *High.* ***Valley***, carrying River Truim in Badenoch and Strathspey district and running N from Pass of Drumochter to River Spey, 5m/8km SW of Kingussie. **40 B1** NN6789.
Glen Tulchan *High.* ***Valley***, partly forested steep-sided valley carrying Burn of Tulchan SE to River Spey. **52 C1** NJ1036.
Glen Turret *P. & K.* ***Valley***, carrying Turret Burn and running SE above and below Loch Turret Reservoir to Strathearn at Crieff. Falls of Turret 2m/3km below Loch Turret Reservoir dam. Distillery at Hosh near foot of glen. **32 D2** NN8225.
Glen Uig *Angus* ***Valley***, small, narrow, steep-sided valley which runs SE, 3m/4km W of Easter Lednathie. **42 B3** NO3163.
Glen Uig *High.* ***Valley***, carrying River Conon, to E of Uig, Skye. NG3963.
Glen Ure *Arg. & B.* ***Valley***, carrying River Ure W into Glen Creran, 3m/5km NE of head of Loch Creran, Argyll. **38 C5** NN0647.
Glen Urquhart *High.* ***Valley***, carrying River Enrick, in Inverness district, on W side of Loch Ness above Drumnadrochit. **50 D1** NH4430.
Glen Varragill *High.* ***Valley***, on Skye, carrying Varragill River through Glen Varragill Forest and Portree Forest. **48 A1** NG4735.
Glen Village *Falk.* ***Village***, 1m/2km S of Falkirk, between Callendar Park and Union Canal. NS8878.
Glenacardoch Point *Arg. & B.* ***Coastal feature***, headland on W coast of Kintyre, 1m/2km NW of Glenbarr. **12 B2** NR6538.
Glenae *D. & G.* ***Settlement***, 3m/4km N of Locharbriggs. **9 D2** NX9984.
Glenaffric Forest *High.* ***Open space***, deer forest astride upper reaches of River Affric above Loch Affric, Inverness district. Contains last remnants of Caledonian Forest, natural vegetation of Highlands. NH1120.
Glenaladale *High.* ***River***, in Lochaber district running S to Loch Shiel 7m/11km from Glenfinnan. NM8274.
Glenaladale *High.* ***Settlement***, on E bank of Glenaladale River, 1m/2km NW of Scamodale across Loch Shiel. **38 A2** NM8274.
Glenald *Arg. & B.* ***Settlement***, 1km SW of Garelochhead. **31 E5** NS2390.
Glenalmond College *P. & K. Alternative name for Trinity College, qv.*
Glenamachrie *Arg. & B.* ***Settlement***, in Glen Lonan, 4m/6km E of Oban. **30 B2** NM9228.
Glenancross *High.* ***Locality***, near coast of Lochaber district, 3m/5km N of Arisaig. NM6691.
Glenapp Castle *S.Ayr.* ***Historic house***, 19c mansion, 1m/2km S of Ballantrae. **6 B2** NX0980.
Glenarm *Angus* ***Settlement***, 3m/5km N of Dykehead. **42 B3** NO3764.
Glenashdale Burn *N.Ayr.* ***River***, on Arran, running E down Glen Ashdale to Whiting Bay. Glenashdale Falls, waterfalls just over 1m/2km above mouth. NS0425.
Glenashdale Falls *N.Ayr. See Glenashdale Burn.*
Glenastle Loch (Also known as Loch Glenastle.) *Arg. & B.* ***Lake/loch***, small loch on The Oa, Islay, 2m/3km S of Rubha Mòr. NR3044.
Glenbarr *Arg. & B.* ***Village***, near W coast of Kintyre, 10m/16km N of Machrihanish. **12 B2** NR6636.
Glenbatrick *Arg. & B.* ***Settlement***, on coast, to N of Jura Forest, 9m/13km N of Craighouse, Jura. **20 D2** NR5179.
Glenbeg *High.* ***Settlement***, 14m/22km SE of Ullapool. Inaccessible by road. **60 C1** NH3183.
Glenbeg *High.* ***Settlement***, 1m/2km W of Grantown-on-Spey. **52 C2** NJ0027.
Glenbeg *High.* ***Settlement***, on Ardnamurchan peninsula, 1m/2km NW of Glenborrodale. **37 E3** NM5862.
Glenbeich *Stir.* ***Settlement***, on N side of Loch Earn, 2m/3km E of Lochearnhead. **32 B2** NN6124.
Glenbervie *Aber.* ***Village***, 7m/12km SW of Stonehaven. **43 F1** NO7680.
Glenbervie *Falk.* ***Locality***, dispersed settlement on E edge of golf course, 1m/2km NW of Larbert. **24 C1** NS8484.
Glenbervie House *Aber.* ***Historic house***, fortified mansion to S of Glenbervie. NO7680.
Glenboig *N.Lan.* Population: 2038. ***Village***, 2m/3km N of Coatbridge. **24 B3** NS7268.
Glenborrodale *High.* ***Settlement***, on Ardnamurchan peninsula, in Lochaber district, 5m/9km SW of Salen. **37 F3** NM6161.
Glenborrodale Bay *High.* ***Bay***, small bay on Ardnamurchan peninsula, in Lochaber district, at foot of Glen Borrodale. NM6060.
Glenborrodale Castle *High.* ***Castle***, to W of Glen Borrodale. NM6061.
Glenbranter *Arg. & B.* ***Hamlet***, 3m/4km SE of Strachur. **30 D5** NS1197.
Glenbranter Forest *Arg. & B.* ***Forest/woodland***, in Argyll round about head of Loch Eck, forming part of Argyll Forest Park. NS1097.
Glenbreck *Sc.Bord.* ***Settlement***, 3m/4km SW of Tweedsmuir in Tweeddale. **16 B3** NT0621.
Glenbrittle *High.* ***Settlement***, 1km N of head of Loch Brittle, Skye. **48 A2** NG4121.
Glenbuchat *Aber.* ***Locality***, parish in Glen Buchat comprising Kirkton of Glenbuchat, Mains of Glenbuchat and Glenbuchat Castle, 13m/20km W of Alford. NJ3716.
Glenbuchat Castle *Aber.* ***Castle***, stronghold of Gordons, dating from 1590 (Historic Scotland), 4m/6km SW of Kildrummy. **53 F3** NJ3716.
Glenbuck *E.Ayr.* ***Village***, 6m/9km W of Douglas. **15 F3** NS7429.
Glenbuck Loch *E.Ayr.* ***Lake/loch***, small loch on border with South Lanarkshire, 1km SE of Glenbuck. NS7528.
Glenburn *Renf.* ***Suburb***, 2m/3km S of Paisley. NS4761.
Glenburn Reservoir *Renf.* ***Reservoir***, on Brownside Braes, 2m/4km S of Paisley. NS4760.
Glenbyre *Arg. & B.* ***Settlement***, on NW shore of Loch Buie, Mull, 2m/3km SW of Lochbuie. **29 E2** NM5823.
Glencairn Castle *D. & G. See Maxwelton House.*
Glencallum Bay *Arg. & B.* ***Bay***, small bay on S coast of Bute, 1m/2km NE of Garroch Head. NS1152.
Glencalvie Forest *High.* ***Open space***, deer forest to W of Glen Calvie. **60 D1** NH4687.
Glencanisp Forest *High.* ***Open space***, deer forest SE of Lochinver, Sutherland district. Includes mountain of Canisp. **70 D2** NC1419.
Glencannel *Arg. & B.* ***River***, on Mull running N down Glen Cannel to head of Loch Bà. NM5836.
Glencannich Forest *High.* ***Open space***, deer forest in Inverness district SE of Loch Monar. **50 B1** NH2433.
Glencaple *D. & G.* ***Village***, on E bank of River Nith estuary, 5m/8km S of Dumfries. **9 D4** NX9968.
Glencarron and Glenuig Forest *High.* ***Open space***, deer forest S of Loch Sgamhain. **60 A5** NH1149.
Glencarse *P. & K.* ***Village***, 5m/8km E of Perth. **33 G2** NO1921.
Glencat *Aber.* ***Settlement***, 3m/5km SW of Marywell. **54 A5** NO5493.
Glenceitlein *High.* ***Settlement***, on SE side of Glen Etive, 3m/4km NE of head of Loch Etive. **39 D5** NN1447.
Glencloy *N.Ayr.* ***Settlement***, on Arran, 1m/2km W of Brodick. **13 F2** NS0035.
Glencoe *High.* ***Village***, at foot of Glen Coe valley. **38 D4** NN1557.
Glencoe (Whitecorries) Chairlift and Ski Area *High.* ***Leisure/recreation***, 8m/13km SE of Kinlochleven. Commercial skiing in Scotland began here. Lift travels approximately 2400 feet or 730 metres to Meall a' Bhùiridh. **39 E4** NN2652.
Glenconglass *Moray* ***Settlement***, 3m/5km E of Bridge of Brown. **53 D2** NJ1722.
Glencorse *Midloth.* ***Locality***, 2m/3km N of Penicuik. Barracks of Royal Scots Regiment. 1m/2km NW, on S side of Castlelaw Hill, is Castlelaw Fort (Historic Scotland), Iron Age fort enclosing an earth house. NT2462.
Glencorse Reservoir *Midloth.* ***Reservoir***, on Pentland Hills 2m/3km W of Glencorse. **25 G3** NT2462.
Glencraig *Fife* ***Village***, 1m/2km N of Lochgelly. **33 G5** NT1895.
Glencripesdale *High.* ***Settlement***, in Morvern, Lochaber district, near S shore of Loch Sunart, 4m/6km SE of Glenborrodale across loch. **37 F4** NM6659.
Glencrosh *D. & G.* ***Settlement***, 1m/2km S of Moniaive. **8 B2** NX7689.
Glencruittein *Arg. & B.* ***Settlement***, 1m/2km E of Oban. **30 A2** NM8729.
Glencuie *Aber.* ***Settlement***, on N side of Kindie Burn, 5m/8km NE of Strathdon. **53 G3** NJ4216.

Glendaruel *Arg. & B.* ***Valley***, carrying River Ruel in Argyll and running S to head of Loch Riddon. **22 A1** NR9985.
Glendaruel Forest *Arg. & B.* ***Forest/woodland***, bordering Glendaruel, 9m/14km N of Tighnabruaich. NR9985.
Glendearg *D. & G.* ***Settlement***, 2m/3km N of Davington. **16 D5** NT2305.
Glendearg *Sc.Bord.* ***Hamlet***, 2m/3km NE of Galashiels. **17 G2** NT5138.
Glendebadel Bay *Arg. & B.* ***Bay***, on NW coast of Jura, 2m/3km SW of Glengarrisdale Bay. **29 F5** NR6295.
Glendessary *High.* ***Settlement***, in Glen Dessary, 2m/3km NW of head of Loch Arkaig, Lochaber district. **49 F5** NM9692.
Glendevon *P. & K.* ***Village***, in Glen Devon, 6m/10km SE of Auchterarder. **33 E4** NN9505.
Glendevon Castle *P. & K.* ***Historic house***, 15c-16c castle, now a farm, 1m/2km NW of Glendevon. NN9705.
Glendevon Forest *P. & K.* ***Forest/woodland***, to NE of Glendevon. **33 E4** NN9504.
Glendevon Reservoirs *P. & K.* ***Reservoir***, consisting of Upper Glendevon Reservoir and Lower Glendevon Reservoir in Ochil Hills, 3m/5km SE of Blackford. **33 E4** NN9004.
Glendhu Forest *High.* ***Open space***, upland moorland area in Sutherland district to N of Loch Glendhu. **74 B5** NC2634.
Glendoe Forest *High.* ***Open space***, deer forest, on which Allt Doe stream rises, to S of Glendoebeg. **50 D4** NH4108.
Glendoebeg *High.* ***Settlement***, 2m/3km E of Fort Augustus. **50 D4** NH4109.
Glendoick *P. & K.* ***Settlement***, 1m/2km NE of St. Madoes. **34 A2** NO2022.
Glendoll Lodge *Angus* ***Other building***, youth hostel and Mountain Rescue Post at foot of Glen Doll, 4m/6km NW of Clova. **42 A2** NO2776.
Glendoune *S.Ayr.* ***Settlement***, adjoining to SE of Girvan. **6 C1** NX1996.
Glendrissaig *S.Ayr.* ***Settlement***, 1m/2km S of Girvan. **6 C1** NX1994.
Glendronach Distillery *Aber.* ***Other feature of interest***, distillery built in 1926 in Glen Dronach, 6m/10km NE of Huntly, draws its water from Dronach Burn, which has previously made its way through rich peat beds. **64 B5** NJ6243.
Glenduckie *Fife* ***Settlement***, on S side of Glenduckie Hill, 3m/5km E of Newburgh. **34 A3** NO2818.
Glenduckie Hill *Fife* ***Hill***, 3m/5km E of Newburgh. Height 715 feet or 218 metres. **34 A3** NO2819.
Glenduisk *S.Ayr.* ***Settlement***, on E bank of Duisk River, 3m/4km NW of Barrhill. **6 D2** NX2085.
Glenduror Forest *High.* ***Forest/woodland***, astride Glen Duror, 3m/4km SE of Kentallen. **38 C4** NN0154.
Glendye Lodge *Aber.* ***Settlement***, to NW of Bridge of Dye. **43 E1** NO6486.
Gleneagles *P. & K.* ***Settlement***, at foot of Glen Eagles, 3m/4km SW of Auchterarder. **33 E4** NN9308.
Gleneagles Castle *P. & K.* ***Castle***, remains of castle at foot of Glen Eagles, 2m/4km SW of Auchterader. NN9209.
Gleneagles Hotel *P. & K.* ***Other building***, palatial hotel with two well-known golf-courses, to N of Gleneagles, 2m/3km W of Auchterarder. **33 E3** NN9111.
Glenearn *P. & K.* ***Settlement***, 2m/3km SE of Forgandenny. **33 G3** NO1016.
Glenegedale *Arg. & B.* ***Settlement***, on Islay, 4m/7km NW of Port Ellen. To W beside Laggan Bay is Islay (Port Ellen) Airport. **20 B4** NR3351.
Glenelg *High.* ***Village***, in Lochaber district on Glenelg Bay. **49 E3** NG8119.
Glenelg Bay *High.* ***Bay***, on mainland, at head of Sound of Sleat, 5m/8km SE of Kyle of Lochalsh across Loch Alsh. **49 D3** NG8119.
Glenelg Brochs *High.* ***Historic/prehistoric site***, prehistoric fortifications (Historic Scotland), in Gleann Beag 2m/3km SE of Glenelg. **49 E3** NG8119.
Glenetive Forest *High.* ***Forest/woodland***, to W of Glen Etive. NN1248.
Glenfarclas Distillery *Moray* ***Other feature of interest***, distillery on open moorland below lower slopes of Ben Rinnes, 4m/7km SW of Charlestown of Aberlour. Established in 1836, it draws its water from Green Burn. Exhibits include old Highland pot still. **53 E1** NJ2138.
Glenfarg *P. & K.* ***Village***, on River Farg, at head of a narrow pass, 8m/13km S of Perth. **33 G3** NO1513.
Glenfarg Reservoir *P. & K.* ***Reservoir***, near source of River Farg, 2m/3km W of Glenfarg. **33 F3** NO1513.
Glenfeochan *Arg. & B.* ***Settlement***, 1km S of Kilmore. **30 A2** NM8824.
Glenfeshie Forest *High.* ***Open space***, deer forest astride head of Glen Feshie. **52 A5** NN8594.
Glenfiddich Distillery *Moray* ***Other feature of interest***, distillery on NE side of Dufftown. Founded by William Grant in 1886 and enlarged in 1955 to become one of biggest malt whisky distilleries in Scotland. **63 F5** NJ3340.
Glenfiddich Forest *Moray* ***Open space***, moorland tract surrounding source of River Fiddich. **53 E1** NJ3030.
Glenfinart Forest *Arg. & B.* ***Forest/woodland***, surrounding Glen Finart. NS1790.
Glenfinnan *High.* ***Village***, at foot of Glen Finnan. Glenfinnan Monument (National Trust for Scotland) to E. **38 B1** NM9083.
Glenfinnan Monument *High.* ***Other feature of interest***, to E of Glenfinnan at head of Loch Shiel. Commemorates uprising in 1745 of Jacobites who met at this spot and raised the standard of Charles Edward Stuart (Bonnie Prince Charlie), before challenging English throne. Visitor centre, with exposition of the campaign. **38 B1** NM9080.
Glenfintaig *High.* ***Locality***, with house and lodge in Lochaber district 1m/2km S of SE shore of Loch Lochy at Invergloy. NN2286.
Glenfoot *P. & K.* ***Hamlet***, 1km SW of Abernethy. **33 G3** NO1715.
Glengalmadale *High.* ***River***, in Lochaber district running S from Creach Bheinn to Loch Linnhe on E side of Loch a' Choire. NM8652.
Glengalmadale *High.* ***Settlement***, in Lochaber district, 1km NW of Rubha na h-Airde Uinnsinn. **38 A4** NM8653.
Glengap *D. & G.* ***Settlement***, 4m/6km NE of Gatehouse of Fleet. **8 A5** NX6559.
Glengap Forest *D. & G.* ***Forest/woodland***, 3m/5km NE of Gatehouse of Fleet. NX6459.
Glengarioch Distillery *Aber.* ***Other feature of interest***, one of Scotland's oldest distilleries, founded in 1797 at Oldmeldrum, in granite building lying at one end of Garioch valley. It draws its water from springs on Percock Hill. **54 D2** NJ8027.
Glengarnock *N.Ayr.* ***Hamlet***, 1m/2km SE of Kilbirnie across River Garnock. **23 E4** NS3252.
Glengarrisdale *Arg. & B.* ***Settlement***, on N coast of Jura, 6m/9km N of Ardlussa. No road access. **29 F5** NR6496.
Glengarrisdale Bay *Arg. & B.* ***Bay***, on NW coast of Jura. **29 F5** NR6497.
Glengarry Forest *High.* ***Open space***, deer forest to S of Glen Garry between Lochs Garry and Lochy. **50 B5** NH1300.
Glengavel Reservoir *S.Lan.* ***Reservoir***, at head of Glengavel Water, 5m/8km NW of Muirkirk. **15 E2** NS6634.
Glengavel Water *S.Lan.* ***River***, issuing from Glengavel Reservoir and flowing N to Avon Water 5m/9km E of Darvel. **15 E2** NS6438.
Glengennet *S.Ayr.* ***Settlement***, 2m/3km SE of Penwhapple Reservoir and 6m/10km E of Girvan. **7 D1** NX2895.
Glengenny Muir *D. & G.* ***Open space***, moorland above River Nith, 4m/6km SE of Sanquhar. **15 G5** NS8105.
Glengolly *High.* ***Settlement***, 1m/2km SW of Thurso. **76 D2** ND1066.
Glengoulandie Deer Park *P. & K.* ***Leisure/recreation***, endangered species, herds of red deer and Highland cattle kept under natural conditions, 4m/7km S of Tummel Bridge. **40 C4** NN7652.
Glengrasco *High.* ***Settlement***, on Skye, 3m/4km NW of Portree. **58 A5** NG4444.
Glengyle *Stir.* ***Settlement***, at NW end of Loch Katrine, 2m/3km N of Stronachlachar. **31 F3** NN3813.
Glengyle Water *Stir.* ***River***, running SE down Glen Gyle to head of Loch Katrine. NN3813.
Glenhead *D. & G.* ***Settlement***, 2m/4km NE of Dunscore. **8 C2** NX8987.
Glenhead Farm *Angus* ***Settlement***, at N end of Backwater Reservoir at foot of Cuilt Hill, 4m/7km SW of Balnaboth. **42 A3** NO2562.
Glenhurich *High.* ***Settlement***, on N bank of River Hurich, 3m/4km E of Pollock, Lochaber district. **38 A3** NM8368.
Glenhurich Forest *High.* ***Forest/woodland***, astride Glen Hurich. NM8468.
Gleniffer Braes *Renf.* ***Open space***, N facing hillslope 3m/4km SW of Paisley. Gleniffer Braes Country Park to E, with extensive views N over lower Clyde area and into Highlands. **23 F3** NS4460.
Glenisla Forest *Angus* ***Forest/woodland***, around head of Backwater Reservoir. **42 A3** NO2563.
Glenkerry *Sc.Bord.* ***Settlement***, 3m/4km S of Ettrick, on Tima Water. **17 D4** NT2810.
Glenkiln *N.Ayr.* ***Settlement***, on Arran, 1km SW of Lamlash. **13 F2** NS0130.
Glenkiln Reservoir *D. & G.* ***Reservoir***, small reservoir 3m/5km N of Crocketford. **8 C3** NX8477.
Glenkin *Arg. & B.* ***Settlement***, in Glen Kin, 2m/3km W of Sandbank. **22 C2** NS1279.
Glenkinchie *E.Loth.* *See Pencaitland.*
Glenkindie *Aber.* ***Village***, on River Don, 6m/9km SW of Lumsden. **53 G3** NJ4313.
Glenkinnon Burn *Sc.Bord.* ***River***, rising in mountains, 4m/7km NW of Selkirk, and flowing NE to River Tweed 1m/2km W of Caddonfoot. **17 E2** NT4335.
Glenlair *D. & G.* ***Settlement***, 2m/4km S of Corsock. **8 B3** NX7572.
Glenlatterach *Moray* ***Settlement***, 1km N of Glenlatterach Reservoir, 6m/9km S of Elgin. **63 E4** NJ1954.
Glenlatterach Reservoir *Moray* ***Reservoir***, 6m/10km S of Elgin. **63 D4** NJ1953.
Glenlean *Arg. & B.* ***Settlement***, at head of Glen Lean, below SE arm of Loch Tarsan, 2m/3km NE of Ardtaraig. **22 B1** NS0883.
Glenlee *Angus* ***Settlement***, at NW end of Loch Lee, 2m/3km W of Kirkton. **42 C1** NO4179.
Glenlee *D. & G.* ***Settlement***, 1m/2km SW of St. John's Town of Dalry. **8 A2** NX6080.
Glenlee Burn *D. & G.* ***River***, stream running E to confluence with Garroch Burn, 1m/2km W of St. John's Town of Dalry. NX6081.
Glenleith Fell *D. & G.* ***Mountain***, in Lowther Hills, 2m/3km SE of Durisdeer. Height 2004 feet or 611 metres. NS9202.
Glenlichorn *P. & K.* ***Settlement***, 7m/11km N of Dunblane. **32 C3** NN7912.
Glenlivet *Moray* ***Settlement***, 3m/4km NW of Tomnavoulin. **53 D2** NJ1929.
Glenlivet *Moray* ***Valley***, carrying Livet Water, or River Livet, and running NW to River Avon 8m/12km N of Tomintoul. **53 E2** NJ2126.
Glenlivet Forest *Moray* ***Forest/woodland***, to W of Glenlivet. NJ2126.
Glenlochar *D. & G.* ***Locality***, on River Dee, 3m/4km NW of Castle Douglas. Site of Roman fort on E bank of river. **8 B4** NX7364.
Glenlood Hill *Sc.Bord.* ***Mountain***, 3m/4km NW of Tweedsmuir. Height 1856 feet or 566 metres. **16 B3** NT0828.
Glenluce *D. & G.* ***Village***, on E side of Water of Luce near its mouth, and 9m/14km E of Stranraer. 16c Castle of Park 1km W. **6 C5** NX1957.
Glenluce Abbey *D. & G.* ***Ecclesiastical building***, remains of abbey (Historic Scotland), 1m/2km NW of Glenluce, dates in part from 12c; chapter house of 1470. **6 C5** NX1957.
Glenlussa Water *Arg. & B.* ***River***, in Kintyre issuing from Lussa Loch and running SE into Ardnacross Bay, 4m/7km NE of Campbeltown. NR7625.
Glenmallan *Arg. & B.* ***Settlement***, with jetty, on E shore of Loch Long, 3m/5km NE of Garelochhead. **31 E5** NS2496.
Glenmanna *D. & G.* ***Settlement***, below steep NE slopes of Dalzean Snout, 5m/8km S of Sanquhar. **15 F5** NS7601.
Glenmavis *N.Lan.* Population: 2332. ***Village***, 2m/3km NW of Airdrie. **24 B3** NS7467.
Glenmeanie *High.* ***Settlement***, in valley of River Muig, 2m/3km SW of Milton. **60 B4** NH2852.
Glenmore *Arg. & B.* ***Settlement***, in Glen More on Bute, 5m/8km NW of Rothesay. **22 B3** NS0269.
Glenmore *High.* ***River***, flowing NW into River Snizort, 1m/2km NE of Loch Duagrich, Skye. NG4240.
Glenmore *High.* ***River***, in Lochaber district, running NW into Sound of Sleat on N side of Glenelg. NG8119.
Glenmore *High.* ***Settlement***, on Skye, 3m/5km SW of Portree. **58 A5** NG4340.
Glenmore Bay *High.* ***Bay***, on S side of Ardnamurchan peninsula in Lochaber district, 6m/10km W of Salen. NM5961.
Glenmore Burn *Arg. & B.* ***River***, running S down Glen More to Ettrick Bay, Bute. NS0366.
Glenmore Forest Park *High.* ***Leisure/recreation***, to E of Aviemore, surrounding Glen More. Scottish Centre of Outdoor Training; ski school and camping available. **52 B3** NH9808.
Glenmore Forest Park Reindeer House *High.* ***Other feature of interest***, in Glenmore Forest Park, where visitors can view Britain's only free-ranging reindeer herd. **52 B3** NH9709.
Glenmore Lodge *High.* ***Other building***, in Glenmore Forest Park, 5m/8km SE of Aviemore. Houses National Outdoor Training Centre; includes mountain rescue post. **52 B4** NH9809.
Glenmore Natural History Centre *High.* ***Other feature of interest***, centre with wildlife exhibitions situated at Glenmore on Ardnamurchan peninsula. **37 E3** NM5862.
Glenmoy *Angus* ***Settlement***, next to Burn of Glenmoye, 3m/5km NE of Dykehead. **42 C3** NO4064.
Glenmuck Height *Sc.Bord.* ***Mountain***, 1m/2km W of Tweedsmuir. Height 1519 feet or 463 metres. **16 B3** NT0724.
Glenmuick *High.* ***Settlement***, at confluence of Abhainn Gleann na Muic and River Cassley, 3m/4km S of Duchally. **71 F3** NC3912.
Glenmuir Water *E.Ayr.* ***River***, rising on W slopes of Stony Hill and running W to Dalblair where it is joined by Guelt Water. It then continues NW to join Bellow Water and form Lugar Water 1km E of Lugar. **15 F4** NS5921.
Glennoe *Arg. & B.* ***Settlement***, on SW side of Loch Etive, 4m/6km NE of Taynuilt. **30 C1** NN0534.
Glenochar *S.Lan.* ***Settlement***, 2m/3km S of Elvanfoot. **16 A4** NS9513.
Glenogil *Angus* ***Hamlet***, 4m/7km NE of Dykehead, in valley of Noran Water. **42 C3** NO4463.
Glenogil Reservoir *Angus* ***Reservoir***, small reservoir in Glen Ogil, valley of Noran Water, 4m/7km NW of Tannadice. NO4464.

Glenprosen *Angus* ***Village***, 1m/2km SE of Balnaboth, in Glen Prosen. **42 B3** NO3265.
Glenquey Reservoir *P. & K.* ***Reservoir***, small reservoir 1m/2km SW of Glendevon. **33 E4** NN9802.
Glenquicken Moor *D. & G.* ***Open space***, moorland 3m/5km E of Creetown. **7 G5** NX5259.
Glenquiech *Angus* ***Settlement***, 3m/4km NE of Dykehead. **42 C3** NO4261.
Glenquoich Forest *High.* ***Open space***, deer forest between Loch Quoich and Loch Loyne. **49 G4** NH0107.
Glenramskill *Arg. & B.* ***Settlement***, on Kintyre, on S shore of Campbeltown Loch, 1m/2km SE of Campbeltown. **12 C4** NR7319.
Glenrazie *D. & G.* ***Settlement***, 3m/5km NW of Newton Stewart. **7 E4** NX3668.
Glenrigh Forest *High.* ***Forest/woodland***, astride Glen Righ. **38 C3** NN0563.
Glenrisdell *Arg. & B.* ***Settlement***, on Kintyre, 1m/2km N of Claonaig. **21 G4** NR8657.
Glenrosa Water *N.Ayr.* ***River***, on Arran, running SE down Glen Rosa to Brodick Bay. NS0136.
Glenrossal *High.* ***Settlement***, on E side of River Cassley, 1m/2km NW of Invercassley. **71 G4** NC4604.
Glenrothes *Fife* Population: 38,650. ***Town***, New Town, designated 1948, 16m/25km NE of Forth road bridge. **34 A4** NO2600.
Glenruthven Weaving Mill *P. & K.* ***Other feature of interest***, mill at Auchterarder, housing Scotland's only working steam textile engine. Weaving demonstrations and exhibits on history of steam and weaving. **33 E3** NN9412.
Glens of Foudland *Aber.* ***Valley***, carrying Glen Water between Hill of Bainshole to N and Hill of Foudland to S, 6m/9km SE of Huntly. **54 A1** NJ6034.
Glensanda *High.* ***Settlement***, on NW shore of Loch Linnhe opposite Lismore, 5m/8km SW of Rubha na h-Airde Uinnsinn. **38 A5** NM8246.
Glensaugh *Aber.* ***Hamlet***, 3m/5km NE of Fettercairn, to W of Strathfinella Hill. **43 E2** NO6778.
Glensax Burn *Sc.Bord.* ***River***, rising on slopes of Dun Rig, and flowing N to join River Tweed, 2m/3km SE of Peebles. **17 D2** NT2739.
Glensgaich *High.* ***Settlement***, 6m/9km W of Dingwall. **61 D3** NH4561.
Glenshalg *Aber.* ***Settlement***, 1m/2km N of Lumphanan. **54 A4** NJ5806.
Glenshee *P. & K.* ***Settlement***, 6m/9km NW of Methven. **33 E1** NN9834.
Glenshee Chairlifts and Ski Centre *Aber.* ***Other feature of interest***, large skiing area 6m/9km NE of Spittal of Glenshee, particularly good for beginners. **41 G2** NO1378.
Glenshellish *Arg. & B.* ***Settlement***, just to S of Glenbranter. **30 D5** NS1197.
Glenshieldaig Forest *High.* ***Open space***, deer forest in Ross and Cromarty district S of Loch Shieldaig. **59 E4** NG8350.
Glensluan *Arg. & B.* ***Settlement***, 1m/2km S of Strachur. **30 C5** NS0999.
Glenstrathfarrar Forest *High.* ***Open space***, deer forest about valley of River Farrar in Inverness district. NH3039.
Glentaggart *S.Lan.* ***Settlement***, 2m/4km S of Glespin. **15 G3** NS8125.
Glentanar *Aber.* ***Locality***, near foot of Glen Tanar, to SW of Aboyne. Forest of Glentanar is on either side of glen. NO4795.
Glentenmont Height *D. & G.* ***Mountain***, on S side of woodland, 4m/7km W of Langholm. Height 1351 feet or 412 metres. **9 G2** NY2885.
Glenton *Aber.* ***Settlement***, on N bank of River Don, 5m/8km NE of Alford. **54 B2** NJ6420.
Glentoo Loch *D. & G.* ***Lake/loch***, small loch 4m/6km W of Castle Douglas. NX7062.
Glentress *Sc.Bord.* ***Hamlet***, 3m/4km SE of Peebles. **17 D2** NT2839.
Glentress Forest *Sc.Bord.* ***Forest/woodland***, 2m/3km E of Peebles. **25 G5** NT2742.
Glentrool Forest *D. & G.* ***Forest/woodland***, part of Galloway Forest Park, 11m/18km N of Newton Stewart. Forest trails, camp sites and picnic areas along Glen Trool. NX3581.
Glentrool Village *D. & G.* ***Village***, forestry village, 3m/5km W of Loch Trool. Glen Trool is valley of Water of Trool. **7 E3** NX3578.
Glentrosdale Bay *Arg. & B.* ***Bay***, small bay 1m/2km SW of N point of Jura. NM6700.
Glenturret Distillery *P. & K.* ***Other feature of interest***, one of Scotland's oldest distilleries, 1km N of Crieff. **33 D2** NN8523.
Glenuachdarach *High.* ***Settlement***, on Trotternish peninsula, Skye, 4m/6km SE of Uig. **58 A4** NG4258.
Glenuig *High.* ***Settlement***, at head of Glenuig Bay, Lochaber district. NM6777.
Glenuig Bay *High.* ***Bay***, small bay in Lochaber district, on S side of Sound of Arisaig, 2m/4km W of Roshven. **37 F2** NM6777.
Glenuig Hill *High.* ***Hill***, 2m/3km SW of Roshven, Lochaber district. Height 984 feet or 300 metres. **37 F2** NM6876.
Glenure *Arg. & B.* ***Settlement***, in Glen Creran, 3m/5km NE of head of Glen Creran. **38 C5** NN0448.
Glenurquhart *High.* ***Settlement***, on Black Isle, 4m/6km SW of Cromarty. **61 G3** NH7462.
Glenurquhart Forest *High.* ***Forest/woodland***, astride River Enrick. **50 D2** NH4430.
Glenury Viaduct *Aber.* ***Other feature of interest***, railway viaduct carrying line over Cowie Water, N of Stonehaven. NO8686.
Glenwhappen Rig *Sc.Bord.* ***Inland physical feature***, saddle at height of 1968 feet or 600 metres between Gathersnow Hill and Coomb Hill, 2m/3km NW of Tweedsmuir. **16 B3** NT0625.
Glenwhilly *D. & G.* ***Settlement***, 7m/11km E of Cairnryan. **6 C3** NX1771.
Gleouraich *High.* ***Mountain***, peak on Glenquoich Forest, Lochaber district, 3m/4km NW of dam of Loch Quoich. Munro: height 3395 feet or 1035 metres. **49 G4** NH0305.
Glespin *S.Lan.* ***Hamlet***, 3m/4km SW of Douglas. **15 G3** NS8028.
Glespin Burn *S.Lan.* ***River***, rising to S of Mosscastle Hill, 3m/4km W of Crawfordjohn, and flowing N to Douglas Water 1km E of Glespin. **15 G3** NS8128.
Glet Ness *Shet.* ***Coastal feature***, spit of land on E coast of Mainland, running SW to NE along E side of small inlet, North Voe of Gletness. HU4751.
Gletness *Shet.* ***Settlement***, on South Voe of Gletness, to SW of Glet Ness headland, on E coast of Mainland. **83 D2** HU4751.
Glimps Holm *Ork.* ***Island***, small uninhabited island between islands of Burray and Mainland, linked to both by Churchill Barrier. **78 D3** ND4799.
Gloup *Shet.* ***Settlement***, on Yell, on W side of Gloup Voe. **85 E2** HP5004.
Gloup Holm *Shet.* ***Island***, small island off N coast of Yell. **85 D2** HP4806.
Gloup Ness *Shet.* ***Coastal feature***, headland on N coast of Yell, on E side of entrance to Gloup Voe. **85 E2** HP5005.
Gloup Voe *Shet.* ***Sea feature***, narrow inlet 2m/3km long on N coast of Yell. HP5005.
Gloy *High.* ***River***, in Lochaber district, running SW down Glen Gloy and N into Loch Lochy at Invergloy, 4m/6km NE of foot of loch. NN2288.
Glumaig Harbour *W.Isles* ***Sea feature***, inlet on S side of Stornoway Harbour, Isle of Lewis. NB4230.
Glunimore Island *Arg. & B.* ***Island***, islet lying 1km SE of Sheep Island off S coast of Kintyre. NR7405.
Gluss *Shet.* ***Settlement***, comprises North and South Gluss, 1km from E coast of Mainland, near Gluss Voe. **84 C5** HU3477.
Gluss Isle *Shet.* ***Coastal feature***, peninsula on NE coast of Mainland on W side of entrance to Sullom Voe. Narrow neck of land joins it to rest of Mainland and separates Sullom Voe from Gluss Voe, inlet to W. **84 C5** HU3778.
Gluss Voe *Shet.* ***Sea feature***, inlet to W of Gluss Isle on Mainland, separated from Sullom Voe by narrow isthmus. HU3678.
Glutt Water *High.* ***River***, in Caithness district, flowing N and joining Rumsdale Water to form River Thurso 4m/7km S of Altnabreac. **76 B5** ND0039.
Goat Fell *N.Ayr.* ***Mountain***, summit (National Trust for Scotland) of Arran, 4m/6km N of Brodick. Height 2867 feet or 874 metres. **22 A5** NR9941.
Goatfield *Arg. & B.* ***Settlement***, adjoining to NW of Furnace, on N shore of Loch Fyne. **30 C4** NN0100.
Gob na h-Airde Mòire *W.Isles* ***Coastal feature***, headland on W coast of Isle of Lewis N of Loch Resort, opposite Scarp. **66 B2** NB0117.
Gob na Milaid *W.Isles* ***Coastal feature***, headland with beacon on E coast of Isle of Lewis, 1m/2km S of Kebock Head. **67 G2** NB4211.
Gob Rubh' Uisenis *W.Isles* ***Coastal feature***, headland with lighthouse, at SE tip of Isle of Lewis, 4m/7km S of entrance to Loch Shell. **67 F3** NB3503.
Gobernuisgeach *High.* ***Settlement***, in Caithness district, on Berriedale Water, 7m/12km E of Kinbrace. **76 B5** NC9831.
Gobhaig (Anglicised form: Govig.) *W.Isles* ***Settlement***, on coast of North Harris, 2m/4km SE of Huisinis. **66 C3** NB0109.
Goblin's Cave (Gaelic name: Corrie na Urisgean.) *Stir.* ***Cave***, near E end of Loch Katrine. **31 G4** NN4807.
Gòdag *High.* ***Island***, islet 1km N of Muck. **36 D1** NM4181.
Gogar *Edin.* ***Hamlet***, 1m/2km SE of Edinburgh (Turnhouse) Airport. **25 F2** NT1672.
Gogar Burn *Edin.* ***River***, rising 2m/3km S of East Calder and flowing NE to Union Canal, under which it passes, then N and W, sometimes underground, to River Almond, 1m/2km E of Kirkliston. **25 E3** NT1374.
Gogarbank *Edin.* ***Locality***, 1m/2km S of Gogar. NT1770.
Gogo Water *N.Ayr.* ***River***, rising on hills 4m/6km E of Largs and flowing through town to Firth of Clyde. **22 D4** NS2059.
Goil *Arg. & B.* ***River***, in Argyll flowing S to head of Loch Goil. **31 D4** NN1901.
Goile Chroic *W.Isles* ***Bay***, small bay on NW coast of Isle of Lewis to N of Bru. **69 E2** NB3451.
Goirtean a' Chladaich *High.* ***Settlement***, on NW shore of Loch Linnhe, 3m/5km SW of Fort William across Loch Linnhe. **38 C2** NN0570.
Goirtein *Arg. & B.* ***Settlement***, on SE shore of Loch Fyne, 5m/8km E of Lochgilphead across loch. **22 A1** NR9589.
Goldenacre *Edin.* ***Suburb***, 1m/2km N of Edinburgh city centre. NT2475.
Goldielea *D. & G.* ***Settlement***, 3m/5km SW of Dumfries. **8 D3** NX9373.
Gollanfield *High.* ***Settlement***, 2m/3km SE of Ardersier. **62 A4** NH8053.
Golspie *High.* Population: 1434. ***Village***, on E coast of Sutherland district, 15m/24km SW of Helmsdale. 3m/5km to NE, on S side of Dunrobin Wood, is Carn Liath (Historic Scotland), a broch surviving to first-floor level. **72 D5** NH8399.
Golspie Burn *High.* ***River***, flowing SE to E coast of Sutherland district, NE of Golspie. **72 D4** NC8300.
Golval *High.* ***Settlement***, on E bank of Halladale River, 1m/2km SE of Melvich. **76 A2** NC8962.
Gometra *Arg. & B.* ***Island***, small sparsely populated island off W end of Ulva. Steep cliffs with columns of basalt in places. Road bridge connection with Ulva. **36 C5** NM3641.
Gometra House *Arg. & B.* ***Settlement***, on Gometra, 1km NE of Rubha Maol na Mine. **36 C5** NM3540.
Gon Firth *Shet.* ***Sea feature***, inlet on W coast of Mainland, 3m/4km W of Hillside. HU3661.
Gonachan *Stir.* ***Settlement***, 1m/2km E of Fintry, at crossing point of Endrick Water. **24 A1** NS6386.
Gonachan Burn *Stir.* ***River***, stream rising on Campsie Fells and flowing down Gonachan Glen to join Endrick Water 1m/2km SE of Fintry. **24 A1** NS6386.
Gonfirth *Shet.* ***Settlement***, at head of Gon Firth, 2m/4km SW of Voe. **82 C1** HU3761.
Goodbush Hill ***Mountain***, on border of East Ayrshire and South Lanarkshire, 6m/10km S of Strathaven. Height 1558 feet or 475 metres. **15 F2** NS7035.
Goodie Water *Stir.* ***River***, flowing SE from Lake of Menteith into River Forth, 6m/10km NW of Stirling. **32 B5** NS7096.
Gorbals *Glas.* ***Suburb***, on S bank of River Clyde, to S of Glasgow city centre. NS5964.
Gordon *Sc.Bord.* ***Village***, 8m/13km NW of Kelso. **26 D5** NT6443.
Gordon Castle *Moray* ***Castle***, partly ruined castle in valley of River Spey, 1km NE of Fochabers. NJ3559.
Gordon Highlanders Regimental Museum *Aberdeen* ***Other feature of interest***, museum in SW Aberdeen, commemorating regiment first raised by Duke of Gordon in 1794. Situated in former home of Victorian artist, Sir George Reid. **55 E4** NJ9004.
Gordonbush *High.* ***Settlement***, on E coast in Sutherland district, near head of Loch Brora, 5m/8km NW of Brora village. **72 D4** NC8409.
Gordonsburgh *Moray* ***Suburb***, on E side of Buckie, on N coast. Harbour and lighthouse. NJ4366.
Gordonstoun *Moray* ***Educational establishment***, coeducational public school 4m/6km W of Lossiemouth. Attended by Prince Charles. **63 D3** NJ1868.
Gordonstown *Aber.* ***Settlement***, 9m/15km SW of Banff. **64 A4** NJ5656.
Gordonstown *Aber.* ***Village***, 7m/12km S of Turriff. **54 C1** NJ7138.
Gore Water *Midloth.* ***River***, stream flowing NW into River South Esk 1m/2km W of Gorebridge. NT3361.
Gorebridge *Midloth.* Population: 5888. ***Small town***, 4m/6km S of Dalkeith. Situated on Gore Water. **26 A3** NT3461.
Gorgie *Edin.* ***Suburb***, 2m/4km SW of Edinburgh city centre. NT2272.
Gorm Loch *High.* ***Lake/loch***, small loch 4m/6km E of Scourie, Sutherland district. **74 B4** NC2144.
Gorm-loch Beag *High.* ***Lake/loch***, small loch to E of Ben Armine. **72 C2** NC7027.
Gorm Loch Mòr *High.* ***Lake/loch***, 4m/7km E of Loch Assynt. **71 F2** NC3125.
Gorm-loch Mòr *High.* ***Lake/loch***, small loch in Ben Armine Forest, to E of Creag Mhòr. **72 C2** NC7123.
Gormack Burn ***River***, rising on Hill of Fare and flowing NE through Midmar Forest, before turning E to join River Dee S of Peterculter. NJ8201.
Gorrachie *Aber.* ***Settlement***, 5m/8km N of Turriff. **64 C4** NJ7358.
Gorseness *Ork.* ***Settlement***, 1km NE of Bay of Isbister, Mainland. **80 C5** HY4119.
Gorstan *High.* ***Settlement***, in Ross and Cromarty district, 10m/15km W of Dingwall. **60 C3** NH3862.
Gorstanvorran *High.* ***Settlement***, on S shore of Loch Shiel, 2m/3km NE of Pollock, Lochaber district. **38 A2** NM8071.
Gortantaoid Point *Arg. & B.* ***Coastal feature***, headland on N coast of Islay, on E side of wide bay at entrance to Loch Gruinart. **20 B2** NR3374.
Gorten *Arg. & B.* ***Settlement***, on Mull, 1km N of Grass Point across Loch Don. **29 G1** NM7432.
Gortenbuie *Arg. & B.* ***Settlement***, in Glen Cannel, 1m/2km S of head of Loch Bà, Mull. **29 E1** NM5933.

Gorteneorn *High.* ***Settlement***, on Kentra Bay, 3m/4km W of Acharacle. **37 F3** NM6367.
Gorthleck *High. Alternative name for Lyne of Gorthleck, qv.*
Gorthlick *High. Alternative name for Lyne of Gorthleck, qv.*
Gorton *Arg. & B.* ***Settlement***, at head of Loch Gorton, on S coast of Coll. **36 A4** NM1753.
Goseland Hill *Sc.Bord.* ***Mountain***, 3m/4km SE of Biggar. Height 1427 feet or 435 metres. **16 B2** NT0735.
Gosford Bay *E.Loth.* ***Bay***, W facing bay on Firth of Forth, 1m/2km SW of Aberlady. **26 B2** NT4478.
Gosford House *E.Loth.* ***Historic house***, overlooking Gosford Bay on Firth of Forth, 2m/3km NE of Longniddry. Central block remains but wings destroyed in 19c. House restored following fire in 1940 and gardens are being re-developed. **26 B2** NT4578.
Gossa Water *Shet.* ***Lake/loch***, 1km NW of Easter Skeld, Mainland. **82 C3** HU3046.
Gossa Water *Shet.* ***Lake/loch***, 3m/4km SE of Voe, Mainland. **82 D1** HU4360.
Gossa Water *Shet.* ***Lake/loch***, in N part of Yell 1m/2km NW of Dalsetter. **85 D3** HU4899.
Gossabrough *Shet.* ***Settlement***, near E coast of Yell, 2m/4km N of Burravoe. **85 E4** HU5383.
Gott *Shet.* ***Settlement***, 1km E of Tingwall Airport, Mainland. **82 D3** HU4345.
Gott Bay *Arg. & B.* ***Bay***, wide bay on S coast of Tiree, NE of Scarinish. **36 B2** NM0546.
Gour *High.* ***River***, in Ardgour, Lochaber district, running E down Glen Gour to Loch Linnhe at Camas Shallachain, on W side of Sallachan Point. NM9862.
Gourdas *Aber.* ***Locality***, to SE of Steinman Hill, 3m/4km N of Fyvie. **64 C5** NJ7741.
Gourdon *Aber.* ***Village***, fishing village on E coast 1m/2km S of Inverbervie. **43 G2** NO8270.
Gourock *Inclyde* Population: 11,743. ***Town***, resort and passenger boat terminus on Firth of Clyde, 2m/4km W of Greenock and due S of Kilcreggan across firth. Popular yachting centre. **22 D2** NS2477.
Gourock Bay *Inclyde* ***Bay***, to E of Gourock, on S side of Firth of Clyde. **22 D2** NS2477.
Gousam *W.Isles* ***Island***, islet in Loch Roag, W coast of Isle of Lewis, 2m/3km E of Miabhig. NB1033.
Govan *Glas.* ***Suburb***, on S side of River Clyde, 2m/4km W of Glasgow city centre. Car ferry across river. **23 G3** NS5565.
Govanhill *Glas.* ***Suburb***, 2m/3km S of Glasgow city centre. NS5862.
Govig *W.Isles Anglicised form of Gobhaig, qv.*
Gowanhill *Aber.* ***Settlement***, 3m/5km SE of Fraserburgh. **65 F3** NK0363.
Gowkhall *Fife* ***Village***, 3m/4km W of Dunfermline. **25 E1** NT0589.
Gowkthrapple *N.Lan.* ***Locality***, on S side of Wishaw. NS7953.
Goyle Hill *Aber.* ***Mountain***, 3m/5km SE of Bridge of Dye. Height 1522 feet or 464 metres. **43 E1** NO6882.
Grabhair (Anglicised form: Gravir.) *W.Isles* ***Village***, near E coast of Isle of Lewis at head of Loch Odhairn, 3m/5km W of Kebock Head. **67 F2** NB3715.
Gracemount *Edin.* ***Suburb***, 4m/6km SE of Edinburgh city centre. NT2768.
Graemsay *Ork.* ***Island***, sparsely inhabited island of about 250 acres or 100 hectares, situated in Hoy Sound S of Stromness, Mainland. Two lighthouses, at NE and NW ends. **78 B2** HY2605.
Graemshall House *Ork.* ***Other feature of interest***, house on S coast of Mainland, 1km E of St. Mary's, containing Norwood collection of antiques including furniture, clocks, watches and fine china collected over 50 years by Norris Wood. **79 D2** HY4801.
Graham Cunninghame Memorial *Stir.* ***Other feature of interest***, cairn (National Trust for Scotland) to N of Gartmore, 2m/3km SW of Aberfoyle, commemorating life of R.B. Graham Cunninghame (1852-1936), a radical politician, writer, traveller and renowned horseman. **32 A5** NS5297.
Grain Earth House *Ork.* ***Historic/prehistoric site***, prehistoric earth house (Historic Scotland) opposite Kirkwall, Mainland, across head of Bay of Kirkwall. **80 C5** HY4411.
Grainel *Arg. & B.* ***Settlement***, on Islay, 4m/7km NW of Bridgend. **20 A3** NR2666.
Grainhow *Aber.* ***Settlement***, 2m/3km W of New Deer. **65 D5** NJ8546.
Gramisdale *W.Isles Anglicised form of Gramsdal, qv.*
Grampian Mountains ***Large natural feature***, great mountain system of Scotland, extending from Oban in SW to Huntly in NE, its southern edge forming natural boundary between Highlands and Lowlands, and N edge being Great Glen fault line. Includes several smaller chains and groups. Highest point is Ben Nevis, 4406 feet or 1343 metres. **40 A2** NN7080.
Grampian Transport Museum *Aber.* ***Other feature of interest***, museum in Alford, with historic vehicles of every description. Includes driving simulator and video bus providing histories of road transport and motor sport. **54 A3** NJ5716.
Gramsdal (Anglicised form: Gramisdale.) *W.Isles* ***Settlement***, at N end of Benbecula, 2m/3km E of Benbecula (Baile a' Mhanaich) Aerodrome. **45 G4** NF8155.
Grandhome *Aberdeen* ***Locality***, comprising Grandhome House, Mains of Grandhome and Grandhome Moss, 4m/7km NW of Aberdeen. NJ9011.
Grandtully *P. & K.* ***Settlement***, in upper valley of River Tay, 4m/6km SW of Pitlochry. **41 E4** NN9152.
Grandtully Castle *P. & K.* ***Castle***, dating from 1560, with later additions, in Strath Tay 3m/4km NE of Aberfeldy. **41 D4** NN8951.
Grandtully Hill *P. & K.* ***Mountain***, in forested area 3m/5km SE of Aberfeldy. Height 1745 feet or 532 metres. **41 E5** NN9147.
Grange *E.Ayr.* ***Suburb***, W district of Kilmarnock. NS4137.
Grange *Edin.* ***Suburb***, 1m/2km S of Edinburgh city centre. NT2571.
Grange *High.* ***Settlement***, in Inverness district, 8m/13km W of Drumnadrochit. **50 C1** NH3730.
Grange *Moray* ***Locality***, comprising Davoch of Grange and Haughs of Grange in Strath Isla, 4m/7km E of Keith. NJ4851.
Grange *P. & K.* ***Settlement***, in Carse of Gowrie, 2m/3km NE of Errol. **34 A2** NO2725.
Grange Crossroads *Moray* ***Settlement***, at crossroads, 4m/6km NE of Keith. **63 G4** NJ4754.
Grange Fell *D. & G.* ***Mountain***, 3m/5km E of Bankshill. Height 1046 feet or 319 metres. **9 G2** NY2481.
Grange Hall *Moray* ***Settlement***, 2m/3km NE of Forres. **62 C3** NJ0660.
Grange of Lindores *Fife* ***Hamlet***, 2m/3km SE of Newburgh. **34 A3** NO2516.
Grangemouth *Falk.* Population: 18,739. ***Town***, industrial town and container port on S side of Firth of Forth, 3m/5km E of Falkirk. E terminus of Forth and Clyde Canal (disused). **24 D1** NS9281.
Grangemuir *Fife* ***Hamlet***, 1m/2km NW of Pittenweem. **34 D4** NO5303.
Grangeston *S.Ayr.* ***Locality***, including Girvan distillery, 2m/3km NE of Girvan. **6 D1** NX2099.
Granish *High.* ***Settlement***, 1m/2km NE of Aviemore. **52 B3** NH9014.
Grantlodge *Aber.* ***Settlement***, 1m/2km W of Kemnay. **54 C3** NJ7017.
Granton *Edin.* ***Suburb***, 2m/4km NW of Edinburgh city centre. Harbour on Firth of Forth. NT2376.
Granton House *D. & G.* ***Settlement***, 3m/4km N of Moffat. **16 B5** NT0709.
Grantown-on-Spey *High.* Population: 2391. ***Small town***, market town and resort, 19m/31km S of Forres. Castle Grant, 2m/3km N, dating in part from 16c, was formerly home of chiefs of Grant, Earls of Seafield. **52 C2** NJ0327.
Grantshouse *Sc.Bord.* ***Village***, on Eye Water, 8m/13km W of Eyemouth. **27 F3** NT8065.
Grass Holm *Ork.* ***Island***, islet off W coast of Shapinsay opposite Salt Ness. HY4719.
Grass Point *Arg. & B.* ***Coastal feature***, headland on E coast of Mull, on S side of entrance to Loch Don. **29 G1** NM7430.
Graven *Shet.* ***Settlement***, on Mainland, at head of Garths Voe. **84 D5** HU4073.
Gravir *W.Isles Anglicised form of Grabhair, qv.*
Greanamul *W.Isles* ***Island***, islet 2m/3km E of Barra (Tràigh Mhòr) Airport. **44 C3** NF7305.
Greanamul *W.Isles* ***Island***, islet midway between Pabbay and Sandray. NL6289.
Great Bernera *W.Isles* ***Island***, in Loch Roag, W coast of Isle of Lewis, 6m/9km N to S and from 1m/2km to 2m/4km in width. Connected to Crulabhig on Isle of Lewis by road bridge at S end. **68 C4** NB1030.
Great Cumbrae *N.Ayr.* ***Island***, in Firth of Clyde, lying about 1m/2km off mainland across Fairlie Roads. Measures about 3m/5km N to S and 2m/3km E to W. Landing stage at Keppel Pier, Millport. **22 C4** NS1656.
Great Glen *High. See Glen Mòr.*
Great Glen Exhibition Centre *High.* ***Other feature of interest***, in Fort Augustus, at SW end of Loch Ness. Demonstrations, in authentic surroundings, of 17c Scottish Highland life. **50 C4** NH3709.
Great Hill *D. & G.* ***Mountain***, with mast at summit, 4m/7km SE of Thornhill. Height 1158 feet or 353 metres. **9 D1** NX9492.
Great Law *Sc.Bord.* ***Mountain***, 4m/6km SW of Stow. Height 1666 feet or 508 metres. **26 B5** NT4041.
Greatmoor Hill *Sc.Bord.* ***Mountain***, 6m/10km SE of Teviothead. Height 1965 feet or 599 metres. **17 F5** NT4800.
Green Head *Ork.* ***Coastal feature***, headland on E coast of Hoy opposite Cava. **78 C3** ND3099.
Green Hill *Angus* ***Mountain***, 2m/3km NE of Clova. Height 2854 feet or 870 metres. **42 B2** NO3475.
Green Holm *Shet.* ***Island***, rock off Burra Ness on S coast of Yell. HU5178.
Green Island *High.* ***Island***, islet in Enard Bay off NW coast of Ross and Cromarty district, 1m/2km S of Eilean Mòr. NC0515.
Green Isle *Shet.* ***Island***, tiny island off E coast of Mainland in Dury Voe. HU4861.
Green Law *Sc.Bord.* ***Mountain***, in Wauchope Forest area of Cheviot Hills, 4m/7km SW of Carter Bar. Height 1207 feet or 368 metres. **11 E1** NT6304.
Green Lowther *S.Lan.* ***Mountain***, summit of Lowther Hills, 2m/3km SE of Leadhills. Mast at summit. Height 2401 feet or 732 metres. **16 A4** NS9012.
Greena *Shet.* ***Island***, small island at entrance to Weisdale Voe, Mainland. HU3747.
Greenbank *Edin.* ***Suburb***, 3m/4km S of Edinburgh city centre. NT2369.
Greenburn *Angus* ***Settlement***, 1m/2km NW of Monikie. **34 C1** NO4839.
Greendams *Aber.* ***Settlement***, 3m/4km N of Bridge of Dye. **54 B5** NO6490.
Greenfaulds *N.Lan.* ***Suburb***, 1m/2km S of Cumbernauld town centre. NS7573.
Greenfield *High.* ***Settlement***, on S side of Loch Garry, 6m/10km W of Invergarry. **50 B4** NH2000.
Greengairs *N.Lan.* ***Village***, 3m/5km SE of Cumbernauld. **24 B2** NS7870.
Greenhall *Aber.* ***Settlement***, 1m/2km NE of Insch. **54 B2** NJ6329.
Greenheads *Aber.* ***Settlement***, 1m/2km NW of Hatton. **55 F1** NK0339.
Greenhill *Falk.* ***Settlement***, 1m/2km S of Bonnybridge. NS8278.
Greenhill *High.* ***Settlement***, 1m/2km N of Brora, Sutherland district. **73 E4** NC9106.
Greenhill Covenanters' House *S.Lan.* ***Historic house***, in Biggar. 17c farmhouse re-erected in town, now a museum of 17c life, which explores Covenanting movement and religious conflict which resulted. **16 B2** NT0237.
Greenhills *S.Lan.* ***Suburb***, S district of East Kilbride. NS6252.
Greenhillstairs *D. & G.* ***Open space***, W facing valley side of Evan Water, below Greenhill, 4m/6km NW of Moffat. **16 B4** NT0410.
Greenholm *E.Ayr.* ***Village***, adjoining to E of Newmilns. Dry ski slope to N. **14 D2** NS5337.
Greenigo *Ork.* ***Settlement***, 3m/5km SW of Kirkwall. **78 D2** HY4107.
Greenknowe Tower *Sc.Bord.* ***Historic/prehistoric site***, attractive and well preserved turreted tower house (Historic Scotland) dating from 1581, 1km W of Gordon. **26 D5** NT6342.
Greenland *High.* ***Locality***, in Caithness district, 3m/4km SE of Dunnet. **77 E2** ND2467.
Greenlaw *Aber.* ***Settlement***, 4m/6km S of Banff. **64 B4** NJ6758.
Greenlaw *Sc.Bord.* ***Village***, on Blackadder Water, 7m/11km SW of Duns. **27 E5** NT7146.
Greenlaw Moor *Sc.Bord.* ***Open space***, moorland 2m/3km N of Greenlaw. **27 E5** NT7048.
Greenli Ness *Ork.* ***Coastal feature***, headland on S coast of Stronsay on W side of entrance to Bay of Holland. **81 E4** HY6221.
Greenloaning *P. & K.* ***Settlement***, 5m/8km NE of Dunblane. **32 D4** NN8307.
Greenmyre *Aber.* ***Settlement***, 4m/6km E of Fyvie. **54 D1** NJ8236.
Greenock *Inclyde* Population: 50,013. ***Town***, industrial town and port on S side of Firth of Clyde, 2m/3km W of Glasgow. Birthplace of James Watt, 1736-1819. Large harbour and docks. **23 D2** NS2776.
Greenock Water *E.Ayr.* ***River***, running SW to River Ayr 4m/7km W of Muirkirk. **15 E3** NS6226.
Greens *Aber.* ***Locality***, 4m/6km W of New Deer. NJ8245.
Greenscares *P. & K.* ***Settlement***, 3m/5km NW of Braco. **32 C3** NN8012.
Greenside Reservoir *W.Dun.* ***Reservoir***, small reservoir on Kilpatrick Hills 5m/8km E of Dumbarton. NS4775.
Greenskares *Aber.* ***Settlement***, 1m/2km SW of Gardenstown. **64 C3** NJ7763.
Greenstone Point (Also known as Rubha na Lice Uaine.) *High.* ***Coastal feature***, headland on W coast of Ross and Cromarty district, 11m/18km N of Poolewe. **70 A5** NG8598.
Greeta *W.Isles Alternative name for (River) Creed, qv.*
Greg Ness *Aberdeen* ***Coastal feature***, headland on E coast at S end of Nigg Bay, Aberdeen. **55 E4** NJ9704.
Greian Head *W.Isles* ***Coastal feature***, headland on NW coast of Barra, 4m/7km SW of Scurrival Point. **44 B3** NF6404.
Greine Sgeir *W.Isles* ***Island***, rock island off W coast of Isle of Lewis opposite entrance to Loch Resort. NB0015.
Greineim *W.Isles* ***Island***, islet nearly 1km off W coast of Isle of Lewis, 1m/2km N of Mealasta Island. NA9824.
Greinetobht (Anglicised form: Grenetote.) *W.Isles* ***Settlement***, at N end of North Uist, 1m/2km E of Solas. **45 G2** NF8275.
Grenetote *W.Isles Anglicised form of Greinetobht, qv.*
Greosabhagh (Anglicised form: Grosebay.) *W.Isles* ***Settlement***, at head of Loch Grosebay, on SE coast of South Harris, 4m/7km S of Tarbert. **67 D4** NG1592.

G

Greshornish *High.* ***Locality***, on W side of Loch Greshornish, N coast of Skye. **57 G4** NG3353.
Greshornish Point *High.* ***Coastal feature***, headland on Skye, 2m/3km NE of Greshornish at entrance to Loch Greshornish. **57 G4** NG3353.
Greskine Forest *D. & G.* ***Forest/woodland***, 4m/6km NW of Moffat. NT0307.
Gress *W.Isles Anglicised form of Griais (village), qv.*
Gress (Gaelic form: Abhainn Ghriais.) *W.Isles* ***River***, on Isle of Lewis, rising 6m/9km NW of Griais and flowing S into Loch a' Tuath 1m/2km S of village. NB4941.
Gretna *D. & G.* Population: 3149. ***Village***, 8m/12km E of Annan. **10 B5** NY3167.
Gretna Green *D. & G.* ***Village***, 1km N of Gretna, famous for runaway marriages in former times. **10 B5** NY3167.
Gretna Green Services *D. & G.* ***Other building***, motorway service station on A74(M), 1m/2km NW of Gretna. **9 G4** NY3068.
Grey Cairns of Camster *High.* ***Historic/prehistoric site***, Neolithic chambered burial cairns (Historic Scotland), 1m/2km N of Upper Camster. **77 E4** ND2544.
Grey Head *Ork.* ***Coastal feature***, headland at N end of Calf of Eday. **81 D2** HY5740.
Grey Hill *S.Ayr.* ***Hill***, 3m/5km S of Girvan. Height 974 feet or 297 metres. **6 C1** NX1692.
Grey Mare's Tail *D. & G.* ***Waterfall***, spectacular waterfall (National Trust for Scotland), 200 feet or over 60 metres high, 9m/14km NE of Moffat. **16 C4** NT1815.
Grey Mare's Tail *D. & G.* ***Waterfall***, upstream of Crichope Linn waterfall, 3m/5km E of Thornhill. NX9296.
Grey Mare's Tail *High.* ***Waterfall***, high waterfall in course of Allt Coire na Bà, to N of Kinlochleven, Lochaber district. NN1862.
Greystone *Aber.* ***Settlement***, 2m/3km E of Crathie. **53 E5** NO2995.
Greystone *Angus* ***Village***, 7m/11km W of Arbroath. **42 D5** NO5343.
Griais (Anglicised form: Gress.) *W.Isles* ***Village***, near E coast of Isle of Lewis, 7m/12km NE of Stornoway. **69 F3** NB4942.
Grianan *W.Isles* ***Settlement***, on Isle of Lewis, 2m/3km N of Stornoway. NB4135.
Gribton *D. & G.* ***Settlement***, 5m/8km NW of Dumfries. **8 D2** NX9280.
Gribun *Arg. & B.* ***Locality***, on W coast of Mull, 2m/3km S of entrance to Loch na Keal. Coast road passes below Gribun Rocks. NM4533.
Gribun Rocks *Arg. & B.* ***Coastal feature***, range of overhanging cliffs on W coast of Mull. NM4533.
Grice Ness *Ork.* ***Coastal feature***, headland on E coast of Stronsay at N end of Mill Bay. HY6728.
Grif Skerry *Shet.* ***Island***, rock island 1km E of East Linga and 3m/5km SE of Skaw Taing, headland at NE end of Whalsay. **83 F1** HU6362.
Grigadale *High.* ***Settlement***, on Ardnamurchan peninsula, 1m/2km E of Point of Ardnamurchan. **36 D3** NM4367.
Grim Ness *Ork.* ***Coastal feature***, headland at E extremity of St. Margaret's Hope. **79 D3** ND4992.
Grimbister *Ork.* ***Settlement***, on Mainland, on S side of Bay of Firth, 1m/2km SE of Finstown. HY3712.
Grimersta *W.Isles Anglicised form of Griomarstaidh, qv.*
Griminis (Anglicised form: Griminish.) *W.Isles* ***Settlement***, near W coast of Benbecula, 2m/3km S of Balivanich. **45 F4** NF7751.
Griminis Point (Anglicised form: Griminish Point.) *W.Isles* ***Coastal feature***, headland at NW end of North Uist. **45 F2** NF7276.
Griminish *W.Isles Anglicised form of Griminis, qv.*
Griminish Point *W.Isles Anglicised form of Griminis Point, qv.*
Grimister *Shet.* ***Hamlet***, on Yell, on S side of Whale Firth. **85 D3** HU4693.
Grimmet *S.Ayr.* ***Settlement***, 1m/2km E of Maybole. **14 B4** NS3210.
Grimness *Ork.* ***Settlement***, in NE of South Ronaldsay, 2m/3km E of St. Margaret's Hope. **79 D3** ND4893.
Grimsay (Gaelic form: Griomasaigh.) *W.Isles* ***Island***, of about 3 square miles or 8 square km between North Uist and Benbecula, with causeway connection to both. **45 G4** NF8656.
Grimshader *W.Isles Anglicised form of Grimsiadar, qv.*
Grimsiadar (Anglicised form: Grimshader.) *W.Isles* ***Village***, on E coast of Isle of Lewis, at head of long narrow inlet, Loch Grimsiadar, 5m/8km S of Stornoway. **69 F5** NB4025.
Grindiscol *Shet.* ***Settlement***, near W coast of Bressay. **83 D4** HU4939.
Grindstone Law *Sc.Bord.* ***Mountain***, in Cheviot Hills, 3m/5km N of Byrness. Height 1535 feet or 468 metres. **11 F1** NT7607.
Griomarstaidh (Anglicised form: Grimersta.) *W.Isles* ***Settlement***, 1m/2km S of Linisiadar, on W shore of Loch Cean Thulabhaig, Isle of Lewis. **68 D4** NB2130.
Griomasaigh *W.Isles Gaelic form of Grimsay, qv.*
Griomaval *W.Isles* ***Mountain***, near W coast of Isle of Lewis, 4m/6km N of entrance to Loch Resort. Height 1630 feet or 497 metres. **68 B5** NB0122.
Grishipoll *Arg. & B.* ***Locality***, on Coll near NW coast at Grishipoll Bay. **36 A4** NM1959.
Grishipoll Bay *Arg. & B.* ***Bay***, on NW coast of Coll. **36 A4** NM1959.
Grishipoll Point *Arg. & B.* ***Coastal feature***, headland on Coll at W end of Grishipoll Bay. NM1859.
Griskerry *Shet.* ***Island***, islet close to W coast of Mainland, 1m/2km NW of Bigton. **82 C5** HU3622.
Gritley *Ork.* ***Settlement***, 1km NE of St. Peter's Bay, Mainland. **79 E2** HY5605.
Groay *W.Isles* ***Island***, small uninhabited island at SE end of Sound of Harris, 4m/7km off E coast of North Uist. **56 C2** NG0079.
Grob Bagh *Arg. & B.* ***Bay***, at S end of Gigha. **21 E5** NR6346.
Groban *High.* ***Mountain***, rounded summit in Ross and Cromarty district, 7m/11km NW of Kinlochewe. Height 2453 feet or 748 metres. **59 G2** NH0970.
Grobister *Ork.* ***Settlement***, 1m/2km NW of Dishes, Stronsay. **81 E4** HY6524.
Grogport *Arg. & B.* ***Settlement***, on Garrachcroit Bàgh, on E coast of Kintyre, Argyll, 4m/7km N of Dippen. **21 G5** NR8044.
Groigearraidh *W.Isles* ***Settlement***, 1km S of Drimore, South Uist. **46 A1** NF7739.
Grosebay *W.Isles Anglicised form of Greosabhagh, qv.*
Grotaig *High.* ***Settlement***, 4m/6km SW of Drumnadrochit. **51 D2** NH4923.
Groundistone Heights *Sc.Bord.* ***Settlement***, 3m/5km N of Hawick. **17 F4** NT4919.
Grudie *High.* ***River***, flows E into Kyle of Durness, Sutherland district. **74 C2** NC3562.
Grudie *High.* ***River***, flowing from E end of Loch Fannich SE to its confluence with River Bran, 1km W of Loch Luichart. **60 B3** NH3062.
Grudie Burn *High.* ***River***, in Sutherland district rising between Loch Shin and Glen Cassley and running SE into River Shin 3m/5km S of Lairg. **72 A4** NC5702.
Gruids *High.* ***Locality***, in Sutherland district 2m/3km SW of Lairg. **72 A4** NC5604.
Gruinard *High.* ***River***, flows N into Gruinard Bay from Loch na Sealga. **59 F1** NG9494.
Gruinard Bay *High.* ***Bay***, on W coast of Ross and Cromarty district, between Greenstone Point and Stattic Point. **70 B5** NG9494.
Gruinard Forest *High.* ***Open space***, mountainous and moorland area to S of Little Loch Broom. **59 G1** NH0286.
Gruinard Island *High.* ***Island***, uninhabited island, property of Ministry of Defence, in Gruinard Bay on W coast of Ross and Cromarty district, between Greenstone Point and Stattic Point. Area about 520 acres or 210 hectares. Formerly site of biological warfare testing. **70 B5** NG9494.
Gruinart *Arg. & B.* ***Locality***, at head of Loch Gruinart on Islay. Here in 1598 Macdonalds repelled invasion of Macleans of Mull. NR2866.
Gruinart Flats *Arg. & B.* ***Locality***, to S of Loch Gruinart, Islay. **20 A3** NR2866.
Grula *High.* ***Settlement***, at head of Loch Eynort, SW coast of Skye. NG3826.
Gruline *Arg. & B.* ***Locality***, at head of Loch na Keal, Mull, 3m/5km SW of Salen. Mausoleum in grounds of Gruline House commemorates Lachlan Macquarie, first governor of New South Wales, Australia. **29 E1** NM5440.
Grumby Rock *High.* ***Hill***, 1m/2km NE of West Langwell, on S side of Strath Brora. Height 981 feet or 299 metres. **72 B3** NC7010.
Gruna Stack *Shet.* ***Island***, rock island off NW coast of Mainland, 1m/2km NE of entrance to Ronas Voe. HU2886.
Grunasound *Shet.* ***Locality***, on West Burra, 1m/2km S of Hamnavoe. HU3733.
Grunay *Shet.* ***Island***, third largest in Out Skerries group of islands, NE of Whalsay. **85 F5** HU6971.
Grundcruie *P. & K.* ***Settlement***, 1m/2km NW of Methven. **33 F2** NO0026.
Gruney *Shet.* ***Island***, uninhabited island nearly 1m/2km N of Point of Fethaland. **84 C3** HU3896.
Grunka Hellier *Shet.* ***Coastal feature***, point on NW coast of Unst. **85 E1** HP5815.
Gruting *Shet.* ***Settlement***, in W part of Mainland, on E side of Gruting Voe. **82 B3** HU2749.
Gruting Voe *Shet.* ***Sea feature***, large inlet whose entrance is on E side of Vaila. **82 B3** HU2749.
Grutness *Shet.* ***Settlement***, on SE side of Grutness Voe, 1m/2km N of Sumburgh Head, Mainland. **83 G5** HU4009.
Gryfe ***River***, rising on hills S of Greenock and running N to Gryfe Reservoirs, then SE down Strath Gryfe to Bridge of Weir, then E to Black Cart Water 2m/4km NW of Paisley. **23 F3** NS4666.
Gryfe Reservoirs *Inclyde* ***Reservoir***, pair of reservoirs 3m/5km S of Greenock. **23 D2** NS2871.
Gualachulain *High.* ***Settlement***, at head of Loch Etive, 11m/18km NE of Taynuilt. **38 D5** NN1145.
Gualann *W.Isles* ***Coastal feature***, narrow strip of land 2m/3km long, between Benbecula and South Uist. Joined to latter at low tide. **45 F5** NF7747.
Guardbridge *Fife* ***Village***, at head of River Eden estuary, with modern road bridge across river beside old 15c bridge, 2m/3km S of Leuchars. Large paper mill. **34 C3** NO4518.
Guarsay Mòr *W.Isles* ***Coastal feature***, headland on NW coast of Mingulay. **44 A5** NL5484.
Guay *P. & K.* ***Hamlet***, in Strath Tay, 3m/5km S of Ballinluig. **41 F5** NO0049.
Guelt Water *E.Ayr.* ***River***, running NW to Glenmuir Water between Kyle Castle and Dalblair, 5m/8km E of Cumnock. NS6419.
Guibean Uluvailt *Arg. & B.* ***Mountain***, 2m/3km SE of Ben More, Mull. Height 1076 feet or 328 metres. **29 E1** NM5531.
Guildtown *P. & K.* ***Village***, 5m/8km N of Perth. **33 G1** NO1331.
Guillamon Island *High.* ***Island***, islet 1km off SE coast of Scalpay. NG6327.
Guirasdeal *Arg. & B.* ***Island***, small island off SW shore of Lunga. **29 F4** NM6907.
Guisachan Fall *High.* ***Waterfall***, in Guisachan Forest, 6m/9km SW of Cannich. NH2924.
Guisachan Forest *High.* ***Open space***, deer forest to S of Glen Affric in Inverness district. **50 B2** NH2520.
Guith *Ork.* ***Settlement***, on Eday, overlooking Ferness Bay. **81 D3** HY5536.
Gulber Wick *Shet.* ***Sea feature***, large inlet on E coast of Mainland, 3m/4km SW of Lerwick. HU4438.
Gulberwick *Shet.* ***Village***, on Mainland, at head of Gulber Wick. **82 D4** HU4438.
Gulf of Corryvreckan *Arg. & B. See Strait of Corryvreckan.*
Gull Point *N.Ayr.* ***Coastal feature***, headland at S end of Little Cumbrae. **22 C5** NS1450.
Gullane *E.Loth.* Population: 2229. ***Small town***, resort on Gullane Bay, on Firth of Forth, 4m/7km SW of North Berwick. Championship golf course (Muirfield) to N. **26 B1** NT4882.
Gullane Bay *E.Loth.* ***Bay***, on Firth of Forth, 4m/7km SW of North Berwick. **26 B1** NT4882.
Gullane Bents *E.Loth.* ***Other feature of interest***, area of heath and grass adjacent to Gullane Bay on Firth of Forth, 4m/7km SW of North Berwick. **26 B1** NT4783.
Gullane Point *E.Loth.* ***Coastal feature***, headland at W end of Gullane Bay. **26 B1** NT4882.
Gullane Sands *E.Loth.* ***Nature reserve***, to S of Gullane Point in Aberlady Bay. NT4581.
Gulvain (Gaelic form: Gaor Bheinn.) *High.* ***Mountain***, in Lochaber district 2m/4km S of head of Loch Arkaig. Height of N summit, a Munro, 3237 feet or 987 metres; S summit 3155 feet or 962 metres. **38 C1** NM9986.
Gunna *Arg. & B.* ***Island***, 1m/2km long E to W, lying off SW end of Coll across Caolas Bàn. **36 B1** NM1051.
Gunnista *Shet.* ***Settlement***, near N coast of Bressay. **83 D3** HU4943.
Gunnister *Shet.* ***Settlement***, in N part of Mainland, 2m/4km N of Mangaster, at head of Gunnister Voe. HU3274.
Gunnister *Shet.* ***Settlement***, near N coast of Bressay, opposite small island of Holm of Gunnister. HU5043.
Gunnister Voe *Shet.* ***Sea feature***, inlet on W coast of Mainland, 3m/4km SE of Hillswick. HU3174.
Gutcher *Shet.* ***Settlement***, on Wick of Gutcher, on E coast of Yell. Vehicle ferry to Wick of Belmont, on Unst. **85 E3** HU5499.
Guthrie *Angus* ***Village***, 7m/11km E of Forfar. **43 D4** NO5650.
Guthrie Castle *Angus* ***Castle***, with 15c tower and notable gardens, 4m/6km E of Forfar. NO5650.
Guynd *Angus* ***Settlement***, 5m/8km W of Arbroath. **43 D5** NO5641.
Gylen Castle *Arg. & B.* ***Castle***, ruined castle at S end of Kerrera. Destroyed by Cromwell's troops in 1645. **30 A2** NM8026.
Gyre *Ork.* ***Settlement***, to NE of Orphir Bay, on S coast of Mainland. **78 C2** HY3404.

H

Haaf Gruney *Shet.* ***Island***, uninhabited island lying nearly 1m/2km off SE coast of Unst. Area about 50 acres or 20 hectares. Nature reserve. **85 F3** HU6398.
Habbies Howe *Sc.Bord.* ***Locality***, wooded area along banks of River North Esk, 1km NE of Carlops. **25 F4** NT1756.
Habost *W.Isles Anglicised form of Tabost (Loch Erisort), qv.*
Habost *W.Isles Anglicised form of Tabost (Butt of Lewis), qv.*
Hackland *Ork.* ***Settlement***, 1m/2km N of Bay of Isbister. **80 B4** HY3920.
Hacklete *W.Isles Anglicised form of Tacleit, qv.*
Hackley Bay *Aber.* ***Bay***, small bay N of mouth of River Ythan, between Collieston and Newburgh Bar. NK0226.
Hackley Head *Aber. Alternative name for Forvie Ness, qv.*
Hackness *Ork.* ***Settlement***, at NE end of peninsula of South Walls, Hoy. **78 C3** ND3390.

G
H

Hackness Martello Tower *Ork.* ***Other building***, impressive tower (Historic Scotland) built during Napoleonic Wars to protect Baltic convoys assembling in Longhope inlet on N coast of South Walls peninsula, Hoy. Renovated in 1866 and used again during First World War. **78 C3** ND3391.
Hacks Ness *Ork.* ***Coastal feature***, headland on S coast of Sanday, 1km E of Spur Ness. HY6134.
Haco's Ness *Ork.* ***Coastal feature***, headland at SE end of Shapinsay on Shapinsay Sound. **80 D5** HY5214.
Hadden *Sc.Bord.* ***Hamlet***, 2m/3km NE of Sprouston. **18 B3** NT7836.
Haddington *E.Loth.* Population: 8844. ***Small town***, historic town on River Tyne, 16m/26km E of Edinburgh. Birthplace of John Knox, 1505. Ruined nave of St. Martin's Church (Historic Scotland), altered in 13c. Lauderdale Aisle (Historic Scotland), former sacristy of the great 15c parish church of St. Mary, contains splendid 17c marble monument. **26 C2** NT5173.
Haddo House *Aber.* ***Historic house***, elegant mansion of 1731 (National Trust for Scotland) designed by William Adam, 6m/10km NW of Ellon. Seat of Marquess of Aberdeen. Houses permanent exhibition of James Giles' paintings; beautiful library. **55 D1** NJ8634.
Hadyard Hill *S.Ayr.* ***Mountain***, 6m/9km E of Girvan. Height 1059 feet or 323 metres. **7 D1** NX2799.
Haggersta *Shet.* ***Settlement***, on Mainland, between Weisdale Voe and Loch of Strom. HU3848.
Haggrister *Shet.* ***Settlement***, on Mainland, on W side of Sullom Voe, near head of inlet. HU3470.
Haggs *Falk.* Population: 1013. ***Locality***, 2m/4km W of Bonnybridge. **24 B2** NS7979.
Haghill *Glas.* ***Suburb***, 3m/4km E of Glasgow city centre in Dennistoun district. NS6265.
Hailes Castle *E.Loth.* ***Castle***, ruined castle of 13c-15c (Historic Scotland) on S bank of River Tyne, 1m/2km SW of East Linton. Includes fine 16c chapel and two vaulted pit-prisons. **26 C2** NT5775.
Haimer *High.* ***Settlement***, 1m/2km SE of Thurso. **76 D2** ND1367.
Halbeath *Fife* ***Hamlet***, 2m/4km E of Dunfermline. **25 F1** NT1288.
Halberry Head *High.* ***Coastal feature***, headland on E coast of Caithness district, 4m/6km E of Lybster. ND3037.
Halcro *High.* ***Locality***, in Caithness district, 5m/8km SE of Castletown. **77 E2** ND2360.
Halcro Head *Ork.* ***Coastal feature***, headland on E coast of South Ronaldsay, 3m/4km NE of Brough Ness. **79 D4** ND4785.
Halfmerk Hill ***Mountain***, on border of Dumfries & Galloway and East Ayrshire, 3m/5km NW of Kirkconnel. Height 1479 feet or 451 metres. **15 E4** NS7016.
Halfwayhouse *Glas.* ***Suburb***, 4m/6km SW of Glasgow city centre, in Cardonald district. NS5363.
Halistra *High.* ***Locality***, on Vaternish peninsula, Skye, comprising settlements of Upper and Lower Halistra, 5m/8km S of Vaternish Point. **57 F4** NG2459.
Halket *E.Ayr.* ***Settlement***, 1m/2km E of Lugton. NS4252.
Halkirk *High.* ***Village***, on River Thurso, 6m/9km S of Thurso, Caithness district. **76 D3** ND1359.
Hall *E.Renf.* ***Settlement***, 1m/2km W of Uplawmoor. **23 F4** NS4154.
Halladale *High.* ***River***, in Caithness district, running N down Strath Halladale to Melvich Bay on N coast. **76 A3** NC8965.
Hallhills Loch *D. & G.* ***Lake/loch***, small loch 5m/8km N of Lockerbie. NY1688.
Halliman Skerries *Moray* ***Island***, island group with lighthouse, 1km off N coast and 1m/2km W of Lossiemouth. **63 E2** NJ2172.
Hallin *High.* ***Settlement***, near NW coast of Skye, 5m/8km S of Vaternish Point. **57 F4** NG2558.
Hallival *High.* ***Mountain***, 2m/3km S of Kinloch, Rum. Height 2371 feet or 723 metres. **47 G5** NM3996.
Halliwell's House Museum and Art Gallery *Sc.Bord.* ***Other feature of interest***, local history exhibitions in restored buildings in Selkirk, showing town's development. **17 F3** NT4628.
Hallrule *Sc.Bord.* ***Hamlet***, 1m/2km N of Bonchester Bridge. **17 G4** NT5914.
Halls *E.Loth.* ***Hamlet***, 2m/3km SE of Stenton. **27 D2** NT6572.
Hallyburton Forest *P. & K.* ***Forest/woodland***, 4m/6km S of Coupar Angus. **34 A1** NO2334.
Hallyne *Sc.Bord.* ***Settlement***, on Lyne Water, 4m/6km W of Peebles. Sites of Roman forts on both sides of river. NT1940.
Halmadarie Burn *High.* ***River***, rising on NE slopes of Meall nan Aighean and flowing into Loch Truderscaig. **75 F5** NC7032.
Halmyre Mains *Sc.Bord.* ***Hamlet***, 2m/3km SE of West Linton. **25 F5** NT1749.
Ham *High.* ***Settlement***, on N coast, 3m/5km SE of Dunnet Head. **77 E1** ND2373.
Ham *Shet.* ***Settlement***, chief settlement of Foula. It is situated on E coast on island's only harbour, Ham Voe. **82 B5** HT9738.
Ham *Shet.* ***Settlement***, on Bressay, 1m/2km SE of Lerwick across Bressay Sound. HU4939.
Ham Voe *Shet.* ***Sea feature***, small inlet on E coast of Foula; only harbour on island. HT9738.
Hamara *High.* ***River***, running NW into Loch Pooltiel on NW coast of Skye. NG1649.
Hamars Ness *Shet.* ***Coastal feature***, headland at NW corner of Fetlar. **85 E3** HU5894.
Hamarsay *W.Isles* ***Island***, islet off South Harris in East Loch Tarbert, to W of Scalpay. NG2194.
Hamilton *S.Lan.* Population: 49,991. ***Town***, administrative and commercial town, 11m/17km SE of Glasgow and 1m/2km W of confluence of Rivers Avon and Clyde. Formerly a significant coalmining area in Scotland. Racecourse. **24 B4** NS7255.
Hamilton House *E.Loth.* *See Prestonpans.*
Hamilton Racecourse *S.Lan.* ***Racecourse***, to N of Hamilton town centre. Flat-racing course with seventeen race days and four evening meetings a year, including Saints and Sinners meeting. **24 B4** NS7156.
Hamilton Services *S.Lan.* ***Other building***, motorway service station on northbound carriageway of M74, 1m/2km NE of Hamilton. **24 B4** NS7256.
Hamiltonhill *Glas.* ***Suburb***, 1m/2km N of Glasgow city centre. NS5867.
Hamna Voe *Shet.* ***Bay***, at NW end of West Burra. Forms a natural harbour for Hamnavoe. HU3635.
Hamna Voe *Shet.* ***Sea feature***, inlet on NW coast of Mainland, 3m/5km NW of Hillswick. HU2379.
Hamna Voe *Shet.* ***Sea feature***, inlet on S coast of Yell. **85 D5** HU4980.
Hamnavoe *Shet.* ***Settlement***, situated N of Hamna Voe on W coast of Mainland. **84 B4** HU2380.
Hamnavoe *Shet.* ***Settlement***, on W side of Lunna Ness, Mainland. **85 D5** HU4971.
Hamnavoe *Shet.* ***Settlement***, at head of Hamna Voe. **85 D4** HU4980.
Hamnavoe *Shet.* ***Village***, fishing village at N end of West Burra, with natural harbour formed by bay of Hamna Voe. Connected to Mainland via road bridges at either end of Trondra. **82 C4** HU3635.
Handa Island *High.* ***Island***, of about 1 square mile or 3 square km, including bird sanctuary, off W coast of Sutherland district, to W of locality of Tarbet across Sound of Handa. **74 A4** NC1348.
Hangingshaw *D. & G.* ***Settlement***, 6m/9km N of Lockerbie. **9 F2** NY1089.
Hangingshaw *Glas.* ***Suburb***, 2m/4km S of Glasgow city centre. NS5961.
Happendon Services *S.Lan.* ***Other building***, motorway service station on M74, 2m/4km NE of Douglas. **15 G2** NS8433.
Harburn *W.Loth.* ***Settlement***, 2m/3km SE of West Calder. **25 E3** NT0461.
Hardgate *Aber.* ***Settlement***, 3m/5km W of Peterculter. **54 C4** NJ7801.
Hare Cairn *Angus* ***Mountain***, to NW of Backwater Reservoir, 2m/3km NE of Kirkton of Glenisla. Height 1692 feet or 516 metres. **42 A3** NO2462.
Hare Hill *E.Ayr.* ***Mountain***, rising to over 600 metres, 3m/5km SE of New Cumnock. **15 E5** NS6509.
Hare Hill *S.Lan.* ***Mountain***, 2m/3km W of Forth. Height 1030 feet or 314 metres. **24 D4** NS9053.
Hare Ness *Aber.* ***Coastal feature***, headland on E coast, 4m/6km S of Aberdeen. NO9599.
Harelaw *S.Lan.* ***Settlement***, 2m/3km NW of Carstairs. **24 D5** NS9147.
Harelaw Dam *E.Renf.* ***Reservoir***, 2m/4km S of Neilston. **23 F4** NS4753.
Harelaw Reservoir *E.Renf.* ***Reservoir***, small reservoir 1m/2km NW of Barrhead. NS4859.
Harelaw Reservoir *Inclyde* ***Reservoir***, small reservoir 1m/2km SW of Port Glasgow. NS3173.
Hareshaw *N.Lan.* ***Settlement***, 4m/7km SE of Airdrie. NS8160.
Hareshaw *S.Lan.* ***Settlement***, 4m/7km SW of Strathaven. **24 A5** NS6241.
Harestanes (Woodland Centre) *Sc.Bord.* ***Other feature of interest***, 1m/2km E of Ancrum, with displays on timber and woodland management. **18 A4** NT6424.
Harlaw Muir *Sc.Bord.* ***Locality***, 4m/7km SW of Penicuik. **25 F4** NT1855.
Harlaw Reservoir *Edin.* ***Reservoir***, 1m/2km SE of Balerno. **25 F3** NT1864.
Harleburn Head *S.Lan.* ***Mountain***, 3m/5km E of Elvanfoot. Height 1781 feet or 543 metres. **16 A4** NT0017.
Harleyholm *S.Lan.* ***Hamlet***, 3m/4km SE of Hyndford Bridge. **16 A2** NS9238.
Harlosh *High.* ***Settlement***, on peninsula protruding southwards into Loch Bracadale, Skye, 4m/7km SE of Dunvegan. **57 F5** NG2841.
Harlosh Island *High.* ***Island***, small uninhabited island off headland in Loch Bracadale, Skye. **47 F1** NG2841.
Harlosh Point *High.* ***Coastal feature***, at end of peninsula protruding into Loch Bracadale, Skye. **57 F5** NG2841.
Harold's Wick *Shet.* ***Sea feature***, inlet on E coast of Unst. **85 F1** HP6312.
Haroldswick *Shet.* ***Village***, fishing village at head of Harold's Wick, Unst. **85 F1** HP6312.
Harperleas Reservoir *Fife* ***Reservoir***, small reservoir 3m/5km NW of Leslie. **33 G4** NO2105.
Harperrig Reservoir *W.Loth.* ***Reservoir***, 4m/7km S of Mid Calder. **25 E3** NT0961.
Harpsdale *High.* ***Settlement***, 2m/3km S of Halkirk. **76 D3** ND1356.
Harrabol *High.* *Alternative name for Harrapool, qv.*
Harrapool (Also known as Harrabol.) *High.* ***Locality***, on coast of Skye, adjoining to E of Broadford. **48 C2** NG6523.
Harray *Ork.* ***Locality***, on Mainland, 3m/5km NW of Finstown. To W is large Loch of Harray. HY3217.
Harrietfield *P. & K.* ***Village***, on N side of River Almond, 9m/15km NE of Crieff. **33 E1** NN9829.
Harris *High.* ***Settlement***, near SW coast of Rum, 4m/6km NW of Rubha nam Meirleach. **47 G5** NM3395.
Harrow *High.* ***Settlement***, on N coast, 5m/8km SE of Dunnet Head. **77 E1** ND2774.
Harrows Law *S.Lan.* ***Mountain***, in Pentland Hills, 3m/5km NW of Dunsyre. Height 1361 feet or 415 metres. **25 E4** NT0553.
Harsgeir *W.Isles* ***Island***, islet off W coast of Isle of Lewis, at entrance to West Loch Roag. NB1140.
Hart Fell ***Mountain***, on border of Dumfries & Galloway and Scottish Borders, 6m/9km N of Moffat. Height 2650 feet or 808 metres. **16 C4** NT1113.
Hart Fell *D. & G.* ***Mountain***, 4m/6km E of Boreland. Height 1086 feet or 331 metres. **9 G2** NY2388.
Hart Hill *E.Dun.* ***Mountain***, part of Campsie Fells on border with Stirling, 4m/6km NW of Lennoxtown. Height 1699 feet or 518 metres. **24 A1** NS6082.
Hart Hill *Stir.* ***Mountain***, 5m/8km E of Fintry. Height 1430 feet or 436 metres. **24 A1** NS6988.
Harta Corrie *High.* ***Valley***, 1m/2km N of Loch Coruisk, Skye. **48 A2** NG4723.
Hartamul *W.Isles* ***Island***, islet lying nearly 1m/2km off SE point of South Uist and nearly 2m/3km E of Eriskay. **46 B3** NF8311.
Hartaval *High.* ***Mountain***, 1m/2km NW of The Storr, Skye. Height 2191 feet or 668 metres. **58 A4** NG4855.
Hartfield *High.* ***Settlement***, 1m/2km NE of Applecross. **58 D5** NG7246.
Harthill *W.Loth.* Population: 2904. ***Village***, 5m/8km SW of Bathgate. Service area on M8 motorway. **24 D3** NS9064.
Harthill Castle *Aber.* ***Castle***, ruined castle 1m/2km SE of Oyne. NJ6825.
Harthill Services *N.Lan.* ***Other building***, motorway service station on M8 to N of Harthill. **24 C3** NS9064.
Hartrigge *Sc.Bord.* ***Settlement***, to NW of Jedburgh. **18 A4** NT6621.
Hartsgarth Fell *Sc.Bord.* ***Open space***, moorland at head of Tarras Water, 4m/7km NW of Newcastleton. **10 C2** NY4594.
Hartshorn Pike *Sc.Bord.* ***Mountain***, in Cheviot Hills, 3m/5km E of Singdean. Height 1788 feet or 545 metres. **11 E1** NT6201.
Hartwood *N.Lan.* ***Hamlet***, 4m/7km NE of Wishaw. **24 C4** NS8459.
Harwood on Teviot *Sc.Bord.* ***Settlement***, 2m/3km SW of Branxholme. **17 F5** NT4409.
Hascosay *Shet.* ***Island***, between Yell and Fetlar. Sea birds abound. **85 E3** HU5592.
Hascosay Sound *Shet.* ***Sea feature***, runs between Hascosay and Yell. **85 E3** HU5592.
Haskeir Eagach (Also known as Heisgeir Eagach.) *W.Isles* ***Island***, group of rocks about 1m/2km SW of Haskeir Island. **45 D1** NF6182.
Haskeir Island (Also known as Heisgeir Island.) *W.Isles* ***Island***, small rocky uninhabited island 8m/13km NW of Griminis Point, North Uist. Seal sanctuary. **45 E1** NF6182.
Hassendean *Sc.Bord.* ***Settlement***, 5m/7km NE of Hawick. **17 G3** NT5420.
Haster *High.* ***Settlement***, 3m/4km W of Wick. **77 F3** ND3251.
Hastigrow *High.* ***Settlement***, in Caithness district, 6m/10km SE of Castletown. **77 E2** ND2661.
Hatton *Aber.* ***Village***, near E coast, 8m/12km SW of Peterhead. **55 F1** NK0537.
Hatton Castle *Aber.* ***Castle***, residence comprising remains of ancient castle of Balquholly, 3m/5km SE of Turriff. **64 C5** NJ7546.
Hatton of Fintray *Aber.* ***Village***, 5m/9km SE of Inverurie. **54 D3** NJ8416.
Hattoncrook *Aber.* ***Settlement***, 3m/4km SE of Oldmeldrum. **54 D2** NJ8424.
Haugh of Glass *Moray* ***Settlement***, 7m/11km W of Huntly. **53 G1** NJ4239.
Haugh of Urr *D. & G.* ***Village***, 4m/6km N of Dalbeattie. **8 C4** NX8066.
Haughhead *E.Dun.* ***Settlement***, 2m/3km NW of Lennoxtown. **24 A2** NS6079.
Haughs *Aber.* ***Settlement***, on W bank of River Isla, 1m/2km N of Ruthven. **64 A5** NJ5049.
Haughs of Cromdale *High.* ***Open space***, tract between Cromdale and NW side of Hills of Cromdale, 4m/6km E of Grantown-on-Spey. **52 C2** NJ0726.

H

Haughton House Country Park *Aber.* ***Leisure/recreation***, 48 acre country park surrounding 19c house, 1km NE of Alford. Consists chiefly of woodland with gardens, aviary and adventure playground. **54 A3** NJ5816.
Haultin *High.* ***River***, on Skye, running W into Loch Eyre 7m/11km NW of Portree. NG4151.
Haun *W.Isles Anglicised form of Haunn, qv.*
Haunn (Anglicised form: Haun.) *W.Isles* ***Settlement***, on bay of same name, on N coast of Eriskay. Ferry to Ludag on South Uist. **44 C2** NF7912.
Hawick *Sc.Bord.* Population: 15,812. ***Town***, on River Teviot, 39m/63km S of Edinburgh and 37m/59km N of Carlisle. Centre for knitwear and tourism. **17 G4** NT5014.
Hawick Museum and Scott Gallery *Sc.Bord.* ***Other feature of interest***, in Hawick, with exhibitions on local, social and industrial history, with some Scottish artwork on display in gallery. **17 F4** NT4914.
Hawkcraig Point *Fife* ***Coastal feature***, headland on Firth of Forth on E side of Aberdour. **25 G1** NT2084.
Hawks Ness *Shet.* ***Coastal feature***, headland on E coast of Mainland, 5m/8km N of Lerwick. **83 D3** HU4649.
Hawksland *S.Lan.* ***Settlement***, 2m/4km E of Lesmahagow. **15 G2** NS8439.
Hawthorn *Glas.* ***Suburb***, 2m/3km N of Glasgow city centre. NS5968.
Hayfield *Arg. & B.* ***Settlement***, on N side of Loch Awe, 3m/4km E of Kilchrenan. **30 C2** NN0723.
Hayfield *Fife* ***Suburb***, to N of Kirkcaldy town centre. NT2792.
Hayfield *High.* ***Settlement***, 1km S of Castletown. **77 D2** ND1966.
Hayhillock *Angus* ***Settlement***, 3m/4km NE of Monikie. **42 D5** NO5242.
Haymarket *Edin.* ***Locality***, with railway station, 1m/2km W of Edinburgh city centre. NT2473.
Hayton *Aberdeen* ***Suburb***, N district of Aberdeen. NJ9208.
Hazelbank *Arg. & B.* ***Settlement***, on SE shore of Loch Fyne, 3m/4km S of Inveraray across loch. **30 C4** NN0904.
Hazelbank *S.Lan.* ***Village***, on River Clyde, 3m/5km NW of Lanark. **24 C5** NS8345.
Hazelhead *Aberdeen* ***Locality***, 3m/5km W of Aberdeen city centre. **55 D4** NJ8805.
Hazelhead Park and Zoo *Aberdeen* ***Leisure/recreation***, 2m/3km W of Aberdeen, comprising woodland and gardens, with children's area, aviary and maze. **55 D4** NJ8705.
Hazelside *S.Lan.* ***Settlement***, 1km NE of Glespin and 2m/3km SW of Douglas. **15 G3** NS8128.
Hazelton Walls *Fife* ***Settlement***, 5m/8km NW of Cupar. **34 B2** NO3321.
Hazelwood *Glas.* ***Suburb***, 3m/4km SW of Glasgow city centre. NS5563.
Hazlefield *D. & G.* ***Locality***, 2m/3km NE of Dundrennan. **4 A2** NX7749.
Head of Brough *Shet.* ***Coastal feature***, headland on W coast of Yell, 2m/3km S of West Sandwick. **84 D4** HU4485.
Head of Crees *High.* ***Coastal feature***, headland on N coast, 1km SE of St. John's Point. **77 F1** ND3174.
Head of Garness *Aber.* ***Coastal feature***, headland on N coast, 3m/4km E of Macduff. **64 C3** NJ7464.
Head of Hesta *Shet.* ***Coastal feature***, headland at easternmost point of Fetlar. **85 F3** HU6791.
Head of Holland *Ork.* ***Coastal feature***, headland on Mainland, 3m/4km E of Kirkwall between Bay of Meil and Inganess Bay. **80 C5** HY4912.
Head of Lambhoga *Shet.* ***Coastal feature***, headland on Fetlar at SE end of Lamb Hoga peninsula. HU6287.
Head of Moclett *Ork.* ***Coastal feature***, to S of Papa Westray. **80 D2** HY4949.
Head of Stanshi *Shet.* ***Coastal feature***, small promontory on N coast of Esha Ness, Mainland. **84 A4** HU2180.
Head of Work *Ork.* ***Coastal feature***, headland on coast of Mainland opposite Shapinsay, 3m/5km NE of Kirkwall. HY4813.
Heads of Ayr *S.Ayr.* ***Coastal feature***, headland at S end of Firth of Clyde, 4m/7km SW of Ayr. Holiday camp to E. **14 A4** NS2818.
Healabhal Bheag (Macleod's Table South or Healaval Beg.) *High.* ***Mountain***, flat-topped mountain 4m/6km SW of Dunvegan, Skye. Height 1601 feet or 488 metres. **57 F5** NG2242.
Healabhal Mhòr (Macleod's Table North or Healaval More.) *High.* ***Mountain***, flat-topped mountain 3m/5km SW of Dunvegan, Skye. Height 1535 feet or 468 metres. **57 F5** NG2144.
Healaval Beg *High. Anglicised form of Healabhal Bheag, qv.*
Healaval More *High. Anglicised form of Healabhal Mhòr, qv.*
Heanish *Arg. & B.* ***Settlement***, on S coast of Tiree, 1km SW of Scarinish. **36 B2** NM0343.
Hearnish *W.Isles* ***Coastal feature***, headland on Ceann Iar, one of Heisker Islands group to W of North Uist. **45 E3** NF6263.
Heart Law *E.Loth.* ***Mountain***, 4m/6km NW of Abbey St. Bathans. Height 1286 feet or 392 metres. **27 E3** NT7166.
Hearthstane *Sc.Bord.* ***Settlement***, in Tweeddale, 1m/2km N of Tweedsmuir. **16 C3** NT1125.
Heast *High.* ***Settlement***, 4m/6km S of Broadford, Skye. Uninhabited island of Eilean Heast 1km off shore to S. **48 C3** NG6417.
Heathcot *Aber.* ***Settlement***, 3m/5km E of Peterculter. **55 D4** NJ8900.
Heathfield *S.Ayr.* ***Suburb***, N district of Ayr. NS3523.
Heaval *W.Isles* ***Mountain***, on Barra 1m/2km NE of Castlebay. Height 1256 feet or 383 metres. **44 B4** NL6799.
Heck *D. & G.* ***Settlement***, 2m/3km SE of Lochmaben, beyond Castle Loch. **9 E2** NY0980.
Hecla *W.Isles* ***Mountain***, on South Uist 2m/4km S of Loch Sgioport. Height 1988 feet or 606 metres. **46 B1** NF8234.
Heddle *Ork.* ***Settlement***, 1m/2km S of Finstown. **80 B5** HY3512.
Heglibister *Shet.* ***Settlement***, on W side of Weisdale Voe, 1km NE of Sound, Mainland. **82 C2** HU3851.
Heights of Brae *High.* ***Settlement***, 2m/3km NW of Dingwall. **61 E3** NH5161.
Heights of Kinlochewe *High.* ***Settlement***, in Ross and Cromarty district, 3m/4km NE of Kinlochewe. **59 G3** NH0764.
Heilam *High.* ***Settlement***, on E side of Loch Eriboll. Ben Sgeireach lies to NW. **75 D2** NC4560.
Heileasbhal Mòr *W.Isles* ***Mountain***, 3m/4km S of Seilebost, South Harris. Height 1260 feet or 384 metres. **66 C4** NG0792.
Heinish *W.Isles* ***Coastal feature***, headland on W coast of Eriskay, 2m/3km S of Haunn. **44 C3** NF7809.
Heisgeir Eagach *W.Isles Alternative name for Haskeir Eagach, qv.*
Heisgeir Island *W.Isles Alternative name for Haskeir Island, qv.*
Heishival Mòr *W.Isles* ***Hill***, highest point on Vatersay. Height 623 feet or 190 metres. **44 B4** NL6296.
Heisker Islands (Also known as Monach Islands.) *W.Isles* ***Island***, group of low-lying islands 8m/13km SW of Aird an Rùnair, W coast of North Uist. Total area about 600 acres or 240 hectares. No permanent population. See Ceann Ear, Ceann Iar, Shillay and Stockay. **45 E3** NF6262.
Heithat *D. & G.* ***Settlement***, 3m/4km SE of Boreland. **9 F2** NY1988.
Heiton *Sc.Bord.* ***Village***, 2m/4km S of Kelso. **18 B3** NT7130.
Heldale Water *Ork.* ***Lake/loch***, on Hoy, 2m/4km N of Tor Ness. Length 1m/2km. **78 B3** ND2592.
Heldon Hill *Moray* ***Hill***, in wooded area, with steep scarp slope to SE, 6m/10km SW of Elgin. Height 768 feet or 234 metres. **62 D4** NJ1257.
Helensburgh *Arg. & B.* Population: 15,852. ***Town***, on N shore of Firth of Clyde, 8m/12km NW of Dumbarton. Noted yachting centre. Birthplace of J.L. Baird, 1888-1946, pioneer of television. **23 D1** NS2982.
Hellabrick's Wick *Shet.* ***Bay***, wide bay to S of Foula. South Ness lies to S. **82 B5** HT9636.
Helli Ness *Shet.* ***Coastal feature***, headland on E coast of Mainland, 8m/13km S of Lerwick. **83 D5** HU4628.
Helliar Holm (Also spelled Hellyar Holm.) *Ork.* ***Island***, small uninhabited island off S coast of Shapinsay opposite Balfour. Lighthouse at S end. **80 C5** HY4815.
Helliers Ness *Shet.* ***Coastal feature***, headland on SW coast of Fetlar, 1km NW of Rams Ness. HU6087.
Hellir *Shet.* ***Coastal feature***, small promontory on NE coast of Mainland, 2m/3km NE of North Roe. **84 C3** HU3892.
Hellisay *W.Isles* ***Island***, uninhabited island lying 3m/4km E of Northbay, Barra. **44 C3** NF7504.
Hellister *Shet.* ***Village***, on Mainland, on E side of Weisdale Voe. **82 C3** HU3849.
Hellmoor Loch *Sc.Bord.* ***Lake/loch***, small loch 7m/12km W of Hawick. **17 E4** NT3816.
Hell's Glen (Gleann Beag). *Arg. & B.* ***Valley***, running SE into River Goil, 3m/4km N of Lochgoilhead. **31 D4** NN1707.
Hellyar Holm *Ork. Alternative spelling of Helliar Holm, qv.*
Helman Head *High.* ***Coastal feature***, headland on E coast of Caithness district, 3m/4km S of Wick. ND3646.
Helmsdale *High.* ***River***, rising from Loch Badanloch and flowing SE to coast of Sutherland district at Helmsdale. **72 C2** ND0215.
Helmsdale *High.* ***Village***, on E coast of Sutherland district, at mouth of River Helmsdale, 15m/24km NE of Golspie. River runs SE from Loch Badanloch down Strath Kildonan. **73 F3** ND0215.
Hempriggs *Moray* ***Settlement***, 3m/5km S of Burghead. **62 D3** NJ1063.
Hempriggs House *High.* ***Settlement***, on E side of Loch Hempriggs. **77 F4** ND3447.
Henderland *D. & G.* ***Settlement***, 6m/10km W of Dumfries. **8 C3** NX8774.
Henderson's Rock *Arg. & B.* ***Coastal feature***, rock off W coast of Seil, 1m/2km S of Easdale. **29 G3** NM7415.
Hendersyde Park *Sc.Bord.* ***Settlement***, 1m/2km NE of Kelso. **18 B3** NT7435.
Heoga Ness *Shet.* ***Coastal feature***, headland at SE end of Yell. HU5278.
Heogan *Shet.* ***Settlement***, on NW coast of Bressay, on small Bay of Heogan. **83 D3** HU4743.
Heriot *Sc.Bord.* ***Locality***, on Heriot Water, 7m/11km NW of Stow. **26 A4** NT3952.
Heriot Water *Sc.Bord.* ***River***, originating in several headstreams on Moorfoot Hills and running E into Gala Water 2m/3km E of Heriot. **26 A4** NT3952.
Herma Ness *Shet.* ***Coastal feature***, headland at NW end of Unst. **85 E1** HP5918.
Herman Law *Sc.Bord.* ***Mountain***, 1km E of Birkhill. Height 2014 feet or 614 metres. **16 D4** NT2115.
Hermaness Hill *Shet.* ***Hill***, at NW end of Unst, to E of Herma Ness. Height 656 feet or 200 metres. HP5918.
Hermetray *W.Isles* ***Island***, small uninhabited island at S end of Sound of Harris, 1km off NE coast of North Uist. **56 C2** NF9874.
Hermiston *Edin.* ***Village***, on outskirts of Edinburgh, 6m/9km SW of city centre. **25 F2** NT1770.
Hermitage *D. & G.* ***Settlement***, 1m/2km NW of Haugh of Urr. **8 C4** NX8068.
Hermitage *Sc.Bord.* ***Settlement***, on Whitrope Burn, 5m/8km N of Newcastleton. **10 D2** NY5095.
Hermitage Castle *Sc.Bord.* ***Castle***, ruined 13c castle (Historic Scotland) on Hermitage Water, 5m/8km N of Newcastleton. **10 C2** NY4996.
Hermitage Water *Sc.Bord.* ***River***, flowing E to Hermitage Castle, then S to Liddel Water 2m/3km NE of Newcastleton. **10 C2** NY4996.
Herscha Hill *Aber.* ***Hill***, 2m/3km W of Glenbervie. Height 731 feet or 223 metres. **43 F1** NO7380.
Herston *Ork.* ***Settlement***, on SW side of Widewall Bay, South Ronaldsay, 1km W of Widewall across bay. **78 D3** ND4291.
Herston Head *Ork.* ***Coastal feature***, headland on W coast of South Ronaldsay to S of Widewall Bay. **78 C3** ND4191.
Hestan Island *D. & G.* ***Island***, small island with lighthouse at entrance to Auchencairn Bay on Solway Firth, S of Dalbeattie. **8 C5** NX8350.
Heugh-head *Aber.* ***Settlement***, 2m/3km SE of Strathdon. **53 F3** NJ3811.
Heugh-head *Aber.* ***Settlement***, 1m/2km W of Aboyne. **54 A5** NO5099.
Hevdadale Head *Shet.* ***Coastal feature***, headland on NW coast of Mainland, 4m/6km W of Burra Voe. **84 B4** HU3089.
Hevden Ness *Shet.* ***Coastal feature***, headland on Mainland on E side of entrance to Busta Voe. HU3565.
Heylipoll *Arg. & B.* ***Settlement***, on Tiree, 4m/7km W of Scarinish. **36 A2** NL9743.
Heylor *Shet.* ***Settlement***, on Mainland, on S shore of Ronas Voe. **84 B4** HU2980.
High Balantyre *Arg. & B.* ***Settlement***, 3m/4km NW of Inveraray. **30 C3** NN0711.
High Blantyre *S.Lan.* ***Suburb***, to SW of Blantyre town centre. **24 A4** NS6756.
High Bonnybridge *Falk.* ***Village***, to SE of Bonnybridge across railway, 3m/5km W of Falkirk. **24 C2** NS8379.
High Borgue *D. & G.* ***Settlement***, 2m/4km W of Kirkcudbright. **8 A5** NX6451.
High Borve *W.Isles* ***Settlement***, near NW coast of Isle of Lewis, 5m/9km NE of Barvas. NB4156.
High Possil *Glas.* ***Suburb***, to N of Possil Park, 2m/3km N of Glasgow city centre. NS5968.
High Seat *Sc.Bord.* ***Mountain***, 3m/4km N of Teviothead. Height 1138 feet or 347 metres. **17 F5** NT4009.
Highfield *N.Ayr.* ***Settlement***, 1m/2km E of Dalry. **23 E4** NS3050.
Highland Folk Museum *High.* ***Other feature of interest***, exhibitions of Highland agriculture, housing and culture, situated in Kingussie. **51 G4** NH7500.
Highland Wildlife Park *High.* ***Leisure/recreation***, wildlife park 4m/6km NE of Kingussie, with breeding groups of Scottish mammals and birds, including some now extinct in the wild in Scotland. Visitor Centre includes exhibition on effects on man in region. **52 A4** NH8004.
Hightae *D. & G.* ***Village***, 3m/4km S of Lochmaben. **9 E3** NY0978.
Hightae Mill Loch *D. & G.* ***Lake/loch***, small loch and nature reserve, 1m/2km N of Hightae. NY0880.
Hildasay *Shet.* ***Island***, uninhabited island of 255 acres or 103 hectares 3m/5km W of Scalloway, Mainland. **82 C3** HU3540.
Hill End *Fife* ***Hamlet***, 2m/3km SE of Powmill. **33 F5** NT0395.
Hill House *Arg. & B.* ***Historic house***, National Trust for Scotland property to N of Helensburgh. Built at beginning of 20c for Walter Blackie, an excellent example of domestic architecture by Charles Rennie Mackintosh. **23 D1** NS3088.
Hill o' Many Stanes *High.* ***Historic/prehistoric site***, prehistoric arrangement (Historic Scotland) of about 200 stones in parallel rows, situated NE of Mid Clyth on Hill of Mid Clyth, 9m/14km SW of Wick. **77 E5** ND2938.

Hill of Achmore *Moray* **Mountain**, N flank of Muckle Lapprach, 7m/11km W of Bridgend. Height 1673 feet or 510 metres. **53 E1** NJ2630.
Hill of Aitnoch *High.* **Mountain**, in Nairn district, 3m/5km S of Ferness. Height 1355 feet or 413 metres. **52 B1** NH9739.
Hill of Alyth *P. & K.* **Hill**, to N of Alyth. Height 968 feet or 295 metres. **42 A4** NO2450.
Hill of Arisdale *Shet.* **Hill**, running SW to NE, above Aris Dale valley to E, and 1km SW of Ward of Otterswick. Height 689 feet or 210 metres. **85 D4** HU4984.
Hill of Auchlee *Aber.* **Hill**, with Boswell's Monument at summit, 2m/3km W of Portlethen. Height 492 feet or 150 metres. **55 D5** NO8897.
Hill of Barra *Aber.* **Hill**, 1km S of Oldmeldrum. Height 633 feet or 193 metres. **54 D2** NJ8025.
Hill of Beath *Fife* **Locality**, adjoining to SW of Cowdenbeath. **33 G5** NT1590.
Hill of Berran *Angus* **Mountain**, 6m/10km NW of Bridgend, above Waterhead. Height 2001 feet or 610 metres. **42 C2** NO4471.
Hill of Carlincraig *Aber.* **Hill**, 4m/7km SW of Turriff. Height 630 feet or 192 metres. **64 B5** NJ6744.
Hill of Cat **Mountain**, 3m/5km SW of Ballochan, with summit on border of Aberdeenshire and Angus. Height 2434 feet or 742 metres. **42 C1** NO4887.
Hill of Christ's Kirk *Aber.* **Mountain**, with ancient hillfort, to N of Christskirk. Height 1020 feet or 311 metres. **54 B2** NJ6027.
Hill of Corsegight *Aber.* **Hill**, 3m/5km NW of New Deer. Height 617 feet or 188 metres. **65 D4** NJ8550.
Hill of Couternach *Angus* **Mountain**, 2m/3km E of Glenprosen. Height 1679 feet or 512 metres. **42 B3** NO3565.
Hill of Culbirnie *Aber.* **Hill**, 4m/6km SW of Banff. Height 518 feet or 158 metres. **64 B3** NJ6360.
Hill of Dudwick *Aber.* **Hill**, 4m/7km W of Hatton. Height 571 feet or 174 metres. **55 E1** NJ9737.
Hill of Edendocher *Aber.* **Mountain**, 3m/5km W of Bridge of Dye. Height 1893 feet or 577 metres. **43 D1** NO6085.
Hill of Fare *Aber.* **Mountain**, 5m/7km N of Banchory. Height 1545 feet or 471 metres. **54 B4** NJ6803.
Hill of Fearn *High.* **Village**, near E coast of Ross and Cromarty district, 4m/7km SE of Tain. **62 A2** NH8377.
Hill of Finavon *Angus* **Hill**, 1m/2km S of Finavon. Height 722 feet or 220 metres. **42 C4** NO4855.
Hill of Fingray **Mountain**, 3m/4km NE of Fernybank, with summit on border of Aberdeenshire and Angus. Height 1558 feet or 475 metres. **43 D1** NO5781.
Hill of Fishrie *Aber.* **Hill**, 4m/7km S of Gardenstown. Height 745 feet or 227 metres. **64 D4** NJ8257.
Hill of Formal *Angus* **Mountain**, 1m/2km N of Bridgend, above West Water. Height 1115 feet or 340 metres. **42 D2** NO5370.
Hill of Foudland *Aber.* **Mountain**, 6m/10km SE of Huntly. Worked-out quarries on N slopes. Glens of Foudland is valley on N side; Skirts of Foudland are S slopes. Height 1532 feet or 467 metres. **54 B1** NJ6033.
Hill of Garbet *Angus* **Mountain**, 4m/7km W of Bridgend. Height 1906 feet or 581 metres. **42 C3** NO4668.
Hill of Glansie *Angus* **Mountain**, 4m/6km E of Rottal in Glen Clova. Height 2381 feet or 726 metres. **42 C3** NO4369.
Hill of Goauch *Aber.* **Mountain**, 1m/2km NW of Strachan and 3m/4km SW of Banchory. Height 1105 feet or 337 metres. **54 B5** NO6694.
Hill of Hobseat *Aber.* **Hill**, in Fetteresso Forest, 4m/7km N of Glenbervie. Height 813 feet or 248 metres. **43 F1** NO7587.
Hill of John Cairns *Aber.* **Mountain**, 6m/9km SW of Rhynie. Height 1745 feet or 532 metres. **53 G2** NJ4320.
Hill of Maud *Moray* **Hill**, 3m/4km SE of Buckie. Height 899 feet or 274 metres. **63 G3** NJ4663.
Hill of Menmuir *Angus* **Hill**, to NW of Kirkton of Menmuir. Height 889 feet or 271 metres. **42 D3** NO5265.
Hill of Miffia *Ork.* **Hill**, 3m/4km N of Stromness, Mainland. Height 518 feet or 158 metres. **80 A5** HY2313.
Hill of Mulderie *Moray* **Mountain**, 3m/4km W of Keith. Height 1020 feet or 311 metres. **63 F4** NJ3851.
Hill of Nigg *High.* **Hill**, 4m/6km SW of Balintore. Height 656 feet or 200 metres. **62 A2** NH8270.
Hill of Rubislaw *Aberdeen* **Hill**, rising to over 80 metres, 2m/3km W of Aberdeen city centre. Rubislaw Quarry is chief source of granite in area. NJ9005.
Hill of Saughs *Angus* **Mountain**, 3m/5km N of Auchronie. Height 2132 feet or 650 metres. **42 C1** NO4485.
Hill of Skilmafilly *Aber.* **Hill**, 3m/5km NE of Methlick. Height 577 feet or 176 metres. **65 D5** NJ8940.
Hill of Stake *Renf.* **Mountain**, summit of hills to NE of Largs. Height 1712 feet or 522 metres. **23 D3** NS2763.
Hill of Stob *Moray* **Mountain**, 4m/6km W of Rothes. Height 1010 feet or 308 metres. **63 E5** NJ2147.
Hill of Strone *Angus* **Mountain**, 2m/3km W of Clova. Height 2788 feet or 850 metres. **42 A2** NO2872.
Hill of Tarvit Mansion House *Fife* **Historic house**, National Trust for Scotland property built late 17c and remodelled early 20c, 2m/3km S of Cupar. Furniture collection, restored Elizabethan laundry house and gardens. 15c Scotstarvit Tower (Historic Scotland) 1km SW. **34 B3** NO3811.
Hill of the Wangie *Moray* **Mountain**, on N side of River Lossie, 7m/11km SW of Elgin. Height 1046 feet or 319 metres. **62 D4** NJ1353.
Hill of Three Stones *Moray* **Mountain**, 4m/6km SW of Cabrach. Height 2073 feet or 632 metres. **53 F2** NJ3422.
Hill of Tillymorgan *Aber.* **Mountain**, 1m/2km N of Kirkton of Culsalmond. Height 1250 feet or 381 metres. **54 B1** NJ6534.
Hill of Tomechole *Moray* **Mountain**, 6m/10km SE of Forres. Height 1128 feet or 344 metres. **62 C5** NJ0649.
Hill of Towie *Moray* **Mountain**, 4m/6km SW of Keith. Height 1112 feet or 339 metres. **63 F5** NJ3847.
Hill of Trusta *Aber.* **Mountain**, surrounded by Fetteresso Forest, 6m/9km W of Stonehaven. Height 1053 feet or 321 metres. **43 F1** NO7886.
Hill of Wirren *Angus* **Inland physical feature**, mountain ridge 6m/9km NW of Edzell. **42 D2** NO5273.
Hill of Yarrows *High.* **Hill**, 1km SW of Loch of Yarrows. Height 695 feet or 212 metres. **77 E4** ND2942.
Hillbrae *Aber.* **Settlement**, on E side of Hill of Craigmancie, 3m/5km E of Milltown of Rothiemay. **64 B5** NJ6047.
Hillbrae *Aber.* **Settlement**, 2m/3km NE of Inverurie. **54 C2** NJ7923.
Hillbrae *Aber.* **Settlement**, 4m/7km SE of Fyvie. **54 D1** NJ8334.
Hillend *Aber.* **Settlement**, on NW side of Hill of Janetstown, 4m/6km S of Keith. **63 G5** NJ4144.
Hillend *Fife* **Village**, 1m/2km NE of Inverkeithing. **25 F1** NT1483.
Hillend *Midloth.* **Settlement**, at N end of Pentland Hills, 5m/7km S of Edinburgh. Chair lift to artificial ski-slope. **25 G3** NT2566.
Hillend *N.Lan.* **Settlement**, 1km SE of Caldercruix, at W end of Hillend Reservoir. NS8267.
Hillend Reservoir *N.Lan.* **Reservoir**, to E of Caldercruix. **24 C3** NS8267.
Hillend Ski Centre Country Park *Edin.* **Leisure/recreation**, longest dry-ski slope in Britain, located on S outskirts of Edinburgh, 1m/2km S of Fairmilehead suburb. Includes chairlift (open to non-skiers) to viewpoint. **25 G3** NT2466.
Hillhead *Glas.* **Suburb**, 1m/2km NW of Glasgow city centre, to N of University of Glasgow. NS5667.
Hillhead (Also known as Hillhead of New Coylton.) *S.Ayr.* **Village**, 6m/9km E of Ayr, adjoining to E of Coylton. NS4219.
Hillhead of Auchentumb *Aber.* **Locality**, 3m/4km NW of Strichen. **65 E4** NJ9258.
Hillhead of Cocklaw *Aber.* **Settlement**, 3m/4km SW of Peterhead. **65 F5** NK0844.
Hillhead of New Coylton *S.Ayr. Alternative name for Hillhead, qv.*
Hilliclay *High.* **Locality**, 3m/5km SE of Thurso. **77 D2** ND1764.
Hillington *Glas.* **Suburb**, on S side of River Clyde, 4m/6km W of Glasgow city centre. NS5164.
Hillington Industrial Estate *Renf.* **Locality**, adjoining to N of Hillington, 5m/8km W of Glasgow city centre. NS5165.
Hillockhead *Aber.* **Settlement**, 6m/10km SE of Strathdon. **53 F4** NJ3809.
Hillockhead *Aber.* **Settlement**, 5m/8km N of Tarland. **53 G3** NJ4912.
Hillowton *D. & G.* **Settlement**, 1km N of Castle Douglas. **8 B4** NX7763.
Hillpark *Glas.* **Suburb**, in Pollokshaws district of Glasgow, 4m/6km SW of city centre. NS5559.
Hills of Cromdale **Large natural feature**, range of hills on border of Highland and Moray, 3m/4km SE of Cromdale, between River Spey to W and River Avon to E. Highest point is Creagan a' Chaise (2368 feet or 722 metres). **52 C2** NJ1124.
Hillside *Aber.* **Locality**, near E coast, 5m/8km S of Aberdeen. **55 E5** NO9297.
Hillside *Angus* Population: 1033. **Village**, 2m/4km N of Montrose. **43 F3** NO7061.
Hillside *Moray* **Settlement**, 4m/6km W of Elgin. **63 D3** NJ1560.
Hillside *Shet.* **Settlement**, adjacent to Voe, Mainland. **82 D1** HU4063.
Hillswick *Shet.* **Village**, on Mainland on W shore of Ura Firth, at neck of peninsula called Ness of Hillswick. **84 B5** HU2877.
Hillwell *Shet.* **Settlement**, adjacent to Ringasta, in S of Mainland. **83 F4** HU3714.
Hilton *Aber.* **Settlement**, 3m/4km N of Ellon. **55 E1** NJ9434.
Hilton *High.* **Settlement**, 1km NE of Portmahomack. **62 B1** NH9285.
Hilton Bay *Sc.Bord.* **Bay**, small rocky cove, 4m/7km NW of Berwick-upon-Tweed. **27 G3** NT9659.
Hilton of Cadboll *High.* **Village**, on E coast of Ross and Cromarty district, 1km NE of Balintore. Foundation remains of small rectangular chapel (Historic Scotland). **62 A2** NH8776.
Hilton of Delnies *High.* **Settlement**, 2m/3km W of Nairn. **62 A4** NH8456.
Hinnisdal *High.* **River**, running W into Loch Snizort, N coast of Skye, at entrance to Loch Snizort Beag. NG3857.
Hirn *Aber.* **Settlement**, 3m/5km NE of Banchory. **54 C4** NJ7300.
Hirta *W.Isles Alternative name for St. Kilda, qv.*
Hobbister *Ork.* **Settlement**, 1km to E of S end of Loch of Kirkbister, Mainland. **78 C2** HY3807.
Hobkirk *Sc.Bord.* **Settlement**, 1km S of Bonchester Bridge. **17 G4** NT5810.
Hoddam Castle *D. & G.* **Castle**, ruined 15c stronghold of Maxwells, in loop of River Annan, 3m/4km SW of Ecclefechan. NY1573.
Hoe Rape *High.* **Coastal feature**, headland on W coast of Skye at S end of Moonen Bay. **57 E5** NG1543.
Hog Fell *D. & G.* **Mountain**, 4m/6km NE of Langholm. Height 1217 feet or 371 metres. **10 B3** NY3989.
Hog Hill *D. & G.* **Mountain**, to E of Castle O'er Forest, 4m/6km NW of Bentpath. Height 1096 feet or 334 metres. **9 G1** NY2895.
Hogganfield *Glas.* **Suburb**, 3m/5km NE of Glasgow city centre. NS6466.
Hogganfield Loch *Glas.* **Lake/loch**, in Hogganfield Park; island in loch is a bird sanctuary. NS6467.
Hoggie *Moray* **Settlement**, 1m/2km SE of Kirktown of Deskford, 4m/7km S of Cullen. **64 A3** NJ5160.
Hogh Bay *Arg. & B.* **Bay**, on NW coast of Coll, 4m/6km W of Arinagour. **36 A4** NM1657.
Hogha Gearraidh (Anglicised form: Hougharry.) *W.Isles* **Village**, on NW coast of North Uist, 4m/6km S of Griminis Point. **45 F2** NF7071.
Hogs Law *Sc.Bord.* **Mountain**, in Lammermuir Hills, 3m/5km NE of Carfraemill. Cairn at summit. Height 1469 feet or 448 metres. **26 C4** NT5555.
Holborn Head *High.* **Coastal feature**, headland on N coast of Caithness district, 2m/3km N of Thurso. Lighthouse 1km S at entrance to Thurso Bay. **76 D1** ND1071.
Holehouse Hill *D. & G.* **Mountain**, on Forest of Ae, 6m/10km SW of Beattock. Height 1305 feet or 398 metres. **9 E1** NY0094.
Holes of Scraada *Shet.* **Cave**, landward end of subterranean cavern, situated on Esha Ness, Mainland. Sea penetrates cave and may be observed from open top. HU2179.
Holl Reservoir *Fife* **Reservoir**, small reservoir 2m/3km NW of Leslie. **34 A4** NO2203.
Holland *Ork.* **Settlement**, in centre of Papa Westray. **80 C1** HY4851.
Holland *Ork.* **Settlement**, in S of Stronsay, 1km S of Dishes. **81 E4** HY6622.
Holland Isle *D. & G.* **Island**, in course of River Dee 2m/3km W of Parton. NX6669.
Hollandstoun *Ork.* **Locality**, near SW end of North Ronaldsay. **81 F1** HY7553.
Hollee *D. & G.* **Settlement**, on W side of woodland, 1km S of Kirkpatrick-Fleming. **9 G4** NY2769.
Hollows Tower (The Holehouse). *D. & G.* **Historic house**, tower on W bank of River Esk, 2m/3km N of Canonbie. Dating from 16c, refuge of Johnnie Armstrong, a Borders bandit, later hanged by James V. **10 B4** NY3878.
Hollybush *E.Ayr.* **Village**, 3m/5km NW of Patna. **14 B4** NS3914.
Holm *D. & G.* **Settlement**, on W side of White Esk River, to NW of Eskdalemuir. **9 G1** NY2598.
Holm *W.Isles* **Settlement**, on Isle of Lewis, 2m/4km SE of Stornoway. NB4531.
Holm Bay *W.Isles* **Bay**, small bay on Isle of Lewis, to E of Holm Island. NB4530.
Holm Island *High.* **Island**, islet off E coast of Skye, 6m/9km NE of Portree. NG5251.
Holm Island *W.Isles* **Island**, small uninhabited island off Isle of Lewis to E of Holm Point. NB4430.
Holm of Aikerness *Ork.* **Island**, small island to E of Aikerness peninsula on Westray. HY4652.
Holm of Boray *Ork.* **Island**, islet off S coast of Gairsay. HY4520.
Holm of Dalry *D. & G.* **Locality**, low-lying area in loop of Water of Ken, on SW side of St. John's Town of Dalry. NX6180.
Holm of Drumlanrig *D. & G.* **Settlement**, 3m/5km NW of Thornhill. **8 C1** NX8398.
Holm of Elsness *Ork.* **Island**, rocky islet off S coast of Sanday to W of Els Ness peninsula. HY6637.
Holm of Faray *Ork.* **Island**, narrow uninhabited island less than 1m/2km in length N to S, lying between Faray to S and Westray to N. HY5238.
Holm of Grimbister *Ork.* **Island**, small uninhabited island in Bay of Firth, 1m/2km E of Finstown, Mainland. HY3713.

Holm of Gunnister *Shet.* ***Island***, small island off N coast of Bressay. HU5044.
Holm of Heogland *Shet.* ***Island***, small island at S end of Unst, 1m/2km W of Uyea. HU5799.
Holm of Houton *Ork.* ***Island***, small uninhabited island at entrance to Bay of Houton, 2m/3km NE of coast of Hoy across Bring Deeps. HY3103.
Holm of Huip *Ork.* ***Island***, small uninhabited island off N coast of Stronsay across Huip Sound. **81 E3** HY6231.
Holm of Melby *Shet.* ***Island***, small island to N of Melby in Sound of Papa. HU1958.
Holm of Noss *Shet.* ***Coastal feature***, flat-topped turf-covered sheer column of rock off SE coast of Isle of Noss. Height about 160 feet or 50 metres. HU5539.
Holm of Odness *Ork.* ***Island***, islet off E coast of Stronsay on S side of entrance to Mill Bay. HY6926.
Holm of Papa *Ork.* ***Island***, small uninhabited island off E coast of Papa Westray. Large chambered cairn (Historic Scotland) with triple central chamber. **80 D1** HY5051.
Holm of Papa Chambered Cairn *Ork.* ***Historic/prehistoric site***, situated on Holm of Papa, off E coast of Papa Westray. Massive tomb (Historic Scotland) with long narrow chamber and 14 side chambers; rare carvings on walls. **80 D1** HY5051.
Holm of Scockness *Ork.* ***Island***, small uninhabited island at N end of Rousay Sound between Rousay and Egilsay. HY4531.
Holm of Skaw *Shet.* ***Island***, narrowly separated from N coast of Unst. **85 F1** HP6616.
Holm of Tressaness *Shet.* ***Island***, rock off N coast of Fetlar, opposite Tressa Ness. HU6294.
Holm of West Sandwick *Shet.* ***Island***, small uninhabited island 1km offshore of West Sandwick, Yell. HU4389.
Holm Point *W.Isles* ***Coastal feature***, headland on Isle of Lewis, 1m/2km SW of Holm at entrance to Stornoway Harbour. NB4430.
Holm Sound *Ork.* ***Sea feature***, strait dividing S part of Mainland from NE coast of Burray. **79 D3** ND4999.
Holmhead *D. & G.* ***Settlement***, 6m/10km NE of St. John's Town of Dalry. **8 B2** NX7085.
Holmhead *E.Ayr.* ***Locality***, 1km NW of Cumnock across Lugar Water. **15 D3** NS5620.
Holms of Ire *Ork.* ***Island***, two small islands off Whale Point at NW end of Sanday. **81 E2** HY6446.
Holms of Spurness *Ork.* ***Island***, three islets off Spur Ness, SW tip of Sanday. HY6032.
Holms Water *Sc.Bord.* ***River***, rising in mountains 3m/5km NW of Tweedsmuir and flowing NE to Biggar Water, 1m/2km SE of Broughton, and into River Tweed. **16 B3** NT1234.
Holmsgarth *Shet.* ***Village***, on Mainland, adjoining to NW of Lerwick. **83 D3** HU4642.
Holmston *S.Ayr.* ***Suburb***, 1m/2km E of Ayr town centre. **14 B3** NS3520.
Holoman Bay *High.* ***Bay***, on W coast of Raasay, 3m/5km from S end of island. **48 B1** NG5439.
Holoman Island *High.* ***Island***, islet off W coast of Raasay at N end of Holoman Bay. NG5440.
Holy Island *N.Ayr.* ***Island***, sparsely inhabited island lying across entrance to Lamlash Bay, E coast of Arran. Measures 2m/3km N to S and about 1km across. Rises to 1030 feet or 314 metres. Lighthouses on either side of S end of island. **13 F2** NS0632.
Holy Loch *Arg. & B.* ***Sea feature***, inlet in Argyll running up to Ardbeg from between Stone Point and Hunter's Quay, N of Dunoon. **22 C1** NS1780.
Holytown *N.Lan.* Population: 5820. ***Village***, 2m/4km NE of Hamilton. Newhouse Industrial Estate 1km NE. **24 B3** NS7660.
Holywood *D. & G.* ***Village***, 4m/6km NW of Dumfries. **8 D2** NX9480.
Home Law *Sc.Bord.* ***Mountain***, 3m/5km E of Ettrick. Height 1351 feet or 412 metres. **17 E4** NT3215.
Hope *High.* ***River***, in Sutherland district, running N from Loch Hope into Loch Eriboll and then into Atlantic Ocean. NC4762.
Hopehouse *Sc.Bord.* ***Hamlet***, 2m/3km NE of Ettrick. **17 D4** NT2916.
Hopeman *Moray* Population: 1461. ***Village***, fishing village and resort on N coast, 6m/9km W of Lossiemouth. **62 D3** NJ1469.
Hopes Reservoir *E.Loth.* ***Reservoir***, small reservoir on Lammermuir Hills, 4m/6km S of Gifford. **26 C3** NT5462.
Hopes Water *E.Loth.* ***River***, rising in Lammermuir Hills, flowing NE through Hopes Reservoir and then N to join Gifford Water 1m/2km SE of Gifford. **26 C3** NT5567.
Hopetoun House *W.Loth.* ***Historic house***, 17c mansion on S side of Firth of Forth, 2m/4km W of Forth Road Bridge. **25 E2** NT0879.
Horndean *Sc.Bord.* ***Settlement***, 1m/2km N of Norham. **27 F5** NT8949.
Horniehaugh *Angus* ***Settlement***, 2m/3km NE of Dykehead. **42 C3** NO4161.
Hornish *W.Isles* ***Coastal feature***, headland at northernmost point of Fuday. **44 C3** NF7309.
Hornish Point *W.Isles* ***Coastal feature***, headland on N coast of South Uist, 1m/2km NE of Ardivachar Point. **45 F5** NF7547.
Horsanish *W.Isles* ***Coastal feature***, headland on W coast of North Harris, 2m/3km SE of Huisinis. **66 B3** NA9908.
Horse Hope Hill *Sc.Bord.* ***Mountain***, 6m/9km NW of St. Mary's Loch. Height 1938 feet or 591 metres. **16 D2** NT2030.
Horse Island *High.* ***Island***, one of Summer Isles group. Lies 1m/2km W of NW coast of Ross and Cromarty district across Horse Sound. Area about 350 acres or 140 hectares. **70 C4** NC0204.
Horse Island *Shet.* ***Island***, rock island lying off S coast of Mainland, 1m/2km W of Sumburgh Head. HU3807.
Horse Isle *N.Ayr.* ***Island***, with bird sanctuary, lying 1km out from Ardrossan harbour in Firth of Clyde. **22 C5** NS2142.
Horse of Copinsay *Ork.* ***Island***, turf-covered rocky islet 1km NE of Copinsay. HY6202.
Horse Sound *High.* ***Sea feature***, sea passage between Horse Island and NW coast of Ross and Cromarty district, 2m/3km SE of Achiltibuie. **70 C4** NC0304.
Horseley Hill *Sc.Bord.* ***Hill***, with mast and hillfort, 3m/4km SE of Grantshouse. Height 859 feet or 262 metres. **27 F3** NT8362.
Horsleyhill *Sc.Bord.* ***Hamlet***, 4m/6km NE of Hawick. NT5319.
Hos Wick *Shet.* ***Bay***, S facing bay on E coast of Mainland, 12m/20km S of Lerwick. HU4123.
Hoselaw Loch *Sc.Bord.* ***Lake/loch***, small loch 3m/4km N of Kirk Yetholm. NT8031.
Hosh *P. & K.* ***Village***, with distillery at foot of Glen Turret, 1m/2km NW of Crieff. **33 D2** NN8523.
Hosta *W.Isles* ***Settlement***, near NW coast of North Uist, 3m/4km S of Griminis Point. **45 F2** NF7272.
Hoswick *Shet.* ***Village***, at head of Hos Wick. **82 D5** HU4123.
Hott Hill *Sc.Bord.* ***Mountain***, 3m/4km SW of Branxholme. Height 1023 feet or 312 metres. **17 F4** NT4210.
Houbie *Shet.* ***Settlement***, on S coast of Fetlar, at head of Wick of Houbie. **85 F3** HU6290.
Houdston *S.Ayr.* ***Settlement***, adjoining to E of Girvan. NX1998.
Hough Bay *Arg. & B.* ***Bay***, at W end of Tiree, on N side of Rubha Chràiginis. **36 A2** NL9346.
Hough Skerries *Arg. & B.* ***Island***, group of island rocks lying 1m/2km NW of Hough Bay at W end of Tiree. NL9247.
Hougharry *W.Isles Anglicised form of Hogha Gearraidh, qv.*
Hound Hillock *Aber.* ***Mountain***, 4m/6km NW of Fettercairn. Height 1699 feet or 518 metres. **43 E2** NO6279.
Hound Point *Edin.* ***Coastal feature***, headland on S side of Firth of Forth, 1m/2km E of Forth Bridge. **25 F2** NT1579.
Houndslow *Sc.Bord.* ***Hamlet***, 5m/8km W of Greenlaw. **26 D5** NT6247.
Houndwood *Sc.Bord.* ***Settlement***, on Eye Water, 2m/4km SE of Grantshouse. **27 F3** NT8463.
Housa Wick *Shet.* ***Bay***, on S coast of Hascosay. HU5591.
Housay *Shet.* ***Island***, main island in Out Skerries group, NE of Whalsay. Island is connected to Bruray by road bridge. **85 F5** HU6671.
Housay *W.Isles* ***River***, in North Harris rising as Ulladale River in Forest of Harris and flowing NE to head of Loch Resort. NB1017.
House of Dun *Angus* ***Historic house***, 18c Palladian house (National Trust for Scotland) built for David Erskine, 3m/5km NW of Montrose. **43 E4** NO6759.
House of the Binns *W.Loth. Alternative name for The Binns, qv.*
Housebay *Ork.* ***Settlement***, on Bay of Houseby, on S coast of Stronsay. HY6721.
Househill *High.* ***Settlement***, 1km from Nairn across River Nairn. **62 A4** NH8855.
Housetter *Shet.* ***Settlement***, on Mainland, 1km N of Colla Firth. **84 C4** HU3684.
Houss *Shet.* ***Settlement***, on East Burra, 1m/2km S of bridge connection with West Burra. HU3731.
Houss Ness *Shet.* ***Locality***, in S part of East Burra. **82 C5** HU3728.
Houston *Renf.* Population: 5479. ***Village***, 3m/5km NW of Johnstone. **23 F3** NS4066.
Houston Industrial Estate *W.Loth.* ***Locality***, to N of Livingston town centre. NT0569.
Houstry *High.* ***Settlement***, in Caithness district, 3m/5km NW of Latheron. **77 D5** ND1535.
Houstry of Dunn *High.* ***Settlement***, just N of Backlass, 2m/3km W of Watten. **77 E3** ND2054.
Houton *Ork.* ***Settlement***, on Bay of Houton, on S coast of Mainland. **78 C2** HY3104.
Houton Head *Ork.* ***Coastal feature***, headland on Mainland, 2m/3km NE of Scad Head on Hoy across Bring Deeps. To E is Holm of Houton at entrance to Bay of Houton. **78 B2** HY3003.
Howat's Hill *D. & G.* ***Hill***, with Torbeckhill Reservoir to NE, 3m/5km NE of Ecclefechan. Height 810 feet or 247 metres. **9 G3** NY2279.
Howden *W.Loth.* ***Suburb***, residential area to SW of Livingston town centre. NT0567.
Howe *High.* ***Settlement***, in Caithness district, 8m/13km NW of Wick. Ruthers of Howe is settlement 1km N. **77 F2** ND3062.
Howe of Alford *Aber.* ***Valley***, broad section of valley carrying River Don in vicinity of Alford. **54 A3** NJ5716.
Howe of Fife *Fife* ***Valley***, fertile area astride River Eden, between Strathmiglo and Cupar. **34 A3** NO2910.
Howe of Teuchar *Aber.* ***Locality***, 2m/3km S of Cuminestown. **64 C5** NJ7947.
Howe of the Mearns *Aber.* ***Valley***, fertile tract to E of Fettercairn. **43 E3** NO6974.
Howequoy Head *Ork.* ***Coastal feature***, headland on S coast of Mainland and on E shore of Scapa Flow, 1km SW of St. Mary's. HY4600.
Howgate *Midloth.* ***Village***, 1m/2km SE of Penicuik. **25 G4** NT2458.
Howmore *W.Isles Anglicised form of Tobha Mòr, qv.*
Hownam *Sc.Bord.* ***Village***, on Kale Water, 8m/13km E of Jedburgh. **18 B5** NT7719.
Hownam Law *Sc.Bord.* ***Mountain***, 3m/4km SE of Morebattle. Height 1473 feet or 449 metres. **18 B4** NT7921.
Hownam Mains *Sc.Bord.* ***Settlement***, 3m/5km S of Morebattle. **18 B4** NT7720.
Howpasley *Sc.Bord.* ***Hamlet***, 1km SW of Craik. **17 E5** NT3407.
Howwood *Renf.* Population: 1036. ***Village***, 3m/4km SW of Johnstone. **23 F3** NS3960.
Hoxa *Ork.* ***Settlement***, on NW peninsula of South Ronaldsay, 2m/3km W of St. Margaret's Hope. **78 D3** ND4293.
Hoxa Head *Ork.* ***Coastal feature***, headland at W extremity of South Ronaldsay, opposite Flotta across Sound of Hoxa. ND4092.
Hoy *High.* ***Settlement***, 3m/4km SE of Castletown. **77 E2** ND2164.
Hoy *Ork.* ***Island***, second largest of Orkney group of islands after Mainland, lying on W side of Scapa Flow and SW of Mainland across Hoy Sound and Bring Deeps. Island is 14m/22km NW to SE and 6m/10km NE to SW. Rugged, rocky landscape of Old Red Sandstone with steep cliffs to W and stack of Old Man of Hoy, rising to 449 feet or 137 metres, on NW coast. **78 B3** ND2597.
Hoy Sound *Ork.* ***Sea feature***, channel to N of Hoy dividing it from Mainland. HY2307.
Hudderstone *S.Lan.* ***Mountain***, 4m/7km S of Coulter. Height 2053 feet or 626 metres. **16 B3** NT0227.
Hugh Miller's Cottage *High.* ***Other feature of interest***, late 17c thatched cottage (National Trust for Scotland) in Church Street, Cromarty, with restored cottage garden. Birthplace in 1802 of eminent geologist and stonemason, Hugh Miller. Contains fine fossil collection and exhibition of Miller's life and work. **61 G3** NH7867.
Huilish Point *W.Isles* ***Coastal feature***, headland 1km NE of Veilish Point on North Uist. **45 G2** NF8278.
Huip Ness *Ork.* ***Coastal feature***, headland on N of Stronsay, bending round to almost enclose Oyce of Huip. **81 E3** HY6430.
Huip Sound *Ork.* ***Sea feature***, channel between Holm of Huip and Stronsay. **81 E3** HY6231.
Huisinis (Anglicised form: Hushinish.) *W.Isles* ***Settlement***, on W coast of North Harris, on Hushinish Bay. **66 B2** NA9812.
Hule Moss *Sc.Bord.* ***Lake/loch***, tarn on Greenlaw Moor 2m/3km N of Greenlaw. **27 E5** NT7149.
Humbie *E.Loth.* ***Village***, on Humbie Water, 8m/13km SW of Haddington. **26 B3** NT4562.
Humbie Water *E.Loth.* ***River***, flowing N into Birns Water 2m/3km N of Humbie. NT4566.
Hume *Sc.Bord.* ***Village***, 3m/5km S of Greenlaw. Ruins of 13c castle, formerly seat of Earls of Home. **27 E5** NT7041.
Hume Castle *Sc.Bord.* ***Castle***, ruins of 13c high-walled enclosure castle, 3m/5km S of Greenlaw. **27 E5** NT7041.
Humehall *Sc.Bord.* ***Settlement***, 3m/4km S of Greenlaw. **27 E5** NT7141.
Humla *High.* ***Island***, rock in Inner Hebrides lying 3m/5km S of W end of Canna. **47 F4** NG1900.
Huna *High.* ***Settlement***, on N coast of Caithness district, 3m/5km W of Duncansby Head. Ness of Huna is headland to NE. **77 F1** ND3673.
Hunda *Ork.* ***Island***, sparsely populated island of about 56 acres or 23 hectares, off W end of Burray. **78 D3** ND4396.
Hundalee *Sc.Bord.* ***Hamlet***, 1m/2km S of Jedburgh. **18 A5** NT6418.
Hunder Holm *Shet.* ***Island***, small uninhabited island off E coast of Mainland at S end of Lunning Sound and 2m/3km NW of Symbister, Whalsay. HU5163.
Hundleshope Heights *Sc.Bord.* ***Mountain***, 4m/7km S of Peebles. Height 2247 feet or 685 metres. **16 D2** NT2333.
Huney *Shet.* ***Island***, uninhabited island SW of Balta, off E coast of Unst. **85 F2** HP6406.

H

Hunglader *High.* ***Settlement***, near N coast of Skye, 5m/8km N of Uig. Monument to Flora Macdonald 1m/2km NE. **57 G2** NG3871.
Hunspow *High.* ***Settlement***, on N coast, 3m/4km S of Dunnet Head. **77 E1** ND2172.
Hunt Hill *Angus* ***Mountain***, 3m/5km NW of Runtaleave. Height 2408 feet or 734 metres. **42 A2** NO2671.
Hunt Hill *Moray* ***Mountain***, 3m/5km SW of Rothes. Height 1197 feet or 365 metres. **63 E5** NJ2346.
Hunt Law *Sc.Bord.* ***Mountain***, in Lammermuir Hills, 3m/5km SE of Hopes Reservoir. Height 1624 feet or 495 metres. **26 C4** NT5758.
Hunter's Quay *Arg. & B.* ***Locality***, with landing stage, on W side of Firth of Clyde, at entrance to Holy Loch, 2m/3km N of Dunoon, Argyll. **22 C2** NS1879.
Hunterston *N.Ayr.* ***Locality***, on Firth of Clyde, opposite Little Cumbrae. Site of atomic power station. Castle with 16c tower. **22 C4** NS1851.
Hunterston House *N.Ayr.* ***Historic house***, 19c home of Hunter family, with ancient castle of Hunterston in grounds, 2m/3km NW of West Kilbride. **22 C4** NS1951.
Huntford *Sc.Bord.* ***Settlement***, 1m/2km NW of Carter Bar. **11 E1** NT6808.
Huntingtower *P. & K.* ***Village***, 3m/5km NW of Perth. **33 F2** NO0725.
Huntingtower Castle *P. & K.* ***Castle***, Historic Scotland property of unusual construction comprising two 15c round towers only 10 feet or 3 metres apart, united by a late 17c building, 3m/4km NW of Perth. **33 F2** NO0725.
Huntly *Aber.* Population: 4230. ***Small town***, near confluence of Rivers Deveron and Bogie, 24m/39km SE of Elgin and 33m/53km NW of Aberdeen. **64 A5** NJ5339.
Huntly Castle *Aber.* ***Castle***, to N of Huntly beside River Deveron are remains of castle (Historic Scotland), partly 12c but mainly 16c. **64 A5** NJ5339.
Huntlywood *Sc.Bord.* ***Hamlet***, 2m/3km W of Gordon. **26 D5** NT6143.
Hurich *High.* ***River***, in Lochaber district running SW from Lochan Dubh down Glen Hurich to Loch Doilet. NM8167.
Hurlet *Glas.* ***Suburb***, 6m/9km SW of Glasgow city centre in Nitshill district. NS5161.
Hurlford *E.Ayr.* Population: 5396. ***Suburb***, 2m/3km E of Kilmarnock across River Irvine. **14 C2** NS4536.
Hurliness *Ork.* ***Settlement***, on Hoy, 1km E of Melsetter. **78 B4** ND2889.
Husabost *High.* ***Settlement***, on W coast of Loch Dunvegan, 4m/6km NW of Dunvegan, Skye. **57 F4** NG2051.
Hushinish *W.Isles Anglicised form of Huisinis, qv.*
Hushinish Bay (Bàgh Huisinis). *W.Isles* ***Bay***, to S of Huisinis, on W coast of North Harris. **66 B3** NA9911.
Hushinish Glorigs *W.Isles* ***Island***, group of rocks 1m/2km S of Hushinish Point, North Harris. NA9809.
Hushinish Point *W.Isles* ***Coastal feature***, headland on W side of Hushinish Bay, North Harris, and 1m/2km S of Scarp. **66 B2** NA9911.
Husival Mòr *W.Isles* ***Mountain***, near W coast of North Harris, 2m/3km E of Huisinis. Height 1604 feet or 489 metres. **66 C2** NB0211.
Huskeiran *W.Isles* ***Island***, small group of islets 2m/3km NW of Heisker Islands group, to W of North Uist. **45 D3** NF5764.
Hutchesontown *Glas.* ***Suburb***, 1m/2km S of Glasgow city centre. NS5963.
Hutton *D. & G.* ***Locality***, with remains of Hutton Mote, 6m/10km NE of Lockerbie. NY1689.
Hutton *Sc.Bord.* ***Village***, 6m/9km W of Berwick-upon-Tweed. **27 G4** NT9053.
Hutton Castle (Also known as Hutton Hall.) *Sc.Bord.* ***Historic house***, 16c building, considerably altered, 1m/2km NW of Hutton. NT8854.
Hutton Hall *Sc.Bord. Alternative name for Hutton Castle, qv.*
Huxter *Shet.* ***Settlement***, 1km N of Hellister, on E side of Weisdale Voe, Mainland. **82 C2** HU3950.
Huxter *Shet.* ***Settlement***, to N of Loch of Huxter, 1m/2km W of Symbister, Whalsay. **83 E1** HU5662.
Hydro-Electric Visitor Centre and Fish Ladder *P. & K.* ***Other feature of interest***, in Pitlochry. Exhibition on development of hydro-electric power in Scotland. Fish ladder with viewing point between River Tummel and Loch Faskally. **41 E4** NN9457.
Hyndford Bridge *S.Lan.* ***Bridge***, road bridge over River Clyde 3m/4km SE of Lanark. **24 D5** NS9141.
Hyndland *Glas.* ***Suburb***, 3m/4km NW of Glasgow city centre, in Partick district. NS5567.
Hyndlee *Sc.Bord.* ***Settlement***, in Wauchope Forest area of Cheviot Hills, 3m/4km S of Hobkirk. **17 G5** NT5806.
Hynish *Arg. & B.* ***Settlement***, at SW end of Hynish Bay, Tiree. **36 A3** NL9839.
Hynish Bay *Arg. & B.* ***Bay***, wide bay on S coast of Tiree. **36 B2** NM0042.
Hyskeir *High. Alternative name for Oigh-sgeir, qv.*
Hythie *Aber.* ***Settlement***, 5m/7km SE of Strichen. **65 F4** NK0051.
Hyvots Bank *Edin.* ***Suburb***, 4m/7km SE of Edinburgh city centre. NT2868.

I

Ianstown *Moray* ***Suburb***, E district of Buckie, on N coast. **63 G3** NJ4366.
Iarsiadar *W.Isles Gaelic form of Earshader, qv.*
Ibrox *Glas.* ***Suburb***, 2m/3km W of Glasgow city centre in Govan district. NS5564.
Idoch Water *Aber.* ***River***, running SW through Cuminestown and turning NW 2m/3km SE of Turriff, then flowing NW into River Deveron on W side of town. **64 C5** NJ7150.
Idrigil *High.* ***Settlement***, 1km W of Uig, Skye. **57 G3** NG3863.
Idrigill Point *High.* ***Coastal feature***, headland on Skye at NW entrance to Loch Bracadale. **47 F1** NG2536.
Idvies *Angus* ***Hamlet***, 1km S of Letham. **42 D5** NO5347.
Imachar *N.Ayr.* ***Locality***, on W side of Arran, 2m/4km S of Pirnmill. **21 G5** NR8640.
Imachar Point *N.Ayr.* ***Coastal feature***, headland to W of Imachar on Arran, 8m/12km SW of Lochranza. NR8640.
Immeroin *Stir.* ***Settlement***, on E side of Glen Buckie, 2m/3km S of Balqhidder. **32 A3** NN5317.
Inch *Aber.* ***Settlement***, 2m/4km SW of Fettercairn. **43 E2** NO6271.
Inch *Edin.* ***Suburb***, 3m/4km SE of Edinburgh city centre. NT2770.
Inch Buie *Stir.* ***Island***, lower of two islands in River Dochart at Killin. Former burial place of Clan MacNab. NN5732.
Inch Garvie *Edin.* ***Island***, islet with lighthouse in Firth of Forth beneath Forth Railway Bridge. **25 F2** NT1379.
Inch Kenneth *Arg. & B.* ***Island***, of about 200 acres or 80 hectares at entrance to Loch na Keal, W coast of Mull. Remains of 12c chapel (Historic Scotland). **28 D1** NM4335.
Inch Kenneth Chapel *Arg. & B.* ***Ecclesiastical building***, chapel (Historic Scotland), on Inch Kenneth, 1m/2km NW of Balnahard off W coast of Mull. Medieval monuments in graveyard. **28 D1** NM4335.
Inch Talla *Stir.* ***Island***, islet in Lake of Menteith, with remains of medieval castle. NN5700.
Inchaffray Abbey *P. & K.* ***Ecclesiastical building***, scant remains of early 13c abbey, 6m/9km E of Crieff. **33 E2** NN9522.
Inchbae Forest *High.* ***Open space***, deer forest in Ross and Cromarty district E of Loch Vaich. Inchbae Lodge at junction of River Glascarnoch and Strath Rannoch at S end of forest. **60 C2** NH3778.
Inchbae Lodge *High.* ***Settlement***, at junction of River Glascarnoch and Strath Rannoch, at S end of Inchbae Forest. NH3969.
Inchbare *Angus* ***Settlement***, on West Water, 2m/3km S of Edzell. **43 E3** NO6065.
Inchberry *Moray* ***Settlement***, 7m/12km SE of Elgin. **63 F4** NJ3155.
Inchbraoch (Also known as Inchbrayock or Rossie Island.) *Angus* ***Locality***, on S side of Montrose Basin, connected by road and railway bridges to Montrose. **43 F4** NO7056.
Inchbrayock *Angus Alternative name for Inchbraoch, qv.*
Inchcailleach *Stir. Alternative spelling of Inchcailloch, qv.*
Inchcailleoch *Stir. Alternative spelling of Inchcailloch, qv.*
Inchcailliach *Stir. Alternative spelling of Inchcailloch, qv.*
Inchcailloch *Stir.* ***Island***, off E shore of Loch Lomond opposite Balmaha. Part of nature reserve comprising also Clairinch and Torrinch. Other spellings include Inchcailleach, Inchcailleoch, and Inchcailliach. **31 G5** NS4090.
Inchcape Rock (Also known as Bell Rock.) *Angus* ***Coastal feature***, reef with lighthouse off E coast, 11m/18km SE of Arbroath. **35 F2** NO7627.
Inchcolm *Fife* ***Island***, in Firth of Forth 1m/2km E of Dalgety Bay. Ruins of medieval abbey (Historic Scotland) founded in 12c including 13c octagonal chapter house. Best preserved group of monastic buildings in Scotland. **25 F1** NT1882.
Inchconnachan *Arg. & B.* ***Island***, in Loch Lomond 1m/2km SE of Luss. **31 F5** NS3792.
Inchcruin *Stir.* ***Island***, in Loch Lomond 2m/3km W of Balmaha. **31 F5** NS3891.
Inchfad *Stir.* ***Island***, in Loch Lomond 1m/2km W of Balmaha. **31 G5** NS3990.
Inchgalbraith *Arg. & B.* ***Island***, islet with remains of castle, in Loch Lomond 1km NE of Rossdhu House. NS3690.
Inchgrundle *Angus* ***Settlement***, at SW end of Loch Lee. **42 C2** NO4179.
Inchindown *High.* ***Settlement***, 3m/5km N of Invergordon. **61 F2** NH6974.
Inchinnan *Renf.* Population: 1815. ***Village***, 3m/5km N of Paisley. **23 F3** NS4868.
Inchkeith *Fife* ***Island***, narrow island, just over 1km long from N to S, in Firth of Forth 3m/4km SE of Kinghorn. Lighthouse near N end. **25 G1** NT2982.
Inchkeith Hill *Sc.Bord.* ***Mountain***, 3m/5km NW of Lauder. Height 1197 feet or 365 metres. **26 B5** NT4848.
Inchkinloch *High.* ***Settlement***, 1km W of S end of Loch Loyal. **75 F4** NC6044.
Inchlaggan *High.* ***Locality***, in Glen Garry, Lochaber district, 8m/13km W of Invergarry. **50 A4** NH1701.
Inchlonaig *Arg. & B.* ***Island***, in Loch Lomond opposite Luss. **31 F5** NS3893.
Inchlumpie *High.* ***Settlement***, 5m/8km NW of Alness. **61 E2** NH5875.
Inchmahome *Stir.* ***Island***, in Lake of Menteith. Remains of 13c priory (Historic Scotland). NN5700.
Inchmahome Priory *Stir.* ***Ecclesiastical building***, remains of Augustinian monastery (Historic Scotland), founded 1238, on Inchmahome in Lake of Menteith. Mary, Queen of Scots lay hidden here, 1547-8. **32 A4** NN5700.
Inchmarlo *Aber.* ***Settlement***, 2m/3km W of Banchory, on N side of River Dee. **54 B5** NO6796.
Inchmarnock *Arg. & B.* ***Island***, sparsely populated low-lying island 1m/2km W of Bute off St. Ninian's Point. Measures about 2m/3km N to S and about 1km across. **22 B4** NS0259.
Inchmickery *Edin.* ***Island***, islet in Firth of Forth, 3m/4km NW of Granton Harbour. **25 G1** NT2080.
Inchmoan *Arg. & B.* ***Island***, in Loch Lomond, 1m/2km NE of Rossdhu House. **31 F5** NS3790.
Inchmurrin *W.Dun.* ***Island***, largest island in Loch Lomond, 3m/4km N of Balloch. Ruins of old Lennox Castle at SW end of island. **23 E1** NS3887.
Inchnabobart *Aber.* ***Settlement***, 2m/3km N of Spittal of Glenmuick, in Glen Muick. **42 B1** NO3087.
Inchnacardoch Forest *High.* ***Open space***, deer forest in Inverness district W of Fort Augustus. NH3409.
Inchnacardoch Hotel *High.* ***Other building***, adjoining to Fort Augustus, at SW end of Loch Ness. **50 C3** NH3710.
Inchnadamph *High.* ***Village***, in Sutherland district, at head of Loch Assynt. Extensive cave system in valley of River Traligill to SE. **71 E2** NC2521.
Inchnadamph Forest *High.* ***Open space***, deer forest to E of Inchnadamph. **71 E2** NC2521.
Inchock *Angus* ***Settlement***, 1m/2km SE of Inverkeilor. **43 E5** NO6848.
Inchrory *Moray* ***Settlement***, on E bank of River Avon, 7m/11km S of Tomintoul. **53 D4** NJ1708.
Inchtavannach *Arg. & B.* ***Island***, close to W shore of Loch Lomond between Luss and Rossdhu House. **31 F5** NS3691.
Inchture *P. & K.* ***Village***, 8m/12km W of Dundee. **34 A2** NO2828.
Inchtuthill *P. & K.* ***Historic/prehistoric site***, site of Roman fortress on N side of River Tay, 1m/2km SE of Spittalfield, built about AD 83 but soon abandoned. NO1239.
Inchvuilt *High.* ***Locality***, on River Farrar, in Inverness district, nearly 2m/3km E of dam of Loch Monar. **50 B1** NH2238.
Inchyra *P. & K.* ***Settlement***, on N bank of River Tay, 5m/8km E of Perth. **33 G3** NO1820.
Inerval *Arg. & B.* ***Settlement***, on The Oa, Islay, 3m/5km SW of Port Ellen. **20 B5** NR3241.
Inga Ness *Ork.* ***Coastal feature***, headland on W coast of Westray, 4m/7km SE of Noup Head. **80 C2** HY4143.
Ingale Skerry *Ork.* ***Island***, rock island off S coast of Stronsay, 1m/2km SW of Lamb Head and 1m/2km SE of Tor Ness across Ingale Sound. **81 E5** HY6719.
Ingale Sound *Ork.* ***Sea feature***, channel between Ingale Skerry and S coast of Stronsay. HY6720.
Inganess Bay *Ork.* ***Bay***, large bay on N coast of Mainland, 2m/3km E of Kirkwall. Kirkwall Airport at head of bay. **80 C5** HY4808.
Inglismaldie Forest *Aber.* ***Forest/woodland***, midway between Edzell and Marykirk. **43 E3** NO6467.
Ingliston *Edin.* ***Locality***, site of Royal Highland Showground, 7m/11km W of Edinburgh and 1km SW of Edinburgh Airport. Motor-racing circuit. NT1372.
Ingliston Motor Racing Ciruit *Edin.* ***Motor racing circuit***, 1km NE of Ratho and 7m/11km W of Edinburgh. **25 F2** NT1473.
Ingstag *High. Alternative spelling of Inkstack, qv.*
Inishail (Sometimes spelled Innishail.) *Arg. & B.* ***Island***, in Loch Awe at entrance to arm of loch running NW to Pass of Brander in Argyll. Ruined church of St. Pindoca. **30 C2** NN1024.
Inistrynich *Arg. & B.* ***Settlement***, on small peninsula, extending into N part of Loch Awe, 4m/6km SW of Dalmally. **30 D2** NN1023.
Inkhorn *Aber.* ***Locality***, comprises Milton of Inkhorn and Mains of Inkhorn, 1m/2km S of Auchnagatt. **55 E1** NJ9239.
Inkstack (Also spelled Ingstag.) *High.* ***Settlement***, near N coast of Caithness district, 4m/7km E of Castletown. **77 E1** ND2570.
Innellan *Arg. & B.* Population: 1142. ***Village***, and resort in Argyll, on W shore of Firth of Clyde, 4m/7km S of Dunoon. **22 C3** NS1470.
Inner Brigurd Point *N.Ayr.* ***Coastal feature***, small headland 1km NW of Hunterston. **22 C4** NS1852.
Inner Hebrides ***Island***, group of islands off W coast of Scotland, the chief islands being Skye (with Raasay), Canna, Rum, Eigg, Muck, Coll, Tiree, Mull (with Iona), Colonsay, Jura and Islay. NM3950.

Inner Holm *Ork.* ***Island***, islet on E side of Stromness Harbour, Mainland, to N of Outer Holm. HY2508.
Inner Score *Shet.* ***Island***, small uninhabited island between N end of Bressay and Outer Score. HU5145.
Inner Sound *High.* ***Sea feature***, strait dividing N coast of Scottish mainland from Island of Stroma. **77 F1** ND3576.
Inner Sound *High.* ***Sea feature***, sea channel between W coast of Ross and Cromarty district and islands of Raasay and Rona. Width from 4m/7km to 7m/11km. **58 C5** NG6441.
Innerdouny Hill *P. & K.* ***Mountain***, in Ochil Hills, 3m/5km NW of Carnbo. Height 1630 feet or 497 metres. **33 F4** NO0307.
Innerdownie *P. & K.* ***Mountain***, in Ochil Hills, 3m/5km N of Dollar. Height 2004 feet or 611 metres. **33 E4** NN9603.
Innergellie *Fife* ***Settlement***, to N of Kilrenny. **35 D4** NO5705.
Innerleithen *Sc.Bord.* Population: 2515. ***Small town***, at confluence of Leithen Water and River Tweed, 6m/9km SE of Peebles. Site of Roman camp on SW side. Robert Smail's Printing Works (National Trust for Scotland) in High Street is restored printing works using machinery and methods of early 20c. **17 E2** NT3336.
Innerleven *Fife* ***Locality***, docks area in Methil, at mouth of River Leven. **34 B4** NO3700.
Innermessan *D. & G.* ***Settlement***, on E side of Loch Ryan, 2m/3km NE of Stranraer. **6 B4** NX0863.
Innerpeffray *P. & K.* ***Settlement***, 3m/5km SE of Crieff. Castle is ruined 17c tower house. Innerpeffray Chapel (Historic Scotland) is rectangular collegiate church founded 1508, still retaining its altar. Several Roman sites in vicinity. NN9018.
Innerpeffray Library *P. & K.* ***Other feature of interest***, oldest public lending library in Scotland, founded in 1680 and housed in 18c building. **33 E3** NN9018.
Innertown *Ork.* ***Locality***, on Mainland, just W of Stromness. HY2409.
Innerwell Port *D. & G.* ***Bay***, small bay 2m/3km N of Garlieston, on W side of Wigtown Bay. **3 E2** NX4849.
Innerwick *E.Loth.* ***Village***, 4m/6km SE of Dunbar. **27 E2** NT7273.
Innerwick *P. & K.* ***Settlement***, in Glen Lyon, 1km NE of Bridge of Balgie. **40 A5** NN5847.
Innes Canal *Moray* ***Canal***, running from 3m/4km W of Garmouth, then skirting disused airfield, before running parallel to River Lossie and joining river 1m/2km SE of Lossiemouth. **63 E3** NJ2569.
Innes House *Moray* ***Garden***, formal walled garden laid out in 1910 with wide borders, yew hedges and ponds set in large park with many unusual trees, 4m/6km W of Garmouth. House is 17c with Edwardian additions. **63 E3** NJ2765.
Innes Links *Moray* ***Coastal feature***, forested coastal area, 3m/5km NW of Garmouth. **63 E3** NJ2867.
Inninbeg *High.* ***Settlement***, on Ardtornish Bay, 1km N of Ardtornish Point, Lochaber district. **37 G5** NM6943.
Inninmore Bay *High.* ***Bay***, on Sound of Mull, extending NW from Rubha and Ridire, Lochaber district. **37 G5** NM7241.
Innis Bheag *High.* ***Island***, sandy island 3m/4km W of Portmahomack. **62 A1** NH8684.
Innis Chonain *Arg. & B.* ***Island***, off W shore of Loch Awe in Argyll, 1m/2km SW of Lochawe. Connected to shore by bridge. **30 D2** NN1025.
Innis Chonnell *Arg. & B.* ***Island***, islet near E shore of Loch Awe in Argyll, opposite Dalavich. Ruins of Ardchonnell Castle, 15c stronghold of the Campbells. NM9711.
Innis Mhòr *High.* ***Island***, sandy island at mouth of Dornoch Firth, 5m/8km NE of Tain. **62 A1** NH8586.
Innis Shearraich *Arg. & B.* ***Island***, islet off E shore of Loch Awe in Argyll, opposite Portinnisherrich. Stepping-stones give access at low water. 13c chapel. NM9711.
Innishail *Arg. & B.* *Occasional spelling of Inishail, qv.*
Insch *Aber.* Population: 1541. ***Village***, 10m/16km NW of Inverurie. Picardy Stone (Historic Scotland), 2m/3km NW. **54 B2** NJ6328.
Insh *High.* ***Village***, in Badenoch and Strathspey district, 4m/6km E of Kingussie. **52 A4** NH8101.
Insh Island *Arg. & B.* ***Island***, uninhabited island in Firth of Lorn, 1m/2km W of Seil, from which it is separated by Sound of Insh. **29 G3** NM7319.
Inshegra *High.* ***Settlement***, on N side of Loch Inchard, W coast of Sutherland district. NC2455.
Inshore *High.* ***Settlement***, overlooking Loch Inshore, 2m/3km NW of Achiemore, Sutherland district. **74 C2** NC3269.
Inshriach Forest *High.* ***Forest/woodland***, to NE of Insh. **52 A4** NH8101.
Inver *Aber.* ***Settlement***, 1m/2km SW of Balmoral Castle, in River Dee valley. **53 E5** NO2293.
Inver *Arg. & B.* ***Settlement***, on N shore of Loch Creran, 1m/2km E of Creagan. **38 B5** NM9945.
Inver *High.* ***River***, in Sutherland district, flowing W from Loch Assynt to Loch Inver. NC0923.
Inver *High.* ***Settlement***, to NE of Dunbeath. **77 D5** ND1630.
Inver *High.* ***Village***, in Ross and Cromarty district, on S shore of Dornoch Firth, 5m/8km E of Tain. **62 A1** NH8682.
Inver *P. & K.* ***Hamlet***, 1km SW of Dunkeld, over River Tay. **41 F5** NO0142.
Inver Bay *High.* ***Sea feature***, inlet on N side of Inver. **62 A1** NH8682.
Inver Dalavil *High.* ***Bay***, on W coast of Sleat peninsula, Skye, 4m/6km N of Point of Sleat. **48 B4** NG5705.
Inver Mallie *High.* ***Settlement***, at mouth of River Mallie on S shore of Loch Arkaig, 4m/6km NW of Gairlochy. **38 D1** NN1388.
Inverailort *High.* ***Settlement***, with jetty, at head of Loch Ailort, Lochaber district. **37 G1** NM7681.
Inveralligin (Alligin). *High.* ***Village***, on N shore of Upper Loch Torridon, Ross and Cromarty district. **59 E4** NG8457.
Inverallochy *Aber.* Population: 1410. ***Village***, on NE coast, 3m/5km E of Fraserburgh. **65 F3** NK0465.
Inveran *High.* ***Locality***, location of power station (Shin Hydro-Electricity Scheme) at confluence of Rivers Shin and Oykel in Sutherland district, 4m/6km NW of Bonar Bridge. **72 A5** NH5797.
Inveraray *Arg. & B.* ***Small town***, in Argyll on W shore of Loch Fyne, 6m/10km SW of head of loch and 19m/31km NE of Lochgilphead. **30 C4** NN0908.
Inveraray Castle *Arg. & B.* ***Castle***, to N of Inveraray, seat of the Dukes of Argyll, dates mainly from 18c; damaged by fire in 1975. **30 C4** NN0908.
Inveraray Jail *Arg. & B.* ***Other feature of interest***, in Inveraray, on NW shore of Loch Fyne. An imaginative exhibition re-creating 19c prison and courtroom life. **30 C4** NN0908.
Inverardoch Mains *Stir.* ***Settlement***, 1km SE of Doune. **32 C4** NN7300.
Inverardran *Stir.* ***Settlement***, 1km E of Crianlarich. **31 F2** NN3924.
Inverarish *High.* ***Settlement***, on SW coast of Raasay, 2m/3km NW of Eyre Point. **48 B1** NG5635.
Inverarity *Angus* ***Settlement***, 4m/6km S of Forfar. **42 C5** NO4544.
Inverarnan *Stir.* ***Settlement***, on River Falloch, 2m/3km N of Ardlui, at head of Loch Lomond. **31 F3** NN3118.
Inverasdale *High.* ***Locality***, on W side of Loch Ewe, W coast of Ross and Cromarty district, 4m/7km NW of Poolewe. **59 E1** NG8186.
Inverbain *High.* ***Settlement***, on W coast of Loch Shieldaig, 7m/11km W of Torridon, Ross and Cromarty district. **59 D4** NG7854.
Inverbeg *Arg. & B.* ***Locality***, on W side of Loch Lomond, 3m/5km N of Luss. Ferry for pedestrians to Rowardennan. **31 F5** NS3497.
Inverbervie *Aber.* Population: 1879. ***Small town***, at mouth of Bervie Water, on E coast, 9m/14km S of Stonehaven. A royal burgh since 1342. **43 G2** NO8372.
Inverboyndie *Aber.* ***Locality***, 1m/2km W of Banff. NJ6664.
Inverbroom *High.* ***Settlement***, in valley of River Broom, 1m/2km S of head of Loch Broom. **60 A1** NH1883.
Inverbrough *High.* ***Settlement***, 1m/2km NE of Tomatin. **52 A2** NH8129.
Invercassley *High.* ***Settlement***, 1km N of confluence of River Cassley and River Oykel. **71 G4** NC4702.
Invercauld Bridge *Aber.* ***Historic/prehistoric site***, on River Dee, 2m/3km E of Braemar. Built by Prince Albert when old bridge, dating from 1752, became royal property and road through Balmoral estate was closed. **53 D5** NO1891.
Invercauld Forest *Aber.* ***Open space***, area of mountain and forest on N side of River Dee, opposite Braemar. **52 D5** NO1395.
Inverchaolain *Arg. & B.* ***Locality***, on E shore of Loch Striven, Argyll, 4m/7km N of Ardyne Point. **22 B2** NS0975.
Invercharnan *High.* ***Settlement***, in Glen Etive, 3m/4km NE of head of Loch Etive. **38 D5** NN1448.
Inverchorachan *Arg. & B.* ***Settlement***, in Glen Fyne, 4m/7km NE of head of Loch Fyne. **31 E3** NN2217.
Inverchoran *High.* ***Settlement***, in valley of River Meig, 8m/12km SE of Achnasheen. **60 B4** NH2550.
Invercloy *N.Ayr.* *Former name of Brodick, qv.*
Invercreran *Arg. & B.* ***Settlement***, 1m/2km NE of head of Loch Creran. **38 C5** NN0146.
Inverdruie *High.* ***Hamlet***, near mouth of River Druie, in Badenoch and Strathspey district, 1m/2km SE of Aviemore. **52 B3** NH9010.
Inverebrie *Aber.* ***Settlement***, on W side of Ebrie Burn, 3m/5km NW of Ellon. **55 E1** NJ9233.
Invereen *High.* ***Settlement***, 3m/5km SE of Moy. **52 A1** NH7931.
Invererne *Moray* ***Settlement***, 1m/2km N of Forres. **62 C3** NJ0360.
Inveresk *E.Loth.* ***Suburb***, to S of Musselburgh, on site of Roman station. **26 A2** NT3472.
Inveresk Lodge Garden *E.Loth.* ***Garden***, National Trust for Scotland property on E bank of River Esk at Inveresk, 1km S of Musselburgh. Specialises in plants for small gardens. **26 A2** NT3471.
Inverewe *High.* *See Poolewe.*
Inverewe Gardens *High.* ***Garden***, exotic collection of plants in themed gardens designed by Osgood Mackenzie in 19c on his peninsula estate, 1km N of Poolewe, Ross and Cromarty district. Gardens thrived due to temperate local climate resulting from Gulf Stream. After Mackenzie's death in 1922, National Trust for Scotland took over ownership. Features include rhododendrons, Victorian and walled gardens, giant eucalypts and visitor centre. **59 E1** NG8581.
Inverey *Aber.* ***Settlement***, at foot of Glen Ey, 4m/7km W of Braemar. **41 F1** NO0889.
Inverfarigaig *High.* ***Settlement***, on SE shore of Loch Ness, at mouth of River Farigaig, 2m/4km NE of Foyers, Inverness district. **51 E2** NH5123.
Invergarry *High.* ***Village***, at foot of Glen Garry, in Lochaber district. **50 C4** NH3001.
Invergarry Castle *High.* ***Castle***, 17c L-plan ruin on shore of Loch Oich, to SE of Invergarry. **50 C4** NH3001.
Invergelder *Aber.* ***Settlement***, 1m/2km SW of Balmoral Castle. **53 E5** NO2393.
Invergeldie *P. & K.* ***Settlement***, in Glen Lednock, 4m/6km NW of Comrie. **32 C2** NN7427.
Invergeldie Burn *P. & K.* ***River***, stream flowing SW into River Lednock, 3m/5km NW of Comrie. **32 C2** NN7326.
Invergloy *High.* ***Locality***, in Lochaber district, at mouth of River Gloy, on SE shore of Loch Lochy. **39 E1** NN2288.
Invergordon *High.* Population: 3929. ***Small town***, port and former naval base on N shore of Cromarty Firth, Ross and Cromarty district, 11m/18km NE of Dingwall. Development in connection with North Sea oil. **61 G3** NH7068.
Invergowrie *P. & K.* ***Suburb***, 4m/6km W of Dundee city centre, on Firth of Tay. **34 B1** NO3430.
Inverguseran *High.* ***Locality***, on NW coast of Knoydart, Lochaber district, at foot of Glen Guseran. **48 D4** NG7407.
Inverhadden *P. & K.* ***Settlement***, 1km SE of Kinloch Rannoch. **40 B4** NN6757.
Inverhadden Burn *P. & K.* ***River***, flowing N into Dunalastair Water, 1m/2km E of Kinloch Rannoch. NN6758.
Inverharroch *Moray* ***Settlement***, 1km SE of Bridgend. **53 F1** NJ3831.
Inverherive *Stir.* ***Settlement***, in Strath Fillan, 1m/2km NW of Crianlarich. **31 F2** NN3626.
Inverhope *High.* ***Settlement***, at mouth of River Hope, 4m/7km SW of Whiten Head. **75 D2** NC4761.
Inverie *High.* ***River***, flowing W into Inverie Bay 1m/2km SE of Inverie village, Lochaber district. **49 E5** NM7798.
Inverie *High.* ***Village***, in Lochaber district, on S side of Knoydart. Village is situated on Inverie Bay, on N side of Loch Nevis. Inverie River flows W into bay 1m/2km SE of village. **49 D4** NG7600.
Inverie Bay *High.* ***Bay***, on S coast of Knoydart peninsula, on N side of Loch Nevis. **49 D5** NG7600.
Inverinan *Arg. & B.* ***Settlement***, on W side of Loch Awe, in Argyll, surrounded by Inverinan Forest. **30 B3** NM9917.
Inverinan Forest *Arg. & B.* ***Forest/woodland***, surrounding locality of Inverinan on W side of Loch Awe in Argyll and to N of Inverliever Forest. Information centre and nature trails. **30 B3** NM9917.
Inverinate *High.* ***Village***, Forestry Commission village surrounded by woodland on E bank of Loch Duich, Skye and Lochalsh district, 2m/3km from head of loch. **49 F2** NG9122.
Inverkeilor *Angus* ***Village***, 6m/9km N of Arbroath. **43 E5** NO6649.
Inverkeithing *Fife* Population: 6001. ***Small town***, on Inverkeithing Bay on N side of Firth of Forth, 4m/6km SE of Dunfermline. Ancient royal burgh with charter dating from 1165. **25 F1** NT1383.
Inverkeithing Bay *Fife* ***Bay***, on N side of Firth of Forth, 4m/6km SE of Dunfermline. **25 F1** NT1383.
Inverkeithny *Aber.* ***Village***, on Burn of Forgue, near its confluence with River Deveron, 4m/6km S of Aberchirder. **64 B5** NJ6246.
Inverkip *Inclyde* Population: 1258. ***Village***, on Firth of Clyde, 5m/8km SW of Greenock. **22 D2** NS2072.
Inverkirkaig *High.* ***Hamlet***, in Sutherland district, at head of Loch Kirkaig on W coast, 2m/3km SW of Lochinver. **70 C3** NC0719.
Inverlael *High.* ***Settlement***, at head of Loch Broom, Ross and Cromarty district. **60 A1** NH1885.
Inverlael Forest *High.* ***Open space***, deer forest to E of Inverlael. **60 A1** NH1886.
Inverlauren *Arg. & B.* ***Settlement***, 3m/4km NE of Helensburgh. **23 E1** NS3185.
Inverleith *Edin.* ***Suburb***, 1m/2km NW of Edinburgh city centre. Contains Royal Botanic Garden. NT2475.
Inverliever *Arg. & B.* ***Settlement***, 2m/3km NE of Ford, on N shore of Loch Awe. **30 A4** NM8905.
Inverliever Forest *Arg. & B.* ***Forest/woodland***, on W side of Loch Awe in Argyll, to S of Inverinan Forest and Dalavich. Information centre and nature trails. **30 B4** NM9409.

I

Inverliver *Arg. & B.* ***Settlement***, on Inverliver Bay, E side of Loch Etive, Argyll, 4m/6km NE of Bonawe. Inverliver Bay is small bay on shore of Loch Etive to N. **30 C1** NN0635.
Inverlochlarig *Stir.* ***Settlement***, in valley of River Larig, 6m/9km SE of Crianlarich. **31 G3** NN4317.
Inverlochy *Arg. & B.* ***Settlement***, 2m/3km E of Dalmally. **31 D2** NN1927.
Inverlochy *High.* ***Locality***, at mouth of River Lochy in Lochaber district, 1m/2km NE of Fort William. Well-preserved 13c square castle with round towers (Historic Scotland) near mouth of river; present-day castle 1m/2km NE. NN1174.
Inverlussa *Arg. & B.* ***Locality***, at mouth of Lussa River, on E coast of Jura. **21 E1** NR6486.
Invermark Castle *Angus* ***Castle***, ruined 16c-17c castle, former residence of Stirlings, at foot of Glen Lee, 3m/5km W of Tarfside. NO4480.
Invermay *P. & K.* ***Settlement***, on S bank of Water of May, 3m/5km NE of Dunning. **33 F3** NO0616.
Invermoriston *High.* ***Village***, in Inverness district, on River Moriston, 1km above mouth of river. **50 D3** NH4216.
Invermoriston Forest *High.* ***Open space***, deer forest to N of Invermoriston. NH4216.
Invernaver *High.* ***Settlement***, near N coast of Caithness district, 1m/2km S of Bettyhill. **75 G2** NC7060.
Inverneil *Arg. & B.* ***Settlement***, on W side of Loch Fyne, 3m/4km S of Ardrishaig. **21 G1** NR8481.
Inverness *High.* Population: 41,234. ***Town***, at mouth of River Ness at entrance to Beauly Firth, 105m/169km NW of Aberdeen and 113m/181km NW of Edinburgh. Administrative, commercial and tourist centre. Caledonian Canal passes to W of town. Inverness Museum and Art Gallery depicts history of Highlands. University of the Highlands and Islands. Airport at locality of Dalcross, 7m/11km NE of town. **61 F5** NH6645.
Inverness Airport (Formerly known as Dalcross Airport.) *High.* ***Airport/airfield***, airport on E side of Inner Moray Firth, 8m/13km NE of Inverness. **61 G4** NH7752.
Inverness Museum and Art Gallery *High.* ***Other feature of interest***, in centre of Inverness, with exhibitions of archaeology, natural history and culture of the Highlands. **61 F5** NH6644.
Invernettie *Aber.* ***Hamlet***, 1m/2km S of Peterhead. **65 G5** NK1244.
Invernoaden *Arg. & B.* ***Settlement***, 1km E of Glenbranter. **30 D5** NS1297.
Inveroran Hotel *Arg. & B.* ***Other building***, 2m/3km NW of Bridge of Orchy. **39 E5** NN2741.
Inverorar *Arg. & B.* ***Locality***, at SW corner of Loch Tulla in Argyll. NN2741.
Inverpolly Forest *High.* ***Open space***, upland area, part of Inverpolly National Nature Reserve near NW coast of Ross and Cromarty district, 7m/11km S of Lochinver. **70 C3** NC0912.
Inverpolly National Nature Reserve *High.* ***Nature reserve***, 7m/11km S of Shieldaig, a wilderness of mountains, moorland, woodland, lochs and bogs. Over 100 bird species recorded. **71 D3** NC1910.
Inverquharity *Angus* ***Settlement***, 3m/4km N of Kirriemuir. **42 C4** NO4057.
Inverquhomery *Aber.* ***Settlement***, 1m/2km SW of Longside. **65 F5** NK0246.
Inverroy *High.* ***Settlement***, in Lochaber district, between Roybridge and Spean Bridge. **39 E1** NN2581.
Inversanda *High.* ***Settlement***, on W side of Loch Linnhe in Lochaber district, at foot of Glen Tarbert. **38 B4** NM9359.
Inversanda Bay *High.* ***Bay***, to E of Inversanda, at mouth of River Tarbert, on Loch Linnhe. **38 B4** NM9359.
Inverscaddle Bay *High.* ***Bay***, containing marsh, sand and shingle on W shore of Loch Linnhe, Lochaber district, at mouth of River Scaddle. **38 C3** NN0268.
Invershiel *High.* ***Settlement***, in Skye and Lochalsh district, at head of Loch Duich. **49 F3** NG9319.
Invershin *High.* ***Locality***, with railway station, in Sutherland district, at confluence of Rivers Oykel and Shin, 4m/6km NW of Bonar Bridge. **72 A5** NH5796.
Invershore *High.* ***Settlement***, on E coast of Caithness district, 1km SW of Lybster. ND2434.
Inversnaid *Stir.* ***Settlement***, on E shore of Loch Lomond, opposite Inveruglas. Garrison of Inversnaid, to NE up glen towards Loch Arklet, is farm incorporating remains of fort built in 1713 as deterrent to clan Macgregor. NN3308.
Inversnaid Hotel *Stir.* ***Other building***, on E shore of Loch Lomond, 3m/5km NE of Tarbet across loch. **31 F4** NN3308.
Invertrossachs *Stir.* ***Settlement***, on S side of Loch Venachar, 3m/5km NE of Aberfoyle. **32 A4** NN5604.
Inverugie *Aber.* ***Hamlet***, on River Ugie, 2m/4km NW of Peterhead. Ruined castle of the Keiths, Earls Marischal. **65 G5** NK1048.
Inveruglas *Arg. & B.* ***Locality***, on W shore of Loch Lomond, 3m/5km N of Tarbet, at mouth of Inveruglas Water. Power station operated by water conveyed from Loch Sloy by aqueduct. **31 F4** NN3109.
Inveruglas Isle *Arg. & B.* ***Island***, islet in Loch Lomond, with remains of castle. NN3209.
Inveruglas Water *Arg. & B.* ***River***, stream descending from Loch Sloy to W shore of Loch Lomond. **31 E4** NN3109.
Inveruglass *High.* ***Settlement***, 3m/5km E of Kingussie. **52 A4** NH8001.
Inverurie *Aber.* Population: 9567. ***Small town***, near confluence of Rivers Don and Urie, 14m/22km NW of Aberdeen. Stone circle (Historic Scotland) at Easter Aquhorthies, 3m/5km W. **54 C2** NJ7721.
Inverurie Museum *Aber.* ***Other feature of interest***, museum in Inverurie, with archaeological and geological finds. **54 C2** NJ7721.
Invervar *P. & K.* ***Settlement***, at foot of Invervar Burn, on N side of Glen Lyon, 5m/8km W of Fortingall. **40 B5** NN6648.
Invervar Burn *P. & K.* ***River***, on N side of Glen Lyon, 5m/8km W of Fortingall. NN6647.
Invervegain *Arg. & B.* ***Settlement***, on E coast of Loch Striven, 2m/4km N of Inverchaolain. **22 B2** NS0878.
Inverwick Forest *High.* ***Open space***, deer forest in Inverness district, 3m/5km NW of Fort Augustus. **50 C3** NH3413.
Invery House *Aber.* ***Settlement***, 1m/2km S of Banchory, on W side of Water of Feugh. **54 B5** NO6993.
Inverythan *Aber.* ***Settlement***, on W bank of River Ythan, 3m/4km N of Fyvie. **64 C5** NJ7541.
Inzie Head *Aber.* ***Coastal feature***, headland on NE coast, at NW end of Strathbeg Bay, 2m/3km SE of Inverallochy. **65 F3** NK0662.
Iochda (Anglicised form: Eochar.) *W.Isles* ***Settlement***, 2m/4km E of Ardivachar Point on South Uist. **45 F5** NF7746.
Iona *Arg. & B.* ***Island***, about 3m/5km long NE to SW and over 1m/2km wide, lying nearly 1m/2km off W end of Ross of Mull across Sound of Iona. Site of monastery founded by St. Columba in 6c. Remains of 13c convent. Cathedral mainly 16c, restored. Tombs of the Kings, where several kings lie buried; grave of John Smith, former Labour leader, also on Iona. Island is owned by National Trust for Scotland and is much visited in summer. Ferry connection with Fionnphort on Mull. Iona Heritage Centre (National Trust for Scotland) situated in old Telford Manse, with displays illustrating lives of islanders over past 200 years. **28 B2** NM2723.
Iona Abbey *Arg. & B.* ***Ecclesiastical building***, site of monastery founded in AD 563 by St. Columba to N of Baile Mòr on E coast of Iona. Frequently attacked by raiders, it was replaced in 1203 by Benedictine monastery which subsequently became a ruin during Reformation. Mainly 16c cathedral on site has notable carvings and interior. Restoration of monastery and cathedral started in 20c, and buildings are now home to Iona community. Grounds also include Tomb of the Kings, restored St. Oran's Chapel, 10c St. Martin's Cross and Abbey Museum. **28 B2** NM2824.
Iorsa Water *N.Ayr.* ***River***, on Arran rising to W of Casteal Abhail and running SW down Glen Iorsa into Kilbrannan Sound at N end of Machrie Bay. **13 E2** NR8836.
Ireland *Ork.* ***Locality***, on Mainland, 5m/8km SW of Finstown, on E side of Bay of Ireland. **78 C2** HY3009.
Ireland *Shet.* ***Settlement***, on W coast of Mainland, 9m/14km N of Sumburgh Head. **82 C5** HU3722.
Ires Geo *High.* ***Coastal feature***, small indentation on E coast 1m/2km W of Thrumster. **77 F4** ND3545.
Irish Law *N.Ayr.* ***Mountain***, 4m/6km E of Largs. Height 1588 feet or 484 metres. **23 D4** NS2559.
Ironmill Bay *Fife* ***Bay***, on N side of Firth of Forth, to W of Charlestown. Long pier on W side of bay. NT0584.
Ironside *Aber.* ***Locality***, comprising Upper Ironside and Backhill of Ironside, 1m/2km E of Fedderate Reservoir and 2m/3km S of New Pitsligo. **65 D4** NJ8852.
Irvine *E.Ayr.* ***River***, flowing W to Galston, and passing S of Kilmarnock to Irvine and Irvine Bay. **14 C2** NS3239.
Irvine *N.Ayr.* Population: 32,988. ***Town***, port (and New Town, designated 1965) on and near mouth of River Irvine, 7m/11km W of Kilmarnock. Originally main port for trade between Scotland and Ireland. **14 B2** NS3239.
Irvine Bay *N.Ayr.* ***Bay***, wide bay to W of Irvine. **14 A2** NS3038.
Isauld *High.* ***Settlement***, near N coast of Caithness district, 1km E of Reay. **76 B2** NC9765.
Isauld Burn *High.* ***River***, rising in Loch Saorach and flowing NW into Sandside Bay on N coast. ND0063.
Isay *High.* ***Island***, uninhabited island in Loch Dunvegan, Skye, 2m/4km E of Dunvegan Head. **57 F4** NG2157.
Isay *W.Isles* ***Island***, islet in West Loch Tarbert 3m/5km NW of Tarbert, North Harris. NB1002.
Isbister *Ork.* ***Locality***, on Mainland, at head of Bay of Isbister. **80 B5** HY3918.
Isbister *Ork.* ***Settlement***, to SE of Loch of Isbister, in NW of Mainland. Disused airfield to S. **80 A4** HY2623.
Isbister *Shet.* ***Settlement***, on Mainland, 3m/4km S of Point of Fethaland. Northern terminus of road. **84 C3** HU3790.
Isbister *Shet.* ***Settlement***, near E coast of Whalsay, 3m/4km SW of Skaw Taing. **83 E1** HU5764.
Isbister Holm *Shet.* ***Island***, small uninhabited island 1m/2km off Whalsay coast to E of Isbister. HU6064.
Ishriff *Arg. & B.* ***Settlement***, 4m/6km N of Lochbuie, Mull. **29 F1** NM6331.
Isla ***River***, rising 3m/4km NE of Dufftown and flowing NE to Keith, then E to Nethermills before turning SE to join River Deveron 5m/8km N of Huntly. Noted for trout. **63 F5** NJ5347.
Isla ***River***, rising S of Braemar and running S down Glen Isla to Airlie Castle, then on to River Tay 4m/7km W of Coupar Angus. **42 A4** NO1637.
Island I Vow *Arg. & B. Alternative name for Eilean Vow, qv.*
Island Macaskin (Macaskin Island). *Arg. & B.* ***Island***, 1m/2km long NE to SW in Loch Craignish in Argyll, near entrance to loch. **29 G5** NR7899.
Island of Danna *Arg. & B. Alternative name for Danna Island, qv.*
Island of Raasay *High. See Raasay.*
Island of Rona *High. Alternative name for Rona, qv.*
Island of Stroma (Stroma). *High.* ***Island***, 2m/3km N to S and 1m/2km E to W, lying in Pentland Firth 2m/3km E of St. John's Point and 4m/6km NW of Duncansby Head. Island is sparsely populated. Disused harbour on S coast. Lighthouse at N point. **77 F1** ND3577.
Islands of Fleet *D. & G.* ***Island***, group of small islands comprising the islands of Ardwell, Barlocco and Murray's, on E side of Wigtown Bay, near entrance to Fleet Bay. **3 F2** NX5749.
Islay *Arg. & B.* ***Island***, most southerly of Inner Hebrides and third in size, measuring 25m/40km N to S and 20m/32km E to W; lies off SW coast of Jura, from which it is separated by narrow Sound of Islay. Mainly low-lying and fertile. Numerous species of birds; large herds of deer in W. Port Ellen is chief town and port. Airport at Glenegedale. Port Askaig on Sound of Islay has ferries to Kintyre and Jura. **20 A3** NR3760.
Islay Airport *Arg. & B.* ***Airport/airfield***, at Glenegedale, 5m/7km NW of Port Ellen, Islay. **20 B4** NR3251.
Islay House *Arg. & B.* ***Settlement***, adjoining to N of Bridgend, Islay. **20 B3** NR3362.
Isle Martin *High.* ***Island***, uninhabited island, outlier of Summer Isles group, off W coast of Ross and Cromarty district 3m/5km NW of Ullapool. Area about 600 acres or 240 hectares. **70 C5** NH0999.
Isle of Arran Heritage Museum *N.Ayr.* ***Other feature of interest***, 18c farm 1m/2km NW of Brodick, with exhibits including a blacksmith's and local industrial history displays. **13 F2** NS0036.
Isle of Ewe *High.* ***Island***, sparsely inhabited island in Loch Ewe, W coast of Ross and Cromarty district, opposite Aultbea on E shore of loch. Area about 900 acres or 365 hectares. **59 E1** NG8588.
Isle of Gunnister *Shet.* ***Island***, rock island at entrance to Gunnister Voe inlet, Mainland. HU3073.
Isle of Lewis (Gaelic form: Eilean Leodhais.) *W.Isles* ***Island***, largest and most northerly island of the Outer Hebrides, measuring 61m/99km NE to SW and a maximum of half that distance NW to SE. The name Lewis is generally applied to N part of island as distinct from North and South Harris, areas forming S part of island. In this sense Isle of Lewis consists largely of peaty uplands containing innumerable, mostly small, lochs and streams in which salmon and trout abound. Some moorland has been reclaimed for farming, with barley and potatoes being main crops. Chief occupations of islanders are fishing and cloth manufacture. Butt of Lewis is most northerly point. Stornoway is chief town. **69 D3** NB3035.
Isle of Man *D. & G.* ***Locality***, to N of Craigs Moss, 2m/4km E of Dumfries. NY0075.
Isle of May *Fife* ***Island***, narrow island 1m/2km long NW to SE, lying 6m/10km SE of Anstruther at entrance to Firth of Forth. Ruins of medieval priory. Relic of first Scottish lighthouse (1636). Present lighthouse built 1816 by Robert, father of Robert Louis Stevenson. Bird observatory. **35 E5** NT6599.
Isle of Nibon *Shet.* ***Island***, located off W coast of N part of Mainland. **84 B5** HU3073.
Isle of Noss *Shet.* ***Island***, uninhabited island and bird sanctuary of about 1 square mile or 3 square km, off E coast of Bressay across Noss Sound. **83 E3** HU5440.
Isle of Stenness *Shet.* ***Island***, to SW of Stenness, off S end of Esha Ness, Mainland. HU2076.
Isle of Whithorn *D. & G.* ***Small town***, small port on rocky coast, 3m/5km SE of Whithorn. St. Ninian's Chapel (Historic Scotland) is nearby. **3 E3** NX4736.
Isle Ornsay *High. Alternative name for Eilean Iarmain, qv.*
Isle Ornsay *High.* ***Island***, small uninhabited island off E coast of Sleat peninsula, Skye, opposite village of Eilean Iarmain. Island forms E side of village harbour. **48 D3** NG7112.
Isle Ristol (Ristol). *High.* ***Island***, one of Summer Isles group. Lies close to NW coast of Ross and Cromarty district 4m/7km S of Rubha Coigeach. Area about 560 acres or 225 hectares. **70 B3** NB9711.

I

Isle Tower *D. & G.* ***Historic house***, 16c tower house on W bank of River Nith, 5m/8km NW of Dumfries. Formerly on an island in river. NX9383.
Isleornsay *High. Alternative name for Eilean Iarmain, qv.*
Isles of the Sea *Arg. & B. Alternative name for Garvellachs, qv.*
Islesburgh *Shet.* ***Settlement***, on Mainland, just S of Mangaster Voe. **82 C1** HU3369.
Islesteps *D. & G.* ***Locality***, 2m/4km S of Dumfries. NX9672.
Islibhig (Anglicised form: Islivig.) *W.Isles* ***Village***, near W coast of Isle of Lewis, 6m/9km SW of Timsgearraidh. **68 A5** NA9927.
Islivig *W.Isles Anglicised form of Islibhig, qv.*
Italian Chapel *Ork.* ***Ecclesiastical building***, beautiful chapel on small island of Lamb Holm, which lies between Mainland and Burray. Created from Nissen hut by Italian prisoners of war. **79 D2** HY4800.

J

Jackstown *Aber.* ***Settlement***, 4m/7km S of Fyvie. **54 C1** NJ7531.
Jackton *S.Lan.* ***Settlement***, 3m/4km E of East Kilbride. **23 G4** NS5952.
James Dun's House *Aberdeen* ***Other feature of interest***, museum and gallery in Aberdeen city centre, sited in Georgian house originally built in 1769 for rector of Aberdeen Grammar School, James Dun. **55 E4** NJ9306.
James Hogg Monument *Sc.Bord.* ***Other feature of interest***, 1km W of Ettrick. Monument commemorates birthplace of James Hogg. **17 D4** NT2613.
Jamestown *D. & G.* ***Settlement***, on W bank of Meggat Water, 4m/7km N of Bentpath. **10 B2** NY2996.
Jamestown *High.* ***Settlement***, in Ross and Cromarty district, 1m/2km S of Strathpeffer. **61 D4** NH4756.
Jamestown *W.Dun.* ***Locality***, 4m/6km N of Dumbarton. **23 E1** NS3981.
Janefield *High.* ***Settlement***, on Black Isle, 1m/2km N of Fortrose. **61 G4** NH7259.
Janetstown *High. Alternative name for Latheronwheel, qv.*
Janetstown *High.* ***Settlement***, 2m/3km SW of Thurso. **76 C2** ND0866.
Janetstown *High.* ***Settlement***, in Caithness district, adjoining to W of Wick. ND3550.
Jarlshof *Shet.* ***Historic/prehistoric site***, important site of prehistoric settlement (Historic Scotland) on E side of West Voe of Sumburgh, Mainland. Contains relics of Bronze, Iron, Dark and Middle Ages. **83 G5** HU3909.
Jawcraig *Falk.* ***Settlement***, 2m/3km N of Slamannan. Settlements of Easter and Wester Jawcraig either side. **24 C2** NS8475.
Jed Water *Sc.Bord.* ***River***, rising in Wauchope Forest and flowing N through Jedburgh to River Teviot 3m/4km N of town. **11 E1** NT6624.
Jedburgh *Sc.Bord.* Population: 4118. ***Small town***, on Jed Water, 10m/16km NE of Hawick. Red sandstone ruins (Historic Scotland) of abbey founded in 12c. Site of Roman fort 3m/5km E. **18 A4** NT6520.
Jedburgh Abbey *Sc.Bord.* ***Ecclesiastical building***, one of four great Border abbeys (Historic Scotland) founded by David I for Augustinian canons, situated on W side of Jedburgh. Dates from 1118 and now extensive ruin, including fine rose window on W front. Visitor Centre with exhibition portraying monastic life. **18 A5** NT6420.
Jemimaville *High.* ***Village***, on S side of Cromarty Firth, Ross and Cromarty district, 4m/7km W of Cromarty. **61 G3** NH7265.
Jersay *N.Lan.* ***Settlement***, 3m/5km N of Newmains. **24 C3** NS8361.
Jerviswood *S.Lan.* ***Settlement***, 1m/2km N of Lanark. **24 C5** NS8845.
Jock's Shoulder *D. & G.* ***Mountain***, in Eskdalemuir Forest, 4m/6km W of Davington. Height 1755 feet or 535 metres. **16 C5** NT1702.
John Buchan Centre *Sc.Bord.* ***Other feature of interest***, in old church, 1km S of Broughton, with exhibits on novelist John Buchan. **16 C2** NT1135.
John Muir Country Park *E.Loth.* ***Leisure/recreation***, adjacent to North Sea coast, 2m/3km W of Dunbar. 1668 acre country park named in honour of one of founders of conservation movement. Park extends over 8m/12km of coast and attracts over 220 species of bird. **26 D2** NT6479.
John o' Groats *High.* ***Village***, in NE corner of Caithness district, nearly 2m/3km W of Duncansby Head. Traditionally referred to as NE end of British mainland. **77 F1** ND3773.
Johnshaven *Aber.* ***Village***, on rocky part of E coast, 4m/7km SW of Inverbervie. **43 F3** NO7967.
Johnston Mains *Aber.* ***Hamlet***, 1km S of Laurencekirk. **43 F3** NO7270.
Johnstone *Renf.* Population: 18,635. ***Town***, 4m/6km W of Paisley. **23 F3** NS4263.
Johnstone Castle *Renf.* ***Historic house***, 15c tower house, 1km SW of Johnstone town centre. Visited by Chopin in 1848. **23 F3** NS4262.
Johnstonebridge *D. & G.* ***Settlement***, and road bridge over River Annan, 7m/11km N of Lockerbie. **9 E1** NY1092.
Johnstons Cashmere Visitor Centre *Moray* ***Other feature of interest***, exhibition at Elgin, showing story of cashmere. Displays of over 200 years of cashmere manufacture. Mill tours. **63 E3** NJ2162.
Joppa *Edin.* ***Suburb***, of Edinburgh, adjoining to SE of Portobello. **26 A2** NT3173.
Joppa *S.Ayr.* ***Hamlet***, 1km W of Coylton. **14 C4** NS4019.
Jordanhill *Glas.* ***Suburb***, 4m/6km NW of Glasgow city centre. NS5368.
Jordanstone *P. & K.* ***Settlement***, 2m/3km SE of Alyth. **42 A5** NO2747.
Juniper Green *Edin.* ***Suburb***, 5m/8km SW of Edinburgh city centre. **25 F3** NT1968.
Jura *Arg. & B.* ***Island***, fourth in size of Inner Hebrides, measuring 28m/45km NE to SW and 8m/13km at its widest in S, situated between Islay and Scottish mainland. A mountain ridge runs almost entire length, although interrupted by long inlet of Loch Tarbert on W coast, which nearly bisects island. Deer are numerous. Craighouse is chief port. **21 D1** NR5379.
Jura Forest *Arg. & B.* ***Open space***, deer forest around Paps of Jura in S part of Jura. **20 D2** NR5075.
Jura House *Arg. & B.* ***Settlement***, on Jura, 3m/5km SW of Craighouse. **20 C3** NR4863.

K

Kailzie Gardens *Sc.Bord.* ***Garden***, 3m/4km SE of Peebles, S of River Tweed. Walled garden dates from 1812. **17 D2** NT2738.
Kaim Hill *N.Ayr.* ***Mountain***, 4m/6km SE of Largs. Height 1269 feet or 387 metres. **22 D4** NS2253.
Kaimes *Edin.* ***Suburb***, 4m/6km S of Edinburgh city centre. **25 G3** NT2768.
Kaimhill *Aberdeen* ***Suburb***, 2m/3km SW of Aberdeen city centre. NJ9203.
Kale Water *Sc.Bord.* ***River***, rising on Cheviot Hills and flowing N to Hownam and Morebattle, where it turns W to run into River Teviot 4m/7km S of Kelso. **18 B4** NT7027.
Kallin *W.Isles Anglicised form of Ceallan, qv.*
Kalm Dam *Renf.* ***Reservoir***, 2m/4km N of Lochwinnoch. NS3462.
Kalnakill *High.* ***Settlement***, on W coast of Ross and Cromarty district, 3m/5km S of Rubha Chuaig. **58 C4** NG6954.
Kame of Foula *Shet. Alternative name for The Kame, qv.*
Kame of Hoy *Ork.* ***Coastal feature***, rocky headland on NW coast of Hoy. **78 A2** HY1905.
Kame of Sandwick *Shet.* ***Hill***, 2m/3km E of West Sandwick. Height 548 feet or 167 metres. **85 D4** HU4787.
Kames *Arg. & B.* ***Settlement***, on S shore of Loch Melfort, 2m/3km SW of Melfort across loch. **30 A3** NM8111.
Kames *Arg. & B.* ***Village***, in Argyll on W side of Kyles of Bute, 5m/8km N of Ardlamont Point. **22 A2** NR9771.
Kames *E.Ayr.* ***Settlement***, 1km S of Muirkirk. **15 E3** NS6926.
Kames Bay *Arg. & B.* ***Bay***, on E coast of Bute, 2m/3km N of Rothesay, with Port Bannatyne on S side. **22 B3** NS0667.
Kames Castle *Arg. & B.* ***Castle***, at head of Kames Bay with tower said to date from 14c. NS0667.
Kames Hill *Arg. & B.* ***Hill***, part of group of hills on N Bute, 4m/6km NW of Rothesay. Height 882 feet or 269 metres. **22 B3** NS0569.
Kanaird *High.* ***River***, running W from Loch a' Chroisg to Loch Kanaird, W coast of Ross and Cromarty district. **71 D4** NH1199.
Kay Holm *Shet.* ***Island***, small island off E coast of Yell at entrance to Mid Yell Voe. HU5291.
Kealasay *W.Isles* ***Island***, small uninhabited island off W coast of Isle of Lewis, 1m/2km N of Great Bernera, with Little Bernera in between. NB1441.
Keallasay Beg *W.Isles* ***Island***, small island 1m/2km N of Lochmaddy, North Uist. **56 C2** NF9171.
Keallasay More *W.Isles* ***Island***, small island 2m/4km N of Lochmaddy, North Uist. **56 C2** NF9172.
Kearnaval *W.Isles* ***Mountain***, 3m/4km NE of head of Loch Langavat. Height 1240 feet or 378 metres. **67 D2** NB1815.
Kearstay *W.Isles* ***Island***, small uninhabited island off N coast of Scarp. **66 B2** NA9617.
Kearvaig *High.* ***River***, in Sutherland district, running N into sea 2m/4km SE of Cape Wrath. NC2872.
Kearvaig *High.* ***Settlement***, 3m/4km SE of Cape Wrath, on N coast of Sutherland district. **74 B1** NC2972.
Keava *W.Isles* ***Island***, small uninhabited island in East Loch Roag opposite Breascleit on W coast of Isle of Lewis. NB1935.
Kebholes *Aber.* ***Settlement***, 3m/4km NE of Aberchirder. **64 B4** NJ6455.
Kebister Ness *Shet.* ***Coastal feature***, headland on E coast of Mainland on E side of entrance to Dales Voe, 4m/6km N of Lerwick. **83 D3** HU4746.
Kebock Head *W.Isles* ***Coastal feature***, headland on E coast of Isle of Lewis 12m/19km S of Stornoway. **67 G2** NB4213.
Keelylang Hill *Ork.* ***Hill***, 3m/4km SE of Finstown. Height 725 feet or 221 metres. **80 B5** HY3710.
Keig *Aber.* ***Village***, 3m/5km NE of Alford. **54 B3** NJ6119.
Keil *Arg. & B.* ***Settlement***, 1m/2km SW of Southend on Kintyre peninsula. **12 B5** NR6707.
Keil *High.* ***Settlement***, on SE shore of Loch Linnhe, on S side of Cuil Bay, 1m/2km SE of Rubha Mòr. Burial place of James Stewart, known as James of the Glens, wrongly hanged for Appin Murder of 1752. **38 B4** NM9753.
Keilarsbrae *Clack.* ***Locality***, between Alloa and New Sauchie. NS8993.
Keilhill *Aber.* ***Settlement***, 3m/5km S of Macduff. **64 C4** NJ7159.
Keillmore *Arg. & B.* ***Settlement***, on N coast of Loch na Cille, 5m/8km SW of Tayvallich. Keills Chapel (Historic Scotland) houses collection of grave slabs and Keills Cross. **21 E1** NR6880.
Keillor *P. & K.* ***Hamlet***, 3m/5km E of Coupar Angus. **42 A5** NO2640.
Keillour *P. & K.* ***Locality***, 3m/5km W of Methven. **33 E2** NN9725.
Keillour Forest *P. & K.* ***Forest/woodland***, tract between Crieff and Methven. **33 E2** NN9523.
Keills *Arg. & B.* ***Hamlet***, on E side of Islay, 1m/2km SW of Port Askaig. **20 C3** NR4168.
Keils *Arg. & B.* ***Settlement***, on SE coast of Jura, 1km N of Craighouse. **20 D3** NR5267.
Keir *Stir.* ***Settlement***, 4m/6km NW of Stirling. **32 C5** NS7698.
Keir Hills *D. & G.* ***Large natural feature***, range of hills, 4m/7km E of Moniaive. **8 C1** NX8490.
Keir Mill *D. & G.* ***Village***, 1m/2km SE of Penpont. **8 C1** NX8593.
Keirs Hill *E.Ayr.* ***Open space***, partly wooded hillslope on NE side of Green Hill, 1m/2km SW of Waterside. **14 C5** NS4107.
Keiss *High.* ***Village***, on E coast of Caithness district, 6m/10km N of Wick. Ruined castle. **77 F2** ND3461.
Keith *Moray* Population: 4793. ***Small town***, on right bank of River Isla, 15m/24km SE of Elgin. Dating from 8c but rebuilt in mid 18c. Birthplace of 17c cartographer Sir John Ogilvie. **63 G4** NJ4350.
Keith Hall *Aber.* ***Historic house***, 16c house on estate, 1m/2km E of Inverurie across River Urie. NJ7821.
Keith Inch *Aber.* ***Island***, former island off coast at Peterhead, bridge connections now making it part of town. Lies on NE side of Peterhead Bay and is most easterly point of Scotland, excluding Shetland. **65 G5** NK1345.
Keithick *P. & K.* ***Settlement***, 1m/2km N of Burrelton. **34 A1** NO2038.
Keithmore *Moray* ***Settlement***, 2m/3km E of Dufftown. **53 F1** NJ3539.
Keithock *Angus* ***Locality***, comprises settlements of Keithock, Little Keithock and East Mains of Keithock, 2m/3km N of Brechin. **43 E3** NO6063.
Kelburn Castle *N.Ayr.* ***Castle***, 16c castle with later additions, 2m/3km S of Largs. Home of Boyle family. NS2156.
Kelburn Country Centre *N.Ayr.* ***Leisure/recreation***, woodland surrounding Kelburn Castle, 2m/3km SE of Largs. Includes The Kelburn Story Cartoon Exhibition and displays of birds of prey in summer. **22 D4** NS2256.
Kellan *Arg. & B.* ***Settlement***, on Mull, 2m/3km W of Gruline, to N of Loch na Keal. **37 E5** NM5140.
Kellas *Angus* ***Village***, 3m/5km N of Broughty Ferry. **34 C1** NO4535.
Kellas *Moray* ***Settlement***, 3m/5km E of Dallas. **63 D4** NJ1654.
Kellie Castle *Angus See Arbirlot.*
Kellie Castle *Fife* ***Historic house***, mainly 16c-17c house (National Trust for Scotland), 2m/4km N of St. Monans. Parts date from 14c; house restored in 19c. Grounds feature herbaceous plants and old roses in late Victorian gardens. **34 D4** NO5105.
Kellie Law *Fife* ***Hill***, 3m/5km NW of Pittenweem. Height 597 feet or 182 metres. **34 D4** NO5106.
Kellie Reservoir *Inclyde* ***Reservoir***, small reservoir bordering North Ayrshire, in course of Kellie Burn, 2m/3km E of Wemyss Bay. NS2268.
Kello Water ***River***, rising on N slopes of Blacklorg Hill and flowing NE, then turning E to join River Nith 1m/2km E of Kirkconnel. **15 F5** NS7411.
Kelloholm *D. & G.* ***Village***, adjoining to SE of Kirkconnel across River Nith. **15 F4** NS7411.
Kelsay *Arg. & B.* ***Settlement***, on Rinns of Islay, 3m/4km NE of Portnahaven. **20 A4** NR1956.
Kelso *Sc.Bord.* Population: 5989. ***Small town***, market town opposite confluence of Rivers Teviot and Tweed, 18m/29km NE of Hawick and 20m/32km SW of Berwick-upon-Tweed. Large Georgian square. Bridge by Rennie, 1801. Remains of 12c Abbey (Historic Scotland). **18 B3** NT7233.

Kelso Abbey *Sc.Bord.* ***Ecclesiastical building***, ruined W end of large abbey church of the Tironensians (Historic Scotland), founded by David I in 1128 in Kelso and still showing suberb architecture. **18 B3** NT7333.
Kelso Museum *Sc.Bord.* ***Other feature of interest***, local history museum in Kelso. **18 B3** NT7334.
Kelso Racecourse *Sc.Bord.* ***Racecourse***, at N side of Kelso. National Hunt course, with twelve race days a year. **18 B3** NT7235.
Keltie Water *Stir.* ***River***, flowing S into River Teith, 2m/3km SE of Callander. NN6504.
Keltney Burn *P. & K.* ***River***, stream which rises as Allt Mòr and runs down Gleann Mòr, then turns S as Keltney Burn to run into River Lyon at Keltneyburn. Falls of Keltney, waterfall near mouth. **40 C4** NN7748.
Keltneyburn *P. & K.* ***Settlement***, 5m/8km W of Aberfeldy. **40 C5** NN7749.
Kelton *D. & G.* ***Settlement***, on E bank of River Nith, 3m/5km S of Dumfries. **9 D3** NX9970.
Kelton Hill *D. & G. Alternative name for Rhonehouse, qv.*
Kelty *Fife* Population: 5461. ***Small town***, 2m/3km N of Cowdenbeath and 4m/6km S of Loch Leven. **33 G5** NT1494.
Kelty Water *Stir.* ***River***, running E through Loch Ard Forest to River Forth, 3m/5km SE of Aberfoyle. **31 G5** NS5596.
Kelvin ***River***, rising 3m/5km E of Kilsyth and flowing W, then SW through NW part of Glasgow to River Clyde, 2m/3km W of city centre. **24 B2** NS5565.
Kelvin *S.Lan.* ***Locality***, industrial estate in S part of East Kilbride. NS6352.
Kelvindale *Glas.* ***Suburb***, 3m/5km NW of Glasgow city centre, in Kelvinside district. NS5568.
Kelvingrove Art Gallery and Museum *Glas.* ***Other feature of interest***, to S of River Kelvin, 1m/2km W of Glasgow city centre. Includes Scottish Natural History display, British and Italian paintings, as well as Scottish and 18c European artists' work and The Glasgow Boys. **23 G3** NS5766.
Kelvingrove Park *Glas. See Glasgow.*
Kelvinhaugh *Glas.* ***Suburb***, 1m/2km W of Glasgow city centre. NS5666.
Kelvinside *Glas.* ***Suburb***, 2m/4km NW of Glasgow city centre. NS5667.
Kemback *Fife* ***Village***, 3m/5km E of Cupar. **34 C3** NO4115.
Kemnay *Aber.* Population: 3157. ***Village***, on River Don, 4m/7km SW of Inverurie. **54 C3** NJ7316.
Kemnay Forest *Aber.* ***Forest/woodland***, to N of Kemnay, forming part of Bennachie Forest. **54 C3** NJ7316.
Kempock Point *Inclyde* ***Coastal feature***, headland on Firth of Clyde at Gourock, opposite Kilcreggan. NS2477.
Kendoon Loch *D. & G.* ***Lake/loch***, meeting point of several streams running into Water of Ken, in Dundeugh Forest, 6m/9km N of St. John's Town of Dalry. **7 G1** NX6090.
Kenknock *P. & K.* ***Settlement***, in Glen Lyon, 4m/6km SW of Bridge of Balgie. **40 A5** NN5243.
Kenknock *Stir.* ***Settlement***, in Glen Lochay, 7m/11km NW of Killin. **31 G1** NN4636.
Kenly Burn *Fife* ***River***, rising from Cameron and Kinaldy Burns, and flowing NE to North Sea, 4m/6km SE of St. Andrews. **34 D3** NO5411.
Kenmore *Arg. & B.* ***Settlement***, on NE side of Loch Fyne, 4m/7km SW of Inveraray. **30 C4** NN0601.
Kenmore *High.* ***Settlement***, on Loch a' Chracaich, on SW side of Loch Torridon, Ross and Cromarty district, 4m/7km NW of Shieldaig. **59 D4** NG7557.
Kenmore *P. & K.* ***Village***, at foot of Loch Tay, 6m/9km SW of Aberfeldy. On islet in loch is a ruined 12c priory. **40 C5** NN7745.
Kenmore *W.Isles* ***Settlement***, on E shore of Loch Seaforth, 2m/3km W of head of Loch Claidh. **67 E3** NB2206.
Kenmore Wood *Arg. & B.* ***Forest/woodland***, on W side of Loch Lomond, and just to N of Loch Long. **31 F4** NN3207.
Kenmure Castle *D. & G.* ***Castle***, of 15c-17c, seat of the Gordons, 1m/2km S of New Galloway. **8 A3** NX6376.
Kennacley (Gaelic form: Ceann-na-Cleithe.) *W.Isles* ***Settlement***, on W shore of East Loch Tarbert, South Harris, 4m/6km SE of Tarbert. NG1794.
Kennacraig *Arg. & B.* ***Settlement***, on SE coast of West Loch Tarbert, 5m/8km SW of Tarbert. **21 G3** NR8262.
Kennavay *W.Isles* ***Settlement***, on S coast of Scalpay. **67 E4** NG2394.
Kennedy's Pass *S.Ayr.* ***Other feature of interest***, small pass through rock adjacent to coast carrying A77(T) road, 3m/5km SW of Girvan. **6 C1** NX1493.
Kennerty *Aber.* ***Settlement***, 3m/5km NW of Banchory. **54 B5** NO6799.
Kennet *Clack.* ***Settlement***, 1m/2km SE of Clackmannan. **33 E5** NS9290.
Kennethmont *Aber.* ***Locality***, parish containing village of Kennethmont, 3m/5km NE of Rhynie. **54 A2** NJ5328.
Kennethmont (Also known as Kirkhill of Kennethmont.) *Aber.* ***Village***, 7m/11km S of Huntly. Leith Hall (National Trust for Scotland) 1km NE. **54 A2** NJ5328.
Kennishead *Glas.* ***Suburb***, 5m/7km SW of Glasgow city centre, in Carnwadric district. NS5460.
Kennoway *Fife* Population: 4609. ***Small town***, 2m/4km NW of Leven. **34 B4** NO3502.
Kenovay *Arg. & B.* ***Settlement***, on Tiree, 3m/5km W of Scarinish. NL9946.
Kensaleyre *High.* ***Settlement***, at head of Loch Eyre, Skye, 7m/11km NW of Portree. **58 A4** NG4251.
Kentallen *High.* ***Settlement***, at head of narrow Kentallen Bay on Loch Linnhe, Lochaber district, 3m/5km SW of Ballachulish. **38 C4** NN0057.
Kentallen Bay *High.* ***Bay***, narrow bay on Loch Linnhe, Lochaber district, 3m/5km SW of Ballachulish. NN0057.
Kentra *High.* ***Settlement***, in Lochaber district, on E side of Kentra Bay, 4m/6km NW of Salen. **37 F3** NM6569.
Kentra Bay *High.* ***Bay***, sheltered bay on N coast of Ardnamurchan peninsula, 3m/4km W of Acharacle. Large expanse of sand at low tide. **37 F3** NM6569.
Keoldale *High.* ***Settlement***, on E side of Kyle of Durness, Sutherland district, 2m/3km SW of Durness. Ancient cairns and standing stones to E. **74 C2** NC3866.
Keose *W.Isles Anglicised form of Ceos, qv.*
Keose Glebe *W.Isles* ***Settlement***, on Isle of Lewis, adjoining to E of Ceos. NB3521.
Keose Island (Gaelic form: Eilean Cheois.) *W.Isles* ***Island***, islet 1km SE of Keose Glebe, in Loch Erisort. NB3621.
Keppanach *High.* ***Settlement***, 2m/3km NW of North Ballachulish. **38 C3** NN0262.
Keppel Pier *N.Ayr.* ***Other feature of interest***, landing stage on SE coast of Great Cumbrae, 1m/2km E of Millport. Scottish Marine Biological Station, with museum and aquarium. NS1754.
Keppoch *Arg. & B.* ***Settlement***, 2m/3km NW of Cardross. **23 E2** NS3279.
Keppoch *High.* ***Locality***, in Lochaber district on N side of Loch nan Ceall, W of Arisaig. Back of Keppoch is settlement to N. NM6486.
Keppoch *High.* ***Settlement***, near NE coast of Loch Duich, 2m/3km SE of Dornie. **49 E2** NG9024.
Keprigan *Arg. & B.* ***Settlement***, near S tip of Kintyre, 1m/2km N of Southend. **12 B4** NR6910.
Kerloch *Aber.* ***Mountain***, 3m/5km NE of Bridge of Dye. Height 1752 feet or 534 metres. **43 E1** NO6987.
Kerrera *Arg. & B.* ***Island***, 5m/7km long NE to SW and 2m/3km at widest point, lying to SW of Oban, from which it is separated by Kerrera Sound. Ruined Gylen Castle at S end of island. **30 A2** NM8128.
Kerry *High.* ***River***, in Ross and Cromarty district, flowing W into Loch Kerry, 2m/3km S of Gairloch. **59 E2** NG8173.
Kerrycroy *Arg. & B.* ***Village***, model village on Kerrycroy Bay, on E coast of Bute, 1m/2km S of Ascog and at N entrance to estate of Mountstuart. **22 C3** NS1061.
Kerrycroy Bay *Arg. & B.* ***Bay***, on E coast of Bute, 1m/2km S of Ascog and at N entrance to estate of Mountstuart. NS1061.
Kerrysdale *High.* ***Settlement***, in Ross and Cromarty district, 3m/4km SE of Gairloch. **59 E2** NG8273.
Kerrytonlia Point *Arg. & B.* ***Coastal feature***, headland on E coast of Bute, at NE end of Kilchattan Bay. NS1156.
Kershader *W.Isles Anglicised form of Cearsiadar, qv.*
Kershope Burn ***River***, rising on borders of England and Scotland, 5m/8km E of Newcastleton, and flowing SW along border into Liddel Water at Kershopefoot. **10 D3** NY4782.
Kessock Bridge *High.* ***Bridge***, road bridge carrying A9 across W end of Moray Firth, linking Inverness with North Kessock. NH6647.
Ketligill Head *Shet.* ***Coastal feature***, headland on NW coast of Mainland, on E side of Ronas Voe near its entrance. HU2784.
Kettins *P. & K.* ***Village***, 1m/2km SE of Coupar Angus. **34 A1** NO2339.
Kettla Ness *Shet.* ***Coastal feature***, headland at S end of West Burra. **82 C5** HU3429.
Kettlebridge *Fife* ***Hamlet***, 1m/2km S of Ladybank. **34 B4** NO3007.
Kettlehill *Fife* ***Hamlet***, 2m/3km SE of Ladybank. NO3207.
Kettleholm *D. & G.* ***Settlement***, 3m/5km S of Lockerbie. **9 F3** NY1476.
Kettlester *Shet.* ***Locality***, near S coast of Yell, adjoining to NW of Burravoe. HU5179.
Kettletoft *Ork.* ***Settlement***, and promontory on S coast of Sanday, between Backaskail Bay to W and Kettletoft Bay to E. **81 E3** HY6538.
Kettletoft Bay *Ork.* ***Bay***, on Sanday to E of Kettletoft, with a landing stage. HY6538.
Kevock *Midloth.* ***Suburb***, in W part of Bonnyrigg and Lasswade. NT2965.
Kiachnish *High.* ***River***, in Lochaber district running N from Lochan Lùnn Dà-Bhrà then turning W and running into Loch Linnhe, 4m/6km SW of Fort William. NN0669.
Kidsdale *D. & G.* ***Settlement***, 3m/4km S of Whithorn. **3 E3** NX4336.
Kiel Crofts *Arg. & B.* ***Settlement***, adjoining to NW of Benderloch. **30 B1** NM9039.
Kiells *Arg. & B.* ***Hamlet***, on Islay, 1m/2km SW of Port Askaig. NR4168.
Kiessimul (Also spelled Kisimul.) *W.Isles* ***Island***, tiny islet in Castle Bay, S coast of Barra, on which stands Kiessimul Castle, ancient stronghold of Clan Macneil of Barra. NL6697.
Kiessimul Castle (Also spelled Kisimul Castle.) *W.Isles* ***Castle***, on tiny islet of Kiessimul in Castle Bay, S coast of Barra. Ancient stronghold of Clan Macneil of Barra. **44 B4** NL6697.
Kilantringan Loch *S.Ayr.* ***Lake/loch***, small loch 2m/4km S of Ballantrae. **6 B3** NX0979.
Kilbagie *Clack.* ***Other building***, paper mill 2m/3km N of Kincardine. NS9289.
Kilbarchan *Renf.* Population: 3846. ***Small town***, 2m/3km W of Johnstone, formerly noted for tartan weaving. 18c weaver's cottage (National Trust for Scotland). **23 F3** NS4063.
Kilbeg *High.* ***Locality***, on E coast of Sleat peninsula, Skye, 2m/4km NE of Ardvasar. **48 C4** NG6506.
Kilberry *Arg. & B.* ***Village***, near W coast of Knapdale, Argyll, 4m/6km NW of Ardpatrick Point. **21 F3** NR7164.
Kilberry Bay *Arg. & B.* ***Bay***, situated to S of Kilberry Head on Kintyre, 10m/18km W of Tarbert. NR7063.
Kilberry Crosses *Arg. & B.* ***Historic/prehistoric site***, collection of late medieval sculptured stones (Historic Scotland) gathered from Kilberry estate at Kilberry Castle on W coast of Kintyre, 1km W of Kilberry. **21 F3** NR7064.
Kilberry Head *Arg. & B.* ***Coastal feature***, headland nearly 1m/2km W of Kilberry, to N of Kilberry Bay. **21 E3** NR7164.
Kilbirnie *N.Ayr.* Population: 8060. ***Small town***, with notable medieval church, on River Garnock, 9m/15km NE of Ardrossan. **23 E4** NS3154.
Kilbirnie Loch *N.Ayr.* ***Lake/loch***, 1m/2km E of Kilbirnie. **23 E4** NS3154.
Kilblaan *Arg. & B.* ***Settlement***, in Glen Shira, 4m/6km NE of Inveraray. **30 D3** NN1213.
Kilblaan Burn *Arg. & B.* ***River***, running E into Glen Shira, 4m/6km NE of Inveraray. **30 D3** NN1213.
Kilbowie *Renf.* ***Suburb***, on N side of Clydebank. NS5071.
Kilbrannan Sound *Arg. & B.* ***Sea feature***, sea passage between Arran and Kintyre. Width between 3m/5km and 8m/13km. **12 D2** NR8441.
Kilbraur *High.* ***Settlement***, 1m/2km W of Gordonbush, to S of River Brora. **72 D3** NC8210.
Kilbraur Hill *High.* ***Mountain***, 1m/2km S of Kilbraur, Sutherland district. Height 1059 feet or 323 metres. **72 D4** NC8208.
Kilbrenan *Arg. & B.* ***Settlement***, on Mull, 2m/3km SE of Fanmore. **36 D5** NM4342.
Kilbride *Arg. & B.* ***Settlement***, in Argyll 3m/4km S of Oban. **30 A2** NM8525.
Kilbride *Arg. & B.* ***Settlement***, on lower slopes of Kilbride Hill, 1m/2km N of Ettrick Bay, Bute. **22 B3** NS0367.
Kilbride *High.* ***Settlement***, 1km E of Torrin, Skye. **48 B2** NG5820.
Kilbride *W.Isles Anglicised form of Cille Bhrighde, qv.*
Kilbride Bay *Arg. & B.* ***Bay***, in Argyll at entrance to Loch Fyne, 2m/4km NW of Ardlamont Point. **22 A3** NR9666.
Kilbride Farm *Arg. & B.* ***Settlement***, 3m/5km SW of Tighnabruaich. **22 A3** NR9668.
Kilbride Point *High.* ***Coastal feature***, headland on E shore of Loch Snizort, Skye, 2m/4km NW of Uig. **57 G3** NG3766.
Kilbridemore *Arg. & B.* ***Settlement***, 5m/8km NE of Clachan of Glendaruel. **30 C5** NS0390.
Kilbryde Castle *Stir.* ***Castle***, dating from 15c on Ardoch Burn, 2m/4km NW of Dunblane. NN7503.
Kilbucho *Sc.Bord.* ***Locality***, 2m/3km SW of Broughton. NT0835.
Kilcadzow *S.Lan.* ***Settlement***, 3m/4km SE of Carluke. **24 C5** NS8848.
Kilchattan *Arg. & B.* ***Village***, on S side of the wide Kilchattan Bay on E coast of Bute, 2m/4km N of Garroch Head. **22 C4** NS1055.
Kilchattan Bay *Arg. & B.* ***Bay***, on E coast of Bute, 2m/4km N of Garroch Head. **22 C4** NS1055.
Kilchenzie *Arg. & B.* ***Village***, in Kintyre, 4m/6km NW of Campbeltown. **12 B3** NR6724.
Kilcheran *Arg. & B.* ***Settlement***, on Lismore, 3m/5km NE of Rubha Fiart. **30 A1** NM8238.
Kilcheran Loch *Arg. & B.* ***Lake/loch***, small loch on Lismore, 2m/3km SW of Achnacroish. Port Kilcheran is small bay to S. NM8239.
Kilchiaran *Arg. & B.* ***Settlement***, near W coast of Rinns of Islay, at Kilchiaran Bay. **20 A4** NR2060.
Kilchiaran Bay *Arg. & B.* ***Bay***, on W coast of Rinns of Islay. **20 A4** NR2060.

K

Kilchoan *Arg. & B.* ***Settlement***, on N shore of Loch Melfort, 3m/5km W of Kilmelford. **29 G3** NM7913.
Kilchoan *High.* ***Village***, on S side of Ardnamurchan peninsula, in Lochaber district, 5m/8km SE of Point of Ardnamurchan. **37 D3** NM4863.
Kilchoan Bay *Arg. & B.* ***Bay***, on N side of Loch Melfort, Argyll. NM7913.
Kilchoan Bay *High.* ***Bay***, to W of Kilchoan village, on S side of Ardnamurchan peninsula. **37 D3** NM4863.
Kilchoan Lochs *Arg. & B.* ***Lake/loch***, two small lochs to N of Kilchoan Bay. NM7914.
Kilchoman *Arg. & B.* ***Settlement***, 1km inland from Machir Bay, on W coast of Islay. **20 A3** NR2163.
Kilchrenan *Arg. & B.* ***Village***, in Argyll, 6m/10km SE of Taynuilt. **30 C2** NN0322.
Kilchrist *Arg. & B.* ***Locality***, on Kintyre, 3m/4km SW of Campbeltown. **12 B4** NR6917.
Kilchurn Castle *Arg. & B.* ***Castle***, remains of castle (Historic Scotland), dating partly from 15c, at NE end of Loch Awe 2m/3km W of Dalmally, Argyll. **30 D2** NN1327.
Kilconquhar *Fife* ***Village***, 1m/2km N of Elie. **34 C4** NO4802.
Kilconquhar Loch *Fife* ***Lake/loch***, small circular loch on S side of Kilconquhar. NO4801.
Kilcoy *High.* ***Locality***, in Ross and Cromarty district, 3m/5km E of Muir of Ord. **61 E4** NH5751.
Kilcoy Castle *High.* ***Castle***, 17c Z-plan castle, now restored, to W of Kilcoy. Belonged to Mackenzies of Kintail. NH5751.
Kilcreggan *Arg. & B.* Population: 1586. ***Village***, at S end of peninsula between Gare Loch and Loch Long, opposite Gourock across Firth of Clyde. Ferry for pedestrians to Gourock. **22 D1** NS2380.
Kildalton *Arg. & B.* ***Locality***, at SE end of Islay, 1m/2km NE of Ardbeg. Celtic cross (Historic Scotland) in churchyard. NR4347.
Kildalton Church and Crosses *Arg. & B.* ***Ecclesiastical building***, 7m/11km NE of Port Ellen, Islay. Churchyard contains intact High Cross (Historic Scotland) carved in 8c and reputedly finest in Scotland. **20 C5** NR4550.
Kildary *High.* ***Hamlet***, 6m/9km NE of Invergordon. **61 G2** NH7675.
Kildavanan Point *Arg. & B.* ***Coastal feature***, headland on W coast of Bute, at entrance to W arm of Kyles of Bute and at NW end of Ettrick Bay. NS0266.
Kildavie *Arg. & B.* ***Settlement***, at S end of Kintyre, 3m/4km NE of Southend. **12 C4** NR7210.
Kildermorie Forest *High.* ***Open space***, deer forest in Ross and Cromarty district to W of Loch Morie. **60 D2** NH4678.
Kildermorie Lodge *High.* ***Settlement***, 9m/15km NW of Alness. **61 E2** NH5177.
Kildonan *N.Ayr.* ***Locality***, at S end of Arran, 1m/2km SW of Dippin Head. **13 F3** NS0321.
Kildonan Burn *High.* ***River***, in Sutherland district, flowing into River Helmsdale, 1km S of Kildonan Lodge. Gold deposits found here in 19c. **73 E2** NC9120.
Kildonan Castle *N.Ayr.* ***Castle***, ruined keep on rocky cliff to E of Kildonan, Arran. **13 F3** NS0320.
Kildonan Lodge *High.* ***Settlement***, in Strath of Kildonan, Sutherland district, 8m/13km NW of Helmsdale. **73 E2** NC9120.
Kildonnan *High.* ***Locality***, on E coast of Eigg. **37 D1** NM4985.
Kildrochet *D. & G.* ***Settlement***, 3m/5km S of Stranraer. **6 B5** NX0856.
Kildrum *N.Lan.* ***Suburb***, to E of Cumbernauld town centre. NS7675.
Kildrummy *Aber.* ***Locality***, 3m/4km S of Lumsden. **53 G3** NJ4717.
Kildrummy Castle *Aber.* ***Castle***, ruined 13c castle (Historic Scotland) 1m/2km SW of Kildrummy, dismantled after Jacobite rising of 1715. Gardens notable for shrubs and alpines, and include ancient quarry and water gardens. **53 G3** NJ4516.
Kilennan *Arg. & B.* ***River***, flowing generally W from slopes of Beinn Bheigier into River Laggan, 9m/13km N of Port Ellen, Islay. **20 B4** NR3558.
Kilfinan *Arg. & B.* ***Village***, on E side of Loch Fyne, Argyll, 4m/7km NW of Tighnabruaich on Kyles of Bute. **22 A2** NR9378.
Kilfinan Bay *Arg. & B.* ***Bay***, 1m/2km W of Kilfinan, at mouth of Kilfinan Burn, on E side of Loch Fyne. **22 A2** NR9378.
Kilfinan Burn *Arg. & B.* ***River***, stream flowing past Kilfinan to sea at Kilfinan Bay, 1m/2km W of village. NR9378.
Kilfinichen Bay *Arg. & B.* ***Bay***, on N side of Loch Scridain on Mull, with headland of Aird Kilfinichen to E. **29 D2** NM4828.
Kilfinnan *High.* ***Settlement***, at NE end of Loch Lochy, 1m/2km SW of Laggan. **50 B5** NN2795.
Kili Holm *Ork.* ***Island***, small uninhabited island lying off N end of Egilsay. **80 C3** HY4732.
Kilkenneth *Arg. & B.* ***Settlement***, 1km NE of Middleton, near W coast of Tiree. **36 A2** NL9444.
Kilkerran *Arg. & B.* ***Settlement***, on Kintyre, adjoining to SE of Campbeltown. **12 C4** NR7219.
Kilkerran *S.Ayr.* ***Locality***, house and estate 4m/7km S of Maybole. **14 B5** NS3003.
Killantringan Bay *D. & G.* *See Black Head.*
Killantringan Lighthouse *D. & G.* *See Black Head.*
Killbeg *Arg. & B.* ***Settlement***, on Mull, 2m/3km SE of Salen. **37 F5** NM6041.
Killean *Arg. & B.* ***Settlement***, 4m/6km SW of Inveraray. **30 C4** NN0404.
Killean *Arg. & B.* ***Settlement***, on W side of Kintyre, Argyll, 1km S of Tayinloan. Remains of medieval church. **21 E5** NR6944.
Killearn *Stir.* Population: 1816. ***Village***, 5m/8km NW of Strathblane. Obelisk commemorates George Buchanan, 16c reformer, and tutor to James VI of Scotland. **23 G1** NS5286.
Killegray *W.Isles* ***Island***, uninhabited island in Sound of Harris, 3m/5km SW of Leverburgh, W coast of Harris. Nearly 3km long NW to SE and nearly 1km wide. **66 B5** NF9783.
Killellan *Arg. & B.* ***Locality***, on Kintyre, 4m/6km SW of Campbeltown. **12 B4** NR6815.
Killen *High.* ***Settlement***, on Black Isle, Ross and Cromarty district, 3m/5km W of Fortrose. **61 F4** NH6758.
Killichonan *P. & K.* ***Village***, on N side of Loch Rannoch, 3m/4km from head of reservoir. Waterfall in burn to E. **40 A4** NN5458.
Killichonan Burn *P. & K.* ***River***, flowing SW into Loch Rannoch at Killichonan. **40 A4** NN5457.
Killichronan *Arg. & B.* ***Settlement***, on Mull, 1km N of Gruline. **37 E5** NM5441.
Killiechanate *High.* ***Settlement***, 1m/2km E of Spean Bridge. **39 E1** NN2481.
Killiechonate Forest *High.* ***Open space***, deer forest in Lochaber district NE of Ben Nevis. **39 E2** NN2174.
Killiecrankie *P. & K.* ***Village***, on River Garry, 3m/5km SE of Blair Atholl, at head of Pass of Killiecrankie (National Trust for Scotland), wooded gorge. To NW is site of battle of 1689 in which troops of King William III were defeated by Jacobites under Graham of Claverhouse ('Bonnie Dundee') who, however, was mortally wounded in the battle. **41 E3** NN9162.
Killiehuntly *High.* ***Settlement***, 3m/4km SE of Kingussie. **51 G5** NN7998.
Killiemor *Arg. & B.* ***Settlement***, 3m/4km W of Gruline, Mull. **29 D1** NM5040.
Killilan *High.* ***Settlement***, in Skye and Lochalsh district, 1m/2km E of head of Loch Long. **49 F1** NG9430.
Killilan Forest *High.* ***Open space***, deer forest to E of Killilan. **49 G1** NG9430.
Killimster *High.* ***Locality***, in Caithness district, 5m/8km NW of Wick. **77 F3** ND3156.
Killin *High.* ***River***, formed from confluence of several tributaries between Meall nan Ruadhag and Carn a' Choire Ghlaise, and flowing N into Loch Killin. NH5309.
Killin *High.* ***Settlement***, to E of Loch Brora, 2m/3km SE of Gordonbush, Sutherland district. **73 D4** NC8507.
Killin *Stir.* ***Village***, at confluence of Rivers Dochart and Lochay, at head of Loch Tay. Moirlanich Longhouse (National Trust for Scotland), 1m/2km NW, is outstanding example of traditional 19c cruck-frame cottage and byre. House retains many original features. **32 A1** NN5732.
Killin Rock *High.* ***Hill***, with rock outcrops to S and W, 1m/2km SE of Killin. Height 705 feet or 215 metres. **72 D4** NC8605.
Killinallan *Arg. & B.* ***Settlement***, on N coast of Islay, 5m/9km N of Bridgend. **20 B2** NR3171.
Killinallan Point *Arg. & B.* ***Coastal feature***, headland on E side of Loch Gruinart on N coast of Islay, before loch widens out into bay enclosed by Ardnave Point and Gortantaoid Point. **20 A2** NR3072.
Killochan Castle *S.Ayr.* ***Historic house***, 16c mansion on N side of Water of Girvan 3m/5km NE of Girvan. **6 D1** NS2200.
Killochyett *Sc.Bord.* ***Locality***, on Gala Water, adjoining to N of Stow. **26 B5** NT4545.
Killocraw *Arg. & B.* ***Settlement***, on W coast of Kintyre, 7m/11km NW of Campbeltown. **12 B3** NR6630.
Killunaig *Arg. & B.* ***Settlement***, on S side of Loch Scridain, 1m/2km W of Pennyghael, Mull. **29 D2** NM4925.
Killundine *High.* ***Settlement***, on E shore on Sound of Mull, 4m/6km SE of Drimnin, Lochaber district. **37 E5** NM5849.
Killypole Loch *Arg. & B.* ***Lake/loch***, small loch or tarn in Kintyre 2m/3km S of Machrihanish. NR6417.
Kilmacolm *Inclyde* Population: 4343. ***Small town***, former weaving centre, 6m/10km SE of Greenock. **23 E3** NS3569.
Kilmaha *Arg. & B.* ***Settlement***, 3m/5km SW of Dalavich. **30 B4** NM9408.
Kilmahog *Stir.* ***Settlement***, on N bank of River Leny, 1m/2km W of Callander. Site of Roman fort on S bank, towards town. **32 B4** NN6108.
Kilmalieu *High.* ***Settlement***, near NW shore of Loch Linnhe, 3m/4km NE of Rubha na h-Airde Uinnsinn. **38 A4** NM8955.
Kilmaluag *High.* ***Locality***, near N coast of Skye, 2m/3km S of Rubha na h-Aiseig. **58 A2** NG4273.
Kilmaluag Bay *High.* ***Bay***, 1m/2km NE of Kilmaluag, Skye. **58 A2** NG4374.
Kilmannan Reservoir *W.Dun.* ***Reservoir***, on border with Stirling, 4m/7km W of Strathblane. NS4978.
Kilmany *Fife* ***Village***, 4m/7km SW of Newport-on-Tay. **34 B2** NO3821.
Kilmarie *High.* ***Locality***, on E side of Strathaird peninsula, Skye, 4m/7km N of Strathaird Point. **48 B3** NG5517.
Kilmarnock *E.Ayr.* Population: 44,307. ***Town***, 19m/31km SW of Glasgow. Once known for a variety of industries, including locomotive-building and distilling. Associations with Robert Burns; Burns monument and museum. Dean Castle, dating from 14c, is now a museum. **14 C2** NS4237.
Kilmarnock Hill *Arg. & B.* ***Mountain***, 2m/3km SW of Black Craig. Height 1296 feet or 395 metres. **22 C2** NS1073.
Kilmarnock Water *E.Ayr.* ***River***, running SW through Kilmarnock to confluence with River Irvine, 1m/2km S of town centre. NS4236.
Kilmartin *Arg. & B.* ***Village***, in Argyll, 3m/5km NE of Crinan Loch. Kilmartin Sculptured Stones (Historic Scotland) in churchyard. Remains of 16c castle keep. Kilmartin Burn flows S past village to River Add, 3m/5km S. Many prehistoric remains in vicinity, including Bronze Age burial chambers of Dunchraigaig Cairn, Glebe Cairn and Nether Largie Cairns (all Historic Scotland). The latter of these comprises one Neolithic and two Bronze Age cairns, with access to chamber in N cairn. **30 A5** NR8398.
Kilmartin Castle *Arg. & B.* ***Castle***, ruins of castle on edge of Kilmartin village, 7m/11km N of Lochgilphead. **30 A5** NR8399.
Kilmartin Glen Monuments (Also known as Poltalloch Monuments.) *Arg. & B.* ***Historic/prehistoric site***, area concentrated in Kilmartin Glen, 6m/10km NW of Lochgilphead, with numerous prehistoric sites and monuments including cup and ring marks, standing stones, cairns and sculptured stones. **30 A5** NR8396.
Kilmartin House *Arg. & B.* ***Other feature of interest***, museum centre at Kilmartin, 8m/12km N of Lochgilphead. Specializes in interpreting local ancient monuments and rich archaeological landscape of Kilmartin Glen via reconstructions and audio-visual displays. **30 A5** NR8398.
Kilmartin Sculptured Stones *Arg. & B.* ***Historic/prehistoric site***, two groups of sculptured stones (Historic Scotland) at Kilmartin Church, 8m/12km N of Lochgilphead. Stone shelter houses weathered Kilmartin crosses which include a 16c example. Churchyard contains collection of 13c-17c graveslabs, known as Poltalloch Stones, most of which were carved locally in West Highland tradition and feature armed warriors, swords and foliage. **30 A5** NR8398.
Kilmaurs *E.Ayr.* Population: 2744. ***Village***, 2m/4km NW of Kilmarnock. **23 F5** NS4141.
Kilmein Hill *E.Ayr.* ***Mountain***, 3m/4km E of Patna. Height 1407 feet or 429 metres. **14 C4** NS4511.
Kilmelford *Arg. & B.* ***Village***, in Argyll, at head of Loch Melfort. **30 A3** NM8413.
Kilmeny *Arg. & B.* ***Settlement***, on Islay, 1km SW of Ballygrant. NR3965.
Kilmichael *Arg. & B.* ***Settlement***, on Kintyre, 2m/3km NW of Campbeltown. **12 B3** NR6922.
Kilmichael Forest *Arg. & B.* ***Open space***, moorland area to NE of Kilmichael Glassary. NR8593.
Kilmichael Glassary *Arg. & B.* ***Village***, in Argyll, 4m/6km N of Lochgilphead across River Add. Cup and ring marked rocks (Historic Scotland). To NE is moorland area of Kilmichael Forest. **30 A5** NR8593.
Kilmichael of Inverlussa *Arg. & B.* ***Settlement***, on E side of Loch Sween in Knapdale, Argyll, 5m/8km S of Crinan. **21 F1** NR7785.
Kilmorack *High.* ***Village***, on River Beauly, 2m/3km SW of Beauly town, in Inverness district. **61 D5** NH4944.
Kilmore *Arg. & B.* ***Settlement***, in Argyll, 4m/6km SE of Oban. **30 A2** NM8825.
Kilmore *High.* ***Settlement***, on E coast of Sleat peninsula, Skye, 1m/2km SW of Teangue. Site of Sleat parish church. **48 C4** NG6507.
Kilmory *Arg. & B.* ***Settlement***, in Knapdale, Argyll, 2m/3km N of Point of Knap. **21 F2** NR7075.
Kilmory *Arg. & B.* ***Settlement***, on shore of Linne Mhuirich, 3m/4km SW of Tayvallich. **21 F1** NR7283.
Kilmory *High.* ***River***, flowing N into sea on N coast of Rum. **47 G4** NG3603.
Kilmory *High.* ***Settlement***, at mouth of Kilmory River, on N coast of Rum. **47 G4** NG3603.
Kilmory *High.* ***Settlement***, on Ardnamurchan, Lochaber district, 4m/6km SW of Rubha Aird Druimnich. **37 E3** NM5270.
Kilmory *N.Ayr.* ***Hamlet***, near S coast of Arran, 7m/11km SW of Lamlash. NR9621.
Kilmory Bay *Arg. & B.* ***Bay***, small bay to SW of Kilmory, 12m/20km SW of Lochgilphead. **21 E2** NR7075.

K

Kilmory Chapel *Arg. & B.* ***Historic/prehistoric site***, 13c chapel containing collection of Celtic and later sculptured stones. Macmillan's Cross (Historic Scotland), late 15c sculptured cross outside chapel. **21 F2** NR7075.
Kilmory Water *N.Ayr.* ***River***, running SW past Kilmory to sea 1km to SW. **13 E3** NR9521.
Kilmote *High.* ***Settlement***, 2m/3km NE of Lothbeg, Sutherland district. **73 E3** NC9711.
Kilmuir *High.* ***Settlement***, to SE of Dunvegan, Skye. **57 F5** NG2547.
Kilmuir *High.* ***Settlement***, near N coast of Skye, 5m/7km N of Uig. **57 G2** NG3770.
Kilmuir *High.* ***Settlement***, 2m/4km N of Inverness across Moray Firth. **61 F5** NH6649.
Kilmuir *High.* ***Settlement***, on Nigg Bay, N side of Cromarty Firth, 4m/7km NE of Invergordon, Ross and Cromarty district. **61 G2** NH7573.
Kilmun *Arg. & B.* ***Village***, on N side of Holy Loch, in Argyll, 1m/2km NW of Strone Point. **22 C1** NS1781.
Kilmux *Fife* ***Settlement***, 2m/3km NE of Kennoway. **34 B4** NO3604.
Kilnave *Arg. & B.* ***Locality***, on W side of Loch Gruinart, on N coast of Islay. **20 A2** NR2870.
Kilneuair *Arg. & B.* ***Locality***, with ruined church on E side of Loch Awe in Argyll, 1m/2km E of head of loch. NM8803.
Kilninian *Arg. & B.* ***Village***, on N side of Loch Tuath, Mull, 4m/6km S of Calgary. **36 D5** NM3945.
Kilninver *Arg. & B.* ***Village***, in Argyll, 6m/9km S of Oban across Loch Feochan. **30 A2** NM8221.
Kiloran *Arg. & B.* ***Settlement***, on Colonsay, 2m/3km N of Scalasaig. **28 C5** NR3996.
Kiloran Bay *Arg. & B.* ***Bay***, 1m/2km N of Kiloran, on NW coast of Colonsay. **28 C5** NR3996.
Kiloran Gardens *Arg. & B.* ***Garden***, on N part of Colonsay. Contains sub-tropical plants. **28 C5** NR3996.
Kilpatrick *N.Ayr.* ***Settlement***, on W coast of Arran at Kilpatrick Point, 1km S of Blackwaterfoot. Ruins of circular dry-stone homestead of Kilpatrick Dun (Historic Scotland). **13 E3** NR9027.
Kilpatrick Hills *W.Dun.* ***Large natural feature***, range of low hills to E of Dumbarton. Summit is Duncolm, 1316 feet or 401 metres. **23 F2** NS4676.
Kilpatrick Point *N.Ayr.* ***Coastal feature***, headland at S end of Drumadoon Bay, on W coast of Arran, 1m/2km S of Blackwaterfoot. NR9027.
Kilpheder *W.Isles Anglicised form of Cille Pheadair, qv.*
Kilphedir *High.* ***Settlement***, at confluence of Allt Cille Pheadair and River Helmsdale, 3m/5km NW of Helmsdale. **73 E3** NC9818.
Kilravock Castle *High.* ***Castle***, partly 15c castle in Nairn district 6m/10km SW of Nairn. NH8149.
Kilrenny *Fife* ***Village***, 1m/2km NE of Anstruther. Forms part of Royal Burgh of Kilrenny, Anstruther Easter and Anstruther Wester. **35 D4** NO5704.
Kilspindie *P. & K.* ***Village***, 7m/11km E of Perth. **34 A2** NO2225.
Kilstay *D. & G.* ***Settlement***, 1m/2km N of Drummore on W side of Luce Bay. **2 B3** NX1238.
Kilstay Bay *D. & G.* ***Bay***, on E coast of Rinns of Galloway, 1m/2km N of Drummore. NX1338.
Kilsyth *N.Lan.* Population: 9918. ***Small town***, 3m/5km NW of Cumbernauld. 1m/2km E is site, now submerged by reservoir, of battle of 1645 in which Montrose defeated Covenanters. **24 B2** NS7178.
Kilsyth Hills *N.Lan.* ***Large natural feature***, upland area running NE from Campsie Fells, to NW of Kilsyth. Bounded by Carron Valley Reservoir to N and River Kelvin valley to S. Notable peaks include Garrel Muir at 1502 feet or 458 metres, Tomtain at 1486 feet or 453 metres and Laird's Hill at 1394 feet or 425 metres. **24 A2** NS6679.
Kiltarlity *High.* ***Village***, in Inverness district, 3m/5km S of Beauly. **61 E5** NH5041.
Kiltyre *P. & K.* ***Settlement***, on N side of Loch Tay, 4m/7km NE of Killin. **32 B1** NN6236.
Kilvaxter *High.* ***Settlement***, on Skye, 4m/7km N of Uig. **57 G3** NG3869.
Kilwinning *N.Ayr.* Population: 15,479. ***Town***, 5m/7km E of Ardrossan. Ruined 12c-13c abbey (Historic Scotland). Dalgaven Mill dates from 1620. **23 E5** NS3043.
Kilwinning Abbey *N.Ayr.* ***Ecclesiastical building***, scant remains of Tironensian-Benedictine abbey (Historic Scotland) founded in 12c-13c at Kilwinning. Parts of church and chapter house survive. **23 E5** NS3043.
Kinaldy *Fife* ***Settlement***, 4m/6km S of St. Andrews. **34 D3** NO5110.
Kinaldy Burn *Fife* ***River***, small stream, which is a continuation of Lathockar Burn, flowing NE to join with Cameron Burn to form Kenly Water, 4m/6km SE of St. Andrews and 3m/5km from where Kenley Water flows into North Sea. **34 D4** NO5411.
Kinblethmont *Angus* ***Locality***, 4m/6km N of Arbroath. **43 E5** NO6346.
Kinbrace *High.* ***Village***, in Sutherland district, 15m/24km NW of Helmsdale. **76 A5** NC8631.
Kinbrace Burn *High.* ***River***, in Sutherland district, flowing W into River Helmsdale, 1m/2km S of Burnfoot. **73 E1** NC8628.
Kinbreack *High.* ***Settlement***, near head of Glen Kingie, 14m/24km NW of Fort William. **49 G5** NN0096.
Kinbuck *Stir.* ***Village***, on Allan Water, 3m/4km N of Dunblane. **32 C4** NN7905.
Kincaldrum *Angus* ***Settlement***, 4m/6km S of Forfar. **42 C5** NO4344.
Kincaple *Fife* ***Settlement***, 3m/5km NW of St. Andrews. **34 C3** NO4618.
Kincardine (Also known as Kincardine-on-Forth.) *Fife* Population: 3184. ***Small town***, former ship-building centre and port on River Forth, 4m/7km SE of Alloa. Ruined Tulliallan Castle dates from 15c. **24 D1** NS9387.
Kincardine *High.* ***Village***, near head of Dornoch Firth, 1m/2km S of Ardgay, Sutherland district. **61 F1** NH6089.
Kincardine Bridge ***Bridge***, swing road bridge carrying A876 NE across River Forth to Kincardine. NS9387.
Kincardine Castle *Aber.* ***Castle***, ruin of former royal residence, 2m/3km NE of Fettercairn. NO6775.
Kincardine Castle *P. & K.* ***Historic house***, 19c mansion beside Ruthven Water, 1m/2km S of Auchterarder. To SW is fragment of old castle, dismantled in 1645. **33 E4** NN9411.
Kincardine-on-Forth *Fife Alternative name for Kincardine, qv.*
Kincardine O'Neil *Aber.* ***Village***, on N side of River Dee, 7m/11km W of Banchory. **54 A5** NO5999.
Kinclaven *P. & K.* ***Settlement***, 1m/2km SW of Meikleour across River Tay. **33 G1** NO1538.
Kinclaven Castle *P. & K.* ***Castle***, ruined medieval castle on bank of River Tay, to SE of Kinclaven. NO1537.
Kincorth *Aberdeen* ***Suburb***, 2m/3km S of Aberdeen city centre across River Dee. **55 E4** NJ9303.
Kincraig *Aber.* ***Settlement***, 3m/4km W of Newburgh. **55 E2** NJ9624.
Kincraig *High.* ***Village***, on River Spey, in Badenoch and Strathspey district, 6m/9km NE of Kingussie. **52 A4** NH8305.
Kincraig Point *Fife* ***Coastal feature***, headland at E end of Largo Bay. **34 C5** NT4699.
Kincraigie *P. & K.* ***Settlement***, on W side of Strath Tay, 6m/10km SE of Pitlochry. **41 E5** NN9849.
Kindallachan *P. & K.* ***Village***, in Strath Tay, 5m/8km N of Dunkeld. **41 E5** NN9949.
Kindrochit Castle *Aber.* ***Castle***, ruined 14c castle, originally a hunting lodge at S side of Braemar on E side of Clunie Water. **53 D5** NO1591.
Kindrogan Field Centre *P. & K.* ***Other feature of interest***, 3m/4km NW of Kirkmichael, in River Ardle valley, to NE of Kindrogan Hill and Kindrogan Wood. Owned by Scottish Field Studies Association, it offers field courses on the natural environment. **41 F3** NO0562.
Kindrogan Hill *P. & K.* ***Mountain***, above Kindrogan in Strathardle, 3m/4km NW of Kirkmichael. Forested, with viewpoint on summit. Height 1624 feet or 495 metres. NO0462.
Kinellar *Aber.* ***Locality***, includes Muir of Kinellar and Kinellar House, 1km W of Blackburn. **54 D3** NJ8112.
Kinfauns *P. & K.* ***Village***, 3m/5km E of Perth across River Tay. **33 G2** NO1622.
Kinfauns Castle *P. & K.* ***Historic house***, Gothic-style mansion, 3m/4km E of Perth. NO1622.
Kinfauns Forest *P. & K.* ***Forest/woodland***, to NE of Kinfauns. **33 G2** NO1622.
King Edward *Aber.* ***Locality***, 4m/7km S of Banff. Castle of King Edward, medieval ruin 1m/2km S. NJ7157.
Kingarth *Arg. & B.* ***Village***, on Bute 3m/5km N of Garroch Head. Ruins of 12c St. Blane's Church (Historic Scotland) 2m/3km S. **22 B4** NS0956.
Kingholm Quay *D. & G.* ***Hamlet***, on E bank of River Nith, 2m/3km S of Dumfries. **9 D3** NX9773.
Kinghorn *Fife* Population: 2931. ***Small town***, popular small resort on Firth of Forth, 2m/3km E of Burntisland. Last Celtic King of Scotland, Alexander, died here in 1286. **25 G1** NT2686.
Kinghorn Loch *Fife* ***Lake/loch***, 1km W of Kinghorn. **25 G1** NT2587.
Kingie *High.* ***River***, in Lochaber district running E down Glen Kingie to River Garry, 2m/3km SE of dam of Loch Quoich. **49 G5** NH1000.
Kingie Pool *High.* ***River***, widening of Rivers Kingie and Garry at their confluence, 2m/3km SE of dam of Loch Quoich. NH1000.
Kinglas Water *Arg. & B.* ***River***, in Argyll, running W down Glen Kinglas to Loch Fyne at Cairndow, near head of loch. NN1710.
Kinglass *Arg. & B.* ***River***, in Argyll, rising on S side of Glas Bheinn Mhòr and running S, then W down Glen Kinglass to Loch Etive on S side of Ardmaddy Bay. NN0737.
Kinglassie *Fife* Population: 1419. ***Village***, 2m/3km SW of Leslie. **34 A5** NT2398.
Kingledores Burn *Sc.Bord.* ***River***, rising on slopes of Coomb Dod, 3m/5km W of Tweedsmuir and flowing NE to River Tweed at Kingledores, 3m/4km N of Tweedsmuir. **16 B3** NT1028.
Kingoodie *P. & K.* ***Locality***, on N side of Firth of Tay, 4m/7km W of Dundee. **34 B2** NO3329.
King's Cave *N.Ayr.* ***Other feature of interest***, cave on Arran, 1km NW of Torbeg and 2m/3km N of Blackwaterfoot. Possible setting for legend of Robert the Bruce and the spider; carvings on walls. **13 D2** NR8830.
Kings Muir *Sc.Bord.* ***Locality***, adjoining to S of Peebles. **17 D2** NT2539.
King's Park *Glas.* ***Suburb***, 3m/5km S of Glasgow city centre. NS5961.
King's Seat *P. & K.* ***Mountain***, 3m/5km SE of Burrelton. Height 1237 feet or 377 metres. **34 A1** NO2233.
King's Seat Hill *Clack.* ***Mountain***, on S edge of Ochil Hills, rising steeply 2m/4km NW of Dollar. Height 2125 feet or 648 metres. **33 E5** NS9399.
Kingsbarns *Fife* ***Village***, near coast, 3m/5km N of Crail. **35 D3** NO5912.
Kingsburgh *High.* ***Locality***, on E shore of Loch Snizort Beag, Skye. **57 G4** NG3955.
Kingscavil *W.Loth.* ***Settlement***, 2m/3km E of Linlithgow. **25 E2** NT0376.
Kingscross *N.Ayr.* ***Settlement***, near E coast of Arran, at S end of Lamlash Bay. **13 F3** NS0528.
Kingscross Point *N.Ayr.* ***Coastal feature***, headland to E of Kingscross on Arran. Site of Viking burial ground. **13 F3** NS0428.
Kingsdale *Fife* ***Suburb***, adjoining to S of Kennoway. **34 B4** NO3401.
Kingseat *Fife* ***Village***, 3m/5km NE of Dunfermline. **33 G5** NT1290.
Kingsford *Aberdeen* ***Settlement***, 1m/2km E of Westhill. **54 D4** NJ8406.
Kingsford *Aber.* ***Settlement***, 1m/2km SW of Alford. **54 A3** NJ5614.
Kingsford *Aber.* ***Settlement***, 3m/5km S of Turriff. **64 C5** NJ7244.
Kingsford *E.Ayr.* ***Settlement***, 3m/4km NE of Stewarton. **23 F5** NS4448.
Kingshouse *Stir.* ***Settlement***, 3m/4km SW of Lochearnhead. **32 A2** NN5620.
Kingshouse Hotel *High.* ***Settlement***, on W side of Rannoch Moor, 6m/10km SE of Kinlochleven. **39 E4** NN2654.
Kingskettle *Fife* ***Village***, 1m/2km S of Ladybank. **34 B4** NO3008.
Kingsmuir *Angus* ***Village***, 2m/3km SE of Forfar. **42 C5** NO4749.
Kingsmuir *Fife* ***Settlement***, 4m/7km W of Crail. NO5308.
Kingsteps *High.* ***Settlement***, dispersed settlement, 1m/2km E of Nairn. **62 B4** NH9057.
Kingston *E.Loth.* ***Settlement***, 2m/3km S of North Berwick. Ruins of 16c Fenton Tower. **26 C1** NT5482.
Kingston *Glas.* ***Suburb***, on S side of River Clyde, to SW of Glasgow city centre. Kingston Bridge carries M8 across River Clyde. NS5864.
Kingston *Moray* ***Village***, on Spey Bay, on W side of mouth of River Spey. **63 F3** NJ3365.
Kingsway East *Dundee* ***Locality***, industrial estate 2m/3km NE of Dundee city centre. NO4231.
Kingswell *E.Ayr.* ***Settlement***, 5m/8km SW of Eaglesham. **23 G5** NS5047.
Kingswells *Aberdeen* Population: 1120. ***Village***, 5m/7km W of Aberdeen. **55 D4** NJ8606.
Kingussie *High.* Population: 1298. ***Small town***, and tourist centre of River Spey 28m/45km S of Inverness. Highland Folk Museum. **51 G4** NH7500.
Kinharrachie *Aber.* ***Locality***, includes West Kinharrachie and East Kinharrachie, 2m/3km W of Ellon. **55 E1** NJ9231.
Kinharvie *D. & G.* ***Settlement***, 3m/4km W of New Abbey. **8 D4** NX9266.
Kinkell *Aber.* ***Locality***, with remains of 16c church (Historic Scotland), 2m/3km S of Inverurie. NJ7819.
Kinkell *E.Dun.* ***Settlement***, 2m/3km NW of Kirkintilloch. **24 A2** NS6375.
Kinkell Bridge *P. & K.* ***Settlement***, in Strathearn, 5m/8km SE of Crieff. **33 E3** NN9317.
Kinkell Church *Aber.* ***Ecclesiastical building***, ruins of 16c parish church with fine sacrament house (Historic Scotland) on E side of River Don, 1m/2km S of Inverurie. Includes grave slab of Gilbert of Greenlaw, killed in battle, 1411. **54 C3** NJ7819.
Kinkell Ness *Fife* ***Coastal feature***, small rocky headland, 2m/3km SE of St. Andrews. **34 D3** NO5315.
Kinknockie *Aber.* ***Locality***, 4m/7km S of Mintlaw. **65 F5** NK0041.
Kinloch *Fife* ***Hamlet***, 2m/3km NW of Ladybank. **34 A3** NO2712.
Kinloch *High.* ***River***, in Caithness district running NE into Kyle of Tongue. NC5553.
Kinloch *High.* ***River***, on Rum, flowing E to Kinloch at head of Loch Scresort on E coast of island. NM4099.
Kinloch *High.* ***Settlement***, at head of Loch More, Sutherland district. **74 C5** NC3434.

K

Kinloch *High.* ***Settlement***, at SE end of Loch Glass, 5m/7km NW of Evanton. **61 E2** NH5370.
Kinloch *High.* ***Settlement***, in Morvern, Lochaber district, on N bank of Kinloch River, near head of Loch Teacuis. **37 F4** NM6554.
Kinloch *High.* ***Village***, at head of Loch Scresort, on E coast of Rum. **48 A5** NM4099.
Kinloch *P. & K.* ***Hamlet***, 1m/2km W of Meigle. **42 A5** NO2644.
Kinloch *P. & K.* ***Village***, 2m/3km W of Blairgowrie. **41 G5** NO1444.
Kinloch Castle *High.* ***Castle***, at Kinloch on E coast of Rum. Early 20c red sandstone castle in Gothic style, built by Sir George Bullough, and now a hotel. **48 A5** NM4099.
Kinloch Hourn *High.* ***Locality***, in Lochaber district, at head of Loch Hourn. **49 F4** NG9507.
Kinloch Laggan *High.* ***Settlement***, at NE end of Loch Laggan, in Badenoch and Strathspey district. **40 A1** NN5489.
Kinloch Rannoch *P. & K.* ***Village***, at foot of Loch Rannoch. **40 B4** NN6658.
Kinlochaline Castle *High.* ***Castle***, at head of Loch Aline in Lochaber district. 15c square turreted tower, stronghold of Clan MacInnes. Now a ruin. **37 F5** NM6947.
Kinlochan *High.* ***Settlement***, in Sunart at head of Loch Doilet, 4m/6km N of Strontian. **38 A3** NM8167.
Kinlochard *Stir.* ***Settlement***, at head of Loch Ard, 4m/7km W of Aberfoyle. **31 G4** NN4502.
Kinlocharkaig *High.* ***Settlement***, near head of Loch Arkaig, Lochaber district. **49 F5** NM9890.
Kinlochbeoraid *High.* ***Settlement***, at head of Loch Beoraid, Lochaber district. **38 A1** NM8585.
Kinlochbervie *High.* ***Village***, on N side of Loch Inchard, W coast of Sutherland district. **74 B3** NC2256.
Kinlocheil *High.* ***Village***, in Lochaber district, near head of Loch Eil, on N shore. **38 B2** NM9779.
Kinlochetive *High.* ***Settlement***, near mouth of River Etive, 1km N of head of Loch Etive. **38 D5** NN1245.
Kinlochewe *High.* ***River***, running 2m/3km NW from village of Kinlochewe into Loch Maree. NH0261.
Kinlochewe *High.* ***Settlement***, in Ross and Cromarty district, 2m/3km SE of head of Loch Maree. **59 G3** NH0261.
Kinlochewe Forest *High.* ***Open space***, deer forest to N and W of Kinlochewe. **59 G3** NH0261.
Kinlochlaich *Arg. & B.* ***Settlement***, 1m/2km SE of Portnacroish. **38 B5** NM9346.
Kinlochleven *High.* Population: 1076. ***Small town***, in Lochaber district, at head of Loch Leven. Former industry was aluminium smelting. **39 D3** NN1861.
Kinlochluichart Forest *High.* ***Open space***, deer forest in Ross and Cromarty district between Loch Fannich and Loch Glascarnoch. **60 B2** NH2769.
Kinlochmoidart *High.* ***Locality***, at head of Loch Moidart, in Lochaber district. **37 G2** NM7072.
Kinlochmorar *High.* ***Settlement***, at head of Loch Morar, Lochaber district. **49 E5** NM8691.
Kinlochmore *High.* ***Village***, in Lochaber district, on E side of Kinlochleven. **39 D3** NN1962.
Kinlochnanuagh *High.* ***Locality***, in Lochaber district, 1km above head of Loch nan Uamh and 5m/8km E of Arisaig. NM7384.
Kinlochspelve *Arg. & B.* ***Settlement***, 3m/5km E of Lochbuie, near head of Loch Spelve, Mull. **29 F2** NM6526.
Kinloss *Moray* Population: 2281. ***Village***, near N coast, 3m/4km NE of Forres. Airfield to N. Ruins of 12c abbey. **62 C3** NJ0661.
Kinmount Gardens *D. & G.* ***Garden***, woodland and lakeside walks at Kinmount House, 4m/6km W of Annan. **9 F4** NY1468.
Kinmuck *Aber.* ***Hamlet***, 3m/5km E of Inverurie. **54 D3** NJ8119.
Kinnaber *Angus* ***Settlement***, near E coast, 3m/4km N of Montrose. 1m/2km W is site of former railway junction famous in days of 'Railway race to the North'. NO7261.
Kinnadie *Aber.* ***Settlement***, 2m/3km S of Stuartfield. **65 E5** NJ9743.
Kinnaird *P. & K.* ***Village***, 10m/16km W of Dundee. **34 A2** NO2428.
Kinnaird Castle *Angus* ***Historic house***, 19c mansion surrounded by deer park, 3m/5km SE of Brechin. NO6357.
Kinnaird Castle *P. & K.* ***Castle***, restored 15c tower on hill above village of Kinnaird, 9m/14km NE of Perth. NO2428.
Kinnairds Head *Aber.* ***Coastal feature***, headland to N of harbour at Fraserburgh. First lighthouse (Historic Scotland) built by Northern Lighthouse Company, contained within 16c castle built for Fraser family. **65 E3** NJ9967.
Kinnairdy Castle *Aber.* ***Historic house***, castellated mansion 2m/3km SW of Aberchirder. NJ6049.
Kinneff *Aber.* ***Settlement***, on E coast, 2m/4km NE of Inverbervie. **43 G2** NO8574.
Kinneff Church *Aber.* ***Ecclesiastical building***, 2m/3km NE of Inverbervie. Part of church formed hiding place for Scottish crown jewels smuggled from Dunnottar castle whilst under seige from Cromwell in 1651. **43 G2** NO8574.
Kinneil House *Falk.* ***Historic house***, mansion (Historic Scotland) of 16-17c, 1m/2km SW of Bo'ness. **25 D1** NS9880.
Kinnel Water *D. & G.* ***River***, rising N of Queensberry and running SE to River Annan, 1m/2km NE of Lochmaben. **9 E2** NY0983.
Kinnelhead *D. & G.* ***Settlement***, 4m/6km SW of Moffat. **16 B5** NT0201.
Kinnell *Angus* ***Settlement***, 1km E of Friockheim. **43 E4** NO6050.
Kinnell *Stir.* ***Settlement***, to E of Killin across River Dochart. **32 A1** NN5732.
Kinnesswood *P. & K.* ***Village***, 4m/6km SE of Milnathort. **33 G4** NO1702.
Kinnettles *Angus* ***Locality***, 3m/5km SW of Forfar. **42 C5** NO4346.
Kinning Park *Glas.* ***Suburb***, 1m/2km SW of Glasgow city centre. NS5664.
Kinnordy *Angus* ***Settlement***, 1m/2km NW of Kirriemuir. Loch of Kinnordy is marsh to SW. **42 B4** NO3655.
Kinnoull Hill *P. & K.* ***Hill***, 1m/2km E of Perth across River Tay, at SW end of Sidlaw Hills. Noted viewpoint. Height 728 feet or 222 metres. **33 G2** NO1322.
Kinpurney Hill *Angus* ***Mountain***, with tower at summit, and hillfort, 1m/2km E of Newtyle. Height 1132 feet or 345 metres. **42 B5** NO3141.
Kinrara *High.* ***Settlement***, 3m/5km S of Aviemore. **52 A4** NH8708.
Kinross *P. & K.* Population: 4552. ***Small town***, and resort on W side of Loch Leven, 9m/15km N of Dunfermline. **33 G4** NO1102.
Kinross House *P. & K.* ***Historic house***, late 17c house on shore of Loch Leven, to E of Kinross. **33 G4** NO1102.
Kinross Sevices *P. & K.* ***Other building***, service station to W of Kinross on A977 road near junction 6 of M90. **33 G4** NO1003.
Kinrossie *P. & K.* ***Village***, 7m/11km NE of Perth. **33 G1** NO1832.
Kintail Estate *High.* ***Open space***, mountainous area (National Trust for Scotland) extending N from Glen Shiel in Skye and Lochalsh district. It encompasses Five Sisters, part of Kintail Forest, Beinn Fhada and Falls of Glomach. Regarded as an excellent upland walking area, it is renowned for wildlife and magnificent scenery. NH0218.
Kintail Forest *High.* ***Open space***, mountainous tract in Skye and Lochalsh district, to NE of Glen Shiel. Mostly within Kintail Estate (National Trust for Scotland). Includes Five Sisters and Beinn Fhada. Herds of red deer and wild goats in area. **49 G3** NG9917.
Kintarvie *W.Isles* ***Settlement***, on Isle of Lewis, 3m/4km SW of head of Loch Erisort, to NW of Loch Seaforth. **67 E2** NB2217.
Kintessack *Moray* ***Settlement***, on edge of Culbin Forest, 3m/4km W of Forres. **62 B3** NJ0060.
Kintillo *P. & K.* ***Suburb***, at S side of Bridge of Earn. **33 G3** NO1317.
Kintocher *Aber.* ***Settlement***, 4m/6km S of Alford. **54 A4** NJ5709.
Kintore *Aber.* Population: 2028. ***Village***, on River Don, 4m/6km S of Inverurie. Site of Roman camp on W side of village. **54 C3** NJ7916.
Kintour *Arg. & B.* ***River***, flowing into Aros Bay on E coast of Islay. **20 C4** NR4651.
Kintour *Arg. & B.* ***Settlement***, on SE side of Islay, 8m/11km NE of Port Ellen. **20 C4** NR4551.
Kintra *Arg. & B.* ***Settlement***, 1km SW of Rubha nan Cearc, Mull. **28 C2** NM3125.
Kintra *Arg. & B.* ***Settlement***, at S end of Laggan Bay, Islay. **20 B5** NR3248.
Kintradwell *High.* ***Settlement***, 3m/4km N of Brora, Sutherland district. **73 E4** NC9107.
Kintraw *Arg. & B.* ***Settlement***, at head of Loch Craignish, to E of mouth of Barbreck River. **30 A4** NM8205.
Kintyre *Arg. & B.* ***Coastal feature***, peninsula in Argyll running S to Mull of Kintyre from narrow isthmus between East and West Loch Tarbert. Length 40m/64km; average width 8m/13km. Chief town is Campbeltown. Airfield at Machrihanish. **12 C2** NR7236.
Kinuachdrach *Arg. & B.* ***Locality***, near NE coast of Jura, 2m/3km from N end of island, with headland of Aird of Kinuachdrach to E. **29 G5** NR7098.
Kinuachdrach Harbour *Arg. & B.* ***Bay***, to SE of Kinuachdrach on E coast of Jura, 1m/2km from N end of island and at S end of Aird of Kinuachdrach. **29 G5** NR7098.
Kinveachy *High.* ***Settlement***, in Badenoch and Strathspey district, 4m/6km N of Aviemore. **52 B3** NH9118.
Kiplaw Croft *Aber.* ***Settlement***, 3m/4km SW of Cruden Bay. **55 F1** NK0533.
Kipp *Stir.* ***Settlement***, in valley of River Balvag, 1km S of Strathyre. **32 A3** NN5516.
Kippen *P. & K.* ***Settlement***, 1m/2km S of Dunning. **33 F3** NO0112.
Kippen *Stir.* ***Village***, 9m/15km W of Stirling. **32 B5** NS6594.
Kippenross House *Stir.* ***Other building***, Georgian house, now a guest house, adjoining to S of Dunblane. **32 C4** NN7800.
Kippford (Also known as Scaur.) *D. & G.* ***Village***, on E side of Urr Water estuary, 4m/6km S of Dalbeattie. **8 C5** NX8354.
Kippo Burn *Fife* ***River***, small stream flowing NE from 1km W of Kippo Farm to North Sea at Cambo Ness, 3m/4km NW of Fife Ness. **35 D4** NO6011.
Kirbister *Ork.* ***Locality***, on Mainland, on W side of Loch of Stenness. HY2514.
Kirbister *Ork.* ***Locality***, on Mainland, 4m/7km S of Finstown and 6m/9km W of Kirkwall, on W side of Loch of Kirbister. **78 C2** HY3607.
Kirbister *Ork.* ***Settlement***, 1m/2km E of Dishes, Stronsay. **81 E4** HY6824.
Kirbuster *Ork.* ***Settlement***, situated between Loch of Boardhouse and Loch of Hundland, in N Mainland. **80 A4** HY2825.
Kirivick *W.Isles* *Anglicised form of Cirbhig, qv.*
Kirk *High.* ***Settlement***, in Caithness district, 4m/6km NE of Watten. **77 E3** ND2859.
Kirk Burn *High.* ***River***, flowing first W then S to Sortat to become Burn of Lyth. **77 E2** ND3164.
Kirk Hill *S.Ayr.* ***Hill***, 2m/3km N of Dailly. Height 817 feet or 249 metres. **14 A5** NS2604.
Kirk Loch *D. & G.* ***Lake/loch***, small lake on SW side of Lochmaben. **9 E2** NY0782.
Kirk Ness *Shet.* ***Coastal feature***, promontory to N of Brough village, connected by narrow neck of land to N coast of Whalsay. HU5565.
Kirk of Mochrum *D. & G.* *Alternative name for Mochrum, qv.*
Kirk of Shotts (Also spelled Kirk o'Shotts.) *N.Lan.* ***Settlement***, 4m/7km W of Harthill. **24 C3** NS8462.
Kirk o'Shotts *N.Lan.* *Alternative spelling of Kirk of Shotts, qv.*
Kirk Yetholm *Sc.Bord.* ***Village***, on E side of Bowmont Water, 7m/12km SE of Kelso. N terminus of The Pennine Way. **18 C4** NT8228.
Kirkabister *Shet.* ***Settlement***, on SW coast of Bressay, 1m/2km S of Grindiscol. **83 D4** HU4837.
Kirkabister Ness *Shet.* ***Coastal feature***, low headland with lighthouse at SW point of Bressay. HU4837.
Kirkaig *High.* ***River***, on border of Ross and Cromarty and Sutherland districts, flowing NW into inlet of Loch Kirkaig on W coast. NC0719.
Kirkaig Point *High.* ***Coastal feature***, headland on W coast of Sutherland district between Lochs Inver and Kirkaig, 2m/4km SW of Lochinver. **70 C2** NC0521.
Kirkandrews *D. & G.* ***Settlement***, 5m/8km S of Gatehouse of Fleet. Cup and ring marked rock to NE. **3 G2** NX6048.
Kirkapoll *Arg. & B.* ***Locality***, on Gott Bay, Tiree, nearly 2m/3km N of Scarinish. NM0447.
Kirkbean *D. & G.* ***Village***, near Solway Firth, 11m/17km S of Dumfries. **9 D5** NX9759.
Kirkbuddo *Angus* ***Locality***, 4m/6km SW of Letham. **42 C5** NO5043.
Kirkburn *Sc.Bord.* ***Locality***, 3m/5km SE of Peebles. **17 D2** NT2938.
Kirkcaldy *Fife* Population: 47,155. ***Town***, port and resort, 11m/17km N of Edinburgh across Firth of Forth. Former textile and pottery town, with now more varied industries. Birthplace of economist Adam Smith, 1723, and architect Robert Adam, 1728. Links Market, held annually in April. 15c Ravenscraig Castle to N. **34 A5** NT2791.
Kirkcaldy Museum and Art Gallery *Fife* ***Other feature of interest***, in Kirkcaldy town centre. Gallery includes work by Camden Town Group, with local history exhibition in museum. **34 A5** NT2792.
Kirkcolm *D. & G.* ***Village***, on Rinns of Galloway, 5m/9km N of Stranraer. **6 B4** NX0268.
Kirkconnel *D. & G.* Population: 2329. ***Small town***, on River Nith, 3m/5km NW of Sanquhar. **15 F4** NS7312.
Kirkconnell *D. & G.* ***Settlement***, 2m/3km NE of New Abbey. **9 D4** NX9767.
Kirkconnell Tower *D. & G.* ***Historic house***, 2m/3km NE of New Abbey. Tower originally part of Kirkconnell House built in 1410; rest of house destroyed in 1570 by English army. NY9768.
Kirkcowan *D. & G.* ***Village***, 6m/10km SW of Newton Stewart. **7 E4** NX3260.
Kirkcudbright (Also known as Castledykes.) *D. & G.* Population: 3588. ***Small town***, on River Dee estuary at head of Kirkcudbright Bay. Site of 13c castle to W beside river. Ruins of MacLellan's Castle (Historic Scotland), 16c mansion, near main square. **8 A5** NX6850.
Kirkcudbright Bay *D. & G.* ***Bay***, on River Dee estuary, to S of Kirkcudbright, on N side of Solway Firth. **3 G2** NX6850.

K

Kirkdale *D. & G.* ***Settlement***, 4m/6km SE of Creetown. **7 G5** NX5153.
Kirkdean *Sc.Bord.* ***Settlement***, 1m/2km SW of Blyth Bridge. **25 F5** NT1244.
Kirkfield *S.Lan.* ***Locality***, adjoining to NW of Bothwell, 3m/4km NW of Hamilton. NS7059.
Kirkfieldbank *S.Lan.* ***Village***, 1m/2km W of Lanark across River Clyde. **24 C5** NS8643.
Kirkgunzeon *D. & G.* ***Village***, 4m/7km NE of Dalbeattie. **8 C4** NX8666.
Kirkgunzeon Lane *D. & G.* ***River***, issuing from Lochaber Loch and flowing SW through Kirkgunzeon village, then through Dalbeattie to Urr Water, 1km S of Dalbeattie. NX8260.
Kirkhill *Angus* ***Hamlet***, 3m/4km NW of Montrose. **43 E3** NO6860.
Kirkhill *High.* ***Village***, in Inverness district, 7m/11km W of Inverness. **61 E5** NH5545.
Kirkhill *Moray* ***Settlement***, 2m/3km NE of Rothes, on W side of River Spey. **63 F4** NJ3051.
Kirkhill Castle *S.Ayr.* ***Historic house***, late 16c house at Colmonell. NX1485.
Kirkhill Forest *Aberdeen* ***Forest/woodland***, NW of Aberdeen and 2m/3km W of Dyce Airport. NJ8412.
Kirkhill of Kennethmont *Aber. Alternative name for Kennethmont (village), qv.*
Kirkhope *Sc.Bord.* ***Settlement***, on Ettrick Water, 1km SW of Ettrickbridge. **17 E3** NT3823.
Kirkibost *High.* ***Locality***, on E side of Strathaird peninsula, Skye, 4m/7km N of Strathaird Point. **48 B3** NG5517.
Kirkibost *W.Isles* ***Settlement***, on Great Bernera, opposite Breasclete on W coast of Isle of Lewis, across East Loch Roag. **68 C4** NB1835.
Kirkibost Island *W.Isles* ***Island***, low-lying uninhabited island off W coast of North Uist 5m/8km SE of Aird an Rùnair. **45 F3** NF7565.
Kirkinch *Angus* ***Settlement***, 2m/3km E of Meigle. **42 B5** NO3144.
Kirkinner *D. & G.* ***Village***, 3m/4km S of Wigtown. **7 F5** NX4251.
Kirkintilloch *E.Dun.* Population: 20,780. ***Town***, on line of Antonine Wall, 7m/11km NE of Glasgow. Formerly a weaving and coalmining centre. **24 A2** NS6573.
Kirkland *D. & G.* ***Settlement***, 2m/3km NW of Kirkconnel. **15 F4** NS7214.
Kirkland *D. & G.* ***Settlement***, to SE of Forest of Ae, 2m/3km NE of Parkgate. **9 E2** NY0389.
Kirkland *D. & G.* ***Village***, 2m/3km E of Moniaive. **8 C1** NX8090.
Kirkland *Fife* ***Suburb***, N district of Methil. NO3600.
Kirkland Hill *D. & G.* ***Mountain***, 3m/4km N of Kirkconnel. Height 1676 feet or 511 metres. NS7316.
Kirkland of Longcastle *D. & G.* ***Settlement***, 4m/7km N of Monreith. **3 D2** NX3747.
Kirkleegreen Reservoir *N.Ayr.* ***Reservoir***, small reservoir 2m/4km NE of Beith. NS3855.
Kirkliston *Edin.* Population: 2739. ***Village***, 3m/4km S of South Queensferry. **25 F2** NT1274.
Kirkmadrine Stones *D. & G.* ***Historic/prehistoric site***, early Christian carved stones (Historic Scotland), some with Latin inscriptions, in churchyard of Kirkmadrine Church on Rinns of Galloway, 1m/2km SW of Sandhead. **2 A2** NX0848.
Kirkmaiden *D. & G.* ***Village***, on Rinns of Galloway, nearly 1m/2km W of Drummore. **2 B3** NX1236.
Kirkmichael *P. & K.* ***Village***, in Strathardle, 9m/14km E of Pitlochry. **41 F3** NO0860.
Kirkmichael *S.Ayr.* ***Village***, 3m/5km E of Maybole. **14 B5** NS3408.
Kirkmuirhill *S.Lan.* Population: 1900. ***Village***, adjoining to S of Blackwood, 6m/9km W of Lanark. **24 B5** NS7943.
Kirknewton *W.Loth.* Population: 1363. ***Village***, 10m/16km SW of Edinburgh. **25 F3** NT1166.
Kirknewton Station *W.Loth.* ***Other building***, railway station at W end of Kirknewton. **25 F3** NT1067.
Kirkney *Aber.* ***Settlement***, 5m/8km S of Huntly. **54 A1** NJ5132.
Kirkney Water *Aber.* ***River***, stream running NE into River Bogie, 1km NE of Kirkney. **53 G1** NJ5133.
Kirkoswald *S.Ayr.* ***Village***, 4m/7km W of Maybole. Souter Johnnie's Cottage (National Trust for Scotland), former home of John Davidson, the original Souter Johnnie of Burns' poem, Tam o' Shanter. **14 A5** NS2307.
Kirkpatrick Durham *D. & G.* ***Village***, 5m/8km N of Castle Douglas. **8 B3** NX7870.
Kirkpatrick-Fleming *D. & G.* ***Village***, 6m/10km SE of Ecclefechan. Bruce's Cave 1km W. 15c Merkland Cross (Historic Scotland) 2m/3km NW. **9 G3** NY2770.
Kirkstile *Aber.* ***Settlement***, 3m/5km S of Huntly. **54 A1** NJ5235.
Kirkstile *D. & G.* ***Village***, on Ewes Water, 4m/6km N of Langholm. **10 B2** NY3690.
Kirkstyle *High.* ***Hamlet***, on Pentland Firth, 4m/6km W of Duncansby Head. ND3472.
Kirkton *Aber.* ***Settlement***, 1m/2km NE of Auchleven. **54 B2** NJ6425.
Kirkton *Aber.* ***Settlement***, 2m/3km W of Turriff. **64 B4** NJ6950.
Kirkton *Aber.* ***Village***, 3m/5km SE of Alford. **54 B3** NJ6113.
Kirkton *Angus* ***Hamlet***, 3m/5km SW of Forfar. **42 C5** NO4246.
Kirkton *Arg. & B.* ***Settlement***, 1km E of Craignish Castle. **29 G4** NM7701.
Kirkton *D. & G.* ***Village***, 4m/6km N of Dumfries. Remains of Roman fort to NW. **9 D2** NX9781.
Kirkton *Fife* ***Settlement***, on Firth of Tay, 2m/4km W of Wormit. **34 B2** NO3625.
Kirkton *High.* ***Locality***, in Inverness district, 1km N of NE end of Loch Ness. **51 F1** NH6038.
Kirkton *High.* ***Settlement***, 1m/2km S of Melvich, Caithness district. **76 A2** NC8962.
Kirkton *High.* ***Settlement***, on N side of Loch Alsh, in Skye and Lochalsh district, 4m/6km W of Dornie. **49 E2** NG8327.
Kirkton *High.* ***Settlement***, 1m/2km N of Ardersier. **61 G4** NH7856.
Kirkton *High.* ***Settlement***, 6m/9km N of Dornoch across Loch Fleet. **72 C5** NH7999.
Kirkton *P. & K.* ***Settlement***, 4m/6km NE of Auchterarder. **33 E3** NN9618.
Kirkton *Sc.Bord.* ***Locality***, 3m/4km E of Hawick. **17 G4** NT5413.
Kirkton *W.Loth.* ***Locality***, in Livingston, 2m/3km SW of town centre. NT0366.
Kirkton Head *Aber.* ***Coastal feature***, headland on NE coast, 3m/5km N of Peterhead. **65 G4** NK1150.
Kirkton Manor *Sc.Bord.* ***Settlement***, 3m/4km SW of Peebles. **16 D2** NT2237.
Kirkton of Airlie *Angus* ***Locality***, 5m/8km W of Kirriemuir. **42 B4** NO3151.
Kirkton of Auchterhouse *Angus* ***Village***, 6m/10km NW of Dundee. **34 B1** NO3438.
Kirkton of Barevan *High.* ***Settlement***, 2m/3km S of Cawdor. **62 A5** NH8347.
Kirkton of Bourtie *Aber.* ***Settlement***, 1m/2km S of Oldmeldrum. **54 D2** NJ8024.
Kirkton of Collace *P. & K.* ***Settlement***, 1km SW of Collace and 7m/11km NE of Perth. **33 G1** NO1931.
Kirkton of Craig *Angus* ***Village***, 1m/2km SW of Montrose. **43 F4** NO7055.
Kirkton of Culsalmond (Also known as Culsalmond.) *Aber.* ***Village***, 9m/14km SE of Huntly. **54 B1** NJ6432.
Kirkton of Durris *Aber.* ***Village***, 5m/8km E of Banchory. **54 C5** NO7796.
Kirkton of Glenbuchat *Aber.* ***Settlement***, on S slopes of Glen Buchat below Ben Newe, 2m/3km NE of Strathdon. **53 F3** NJ3715.
Kirkton of Glenisla *Angus* ***Village***, on River Isla, 8m/12km N of Alyth. **42 A3** NO2160.
Kirkton of Kingoldrum *Angus* ***Village***, 3m/5km W of Kirriemuir. Site of Balfour Castle to S. **42 B4** NO3355.
Kirkton of Largo *Fife Alternative name for Upper Largo, qv.*
Kirkton of Lethendy *P. & K.* ***Settlement***, 4m/6km SW of Blairgowrie. **41 G5** NO1241.
Kirkton of Logie Buchan *Aber.* ***Village***, 2m/3km E of Ellon across River Ythan. **55 E2** NJ9829.
Kirkton of Maryculter (Also known as Maryculter.) *Aber.* ***Village***, 1m/2km SE of Peterculter across River Dee. **55 D5** NO8599.
Kirkton of Menmuir *Angus* ***Village***, 5m/8km NW of Brechin. **42 D3** NO5364.
Kirkton of Monikie *Angus* ***Settlement***, 4m/6km NW of Carnoustie. **34 D1** NO5138.
Kirkton of Oyne *Aber.* ***Locality***, 1km E of Oyne and 6m/9km NW of Inverurie. NJ6825.
Kirkton of Rayne (Also known as Rayne.) *Aber.* ***Village***, 8m/12km NW of Inverurie. **54 B1** NJ6930.
Kirkton of Skene *Aber.* ***Village***, 9m/14km W of Aberdeen. **54 D4** NJ8007.
Kirkton of Strathmartine *Angus* ***Village***, 4m/6km NW of Dundee. **34 B1** NO3735.
Kirkton of Tealing (Also known as Tealing.) *Angus* ***Hamlet***, 5m/7km N of Dundee. Mast to NW. Tealing House to E has unusual dovecote; also souterrain or earth-house (Historic Scotland). **34 C1** NO4138.
Kirkton Sculptured Stones *Arg. & B.* ***Historic/prehistoric site***, 1km E of Craignish Castle, 2m/3km SW of Adfern. **29 G4** NM7701.
Kirktonhill *Aber.* ***Hamlet***, 1km NE of Marykirk. **43 E3** NO6965.
Kirktonhill *W.Dun.* ***Suburb***, W district of Dumbarton. NS3975.
Kirktown *Aber.* ***Locality***, 1m/2km S of Fraserburgh. NJ9965.
Kirktown *Aber.* ***Suburb***, S district of Peterhead. **65 F4** NK1346.
Kirktown of Alvah *Aber.* ***Village***, near N coast, 2m/4km S of Banff. **64 B3** NJ6760.
Kirktown of Auchterless (Also known as Auchterless.) *Aber.* ***Village***, 5m/8km S of Turriff. **64 C5** NJ7141.
Kirktown of Clatt *Aber. Alternative name for Clatt, qv.*
Kirktown of Deskford *Moray* ***Village***, near N coast, 4m/6km S of Cullen. Ruined church (Historic Scotland). **64 A3** NJ5061.
Kirktown of Fetteresso *Aber.* ***Village***, on E side of Fetteresso Forest, 1m/2km W of Stonehaven. **43 G1** NO8585.
Kirktown of Slains *Aber.* ***Locality***, adjoining to N of Collieston, 5m/9km E of Ellon. Remains of Old Castle of Slains 1m/2km NE of Collieston. **55 F2** NK0428.
Kirkwall *Ork.* Population: 6469. ***Small town***, chief town and port of Mainland and capital of Orkney, situated at N end of narrow neck of land between Wide Firth to N and Scapa Flow to S, 24m/38km N of Scottish mainland at Duncansby Head. Location of 12c Bishop's Palace (Historic Scotland), with later additions including 16c round tower, and 17c Renaissance style Earl's Palace (Historic Scotland). **80 C5** HY4411.
Kirkwall Airport *Ork.* ***Airport/airfield***, on Mainland, situated 3m/4km SE of Kirkwall, at head of Inganess Bay. **79 D2** HY4808.
Kirn *Arg. & B.* ***Locality***, in Argyll, adjoining to N of Dunoon, on W shore of Firth of Clyde. **22 C2** NS1878.
Kirriemuir *Angus* Population: 5571. ***Small town***, former linen-weaving centre, 5m/8km NW of Forfar. The Thrums of Barrie's novels, whose birthplace here houses a museum (National Trust for Scotland). **42 B4** NO3854.
Kirriereoch Hill *D. & G.* ***Mountain***, in Glentrool Forest Park on border with South Ayrshire, 4m/7km N of Loch Trool and 1m/2km NW of Merrick. Height 2578 feet or 786 metres. **7 F2** NX4287.
Kirriereoch Loch *D. & G.* ***Lake/loch***, in Glentrool Forest, 5m/8km NW of Loch Trool. **7 E2** NX3686.
Kirroughtree Forest *D. & G.* ***Forest/woodland***, 4m/7km NE of Newton Stewart. NX4473.
Kirtle Water *D. & G.* ***River***, rising 6m/10km W of Langholm and running S to Kirtlebridge, then SE to Solway Firth 1m/2km S of Gretna. **9 G3** NY3165.
Kirtlebridge *D. & G.* ***Village***, 3m/5km SE of Ecclefechan. **9 G3** NY2372.
Kirtleton *D. & G.* ***Settlement***, 6m/9km NE of Ecclefechan. NY2680.
Kirtomy *High.* ***Village***, near N coast of Caithness district, 3m/4km E of Bettyhill. **75 G2** NC7463.
Kirtomy Bay *High.* ***Bay***, 1km N of Kirtomy, on N coast of Caithness district, 3m/4km NE of Bettyhill. **75 G2** NC7464.
Kirtomy Point *High.* ***Coastal feature***, headland 1m/2km N of Kirtomy. **75 G2** NC7463.
Kiscadale *N.Ayr.* ***Locality***, two localities, North and South Kiscadale, on Whiting Bay, E coast of Arran. **13 F3** NS0426.
Kishorn *High.* ***Locality***, in Ross and Cromarty district, at head of Loch Kishorn. NG8340.
Kishorn *High.* ***River***, running S to head of Loch Kishorn. **59 E5** NG8340.
Kishorn Island *High.* ***Island***, small uninhabited island at entrance to Loch Kishorn. NG8037.
Kisimul *W.Isles Alternative spelling of Kiessimul, qv.*
Kisimul Castle *W.Isles Alternative spelling of Kiessimul Castle, qv.*
Kitchener's Monument *Ork.* ***Other feature of interest***, situated on Marwick Head, 1m/2km NW of Marwick on W coast of Mainland. Memorial to crew of HMS Hampshire and Lord Kitchener, whose boat sank off coast in 1916. **80 A4** HY2225.
Kittybrewster *Aberdeen* ***Suburb***, 1m/2km NW of Aberdeen city centre. NJ9207.
Klibreck *High.* ***Settlement***, 1m/2km SE of Altnaharra, on S shore of Loch Naver. **75 E5** NC5834.
Klibreck Burn *High.* ***River***, flowing NE into Loch Naver, 1m/2km E of Altnaharra. **75 E5** NC5934.
Knabbygates *Moray* ***Settlement***, 3m/4km N of Milltown of Rothiemay. **64 A4** NJ5552.
Knaik *P. & K.* ***River***, running SE to Allan Water, 1m/2km S of Braco. **32 C3** NN8307.
Knap of Howar *Ork.* ***Historic/prehistoric site***, site of prehistoric stone dwellings (Historic Scotland) on W coast of Papa Westray. Remains date from between 2400 BC and 2800 BC. **80 C1** HY4851.
Knap of Trowieglen *Ork.* ***Mountain***, 3m/4km E of Rackwick. Height 1309 feet or 399 metres. **78 B3** ND2498.
Knapdale *Arg. & B.* ***Locality***, area of Argyll, bounded by Crinan Canal to N, and East and West Loch Tarbert to S. Largely moorland, with many small lochs. **21 F3** NR8078.
Knapdale Forest *Arg. & B.* ***Forest/woodland***, at NW end of Knapdale. **21 F1** NR8176.
Knapp *Dundee* ***Hamlet***, 2m/3km NW of Longforgan. **34 A1** NO2831.
Knapps Loch *Inclyde* ***Lake/loch***, small loch 1m/2km SE of Kilmacolm. NS3658.
Knarie Burn *D. & G.* ***River***, rising on E side of Brockloch Hill and flowing SW to join Urr Water, 1km SE of Corsock. **8 B3** NX7675.
Knarston *Ork.* ***Settlement***, on Mainland, 1km E of Dounby. HY3020.
Knaven *Aber.* ***Locality***, comprises many dispersed settlements, 3m/4km S of New Deer. **65 D5** NJ8843.
Knightsridge *W.Loth.* ***Suburb***, to NW of Livingston town centre. NT0469.

Knightswood *Glas.* ***Suburb***, 4m/7km NW of Glasgow city centre. NS5369.
Knipoch *Arg. & B.* ***Settlement***, on S shore of Loch Feochan, 2m/3km NE of Kilninver. **30 A2** NM8522.
Knock *Arg. & B.* ***Settlement***, on S bank of River Bà, 1km S of Gruline, Mull. **29 E1** NM5438.
Knock (Gaelic form: Cnoc Uaine.) *High.* ***Settlement***, on Knock Bay, Skye, on E coast of Sleat peninsula, adjoining to E of Teangue. NG6709.
Knock *Moray* ***Settlement***, 7m/12km E of Keith. **64 A4** NJ5452.
Knock *W.Isles Anglicised form of Cnoc, qv.*
Knock Bay *High.* ***Bay***, on E coast of Sleat peninsula, Skye. **48 C4** NG6709.
Knock Castle (Also known as Camus Castle.) *High.* ***Castle***, on Skye, at E end of bay, also called Camus Castle, ruined castle of Barons of Sleat. **48 C4** NG6709.
Knock Fell *D. & G.* ***Hill***, adjacent to W of Knock of Luce, 4m/6km E of Glenluce. Fort at summit. Height 574 feet or 175 metres. **6 D5** NX2555.
Knock Head *Aber.* ***Coastal feature***, headland on N coast, 2m/4km NW of Banff. **64 B3** NJ6566.
Knock Hill *Aber.* ***Mountain***, to N of Knock. Height 1410 feet or 430 metres. **64 A4** NJ5452.
Knock Hill *Fife* ***Mountain***, 2m/3km NE of Saline. Height 1194 feet or 364 metres. **33 F5** NT0593.
Knock More *Moray* ***Mountain***, in wooded area, 3m/4km E of Rothes. Height 1168 feet or 356 metres. **63 F4** NJ3150.
Knock Moss *D. & G.* ***Open space***, afforested area adjoining to S of Dernaglar Loch, 4m/7km E of Glenluce. **6 D5** NX2657.
Knock of Auchnahannet *High.* ***Settlement***, 4m/6km N of Grantown-on-Spey. **52 C1** NJ0633.
Knock of Balmyle *P. & K.* ***Mountain***, to E of Balmyle, 3m/5km NW of Bridge of Cally. Height 1456 feet or 444 metres. **41 G4** NO1156.
Knock of Braemoray *Moray* ***Mountain***, 2m/3km N of Dava. Height 1496 feet or 456 metres. **62 C5** NJ0141.
Knock of Crieff *P. & K.* ***Hill***, with notable viewpoint, 1m/2km N of Crieff. Height 912 feet or 278 metres. NN8622.
Knock Saul *Aber.* ***Mountain***, surrounded by Whitehaugh Forest, 5m/7km N of Alford. Height 1351 feet or 412 metres. **54 A2** NJ5723.
Knockaird *W.Isles* ***Settlement***, near N end of Isle of Lewis, 1km NW of Port Nis. NB5364.
Knockalava *Arg. & B.* ***Settlement***, 6m/10km NE of Lochgilphead. **30 B5** NR9196.
Knockally *High.* ***Settlement***, 1km SW of Dunbeath. **73 G2** ND1429.
Knockan *High.* ***Hamlet***, in Sutherland district, adjoining to S of Elphin, 8m/12km S of Inchnadamph. **71 E3** NC2110.
Knockan *Moray* ***Mountain***, 5m/8km NE of Charlestown of Aberlour. Height 1220 feet or 372 metres. **63 F5** NJ3546.
Knockandhu *Moray* ***Village***, 4m/7km NE of Tomintoul. **53 E2** NJ2123.
Knockando *Moray* ***Locality***, on N bank of River Spey, 7m/11km W of Craigellachie. Includes Knockando Distillery. **63 D5** NJ1941.
Knockando Distillery *Moray* ***Other feature of interest***, distillery in glen of Knockando Burn, near N bank of River Spey and 1m/2km S of Upper Knockando. Originally built in 1898, it produces whisky predominantly for blending. **63 D5** NJ1841.
Knockandy Hill *Aber.* ***Mountain***, 2m/3km SW of Gartly. Height 1424 feet or 434 metres. **54 A1** NJ5431.
Knockarthur *High.* ***Settlement***, in Sutherland district, 7m/11km NW of Golspie. NC7506.
Knockbain *High.* ***Settlement***, 3m/4km NW of Munlochy. **61 F4** NH6256.
Knockban *High.* ***Locality***, in Strath Bran, 4m/7km E of Achnasheen. **60 B3** NH2161.
Knockbreck *High.* ***Settlement***, adjoining to SE of Tain. **61 G1** NH7981.
Knockbrex *D. & G.* ***Settlement***, overlooking Andwall Isle, on E side of Wigtown Bay, 4m/7km S of Gatehouse of Fleet. **3 F2** NX5849.
Knockdamph *High.* ***Settlement***, 10m/16km E of Ullapool. Inaccessible by road. **71 E5** NH2895.
Knockdee *High.* ***Settlement***, 3m/4km NE of Halkirk. **77 D2** ND1661.
Knockdolian *S.Ayr.* ***Hill***, prominent hill 2m/4km NE of Ballantrae. Height 869 feet or 265 metres. **6 B2** NX1184.
Knockdow *Arg. & B.* ***Settlement***, 2m/3km N of Ardyne Point. **22 C2** NS1070.
Knockencorsan *N.Ayr.* ***Mountain***, elongated mass aligned NE to SW, rising to over 330 metres at head of Noddsdale Water, 3m/5km E of Skelmorlie. **22 D3** NS2366.
Knockendon Reservoir *N.Ayr.* ***Reservoir***, 4m/6km NW of Dalry. **22 D4** NS2452.
Knockenkelly *N.Ayr.* ***Settlement***, on E coast of Arran, towards N end of Whiting Bay. **13 F3** NS0427.
Knockentiber *E.Ayr.* ***Hamlet***, 2m/3km NW of Kilmarnock. **14 C2** NS3939.
Knockfin *High.* ***Settlement***, 4m/6km SW of Cannich. **50 B2** NH2926.
Knockfin Heights *High.* ***Open space***, high ground on border of Sutherland and Caithness districts, rising to 1404 feet or 428m. Marshland and numerous small lochs. **76 B5** NC9134.
Knockgray *D. & G.* ***Settlement***, 1m/2km E of Carsphairn. **7 G1** NX5793.
Knockhill Motor Racing Circuit *Fife* ***Motor racing circuit***, 5m/8km N of Dunfermline. **33 F5** NT0693.
Knockinlaw *E.Ayr.* ***Suburb***, N district of Kilmarnock. NS4239.
Knocklearn *D. & G.* ***Settlement***, 2m/3km N of Corsock. **8 B3** NX7579.
Knocknagael Boar Stone *High.* ***Historic/prehistoric site***, 7c or 8c Pictish stone (Historic Scotland), bearing outline of wild boar, situated 3m/4km S of Inverness. **61 F5** NH6541.
Knocknaha *Arg. & B.* ***Settlement***, on Kintyre, 3m/4km SW of Campbeltown. **12 B4** NR6818.
Knocknain *D. & G.* ***Settlement***, 6m/9km W of Stranraer. **6 A4** NW9764.
Knocknairshill Reservoir *Inclyde* ***Reservoir***, small reservoir 3m/5km SE of Greenock. NS3073.
Knocknalling *D. & G.* ***Settlement***, 3m/4km NW of St. John's Town of Dalry. **7 G2** NX5984.
Knockrome *Arg. & B.* ***Settlement***, adjoining to W of Ardfernal, Jura. **21 D2** NR5571.
Knockruan Loch *Arg. & B.* ***Lake/loch***, small loch or tarn in Kintyre 2m/3km NE of Campbeltown. NR7322.
Knocksting Loch *D. & G.* ***Lake/loch***, small loch or tarn 5m/8km W of Moniaive. NX6988.
Knockton *Angus* ***Mountain***, in Forest of Alyth, 3m/4km W of Bellaty. Height 1604 feet or 489 metres. **41 G4** NO1958.
Knockville *D. & G.* ***Settlement***, 6m/9km NW of Newton Stewart. **7 E3** NX3672.
Knockvologan *Arg. & B.* ***Settlement***, 3m/4km S of Fionnphort, Ross of Mull. **28 C3** NM3119.
Knowe *D. & G.* ***Settlement***, 7m/12km NW of Newton Stewart. **7 E3** NX3171.
Knowe of Onstan Chambered Cairn *Ork.* ***Historic/prehistoric site***, chambered cairn (Historic Scotland) at Knowe of Onstan on S side of Loch of Stenness, Mainland, 3m/4km NE of Stromness. **80 A5** HY2811.
Knowe of Yarso Chambered Cairn *Ork.* ***Historic/prehistoric site***, site of Neolithic communal burial-chamber (Historic Scotland) at Knowe of Yarso, on Rousay, 2m/3km W of Brinyan. **80 C4** HY4028.
Knowes Hill *Sc.Bord.* ***Mountain***, 1m/2km NW of Clovenfords. Height 1220 feet or 372 metres. **17 F2** NT4338.
Knowes of Elrick *Aber.* ***Settlement***, 1m/2km NW of Aberchirder. **64 B4** NJ6053.
Knoweside *S.Ayr.* ***Settlement***, 3m/5km NW of Maybole. **14 A4** NS2512.
Knowetownhead *Sc.Bord.* ***Hamlet***, 4m/6km NE of Hawick. **17 G4** NT5418.
Knowhead *Aber.* ***Settlement***, 1m/2km W of Strichen. **65 E4** NJ9255.
Knox Hill *Aber.* ***Hill***, 1m/2km SW of Inverbervie. Height 522 feet or 159 metres. **43 G2** NO8171.
Knox Knowe *Sc.Bord.* ***Mountain***, on W side of Carter Fell in Cheviot Hills, 4m/6km SW of Carter Bar. Height 1637 feet or 499 metres. **11 E1** NT6402.
Knoydart *High.* ***Large natural feature***, mountainous area of Lochaber district between Lochs Hourn and Nevis, bordering Sound of Sleat between Mainland and Isle of Skye. **48 D4** NG8301.
Kyle *E.Ayr.* ***Locality***, area of land between Ayr in W and Cumnock in E. **14 D2** NS5021.
Kyle Akin *High.* ***Sea feature***, narrow strait between Kyleakin, village on Skye, and Kyle of Lochalsh on Scottish mainland, at mouth of Loch Alsh. Crossed by toll road bridge. **48 D2** NG7526.
Kyle Castle *E.Ayr.* ***Castle***, ruined castle at confluence of Guelt Water and Glenmuir Water, 5m/8km E of Cumnock. NS6419.
Kyle Forest *E.Ayr.* ***Forest/woodland***, 3m/5km N of Dalmellington. NS4911.
Kyle More (Also known as Caol Mòr.) *High.* ***Sea feature***, sea channel between Raasay and Scalpay. **48 B1** NG5833.
Kyle of Durness *High.* ***Sea feature***, estuary of River Dionard running into Balnakeil Bay on N coast of Sutherland district, to W of Durness. **74 C2** NC3668.
Kyle of Lochalsh *High.* ***Village***, port in Skye and Lochalsh district, on N side of entrance to Loch Alsh. Road bridge to Kyleakin on Skye across narrow strait of Kyle Akin. **49 D2** NG7627.
Kyle of Sutherland *High.* ***Sea feature***, narrows between Invershin and Bonar Bridge, Sutherland district, at head of Dornoch Firth. **72 A5** NH5795.
Kyle of Tongue *High.* ***Sea feature***, estuarial inlet on N coast of Caithness district running out into Tongue Bay. Village of Tongue on E side of inlet. **75 E3** NC5859.
Kyle Rhea *High.* ***Sea feature***, narrow strait between E end of Skye and W coast of Scottish mainland, connecting Loch Alsh to N with Sound of Sleat to S. Vehicle ferry at S end of strait. **49 D2** NG7922.
Kyle Rona (Also known as Caol Rona.) *High.* ***Sea feature***, strait separating islands of Raasay and Rona. **58 C4** NG6154.
Kyleakin *High.* ***Village***, on Skye, 1km SW of Kyle of Lochalsh across Kyle Akin. **49 D2** NG7526.
Kylerhea *High.* ***Settlement***, at E end of Skye, on Kyle Rhea, 4m/7km SE of Kyleakin. Vehicle ferry across strait to Scottish mainland. **49 D2** NG7820.
Kyles of Bute *Arg. & B.* ***Sea feature***, narrow channel surrounding N part of Bute and separating it from mainland of Argyll. **22 B2** NS0175.
Kyles Scalpay *W.Isles Anglicised form of Caolas Scalpaigh, qv.*
Kyles Stockinish *W.Isles* ***Village***, on E side of entrance to Loch Stockinish, on SE coast of South Harris, 6m/9km S of Tarbert. NG1391.
Kylesbeg *High.* ***Settlement***, on N shore of Loch Moidart, opposite E end of Shona Beag. **37 F2** NM6773.
Kylesknoydart *High.* ***Locality***, on N shore of Loch Nevis, Lochaber district, at S end of Knoydart. Loch narrows considerably above this point. **49 E5** NM8093.
Kylesku *High.* ***Hamlet***, at W end of Loch Glendhu, 1km NW of Unapool. NC2233.
Kylesmorar *High.* ***Locality***, 1m/2km NE of Tarbet on N side of North Morar, on S shore of Loch Nevis, Lochaber district. **49 E5** NM8093.
Kylestrome *High.* ***Settlement***, on N side of Loch a' Chàirn Bhàin, W coast of Sutherland district. **74 B5** NC2134.
Kyloag *High.* ***Settlement***, 3m/5km E of Bonar Bridge. **72 B5** NH6691.
Kype Muir *S.Lan.* ***Open space***, upland moorland 4m/6km S of Strathaven, below peaks of Middle Rig and Martinside. **15 F2** NS7038.
Kype Reservoir *S.Lan.* ***Reservoir***, in course of Kype Water, 4m/6km SE of Strathaven. NS7338.
Kype Water *S.Lan.* ***River***, issuing from Kype Reservoir and flowing N, then NW to Avon Water 1m/2km SE of Strathaven. **15 F2** NS7143.

L

Labost *W.Isles* ***Settlement***, near NW coast of Isle of Lewis, 1m/2km NW of Bragar. **69 D3** NB2749.
Lacasaigh (Anglicised form: Laxay.) *W.Isles* ***Village***, near E coast of Isle of Lewis, on N side of Loch Erisort. **69 E5** NB3321.
Lacasdal *W.Isles Gaelic form of Laxdale (village), qv.*
Lachlan Castle *Arg. & B. Alternative name for Castle Lachlan, qv.*
Lackalee *W.Isles Anglicised form of Leac a' Li, qv.*
Ladder Hills *Aber.* ***Large natural feature***, range of hills, 6m/10km E of Tomintoul. Summit at Carn Mòr, 2636 feet or 804 metres. **53 E3** NJ2718.
Ladhar Bheinn *High.* ***Mountain***, in Knoydart, in Lochaber district, 4m/7km NE of Inverie. Munro: height 3346 feet or 1020 metres. **49 E4** NG8203.
Lady Gifford's Well *Sc.Bord.* ***Other feature of interest***, well at West Linton, topped by figure of Lady Gifford, carved 1666. **25 F4** NT1452.
Lady Isle *S.Ayr.* ***Island***, small island with lighthouse in Firth of Clyde 3m/5km W of Troon. **14 A3** NS2729.
Lady Kirk *Ork.* ***Ecclesiastical building***, remains of 17c church at Pierowall on shore of Pierowall Bay, Westray. **80 C2** HY4348.
Ladybank *Fife* Population: 1373. ***Small town***, 5m/8km SW of Cupar. **34 A3** NO3009.
Ladyfield *Arg. & B.* ***Settlement***, in Glen Aray, 4m/7km N of Inveraray. **30 C3** NN0915.
Ladykirk *Sc.Bord.* ***Village***, on River Tweed, 6m/9km NE of Coldstream. **27 F5** NT8847.
Ladykirk Church *Sc.Bord.* ***Ecclesiastical building***, 1km W of Norham, W of River Tweed. Built by James IV in 1500. All stone construction to preserve it from border disputes. **27 F5** NT8847.
Ladylea Hill *Aber.* ***Mountain***, 3m/4km N of Strathdon. Height 1998 feet or 609 metres. **53 F3** NJ3416.
Lady's Holm *Shet.* ***Island***, small uninhabited island lying off S coast of Mainland 2m/4km NW of Sumburgh Head. **83 F5** HU3709.
Lady's Rock *Arg. & B.* ***Island***, rock marked by beacon, lying between Eilean Musdile and E coast of Mull. **29 G1** NM7734.
Ladysford *Aber.* ***Settlement***, 7m/12km SW of Fraserburgh. **65 E3** NJ8960.
Ladyside Height *Sc.Bord.* ***Mountain***, on N flank of Eastside Heights, 1m/2km SE of Dewar. Height 1771 feet or 540 metres. **26 A5** NT3647.
Ladywell *W.Loth.* ***Suburb***, near Livingston town centre. NT0568.
Lael *High.* ***River***, rising on N slope of Beinn Dearg and flowing NW, then W into Loch Broom. **60 B1** NH1785.
Lael Forest *High.* ***Forest/woodland***, above head of Loch Broom, Ross and Cromarty district. NH1982.
Lag Burn *Aber.* ***River***, rising on N slopes of Long Bank and flowing NE to join River Bogie, 3m/4km S of Huntly. **53 G1** NJ5235.

Laga *High.* ***Settlement***, 1m/2km E of Glenborrodale, Lochaber district. **37 F3** NM6360.
Lagalochan *Arg. & B.* ***Settlement***, 2m/3km SE of Kilmelford. **30 A3** NM8711.
Lagavulin *Arg. & B.* ***Village***, on S coast of Islay, 1km W of Ardbeg. Distillery. **20 C5** NR4045.
Lagg *Arg. & B.* ***Locality***, on Lagg Bay, on E coast of Jura, 3m/5km S of head of Loch Tarbert. **21 D2** NR5978.
Lagg *N.Ayr.* ***Settlement***, near S coast of Arran, 7m/12km SW of Lamlash. **13 E3** NR9521.
Lagg *S.Ayr.* ***Settlement***, 2m/3km NE of Dunure. **14 A4** NS2717.
Lagg Bay *Arg. & B.* ***Bay***, on E coast of Jura, 3m/5km S of head of Loch Tarbert. NR5978.
Laggan *Arg. & B.* ***River***, on Islay rising near E coast and running W to Laggan Bay, 1m/2km E of Laggan Point. **20 B4** NR2955.
Laggan *Arg. & B.* ***Settlement***, on N side of Laggan Bay, Islay. **20 A4** NR2855.
Laggan *High.* ***Settlement***, at NE end of Loch Lochy, 1km N of South Laggan and 3m/5km SW of Invergarry. Laggan Swing Bridge 1km N. **50 B5** NN2997.
Laggan *High.* ***Village***, on River Spey, in Badenoch and Strathspey district, 6m/10km N of Dalwhinnie. **51 F5** NN6194.
Laggan *Moray* ***Settlement***, on W side of River Fiddich, 2m/3km SE of Dufftown. **53 F1** NJ3436.
Laggan *Stir.* ***Settlement***, on W side of Loch Lubnaig, 1m/2km S of Strathyre. **32 A3** NN5614.
Laggan Bay *Arg. & B.* ***Bay***, small bay at SE end of Loch Tuath, W coast of Mull. **36 D5** NM4540.
Laggan Bay *Arg. & B.* ***Bay***, on Islay, 5m/8km wide, extending S from Laggan Point to Rubha Mòr. **20 A4** NR2955.
Laggan Bridge *High.* ***Bridge***, spans River Spey at Laggan, 7m/11km SW of Newtonmore. NN6194.
Laggan Deer Forest *Arg. & B.* ***Open space***, deer forest on E side of Loch Buie, Mull. NM6221.
Laggan Point *Arg. & B.* ***Coastal feature***, headland on Islay at entrance to Loch Indaal, 3m/5km SW of Bowmore. NR2755.
Laggan Swing Bridge *High.* ***Bridge***, swing bridge carrying road across Caledonian Canal at SW end of Loch Oich. **50 B5** NN2999.
Laggangairn Standing Stones *D. & G.* ***Historic/prehistoric site***, two Bronze Age standing stones (Historic Scotland) on Southern Upland Way near Killgallioch, 7m/11km S of Barrhill. One has Early Christian incised cross. **6 D3** NX2272.
Laggantalluch Head *D. & G.* ***Coastal feature***, headland on W coast of Rinns of Galloway, 3m/5km W of Drummore. **2 A3** NX0836.
Lagganulva *Arg. & B.* ***Settlement***, near head of Loch Tuath, Mull, 4m/7km SE of Kilninian. **37 D5** NM4541.
Lagganvoulin *Moray* ***Settlement***, 1m/2km SE of Tomintoul. **53 D3** NJ1817.
Laglingarten *Arg. & B.* ***Settlement***, 3m/5km E of Inveraray across Loch Fyne. **30 D4** NN1408.
Lagnalean *High.* ***Settlement***, 3m/5km SW of Inverness. **61 F5** NH6241.
Lagrae *D. & G.* ***Settlement***, 2m/3km NW of Kirkconnel. **15 F4** NS7013.
Laguna *P. & K.* ***Settlement***, 3m/4km N of Stanley. **33 G1** NO1036.
Lahill *Fife* ***Locality***, includes Lahill House, Lahill Mains and Lahill Craig, 2m/3km NE of Lower Largo. **34 C4** NO4403.
Laid *High.* ***Settlement***, in Sutherland district, 5m/8km S of Durness. **74 D3** NC4159.
Laide *High.* ***Village***, in Ross and Cromarty district 5m/8km SE of Greenstone Point on W coast. **70 A5** NG8991.
Laig *High.* ***Settlement***, on Eigg, 1km SW of Cleadale. **37 D1** NM4687.
Laighstonehall *S.Lan.* ***Suburb***, SW district of Hamilton. NS7054.
Laight *E.Ayr.* ***Settlement***, 1m/2km SW of New Cumnock. **15 E4** NS6111.
Laiken Forest *High.* ***Forest/woodland***, 3m/4km SE of Nairn. **62 B4** NH9053.
Laimhrig *W.Isles* ***Coastal feature***, headland on E coast of Isle of Lewis, 1m/2km N of Cellar Head. **69 G2** NB5558.
Lainchoil *High.* ***Settlement***, 4m/6km SE of Nethy Bridge. **52 C3** NJ0618.
Lair *P. & K.* ***Settlement***, in Glen Shee, over Shee Water from Cray. **41 G3** NO1463.
Lair of Aldararie ***Mountain***, 3m/5km N of Clova. Summit on border of Aberdeenshire and Angus. Height 2729 feet or 832 metres. **42 B2** NO3178.
Laird's Seat *Moray* ***Mountain***, on W side of Glen Fiddich, 3m/5km S of Dufftown. Height 1499 feet or 457 metres. **53 F1** NJ3134.
Laird's Seat *S.Lan.* ***Mountain***, 4m/7km SE of Eaglesham. Height 1184 feet or 361 metres. **24 A5** NS6045.
Lairg *High.* ***Village***, at SE end of Loch Shin, in Sutherland district, 17m/27km W of Golspie on E coast. **72 A4** NC5806.
Lairg Lodge *High.* ***Settlement***, on NE shore of Loch Shin, 1km NW of Lairg. **72 A4** NC5707.
Lairg Station *High.* ***Other building***, railway station 2m/3km S of Lairg. **72 A4** NC5804.
Lairgs of Tain *High.* ***Open space***, S slopes of Morangie Forest, 4m/6km SW of Tain. **61 G1** NH7279.
Lairig an Laoigh *High.* ***Other feature of interest***, 30m/48km route, part footpath, part mountain pass, traversing Cairngorm Mountains from Braemar to Nethy Bridge. **52 C4** NJ0209.
Lairig Breisleich ***Other feature of interest***, mountain pass on border of Perth & Kinross and Stirling, 4m/6km SW of Bridge of Balgie. **40 A5** NN5541.
Lairig Ghru ***Inland physical feature***, deep defile creating a mountain pass between Braeriach and Cairn Gorm, dividing Cairngorm Mountains into E and W ranges. **52 B4** NH9603.
Lairig Leacach *High.* ***Valley***, carrying Allt na Lairige SE into S end of Loch Treig. **39 E2** NN2874.
Lairigmor *High.* ***Settlement***, on West Highland Way, 4m/7km NW of Kinlochleven. **38 D3** NN1264.
Laithers *Aber.* ***Locality***, comprises Hill of Laithers, Mains of Laithers and Mill of Laithers on S bank of River Deveron, 3m/5km W of Turriff. **64 B5** NJ6749.
Lake of Menteith *Stir.* ***Lake/loch***, to S of Menteith Hills, 5m/8km SW of Callander. Remains of medieval priory (Historic Scotland) on Inchmahome island and ruins of medieval castle on smaller Inch Talla island. **32 A5** NN5700.
Lamachan Hill *D. & G.* ***Mountain***, in Glentrool Forest Park 2m/4km SE of Loch Trool. Height 2348 feet or 716 metres. **7 F3** NX4377.
Lamahip *Aber.* ***Mountain***, 4m/6km SE of Aboyne. Height 1325 feet or 404 metres. **54 A5** NO5592.
Lamancha *Sc.Bord.* ***Settlement***, 3m/5km SW of Leadburn. **25 G4** NT1952.
Lamb *E.Loth.* ***Island***, islet 1m/2km W of North Berwick. Haunt of sea birds. **26 C1** NT5386.
Lamb Head *Ork.* ***Coastal feature***, headland at SE end of Stronsay. **81 E4** HY6921.
Lamb Hoga *Shet.* ***Coastal feature***, peninsula at SW corner of Fetlar between Wick of Tresta and Colgrave Sound. **85 F4** HU6088.
Lamb Holm *Ork.* ***Island***, small uninhabited island off S coast of Mainland to SE of St. Mary's, joined to Mainland by road causeway, first part of Churchill Barrier. **79 D2** HY4800.
Lamba *Shet.* ***Island***, uninhabited island in Yell Sound 1m/2km N of entrance to Sullom Voe. Area about 120 acres or 48 hectares. **84 C4** HU3981.
Lamba Ness *Ork.* ***Coastal feature***, headland on SW coast of Sanday, 3m/5km N of Spur Ness. HY6138.
Lamba Ness *Shet.* ***Coastal feature***, headland on NE coast of Unst. **85 F1** HP6715.
Lamba Taing *Shet.* ***Coastal feature***, headland on E coast of Mainland, 1km N of Leebotten. **82 D5** HU4326.
Lambaness *Ork.* ***Village***, on SW coast of Sanday, inland from headland at Lamba Ness. HY6137.
Lambden *Sc.Bord.* ***Hamlet***, 2m/3km NW of Eccles. NT7443.
Lamberton *Sc.Bord.* ***Settlement***, 3m/5km NW of Berwick-upon-Tweed. **27 G4** NT9657.
Lamberton Beach *Sc.Bord.* ***Coastal feature***, area of rocky coastline to NE of Lamberton, 4m/6km NW of Berwick-upon-Tweed. **27 G4** NT9758.
Lambgarth Head *Shet.* ***Coastal feature***, headland on E coast of Mainland, 6m/9km N of Lerwick. HU4550.
Lambhill *Glas.* ***Suburb***, 2m/4km N of Glasgow city centre. NS5769.
Lambhoga Head *Shet.* ***Coastal feature***, headland on E coast of Mainland, 1m/2km SE of Boddam. **83 G4** HU4013.
Lamblair Knowe *D. & G.* ***Mountain***, on Eskdalemuir Forest, 4m/7km NE of Eskdalemuir. Height 1332 feet or 406 metres. **17 D5** NT2903.
Lamh Dhearg *P. & K.* ***Mountain***, to W of Glen Shee, 1m/2km W of Cray. Height 1886 feet or 575 metres. **41 G3** NO1263.
Lamington *High.* ***Village***, 4m/6km SW of Tain. **61 G2** NH7476.
Lamington *S.Lan.* ***Village***, 6m/9km SW of Biggar. **16 A2** NS9831.
Lamlash *N.Ayr.* ***Village***, and small port on Lamlash Bay, on E coast of Arran, 3m/5km S of Brodick. **13 F2** NS0231.
Lamlash Bay *N.Ayr.* ***Bay***, on E coast of Arran, 3m/5km S of Brodick. **13 F2** NS0231.
Lamloch *D. & G.* ***Settlement***, 6m/10km SE of Dalmellington. **7 G1** NX5296.
Lammer Law *E.Loth.* ***Mountain***, peak on Lammermuir Hills, 4m/6km S of Gifford. Height 1732 feet or 528 metres. **26 C3** NT5261.
Lammermuir ***Locality***, large upland area straddling borders of Lothian and Scottish Borders, extending W from St. Abb's Head and culminating in Lammermuir Hills. **27 D4** NT7560.
Lammermuir Hills ***Large natural feature***, range of hills with SW to NE axis, summit of which is Meikle Says Law, 1755 feet or 535 metres high. **26 B4** NT5861.
Lampay Islands *High.* ***Island***, two islets on E side of Loch Dunvegan, Skye, 3m/5km E of Dunvegan Head. **57 F4** NG2255.
Lanark *S.Lan.* Population: 8877. ***Small town***, market town above E bank of River Clyde, 11m/18km SE of Motherwell. **24 C5** NS8843.
Landerberry *Aber.* ***Locality***, 1km S of Echt. **54 C4** NJ7404.
Landhallow *High.* ***Settlement***, near E coast of Caithness, 1km W of Latheron. ND1833.
Landmark *High.* ***Other feature of interest***, forest heritage park situated at Carrbridge, 7m/11km N of Aviemore, with woodland walks, adventure playground, tree top trails and 70 foot or 21 metre wooden viewing tower. Attractions also include waterflume ride, maze, working steam-powered sawmill, exhibitions and audio-visual show about forest. **52 B2** NH9022.
Lang Craig *Angus* ***Coastal feature***, rock headland at S end of Lunan Bay to E of Ethie Haven, 3m/4km E of Inverkeilor. **43 F5** NO7048.
Lang Stane o'Craigearn *Aber.* *See Craigearn.*
Langais (Anglicised form: Langass.) *W.Isles* ***Settlement***, on North Uist, 1m/2km NW of Locheport. **45 G3** NF8365.
Langamull *Arg. & B.* ***Settlement***, on Mull, 1m/2km NE of Calgary. **36 C4** NM3853.
Langass *W.Isles* *Anglicised form of Langais, qv.*
Langaton Point *High.* ***Coastal feature***, headland at NW end of Stroma in Pentland Firth. **77 F1** ND3479.
Langbank *Renf.* ***Village***, on S bank of River Clyde, opposite Dumbarton. **23 E2** NS3873.
Langdale Burn *High.* ***River***, rising from Loch Syre and flowing E to join River Naver. NC6944.
Langdyke *Fife* ***Hamlet***, 2m/3km NW of Kennoway. **34 B4** NO3304.
Langholm *D. & G.* Population: 2538. ***Small town***, former mill town on River Esk, 15m/24km E of Lockerbie and 18m/29km N of Carlisle. Birthplace of poet, Hugh MacDiarmid. **10 B3** NY3684.
Langhope Burn *Sc.Bord.* ***River***, flowing E from Shaws Under Loch to Ale Water, 2m/3km SW of Ashkirk. **17 F4** NT4520.
Langlands *D. & G.* ***Settlement***, 2m/3km W of Kirkcudbright. **8 A5** NX6552.
Langlee *Sc.Bord.* ***Hamlet***, 2m/3km S of Jedburgh. **18 A5** NT6417.
Langshaw *Sc.Bord.* ***Settlement***, 3m/4km NE of Galashiels. **17 G2** NT5139.
Langshawburn *D. & G.* ***Settlement***, 4m/6km NE of Garwaldwaterfoot, accessible only by track. **17 D5** NT2904.
Langside *Glas.* ***Suburb***, 3m/4km SW of Glasgow city centre. NS5761.
Langside *P. & K.* ***Settlement***, 8m/12km N of Dunblane. **32 C3** NN7913.
Langskaill *Ork.* ***Settlement***, 1km N of Bakie Skerry, on S coast of Westray. **80 C2** HY4342.
Langwell *High.* ***Settlement***, on S side of River Oykel, 2m/3km E of Oykel Bridge. **71 G4** NC4101.
Langwell Forest *High.* ***Open space***, moorland area astride Langwell Water, in Caithness district, W and NW of Berriedale. **73 F2** ND0425.
Langwell House *High.* ***Settlement***, 1km W of Berriedale. **73 G2** ND1022.
Langwell Water *High.* ***River***, in Caithness district, rising on Langwell Forest and flowing E to coast at Berriedale. **73 F2** ND1122.
Lanrick Castle *Stir.* ***Historic house***, mansion on S bank of River Teith 3m/4km NW of Doune. NN6803.
Lantern of the North *Moray* *See Elgin Cathedral.*
Lanton *Sc.Bord.* ***Village***, 2m/3km NW of Jedburgh. **18 A4** NT6221.
Laphroaig *Arg. & B.* ***Village***, on S coast of Islay, 1m/2km E of Port Ellen. Distillery. **20 B5** NR3845.
Lapidary Workshops *Aber.* ***Other feature of interest***, gemstone workshops at Garlogie, 3m/5km E of Echt. **54 C4** NJ7704.
Larach na Gaibhre *Arg. & B.* ***Settlement***, on W coast of Kintyre, 9m/14km W of Tarbert. **21 F3** NR7269.
Larachbeg *High.* ***Settlement***, 1km N of head of Loch Aline, Lochaber district. **37 F5** NM6948.
Larbert *Falk.* ***Town***, former iron-working town, 2m/4km NW of Falkirk. **24 C1** NS8582.
Larg *D. & G.* ***Settlement***, at confluence of Water of Minnoch and River Cree, 7m/11km NW of Newton Stewart. **7 E3** NX3674.
Larg Hill *D. & G.* ***Mountain***, 7m/11km N of Newton Stewart. Height 2214 feet or 675 metres. **7 F3** NX4275.
Largie *Aber.* ***Settlement***, 7m/12km SE of Huntly. **54 B1** NJ6131.
Largiemore *Arg. & B.* ***Hamlet***, on SE coast of Loch Fyne, 5m/8km E of Lochgilphead. **22 A1** NR9486.
Larglear Hill *D. & G.* ***Hill***, 3m/5km W of Corsock. Height 925 feet or 282 metres. **8 B3** NX7176.
Largo *Fife* ***Locality***, consists of two adjacent villages: Lower Largo on Largo Bay, 3m/4km NE of Leven, and Upper Largo, 1km further NE. NO4102.

L

Largo Bay *Fife* ***Bay***, on Firth of Forth, extending E from Buckhaven and Methil to Kincraig Point. **34 C4** NO4202.
Largo Law *Fife* ***Hill***, 1m/2km N of Upper Largo. Height 951 feet or 290 metres. **34 C4** NO4204.
Largo Ward *Fife Alternative spelling of Largoward, qv.*
Largoward (Also spelled Largo Ward.) *Fife* ***Village***, 4m/6km NE of Upper Largo. **34 C4** NO4607.
Largs *N.Ayr.* Population: 10,925. ***Town***, old weaving town and resort on Largs Bay, on Firth of Clyde opposite N end of Great Cumbrae. Formerly a major fishing port. Largs Old Kirk (Historic Scotland) is mausoleum added to parish church in 1636; it features painted ceiling depicting the four seasons, and elaborate carved stone tomb in Renaissance style. **22 D4** NS2059.
Largs Bay *N.Ayr.* ***Bay***, on Firth of Clyde, opposite N end of Great Cumbrae. NS2059.
Largue *Aber.* ***Settlement***, 4m/6km S of Inverkeithny. **64 B5** NJ6441.
Largybaan *Arg. & B.* ***Settlement***, on S part of Kintyre, 6m/9km NW of Southend. **12 B4** NR6114.
Largybeg *N.Ayr.* ***Settlement***, on SE coast of Arran, to W and above Largybeg Point. **13 F3** NS0523.
Largybeg Point *N.Ayr.* ***Coastal feature***, headland on E coast of Arran at S end of Whiting Bay. Standing stones. **13 F3** NS0523.
Largymore *N.Ayr.* ***Settlement***, on E coast of Arran, 1km S of Whiting Bay. **13 F3** NS0424.
Larig Hill *High.* ***Mountain***, 5m/8km E of Dava. Height 1788 feet or 545 metres. **62 C5** NJ0840.
Larkfield *Inclyde* ***Suburb***, 1m/2km S of Gourock. NS2375.
Larkhall *S.Lan.* Population: 15,493. ***Town***, 4m/6km SE of Hamilton. **24 B4** NS7651.
Laroch *High.* ***River***, in Lochaber district, flowing NE below Beinn a' Bheithir to S shore of Loch Leven at Ballachulish. **38 C4** NN0858.
Larriston *Sc.Bord.* ***Settlement***, in valley of Liddel Water, 6m/9km NE of Newcastleton. **10 D2** NY5494.
Larriston Fells *Sc.Bord.* ***Open space***, 4m/6km W of Kielder, on W side of Kielder Forest, with many streams running down W slopes into Larriston Burn. Highest point is 1679 feet or 512 metres. **11 D2** NY5692.
Lary *Aber.* ***Settlement***, at foot of Lary Hill, 3m/5km NW of Ballater. **53 F4** NJ3300.
Lassintullich *P. & K.* ***Settlement***, on S side of Dunalastair Water, 2m/3km SE of Kinloch Rannoch. **40 C4** NN6957.
Lassodie *Fife* ***Settlement***, 2m/3km SW of Kelty. **33 G5** NT1292.
Lasswade *Midloth.* ***Town***, adjoining Bonnyrigg 2m/3km SW of Dalkeith. **26 A3** NT3066.
Lathallan Mill *Fife* ***Settlement***, 4m/6km NE of Lower Largo. **34 C4** NO4605.
Latheron *High.* ***Village***, near E coast of Caithness district, 15m/24km SW of Wick. **77 D5** ND1933.
Latheronwheel (Also known as Janetstown.) *High.* ***Village***, near E coast of Caithness district, 1m/2km SW of Latheron. **77 D5** ND1832.
Lathockar *Fife* ***Settlement***, 4m/6km S of St. Andrews. **34 C3** NO4910.
Lathones *Fife* ***Settlement***, 1m/2km NE of Largoward. **34 C4** NO4708.
Lathrisk *Fife* ***Settlement***, 1m/2km NE of Falkland. **34 A4** NO2708.
Lauchentyre *D. & G.* ***Settlement***, 3m/4km W of Gatehouse of Fleet. **7 G5** NX5557.
Lauchintilly *Aber.* ***Settlement***, 4m/6km SW of Kintore. **54 C3** NJ7512.
Lauder *Sc.Bord.* Population: 1064. ***Small town***, on Leader Water, 9m/14km N of Melrose. Thirlestane Castle to NE. **26 C5** NT5347.
Lauder Common *Sc.Bord.* ***Open space***, moorland 2m/3km SW of Lauder. **26 B5** NT4946.
Lauderdale *Sc.Bord.* ***Valley***, carrying Leader Water and running SE from Oxton, through Lauder and Earlston, to its confluence with River Tweed at Leaderfoot. **26 C4** NT5348.
Laughing Law *Sc.Bord.* ***Mountain***, 2m/3km NW of Abbey St. Bathans. Height 1010 feet or 308 metres. **27 E3** NT7364.
Laurencekirk *Aber.* Population: 1611. ***Small town***, market town 10m/16km NE of Brechin. Formerly noted for manufacture of snuff-boxes. **43 F2** NO7171.
Laurieston *D. & G.* ***Village***, 9m/14km N of Kirkcudbright. **8 A4** NX6864.
Laurieston *Falk.* ***Locality***, 1m/2km E of Falkirk. Site of Roman fort on line of Antonine Wall to E. **24 D2** NS9179.
Laurieston Forest *D. & G.* ***Forest/woodland***, to W of Laurieston. NX6464.
Lauriston Castle *Edin.* ***Castle***, 4m/6km NW of Edinburgh city centre, dating in part from late 16c. Grounds overlook Firth of Forth. **25 G2** NT2076.
Laverhay *D. & G.* ***Settlement***, on hillside, 4m/7km SE of Beattock. **9 F1** NY1498.
Laverhay Height *D. & G.* ***Mountain***, 5m/8km SE of Beattock. Height 1588 feet or 484 metres. **9 F1** NY1598.
Law *S.Lan.* Population: 2900. ***Village***, 2m/4km NW of Carluke. **24 C4** NS8152.
Law Castle *N.Ayr.* ***Castle***, with late 15c tower at West Kilbride. NS2148.
Law Kneis *Sc.Bord.* ***Mountain***, 2m/3km SE of Ettrick. Height 1633 feet or 498 metres. **17 D4** NT2913.
Lawers *P. & K.* ***Settlement***, 1m/2km NE of Comrie. **32 C2** NN7923.
Lawers *P. & K.* ***Village***, on N side of Loch Tay, 7m/11km SW of Kenmore, near mouth of Lawers Burn. **32 B1** NN6739.
Lawers Burn *P. & K.* ***River***, on N side of Loch Tay. **40 B5** NN6739.
Laws *Angus* ***Hamlet***, 2m/3km N of Monifieth. Prehistoric fort and broch to SW. **34 C1** NO4935.
Lax Firth *Shet.* ***Sea feature***, inlet on E coast of Mainland, 5m/8km N of Lerwick. **82 D3** HU4447.
Laxa Burn *Shet.* ***River***, stream on Yell running N into head of Mid Yell Voe. **85 D4** HU5091.
Laxadale Lochs *W.Isles* ***Lake/loch***, series of three lochs running N from Urgha on N shore of East Loch Tarbert, North Harris. **67 D3** NB1801.
Laxay *W.Isles Anglicised form of Lacasaigh, qv.*
Laxdale *W.Isles* ***River***, rising 5m/8km NW of Laxdale and flowing past village into Loch a' Tuath, Isle of Lewis. **69 E4** NB4234.
Laxdale (Gaelic form: Lacasdal.) *W.Isles* Population: 1258. ***Village***, at head of River Laxdale estuary, 1m/2km N of Stornoway, Isle of Lewis. **69 F4** NB4234.
Laxfirth *Shet.* ***Settlement***, on Mainland, at head of inlet of Lax Firth. **82 D3** HU4446.
Laxfirth *Shet.* ***Settlement***, on Mainland, on S side of Dury Voe. **83 D2** HU4759.
Laxford *High.* ***River***, in Sutherland district, running from Loch Stack NW to Loch Laxford. NC2347.
Laxford Bridge *High.* ***Bridge***, road junction and bridge over River Laxford at head of Loch Laxford on W coast of Sutherland district. **74 B4** NC2346.
Laxo *Shet.* ***Settlement***, on E coast of Mainland, at head of Dury Voe. **82 D1** HU4463.
Laxo Water *Shet.* ***Lake/loch***, on Mainland, 1km N of Laxo. HU4464.
Lea Taing *Ork.* ***Coastal feature***, small rocky promontory 1m/2km S of Rerwick Head on Mainland. **80 D5** HY5410.
Leabaidh an Daimh Bhuidhe ***Mountain***, summit of Ben Avon massif, on border of Aberdeenshire and Moray, N of Braemar. Munro: height 3841 feet or 1171 metres. **52 D4** NJ1301.
Leac a' Li (Anglicised form: Lackalee.) *W.Isles* ***Settlement***, 1m/2km W of Greosabhagh, South Harris. **66 D4** NG1292.
Leac Dhonn *High.* ***Coastal feature***, rocky headland at NW end of Annat Bay, 8m/12km NW of Ullapool, Ross and Cromarty district. **70 B5** NH0199.
Leac Mhòr *High.* ***Coastal feature***, flat rock on coast, N of Opinan and 1m/2km SE of Greenstone Point, Ross and Cromarty district. **70 A5** NG8897.
Leac na Hoe *W.Isles* ***Coastal feature***, headland, easternmost point of North Uist, 3m/4km E of Lochportain. **56 C2** NF9872.
Leac nam Faoileann *High.* ***Coastal feature***, headland at westernmost point of Soay, and 1m/2km S of Skye across Soay Sound. **48 A3** NG4214.
Leac Shoilleir *High.* ***Mountain***, 3m/5km N of Glenborrodale. Height 1443 feet or 440 metres. **37 F3** NM6065.
Leac Tressirnish *High.* ***Coastal feature***, headland on E coast of Skye, 3m/4km NE of The Storr. **58 B4** NG5257.
Leacann Doire Bainneir *High.* ***Mountain***, on E side of NE end of Loch Lochy, 2m/3km SE of Laggan. Height 2099 feet or 640 metres. **50 C5** NN3094.
Leacann nan Gall *Arg. & B.* ***Mountain***, at head of Inverchaolain Glen, 4m/7km NW of Dunoon. Height 1863 feet or 568 metres. **22 C2** NS1078.
Leacann Water *Arg. & B.* ***River***, stream in Argyll running E from Loch Leacann, then S to Loch Fyne at Furnace. NN0200.
Leachie Hill *Aber.* ***Mountain***, 4m/6km NW of Glenbervie. Height 1299 feet or 396 metres. **43 F1** NO7385.
Leachkin *High.* ***Locality***, in Inverness district, 2m/3km W of Inverness. **61 F5** NH6444.
Leack *Arg. & B.* ***Settlement***, on S shore of Loch Fyne, 4m/6km SW of Strachur. **30 C5** NS0498.
Leadburn *Midloth.* ***Hamlet***, 3m/4km S of Penicuik. **25 G4** NT2355.
Leader Water *Sc.Bord.* ***River***, rising on Lammermuir Hills and flowing S down Lauderdale to River Tweed at Leaderfoot, 2m/3km E of Melrose. **26 C4** NT5734.
Leaderfoot *Sc.Bord.* ***Settlement***, 2m/3km E of Melrose, at confluence of Leader Water and River Tweed. NT5734.
Leadhills *S.Lan.* ***Town***, former lead-mining town 6m/10km SW of Abington. **15 G4** NS8815.
Leagach *High. Anglicised form of Liathach, qv.*
Leagag *P. & K.* ***Mountain***, rising to over 600 metres in Rannoch district, 2m/3km SE of Bridge of Gaur. **40 A4** NN5153.
Lealt *Arg. & B.* ***Settlement***, in Glen Lealt, on E coast of Jura, 2m/3km N of Ardlussa. **29 F5** NR6690.
Lealt *High.* ***Settlement***, near NE coast of Skye, 11m/17km N of Portree. **58 B3** NG5060.
Lealt Burn *Arg. & B.* ***River***, running through Glen Lealt into Sound of Jura, on E coast of Jura. **29 F5** NR6690.
Leana Mhòr *High.* ***Mountain***, in Lochaber district, on E side of Glen Roy, 4m/7km N of Roybridge. Height 2247 feet or 685 metres. **39 E1** NN2887.
Leana Mhòr *High.* ***Mountain***, on E side of Glen Roy, 5m/8km NE of Roybridge. Height 2224 feet or 678 metres. **39 F1** NN3087.
Leanach *Arg. & B.* ***Settlement***, 4m/7km SW of Strachur. **30 C5** NS0497.
Leanach *High.* ***Locality***, 6m/10km E of Inverness. **61 G5** NH7544.
Leanachan Forest *High.* ***Forest/woodland***, in Lochaber district 4m/6km SW of Spean Bridge. **39 D2** NN1977.
Leanaig *High.* ***Settlement***, 1m/2km SE of Conon Bridge. **61 E4** NH5654.
Leanoch *Moray* ***Settlement***, on W bank of River Lossie, 1m/2km E of Kellas. **63 D4** NJ1954.
Leanoch Burn *Moray* ***River***, stream flowing N down Glen Latterach into Glenlatterach Reservoir, 6m/10km S of Elgin. **63 D4** NJ1852.
Leap Moor *Inclyde* ***Open space***, moorland area, to E of Wemyss Bay. **22 D3** NS2369.
Leapmoor Forest *Inclyde* ***Forest/woodland***, on W side of Leap Moor. NS2270.
Leargybreck *Arg. & B.* ***Locality***, on E coast of Jura, 3m/4km N of Craighouse. **20 D2** NR5371.
Leask *Aber.* ***Locality***, comprises many dispersed settlements, 4m/6km E of Ellon. **55 F1** NK0232.
Leathad an Taobhain *High.* ***Mountain***, 4m/6km E of Loch an t-Seilich. Height 2959 feet or 902 metres. NN8185.
Leathad Dail nan Cliabh *High.* ***Mountain***, 1m/2km SW of Duchally, to W of Glen Cassley. Height 1079 feet or 329 metres. **71 F3** NC3715.
Lecht Ski Centre *Moray* ***Other feature of interest***, centre providing dry slope, winter and floodlit skiing, 6m/10km SE of Tomintoul. **53 E3** NJ2413.
Lechuary *Arg. & B.* ***Settlement***, in valley of River Add, 4m/7km N of Lochgilphead. **30 A5** NR8795.
Lecket Hill *E.Dun.* ***Mountain***, on Campsie Fells, 2m/4km NE of Lennoxtown. Height 1791 feet or 546 metres. **24 A1** NS6481.
Leckfurin *High.* ***Settlement***, near N coast of Caithness district, 1m/2km S of Bettyhill. **75 G3** NC7059.
Leckgruinart *Arg. & B.* ***Locality***, on Islay, 4m/6km S of Ardnave Point. **20 A3** NR2769.
Leckie *High.* ***Settlement***, 4m/7km NE of Kinlochewe. **59 G3** NH0864.
Leckie *Stir.* ***Locality***, comprises Inch of Leckie, Wester Leckie and Old Leckie, 1m/2km W of Gargunnock. **32 B5** NS6894.
Leckmelm *High.* ***Locality***, on E shore of Loch Broom, Ross and Cromarty district, 4m/6km SE of Ullapool. **71 D5** NH1690.
Leckroy *High.* ***Settlement***, in upper part of Glen Roy, 9m/14km NE of Roybridge. **50 C5** NN3592.
Ledaig *Arg. & B.* ***Locality***, adjoining to S of Tobermory, Mull. NM5055.
Ledaig *Arg. & B.* ***Settlement***, on Ardmucknish Bay, 2m/3km N of Connel, Argyll. **30 B1** NM9037.
Ledaig Point *Arg. & B.* ***Coastal feature***, headland on S end of Ardmucknish Bay and on N side of entrance to Loch Etive. NM8935.
Ledard *Stir.* ***Settlement***, on N shore of Loch Ard, 4m/7km NW of Aberfoyle. **31 G4** NN4602.
Ledbeg *High.* ***Settlement***, on Ledbeg River, 1m/2km E of Cam Loch. **71 E3** NC2413.
Ledcharrie *Stir.* ***Settlement***, in Glen Dochart, 5m/8km SW of Killin. **32 A2** NN5028.
Ledgowan Forest *High.* ***Open space***, deer forest S of Loch a' Chroisg in Ross and Cromarty district. **59 G4** NH1256.
Ledmore *Arg. & B.* ***Settlement***, at S end of Loch Frisa, 4m/6km NW of Salen, Mull. **37 E5** NM5246.
Ledmore *High.* ***Settlement***, in Sutherland district, 6m/10km S of Inchnadamph. **71 E3** NC2412.
Lednagullin *High.* ***Settlement***, 1km E of Armadale, near N coast of Caithness district. **75 G2** NC8064.
Lednock *P. & K.* ***River***, running SE down Glen Lednock to River Earn at Comrie. Falls of Lednock at Deil's Caldron, 1m/2km N of Comrie. **32 C2** NN7722.
Lee *Arg. & B.* ***Settlement***, on Mull, 1m/2km E of Bunessan. **28 D2** NM4021.
Lee Pen *Sc.Bord.* ***Mountain***, 1m/2km N of Innerleithen. Height 1647 feet or 502 metres. **17 E2** NT3238.
Leebotten *Shet.* ***Settlement***, 1km N of Sandwick, on E coast of Mainland. **82 D5** HU4324.
Leet Water *Sc.Bord.* ***River***, rising N of Whitsome and flowing S to join River Tweed at Coldstream. **27 F5** NT8439.
Leetown *P. & K.* ***Hamlet***, 3m/4km W of Errol. NO2121.
Left Law *S.Lan.* ***Mountain***, 2m/3km NW of Dunsyre. Height 1181 feet or 360 metres. **25 E4** NT0550.

Legars *Sc.Bord.* ***Settlement***, 4m/6km S of Greenlaw. **27 E5** NT7140.
Legerwood *Sc.Bord.* ***Village***, 4m/7km SE of Lauder. **26 C5** NT5843.
Leideag *W.Isles* ***Settlement***, adjoining to SE of Castlebay, Barra. **44 B4** NL6697.
Leidle *Arg. & B.* ***River***, stream on Mull, rising on Beinn na Croise and running S, W, and finally NW down Glen Leidle into Loch Scridain at Pennyghael. **29 E2** NM5126.
Leir Mhaodail *High.* ***Coastal feature***, headland at S end of Sleat peninsula, Skye, 1km E of Point of Sleat. NM5799.
Leirinmore *High.* ***Hamlet***, near N coast of Sutherland district, 1m/2km SE of Durness. **74 D2** NC4166.
Leitfie *P. & K.* ***Hamlet***, 2m/3km S of Alyth. **42 A5** NO2545.
Leith *Edin.* ***Suburb***, 2m/3km N of Edinburgh city centre. Harbour and docks on Firth of Forth. **25 G2** NT2676.
Leith Hall *Aber.* ***Historic house***, National Trust for Scotland property built round central courtyard 1km NE of Kirkhill of Kennethmont, and 7m/11km S of Huntly. Home of head of Leith family since 1650. **54 A2** NJ5429.
Leithen Water *Sc.Bord.* ***River***, rising on Moorfoot Hills, 3m/4km E of Eddleston, and flowing S to River Tweed at Innerleithen. **26 A5** NT3336.
Leitholm *Sc.Bord.* ***Village***, 4m/7km NW of Coldstream. **27 E5** NT7944.
Leithope Forest *Sc.Bord.* ***Forest/woodland***, large area of coniferous forest in Cheviot Hills, to NE of Carter Bar. **11 F1** NT7209.
Lemnas *Aber.* ***Settlement***, 2m/3km S of Pennan Bay and 3m/4km W of New Aberdour. **64 D3** NJ8462.
Lempitlaw *Sc.Bord.* ***Settlement***, 3m/5km E of Kelso. **18 B3** NT7832.
Lemreway *W.Isles Anglicised form of Leumrabhagh, qv.*
Lendalfoot *S.Ayr.* ***Village***, coastal village, 6m/10km SW of Girvan. **6 C2** NX1390.
Lendrick *Stir.* ***Settlement***, at W end of Loch Venachar, 4m/6km NE of Aberfoyle. **32 A4** NN5406.
Lendrick Hill *P. & K.* ***Mountain***, 2m/3km NE of Pool of Muckhart. Height 1496 feet or 456 metres. **33 F4** NO0103.
Lenie *High.* ***Locality***, comprising Upper Lenie and Lower Lenie, on NW shore of Loch Ness, 2m/3km S of Drumnadrochit, Inverness district. **51 E2** NH5126.
Lenimore (Also known as North Thundergay.) *N.Ayr.* ***Settlement***, on NW coast of Arran, 3m/4km NE of Pirnmill. **21 G5** NR8847.
Lennel *Sc.Bord.* ***Village***, on River Tweed, 1m/2km NE of Coldstream. **27 F5** NT8540.
Lennox Forest *E.Dun.* ***Forest/woodland***, 1m/2km W of Lennoxtown. **23 G2** NS6077.
Lennox Plunton *D. & G.* ***Settlement***, 3m/5km S of Gatehouse of Fleet. **8 A5** NX6051.
Lennoxlove House *E.Loth.* ***Historic house***, mansion of 14c with later additions, 1m/2km S of Haddington. **26 C2** NT5172.
Lennoxtown *E.Dun.* Population: 4524. ***Small town***, 8m/13km N of Glasgow. **24 A2** NS6277.
Lentran *High.* ***Settlement***, in Inverness district, 5m/8km W of Inverness. NH5845.
Lentran Point *High.* ***Coastal feature***, headland to N of Lentran on Beauly Firth. NH5846.
Leny *Stir.* ***River***, running SE from Loch Lubnaig to River Teith at Callander. Falls of Leny 2m/4km W of Callander at Pass of Leny. NN6207.
Lenzie *E.Dun.* Population: 9924. ***Locality***, adjoining to S of Kirkintilloch. **24 A2** NS6571.
Lenziemill *N.Lan.* ***Suburb***, 1km S of Cumbernauld town centre. NS7673.
Leoch *Angus* ***Hamlet***, 1m/2km SE of Kirkton of Auchterhouse. **34 B1** NO3536.
Leochel-Cushnie *Aber.* ***Village***, 5m/7km SW of Alford. **54 A3** NJ5210.
Leonach Burn *High.* ***River***, rising on E slopes of Carn an t-Sean-liathanaich and flowing N into River Findhorn, 4m/6km SW of Ferness. Waterfalls in lower course. **52 B1** NH9240.
Leorin *Arg. & B.* ***Settlement***, 3m/4km NW of Port Ellen, Islay. **20 B5** NR3548.
Leorin Lochs *Arg. & B.* ***Lake/loch***, group of small lochs at S end of Islay, 2m/3km N of Port Ellen. **20 B5** NR3748.
Leosaval *W.Isles* ***Mountain***, in Forest of Harris, 3m/5km SE of Huisinis. Height 1351 feet or 412 metres. **66 C3** NB0309.
Leperstone Reservoir *Inclyde* ***Reservoir***, small reservoir 1m/2km N of Kilmacolm. NS3571.
Lephin *High.* ***Settlement***, near W coast of Skye, 5m/8km W of Dunvegan. NG1749.
Lephinchapel *Arg. & B.* ***Settlement***, on SW side of Loch Fyne, 3m/5km E of Lochgair across loch. **30 B5** NR9690.
Lephinmore *Arg. & B.* ***Settlement***, on N of Cowal peninsula, 12m/19km N of Tighnabruaich. **30 B5** NR9892.
Lerags *Arg. & B.* ***Locality***, 3m/4km NE of Kilninver, on N shore of Loch Feochan. **30 A2** NM8424.
Lerags Cross *Arg. & B.* ***Historic/prehistoric site***, restored 16c cross on a mound to E of Kilbride, in Argyll, 3m/4km S of Oban. NM8525.
Lerwick *Shet.* Population: 7336. ***Small town***, chief town of Mainland and of Shetland, situated on Bressay Sound 22m/35km N of Sumburgh Head. Fishing port, service base for North Sea oilfields and terminus of passenger boat services from Scottish mainland. Annual festival of Up-Helly-Aa, of pagan origin, held on last Tuesday in January. Fort Charlotte (Historic Scotland), 17c fort. **83 D3** HU4741.
Leschangie *Aber.* ***Locality***, 1m/2km S of Kemnay. **54 C3** NJ7314.
Leslie *Aber.* ***Village***, 3m/5km SW of Insch. **54 A2** NJ5924.
Leslie *Fife* Population: 3062. ***Small town***, 2m/3km NW of Glenrothes. **34 A4** NO2401.
Leslie Castle *Aber.* ***Castle***, ruined 17c tower house just E of Leslie, 6m/10km SE of Huntly. NJ5924.
Lesmahagow (Also known as Abbey Green.) *S.Lan.* Population: 3266. ***Small town***, former mining town on River Nethan, 5m/8km SW of Lanark. Ruins of 12c priory. **15 G2** NS8139.
Lessendrum *Aber.* ***Settlement***, to N of Newtongarry Hill, 3m/5km NE of Huntly. **64 A5** NJ5741.
Leswalt *D. & G.* ***Village***, on Rinns of Galloway, 3m/5km NW of Stranraer. **6 B4** NX0163.
Leth Meadhanach (Anglicised form: South Boisdale.) *W.Isles* ***Village***, 1m/2km SE of Baghasdal. **44 C2** NF7417.
Letham *Angus* Population: 1247. ***Village***, 5m/8km E of Forfar. **42 D5** NO5248.
Letham *Falk.* ***Hamlet***, 1m/2km S of Airth. NS8985.
Letham *Fife* ***Village***, 4m/7km W of Cupar. **34 B3** NO3014.
Letham *P. & K.* ***Suburb***, NW district of Perth. NO0924.
Lethanhill *E.Ayr.* ***Locality***, 1m/2km E of Patna. **14 C4** NS4310.
Lethans Muir *Fife* ***Open space***, moorland to NE of Knock Hill, 4m/6km W of Kelty. **33 F5** NT0794.
Lethen Bar *High.* ***Hill***, in Nairn district, 6m/10km SE of Nairn. Height 846 feet or 258 metres. **62 B5** NH9449.
Lethendy *P. & K.* ***Locality***, 2m/3km NW of Meikleour. 17c tower house. NO1341.
Lethendy *P. & K.* ***Settlement***, 1m/2km NW of New Scone. **33 G2** NO1228.
Lethenty *Aber.* ***Settlement***, 3m/5km NE of Fyvie. **64 D5** NJ8041.
Letter Finlay *High.* ***Settlement***, on SE side of Loch Lochy, 4m/7km SW of Laggan. **50 B5** NN2591.
Letterach *Moray* ***Mountain***, 7m/11km NW of Strathdon. Height 2581 feet or 787 metres. **53 E2** NJ2820.
Letterewe *High.* ***Settlement***, on NE shore of Loch Maree, Ross and Cromarty district, 6m/10km NW of head of loch. **59 F2** NG9571.
Letterewe Forest *High.* ***Open space***, deer forest to NE of Letterewe. NG9872.
Letterfearn *High.* ***Settlement***, on W shore of Loch Duich, Skye and Lochalsh district, 1m/2km from mouth of loch. **49 E2** NG8823.
Lettermorar *High.* ***Settlement***, on S side of Loch Morar, in Lochaber district, 4m/6km SE of Morar. **37 G1** NM7389.
Lettermore *Arg. & B.* ***Settlement***, on NE shore of Loch Frisa, 6m/9km NW of Salen, Mull. **37 E5** NM4948.
Lettermore *High.* ***Settlement***, 2m/3km NE of Inchkinloch, on W side of Loch Loyal. **75 F4** NC6147.
Letters *High.* ***Settlement***, on W side of Loch Broom, Ross and Cromarty district, 2m/3km from head of loch. **60 A1** NH1687.
Lettershaws *S.Lan.* ***Settlement***, 3m/4km SW of Abington. **15 G3** NS9020.
Lettoch *High.* ***Settlement***, 2m/3km SE of Nethy Bridge. **52 C3** NJ0219.
Lettoch *High.* ***Settlement***, 5m/8km NE of Grantown-on-Spey. **52 C1** NJ0932.
Leuchar Burn ***River***, stream running from Loch of Skene and flowing S to Garlogie, then SE to join Gormack Burn 1km W of Peterculter. NJ8400.
Leuchars *Fife* Population: 2991. ***Village***, 5m/7km S of Tayport, on N side of River Eden estuary. **34 C2** NO4521.
Leum Uilleim *High.* ***Mountain***, in Lochaber district 3m/5km S of head of Loch Treig. Height 2972 feet or 906 metres. **39 F3** NN3364.
Leumrabhagh (Anglicised form: Lemreway.) *W.Isles* ***Village***, near E coast of Isle of Lewis, on N side of Loch Shell, 3m/5km SW of Kebock Head. **67 F2** NB3711.
Leurbost *W.Isles Anglicised form of Liurbost, qv.*
Leven ***River***, issuing from Loch Leven and flowing E to Largo Bay between towns of Leven and Methil. **34 A4** NO3800.
Leven *Fife* Population: 8317. ***Small town***, resort and former mining town on W side of Largo Bay. Docks at Methil. **34 B4** NO3800.
Leven *High.* ***River***, in Lochaber district, running W from Blackwater Reservoir to head of Loch Leven at Kinlochleven. **39 E3** NN1762.
Leven *W.Dun.* ***River***, running S from foot of Loch Lomond at Balloch to River Clyde at Dumbarton. NS3974.
Leven Wick *Shet.* ***Bay***, on E coast of Mainland, 9m/14km N of Sumburgh Head. HU4121.
Levencorroch *N.Ayr.* ***Settlement***, above rocky cliff on S coast of Arran, 1m/2km NW of Kildonan. **13 F3** NS0021.
Levenhall *E.Loth.* ***Suburb***, on E side of Musselburgh. **26 A2** NT3673.
Levenish *W.Isles* ***Island***, rock islet (National Trust for Scotland) in St. Kilda group lying 2m/3km SE of E end of St. Kilda itself. Haunt of sea birds. NF1396.
Levenwick *Shet.* ***Village***, on W side of Leven Wick bay, on E coast of mainland. **82 D5** HU4021.
Levenwick Ness *Shet.* ***Coastal feature***, headland to E of Leven Wick, on E coast of Mainland. HU4121.
Leverburgh (Gaelic form: An T-òb. Formerly named Obbe.) *W.Isles* ***Village***, on SW coast of South Harris, 4m/6km NW of Renish Point. Village and harbour date from industrial development of Isle of Lewis by Lord Leverhulme in 1920s. Lighthouse. **66 C5** NG0186.
Levishie *High.* ***Settlement***, 1m/2km NW of Invermoriston. **50 D3** NH4018.
Levishie Forest *High.* ***Open space***, mountainous area on NW side of Loch Ness, 6m/10km N of Fort Augustus. **50 C3** NH4019.
Lewis *W.Isles See Isle of Lewis.*
Lewiston *High.* ***Village***, on River Coiltie, 1m/2km W of Urquhart Bay on Loch Ness, Inverness district. **51 E2** NH5129.
Lews Castle Gardens *W.Isles* ***Garden***, surrounding Lews Castle on W side of Stornoway Harbour, Isle of Lewis. Soil imported from mainland to create gardens also led to formation of large wooded area. **69 F4** NB4133.
Ley *Aber.* ***Settlement***, 3m/5km SW of Alford. **54 A3** NJ5312.
Leylodge *Aber.* ***Settlement***, 2m/4km SW of Kintore. **54 C3** NJ7713.
Leys *Aber.* ***Settlement***, 1m/2km SW of Tarland. **53 G4** NJ4602.
Leys *Aber.* ***Settlement***, 3m/4km N of Mintlaw. **65 F4** NK0052.
Leys *P. & K.* ***Settlement***, 3m/4km SE of Coupar Angus. **34 A1** NO2537.
Leys of Cossans *Angus* ***Settlement***, 2m/3km N of Glamis. **42 B5** NO3749.
Leysmill *Angus* ***Village***, 5m/8km NW of Arbroath. **43 E5** NO6047.
Lhaidhay Croft Museum *High.* ***Other feature of interest***, mid 19c croft complex in Dunbeath. House and byre under one roof, with adjacent barn being fine example of cruck roof construction. **77 D5** ND1530.
Lhanbryde *Moray* Population: 1998. ***Village***, 4m/6km E of Elgin. **63 E3** NJ2761.
Liath Eilean *Arg. & B.* ***Island***, in Loch Fyne, on E side of Eilean Mòr and 3m/5km SE of Lochgilphead, Argyll. NR8883.
Liathach (Anglicised form: Leagach.) *High.* ***Large natural feature***, mountain mass in Torridon Forest, Ross and Cromarty district, N of Torridon. Highest point is Spidean a' Choire Leith, a Munro at 3456 feet or 1054 metres. **59 F4** NG9257.
Liatrie *High.* ***Settlement***, 6m/9km W of Cannich. **50 B1** NH2432.
Libberton *S.Lan.* ***Village***, 2m/4km S of Carnwath. **25 D5** NS9846.
Liberton *Edin.* ***Suburb***, 3m/5km SE of Edinburgh city centre. **25 G3** NT2769.
Liceasto (Anglicised form: Likisto.) *W.Isles* ***Settlement***, near head of Loch Stockinish, South Harris, 2m/3km W of Greosabhagh. **66 D4** NG1192.
Liddel *Ork.* ***Locality***, in SE corner of South Ronaldsay, 2m/3km E of Burwick. **79 D4** ND4683.
Liddel Water ***River***, rising on Cheviot Hills, 8m/13km SW of Carter Bar, and running SW down Liddesdale to border with England at Kershopefoot. It then continues SW along England-Scotland border to its confluence with River Esk, 2m/3km S of Canonbie. **10 C4** NY3973.
Liddesdale *High.* ***Settlement***, on S shore of Loch Sunart, 3m/4km SW of Strontian across loch. **37 G4** NM7759.
Liddesdale *Sc.Bord.* ***Valley***, carrying Liddel Water SW from Saughtree, through village of Newcastleton towards Caulside. **10 C3** NY4888.
Lienassie *High.* ***Settlement***, in Skye and Lochalsh district, 3m/4km NE of Shiel Bridge. **49 F2** NG9621.
Lieurary *High.* ***Locality***, to N of Loch Calder. **76 C2** ND0662.
Liever *Arg. & B.* ***River***, in Argyll running S down Glen Liever to Loch Awe, 1m/2km E of head of loch. NM8905.
Liff *Angus* ***Village***, 5m/8km NW of Dundee. **34 B1** NO3333.
Lighthill (Gaelic form: Cnoc an t-Soluis.) *W.Isles* ***Settlement***, adjoining to W of Bac, near E coast of Isle of Lewis. NB4740.

L

Likisto *W.Isles Anglicised form of Liceasto, qv.*
Lillie Art Gallery *E.Dun.* ***Other feature of interest***, to N of Milngavie town centre, exhibiting work of 20c Scottish painters and craftwork. **23 G2** NS5575.
Lilliesleaf *Sc.Bord.* ***Village***, 7m/11km N of Hawick. **17 G3** NT5325.
Lilly Loch *N.Lan.* ***Lake/loch***, small loch 1km S of Caldercruix. NS8266.
Lily Loch *W.Dun.* ***Lake/loch***, small loch in Kilpatrick Hills, 1m/2km NE of Loch Humphrey. NS4777.
Lilybank *Inclyde* ***Suburb***, between Greenock and Port Glasgow. Site of small Roman fort 1m/2km SW. NS3074.
Limehillock *Moray* ***Settlement***, on W side of Sillyearn Wood, 3m/5km NW of Milltown of Rothiemay. **64 A4** NJ5152.
Limekilnburn *S.Lan.* ***Locality***, 3m/5km S of Hamilton. **24 B4** NS7050.
Limekilns *Fife* Population: 1620. ***Village***, on N bank of Firth of Forth, 3m/5km W of Inverkeithing. **25 E1** NT0783.
Limerigg *Falk.* ***Hamlet***, 1m/2km S of Slamannan. **24 C2** NS8570.
Lincluden *D. & G.* ***Suburb***, NW district of Dumfries. 14c collegiate church (Historic Scotland) to E. NX9677.
Lincluden College *D. & G.* ***Ecclesiastical building***, remains of collegiate church (Historic Scotland) founded in 1389 by Archibald the Grim, at confluence of Cluden Water and River Nith, 1m/2km N of Dumfries. Includes splendid chancel housing fine monumental tomb of his wife, Princess Margaret, daughter of Robert III. **9 D3** NX9677.
Lindean *Sc.Bord.* ***Hamlet***, 2m/3km NE of Selkirk. **17 F2** NT4931.
Lindertis *Angus* ***Settlement***, 3m/5km SW of Kirriemuir. **42 B4** NO3351.
Lindifferon *Fife* ***Settlement***, 4m/6km NW of Cupar. **34 B3** NO3116.
Lindores *Fife* ***Village***, 2m/3km SE of Newburgh. **34 A3** NO2616.
Lindores Abbey *Fife* ***Ecclesiastical building***, scant remains of abbey founded in 1191 and situated on E side of Newburgh. **34 A3** NO2418.
Lindores Loch *Fife* ***Lake/loch***, small loch on S side of Lindores. **34 A3** NO2616.
Lindsaig *Arg. & B.* ***Settlement***, on Cowal peninsula, 5m/8km NW of Tighnabruaich. **22 A2** NR9379.
Linfern Loch *S.Ayr.* ***Lake/loch***, 4m/7km S of Straiton. **7 E1** NX3697.
Ling *High.* ***River***, in Skye and Lochalsh district, running SW to head of Loch Long. **49 F1** NG9330.
Ling Hill *Stir.* ***Mountain***, 4m/6km NE of Fintry. Height 1364 feet or 416 metres. **24 A1** NS6789.
Ling Ness *Shet.* ***Coastal feature***, headland attached to E coast of Mainland by narrow neck of land. **83 D2** HU4954.
Linga *Shet.* ***Island***, small uninhabited island in Vaila Sound between Vaila and Walls, Mainland. HU2348.
Linga *Shet.* ***Island***, uninhabited island of about 170 acres or 70 hectares off W coast of Mainland between Muckle Roe and the entrance to Olna Firth. **82 C1** HU3563.
Linga *Shet.* ***Island***, uninhabited island off E coast of Mainland opposite Firth Ness. **85 D5** HU4673.
Linga *Shet.* ***Island***, narrow uninhabited island, 1m/2km long, at S end of Bluemull Sound between Yell and Unst. **85 E3** HU5598.
Linga Holm *Ork.* ***Island***, small uninhabited island off W coast of Stronsay at entrance to St. Catherine's Bay. **81 E4** HY6127.
Linga Sound *Shet.* ***Sea feature***, separates West Linga from W coast of Whalsay. **83 E1** HU5364.
Lingara Bay *W.Isles* ***Bay***, small bay on SE coast of South Harris containing islet of Lingarabay Island, 4m/6km SW of Manais. NG0684.
Lingarabay *W.Isles Anglicised form of Ceann a' Bháigh, qv.*
Lingarabay Island *W.Isles* ***Island***, islet in Lingara Bay, off SE coast of South Harris. **66 C5** NG0684.
Lingay *W.Isles* ***Island***, small uninhabited island 2m/3km SW of Ludag, on S coast of South Uist. **44 C2** NF7511.
Lingay *W.Isles* ***Island***, small uninhabited island off N coast of North Uist nearly 1m/2km SE of Boreray. **45 G2** NF8778.
Lingay *W.Isles* ***Island***, small uninhabited island at SE end of Sound of Harris, 4m/7km off E coast of North Uist. **56 D2** NG0179.
Lingay *W.Isles* ***Island***, small uninhabited island 1km N of Pabbay and 2m/3km SW of Sandray. **44 A5** NL6089.
Linhead *Aber.* ***Settlement***, on N side of Rosy Burn, 5m/8km NW of Turriff. **64 B4** NJ6755.
Linhope *Sc.Bord.* ***Settlement***, 3m/4km S of Teviothead, where Linhope Burn joins Frostlie Burn. **17 F5** NT4001.
Linhouse Water *W.Loth.* ***River***, stream running N from Pentland Hills to River Almond on E side of Livingston. **25 E3** NT0767.
Liniclett *W.Isles Anglicised form of Lionacleit, qv.*
Linicro *High.* ***Settlement***, on Skye, 2m/4km N of Uig. **57 G3** NG3867.
Linklater *Ork.* ***Settlement***, 1km S of Ward Hill, South Ronaldsay, above Wind Wick bay. **79 D4** ND4587.
Linklet Bay *Ork.* ***Bay***, wide bay on E side of North Ronaldsay, extending SW from Dennis Head. **81 F1** HY7754.
Links Bay *Aber.* ***Bay***, small bay on N coast of Banff and Buchan district, on E side of Portsoy. NJ5966.
Links Ness *Ork.* ***Coastal feature***, headland at NW end of Stronsay. **81 D4** HY6129.
Links of Dunnet *High.* ***Coastal feature***, undulating sandy area on E shore of Dunnet Bay and to S of Dunnet Head. Partly within Dunnet Forest. **77 E2** ND2270.
Linksness *Ork.* ***Locality***, including headland with landing stage, at N end of Hoy on Burra Sound, opposite Graemsay. **78 B2** HY2403.
Linksness *Ork.* ***Settlement***, 1m/2km SW of Rerwick Head, on Mainland. **80 D5** HY5310.
Linktown *Fife* ***Suburb***, S district of Kirkcaldy. **34 A5** NT2790.
Linkwood *Moray* ***Locality***, 1m/2km SE of Elgin. NJ2361.
Linlithgow *W.Loth.* Population: 11,866. ***Town***, historic town, 16m/26km W of Edinburgh. Formerly an important industrial area. 15c Linlithgow Palace (Historic Scotland) on side of Linlithgow Loch. 18c Annet House contains Linlithgow Story Museum. The Binns (National Trust for Scotland) 3m/5km E. **25 D2** NS9977.
Linlithgow Bridge *W.Loth.* ***Locality***, adjoining to W of Linlithgow, below high railway viaduct. **25 D2** NS9977.
Linlithgow Loch *W.Loth.* ***Lake/loch***, to N of Linlithgow. NT0077.
Linlithgow Palace *W.Loth.* ***Historic/prehistoric site***, ruins (Historic Scotland) stand on high ground in parkland on S side of Linlithgow Loch, to N of Linlithgow. Birthplace in 1542 of Mary, Queen of Scots and home to all Stewart kings. **25 E2** NS9977.
Linn of Barhoise *D. & G.* ***Waterfall***, in course of River Bladnoch, 1m/2km N of Kirkcowan. **7 E4** NX3362.
Linn of Corriemulzie *Aber.* ***Waterfall***, series of small waterfalls in a ravine in course of Corriemulzie Burn, 3m/5km SW of Braemar. **41 F1** NO1189.
Linn of Dee *Aber.* ***Waterfall***, cascades in narrow cleft in course of River Dee, 1m/2km W of Inverey. **41 F1** NO0689.
Linn of Muick *Aber.* ***Waterfall***, in course of River Muick, 4m/7km SW of Ballater. NO3389.
Linn of Muick Cottage *Aber.* ***Settlement***, 4m/7km SW of Ballater, in Glen Muick. **42 B1** NO3389.
Linn of Pattack *High.* ***Lake/loch***, pool in course of River Pattack, 2m/3km SE of Kinloch Laggan. **40 A1** NN5587.
Linn of Quoich *Aber.* ***Waterfall***, in course of Quoich Water, 1km NW of its confluence with River Dee. **52 D5** NO1191.
Linn of Tummel *P. & K.* ***Waterfall***, National Trust for Scotland property in River Tummel near its confluence with River Garry 2m/3km S of Killiecrankie. **41 E3** NN9060.
Linne Mhuirich *Arg. & B.* ***Sea feature***, western arm of Loch Sween, Argyll, running N from Taynish. NR7284.
Linne nam Beathach *Arg. & B.* ***River***, in Argyll, running E from Loch Dochard to Loch Tulla. NN2742.
Linngeam *W.Isles* ***Island***, islet in Loch Roag, W coast of Isle of Lewis, 1m/2km NE of entrance to Little Loch Roag. NB1433.
Linnvale *Renf.* ***Suburb***, 1m/2km E of Clydebank town centre across Forth and Clyde canal. NS5170.
Linshader *W.Isles Anglicised form of Linsiadar, qv.*
Linsiadar (Anglicised form: Linshader.) *W.Isles* ***Settlement***, 3m/5km SE of Earshader, at entrance to Loch Cean Thulabhig, Isle of Lewis. **68 D4** NB2031.
Linsidemore *High.* ***Settlement***, in Sutherland district, 6m/10km NW of Bonar Bridge. **72 A5** NH5499.
Lintlaw *Sc.Bord.* ***Village***, 4m/6km NE of Duns. **27 F4** NT8258.
Lintmill *Moray* ***Village***, near N coast 1m/2km S of Cullen. **64 A3** NJ5165.
Linton *Sc.Bord.* ***Settlement***, nearly 1m/2km N of Morebattle. **18 B4** NT7726.
Linton Hill *Sc.Bord.* ***Hill***, 2m/3km W of Town Yetholm. Height 925 feet or 282 metres. **18 B4** NT7827.
Linwood *Renf.* Population: 10,183. ***Locality***, large residential development, 1m/2km NE of Johnstone. **23 F3** NS4464.
Lionacleit (Anglicised form: Liniclett.) *W.Isles* ***Village***, on SW coast of Benbecula, 4m/6km S of Benbecula (Baile a' Mhanaich) Aerodrome. **45 F5** NF7949.
Lional (Anglicised form: Lionel.) *W.Isles* ***Village***, near N end of Isle of Lewis, 1km W of Port Nis. **69 G1** NB5263.
Lionel *W.Isles Anglicised form of Lional, qv.*
Liongam *W.Isles* ***Island***, small uninhabited island off W coast of Isle of Lewis, 2m/4km NE of Scarp. **66 B2** NA9919.
Lion's Head *Aber.* ***Coastal feature***, headland on N coast, 1m/2km SE of Troup Head. NJ8366.
Liquo *N.Lan. Alternative name for Bowhousebog, qv.*
Lismore *Arg. & B.* ***Island***, long, narrow and fertile island in Loch Linnhe, extending 10m/15km from Rubha Fiart NE to a point opposite Port Appin on mainland to E. Ferry to Port Appin. **30 A1** NM8440.
Little *High.* ***River***, flowing N and then NW to join River Thurso just E of Dalemore. **76 D4** ND1548.
Little Assynt *High.* ***Settlement***, on N side of Lochan an Iasgaich, W of Loch Assynt. **70 D2** NC1525.
Little Ballinluig *P. & K.* ***Settlement***, on River Tay, 4m/7km W of Ballinluig. **41 E4** NN9152.
Little Bernera *W.Isles* ***Island***, off W coast of Isle of Lewis between entrances to East and West Loch Roag and off N shore of Great Bernera. Measures about 1m/2km E to W and an average of 1m/2km N to S. **68 C3** NB1440.
Little Brechin *Angus* ***Village***, 2m/3km NW of Brechin. **43 D3** NO5960.
Little Carleton Motte *S.Ayr.* ***Historic/prehistoric site***, adjoining to E of Little Carleton, 6m/10km SW of Girvan. **6 C2** NX1389.
Little Colonsay *Arg. & B.* ***Island***, uninhabited island of about 200 acres or 80 hectares, lying 1m/2km off SW coast of Ulva. **28 C1** NM3736.
Little Creich *High.* ***Settlement***, in Sutherland district, on N shore of Dornoch Firth, 2m/4km SE of Bonar Bridge. **61 F1** NH6389.
Little Cumbrae *N.Ayr.* ***Island***, lying 1km S of Great Cumbrae. Measures nearly 2m/3km N to S by nearly 1m/2km E to W. Lighthouse on W side. **22 C4** NS1451.
Little Dens *Aber.* ***Settlement***, 4m/6km SW of Peterhead. **65 F5** NK0743.
Little Dunkeld *P. & K.* ***Village***, across River Tay, to S of Dunkeld (road bridge by Telford, 1809). **41 F5** NO0242.
Little Eachaig *Arg. & B.* ***River***, in Argyll, running E down Glen Lean to Clachaig and continuing E to River Eachaig at head of Holy Loch. NS1582.
Little France *Edin.* ***Suburb***, 3m/5km SE of Edinburgh city centre. NT2870.
Little Green Holm *Ork.* ***Island***, islet to S of Muckle Green Holm across narrow Sound of the Green Holms. HY5226.
Little Gruinard *High.* ***River***, flows N into Gruinard Bay from Fionn Loch. **59 F1** NG9494.
Little Gruinard *High.* ***Settlement***, on coast of Ross and Cromarty district, 3m/4km SE of Laide. **59 F1** NG9489.
Little Gruna Stacks *Shet.* ***Coastal feature***, group of rocks on S side of Gruna Stack, off NW coast of Mainland. HU2886.
Little Havra *Shet.* ***Island***, small uninhabited island lying off W coast of South Havra. HU3526.
Little Holm *Shet.* ***Island***, rock island in Yell Sound 3m/4km SE of Burra Voe. HU4086.
Little Idoch *Aber.* ***Settlement***, on S side of Idoch Water, 3m/4km E of Turriff. **64 C5** NJ7649.
Little Ley *Aber.* ***Settlement***, 3m/5km SW of Monymusk. **54 B3** NJ6511.
Little Linga *Ork.* ***Island***, small islet off Links Ness at NW point of Stronsay. HY6030.
Little Linga *Shet.* ***Island***, small island among several others between West Linga and Mainland. HU5265.
Little Loch Broom *High.* ***Sea feature***, inlet to W of Loch Broom, running parallel to it. **70 C5** NH1392.
Little Loch Roag (Gaelic form: Loch Ròg Beag.) *W.Isles* ***Lake/loch***, narrow loch, 5m/8km long, opening at its N end into Loch Roag, W coast of Isle of Lewis. **68 C5** NB1228.
Little Loch Shin *High.* ***Reservoir***, formed by damming River Shin below Loch Shin dam, to W of Lairg. NC5806.
Little Loch Skiach *P. & K.* ***Lake/loch***, to S of Loch Skiach, 5m/8km NW of Dunkeld. NN9546.
Little Minch ***Sea feature***, sea passage between Western Isles and Skye. **56 C5** NG1060.
Little Ossa *Shet.* ***Island***, rock off NW coast of Mainland 2m/4km W of The Faither. Muckle Ossa rock is adjacent to N. HU2184.
Little Rack Wick *Ork.* ***Bay***, on W coast of Hoy, 2m/3km SE of Sneuk Head. **78 B3** ND2392.
Little Roe *Shet.* ***Island***, uninhabited island of about 70 acres or 30 hectares at S end of Yell Sound 2m/4km E of Ollaberry, Mainland. **84 D5** HU4079.
Little Rogart *High.* ***Settlement***, 1m/2km N of Rogart Station, Sutherland district. **72 C4** NC7204.
Little Ross *D. & G.* ***Island***, with lighthouse at entrance to Kirkcudbright Bay, at E extremity of Wigtown Bay. **3 G2** NX6543.
Little Scatwell *High.* ***Settlement***, at confluence of Rivers Conan and Meig, below Loch Luichart, Ross and Cromarty district. **60 C4** NH3956.
Little Shillay *W.Isles* ***Island***, islet to SW of Shillay. NF8790.
Little Skerry *Ork.* ***Island***, most southerly of Pentland Skerries. ND4776.
Little Torboll *High.* ***Settlement***, 5m/8km W of Golspie. **72 C5** NH7598.

Little Water *Aber.* ***River***, running S to join River Ythan near Chapelhaugh, 2m/3km NW of Methlick. **64 D5** NJ8439.

Little Water of Fleet *D. & G.* ***River***, running S from Loch Fleet into Water of Fleet, 3m/5km N of Gatehouse of Fleet. **7 G4** NX5860.

Little Wyvis *High.* ***Mountain***, in Strathgarve Forest, Ross and Cromarty district, 3m/5km NE of Garve. Height 2506 feet or 764 metres. **60 D3** NH4264.

Littleferry *High.* ***Locality***, in Sutherland district, on N side of entrance to Loch Fleet, 3m/5km SW of Golspie. **72 D5** NH8095.

Littlemill *E.Ayr.* ***Settlement***, 2m/3km S of Drongan. **14 C4** NS4515.

Littlemill *High.* ***Settlement***, in Nairn district, 4m/7km SE of Nairn. **62 B4** NH9150.

Littleton *Dundee* ***Settlement***, in Sidlaw Hills, 4m/6km NW of Longforgan. **34 A1** NO2633.

Liurbost (Anglicised form: Leurbost.) *W.Isles* ***Village***, on Isle of Lewis, 6m/9km SW of Stornoway, near head of long inlet, Loch Leurbost. **69 E5** NB3725.

Liuthaid *W.Isles* ***Mountain***, 1m/2km E of head of Loch Langavat. Height 1614 feet or 492 metres. **67 D2** NB1713.

Liver *Arg. & B.* ***River***, running W down Glen Liver into Loch Etive, Argyll, on S side of Inverliver Bay, 4m/6km NE of Bonawe. **30 D1** NN0635.

Livet (Also known as Livet Water.) ***River***, rising in Blackwater Forest and flowing NW down Glenlivet to River Avon, 8m/12km N of Tomintoul. **53 E2** NJ1830.

Livet Water *Alternative name for (River) Livet, qv.*

Livingston *W.Loth.* Population: 41,647. ***Town***, manufacturing town, 13m/21km W of Edinburgh. New town, designated 1962, now noted for hi-tech industries. Calder House has links with John Knox. **25 E3** NT0568.

Livingston Mill Farm *W.Loth. Alternative name for Almond Valley Heritage Centre, qv.*

Livingston South Station *W.Loth.* ***Other building***, railway station to S of Livingston, in suburb of Nether Williamston. **25 E3** NT0665.

Livingston Station *W.Loth.* ***Locality***, 2m/4km W of Livingston town centre. NT0568.

Livingston Village *W.Loth.* ***Village***, 1m/2km SW of Livingston. **25 E3** NT0568.

Loanan *High.* ***River***, issuing from Loch Awe and flowing N into Loch Assynt. NC2421.

Loandhu *High.* ***Settlement***, 3m/5km SE of Tain. **62 A2** NH8178.

Loanhead *Aber.* ***Settlement***, 3m/4km S of Auchnagatt. **55 E1** NJ9138.

Loanhead *Midloth.* Population: 5659. ***Small town***, former mining town with industrial estates, 6m/9km S of Edinburgh. **25 G3** NT2865.

Loanhead Stone Circle *Aber.* ***Historic/prehistoric site***, Bronze Age stone circle (Historic Scotland) enclosing ring cairn, 1km N of Daviot. Small burial enclosure nearby. **54 C2** NJ7428.

Loans *S.Ayr.* ***Village***, 2m/3km E of Troon. **14 B2** NS3431.

Loch a' Bhaid-luachraich *High.* ***Lake/loch***, near W coast of Ross and Cromarty district 4m/6km NE of Poolewe. **59 E1** NG8986.

Loch a' Bhaile *W.Isles* ***Lake/loch***, freshwater loch on NW coast of Isle of Lewis on N side of Siabost. NB2547.

Loch a' Bhaile-Mhargaidh *Arg. & B.* ***Lake/loch***, small loch on Jura 2m/3km W of Craighouse. NR4966.

Loch a' Bhainne *High.* ***Lake/loch***, small loch 3m/5km NW of Invergarry. **50 B4** NH2704.

Loch a' Bhàna *High.* ***Lake/loch***, small loch in Inverness district immediately below dam of Loch Mullardoch. NH2231.

Loch a' Bharpa *W.Isles* ***Lake/loch***, small loch on North Uist, 2m/4km NW of Locheport. **45 G3** NF8366.

Loch a' Bhealaich *Arg. & B. See Tayvallich.*

Loch a' Bhealaich (Anglicised form: Loch a' Vellich.) *High.* ***Lake/loch***, in Caithness district running into SW end of Loch Choire. **72 A2** NC5926.

Loch a' Bhealaich (Also known as Loch Vallich.) *High.* ***Lake/loch***, 2m/3km in length E to W, 4m/7km N of Upper Loch Torridon, Ross and Cromarty district. **59 E3** NG8664.

Loch a' Bhealaich *High.* ***Lake/loch***, National Trust for Scotland property 5m/8km E of head of Loch Duich, in Skye and Lochalsh district. **49 G2** NH0221.

Loch a' Bhealaich Bheithe *High.* ***Lake/loch***, mountain loch in Badenoch and Strathspey district between Ben Alder and Loch Ericht. **40 A2** NN5171.

Loch a' Bhlàir *High.* ***Lake/loch***, small loch in Lochaber district, 1m/2km N of Loch Arkaig below W slopes of Meall a' Bhlàir. **49 G5** NN0594.

Loch a' Bhràighe *High.* ***Bay***, facing NW at N end of Rona. **58 C3** NG6260.

Loch a' Bhraoin *High.* ***Lake/loch***, in Ross and Cromarty district 7m/11km S of head of Loch Broom. **60 A2** NH1374.

Loch a' Chadh-Fi *High.* ***Sea feature***, inlet off N side of Loch Laxford, W coast of Sutherland district. NC2050.

Loch a' Chàirn Bhàin (Anglicised form: Loch Cairnbawn.) *High.* ***Sea feature***, inlet on W coast of Sutherland district, running out into Eddrachillis Bay. **74 A5** NC1934.

Loch a' Chaorainn *High.* ***Lake/loch***, small loch on Kildermorie Forest 3m/5km W of Loch Morie, Ross and Cromarty district. **61 D2** NH4678.

Loch a' Chaoruinn *Arg. & B.* ***Lake/loch***, small loch in Knapdale, Argyll, 4m/7km W of West Tarbert. **21 F3** NR7866.

Loch a' Chlachain *High.* ***Lake/loch***, small loch in Inverness district 8m/13km S of Inverness and close to NE end of Loch Duntelchaig. NH6532.

Loch a' Chlaidheimh *High.* ***Lake/loch***, small corrie lake on NE slopes of Maoile Lunndaidh. Issuing stream flows into Loch Monar 2m/4km S. **60 A5** NH1446.

Loch a' Chnuic Bhric *Arg. & B.* ***Lake/loch***, small loch near W coast of Jura, 3m/4km W of Beinn a' Chaolais. **20 C2** NR4473.

Loch a' Choire *High.* ***Lake/loch***, small loch in Inverness district 4m/6km SE of Dores. **51 F2** NH6229.

Loch a' Choire *High.* ***Sea feature***, inlet on NW shore of Loch Linnhe, opposite Shuna Island. **38 A4** NM8452.

Loch a' Choire Mhòir *High.* ***Lake/loch***, small loch at head of Strath Mulzie, Sutherland district, to E of Seana Bhraigh. **60 B1** NH3088.

Loch a' Choire Riabhaich *High.* ***Lake/loch***, small loch in South Morar, 4m/6km W of Arisaig. **37 G1** NM7287.

Loch a' Chracaich *High. Gaelic form of Loch a' Creagach, qv.*

Loch a' Chràthaich *High.* ***Lake/loch***, small loch in Inverness district 4m/7km NW of Invermoriston. **50 C2** NH3621.

Loch a' Chroisg (Anglicised form: Loch Rosque.) *High.* ***Lake/loch***, in Ross and Cromarty district, 1m/2km W of Achnasheen. Length 3m/5km E to W. **60 A4** NH1258.

Loch a' Chuilinn (Also known as Loch Culen.) *High.* ***Lake/loch***, small loch in course of River Bran in Ross and Cromarty district, 1m/2km W of head of Loch Luichart. **60 B3** NH2961.

Loch a' Chumhainn *Arg. & B.* ***Sea feature***, long narrow inlet on NW coast of Mull, running up to Dervaig. NM4252.

Loch a' Creagach (Gaelic form: Loch a' Chracaich.) *High.* ***Bay***, on SW side of Loch Torridon, Ross and Cromarty district, 4m/6km NW of Shieldaig. **59 D4** NG7657.

Loch a' Gharbh Bhaid Mhòir *High.* ***Lake/loch***, narrow loch 2m/3km SE of Rhiconich, Sutherland district. **74 B4** NC2748.

Loch a' Gharbhrain *High.* ***Lake/loch***, small loch in Strathvaich Forest, 1km NW of W end of Loch Glascarnoch. **60 B2** NH2876.

Loch a' Ghille Ghobaich *High.* ***Lake/loch***, near coast of Lochaber district, 2m/3km S of Mallaig. **48 C5** NM6894.

Loch a' Ghleannain *Arg. & B.* ***Lake/loch***, small loch on Mull 1m/2km S of Lochdon. NM7231.

Loch a' Ghlinne *High.* ***Lake/loch***, small loch 3m/5km N of Aird of Sleat, Skye. **48 B4** NG5905.

Loch a' Ghlinne (Glen Bay). *W.Isles* ***Lake/loch***, on N coast of St. Kilda. NA0800.

Loch a' Ghlinne *W.Isles* ***Lake/loch***, near W coast of North Harris, 1km N of Husival Mòr. **66 C2** NB0212.

Loch a' Ghobha-Dhuibh *High.* ***Lake/loch***, one of two small lochs on E side of Ben Hope. **75 D4** NC4949.

Loch a' Ghobhainn *High.* ***Lake/loch***, small loch in Shieldaig Forest, 5m/8km SW of Talladale, Ross and Cromarty district. **59 E3** NG8365.

Loch a' Ghorm-choire *High.* ***Lake/loch***, 1m/2km N of Loch Fiag. Ben Hee rises steeply to NW. **74 D5** NC4433.

Loch a' Ghriama *High.* ***Lake/loch***, in Sutherland district running N to S at head of Loch Shin. **71 F2** NC3926.

Loch a' Laip *W.Isles* ***Sea feature***, stretch of water separating Benbecula and Wiay. **45 G5** NF8647.

Loch a' Mhadaidh *High.* ***Lake/loch***, corrie loch below Sgurr Mòr in Ross and Cromarty district, 3m/5km S of Corrieshalloch Gorge. **60 B2** NH1973.

Loch a' Mhuilinn *High. Alternative name for Loch a' Mhuillidh, qv.*

Loch a' Mhuilinn *High.* ***Lake/loch***, small loch 3m/4km SE of Altnabreac Station. **76 C4** ND0142.

Loch a' Mhuillidh (Also known as Loch a' Mhuilinn.) *High.* ***Lake/loch***, small loch in course of River Farrar in Inverness district 4m/7km below Loch Monar. **50 B1** NH2738.

Loch a' Phearsain *Arg. & B.* ***Lake/loch***, to NE of Kilmelford. **30 A3** NM8513.

Loch a' Phuill *Arg. & B.* ***Lake/loch***, near W end of Tiree 2m/3km NE of Rinn Thorbhais. NL9541.

Loch a' Sguirr *High.* ***Bay***, W facing bay at N end of Raasay. **58 B4** NG6052.

Loch a' Tuath (Also known as Broad Bay.) *W.Isles* ***Bay***, large bay on E coast of Isle of Lewis, extending from Tolsta Head to Tiumpan Head on Eye Peninsula, and SW to Laxdale, N of Stornoway. **69 F4** NB4936.

Loch a' Vellich *High. Anglicised form of Loch a' Bhealaich, qv.*

Loch Achaidh na h-Inich *High.* ***Lake/loch***, small loch 2m/3km S of Plockton, Skye and Lochalsh district. **49 E1** NG8130.

Loch Achall *High.* ***Lake/loch***, at foot of Glen Achall, Ross and Cromarty district, 2m/4km E of Ullapool. **71 D5** NH1795.

Loch Achanalt *High.* ***Lake/loch***, small loch in course of River Bran in Ross and Cromarty district 3m/5km W of head of Loch Luichart. **60 B3** NH2761.

Loch Achilty *High.* ***Lake/loch***, small loch in Ross and Cromarty district 3m/5km W of Strathpeffer. **60 D4** NH4356.

Loch Achnamoine *High.* ***Lake/loch***, 1m/2km SE of Badanloch Lodge, in course of River Helmsdale, Sutherland district. **75 G5** NC8032.

Loch Achonachie *High.* ***Lake/loch***, and reservoir in course of River Conon, Ross and Cromarty district, 3m/5km SW of Strathpeffer. **60 D4** NH4354.

Loch Achray *Stir.* ***Lake/loch***, small loch in Achray Forest, within Queen Elizabeth Forest Park, 7m/11km W of Callander. **32 A4** NN5106.

Loch Affric *High.* ***Lake/loch***, in course of River Affric in Inverness district 12m/19km SW of Cannich. **50 A2** NH1522.

Loch Ailort *High.* ***Sea feature***, arm of Sound of Arisaig passing to S of peninsula of Ardnish in Lochaber district. **37 G1** NM7379.

Loch Ailsh *High.* ***Lake/loch***, in Sutherland district 8m/12km SE of Inchnadamph. **71 F3** NC3110.

Loch Ainort *High.* ***Sea feature***, inlet on E coast of Skye opposite Scalpay. **48 B2** NG5528.

Loch Airdeglais *Arg. & B.* ***Lake/loch***, highest and largest of chain of small lochs in upper reaches of Lussa River, Mull, 2m/3km N of Loch Buie. Others, in order of descent, are Loch an Ellen, Loch an Eilein and Loch Sguabain. **29 F2** NM6228.

Loch Airigh a' Phuill *High.* ***Lake/loch***, small loch in Ross and Cromarty district, 2m/3km E of Charlestown and head of Gair Loch. **59 E2** NG8475.

Loch Airigh na Beinne *High.* ***Lake/loch***, small loch at base of E slopes of Fashven, Sutherland district. **74 C2** NC3266.

Loch Airigh na h-Airde *W.Isles* ***Lake/loch***, 4m/7km E of head of Little Loch Roag, Isle of Lewis. **68 C5** NB2123.

Loch Airigh nan Sloc *W.Isles* ***Lake/loch***, small loch 8m/13km W of Stornoway, Isle of Lewis. **69 D4** NB2833.

Loch Akran *High.* ***Lake/loch***, small loch in Sutherland district, 3m/5km SW of Reay. **76 B2** NC9260.

Loch Aline *High.* ***Lake/loch***, in Lochaber district, running out into Sound of Mull. Deposits of silica sand on W shore. NM6845.

Loch Alsh *High.* ***Sea feature***, arm of sea between Skye and Scottish mainland, penetrating inland to Eilean Donan, where Loch Duich runs into it from SE and Loch Long from NE. **49 D2** NG8125.

Loch Alvie *High.* ***Lake/loch***, small loch in Badenoch and Strathspey district 2m/4km SW of Aviemore. **52 A4** NH8609.

Loch an Aircill *Arg. & B.* ***Lake/loch***, small loch on Jura, 1m/2km N of Beinn an Oir. NR5076.

Loch an Alltain Duibh *High.* ***Bay***, on W coast of Ross and Cromarty district, 1m/2km NW of Polbain. **70 B3** NB9812.

Loch an Alltan Fheàrna *High.* ***Lake/loch***, small loch in Sutherland district, 1km S of Loch nan Clàr and between Lochs Badanloch and Rimsdale. **75 G5** NC7433.

Loch an Daimh *High.* ***Lake/loch***, in Ross and Cromarty district 9m/14km E of Ullapool. **71 E5** NH2794.

Loch an Daimh *P. & K.* ***Lake/loch***, and reservoir 3m/4km NE of Loch Lyon. Formed out of two smaller lochs, Loch Giorra and Loch Daimh, when water level was raised. **39 G5** NN4846.

Loch an Deerie *High. Alternative name for Loch an Dherue, qv.*

Loch an Dherue (Also known as Loch an Deerie.) *High.* ***Lake/loch***, in Caithness district 3m/5km S of head of Kyle of Tongue. **75 E4** NC5448.

Loch an Doire Dhuibh *High.* ***Lake/loch***, just to S of Loch Sionascaig. **70 D3** NC1311.

Loch an Draing *High.* ***Lake/loch***, small loch in Ross and Cromarty district, 3m/5km NE of Melvaig. **70 A5** NG7790.

Loch an Droighinn *Arg. & B.* ***Lake/loch***, small loch 1m/2km NW of Kilchrenan, Argyll. NN0224.

Loch an Dubh-Lochain *High.* ***Lake/loch***, small loch in Gleann an Dubh-Lochain. NG8200.

Loch an Dùin ***Lake/loch***, small deep loch on border of Highland and Perth & Kinross, 6m/10km SE of Dalwhinnie. **40 C2** NN7279.

Loch an Easain Uaine *High.* ***Lake/loch***, small loch in Reay Forest, Sutherland district, 3m/4km S of Foinaven. **74 C4** NC3246.

Loch an Eilein *Arg. & B. See Loch Airdeglais.*

Loch an Eilein *High.* ***Lake/loch***, small loch in Rothiemurchus Forest, Badenoch and Strathspey district, 3m/5km S of Aviemore. Noted for triple echo. Remains of medieval castle on islet in loch. **52 A4** NH8907.

L

Loch an Eilein Castle *High.* ***Castle***, ruined 15c castle, later enlarged, in Loch an Eilein, 3m/5km S of Aviemore. **52 A4** NH8908.
Loch an Eilein Visitor Centre and Forest Trail *High.* ***Other feature of interest***, cottage by Loch an Eilein, with exhibition on management and conservation of native pine forest, 3m/4km S of Aviemore. **52 A4** NH8908.
Loch an Eircill *High.* ***Lake/loch***, at SE end of Glen Coul. **71 F2** NC3027.
Loch an Ellen *Arg. & B. See Loch Airdeglais.*
Loch an Eòin *High.* ***Lake/loch***, small loch in Ross and Cromarty district, 5m/8km N of head of Loch Carron. **59 F4** NG9251.
Loch an Fhiarlaid *High.* ***Lake/loch***, small loch in Ross and Cromarty district 4m/6km S of Kinlochewe. **59 G4** NH0556.
Loch an Fhir Mhaoil *W.Isles* ***Lake/loch***, small loch on Isle of Lewis, 5m/8km S of Earshader. **68 C5** NB1826.
Loch an Iasaich *High.* ***Lake/loch***, small loch 3m/4km SE of Attadale, Ross and Cromarty district. **49 F1** NG9535.
Loch an Lagain *High.* ***Lake/loch***, small loch 4m/6km NE of Bonar Bridge. **72 B5** NH6595.
Loch an Laig Aird *High.* ***Lake/loch***, small, irregular-shaped loch, 1m/2km NE of Scourie, Sutherland district. **74 A4** NC1746.
Loch an Laoigh *High.* ***Lake/loch***, on border of Ross and Cromarty and Skye and Lochalsh districts, 4m/6km S of Achnashellach Station. **59 G5** NH0241.
Loch an Leathaid Bhuain *High.* ***Lake/loch***, in Sutherland district adjoining Loch na Creige Duibhe, to W of Loch More. **74 B5** NC2736.
Loch an Leoid *Arg. & B.* ***Lake/loch***, small loch in Argyll, 1m/2km NW of Kilchrenan. **30 C2** NN0124.
Loch an Leothaid *High.* ***Lake/loch***, 2m/3km N of Loch Assynt. **71 E2** NC1630.
Loch an Nostarie *High.* ***Lake/loch***, near coast of Lochaber district, 1m/2km SE of Mallaig. **48 C5** NM6995.
Loch an Ruathair *High.* ***Lake/loch***, in Sutherland district 3m/4km N of Kinbrace. **76 A5** NC8636.
Loch an Sgòir *High.* ***Lake/loch***, small mountain loch, 2m/3km N of Ben Alder. **39 G2** NN4975.
Loch an Sgoltaire *Arg. & B.* ***Lake/loch***, small loch on Colonsay 1km SW of Kiloran Bay. **28 C5** NR3897.
Loch an t-Seilg *High.* ***Lake/loch***, in Sutherland district, 3m/4km NE of Loch Merkland. **74 D5** NC4136.
Loch an t-Seilich *High.* ***Lake/loch***, in course of River Tromie on Gaick Forest, in Badenoch and Strathspey district, 9m/14km S of Kingussie. **40 C1** NN7586.
Loch an t-Siob *Arg. & B.* ***Lake/loch***, on Jura, to S of Beinn Shiantaidh in Paps of Jura. **20 D2** NR5173.
Loch an Tachdaidh *High.* ***Lake/loch***, small loch on low plateau, 10m/16km E of Attadale. **49 G1** NH0938.
Loch an Tairbeart *W.Isles* ***Lake/loch***, small loch, almost surrounded by woodland, 3m/4km SE of Breascleit, Isle of Lewis. **69 D4** NB2532.
Loch an Tobair *W.Isles* ***Lake/loch***, small loch 8m/13km N of Stornoway, Isle of Lewis. **69 F3** NB4345.
Loch an Torr *Arg. & B.* ***Lake/loch***, small loch on Mull, 1m/2km E of Dervaig. NM4552.
Loch an Ulbhaidh *High.* ***Lake/loch***, small loch in course of Allt Loch an Ulbhaidh, 2m/3km N of Loch Shin. **71 G2** NC4922.
Loch Ard *Stir.* ***Lake/loch***, 3m/5km W of Aberfoyle. Remains of medieval castle on islet near S shore. **31 G4** NN4601.
Loch Ard Forest *Stir.* ***Forest/woodland***, S of Loch Ard, forming part of Queen Elizabeth Forest Park. **31 G5** NS4898.
Loch Ardbhair *High. Gaelic form of Loch Ardvar, qv.*
Loch Ardinning *Stir.* ***Lake/loch***, small loch 1m/2km S of Strathblane. NS5677.
Loch Ardnahoe *Arg. & B. See Ardnahoe Loch.*
Loch Ardvar (Gaelic form: Loch Ardbhair.) *High.* ***Sea feature***, inlet on S side of Eddrachillis Bay, to W of Loch a' Chàirn Bhàin on W coast of Sutherland district. NC1633.
Loch Arichlinie *High.* ***Lake/loch***, small loch in Sutherland district, 2m/3km NW of Kinbrace. **76 A5** NC8435.
Loch Arienas *High.* ***Lake/loch***, in Morvern, Lochaber district, 4m/6km N of Lochaline. **37 F4** NM6851.
Loch Arkaig *High.* ***Lake/loch***, in Lochaber district running about 12m/19km W to E from 1km below confluence of Rivers Dessary and Pean to 1m/2km NW of Bunarkaig on Loch Lochy. **49 G5** NN0891.
Loch Arklet *Stir.* ***Lake/loch***, and reservoir between Loch Katrine and Loch Lomond, 1m/2km E of Inversnaid. **31 F4** NN3709.
Loch Arnicle *Arg. & B.* ***Lake/loch***, small loch or tarn in Kintyre 3m/4km E of Glenbarr. NR7135.
Loch Arnish *High.* ***Bay***, on W coast of Raasay, 3m/5km from N end of island. **58 B5** NG5948.
Loch Arnol *W.Isles* ***Lake/loch***, on NW coast of Isle of Lewis 1km W of Arnol village. River Arnol runs into loch from S and out into Port Arnol to N. NB3148.
Loch Arthur *D. & G.* ***Lake/loch***, small loch 1km E of Beeswing and 6m/10km SW of Dumfries. **8 D4** NX9068.
Loch Ascaig *High.* ***Lake/loch***, in Sutherland district, 2m/4km E of Altanduin. **72 D2** NC8425.
Loch Ascog *Arg. & B.* ***Lake/loch***, small loch on Bute, 1m/2km S of Rothesay. **22 B3** NS0962.
Loch Ashie *High.* ***Lake/loch***, in Inverness district 6m/10km S of Inverness. Area about 390 acres or 160 hectares. **51 F1** NH6234.
Loch Assapol *Arg. & B.* ***Lake/loch***, on Ross of Mull, 1m/2km SE of Bunessan. **28 D2** NM4020.
Loch Assynt *High.* ***Lake/loch***, in Sutherland district, over 6m/10km NW to SE and 282 feet or 86 metres at maximum depth, 5m/7km E of Lochinver. Village of Inchnadamph at head of loch. **71 D2** NC2124.
Loch Aulasary *W.Isles* ***Sea feature***, large inlet on NE coast of North Uist, 1km N of Lochportain. **56 C2** NF9474.
Loch Avail (Also known as Loch Ellen.) *Arg. & B.* ***Lake/loch***, small loch in Knapdale, Argyll, 2m/3km NE of Achahoish. NR8079.
Loch Avich *Arg. & B.* ***Lake/loch***, 2m/3km NW of Dalavich on W side of Loch Awe, Argyll. **30 B3** NM9314.
Loch Avon *Moray* ***Lake/loch***, below SE slope of Cairn Gorm. River Avon flows from foot of loch. **52 C4** NJ0102.
Loch Awe *Arg. & B.* ***Lake/loch***, narrow loch 24m/39km long SW to NE in Argyll. Runs from Ford to Pass of Brander and discharges by River Awe to Loch Etive. Maximum depth over 300 feet or 90 metres. **30 B4** NM9610.
Loch Awe *High.* ***Lake/loch***, at head of River Loanan, 4m/6km S of Loch Assynt. **71 E3** NC2415.
Loch Bà *Arg. & B.* ***Lake/loch***, source of River Bà on Mull, 3m/5km S of Salen. Length 3m/5km SE to NW. **29 E1** NM5638.
Loch Bà *High.* ***Lake/loch***, on Rannoch Moor in Lochaber district, from which River Bà flows into head of Loch Laidon. **39 F5** NN3250.
Loch Bad a' Bhàthaich *High.* ***Lake/loch***, small loch in Ross and Cromarty district, 1m/2km N of Loch Morie. NH5378.
Loch Bad a' Ghaill (Anglicised form: Loch Baddagyle.) *High.* ***Lake/loch***, near NW coast of Ross and Cromarty district 8m/12km S of Lochinver. **70 C4** NC0710.
Loch Bad an Sgalaig *High.* ***Lake/loch***, near W coast of Ross and Cromarty district 4m/7km SE of Gairloch. Upper part of loch is known as Dubh Loch. **59 E2** NG8470.
Loch Badanloch *High.* ***Lake/loch***, S part of a double loch in Sutherland district 5m/8km W of Kinbrace. N part of loch is known as Loch nan Clàr. **75 G5** NC7734.
Loch Baddagyle *High. Anglicised form of Loch Bad a' Ghaill, qv.*
Loch Baghasdail *W.Isles Gaelic form of Lochboisdale (village), qv.*
Loch Baghasdail (Anglicised form: Loch Boisdale.) *W.Isles* ***Sea feature***, inlet containing several small islands, near S end of South Uist on E side. **44 D2** NF7919.
Loch Baile Mhic Chailein *Arg. & B.* ***Lake/loch***, small loch in course of River Creran, 2m/3km NW of mouth of river at head of Loch Creran, Argyll. **38 C5** NN0247.
Loch Ballygrant *Arg. & B.* ***Lake/loch***, small loch to E of Ballygrant village on Islay, 3m/4km SW of Port Askaig. **20 C3** NR4066.
Loch Baravaig *High. See Baravaig.*
Loch Bay *High.* ***Sea feature***, inlet on NW coast of Skye, 4m/7km N of Dunvegan. **57 F4** NG2655.
Loch Beag *High.* ***Sea feature***, small inlet at head of Loch nan Uamh, on N side of Ardnish peninsula in Lochaber district. **37 G1** NM7283.
Loch Bealach Cùlaidh *High.* ***Lake/loch***, small narrow loch in Wyvis Forest, 7m/11km NE of Gorstan. **60 D2** NH4471.
Loch Beanie *P. & K.* ***Lake/loch***, small loch or tarn, 3m/5km E of Spittal of Glenshee. **41 G3** NO1668.
Loch Beannach *High.* ***Lake/loch***, 3m/5km NE of Lochinver. **70 D2** NC1326.
Loch Beannach *High.* ***Lake/loch***, in Sutherland district, 4m/6km N of Lairg. **72 B3** NC5912.
Loch Beannach *High.* ***Lake/loch***, small loch, N of River Brora and 3m/5km E of Dalnessie. **72 B3** NC6814.
Loch Beannachan (Also known as Loch Beannacharain.) *High.* ***Lake/loch***, small but deep loch in course of River Meig on Strathconon Forest in Ross and Cromarty district. **60 B4** NH2351.
Loch Beannacharain *High. Alternative name for Loch Beannachan, qv.*
Loch Beannacharan (Also known as Loch Bunacharan.) *High.* ***Lake/loch***, small but deep loch in course of River Farrar in Inverness district 6m/9km above Struy Bridge. **50 C1** NH3038.
Loch Bee *W.Isles* ***Lake/loch***, large loch at N end of South Uist. **45 F5** NF7743.
Loch Beg *Arg. & B.* ***Sea feature***, inlet at head of Loch Scridain, Mull. **29 E2** NM5229.
Loch Beinn a' Mheadhoin (Also known as Loch Beneveian.) *High.* ***Lake/loch***, and reservoir in Glen Affric, Inverness district. Length 6m/9km SW to NE. **50 B2** NH2425.
Loch Belivat *High.* ***Lake/loch***, small loch in Nairn district 7m/11km SE of Nairn. NH9547.
Loch Ben Harrald *High.* ***Lake/loch***, 3m/5km SW of Altnaharra, Sutherland district. **75 E5** NC5133.
Loch Benachally *P. & K.* ***Lake/loch***, small loch 4m/7km W of Bridge of Cally. **41 F4** NO0750.
Loch Beneveian *High. Alternative name for Loch Beinn a' Mheadhoin, qv.*
Loch Benisval *W.Isles* ***Lake/loch***, small loch 1m/2km NW of head of Loch Resort, Isle of Lewis. **66 C2** NB0818.
Loch Beoraid *High.* ***Lake/loch***, narrow but deep loch in South Morar, Lochaber district, between Loch Morar and Loch Eilt. Length 3m/5km E to W. **38 A1** NM8285.
Loch Bhac *P. & K.* ***Lake/loch***, small loch 4m/6km SW of Blair Atholl. **40 D3** NN8262.
Loch Bhad Ghaineamhaich *High.* ***Lake/loch***, small loch 3m/4km NE of Milton. **60 C4** NH3259.
Loch Bharanaichd *High.* ***Lake/loch***, small loch 5m/8km E of Torridon. **59 F4** NG9757.
Loch Bhasapoll *Arg. & B.* ***Lake/loch***, near N coast of Tiree 5m/8km W of Scarinish. NL9747.
Loch Bhrodainn *High.* ***Lake/loch***, in Gaick Forest, 7m/11km E of Dalwhinnie. **40 C1** NN7483.
Loch Bhrollum *W.Isles* ***Sea feature***, inlet on SE coast of Isle of Lewis, 2m/4km to E of Loch Claidh. **67 F3** NB3102.
Loch Bhruthaich *High. Alternative name for Loch Bruicheach, qv.*
Loch Bodavat *W.Isles* ***Lake/loch***, small loch 2m/3km E of Aird Bheag and 1km N of Loch Resort, Isle of Lewis. **66 C2** NB0619.
Loch Bog *P. & K. Alternative name for Stormont Loch, qv.*
Loch Boisdale *W.Isles Anglicised form of Loch Baghasdail (sea-loch), qv.*
Loch Boltachan *P. & K.* ***Lake/loch***, small loch or tarn 1m/2km N of St. Fillans. **32 B2** NN6926.
Loch Bornish *W.Isles* ***Lake/loch***, on South Uist, 1m/2km E of Rubha Ardvule. NF7329.
Loch Borralan *High.* ***Lake/loch***, small loch in Sutherland district 7m/11km S of Inchnadamph. **71 E3** NC2610.
Loch Bracadale *High.* ***Sea feature***, wide inlet on SW coast of Skye between Idrigill Point and Rubha nan Clach. **47 F1** NG2837.
Loch Bradan Reservoir *S.Ayr.* ***Reservoir***, within Glen Trool Forest Park, 7m/11km SW of Dalmellington. **7 F1** NX4297.
Loch Branahuie *W.Isles* ***Lake/loch***, small lake to E of Branahuie, on spit of land connecting Eye Peninsula to rest of Isle of Lewis. NB4732.
Loch Brandy *Angus* ***Lake/loch***, mountain loch 1m/2km N of Clova. **42 B2** NO3375.
Loch Breachacha *Arg. & B.* ***Sea feature***, large inlet on S coast of Coll, 5m/7km SW of Arinagour. **36 A4** NM1653.
Loch Breivat *W.Isles* ***Lake/loch***, near NW coast of Isle of Lewis 2m/3km SE of Arnol. **69 E3** NB3345.
Loch Brittle *High.* ***Sea feature***, inlet on SW coast of Skye, 4m/6km SE of Loch Eynort. **47 G3** NG4019.
Loch Broom *High.* ***Sea feature***, long inlet on which small town of Ullapool is situated, on W coast of Ross and Cromarty district. **70 C5** NH1392.
Loch Broom *P. & K.* ***Lake/loch***, small loch 4m/7km E of Pitlochry. **41 F4** NO0057.
Loch Brora *High.* ***Lake/loch***, in course of River Brora, Sutherland district, 4m/6km NW of Brora village. **72 D4** NC8507.
Loch Bruicheach (Also known as Loch Bhruthaich.) *High.* ***Lake/loch***, small loch in Inverness district 5m/8km NW of Drumnadrochit. **51 D1** NH4536.
Loch Buidhe *High.* ***Lake/loch***, small loch 1km E of Coldbackie, Caithness district. **75 F2** NC6359.
Loch Buidhe *High.* ***Lake/loch***, in Sutherland district 5m/8km NE of Bonar Bridge. **72 B5** NH6698.
Loch Buidhe *High.* ***Lake/loch***, small loch in course of River Bà 5m/9km N of Bridge of Orchy. NN2948.
Loch Buidhe Mòr *High.* ***Lake/loch***, small loch 1m/2km W of Strathy Forest, Caithness district. **75 G3** NC7758.
Loch Buie *Arg. & B.* ***Sea feature***, large inlet on S coast of Mull. **29 F2** NM6025.
Loch Builg *Moray* ***Lake/loch***, small loch, source of Builg Burn, 6m/9km SW of Cock Bridge. **53 D4** NJ1803.
Loch Bun Abhainn-eadar *W.Isles* ***Sea feature***, inlet on N side of West Loch Tarbert, W coast of North Harris. NB1203.
Loch Bunacharan *High. Alternative name for Loch Beannacharan, qv.*
Loch Bunachton *High.* ***Lake/loch***, small loch in Inverness district 6m/10km S of Inverness and 2m/3km E of Loch Ashie. NH6635.
Loch Cairnbawn *High. Anglicised form of Loch a' Chàirn Bhàin, qv.*
Loch Calavie *High.* ***Lake/loch***, small loch in Skye and Lochalsh district 3m/5km SW of head of Loch Monar. **49 G1** NH0538.
Loch Calder *High.* ***Lake/loch***, in Caithness district, 2m/4km long N to S and nearly 1m/2km wide, 5m/8km SW of Thurso. **76 C3** ND0760.

L

Loch Callater *Aber.* ***Lake/loch***, small loch in Glen Callater 5m/8km S of Braemar. **41 G1** NO1884.
Loch Caluim *High.* ***Lake/loch***, 2m/3km SE of Loch Scye. Loch is approximately 1km N to S. **76 C3** ND0152.
Loch Càm *Arg. & B.* ***Lake/loch***, small loch on Islay, 3m/4km N of Bridgend. **20 B3** NR3466.
Loch Caoldair *High.* ***Lake/loch***, small loch in Badenoch and Strathspey district 3m/5km NW of Dalwhinnie. **40 B1** NN6189.
Loch Caolisport *Arg. & B.* ***Sea feature***, sea-loch in Argyll, running NE from Point of Knap to Achahoish. **21 F2** NR7374.
Loch Caravat *W.Isles* ***Lake/loch***, on S of North Uist, 1m/2km E of Corúna. **45 G3** NF8461.
Loch Carlabhagh (Anglicised form: Loch Carloway.) *W.Isles* ***Sea feature***, inlet and estuary of Carloway River, on W coast of Isle of Lewis, to W of Carloway village. **68 C3** NB1842.
Loch Carloway *W.Isles Anglicised form of Loch Carlabhagh, qv.*
Loch Càrn a' Mhaoil *Arg. & B.* ***Lake/loch***, small loch on Islay, 3m/4km W of Ardmore Point. NR4350.
Loch Carnan *W.Isles* ***Sea feature***, inlet on NE coast of South Uist. **45 G5** NF8243.
Loch Caroy *High.* ***Sea feature***, inlet of Loch Bracadale, Skye, 4m/7km NW of Bracadale village. **57 F5** NG3043.
Loch Carrie *High.* ***Lake/loch***, small loch in course of River Cannich 3m/5km below dam of Loch Mullardoch in Inverness district. **50 B1** NH2633.
Loch Carron *High.* ***Sea feature***, long inlet in Ross and Cromarty district, extending from S end of Inner Sound on N side of Kyle of Lochalsh to foot of Glen Carron. Vehicle ferry across narrows at Stromeferry. **49 F1** NG8735.
Loch Casgro *W.Isles* ***Lake/loch***, small loch 3m/5km E of Bragar, Isle of Lewis. **69 E3** NB3347.
Loch Cean Thulabhig (Anglicised form: Loch Ceann Hulavig.) *W.Isles* ***Sea feature***, inlet on NW coast of Isle of Lewis, 3m/4km S of Breascleit. **68 D4** NB2131.
Loch Ceann Dibig *W.Isles* ***Sea feature***, inlet on E coast of South Harris, 1m/2km S of Tarbert. **67 D4** NG1597.
Loch Ceann Hulavig *W.Isles Anglicised form of Loch Cean Thulabhaig, qv.*
Loch Ceo Ghlas *High. Alternative spelling of Loch Ceo Glais, qv.*
Loch Ceo Glais (Also spelled Loch Ceo Ghlas or Loch Ceo Glas.) *High.* ***Lake/loch***, small loch in Inverness district nearly 1km SW of Loch Duntelchaig. **51 E2** NH5828.
Loch Ceo Glas *High. Alternative spelling of Loch Ceo Glais, qv.*
Loch Chaorunn *Arg. & B.* ***Lake/loch***, small loch in Knapdale, Argyll, 3m/4km NW of Tarbert. **21 G2** NR8371.
Loch Chiarain *High.* ***Lake/loch***, small loch in course of Ciaran Water, Lochaber district, 3m/5km NE of dam of Blackwater Reservoir. NN2963.
Loch Choire *High.* ***Lake/loch***, in Caithness district 6m/9km SE of Altnaharra. **72 A2** NC6328.
Loch Choire Forest *High.* ***Open space***, deer forest in Caithness district surrounding Loch Choire. **72 A2** NC6328.
Loch Choire Lodge *High.* ***Settlement***, at NE end of Loch Choire, Sutherland district. **75 F5** NC6530.
Loch Chon *Stir.* ***Lake/loch***, 4m/6km E of Ben Lomond. **31 G4** NN4205.
Loch Ciaran *Arg. & B.* ***Lake/loch***, small loch in Kintyre, Argyll, 1m/2km S of Clachan. **21 F4** NR7754.
Loch Cill Chriosd *High.* ***Lake/loch***, small loch on Skye, 3m/4km SW of Broadford. **48 B2** NG6120.
Loch Claidh *W.Isles* ***Sea feature***, large inlet on S coast of Isle of Lewis, to E of Loch Seaforth. **67 E3** NB2603.
Loch Clàir *High.* ***Lake/loch***, small loch in Ross and Cromarty district, 1m/2km SE of Port Henderson. **59 D2** NG7771.
Loch Clair *High.* ***Lake/loch***, small loch in Ross and Cromarty district 3m/5km SW of Kinlochewe. NH0057.
Loch Clash *High.* ***Sea feature***, on W coast of Sutherland district. Kinlochbervie lies at its head. **74 A3** NC2056.
Loch Cleap *High.* ***Lake/loch***, small loch 2m/3km N of Beinn Edra, Skye. **58 A3** NG4666.
Loch Cleit Steirmeis *W.Isles* ***Lake/loch***, small loch, 2m/3km S of head of Loch Cean Thulabhig. **68 D5** NB2326.
Loch Cliad *Arg. & B.* ***Lake/loch***, largest of numerous lochs on Coll, 1m/2km S of Cliad Bay and 1m/2km NW of Arinagour. **36 B4** NM2058.
Loch Cluanie *High.* ***Lake/loch***, and reservoir, partly in Skye and Lochalsh district and partly in Inverness district. Runs E for about 7m/11km from foot of Glen Shiel. **50 A3** NH1409.
Loch Cnoc an Loch *N.Ayr.* ***Lake/loch***, small loch or tarn on Arran 3m/4km E of Blackwaterfoot. NR9328.
Loch Coire Lair *High.* ***Lake/loch***, small narrow loch in Ross and Cromarty district 2m/3km N of head of Loch Glascarnoch. **60 B2** NH2878.
Loch Coire Mhic Fhearchair *High.* ***Lake/loch***, small loch in spectacular corrie on N side of Beinn Eighe, in Ross and Cromarty district. NG9460.
Loch Coire na Saighe Duibhe *High.* ***Lake/loch***, 2m/3km N of Loch a' Ghorm-choire. **74 D5** NC4436.
Loch Coire nam Mang *High.* ***Lake/loch***, in Sutherland district adjacent to, and W of, Loch Druim a' Chliabhain. **75 G4** NC8040.
Loch Coirigerod *W.Isles* ***Lake/loch***, small loch 3m/4km SE of head of Little Loch Roag, Isle of Lewis. **68 C5** NB1721.
Loch Con *P. & K.* ***Lake/loch***, small loch between Loch Errochty and Glen Garry. **40 B3** NN6867.
Loch Connan *High.* ***Lake/loch***, small loch 4m/6km NE of Bracadale, Skye. **57 G5** NG3842.
Loch Connell *D. & G.* ***Lake/loch***, small loch 1km W of Kirkcolm. **6 B4** NX0168.
Loch Corodale *W.Isles* ***Lake/loch***, small loch on South Uist, 2m/3km NE of Beinn Mhòr. **46 B1** NF8333.
Loch Corr *Arg. & B.* ***Lake/loch***, small loch near NW coast of Islay, 1m/2km S of Tòn Mhòr. NR2269.
Loch Coruisk *High.* ***Lake/loch***, on Skye below Cuillin Hills running into Loch na Cuilce and thence into Loch Scavaig. **48 A2** NG4820.
Loch Coulin *High.* ***Lake/loch***, small loch in Ross and Cromarty district 5m/7km S of Kinlochewe. **59 G4** NH0155.
Loch Coulside *High.* ***Lake/loch***, small narrow loch 1m/2km W of S end of Loch Loyal. **75 E4** NC5743.
Loch Coulter Reservoir *Stir.* ***Lake/loch***, small loch and reservoir 5m/8km SW of Stirling. **24 B1** NS7686.
Loch Coultrie *High.* ***Lake/loch***, in Ross and Cromarty district running into head of Loch Damh. **59 E5** NG8545.
Loch Cracail Mòr *High.* ***Lake/loch***, small loch 4m/6km SE of Lairg. **72 B4** NC6202.
Loch Craggie *High.* ***Lake/loch***, 1km S of Glen Oykel in Sutherland district. **71 F4** NC3205.
Loch Craggie *High.* ***Lake/loch***, in course of River Borgie 4m/6km SE of Tongue, in Caithness district. **75 F3** NC6152.
Loch Craggie *High.* ***Lake/loch***, in Sutherland district 3m/5km E of Lairg. **72 B4** NC6207.
Loch Craignish *Arg. & B.* ***Sea feature***, long inlet on coast of Argyll, at N end of Sound of Jura and on E side of peninsula, comprising parish of Craignish. Large standing stone and remains of two burial cairns at head of loch. NM7800.
Loch Cravadale *W.Isles* ***Bay***, N facing bay on W coast of North Harris, 2m/3km NE of Huisinis. **66 B2** NB0113.
Loch Creagh *P. & K.* ***Lake/loch***, small loch or tarn 4m/7km SE of Aberfeldy. NN9044.
Loch Creran *Arg. & B.* ***Sea feature***, arm of Loch Linnhe extending 7m/11km from Lynn of Lorn to foot of Glen Creran. Width varies from nearly 1m/2km in places to about 100 metres at Dallachoilish. **38 B5** NM9442.
Loch Crinan *Arg. & B. Alternative name for Crinan Loch, qv.*
Loch Cròcach *High.* ***Lake/loch***, 2m/3km N of Lochinver. **70 C2** NC1027.
Loch Cròcach *High.* ***Lake/loch***, 3m/4km N of Loch a' Chàirn Bhàin, Sutherland district. **74 A4** NC1939.
Loch Cròcach *High.* ***Lake/loch***, 2m/3km S of Kinlochbervie, Sutherland district. **74 B3** NC2152.
Loch Cròcach *High.* ***Lake/loch***, small loch 1m/2km SW of S end of Loch Hope. **74 D4** NC4249.
Loch Cròcach *High.* ***Lake/loch***, small loch, 1km N of Loch Druim a' Chliabhain, Caithness district. **76 A4** NC8044.
Loch Croistean *W.Isles* ***Lake/loch***, small loch 3m/4km S of Cairisiadar and 1km W of Little Loch Roag, Isle of Lewis. **68 B5** NB1129.
Loch Cromore *W.Isles* ***Lake/loch***, small loch S of Gleann Ghrabhair, near E coast of Isle of Lewis. NB4020.
Loch Crongart *S.Ayr.* ***Lake/loch***, small loch 3m/5km E of Barrhill. NX2882.
Loch Crunachdan *High.* ***Lake/loch***, small loch in Badenoch and Strathspey district 4m/7km W of Laggan Bridge. **51 E5** NN5492.
Loch Cruoshie *High.* ***Lake/loch***, small loch on plateau, 5m/8km NW of W end of Loch Mullardoch, in Skye and Lochalsh district. **49 G1** NH0536.
Loch Cuaich *High.* ***Lake/loch***, 4m/6km NE of Dalwhinnie. **40 B1** NN6987.
Loch Culag *High.* ***Lake/loch***, small loch just S of Loch Inver. **70 C2** NC0921.
Loch Culen *High. Alternative name for Loch a' Chuilinn, qv.*
Loch Daimh *P. & K. See Loch an Daimh.*
Loch Dallas *Moray* ***Lake/loch***, small loch 4m/6km SW of Dallas. **62 C5** NJ0947.
Loch Damh *High.* ***Lake/loch***, in Ross and Cromarty district, 4m/6km long N to S, running out into S side of Upper Loch Torridon. **59 E4** NG8650.
Loch Davan *Aber.* ***Lake/loch***, small loch 1m/2km NW of Dinnet. **53 G4** NJ4400.
Loch Dee *D. & G.* ***Lake/loch***, 4m/7km W of Clatteringshaws Loch. **7 F3** NX4678.
Loch Derculich *P. & K.* ***Lake/loch***, small loch 4m/6km N of Aberfeldy. **40 D4** NN8655.
Loch Derry *D. & G.* ***Lake/loch***, small loch or tarn 2m/4km SW of Loch Maberry. NX2573.
Loch Diabaig *High.* ***Sea feature***, inlet on NE side of Loch Torridon, W coast of Ross and Cromarty district. **59 D3** NG7959.
Loch Diabaigas Airde *High.* ***Lake/loch***, in Ross and Cromarty district 2m/3km N of mouth of Upper Loch Torridon. **59 E4** NG8159.
Loch Dibadale *W.Isles* ***Lake/loch***, small loch on Isle of Lewis, 1m/2km S of Tahaval. **68 B5** NB0423.
Loch Dionard *High.* ***Lake/loch***, small loch at head of River Dionard, 4m/6km SW of head of Loch Eriboll. **74 C4** NC3549.
Loch Dochard *Arg. & B.* ***Lake/loch***, small loch in Argyll 4m/6km W of Loch Tulla. **39 E5** NN2141.
Loch Dochart *Stir.* ***Lake/loch***, small loch in course of River Fillan, 1m/2km E of Crianlarich. Ruined castle on islet in middle of loch. **31 G2** NN4025.
Loch Dochfour *High.* ***Lake/loch***, small loch at N end of Loch Ness, 5m/8km SW of Inverness. **51 F1** NH6039.
Loch Doilet *High.* ***Lake/loch***, small loch in course of River Hurich in Glenhurich Forest, Lochaber district. NM8067.
Loch Doine *Stir.* ***Lake/loch***, small loch 4m/7km W of Balquhidder. **31 G3** NN4719.
Loch Doir a' Ghearrin *High.* ***Lake/loch***, in Lochaber district on Ardnish peninsula. **37 G1** NM7281.
Loch Doire nam Mart *High.* ***Lake/loch***, small loch in Morvern, Lochaber district 5m/8km N of Lochaline. NM6652.
Loch Don *Arg. & B.* ***Sea feature***, inlet on E coast of Mull. **29 G1** NM7333.
Loch Doon *E.Ayr.* ***Lake/loch***, large loch and reservoir at head of River Doon 4m/7km S of Dalmellington. **7 F1** NX4998.
Loch Doon Castle *E.Ayr.* ***Castle***, remains (Historic Scotland), formerly on islet in loch, re-erected on W bank of Loch Doon reservoir. **7 F1** NX4998.
Loch Dornal *S.Ayr.* ***Lake/loch***, on border with Dumfries & Galloway, 5m/8km SE of Barrhill and adjacent to NE of Loch Maberry. **7 D3** NX2976.
Loch Doule *High. Alternative name for Loch Dùghaill, qv.*
Loch Droma *High.* ***Lake/loch***, small loch in Ross and Cromarty district, 1m/2km W of head of Loch Glascarnoch. **60 B2** NH2675.
Loch Druidibeg *W.Isles* ***Lake/loch***, large loch on South Uist 4m/6km N of Beinn Mhòr. Nature reserve. **46 A1** NF8031.
Loch Druim a' Chliabhain *High.* ***Lake/loch***, in Sutherland district below Ben Griam Beg and 5m/8km W of Forsinard railway station. **76 A4** NC8141.
Loch Drunkie *Stir.* ***Lake/loch***, at E edge of Achray Forest, S of Loch Venachar. **32 A4** NN5404.
Loch Duagrich *High.* ***Lake/loch***, small loch 3m/5km E of Bracadale, Skye. **48 A1** NG3939.
Loch Dubh *High.* ***Lake/loch***, corrie lake on SE slope of Carn Deag, 5m/8km NE of Newtonmore. **51 F4** NH6301.
Loch Dubh a' Chuail *High.* ***Lake/loch***, corrie loch below Meallan a' Chuail which feeds Abhainn a' Choire. **71 F2** NC3428.
Loch Dùghaill (Also known as Loch Doule.) *High.* ***Lake/loch***, small loch in Glen Carron 5m/8km NE of head of Loch Carron. **59 F5** NG9947.
Loch Dùghaill *High.* ***Sea feature***, inlet on W coast of Sutherland district, 4m/6km W of Rhiconich. **74 A3** NC1952.
Loch Duibaig *High.* ***Sea feature***, small inlet on E coast of Vaternish peninsula, Skye, 2m/3km SW of Greshornish Point. **57 G4** NG3354.
Loch Duich *High.* ***Lake/loch***, 5m/8km long, in Skye and Lochalsh district, running NW into head of Loch Alsh. **49 E2** NG9022.
Loch Dùn na Cille *W.Isles* ***Lake/loch***, small loch near W coast of South Uist, 1m/2km S of Dalabrog. **44 C2** NF7418.
Loch Dungeon *D. & G.* ***Lake/loch***, on E side of Rhinns of Kells, 4m/6km N of Clatteringshaws Loch. **7 G2** NX5284.
Loch Duntelchaig *High.* ***Lake/loch***, in Inverness district 8m/13km S of Inverness and 2m/3km SE of Dores. **51 F1** NH6231.
Loch Dunvegan *High.* ***Sea feature***, sea-loch on NW coast of Skye. **57 F4** NG2547.
Loch Earn ***Lake/loch***, on border of Perth & Kinross and Stirling, extending over 6m/10km W to E, from Lochearnhead to St. Fillans. Width about 1km. Facilities for water sports, including sailing and water-skiing. **32 B2** NN6423.
Loch Eatharna *Arg. & B.* ***Sea feature***, inlet on SE coast of Coll, with port of Arinagour on W side. **36 B4** NM2256.
Loch Eck *Arg. & B.* ***Lake/loch***, narrow loch in Argyll running 6m/10km N to S, within Argyll Forest Park. S end is 7m/11km N of Dunoon. **30 D5** NS1391.
Loch Eck Forest *Arg. & B.* ***Forest/woodland***, on E shore of Loch Eck, Argyll Forest Park. NS1391.
Loch Ederline *Arg. & B.* ***Lake/loch***, small loch in Argyll, 1m/2km S of head of Loch Awe. **30 A4** NM8602.

L

Loch Eigheach *P. & K.* ***Lake/loch***, and reservoir 1m/2km E of Rannoch railway station. Power station near dam at E end. **39 G4** NN4556.
Loch Eil *High.* ***Lake/loch***, in Lochaber district running 8m/13km W to E, from Kinlocheil to Corpach, where it turns S into head of Loch Linnhe. **38 C2** NN0277.
Loch Eil Centre (Achdalieu Lodge). *High.* ***Other building***, Outward Bound centre 4m/7km NW of Fort William across head of Loch Linnhe. **38 C2** NN0578.
Loch Eilde Beag *High.* ***Lake/loch***, a short distance upstream to NE of Loch Eilde Mòr. **39 E3** NN2364.
Loch Eilde Mòr *High.* ***Lake/loch***, on E side of Mamore Forest in Lochaber district, 3m/4km NE of Kinlochleven. **39 E3** NN2364.
Loch Eileanach *High.* ***Lake/loch***, small loch 5m/8km SW of S end of Loch Loyal, Caithness district. **75 E4** NC5940.
Loch Eileanach *High.* ***Lake/loch***, 1km long N to S, just NW of Loch More. **76 C4** ND0647.
Loch Eilt *High.* ***Lake/loch***, narrow loch in Lochaber district between Lochailort and Glenfinnan. Length over 3m/5km E to W. **38 A1** NM8182.
Loch Einich *High.* ***Lake/loch***, in Cairngorm Mountains, in Badenoch and Strathspey district, 8m/13km S of Aviemore. **52 B5** NN9199.
Loch Eishort *High.* ***Sea feature***, large inlet on SW coast of Skye, to N of Sleat peninsula. **48 C3** NG6014.
Loch Ellen *Arg. & B. Alternative name for Loch Avail, qv.*
Loch Enoch *D. & G.* ***Lake/loch***, in Glentrool Forest Park, 1m/2km E of Merrick. **7 F2** NX4485.
Loch Eport *W.Isles Anglicised form of Loch Euphoirt, qv.*
Loch Eriboll *High.* ***Sea feature***, long inlet on N coast of Sutherland district to E of Durness, penetrating 9m/15km inland and varying in width from 1m/2km to 2m/3km. **74 D3** NC4360.
Loch Ericht *High.* ***Lake/loch***, on border with Perth & Kinross and running 15m/24km from near Dalwhinnie to dam at S end, from where tunnel aqueduct conveys water to power station on Loch Rannoch. **40 A3** NN5371.
Loch Ericht Forest *High.* ***Forest/woodland***, on NW side of Loch Ericht, at NE end of loch. **40 A1** NN5779.
Loch Erisort *W.Isles* ***Sea feature***, inlet on E coast of Isle of Lewis, penetrating 8m/13km inland. Entrance is 7m/11km S of Stornoway. **69 E5** NB3420.
Loch Errochty *P. & K.* ***Lake/loch***, and reservoir at head of Glen Errochty, 10m/16km W of Blair Atholl. **40 B3** NN6965.
Loch Esk *Angus* ***Lake/loch***, small loch or tarn near head of River South Esk 9m/15km SE of Braemar. NO2379.
Loch Essan *Stir.* ***Lake/loch***, 3m/4km NE of Crianlarich. **31 G2** NN4128.
Loch Etchachan *Aber.* ***Lake/loch***, small loch on NE side of Ben Macdui in Cairngorm Mountains. **52 C4** NJ0000.
Loch Etive ***Sea feature***, sea-loch extending 18m/29km from Ledaig Point to foot of Glen Etive. Wild, mountainous scenery in upper reaches. Road bridge spans loch at Connel, near mouth. **30 B1** NN0434.
Loch Ettrick *D. & G.* ***Lake/loch***, small loch 3m/5km E of Closeburn. **8 D1** NX9493.
Loch Euphoirt (Anglicised form: Loch Eport.) *W.Isles* ***Sea feature***, long narrow inlet on E coast of North Uist, 3m/5km S of Lochmaddy. **45 G3** NF8963.
Loch Ewe *High.* ***Sea feature***, large inlet on W coast of Ross and Cromarty district. Village of Poolewe at head of loch. **59 E1** NG8387.
Loch Eye *High.* ***Lake/loch***, in Ross and Cromarty district 3m/5km SE of Tain. NH8379.
Loch Eynort *High.* ***Sea feature***, large inlet on SW coast of Skye, extending inland to locality of Grula and mouth of Eynort River. **47 G2** NG3724.
Loch Eynort *W.Isles* ***Sea feature***, long inlet on E coast of South Uist, 5m/8km N of Lochboisdale. **46 B2** NF8026.
Loch Eyre *High.* ***Sea feature***, inlet at head of Loch Snizort Beag, Skye, 7m/11km NW of Portree. **58 A4** NG4152.
Loch Fad *Arg. & B.* ***Lake/loch***, on Bute, 2m/3km S of Rothesay. **22 B3** NS0761.
Loch Fada *Arg. & B.* ***Lake/loch***, in N part of Coll, 4m/6km NE of Arinagour. **36 B3** NM2561.
Loch Fada *Arg. & B.* ***Lake/loch***, on Colonsay, 1m/2km N of Scalasaig. **28 C5** NR3895.
Loch Fada *High.* ***Lake/loch***, on Skye 3m/5km N of Portree. Runs into Loch Leathan. **58 A5** NG4949.
Loch Fada *High.* ***Lake/loch***, small loch near E coast of Skye, 4m/6km SE of Portree. **48 A1** NG5037.
Loch Fada *High.* ***Lake/loch***, near W coast of Ross and Cromarty district 4m/7km NE of Poolewe. **59 F1** NG9086.
Loch Fada *W.Isles* ***Lake/loch***, small loch 2m/3km NW of Lacasaigh, Isle of Lewis. **69 E5** NB3124.
Loch Fada *W.Isles* ***Lake/loch***, on North Uist, 1m/2km S of Crogary Mòr. **45 G2** NF8770.
Loch Fadagoa *W.Isles* ***Lake/loch***, 3m/5km NW of Baile Ailein, Isle of Lewis. **68 D5** NB2423.
Loch Fannich *High.* ***Reservoir***, large reservoir in Ross and Cromarty district, 18m/29km W of Dingwall. Length 7m/11km E to W. **60 A3** NH2666.
Loch Farr *High.* ***Lake/loch***, small loch in Strathnairn Forest, Inverness district, 1m/2km S of Farr and 9m/15km S of Inverness. **51 F1** NH6830.
Loch Farroch *S.Ayr.* ***Lake/loch***, small loch 2m/4km NE of Barrhill. NX2585.
Loch Faskally *P. & K.* ***Lake/loch***, and reservoir in course of River Tummel above Pitlochry. **41 E4** NN9258.
Loch Fearna *High.* ***Lake/loch***, small corrie loch below Spidean Mialach, in Lochaber district, which feeds short stream flowing S to Loch Quoich. **49 G4** NH0503.
Loch Féith an Leòthaid *High.* ***Lake/loch***, 1m/2km S of Loch Assynt. **71 D2** NC1822.
Loch Fell *D. & G.* ***Mountain***, 5m/9km E of Moffat. Height 2257 feet or 688 metres. **16 C5** NT1704.
Loch Fender *P. & K.* ***Lake/loch***, small loch or tarn 5m/8km S of Aberfeldy. **41 D5** NN8741.
Loch Feochan *Arg. & B.* ***Sea feature***, inlet on coast of Argyll, 4m/6km long and 4m/6km S of Oban. **30 A2** NM8423.
Loch Fern *D. & G.* ***Lake/loch***, 2m/3km NE of Dalbeattie. **8 C4** NX8662.
Loch Fiag *High.* ***Lake/loch***, in Sutherland district 8m/13km SW of Altnaharra. **71 G2** NC4429.
Loch Fiart *Arg. & B.* ***Lake/loch***, small loch on Lismore, 2m/3km NE of Rubha Fiart. **30 A1** NM8037.
Loch Finlaggan *Arg. & B.* ***Lake/loch***, on Islay 3m/5km SW of Port Askaig. On islet at N end of loch are ruins of castle of the Macdonalds, Lords of the Isles. **20 B3** NR3867.
Loch Finlas *E.Ayr.* ***Lake/loch***, 5m/8km S of Dalmellington, to W of Loch Doon. **7 F1** NX4598.
Loch Finnart *P. & K.* ***Lake/loch***, small loch 1m/2km S of Finnart. NN5255.
Loch Finsbay *W.Isles* ***Sea feature***, inlet on SE coast of South Harris, 2m/3km SW of Manais. **66 C5** NG0886.
Loch Fithie *Angus* ***Lake/loch***, lochan, 2m/3km E of Forfar. **42 C4** NO4951.
Loch Fitty *Fife* ***Lake/loch***, small loch 3m/4km W of Cowdenbeath. **33 G5** NT1291.
Loch Fleet *D. & G.* ***Lake/loch***, 7m/11km SW of New Galloway. **7 G4** NX5669.
Loch Fleet *High.* ***Sea feature***, inlet on E coast of Sutherland district formed by estuary of River Fleet, 4m/6km N of Dornoch. **72 C5** NH7896.
Loch Flemington *High.* ***Lake/loch***, small loch on border of Inverness and Nairn districts 5m/8km SW of Nairn. **62 A4** NH8152.
Loch Fleoideabhagh (Anglicised form: Loch Flodabay.) *W.Isles* ***Sea feature***, inlet on SE coast of South Harris, 2m/3km SW of Manais. **66 D5** NG0886.
Loch Flodabay *W.Isles Anglicised form of Loch Fleoideabhagh, qv.*
Loch Freuchie *P. & K.* ***Lake/loch***, in Glen Quaich nearly 2m/3km long NW of SE, and nearly 2m/3km W of Amulree. **32 D1** NN8637.
Loch Frisa *Arg. & B.* ***Lake/loch***, in N part of Mull, 4m/6km S of Tobermory. **37 D4** NM4848.
Loch Fuar-Bheinne *Arg. & B.* ***Lake/loch***, small loch in Knapdale, Argyll, 2m/3km E of Achahoish. **21 G2** NR8178.
Loch Fuaron *Arg. & B.* ***Lake/loch***, on Mull 2m/3km NW of Lochbuie. **29 E2** NM5826.
Loch Fyne *Arg. & B.* ***Sea feature***, long sea-loch in Argyll running N from Sound of Bute and penetrating inland to foot of Glen Fyne, NE of Inveraray. **21 G1** NR9591.
Loch Gaineamhach *Arg. & B.* ***Lake/loch***, 3m/5km SE of Ford. **30 B4** NM9100.
Loch Gaineamhach *High.* ***Lake/loch***, small loch 7m/11km S of Altnaharra, to SW of Loch a' Bhealaich, Sutherland district. **72 A2** NC5824.
Loch Gaineamhach *High.* ***Lake/loch***, small loch in Ross and Cromarty district, 4m/6km W of Shieldaig. **59 D4** NG7553.
Loch Gaineamhach *High.* ***Lake/loch***, small loch in Ross and Cromarty district, 1m/2km NW of Loch a' Ghobhainn. **59 E3** NG8367.
Loch Gaineimh *High.* ***Lake/loch***, small loch 2m/3km N of West Langwell and 4m/6km SW of Dalbreck, Sutherland district. **72 C3** NC6912.
Loch Gair *Arg. & B.* ***Sea feature***, inlet on W side of Loch Fyne in Argyll, 5m/7km E of Lochgilphead. **22 A1** NR9290.
Loch Gamhna *High.* ***Lake/loch***, small loch 4m/6km S of Aviemore. **52 A4** NH8906.
Loch Gaorsaic *High.* ***Lake/loch***, small loch in NE part of Kintail Estate, Skye and Lochalsh district. **49 G2** NH0222.
Loch Garasdale *Arg. & B.* ***Lake/loch***, small loch in Kintyre, Argyll, 3m/5km S of Clachan. **21 F4** NR7651.
Loch Garbhaig *High.* ***Lake/loch***, small loch 3m/4km E of Letterewe, Ross and Cromarty district. **59 G2** NG9970.
Loch Garry *High.* ***Lake/loch***, and reservoir in course of River Garry, Lochaber district, 2m/4km W of Invergarry. Length 5m/7km. **50 B4** NH2302.
Loch Garry *P. & K.* ***Lake/loch***, narrow deep loch 3m/4km long N to S, at head of Glen Garry, Atholl. **40 B3** NN6270.
Loch Garten *High.* ***Lake/loch***, small loch in Abernethy Forest, in Badenoch and Strathspey district, 4m/6km E of Boat of Garten. Nature trail in vicinity. **52 B3** NJ9718.
Loch Garten Nature Reserve *High.* ***Nature reserve***, Royal Society for the Protection of Birds reserve, 2m/3km SE of Boat of Garten. Particularly noted for nesting ospreys which can be observed from a special hide. **52 B3** NH9718.
Loch Garve *High.* ***Lake/loch***, small but deep loch in Ross and Cromarty district 4m/7km W of Strathpeffer. **60 D3** NH4159.
Loch Gearach *Arg. & B.* ***Lake/loch***, small loch on Rinns of Islay 2m/3km E of Kilchiaran Bay. NR2259.
Loch Gelly *Fife* ***Lake/loch***, small loch to SE of Lochgelly. **33 G5** NT1893.
Loch Ghabhaig *High.* ***Lake/loch***, small loch 1m/2km SW of Talladale, Ross and Cromarty district. **59 F3** NG8969.
Loch Ghuilbinn (Anglicised form: Loch Gulbin.) *High.* ***Lake/loch***, small loch in Lochaber district, 3m/4km N of foot of Loch Ossian. **39 G2** NN4174.
Loch Gilp *Arg. & B.* ***Sea feature***, inlet of Loch Fyne, running past Ardrishaig to Lochgilphead in Argyll. **21 G1** NR8584.
Loch Giorra *P. & K. See Loch an Daimh.*
Loch Glascarnoch *High.* ***Reservoir***, in Ross and Cromarty district, 14m/23km NW of Dingwall. **60 C2** NH3470.
Loch Glashan *Arg. & B.* ***Lake/loch***, and reservoir in Asknish Forest 4m/7km NE of Lochgilphead, Argyll. **30 B5** NR9193.
Loch Glass *High.* ***Lake/loch***, in Ross and Cromarty district 8m/12km W of Alness. **61 D2** NH5172.
Loch Glassie *P. & K.* ***Lake/loch***, small loch, 2m/3km N of Aberfeldy. **40 D4** NN8552.
Loch Glenastle *Arg. & B. Alternative name for Glenastle Loch, qv.*
Loch Glencoul *High.* ***Lake/loch***, running NW to join Loch Glendhu, past Kylesku into Loch a' Chàirn Bhàin and then into Eddrachillis Bay, W coast of Sutherland district. **74 B5** NC2531.
Loch Glendhu *High.* ***Lake/loch***, running W to join Loch Glencoul, past Kylesku into Loch a' Chàirn Bhàin and then into Eddrachillis Bay, W coast of Sutherland district. **74 B5** NC2533.
Loch Glow *Fife* ***Lake/loch***, small loch in Cleish Hills 3m/5km W of Kelty. **33 F5** NT0895.
Loch Goil *Arg. & B.* ***Sea feature***, sea-loch in Argyll, running 6m/10km N to S from Lochgoilhead to Loch Long. **31 D5** NS2097.
Loch Goosey *S.Ayr.* ***Lake/loch***, small loch 4m/7km E of Barrhill. **7 D2** NX2982.
Loch Goosie *S.Ayr.* ***Lake/loch***, small loch 1km N of Loch Riecawr. NX4494.
Loch Gorm *Arg. & B.* ***Lake/loch***, near W coast of Islay 3m/5km NW of Bruichladdich. On islet towards E side of loch are ruins of a Macdonald stronghold. **20 A3** NR2365.
Loch Gorm *High.* ***Lake/loch***, corrie lake to N of An Coileachan, 2m/4km NE of Loch Fannich. **60 B3** NH2369.
Loch Gowan *High.* ***Lake/loch***, small loch 1m/2km S of Achnasheen, Ross and Cromarty district. **60 A4** NH1456.
Loch Grannoch (Also spelled Loch Grennoch.) *D. & G.* ***Lake/loch***, 7m/11km SW of New Galloway. **7 G4** NX5469.
Loch Grennoch *D. & G. Alternative spelling of Loch Grannoch, qv.*
Loch Greshornish *High.* ***Sea feature***, inlet of Loch Snizort on N coast of Skye, 6m/10km NE of Dunvegan. **57 G4** NG3454.
Loch Gress *W.Isles* ***Lake/loch***, small loch on Isle of Lewis, 6m/9km E of Barvas. **69 F2** NB4450.
Loch Grimshader *W.Isles Anglicised form of Loch Grimsiadar, qv.*
Loch Grimsiadar (Anglicised form: Loch Grimshader.) *W.Isles* ***Sea feature***, long narrow inlet on E coast of Isle of Lewis. Village of Grimsiadar at head of inlet, 5m/8km S of Stornoway. **69 F5** NB4125.
Loch Grosebay *W.Isles* ***Sea feature***, inlet on SE coast of South Harris, 5m/8km S of Tarbert. **67 D4** NG1592.
Loch Gruinart *Arg. & B.* ***Sea feature***, deep inlet on N coast of Islay. **20 A3** NR2971.
Loch Grunavat *W.Isles* ***Lake/loch***, about 2m/4km N to S near W coast of Isle of Lewis, 2m/4km W of Little Loch Roag. **68 B5** NB0827.
Loch Guinach *High. Alternative name for Loch Gynack, qv.*
Loch Gulbin *High. Anglicised form of Loch Ghuilbinn, qv.*
Loch Gynack (Also known as Loch Guinach.) *High.* ***Lake/loch***, small loch in Badenoch and Strathspey district, 1m/2km NW of Kingussie. **51 G4** NH7402.
Loch Hallan *W.Isles* ***Lake/loch***, small loch near to coast of South Uist, 1m/2km NW of Dalabrog. **44 C1** NF7322.
Loch Haluim *High.* ***Lake/loch***, small irregular-shaped loch 3m/5km W of Loch Loyal, Caithness district. **75 E4** NC5545.

L

Loch Harport *High.* ***Sea feature***, long narrow inlet of Loch Bracadale on Skye, running up to Drynoch, W of Sligachan. **47 G1** NG3634.
Loch Harrow *D. & G.* ***Lake/loch***, 2m/3km E of Corserine, summit of Rhinns of Kells. **7 G2** NX5866.
Loch Head *D. & G.* ***Settlement***, on NW shore of Elrig Loch, 4m/6km N of Port William. **2 D2** NX3249.
Loch Head *D. & G.* ***Settlement***, at S end of Loch Doon, 5m/8km W of Carsphairn. **7 F1** NX4892.
Loch Heilen *High.* ***Lake/loch***, in Caithness district 3m/4km SE of Dunnet. **77 E2** ND2568.
Loch Hempriggs *High.* ***Lake/loch***, in Caithness district 2m/4km S of Wick. **77 F4** ND3447.
Loch Heron *D. & G.* ***Lake/loch***, small loch adjoining to NE of Loch Ronald, 4m/7km NW of Kirkcowan. NX2764.
Loch Hirta (Also known as Village Bay.) *W.Isles* ***Bay***, on SE coast of St. Kilda. NF1098.
Loch Hoil *P. & K.* ***Lake/loch***, small loch or tarn 4m/6km S of Aberfeldy. **41 D5** NN8643.
Loch Hope *High.* ***Lake/loch***, narrow loch in Sutherland district, some 6m/10km long N to S, 1m/2km E of Loch Eriboll at nearest point. **75 D3** NC4654.
Loch Horn *High.* ***Lake/loch***, small loch 1km W of Ben Horn, 4m/7km NW of Golspie. **72 C4** NC7906.
Loch Hosta *W.Isles* ***Lake/loch***, small loch near NW coast of North Uist to N of Hosta. **45 F2** NF7272.
Loch Hourn *High.* ***Sea feature***, long inlet of Sound of Sleat, penetrating inland to Kinloch Hourn, 5m/8km N of head of Loch Quoich, Lochaber district. **49 D3** NG8506.
Loch Howie *D. & G.* ***Lake/loch***, 5m/8km E of St. John's Town of Dalry. **8 B2** NX6983.
Loch Humphrey *W.Dun.* ***Lake/loch***, small loch on Kilpatrick Hills 4m/6km E of Dumbarton. **23 F2** NS4576.
Loch Huna *W.Isles* ***Lake/loch***, small loch on North Uist, 5m/8km S of Solas. **45 G3** NF8166.
Loch Hunder *W.Isles* ***Lake/loch***, small loch on North Uist, 2m/3km S of Loch na Madadh inlet. **56 C3** NF9065.
Loch Hunish *High.* ***Bay***, on S side of Rubha Hunish, at N tip of Skye. **57 G2** NG4076.
Loch Inchard *High.* ***Sea feature***, large inlet on W coast of Sutherland district. River Rhiconich flows into head of loch at Rhiconich. **74 B3** NC2355.
Loch Indaal *Arg. & B.* ***Sea feature***, large arm of sea on E side of Rinns of Islay, extending N to within 2m/4km of Loch Gruinart. **20 A4** NR2758.
Loch Insh *High.* ***Lake/loch***, small loch in course of River Spey in Badenoch and Strathspey district, 5m/8km NE of Kingussie. **52 A4** NH8304.
Loch Inshore *High.* ***Lake/loch***, small loch 2m/3km NW of Achiemore, Sutherland district. **74 C2** NC3269.
Loch Inver *High.* ***Sea feature***, inlet on W coast of Sutherland district with port of Lochinver at its head. **70 C2** NC0922.
Loch Isbister *Shet.* ***Lake/loch***, on Whalsay to N of Isbister. HU5764.
Loch Iubhair *Stir.* ***Lake/loch***, in course of River Fillan 2m/4km E of Crianlarich. **31 G2** NN4226.
Loch Kanaird *High.* ***Sea feature***, inlet of Loch Broom, W coast of Ross and Cromarty district, into which River Kanaird flows, on E side of Isle Martin. **70 C5** NH1099.
Loch Katrine *Stir.* ***Lake/loch***, 8m/13km W to E, extending from Glen Gyle to the Trossachs 8m/13km W of Callander. Aqueduct conveys water to Glasgow. **31 G4** NN4409.
Loch Keisgaig *High.* ***Lake/loch***, small loch 4m/7km S of Cape Wrath. **74 B2** NC2668.
Loch Kemp *High.* ***Lake/loch***, small loch on SE side of Loch Ness, 3m/5km across loch from Invermoriston. **51 D3** NH4616.
Loch Ken *D. & G.* ***Lake/loch***, long loch extending 9m/15km S from Kenmure Castle, near New Galloway to Glenlochar. N end of loch is fed by Water of Ken, one of two main tributaries, the other being Black Water of Dee or River Dee which flows into loch below Loch Ken Viaduct. Lower section of loch is also known as River Dee. **8 A3** NX7068.
Loch Kennard *P. & K.* ***Lake/loch***, small loch 4m/6km SE of Aberfeldy. **41 E5** NN9046.
Loch Kernsary *High.* ***Lake/loch***, near W coast of Ross and Cromarty district, 1m/2km E of Poolewe. National Trust for Scotland owns N part of loch and area to N. NG8780.
Loch Kildonan *W.Isles* ***Lake/loch***, and locality near W coast of South Uist, 2m/3km SE of Rubha Ardvule. Ruined building near S end of loch is Flora Macdonald's birthplace (1722). **44 C1** NF7327.
Loch Killin *High.* ***Lake/loch***, small loch in Inverness district 9m/15km E of Fort Augustus. **51 E3** NH5210.
Loch Kinardochy *P. & K.* ***Lake/loch***, small loch 3m/4km S of Tummel Bridge. **40 C4** NN7755.
Loch Kindar *D. & G.* ***Lake/loch***, 1m/2km S of New Abbey. **9 D4** NX9664.
Loch Kinellan *High.* ***Lake/loch***, small loch on SW edge of Strathpeffer. **61 D4** NH4757.
Loch Kinnabus *Arg. & B.* ***Lake/loch***, small loch on The Oa, Islay, 2m/3km E of Mull of Oa. **20 A5** NR3042.
Loch Kinord *Aber.* ***Lake/loch***, small loch 1m/2km W of Dinnet. **53 G4** NO4499.
Loch Kirkaig *High.* ***Sea feature***, inlet on W coast on border of Ross and Cromarty district and Sutherland district, 2m/4km SW of Lochinver. **70 C2** NC0719.
Loch Kishorn *High.* ***Sea feature***, wide inlet on N side of Loch Carron, Ross and Cromarty district, opposite Plockton. **49 E1** NG8138.
Loch Knockie *High.* ***Lake/loch***, small loch in Inverness district 5m/8km NE of Fort Augustus. **51 D3** NH4513.
Loch Knowe *Sc.Bord.* ***Mountain***, on W edge of Kielder Forest, 3m/4km W of Kielder. Height 1322 feet or 403 metres. **11 D2** NY5893.
Loch Laga *High.* ***Lake/loch***, small loch 2m/4km NW of Glenborrodale. **37 F3** NM6463.
Loch Laggan *High.* ***Lake/loch***, and reservoir in Badenoch and Strathspey district, linked to Loch Moy to SW where Laggan Dam is located (Lochaber district). Length 11m/18km NE to SW (including Loch Moy). **39 G1** NN4886.
Loch Laggan *Stir.* ***Lake/loch***, small loch 2m/4km SW of Kippen. NS6292.
Loch Laich *Arg. & B.* ***Sea feature***, inlet on E shore of Loch Linnhe, SW of Portnacroish, Argyll. **38 B5** NM9246.
Loch Laide *High.* ***Lake/loch***, small loch in Inverness district 4m/7km NE of Drumnadrochit. **51 E1** NH5435.
Loch Laidon (Also known as Loch Lydoch.) ***Lake/loch***, narrow loch 5m/8km long SW to NE on border of Highland and Perth & Kinross, 6m/10km W of Loch Rannoch. Rannoch railway station near NE end. **39 F4** NN3854.
Loch Laingeadail *Arg. & B.* ***Lake/loch***, small loch 3m/5km SW of Ardnave Point on N coast of Islay. NR2671.
Loch Lairig Eala *Stir.* ***Lake/loch***, small loch 3m/5km S of Killin. **32 A2** NN5527.
Loch Langavat *W.Isles* ***Lake/loch***, on Isle of Lewis, midway between Loch Erisort to E and Loch Resort to W. 8m/13km long NE to SW, although nowhere more than 1km wide. **67 D2** NB1819.
Loch Langavat *W.Isles* ***Lake/loch***, small loch near E coast of Isle of Lewis, 3m/4km SW of Cellar Head. **69 G2** NB5254.
Loch Langavat *W.Isles* ***Lake/loch***, on South Harris, some 3m/4km in length N to S and 2m/4km NE of Leverburgh. **66 C4** NG0490.
Loch Laoigh *High.* ***Lake/loch***, small loch 5m/8km NW of Dornoch. **72 C5** NH7395.
Loch Laro *High.* ***Lake/loch***, small loch 5m/7km N of Bonar Bridge. **72 B5** NH6099.
Loch Laxford *High.* ***Sea feature***, large inlet on W coast of Sutherland district, 4m/6km NE of Scourie. **74 A3** NC1950.
Loch Leacann *Arg. & B.* ***Lake/loch***, small loch in Argyll 3m/4km NW of Furnace on Loch Fyne. NN0003.
Loch Leathan *Arg. & B.* ***Lake/loch***, small loch, 6m/10km N of Lochgilphead. **30 A5** NR8798.
Loch Leathan *High.* ***Reservoir***, 5m/8km N of Portree, Skye. **58 B4** NG5051.
Loch Lednock Reservoir *P. & K.* ***Reservoir***, near head of Glen Lednock, 5m/8km NW of Comrie. **32 C1** NN7129.
Loch Lee *Angus* ***Lake/loch***, in course of Water of Lee, 4m/6km W of Tarfside. **42 C2** NO4279.
Loch Leurbost *W.Isles* ***Sea feature***, long inlet on E coast of Isle of Lewis. Village of Liurbost is near head of inlet on N side. **69 E5** NB3724.
Loch Leven *High.* ***Lake/loch***, in Lochaber district, running 11m/17km W from Kinlochleven to Loch Linnhe. **38 D4** NN0859.
Loch Leven *P. & K.* ***Lake/loch***, some 10m/16km in circumference, on E side of Kinross. Nature reserve. Ruins of medieval priory on St. Serf's Island and ruins of 15c castle (Historic Scotland) on Castle Island. **33 G4** NO1401.
Loch Leven Castle *P. & K.* ***Castle***, on Castle Island in Loch Leven, 1km from shore at Kinross. Early 15c tower house (Historic Scotland) famous as castle in which Mary, Queen of Scots, was imprisoned in 1567. **33 G4** NO1301.
Loch Libo *E.Renf.* ***Lake/loch***, small loch 3m/5km SW of Neilston. **23 F4** NS4355.
Loch Linnhe ***Sea feature***, long sea-loch running 22m/35km from Fort William to Mull. **38 A5** NM9354.
Loch Loch *P. & K.* ***Lake/loch***, narrow, deep loch 1m/2km long, 9m/14km NE of Blair Atholl. NN9874.
Loch Lochy *High.* ***Lake/loch***, in Glen Mòr in Lochaber district, running 10m/16km SW from Laggan to Gairlochy. Caledonian Canal passes through loch. **39 E1** NN2390.
Loch Lomond ***Lake/loch***, on borders of Argyll & Bute, Stirling and West Dunbartonshire, forming largest stretch of inland water in Britain. Extends 24m/39km from Ardlui in N to Balloch in S. Although generally narrow, the loch widens towards S end where there are a number of wooded islands. **23 E1** NS3598.
Loch Lomond Regional Park ***Leisure/recreation***, regional park surrounding Loch Lomond, Britain's largest stretch of inland water, and including Ben Lomond, Scotland's most southerly mountain over 900 metres. Visitor centre at Luss on W side of loch; West Highland Way long distance path passes along E bank; facilities for cruising and boating. **31 F3** NS3599.
Loch Long *Arg. & B.* ***Sea feature***, narrow sea-loch penetrating 16m/27km inland from head of Firth of Clyde at Kilcreggan on S of Rosneath peninsula and extending NE to Arrochar. **31 E5** NS2192.
Loch Long *High.* ***Lake/loch***, narrow loch in Skye and Lochalsh district running into Loch Alsh at Dornie. **49 F2** NG8928.
Loch Losait *High.* ***Bay***, small bay on E coast of Vaternish peninsula, 6m/9km SE of Vaternish Point, Skye. **57 F3** NG2760.
Loch Loskin *Arg. & B.* ***Lake/loch***, small loch 1m/2km N of Dunoon. **22 C2** NS1678.
Loch Lossit *Arg. & B.* ***Lake/loch***, small loch on Islay 3m/5km SW of Port Askaig. **20 C3** NR4065.
Loch Loy *High.* ***Lake/loch***, small loch in Nairn district 3m/5km E of Nairn. NH9358.
Loch Loyal *High.* ***Lake/loch***, large loch, 4m/7km N to S, in Caithness district 4m/7km S of Tongue. **75 F4** NC6247.
Loch Loyne *High.* ***Lake/loch***, and reservoir on border of Lochaber and Skye and Lochalsh districts between Lochs Cluanie and Garry. **50 A4** NH1705.
Loch Lubnaig *Stir.* ***Lake/loch***, narrow loch, 4m/6km long N to S, 3m/5km NW of Callander. NN5713.
Loch Luichart *High.* ***Lake/loch***, and reservoir 6m/10km W of Strathpeffer, Ross and Cromarty district. Power station below dam. Length of loch 6m/10km NW to SE. **60 C3** NH3562.
Loch Lundie *High.* ***Lake/loch***, small loch 1m/2km S of Plockton, Skye and Lochalsh district. **49 E1** NG8031.
Loch Lundie *High.* ***Lake/loch***, in Ross and Cromarty district 3m/5km S of Shieldaig. **59 D5** NG8049.
Loch Lundie *High.* ***Lake/loch***, and reservoir 1m/2km N of Invergarry in Lochaber district. **50 B4** NH2903.
Loch Lungard *High.* ***Lake/loch***, upper part of Loch Mullardoch in Skye and Lochalsh district. NH0929.
Loch Lunndaidh *High.* ***Lake/loch***, in Sutherland district, 2m/4km W of Golspie. **72 C4** NC7800.
Loch Lurgainn *High.* ***Lake/loch***, in Ross and Cromarty district 8m/13km N of Ullapool. **70 D4** NC1108.
Loch Lydoch *P. & K.* *Alternative name for Loch Laidon, qv.*
Loch Lyon *P. & K.* ***Lake/loch***, large loch and reservoir at head of Glen Lyon. **31 F1** NN4141.
Loch ma Stac *High.* ***Lake/loch***, small loch in Inverness district 6m/10km NW of Invermoriston. **50 C2** NH3421.
Loch Maaruig *W.Isles* ***Sea feature***, inlet on W side of Loch Seaforth, North Harris, between Seaforth Island and mouth of loch. NB1905.
Loch Maberry *D. & G.* ***Lake/loch***, on border with South Ayrshire, 5m/9km SE of Barrhill. Remains of old castle on islet in loch. **7 D3** NX2875.
Loch Macaterick *E.Ayr.* ***Lake/loch***, 4m/6km N of Merrick. **7 F1** NX4491.
Loch Maddy *W.Isles* *Anglicised form of Loch na Madadh (sea-loch), qv.*
Loch Magharaidh *High.* ***Lake/loch***, small loch on Kildermorie Forest, Ross and Cromarty district, 3m/5km NW of Loch Glass. **60 D2** NH4576.
Loch Magillie (Also known as Magillie Loch.) *D. & G.* ***Lake/loch***, small loch 2m/4km E of Stranraer. **6 B5** NX0959.
Loch Mahaick *Stir.* ***Lake/loch***, small loch or tarn 4m/6km N of Doune. **32 C4** NN7006.
Loch Mallachie *High.* ***Lake/loch***, small loch on SW edge of Abernethy Forest, 2m/3km SE of Boat of Garten. **52 B3** NH9617.
Loch Màma *High.* ***Lake/loch***, small loch in South Morar, Lochaber district, 2m/3km NW of Lochailort. Loch na Creige Duibhe to E runs into head of loch. NM7585.
Loch Mannoch *D. & G.* ***Lake/loch***, 6m/10km N of Kirkcudbright. NX6660.
Loch Maoile *High.* ***Lake/loch***, 1km S of Strath Kanaird, Ross and Cromarty district. **71 D5** NC1500.
Loch Maovally *High.* ***Lake/loch***, 1km W of Moine House, 2m/3km E of N end of Loch Hope. **75 E2** NC5060.
Loch Maree *High.* ***Lake/loch***, in W part of Ross and Cromarty district extending 12m/20km NW from near Kinlochewe to near Poolewe, where it runs out into Loch Ewe. Width is mostly about 1km, although the maximum width is over 2m/3km. Maximum depth 367 feet or 112 metres. **59 F2** NG9570.
Loch Mariveg (Gaelic form: Loch Mharabhig.) *W.Isles* ***Sea feature***, inlet to N of Marthig, on E coast of Isle of Lewis. NB4119.
Loch Meadaidh *High.* ***Lake/loch***, small loch 2m/3km S of Durness. **74 C2** NC3964.
Loch Meadie *High.* ***Lake/loch***, 3m/5km N to S, in Caithness district 5m/8km NW to Altnaharra. **75 D4** NC5040.
Loch Meadie *High.* ***Lake/loch***, narrow loch, 2m/3km N to S, 1m/2km S of Kirtomy, Caithness district. **75 G3** NC7560.
Loch Meadie *High.* ***Lake/loch***, 1km NE of Loch Mòr, 1m/2km in length N to S. **76 C4** ND0848.
Loch Meala *High.* ***Lake/loch***, small loch on SW edge of Strathy Forest, Caithness district. **75 G3** NC7857.

L

Loch Mealt *High.* ***Lake/loch***, small loch near NE coast of Skye 7m/11km E of Uig. **58 B3** NG5065.
Loch Meavaig *W.Isles* ***Sea feature***, narrow inlet on W coast of North Harris, 5m/8km NW of Tarbert. NB0905.
Loch Meig *High.* ***Lake/loch***, and reservoir in course of River Meig, 1m/2km above its confluence with River Conon in Ross and Cromarty district. **60 C4** NH3555.
Loch Meiklie *High.* ***Lake/loch***, small loch in Glen Urquhart, Inverness district 4m/7km W of Drumnadrochit. **50 D2** NH4330.
Loch Melfort *Arg. & B.* ***Sea feature***, inlet on coast of Argyll, running up towards Kilmelford. **30 A3** NM8112.
Loch Melldalloch *Arg. & B.* ***Lake/loch***, small loch to E of Melldalloch, 3m/4km NW of Tighnabruaich on Cowal peninsula. NR9374.
Loch Merkland *High.* ***Lake/loch***, in Sutherland district 4m/6km SW of summit of Ben Hee. **74 C5** NC4233.
Loch Mhairc *P. & K.* ***Lake/loch***, small loch in Forest of Atholl, 9m/14km N of Blair Atholl. **41 D2** NN8879.
Loch Mharabhig *W.Isles Gaelic form of Loch Mariveg, qv.*
Loch Mhoicean *High.* ***Lake/loch***, small loch in Skye and Lochalsh district, 2m/3km NW of Loch Mullardoch. **49 G1** NH0731.
Loch Mhòr *High.* ***Lake/loch***, and reservoir in Inverness district on E side of Loch Ness, 10m/16km NE of Fort Augustus. Reservoir used in Foyers Pump Storage Scheme. **51 E3** NH5319.
Loch Mhuilich *High.* ***Lake/loch***, in valley between Bidean an Eòin Deirg and Maoile Lunndaidh, 1km N of W part of Loch Mullardoch. **60 A5** NH1243.
Loch Migdale *High.* ***Lake/loch***, in Sutherland district, 1m/2km E of Bonar Bridge. **72 B5** NH6390.
Loch Minnoch *D. & G.* ***Lake/loch***, small hill loch or tarn on E side of Rhinns of Kells, 6m/10km NW of St. John's Town of Dalry. NX5385.
Loch Moan *D. & G.* ***Lake/loch***, in Glentrool Forest 7m/12km E of Barrhill. **7 E2** NX3485.
Loch Moidart *High.* ***Sea feature***, arm of sea on W coast of Moidart, running up to Kinlochmoidart in Lochaber district. **37 F2** NM6472.
Loch Monaghan *P. & K.* ***Lake/loch***, small loch 2m/3km SE of head of Loch Rannoch. NN5355.
Loch Monar *High.* ***Lake/loch***, and reservoir at head of Glen Farrar on borders of Inverness, Ross and Cromarty, and Skye and Lochalsh districts. Level of loch artificially raised by dam at E end. Length of loch 8m/13km. **60 A5** NH1440.
Loch Mòr *High.* ***Lake/loch***, near W coast of Skye, 7m/11km W of Dunvegan. **57 E5** NG1448.
Loch Mòr an Stàirr *W.Isles* ***Lake/loch***, small loch on Isle of Lewis, 3m/4km E of Beinn Mholach. **69 E4** NB3938.
Loch Mòr Barabhais (Anglicised form: Loch Mòr Barvas.) *W.Isles* ***Lake/loch***, to W of Barvas village, Isle of Lewis, at foot of Gleann Mòr Bharabhais. **69 E2** NB3450.
Loch Mòr Barvas *W.Isles Anglicised form of Loch Mòr Barabhais, qv.*
Loch Mòr na Caorach *High.* ***Lake/loch***, small loch 3m/4km E of Achargary, Caithness district. **75 G3** NC7654.
Loch Mòr Sandavat *W.Isles* ***Lake/loch***, small loch 1km N of Loch an Tobair, Isle of Lewis. **69 F3** NB4346.
Loch Mòr Sandavat *W.Isles* ***Lake/loch***, small loch on Isle of Lewis, 5m/8km NW of Tolsta Head. **69 F2** NB4952.
Loch Moraig *P. & K.* ***Lake/loch***, small loch 2m/4km E of Blair Atholl. **41 E3** NN9066.
Loch Morar *High.* ***Lake/loch***, long, narrow, deep loch and reservoir in Lochaber district. The loch, which divides North Morar from South Morar, runs 11m/18km E to W and almost reaches sea 3m/5km S of Mallaig. Reputed to be deepest loch in Scotland. **48 D5** NM7790.
Loch More *High.* ***Lake/loch***, in Sutherland district 4m/6km long NW to SE, 6m/10km SE of Laxford Bridge. **74 C5** NC3237.
Loch More *High.* ***Lake/loch***, in course of River Thurso, Caithness district, 9m/15km S of Halkirk. **76 C4** ND0745.
Loch Moreef *W.Isles* ***Lake/loch***, near SE coast of South Uist, 4m/6km E of Ludag. **46 B3** NF8314.
Loch Morie *High.* ***Lake/loch***, in Ross and Cromarty district 8m/13km NW of Alness. **61 E2** NH5376.
Loch Morlich *High.* ***Lake/loch***, in The Queen's Forest, Glenmore Forest Park, in Badenoch and Strathspey district, 4m/6km NW of Cairn Gorm. **52 B4** NH9609.
Loch Morsgail *W.Isles* ***Lake/loch***, small loch on Isle of Lewis, 1m/2km S of head of Little Loch Roag. **68 C5** NB1322.
Loch Moy *High.* ***Lake/loch***, in Strathdearn Forest, Inverness district, 9m/15km SE of Inverness. **51 G1** NH7734.
Loch Moy *High.* ***Lake/loch***, and reservoir, partly in Lochaber district and partly in Badenoch and Strathspey district, linked to Loch Laggan to NE. Laggan Dam is sited at SW end. Sometimes loch is considered as part of Loch Laggan. **39 G1** NN4081.
Loch Muck *E.Ayr.* ***Lake/loch***, small loch 4m/6km SE of Dalmellington. NS5100.
Loch Mudle *High.* ***Lake/loch***, small loch on Ardnamurchan peninsula in Lochaber district, 4m/6km NE of Kilchoan. **37 E3** NM5466.
Loch Muick *Aber.* ***Lake/loch***, at head of Glen Muick, 9m/14km SW of Ballater. **42 A1** NO2882.
Loch Mullardoch *High.* ***Lake/loch***, and reservoir on borders of Inverness and Skye and Lochalsh districts 7m/11km W of Cannich. **50 A1** NH1931.
Loch na Beinne Bàine *High.* ***Lake/loch***, small loch in Inverness district 8m/13km W of Invermoriston. **50 B3** NH2819.
Loch na Béiste *High.* ***Sea feature***, inlet of Loch Alsh 1km S of Kyleakin, Skye. **49 D2** NG7525.
Loch na Caillich *High.* ***Lake/loch***, small loch 4m/6km W of Lairg. **72 A4** NC5108.
Loch na Cairidh *High.* ***Sea feature***, strait between Scalpay and Skye. NG5928.
Loch na Caoidhe *High.* ***Lake/loch***, small loch in course of River Orrin, Ross and Cromarty district, 6m/10km W of head of Orrin Reservoir. **60 B5** NH2246.
Loch na Cille *Arg. & B.* ***Sea feature***, inlet at S end of peninsula in Argyll, situated between Loch Sween and Sound of Jura. **21 E2** NR6980.
Loch na Claise Càrnaich *High.* ***Lake/loch***, in Sutherland district, 1m/2km E of Rhiconich. **74 B3** NC2752.
Loch na Claise Mòire *High.* ***Lake/loch***, 3m/4km N of Oykel Bridge. **71 F4** NC3805.
Loch na Craige *P. & K.* ***Lake/loch***, small loch or tarn 3m/5km SE of Aberfeldy. **41 D5** NN8845.
Loch na Craobhaig *W.Isles* ***Lake/loch***, small loch 1m/2km E of head of Loch Tamanavay, Isle of Lewis. **68 B5** NB0620.
Loch na Creige Duibhe *High.* ***Lake/loch***, in Sutherland district adjoining Loch an Leathaid Bhuain, to W of Loch More. **74 B5** NC2836.
Loch na Creige Duibhe *High.* ***Lake/loch***, small loch in South Morar, Lochaber district, 2m/3km N of Lochailort. Runs W into Loch Màma. NM7685.
Loch na Creitheach *High.* ***Lake/loch***, near S coast of Skye 4m/6km N of Elgol. **48 B2** NG5120.
Loch na Cròic *High.* ***Lake/loch***, small loch in Ross and Cromarty district in course of Black Water below Loch Garve. NH4359.
Loch na Cuaich *High.* ***Lake/loch***, small loch in Badenoch and Strathspey district 4m/6km NE of Dalwhinnie. NN6987.
Loch na Cuilce *Arg. & B.* ***Lake/loch***, small loch on Mull, on S side of Dervaig. NM4351.
Loch na Cuilce *High.* ***Sea feature***, small inlet on coast of Skye, S of Loch Coruisk. **48 A3** NG4819.
Loch na Curra *High.* ***Lake/loch***, small loch in Ross and Cromarty district, 2m/3km W of Poolewe. **59 E2** NG8280.
Loch na Dal *High.* ***Sea feature***, inlet of Sound of Sleat, at head of Sleat peninsula, Skye. **48 D3** NG7015.
Loch na Droma Buidhe *High.* ***Sea feature***, inlet on S side of Oronsay. NM5958.
Loch na Dubhcha *W.Isles* ***Lake/loch***, small loch on North Uist, 1km NE of Lochportain. **56 C2** NF9572.
Loch na Fuaralaich *High.* ***Lake/loch***, 6m/9km W of Lairg and to W of Strath Grudie. **71 G4** NC4806.
Loch na Fùdarlaich *Arg. & B.* ***Lake/loch***, small loch on Jura, 1m/2km NE of Beinn Shiantaidh. NR5376.
Loch na Gaineimh *High.* ***Lake/loch***, small loch 2m/3km S of Loch Badanloch, Sutherland district. **75 G5** NC7630.
Loch na Gainimh *High.* ***Lake/loch***, 1m/2km W of Canisp in Glencanisp Forest. **71 D3** NC1719.
Loch na Gainimh *High.* ***Lake/loch***, small loch in Sutherland district 1km NE of Blairmore. **74 A2** NC2061.
Loch na Gainimh *High.* ***Lake/loch***, small loch in Sutherland district, 3m/4km E of Kinlochbervie. **74 B3** NC2656.
Loch na Gainmhich *High.* ***Lake/loch***, 1m/2km S of Loch Glencoul, Sutherland district. **71 E2** NC2429.
Loch na h-Oidhche *High.* ***Lake/loch***, in W part of Ross and Cromarty district 4m/7km N of head of Upper Loch Torridon. **59 E3** NG8865.
Loch na h-Ula *High.* ***Lake/loch***, 1km S of Rhiconich, Sutherland district. **74 B3** NC2550.
Loch na Keal *Arg. & B.* ***Sea feature***, large inlet on W coast of Mull, head of which reaches to within 3m/4km of E coast at Salen. **29 E1** NM5038.
Loch na Lairige *High.* ***Lake/loch***, small loch in Inverness district, 1m/2km N of Geal Charn and 9m/15km W of Newtonmore. **51 E4** NH5601.
Loch na Lap *High.* ***Lake/loch***, small loch or tarn in Lochaber district, 1m/2km NW of foot of Loch Ossian. NN3971.
Loch na Lathaich *Arg. & B.* ***Bay***, large bay on N coast of Ross of Mull. Village of Bunessan is at SE corner. **28 C2** NM3623.
Loch na Leitreach *High.* ***Lake/loch***, small but deep loch in Skye and Lochalsh district 6m/9km E of head of Loch Long. **49 G2** NH0227.
Loch na Madadh *W.Isles Gaelic form of Lochmaddy (village), qv.*
Loch na Madadh (Anglicised form: Loch Maddy.) *W.Isles* ***Sea feature***, large inlet and anchorage on E coast of North Uist, containing innumerable islets. On W shore is village and port of Lochmaddy. **56 C3** NF9369.
Loch na Mile *Arg. & B.* ***Bay***, on E coast of Jura, at mouth of Corran River, 3m/4km N of Craighouse. **20 D2** NR5470.
Loch na Mòine *High.* ***Lake/loch***, small loch 1km NE of N end of Loch Loyal. **75 F3** NC6251.
Loch na Mòine *High.* ***Lake/loch***, small loch 4m/7km SE of Poolewe, Ross and Cromarty district. **59 F2** NG9278.
Loch na Saobhaidhe *High.* ***Lake/loch***, small loch 1m/2km E of Loch Strathy. **76 A4** NC7947.
Loch na Scaravat *W.Isles* ***Lake/loch***, small loch, 1km N of Beinn Mholach, Isle of Lewis. **69 E3** NB3540.
Loch na Sealga *High.* ***Lake/loch***, in W part of Ross and Cromarty district 4m/7km SW of Little Loch Broom. **59 G1** NH0382.
Loch na Seilg *High.* ***Lake/loch***, one of two small lochs on E side of Ben Hope. **75 D3** NC4951.
Loch na Seilge *High.* ***Lake/loch***, small loch 1m/2km E of Achiemore, Caithness district. **76 B3** NC9158.
Loch na Sgeallaig *High.* ***Lake/loch***, 1km S of W end of Loch Ossian, and 1km SE of Corrour Station. **39 F3** NN3665.
Loch na Sreinge *Arg. & B.* ***Lake/loch***, small loch 1m/2km N of Loch Avich. **30 B3** NM9216.
Loch na Tuadh *High.* ***Lake/loch***, small loch in Reay Forest, Sutherland district, 2m/3km S of Foinaven. **74 C4** NC3147.
Loch nam Bonnach *High.* ***Lake/loch***, small loch in Inverness district 3m/5km NW of Beauly. **61 D5** NH4848.
Loch nam Brac *High.* ***Lake/loch***, in Caithness district, 1km E of Tarbet. **74 A4** NC1748.
Loch nam Breac *High.* ***Lake/loch***, small loch 3m/5km E of Loch Strathy, Caithness district. **76 A4** NC8248.
Loch nam Breac *W.Isles* ***Lake/loch***, small loch 4m/7km E of Breascleit, Isle of Lewis. **69 D4** NB2837.
Loch nam Breac Dearga *High.* ***Lake/loch***, small loch in Inverness district 4m/6km NE of Invermoriston. **50 D2** NH4522.
Loch nam Falcag *W.Isles* ***Lake/loch***, small loch, 4m/6km W of Liurbost, Isle of Lewis. **69 E5** NB2926.
Loch nam Fiadh *High.* ***Lake/loch***, small loch 5m/8km NW of Garve. **60 C3** NH3164.
Loch nam Meur *High.* ***Lake/loch***, small loch in Inverness district, 4m/7km N of Invermoriston. Another small loch of same name 1m/2km N. **50 C2** NH3923.
Loch nam Uamh *High.* ***Lake/loch***, small loch on Sleat peninsula, 3m/4km E of Tarskavaig, Skye. **48 C4** NG6308.
Loch nan Ceall *High.* ***Sea feature***, inlet on coast of Lochaber district, running up to Arisaig. **37 F1** NM6486.
Loch nan Clach *High.* ***Lake/loch***, small loch in afforested area, 1km S of Loch Mòr na Caorach, 4m/6km SE of Skelpick, Caithness district. **75 G3** NC7653.
Loch nan Clach *High.* ***Lake/loch***, small loch in Morvern, Lochaber district, 5m/8km NE of Rubha an Ridire. **37 G5** NM7846.
Loch nan Clàr *High.* ***Lake/loch***, N part of a double loch in Sutherland district, 6m/10km W of Kinbrace. S part of loch is known as Loch Badanloch. **75 G5** NC7635.
Loch nan Cuinne *High. Alternative name for Loch Rimsdale, qv.*
Loch nan Ealachan *High.* ***Lake/loch***, small loch just E of Borgie Forest, Caithness district. **75 F3** NC6752.
Loch nan Eun *High.* ***Lake/loch***, small loch in Ross and Cromarty district, 3m/4km N of Applecross. **58 D5** NG7048.
Loch nan Eun *High.* ***Lake/loch***, small loch in Skye and Lochalsh district, 4m/7km E of Dornie. **49 F2** NG9426.
Loch nan Eun *High.* ***Lake/loch***, small loch in Inverness district 7m/12km NW of Invermoriston. **50 C2** NH3120.
Loch nan Eun *High.* ***Lake/loch***, small loch 5m/8km E of Fort Augustus. **51 D4** NH4510.
Loch nan Eun *High.* ***Lake/loch***, small loch on border of Inverness and Ross and Cromarty districts 4m/6km W of Muir of Ord. **61 D5** NH4648.
Loch nan Eun *P. & K.* ***Lake/loch***, small loch or tarn, 6m/9km NW of Spittal of Glenshee. NO0678.
Loch nan Eun *W.Isles* ***Lake/loch***, on North Uist, 3m/4km N of Locheport. **45 G3** NF8367.
Loch nan Gall *High.* ***Lake/loch***, small loch 2m/3km W of Achiemore, Caithness district. **76 A3** NC8658.
Loch nan Geireann *W.Isles* ***Lake/loch***, on North Uist, 2m/3km SE of Solas. **45 G2** NF8472.
Loch nan Nighean *P. & K.* ***Lake/loch***, small loch 3m/5km SW of Blair Atholl. NN8461.
Loch nan Stearnag *W.Isles* ***Lake/loch***, small loch, 6m/10km E of Breascleit, Isle of Lewis. **69 E4** NB3137.
Loch nan Torran *Arg. & B.* ***Lake/loch***, small loch in Knapdale, Argyll, 3m/4km SE of Ormsary. **21 F3** NR7568.
Loch nan Uamh *High.* ***Sea feature***, inlet of Sound of Arisaig on N side of peninsula of Ardnish, on coast of Lochaber district. **37 F1** NM6982.

Loch nan Uan *High.* ***Lake/loch***, small loch on W slope of Ben Klibreck, 4m/6km S of Altnaharra. **75 E5** NC5629.
Loch Nant *Arg. & B.* ***Lake/loch***, and reservoir 2m/4km NW of Kilchrenan in Argyll. **30 B2** NN0024.
Loch Naver *High.* ***Lake/loch***, in Caithness district extending 6m/10km E from Altnaharra. **75 E5** NC6136.
Loch Neaty *High.* ***Lake/loch***, small loch in Inverness district 3m/5km SE of Struy Bridge. **50 D1** NH4336.
Loch Nedd *High.* ***Sea feature***, inlet on S side of Eddrachillis Bay, W coast of Sutherland district. **74 A5** NC1333.
Loch Neldricken *D. & G.* ***Lake/loch***, in Glentrool Forest Park, 2m/3km SE of Merrick. **7 F2** NX4482.
Loch Nell *Arg. & B.* ***Lake/loch***, in Argyll 2m/4km SE of Oban. **30 A2** NM8927.
Loch Ness *High.* ***Lake/loch***, in Inverness district extending NE from Fort Augustus to a point 6m/10km SW of Inverness. Length 23m/36km. Average width about 1m/2km. Maximum depth 754 feet or 230 metres. Loch forms part of course of Caledonian Canal. **50 D3** NH5023.
Loch Ness Monster Exhibition Centre *High.* ***Other feature of interest***, in Drumnadrochit, 13m/22km SW of Inverness, exhibiting images of Loch Ness Monster and contentious film of mysterious humps moving through the water. **51 E2** NH5030.
Loch Nevis *High.* ***Sea feature***, long inlet of Sound of Sleat, between Knoydart and North Morar in Lochaber district. Narrows considerably above Kylesknoydart. Total length about 13m/21km. **49 D5** NM7695.
Loch Nisreaval *W.Isles* ***Lake/loch***, small loch on Isle of Lewis, 6m/10km SW of Stornoway. **69 E5** NB3326.
Loch o' th' Lowes *E.Ayr.* ***Lake/loch***, small loch 1m/2km NW of New Cumnock. NS6014.
Loch Obisary *W.Isles* ***Lake/loch***, in SE part of North Uist, to N and W of Eaval. **45 G3** NF8861.
Loch Ochiltree *D. & G.* ***Lake/loch***, 8m/13km NW of Newton Stewart. **7 E3** NX3174.
Loch Odhairn *W.Isles* ***Sea feature***, inlet on E coast of Isle of Lewis, extending from Grabhair to Kebock Head. **67 G2** NB4014.
Loch of Aboyne *Aber.* ***Lake/loch***, small loch 1m/2km NE of Aboyne. NO5399.
Loch of Aithsness *Shet.* ***Lake/loch***, on Mainland to SW of Aith Ness. HU3258.
Loch of Benston *Shet.* ***Lake/loch***, to S of Benston, separated by narrow neck of land from Vassa Voe. HU4653.
Loch of Blairs *Moray* ***Lake/loch***, small loch 2m/3km S of Forres. **62 C4** NJ0255.
Loch of Boardhouse *Ork.* ***Lake/loch***, large loch in NW Mainland 2m/3km SE of Brough Head. Named after locality at its NW end. **80 A4** HY2625.
Loch of Boath *High.* ***Lake/loch***, small loch in Nairn district 7m/11km S of Nairn. NH8845.
Loch of Bosquoy *Ork.* ***Lake/loch***, small loch 1m/2km SE of Dounby, Mainland. HY3018.
Loch of Brindister *Shet.* ***Lake/loch***, to W of Brindister, Mainland. HU4336.
Loch of Butterstone *P. & K.* ***Lake/loch***, small loch SW of Butterstone and 2m/4km NE of Dunkeld. **41 F5** NO0544.
Loch of Cliff *Shet.* ***Lake/loch***, long narrow loch S of Burrafirth, Unst. **85 E1** HP6012.
Loch of Clunie *P. & K.* ***Lake/loch***, small loch 4m/6km W of Blairgowrie. On island in loch are remains of Clunie Castle, built about 1500. **41 G5** NO1144.
Loch of Craiglush *P. & K.* ***Lake/loch***, small loch 1m/2km NE of Dunkeld. **41 F5** NO0444.
Loch of Drumellie (Also known as Loch of Marlee.) *P. & K.* ***Lake/loch***, small loch 2m/3km W of Blairgowrie. **41 G5** NO1444.
Loch of Fladdabister *Shet.* ***Lake/loch***, 1km N of Fladdabister, Mainland. HU4333.
Loch of Flugarth *Shet.* ***Lake/loch***, on Mainland 1km N of Burra Voe. HU3690.
Loch of Forfar *Angus* ***Lake/loch***, small loch on W side of Forfar. **42 C5** NO4450.
Loch of Girlsta *Shet.* ***Lake/loch***, deep freshwater loch on E coast of Mainland 6m/10km N of Lerwick. **82 D2** HU4350.
Loch of Gonfirth *Shet.* ***Lake/loch***, to E of Gon Firth towards village of Voe, Mainland. HU3862.
Loch of Grandtully *P. & K.* ***Lake/loch***, small loch or tarn 4m/6km E of Aberfeldy. NN9150.
Loch of Haggrister *Shet.* ***Lake/loch***, to W of Haggrister, Mainland. HU3470.
Loch of Harray *Ork.* ***Lake/loch***, large loch, nearly 5m/8km N to S, to S of Dounby on Mainland. S end is separated from Loch of Stenness by narrow tongue of land and causeway. **80 A5** HY2915.
Loch of Hellister *Shet.* ***Lake/loch***, small loch to E of Hellister, Mainland. HU3849.
Loch of Housetter *Shet.* ***Lake/loch***, small loch to N of Housetter, Mainland. HU3685.
Loch of Hundland *Ork.* ***Lake/loch***, at N end of Mainland 3m/5km N of Dounby. **80 B4** HY2925.
Loch of Isbister *Ork.* ***Lake/loch***, small loch on Mainland 3m/5km NW of Dounby. HY2523.
Loch of Kettlester *Shet.* ***Lake/loch***, to N of Kettlester, Yell. HU5180.
Loch of Kinnordy *Angus See Kinnordy.*
Loch of Kirbister *Ork.* ***Lake/loch***, 3m/5km S of Finstown, on N side of road running W from Kirkwall. **78 C2** HY3607.
Loch of Lintrathen *Angus* ***Lake/loch***, and reservoir, 6m/10km W of Kirriemuir. **42 A4** NO2754.
Loch of Lowes *P. & K.* ***Lake/loch***, small loch 1m/2km NE of Dunkeld. Reserve of Scottish Wildlife Trust. **41 F5** NO0443.
Loch of Lunnister *Shet.* ***Lake/loch***, small loch to W of Lunnister, Mainland. HU3471.
Loch of Marlee *P. & K. Alternative name for Loch of Drumellie, qv.*
Loch of Mey *High.* ***Lake/loch***, small loch near N coast, 4m/7km SE of Dunnet Head. **77 E1** ND2673.
Loch of Murraster *Shet.* ***Lake/loch***, 1m/2km NE of Bridge of Walls, Mainland. HU2751.
Loch of Sabiston *Ork.* ***Lake/loch***, small loch on Mainland, 1m/2km N of Dounby. Named after settlement to S towards Dounby. HY2922.
Loch of Skaill *Ork.* ***Lake/loch***, near W coast of Mainland 1km E of Skara Brae. **80 A5** HY2418.
Loch of Skellister *Shet.* ***Lake/loch***, to N of Skellister, Mainland. HU4656.
Loch of Skene *Aber.* ***Lake/loch***, small round loch 9m/15km W of Aberdeen. **54 C4** NJ7807.
Loch of Snarravoe *Shet.* ***Lake/loch***, near SW end of Unst, 1m/2km W of Uyeasound. HP5701.
Loch of Spiggie *Shet.* ***Lake/loch***, on Mainland 2m/4km NE of Fitful Head. **83 F4** HU3716.
Loch of Stenness *Ork.* ***Lake/loch***, large loch on Mainland 4m/6km W of Finstown. Separated at E end from Loch of Harray by narrow tongue of land and causeway. **80 A5** HY2812.
Loch of Strathbeg *Aber.* ***Lake/loch***, near NE coast behind Strathbeg Bay, 2m/3km long NW to SE. **65 F4** NK0758.
Loch of Strom *Shet.* ***Lake/loch***, long narrow loch on Mainland in course of Burn of Sandwater, emptying into Stromness Voe, E of Weisdale Voe. **82 C3** HU4048.
Loch of Swannay *Ork.* ***Lake/loch***, large loch at N end of Mainland 5m/8km E of Brough Head. **80 B4** HY3128.
Loch of Tankerness *Ork.* ***Lake/loch***, on Mainland 2m/3km SW of Rerwick Head. HY5109.
Loch of the Lowes *Sc.Bord.* ***Lake/loch***, small loch running into head of St. Mary's Loch in Ettrick Forest. **16 D4** NT2319.
Loch of Tingwall *Shet.* ***Lake/loch***, on Mainland 2m/3km N of Scalloway. At N end of loch is small island traditionally held to be site of old Norse open-air parliament. **82 C3** HU4142.
Loch of Toftingall *High.* ***Lake/loch***, in Caithness district 4m/6km W of Watten. **77 D3** ND1952.
Loch of Trebister *Shet.* ***Lake/loch***, small loch to NE of Trebister, Mainland. HU4539.
Loch of Urafirth *Shet.* ***Lake/loch***, to N of Ura Firth, Mainland. HU3079.
Loch of Vatsetter *Shet.* ***Lake/loch***, small loch on Yell to W of Vatsetter, separated from Wick of Vatsetter by narrow causeway. HU5389.
Loch of Voe *Shet.* ***Lake/loch***, 1km E of Voe, Mainland. HU4162.
Loch of Watlee *Shet.* ***Lake/loch***, on Unst 2m/4km N of Uyeasound. **85 E2** HP5905.
Loch of Wester *High.* ***Lake/loch***, in Caithness district 6m/10km N of Wick. **77 F3** ND3259.
Loch of Westerwick *Shet.* ***Lake/loch***, on Mainland to N of Wester Wick. HU2843.
Loch of Winless *High.* ***Lake/loch***, narrow loch to W of Winless. **77 E3** ND2954.
Loch of Yarehouse *High. Alternative name for Loch of Yarrows, qv.*
Loch of Yarrows (Also known as Loch of Yarehouse.) *High.* ***Lake/loch***, in Caithness district 5m/9km SW of Wick. **77 F4** ND3043.
Loch Oich *High.* ***Lake/loch***, narrow loch in Lochaber district between Loch Lochy and Loch Ness. Caledonian Canal passes through loch. NE end of loch is in Inverness district. **50 C5** NH3100.
Loch Olavat *W.Isles* ***Lake/loch***, small loch on Benbecula, 2m/3km N of Creag Ghoraidh. **45 G4** NF8050.
Loch Olavat *W.Isles* ***Lake/loch***, small loch near N coast of Benbecula, 3m/4km E of Balivanich. **45 G5** NF8154.
Loch Olginey *High.* ***Lake/loch***, in Caithness district 3m/5km SW of Halkirk. **76 C3** ND0957.
Loch Orasay *W.Isles* ***Lake/loch***, on Isle of Lewis, 5m/8km E of Achadh Mòr. Contains small island, Eilean Mòr. **69 E5** NB3828.
Loch Ordie *P. & K.* ***Lake/loch***, small loch 4m/6km SE of Ballinluig. **41 F4** NO0350.
Loch Ore *Fife* ***Lake/loch***, to SW of Lochore, 2m/4km N of Cowdenbeath. NT1695.
Loch Osgaig (Also known as Loch Owskeich.) *High.* ***Lake/loch***, near NW coast of Ross and Cromarty district 1km S of Enard Bay. **70 C3** NC0412.
Loch Ossian *High.* ***Lake/loch***, in Lochaber district between head of Loch Treig and head of Loch Ericht. Deer sanctuary to N. **39 F3** NN3968.
Loch Owskeich *High. Alternative name for Loch Osgaig, qv.*
Loch Park *Moray* ***Lake/loch***, small loch 3m/4km NE of Dufftown. **63 F5** NJ3543.
Loch Pattack *High.* ***Lake/loch***, small loch in Badenoch and Strathspey district, from which River Pattack flows N then W to head of Loch Laggan. **40 A2** NN5379.
Loch Peallach *Arg. & B.* ***Lake/loch***, on Mull 2m/3km SW of Tobermory. NM4853.
Loch Pityoulish *High.* ***Lake/loch***, small loch in Badenoch and Strathspey district, 2m/3km NE of Aviemore across River Spey. **52 B3** NH9213.
Loch Poit na h-I *Arg. & B.* ***Lake/loch***, 1km E of Fionnphort, Ross of Mull. NM3122.
Loch Poll *High.* ***Lake/loch***, 1m/2km long N to S, situated 1m/2km SW of Drumbeg, Sutherland district. **70 D1** NC0931.
Loch Poll Dhaidh *High.* ***Lake/loch***, 3m/4km SE of Clashnessie, Sutherland district. **70 C2** NC0729.
Loch Polly *High. Alternative name for Polly Bay, qv.*
Loch Pooltiel *High.* ***Sea feature***, on NW coast of Skye, 4m/6km S of Dunvegan Head. **57 E4** NG1650.
Loch Portain *W.Isles* ***Sea feature***, inlet 2m/4km NE of Lochmaddy, North Uist. **56 C2** NF9471.
Loch Portree *High.* ***Sea feature***, on E coast of Skye. Town of Portree is situated on N side of loch. **58 A5** NG4842.
Loch Poulary *High.* ***Lake/loch***, narrow loch in course of River Garry in Lochaber district, 1m/2km below confluence of Rivers Garry and Kingie. NH1201.
Loch Quien *Arg. & B.* ***Lake/loch***, small loch on Bute 1km NE of Scalpsie Bay. **22 B4** NS0659.
Loch Quoich *High.* ***Lake/loch***, and reservoir in Lochaber district at head of Glen Garry. Length about 9m/14km. **49 F4** NH0102.
Loch Rangag *High.* ***Lake/loch***, in Caithness district 5m/9km NW of Lybster. **77 D4** ND1741.
Loch Rannoch *P. & K.* ***Lake/loch***, and reservoir, 10m/16km long W to E. Dam at Kinloch Rannoch at E end. **40 A4** NN5957.
Loch Ranza *N.Ayr.* ***Sea feature***, sea-loch on N coast of Arran. Village of Lochranza on SW side of loch. **22 A4** NR9350.
Loch Raonasgail *W.Isles* ***Lake/loch***, small loch on Isle of Lewis, 1km NW of Tahaval. **68 B5** NB0327.
Loch Recar *S.Ayr. Alternative spelling of Loch Riecawr, qv.*
Loch Ree *D. & G.* ***Lake/loch***, small loch 5m/9km NW of New Luce. NX1069.
Loch Reraig *High.* ***Sea feature***, small inlet on N shore of Loch Carron, 2m/3km NE of Plockton. **49 E1** NG8135.
Loch Resort *W.Isles* ***Sea feature***, long narrow inlet on W coast of Isle of Lewis, opposite Scarp. **66 C2** NB0616.
Loch Restil *Arg. & B.* ***Lake/loch***, small loch in Argyll immediately N of Rest and be thankful. NN2207.
Loch Riddon (Also known as Loch Ruel.) *Arg. & B.* ***Sea feature***, inlet in Argyll running N from Kyles of Bute opposite Buttock Point. **22 B2** NS0076.
Loch Riecawr (Also spelled Loch Recar.) *S.Ayr.* ***Lake/loch***, 3m/4km W of S end of Loch Doon. **7 F1** NX4393.
Loch Rifa-gil *High.* ***Lake/loch***, small loch 1m/2km SE of Rhifail, Caithness district. **75 G4** NC7448.
Loch Righ Mòr *Arg. & B.* ***Lake/loch***, on Jura 2m/3km N of Loch Tarbert. **20 D1** NR5485.
Loch Rimsdale (Also known as Loch nan Cuinne.) *High.* ***Lake/loch***, adjoining to W of Loch nan Clar, 8m/13km W of Kinbrace. Border between Caithness and Sutherland districts runs down centre of loch. **75 G5** NC7335.
Loch Roag (Gaelic form: Loch Ròg.) *W.Isles* ***Sea feature***, sea-loch off NW coast of Isle of Lewis to SW of Great Bernera, connected to Little, West and East Loch Roag. Contains many islands and islets. NB1233.
Loch Roan *D. & G.* ***Lake/loch***, small loch 4m/7km N of Castle Douglas. **8 B4** NX7469.
Loch Rodel *W.Isles* ***Sea feature***, inlet at S end of South Harris, 1km N of Renish Point. NG0482.
Loch Ròg *W.Isles Gaelic form of Loach Roag, qv.*
Loch Ròg Beag *W.Isles Gaelic form of Little Loch Roag, qv.*
Loch Ronald *D. & G.* ***Lake/loch***, 4m/7km NW of Kirkcowan. **7 D4** NX2664.
Loch Rosail *High.* ***Lake/loch***, 1m/2km E of Naver Forest, Caithness district. **75 F4** NC7140.
Loch Rosque *High. Anglicised form of Loch a' Chroisg, qv.*
Loch Ruard *High.* ***Lake/loch***, in Caithness district 8m/13km NW of Lybster. **76 D4** ND1443.
Loch Ruel *Arg. & B. Alternative name for Loch Riddon, qv.*
Loch Rusky *Stir.* ***Lake/loch***, small loch or tarn 3m/5km S of Callander. **32 B4** NN6103.
Loch Ruthven *High.* ***Lake/loch***, in Inverness district 4m/7km S of Dores. **51 F2** NH6127.
Loch Ryan *D. & G.* ***Sea feature***, large inlet and anchorage running from Milleur Point, at N end of Rinns of Galloway, to Stranraer at head of loch. **6 B3** NX0465.
Loch Sand *High.* ***Lake/loch***, in Caithness district 8m/12km NW of Latheron. **76 C4** ND0941.

L

Loch Saugh *Aber.* ***Lake/loch***, small loch 4m/6km NE of Fettercairn. NO6778.
Loch Scadavay *W.Isles* ***Lake/loch***, on North Uist 4m/6km W of Lochmaddy. **45 G3** NF8668.
Loch Scadavay *W.Isles* ***Lake/loch***, irregular shaped loch on North Uist, 1m/2km NW of Locheport. **45 G3** NF8766.
Loch Scalabsdale *High.* ***Lake/loch***, small loch in Caithness district, 4m/6km SW of Morven. **73 E2** NC9624.
Loch Scalloch *S.Ayr.* ***Lake/loch***, small loch or tarn 3m/5km S of Barr. NX2889.
Loch Scammadale *Arg. & B.* ***Lake/loch***, small but deep loch in Argyll, 6m/10km S of Oban. **30 A3** NM8920.
Loch Scarmclate *High.* ***Lake/loch***, in Caithness district 7m/11km SE of Thurso. **77 D3** ND1859.
Loch Scaslavat *W.Isles Anglicised form of Loch Sgaslabhat, qv.*
Loch Scavaig *High.* ***Sea feature***, large bay on S coast of Skye, between Elgol and Soay. Cuillin Hills rise steeply from N shore. **48 A3** NG4916.
Loch Scaven *High. Alternative name for Loch Sgamhain, qv.*
Loch Scoly *P. & K.* ***Lake/loch***, small loch or tarn 4m/7km E of Aberfeldy. NN9147.
Loch Scresort *High.* ***Sea feature***, inlet on E coast of Rum, containing only landing place on island. Village of Kinloch at head of inlet. NM4199.
Loch Scridain *Arg. & B.* ***Sea feature***, long inlet on W coast of Mull, penetrating to foot of Glen More. **28 D2** NM4525.
Loch Scye *High.* ***Lake/loch***, small loch to E of Beinn nam Bad Mòr. **76 C3** ND0055.
Loch Seaforth *W.Isles* ***Sea feature***, narrow inlet 14m/23km long, penetrating deep into SE coast of North Harris, to NE of Tarbert. Contains steep and uninhabited Seaforth Island. **67 E3** NB2107.
Loch Sealbhanach *High.* ***Lake/loch***, small loch in course of River Cannich in Inverness district below Loch Mullardoch. NH2331.
Loch Sealg *W.Isles Alternative name for Loch Shell, qv.*
Loch Seil *Arg. & B.* ***Lake/loch***, small loch in Argyll, 1m/2km SW of Kilninver. NM8020.
Loch Sgamhain (Also known as Loch Scaven.) *High.* ***Lake/loch***, small loch in Ross and Cromarty district 5m/8km SW of Achnasheen. **60 A4** NH0952.
Loch Sgaslabhat (Anglicised form: Loch Scaslavat.) *W.Isles* ***Lake/loch***, near W coast of Isle of Lewis, 1km S of Camas Uig bay. **68 B4** NB0231.
Loch Sgeireach *High.* ***Lake/loch***, corrie loch below Ben Sgeireach, 3m/5km W of Loch Shin. **71 G3** NC4611.
Loch Sgeireach Mòr *W.Isles* ***Lake/loch***, small loch 2m/3km S of Muirneag and 4m/7km W of Tolsta Head, Isle of Lewis. **69 F3** NB4945.
Loch Sgibacleit *W.Isles* ***Lake/loch***, small loch to E of head of Loch Seaforth, Isle of Lewis. **67 F2** NB3016.
Loch Sgioport (Anglicised form: Loch Skiport.) *W.Isles* ***Sea feature***, inlet on E coast of South Uist, 12m/20km N of Lochboisdale. **46 B1** NF8438.
Loch Sgioport (Anglicised form: Lochskipport.) *W.Isles* ***Settlement***, on South Uist at head of Loch Sgioport, 2m/4km N of Hecla. **46 B1** NF8238.
Loch Sguabain *Arg. & B. See Loch Airdeglais.*
Loch Sguadaig *High.* ***Lake/loch***, to N of Beinn Teallach, 5m/7km N of Tulloch Station. **39 F1** NN3687.
Loch Sguod *High.* ***Lake/loch***, small loch in Ross and Cromarty district, 5m/8km SE of Rubha Réidh. **59 E1** NG8087.
Loch Shandra *Angus* ***Lake/loch***, tarn on W edge of Glenisla Forest, 1m/2km N of Kirkton of Glenisla. NO2162.
Loch Shanndabhat *W.Isles* ***Lake/loch***, small loch on Isle of Lewis, 2m/3km NW of Leumrabhagh. **67 F2** NB3413.
Loch Shawbost *W.Isles* ***Bay***, on NW coast of Isle of Lewis, 1km N of Siabost across Loch a' Bhaile. NB2548.
Loch Sheilavaig *W.Isles* ***Sea feature***, inlet on E coast of South Uist, 1m/2km N of Loch Sgioport. **46 B1** NF8340.
Loch Shell (Also known as Loch Sealg.) *W.Isles* ***Sea feature***, large inlet on E coast of Isle of Lewis to SW of Kebock Head. **67 F2** NB3410.
Loch Shiel *High.* ***Lake/loch***, narrow loch, 17m/27km long, in Lochaber district, extending SW from Glenfinnan to Acharacle, between Moidart and Sunart. **38 A2** NM8072.
Loch Shieldaig *High.* ***Sea feature***, arm of Loch Torridon, W coast of Ross and Cromarty district. Village of Shieldaig at head of loch. **59 D4** NG7955.
Loch Shieldaig *High.* ***Sea feature***, inlet of Gair Loch on W coast of Ross and Cromarty district, 3m/4km S of Gairloch village. NG8072.
Loch Shin *High.* ***Lake/loch***, in Sutherland district, 17m/27km NW to SE at Lairg. Width varies from under 1km to just over 1m/2km. Maximum depth about 195 feet or 60 metres. Water level raised by concrete dam at SE end. **71 G2** NC4816.
Loch Shira *Arg. & B.* ***Sea feature***, inlet of Loch Fyne, to N of Inveraray in Argyll. NN1009.
Loch Shurrery *High.* ***Lake/loch***, in Caithness district 9m/15km SW of Thurso. **76 C3** ND0455.
Loch Sionascaig *High.* ***Lake/loch***, near NW coast of Ross and Cromarty district 5m/8km S of Lochinver. **70 D3** NC1213.
Loch Skealtar *W.Isles* ***Lake/loch***, small loch on North Uist, 4m/6km NE of Locheport. **45 G3** NF8968.
Loch Skeen *D. & G.* ***Lake/loch***, small loch in hills NE of Moffat, 1m/2km N of White Coomb. **16 C4** NT1716.
Loch Skerrow *D. & G.* ***Lake/loch***, 7m/11km N of Gatehouse of Fleet. **8 A4** NX6068.
Loch Skiach *P. & K.* ***Lake/loch***, small loch 4m/6km SW of Ballinluig. **41 E5** NN9547.
Loch Skiport *W.Isles Anglicised form of Loch Sgioport, qv.*
Loch Slaim *High.* ***Lake/loch***, small loch at N end of Loch Craggie, Caithness district. **75 F3** NC6253.
Loch Slapin *High.* ***Sea feature***, inlet on S coast of Skye, on E side of Strathaird peninsula. **48 B3** NG5717.
Loch Sletill *High.* ***Lake/loch***, small loch 2m/3km E of Sletill Hill, 11m/18km S of Reay in Sutherland district. **76 B4** NC9547.
Loch Sligachan *High.* ***Sea feature***, inlet on E coast of Skye, 7m/11km S of Portree. **48 B1** NG5132.
Loch Sloy *Arg. & B.* ***Lake/loch***, and reservoir on W side of Ben Vorlich, 3m/5km SW of Ardlui. Tunnel aqueduct to Inveruglas on W shore of Loch Lomond. **31 E3** NN2812.
Loch Smigeadail *Arg. & B.* ***Lake/loch***, small loch or tarn near N coast of Islay, 2m/3km S of Rubha Bholsa. NR3875.
Loch Sneosdal *High.* ***Lake/loch***, small loch 1km NE of Suidh' a' Mhinn, Skye. **58 A3** NG4169.
Loch Snigisclett *W.Isles* ***Lake/loch***, small loch on South Uist, 3m/5km W of Mingearraidh. **46 B2** NF8025.
Loch Snizort *High.* ***Sea feature***, on N coast of Skye, between Trotternish and Vaternish. **57 G3** NG3261.
Loch Snizort Beag *High.* ***Sea feature***, long narrow inlet at SE corner of Loch Snizort, penetrating 6m/10km inland. **57 G4** NG3261.
Loch Spallander Reservoir *S.Ayr.* ***Reservoir***, 6m/9km E of Maybole. **14 B5** NS3908.
Loch Spelve *Arg. & B.* ***Sea feature***, large inlet with narrow entrance on SE coast of Mull. **29 F2** NM6927.
Loch Spey *High.* ***Lake/loch***, small loch, or tarn, in Badenoch and Strathspey district near source of River Spey, 10m/16km S of Fort Augustus. NN4293.
Loch Spotal *W.Isles* ***Lake/loch***, small loch on South Uist, 1m/2km N of Hecla. **46 B1** NF8336.
Loch Spynie *Moray* ***Lake/loch***, small loch 3m/4km S of Lossiemouth. **63 E3** NJ2366.
Loch Stack *High.* ***Lake/loch***, in Sutherland district, in course of River Laxford between Loch More and Loch Laxford. **74 B4** NC2942.
Loch Staing *High.* ***Lake/loch***, small loch 3m/5km SW of S end of Loch Loyal, Caithness district. **75 E4** NC5740.
Loch Staoisha *Arg. & B.* ***Lake/loch***, small loch on Islay 2m/3km NW of Port Askaig. **20 B2** NR4071.
Loch Staosnaig *Arg. & B.* ***Bay***, on E coast of Colonsay, to S of Scalasaig. NR3993.
Loch Steisevat *W.Isles* ***Lake/loch***, near SW coast of South Harris on N side of Leverburgh. **66 C5** NG0187.
Loch Stemster *High.* ***Lake/loch***, 8m/13km NE of Dunbeath. **77 D4** ND1842.
Loch Stochy *S.Ayr.* ***Marsh/bog***, marshland 1km SW of Loch Riecawr. NX4292.
Loch Stockinish *W.Isles* ***Sea feature***, inlet on SE coast of South Harris, 5m/8km S of Tarbert. **66 D4** NG1292.
Loch Stornoway *Arg. & B.* ***Sea feature***, on S coast of Knapdale, Argyll, 2m/3km N of Ardpatrick Point. **21 F4** NR7361.
Loch Strandavat *W.Isles* ***Lake/loch***, narrow loch on Isle of Lewis, 1m/2km long N to S and 1m/2km W of head of Loch Erisort. **67 E2** NB2519.
Loch Strathy *High.* ***Lake/loch***, small loch within Caithness district, 3m/5km SE of Rhifail; Meall Bad na Cuaiche rising to W. **75 G4** NC7747.
Loch Striven *Arg. & B.* ***Sea feature***, sea-loch in Argyll, running N for 8m/13km from Strone Point, Kyles of Bute. **22 B1** NS0777.
Loch Stulaval *W.Isles* ***Lake/loch***, on South Uist, 2m/3km N of Lochboisdale. **46 B2** NF8022.
Loch Suainaval *W.Isles* ***Lake/loch***, long narrow loch, nearly 4m/6km N to S, near W coast of Isle of Lewis S of Timsgearraidh. **68 B5** NB0629.
Loch Sunart *High.* ***Sea feature***, long arm of sea on W coast in Lochaber district, between Ardnamurchan and Sunart to N and Morvern to S. **37 F3** NM7262.
Loch Sween *Arg. & B.* ***Sea feature***, sea-loch running NE from Danna Island to Knapdale Forest, Argyll. Afforestation on banks. **21 F2** NR7383.
Loch Syre *High.* ***Lake/loch***, irregular-shaped loch, containing a number of small islands, 2m/3km E of S end of Loch Loyal. **75 F4** NC6645.
Loch Tamanavay (Gaelic form: Loch Tamnabhaigh.) *W.Isles* ***Sea feature***, inlet on W coast of Isle of Lewis, 4m/7km S of Mealisval mountain. Tamanavay River flows into loch from E. **66 C2** NB0320.
Loch Tamnabhaigh *W.Isles Gaelic form of Loch Tamanavay, qv.*
Loch Tanna *N.Ayr.* ***Lake/loch***, on Arran 3m/5km E of Pirnmill. **22 A5** NR9242.
Loch Tarbert *Arg. & B.* ***Sea feature***, long inlet on W coast of Jura, almost bisecting the island. **20 D1** NR5481.
Loch Tarbhaidh *High.* ***Lake/loch***, small loch 3m/5km NE of Rhiconich. **74 C3** NC2955.
Loch Tarff *High.* ***Lake/loch***, small loch in Inverness district 3m/5km E of Fort Augustus. **50 D3** NH4210.
Loch Tarsan *Arg. & B.* ***Lake/loch***, and reservoir in Argyll, 1m/2km E of head of Loch Striven. **22 B1** NS0784.
Loch Tay *P. & K.* ***Lake/loch***, 15m/24km long from Killin in SW to Kenmore in NE, and in places over 500 feet (over 150 metres) deep. Noted for salmon. **32 B1** NN6838.
Loch Teacuis *High.* ***Sea feature***, long inlet on N coast of Morvern, in Lochaber district. **37 F4** NM6356.
Loch Tealasavay *W.Isles Anglicised form of Loch Thealasbhaidh, qv.*
Loch Teàrnait *High.* ***Lake/loch***, small loch in Morvern, Lochaber district, 4m/7km N of Rubha an Ridire. **37 G5** NM7447.
Loch Thealasbhaidh (Anglicised form: Loch Tealasavay.) *W.Isles* ***Sea feature***, inlet on W coast of Isle of Lewis, between Loch Tamanavay and Loch Resort. **66 C2** NB0218.
Loch Thom *Inclyde* ***Lake/loch***, and reservoir 3m/4km SW of Greenock. **22 D2** NS2572.
Loch Thota Bridein *W.Isles* ***Lake/loch***, small loch 6m/10km SW of Stornoway, Isle of Lewis. **69 E5** NB3327.
Loch Thulachan *High. Alternative name for Lochan Thulachan, qv.*
Loch Thùrnaig *High.* ***Sea feature***, inlet on E side of Loch Ewe, 2m/3km N of Poolewe, Ross and Cromarty district. **59 E1** NG8684.
Loch Tinker *Stir.* ***Lake/loch***, small loch, 4m/6km SE of Stronachlachar. NN4406.
Loch Tollaidh (Also known as Loch Tollie.) *High.* ***Lake/loch***, near W coast of Ross and Cromarty district 3m/5km E of Gairloch. **59 E2** NG8478.
Loch Tollie *High. Alternative name for Loch Tollaidh, qv.*
Loch Torridon *High.* ***Sea feature***, wide inlet on W coast of Ross and Cromarty district between Red Point and Rubha na Fearn. **58 D3** NG7560.
Loch Toscaig *High.* ***Sea feature***, inlet on W coast of Ross and Cromarty district, 4m/7km S of Applecross. **48 D1** NG7137.
Loch Tralaig *Arg. & B.* ***Lake/loch***, small loch and reservoir in Argyll 3m/5km NE of head of Loch Melfort. **30 A3** NM8816.
Loch Trealaval *W.Isles* ***Lake/loch***, large loch 2m/3km NW of Baile Ailein, Isle of Lewis. **69 D5** NB2723.
Loch Treaslane *High.* ***Sea feature***, inlet of Loch Snizort Beag on N coast of Skye, 8m/12km NW of Portree. NG3952.
Loch Treig *High.* ***Lake/loch***, and reservoir in Lochaber district, 5m/9km long N to S, 14m/23km E of Fort William. Supplies water to aluminium works at Fort William by tunnel under Ben Nevis. Glasgow-Fort William railway runs along E side of loch. Length of dam at N end 440 feet or 134 metres. **39 F3** NN3372.
Loch Triochatan *High.* ***Lake/loch***, small loch in Glen Coe in Lochaber district, 4m/7km SW of Kinlochleven. Ossian, legendary Gaelic warrior and bard, supposedly of 3c, is said to have been born beside its waters. NN1456.
Loch Trollamarig *W.Isles* ***Sea feature***, inlet on SE coast of North Harris, on W side of entrance to Loch Seaforth. NB2201.
Loch Tromlee *Arg. & B.* ***Lake/loch***, small loch in Argyll, 1m/2km N of Kilchrenan. **30 C2** NN0425.
Loch Trool *D. & G.* ***Lake/loch***, in Glentrool Forest Park 8m/13km N of Newton Stewart. **7 F3** NX4179.
Loch Truderscaig *High.* ***Lake/loch***, small loch 1m/2km SW of Loch Rimsdale. Border of Caithness and Sutherland districts runs down centre of loch. **75 G5** NC7132.
Loch Tuath *Arg. & B.* ***Sea feature***, arm of sea on W of Mull, with main island to N and Gometra and Ulva to S. **36 C5** NM3943.
Loch Tuill Bhearnach *High.* ***Lake/loch***, small loch in Ross and Cromarty district 1km SE of summit of Sgurr na Lapaich. NH1634.
Loch Tuim Ghlais *High.* ***Lake/loch***, small loch in Caithness district, 4m/7km NW of Altnabreac. **76 B3** NC9752.
Loch Tulla *Arg. & B.* ***Lake/loch***, in Argyll 2m/3km N of Bridge of Orchy. **39 E5** NN2942.
Loch Tummel *P. & K.* ***Lake/loch***, and reservoir 7m/11km long W to E. The dam at E end is 4m/6km NW of Pitlochry. **40 D4** NN8259.
Loch Tungavat *W.Isles* ***Lake/loch***, small loch 3m/5km S of Earshader, Isle of Lewis. **68 C5** NB1529.
Loch Turret Reservoir *P. & K.* ***Reservoir***, in Glen Turret, 5m/8km NW of Crieff. **32 D2** NN8027.
Loch Uidh an Tuim *High.* ***Lake/loch***, small loch 3m/5km SE of Loch Inchard in Sutherland district. **74 B3** NC2949.
Loch Uigeadail *Arg. & B.* ***Lake/loch***, small loch on Islay, 3m/4km N of Ardbeg. **20 C4** NR4050.

L

Loch Uisg *Arg. & B.* ***Lake/loch***, nearly 2m/3km long between Loch Buie and Loch Spelve, Mull. **29 F2** NM6425.
Loch Uisge *High.* ***Lake/loch***, small loch in Morvern, Lochaber district, 3m/4km NW of Loch a' Choire. **38 A4** NM8055.
Loch Uisgebhagh (Anglicised form: Loch Uskavagh.) *W.Isles* ***Sea feature***, containing numerous islets, on E coast of Benbecula. **45 G4** NF8551.
Loch Uraraidh *Arg. & B.* ***Lake/loch***, small loch on Islay 4m/7km N of Ardbeg. **20 C4** NR4053.
Loch Uraval *W.Isles* ***Lake/loch***, small loch, 7m/12km W of Stornoway, Isle of Lewis. **69 E4** NB3032.
Loch Urigill *High.* ***Lake/loch***, in Sutherland district 7m/11km S of Inchnadamph. **71 E4** NC2410.
Loch Urr *D. & G.* ***Lake/loch***, 4m/7km S of Moniaive. **8 B2** NX7684.
Loch Urrahag *W.Isles* ***Lake/loch***, 1m/2km long N to S, near NW coast of Isle of Lewis, to E and SE of Arnol village. **69 E3** NB3247.
Loch Uskavagh *W.Isles Anglicised form of Loch Uisgebhagh, qv.*
Loch Ussie *High.* ***Lake/loch***, roughly circular in shape, 3m/4km W of Dingwall in Ross and Cromarty district. **61 E4** NH5057.
Loch Vaa *High.* ***Lake/loch***, small loch 3m/5km N of Aviemore. **52 B3** NH9117.
Loch Vaich *High.* ***Reservoir***, in Ross and Cromarty district, 16m/25km NW of Dingwall. **60 C2** NH3475.
Loch Valigan *P. & K.* ***Lake/loch***, tarn 3m/4km S of summit of Beinn a' Ghlo. NN9769.
Loch Valley *D. & G.* ***Lake/loch***, in Glentrool Forest Park, 2m/3km NE of Loch Trool. **7 F2** NX4481.
Loch Vallich *High. Alternative name for Loch a' Bhealaich, qv.*
Loch Varkasaig *High.* ***Sea feature***, inlet of Loch Bracadale, 3m/5km S of Dunvegan, Skye. **57 F5** NG2542.
Loch Vatandip *W.Isles* ***Lake/loch***, small loch on Isle of Lewis, 4m/6km W of Stornoway. **69 E4** NB3433.
Loch Vatten *High.* ***Sea feature***, on Skye, 3m/5km SE of Dunvegan. **57 F5** NG2843.
Loch Venachar *Stir.* ***Lake/loch***, extending nearly 4m/6km W to E, 2m/4km W of Callander. **32 A4** NN5705.
Loch Veyatie *High.* ***Lake/loch***, narrow loch, 4m/6km long NW to SE, 7m/11km SW of Inchnadamph. Border of Ross and Cromarty and Sutherland districts runs down centre of loch. **71 D3** NC1713.
Loch Voil *Stir.* ***Lake/loch***, narrow loch, nearly 4m/6km long W to E. Village of Balquhidder at E end. **32 A3** NN5019.
Loch Voshimid *W.Isles* ***Lake/loch***, small loch 3m/4km S of head of Loch Resort. **66 D2** NB1013.
Loch Watston *Stir.* ***Lake/loch***, small loch 1m/2km SW of Doune. NN7100.
Loch Watten *High.* ***Lake/loch***, to N of Watten; 3m/5km long running NW to SE. **77 E3** ND2355.
Loch Wharral *Angus* ***Lake/loch***, small loch or tarn 2m/3km NE of Clova. **42 B2** NO3574.
Loch Whinyeon *D. & G.* ***Lake/loch***, 3m/5km NE of Gatehouse of Fleet. **8 A4** NX6260.
Lochaber *High.* ***Locality***, mountainous moorland region of W Scotland, spanning Great Glen from Knoydart and North and South Morar in W, to Monadhliath Mountains and Glen Spean in E. Deeply incised by Lochs Arkaig, Eil, Linnhe, Lochy and Quoich. **49 F5** NM8797.
Lochaber Loch *D. & G.* ***Lake/loch***, small loch 5m/8km SW of Dumfries. **8 D3** NX9270.
Lochailort *High.* ***Locality***, at head of Loch Ailort. **37 G1** NM7682.
Lochaline *High.* ***Village***, in Lochaber district, on W side of entrance to Loch Aline. **37 F5** NM6744.
Lochalsh Woodland Garden *High.* ***Garden***, wooded lochside garden on Balmacara Estate by N shore of Loch Alsh, 2m/3km E of Kyle of Lochalsh. **49 E2** NG8027.
Lochan a' Bhealaich *P. & K.* ***Lake/loch***, small loch or tarn near border with Highland region 4m/6km SW of Ben Alder. NN4568.
Lochan a' Bhruic *Arg. & B.* ***Lake/loch***, small loch in Inverliever Forest, 6m/9km NE of Ford. **30 B3** NM9109.
Lochan a' Chlaidheimh *P. & K.* ***Lake/loch***, small loch or tarn near source of Black Water, E of Blackwater Reservoir. NN4060.
Lochan a' Chreachain *Arg. & B.* ***Lake/loch***, small mountain loch or tarn in Argyll on NW side of Beinn a' Chreachain. NN3644.
Lochan a' Mhadaidh Riabhaich *High.* ***Lake/loch***, small loch on Ardnamurchan peninsula in Lochaber district, 1km E of Loch Mudle. NM5565.
Lochan a' Mhuilinn *P. & K.* ***Lake/loch***, tarn 3m/5km W of Amulree. NN8435.
Lochan an Tairt *High.* ***Lake/loch***, small loch above N side of Glen Urquhart, 4m/7km NW of Drumnadrochit. **50 D1** NH4433.
Lochan Balloch *Stir.* ***Lake/loch***, tarn 3m/5km SW of Callander. NN5904.
Lochan Beannach *High.* ***Lake/loch***, comprises two lochs below Beinn Airigh Mòr, Lochan Beannach Mòr and Lochan Beannach Beag, to W and E respectively. They are connected by narrow stretch of water and drain into Fionn Loch. **59 F2** NG9477.
Lochan Breaclaich *Stir.* ***Reservoir***, small reservoir 3m/5km E of Killin. **32 B1** NN6231.
Lochan Buidhe *Moray* ***Lake/loch***, small loch or tarn 1m/2km N of Ben Macdui. Highest lake in Britain at 3598 feet or 1097 metres. NH9801.
Lochan Coire an Lochain *High.* ***Lake/loch***, small loch or tarn 1m/2km W of Chno Dearg. NN3674.
Lochan Dubh *High.* ***Lake/loch***, small mountain loch at head of Glen Hurich in Lochaber district. NM8971.
Lochan Dubh *High.* ***Lake/loch***, in Lochaber district, between Loch Arkaig and Glen Kingie. **49 G5** NN0695.
Lochan Dubh nan Geodh *High.* ***Lake/loch***, 1m/2km NW of Loch More. **76 C4** ND0547.
Lochan Fada *High.* ***Lake/loch***, narrow loch, 1m/2km N of Cam Loch. The summit of Canisp lies 1m/2km N. **71 E3** NC2016.
Lochan Fada *High.* ***Lake/loch***, in W part of Ross and Cromarty, 4m/6km NE of head of Loch Maree. **59 G2** NH0271.
Lochan Fada *High.* ***Lake/loch***, small narrow loch in Erchless Forest, 2m/3km NE of Erchless Castle. **60 D5** NH4243.
Lochan Gaineamhach *High.* ***Lake/loch***, small loch or tarn 2m/3km NW of Loch Bà. **39 E4** NN3053.
Lochan Gleann Astaile *Arg. & B.* ***Lake/loch***, small loch on Jura, 1m/2km SW of Beinn a' Chaolais. NR4771.
Lochan Hakel *High.* ***Lake/loch***, small loch 1km E of S end of Kyle of Tongue. **75 E3** NC5653.
Lochan Loin nan Donnlaich *P. & K.* ***Lake/loch***, small loch 2m/4km NE of Loch Eigheach. **39 G3** NN4661.
Lochan Long *Arg. & B.* ***Lake/loch***, 4m/6km SE of Dalavich across Loch Awe. **30 C4** NN0209.
Lochan Lùnn Dà-Bhrà *High.* ***Lake/loch***, small loch in Lochaber district, 5m/8km S of Fort William. **38 C3** NN0866.
Lochan Mathair Eite *High.* ***Lake/loch***, small loch or tarn 5m/7km SE of dam of Blackwater Reservoir. NN2854.
Lochan Mhic Pheadair Ruaidh *High.* ***Lake/loch***, small loch or tarn on Black Mount, Lochaber district, 3m/5km N of Loch Tulla. Drains into River Bà to N. NN2847.
Lochan na Bi *Arg. & B.* ***Lake/loch***, small loch in Argyll in course of River Lochy, 1m/2km NW of Tyndrum. **31 F1** NN3031.
Lochan na h-Achlaise *High.* ***Lake/loch***, small loch on Black Mount in Lochaber district, 2m/3km N of Loch Tulla. **39 F5** NN3148.
Lochan na h-Earba *High.* ***Lake/loch***, narrow loch in Badenoch and Strathspey district running parallel to, and about 1m/2km SE of, Loch Laggan. **39 G1** NN4883.
Lochan na Lairige *P. & K.* ***Reservoir***, 1m/2km long N to S, 4m/6km N of head of Loch Tay. **40 A5** NN5940.
Lochan na Stainge *High.* ***Lake/loch***, small loch in Lochaber district in course of River Bà, between Loch Buidhe and Loch Bà. **39 E5** NN3049.
Lochan na Stairne *High.* ***Lake/loch***, small loch in Glendoe Forest, 4m/7km SE of Fort Augustus. **50 D4** NH4405.
Lochan nam Breac *High.* ***Lake/loch***, small loch in Lochaber district, 1m/2km W of head of Loch Quoich. NM9199.
Lochan nam Fiann *High.* ***Lake/loch***, small loch on Ardnamurchan peninsula, 2m/3km N of Glenborrodale. **37 F3** NM6164.
Lochan nan Carn *High.* ***Lake/loch***, 1km E of Borgie Forest, Caithness district. **75 F3** NC6953.
Lochan nan Cat *P. & K.* ***Lake/loch***, small mountain loch or tarn in corrie on E side of Stuchd an Lochain. NN4844.
Lochan nan Cat *P. & K.* ***Lake/loch***, small mountain loch in corrie, nearly 1m/2km NE of Ben Lawers. NN6442.
Lochan Oisinneach Beag *P. & K.* ***Lake/loch***, small tarn 1km NE of Lochan Oisinneach Mòr. NO0355.
Lochan Oisinneach Mòr *P. & K.* ***Lake/loch***, small loch 4m/6km NE of Ballinluig. NO0354.
Lochan Shira *Arg. & B.* ***Lake/loch***, and reservoir 4m/6km S of Dalmally in Argyll. **31 D2** NN1620.
Lochan Spling *Stir.* ***Lake/loch***, tarn in Loch Ard Forest, 1m/2km W of Aberfoyle. NN5000.
Lochan Sròn Mòr *Arg. & B.* ***Lake/loch***, and reservoir in Argyll below dam of Lochan Shira, 8m/13km NE of Inveraray. **30 D3** NN1619.
Lochan Sròn Smeur *P. & K.* ***Lake/loch***, small loch 2m/3km N of Loch Eigheach. **39 G3** NN4560.
Lochan Thulachan (Also known as Loch Thulachan.) *High.* ***Lake/loch***, in Caithness district 8m/12km NW of Latheron. **76 D4** ND1041.
Lochan Uaine *High.* ***Lake/loch***, small loch in Ross and Cromarty district, 4m/7km SE of Torridon. **59 F4** NG9652.
Lochans *D. & G.* ***Village***, 3m/4km S of Stranraer. **6 B5** NX0656.
Lochar Moss *D. & G.* ***Open space***, low-lying region to E and SE of Dumfries, traversed and drained by Lochar Water. NY0371.
Lochar Water *D. & G.* ***River***, rising N of Dumfries and flowing into Solway Firth to SW of Cummertrees. Traverses and drains low-lying region of Lochar Moss. **9 E3** NY0371.
Locharbriggs *D. & G.* Population: 5383. ***Small town***, 3m/4km NE of Dumfries. **9 D2** NX9980.
Lochawe *Arg. & B.* ***Village***, on W bank of Loch Awe in Argyll, 3m/4km W of Dalmally. **30 D2** NN1227.
Lochay *Stir.* ***River***, running W down Glen Lochay to join River Dochart at head of Loch Tay. NN5733.
Lochboisdale (Gaelic form: Loch Baghasdail.) *W.Isles* ***Village***, port on N shore of Loch Baghasdail, inlet on E coast of South Uist. **44 C2** NF7919.
Lochbroom Burn *P. & K.* ***River***, flowing SW from Loch Broom into River Tay, 3m/4km SE of Pitlochry. **41 E4** NN9654.
Lochbuie *Arg. & B.* ***Village***, on S coast of Mull, at head of large inlet of Loch Buie. Ruined keep of Castle Moy. Ancient stone circle to E. **29 F2** NM6025.
Lochcarron *High.* ***Village***, on N shore of Loch Carron, 2m/3km below head of loch. **49 E1** NG8735.
Lochcote Reservoir *W.Loth.* ***Reservoir***, small reservoir 2m/4km SW of Linlithgow. NS9773.
Lochcraig Head *Sc.Bord.* ***Mountain***, rising above N shore of Loch Skeen, 5m/8km SW of St. Mary's Loch. Height 2624 feet or 800 metres. **16 C4** NT1618.
Lochcraig Reservoir *E.Renf.* ***Reservoir***, 3m/5km W of Eaglesham. NS5350.
Lochdhu Hotel *High.* ***Other building***, hotel situated on E side of Loch Dubh, 1m/2km S of Altnabreac station. **76 C4** ND0144.
Lochdon *Arg. & B.* ***Village***, at head of Loch Don, inlet on E coast of Mull. **29 G1** NM7333.
Lochdrum *High.* ***Settlement***, in Dirrie More, 4m/6km E of Corrieshalloch Gorge. **60 B2** NH2475.
Lochearnhead *Stir.* ***Village***, at head, or W end, of Loch Earn, 6m/10km S of Killin. **32 A2** NN5823.
Lochee *Dundee* ***Suburb***, 2m/3km NW of Dundee city centre. **34 B1** NO3731.
Locheil Forest *High.* ***Open space***, deer forest extending N of Loch Eil to Loch Arkaig. **38 C1** NN0277.
Locheilside Station *High.* ***Other building***, railway station on N shore of Loch Eil, 1km E of Kinlocheil, Lochaber district. **38 B2** NM9978.
Lochenbreck Loch *D. & G.* ***Lake/loch***, small loch on N side of Laurieston Forest, 3m/4km W of Laurieston. NX6465.
Lochend *Edin.* ***Suburb***, 2m/3km NE of Edinburgh city centre. NT2774.
Lochend *High.* ***Settlement***, in Caithness district, on E side of Loch Heilen, 4m/6km SE of Dunnet. **77 E2** ND2668.
Lochend *High.* ***Settlement***, at NE end of Loch Ness, Inverness district. **51 E1** NH5937.
Lochend Loch *N.Lan.* ***Lake/loch***, small loch 1m/2km W of Coatbridge. NS7066.
Locheport *W.Isles* ***Settlement***, on North Uist, on S shore of Loch Euphoirt, 5m/7km from mouth. NF8563.
Lochfoot *D. & G.* ***Village***, at N end of Lochrutton Loch, 5m/8km W of Dumfries. **8 D3** NX8973.
Lochgair *Arg. & B.* ***Village***, 4m/6km NE of Lochgilphead, on Loch Gair, a small inlet on Loch Fyne. **30 B5** NR9290.
Lochgarthside *High.* ***Settlement***, in Inverness district, on NW shore of Loch Mhòr. **51 E3** NH5219.
Lochgelly *Fife* Population: 7044. ***Small town***, former mining town, 7m/11km SW of Glenrothes. **33 G5** NT1893.
Lochgilphead *Arg. & B.* Population: 2421. ***Small town***, at head of Loch Gilp in Argyll. Tourist and shopping centre. Former fishing village which developed with opening of Crinan Canal. **21 G1** NR8687.
Lochgoilhead *Arg. & B.* ***Village***, at head of Loch Goil in Argyll. **31 E4** NN1901.
Lochgoin *E.Ayr.* ***Settlement***, 4m/7km SW of Eaglesham. **23 G5** NS5346.
Lochgoin Reservoir *E.Ayr.* ***Reservoir***, 4m/6km SW of Eaglesham. **23 G5** NS5347.
Lochhill *E.Ayr.* ***Settlement***, 2m/3km NW of New Cumnock. **15 E4** NS6015.
Lochhill *Moray* ***Settlement***, 3m/5km W of Garmouth. **63 E3** NJ2965.
Lochinch Castle *D. & G.* ***Historic house***, 19c mansion 3m/5km E of Stranraer. Grounds contain pinetum, two lochs (White Loch and Black Loch, the latter being more easterly), and, on isthmus between them, ruins of Castle Kennedy, late 16c castle destroyed by fire in 1715. **6 C4** NX1061.
Lochindorb *High.* ***Lake/loch***, 8m/13km N of Carrbridge and 6m/10km NW of Grantown-on-Spey. Medieval castle on island in loch. **52 B1** NH9736.
Lochindorb Castle *High.* ***Castle***, ruins of early 13c castle on island in Lochindorb, 6m/10km NW of Grantown-on-Spey. **52 B1** NH9736.
Lochinvar *D. & G.* ***Lake/loch***, 3m/5km NE of St. John's Town of Dalry. Ruins of old castle on islet in loch, home of 'Young Lochinvar'. NX6585.

L

Lochinver *High.* ***Small town***, fishing port and resort on W coast of Sutherland district at head of Loch Inver 18m/29km N of Ullapool. **70 C2** NC0922.
Lochlair *Angus* ***Settlement***, 3m/5km S of Letham. **42 D5** NO5243.
Lochlands Hill *N.Ayr.* ***Hill***, 2m/3km NE of Beith. Height 689 feet or 210 metres. **23 E4** NS3755.
Lochlane *P. & K.* ***Locality***, in valley of River Earn, 1m/2km W of Crieff. **32 D2** NN8321.
Lochlea *S.Ayr.* ***Settlement***, 3m/4km NE of Tarbolton. **14 C3** NS4530.
Lochluichart *High.* ***Settlement***, on N shore of Loch Luichart, at W end of loch, 4m/6km W of Gorstan. **60 C3** NH3363.
Lochluichart Station *High.* ***Other building***, railway station on route from Inverness to Kyle of Lochalsh, 4m/6km W of Gorstan. **60 C3** NH3262.
Lochmaben *D. & G.* Population: 2024. ***Small town***, royal burgh 8m/13km NE of Dumfries, surrounded by several small lochs. Reputed birthplace of Robert the Bruce. Ruined 13c castle (Historic Scotland) on Castle Loch supplied building stone for many of town's houses. **9 E2** NY0882.
Lochmaben Castle *D. & G.* ***Castle***, 14c ruins of royal castle (Historic Scotland) on S shore of Castle Loch, to S of Lochmaben. Originally built by English, it was extensively rebuilt during reign of James VI; said to be birthplace of Robert the Bruce. **9 E2** NY0881.
Lochmaddy (Gaelic form: Loch na Madadh.) *W.Isles* ***Village***, port on W shore of Loch na Madadh. **56 C3** NF9369.
Lochnagar *Aber.* ***Inland physical feature***, mountain ridge with steep NE facing cliffs, comprising four distinct peaks above Lochnagar Loch, 3m/4km NW of Loch Muick. Peaks are Cac Carn Beag, a Munro at 3788 feet or 1155 metres, Cac Carn Mòr at 3772 feet or 1150 metres, Cuidhe Cròm at 3552 feet or 1083 metres and Meikle Pap at 3214 feet or 980 metres. **42 A1** NO2585.
Lochnagar *Aber.* ***Lake/loch***, small loch or tarn below mountain ridge of same name, 7m/11km SE of Braemar. Summit of ridge is Cac Carn Beag. NO2585.
Lochnaw Castle *D. & G.* ***Castle***, mainly 17c castle, incorporating 16c tower, on S side of small loch, 5m/7km W of Stranraer. Former seat of Agnews. **6 A4** NW9962.
Lochore *Fife* ***Town***, former mining town, 3m/5km N of Cowdenbeath. **33 G5** NT1796.
Lochore Meadows Country Park *Fife* ***Leisure/recreation***, on N side of Loch Ore, 1km SW of Lochore. Focal point of park is loch, with emphasis on watersports and fishing, although there is also a golf course and extensive woodlands. **33 G5** NT1695.
Lochportain *W.Isles* ***Settlement***, on North Uist, on N shore of Loch Portain. **56 C2** NF9471.
Lochranza *N.Ayr.* ***Village***, and resort on W side of Loch Ranza, inlet at N end of Arran. Castle (Historic Scotland) dates from 13c. **22 A5** NR9250.
Lochranza Castle *N.Ayr.* ***Castle***, ruined castle built 13c-14c on promontory in Loch Ranza on N coast of Arran. **22 A4** NR9350.
Lochrosque Forest *High.* ***Open space***, deer forest to NE of Loch Rosque. **60 A3** NH1258.
Lochrutton Loch *D. & G.* ***Lake/loch***, 5m/8km W of Dumfries. **8 C3** NX8972.
Lochs of Lumbister *Shet.* ***Lake/loch***, series of lochs in N part of Yell. **85 D3** HU4896.
Lochside *Aber.* ***Hamlet***, 1km W of St. Cyrus. **43 F3** NO7364.
Lochside *D. & G.* ***Suburb***, NW district of Dumfries. NX9577.
Lochside *High.* ***Settlement***, on E shore of N end of Loch Hope. **75 D3** NC4759.
Lochside *High.* ***Settlement***, in Sutherland district, to SE of Loch an Ruathair. **76 A5** NC8735.
Lochside *High.* ***Settlement***, 1m/2km SE of Castletown. **77 E2** ND2165.
Lochskipport *W.Isles* *Anglicised form of Loch Sgioport (settlement), qv.*
Lochslin *High.* ***Settlement***, 3m/5km E of Tain. **62 A1** NH8380.
Lochton *S.Ayr.* ***Settlement***, 2m/3km SE of Barrhill. **7 D2** NX2580.
Lochty *Fife* ***Settlement***, 4m/6km NW of Anstruther. **34 D4** NO5208.
Lochuisge *High.* ***Settlement***, 1km W of Loch Uisge, Lochaber district. **37 G4** NM7955.
Lochurr *D. & G.* ***Settlement***, 4m/6km S of Moniaive. **8 B2** NX7685.
Lochussie *High.* ***Settlement***, 1m/2km SW of Strathpeffer. **61 D4** NH4956.
Lochwinnoch *Renf.* Population: 2347. ***Small town***, residential town, 12m/19km SW of Paisley, formerly a weaving centre. Clyde Muirshiel Regional Park contains RSPB reserve. **23 E4** NS3558.
Lochy *Arg. & B.* ***River***, in Argyll, running W down Glen Lochy to River Orchy 2m/3km E of Dalmally. NN1927.
Lochy *High.* ***River***, in Lochaber district, running SW from Loch Lochy to head of Loch Linnhe. NN1175.
Lochy Burn *Alternative name for Burn of Lochy, qv.*
Lockerbie *D. & G.* Population: 3982. ***Small town***, market town founded in 17c, 11m/17km E of Dumfries. Agricultural centre for surrounding area. Lockerbie Air Disaster Memorial, sited at Lockerbie City Cemetery, commemorates all victims who died in Lockerbie Air Disaster, December 1988. **9 F2** NY1381.
Loder Head *Shet.* ***Coastal feature***, headland on E coast of Bressay at entrance to Voe of Cullingsburgh. **83 E3** HU5243.
Lodge Island *D. & G.* ***Island***, in River Dee, connected to E bank by causeway, 2m/3km SW of Castle Douglas. NX7361.
Logan *D. & G.* ***Locality***, 4m/7km S of Sandhead, includes Logan Mains, Logan House and Logan Botanic Gardens. **2 A2** NX0943.
Logan *E.Ayr.* Population: 1214. ***Village***, 1m/2km E of Cumnock. **15 D3** NS5820.
Logan Botanic Gardens *D. & G.* ***Garden***, 1m/2km N of Port Logan. Exotic ferns, plants, palms, shrubs and perennials planted outside. **2 A2** NX0942.
Logan Reservoir *S.Lan.* ***Reservoir***, in course of Logan Water and beneath NE slopes of Spirebush Hill. NS7435.
Logan Water *S.Lan.* ***River***, rising on Spirebush Hill and running E to River Nethan 2m/3km SW of Lesmahagow. **15 F2** NS7936.
Loganlea *W.Loth.* ***Hamlet***, adjoining to W of Addiewell, 4m/7km S of Bathgate. **25 D3** NS9862.
Loganlea Reservoir *Midloth.* ***Reservoir***, small reservoir on Pentland Hills, 3m/5km NW of Penicuik. **25 F3** NT1962.
Loggie *High.* ***Settlement***, on W shore of Loch Broom, Ross and Cromarty district, 4m/6km from head of loch. **70 D5** NH1490.
Logie *Angus* ***Settlement***, 1m/2km S of Kirriemuir. **42 B4** NO3952.
Logie *Angus* ***Settlement***, 4m/6km N of Montrose. **43 E3** NO6963.
Logie *Fife* ***Village***, 3m/5km W of Leuchars. **34 C2** NO4020.
Logie *Moray* ***Settlement***, 5m/8km S of Forres. **62 C4** NJ0150.
Logie Buchan *Aber.* ***Locality***, parish containing Kirkton of Logie Buchan. NJ9829.
Logie Coldstone *Aber.* ***Village***, adjoining to small lake, 4m/6km NW of Dinnet and 7m/11km NE of Ballater. **53 G4** NJ4304.
Logie Head *Aber.* ***Coastal feature***, headland on N coast, 1m/2km NE of Cullen. **64 A3** NJ5268.
Logie Hill *High.* ***Settlement***, 6m/10km NE of Invergordon. **61 G2** NH7676.
Logie Newton *Aber.* ***Settlement***, 4m/6km N of Kirkton of Culsalmond. **54 B1** NJ6638.
Logie Pert *Angus* ***Village***, 5m/8km NW of Montrose. Cottage within parish, to NW of village, is birthplace of James Mill, 1773-1836. **43 E3** NO6664.
Logiealmond *P. & K.* ***Locality***, on N slope of Glen Almond, 8m/12km NW of Perth. **33 E1** NN9930.
Logierait *P. & K.* ***Village***, 4m/7km SE of Pitlochry, near confluence of Rivers Tay and Tummel. **41 E4** NN9651.
Loin Water *Arg. & B.* ***River***, running S down Glen Loin to head of Loch Long. NN2904.
Loirston Country Park *Aberdeen* ***Leisure/recreation***, country park with 620 acres of coastal walks to S of River Dee, 2m/3km SE of Aberdeen harbour. Attracts a wide variety of seabirds and other wildlife. Includes Girdle Ness lighthouse. **55 E4** NJ9302.
Loirston Loch *Aberdeen* ***Lake/loch***, small loch 1m/2km W of Cove Bay and 3m/5km S of Aberdeen. NJ9301.
Lomond Hills *Fife* ***Large natural feature***, range of hills NE of Loch Leven. Summit is West Lomond, 1712 feet or 522 metres. **34 A4** NO2106.
Lòn Mòr *High.* ***River***, flowing SW and joining River Haultin, 1m/2km E of head of Loch Eyre. **58 A4** NG4351.
Lonan *Arg. & B.* ***River***, in Argyll, running W down Glen Lonan to head of Loch Nell, 3m/5km E of Oban. **30 B2** NM9028.
Lonbain *High.* ***Locality***, in Ross and Cromarty district, 6m/9km N of Applecross. **58 C4** NG6853.
Londubh *High.* ***Settlement***, adjoining to E of Poolewe, Ross and Cromarty district. **59 E1** NG8681.
Lonemore *High.* ***Settlement***, on N shore of Dornoch Firth, 2m/3km W of Dornoch. **61 G1** NH7688.
Long Craig *Angus* ***Coastal feature***, small peninsula of rock on North Sea coast, 2m/3km SE of Montrose. **43 F4** NO7254.
Long Geo *Ork.* ***Coastal feature***, on W coast of S part of Mainland, 3m/5km S of Kirkwall. **78 D2** HY4404.
Long Haven *Aber.* ***Bay***, small bay on E coast of Buchan, 4m/6km S of Peterhead. NK1240.
Long Head *Moray* ***Coastal feature***, headland at N end of Findochty on N coast. NJ4668.
Long Hermiston *Edin.* ***Locality***, 5m/8km SW of Edinburgh. NT1770.
Long Hope *Ork.* ***Sea feature***, strait separating SE coast of Hoy from N coast of South Walls peninsula. ND3091.
Long Loch *Angus* ***Lake/loch***, small loch 2m/3km S of Newtyle. **34 A1** NO2838.
Long Loch *E.Renf.* ***Lake/loch***, 3m/5km S of Neilston. **23 F4** NS4752.
Long Taing of Newark *Ork.* ***Coastal feature***, promontory on E coast of Sanday at Newark, protruding E between Bay of Newark and Bay of Lopness. HY7242.
Longa Island *High.* ***Island***, uninhabited island of about 360 acres or 145 hectares at mouth of Gair Loch, W coast of Ross and Cromarty district, 1m/2km S of Rubha Bàn. **58 D2** NG7377.
Longannet *Fife* ***Other building***, power station on N bank of River Forth, 2m/4km W of Culross. NS9585.
Longay *High.* ***Island***, uninhabited island of about 150 acres or 60 hectares, lying 1m/2km E of Scalpay at S end of Inner Sound. **48 C1** NG6531.
Longcroft *Falk.* ***Village***, 4m/6km NE of Cumbernauld. NS7979.
Longdrum *Aber.* ***Settlement***, 3m/5km SE of Newmachar and 2m/4km W of Balmedie. **55 E3** NJ9217.
Longforgan *P. & K.* ***Village***, 6m/10km W of Dundee. **34 B2** NO3129.
Longformacus *Sc.Bord.* ***Village***, on Dye Water, 6m/10km W of Duns. **27 D4** NT6957.
Longgrain Head *D. & G.* ***Mountain***, on uplands to S of Craik Forest, 5m/8km N of Langholm. Height 1535 feet or 468 metres. **10 B2** NY3592.
Longhill *Aber.* ***Settlement***, just S of New Leeds, 4m/6km N of Mintlaw. **65 E4** NJ9953.
Longhope *Ork.* ***Settlement***, on N coast of South Walls peninsula, Hoy, overlooking North Bay. **78 C3** ND3090.
Longlands *Aber.* ***Settlement***, 3m/5km W of Rhynie. **53 G2** NJ4525.
Longman Point *High.* ***Coastal feature***, shingle point to N of Inverness, extending into Moray Firth. **61 F5** NH6647.
Longmanhill *Aber.* ***Locality***, near N coast, 3m/4km SE of Macduff. **64 C3** NJ7362.
Longmorn *Moray* ***Village***, 3m/5km S of Elgin. **63 E4** NJ2358.
Longnewton *Sc.Bord.* ***Settlement***, 3m/4km S of Newtown St. Boswells. **17 G3** NT5827.
Longniddry *E.Loth.* Population: 2933. ***Village***, 3m/4km SW of Aberlady. **26 B2** NT4476.
Longniddry Bents *E.Loth.* ***Other feature of interest***, area of heath and grass to NW of Longniddry along Firth of Forth coast, 12m/20km NE of Edinburgh city centre. **26 B2** NT4276.
Longridge *W.Loth.* ***Village***, 2m/3km S of Whitburn. **24 D3** NS9462.
Longriggend *N.Lan.* ***Village***, 5m/8km NE of Airdrie. **24 C2** NS8270.
Longside *Aber.* ***Village***, 6m/10km W of Peterhead. **65 F5** NK0347.
Longstone *Edin.* ***Suburb***, 3m/5km SW of Edinburgh city centre. NT2170.
Longyester *E.Loth.* ***Hamlet***, 2m/3km SE of Gifford. **26 C3** NT5465.
Lonmay *Aber.* ***Settlement***, 5m/8km S of Fraserburgh. NK0158.
Lonmore *High.* ***Settlement***, 1m/2km SE of Dunvegan, Skye. **57 F5** NG2646.
Lop Ness *Ork.* ***Coastal feature***, headland on Sanday at E end of Bay of Lopness and 2m/3km W of Start Point. HY7643.
Lord Arthur's Cairn *Aber.* ***Mountain***, 4m/7km NW of Alford. Height 1699 feet or 518 metres. **54 A3** NJ5119.
Lord Lovat's Bay *Arg. & B.* ***Bay***, small bay to E of entrance to Loch Buie, Mull. NM6020.
Lord Lovat's Cave *Arg. & B.* ***Cave***, on Lord Lovat's Bay, to E of entrance to Loch Buie, Mull. NM6020.
Lord Macdonald's Forest *High.* ***Open space***, mountainous tract S of Loch Sligachan, Skye. NG5128.
Lord Macdonald's Table *High.* ***Island***, one of a group of islets 3m/5km NW of Rubha Hunish at N tip of Skye. See also Gaeilavore Island, and Gearran Island. NG3679.
Loretto *E.Loth.* ***Educational establishment***, boy's public school at Musselburgh. NT3373.
Lorgill *High.* ***Locality***, 6m/9km NW of Idrigill Point, Skye. **57 E5** NG1741.
Lorn *Arg. & B.* ***Locality***, area of Argyll bounded by Loch Awe, Loch Etive and W coast adjoining Firth of Lorn. **30 B2** NN0834.
Lorn *W.Dun.* ***Settlement***, above S shore of Loch Lomond, 2m/3km W of Gartocharn. **23 E1** NS3985.
Lornty *P. & K.* ***Settlement***, on Lornty Burn, 1m/2km NW of Blairgowrie. **41 G5** NO1646.
Lornty Burn *P. & K.* ***River***, rising in Forest of Clunie and flowing SE to River Ericht, 1m/2km N of Blairgowrie. **41 G5** NO1746.
Losgaintir (Anglicised form: Luskentyre.) *W.Isles* ***Settlement***, on W coast of South Harris, 5m/8km W of Tarbert. **66 C4** NG0799.
Lossie *Moray* ***River***, rising at The Seven Sisters below NE slopes of Carn Kitty and flowing N along Glen Lossie to Dallas, then E through Kellas, and N again to Elgin where it turns E, then finally N to enter Moray Firth at Lossiemouth. **63 E3** NJ2370.

Lossie Forest *Moray* ***Forest/woodland***, bordering N coast on E side of Lossiemouth. **63 E3** NJ2767.
Lossiemouth *Moray* Population: 7184. ***Small town***, fishing port and resort on N coast, 5m/8km N of Elgin. Ramsay MacDonald, first Labour prime minister, born here in 1866. **63 E2** NJ2370.
Lossiemouth Fisheries and Communities Museum *Moray* ***Other feature of interest***, museum at Lossiemouth Harbour, detailing history of fishing and community. Includes history of Ramsay MacDonald who was born here in 1866. **63 E2** NJ2370.
Lossit *Arg. & B.* ***Settlement***, on Rinns of Islay, 3m/4km NE of Portnahaven. **20 A4** NR1856.
Lossit Bay *Arg. & B.* ***Bay***, on W side of Rinns of Islay, 3m/5km N of Rinns Point. **20 A4** NR1756.
Lossit Point *Arg. & B.* ***Coastal feature***, headland on N side of Lossit Bay, W coast of Rinns of Islay. NR1756.
Loth *Ork.* ***Coastal feature***, cliffs on W coast of Spur Ness, Sanday. **81 D3** HY6034.
Lothbeg *High.* ***Settlement***, near E coast of Sutherland district, 6m/10km SW of Helmsdale. **73 E3** NC9410.
Lothbeg Point *High.* ***Coastal feature***, headland on E coast, 1m/2km SE of Lothbeg. **73 E4** NC9410.
Lothianbridge *Midloth.* ***Locality***, on River South Esk, 1km NW of Newtongrange. NT3264.
Lothmore *High.* ***Settlement***, near E coast of Sutherland district, 5m/7km SW of Helmsdale. **73 E3** NC9611.
Lothrie Burn *Fife* ***River***, stream which flows E from Holl Reservoir to join River Leven at Glenrothes. NO2601.
Lotus Hill *D. & G.* ***Mountain***, 1km S of Loch Arthur, 6m/10km NE of Dalbeattie. Height 1053 feet or 321 metres. **8 C4** NX9067.
Loudoun Castle Park *E.Ayr.* ***Leisure/recreation***, surrounding ruins of Loudoun Castle, 1km N of Galston. Scotland's largest theme park featuring a variety of rides, including Scotland's highest roller-coaster. 500 acre park also contains large areas of woodland. **14 D2** NS5037.
Loudoun Hall *S.Ayr.* ***Historic house***, restored merchant's house dating from 15c-16c and oldest house in Ayr. **14 B3** NS3420.
Loudoun Hill *E.Ayr.* ***Mountain***, summit is rocky knoll 3m/5km E of Darvel. Height 1036 feet or 316 metres. To S across River Irvine, is site of Battle of Loudoun Hill 1307. NS6037.
Loup of Fintry *Stir.* ***Mountain***, with steep slope on S side, in SE part of Fintry Hills. Height 1515 feet or 462 metres. **24 A1** NS6687.
Lour *Angus* ***Settlement***, 3m/5km S of Forfar. **42 C5** NO4746.
Lousie Wood Law *S.Lan.* ***Mountain***, in Lowther Hills, 2m/3km SW of Elvanfoot. Height 2027 feet or 618 metres. NS9315.
Louther Skerry *Ork.* ***Island***, one of Pentland Skerries, lying between Little Skerry and Clettack Skerry. ND4777.
Lovaig Bay *High.* ***Bay***, 1km SW of Rubha Maol, Skye. **57 F4** NG2355.
Low Ballivain *Arg. & B.* ***Settlement***, on N edge of Machrihanish Bay, Kintyre, 5m/7km NW of Campbeltown. **12 B3** NR6525.
Low Blantyre *S.Lan.* ***Suburb***, to E of Blantyre town centre. NS6957.
Low Craighead *S.Ayr.* ***Settlement***, 3m/5km NE of Girvan. **14 A5** NS2301.
Low Stillaig *Arg. & B.* ***Settlement***, on SW tip of Cowal peninsula, 4m/6km SW of Tighnabruaich. **22 A3** NR9267.
Low Torry *Fife* ***Locality***, 3m/4km E of Culross. **25 E1** NT0186.
Low Waters *S.Lan.* ***Suburb***, S district of Hamilton. **24 B4** NS7253.
Lower Auchalick *Arg. & B.* ***Settlement***, on W coast of Cowal, 4m/6km W of Tighnabruaich. **22 A2** NR9174.
Lower Banavie *High.* ***Locality***, adjacent to Banavie in Lochaber district, beside Caledonian Canal, 2m/3km N of Fort William. Series of locks on canal. NN1177.
Lower Barvas *W.Isles* ***Settlement***, on Isle of Lewis, 1km W of Barvas. NB3549.
Lower Bayble *W.Isles Anglicised form of Pabail Iarach, qv.*
Lower Breakish *High.* ***Settlement***, on Skye, to N of Broadford, on inlet of Ob Breakish. **48 C2** NG6723.
Lower Camster *High.* ***Settlement***, 1km N of Grey Cairns of Camster. **77 E4** ND2545.
Lower City Mills *P. & K.* ***Other feature of interest***, working Victorian oatmeal mill in central Perth. Massive internal waterwheel and exhibition telling story of Perth town mills. **33 G2** NO1023.
Lower Diabaig *High.* ***Settlement***, with landing stage on Loch Diabaig, arm on NE side of larger Loch Torridon, Ross and Cromarty district. **59 D3** NG8160.
Lower Gledfield *High.* ***Hamlet***, in Sutherland district, 1m/2km W of Bonar Bridge. **72 A5** NH5990.
Lower Glendevon Reservoir *P. & K.* ***Reservoir***, near head of Glen Devon, to W of Glendevon. NN9304.
Lower Halistra *High.* ***Settlement***, adjoining Upper Halistra, 5m/8km S of Vaternish Point, Skye. NG2459.
Lower Kilchattan *Arg. & B.* ***Settlement***, adjoining to SW of Upper Kilchattan. **28 C5** NR3694.
Lower Killeyan *Arg. & B.* ***Locality***, on W side of The Oa, Islay, 1m/2km N of Mull of Oa. **20 A5** NR2743.
Lower Kinchrackine *Arg. & B.* ***Locality***, in Strath of Orchy in Argyll, 1m/2km W of Dalmally. NN1527.
Lower Largo *Fife* ***Village***, on Largo Bay, 2m/4km NE of Leven. Forms locality of Largo with adjacent village of Upper Largo. **34 C4** NO4202.
Lower Milovaig *High.* ***Settlement***, on Skye, forming locality of Milovaig, along with Upper Milovaig, 6m/10km W of Dunvegan. NG1450.
Lower Oakfield *Fife* ***Suburb***, S district of Kelty. **33 G5** NT1493.
Lower Ollach *High.* ***Settlement***, on Skye, nearly 1m/2km NW of Ollach. **48 B1** NG5137.
Lower Shader *W.Isles Anglicised form of Siadar Iarach, qv.*
Lower Whitehall *Ork.* ***Locality***, adjoining to E of Whitehall, Stronsay. HY6628.
Lowertown *Ork.* ***Settlement***, on N coast of South Ronaldsay, 1m/2km NW of St. Margaret's Hope. ND4394.
Lowlandman's Bay *Arg. & B.* ***Bay***, with landing stage on E coast of Jura, 4m/6km S of Lagg. Long rocky promontory on SE side almost closes entrance. **21 D2** NR5672.
Lownie Moor *Angus* ***Hamlet***, 2m/3km SE of Forfar. **42 C5** NO4848.
Lowther Hill *S.Lan.* ***Mountain***, on border with Dumfries & Galloway, 7m/11km E of Sanquhar. Second highest of Lowther Hills. Mast at summit. Height 2378 feet or 725 metres. See also Green Lowther. **15 G4** NS8810.
Lowther Hills ***Large natural feature***, mountain range forming part of Southern Uplands, framed by Nithsdale to W, Tweeddale and Annandale to E. Range is traversed by Roman Roads with notable Mennock and Dalveen Passes. Former centre of lead mining, especially to N of range around Wanlockhead and Leadhills. Southern Upland Way lies along part of range, including Lowther Hill, second highest peak at 2378 feet or 725 metres. Other notable peaks are Green Lowther at 2401 feet or 732 metres; East Mount Lowther, with its excellent viewpoint at 2070 feet or 631 metres; and Ballencleuch Law at 2266 feet or 691 metres. **15 G4** NS8615.
Loy *High.* ***River***, in Lochaber district rising on Locheil Forest and running SE down Glen Loy into River Lochy 2m/4km SW of Gairlochy. NN1581.
Loyne *High.* ***River***, rising on E slopes of Glenquoich Forest and flowing N, then E into Loch Loyne. **49 G4** NH0706.
Lùb a' Sgiathain *High.* ***Bay***, on N coast of Skye, to E of Rubha Hunish. NG4176.
Lùb Score *High. Alternative name for Score Bay, qv.*
Lubachoinnich *High.* ***Settlement***, in Strath Cuileannach, 5m/8km SW of Invercassley. **71 G5** NH4195.
Lubcroy *High.* ***Settlement***, near confluence of River Oykel and Garbh Allt. **71 F4** NC3501.
Lubfearn *High.* ***Settlement***, 5m/8km N of Gorstan. **60 C2** NH3870.
Lubmore *High.* ***Settlement***, at W end of Loch a' Chroisg, 4m/6km W of Achnasheen. **59 G4** NH0958.
Lubreoch *P. & K.* ***Settlement***, in Glen Lyon, adjacent to dam at E end of Loch Lyon. **39 G5** NN4441.
Luce Bay *D. & G.* ***Bay***, large bay on S coast of Scotland, extending E from Mull of Galloway to Burrow Head, and N to mouth of Water of Luce. **2 B2** NX2244.
Lucklaw Hill *Fife* ***Hill***, 2m/3km W of Leuchars. Height 623 feet or 190 metres. NO4121.
Lucklawhill *Fife* ***Settlement***, below Lucklaw Hill, 2m/3km W of Leuchars. **34 C2** NO4221.
Ludac *W.Isles Anglicised form of Ludag, qv.*
Ludag (Anglicised form: Ludac.) *W.Isles* ***Village***, on S coast of South Uist, 1m/2km E of Cille Bhrighde. Ferry for pedestrians to Eriskay. **44 C2** NF7714.
Luffness *E.Loth.* ***Locality***, to NE of Aberlady, 5m/8km SW of North Berwick. **26 B1** NT4780.
Luffness Castle *E.Loth.* ***Castle***, on S side of Aberlady Bay, W of Luffness. 16c house with castle inside fortifications. **26 B1** NT4680.
Luffness Convent *E.Loth.* ***Ecclesiastical building***, 1m/2km E of Aberlady. **26 B1** NT4580.
Lugar *E.Ayr.* ***Village***, 2m/3km E of Cumnock. **15 D3** NS5921.
Lugar Water *E.Ayr.* ***River***, running W past Lugar and Cumnock to Ochiltree, then N to River Ayr 1m/2km S of Mauchline. **14 D3** NS4925.
Lugate Water *Sc.Bord.* ***River***, arising from numerous streams in mountains W of Stow, and flowing SE into Gala Water, 1m/2km S of Stow. **26 B5** NT4543.
Luggate *E.Loth.* ***Hamlet***, 2m/3km S of East Linton. NT5974.
Luggate Burn *E.Loth.* ***Hamlet***, S of Luggate, 1m/2km W of Stenton. NT5974.
Luggie Water ***River***, rising on hills S of Cumbernauld, past which river flows, before joining River Kelvin at Kirkintilloch. NS6574.
Luggiebank *N.Lan.* ***Suburb***, 1m/2km S of Cumbernauld town centre. **24 B2** NS7672.
Lugton *E.Ayr.* ***Village***, 4m/7km N of Stewarton. **23 F4** NS4152.
Lui Water *Aber.* ***River***, running SE down Glen Lui to River Dee, 5m/8km W of Braemar. **52 C5** NO0789.
Luib *High.* ***Settlement***, on S shore of Loch Ainort, Skye. **48 B2** NG5627.
Luibeilt *High.* ***Settlement***, in Mamore Forest, 6m/10km NE of Kinlochleven. **39 E3** NN2668.
Luineag *High.* ***River***, flowing W from Loch Morlich and into River Druie at Coylumbridge. **52 B4** NH9110.
Luing *Arg. & B.* ***Island***, lying between Seil and Scarba, 6m/9km long N to S and about 1km wide. Formerly noted for slate-quarrying. **29 G3** NM7410.
Luinga Bheag *High.* ***Island***, to NE of Luinga Mhòr, off W coast of Lochaber district, 3m/4km W of Arisaig. NM6187.
Luinga Mhòr *High.* ***Island***, small uninhabited island off W coast of Lochaber district, 3m/5km W of Arisaig. **37 E1** NM6085.
Luinne Bheinn *High.* ***Mountain***, in Knoydart, Lochaber district, 3m/4km S of Barrisdale. Munro: height 3080 feet or 939 metres. **49 E4** NG8600.
Lumphanan *Aber.* ***Village***, 9m/15km NW of Banchory. Macbeth is reputed to have died here; commemorative cairn 1km NW. Peel Ring of Lumphanan (Historic Scotland), 1km SW, site of medieval castle. **54 A4** NJ5703.
Lumphinnans *Fife* ***Locality***, between Cowdenbeath and Lochgelly. **33 G5** NT1792.
Lumsdaine *Sc.Bord.* ***Hamlet***, 3m/5km NW of Coldingham. **27 F3** NT8769.
Lumsden *Aber.* ***Village***, 4m/6km S of Rhynie. St. Mary's Kirk (Historic Scotland) at Auchindoir, 2m/3km N. **53 G2** NJ4721.
Lunan *Angus* ***Village***, small village near mouth of Lunan Water, 4m/7km SW of Montrose. **43 E4** NO6851.
Lunan Bay *Angus* ***Bay***, 4m/7km S of Montrose. **43 F4** NO6951.
Lunan Burn *P. & K.* ***River***, rising on Craig More, 3m/4km NE of Dunkeld, and flowing E through a series of five small lochs to River Isla, 3m/4km NE of confluence of River Isla with River Tay. **41 G5** NO1839.
Lunan Castle *Angus* ***Castle***, ruin overlooking Lunan Bay. NO6951.
Lunan Water *Angus* ***River***, running E to Lunan Bay, 4m/7km S of Montrose. **43 E5** NO6951.
Lunanhead *Angus* ***Village***, 1m/2km NE of Forfar. **42 C4** NO4752.
Luncarty *P. & K.* Population: 1190. ***Village***, 4m/7km N of Perth. Site of battle of 990 in which Scots defeated Danes. **33 F2** NO0929.
Lund *Shet.* ***Settlement***, overlooking Lunda Wick, on W coast of Unst. **85 E2** HP5703.
Lunda Wick *Shet.* ***Bay***, on W coast of Unst, 2m/4km NW of Uyeasound. HP5604.
Lundavra *High.* ***Settlement***, on N shore of Lochan Lùnn Dà-Bhrà, 4m/7km NE of North Ballachulish. **38 C3** NN0866.
Lunderston Bay *Inclyde* ***Bay***, W facing bay on Firth of Clyde, 1m/2km N of Inverkip. **22 C2** NS2073.
Lunderton *Aber.* ***Settlement***, 3m/4km NW of Peterhead. **65 G5** NK1049.
Lundie *Angus* ***Village***, 3m/5km S of Newtyle. **34 A1** NO2936.
Lundie *High.* ***Locality***, on N shore of Loch Cluanie, 10m/15km W of Dalchreichart. **50 A3** NH1410.
Lundin Links *Fife* Population: 2375. ***Village***, on Largo Bay, on W side of Lower Largo. Three large standing stones on golf-course to N of A915 road. **34 C4** NO4002.
Lundy *High.* ***River***, in Lochaber district, running W into River Lochy 2m/3km NE of Fort William. NN1276.
Lunga *Arg. & B.* ***Island***, largest island in Treshnish Isles group, situated at mid point of chain. Its summit, Cruachan, is also highest point of Treshnish Isles; 337 feet or 103 metres. **36 B5** NM2741.
Lunga *Arg. & B.* ***Island***, uninhabited island immediately N of Scarba, and W of Luing across Sound of Luing. Area about 500 acres or 200 hectares. **29 F4** NM7008.
Lunga *Arg. & B.* ***Settlement***, 3m/4km S of Arduaine. **29 G4** NM7906.
Lunna *Shet.* ***Village***, on Mainland, on narrow neck of land between two small bays of East and West Lunna Voe, 4m/6km SW of Lunna Ness. **83 D1** HU4869.
Lunna Holm *Shet.* ***Island***, small uninhabited island off Lunna Ness on NE coast of Mainland. **85 E5** HU5274.
Lunna Ness *Shet.* ***Coastal feature***, peninsula on E coast of Mainland, extending NE to its headland 4m/6km NE of Lunna. **85 E5** HU5071.
Lunnasting *Shet.* ***Locality***, district of Mainland, extending S from Lunna Ness to Dury Voe on E coast. **83 D1** HU4765.
Lunning *Shet.* ***Settlement***, near E coast of Mainland, 4m/7km NE of Laxo. **83 E1** HU5066.
Lunning Head *Shet.* ***Coastal feature***, headland to NE of Lunning, Mainland. HU5167.

Lunning Sound *Shet.* ***Sea feature***, sea passage between Mainland and West Linga, to S of Lunning. **83 E1** HU5066.
Lunnister *Shet.* ***Settlement***, on Mainland, 1m/2km S of Sullom, on W side of Sullom Voe. HU3471.
Lurg Hill *Moray* ***Mountain***, 5m/8km W of Cornhill. Height 1027 feet or 313 metres. **64 A4** NJ5057.
Lurg Mhòr *High.* ***Mountain***, on border of Skye and Lochalsh and Ross and Cromarty districts, 6m/10km SE of Achnashellach Station. Munro: height 3234 feet or 986 metres. **59 G5** NH0640.
Lurg Moor *Inclyde* ***Open space***, moorland 2m/3km SE of Greenock. **23 D2** NS2973.
Lurignich *Arg. & B.* ***Settlement***, on SE shore of Loch Linnhe, 3m/4km NE of Portnacroish. **38 B4** NM9451.
Luskentyre *W.Isles Anglicised form of Losgaintir, qv.*
Luss *Arg. & B.* ***Village***, on W shore of Loch Lomond, 8m/12km S of Tarbet. **31 F5** NS3592.
Luss Water *Arg. & B.* ***River***, rising on S slope of Cruach an t-Sithein and running down Glen Luss into Loch Lomond on S side of Luss. NS3692.
Lussa *Arg. & B.* ***River***, on Mull, running E down Glen More to head of Loch Spelve. NM6930.
Lussa *Arg. & B.* ***River***, on Jura, running S to Lussa Bay on E coast. **29 F5** NR6486.
Lussa Bay *Arg. & B.* ***Bay***, on E coast of Jura, just E of Lussagiven. NR6486.
Lussa Loch *Arg. & B.* ***Lake/loch***, large loch in Kintyre 5m/8km N of Campbeltown. **12 C2** NR7130.
Lussa Point *Arg. & B.* ***Coastal feature***, headland to E of Lussa Bay, on E coast of Jura. **21 E1** NR6486.
Lussagiven *Arg. & B.* ***Settlement***, on E coast of Jura, 3m/5km NE of Tarbert. **21 E1** NR6386.
Lusta *High.* ***Village***, on Vaternish peninsula, Skye, 4m/7km SE of Ardmore Point. **57 F4** NG2756.
Luther Bridge *Aber.* ***Bridge***, road bridge over Luther Water, 2m/3km NW of Marykirk. Site of Roman camp nearly 1km E. NO6566.
Luther Water *Aber.* ***River***, rising in Drumtochty Forest and running S to River North Esk, 2m/3km W of Marykirk. **43 E3** NO6566.
Luthermuir *Aber.* ***Village***, on W side of Luther Water, 3m/4km NW of Marykirk. **43 E3** NO6568.
Luthrie *Fife* ***Village***, 4m/7km NW of Cupar. **34 B3** NO3319.
Lybster *High.* ***Settlement***, 6m/9km W of Thurso. **76 C2** ND0268.
Lybster *High.* ***Village***, in Caithness district, 12m/20km SW of Wick. **77 E5** ND2435.
Lymekilns *S.Lan.* ***Suburb***, to NW of East Kilbride town centre. **24 A4** NS6254.
Lynaberack *High.* ***Settlement***, in valley of River Tromie, 4m/6km S of Kingussie. **51 G5** NN7694.
Lynchat *High.* ***Settlement***, in Badenoch and Strathspey district, 2m/3km NE of Kingussie. **51 G4** NH7801.
Lyndale Point *High.* ***Coastal feature***, headland on Loch Snizort, N coast of Skye, between entrances to Lochs Greshornish and Snizort Beag. **57 G4** NG3657.
Lyne *Aber.* ***Locality***, comprising Lyne of Linton and Mill of Lyne, 1m/2km S of Sauchen. **54 C4** NJ7008.
Lyne *Sc.Bord.* ***Settlement***, 3m/5km W of Peebles. Site of Roman camp. **25 G5** NT2041.
Lyne of Gorthleck (Also known as Gorthleck or Gorthlick.) *High.* ***Settlement***, on W side of Loch Mhòr, in Inverness district, 3m/5km E of Foyers. **51 E2** NH5420.
Lyne of Skene *Aber.* ***Village***, 4m/7km SW of Kintore. **54 C3** NJ7610.
Lyne Station *Sc.Bord.* ***Hamlet***, 3m/4km W of Peebles. **16 D2** NT2039.
Lyne Water *Sc.Bord.* ***River***, rising on Pentland Hills and flowing S to River Tweed 3m/4km W of Peebles. **25 F5** NT2139.
Lynedale House *High.* ***Settlement***, 3m/4km S of Lyndale Point, Skye. **57 G4** NG3654.
Lynegar *High.* ***Settlement***, to N of Loch Watten. **77 E3** ND2257.
Lynemore *High.* ***Settlement***, 3m/5km SE of Grantown-on-Spey. **52 C2** NJ0624.
Lynemore *Moray* ***Settlement***, in Glen Gheallaidh, 4m/6km SW of Upper Knockando. **52 D1** NJ1438.
Lyness *Ork.* ***Settlement***, with oil service base, on Hoy, opposite S end of Fara. **78 C3** ND3094.
Lynn of Lorn *Arg. & B.* ***Sea feature***, strait in Loch Linnhe between Lismore and mainland to E. **38 A5** NM8741.
Lynn of Morvern ***Sea feature***, strait in Loch Linnhe running between Morvern in Lochaber district, Highland, and Lismore, Argyll & Bute. **37 G5** NM7740.
Lyon *P. & K.* ***River***, running E from Loch Lyon down Glen Lyon to River Tay, 4m/6km W of Aberfeldy. **40 B5** NN7947.
Lyrabus *Arg. & B.* ***Settlement***, on Islay, 3m/5km NW of Bridgend. **20 A3** NR2964.
Lyrawa Burn *Ork.* ***River***, rising in central Hoy and flowing E to Lyrawa Bay on E coast. **78 B3** ND2599.
Lyth *High.* ***Settlement***, in Caithness district, 6m/10km SE of Castletown. **77 E2** ND2863.
Lythes *Ork.* ***Settlement***, on South Ronaldsay, 2m/4km S of St. Margaret's Hope. **79 D4** ND4589.
Lythmore *High.* ***Settlement***, 4m/6km SW of Thurso. **76 C2** ND0466.

M

Maari *W.Isles* ***Hill***, on North Uist, 3m/5km SE of Solas. Height 561 feet or 171 metres. **45 G2** NF8672.
Maaruig *W.Isles Anglicised form of Maruig, qv.*
Maaruig Island *W.Isles* ***Island***, tiny islet to E of Maruig in Loch Seaforth, North Harris. NB2006.
Mabie Forest *D. & G.* ***Forest/woodland***, 4m/7km SW of Dumfries. NX9370.
Mabie Hotel *D. & G.* ***Other building***, 4m/6km SW of Dumfries, at E side of Mabie Forest. **8 D3** NX9470.
Macaskin Island *Arg. & B. See Island Macaskin.*
Macbeth's Hillock *Moray* ***Hill***, small hill 5m/8km E of Nairn. Height 161 feet or 49 metres. **62 B4** NH9557.
Macduff *Aber.* Population: 3894. ***Small town***, small fishing town on E side of Banff Bay, 1m/2km E of Banff. **64 C3** NJ7064.
Macduff's Castle *Fife* ***Castle***, late 14c ruin on E side of East Wemyss, supposed former stronghold of Thanes of Fife. **34 B5** NT3497.
Macedonia *Fife* ***Suburb***, W district of Glenrothes. NO2501.
Macgregor's Leap *P. & K.* ***Other feature of interest***, narrowest point in Pass of Lyon, in Glen Lyon, 1m/2km W of Fortingall. NN7247.
Machan *S.Lan.* ***Locality***, adjoining to S of Larkhall. **24 B4** NS7650.
Machany *P. & K.* ***Settlement***, 3m/5km NE of Auchterarder. **33 E3** NN9015.
Machany Water *P. & K.* ***River***, running E to River Earn 3m/4km N of Auchterarder. **32 D3** NN9412.
Macharioch *Arg. & B.* ***Settlement***, on Kintyre, 3m/5km E of Southend. **12 C5** NR7309.
Machir *Arg. & B.* ***Settlement***, on Rinns of Islay, 9m/13km W of Bridgend. **20 A3** NR2063.
Machir Bay *Arg. & B.* ***Bay***, on W coast of Islay, on S side of Coul Point. **20 A3** NR2063.
Machrie *Arg. & B.* ***River***, flowing E into Laggan Bay, Islay, 4m/7km NW of Port Ellen. **20 B5** NR3250.
Machrie *Arg. & B.* ***Settlement***, on Islay, 3m/5km NW of Port Ellen. **20 B5** NR3249.
Machrie *N.Ayr.* ***Locality***, on Machrie Bay, on W coast of Arran, 4m/6km N of Blackwaterfoot. **13 E2** NR8934.
Machrie Bay *N.Ayr.* ***Bay***, on W coast of Arran, 4m/6km N of Blackwaterfoot. **13 D2** NR8934.
Machrie Moor Stone Circles *N.Ayr.* ***Historic/prehistoric site***, remains of five Bronze Age stone circles (Historic Scotland) 3m/4km N of Blackwaterfoot on Arran, with standing stones up to 15 feet or 2.5 metres high, although some have fallen. Considered to be among most important sites of its kind in Britain. **13 E2** NR9132.
Machrie Water *N.Ayr.* ***River***, running W into Machrie Bay. **13 E2** NR8934.
Machrihanish *Arg. & B.* ***Village***, on Machrihanish Bay, on W coast of Kintyre, 5m/8km W of Campbeltown. **12 B4** NR6320.
Machrihanish Bay *Arg. & B.* ***Bay***, on W coast of Kintyre, 5m/8km W of Campbeltown. **12 B3** NR6320.
Machrihanish Water *Arg. & B.* ***River***, flowing W into bay on E side of Machrihanish village. NR6421.
Machrins *Arg. & B.* ***Settlement***, on Colonsay, 1m/2km W of Scalasaig. **28 C5** NR3693.
MacIntyre Monument *Arg. & B.* ***Other feature of interest***, 1m/2km SW of Dalmally. Monument to Duncan Ban MacIntyre (1724-1812), known as the Burns of the Highlands. **31 D2** NN1425.
Maclaurin Gallery and Rozelle House *S.Ayr.* ***Other feature of interest***, 18c Rozelle House situated in parkland 2m/3km S of Ayr. Maclaurin Gallery is housed in former stables and servant quarters; exhibitions of contemporary art, sculpture and crafts. Location of Ayrshire Yeomanry Museum. **14 B4** NS3319.
Maclean's Cross *Arg. & B.* ***Historic/prehistoric site***, 15c Celtic cross (Historic Scotland) at Baile Mòr, Iona. **28 B2** NM2824.
Maclean's Nose *High.* ***Coastal feature***, headland on S coast of Ardnamurchan peninsula in Lochaber district, 3m/5km SE of Kilchoan. **37 E3** NM5361.
Maclean's Towel (Also known as Tubhailt Mhic 'ic Eoghain.) *High.* ***Waterfall***, in Lochaber district 2m/4km N of Sallachan Point on Loch Linnhe. NM9964.
MacLellan's Castle *D. & G.* ***Castle***, elegant 16c L-plan castellated and turreted mansion (Historic Scotland) overlooking harbour in Kirkcudbright. Ruined since 1752; complete except for roof. **8 A5** NX6851.
MacLeod's Maidens *High.* ***Coastal feature***, three rocks off Idrigill Point on SW coast of Skye. **47 F1** NG2436.
Macleod's Table North *High. Alternative name for Healabhal Mhòr, qv.*
Macleod's Table South *High. Alternative name for Healabhal Bheag, qv.*
Macmerry *E.Loth.* Population: 1173. ***Village***, 2m/3km E of Tranent. **26 B2** NT4372.
Macmillan's Cross *Arg. & B. See Kilmory Chapel.*
Macphee's Hill *W.Isles* ***Hill***, on Mingulay, overlooking NE coast. Height 735 feet or 224 metres. **44 A5** NL5684.
Macringan's Point *Arg. & B.* ***Coastal feature***, headland on E coast of Kintyre on N side of entrance to Campbeltown Loch. NR7521.
Macterry *Aber.* ***Settlement***, 3m/5km NE of Fyvie. **64 C5** NJ7842.
Madderty *P. & K.* ***Locality***, 5m/9km E of Crieff. **33 E2** NN9521.
Maddiston *Falk.* ***Village***, 4m/6km W of Linlithgow. **24 D2** NS9476.
Made in Scotland *High.* ***Other feature of interest***, craft centre at Beauly producing gifts, crafts, jewellery, knitwear and textiles. Hosts Scotland's International Trade Fair and Highland Trade Fair. **61 E5** NH5246.
Mae Ness *Ork.* ***Coastal feature***, headland at easternmost point of Egilsay. **80 C3** HY4831.
Maes Howe *Ork.* ***Historic/prehistoric site***, site of Neolithic communal burial-chamber (Historic Scotland) near S end of Loch of Harray 3m/4km W of Finstown, Mainland. Viking runes carved on walls. Reputed to be finest megalithic tomb in British Isles. **80 B5** HY3112.
Maggieknockater *Moray* ***Locality***, 2m/3km E of Craigellachie. **63 F5** NJ3145.
Maghannan *W.Isles* ***Open space***, hillslope below Beinn Mheadhonach, 3m/4km E of head of Loch Tamanavay. **68 B5** NB0721.
Magillie Loch *D. & G. Alternative name for Loch Magillie, qv.*
Magus Muir *Fife* ***Settlement***, 1m/2km SW of Strathkinness. **34 C3** NO4515.
Maich Water *Renf.* ***River***, rising on SE slopes of Misty Law and flowing SE to Kilbirnie Loch. **23 E3** NS3355.
Maiden Island *Arg. & B.* ***Island***, islet 1m/2km N of Oban, Argyll. **30 A1** NM8431.
Maiden Pap *High.* ***Mountain***, 3m/4km E of Morven. Height 1588 feet or 484 metres. **73 F2** ND0429.
Maiden Paps *Sc.Bord.* ***Mountain***, 3m/4km SW of Shankend. Height 1676 feet or 511 metres. **17 F5** NT5002.
Maiden Stone *Aber.* ***Historic/prehistoric site***, 10 foot high 9c red granite Pictish symbol stone (Historic Scotland), 2m/3km E of Oyne. Pictish symbols carved on one side, Celtic cross on other. **54 C2** NJ7024.
Maidenhead Bay *S.Ayr.* ***Bay***, between Culzean and Turnberry. **14 A5** NS2108.
Maidens *S.Ayr.* ***Village***, fishing village on Maidenhead Bay, 5m/9km W of Maybole. **14 A5** NS2107.
Maids of Bute *Arg. & B.* ***Coastal feature***, two rocks at N end of Bute near Buttock Point. NS0174.
Mail *Shet.* ***Settlement***, on E coast of Mainland, 1m/2km S of Starkigarth. **82 D5** HU4327.
Main Water of Luce *D. & G.* ***River***, rising 4m/7km SE of Ballantrae, and flowing S to join Cross Water of Luce at New Luce, to form Water of Luce. **6 C4** NX1764.
Mainland (Formerly known as Pomona.) *Ork.* ***Island***, largest island of Orkney group, being 26m/42km long from Brough Head in NW to Rose Ness in SE, and of irregular shape. Kirkwall, chief town of island and of group, is 24m/38km N of Duncansby Head on Scottish mainland across Scapa Flow and Pentland Firth. Kirkwall Airport 3m/4km SE of Kirkwall. **80 A5** HY4010.
Mainland *Shet.* ***Island***, largest island of Shetland, containing Lerwick, the capital, on E coast. Island is 56m/90km long N to S, and generally narrow E to W, being much indented by inlets or voes. **82 C1** HU4149.
Mains *S.Lan.* ***Suburb***, comprised of East Mains and West Mains, to N of East Kilbride town centre. NS6354.
Mains Castle *S.Lan.* ***Castle***, late 15c tower to N of East Kilbride. NS6256.
Mains of Ardestie *Angus* ***Hamlet***, 1m/2km N of Monifieth. **34 D1** NO5034.
Mains of Balhall *Angus* ***Hamlet***, 1m/2km SW of Kirkton of Menmuir. **42 D3** NO5163.
Mains of Ballindarg *Angus* ***Hamlet***, 2m/3km SE of Kirriemuir. **42 C4** NO4051.
Mains of Burgie *Moray* ***Settlement***, 3m/5km E of Forres. **62 C4** NJ0959.
Mains of Culsh *Aber.* ***Settlement***, 1m/2km N of New Deer. **65 D5** NJ8848.
Mains of Dillavaird *Aber.* ***Settlement***, 2m/3km NW of Glenbervie. **43 F1** NO7381.
Mains of Drum *Aber.* ***Settlement***, 5m/8km W of Peterculter. **54 D4** NO8099.
Mains of Dudwick *Aber.* ***Settlement***, 4m/7km W of Hatton. **55 E1** NJ9737.
Mains of Faillie *High.* ***Settlement***, 2m/3km SW of Daviot. **51 G1** NH7037.
Mains of Fedderate *Aber.* ***Settlement***, 3m/4km NW of Maud. **65 D5** NJ8950.
Mains of Glenbuchat *Aber.* ***Settlement***, on W side of River Don, 3m/5km NE of Strathdon. Ruins of Glenbuchat Castle, built 1590, nearby. **53 F3** NJ3914.

Mains of Linton *Aber.* ***Settlement***, 1km SE of Sauchen. **54 C4** NJ7010.
Mains of Melgund *Angus* ***Hamlet***, 3m/5km E of Finavon. **42 D4** NO5456.
Mains of Pitfour *Aber.* ***Settlement***, 1m/2km NW of Mintlaw. **65 E5** NJ9849.
Mains of Pittrichie *Aber.* ***Settlement***, 4m/6km SE of Oldmeldrum. **55 D2** NJ8624.
Mains of Sluie *Moray* ***Settlement***, on E bank of River Findhorn, 4m/6km SW of Forres. **62 C4** NJ0053.
Mains of Tannachy *Moray* ***Settlement***, near N coast, 1km W of Portgordon. **63 F3** NJ3863.
Mains of Thornton *Aber.* ***Settlement***, 2m/3km SE of Fettercairn. **43 E2** NO6871.
Mains of Tig *S.Ayr.* ***Settlement***, 3m/4km E of Ballantrae. **6 C2** NX1283.
Mains of Watten *High.* ***Settlement***, 1m/2km NE of Watten, on N side of Loch Watten. **77 E3** ND2456.
Mainsriddle *D. & G.* ***Settlement***, 2m/3km NW of Southerness. **8 D5** NX9456.
Maisgeir *Arg. & B.* ***Island***, rock island off SW coast of Gometra, Mull. **28 C1** NM3439.
Makerstoun *Sc.Bord.* ***Settlement***, 4m/6km W of Kelso. **18 A3** NT6732.
Malacleit (Anglicised form: Malaclete.) *W.Isles* ***Settlement***, on North Uist, 1m/2km SW of Solas. **45 F2** NF7974.
Malaclete *W.Isles Anglicised form of Malacleit, qv.*
Malasgair *W.Isles* ***Hill***, NE of head of Loch Seaforth, Isle of Lewis. Height 564 feet or 172 metres. **67 E2** NB2917.
Malcolm's Head *Shet.* ***Coastal feature***, headland on NW coast of Fair Isle. **82 A5** HZ1970.
Malcolm's Point *Arg. & B.* ***Coastal feature***, headland on S coast of Ross of Mull, 3m/5km SW of Carsaig. **29 D3** NM4918.
Maligar *High.* ***Settlement***, 1m/2km S of Staffin, Skye. **58 A3** NG4864.
Mallaig *High.* ***Town***, small fishing port and railway terminus on coast of Lochaber district at entrance to Sound of Sleat, and S of entrance to Loch Inver. Vehicle ferry to Armadale, Skye. **48 C5** NM6796.
Mallaigmore *High.* ***Settlement***, on N coast of North Morar, 1m/2km W of Mallaig. **48 D5** NM6997.
Mallaigvaig *High.* ***Locality***, on coast of Lochaber district, 1m/2km NE of Mallaig. **48 C5** NM6997.
Mallart *High.* ***River***, running N through Loch Choire into River Naver below Loch Naver in Caithness district. **75 F5** NC6737.
Malleny House *Edin.* ***Garden***, surrounding 17c house at Balerno. Garden (National Trust for Scotland) includes National Collection of Bonsai and display of shrub roses. **25 F3** NT1666.
Malleny Mills *Edin.* ***Hamlet***, 1km SE of Balerno. **25 F3** NT1665.
Malletsheugh *E.Renf.* ***Settlement***, 1km W of Newton Mearns. **23 G4** NS5255.
Mallie *High.* ***River***, in Lochaber district, rising on Locheil Forest and running E down Glen Mallie into S side of Loch Arkaig, 2m/3km W of foot of loch. NN1388.
Malling *Stir.* ***Settlement***, on W side of Lake of Menteith, 3m/4km E of Aberfoyle. **32 A4** NN5600.
Mam a' Chullaich *High.* ***Mountain***, 2m/3km N of Rubha an Ridire. Height 1515 feet or 462 metres. **37 G5** NM7443.
Mam na Gualainn *High.* ***Mountain***, in Lochaber district on N side of Loch Leven and 4m/7km W of Kinlochleven. Height 2611 feet or 796 metres. **38 D3** NN1162.
Mam nan Carn *P. & K.* ***Mountain***, 7m/12km S of Inverey. Height 3234 feet or 986 metres. NO0477.
Mam Ratagain *High. Alternative name for Mam Rattachan, qv.*
Mam Rattachan (Also known as Mam Ratagain.) *High.* ***Other feature of interest***, mountain pass, with road leading from foot of Glen Shiel in Skye and Lochalsh district, to foot of Glen More in Lochaber district. NG9019.
Mam Sodhail (Anglicised form: Mam Soul.) *High.* ***Mountain***, on border of Inverness and Skye and Lochalsh districts 3m/4km NW of Loch Affric. Munro: height 3870 feet or 1180 metres. **50 A2** NH1225.
Mam Soul *High. Anglicised form of Mam Sodhail, qv.*
Màm Suim *High.* ***Open space***, hillslope forming N shoulder of Stac na h-Iolaire, 3m/5km E of Loch Morlich. **52 C4** NJ0108.
Mambeg *Arg. & B.* ***Settlement***, on W shore of Gare Loch, 1m/2km SW of Garelochhead. **22 D1** NS2389.
Mamore Forest *High.* ***Open space***, mountain tract in Lochaber district between Kinlochleven and Glen Nevis. **38 D3** NN1765.
Manais (Anglicised form: Manish.) *W.Isles* ***Settlement***, on SE coast of South Harris, 8m/12km S of Tarbert. **66 D5** NG1089.
Mandally *High.* ***Locality***, containing settlements of Easter Mandally and Wester Mandally across River Garry from Invergarry. **50 B4** NH2900.
Manderston *Sc.Bord.* ***Historic house***, 2m/3km E of Duns. Edwardian country mansion with luxurious interior, unique silver staircase and marble dairy. Includes Biscuit Tin Museum. **27 F4** NT8154.
Maneight *E.Ayr.* ***Settlement***, below Maneight Hill, 4m/7km NE of Dalmellington. **14 D5** NS5409.
Mangaster *Shet.* ***Settlement***, in N part of Mainland, on N side of inlet of St. Magnus Bay called Mangaster Voe. **84 C5** HU3270.
Mangaster Voe *Shet.* ***Sea feature***, inlet of St. Magnus Bay in N part of Mainland. HU3270.
Mangersta *W.Isles Anglicised form of Mangurstadh, qv.*
Mangurstadh (Anglicised form: Mangersta.) *W.Isles* ***Settlement***, on W coast of Isle of Lewis, 6m/9km SW of Gallan Head. **68 B4** NB0031.
Manish *W.Isles Anglicised form of Manais, qv.*
Manish Island *High.* ***Island***, islet off Raasay to SW of Manish Point. NG5648.
Manish Point *High.* ***Coastal feature***, N facing headland on W coast of Raasay, Skye, at entrance to Loch Arnish. **58 B5** NG5648.
Manish Point *W.Isles* ***Coastal feature***, headland on North Uist, 2m/3km NE of Aird an Rùnair. **45 E2** NF7173.
Mannel *Arg. & B.* ***Settlement***, on Hynish Bay, Tiree, 1km S of Balemartine. **36 A2** NL9840.
Mannofield *Aberdeen* ***Suburb***, 2m/3km SW of Aberdeen city centre. **55 E4** NJ9104.
Manor Water *Sc.Bord.* ***River***, rising 2m/3km SE of Dollar Law in Ettrick Forest and running N to join River Tweed 1m/2km SW of Peebles. **16 D2** NT2239.
Mansewood *Glas.* ***Suburb***, 3m/5km SW of Glasgow city centre. NS5660.
Manxman's Lake *D. & G.* ***Sea feature***, arm of Kirkcudbright Bay on E side of St. Mary's Isle. NX6748.
Maodal *W.Isles* ***Hill***, on W coast of South Harris, 3m/4km NW of Leverburgh. Height 823 feet or 251 metres. **66 C4** NF9990.
Maoile Lunndaidh *High.* ***Mountain***, in Ross and Cromarty district 3m/5km N of Loch Monar. Munro: height 3303 feet or 1007 metres. **60 A5** NH1345.
Maol Bàn *Arg. & B.* ***Mountain***, 3m/5km SW of Rubha nan Sailthean, Mull. Height 1109 feet or 338 metres. **29 F2** NM6823.
Maol Breac ***Mountain***, on border of Stirling and Argyll & Bute, 4m/6km W of Ardlui. Height 2116 feet or 645 metres. **31 E3** NN2515.
Maol Buidhe *Arg. & B.* ***Hill***, on The Oa, Islay, 4m/7km W of Port Ellen. Height 541 feet or 165 metres. **20 A5** NR2945.
Maol Chean-dearg *High.* ***Mountain***, on Ben-damph Forest, Ross and Cromarty district, 5m/8km N of head of Loch Carron. Munro: height 3060 feet or 933 metres. **59 F4** NG9249.
Maol Chinn-dearg *High.* ***Mountain***, peak along ridge on border of Lochaber and Skye and Lochalsh district between Loch Quoich and head of Loch Cluanie. Munro: height 3218 feet or 981 metres. **49 G4** NH0308.
Maol Mòr *Stir.* ***Mountain***, 2m/3km NW of Stronachlachar. Height 2250 feet or 686 metres. **31 F3** NN3711.
Maol na Coille Mòire *Arg. & B.* ***Hill***, 3m/4km SW of Ben More, Mull. Height 945 feet or 288 metres. **29 D1** NM4929.
Maol nan Uan *Arg. & B.* ***Hill***, 1m/2km E of Pennyghael, Mull. Height 899 feet or 274 metres. **29 E2** NM5325.
Maol nan Uan *Arg. & B.* ***Mountain***, 3m/5km W of Duart Point, Mull. Radio mast. Height 1407 feet or 429 metres. **29 G1** NM7035.
Maol Odhar *High.* ***Mountain***, rising to over 790 metres, 2m/3km NE of Fuar Bheinn, Lochaber district. **38 B4** NM8857.
Maol Ruadh *High.* ***Inland physical feature***, ridge extending SE to Meall na h-Uamha, 3m/5km S of Port Henderson, in Ross and Cromarty district. **59 D3** NG7568.
Maolachy *Arg. & B.* ***Settlement***, 1m/2km SW of head of Loch Avich. **30 A3** NM8912.
Maovally *High.* ***Hill***, 3m/5km W of mouth of Kyle of Durness. Height 981 feet or 299 metres. **74 C2** NC3069.
Maovally *High.* ***Mountain***, 2m/3km SW of N end of Loch Shin. Height 1679 feet or 512 metres. **71 F2** NC3721.
Mar Forest *Aber.* ***Open space***, deer forest astride Glen Dee on S side of Cairngorm Mountains. **52 C5** NO0291.
Mar Lodge *Aber.* ***Hamlet***, 1m/2km NE of Inverey. **52 C5** NO0990.
Maratz Hill *S.Ayr.* ***Mountain***, rising to over 320 metres, 3m/5km SE of Straiton. **14 C5** NS4302.
March Burn *D. & G.* ***River***, rising on E side of Troston Hill, flowing SE to join New Abbey Pow 1m/2km E of New Abbey and just W of confluence with River Nith. NX9766.
Marchmont *Edin.* ***Suburb***, 1m/2km S of Edinburgh city centre. NT2572.
Marcus *Angus* ***Settlement***, 1m/2km E of Finavon. **42 D4** NO5157.
Mardington *Sc.Bord.* ***Locality***, 4m/6km NW of Berwick-upon-Tweed. NT9456.
Marg na Craige *High.* ***Mountain***, craggy summit, 5m/8km W of Newtonmore. Height 2736 feet or 834 metres. **51 F5** NN6297.
Margadale Hill *Arg. & B.* ***Hill***, near N end of Islay, 4m/7km NW of Port Askaig. Height 928 feet or 283 metres. **20 B2** NR3975.
Margnaheglish *N.Ayr.* ***Village***, on Lamlash Bay on E coast of Arran, adjoining to NE of Lamlash village. **13 F2** NS0331.
Margreig *D. & G.* ***Settlement***, at head of Glenkiln Reservoir, 3m/4km NW of Shawhead. **8 C3** NX8378.
Marishader *High.* ***Settlement***, 3m/5km S of Staffin Bay, Skye. **58 A3** NG4963.
Marjoribanks *D. & G.* ***Locality***, 1km N of Lochmaben. NY0883.
Markdhu *D. & G.* ***Settlement***, 6m/10km SW of Barrhill. **6 C3** NX1873.
Markethill *P. & K.* ***Settlement***, 1km SE of Coupar Angus. **34 A1** NO2239.
Markie Burn *High.* ***River***, stream in Badenoch and Strathspey district, running S into River Spey 1m/2km W of Laggan Bridge. NN5793.
Markinch *Fife* Population: 2176. ***Small town***, on E side of Glenrothes. 12c tower on St. Drosten's Church. **34 A4** NO2901.
Marnoch *Aber.* ***Settlement***, 2m/4km SW of Aberchirder. **64 A4** NJ5950.
Marrel *High.* ***Settlement***, in Sutherland district, 1m/2km N of Helmsdale. **73 F3** ND0117.
Marrister *Shet.* ***Settlement***, close to W coast of Whalsay, 1m/2km NE of Symbister. **83 E1** HU5463.
Marrival *W.Isles* ***Hill***, on North Uist, 3m/5km S of Solas. Height 754 feet or 230 metres. **45 G3** NF8070.
Marscalloch Hill *D. & G.* ***Mountain***, 3m/5km E of Carsphairn. Height 1250 feet or 381 metres. **8 A1** NX6192.
Marsco *High.* ***Mountain***, 3m/4km SW of head of Loch Ainort, Skye. Height 2414 feet or 736 metres. **48 B2** NG5025.
Marthig (Anglicised form: Marvig.) *W.Isles* ***Village***, near E coast of Isle of Lewis, 2m/3km S of entrance to Loch Erisort. **67 G2** NB4119.
Martnaham Loch *E.Ayr.* ***Lake/loch***, 5m/7km SE of Ayr. Remains of castle on islet in loch. **14 C4** NS3917.
Martyrs' Monument *D. & G.* ***Other feature of interest***, memorial stone in Wigtown to two 17c anti-Episcopalian women who were tied to stakes in River Bladnoch to drown in rising tide. **7 F5** NX4355.
Maruig (Anglicised form: Maaruig.) *W.Isles* ***Settlement***, on N side of Loch Maaruig, inlet on W side of Loch Seaforth, North Harris. **67 E3** NB1906.
Marvig *W.Isles Anglicised form of Marthig, qv.*
Marwick *Ork.* ***Settlement***, near W coast of Mainland, 4m/7km NW of Dounby. **80 A4** HY2324.
Marwick Head *Ork.* ***Coastal feature***, headland on NW coast of Mainland, 5m/8km NW of Dounby. Kitchener's Monument commemorates death of Lord Kitchener in 1916 when HMS Hampshire sank after striking a mine in these waters. **80 A4** HY2225.
Mary, Queen of Scots House *Sc.Bord.* ***Historic house***, 16c house where Mary, Queen of Scots stayed on visit to Jedburgh in 1566. Now museum and visitor centre detailing Mary's life and displaying some of her possessions. **18 A4** NT6520.
Marybank *High.* ***Settlement***, in Ross and Cromarty district, 3m/5km S of Strathpeffer. **61 D4** NH4853.
Maryburgh *High.* ***Village***, in Ross and Cromarty district, 2m/3km S of Dingwall. **61 E4** NH5456.
Maryculter *Aber. Alternative name for Kirkton of Maryculter, qv.*
Maryfield *Shet.* ***Settlement***, on W coast of Bressay, overlooking Bressay Sound towards Lerwick, on Mainland. **83 D3** HU4842.
Marygold *Sc.Bord.* ***Settlement***, 4m/7km NE of Duns. **27 F3** NT8160.
Maryhill *Aber.* ***Settlement***, 3m/5km SE of Cuminestown. **64 D5** NJ8245.
Maryhill *Glas.* ***Suburb***, 3m/4km NW of Glasgow city centre. Aqueduct carries Forth and Clyde Canal over River Kelvin. **23 G3** NS5668.
Marykirk *Aber.* ***Village***, on N side of River North Esk, 4m/6km SW of Laurencekirk. **43 E3** NO6865.
Marypark *Moray* ***Locality***, 5m/9km SW of Charlestown of Aberlour. **53 D1** NJ1938.
Maryport *D. & G.* ***Locality***, on Maryport Bay, 3m/4km N of Mull of Galloway. **2 B3** NX1434.
Maryport Bay *D. & G.* ***Bay***, 3m/4km N of Mull of Galloway. NX1434.
Maryton *Angus* ***Settlement***, 2m/4km W of Montrose. **43 E4** NO6856.
Marywell *Aber.* ***Hamlet***, 1m/2km N of Portlethen. **55 E5** NO9298.
Marywell *Aber.* ***Village***, 4m/6km SE of Aboyne. **54 A5** NO5895.
Marywell *Angus* ***Village***, 2m/3km N of Arbroath. **43 E5** NO6544.
Màs a' Chnoic-chuairtich *W.Isles* ***Mountain***, to W of Loch Ulladale, 5m/8km NE of Huisinis, North Harris. Height 1266 feet or 386 metres. **66 C2** NB0614.
Màs Garbh *W.Isles* ***Hill***, rising to over 300 metres, 1km SW of Loch Langavat, South Harris. **66 C5** NG0487.

M

Màs Sgeir *W.Isles* ***Island***, islet off W coast of Isle of Lewis, 2m/4km N of Great Bernera. NB1444.
Mashie *High.* ***River***, flowing NE from Beinn Eildhe into River Spey, 8m/12km SW of Newtonmore. **40 A1** NN6093.
Massacamber *W.Isles* ***Coastal feature***, headland on NE Berneray. **66 B5** NF9482.
Massacre of Glencoe 1692 *High.* ***Battle site***, where Macdonald clan of Glencoe were killed on orders of Sir James Dalrymple for being six days late in signing their peace with William III. Visitor centre tells story, and there are walks in the glen. **38 D4** NN1255.
Massan *Arg. & B.* ***River***, in Argyll, running SE down Glen Massan to River Eachaig, 2m/4km NW of head of Holy Loch. NS1484.
Mastrick *Aberdeen* ***Suburb***, 2m/4km W of Aberdeen city centre. **55 D4** NJ9007.
Mauchline *E.Ayr.* Population: 3931. ***Small town***, 8m/13km SE of Kilmarnock. Burns memorial 1km NW. **14 D3** NS4927.
Maud *Aber.* ***Village***, 3m/4km E of Old Deer and 13m/21km W of Peterhead. **65 E5** NJ9247.
Mauld *High.* ***Settlement***, in Strathglass, 6m/9km NE of Cannich. **50 C1** NH3938.
Mavis Grind *Shet.* ***Coastal feature***, narrow isthmus and former portage on Mainland between Sullom Voe and St. Magnus Bay. **82 C1** HU3468.
Maxton *Sc.Bord.* ***Village***, 5m/8km SE of Melrose. **18 A4** NT6130.
Maxwellheugh *Sc.Bord.* ***Village***, on S side of River Tweed, opposite Kelso. **18 B3** NT7333.
Maxwelltown *D. & G.* ***Suburb***, W part of Dumfries across River Nith. **9 D3** NX9676.
Maxwelton House *D. & G.* ***Historic house***, restored 14c-15c house, incorporating parts of 14c Glencairn Castle, 3m/5km E of Moniaive. House was 17c birthplace of Annie Laurie, immortalised in Scottish ballad of same name. **8 C2** NX8289.
May Wick *Shet.* ***Bay***, small N facing bay on W coast of Mainland, 1m/2km SE of South Havra. HU3724.
Mayar *Angus* ***Mountain***, 5m/9km W of Clova. Munro: height 3044 feet or 928 metres. **42 A2** NO2473.
Maybole *S.Ayr.* Population: 4737. ***Small town***, market town 8m/12km S of Ayr. Restored castle. Remains of 15c collegiate church (Historic Scotland). Former centre for weaving and shoe-making. **14 B5** NS3009.
Maybole Collegiate Church *S.Ayr.* ***Ecclesiastical building***, roofless ruin (Historic Scotland) of 15c church in Maybole, built for small college established in 1373 by John Kennedy of Dunure. **14 B5** NS3009.
Mayen *Moray* ***Settlement***, in loop of River Deveron, 2m/3km E of Milltown of Rothiemay. **64 A5** NJ5747.
Mayfield *Midloth.* Population: 12,103. ***Town***, 3m/4km SE of Dalkeith. **26 A3** NT3564.
Maywick *Shet.* ***Settlement***, on W coast of Mainland, at head of May Wick Bay. **82 C5** HU3724.
McArthur's Head *Arg. & B.* ***Coastal feature***, headland with lighthouse on E coast of Islay, at S end of Sound of Islay. **20 C4** NR4659.
McDougall's Bay *Arg. & B.* ***Bay***, on W coast of Jura, 1km S of Feolin Ferry. NR4468.
McFarquhar's Caves *High.* ***Cave***, group of caves on NE tip of Black Isle, 2m/3km SE of Cromarty. Natural sea arch, McFarquhar's Bed, lies at entrance to caves. **62 A3** NH8065.
McLean Museum and Art Gallery *Inclyde* ***Other feature of interest***, 1km NW of Greenock town centre, showing exhibits on James Watt, shipping, Egyptology and ethnography. **23 D2** NS2776.
McPhail's Anvil *Arg. & B.* ***Island***, one of Torran Rocks group, 4m/6km SW of Mull. **28 B3** NM2613.
Meabhag (Anglicised form: Meavag.) *W.Isles* ***Settlement***, on South Harris, 2m/4km S of Tarbert. **67 D4** NG1596.
Meadowmill *E.Loth.* ***Hamlet***, 1m/2km SE of Prestonpans. **26 B2** NT4073.
Meal Buidhe *High.* ***Mountain***, in Badenoch and Strathspey district, 5m/7km SE of Kingussie. Height 2060 feet or 628 metres. **51 G5** NN7995.
Meal Fuar-mhonaidh *High.* ***Mountain***, in Inverness district on NW side of Loch Ness, 6m/9km SW of Drumnadrochit. Height 2283 feet or 696 metres. **51 D2** NH4522.
Mealabost (Anglicised form: Melbost Borve.) *W.Isles* ***Settlement***, 1km N of High Borve, near NW coast of Isle of Lewis. **69 F2** NB4157.
Mealasta *W.Isles* ***Settlement***, on W coast of Isle of Lewis, 5m/9km NW of entrance to Loch Resort. **68 A5** NA9924.
Mealasta Island *W.Isles* ***Island***, uninhabited island, 1m/2km by 1km in extent, lying 1km off W coast of Isle of Lewis, 3m/4km S of Breanais. **68 A5** NA9821.
Mealdarroch Point *Arg. & B.* ***Coastal feature***, headland on W side of Loch Fyne, Argyll, 1m/2km E of Loch Tarbert. **21 G3** NR8868.
Mealisval *W.Isles* ***Mountain***, near W coast of Isle of Lewis 3m/5km W of S end of Loch Suainaval. Height 1883 feet or 574 metres. **68 B5** NB0227.
Meall a' Bhainne *High.* ***Mountain***, 1m/2km S of Glenfinnan, Lochaber district. Height 1834 feet or 559 metres. **38 B2** NM9078.
Meall a' Bhata *High.* ***Mountain***, to S of Loch Choire. Height 1906 feet or 581 metres. **72 B2** NC6326.
Meall a' Bhealaich *High.* ***Mountain***, 4m/6km E of Ben Griam Beg, Caithness district. Height 1105 feet or 337 metres. **76 A4** NC8940.
Meall a' Bhealaich *P. & K.* ***Mountain***, peak between Loch Ericht and Loch Ossian. Height 2827 feet or 862 metres. **39 G3** NN4569.
Meall a' Bhlàir *High.* ***Mountain***, in Lochaber district 2m/3km N of Loch Arkaig and 5m/7km S of dam of Loch Quoich. Height 2152 feet or 656 metres. **49 G5** NN0795.
Meall a' Bhobuir *P. & K.* ***Mountain***, in Rannoch district, 3m/5km SE of Bridge of Gaur. Height 2148 feet or 655 metres. **40 A4** NN5152.
Meall a' Bhràghaid *High.* ***Mountain***, at the head of Glen Oykel. Height 2257 feet or 688 metres. **71 E3** NC2914.
Meall a' Bhreacraibh *High.* ***Mountain***, in Inverness district, 5m/8km SE of Daviot. Height 1807 feet or 551 metres. **51 G1** NH7835.
Meall a' Bhroin *High.* ***Hill***, on S shore of Loch Sunart, 5m/8km E of Glenborrodale across the loch. Height 994 feet or 303 metres. **37 F4** NM6860.
Meall a' Bhrollaich *High.* ***Hill***, 2m/3km NE of Altnaharra, Sutherland district. Height 741 feet or 226 metres. **75 E5** NC5837.
Meall a' Bhuachaille *High.* ***Mountain***, on N edge of Glenmore Forest Park, in Badenoch and Strathspey district, 5m/8km N of Cairn Gorm. Height 2657 feet or 810 metres. **52 B3** NH9911.
Meall a' Bhùirich *High.* ***Mountain***, in Lochaber district, 4m/6km W of head of Loch Treig. Height 2755 feet or 840 metres. **39 E2** NN2570.
Meall a' Bhùiridh *High.* ***Mountain***, in Lochaber district, 1m/2km NE of Clach Leathad to E of Glen Etive. Munro: height 3634 feet or 1108 metres. **39 E4** NN2550.
Meall a' Chàise *High.* ***Mountain***, in Morvern, Lochaber district, 6m/9km N of Ardtornish. Height 1712 feet or 522 metres. **37 G4** NM7256.
Meall a' Chaorainn ***Mountain***, on border of Highland and Perth & Kinross, 3m/5km SE of Dalwhinnie. Height 2959 feet or 902 metres. **40 B1** NN6680.
Meall a' Chaorainn *High.* ***Mountain***, in Ross and Cromarty district, 2m/3km NW of Achnasheen. Height 2312 feet or 705 metres. **60 A3** NH1360.
Meall a' Chaorainn *High.* ***Mountain***, 4m/6km NE of Rubha an Ridire. Height 1578 feet or 481 metres. **37 G5** NM7644.
Meall a' Chaorainn Loch Uisge *High.* ***Mountain***, 1km S of Luch Uisge. Height 1679 feet or 512 metres. **38 A4** NM8053.
Meall a' Chathaidh *P. & K.* ***Mountain***, between Glen Garry and Glen Errochty. Height 1709 feet or 521 metres. **40 C3** NN7467.
Meall a' Chòcaire *High.* ***Mountain***, in Badenoch and Strathspey district, 4m/6km N of Kingussie. Height 2345 feet or 715 metres. **51 G4** NH7507.
Meall a' Choire Bhuidhe *P. & K.* ***Mountain***, 3m/5km NW of Spittal of Glenshee. Height 2847 feet or 868 metres. **41 F2** NO0670.
Meall a' Choire Chreagaich *P. & K.* ***Mountain***, 3m/4km SE of Kenmore. Height 2181 feet or 665 metres. NN7941.
Meall a' Choire Léith *P. & K.* ***Mountain***, 2m/3km NW of Ben Lawers. Munro: height 3037 feet or 926 metres. **40 B5** NN6143.
Meall a' Choirein Luachraich *High.* ***Mountain***, 3m/5km W of Inversander, Lochaber district. Height 1768 feet or 539 metres. **38 A4** NM8959.
Meall a' Chraidh *High.* ***Mountain***, 3m/4km from W side of Loch Eriboll. Height 1607 feet or 490 metres. **74 C3** NC3759.
Meall a' Chrasgaidh *High.* ***Mountain***, in Ross and Cromarty district, 1m/2km NW of Sgurr Mòr. Munro: height 3064 feet or 934 metres. **60 A2** NH1873.
Meall a' Chràthaich *High.* ***Mountain***, in Inverness district, 11m/18km SW of Drumnadrochit. Height 2227 feet or 679 metres. **50 C2** NH3622.
Meall a' Chuaille *High.* ***Mountain***, in Ross and Cromarty district, 12m/20km NW of Gorstan. Height 2060 feet or 628 metres. **60 C1** NH3482.
Meall a' Churain *Stir.* ***Mountain***, 6m/10km W of Killin. Height 3008 feet or 917 metres. **31 G1** NN4632.
Meall a Fheur Loch *High.* ***Mountain***, 2m/3km W of Loch Merkland. Height 2011 feet or 613 metres. **74 C5** NC3631.
Meall a' Ghiubhais *High.* ***Mountain***, 2m/3km W of head of Loch Maree, Ross and Cromarty district. Height 2880 feet or 878 metres. **59 F3** NG9763.
Meall a' Ghrianain *High.* ***Mountain***, on Inchbae Forest, Ross and Cromarty district, 2m/3km SE of head of Loch Vaich. Height 2532 feet or 772 metres. NH3677.
Meall a' Mhadaidh *Stir.* ***Inland physical feature***, mountain ridge rising to over 550 metres on N side of Loch Earn, 1m/2km NE of Lochearnhead. **32 B2** NN6026.
Meall a' Mhaoil *High.* ***Hill***, 3m/4km NE of head of Loch Ainort. Height 932 feet or 284 metres. **48 B1** NG5530.
Meall a' Mheanbhchruidh *High.* ***Mountain***, in Lochaber district 5m/8km N of middle of Loch Moy. Height 2680 feet or 817 metres. NN3989.
Meall a' Mhuic *P. & K.* ***Mountain***, 4m/6km S of Dall on S side of Loch Rannoch. Height 2444 feet or 745 metres. **40 A4** NN5750.
Meall a' Phiobaire *High.* ***Mountain***, 1km NE of Loch Beannach, Sutherland district. Height 1220 feet or 372 metres. **72 B3** NC6915.
Meall a' Phubuill *High.* ***Mountain***, on Locheil Forest, Lochaber district, 5m/8km NE of Kinlocheil. Height 2539 feet or 774 metres. **38 C1** NN0285.
Meall a' Phuill *P. & K.* ***Mountain***, 1m/2km N of E end of Loch an Daimh. Height 2880 feet or 878 metres. NN5048.
Meall Ailein *High.* ***Mountain***, 4m/6km SE of Altnaharra. Height 2365 feet or 721 metres. **75 F5** NC6131.
Meall A'irigh Mhic Craidh *High.* ***Mountain***, 2m/3km E of Gairloch, Ross and Cromarty district. Height 1145 feet or 349 metres. **59 E2** NG8377.
Meall an Aodainn *High.* ***Mountain***, in Lochaber district, 4m/6km S of Ballachulish. Height 2227 feet or 679 metres. **38 C4** NN0852.
Meall an Araich *Arg. & B.* ***Mountain***, in Argyll, 1m/2km N of Loch Dochard. Height 2837 feet or 865 metres. **39 E5** NN2143.
Meall an Doire Shleaghaich *High.* ***Mountain***, 4m/6km S of Kinlocheil, Lochaber district. Height 1335 feet or 407 metres. **38 B2** NM9873.
Meall an Fharaidh *Arg. & B.* ***Mountain***, with craggy E face, above NW shore of Loch Tarsan. Height 1309 feet or 399 metres. **22 B1** NS0786.
Meall an Fheidh *High.* ***Mountain***, 7m/11km E of Scamodale, Lochaber district. Height 1387 feet or 423 metres. **38 B2** NM9473.
Meall an Fheuraich *Arg. & B.* ***Mountain***, on S side of Glen Kinglass, 6m/9km N of Lochawe. Height 1151 feet or 351 metres. **30 C1** NN1036.
Meall an Fhìar Mhàim *Arg. & B.* ***Mountain***, 5m/8km W of Salen, Mull. Height 1066 feet or 325 metres. **37 D5** NM4843.
Meall an Fhiodhain *Stir.* ***Mountain***, at head of Kirkton Glen, 3m/4km NW of Balquhidder. Height 2594 feet or 791 metres. **32 A2** NN5224.
Meall an Fhuarain *High.* ***Hill***, 4m/6km NE of head of Loch Harport. Height 954 feet or 291 metres. **48 A1** NG4535.
Meall an Fhuarain *High.* ***Mountain***, 4m/7km SE of Loch Urigill, Ross and Cromarty district. Height 1896 feet or 578 metres. **71 E4** NC2802.
Meall an Fhuarain *High.* ***Mountain***, in Sutherland district, 4m/7km SW of Altnaharra. Height 1551 feet or 473 metres. **75 E5** NC5130.
Meall an Fhudair *Arg. & B.* ***Mountain***, in Argyll, 7m/11km NE of head of Loch Fyne. Height 2506 feet or 764 metres. **31 E3** NN2719.
Meall an Inbhire *Arg. & B.* ***Hill***, 3m/4km NW of Tobermory, Mull. Mast on summit. Height 866 feet or 264 metres. **37 D4** NM4656.
Meall an Spothaidh *High.* ***Mountain***, 1km S of Borgie Forest, Caithness district. Height 1207 feet or 368 metres. **75 F4** NC6649.
Meall an t-Seallaidh *Stir.* ***Mountain***, 3m/5km W of Lochearnhead. Height 2795 feet or 852 metres. **32 A2** NN5423.
Meall an t-Sithe *High.* ***Mountain***, in Ross and Cromarty district, 4m/6km W of Corrieshalloch Gorge. Height 1971 feet or 601 metres. **60 A2** NH1476.
Meall an t-Slamain *High.* ***Mountain***, in Ardgour, 2m/3km W of Fort William across Loch Linnhe. Height 1532 feet or 467 metres. **38 C2** NN0773.
Meall an Tarmachain *High.* ***Mountain***, on Ardnamurchan peninsula, 1m/2km N of Kilchoan. Height 1325 feet or 404 metres. **37 D3** NM4966.
Meall an Tuirc *High.* ***Mountain***, in Ross and Cromarty district on NE side of Loch Glass, 5m/9km NW of Evanton. Height 2050 feet or 625 metres. **61 E2** NH5372.
Meall an Uillt Chreagaich *High.* ***Mountain***, on Glenfeshie Forest, Badenoch and Strathspey district, 4m/7km E of Loch an t-Seilich. Height 2778 feet or 847 metres. NN8287.
Meall Aundrary *High.* ***Mountain***, 4m/6km SE of Gairloch, Ross and Cromarty district. Height 1079 feet or 329 metres. **59 E2** NG8472.
Meall Bàn *Arg. & B.* ***Mountain***, 3m/5km S of Duror. Height 2148 feet or 655 metres. **38 B5** NM9949.
Meall Beag *High.* ***Island***, one of two islets in Eddrachillis Bay off W coast of Sutherland district, 2m/4km offshore. **74 A5** NC1237.
Meall Bhalach *High.* ***Mountain***, on S side of Blackwater Reservoir, 5m/8km SE of Kinlochleven. Height 2322 feet or 708 metres. **39 E4** NN2557.
Meall Bhanabhie *High.* ***Mountain***, in Lochaber district, 3m/5km N of Fort William. Height 1073 feet or 327 metres. **38 D2** NN1178.
Meall Bhenneit *High.* ***Mountain***, on border of Ross and Cromarty and Sutherland districts, 7m/11km SW of Bonar Bridge. Height 1745 feet or 532 metres. **61 E1** NH5483.

Meall Breac *P. & K.* ***Mountain***, 6m/10km NE of Blair Atholl. Height 2214 feet or 675 metres. **41 E3** NN9668.

Meall Buidhe ***Mountain***, on border of Argyll & Bute and Perth & Kinross, 2m/3km W of head of Loch an Daimh. Height 2975 feet or 907 metres. **39 G4** NN4244.

Meall Buidhe *Arg. & B.* ***Mountain***, in Argyll 6m/10km N of Dalmally. Height 2043 feet or 623 metres. **31 D1** NN1837.

Meall Buidhe *Arg. & B.* ***Mountain***, on Kintyre, 8m/12km N of Campbeltown. Height 1227 feet or 374 metres. **12 C2** NR7332.

Meall Buidhe *High.* ***Mountain***, in Skye and Lochalsh district, 3m/5km S of Glenelg. Height 1594 feet or 486 metres. **49 E3** NG8014.

Meall Buidhe *High.* ***Mountain***, in Knoydart, in Lochaber district, 5m/8km E of Inverie on Loch Nevis. Munro: height 3103 feet or 946 metres. **49 E5** NM8498.

Meall Buidhe *P. & K.* ***Mountain***, 2m/3km N of Loch an Daimh. Munro: height 3054 feet or 931 metres. **39 G4** NN4949.

Meall Cala *Stir.* ***Mountain***, N of Glen Finglas Reservoir, 4m/7km NW of Brig o' Turk. Height 2211 feet or 674 metres. **32 A3** NN5012.

Meall Challibost *W.Isles* ***Coastal feature***, headland at southermost point of Scalpay. **67 E4** NG2294.

Meall Chuaich *High.* ***Mountain***, in Badenoch and Strathspey district 5m/9km NE of Dalwhinnie. Munro: height 3119 feet or 951 metres. **40 C1** NN7187.

Meall Coire Lochain *High.* ***Mountain***, in Lochaber district 2m/4km N of Clunes on NW shore of Loch Lochy. Height 2972 feet or 906 metres. NN2191.

Meall Coire nan Saobhaidh *High.* ***Mountain***, in Lochaber district 5m/8km N of Bunarkaig on Loch Lochy. Height 2693 feet or 821 metres. **50 A5** NN1795.

Meall Copagach *Arg. & B.* ***Mountain***, in Argyll 2km NE of Beinn Eunaich and 4m/7km N of Dalmally. Height 2657 feet or 810 metres. NN1534.

Meall Corranaich *P. & K.* ***Mountain***, 1m/2km W of Ben Lawers summit and 6m/9km NE of Killin. Munro: height 3506 feet or 1069 metres. **40 B5** NN6140.

Meall Cruaidh *High.* ***Mountain***, in Badenoch and Strathspey district, 4m/7km SW of Dalwhinnie. Height 2942 feet or 897 metres. **40 A1** NN5780.

Meall Cruinn *P. & K.* ***Mountain***, in Rannoch district, 8m/12km W of Bridge of Balgie. Height 2716 feet or 828 metres. **39 G5** NN4547.

Meall Cuanail *Arg. & B.* ***Mountain***, peak on S side of Ben Cruachan in Argyll, 1km from summit. Height 3004 feet or 916 metres. NN0629.

Meall Cuileig *High.* ***Mountain***, in Inverness district, 3m/5km N of Dalchreichart. Height 1453 feet or 443 metres. **50 B3** NH2716.

Meall Daill *P. & K.* ***Mountain***, on N side of Loch Lyon. Height 2857 feet or 871 metres. **39 G5** NN4143.

Meall Damh *High.* ***Mountain***, 3m/4km E of Ardtornish, Lochaber district. Height 1112 feet or 339 metres. **37 G5** NM7348.

Meall Dearg *High.* ***Mountain***, peak towards E end of Aonach Eagach, N of Glen Coe. Munro: height 3119 feet or 951 metres. **39 D4** NN1658.

Meall Dearg *P. & K.* ***Mountain***, 5m/8km SE of Aberfeldy. Height 2263 feet or 690 metres. **41 D5** NN8841.

Meall Dheirgidh *High.* ***Mountain***, in Sutherland district, 10m/16km SW of Lairg. Height 1663 feet or 507 metres. **71 G5** NH4794.

Meall Dhùin Croisg *Stir.* ***Mountain***, 3m/5km NW of Killin. Height 2457 feet or 749 metres. NN5437.

Meall Dola *High.* ***Mountain***, 2m/4km E of Lairg, to S of Loch Craggie. Height 1059 feet or 323 metres. **72 B4** NC6106.

Meall Dubh *Arg. & B.* ***Mountain***, 3m/5km N of Loch Tarsan. Height 1873 feet or 571 metres. **22 B1** NS0789.

Meall Dubh *High.* ***Mountain***, rounded summit in Ross and Cromarty district, 2m/4km E of Leckmelm. Height 2106 feet or 642 metres. **71 E5** NH2089.

Meall Dubh *High.* ***Mountain***, on border of Inverness and Lochaber districts, 3m/5km E of dam of Loch Loyne. Height 2585 feet or 788 metres. **50 B4** NH2407.

Meall Dubh *P. & K.* ***Mountain***, 5m/8km S of Aberfeldy. Height 2020 feet or 616 metres. **41 D5** NN8540.

Meall Dubhag *High.* ***Mountain***, in W part of Cairngorm Mountains, in Badenoch and Strathspey district, 8m/13km SE of Kingussie. Height 3273 feet or 998 metres. **52 A5** NN8895.

Meall Gaothar *High.* ***Mountain***, in Knoydart, Lochaber district, 4m/6km NW of Inverie. Height 1384 feet or 422 metres. **49 D4** NG7405.

Meall Garbh *Arg. & B.* ***Mountain***, in Argyll to E of Glen Kinglass, 6m/9km N of Dalmally. Height 2283 feet or 696 metres. **31 D1** NN1636.

Meall Garbh *High.* ***Mountain***, a peak of Aonach Eagach in Lochaber district, on N side of ridge towards Loch Leven. Height 2840 feet or 866 metres. NN1558.

Meall Garbh *High.* ***Mountain***, in Lochaber district 5m/9km NE of head of Loch Etive. Height 2299 feet or 701 metres. **39 D5** NN1948.

Meall Garbh *P. & K.* ***Mountain***, N shoulder of Ben Lawers. Munro: height 3667 feet or 1118 metres. **40 B5** NN6443.

Meall Garbh *P. & K.* ***Mountain***, in Rannoch district, 4m/7km S of Kinloch Rannoch. Munro: height 3175 feet or 968 metres. **40 B4** NN6551.

Meall Geal *W.Isles* ***Coastal feature***, headland on E coast of Isle of Lewis, 3m/5km N of Cellar Head. **69 G1** NB5660.

Meall Ghaordie ***Mountain***, on border of Perth & Kinross and Stirling, 1m/2km S of Stronwich Reservoir. Munro: height 3408 feet or 1039 metres. **32 A1** NN5139.

Meall Giubhais *High.* ***Mountain***, in Strathconon Forest, Ross and Cromarty district, 3m/5km S of Milton. Height 2171 feet or 662 metres. **60 C4** NH3050.

Meall Glas *Stir.* ***Mountain***, 5m/8km NE of Crianlarich. Munro: height 3139 feet or 957 metres. **31 G1** NN4332.

Meall Glass ***Mountain***, on border of Perth & Kinross and Stirling, 5m/8km N of Killin. Height 2886 feet or 880 metres. **32 A1** NN5639.

Meall Gorm *Aber.* ***Mountain***, 2m/3km N of Bridge of Dee. Height 2024 feet or 617 metres. **53 D5** NO1894.

Meall Gorm *High.* ***Mountain***, 5m/8km SE of Applecross, Ross and Cromarty district. Height 2329 feet or 710 metres. **59 D5** NG7740.

Meall Gorm *High.* ***Mountain***, in Ross and Cromarty district 2m/4km N of Fannich Lodge on N shore of Loch Fannich. Munro: height 3113 feet or 949 metres. **60 B3** NH2269.

Meall Gorm *High.* ***Mountain***, in Inverness district, 3m/5km NW of Drumnadrochit. Height 1355 feet or 413 metres. **51 D1** NH4834.

Meall Greigh *P. & K.* ***Mountain***, 3m/5km NE of Ben Lawers. Munro: height 3283 feet or 1001 metres. **40 B5** NN6743.

Meall Horn *High.* ***Mountain***, 1m/2km SE of Creagan Meall Horn. Height 2549 feet or 777 metres. **74 C4** NC3544.

Meall Leacachain *High.* ***Mountain***, in Ross and Cromarty district, 2m/4km E of Corrieshalloch Gorge. Height 2027 feet or 618 metres. **60 B2** NH2477.

Meall Leathad na Craoibhe *High.* ***Mountain***, 1m/2km SE of Tongue, Caithness district. Height 1017 feet or 310 metres. **75 F3** NC6155.

Meall Leathan Dhail *Stir.* ***Mountain***, 3m/5km NE of Callander. Height 1588 feet or 484 metres. **32 B3** NN6611.

Meall Liath Choire *High.* ***Mountain***, in Ross and Cromarty district, 7m/11km E of Ullapool. Height 1797 feet or 548 metres. **71 E5** NH2296.

Meall Liath Mòr *High.* ***Mountain***, 3m/5km SW of Loch Laggan. Height 1686 feet or 514 metres. **39 F1** NN4080.

Meall Lighiche *High.* ***Mountain***, 4m/6km S of Glencoe village. Height 2532 feet or 772 metres. **38 C4** NN0952.

Meall Loch Airigh Alasdair *High.* ***Mountain***, in Ross and Cromarty district, 2m/3km SE of Toscaig. Height 1155 feet or 352 metres. **48 D1** NG7436.

Meall Luaidhe *P. & K.* ***Mountain***, 2m/3km S of Bridge of Balgie. Height 2558 feet or 780 metres. **40 A5** NN5843.

Meall Meadhonach *High.* ***Mountain***, 3m/5km S of Durness. Height 1384 feet or 422 metres. **74 D2** NC4062.

Meall Mheannaidh *High.* ***Mountain***, 2m/3km N of Letterewe, Ross and Cromarty district. Height 2362 feet or 720 metres. **59 F2** NG9574.

Meall Mhic Iomhair *High.* ***Mountain***, rounded summit in Ross and Cromarty district, 6m/10km NW of Garve. Height 1991 feet or 607 metres. **60 C3** NH3167.

Meall Mòr ***Mountain***, on border of Angus and Perth & Kinross, 3m/4km SE of Cray. Height 1807 feet or 551 metres. **41 G3** NO1760.

Meall Mòr *Arg. & B.* ***Mountain***, on Knapdale, 4m/7km NW of Tarbert. Mast on summit. Height 1574 feet or 480 metres. **21 G2** NR8374.

Meall Mòr *High.* ***Island***, one of two islets in Eddrachillis Bay off W coast of Sutherland district, 2m/4km offshore. **74 A5** NC1237.

Meall Mòr *High.* ***Mountain***, in Ross and Cromarty district between Loch Glass and Loch Morie. Height 2421 feet or 738 metres. **61 E2** NH5174.

Meall Mòr *High.* ***Mountain***, in Inverness district, 3m/4km SE of Daviot. Height 1614 feet or 492 metres. **51 G1** NH7335.

Meall Mòr *High.* ***Mountain***, 3m/5km E of Scamodale, Lochaber district. Height 2490 feet or 759 metres. **38 A2** NM8872.

Meall Mòr *High.* ***Mountain***, 2m/3km S of Glencoe village. Height 2217 feet or 676 metres. **38 D4** NN1055.

Meall Mòr *Stir.* ***Mountain***, 1m/2km N of head of Loch Katrine. Height 2450 feet or 747 metres. **31 F3** NN3815.

Meall Moraig *High.* ***Mountain***, in Sutherland district, 4m/6km NE of Bonar Bridge. Height 1089 feet or 332 metres. **72 B5** NH6694.

Meall na Caorach *Arg. & B.* ***Hill***, rising to over 230 metres in Salen Forest, 3m/5km NW of Salen, Mull. **37 E5** NM5347.

Meall na Caorach *High.* ***Mountain***, rising above Berriedale Water, 3m/5km NW of Berriedale. Height 1299 feet or 396 metres. **73 F2** ND0927.

Meall na Dige *Stir.* ***Mountain***, 5m/9km W of Balquhidder. Height 3168 feet or 966 metres. NN4522.

Meall na Drochaide *High.* ***Mountain***, in Ross and Cromarty district, 9m/14km NE of Garve. Height 2309 feet or 704 metres. **61 E2** NH5069.

Meall na Duibhe *High.* ***Mountain***, 3m/4km E of Kinlochleven. Height 1870 feet or 570 metres. **39 E3** NN2262.

Meall na Faochaig *High.* ***Mountain***, in Ross and Cromarty district, 1m/2km N of Inverchoran. Height 2230 feet or 680 metres. **60 B4** NH2552.

Meall na Fhuaid *High.* ***Mountain***, 4m/7km SW of Ardheslaig, Ross and Cromarty district. Height 1699 feet or 518 metres. **58 D4** NG7350.

Meall na h-Aisre *High.* ***Mountain***, on border of Inverness and Badenoch and Strathspey districts, 10m/17km SE of Fort Augustus. Height 2827 feet or 862 metres. **51 E4** NH5100.

Meall na h-Eilrig *High.* ***Mountain***, in Inverness district, 3m/4km NE of Drumnadrochit. Height 1525 feet or 465 metres. **51 E1** NH5332.

Meall na h-Uamha *High.* ***Hill***, 3m/5km SE of Redpoint, Ross and Cromarty district. Height 945 feet or 288 metres. **59 D3** NG7765.

Meall na Leitreach *High.* ***Mountain***, 2m/3km S of Loch More. Height 1856 feet or 566 metres. **74 C5** NC3432.

Meall na Leitreach *P. & K.* ***Mountain***, on E side of Loch Garry. Height 2542 feet or 775 metres. **40 B2** NN6470.

Meall na Mèine *High.* ***Hill***, 3m/5km E of Poolewe. Height 823 feet or 251 metres. **59 F1** NG9081.

Meall na Moine *High.* ***Mountain***, 1m/2km NW of Creag Riabhach, Sutherland district. Height 1522 feet or 464 metres. **74 B2** NC2862.

Meall na Saobhaidhe *High.* ***Mountain***, 1m/2km SW of Beinn Damh, Ross and Cromarty district. Height 1207 feet or 368 metres. **59 E5** NG8748.

Meall na Speireig *High.* ***Mountain***, rising to over 610 metres, in Ross and Cromarty district, 2m/3km SE of Ben Wyvis. **61 D3** NH4966.

Meall na Suiramach *High.* ***Mountain***, 5m/8km SE of Rubha Hunish, Skye. Height 1781 feet or 543 metres. **58 A3** NG4469.

Meall na Teanga *High.* ***Mountain***, bounded by Allt Coire na Saighe Duibhe to N, and Allt an t-Srath a Dhuibh to S, the two main tributaries of River Mudale. Height 1197 feet or 365 metres. **75 D5** NC4834.

Meall na Teanga *High.* ***Mountain***, on NW side of Loch Lochy, 7m/11km N of Spean Bridge across the loch. Munro: height 3008 feet or 917 metres. **50 B5** NN2192.

Meall nam Bràdhan *High.* ***Mountain***, on borders of Ross and Cromarty and Sutherland districts, 6m/10km E of Leckmelm. Height 2221 feet or 677 metres. **71 E5** NH2690.

Meall nam Fiadh *P. & K.* ***Mountain***, 2m/3km N of St. Fillans. Height 2001 feet or 610 metres. **32 B2** NN6927.

Meall nam Fuaran *P. & K.* ***Mountain***, 5m/8km W of Amulree. Height 2640 feet or 805 metres. **32 D1** NN8236.

Meall nan Aighean *High.* ***Mountain***, 2m/3km SE of Loch Choire Lodge. Height 2276 feet or 694 metres. **72 B2** NC6828.

Meall nan Caorach *High.* ***Mountain***, in Inverness district, 4m/6km NW of Drumnadrochit. Height 1404 feet or 428 metres. **51 D1** NH4735.

Meall nan Caoraich *P. & K.* ***Mountain***, 9m/14km NW of Crieff. Height 2043 feet or 623 metres. **33 E1** NN9234.

Meall nan Ceapraichean *High.* ***Mountain***, in Ross and Cromarty district, 10m/16km SE of Ullapool. Munro: height 3205 feet or 977 metres. **60 B1** NH2582.

Meall nan Con *High.* ***Mountain***, summit of Ben Klibreck, situated 4m/6km S of Altnaharra, Sutherland district. Munro: height 3152 feet or 961 metres. **75 E5** NC5829.

Meall nan Con *High.* ***Mountain***, on Ardnamurchan peninsula, 3m/4km N of Kilchoan. Height 1433 feet or 437 metres. **37 E3** NM5068.

Meall nan Damh *High.* ***Mountain***, in Ross and Cromarty district, 6m/10km SW of Garve. Height 2201 feet or 671 metres. **60 C4** NH3552.

Meall nan Damh *High.* ***Mountain***, 4m/6km S of Glenfinnan, Lochaber district. Height 2371 feet or 723 metres. **38 B2** NM9174.

Meall nan Each *High.* ***Mountain***, 3m/4km N of Rubha na h-Airde Uinnsinn, Lochaber district. Height 1938 feet or 591 metres. **38 A4** NM8856.
Meall nan Eun *Arg. & B.* ***Mountain***, in Argyll 5m/8km E of head of Loch Etive. Munro: height 3037 feet or 926 metres. **39 D5** NN1944.
Meall nan Eun *High.* ***Mountain***, 2m/3km E of mouth of River Barrisdale, to S of Loch Hourn. Height 2184 feet or 666 metres. **49 F4** NG9005.
Meall nan Eun *P. & K.* ***Mountain***, 3m/5km NW of Fortingall. Height 2867 feet or 874 metres. NN7050.
Meall nan Gabhar *High.* ***Island***, small island in Summer Isles group, adjacent to and N of Horse Island, and nearly 1m/2km W of NW coast of Ross and Cromarty district to S of Polglass. NC0205.
Meall nan Ruadhag *High.* ***Mountain***, on NW side of Rannoch Moor, and S of Blackwater Reservoir. Height 2119 feet or 646 metres. **39 E4** NN2957.
Meall nan Sùbh *P. & K.* ***Mountain***, 1m/2km SE of dam of Loch Lyon. Height 2637 feet or 804 metres. **31 G1** NN4639.
Meall nan Tarmachan *P. & K.* ***Mountain***, 4m/6km N of Killin. Munro: height 3421 feet or 1043 metres. **32 A1** NN5839.
Meall nan Tighearn ***Mountain***, on border of Argyll & Bute and Stirling, 5m/9km SE of Dalmally. Height 2424 feet or 739 metres. **31 E2** NN2323.
Meall Odhar ***Mountain***, on border of Perth & Kinross and Stirling, 4m/7km N of Callander. Height 2119 feet or 646 metres. **32 B3** NN6415.
Meall Odhar *High.* ***Mountain***, in Lochaber district, 8m/13km NW of Bridge of Orchy. Height 2873 feet or 876 metres. **39 D5** NN1946.
Meall Odhar *P. & K.* ***Mountain***, on NE side of Loch Tay, 8m/12km SW of Kenmore. Height 1794 feet or 547 metres. **32 B1** NN6640.
Meall Reamhar *Arg. & B.* ***Mountain***, on Kintyre, 5m/8km W of Tarbert. Height 1565 feet or 477 metres. **21 F3** NR7768.
Meall Reamhar *Arg. & B.* ***Mountain***, on Knapdale, 2m/3km NW of Tarbert. Height 1079 feet or 329 metres. **21 G3** NR8369.
Meall Reamhar *P. & K.* ***Mountain***, to S of Loch Earn, 3m/5km SW of St. Fillans. Height 2224 feet or 678 metres. **32 B2** NN6621.
Meall Reamhar *P. & K.* ***Mountain***, rounded summit, 3m/5km N of Blair Atholl. Height 1853 feet or 565 metres. **41 D2** NN8670.
Meall Reamhar *P. & K.* ***Mountain***, on N side of Glen Almond, 3m/5km SW of Amulree. Height 2188 feet or 667 metres. **33 D1** NN8732.
Meall Reamhar *P. & K.* ***Mountain***, 9m/13km S of Pitlochry. Height 1660 feet or 506 metres. **41 E5** NN9346.
Meall Reamhar *P. & K.* ***Mountain***, 4m/7km NE of Ballinluig. Height 1752 feet or 534 metres. **41 F4** NO0356.
Meall Tairneachan *P. & K.* ***Mountain***, 5m/7km NW of Aberfeldy. Height 2558 feet or 780 metres. **40 D4** NN8054.
Meall Tarsuinn *Arg. & B.* ***Mountain***, on border of Argyll and Lochaber districts, nearly 1m/2km W of Meall nan Eun. Height 2870 feet or 875 metres. NN1744.
Meall Tarsuinn *High.* ***Mountain***, in Lochaber district, 5m/8km N of Achnacarry. Height 2165 feet or 660 metres. **50 A5** NN1696.
Meall Tarsuinn *P. & K.* ***Mountain***, 5m/8km N of Crieff. Height 2125 feet or 648 metres. **33 D2** NN8729.
Meall Taurnie ***Mountain***, on border of Perth & Kinross and Stirling, 6m/10km NW of Killin. Height 2578 feet or 786 metres. **31 G1** NN4838.
Meall Thailm *High.* ***Island***, islet off NW coast of Eilean Iosal. NC6266.
Meall Tionail *P. & K.* ***Mountain***, 1m/2km SE of head of Loch Lyon. Height 2936 feet or 895 metres. NN3937.
Meall Tòn Eich *Stir.* ***Mountain***, 4m/7km NW of Killin. Height 2673 feet or 815 metres. NN5538.
Meall Uaine *P. & K.* ***Mountain***, 2m/3km S of Spittal of Glenshee. Height 2604 feet or 794 metres. **41 G3** NO1167.
Meallach Mhòr *High.* ***Mountain***, in Badenoch and Strathspey district 6m/10km S of Kingussie. Height 2522 feet or 769 metres. **51 G5** NN7790.
Meallan a' Chuail *High.* ***Mountain***, rises steeply to N of Loch Dubh a' Chuail, 2m/3km E of Beinn Leòid. Height 2460 feet or 750 metres. **71 F2** NC3429.
Meallan Buidhe *High.* ***Mountain***, rounded summit in Inverness district, 1m/2km S of central part of Loch Monar. Height 1820 feet or 555 metres. **50 A1** NH1337.
Meallan Buidhe *High.* ***Mountain***, in Inverness district, 8m/13km N of Cannich. Height 2512 feet or 766 metres. **60 C5** NH3344.
Meallan Chuaich *High.* ***Mountain***, rounded summit in Ross and Cromarty district, 7m/11km NE of Kinlochewe. Height 2263 feet or 690 metres. **60 A3** NH1168.
Meallan Liath *High.* ***Mountain***, 2m/3km E of Ben Hope. Height 1971 feet or 601 metres. **75 E3** NC5150.
Meallan Liath Beag *High.* ***Mountain***, in Sutherland district, 5m/8km NW of Lothbeg. Height 1571 feet or 479 metres. **73 D3** NC8815.
Meallan Liath Coire Mhic Dhughaill *High.* ***Mountain***, in Reay Forest in Sutherland district, 2m/3km NE of Loch More. Height 2627 feet or 801 metres. **74 C5** NC3539.
Meallan Liath Mòr *High.* ***Mountain***, rises to E of Loch Merkland. Height 2240 feet or 683 metres. **74 D5** NC4032.
Meallan Liath Mòr *High.* ***Mountain***, in Ben Armine Forest, 2m/4km NE of Dalnessie. Height 1512 feet or 461 metres. **72 B3** NC6518.
Meallan nan Uan *High.* ***Mountain***, in Ross and Cromarty district, 3m/4km W of Milton. Height 2755 feet or 840 metres. **60 B4** NH2654.
Meallan Odhar *High.* ***Mountain***, in Inverness district, 2m/3km N of Sgurr na Lapaich. Height 1870 feet or 570 metres. **50 A1** NH1538.
Meallan Odhar *High.* ***Mountain***, rounded summit in Inverness district, 5m/8km N of E end of Loch Cluanie. Height 2004 feet or 611 metres. **50 B3** NH2117.
Meallan Odhar *High.* ***Mountain***, rounded summit in Inverness district, 3m/5km NE of E end of Loch Mullardoch. Height 2276 feet or 694 metres. **50 A1** NH2435.
Mealna Letter (Also known as Duchray Hill.) *P. & K.* ***Mountain***, 4m/6km SE of Spittal of Glenshee. Height 2299 feet or 701 metres. **41 G3** NO1667.
Mearns *E.Renf.* ***Locality***, adjoining to SE of Newton Mearns, 3m/5km NW of Eaglesham. **23 G4** NS5455.
Mearns Castle *E.Renf.* ***Castle***, dates from 15c, 1km E of Mearns. NS5555.
Meaul *D. & G.* ***Mountain***, towards N end of Rhinns of Kells, 4m/7km W of Carsphairn. Height 2280 feet or 695 metres. **7 G1** NX5090.
Meavag *W.Isles Anglicised form of Meabhag, qv.*
Meavaig *W.Isles Anglicised form of Miabhag, qv.*
Meavaig *W.Isles* ***River***, flowing S into Loch Meavaig, North Harris, on N side of West Loch Tarbert. NB1006.
Meavie Point *Aber.* ***Coastal feature***, headland at Banff on N coast. NJ6864.
Medwin Water ***River***, rising in Pentland Hills on N slopes of White Craig and flowing S, forming border between South Lanarkshire and Scottish Borders, before joining with other streams to become South Medwin River. **25 E4** NT0949.
Medwin Water *S.Lan.* ***River***, formed by confluence of North and South Medwin Rivers and flowing W to join River Clyde at The Meetings, 1m/2km S of Carnwath. **25 D5** NS9744.
Meffan Institute *Angus* ***Other feature of interest***, museum and art gallery at Forfar with Neolithic, Pictish and Celtic exhibits, and section on 17c witch-hunting. **42 C4** NO4650.
Meggat Water *D. & G.* ***River***, running S to River Esk, 6m/10km NW of Langholm. **10 A2** NY2991.
Meggernie Castle *P. & K.* ***Historic house***, mansion in Glen Lyon 2m/3km W of Bridge of Balgie. Has a 16c tower of the Menzies. NN5546.
Megget Reservoir *Sc.Bord.* ***Reservoir***, lies on course of Megget Water, 2m/3km W of Cappercleuch. **16 C3** NT2422.
Megget Water *Sc.Bord.* ***River***, running E from Megget Reservoir into St. Mary's Loch near Cappercleuch. NT2422.
Meggethead *Sc.Bord.* ***Settlement***, at W end of Megget Reservoir. **16 C3** NT1621.
Megginch Castle *P. & K.* ***Castle***, 16c castle in Carse of Gowrie, 1m/2km N of Errol. **34 A2** NO2424.
Meg's Craig *Angus* ***Coastal feature***, rock headland at N end of Castlesea Bay, 3m/5km NE of Arbroath. **43 E5** NO6843.
Meig *High.* ***River***, in Ross and Cromarty district, rising on West Monar Forest and running E to join River Conon 1m/2km below Loch Luichart. NH3956.
Meigle *P. & K.* ***Village***, 4m/6km SE of Alyth. Belmont Castle to S. Roman sites to N across Dean Water. **42 A5** NO2844.
Meigle Bay *N.Ayr.* ***Bay***, on Firth of Clyde 1m/2km S of Skelmorlie. **22 C3** NS1965.
Meigle Hill *Sc.Bord.* ***Mountain***, 1m/2km W of Galashiels. Height 1387 feet or 423 metres. **17 F2** NT4636.
Meigle Sculptured Stones *P. & K.* ***Historic/prehistoric site***, Christian and Pictish inscribed stones (Historic Scotland) in Meigle. Meigle Museum also houses around 30 stones from area, from 7c-10c. **42 A5** NO2844.
Meikle Balloch Hill ***Mountain***, on border of Aberdeenshire and Moray, 3m/4km E of Keith. Height 1200 feet or 366 metres. **63 G5** NJ4749.
Meikle Bin *Stir.* ***Mountain***, above Carron Valley Forest, on NE edge of Campsie Fells, 4m/6km N of Milton of Campsie. Height 1870 feet or 570 metres. **24 A1** NS6682.
Meikle Black Law *Sc.Bord.* ***Hill***, 3m/4km NE of Grantshouse. Height 804 feet or 245 metres. **27 F3** NT8268.
Meikle Carewe Hill *Aber.* ***Hill***, 5m/8km NW of Stonehaven. Height 872 feet or 266 metres. **54 D5** NO8292.
Meikle Conval *Moray* ***Mountain***, 3m/4km SW of Dufftown. Height 1866 feet or 569 metres. **53 E1** NJ2937.
Meikle Earnock *S.Lan.* ***Locality***, adjoining to S of Hamilton. **24 B4** NS7153.
Meikle Firbriggs *Moray* ***Mountain***, rising above E side of Black Water valley, 2m/3km NW of Cabrach. Height 1768 feet or 539 metres. **53 F2** NJ3528.
Meikle Grenach *Arg. & B.* ***Settlement***, on Bute, E of Loch Fad, 3m/4km SW of Rothesay. **22 B3** NS0760.
Meikle Hill *Moray* ***Hill***, 2m/3km SE of Dallas and 8m/13km W of Rothes. Height 932 feet or 284 metres. **62 D4** NJ1450.
Meikle Kilmory *Arg. & B.* ***Settlement***, on Bute, 3m/5km SW of Rothesay. **22 B3** NS0561.
Meikle Law *Sc.Bord.* ***Mountain***, in Lammermuir Hills, 4m/6km SW of Whiteadder Reservoir. Height 1535 feet or 468 metres. **26 C3** NT6059.
Meikle Loch *Aber.* ***Lake/loch***, small loch near E coast, 1m/2km N of Kirktown of Slains. **55 F1** NK0230.
Meikle Millyea *D. & G.* ***Mountain***, in Rhinns of Kells, 3m/5km N of NW corner of Clatteringshaws Loch. Height 2447 feet or 746 metres. **7 G2** NX5182.
Meikle Pap *Aber. See Lochnagar.*
Meikle Rahane *Arg. & B.* ***Settlement***, 3m/5km S of Garelochhead. **22 D1** NS2386.
Meikle Says Law *E.Loth.* ***Mountain***, summit of Lammermuir Hills, 5m/8km SE of Gifford. Height 1755 feet or 535 metres. **26 C3** NT5861.
Meikle Strath *Aber.* ***Settlement***, 3m/5km NE of Edzell. **43 E2** NO6471.
Meikle Tarty *Aber.* ***Settlement***, 2m/3km N of Newburgh. **55 E2** NJ9927.
Meikle Wartle *Aber.* ***Hamlet***, 6m/9km NW of Oldmeldrum. **54 C1** NJ7230.
Meikleour *P. & K.* ***Village***, 4m/6km S of Blairgowrie. Beech hedge of Meikleour House borders A93 road S of here for 656 yards or 600 metres. Planted in 1746, it is now 98 feet or 30 metres high. **33 G1** NO1539.
Meikleross Bay *Arg. & B.* ***Bay***, on Firth of Clyde, 2m/3km E of Kilcreggan. NS2680.
Mein Water *D. & G.* ***River***, rising to N of Torbeckhill Reservoir and flowing S then SW to River Annan 1m/2km S of Ecclefechan. NY1872.
Meith Bheinn *High.* ***Mountain***, peak in South Morar, Lochaber district, between Loch Morar and Loch Beoraid. Height 2329 feet or 710 metres. **38 A1** NM8287.
Melbost *W.Isles* ***Village***, on Isle of Lewis, 3m/4km E of Stornoway. Stornoway Airport on W side of village. **69 F4** NB4632.
Melbost Borve *W.Isles Anglicised form of Mealabost, qv.*
Melbost Point *W.Isles* ***Coastal feature***, headland to N of Melbost. **69 F4** NB4632.
Melbost Sands *W.Isles* ***Coastal feature***, on River Laxdale estuary to NW of Melbost, covered at high tide. **69 F4** NB4632.
Melby *Shet.* ***Village***, on W coast of Mainland, opposite Papa Stour. **82 A2** HU1957.
Melfort *Arg. & B.* ***Settlement***, in Argyll, at head of Loch Melfort, 1m/2km NW of Kilmelford. **30 A3** NM8314.
Melgam Water *Angus* ***River***, a continuation of Black Water, which flows SE into Loch of Lintrathen and exits at Bridgend of Lintrathen, then flows S to join River Isla by Airlie Castle, 4m/6km NE of Alyth. **42 A4** NO2952.
Melgarve *High.* ***Settlement***, to S of Corrieyairack Forest, 10m/17km NW of Kinloch Laggan. **51 D5** NN4695.
Melgum *Aber.* ***Settlement***, 1m/2km N of Tarland. **53 G4** NJ4706.
Melgund Castle *Angus* ***Castle***, mid 16c ruined tower house, 4m/7km SW of Brechin. NO5456.
Mell Head *High.* ***Coastal feature***, headland at SW end of Stroma in Pentland Firth. **77 F1** ND3376.
Melldalloch *Arg. & B.* ***Settlement***, in Argyll, 3m/4km S of Kilfinan. **22 A2** NR9274.
Mellerstain House *Sc.Bord.* ***Historic house***, 18c mansion by William and Robert Adam, 6m/10km NW of Kelso. **18 A3** NT6439.
Mellon Charles *High.* ***Settlement***, 2m/3km NW of Aultbea, on W coast of Ross and Cromarty district. **70 A5** NG8591.
Mellon Udrigle *High.* ***Locality***, 3m/4km SE of Greenstone Point, W coast of Ross and Cromarty district. **70 A5** NG8895.
Melowther Hill *E.Renf.* ***Hill***, 2m/3km S of Eaglesham. Height 987 feet or 301 metres. **23 G5** NS5648.
Melrose *Aber.* ***Locality***, comprises Mains of Melrose and Mill of Melrose, 3m/4km E of Macduff. **64 C3** NJ7464.
Melrose *Sc.Bord.* Population: 2270. ***Small town***, on S side of River Tweed 4m/6km E of Galashiels. Ruins of 12c abbey (Historic Scotland). Attractive 19c walled Harmony Garden (National Trust for Scotland) lies opposite abbey. See also Old Melrose. **17 G2** NT5434.

Melrose Abbey *Sc.Bord.* ***Ecclesiastical building***, ruins of Cistercian Abbey (Historic Scotland) founded around 1136 by David I. Almost destroyed during Wars of Independence and current remains, largely 15c, are considered to be the most elegant in Scotland. Robert the Bruce bequeathed his heart to abbey. **17 G2** NT5434.
Melsetter *Ork.* ***Settlement***, at S end of Hoy, 1m/2km NE of Tor Ness. **78 B4** ND2689.
Meluncart *Aber.* ***Mountain***, 3m/5km SW of Bridge of Dye. Height 1722 feet or 525 metres. **43 E1** NO6382.
Melvaig *High.* ***Village***, on W coast of Ross and Cromarty district, 3m/5km S of Rubha Réidh. **58 D1** NG7486.
Melvich *High.* ***Village***, near N coast of Caithness district, 15m/24km W of Thurso. **76 A2** NC8864.
Melvich Bay *High.* ***Bay***, 1km N of Melvich, on N coast of Caithness district. **76 A2** NC8864.
Melville's Monument *P. & K.* ***Other feature of interest***, obelisk on hill, 1m/2km N of Comrie, commemorating Lord Melville, 1742-1811. **32 C2** NN7623.
Memsie *Aber.* ***Village***, 3m/5km SW of Fraserburgh. Bronze Age burial cairn (Historic Scotland). **65 E3** NJ9762.
Memsie Cairn *Aber.* ***Historic/prehistoric site***, fine example of large stone cairn (Historic Scotland), possibly Bronze Age, 3m/5km S of Fraserburgh. **65 E3** NJ9762.
Memus *Angus* ***Village***, 6m/9km NW of Forfar. **42 C4** NO4258.
Men of Mey *High.* ***Coastal feature***, cluster of rocks off St. John's Point on N coast of Caithness district. **77 E1** ND3175.
Mendick Hill *Sc.Bord.* ***Mountain***, 2m/3km SW of West Linton. Height 1479 feet or 451 metres. **25 F4** NT1250.
Menie House *Aber.* ***Settlement***, near small lake, 2m/3km N of Balmedie. **55 E2** NJ9720.
Mennock *D. & G.* ***Village***, 2m/3km SE of Sanquhar, at confluence of River Nith and Mennock Water, which flows SW down Mennock Pass. **15 G5** NS8008.
Mennock Pass *D. & G.* ***Other feature of interest***, pass carrying road over Lowther Hills at height of 676 feet or 206 metres, between Mennock and Wanlockhead. **15 G4** NS8410.
Mennock Water *D. & G.* ***River***, rising 1km S of Wanlockhead and flowing into River Nith at Mennock, 2m/3km SE of Sanquhar. **15 G5** NS8008.
Menstrie *Clack.* Population: 2274. ***Small town***, 4m/6km NE of Stirling. 16c castle was home of Sir William Alexander, 1567-1640, founder of Nova Scotia. **32 D5** NS8496.
Menstrie Castle *Clack.* ***Castle***, late 16c L-plan tower house (National Trust for Scotland) at Menstrie. Birthplace of Sir William Alexander, founder of Nova Scotia. **33 D5** NS8596.
Menteith Hills *Stir.* ***Large natural feature***, range of low hills between Aberfoyle and Callander. **32 A4** NN5603.
Meoble *High.* ***River***, in South Morar, Lochaber district, running N from foot of Loch Beoraid to Loch Morar. Locality of Meoble on right bank 1m/2km above mouth. **38 A1** NM7889.
Meoble *High.* ***Settlement***, on E bank of River Meoble, 4m/6km NE of Lochailort. **37 G1** NM7987.
Meoir Langwell *High.* ***River***, stream formed by many small tributaries, flowing N from slopes of Coire Buidhe into River Oykel, 3m/5km E of Oykel Bridge. **71 G5** NC4301.
Merchiston *Edin.* ***Suburb***, 1m/2km SW of Edinburgh city centre. NT2472.
Mergie *Aber.* ***Settlement***, 1m/2km W of Rickarton. **43 F1** NO7988.
Merkadale *High.* ***Settlement***, on S side of Loch Harport, near head of loch, 1m/2km SE of Carbost, Skye. NG3831.
Merkinch *High.* ***Suburb***, NW district of Inverness. NH6546.
Merkland *D. & G.* ***Settlement***, 2m/3km S of Corsock. **8 B3** NX7473.
Merkland Cross *D. & G.* ***Historic/prehistoric site***, wayside cross (Historic Scotland), 9 feet or 3 metres high and dating from 1494, 2m/3km NW of Kirkpatrick-Fleming. Thought to commemorate death of member of Maxwell family in battle. **9 G3** NY2472.
Merkland Point *N.Ayr.* ***Coastal feature***, headland on E coast of Arran, at N end of Brodick Bay. **13 F2** NS0238.
Merrick *D. & G.* ***Mountain***, in Glentrool Forest Park, 4m/6km N of Loch Trool. Height 2765 feet or 843 metres. **7 F2** NX4285.
Merse *D. & G.* ***Marsh/bog***, marshland on N coast of Solway Firth, on E side of mouth of River Nith. **9 E4** NY0464.
Mersehead Sands *D. & G.* ***Coastal feature***, sandflat in Solway Firth, from Southerness Point in E to Cow's Snout in W. **8 D5** NX9053.
Mertoun House *Sc.Bord.* ***Garden***, on N bank of River Tweed, 3m/4km E of Newtown St. Boswell, with 20 acres of trees and herbaceous plants, as well as walled garden and circular dovecote. **18 A3** NT6131.
Mervinslaw *Sc.Bord.* ***Settlement***, to SW of Camptown, over Jed Water. **18 A5** NT6713.
Methil *Fife* ***Town***, port on N coast of Firth of Forth, 8m/12km NE of Kirkcaldy. Formerly a joint burgh with Buckhaven and busy coal port. **34 B5** NT3799.
Methilhill *Fife* ***Suburb***, W district of Methil. NO0035.
Methlick *Aber.* ***Village***, on River Ythan, 6m/10km S of New Deer. **55 D1** NJ8537.
Methven *P. & K.* Population: 1139. ***Village***, 6m/10km W of Perth. **33 F2** NO0225.
Methven Castle *P. & K.* ***Castle***, 17c tower house, where Queen Margaret Tudor died in 1541, 1m/2km E of Methven. NO0425.
Mey *High.* ***Village***, near N coast of Caithness district, 6m/9km W of John o' Groats. **77 E1** ND2872.
Miabhag (Anglicised form: Meavaig.) *W.Isles* ***Settlement***, on NE shore of Loch Meavaig, North Harris. **66 C3** NB0905.
Miabhig (Anglicised form: Miavaig). *W.Isles* ***Village***, at head of inlet of Loch Roag, near W coast of Isle of Lewis, 4m/6km SE of Gallan Head. **68 B4** NB0834.
Mial *High.* ***Settlement***, 1km NW of Gairloch, Ross and Cromarty district. **59 D2** NG7978.
Miavaig *W.Isles Anglicised form of Miabhig, qv.*
Michael Muir *Aber.* ***Settlement***, 4m/6km NW of Ellon. NJ9033.
Mid Ardlaw *Aber.* ***Settlement***, near N coast, 4m/6km SW of Fraserburgh. **65 E3** NJ9463.
Mid Beltie *Aber.* ***Settlement***, 1m/2km S of Torphins. **54 B4** NJ6200.
Mid Cairncross *Angus* ***Settlement***, in Glen Esk, 1km S of Tarfside. **42 D2** NO4979.
Mid Calder *W.Loth.* ***Village***, 1m/2km SE of Livingston. **25 E3** NT0767.
Mid Clyth *High.* ***Settlement***, on E coast of Caithness district, 2m/3km E of Lybster. To N, on small hill, Hill o' Many Stanes (Historic Scotland). **77 E5** ND2937.
Mid Hill *Angus* ***Mountain***, 3m/5km NE of Auchavan. Height 2539 feet or 774 metres. **42 A2** NO2270.
Mid Hill *E.Ayr.* ***Mountain***, on E side of Blackside, 4m/7km SE of Darvel. Height 1342 feet or 409 metres. **15 D2** NS5830.
Mid Hill *High.* ***Mountain***, 6m/10km W of Berriedale. Height 1023 feet or 312 metres. **73 F2** ND0223.
Mid Howe *Ork. Alternative spelling of Midhowe, qv.*
Mid Kame *Shet.* ***Inland physical feature***, ridge rising to over 180 metres and running N to S, situated to S of Voe, Mainland. **82 D2** HU4058.
Mid Letter *Arg. & B.* ***Settlement***, on S side of Loch Fyne, 2m/3km SW of Strachur. **30 C4** NN0700.
Mid Lix *Stir.* ***Settlement***, 2m/3km SW of Killin. **32 A2** NN5530.
Mid Loch Ollay *W.Isles See Ollay Lochs.*
Mid Sannox *N.Ayr.* ***Locality***, near E coast of Arran, at foot of Glen Sannox. **22 B5** NS0145.
Mid Thundergay *N.Ayr. Alternative name for Thundergay, qv.*
Mid Yell *Shet.* ***Village***, on S side of Mid Yell Voe, on E coast of Yell. **85 E3** HU5191.
Mid Yell Voe *Shet.* ***Sea feature***, large inlet on E coast of Yell, opposite Hascosay. HU5191.
Midbea *Ork.* ***Settlement***, on Westray, 3m/5km S of Pierowall. **80 C2** HY4444.
Middle Drums *Angus* ***Hamlet***, 2m/3km SW of Brechin. **43 D4** NO5957.
Middle Kames *Arg. & B.* ***Settlement***, 3m/5km E of Lochgilphead. **22 A1** NR9189.
Middle Rigg *P. & K.* ***Settlement***, 2m/3km S of Path of Condie. **33 F4** NO0608.
Middlebie *D. & G.* ***Village***, 2m/3km NE of Ecclefechan. Site of Roman camp to N, and Roman fort of Blatobulgium to S. **9 G3** NY2176.
Middlefield *Aberdeen* ***Suburb***, 3m/4km NW of Aberdeen city centre. NJ9108.
Middlefield Law *E.Ayr.* ***Mountain***, with cairn at summit, 2m/4km N of Muirkirk. Height 1528 feet or 466 metres. **15 E2** NS6830.
Middlehill *Aber.* ***Settlement***, 2m/3km SE of Cuminestown. **64 D5** NJ8349.
Middlequarter *W.Isles Anglicised form of Ceathramh Meadhanach, qv.*
Middleton *Aber.* ***Settlement***, 3m/4km W of Newmachar. **54 D3** NJ8419.
Middleton *Angus* ***Hamlet***, 1km SW of Friockheim. **43 D5** NO5848.
Middleton *Arg. & B.* ***Settlement***, near W end of Tiree, 2m/3km SE of Rubha Chràiginis. NL9443.
Middleton *Midloth.* ***Settlement***, 3m/4km SE of Gorebridge. **26 A4** NT3658.
Middleton *P. & K.* ***Settlement***, 3m/5km N of Kinross. **33 G4** NO1206.
Middleton *P. & K.* ***Settlement***, 3m/5km NW of Blairgowrie. **41 G5** NO1447.
Middleton of Potterton *Aber.* ***Settlement***, 1km W of Potterton and 3m/4km SW of Balmedie. **55 E3** NJ9315.
Middleton Park *Aberdeen* ***Suburb***, to NW of Bridge of Don, 3m/5km N of Aberdeen city centre. **55 E3** NJ9211.
Middleyard *E.Ayr.* ***Settlement***, 3m/4km S of Galston. **14 D2** NS5132.
Midfield *High.* ***Settlement***, on N coast of Caithness district, on W side of entrance to Tongue Bay. **75 E2** NC5864.
Midhowe (Sometimes spelled Mid Howe.) *Ork.* ***Historic/prehistoric site***, site of Iron Age broch and Midhowe Stalled Cairn (both Historic Scotland), on W coast of Rousay. Cairn is huge Neolithic chambered tomb in oval mound with 25 stalls; now protected by modern building. **80 B3** HY3730.
Midland Ness *Ork.* ***Coastal feature***, headland on S coast of Mainland, to E of Bay of Houton. **78 C2** HY3203.
Midlem *Sc.Bord.* ***Village***, 4m/6km E of Selkirk. **17 G3** NT5227.
Midlock *S.Lan.* ***River***, rising to W of Clyde Law and flowing NW to join River Clyde to N of Crawford. **16 B4** NS9521.
Midmar *Aber.* ***Locality***, 6m/10km N of Banchory. 16c Midmar Castle and Midmar Forest to SE. NJ6707.
Midmar Forest *Aber.* ***Forest/woodland***, to SE of Midmar. **54 C4** NJ7005.
Midpark *Arg. & B.* ***Settlement***, on E coast of Inchmarnock, 6m/8km SW of Rothesay. **22 B4** NS0259.
Midton *Inclyde* ***Suburb***, S district of Gourock. NS2376.
Midtown *High.* ***Settlement***, in Caithness district, on W side of Kyle of Tongue. **75 E2** NC5861.
Midtown *High.* ***Village***, on W shore of Loch Ewe, Ross and Cromarty district, 4m/6km NW of Poolewe. Settlement of Brae adjoins to W. **59 E1** NG8284.
Midtown of Barras *Aber.* ***Hamlet***, 2m/3km SW of Stonehaven. **43 G1** NO8480.
Migdale *High.* ***Settlement***, in Sutherland district, 1m/2km E of Bonar Bridge and on N side of head of Loch Migdale. **72 B5** NH6292.
Migvie *Aber.* ***Settlement***, 3m/5km NW of Tarland. **53 G4** NJ4306.
Milarrochy *Stir.* ***Settlement***, on E shore of Loch Lomond, 1m/2km NW of Balmaha. **31 G5** NS4092.
Milbethill *Aber.* ***Settlement***, 3m/4km SE of Cornhill. **64 B4** NJ6156.
Mile Hill *Angus* ***Mountain***, 3m/4km NE of Bridgend of Lintrathen. Height 1342 feet or 409 metres. **42 B4** NO3157.
Milesmark *Fife* ***Village***, 2m/3km NW of Dunfermline. **25 E1** NT0688.
Mill Bay *Ork.* ***Bay***, wide bay on E coast of Stronsay, extending S from Grice Ness to Odness. **81 E4** HY6626.
Mill Buie *Moray* ***Mountain***, 6m/10km SE of Forres. Height 1217 feet or 371 metres. **62 C4** NJ0950.
Mill Buie *Moray* ***Mountain***, 2m/3km W of Glenlatterach Reservoir and 1m/2km S of Kellas. Height 1099 feet or 335 metres. **63 D4** NJ1651.
Mill of Colp *Aber.* ***Settlement***, on S side of Idoch Water, 2m/3km SE of Turriff. **64 C5** NJ7447.
Mill of Elrick *Aber.* ***Settlement***, on E side of Ebrie Burn, 1km S of Auchnagatt. **65 E5** NJ9340.
Mill of Fortune *P. & K.* ***Settlement***, 1m/2km SE of Comrie. **32 C2** NN7820.
Mill of Kingoodie *Aber.* ***Settlement***, 2m/3km SE of Oldmeldrum. **54 D2** NJ8325.
Mill of Monquich *Aber.* ***Hamlet***, 1m/2km N of Netherley. **55 D5** NO8595.
Mill of Uras *Aber.* ***Settlement***, 3m/5km S of Stonehaven. **43 G2** NO8679.
Mill Rig *S.Lan.* ***Mountain***, partly wooded peak, 5m/8km SE of Darvel. Height 1099 feet or 335 metres. **15 E2** NS6334.
Millarston *Renf.* ***Suburb***, W district of Paisley. NS4663.
Millbank *Aber.* ***Settlement***, on N side of River Ugie, 1m/2km N of Longside. **65 F5** NK0449.
Millbounds *Ork.* ***Settlement***, on Eday, 1m/2km NE of Eday Airfield. **81 D3** HY5635.
Millbreck *Aber.* ***Settlement***, 2m/3km S of Mintlaw. **65 F5** NK0045.
Millbuie *High.* ***Locality***, comprises central, mainly forested, area of Black Isle in Ross and Cromarty district. **61 F3** NH6257.
Millbuie Forest *High.* ***Forest/woodland***, on Black Isle, Ross and Cromarty district, NW of Fortrose. **61 F3** NH6960.
Millburn *Aber.* ***Settlement***, 1km E of Suie Hill and 4m/6km N of Alford. **54 A2** NJ5722.
Millburn *Aber.* ***Settlement***, 6m/10km E of Huntly. **54 B1** NJ6236.
Millburn Geo *Shet.* ***Coastal feature***, small indentation on E coast of Bressay. **83 E4** HU5239.
Millden *Aber.* ***Settlement***, 1km S of Balmedie. **55 E3** NJ9616.
Milldens *Angus* ***Hamlet***, 3m/5km W of Friockheim. **42 D4** NO5450.
Milldoe *Ork.* ***Hill***, 1m/2km NW of Settiscarth, Mainland. Height 725 feet or 221 metres. **80 B4** HY3520.
Millearn *P. & K.* ***Settlement***, in Strathearn, 5m/8km SE of Crieff. Muir o' Fauld Signal Station (Historic Scotland) is Roman watch tower 1m/2km NE. **33 E3** NN9316.
Millerhill *Midloth.* ***Village***, 1m/2km N of Dalkeith. **26 A3** NT3269.

Millerston *Glas.* **Locality**, 4m/6km E of Glasgow. NS6467.
Millerton Hill *Sc.Bord.* **Hill**, 1m/2km SW of Ayton. Height 433 feet or 132 metres. **27 F4** NT9159.
Milleur Point *D. & G.* **Coastal feature**, headland at N end of Rinns of Galloway, 3m/5km N of Kirkcolm. **6 B3** NX0273.
Millfire *D. & G.* **Mountain**, on Rhinns of Kells, 4m/7km N of Clatteringshaws Loch. Height 2348 feet or 716 metres. **7 G2** NX5084.
Millfore *D. & G.* **Mountain**, 7m/12km NE of Newton Stewart. Height 2152 feet or 656 metres. **7 F3** NX4775.
Millheugh *S.Lan.* **Locality**, adjoining to W of Larkhall. NS7550.
Millhouse *Arg. & B.* **Settlement**, in Argyll, 1m/2km SW of Kames. **22 A2** NR9570.
Millhousebridge *D. & G.* **Settlement**, on River Annan, 3m/5km NW of Lockerbie. **9 F2** NY1085.
Milliganton *D. & G.* **Settlement**, 1m/2km SW of Dunscore. **8 C2** NX8483.
Millikenpark *Renf.* **Suburb**, residential development adjoining to SW of Johnstone. **23 F3** NS4161.
Milljoan Hill *S.Ayr.* **Mountain**, 4m/6km SE of Ballantrae. Height 1322 feet or 403 metres. **6 C3** NX1176.
Millness *High.* **Settlement**, 3m/4km E of Cannich. **50 C1** NH3731.
Millport *N.Ayr.* Population: 1340. **Small town**, resort and port on Millport Bay, at S end of Great Cumbrae, 3m/4km W of Fairlie across Fairlie Roads. **22 C4** NS1655.
Millport Bay *N.Ayr.* **Bay**, at S end of Great Cumbrae, 3m/4km W of Fairlie across Fairlie Roads. Islets in bay are known as The Eileans. **22 C4** NS1655.
Millstone Edge *Sc.Bord.* **Mountain**, 2m/3km SE of Linhope. Height 1853 feet or 565 metres. **17 F5** NT4300.
Millstone Hill *Aber.* **Mountain**, in Bennachie Forest, 3m/5km N of Monymusk. Height 1338 feet or 408 metres. **54 B2** NJ6720.
Millstone Hill *Moray* **Hill**, in woodlands 4m/7km N of Keith. Height 987 feet or 301 metres. **63 G4** NJ4257.
Milltimber *Aberdeen* **Village**, 1m/2km E of Peterculter. **55 D4** NJ8501.
Millton of Noth *Aber.* **Settlement**, 1km N of Rhynie. **54 A2** NJ5028.
Milltown *Aber.* **Settlement**, just E of Cock Bridge, 11m/17km NW of Ballater. NJ2609.
Milltown *D. & G.* **Settlement**, 4m/6km W of Canonbie. **10 B4** NY3375.
Milltown *High.* **Settlement**, in Strathconon, Ross and Cromarty district, 2m/4km above head of Loch Meig. **60 C4** NH3055.
Milltown *High.* **Settlement**, 3m/4km SW of Ferness. **62 B5** NH9441.
Milltown of Aberdalgie *P. & K.* **Hamlet**, to N of Aberdalgie, 3m/5km SW of Perth. **33 F2** NO0720.
Milltown of Auchindoun *Moray* **Settlement**, 2m/3km E of Dufftown. **63 F5** NJ3539.
Milltown of Campfield *Aber.* **Settlement**, 2m/3km SE of Torphins. **54 B4** NJ6400.
Milltown of Craigston *Aber.* **Settlement**, 4m/7km NE of Turriff. **64 C4** NJ7655.
Milltown of Edinvillie *Moray* **Village**, 2m/3km S of Charlestown of Aberlour. **63 E5** NJ2640.
Milltown of Kildrummy *Aber.* **Locality**, 1km S of Kildrummy and 3m/5km S of Lumsden. **53 G3** NJ4716.
Milltown of Rothiemay *Moray* **Village**, 5m/9km N of Huntly. **64 A5** NJ5448.
Milltown of Towie *Aber.* **Settlement**, near bridge over River Don, 7m/11km E of Strathdon. **53 G3** NJ4612.
Milnathort *P. & K.* Population: 1368. **Small town**, with woollen mills, 2m/3km N of Kinross. Burleigh Castle (Historic Scotland) to E. **33 G4** NO1204.
Milnbank *Glas.* **Suburb**, 2m/3km E of Glasgow city centre, in Dennistoun district. NS6165.
Milne Height *D. & G.* **Mountain**, 4m/7km N of Boreland. Height 1381 feet or 421 metres. **9 F1** NY1597.
Milngavie *E.Dun.* Population: 12,592. **Town**, 6m/10km N of Glasgow. Remains of 15c Mugdock Castle on Mugdock Loch to N. **23 G2** NS5574.
Milovaig *High.* **Locality**, on Skye, comprising Upper and Lower Milovaig, 6m/10km W of Dunvegan. **57 E4** NG1549.
Milrig *E.Ayr.* **Settlement**, 2m/3km S of Galston. **14 D2** NS5034.
Milton *Angus* **Hamlet**, 2m/3km S of Glamis, in Glen Ogilvey. **42 B5** NO3743.
Milton *D. & G.* **Hamlet**, 2m/4km SE of Glenluce. NX2154.
Milton *D. & G.* **Village**, 2m/3km SE of Crocketford, with Milton Loch to NW. **8 C3** NX8470.
Milton *Glas.* **Suburb**, 3m/4km N of Glasgow city centre. NS5969.
Milton *High.* **Locality**, consisting of Easter and Wester Milton, 5m/8km SE of Nairn. **62 B4** NH9553.
Milton *High.* **Settlement**, 1km W of Wick. **77 F3** ND3451.
Milton *High.* **Settlement**, on W coast of Ross and Cromarty district, adjoining to S of Applecross. **58 D5** NG7043.
Milton *High.* **Settlement**, in Ross and Cromarty district, on N shore of Beauly Firth, 3m/5km E of Muir of Ord. **61 E5** NH5749.
Milton *High.* **Village**, in Glen Urquhart, in Inverness district, 1m/2km W of Drumnadrochit. **51 D1** NH4930.
Milton *High.* **Village**, in Ross and Cromarty district, 5m/8km NE of Invergordon. **61 G2** NH7674.
Milton *Moray* **Settlement**, near N coast, 3m/4km S of Cullen. **64 A3** NJ5163.
Milton *P. & K.* **Settlement**, in Glen Cochill, 1m/2km NE of Amulree. **33 E1** NN9138.
Milton *Stir.* **Settlement**, 1m/2km W of Aberfoyle. **32 A4** NN5001.
Milton *Stir.* **Settlement**, on N side of Loch Venachar, 3m/5km SW of Callander. **32 A4** NN5706.
Milton *Stir.* **Village**, 2m/4km NW of Drymen. **31 G5** NS4490.
Milton *W.Dun.* Population: 1079. **Village**, 2m/3km E of Dumbarton. **23 F2** NS4274.
Milton *W.Isles Anglicised form of Gearraidh Bhailteas, qv.*
Milton Bridge *Midloth.* **Locality**, 2m/3km NE of Penicuik. **25 G3** NT2562.
Milton Burn *P. & K.* **River**, flowing SE into River Almond, 4m/6km NW of Methven. **33 E1** NN9729.
Milton Coldwells *Aber.* **Settlement**, 3m/4km SE of Auchnagatt. **55 E1** NJ9538.
Milton Eonan *P. & K.* **Locality**, in Glen Lyon above Bridge of Balgie. Waterfall in Allt Bail a' Mhuilinn, stream running into River Lyon here from S. NN5746.
Milton Inveramsay *Aber.* **Settlement**, 3m/5km NW of Inverurie. **54 C2** NJ7325.
Milton Loch *D. & G.* **Lake/loch**, 1km SE of Crocketford. **8 C3** NX8471.
Milton Lockhart *S.Lan.* **Settlement**, above E bank of River Clyde, 2m/3km W of Carluke. **24 C5** NS8149.
Milton Morenish *P. & K.* **Settlement**, on N side of Loch Tay, 3m/5km NE of Killin. **32 B1** NN6136.
Milton Ness *Aber.* **Coastal feature**, headland on E coast, 6m/9km NE of Montrose. **43 F3** NO7764.
Milton of Auchinhove *Aber.* **Settlement**, 2m/3km W of Lumphanan. **54 A4** NJ5503.
Milton of Balgonie *Fife* **Village**, 1m/2km E of Markinch. **34 B4** NS3100.
Milton of Cairnborrow *Aber.* **Settlement**, on N side of River Deveron, 3m/5km E of Haugh of Glass. **63 G5** NJ4740.
Milton of Campsie *E.Dun.* Population: 4056. **Village**, 2m/3km N of Kirkintilloch. **24 A2** NS6576.
Milton of Cullerlie *Aber.* **Settlement**, on N side of Gormack Burn, 3m/4km SE of Echt. **54 C4** NJ7602.
Milton of Cushnie *Aber.* **Village**, 5m/7km SW of Alford. **54 A3** NJ5211.
Milton of Dalcapon *P. & K.* **Settlement**, 3m/5km SE of Pitlochry. **41 E4** NN9755.
Milton of Tullich *Aber.* **Settlement**, on Tullich Burn, 2m/3km NE of Ballater. **53 F5** NO3897.
Milton Tower *Moray* **Other feature of interest**, remains of tower in Keith, built 1480, former home of Oliphant family. **63 G4** NJ4251.
Miltonduff *Moray* **Settlement**, 3m/4km SW of Elgin. **63 D3** NJ1760.
Miltonhill *Moray* **Settlement**, 1m/2km inland from Burghead Bay and 4m/7km NE of Forres. **62 C3** NJ0963.
Miltonise *D. & G.* **Settlement**, 6m/10km SW of Barrhill. **6 C3** NX1873.
Minard *Arg. & B.* **Hamlet**, in Argyll, on W shore of Loch Fyne, 4m/6km SW of Furnace. **30 B5** NR9796.
Minard Castle *Arg. & B.* **Settlement**, on NW coast of Loch Fyne, 1m/2km S of Minard. **30 B5** NR9794.
Minard Forest *Arg. & B.* **Forest/woodland**, to W of Minard. **30 B5** NR9796.
Minard Point *Arg. & B.* **Coastal feature**, headland on N side of entrance to Loch Feochan in Argyll, 5m/8km SW of Oban. **30 A2** NM8123.
Minch Moor *Sc.Bord.* **Mountain**, 3m/5km SE of Innerleithen. Height 1860 feet or 567 metres. **17 E2** NT3533.
Mingarry *W.Isles Anglicised form of Mingearraidh, qv.*
Mingary Castle *High.* **Castle**, ruined 13c castle on S coast Ardnamurchan peninsula in Lochaber district, 1m/2km SE of Kilchoan. **37 E3** NM5063.
Mingay Island *High.* **Island**, small uninhabited island in Loch Dunvegan, 1m/2km S of Ardmore Point, Skye. **57 F4** NG2257.
Mingearraidh (Anglicised form: Mingary.) *W.Isles* **Settlement**, on South Uist, 3m/5km SE of Rubha Ardvule. **44 C1** NF7426.
Minginish *High.* **Locality**, on Skye, lying S of a line from Sligachan to Loch Harport and W of River Sligachan. Includes Cuillin Hills. **47 G2** NG3530.
Mingulay (Gaelic form: Miughalaigh.) *W.Isles* **Island**, gaunt, uninhabited island of about 6 square km, with high cliffs, 2m/3km SW of Pabbay and 6m/10km SW of Vatersay. Haunt of sea birds. **44 A5** NL5582.
Mingulay Bay *W.Isles* **Bay**, on E coast of Mingulay. **44 A5** NL5783.
Minishant *S.Ayr.* **Settlement**, 3m/5km NE of Maybole. **14 B4** NS3314.
Minnes *Aber.* **Locality**, comprises South Minnes, Miltown of Minnes, Mill of Minnes and Hill of Minnes, 4m/6km W of Newburgh. **55 E2** NJ9423.
Minnigaff *D. & G.* **Village**, on E side on Newton Stewart across River Cree. **7 F4** NX4166.
Minnonie *Aber.* **Settlement**, 3m/5km SW of Gardenstown. **64 C3** NJ7760.
Minnygap Height *D. & G.* **Mountain**, on E edge of Forest of Ae, 5m/8km SW of Beattock. Height 1309 feet or 399 metres. **9 E1** NY0296.
Mintlaw *Aber.* Population: 2522. **Village**, 8m/13km W of Peterhead. **65 F5** NK0048.
Minto *Sc.Bord.* **Village**, 5m/9km NE of Hawick. **17 G3** NT5620.
Minto Hills *Sc.Bord.* **Large natural feature**, comprising two distinct summits separated by a saddle, 1km NW of Minto. N summit height is 836 feet or 255 metres, S summit is 905 feet or 276 metres. **17 G3** NT5521.
Mio Ness *Shet.* **Coastal feature**, headland on Mainland at S end of Yell Sound, 1m/2km NW of Brough. HU4279.
Miodar *Arg. & B.* **Settlement**, on N coast of Tiree, 1km NW of Caolas. **36 B2** NM0749.
Mirbister *Ork.* **Settlement**, on Mainland, 1m/2km SE of Dounby. **80 B4** HY3019.
Mire of Midgates *Aber.* **Mountain**, in Correen Hills, 3m/5km SE of Rhynie. Height 1588 feet or 484 metres. **54 A2** NJ5222.
Mireland *High.* **Settlement**, near E coast of Caithness district, 7m/11km NW of Wick. **77 F2** ND3160.
Mirkady Point *Ork.* **Coastal feature**, headland on Mainland on E side of Deer Sound, 4m/7km SW of Mull Head. **79 E2** HY5306.
Mishnish *Arg. & B.* **Locality**, on Mull, 3m/5km W of Tobermory. **36 D4** NM4656.
Mishnish Lochs *Arg. & B.* **Lake/loch**, group of three small lochs, 3m/4km SW of Tobermory. In descending order they are, Loch Carnain an Amais, Loch Meadhoin and Loch Peallach. **37 D4** NM4752.
Misty Law *N.Ayr.* **Mountain**, 6m/10km NE of Largs. Height 1673 feet or 510 metres. **23 D3** NS2961.
Mither Tap *Aber.* **Mountain**, with panoramic viewpoint, 5m/8km W of Inverurie. Height 1699 feet or 518 metres. **54 B2** NJ6822.
Miughalaigh *W.Isles Gaelic form of Mingulay, qv.*
Moar *P. & K.* **Settlement**, in Glen Lyon, 3m/5km SW of Bridge of Balgie. **40 A5** NN5344.
Mochrum (Also known as Kirk of Mochrum.) *D. & G.* **Village**, 2m/3km N of Port William. Restored castle, Old Place of Mochrum, on N shore of Mochrum Loch 6m/9km to NW. **2 D2** NX3446.
Mochrum Hill *S.Ayr.* **Hill**, 2m/3km W of Maybole. Height 886 feet or 270 metres. NS2610.
Mochrum Loch *D. & G.* **Lake/loch**, 8m/13km W of Wigtown. At NE corner of loch stands restored Old Place of Mochrum. **7 D5** NX3053.
Mochrum Loch *S.Ayr.* **Lake/loch**, small loch on S side of Mochrum Hill. NS2709.
Modsarie *High.* **Settlement**, 3m/5km E of Bettyhill, Caithness district. **75 F2** NC6462.
Moffat *D. & G.* Population: 2342. **Small town**, market town and resort on River Annan, 19m/31km NE of Dumfries. Fashionable as spa town in 18c. **16 B5** NT0805.
Moffat Water *D. & G.* **River**, running SW to River Annan 2m/3km S of Moffat. **16 C5** NT0805.
Moidart *High.* **Locality**, part of Lochaber district lying W of Loch Shiel and S of Loch Eilt. Coastline indented by Lochs Ailort and Moidart. **37 G2** NM7472.
Moin' a' choire *Arg. & B.* **Settlement**, 2m/4km NE of Bridgend. **20 B3** NR3664.
Moine House *High.* **Settlement**, 1km E of Loch Maovally, 6m/9km S of Whiten Head. **75 E2** NC5160.
Mòine Mhòr *Arg. & B.* **Open space**, flood plain of River Add which meanders across area to its mouth at head of Loch Crinan. **30 A5** NR8293.
Moinechoill Chambered Cairn *N.Ayr.* **Historic/prehistoric site**, long cairn 5m/7km W of Brodick. **13 E2** NR9435.
Mol a' Tuath *W.Isles* **Sea feature**, inlet on E coast of South Uist, 1km S of Rubha Rossel. **46 B1** NF8535.
Mol-chlach *High.* **Settlement**, on W side of Camas nan Gall inlet, Soay, in Skye and Lochalsh district. **48 A3** NG4513.
Mol Truisg *W.Isles* **Bay**, small bay on SE coast of Isle of Lewis, 1m/2km N of Gob Rubh' Uisenis. **67 F3** NB3505.
Mollance *D. & G.* **Settlement**, 3m/4km N of Castle Douglas. **8 B4** NX7765.
Mollin Burn *D. & G.* **River**, flowing S to join Kinnel Water, 3m/5km NE of Parkgate. **9 E1** NY0593.
Mollinsburn *N.Lan.* **Hamlet**, 4m/6km SW of Cumbernauld. **24 B2** NS7171.
Molls Cleuch Dod *Sc.Bord.* **Mountain**, 5m/8km SE of Tweedsmuir. Height 2572 feet or 784 metres. **16 C4** NT1518.
Monach Islands *W.Isles Alternative name for Heisker Islands, qv.*

Monachyle Glen *Stir.* ***Valley***, carrying Monachyle Burn S into Loch Voil, 4m/6km W of Balquhidder. **31 G2** NN4722.
Monachylemore *Stir.* ***Settlement***, at W end of Loch Voil, 4m/6km W of Balquhidder. **31 G3** NN4719.
Monadh Fergie *Moray* ***Mountain***, 3m/4km SE of Tomintoul. Height 1889 feet or 576 metres. **53 D3** NJ1914.
Monadh Gorm *High.* ***Mountain***, 2m/3km W of Loch Arkaig, Lochaber district. Height 1568 feet or 478 metres. **49 F5** NM9691.
Monadh Mòr ***Mountain***, in Cairngorm Mountains on border of Highland and Aberdeenshire, 4m/7km SW of Ben Macdui. Munro: height 3651 feet or 1113 metres. **52 B5** NN9394.
Monadh nam Mial *P. & K.* ***Mountain***, 3m/4km S of Aberfeldy. Height 1975 feet or 602 metres. **41 D5** NN8644.
Monadhliath Mountains *High.* ***Large natural feature***, range of mountains running NE to SW, astride border between Inverness and Badenoch and Strathspey districts, on W side of upper Strathspey. Summit is Carn Dearg at a height of 3100 feet or 945 metres, 16m/26km S of Inverness. **51 D4** NH6710.
Monamenach ***Mountain***, on border of Angus and Perth & Kinross, 4m/6km E of Spittal of Glenshee. Height 2647 feet or 807 metres. **41 G2** NO1770.
Monaughty Forest *Moray* ***Forest/woodland***, 6m/9km SW of Elgin. **62 D4** NJ1358.
Monawee *Angus* ***Mountain***, 4m/6km S of Mount Keen. Height 2283 feet or 696 metres. **42 C1** NO4080.
Monboddo *Aber.* ***Historic house***, 1m/2km E of Auchenblae. Formerly seat of Burnetts; visited by Johnson and Boswell. NO7478.
Moncreiffe *P. & K.* ***Suburb***, S district of Perth. **33 G3** NO1121.
Moncreiffe Hill *P. & K.* ***Hill***, 2m/3km SE of Moncreiffe. Height 725 feet or 221 metres. **33 G3** NO1121.
Moncreiffe Island *P. & K. Alternative name for Friarton Island, qv.*
Monega Hill *Angus* ***Mountain***, to S of Caenlochan Glen, 3m/5km SE of Glenshee Ski Centre. Height 2978 feet or 908 metres. **41 G2** NO1875.
Monevechadan *Arg. & B.* ***Settlement***, at foot of Hell's Glen, 3m/4km N of Lochgoilhead. **31 D4** NN1805.
Money Head *D. & G.* ***Coastal feature***, headland 4m/7km SE of Portpatrick. **2 A2** NX0448.
Moneydie *P. & K.* ***Settlement***, 5m/8km NW of Perth. **33 F2** NO0629.
Mongour *Aber.* ***Mountain***, 4m/6km S of Crathes. Height 1233 feet or 376 metres. **54 C5** NO7590.
Moniaive *D. & G.* ***Village***, on Dalwhat Water, 7m/11km SW of Thornhill. 3m/5km E is Maxwelton House. **8 B1** NX7790.
Monifieth *Angus* ***Suburb***, on Firth of Tay, 6m/10km E of Dundee. **34 C1** NO4932.
Monikie *Angus* ***Village***, 5m/8km NW of Carnoustie. Reservoir to SE. **34 C1** NO5038.
Monikie Country Park *Angus* ***Leisure/recreation***, at Monikie Reservoir, to SW of Monikie. 185 acre country park with grass and woodland. Watersports on reservoir. **34 C1** NO5038.
Monimail *Fife* ***Village***, 4m/7km W of Cupar. **34 A3** NO2914.
Monivey *Ork.* ***Bay***, to S of Noup Head, Westray. **80 B2** HY4047.
Monk Castle *N.Ayr.* ***Castle***, remains of medieval castle, 1m/2km S of Dalry. NS2947.
Monkshill *Aber.* ***Settlement***, 3m/4km NE of Fyvie. **64 C5** NJ7940.
Monkstadt *High.* ***Settlement***, 3m/4km N of Uig, Skye. **57 G3** NG3767.
Monkstown *Fife* ***Suburb***, adjoining to W of Ladybank. NO3009.
Monkton *S.Ayr.* ***Hamlet***, on N side of Prestwick Airport, 4m/7km N of Ayr. **14 B3** NS3527.
Monktonhall *E.Loth.* ***Suburb***, SW part of Musselburgh. NT3371.
Monreith *D. & G.* ***Village***, on Monreith Bay, 2m/3km SE of Port William. **3 D2** NX3541.
Monreith Bay *D. & G.* ***Bay***, 2m/3km SE of Port William. Ancient cross (Historic Scotland) in grounds of Monreith House to N. **2 D2** NX3541.
Monreith House *D. & G.* ***Historic house***, 1m/2km N of Monreith; grounds contain ancient cross (Historic Scotland). NX3542.
Monteach *Aber.* ***Settlement***, 3m/4km N of Methlick. **65 D5** NJ8640.
Montgarrie *Aber.* ***Village***, 1m/2km N of Alford. **54 A3** NJ5717.
Montgreenan *N.Ayr.* ***Locality***, 2m/4km E of Kilwinning. **23 E5** NS3444.
Montrave *Fife* ***Settlement***, 3m/5km NW of Kennoway. **34 B4** NO3706.
Montreathmont Forest *Angus* ***Forest/woodland***, Forestry Commission coniferous forest, 3m/5km NW of Friockheim. **42 D4** NO5654.
Montreathmont Moor *Angus* ***Forest/woodland***, wooded tract 4m/6km S of Brechin. Radio/TV mast. **43 D4** NO5854.
Montrose *Angus* Population: 11,440. ***Town***, port on E coast, 26m/42km NE of Dundee. Golf course founded 1810. **43 F4** NO7157.
Montrose Basin *Angus* ***Sea feature***, large tidal lagoon to W of Montrose. **43 E4** NO7157.
Montrose Museum and Art Gallery *Angus* ***Other feature of interest***, local history museum in centre of Montrose, with maritime and natural history exhibits. **43 F4** NO7157.
Monymusk *Aber.* ***Village***, 7m/11km SW of Inverurie. **54 B3** NJ6815.
Monynut Edge *E.Loth.* ***Large natural feature***, ridge and watershed in Lammermuir Hills, 7m/11km S of Dunbar. **27 D3** NT7067.
Monynut Water ***River***, running down W side of Monynut Edge to Whiteadder Water at Abbey St. Bathans. **27 E3** NT7067.
Mony's Stone *High.* ***Historic/prehistoric site***, standing stone at Corrimony, 9m/14km W of Drumnadrochit. Reputed to mark spot where Norse raider, Monie, was killed by Highlanders. **50 C1** NH3730.
Monzie *P. & K.* ***Village***, 2m/4km N of Crieff. Falls of Monzie 1m/2km N. **33 D2** NN8725.
Monzie Castle *P. & K.* ***Castle***, to SW of Monzie, 17c castle rebuilt after fire in early 20c. NN8724.
Mooa *Shet.* ***Island***, small uninhabited island off E coast of Whalsay, 1m/2km S of Skaw Taing. HU6065.
Moodiesburn *N.Lan.* Population: 5979. ***Small town***, 4m/7km SW of Cumbernauld. **24 A2** NS6970.
Moodlaw Loch *D. & G.* ***Lake/loch***, small loch in Craik Forest, 3m/5km W of Craik. **17 D5** NT2907.
Moonen Bay *High.* ***Bay***, S facing bay on W coast of Skye, 8m/12km W of Dunvegan. Headland of Neist Point to W. **57 E5** NG1346.
Moonzie *Fife* ***Settlement***, 3m/5km NW of Cupar. **34 B3** NO3417.
Moorbrock Hill *D. & G.* ***Mountain***, 4m/7km NE of Carsphairn. Height 2135 feet or 651 metres. NX6298.
Moorfoot Hills ***Large natural feature***, range of hills, mainly grass-covered, running NE to SW between Tynehead and Peebles. Summit is Blackhope Scar, 2136 feet or 651 metres. **26 A4** NT3050.
Moorpark *Renf.* ***Suburb***, S district of Renfrew. NS5066.
Mòr Mhonadh *W.Isles* ***Mountain***, on North Harris, 2m/3km NE of Muaithabhal. Height 1315 feet or 401 metres. **67 E2** NB2713.
Morangie *High.* ***Settlement***, in Ross and Cromarty district, on S shore of Dornoch Firth, 1m/2km NW of Tain. **61 G1** NH7683.
Morangie Forest *High.* ***Forest/woodland***, to SW of Morangie. **61 G1** NH7683.
Morar *High.* ***Coastal feature***, coastal area of Lochaber district lying between Loch Nevis to N and Loch nan Uamh to S, and divided into North and South Morar by Loch Morar. Village of Morar lies on neck of North Morar between foot of loch and estuary of river. NM7090.
Morar *High.* ***Sea feature***, estuarial river flowing W from dam of Loch Morar, Lochaber district, to sea 3m/4km S of Mallaig. NM6692.
Morar *High.* ***Village***, lies on neck of North Morar, Lochaber district, between foot of Loch Morar and River Morar estuary. **48 C5** NM6792.
Moray Firth *High.* ***Sea feature***, arm of North Sea extending to Inverness from a line drawn from Duncansby Head to Fraserburgh. Above the narrows between Chanonry Point and Fort George, the firth is known as Inner Moray Firth or Inverness Firth, and above Inverness as Beauly Firth, which extends to mouth of River Beauly. Other important inlets on W side of Moray Firth are Dornoch and Cromarty Firths. **62 A3** NH8565.
Moray Motor Museum *Moray* ***Other feature of interest***, unique collection of classic cars and motorbikes in converted mill building in Elgin. **63 E3** NJ2062.
Mordington *Sc.Bord.* ***Settlement***, 2m/3km E of Foulden. **27 G4** NT9456.
More Head *Aber.* ***Coastal feature***, headland on N coast, 5m/8km E of Macduff. NJ7865.
Morebattle *Sc.Bord.* ***Village***, 6m/10km SE of Kelso. 1km SE is Corbet Tower, stronghold of the Kers, destroyed in 16c, restored in 19c. **18 B4** NT7724.
Moredun *Edin.* ***Suburb***, 3m/5km SE of Edinburgh city centre. NT2869.
Morefield *High.* ***Settlement***, on Loch Broom, Ross and Cromarty district, 1m/2km NW of Ullapool. **70 D5** NH1195.
Morenish *P. & K.* ***Settlement***, on N side of Loch Tay, 2m/3km NE of Killin. **32 B1** NN6035.
Morham *E.Loth.* ***Locality***, 3m/5km E of Haddington. NT5571.
Moriston *High.* ***River***, in Inverness district running E from Loch Cluanie down Glen Moriston to Loch Ness. Power station for hydro-electricity scheme at Ceannacroc Bridge. **50 B3** NH4216.
Mormond Hill *Aber.* ***Hill***, 3m/4km NE of Strichen. Height 754 feet or 230 metres. **65 E4** NJ9856.
Morningside *Edin.* ***Suburb***, 1m/2km S of Edinburgh city centre. **25 G2** NT2471.
Morningside *N.Lan.* ***Settlement***, 1m/2km SE of Newmains. **24 C4** NS8355.
Mornish *Arg. & B.* ***Locality***, lying E and SE of Caliach Point, Mull. **36 C4** NM3753.
Morphie *Aber.* ***Hamlet***, 2m/3km SE of Marykirk. **43 F3** NO7164.
Morriston *Sc.Bord.* ***Locality***, formed of East and West Morriston, 2m/3km SE of Legerwood. NT6041.
Morriston *S.Ayr.* ***Settlement***, 1m/2km NE of Maidens. **14 A5** NS2309.
Morroch *High.* ***Settlement***, adjoining to S of Arisaig, Lochaber district. **37 F1** NM6686.
Morrone Hill *Aber.* ***Mountain***, 2m/3km SW of Braemar. Height 2818 feet or 859 metres. **41 G1** NO1388.
Morsgail Forest *W.Isles* ***Forest/woodland***, upland tract, broken up by innumerable streams and small lochs, to W of Loch Langavat, Isle of Lewis. **66 D2** NB1217.
Mortimer's Deep *Fife* ***Sea feature***, passage between Inchcolm and mainland of Fife. **25 F1** NT1883.
Mortlach Church *Moray* ***Ecclesiastical building***, at Kirktown of Mortlach, to S of Dufftown, and believed to be one of oldest churches continually used for public worship. Originally founded c. AD 566 by St. Moluag, building dates from 11c and 12c and includes sculptured stones, fine stained glass, battle stone and old watch tower. **53 F1** NJ3239.
Mortlich *Aber.* ***Mountain***, 2m/3km N of Aboyne. Height 1250 feet or 381 metres. **54 A4** NJ5301.
Morton Castle *D. & G.* ***Castle***, well-preserved ruin of late 13c hall (Historic Scotland) on S shore of small Morton Loch, 3m/4km N of Thornhill. Stronghold of Douglas family. **8 C1** NX8999.
Morton Loch *D. & G.* ***Lake/loch***, small loch, 3m/4km N of Thornhill. Ruins of 13c Morton Castle (Historic Scotland) on S shore. **8 C1** NX8999.
Morton Reservoir *W.Loth.* ***Reservoir***, small reservoir 3m/4km S of Mid Calder. NT0763.
Moruisg *High.* ***Mountain***, on Glencarron and Glenuig Forest, Ross and Cromarty district. Munro: height 3044 feet or 928 metres. **60 A4** NH1050.
Morven *Aber.* ***Mountain***, 5m/8km N of Ballater. Height 2857 feet or 871 metres. **53 F4** NJ3704.
Morven *High.* ***Mountain***, in Caithness district 9m/14km N of Helmsdale. Height 2316 feet or 706 metres. **73 F2** ND0028.
Morvern *High.* ***Locality***, large peninsula in Lochaber district, bounded on N by Loch Sunart, on SW by Sound of Mull and on SE by Loch Linnhe. **37 E4** NM6654.
Morvich *High.* ***Locality***, in Skye and Lochalsh district, near mouth of River Croe, on E side of Loch Duih. Camping site (National Trust for Scotland) for tents and caravans. Adventure camp. **49 F2** NG9620.
Morvich *High.* ***Settlement***, on NE side of River Fleet, 2m/3km SE of Rogart station. **72 C4** NC7500.
Moscow *E.Ayr.* ***Hamlet***, 4m/7km NE of Kilmarnock. **23 F5** NS4840.
Moss *Arg. & B.* ***Settlement***, 1km NE of Middleton, Tiree. **36 A2** NL9644.
Moss Hill *Aber.* ***Mountain***, 4m/6km NW of Strathdon. Height 2158 feet or 658 metres. **53 F3** NJ3117.
Moss of Barmuckity *Moray* ***Settlement***, 2m/3km SE of Elgin. **63 E3** NJ2461.
Moss of Belnagoak *Aber.* ***Open space***, moorland 2m/4km S of New Deer. **65 D5** NJ8742.
Moss of Cruden *Aber.* ***Open space***, moorland 2m/3km N of Hatton. **65 F5** NK0340.
Moss-side *High.* ***Settlement***, 2m/3km SW of Nairn. **62 A4** NH8654.
Moss-side *Moray* ***Settlement***, 1m/2km N of Milltown of Rothiemay. **64 A4** NJ5450.
Mossat *Aber.* ***Settlement***, 2m/3km S of Lumsden. **53 G3** NJ4719.
Mossbank *Shet.* ***Village***, on NE coast of Mainland, opposite Samphrey. **85 D5** HU4575.
Mossblown *S.Ayr.* Population: 2039. ***Village***, 1m/2km N of Annbank. **14 C3** NS4023.
Mossbrae Height *Sc.Bord.* ***Mountain***, 2m/3km E of Newburgh. Height 1528 feet or 466 metres. **17 E4** NT3419.
Mossburnford *Sc.Bord.* ***Settlement***, 3m/5km S of Jedburgh. **18 A5** NT6616.
Mossdale *D. & G.* ***Locality***, at site of former railway station, 5m/8km S of New Galloway. **8 A3** NX6670.
Mossend *N.Lan.* ***Town***, 2m/4km NW of Hamilton. **24 B3** NS7360.
Mossgiel *E.Ayr.* ***Settlement***, 1m/2km NW of Mauchline. **14 C3** NS4828.
Mosshead *Aber.* ***Settlement***, 3m/4km E of Huntly. **54 A1** NJ5639.
Mosside *Angus* ***Settlement***, 2m/3km NW of Forfar. **42 C4** NO4352.
Mosspark *Glas.* ***Suburb***, 3m/5km SW of Glasgow city centre. NS5463.
Mosspaul Hotel *D. & G.* ***Other building***, 4m/6km S of Teviothead, on A74 road. **10 C2** NY4099.
Mosstodloch *Moray* Population: 1066. ***Village***, 1m/2km NW of Fochabers. **63 F3** NJ3360.
Mosston *Angus* ***Hamlet***, 1m/2km W of Redford. **42 D5** NO5444.
Mosstown *Aber.* ***Settlement***, 4m/6km SE of Fraserburgh. NK0362.

Mote of Mark *D. & G.* ***Historic/prehistoric site***, well preserved Celtic hillfort of 5c or 6c (National Trust for Scotland) just W of Rockcliffe, 4m/7km S of Dalbeattie. One of the most important archaeological sites on Solway Firth. **8 C5** NX8454.
Mote of Urr *D. & G.* ***Historic/prehistoric site***, remains of Saxon-early Norman fortification, on W bank of Urr Water 2m/4km N of Dalbeattie. **8 C4** NX8164.
Motherwell *N.Lan.* Population: 30,717. ***Town***, former steel town, 12m/20km SE of Glasgow. **24 B4** NS7557.
Motte of Druchtag *D. & G.* ***Historic/prehistoric site***, early medieval earthwork (Historic Scotland) on NE side of Mochrum, 2m/3km N of Port William. **3 D2** NX3446.
Moul of Eswick *Shet.* ***Coastal feature***, headland 1km E of Eswick. Lighthouse. **83 E2** HU4853.
Moulin *P. & K.* ***Village***, 1km N of Pitlochry. To SE is Caisteal Dubh (or Castle Dhu), ruined former stronghold of the Campbells. **41 E4** NN9459.
Mound Rock *High.* ***Hill***, on NW side of Loch Fleet, 3m/5km W of Golspie. Height 656 feet or 200 metres. **72 C5** NH7798.
Mounie Castle *Aber.* ***Castle***, 17c castle with round tower, 3m/4km NW of Oldmeldrum. Alterations made in late 19c. **54 C2** NJ7628.
Mount *High.* ***Settlement***, 1m/2km NE of Ferness. **62 B5** NH9746.
Mount Battock ***Mountain***, on border of Aberdeenshire and Angus, 5m/8km NE of Tarfside. Height 2555 feet or 779 metres. **42 D1** NO5484.
Mount Blair *P. & K.* ***Mountain***, 1m/2km SW of Forter. Height 2440 feet or 744 metres. **41 G3** NO1662.
Mount Bouie *Angus* ***Mountain***, 2m/3km SW of Clova. Height 1919 feet or 585 metres. **42 B2** NO3070.
Mount Eagle *High.* ***Hill***, on Black Isle in Ross and Cromarty district, 3m/5km N of Munlochy. Height 840 feet or 256 metres. **61 F4** NH6458.
Mount Florida *Glas.* ***Suburb***, 3m/5km S of Glasgow city centre. NS5861.
Mount Hill *Fife* ***Hill***, 3m/5km NW of Cupar. Height 725 feet or 221 metres. **34 B3** NO3216.
Mount Keen ***Mountain***, on border of Aberdeenshire and Angus, 6m/10km SE of Ballater. Munro: height 3080 feet or 939 metres. **42 C1** NO4086.
Mount Meddin ***Mountain***, on border of Aberdeenshire and Moray, 4m/6km S of Cabrach. Height 1935 feet or 590 metres. **53 F2** NJ4021.
Mount of Haddoch *Moray* ***Mountain***, 2m/3km NE of Cabrach. Height 1709 feet or 521 metres. **53 G2** NJ4128.
Mount Oliphant *S.Ayr.* ***Settlement***, 3m/5km SE of Ayr. **14 B4** NS3516.
Mount Stuart *S.Lan.* ***Mountain***, on border with Dumfries & Galloway, at head of Nithsdale, 6m/10km NW of Sanquhar. Height 1568 feet or 478 metres. **15 F4** NS7519.
Mount Vernon *Glas.* ***Suburb***, 4m/7km SE of Glasgow. NS6563.
Mountain Cross *Sc.Bord.* ***Settlement***, 3m/5km S of West Linton. **25 F5** NT1446.
Mountbenger *Sc.Bord.* ***Hamlet***, 3m/5km NE of St. Mary's Loch. **17 E3** NT3125.
Mountblairy *Aber.* ***Locality***, includes Hillhead of Mountblairy, Hill of Mountblairy and Newton of Mountblairy, W of River Deveron and 4m/6km NW of Turriff. **64 B4** NJ6954.
Mountblow *W.Dun.* ***Suburb***, 2m/4km NW of Clydebank town centre. NS4771.
Mountfleurie *Fife* ***Suburb***, W district of Leven. NO3701.
Mountgerald *High.* ***Settlement***, 3m/4km NE of Dingwall. **61 E3** NH5661.
Mountstuart *Arg. & B.* ***Historic house***, Victorian mansion (1877) near E coast of Bute 4m/6km SE of Rothesay. Seat of Marquess of Bute. **22 C4** NS1059.
Mousa *Shet.* ***Island***, uninhabited island of about 3 square km lying 1km off E coast of Mainland across Mousa Sound in vicinity of Sandwick. Broch of Mousa (Historic Scotland) on W coast. **83 D5** HU4624.
Mousa Sound *Shet.* ***Sea feature***, channel between Mousa and Mainland. **82 D5** HU4624.
Mouse Water *S.Lan.* ***River***, rising 2m/3km NE of Forth and running SW into River Clyde 1m/2km W of Lanark. NS8643.
Mouswald *D. & G.* ***Village***, 6m/10km E of Dumfries. **9 E3** NY0672.
Mowhaugh *Sc.Bord.* ***Settlement***, 4m/6km SE of Morebattle. **18 C4** NT8120.
Mowtie *Aber.* ***Settlement***, 3m/5km NW of Stonehaven. **43 G1** NO8388.
Moy *High.* ***Settlement***, on N side of Caledonian Canal, 1m/2km SW of Gairlochy. **39 D1** NN1682.
Moy *High.* ***Settlement***, in Glen Spean, 9m/14km W of Kinloch Laggan. **39 G1** NN4282.
Moy *High.* ***Village***, in Inverness district, on W side of Loch Moy, 9m/15km SE of Inverness. **51 G1** NH7634.
Moy Burn *High.* ***River***, flowing W from S slopes of Beinn Bhreac, then flowing S into Loch Moy, 4m/7km SE of Daviot. **51 G1** NH7734.
Moy Forest *High.* ***Open space***, upland area on N side of Loch Laggan. **39 G1** NN4183.
Moy House *Moray* ***Settlement***, 1m/2km NW of Forres. **62 C3** NJ0160.
Moycroft *Moray* ***Locality***, E district of Elgin. NJ2362.
Mu Ness *Shet.* ***Coastal feature***, headland at SE end of Unst 3m/5km E of Uyeasound. **85 F2** HP6301.
Mu Ness *Shet.* ***Coastal feature***, headland on W coast of Mainland, 4m/6km S of Melby. **82 A2** HU1652.
Muaithabhal *W.Isles* ***Mountain***, 3m/4km W of head of Loch Shell, Isle of Lewis. Height 1391 feet or 424 metres. **67 E2** NB2511.
Muasdale *Arg. & B.* ***Village***, on W coast of Kintyre, 3m/4km N of Glenbarr. **21 E5** NR6740.
Muchalls *Aber.* ***Village***, on E coast, 4m/7km N of Stonehaven. Red sandstone cliffs. Bridge of Muchalls is settlement 1km S. **55 D5** NO9092.
Muchalls Castle *Aber.* ***Castle***, 1km W of Muchalls. 17c castle burnt in second Jacobite uprising and later rebuilt. **55 D5** NO8991.
Muchra *Sc.Bord.* ***Settlement***, 3m/4km S of St. Mary's Loch. **16 D4** NT2217.
Muchrachd *High.* ***Settlement***, in Glen Cannich, 3m/5km NW of Cannich. **50 B1** NH2833.
Muck *High.* ***Island***, sparsely populated island in Inner Hebrides lying 3m/5km SW of Eigg across Sound of Eigg. Area about 2 square miles or 5 square km. Rises to height of 451 feet or 137 metres. **36 D2** NM4179.
Muck Water *S.Ayr.* ***River***, rising on Drumneillie Hill and flowing SW to join Duisk River, 1km SE of Pinwherry. **6 D2** NX2085.
Muckle Burn *Stir.* ***River***, flowing E, then SE into Allan Water 4m/6km NE of Dunblane. **32 C4** NN8106.
Muckle Cairn *Angus* ***Mountain***, 4m/6km NE of Clova. Height 2709 feet or 826 metres. **42 B2** NO3776.
Muckle Flugga *Shet.* ***Island***, small rocky island 1km N of Unst. Lighthouse. **85 E1** HP6019.
Muckle Green Holm *Ork.* ***Island***, small uninhabited island 1m/2km SW of War Ness at S end of Eday. Smaller island of Little Green Holm to S. **80 D4** HY5227.
Muckle Holm *Shet.* ***Island***, small uninhabited island in Yell Sound 2m/3km E of Burra Voe. **84 C4** HU4088.
Muckle Long Hill *Aber.* ***Mountain***, 3m/5km SE of Haugh of Glass. Height 1282 feet or 391 metres. **53 G1** NJ4536.
Muckle Ness *Shet.* ***Coastal feature***, headland on E coast of Mainland on S side of Dury Voe. HU4661.
Muckle Ossa *Shet.* ***Island***, rock off NW coast of Mainland, 2m/4km W of The Faither. Little Ossa rock is adjacent to S. **84 B4** HU2285.
Muckle Roe *Shet.* ***Island***, inhabited island of some 7 square miles or 18 square km off W coast of Mainland in St. Magnus Bay, connected to Mainland by bridge across Roe Sound. Has high, red cliffs. **82 C1** HU3264.
Muckle Skerry *Ork.* ***Island***, largest of Pentland Skerries, with lighthouse. **77 G1** ND4678.
Muckle Skerry *Shet.* ***Island***, isolated group of rock islands 3m/5km off NW coast of Out Skerries island group. **85 F5** HU6273.
Muckle Skerry of Neapaback *Shet.* ***Island***, rock off Heoga Ness at SE end of Yell. HU5378.
Muckle Water *Ork.* ***Lake/loch***, on Rousay, 1m/2km long, aligned NW to SE. **80 B3** HY3930.
Muckletown *Aber.* ***Settlement***, 3m/5km N of Alford. **54 A2** NJ5721.
Mudale *High.* ***River***, running E into head of Loch Naver, in Sutherland district. NC5735.
Mudale *High.* ***Settlement***, to N of River Mudale, 3m/4km W of Loch Naver. **75 E5** NC5336.
Mudlee Bracks ***Mountain***, 3m/5km SW of Ballochan, with summit on border of Aberdeenshire and Angus. Height 2257 feet or 688 metres. **42 D1** NO5185.
Mugdock *Stir.* ***Hamlet***, 2m/3km N of Milngavie and 2m/3km S of Strathblane. NS5576.
Mugdock Castle *Stir.* ***Castle***, remains of castle of W shore of Mugdock Loch, formerly seat of Montrose family. NS5477.
Mugdock Country Park *Stir.* ***Leisure/recreation***, country park surrounding Mugdock Loch and Castle, 1m/2km S of Strathblane. **23 G2** NS5576.
Mugdock Loch *Stir.* ***Lake/loch***, small loch with surrounding country park just 1km W of Mugdock. NS5577.
Mugdock Reservoir *E.Dun.* ***Reservoir***, small reservoir to S of Mugdock. NS5575.
Mugdrum Island *Fife* ***Island***, narrow low-lying island, 1m/2km long E to W, in Firth of Tay NW of Newburgh. **34 A3** NO2218.
Mugeary *High.* ***Settlement***, on Skye, 4m/6km SW of Portree. **48 A1** NG4438.
Muick *Aber.* ***River***, running NE from Loch Muick down Glen Muick to River Dee 1km S of Ballater. **42 B1** NO3694.
Muie *High.* ***Settlement***, in Sutherland district, 6m/9km E of Lairg. **72 B4** NC6704.
Muir *Aber.* ***Settlement***, at bridge over River Dee, 1m/2km W of Inverey. **41 F1** NO0689.
Muir of Dinnet *Aber.* ***Open space***, moorland on N bank of River Dee to W of Dinnet, 5m/8km W of Aboyne. **53 G5** NO4397.
Muir of Fowlis *Aber.* ***Village***, 3m/4km S of Alford. **54 A3** NJ5612.
Muir of Lochs *Moray* ***Settlement***, 3m/4km SW of Garmouth. **63 F3** NJ3062.
Muir of Miltonduff *Moray* ***Locality***, 1km S of Miltonduff and 3m/4km SW of Elgin. NJ1859.
Muir of Orchill *P. & K.* ***Open space***, moorland tract 3m/5km S of Muthill. **33 D3** NN8612.
Muir of Ord *High.* Population: 2033. ***Village***, in Ross and Cromarty district, 3m/4km N of Beauly. **61 E4** NH5250.
Muir of the Clans *High.* ***Open space***, moorland area 4m/6km SW of Nairn. **62 A4** NH8352.
Muir of Thorn *P. & K.* ***Forest/woodland***, wooded area 4m/6km SE of Dunkeld. **33 F1** NO0737.
Muir Park Reservoir *Stir.* ***Reservoir***, small reservoir 2m/4km N of Drymen. NS4892.
Muiravonside Country Park *W.Loth.* ***Leisure/recreation***, country park with 170 acres of parkland, woodland and gardens on W bank of River Avon, 3m/5km SW of Linlithgow. Park includes disused mine shaft. **25 D2** NS9575.
Muirden *Aber.* ***Settlement***, on E side of River Deveron, 3m/4km NW of Turriff. **64 C4** NJ7053.
Muirdrum *Angus* ***Village***, 2m/3km N of Carnoustie. **35 D1** NO5637.
Muiredge *Fife* ***Suburb***, W district of Buckhaven. NT3598.
Muirend *Glas.* ***Suburb***, 4m/6km S of Glasgow city centre, in Cathcart district. NS5760.
Muirfield *E.Loth.* *See Gullane.*
Muirhead *Aber.* ***Settlement***, 3m/5km S of Alford. **54 A3** NJ5611.
Muirhead *Angus* Population: 919. ***Village***, 5m/8km NW of Dundee. **34 B1** NO3434.
Muirhead *Fife* ***Hamlet***, 3m/4km SE of Falkland. **34 A4** NO2805.
Muirhead *Glas.* ***Suburb***, 6m/9km E of Glasgow city centre. NS6763.
Muirhead *Moray* ***Settlement***, 4m/6km NE of Forres. **62 C3** NJ0863.
Muirhead *N.Lan.* Population: 1027. ***Village***, 4m/6km NW of Coatbridge. **24 A3** NS6869.
Muirhead Reservoir *N.Ayr.* ***Reservoir***, 4m/6km SE of Largs. **22 D4** NS2556.
Muirhouse *Edin.* ***Suburb***, 3m/5km NW of Edinburgh city centre. NT2176.
Muirhouses *Falk.* ***Hamlet***, 1m/2km SE of Bo'ness. **25 E1** NT0180.
Muirkirk *E.Ayr.* Population: 1860. ***Small town***, on River Ayr, 9m/15km NE of Cumnock. Cairn to S marks site of McAdam's original tar works. **15 E3** NS6927.
Muirmill *Stir.* ***Settlement***, 1m/2km W of Carron Bridge. **24 B1** NS7283.
Muirneag *W.Isles* ***Hill***, 6m/9km W of Tolsta Head. Height 813 feet or 248 metres. **69 F3** NB4748.
Muirshearlich *High.* ***Locality***, on NW side of Caledonian Canal in Lochaber district, 5m/7km NE of Fort William. NN1380.
Muirshiel Country Park *Renf.* ***Leisure/recreation***, country park with moorland and mixed woodland on slopes above River Calder, 4m/6km NW of Lochwinnoch. Visitor centre, ranger services and walking trails. **23 E3** NS3163.
Muirskie *Aber.* ***Settlement***, 2m/3km NW of Netherley. **54 D5** NO8295.
Muirtack *Aber.* ***Locality***, 3m/5km W of Hatton. **55 E1** NJ9937.
Muirtack *Aber.* ***Settlement***, 3m/4km S of Cuminestown. **64 D5** NJ8146.
Muirton *High.* ***Settlement***, on Black Isle, 4m/5km SW of Cromarty. **61 G3** NH7463.
Muirton *P. & K.* ***Suburb***, N district of Perth. NO1025.
Muirton of Ardblair *P. & K.* ***Village***, 1m/2km S of Blairgowrie. **41 G5** NO1743.
Muirton of Ballochy *Angus* ***Hamlet***, 3m/5km NE of Brechin. **43 E3** NO6462.
Muirtown *High.* ***Locality***, on NW side of Inverness. NH6546.
Muirtown *Moray* ***Settlement***, 3m/4km W of Forres. NH9959.
Muirtown *P. & K.* ***Village***, 2m/3km SW of Auchterarder. **33 E3** NN9211.
Muirtown Basin *High.* ***Other water feature***, entrance to Caledonian Canal from Beauly Firth, 1km W of Inverness centre. NH6546.
Muiryfold *Aber.* ***Settlement***, on N side of Delgaty Forest, 3m/4km E of Turriff. **64 C4** NJ7651.
Mulben *Moray* ***Settlement***, 5m/8km W of Keith. **63 F4** NJ3550.
Muldoanich *W.Isles* ***Island***, uninhabited island lying 2m/3km E of SE point of Vatersay. Attains height of 502 feet or 153 metres. **44 B4** NL6893.
Mulhagery *W.Isles* ***Settlement***, on SE coast of Isle of Lewis, 2m/3km S of entrance to Loch Shell. **67 F3** NB3606.
Mull *Arg. & B.* ***Island***, one of Inner Hebrides lying opposite entrance to Loch Linnhe, off W coast of Scottish mainland, separated by Firth of Lorne and the narrow Sound of Mull. Area about 350 square

M

miles or 910 square km. Coastline rugged, and much indented on W side. Terrain mountainous, reaching 3169 feet or 966 metres at Ben More. Chief town is Tobermory. **29 E1** NM6035.

Mull and West Highland Railway *Arg. & B.* ***Other feature of interest***, Scotland's only island passenger tourist railway, on E coast of Mull, operating between Craignure and Torosay Castle. **29 G1** NM7336.

Mull Head *Ork.* ***Coastal feature***, headland at N end of Papa Westray. **80 D1** HY5055.

Mull Head *Ork.* ***Coastal feature***, headland at E extremity of Mainland beyond Deer Sound. **79 E2** HY5909.

Mull of Cara *Arg. & B.* ***Coastal feature***, headland at S end of Cara. **21 E5** NR6343.

Mull of Galloway *D. & G.* ***Coastal feature***, bold headland, with high cliffs and lighthouse, at S extremity of Rinns of Galloway. Southernmost point of Scotland. **2 B3** NX1530.

Mull of Kintyre *Arg. & B.* ***Coastal feature***, headland at SW end of Kintyre, 9m/14km S of Machrihanish. Mull lighthouse to N. **12 A5** NR5907.

Mull of Logan *D. & G.* ***Coastal feature***, headland to N of Port Logan Bay, 9m/14km SE of Portpatrick. **2 A2** NX0741.

Mull of Oa *Arg. & B.* ***Coastal feature***, headland at SW end of The Oa, Islay. Monument commemorates those who died in two American troopships in 1918. **20 A5** NR2641.

Mulla-fo-dheas *W.Isles* ***Mountain***, on North Harris, 3m/5km S of head of Loch Langavat. Height 2437 feet or 743 metres. **66 D3** NB1407.

Mullach a' Ruisg *W.Isles* ***Mountain***, 1km E of head of Loch Langavat. Height 1551 feet or 473 metres. **67 D2** NB1612.

Mullach an Rathain *High.* ***Mountain***, one of the peaks of Liathach, Ross and Cromarty district. Munro: height 3355 feet or 1023 metres. **59 F4** NG9157.

Mullach Buidhe *N.Ayr.* ***Mountain***, on NW of Arran, 2m/3km SE of Pirnmill. Height 2365 feet or 721 metres. **22 A5** NR9042.

Mullach Charlabhaigh (Anglicised form: Upper Carloway.) *W.Isles* ***Settlement***, adjoining to N of Carloway, Isle of Lewis. **68 D3** NB2043.

Mullach Clach a' Bhlàir *High.* ***Mountain***, in Cairngorm Mountains, in Badenoch and Strathspey district, 8m/12km SW of Ben Macdui. Munro: height 3342 feet or 1019 metres. **52 A5** NN8892.

Mullach Coire a' Chuir *Arg. & B.* ***Mountain***, in Argyll, 3m/4km NW of Lochgoilhead. Height 2096 feet or 639 metres. **31 D4** NN1703.

Mullach Coire Ardachaidh *High.* ***Mountain***, in Lochaber district, between Loch Loyne and Loch Garry. Height 1768 feet or 539 metres. **50 B4** NH2004.

Mullach Coire Mhic Fhearchair *High.* ***Mountain***, in W part of Ross and Cromarty district 3m/5km E of head of Lochan Fada. Munro: height 3342 feet or 1019 metres. **59 G2** NH0573.

Mullach Coire nan Geur-oirean *High.* ***Mountain***, on Locheil Forest, Lochaber district, 4m/7km SE of head of Loch Arkaig. Height 2385 feet or 727 metres. **38 C1** NN0489.

Mullach Fraoch-choire *High.* ***Mountain***, on Glenaffric Forest, Inverness district, 4m/6km SW of head of Loch Affric. Munro: height 3615 feet or 1102 metres. **49 G3** NH0917.

Mullach Lochan nan Gabhar ***Mountain***, NE shoulder of Ben Avon massif, on border of Moray and Aberdeenshire, N of Braemar. Height 3624 feet or 1105 metres. NJ1402.

Mullach Mòr *High.* ***Hill***, 1m/2km NW of Kinloch, Rum. Height 997 feet or 304 metres. **47 G4** NG3801.

Mullach na Càrn *High.* ***Mountain***, highest point on Scalpay, Skye and Lochalsh district. Height 1299 feet or 396 metres. **48 C2** NG6029.

Mullach na Dheiragain *High.* ***Mountain***, in Skye and Lochalsh district, with craggy summit 2m/4km SW of W end of Loch Mullardoch. Munro: height 3221 feet or 982 metres. **49 G2** NH0825.

Mullach na Reidheachd *W.Isles* ***Hill***, 1m/2km E of Màs a' Chnoic-chuairtich. Height 968 feet or 295 metres. **66 C2** NB0914.

Mullach nan Cadhaichean *High.* ***Hill***, 6m/9km E of Redpoint, Ross and Cromarty district. Height 964 feet or 294 metres. **59 E3** NG8269.

Mullach nan Coirean *High.* ***Mountain***, in Lochaber district 5m/8km S of Fort William. Munro: height 3080 feet or 939 metres. **38 D3** NN1266.

Mulldonoch *D. & G.* ***Mountain***, 2m/3km SE of Glen Trool Lodge. Height 1827 feet or 557 metres. **7 F3** NX4278.

Mullwharchar *E.Ayr.* ***Mountain***, 3m/4km W of Corserine. Height 2270 feet or 692 metres. NX4586.

Mundurno *Aberdeen* ***Settlement***, 1m/2km inland and 4m/6km E of Dyce. **55 E3** NJ9412.

Munerigie *High.* ***Settlement***, at E end of Loch Garry, 3m/4km W of Invergarry. **50 B4** NH2602.

Muness Castle *Shet.* ***Castle***, late 16c castle (Historic Scotland), 1km W of Mu Ness. **85 F2** HP6301.

Munga Skerries *Shet.* ***Coastal feature***, group of rocks off NW coast of Mainland 2m/3km NE of entrance to Ronas Voe. HU2987.

Mungasdale *High.* ***Settlement***, 4m/7km E of Laide across Gruinard Bay, Ross and Cromarty district. **70 B5** NG9693.

Mungoswells *E.Loth.* ***Settlement***, 3m/5km NW of Haddington. **26 B2** NT4978.

Munlochy *High.* ***Village***, in Ross and Cromarty district at head of Munlochy Bay, 6m/9km N of Inverness. **61 F4** NH6453.

Munlochy Bay *High.* ***Bay***, inlet on W side of Inner Moray Firth or Inverness Firth, on S side of Black Isle. **61 F4** NH6453.

Munnoch *N.Ayr.* ***Settlement***, 3m/4km W of Dalry. **22 D5** NS2548.

Munnoch Reservoir *N.Ayr.* ***Reservoir***, 4m/6km N of Ardrossan. **22 D5** NS2547.

Murdoch Head *Aber.* ***Coastal feature***, headland on E coast, 4m/7km S of Peterhead. **55 G1** NK1239.

Murdostoun *N.Lan.* ***Locality***, 2m/3km NE of Wishaw. **24 C4** NS8257.

Murieston *W.Loth.* ***Suburb***, 2m/3km S of Livingston town centre. NT0664.

Murkle *High.* ***Settlement***, near N coast of Caithness district, 3m/5km E of Thurso. **77 D2** ND1668.

Murkle Bay *High.* ***Bay***, small bay on SW side of Dunnet Bay. **77 D2** ND1669.

Murlaganmore *Stir.* ***Settlement***, at SE end of Glen Lochay, 2m/3km NW of Killin. **32 A1** NN5434.

Murlaggan *High.* ***Settlement***, on N shore of Loch Arkaig, 12m/20km NW of Fort William. **49 G5** NN0192.

Murlaggan *High.* ***Settlement***, in valley of River Spean, 3m/4km E of Roybridge. **39 F1** NN3181.

Murra *Ork.* ***Settlement***, 1m/2km NW of Orgil, near to N coast of Hoy. **78 B2** HY2104.

Murrayfield *Edin.* ***Suburb***, 2m/3km W of Edinburgh city centre. Scottish Rugby Union football ground in S part of district. NT2273.

Murray's Hill *P. & K.* ***Hill***, low hill 5m/8km NE of Crieff. Height 807 feet or 246 metres. **33 E2** NN9325.

Murray's Isles *D. & G.* ***Island***, two most northerly of Islands of Fleet, at entrance to Fleet Bay from Wigtown Bay. **7 G5** NX5649.

Murrister *Shet.* ***Locality***, on Mainland, 2m/3km N of Gruting. HU2751.

Murroes *Angus* ***Hamlet***, on Sweet Burn, 3m/4km NW of Monifieth. **34 C1** NO4635.

Murthill *Angus* ***Hamlet***, 2m/3km W of Finavon. **42 C4** NO4657.

Murthly *P. & K.* ***Village***, 5m/8km SE of Dunkeld. **33 F1** NO0938.

Murthly Castle *P. & K.* ***Castle***, stands in wooded grounds beside River Tay, 2m/3km NW of Murthly. NO0739.

Musdale *Arg. & B.* ***Settlement***, 3m/4km NE of head of Loch Scammadale. **30 B2** NM9322.

Museum of Scottish Lead Mining *D. & G.* ***Other feature of interest***, in Lowther Hills at Wanlockhead. Museum tracing 300 years of Scottish lead mining. Features heritage trail, beam engine, period cottages and gold panning centre. **15 G4** NS8712.

Muskna Field *Shet.* ***Hill***, 1m/2km W of Fladdabister, Mainland. Height 859 feet or 262 metres. **82 D4** HU4032.

Musselburgh *E.Loth.* Population: 20,630. ***Town***, former trading and fishing port on Firth of Forth at mouth of River Esk, 6m/9km E of Edinburgh. Town contains boys' public school of Loretto. Tolbooth, late 16c. Racecourse. **26 A2** NT3472.

Muthill *P. & K.* ***Village***, 19c conservation village, 3m/5km S of Crieff. Ruined 15c church with 12c tower (Historic Scotland). **33 D3** NN8617.

Muthill Church *P. & K.* ***Historic/prehistoric site***, ruins of 15c parish church with tall Romanesque tower (Historic Scotland) in Muthill, 3m/4km S of Crieff. **33 D3** NN8717.

Muttonhole *Edin.* *Former name of Davidson's Mains, qv.*

Mybster *High.* ***Settlement***, in Caithness district, 5m/8km W of Watten. **77 D3** ND1652.

Myrebird *Aber.* ***Settlement***, 4m/6km NE of Banchory. **54 C5** NO7499.

Myres Castle *Fife* ***Castle***, on S side of Auchtermuchty, dating from 17c. NO2411.

N

Na Binneinean *Arg. & B.* ***Mountain***, rising from NE shore of Loch Bà, 3m/4km SE of Gruline. Height 1076 feet or 328 metres. **29 E1** NM5737.

Na Cruachan *High.* ***Mountain***, in Knoydart, 4m/7km N of Inverie. Height 1912 feet or 583 metres. **49 D4** NG7707.

Na Cùiltean *Arg. & B.* ***Island***, group of rocks with lighthouse, about 1m/2km SE of Rubha na Caillich on E coast of Jura. **21 D3** NR5464.

Na Dromannan *High.* ***Mountain***, 1m/2km SE of Strath Kanaird. Height 1338 feet or 408 metres. **71 E4** NC2001.

Na Glas Leacan *High.* *Alternative name for Eileanan nan Glas Leac, qv.*

Na Gruagaichean *High.* ***Mountain***, on Mamore Forest in Lochaber district 2m/4km NE of Kinlochleven. Munro: height 3460 feet or 1055 metres. **39 E3** NN2065.

Na h-Uamhachan *High.* ***Mountain***, 4m/7km NE of Glenfinnan, Lochaber district. Height 2266 feet or 691 metres. **38 B1** NM9684.

Na Peileirean ***Sea feature***, stretch of sea to N of Nave Island, 9m/15km NW of Bridgend. **20 A2** NR2976.

Na Torrain *Arg. & B.* ***Island***, one of Torran Rocks group, 4m/6km SW of Mull. **28 B3** NM2613.

Naast *High.* ***Settlement***, on W side of Loch Ewe, in Ross and Cromarty district, 3m/4km NW of Poolewe. **59 E1** NG8283.

Nairn *High.* ***River***, rising on slopes of Coile Mhòr and flowing NE through Strathnairn to Daviot, and continuing NE to enter Moray Firth at Nairn. **62 A4** NH8857.

Nairn *High.* Population: 7892. ***Small town***, royal burgh and resort in Nairn district, at mouth of River Nairn on S side of Moray Firth, 7m/12km E of Fort George. Former fishing port with harbour built by Thomas Telford. **62 A4** NH8856.

Naked Tam *Angus* ***Mountain***, 4m/6km NE of Dykehead. Height 1607 feet or 490 metres. **42 C3** NO4264.

Nan Eilean Museum *W.Isles* ***Other feature of interest***, in Stornoway, Isle of Lewis, depicting local history and archaeology of the area. **69 F4** NB4332.

Narachan Hill *Arg. & B.* ***Hill***, on Kintyre, 4m/6km E of Tayinloan. Height 935 feet or 285 metres. **21 F5** NR7547.

Narrachan *Arg. & B.* ***Settlement***, 4m/7km E of Kilmelford, to N of Loch Avich. **30 B3** NM9114.

Narrows of Raasay *High.* ***Sea feature***, strait between Skye and Raasay at S end of Sound of Raasay. Width just over 1km. **48 B1** NG5435.

National Gallery of Modern Art *Edin.* ***Other feature of interest***, 1m/2km W of Edinburgh city centre, with 20c paintings, and sculptures in the park outside. Artists include Vuillard, Bonnard, Matisse, Léger and Picasso. **25 G2** NT2373.

Nave Island *Arg. & B.* ***Island***, small island off Ardnave Point on N coast of Islay, on W side of entrance to Loch Gruinart. **20 A2** NR2875.

Naver *High.* ***River***, in Caithness district running N from Loch Naver down Strathnaver to Torrisdale Bay on N coast. **75 G3** NC6962.

Naver Rock *High.* ***Hill***, 2m/3km S of Bettyhill, Caithness district. Height 554 feet or 169 metres. **75 F3** NC7059.

Navidale *High.* ***Settlement***, just N of Helmsdale. **73 F3** ND0316.

Navity *High.* ***Settlement***, 2m/3km S of Cromarty. **61 G3** NH7865.

Neap *Shet.* ***Settlement***, 1km E of Housabister, Mainland. **83 E2** HU5058.

Neap of Skea *Shet.* ***Coastal feature***, headland 1km SE of Housetter, Mainland. **84 C4** HU3783.

Neaty Burn *High.* ***River***, flowing SE between Carn Bàn and Beinn a' Bha'ach Ard, and into River Farrar 2m/4km SW of Erchless Castles. **60 C5** NH3739.

Neave Island (Also known as Coomb Island.) *High.* ***Island***, small uninhabited island off N coast of Caithness district opposite Skerray. **75 F2** NC6664.

Neban Point *Ork.* ***Coastal feature***, headland on W coast of Mainland, 3m/5km NW of Stromness. **80 A5** HY2113.

Nechtansmere *Angus* *See Dunnichen.*

Nedd *High.* ***Village***, at head of Loch Nedd, 1m/2km SE of Drumbeg, W coast of Sutherland district. **74 A5** NC1331.

Needs Law *Sc.Bord.* ***Mountain***, in Wauchope Forest area of Cheviot Hills, 1m/2km SE of Note o' the Gate. Height 1456 feet or 444 metres. **11 E1** NT6002.

Neidpath Castle *Sc.Bord.* ***Castle***, 14c-16c L-plan tower house, on N bank of River Tweed, 1km W of Peebles. **16 D2** NT2340.

Neilston *E.Renf.* Population: 5260. ***Small town***, 2m/3km SW of Barrhead. **23 F4** NS4757.

Neilston Pad *E.Renf.* ***Hill***, rising to over 260 metres, 1m/2km S of Neilston. Craggy rocks on E face. **23 F4** NS4755.

Neist Point *High.* ***Coastal feature***, headland with lighthouse on W coast of Skye, 8m/13km W of Dunvegan. Most westerly point of Skye. **57 E5** NG1246.

Nemphlar *S.Lan.* ***Settlement***, 2m/3km W of Lanark. **24 C5** NS8544.

Nenthorn *Sc.Bord.* ***Village***, 4m/6km NW of Kelso. **18 A3** NT6837.

Neptune's Staircase *High.* ***Other feature of interest***, 2m/3km N of Fort William. A flight of eight locks built 1805-22, raising Caledonian Canal a total of 64 feet or 20 metres. **38 D2** NN1077.

Nereabolls *Arg. & B.* ***Settlement***, on S coast of Rinns of Islay, 3m/4km SW of Port Charlotte. **20 A4** NR2255.

Neriby *Arg. & B.* ***Settlement***, on Islay, 2m/3km E of Bridgend. **20 B3** NR3660.

M

N

Nerston *S.Lan.* ***Suburb***, to N of East Kilbride town centre. **24 A4** NS6456.
Ness *High.* ***River***, flowing from Loch Dochfour at NE end of Loch Ness, NE through Inverness and into Moray Firth at South Kessock. NH6646.
Ness *W.Isles* ***Locality***, 3m/5km S of Butt of Lewis. **69 G1** NB5261.
Ness Glen *E.Ayr.* ***Valley***, steep-sided wooded valley carrying River Doon N to Dalmellington from N arm of Loch Doon. **14 C5** NS4703.
Ness Head *High.* ***Coastal feature***, headland on E coast of Caithness district, 5m/7km S of Duncansby Head. **77 F2** ND3866.
Ness of Bardister *Shet.* ***Coastal feature***, headland on Sullom Voe to E of Bardister, Mainland. HU3676.
Ness of Bixter *Shet.* ***Coastal feature***, headland on The Firth, to E of Bixter, Mainland. HU3451.
Ness of Brodgar *Ork.* ***Coastal feature***, narrow tongue of land on Mainland, carrying a road between Loch of Harray and Loch of Stenness, 4m/6km W of Finstown. HY3012.
Ness of Brough *Shet.* ***Coastal feature***, headland at westernmost point of Fetlar, opposite Hascosay. HU5792.
Ness of Burgi *Shet.* ***Coastal feature***, headland on W side of West Voe of Sumburgh, opposite Sumburgh Head. Ancient fort (Historic Scotland). **83 F5** HU3808.
Ness of Burravoe *Shet.* ***Coastal feature***, headland 1m/2km NE of Burra Voe, Mainland. HU3890.
Ness of Burwick *Shet.* ***Coastal feature***, headland on N coast of Bur Wick, Mainland. HU3940.
Ness of Copister *Shet.* ***Coastal feature***, headland to E of Copister. HU4978.
Ness of Duncansby *High.* ***Coastal feature***, headland on N coast of Caithness district, 1m/2km W of Duncansby Head. **77 F1** ND3873.
Ness of Gossabrough *Shet.* ***Coastal feature***, headland on E coast of Yell to E of Gossabrough. HU5383.
Ness of Gruting *Shet.* ***Coastal feature***, promontory on Fetlar at centre of Wick of Gruting. HU6591.
Ness of Haggrister *Shet.* ***Coastal feature***, headland to E of Haggrister, Mainland. HU3470.
Ness of Hillswick *Shet.* ***Coastal feature***, peninsula on Mainland on W shore of Ura Firth. HU2877.
Ness of Huna *High.* ***Coastal feature***, headland on N coast of Caithness district, 3m/4km W of Duncansby Head. ND3673.
Ness of Kaywick *Shet.* ***Coastal feature***, promontory on Yell, on N side of entrance to Mid Yell Voe. HU5392.
Ness of Litter *High.* ***Coastal feature***, headland on N coast of Caithness district, 3m/5km NW of Thurso. **76 C1** ND0771.
Ness of Melby *Shet.* ***Coastal feature***, headland on W coast of Mainland to NW of Melby. HU1957.
Ness of Ork *Ork.* ***Coastal feature***, headland at NE end of Shapinsay. **80 D4** HY5422.
Ness of Queyfirth *Shet.* ***Coastal feature***, headland on NE coast of Mainland between Quey Firth and Colla Firth. HU3682.
Ness of Ramnageo *Shet.* ***Coastal feature***, headland on S coast of Unst 2m/4km E of Uyeasound. HU6299.
Ness of Skellister *Shet.* ***Coastal feature***, headland to NE of Skellister, Mainland. HU4795.
Ness of Snabrough *Shet.* ***Coastal feature***, headland on W coast of Fetlar. HU5793.
Ness of Sound *Shet.* ***Coastal feature***, headland with lighthouse on W coast of Yell, 4m/6km S of West Sandwick. **84 D4** HU4482.
Ness of Sound *Shet.* ***Coastal feature***, headland on Mainland to S of Sound, on E side of Voe of Sound. HU4640.
Ness of Tenston *Ork.* ***Settlement***, on headland, on W shore of Loch of Harray, Mainland. **80 A5** HY2816.
Ness of Trebister *Shet.* ***Coastal feature***, headland to SE of Trebister on E side of Gulber Wick, Mainland. HU4438.
Ness of Tuquoy *Ork.* ***Coastal feature***, headland on W side of Bay of Tuquoy, Westray. Ruined 12c Westside Church (Historic Scotland). HY4543.
Ness of Vatsetter *Shet.* ***Coastal feature***, headland to E of Vatsetter, Yell. HU5389.
Ness of West Sandwick *Shet.* ***Coastal feature***, headland on Yell, 1m/2km S of West Sand Wick bay. HU4387.
Nesting *Shet.* ***Locality***, on Mainland, consisting of North and South Nesting and enclosing South Nesting Bay on E coast. HU4554.
Nethan *S.Lan.* ***River***, rising 2m/4km N of Glenbuck and running NE past Lesmahagow, then into River Clyde on N side of Crossford. NS8247.
Nether Auchendrane *S.Ayr.* ***Settlement***, 3m/5km S of Ayr. **14 B4** NS3416.
Nether Barr *D. & G.* ***Settlement***, 1m/2km S of Newton Stewart. **7 F4** NX4263.
Nether Blainslie *Sc.Bord.* ***Hamlet***, 3m/4km SE of Lauder. **26 C5** NT5443.
Nether Boyndlie *Aber.* ***Settlement***, forms locality of Boyndlie with Upper Boyndlie, near N coast, 5m/9km SW of Fraserburgh. NJ9263.
Nether Crimond *Aber.* ***Settlement***, 4m/6km E of Inverurie. **54 D2** NJ8222.
Nether Dalgliesh *Sc.Bord.* ***Settlement***, 3m/5km S of Ettrick on Tima Water. **17 D5** NT2709.
Nether Dallachy *Moray* ***Village***, near N coast, 4m/6km W of Buckie. **63 F3** NJ3663.
Nether Glasslaw *Aber.* ***Settlement***, 3m/4km SW of New Aberdour. **65 D4** NJ8659.
Nether Handwick *Angus* ***Hamlet***, 3m/5km S of Glamis. **42 B5** NO3641.
Nether Kinmundy *Aber.* ***Settlement***, 6m/9km W of Peterhead. **65 F5** NK0443.
Nether Lenshie *Aber.* ***Settlement***, 4m/6km NW of Rothienorman. **64 B5** NJ6840.
Nether Pitforthie *Aber.* ***Settlement***, 3m/5km SE of Glenbervie. **43 G2** NO8179.
Nether Urquhart *Fife* ***Settlement***, 2m/3km SW of Strathmiglo. **33 G4** NO1808.
Nether Wellwood *E.Ayr.* ***Settlement***, 3m/5km SW of Muirkirk. **15 E3** NS6526.
Netherbrae *Aber.* ***Settlement***, near N coast, 3m/5km S of Gardenstown. Locality of Overbrae to E. **64 C4** NJ7959.
Netherbrough *Ork.* ***Settlement***, on Mainland, 4m/6km NW of Finstown. **80 B5** HY3116.
Netherburn *S.Lan.* ***Settlement***, 3m/5km N of Blackwood. **24 C5** NS8047.
Netherfield *S.Lan.* ***Locality***, 2m/3km NE of Strathaven. **24 B5** NS7245.
Netherhall *N.Ayr.* ***Settlement***, 1km N of Largs across Noddsdale Water. **22 D3** NS2060.
Netherley *Aber.* ***Locality***, 4m/7km S of Peterculter. **55 D5** NO8493.
Nethermill *D. & G.* ***Settlement***, 4m/6km NW of Lochmaben. **9 E2** NY0487.
Nethermuir *Aber.* ***Settlement***, 2m/3km SE of New Deer. **65 E5** NJ9044.
Nethershield *E.Ayr.* ***Settlement***, 2m/3km E of Sorn. **15 D3** NS5826.
Netherthird *D. & G.* ***Settlement***, 1m/2km N of Tongland, on E side of Tongland Loch. **8 B5** NX7155.
Netherthird *E.Ayr.* ***Village***, 1m/2km SE of Cumnock. **15 D4** NS5718.
Netherton *Angus* ***Hamlet***, 4m/6km W of Brechin. **42 D4** NO5457.
Netherton *N.Lan.* ***Village***, 1m/2km SW of Wishaw. NS7854.
Netherton *P. & K.* ***Settlement***, just N of Bridge of Cally. **41 G4** NO1452.
Netherton *S.Lan.* ***Settlement***, 2m/3km SW of Forth. **24 D4** NS9250.
Nethertown *High.* ***Settlement***, near N end of Island of Stroma, in Pentland Firth. **77 F1** ND3578.
Netherwood *D. & G.* ***Settlement***, 2m/3km S of Dumfries. **9 D3** NX9872.
Netherwood *E.Ayr.* ***Settlement***, on N bank of Greenock Water, 2m/4km NW of Muirkirk. **15 E3** NS6628.
Nethy *High.* ***River***, in Badenoch and Strathspey district, rising in Cairngorm Mountains and running N to River Spey 4m/7km SW of Grantown-on-Spey. **52 C3** NH9922.
Nethy Bridge *High.* ***Village***, on River Nethy, 1m/2km above mouth. **52 C2** NH9922.
Nev of Stuis *Shet.* ***Coastal feature***, headland on Yell on W side of entrance to Whale Firth. **85 D3** HU4697.
Nevis Forest *High.* ***Forest/woodland***, in Lochaber district on W side of Glen Nevis, SE of Fort William. **38 D2** NN1172.
New Abbey *D. & G. Alternative name for Sweetheart Abbey, qv.*
New Abbey *D. & G.* ***Village***, 6m/10km S of Dumfries. Ruins of Sweetheart Abbey (Historic Scotland). Monument to W of village commemorates Battle of Waterloo. 18c corn mill (Historic Scotland). **9 D4** NX9666.
New Abbey Corn Mill *D. & G.* ***Other feature of interest***, 18c water-powered corn mill (Historic Scotland) in working order, at New Abbey 12m/20km S of Dumfries. **8 D4** NX9666.
New Abbey Pow *D. & G.* ***River***, stream running E through New Abbey to River Nith estuary. NX9865.
New Aberdour *Aber.* ***Village***, 1m/2km S of Aberdour Bay, on N coast, and 4m/7km SW of Rosehearty. **65 D3** NJ8863.
New Alyth *P. & K.* ***Hamlet***, 1km S of Alyth. **42 A5** NO2447.
New Belses *Sc.Bord.* ***Settlement***, 6m/10km SE of Selkirk. **17 G3** NT5725.
New Bridge *D. & G.* ***Hamlet***, at road crossing of Cluden Water, 2m/4km NW of Dumfries. **8 D3** NX9479.
New Byth *Aber.* ***Village***, 7m/11km NE of Turriff. **64 D4** NJ8253.
New Cumnock *E.Ayr.* Population: 3968. ***Small town***, at confluence of Afton Water and River Nith, 5m/8km SE of Cumnock, in former coal-mining area. **15 E4** NS6113.
New Deer *Aber.* ***Village***, 14m/23km SW of Fraserburgh. **65 D5** NJ8846.
New Elgin *Moray* ***Locality***, S district of Elgin. **63 E3** NJ2261.
New England Bay *D. & G.* ***Bay***, 2m/4km S of Ardwell, on W side of Luce Bay. **2 B2** NX1242.
New Galloway *D. & G.* ***Small town***, on W side of Water of Ken valley, 17m/27km N of Kirkcudbright. Smallest royal burgh in Scotland. RSPB reserve on Ken Dee Marshes. **8 A3** NX6377.
New Gilston *Fife* ***Hamlet***, 5m/8km SE of Cupar. **34 C4** NO4308.
New Inn *Fife* ***Settlement***, 3m/4km SE of Falkland. **34 A4** NO2804.
New Kelso *High.* ***Settlement***, in Ross and Cromarty district, 3m/5km NE of Lochcarron. NG9342.
New Lanark *S.Lan.* ***Village***, 1km S of Lanark. **24 C5** NS8842.
New Lanark World Heritage Village *S.Lan.* ***Other feature of interest***, museum in New Lanark, 1km S of Lanark, commemorates model village designed by 19c industrialist, Robert Owen. Exhibits include re-creations of workers' living conditions. **24 C5** NS8742.
New Leeds *Aber.* ***Village***, 3m/5km E of Strichen. **65 E4** NJ9954.
New Leslie *Aber.* ***Settlement***, on SE side of Hill of Newleslie, 3m/5km SW of Insch. **54 A2** NJ5825.
New Luce *D. & G.* ***Village***, 5m/8km N of Glenluce, at confluence of Cross Water of Luce and Main Water of Luce. **6 C4** NX1764.
New Mains *S.Lan.* ***Settlement***, 1m/2km NE of Douglas. **15 G2** NS8431.
New Mains of Ury *Aber.* ***Settlement***, 1m/2km N of Stonehaven. **43 G1** NO8787.
New Mill *Aber.* ***Settlement***, 2m/3km NE of Glenbervie. **43 F1** NO7883.
New Orleans *Arg. & B.* ***Settlement***, at S end of Kintyre, on E coast, 3m/5km SE of Campbeltown. **12 C4** NR7517.
New Pitsligo *Aber.* Population: 1118. ***Village***, 10m/16km SW of Fraserburgh. Ruins of 15c Pitsligo Castle 1km SE of Rosehearty. **65 D4** NJ8855.
New Prestwick *S.Ayr.* ***Suburb***, 2m/3km NE of Ayr town centre. **14 B3** NS3524.
New Sauchie *Clack.* ***Locality***, adjoining to NE of Alloa. **33 D5** NS9094.
New Scone *P. & K.* Population: 4533. ***Village***, 2m/3km NE of Perth. **33 G2** NO1326.
New Shawbost *W.Isles* ***Settlement***, near NW coast of Isle of Lewis, forms locality of Siabost along with North and South Shawbost, 2m/4km W of Bragar. NB2646.
New Stevenston *N.Lan.* ***Suburb***, 2m/3km NE of Motherwell. NS7659.
New Tolsta *W.Isles Anglicised form of Tolastadh Úr, qv.*
New Town *E.Loth.* ***Village***, 3m/5km SE of Tranent. **26 B2** NT4470.
New Ulva *Arg. & B.* ***Settlement***, on S coast of Loch na Cille, 5m/8km SW of Tayvallich. **21 F1** NR7080.
New Valley *W.Isles* ***Village***, on Isle of Lewis, 1m/2km NW of Stornoway. NB4134.
New Winton *E.Loth.* ***Hamlet***, 2m/3km SE of Tranent. 17c Winton House 1m/2km SE. **26 B2** NT4271.
Newark *Ork.* ***Settlement***, on Sanday, at N end of Bay of Newark, 4m/7km SW of Tafts Ness. **81 F2** HY7242.
Newark Bay *Ork.* ***Bay***, on S coast of Mainland, 1m/2km E of St. Peter's Pool. **79 E2** HY5704.
Newark Castle *Inclyde* ***Historic house***, 16c-17c mansion (Historic Scotland) on E side of Port Glasgow. Incorporates 15c tower. **23 E2** NS3374.
Newark Castle *Sc.Bord.* ***Castle***, ruined 15c castle beside Yarrow Water, 3m/5km W of Selkirk. NT4229.
Newarthill *N.Lan.* Population: 6585. ***Village***, 3m/5km NE of Motherwell. **24 B4** NS7859.
Newbattle *Midloth.* ***Village***, 1km S of Dalkeith. NT3366.
Newbattle Abbey *Midloth.* ***Historic house***, dating mainly from 16c on site of abbey founded in 1140, 1km S of Dalkeith. **26 A3** NT3366.
Newbigging *Aber.* ***Settlement***, in Glen Clunie, 4m/6km S of Braemar. **41 G1** NO1485.
Newbigging *Aber.* ***Settlement***, 4m/6km N of Stonehaven. **55 D5** NO8591.
Newbigging *Angus* ***Hamlet***, 4m/6km NE of Broughty Ferry. **34 C1** NO4935.
Newbigging *Angus* ***Settlement***, 1km NW of Newtyle. **42 A5** NO2841.
Newbigging *Angus* ***Settlement***, 5m/8km N of Dundee. **34 C1** NO4237.
Newbigging *S.Lan.* ***Village***, 2m/4km E of Carnwath. **25 E5** NT0145.
Newbridge *Edin.* ***Village***, 3m/5km S of Forth Road Bridge. **25 F2** NT1272.
Newburgh *Aber.* ***Settlement***, to N of Mormond Hill, 3m/4km NE of Strichen. **65 E4** NJ9659.
Newburgh *Aber.* Population: 1401. ***Village***, with quay, on W side of River Ythan estuary, 1m/2km N of Newburgh Bar at mouth of river. Village is 4m/7km SE of Ellon. **55 E2** NJ9925.
Newburgh *Fife* Population: 2032. ***Small town***, former industrial town with small harbour, on S bank of Firth of Tay, 9m/14km W of Cupar. **34 A3** NO2318.
Newburgh *Sc.Bord.* ***Hamlet***, 5m/8km SW of Ettrickbridge. **17 E4** NT3220.
Newburgh Bar *Aber.* ***Coastal feature***, sand bar at mouth of River Ythan, 1m/2km N of Newburgh. **55 F2** NJ9925.

Newcastle *Fife* ***Suburb***, W district of Glenrothes. NO2401.
Newcastleton *Sc.Bord.* ***Village***, 18c symmetrical village on Liddel Water, 17m/27km S of Hawick. Former weaving centre. **10 C3** NY4887.
Newcastleton Forest *Sc.Bord.* ***Forest/woodland***, to E of Newcastleton forms part of Border Forest Park. **10 D3** NY4887.
Newcraighall *Edin.* ***Village***, 1m/2km SE of Portobello. **26 A2** NT3271.
Newfield *High.* ***Settlement***, in Ross and Cromarty district, 3m/5km S of Tain. **61 G2** NH7877.
Newgord *Shet.* ***Settlement***, just N of Westing, on W coast of Unst. **85 E2** HP5705.
Newhailes *E.Loth.* ***Locality***, adjoining to W of Musselburgh. NT3372.
Newhall Point *High.* ***Coastal feature***, N point of Udale Bay on Black Isle, 1km S of Invergordon across Cromarty Firth. **61 G3** NH7067.
Newhaven *Edin.* ***Suburb***, 2m/3km N of Edinburgh city centre. Small harbour on W side of Leith Harbour. NT2577.
Newhouse *N.Lan.* ***Settlement***, 4m/6km SE of Airdrie. **24 B3** NS7961.
Newhouse Industrial Estate *N.Lan. See Holytown.*
Newington *Edin.* ***Suburb***, `m/2km SE of Edinburgh city centre. NT2671.
Newlandrig *Midloth.* ***Hamlet***, 2m/3km NE of Gorebridge. **26 A3** NT3662.
Newlands *Glas.* ***Suburb***, 3m/5km S of Glasgow city centre. NS5760.
Newlands *Sc.Bord.* ***Settlement***, on E bank of Hermitage Water, 4m/7km N of Newcastleton. **10 D2** NY5094.
Newlands Hill *E.Loth.* ***Mountain***, 2m/3km SE of Danskine. Height 1387 feet or 423 metres. **26 C3** NT5865.
Newlands of Geise *High.* ***Settlement***, 2m/3km SW of Thurso. **76 C2** ND0865.
Newlands of Tynet *Moray* ***Hamlet***, near N coast, 4m/6km SW of Buckie. NJ3761.
Newmachar *Aber.* Population: 1504. ***Village***, 9m/14km N of Aberdeen. **55 D3** NJ8819.
Newmains *N.Lan.* Population: 5878. ***Small town***, 2m/3km E of Wishaw. **24 C4** NS8256.
Newmarket *W.Isles* ***Village***, on Isle of Lewis, 2m/3km N of Stornoway, adjoining to N of Laxdale across River Laxdale. **69 F4** NB4235.
Newmill *Aber.* ***Settlement***, 3m/4km E of Inverurie. **54 D2** NJ8122.
Newmill *Aber.* ***Settlement***, 3m/5km SW of New Deer. **65 D5** NJ8543.
Newmill *Moray* ***Village***, 1m/2km N of Keith. **63 G4** NJ4350.
Newmill *Sc.Bord.* ***Settlement***, in Teviotdale, 4m/7km SW of Hawick, at confluence of Allan Water and River Teviot. **17 F4** NT4510.
Newmill of Inshewan *Angus* ***Settlement***, 2m/3km E of Dykehead. **42 C3** NO4260.
Newmills *Edin.* ***Locality***, just N of Balerno across Water of Leith. NT1667.
Newmills *High.* ***Settlement***, on Cromarty Firth in Ross and Cromarty district, 2m/3km SW of Balblair. **61 F3** NH6764.
Newmiln *P. & K.* ***Hamlet***, 3m/4km N of New Scone. **33 G1** NO1230.
Newmiln *P. & K.* ***Settlement***, 2m/3km SW of Methven. **33 F2** NO0122.
Newmilns *E.Ayr.* Population: 3436. ***Small town***, on River Irvine, 7m/11km E of Kilmarnock. Once famous for muslim-weaving and lace. **14 D2** NS5337.
Newnoth *Aber.* ***Settlement***, to E of Hill of Noth, 1m/2km S of Gartly. **54 A1** NJ5130.
Newport *High.* ***Village***, near E coast of Caithness district, 4m/6km SW of Dunbeath. **73 G2** ND1324.
Newport-on-Tay *Fife* Population: 4343. ***Small town***, on S bank of Firth of Tay, opposite Dundee, and connected to it by road and rail bridges. **34 C2** NO4228.
Newseat *Aber.* ***Settlement***, 2m/3km N of Kirktown of Rayne. **54 C1** NJ7032.
Newstead *Sc.Bord.* ***Village***, 1m/2km E of Melrose. Remains of Roman fort of Trimontium to E. **17 G2** NT5634.
Newton *Aber.* ***Settlement***, 4m/7km SE of Keith. **63 G5** NJ4745.
Newton *Aber.* ***Settlement***, 4m/6km S of Mintlaw. **65 F5** NK0142.
Newton *Arg. & B.* ***Settlement***, on Newton Bay, on S shore of Loch Fyne, Argyll, opposite Furnace. **30 C5** NS0498.
Newton *D. & G.* ***Village***, 7m/11km S of Moffat. **9 F1** NY1194.
Newton *High.* ***Settlement***, on SW side of Loch Glencoul, Sutherland district. **74 B5** NC2331.
Newton *High.* ***Settlement***, 1m/2km W of Watten. **77 E3** ND2153.
Newton *High.* ***Settlement***, in Caithness district, 1m/2km SW of Wick. **77 F4** ND3449.
Newton *High.* ***Settlement***, 3m/5km E of Muir of Ord. **61 E4** NH5850.
Newton *High.* ***Settlement***, in Inverness district, near E shore of Inner Moray Firth or Inverness Firth, 2m/3km E of Alturlie Point. **61 G5** NH7448.
Newton *High.* ***Settlement***, in Ross and Cromarty district, 1m/2km SW of Cromarty. **61 G3** NH7766.
Newton *Moray* ***Settlement***, 1m/2km S of Garmouth. **63 F3** NJ3362.
Newton *N.Ayr.* ***Settlement***, on N coast of Arran, 1km NE of Lochranza across Loch Ranza. **22 A4** NR9351.
Newton *P. & K.* ***Settlement***, on N bank of River Almond, 6m/10km N of Crieff. **33 D1** NN8831.
Newton *Sc.Bord.* ***Hamlet***, 3m/5km W of Jedburgh. **18 A4** NT6020.
Newton *S.Lan.* ***Locality***, 6m/9km SE of Glasgow. NS6660.
Newton *S.Lan.* ***Settlement***, 1m/2km W of Wiston. **16 A2** NS9331.
Newton *W.Loth.* ***Settlement***, 2m/3km W of S end of Forth Road Bridge. **25 E2** NT0977.
Newton *W.Isles Anglicised form of Baile Mhic Phail, qv.*
Newton Bay *Arg. & B.* ***Bay***, on S shore of Loch Fyne, Argyll, to N of Newton and opposite Furnace. NS0498.
Newton Mearns *E.Renf.* Population: 19,494. ***Suburb***, 6m/10km SW of Glasgow. **23 G4** NS5355.
Newton of Ardtoe *High.* ***Settlement***, 3m/4km NW of Acharacle, Lochaber district. **37 F2** NM6470.
Newton of Balcanquhal *P. & K.* ***Settlement***, 1m/2km E of Glenfarg. **33 G3** NO1510.
Newton of Dalvey *Moray* ***Settlement***, on E side of River Findhorn, 2m/3km W of Forres. **62 C4** NJ0057.
Newton of Falkland *Fife* ***Village***, 1m/2km E of Falkland. **34 A4** NO2607.
Newton of Leys *High.* ***Settlement***, 3m/5km S of Inverness. **61 F5** NH6739.
Newton Point *N.Ayr.* ***Coastal feature***, headland to W of North and South Newton, at entrance to Loch Ranza, on N coast of Arran. NR9351.
Newton Stewart *D. & G.* Population: 3673. ***Small town***, market town on River Cree, 7m/11km N of Wigtown, and popular holiday resort and fishing centre. **7 F4** NX4165.
Newton upon Ayr *S.Ayr.* ***Suburb***, N district of Ayr. NS3423.
Newtonairds *D. & G.* ***Settlement***, 3m/4km S of Dunscore. **8 C2** NX8880.
Newtonferry *W.Isles Anglicised form of Port nan Long, qv.*
Newtongarry *Aber.* ***Locality***, comprising Mains of Newtongarry and Newtongarry Hill, 3m/5km E of Huntly. NJ5735.
Newtongrange *Midloth.* ***Town***, former mining town, 2m/3km S of Dalkeith. Scottish Mining Museum at Lady Victoria colliery. **26 A3** NT3364.
Newtonhill *Aber.* Population: 2139. ***Village***, on E coast, 5m/8km NE of Stonehaven. **55 E5** NO9193.
Newtonmill *Angus* ***Settlement***, 3m/4km N of Brechin. **43 E3** NO6064.
Newtonmore *High.* Population: 1044. ***Village***, on River Spey, in Badenoch and Strathspey district, 3m/5km W of Kingussie. Holiday and skiing centre. Clan Macpherson Museum. **51 G5** NN7199.
Newtown *Aber.* ***Suburb***, E district of Macduff. **64 C3** NJ7164.
Newtown *High.* ***Locality***, in Invernesss district, 3m/5km SW of Fort Augustus. **50 C4** NH3504.
Newtown *Moray* ***Locality***, on N coast adjoining to W of Hopeman, 6m/9km W of Lossiemouth. NJ1469.
Newtown St. Boswells *Sc.Bord.* Population: 1108. ***Village***, 3m/4km SE of Melrose. **17 G2** NT5731.
Newtyle *Angus* ***Village***, below N side of Newtyle Hill, 9m/15km NW of Dundee. **42 A5** NO2941.
Newtyle Forest *Moray* ***Forest/woodland***, 4m/7km S of Forres. **62 C4** NJ0552.
Newtyle Hill *Angus* ***Hill***, S of Newtyle. Height 882 feet or 269 metres. NO2939.
Newtyle Hill *P. & K.* ***Mountain***, 1m/2km E of Dunkeld. Height 1040 feet or 317 metres. **41 F5** NO0441.
Nibon *Shet.* ***Locality***, on coast in N part of Mainland, 2m/3km NW of Mangaster. Offshore is island called Isle of Nibon. HU3073.
Nick of Kindram *D. & G.* ***Coastal feature***, cliff indentation 3m/5km W of Mull of Galloway. **2 B3** NX1132.
Nick of the Balloch Pass *S.Ayr.* ***Other feature of interest***, mountain road pass between Pinbreck Hill and Glengap Hill, 4m/7km E of Barr. **7 E1** NX3493.
Niddrie *Edin.* ***Suburb***, 3m/5km SE of Edinburgh city centre. **25 G2** NT3071.
Niddry Burn *W.Loth.* ***River***, rising to S of Riccarton Hills and flowing E to Union Canal at Winchburgh. **25 E2** NT0874.
Niddry Castle *W.Loth. See Winchburgh.*
Nigg *Aberdeen* ***Suburb***, 2m/3km S of Aberdeen city centre across River Dee. **55 E4** NJ9403.
Nigg *High.* ***Settlement***, near E side of Nigg Bay, 6m/10km NE of Invergordon, in Ross and Cromarty district. **62 A2** NH8071.
Nigg Bay *Aberdeen* ***Bay***, on E coast between Girdle Ness and Greg Ness, 2m/3km SE of centre of Aberdeen across River Dee. **55 E4** NJ9604.
Nigg Bay *High.* ***Bay***, to E of Invergordon, on N side of Cromarty Firth. At low tide Sands of Nigg are visible. **61 G2** NH8071.
Nine Mile Bar *D. & G. Alternative name for Crocketford, qv.*
Nine Mile Burn *Midloth.* ***Hamlet***, 4m/6km SW of Penicuik. **25 F4** NT1857.
Nisa Mhòr *W.Isles* ***Hill***, 1km NW of Uigen, Isle of Lewis. Height 446 feet or 136 metres. **68 B4** NB0935.
Nisam Point *W.Isles* ***Coastal feature***, headland at easternmost point of Bearnaraigh. **44 A5** NL5780.
Nisbet *Sc.Bord.* ***Village***, 4m/6km N of Jedburgh. **18 A4** NT6725.
Nista *Shet.* ***Island***, small uninhabited island off E coast of Whalsay, 1m/2km S of Skaw Taing. HU6065.
Nith ***River***, rising on Prickery Hill in Carsphairn Forest, 5m/7km E of Dalmellington and flowing through New Cumnock, then past Sanquhar and Thornhill to Dumfries and out to Solway Firth 3m/4km NE of Southerness. **8 C1** NY0057.
Nithsdale *D. & G.* ***Valley***, carrying River Nith from its source, 5m/7km E of Dalmellington, S to Dumfries. **15 F4** NX8791.
Nithside *D. & G.* ***Suburb***, W district of Dumfries. NX9676.
Nitshill *Glas.* ***Suburb***, 5m/8km SW of Glasgow city centre. **23 G3** NS5260.
No Ness *Shet.* ***Coastal feature***, headland on E coast of Mainland, 1m/2km SW of Mousa. **82 D5** HU4421.
Noblehill *D. & G.* ***Suburb***, E district of Dumfries. **9 D3** NX9976.
Noddsdale *N.Ayr.* ***Settlement***, 2m/3km NE of Largs. **22 D3** NS2161.
Noddsdale Water *N.Ayr.* ***River***, rising on NE slopes of Knockencorsan and flowing SW to join sea 1km N of Largs. **22 D3** NS2000.
Noe *Arg. & B.* ***River***, running NW down Glen Noe to Loch Etive, Argyll, 3m/4km E of Bonawe. **30 C1** NN0434.
Noltland Castle *Ork.* ***Castle***, ruins of 16c castle (Historic Scotland) on Westray, W of Pierowall. **80 C2** HY4248.
Noness Head *Shet.* ***Coastal feature***, headland on E coast of Mainland between entrances to Colla Firth and Swining Voe. HU4570.
Noonsbrough *Shet.* ***Settlement***, situated on Ness of Noonsbrough, adjacent to Voe of Clousta, Mainland. **82 B2** HU2957.
Nor Wick *Shet.* ***Bay***, on NE coast of Unst, on which locality of Norwick is situated. **85 F1** HP6514.
Noran Water *Angus* ***River***, running S down Glen Ogil then SE to River South Esk 4m/6km W of Brechin. Falls of Drumly Harry in course of river, 3m/5km NW of Tannadice. **42 C4** NO5358.
Noranside *Angus* ***Hamlet***, 3m/4km NW of Finavon. HM Prison. **42 C3** NO4761.
Normann's Ruh *Arg. & B.* ***Settlement***, on Mull, 1m/2km SE of Kilninian. **36 D5** NM4144.
Norman's Law *Fife* ***Hill***, with hillfort and settlement, 1m/2km SW of Brunton. Height 935 feet or 285 metres. **34 B2** NO3020.
North Ballachulish *High.* ***Village***, on N shore of Loch Leven, in Lochaber district, 8m/13km W of Kinlochleven. Road bridge spans loch. **38 C3** NN0559.
North Balloch *S.Ayr.* ***Settlement***, on N side of River Strinchar, 4m/6km E of Barr. **7 E1** NX3395.
North Bay *Ork.* ***Bay***, large bay on W coast of Sanday, divided from Bay of Brough by Ness of Brough. **81 E2** HY6642.
North Bay *Ork.* ***Bay***, on N side of The Ayre, narrow neck of land connecting peninsula of South Walls to S end of Hoy. **78 B3** ND2890.
North Bay *W.Isles* ***Bay***, to E of Northbay, containing numerous small islands. **44 C3** NF7002.
North Berwick *E.Loth.* Population: 5687. ***Small town***, and resort on S side of entrance to Firth of Forth, 19m/31km E of Edinburgh. **26 C1** NT5585.
North Berwick Law *E.Loth.* ***Hill***, to S of North Berwick, surmounted by ancient fort and ruins of watch-tower built in Napoleonic Wars. Height 613 feet or 187 metres. **26 C1** NT5584.
North Birny Fell *Sc.Bord.* ***Hill***, 3m/4km N of Newcastleton. Height 902 feet or 275 metres. **10 C2** NY4791.
North Bogbain *Moray* ***Settlement***, 3m/4km NW of Keith. **63 F4** NJ3952.
North Boisdale *W.Isles Anglicised form of Baghasdal, qv.*
North Broomage *Falk.* ***Suburb***, on N side of Larbert. NS8583.
North Burnt Hill *N.Ayr.* ***Mountain***, at head of Noddsdale Water, 6m/9km NE of Largs. Height 1414 feet or 431 metres. **23 D3** NS2566.
North Cairn *D. & G.* ***Settlement***, 1m/2km S of Corsewall Point. **6 A3** NW9770.
North Carr *Fife* ***Coastal feature***, offshore rock with beacon, 1m/2km N of Fife Ness. **35 E3** NO6411.
North Collafirth *Shet.* ***Settlement***, at head of Colla Firth inlet, 6m/10km N of Sullom, Mainland. HU3583.
North Commonty *Aber.* ***Settlement***, 1m/2km NW of New Deer. NJ8648.

North Connel Airfield *Arg. & B.* ***Airport/airfield***, on N side of Loch Etive, at S end of Ardmucknish Bay. NM9035.
North Crossaig *Arg. & B.* ***Locality***, adjoining to South Crossaig, on road running beside E coast of Kintyre, Argyll, 4m/7km SW of Claonaig. NR8351.
North Dallens *Arg. & B.* ***Settlement***, on SE shore of Loch Linnhe, opposite Shuna Island. **38 B5** NM9248.
North Dawn *Ork.* ***Settlement***, 1m/2km N of St. Mary's, Mainland. **79 D2** HY4703.
North Deep *Fife* ***Sea feature***, channel in River Tay estuary, between Mugdrum Island and N bank. **34 A3** NO2119.
North Dell *W.Isles* *Anglicised form of Dail Bho Thuath, qv.*
North East Scotland Agricultural Heritage Museum *Aber.* ***Other feature of interest***, museum portraying story of farming in NE Scotland, set in Aden Country Park, 1m/2km W of Mintlaw. **65 E5** NJ9847.
North Erradale *High.* ***Village***, near W coast of Ross and Cromarty district, 4m/7km NW of Gairloch. **58 D1** NG7481.
North Esk ***River***, formed by several streams W of Tarfside and running SE down Glen Esk to Edzell, Marykirk and North Sea between Montrose and St. Cyrus. **43 D2** NO7462.
North Esk ***River***, rising on Pentland Hills near North Esk Reservoir, 1m/2km N of Carlops, and flowing NE to join South Esk River 1m/2km N of Dalkeith; combined river then continues N to Firth of Forth at Musselburgh. **25 F4** NT3368.
North Esk Reservoir *Midloth.* ***Reservoir***, small reservoir in Pentland Hills, bordering Scottish Borders region, 1m/2km N of Carlops. **25 F4** NT1558.
North Essie *Aber.* ***Settlement***, 2m/3km SE of Crimond. **65 F4** NK0755.
North Galson *W.Isles* *Anglicised form of Gabhsunn Bho Thuath, qv.*
North Galson *W.Isles* ***River***, flowing into Atlantic Ocean to NE of Gabhsunn Bho Thuath, Isle of Lewis. NB4459.
North Glen Sannox *N.Ayr.* ***Valley***, to N of Glen Sannox and running E to coast, 1km N of Sannox Bay. **22 A5** NR9944.
North Greens *Moray* ***Locality***, near N coast, 2m/3km W of Lossiemouth. NJ2070.
North Harris (Gaelic form: Ceann a Tuath na Hearadh.) *W.Isles* ***Large natural feature***, southern and more mountainous part of Isle of Lewis, S of Loch Resort and W of Loch Seaforth. Includes Forest of Harris. **66 D2** NB1010.
North Haven *Aber.* ***Bay***, rocky bay, 2m/3km N of Cruden Bay. **55 G1** NK1138.
North Haven Bird Observatory *Shet.* ***Other feature of interest***, bird observatory on E coast of Fair Isle, near Bu Ness. **82 A5** HZ2172.
North Havra *Shet.* ***Island***, small uninhabited island off S end of peninsula of Strom Ness, Mainland. **82 C3** HU3642.
North Head *High.* ***Coastal feature***, headland to N of Wick Bay. **77 F3** ND3850.
North Holms *Shet.* ***Island***, small rocky island off W coast of Unst. HP5611.
North Isle of Gletness *Shet.* ***Island***, one of two small islands to S of Glet Ness headland on E coast of Mainland. HU4751.
North Kessock *High.* ***Village***, in Ross and Cromarty district, on N shore of Beauly Firth, opposite Inverness. **61 F5** NH6547.
North Kiscadale *N.Ayr.* ***Settlement***, forms locality of Kiscadale, along with South Kiscadale, on Whiting bay, E coast of Arran. NS0426.
North Lee *W.Isles* ***Hill***, on North Uist, 1m/2km NE of South Lee. Height 820 feet or 250 metres. **56 C3** NF9366.
North Loch *Ork.* ***Lake/loch***, on NE peninsula of Sanday. **81 F2** HY7545.
North Medwin *S.Lan.* ***River***, rising in Pentland Hills and flowing S to join South Medwin River and become Medwin Water before flowing W into River Clyde, 1m/2km S of Carnwath. **25 E4** NS9844.
North Middleton *Midloth.* ***Village***, 1km NW of Middleton. **26 A4** NT3658.
North Millbrex *Aber.* ***Settlement***, 5m/8km NE of Fyvie. **64 D5** NJ8243.
North Morar *High.* ***Locality***, mountainous coastal area of Lochaber district between Loch Nevis to N and Loch Morar to S. **49 D5** NM7592.
North Mount Vernon *Glas.* ***Suburb***, adjoining to N of Mount Vernon, 4m/7km SE of Glasgow city centre. NS6563.
North Neaps *Shet.* ***Coastal feature***, promontory on N coast of Yell. **85 D2** HP4805.
North Ness *Fife* ***Coastal feature***, rocky headland at N end of Isle of May (Nature Reserve), which lies 5m/8km SE of Anstruther. **35 E4** NO6400.
North Ness *Ork.* ***Coastal feature***, headland and settlement with pier on Hoy, on N side of entrance to North Bay. ND3091.
North Nesting *Shet.* ***Locality***, forms locality of Nesting on Mainland, along with South Nesting. **82 D2** HU4559.
North Newton *N.Ayr.* ***Locality***, at N end of Arran, opposite Lochranza across Loch Ranza. NR9351.
North Queensferry *Fife* Population: 1051. ***Village***, at N end of Forth bridges. **25 F1** NT1380.
North Queensferry Deep Sea World *Fife* ***Other feature of interest***, in North Queensferry, featuring a moving walkway in transparent underwater tunnel to view sharks, piranhas and seahorses, amongst other sea life. **25 F1** NT1381.
North Queich *P. & K.* ***River***, stream rising from smaller streams flowing off Ochil Hills and flowing E to enter Loch Leven to NW of Kinross. **33 F4** NO1303.
North Roe *Shet.* ***Locality***, area to N of Mainland, comprising an abundance of lochs and rivers. **84 C4** HU3487.
North Roe *Shet.* ***Village***, on Mainland, just N of Burra Voe. **84 C4** HU3689.
North Rona *W.Isles* *Alternative name for Rona, qv*
North Ronaldsay *Ork.* ***Island***, most northerly island of Orkney group, 3m/4km N of Sanday across North Ronaldsay Firth. An airfield provides air link with Scottish mainland. Area of island about 3 square miles or 8 square km. **81 F1** HY7553.
North Ronaldsay Airfield *Ork.* ***Airport/airfield***, to N of Hollandstoun, North Ronaldsay. **81 F1** HY7553.
North Ronaldsay Firth *Ork.* ***Sea feature***, stretch of water separating North Ronaldsay and Sanday. **81 F2** HY7553.
North Sandwick *Shet.* ***Settlement***, 1m/2km S of Gutcher, Yell. **85 E3** HU5497.
North Shawbost *W.Isles* ***Settlement***, near NW coast of Isle of Lewis, forms locality of Siabost along with South and New Shawbost, 2m/3km W of Bragar. NB2647.
North Shian *Arg. & B.* ***Locality***, on N shore of Loch Creran, in Argyll. **38 B5** NM9243.
North Sutor *High.* ***Coastal feature***, headland on N side of entrance to Cromarty Firth, Ross and Cromarty district. **62 A3** NH8168.
North Tarbothill *Aberdeen* ***Settlement***, 1km inland from coast and 3m/4km S of Balmedie. **55 E3** NJ9513.
North Third *Stir.* ***Locality***, includes North Third Reservoir, 3m/5km SW of Stirling. **24 B1** NS7489.
North Third Reservoir *Stir.* ***Reservoir***, small reservoir in course of Bannock Burn, 4m/6km SW of Stirling. **24 B1** NS7589.
North Thundergay *N.Ayr.* *Alternative name for Lenimore, qv.*
North Tolsta *W.Isles* *Anglicised form of Tolastadh Bho Thuath, qv.*
North Top *Aber.* ***Mountain***, N summit of Beinn a' Bhùird mass in Grampian Mountains, 6m/10km NW of Braemar. Height 3926 feet or 1197 metres. **52 C4** NJ0900.
North Ugie Water *Aber.* ***River***, rising on E side of Windyheads Hill and flowing SE through Strichen to join South Ugie Water 1m/2km NE of Longside, forming River Ugie. **65 E4** NK0548.
North Uist (Gaelic form: Uibhist a Tuath.) *W.Isles* ***Island***, of about 120 square miles or 310 square km, between South Harris and Benbecula, having innumerable lochs and offshore islands. **45 F2** NF8070.
North Voe of Gletness *Shet.* ***Sea feature***, small inlet on E coast of Mainland. HU4751.
North Water Bridge *Angus* *Alternative spelling of Northwaterbridge, qv.*
North Watten *High.* ***Settlement***, 3m/4km N of Watten. **77 E3** ND2458.
Northbay (Also known as Bayherivagh.) *W.Isles* ***Village***, on Barra, 4m/7km S of Scurrival Point. Barra Airport is 1m/2km N on Tràigh Mhòr. Inlet on which village is situated, is known as Bàgh Hirivagh. NF7002.
Northburnhill *Aber.* ***Settlement***, 2m/3km S of Cuminestown. **64 D5** NJ8147.
Northdyke *Ork.* ***Settlement***, situated on W coast of Mainland, to N of Bay of Skaill. **80 A4** HY2320.
Northfield *Aberdeen* ***Suburb***, NW district of Aberdeen. **55 D4** NJ9008.
Northfield *Aber.* ***Settlement***, 1km S of Troup Head, 2m/3km NE of Gardenstown. **64 D3** NJ8266.
Northfield *Edin.* ***Suburb***, adjoining to W of Portobello, 2m/3km E of Edinburgh city centre. NT2973.
Northfield *High.* ***Settlement***, 1m/2km SW of Wick. **77 F4** ND3548.
Northfield *Sc.Bord.* ***Settlement***, adjoining to W of St. Abbs. **27 G3** NT9167.
Northhouse *Sc.Bord.* ***Settlement***, 3m/4km NE of Teviothead. **17 F5** NT4307.
Northmavine *Shet.* ***Coastal feature***, peninsula district of Mainland lying W of Sullom Voe and Yell Sound. HU3475.
Northmuir *Angus* ***Village***, 1m/2km N of Kirriemuir. **42 B4** NO3855.
Northpunds *Shet.* ***Settlement***, 1m/2km SW of Hoswick, Mainland. **82 D5** HU4022.
Northton (Gaelic form: Taobh Tuath.) *W.Isles* ***Village***, on W coast of South Harris, 4m/6km SE of Toe Head. **66 B5** NF9989.
Northtown *Ork.* ***Settlement***, in N part of Burray, on NE side of Echnaloch Bay. **79 D3** ND4797.
Northwaterbridge (Also spelled North Water Bridge.) *Angus* ***Settlement***, on River North Esk, 5m/8km SW of Laurencekirk. NO6566.
Norwick *Shet.* ***Hamlet***, on NE coast of Unst, on Nor Wick bay. **85 F1** HP6514.
Noss Head *High.* ***Coastal feature***, headland with lighthouse on E coast of Caithness district at S end of Sinclair's Bay. **77 F3** ND3855.
Noss Head *Shet.* ***Coastal feature***, headland on E coast of Isle of Noss, culminating in Noup of Noss. HU5539.
Noss Sound *Shet.* ***Sea feature***, narrow channel separating Bressay from Isle of Noss. HU5240.
Nostie *High.* ***Settlement***, on N side of Loch Alsh, Skye and Lochalsh district, 2m/3km W of Dornie. **49 E2** NG8527.
Nostie Bay *High.* ***Sea feature***, inlet on N shore of Loch Alsh to S of Nostie. NG8526.
Note o' the Gate *Sc.Bord.* ***Mountain***, in Wauchope Forest area of Cheviot Hills, over which passes B6357 road in a N to S direction. Height 1233 feet or 376 metres. **17 G5** NT5803.
Nottingham *High.* ***Settlement***, 1m/2km NE of Latheron. **77 E5** ND2135.
Noup Head *Ork.* ***Coastal feature***, headland with overhanging cliffs at NW end of Westray. Lighthouse. **80 B1** HY3950.
Noup of Noss *Shet.* ***Coastal feature***, sheer cliff on E coast of Isle of Noss, rising from sea to 594 feet or 181 metres. HU5539.
Nousta Ness *Shet.* ***Coastal feature***, headland on E coast of Fetlar, 1km SE of Funzie. HU6689.
Nunraw Abbey *E.Loth.* ***Ecclesiastical building***, built by Cistercian monks in 1948 on site of earlier foundation, 1km SE of Garvald. **26 C2** NT5970.
Nuns' Cave *Arg. & B.* ***Cave***, at Nuns' Pass on S coast of Mull 1m/2km SW of Carsaig Bay. Said to have served as shelter to nuns evicted from Iona during Reformation. NM5220.
Nuns' Pass *Arg. & B.* ***Other feature of interest***, pass on S coast of Mull, 1m/2km SW of Carsaig Bay. **29 E2** NM5220.
Nunton *W.Isles* *Anglicised form of Baile nan Cailleach, qv.*
Nutberry Hill *S.Lan.* ***Mountain***, 6m/10km SW of Lesmahagow. River Nethan rises on S side. Height 1712 feet or 522 metres. **15 F2** NS7433.
Nutberry Moss *D. & G.* ***Open space***, flat area on N side of Solway Firth, 3m/5km W of Gretna. **9 G4** NY2668.
Nyadd *Stir.* ***Settlement***, 4m/7km NW of Stirling. **32 C5** NS7497.
Nybster *High.* ***Settlement***, near E coast of Caithness district, 6m/10km S of John o' Groats. **77 F2** ND3663.

O

Oakbank *Arg. & B.* ***Settlement***, near head of Loch Don, 2m/3km NE of Grass Point, Mull. **29 G1** NM7232.
Oakbank *W.Loth.* ***Settlement***, 1km S of Mid Calder. **25 E3** NT0866.
Oakenhead *Moray* ***Settlement***, 1m/2km S of Lossiemouth. **63 E3** NJ2468.
Oakfield *Fife* ***Suburb***, adjoining to S of Kelty. NT1493.
Oakley *Fife* Population: 4181. ***Village***, 4m/7km W of Dunfermline. **25 E1** NT0289.
Oatfield *Arg. & B.* ***Settlement***, on Kintyre, 3m/4km SW of Campbeltown. **12 B4** NR6817.
Oathlaw *Angus* ***Village***, 4m/6km N of Forfar. **42 C4** NO4756.
Oatlands *Glas.* ***Suburb***, 1m/2km S of Glasgow city centre. NS5963.
Òb Breakish *High.* ***Sea feature***, narrow inlet on which settlement of Lower Breakish is situated, 2m/3km E of Broadford, Skye. NG6723.
Òb Chuaig *High.* ***Bay***, on W coast of Ross and Cromarty district, 2m/3km SW of Rubha na Fearn and entrance to Loch Torridon. NG7059.
Òb Gauscavaig *High.* ***Bay***, on W side of Sleat peninsula, Skye, 1m/2km N of Tarskavaig. Dunscaith Castle at N end of bay. NG5911.
Òb Mheallaidh *High.* ***Sea feature***, inlet on S side of Upper Loch Torridon, Ross and Cromarty district. NG8354.
Ob na h-Uamha *High.* ***Bay***, small bay near entrance to Loch Torridon, 1km SW of Rubha na Fearn. NG7160.
Oban *Arg. & B.* Population: 8203. ***Small town***, port and resort in Argyll on Oban Bay, Sound of Kerrera, 60m/97km NW of Glasgow (93m/150km by road). Ferry services to Inner and Outer Hebrides. Annual Highland Gathering in September. **30 A2** NM8530.
Oban Bay *Arg. & B.* ***Bay***, in Argyll on Sound of Kerrera, to W of Oban. **30 A1** NM8530.
Oban Sea Life Centre *Arg. & B.* ***Other feature of interest***, on S shore of Loch Creran, 1m/2km W of Barcaldine and 9m/14km NE of Oban. Sea life, including octopus and stingray, are returned to sea at end of season. **38 B5** NM9441.
Obbe *W.Isles* *Former name of Leverburgh, qv.*

N

O

Obney Hills *P. & K.* ***Mountain***, with steep slopes and rock outcrops to S and E, 3m/5km NW of Bankfoot and 2m/4km S of Dunkeld. Hillfort at summit. Height 1322 feet or 403 metres. **33 F1** NO0238.
Obsdale *High.* ***Locality***, on E side of Alness, Ross and Cromarty district. NH6669.
Occumster *High.* ***Settlement***, on E coast, to E of Lybster. **77 E5** ND2635.
Ochil Hills ***Large natural feature***, range of hills extending from Bridge of Allan, N of Stirling, to Firth of Tay at Newburgh. Summit is Ben Cleuch, 2363 feet or 720 metres. **33 D4** NO0005.
Ochiltree *E.Ayr.* ***Village***, at confluence of Burnock Water and Lugar Water, 4m/7km W of Cumnock. **14 D3** NS5021.
Ochtermuthill *P. & K.* ***Settlement***, 3m/5km SW of Crieff. **32 D3** NN8316.
Ochtertyre *P. & K.* ***Settlement***, 2m/3km NW of Crieff. **32 D2** NN8323.
Ochtertyre *Stir.* ***Settlement***, 4m/7km NW of Stirling. **32 C5** NS7597.
Ockle *High.* ***Hamlet***, on Ardnamurchan peninsula, 1km SE of Ockle Point. **37 E2** NM5570.
Ockle Point *High.* ***Coastal feature***, headland on N coast of Ardnamurchan peninsula in Lochaber district, 10m/16km NW of Salen. **37 E2** NM5471.
Oddsta *Shet.* ***Locality***, 1m/2km N of Brough Lodge, on NW coast of Fetlar. **85 E3** HU5894.
Odie *Ork.* ***Settlement***, on Stronsay, 1km SE of Links Ness. **81 E4** HY6229.
Odin Bay *Ork.* ***Bay***, on E coast of Stronsay, extending N from Burgh Head. **81 E4** HY6924.
Odness *Ork.* ***Coastal feature***, headland on E coast of Stronsay on S side of entrance to Mill Bay. **81 E4** HY6926.
Ogil *Angus* ***Locality***, comprises Easter Ogil, Mains of Ogil and Milton of Ogil, in valley of Noran Water, 4m/7km E of Dykehead. **42 C3** NO4561.
Ogilvie Castle *P. & K.* ***Castle***, remains of old castle on hillside, 1m/2km SE of Blackford. NN9008.
Oich *High.* ***River***, in Inverness district running NE from Loch Oich to Fort Augustus at head of Loch Ness. **50 C4** NH3809.
Oigh-sgeir (Also known as Hyskeir.) *High.* ***Island***, group of islets in Inner Hebrides, with lighthouse, lying 9m/14km W of Rum. **47 E5** NM1596.
Oisgill Bay *High.* ***Bay***, on W coast of Skye, 7m/12km W of Dunvegan. **57 E5** NG1349.
Oitir Mhòr *W.Isles* ***Coastal feature***, sandbank on North Uist, 5m/8km SE of Aird an Rùnair to N of Kirkibost Island. **45 F3** NF7566.
Oitir Mhòr *W.Isles* ***Coastal feature***, large sandbank, visible at low tide, between North Uist and Benbecula. **45 G4** NF8157.
Oitir Mhòr *W.Isles* ***Sea feature***, stretch of sea separating Fuday and Gighay, NE of Barra. **44 C3** NF7306.
Oitir na Cudaig *W.Isles* ***Coastal feature***, sandbank at small inlet on E coast of South Uist, 4m/6km SE of Lochboisdale. **46 B3** NF8315.
Okraquoy *Shet.* ***Settlement***, overlooking Bay of Okraquoy, 1km S of Fladdabister, Mainland. **82 D4** HU4331.
Old Aberdeen *Aberdeen* ***Suburb***, 1m/2km N of Aberdeen city centre. Includes University of Aberdeen and St. Machar's Cathedral. **55 E4** NJ9408.
Old Belses *Sc.Bord.* ***Settlement***, 6m/10km SE of Selkirk. **17 G3** NT5624.
Old Blair *P. & K.* ***Settlement***, with ruined church, 1m/2km N of Blair Atholl. Burial place of 'Bonnie Dundee' - see Killiecrankie. NN8666.
Old Bridge of Urr *D. & G.* ***Settlement***, and road bridge across Urr Water, 4m/6km N of Castle Douglas. **8 B4** NX7767.
Old Castle of Slains *Aber.* ***Castle***, remains of old castle destroyed by James VI (James I of England), on E coast 4m/7km NE of Newburgh. See also Slains Castle. NK0529.
Old Craig *Aber.* ***Settlement***, 1m/2km SE of Pitmedden. **55 E2** NJ9025.
Old Craighall *E.Loth.* ***Settlement***, 1m/2km S of Musselburgh. **26 A2** NT3370.
Old Crombie *Aber.* ***Settlement***, 2m/3km W of Aberchirder. **64 A4** NJ5951.
Old Dailly *S.Ayr.* ***Village***, 3m/4km E of Girvan. **6 D1** NX2299.
Old Deer *Aber.* ***Village***, on S side of Forest of Deer, 10m/15km W of Peterhead. Ruined 13c abbey (Historic Scotland) 1km NW. **65 E5** NJ9747.
Old Head *Ork.* ***Coastal feature***, headland at SE end of South Ronaldsay. **79 D4** ND4683.
Old Hill *W.Isles* ***Island***, small uninhabited island off W coast of Isle of Lewis, 2m/3km NW of Great Bernera. NB1143.
Old Inverlochy Castle *High.* ***Castle***, ruined 13c building with round corner towers, on bank of River Lochy, 2m/3km NE of Fort William. **38 D2** NN1275.
Old Kilpatrick *W.Dun.* Population: 2408. ***Small town***, on N bank of River Clyde, to N of Erskine Bridge. Site of Roman fort near line of Antonine Wall. **23 F2** NS4673.
Old Kinnernie *Aber.* ***Settlement***, 2m/3km W of Dunecht. **54 C4** NJ7209.
Old Leslie *Aber.* ***Settlement***, 3m/4km SW of Insch. **54 A2** NJ5925.
Old Man of Hoy *Ork.* ***Coastal feature***, massive column of rock rising from foot of cliffs on NW coast of Hoy, 1m/2km N of Rora Head. Height 449 feet or 137 metres. **78 A2** HY1700.
Old Man of Storr *High.* ***Inland physical feature***, column of rock 160 feet or 49 metres high, on E side of The Storr, Skye, 7m/11km N of Portree. NG5053.
Old Man of Wick *High.* *Alternative name for Castle of Old Wick, qv.*
Old Melrose *Sc.Bord.* ***Ecclesiastical building***, site of monastery founded in 7c, in loop of River Tweed, 3m/4km E of Melrose. NT5833.
Old Military Road *High.* ***Other feature of interest***, series of military roads traversing the Highlands, built by Caulfeild, Wade's successor, after 1745 Hanoverian campaign. **52 C1** NJ0035.
Old Philpstoun *W.Loth.* ***Hamlet***, nearly 1m/2km E of Philpstoun. **25 E2** NT0577.
Old Place of Mochrum *D. & G.* ***Castle***, restored castle with 15c and 16c towers, on NE bank of Mochrum Loch, 7m/11km NW of Port William. **7 E5** NX3054.
Old Poltalloch *Arg. & B.* ***Settlement***, 3m/4km S of Ardfern across Loch Craignish. **30 A4** NM8000.
Old Portlethen *Aber.* ***Village***, 1km E of Portlethen on North Sea coast. **55 E5** NO9295.
Old Rattray *Aber.* ***Settlement***, on E side of Loch of Strathbeg, 1m/2km W of Rattray Head. **65 F4** NK0857.
Old Rayne *Aber.* ***Village***, 8m/12km NW of Inverurie. **54 B2** NJ6728.
Old Scone *P. & K.* ***Hamlet***, 2m/3km N of Perth, on E side of River Tay. **33 G2** NO1126.
Old Shields *N.Lan.* ***Settlement***, 3m/5km NE of Cumbernauld. **24 C2** NS8175.
Old Water *D. & G.* ***River***, issuing from Glenkiln Reservoir and joining Cairn Water to E, to form Cluden Water, 6m/10km NW of Dumfries. **8 C3** NX8879.
Old Wick (Also known as Pulteneytown.) *High.* ***Locality***, on S side of Wick, in Caithness district. Ruins of Castle of Old Wick (Historic Scotland), 1m/2km S of Wick. ND3649.
Oldany Island *High.* ***Island***, uninhabited island of about 500 acres or 200 hectares at SW side of entrance to Eddrachillis Bay, W coast of Sutherland district. **70 C1** NC0834.
Oldhall *Aber.* ***Settlement***, 4m/6km W of Aboyne. **53 G5** NO4698.
Oldhall *High.* ***Settlement***, 3m/4km NW of Watten. **77 E3** ND2056.
Oldhall *Renf.* ***Suburb***, 2m/3km E of Paisley. NS5064.
Oldhamstocks *E.Loth.* ***Village***, 6m/10km SE of Dunbar. **27 E2** NT7470.
Oldmeldrum *Aber.* Population: 1976. ***Small town***, 4m/7km NE of Inverurie. **54 D2** NJ8027.
Oldmill *Aber.* ***Settlement***, on S side of Corse Burn, 4m/6km NE of Tarland. **54 A4** NJ5306.
Oldmills Working Mill *Moray* ***Other feature of interest***, 13c oatmeal mill on River Lossie, to W of Elgin. **63 D3** NJ2063.
Oldshore Beg *High.* ***Settlement***, near W coast of Sutherland district, 3m/4km NW of Kinlochbervie. **74 A3** NC1959.
Oldshore More *High.* ***Settlement***, near W coast of Sutherland district, 2m/3km NW of Kinlochbervie. **74 B3** NC2058.
Oldtown *High.* ***Settlement***, in Sutherland district, 1km S of Ardgay, near head of Dornoch Firth. NH5989.
Oldtown of Aigas *High.* ***Settlement***, 5m/8km SW of Beauly. **61 D5** NH4540.
Oldtown of Ord *Aber.* ***Settlement***, 5m/8km SW of Banff. **64 B4** NJ6259.
Oldwhat *Aber.* ***Locality***, 3m/5km SW of New Pitsligo. **65 D4** NJ8651.
Olgrinmore *High.* ***Locality***, to S of Scotscalder Station. **76 C3** ND0955.
Oliver *Sc.Bord.* ***Settlement***, just N of Tweedsmuir, in Tweeddale. **16 C3** NT1025.
Ollaberry *Shet.* ***Village***, on N side of bay of same name, on NE coast of Mainland, 4m/7km N of Sullom. **84 C4** HU3680.
Ollay Lochs *W.Isles* ***Lake/loch***, group of three lochs; West, Mid and East Loch Ollay on South Uist, 3m/5km E of Rubha Ardvule. NF7531.
Olna Firth *Shet.* ***Sea feature***, inlet on W coast of Mainland with village of Voe at its head. **82 C1** HU3864.
Olrig House *High.* ***Settlement***, 1m/2km SW of Castletown. **77 D2** ND1866.
Onich *High.* ***Village***, in Lochaber district, on N side of entrance to Loch Leven, 2m/3km W of North Ballachulish. **38 C3** NN0261.
Opinan *High.* ***Settlement***, 2m/3km SE of Greenstone Point, Ross and Cromarty district. **70 A5** NG8796.
Opinan *High.* ***Village***, on W coast of Ross and Cromarty district, 4m/7km SW of Gairloch across Gair Loch. **58 D2** NG7472.
Opsay *W.Isles* ***Island***, small uninhabited island in Sound of Harris, 4m/6km off NE coast of North Uist. NF9876.
Orange Lane *Sc.Bord.* ***Settlement***, 4m/7km SE of Greenlaw. **27 E5** NT7742.
Orasay Island *W.Isles* ***Island***, small uninhabited island near head of East Loch Roag, W coast of Isle of Lewis. NB2132.
Orasay Island (Gaelic form: Eilean Orasaigh.) *W.Isles* ***Island***, islet at entrance to Loch Leurbost, E coast of Isle of Lewis. NB4024.
Orbliston *Moray* ***Settlement***, 7m/11km SE of Elgin. **63 F4** NJ3057.
Orbost *High.* ***Locality***, on Skye, 3m/5km S of Dunvegan. **57 F5** NG2543.
Orcadia *Arg. & B.* ***Settlement***, on E coast of Bute, 1m/2km E of Rothesay. **22 C3** NS1063.
Orchard *Arg. & B.* ***Settlement***, 1km NW of head of Holy Loch and 4m/7km NW of Dunoon. **22 C1** NS1582.
Orchardton *D. & G.* ***Historic/prehistoric site***, 12c round tower (Historic Scotland) 1m/2km S of Palnackie and 1km N of Orchardton Bay. **8 C5** NX8155.
Orchardton Bay *D. & G.* ***Bay***, small bay on W side of Wigtown Bay, 4m/6km SE of Wigtown. **7 F5** NX4650.
Orchardton Bay *D. & G.* ***Sea feature***, inlet of Auchencairn Bay, 2m/3km S of Palnackie. NX8153.
Orchy *Arg. & B.* ***River***, in Argyll, running SW from Loch Tulla down Glen Orchy to NE end of Loch Awe. **31 E1** NN1327.
Ord *High.* ***River***, flowing NW into Loch Eishort, Skye, 3m/4km NE of Tarskavaig. **48 C3** NG6113.
Ord *High.* ***Settlement***, on S side of Loch Eishort, Sleat peninsula, Skye, 5m/8km W of Eilean Iarmain. **48 C3** NG6113.
Ord of Caithness *High.* ***Viewpoint***, overlooking Ord Point with Helmsdale 3m/4km to SW. **73 F3** ND0517.
Ord Point *High.* ***Coastal feature***, headland on border of Caithness and Sutherland districts, on E coast 3m/4km NE of Helmsdale. ND0617.
Ordhead *Aber.* ***Village***, 7m/11km SE of Alford. **54 B3** NJ6610.
Ordie *Aber.* ***Village***, 2m/3km N of Dinnet. **53 G4** NJ4501.
Ordie Burn *P. & K.* ***River***, rising on hills W of Bankfoot and flowing SE to join River Tay at Luncarty, 4m/6km N of Perth. **33 F1** NO1029.
Ordiequish *Moray* ***Settlement***, on E side of River Spey, 1m/2km S of Fochabers. **63 F4** NJ3357.
Ore *Fife* ***River***, issuing from Loch Ore, N of Cowdenbeath, and flowing E to River Leven to W of Windygates. NO3300.
Oreval *W.Isles* ***Mountain***, 1m/2km N of Cleiseval in Forest of Harris. Height 2171 feet or 662 metres. **66 C2** NB0810.
Orfasay *Shet.* ***Island***, small uninhabited island off S coast of Yell, separated from it by Sound of Orfasay. **85 D5** HU4977.
Orinsay *W.Isles* ***Settlement***, near E coast of Isle of Lewis, on N side of Loch Shell, 1m/2km W of Leumrabhagh. NB3612.
Orinsay Island *W.Isles* *Anglicised form of Eilean Orasaigh, qv.*
Orka Voe *Shet.* ***Sea feature***, inlet on coast of Mainland at S end of Yell Sound. **84 D5** HU4077.
Orknagable *Shet.* ***Coastal feature***, cliffs on W coast of Unst, towards N of island. **85 E1** HP5713.
Ormacleit (Anglicised form: Ormiclate.) *W.Isles* ***Settlement***, 2m/4km NE of Rubha Ardvule, South Uist. **46 A1** NF7431.
Ormiclate *W.Isles* *Anglicised form of Ormacleit, qv.*
Ormidale *Arg. & B.* ***Settlement***, in lower Glendaruel, 2m/3km S of Clachan of Glendaruel. **22 B1** NS0081.
Ormiscaig *High.* ***Settlement***, on E shore of Loch Ewe, Ross and Cromarty district, 1m/2km NW of Aultbea. **70 A5** NG8590.
Ormiston *E.Loth.* Population: 2078. ***Village***, 2m/4km S of Tranent. 15c market cross (Historic Scotland). **26 B3** NT4169.
Ormiston Hill *Fife* ***Hill***, 1km S of Newburgh. Height 777 feet or 237 metres. **34 A3** NO2316.
Ormiston Market Cross *E.Loth.* ***Historic/prehistoric site***, 15c cross (Historic Scotland) on modern base in main street at Ormiston, 2m/3km S of Tranent. Symbol of right of inhabitants to hold a market. **26 B3** NT4169.
Ormlie *High.* ***Locality***, adjacent to SW of Thurso. **76 D2** ND1067.
Ormsaigbeag *High.* ***Locality***, on S coast of Ardnamurchan in Lochaber district, 1km SW of Kilchoan. NM4763.
Ormsaigmore *High.* ***Settlement***, on S coast of Ardnamurchan, in Lochaber district, between Kilchoan and locality of Ormsaigbeag. **37 D3** NM4763.
Ormsary *Arg. & B.* ***Settlement***, in Knapdale, Argyll, on E side of Loch Caolisport, 4m/7km SW of Achahoish. NR7472.
Ornish Island *W.Isles* ***Island***, small uninhabited island at entrance to Loch Sgioport, E coast of North Uist. **46 B1** NF8538.

Oronsay *Arg. & B.* ***Island***, sparsely inhabited island of about 2 square miles or 5 square km off S end of Colonsay, to which it is connected by sands at low tide. Traces of Stone Age settlement. Remains of 14c priory near W coast. **20 B1** NR3588.
Oronsay *High.* ***Island***, small uninhabited island off Ullinish Point, Skye, in Loch Bracadale. **47 G1** NG3136.
Oronsay *High.* ***Island***, small uninhabited island at entrance to Loch Sunart in Lochaber district, W of Carna. **37 E4** NM5959.
Oronsay *W.Isles* ***Island***, low-lying uninhabited island in bay on N coast of North Uist to E of Solas. **45 G2** NF8475.
Oronsay Priory *Arg. & B.* ***Ecclesiastical building***, on Oronsay. Ruins of priory thought to be founded by St. Columba. Present remains are of 14c Augustinian foundation, together with grave slabs and crosses. **20 B1** NR3488.
Orosay *W.Isles* ***Island***, small uninhabited island on E side of Barra (Tràigh Mhòr) Airport. **44 C3** NF7106.
Orosay *W.Isles* ***Island***, small uninhabited island off W coast of South Uist 3m/5km SW of Dalabrog. **44 C2** NF7217.
Orosay *W.Isles* ***Island***, islet off NE coast of Vatersay. NL6497.
Orosay *W.Isles* ***Island***, islet on E side of entrance to Castle Bay on S coast of Barra. NL6697.
Orosay *W.Isles* ***Island***, islet off SE coast of Barra opposite Earsairidh. NL7099.
Orphir *Ork.* ***Locality***, on Mainland, 7m/11km SW of Kirkwall. Scant remains of 12c round church (Historic Scotland). **78 C2** HY3406.
Orphir Round Church and Earl's Bu *Ork.* ***Ecclesiastical building***, remains of only 12c circular church (Historic Scotland) in Scotland, overlooking Orphir Bay on S coast of Mainland. Earl's Bu (also Historic Scotland) are foundation remains of what may have been a Viking palace. **78 C2** HY3304.
Orrin *High.* ***River***, in Ross and Cromarty district, rising on East Monar Forest and running E to River Conon 4m/7km SW of Dingwall. **60 D4** NH5153.
Orrin Reservoir *High.* ***Reservoir***, 5m/8km long and 7m/12km from confluence of River Orrin and River Conon. **60 C5** NH3649.
Orrok House *Aber.* ***Settlement***, 1m/2km N of Balmedie. **55 E3** NJ9619.
Orroland *D. & G.* ***Settlement***, 2m/3km E of Dundrennan. **4 A2** NX7746.
Orsay *Arg. & B.* ***Island***, with lighthouse off S end of Rinns of Islay opposite Port Wemyss. **20 A4** NR1651.
Orval *High.* ***Mountain***, on Rum, 4m/7km W of Kinloch. Height 1873 feet or 571 metres. **47 G5** NM3398.
Ose *High.* ***River***, on Skye, running SW into Loch Bracadale 3m/5km NW of Bracadale village. NG3140.
Ose *High.* ***Settlement***, at mouth of River Ose, Skye, 3m/5km NW of Bracadale. **57 G5** NG3140.
Oskaig *High.* ***Settlement***, on W coast of Raasay, 3m/5km from S end of island. **48 B1** NG5438.
Oskaig Point *High.* ***Coastal feature***, headland on W coast of Raasay, 1km N of Clachan. **48 B1** NG5438.
Osnaburgh *Fife* *Alternative name for Dairsie, qv.*
Ossian *High.* ***River***, in Lochaber district, running N from Loch Ossian down Strath Ossian to Loch Ghuilbinn. **39 G2** NN4174.
Ossian's Cave *High.* ***Cave***, cleft on N face of Aonach Dubh, Lochaber district, one of The Three Sisters. Ossian, legendary Gaelic warrior and bard, is said to have been born beside Loch Triochatan to W. **39 D4** NN1556.
Ostem *W.Isles* ***Island***, islet on W side of Kearstay, small island off N coast of Scarp. NA9617.
Otter *Arg. & B.* ***Settlement***, on Kilfinan Bay, 5m/8km NW of Tighnabruaich. **22 A2** NR9278.
Otter Ferry *Arg. & B.* ***Settlement***, in Argyll, on E side of Loch Fyne, 4m/6km N of Kilfinan. **22 A1** NR9384.
Otter Rock *Arg. & B.* ***Island***, to S of Torran Rocks group, 4m/7km SW of Mull. **28 B3** NM2811.
Otters Wick *Ork.* ***Sea feature***, large inlet on N coast of Sanday. **81 E2** HY6943.
Otters Wick *Shet.* ***Bay***, on E coast of Yell. **85 E4** HU5285.
Otterston Loch *Fife* ***Lake/loch***, small loch 2m/3km W of Aberdour. NT1685.
Otterswick *Shet.* ***Settlement***, at head of Otters Wick bay. **85 E4** HU5285.
Oude *Arg. & B.* ***River***, in Argyll, running W from Loch Tralaig then SW to head of Loch Melfort. NM8314.
Ousdale *High.* ***Settlement***, on Ousdale Burn, 4m/6km SW of Berriedale. **73 F2** ND0620.
Ouse Ness *Ork.* ***Coastal feature***, headland on E coast of Westray, overlooking Papa Sound. **80 C2** HY4549.
Out Head *Fife* ***Coastal feature***, headland on S side of River Eden estuary, 2m/4km N of St. Andrews. **34 C3** NO4919.
Out Skerries (Also known as The Skerries.) *Shet.* ***Island***, group of several small islands, some no more than rocks, lying about 5m/8km NE of Whalsay. Housay and Bruray are inhabited and connected by a road bridge. The extreme eastern island, Bound Skerry, has a lighthouse. **85 F5** HU6771.
Out Skerries Airstrip *Shet.* ***Airport/airfield***, situated on Burray, in the Out Skerries group of islands. **85 F5** HU6872.
Out Stack *Shet.* ***Island***, rock about 1km NE of Muckle Flugga and 1m/2km NE of Herma Ness, Unst. Most northerly point of British Isles. **85 F1** HP6120.
Outer Hebrides *W.Isles See Western Isles administrative area description.*
Outer Holm *Ork.* ***Island***, islet on E side of Stromness Harbour, Mainland. HY2508.
Outer Score *Shet.* ***Island***, small uninhabited island off N end of Bressay. HU5145.
Outertown *Ork.* ***Settlement***, near W coast of Mainland, 1m/2km NW of Stromness. **80 A5** HY2310.
Outerwards Reservoir *N.Ayr.* ***Reservoir***, small reservoir 4m/7km NE of Largs. NS2365.
Outshore Point *Ork.* ***Coastal feature***, headland on W coast of Mainland 2m/3km S of Marwick Head. **80 A4** HY2222.
Over Rankeilour *Fife* ***Settlement***, 3m/5km W of Cupar. **34 B3** NO3213.
Overbister *Ork.* ***Village***, in centre of Sanday, with Lamaness Firth to N and Cata Sand to E. **81 E2** HY6840.
Overbrae *Aber.* ***Locality***, near N coast, 3m/5km S of Gardenstown. Locality of Netherbrae to W. **64 D4** NJ8059.
Overscaig Hotel *High.* ***Other building***, on NE side of Loch Shin. **71 G2** NC4123.
Overton *Aberdeen* ***Settlement***, to NW of Aberdeen Airport, 2m/3km NW of Dyce. **55 D3** NJ8714.
Overton *Aber.* ***Settlement***, on S side of Gallows Hill, 2m/3km NW of Kemnay. **54 C3** NJ7118.
Overtown *Aber.* ***Locality***, just SE of Gordonstown, 9m/15km SW of Banff. NJ5655.
Overtown *N.Lan.* Population: 1972. ***Village***, 1m/2km S of Wishaw. **24 C4** NS8052.
Oxcars *Fife* ***Island***, islet with lighthouse in Firth of Forth 1km SE of Inchcolm and 2m/3km S of Hawkcraig Point. NT2081.
Oxenfoord Castle *Midloth.* ***Castle***, 18c castle built on site of older castle in mansion style designed by Robert Adam, to N of Pathhead, 4m/6km SE of Dalkeith. Now a boarding school. **26 A3** NT3865.
Oxgangs *Edin.* ***Suburb***, 4m/6km S of Edinburgh city centre. NT2368.
Oxna *Shet.* ***Island***, uninhabited island of about 180 acres or 73 hectares 4m/6km SE of Skelda Ness, Mainland, across The Deeps. **82 C4** HU3537.
Oxnam *Sc.Bord.* ***Village***, on Oxnam Water, 4m/6km SE of Jedburgh. **18 A5** NT6918.
Oxnam Water *Sc.Bord.* ***River***, rising near Harkers Hill and flowing W, then N through Oxnam and into River Teviot 4m/6km SE of Jedburgh. **18 B5** NT6918.
Oxton *Sc.Bord.* ***Village***, 4m/7km NW of Lauder. Site of Roman fort 1km N. **26 B4** NT4953.
Oykel *High.* ***River***, in Sutherland district rising S of Ben More Assynt and running SE to Oykel Bridge, then E down Strath Oykel to join River Shin in Kyle of Sutherland, 4m/6km NW of Bonar Bridge. **71 F4** NH5796.
Oykel Bridge *High.* ***Bridge***, road bridge over River Oykel in Sutherland district 13m/21km W of Lairg. **71 F4** NC3800.
Oykel Forest *High.* ***Forest/woodland***, in Sutherland district 7m/11km W of Lairg. **71 G4** NC4802.
Oyne *Aber.* ***Village***, 7m/11km NW of Inverurie. **54 B2** NJ6725.

P

Pabaidh Mòr (Anglicised form: Pabay Mòr.) *W.Isles* ***Island***, uninhabited island in West Loch Roag, 3m/5km E of Gallan Head, Isle of Lewis. **68 C4** NB1038.
Pabaigh *W.Isles Gaelic form of Pabbay, qv.*
Pabail Iarach (Anglicised form: Lower Bayble.) *W.Isles* ***Village***, on Eye Peninsula, Isle of Lewis, 1m/2km S of Garrabost. Adjacent to Pabail Uarach. **69 G4** NB5231.
Pabail Uarach (Anglicised form: Upper Bayble.) *W.Isles* ***Village***, on Eye Peninsula, Isle of Lewis, 1m/2km SE of Garrabost. Adjacent to Pabail Iarach. **69 G4** NB5231.
Pabay *High.* ***Island***, low-lying island of 360 acres or 145 hectares, sparsely inhabited, 3m/4km NE of Broadford, Skye. **48 C2** NG6727.
Pabay Beag *W.Isles* ***Island***, small uninhabited island in West Loch Roag, 3m/5km E of Gallan Head, Isle of Lewis. NB1038.
Pabay Mòr *W.Isles Anglicised form of Pabaidh Mòr, qv.*
Pabbay *W.Isles* ***Island***, uninhabited island at N end of Sound of Harris 5m/8km SW of Toe Head. Pabbay measures 3m/4km by nearly 2m/3km and rises to a height of 642 feet or 196 metres. **66 B5** NF8988.
Pabbay (Gaelic form: Pabaigh.) *W.Isles* ***Island***, uninhabited island of about 560 acres or 225 hectares midway between Mingulay and Sandray. **44 A5** NL6087.
Padanaram *Angus* ***Village***, 2m/3km W of Forfar. **42 C4** NO4251.
Paddockhaugh *Moray* ***Settlement***, on E side of River Lossie, 3m/4km S of Elgin. **63 E4** NJ2058.
Paddockhole *D. & G.* ***Settlement***, at bridge over Water of Milk, 3m/4km NE of Bankshill. **9 G2** NY2383.
Paibeil (Anglicised form: Paible.) *W.Isles* ***Settlement***, near W coast of North Uist, 3m/5km SE of Aird an Rùnair. **45 F3** NF7367.
Paible *W.Isles Anglicised form of Paibeil, qv.*
Paible *W.Isles* ***Settlement***, on SE coast of Tarasaigh. **66 C4** NG0299.
Pairc *W.Isles Gaelic form of Park, qv.*
Paisley *Renf.* Population: 75,526. ***Town***, 7m/11km W of Glasgow. Originally a monastic settlement, with its first church built in 12c; rebuilt 13c church now restored. Formerly known for its linen production, then as a cotton and silk town. University. **23 F3** NS4864.
Paisley Abbey *Renf.* ***Ecclesiastical building***, Cluniac Abbey church founded in Paisley town centre in 1163 and restored following destruction on orders of Edward I. **23 F3** NS4863.
Paisley Museum and Art Gallery *Renf.* ***Other feature of interest***, in Paisley town centre, with collection of shawls, exhibitions on local industrial and natural history, and 19c Scottish art gallery. **23 F3** NS4764.
Palace of Holyroodhouse *Edin.* ***Historic house***, chief royal residence of Scotland dating from 16c, located below Holyrood Park (Historic Scotland) at E end of Royal Mile in Edinburgh city centre. Ruined nave of 12c-13c Holyrood Abbey (Historic Scotland), built for Augustinian canons, is situated in the grounds. **25 G2** NT2773.
Palace of Spynie (Also known as Spynie Palace.) *Moray* ***Historic/prehistoric site***, ruined castle (Historic Scotland), 3m/4km S of Lossiemouth. Built in 14c and dominated by 15c David's Tower, it served as residence to Bishops of Moray until 1686. Affords spectacular views over Spynie Loch and Moray Firth. **63 E3** NJ2365.
Palacerigg Country Park *N.Lan.* ***Leisure/recreation***, 700 acre country park, 2m/3km SE of Cumbernauld. Home to wide variety of animals from Scotland and N Europe, also wild population of bison, lynx and wildcats. **24 B2** NS7873.
Palgowan *D. & G.* ***Locality***, including large traditional sheep farm on E side of Glentrool Forest, 3m/5km N of Glentrool Village. **7 E2** NX3783.
Palmerscross *Moray* ***Settlement***, on SW side of Elgin. **63 E3** NJ2061.
Palnackie *D. & G.* ***Village***, 3m/5km S of Dalbeattie. **8 C5** NX8256.
Palnure *D. & G.* ***Settlement***, 3m/5km SE of Newton Stewart. **7 F4** NX4563.
Palnure Burn *D. & G.* ***River***, rising to S of Clatteringshaws Loch and flowing SW, then S into River Cree at Muirfad Flow 3m/5km SE of Newton Stewart. **7 F4** NX4562.
Pan *Ork.* ***Settlement***, on S side of Pan Hope, Flotta. **78 C3** ND3794.
Panbride *Angus* ***Village***, 1km N of Carnoustie. **35 D1** NO5634.
Panmure Castle *Angus* ***Castle***, scant remains of 13c castle, 2m/4km NW of Carnoustie. Monument to W commemorates Lord Panmure of Brechin (d 1852). NO5437.
Pannanich Hill *Aber.* ***Mountain***, 2m/3km SE of Ballater. Height 1971 feet or 601 metres. **53 F5** NO3895.
Pap of Glencoe (Also known as Sgorr na Ciche.) *High.* ***Mountain***, in Lochaber district nearly 2m/3km E of foot of Glen Coe. Height 2434 feet or 742 metres. **38 D4** NN1259.
Papa *Shet.* ***Island***, small uninhabited island on E side of island of Oxna and 2m/4km W of Scalloway, Mainland. **82 C4** HU3637.
Papa Little *Shet.* ***Island***, situated between Muckle Roe and Mainland, 2m/3km N to S and 1km E to W. **82 C1** HU3360.
Papa Sound *Ork.* ***Sea feature***, sea channel between islands of Westray and Papa Westray. **80 C1** HY4751.
Papa Sound *Ork.* ***Sea feature***, strait separating coast of Stronsay from Papa Stronsay. HY6629.
Papa Stour *Shet.* ***Island***, inhabited island 1m/2km off W coast of Mainland at SW end of St. Magnus Bay. It is roughly 3m/4km E to W and 2m/3km N to S, separated from Mainland by Sound of Papa, 1m/2km wide. Coastline noted for caves. **82 A1** HU1760.
Papa Stour Airstrip *Shet.* ***Airport/airfield***, to S of Biggings, on Papa Stour. **82 A1** HU1760.
Papa Stronsay *Ork.* ***Island***, off NE coast of Stronsay, separated from it by Papa Sound. Lighthouse on far side of island. **81 E3** HY6629.
Papa Westray (Papay). *Ork.* ***Island***, N and E of Westray across Papa Sound. It is some 3m/5km N to S and from 1km to 1m/2km E to W. **80 D1** HY4952.
Papa Westray Airfield *Ork.* ***Airport/airfield***, to N of Holland, Papa Westray. **80 C1** HY4852.
Papay *Ork.* *See Papa Westray.*
Paphrie Burn *Angus* ***River***, stream which flows NE on N side of Hill of Menuir to join West Water 1km S of Bridgend. **42 D3** NO5467.

O P

Papil *Shet.* ***Settlement***, on West Burra, 3m/4km S of Hamnavoe. HU3631.
Papil Water *Shet.* ***Lake/loch***, on Fetlar 1m/2km W of Houbie. HU6090.
Papley *Ork.* ***Locality***, on E side of South Ronaldsay, 2m/3km SE of St. Margaret's Hope. ND4691.
Papple *E.Loth.* ***Settlement***, 3m/5km S of East Linton. **26 C2** NT5972.
Paps of Jura *Arg. & B.* ***Inland physical feature***, three highest peaks of mountain ridge of Jura, situated 5m/8km N of Craighouse. Peaks are Beinn an Oir, Beinn Shiantaidh and Beinn a' Chaol. **20 C2** NR5074.
Parallel Roads of Glen Roy *High. See Glen Roy.*
Parish Holm *S.Lan.* ***Settlement***, 3m/5km W of Glespin. **15 F3** NS7628.
Park *Aber.* ***Locality***, 4m/6km SW of Peterculter. NO7898.
Park *Aber.* ***Settlement***, 1km S of Cornhill. **64 A4** NJ5857.
Park (Gaelic: Pairc.) *W.Isles* ***Locality***, in SE part of Isle of Lewis, between Loch Erisort and Loch Seaforth. **67 E3** NB3212.
Park Burn *D. & G.* ***River***, flowing N from Locharbriggs to join Water of Ae, 1m/2km W of Parkgate. NX9987.
Parkford *Angus* ***Settlement***, 2m/3km SW of Finavon. **42 C4** NO4754.
Parkgate *D. & G.* ***Locality***, 5m/8km NW of Lochmaben. **9 E2** NY0187.
Parkhall *Renf.* ***Suburb***, 2m/3km NW of Clydebank. NS4872.
Parkhead *Glas.* ***Suburb***, 2m/4km E of Glasgow city centre. NS6163.
Parkhill *Angus* ***Settlement***, 3m/4km N of Arbroath. **43 E5** NO6445.
Parkhill *P. & K.* ***Settlement***, 1m/2km NE of Blairgowrie. **41 G5** NO1846.
Parkhouse *Glas.* ***Suburb***, 2m/3km N of Glasgow city centre. NS5968.
Parkmore *Moray* ***Settlement***, 1m/2km NE of Dufftown. **63 F5** NJ3341.
Parkneuk *Aber.* ***Settlement***, 3m/5km NW of Inverbervie. **43 F2** NO7975.
Parkneuk *Fife* ***Suburb***, adjoining to NW of Dunfermline. NT0888.
Parkside *N.Lan.* ***Village***, 3m/4km N of Wishaw. NS8058.
Partick *Glas.* ***Suburb***, 2m/3km W of Glasgow city centre. **23 G3** NS5567.
Partickhill *Glas.* ***Suburb***, 3m/4km NW of Glasgow city centre in Partick district. NS5566.
Parton *D. & G.* ***Village***, 7m/11km NW of Castle Douglas. **8 A3** NX6970.
Pass of Aberfoyle *Stir.* ***Other feature of interest***, road pass at NE end of Loch Ard, 3m/4km NW of Aberfoyle. **31 G4** NN4801.
Pass of Achray *Stir.* ***Other feature of interest***, section of narrow, steep-sided valley carrying Achray Water E from Loch Katrine to Loch Achray, 4m/6km NW of Aberfoyle. **31 G4** NN4806.
Pass of Ballater *Aber.* ***Other feature of interest***, mountain pass carrying minor road, 1km N of Ballater. NO3696.
Pass of Balmaha *Stir.* ***Other feature of interest***, pass to W of Balmaha and to N of Craigie Fort, carrying road at height of 92 feet or 28 metres along E shore of Loch Lomond. **31 G5** NS4191.
Pass of Brander *Arg. & B.* ***Other feature of interest***, pass in Argyll, traversed by River Awe, running from foot of Loch Awe, on SW side of Ben Cruachan. **30 C2** NN0528.
Pass of Drumochter ***Other feature of interest***, mountain pass between Glen Truim and Glen Garry, 6m/9km S of Dalwhinnie. Carries the A9 road and the Perth-Inverness railway, the latter rising to 1484 feet or 452 metres, the summit of the British railway system. **40 B2** NN6275.
Pass of Glencoe *High.* ***Other feature of interest***, mountain pass carrying A82(T) between S slopes of A' Chailleach and N slopes of The Three Sisters, at head of Glen Coe, 3m/5km S of Kinlochleven. **39 D4** NN1557.
Pass of Killiecrankie *P. & K.* ***Other feature of interest***, narrow, wooded pass in valley of River Garry, 3m/4km NW of Pitlochry. Visitor centre gives information on local history and wildlife. **41 E3** NN9161.
Pass of Leny *Stir.* ***Other feature of interest***, wooded defile containing Falls of Leny, below Loch Lubnaig 2m/4km W of Callander. **32 A4** NN5908.
Pass of Lyon *P. & K.* ***Other feature of interest***, deep defile in Glen Lyon, 1m/2km W of Fortingall. At its narrowest point is Macgregor's Leap. NN7247.
Pass of Melfort *Arg. & B.* ***Other feature of interest***, mountain pass 1km N of Melfort. **30 A3** NM8414.
Path of Condie *P. & K.* ***Hamlet***, 4m/6km SE of Dunning. **33 F3** NO0711.
Pather *N.Lan.* ***Suburb***, S district of Wishaw. NS7954.
Pathhead *Aber.* ***Settlement***, 1m/2km SW of St. Cyrus. **43 F3** NO7363.
Pathhead *E.Ayr.* ***Hamlet***, on N bank of River Nith, opposite New Cumnock. **15 E4** NS6114.
Pathhead *Fife* ***Locality***, district of Kirkcaldy, in vicinity of harbour. **34 A5** NT2892.
Pathhead *Midloth.* ***Village***, 4m/7km SE of Dalkeith. **26 A3** NT3964.
Pathstruie *P. & K.* ***Locality***, 4m/6km SE of Dunning. NO0711.
Patna *E.Ayr.* Population: 2387. ***Village***, on River Doon, 5m/8km NW of Dalmellington. **14 C4** NS4110.
Pattack *High.* ***River***, in Badenoch and Strathspey district, running N from Loch Pattack then turning W to head of Loch Laggan. **40 A1** NN5389.
Paul's Hill *Moray* ***Mountain***, rising to over 450 metres, 4m/7km SW of Upper Knockando. **62 D5** NJ1140.
Paxton *Sc.Bord.* ***Village***, 4m/7km W of Berwick-upon-Tweed. **27 G4** NT9353.
Paxton House *Sc.Bord.* ***Historic house***, Palladian mansion built for daughter of Frederick the Great, 1km S of Paxton on W bank of River Tweed. Designed by Adam family, it is well-preserved, furnished by Chippendale and Trotter, and houses a Regency picture gallery. **27 G4** NT9352.
Pean *High.* ***River***, in Lochaber district, running E down Glen Pean to join River Dessary 1km above head of Loch Arkaig. **38 B1** NM9791.
Pearsie *Angus* ***Hamlet***, 4m/6km NW of Kirriemuir. **42 B4** NO3659.
Pease Bay *Sc.Bord.* ***Bay***, small sandy bay with rocky headlands, 1m/2km E of Cockburnspath. **27 E2** NT7971.
Peaston *E.Loth.* ***Hamlet***, 3m/4km SW of Pencaitland. **26 B3** NT4365.
Peastonbank *E.Loth.* ***Hamlet***, 1m/2km S of Pencaitland. **26 B3** NT4466.
Peat Hill *Aber.* ***Mountain***, 6m/9km NE of Strathdon. Height 1856 feet or 566 metres. **53 G3** NJ4119.
Peat Hill *Angus* ***Mountain***, 3m/5km NW of Kirkton of Menmuir. Height 1578 feet or 481 metres. **42 D3** NO5067.
Peat Hill *N.Ayr.* ***Mountain***, 4m/6km NE of Largs. Height 1378 feet or 420 metres. **22 D3** NS2464.
Peat Inn *Fife* ***Village***, 6m/9km SE of Cupar. **34 C4** NO4509.
Peat Law *Sc.Bord.* ***Mountain***, 2m/3km NW of Selkirk. Height 1397 feet or 426 metres. **17 F2** NT4430.
Peathill *Aber.* ***Village***, 1m/2km S of Rosehearty. **65 E3** NJ9365.
Peebles *Sc.Bord.* Population: 7065. ***Small town***, resort on River Tweed, 20m/33km S of Edinburgh. Cross Kirk (Historic Scotland) is ruin dating from 13c. **25 G5** NT2540.
Peel Fell ***Mountain***, on border of Northumberland and Scottish Borders, 4m/6km N of Kielder. Steep-sided to W. Height 1975 feet or 602 metres. **11 E2** NY6399.
Peel Ring of Lumphanan *Aber.* ***Historic/prehistoric site***, moated medieval earthwork (Historic Scotland), 1km SW of Lumphanan, where it is said Macbeth made his last stand. Structure is 120 feet or 36.5 metres in diameter by 18 feet or 5.5 metres high. **54 A4** NJ5703.
Peffer Burn *E.Loth.* ***River***, rising in Garleton Hills, N of Haddington, and flowing NE to North Sea at Peffersíde, 4m/7km NW of Dunbar. **26 C2** NT5678.
Pegal Burn *Ork.* ***River***, rising in central Hoy and flowing E into Pegal Bay. **78 B3** ND2598.
Pegal Head *Ork.* ***Coastal feature***, headland on E coast of Hoy opposite Rysa Little. ND3098.
Peighinn nan Aoireann (Anglicised form: Peninerine.) *W.Isles* ***Settlement***, on South Uist, 1m/2km NE of Rubha Aird-mhicheil. **46 A1** NF7434.
Peinchorran *High.* ***Settlement***, on Skye, on N side of Loch Sligachan, near mouth of loch. **48 B1** NG5233.
Peinlich *High.* ***Settlement***, on Skye, 3m/5km S of Uig. **58 A4** NG4158.
Peinmore *High.* ***Settlement***, on Skye, 5m/8km NW of Portree. NG4248.
Pencaitland *E.Loth.* Population: 1287. ***Locality***, parish containing villages of Easter and Wester Pencaitland, on either side of Tyne Water, 4m/6km SE of Tranent. **26 B3** NT4468.
Penicuik *Midloth.* Population: 17,173. ***Town***, on River North Esk, 9m/14km S of Edinburgh. Edinburgh Crystal Glass Works and Visitor Centre based here. 12c belfry in parish church. **25 G3** NT2359.
Peniel Heugh *Sc.Bord.* ***Hill***, 4m/6km N of Jedburgh, bearing monument raised in 1815 to commemorate Battle of Waterloo. Height 777 feet or 237 metres. **18 A4** NT6526.
Penifiler *High.* ***Settlement***, on Skye, 1m/2km S of Portree across Loch Portree. **58 A5** NG4841.
Penilee *Glas.* ***Suburb***, in Hillington district of Glasgow. NS5164.
Peninerine *W.Isles Anglicised form of Peighinn nan Aoireann, qv.*
Peninver *Arg. & B.* ***Settlement***, on E coast of Kintyre, 4m/6km NE of Campbeltown. **12 C3** NR7524.
Penkill *S.Ayr.* ***Settlement***, 3m/5km E of Girvan. Penkill Castle to S. **6 D1** NX2398.
Penkill Castle *S.Ayr.* ***Castle***, 16c-17c tower keep with 19c alterations, to S of Penkill and 3m/5km E of Girvan. NX2398.
Penkiln Burn *D. & G.* ***River***, rising on S slopes of Lamachan Hill and running S to River Cree at N end of Newton Stewart. **7 F4** NX4166.
Pennan *Aber.* ***Village***, on N coast, at foot of cliffs on Pennan Bay, W of Pennan Head and 2m/3km SE of Troup Head. **64 D3** NJ8465.
Pennan Bay *Aber.* ***Bay***, on N coast of Buchan district, 6m/9km SW of Rosehearty. NJ8465.
Pennan Head *Aber.* ***Coastal feature***, on W of Pennan Bay and 2m/3km SE of Troup Head. **65 D3** NJ8565.
Penninghame *D. & G.* ***Settlement***, 4m/6km NW of Newton Stewart. **7 E4** NX3869.
Penninghame Forest *D. & G.* ***Forest/woodland***, 4m/6km NW of Newton Stewart. NX3568.
Pennyfuir *Arg. & B.* ***Settlement***, 1m/2km NE of Oban. **30 A1** NM8732.
Pennyghael *Arg. & B.* ***Locality***, on S side of Loch Scridain, Mull, 9m/14km E of Bunessan. **29 E2** NM5126.
Pennyglen *S.Ayr.* ***Settlement***, 2m/3km W of Maybole. **14 A4** NS2710.
Pennygown *Arg. & B.* ***Settlement***, on Sound of Mull, 2m/3km E of Salen. Ruined chapel, with decorated Celtic cross shaft, beside road to E. **37 F5** NM5942.
Pennyvenie *E.Ayr.* ***Settlement***, 1m/2km NE of Dalmellington. NS4906.
Penpont *D. & G.* ***Village***, on Scaur Water, 2m/4km W of Thornhill. **8 C1** NX8494.
Penshiel Hill *E.Loth.* ***Mountain***, in Lammermuir Hills, 1m/2km SW of Whiteadder Reservoir. Height 1401 feet or 427 metres. **26 D3** NT6362.
Penston *E.Loth.* ***Hamlet***, 1km E of Macmerry. NT4472.
Pentland Firth ***Sea feature***, sea area between Orkney and N coast of Scottish mainland. **78 B4** ND2682.
Pentland Hills ***Large natural feature***, range of grass-covered hills, designated as Regional Park, largely composed of Old Red Sandstone, running some 16m/26km from S of Edinburgh towards Carnwath. Numerous reservoirs. Summit is Scald Law, 1898 feet or 579 metres. **25 E4** NT1055.
Pentland Skerries *Ork.* ***Island***, group of four small uninhabited islands at E end of Pentland Firth, 3m/5km S of South Ronaldsay. Islands are Muckle Skerry (largest, with lighthouse), Little Skerry, Louther Skerry and Clettack Skerry. **77 G1** ND4678.
Penvalla *Sc.Bord.* ***Mountain***, 3m/4km NW of Stobo. Height 1765 feet or 538 metres. **16 C2** NT1539.
Penwhapple Reservoir *S.Ayr.* ***Reservoir***, 2m/4km N of Barr. **7 D1** NX2697.
Penwhirn Reservoir *D. & G.* ***Reservoir***, 4m/7km NW of New Luce. NX1269.
People's Palace Museum *Glas.* ***Other feature of interest***, on Glasgow Green, 1m/2km SE of Glasgow city centre. Built in red sandstone and opened in 1898 as a cultural and recreational centre for people from Glasgow's E end, it is now a museum charting history and development of city. **24 A3** NS6064.
Peppermill Dam *Fife* ***Lake/loch***, 2m/3km NE of Kincardine. **24 D1** NS9489.
Perceton *N.Ayr.* ***Suburb***, in E part of Irvine. **23 E5** NS3440.
Percie *Aber.* ***Settlement***, 1km W of Finzean. **54 A5** NO5992.
Percyhorner *Aber.* ***Hamlet***, 2m/4km SW of Fraserburgh. NJ9565.
Perkhill *Aber.* ***Settlement***, 1m/2km NW of Lumphanan. **54 A4** NJ5705.
Persey *P. & K.* ***Settlement***, 2m/3km N of Bridge of Cally. **41 G4** NO1354.
Persley *Aberdeen* ***Locality***, on River Don, 3m/5km NW of Aberdeen city centre. NJ9010.
Pert *Angus* ***Hamlet***, to S of North Bridge Water, 2m/3km W of Marykirk. **43 E3** NO6565.
Perth *P. & K.* Population: 41,453. ***City***, ancient cathedral city (Royal Charter granted 1210) on River Tay, 31m/50km N of Edinburgh. Once capital of Medieval Scotland. Centre of livestock trade. Previously cotton manufacturing centre; now important industries include whisky distilling. Airfield (Scone) to NE. **33 G2** NO1123.
Perth Racecourse *P. & K.* ***Racecourse***, to N of Perth, adjacent to Scone Park and on E bank of River Tay. National Hunt course, with ten race days each year. **33 G2** NO1026.
Peter Anderson Woollen Mill *Sc.Bord.* ***Other feature of interest***, woollen mill at Galashiels where processes involved in manufacutre of tweed and tartan can be seen. Also museum of local history. **17 F2** NT4936.
Peter Hill *Aber.* ***Mountain***, 3m/5km SE of Ballochan. Height 2024 feet or 617 metres. **43 D1** NO5788.
Peterburn *High.* ***Settlement***, on W coast of Ross and Cromarty district, 6m/9km S of Rubha Réidh. **58 D1** NG7483.
Peterculter *Aberdeen* ***Village***, with much housing development, at confluence of Leuchar Burn and River Dee, 7m/11km SW of Aberdeen. **54 D4** NJ8400.
Peterhead *Aber.* Population: 18,674. ***Town***, spa town, port and most easterly town on Scottish mainland, located on NE coast, 27m/44km N of Aberdeen. Largest white fish port in Europe. Industrial estate developments at Dales Farm and Upperton to S. **65 G5** NK1346.

Peterhead Bay *Aber.* ***Bay***, forms large harbour to S of Peterhead. **65 G5** NK1245.
Peterhead Maritime Heritage Centre *Aber.* ***Other feature of interest***, museum illustrating importance of maritime industries to Peterhead, with displays on fishing, whaling and oil industries. **65 G5** NK1346.
Peter's Hill *Aber.* ***Mountain***, 3m/5km N of Ballater. Height 1863 feet or 568 metres. **53 F4** NJ3600.
Peterson's Rock *Arg. & B.* ***Island***, rock with beacon lying 1m/2km E of Sanda Island, off S coast of Kintyre. NR7504.
Petta Water *Shet. See Sand Water.*
Pettinain *S.Lan.* ***Village***, 2m/3km S of Carstairs Junction across River Clyde. **25 D5** NS9543.
Petty *Aber.* ***Settlement***, 1km S of Fyvie. **54 C1** NJ7636.
Pettycur *Fife* ***Locality***, with small harbour, at S end of Kinghorn. **25 G1** NT2686.
Pettymuick *Aber.* ***Settlement***, 2m/3km SE of Pitmedden. **55 E2** NJ9024.
Phantassie *E.Loth.* ***Suburb***, on E side of East Linton. Birthplace of Sir John Rennie, 1761-1821, engineer. Notable 16c dovecote (National Trust for Scotland). NT5977.
Pharay *Ork. Alternative spelling of Faray, qv.*
Phesdo *Aber.* ***Settlement***, 2m/3km NE of Fettercairn. **43 E2** NO6775.
Philip Law *Sc.Bord.* ***Mountain***, in Cheviot Hills, 3m/5km NW of Carter Bar. Height 1358 feet or 414 metres. **18 B5** NT7210.
Philiphaugh *Sc.Bord.* ***Locality***, estate to N of confluence of Ettrick Water and Yarrow Water, 2m/3km W of Selkirk. Site of 1645 Battle of Philiphaugh to E. **17 F3** NT4528.
Philorth *Aber.* ***Locality***, comprises Mains of Philorth, Milton of Philorth and Philorth House, 3m/4km S of Fraserburgh. Water of Philorth is stream on E side of locality running NE into Fraserburgh Bay. NK0063.
Philpstoun *W.Loth.* ***Village***, 3m/5km E of Linlithgow. **25 E2** NT0477.
Phones *High.* ***Settlement***, 3m/5km S of Newtonmore. **51 G5** NN7094.
Phorp *Moray* ***Settlement***, 4m/6km S of Forres. **62 C4** NJ0452.
Picardy Stone *Aber.* ***Historic/prehistoric site***, Pictish inscriptions dating from 7c or 8c on stone (Historic Scotland), 2m/3km NW of Insch. **54 B1** NJ6130.
Pickletillem *Fife* ***Hamlet***, 3m/4km N of Leuchars. **34 C2** NO4324.
Pickston *P. & K.* ***Settlement***, 3m/4km NW of Methven. **33 E2** NN9928.
Pictish Wheel House *W.Isles* ***Historic/prehistoric site***, aisled round house near W coast of South Uist, 1m/2km SW of Dalabrog. **44 C2** NF7320.
Pier Arts Centre *Ork.* ***Other feature of interest***, in Stromness, Mainland, exhibiting 20c British art. **78 B2** HY2508.
Pierowall *Ork.* ***Village***, on Bay of Pierowall, on E coast of Westray. Medieval church (Historic Scotland) has finely lettered tombstones. **80 C2** HY4348.
Pike Fell *D. & G.* ***Mountain***, 7m/11km NE of Langholm. Height 1637 feet or 499 metres. **10 C2** NY4193.
Pike Hill *Sc.Bord.* ***Mountain***, 2m/3km S of Craik. Height 1368 feet or 417 metres. **17 E5** NT3505.
Pikey Hill *Moray* ***Mountain***, 4m/6km NW of Rothes. Height 1164 feet or 355 metres. **63 E4** NJ2151.
Pilrig *Edin.* ***Suburb***, 1m/2km NE of Edinburgh city centre. NT2675.
Piltanton Burn *D. & G.* ***River***, rising on Rinns of Galloway, 4m/6km NW of Stranraer, and flowing SE to join Water of Luce at Sands of Luce, S of Glenluce. **6 B5** NX1954.
Pilton *Edin.* ***Suburb***, 2m/3km NW of Edinburgh city centre. NT2376.
Pinderachy *Angus* ***Mountain***, 1m/2km NE of Glenogil. Height 1686 feet or 514 metres. **42 C3** NO4564.
Pinkie House *E.Loth.* ***Historic house***, Jacobean mansion on E side of Musselburgh where Prince Charles Edward Stuart spent night after battle of Prestonpans in 1745. House now used by Loretto School. **26 A2** NT3572.
Pinminnoch *S.Ayr.* ***Settlement***, 3m/4km S of Girvan. **6 C1** NX1893.
Pinmore *S.Ayr.* ***Locality***, 5m/8km S of Girvan. **6 D1** NX2091.
Pinwherry *S.Ayr.* ***Village***, at confluence of River Stinchar and Duisk River, 7m/11km S of Girvan. **6 C2** NX1986.
Piperhall *Arg. & B.* ***Settlement***, on Bute, 4m/6km S of Rothesay. **22 B4** NS0958.
Piperhill *High.* ***Locality***, in Nairn district, 4m/6km S of Nairn. **62 A4** NH8650.
Pirnmill *N.Ayr.* ***Village***, on W coast of Arran, opposite Grogport in Kintyre. **21 G5** NR8744.
Pisgah *Stir.* ***Locality***, adjoining to SE of Dunblane. **32 C4** NN7900.
Pitagowan *P. & K.* ***Settlement***, in valley of River Garry, 3m/5km W of Blair Atholl. **40 D3** NN8265.
Pitblae *Aber.* ***Settlement***, 1m/2km SW of Fraserburgh. **65 E3** NJ9764.
Pitcairley Hill *Fife* ***Hill***, on N edge of Ochil Hills, 1m/2km SE of Abernethy. Height 922 feet or 281 metres. **34 A3** NO2116.
Pitcairngreen *P. & K.* ***Village***, with large green, 4m/6km NW of Perth. **33 F2** NO0627.
Pitcairnie Lake *P. & K.* ***Lake/loch***, small lake to SW of Dupplin Lake, 6m/10km SW of Perth. NO0219.
Pitcairns *P. & K.* ***Settlement***, 1km SE of Dunning. **33 F3** NO0214.
Pitcalnie *High.* ***Hamlet***, in Ross and Cromarty district, 2m/4km N of N side of entrance to Cromarty Firth. NH8072.
Pitcaple *Aber.* ***Village***, 4m/7km NW of Inverurie. **54 C2** NJ7225.
Pitcaple Castle *Aber.* ***Castle***, Z-plan 16c castle, renovated in 19c, 1km NE of Pitcaple. **54 C2** NJ7226.
Pitcarity *Angus* ***Locality***, in Glen Prosen, 8m/13km NW of Kirriemuir. NO3265.
Pitcox *E.Loth.* ***Settlement***, 3m/5km SW of Dunbar. **26 D2** NT6475.
Pitcur *P. & K.* ***Locality***, 3m/4km SE of Coupar Angus. Ancient earth-house. **34 A1** NO2537.
Pitfichie *Aber.* ***Settlement***, and ruined castle, 7m/11km SW of Inverurie. **54 B3** NJ6716.
Pitfichie Forest *Aber.* ***Forest/woodland***, to W of Pitfichie and Monymusk. **54 B3** NJ6415.
Pitfour Castle *P. & K.* ***Hamlet***, 5m/8km E of Perth. NO1920.
Pitgrudy *High.* ***Settlement***, 1km NW of Dornoch. **72 C5** NH7991.
Pitinnan *Aber.* ***Locality***, includes Loanhead of Pitinnan, 4m/6km SE of Rothienorman. **54 C1** NJ7430.
Pitkennedy *Angus* ***Settlement***, to W of Montreathmont Forest, 4m/7km NW of Friockheim. **42 D4** NO5454.
Pitkevy *Fife* ***Settlement***, 3m/4km NW of Glenrothes. **34 A4** NO2403.
Pitlessie *Fife* ***Village***, 4m/6km SW of Cupar. **34 B4** NO3309.
Pitlochry *P. & K.* Population: 2541. ***Small town***, and summer resort on River Tummel 5m/8km NW of its confluence with River Tay and 11m/18km NW of Dunkeld. Festival Theatre. Highland Games in August. **41 E4** NN9458.
Pitmachie *Aber.* ***Settlement***, adjoining to W of Old Rayne across River Urie. NJ6728.
Pitmedden *Aber.* Population: 1082. ***Village***, 5m/9km E of Oldmeldrum. Remains of Tolquhon Castle (Historic Scotland), 1m/2km NW. **55 D2** NJ8927.
Pitmedden Forest *P. & K.* ***Forest/woodland***, to SE of Abernethy. **33 G3** NO2014.
Pitmedden Garden *Aber.* ***Garden***, National Trust for Scotland property, 1km NW of Pitmedden, includes 17c garden designed by Sir Alexander Seton, Baron of Pitmedden, and Museum of Farming Life. **55 D2** NJ8828.
Pitmiddle Wood *P. & K.* ***Forest/woodland***, coniferous wood with small loch at N end, 2m/3km W of Abernyke. **34 A1** NO2230.
Pitmuies *Angus* ***Settlement***, 3m/4km NE of Letham. Includes 18c white harled mansion with gardens featuring kitchen garden, rose garden, trellis walk, hornbeam walk and alpine meadow. **43 D5** NO5649.
Pitmunie *Aber.* ***Settlement***, 1m/2km W of Monymusk. **54 B3** NJ6615.
Pitnacree *P. & K.* ***Settlement***, 3m/5km SW of Pitlochry. **41 E4** NN9253.
Pitroddie *P. & K.* ***Locality***, 6m/10km E of Perth. **34 A2** NO2125.
Pitscottie *Fife* ***Village***, 3m/5km E of Cupar. **34 C3** NO4113.
Pitsligo *Aber.* ***Locality***, parish on N coast containing ruined Pitsligo Castle, dating from 1424, 1km SE of Rosehearty. NJ9366.
Pitsligo Castle *Aber.* ***Castle***, ruined early 15c castle dating from 1424, 1km SE of Rosehearty. **65 E3** NJ9367.
Pittendreich *Moray* ***Settlement***, 1m/2km SW of Elgin. **63 D3** NJ1961.
Pittentrail *High.* ***Settlement***, in Strath Fleet, 1m/2km S of Little Rogart, Sutherland district. **72 C4** NC7202.
Pittenweem *Fife* Population: 1561. ***Small town***, royal burgh and fishing port on Firth of Forth, 1m/2km W of Anstruther. **34 D4** NO5402.
Pitteuchar *Fife* ***Suburb***, in SE part of Glenrothes. NT2799.
Pittodrie House *Aber.* ***Other building***, hotel 2m/3km SE of Oyne. **54 B2** NJ7023.
Pittulie *Aber.* ***Settlement***, on N coast, adjoining to W of Sandhaven, 2m/4km W of Fraserburgh. NJ9667.
Pittulie Castle *Aber.* ***Castle***, 17c rectangular tower block, now in ruins, 1m/2km E of Rosehearty. NJ9467.
Pladda *Arg. & B.* ***Island***, one of Small Isles group off E coast of Jura. NR5468.
Pladda *N.Ayr.* ***Island***, small uninhabited island about 1km off S coast of Arran across Sound of Pladda. **13 F4** NS0219.
Pladda Island *Arg. & B.* ***Island***, islet off S coast of Lismore, nearly 1km S of Eilean Dubh, and on E side of Creag Island. **30 A1** NM8337.
Plaidy *Aber.* ***Settlement***, 3m/5km N of Turriff. **64 C4** NJ7255.
Plains *N.Lan.* Population: 2581. ***Village***, 2m/4km NE of Airdrie. **24 B3** NS7966.
Plasterfield *W.Isles* ***Hamlet***, on Isle of Lewis, 1m/2km E of Stornoway. NB4433.
Plean *Stir.* Population: 1671. ***Village***, 5m/8km SE of Stirling. **24 C1** NS8386.
Pleasance *Fife* ***Hamlet***, 1km N of Auchtermuchty. **34 A3** NO2312.
Pley Moss *E.Ayr.* ***Open space***, plateau, part moorland and part forest, 3m/5km N of Darvel. **23 G5** NS5641.
Plockton *High.* ***Village***, in Skye and Lochalsh district, on S side of Loch Carron, 5m/8km NE of Kyle of Lochalsh. Airfield 1m/2km W. **49 E1** NG8033.
Plocrapool Point *W.Isles* ***Coastal feature***, headland on W side of entrance to East Loch Tarbert, South Harris. NG1893.
Plodda Falls *High.* ***Waterfall***, formed where Eas Socach falls over 70 feet or 20 metres into pool swelled by confluence with Abhainn Deabhag, 6m/10km SW of Cannich. **50 B2** NH2723.
Pluscarden Priory *Moray* ***Ecclesiastical building***, 13c priory near locality of Barnhill, 5m/9km SW of Elgin. Occupied and restored by Benedictine monks since 1943. **62 D4** NJ1457.
Pocan Smoo *High.* ***Coastal feature***, rock on N coast 1m/2km E of Durness, Sutherland district. **74 D2** NC4267.
Point *W.Isles Alternative name for Eye Peninsula, qv.*
Point of Ardnamurchan *High.* ***Coastal feature***, the most westerly point of British mainland. Lighthouse. **36 D3** NM4167.
Point of Ayre *Ork.* ***Coastal feature***, headland on E coast of Mainland, 4m/6km S of Mull Head. **79 E2** HY5903.
Point of Buckquoy (Buckquoy Point). *Ork.* ***Coastal feature***, headland at NW end of Mainland opposite Brough of Birsay. HY2428.
Point of Bugarth *Shet.* ***Coastal feature***, headland on W coast of Yell, 3m/5km N of West Sandwick. HU4493.
Point of Fethaland *Shet.* ***Coastal feature***, headland at northernmost point of Mainland. **84 C3** HU3795.
Point of Grimsetter *Ork.* ***Coastal feature***, headland on Inganess Bay to N of Kirkwall Airport. HY4808.
Point of Hackness *Ork.* ***Coastal feature***, headland on South Walls peninsula of Hoy to N of Hackness. ND3391.
Point of Howana Geo *Ork.* ***Coastal feature***, headland on W coast of Mainland, 3m/5km S of Marwick Head. HY2220.
Point of Huro *Ork.* ***Coastal feature***, headland at S end of Westray. **80 C3** HY4938.
Point of Knap *Arg. & B.* ***Coastal feature***, headland in Knapdale, Argyll, on W side of entrance to Loch Caolisport. **21 E2** NR6972.
Point of Ness *Shet.* ***Coastal feature***, headland on E coast of Yell, on W side of entrance to Basta Voe. HU5394.
Point of Scaraber *Ork.* ***Coastal feature***, promontory at S end of Faray, 1km N of Fers Ness, Eday. HY5335.
Point of Sinsoss *Ork.* ***Coastal feature***, in far NE of North Ronaldsay. Dennis Head lies 1km SE. **81 F1** HY7856.
Point of Sleat *High.* ***Coastal feature***, headland with beacon at S end of Sleat peninsula. Most southerly point of Skye. **48 B5** NM5699.
Point of Stoer *High.* ***Coastal feature***, headland on W coast of Sutherland district, 9m/15km NW of Lochinver. **70 C1** NC0235.
Point of the Graand *Ork.* ***Coastal feature***, headland and southernmost point of Egilsay. HY4726.
Polanach *Arg. & B.* ***Settlement***, on SE shore of Loch Linnhe, 4m/6km NE of Port Appin. **38 B4** NM9350.
Polbae *D. & G.* ***Settlement***, 1m/2km S of Loch Maberry and 6m/10km SE of Barrhill. **7 D3** NX2873.
Polbain *High.* ***Village***, near NW coast of Ross and Cromarty district, 2m/3km NW of Achiltibuie. **70 B3** NC0208.
Polbaith Burn *E.Ayr.* ***River***, rising on slopes E of Sneddon Law and flowing SW to join River Irvine 1m/2km W of Galston. **23 G5** NS4837.
Polbeth *W.Loth.* Population: 2352. ***Hamlet***, 3m/5km SW of Livingston. **25 E3** NT0264.
Polchar *High.* ***Settlement***, 2m/3km S of Aviemore. **52 A4** NH8909.
Poldean *D. & G.* ***Settlement***, on hillside, 2m/3km SE of Beattock. **9 F1** NT1000.
Poldorais *High.* ***Sea feature***, strait between Eilean Flodigarry and NE coast of Skye. NG4771.
Pole Hill *High.* ***Hill***, 2m/3km W of Naver Forest, Caithness district. Height 964 feet or 294 metres. **75 F4** NC6441.
Pole Hill *P. & K.* ***Hill***, in Braes of the Carse, 3m/5km N of St. Madoes. Height 945 feet or 288 metres. **33 G2** NO1926.
Poles *High.* ***Settlement***, 2m/3km NW of Dornoch. **72 C5** NH7893.
Polglass *High.* ***Village***, on NW coast of Ross and Cromarty district, 10m/15km NW of Ullapool. **70 C4** NC0307.
Polgown *D. & G.* ***Settlement***, 5m/8km SW of Sanquhar. **15 F5** NS7103.

Polharrow Burn *D. & G.* ***River***, running E from Loch Harrow to Water of Ken, 2m/4km N of St. John's Town of Dalry. **7 G2** NX6084.
Polin *High.* ***Settlement***, near W coast of Sutherland district, 3m/4km NW of Kinlochbervie. NC1959.
Polkemmet Country Park *W.Loth.* ***Leisure/recreation***, 68 acre country park with woodland, bowling green and golf course, 1m/2km W of Whitburn. **24 D3** NS9265.
Polkemmet Moor *W.Loth.* ***Open space***, partly wooded moorland between Fauldhouse and Harthill. **24 D3** NS9162.
Poll a' Charra (Anglicised form: Pollachar.) *W.Isles* ***Settlement***, near SW coast of South Uist, 4m/6km S of Dalabrog. **44 C2** NF7414.
Poll a' Mhuineil *High.* ***Bay***, small bay on SW shore of Loch Hourn, Lochaber district. Eilean a' Mhuneil is islet off E end of bay. NG8406.
Poll Creadha *High.* ***Sea feature***, inlet on W coast of Ross and Cromarty district, 1m/2km N of Toscaig. **58 C5** NG7140.
Poll na h-Ealaidh *High.* ***Sea feature***, small inlet on W coast of Trotternish peninsula, Skye, 3m/5km S of Uig. **57 G4** NG3759.
Polla *High.* ***Settlement***, at N end of Strath Beag. **74 C3** NC3854.
Pollachar *W.Isles Anglicised form of Poll a' Charra, qv.*
Pollagach Burn *Aber.* ***River***, stream flowing NE to River Dee 4m/6km E of Ballater. **53 G5** NO4296.
Polldubh *High.* ***Settlement***, in Glen Nevis, 5m/8km NW of Kinlochleven. **38 D3** NN1368.
Pollie *High.* ***Settlement***, 1m/2km E of Dalbreck, to N of Black Water river, Sutherland district. **72 C3** NC7515.
Polliwilline Bay *Arg. & B.* ***Bay***, on E coast of Kintyre, 3m/5km E of Southend. **12 C5** NR7409.
Polloch *High.* ***Settlement***, in Lochaber district, on river of same name, which runs NW from Loch Doilet to Loch Shiel. **37 G3** NM7968.
Pollok *Glas.* ***Suburb***, 4m/7km SW of Glasgow city centre. NS5362.
Pollok Grounds *Glas.* ***Open space***, to E of Pollok across White Cart Water. Includes Pollok Country Park, with sports facilities. NS5562.
Pollok House *Glas.* ***Historic house***, dating from 1750, former home of Maxwells is now owned by city of Glasgow. Situated by White Cart Water and surrounded by 361 acres of parkland and gardens to form Pollok Grounds, 3m/5km SW of Glasgow city centre. Stirling Maxwell collection of Spanish paintings is housed here. **23 G3** NS5561.
Pollokshaws *Glas.* ***Suburb***, 3m/5km SW of Glasgow city centre. **23 G3** NS5661.
Pollokshields *Glas.* ***Suburb***, 2m/3km SW of Glasgow city centre. NS5763.
Polly *High.* ***River***, flowing W from Loch Sionascaig to Polly Bay. NC0614.
Polly Bay (Also known as Loch Polly.) *High.* ***Sea feature***, inlet in Enard Bay, NW coast of Ross and Cromarty district 2m/4km W of Loch Sionascaig. **70 C3** NC0714.
Polmaddie Hill *S.Ayr.* ***Mountain***, 4m/6km SE of Barr. Height 1853 feet or 565 metres. **7 E1** NX3391.
Polmaddy Burn *D. & G.* ***River***, rising on E slopes of Corserine and flowing E to Water of Ken, 4m/7km SE of Carsphairn. **7 G2** NX6088.
Polmadie *Glas.* ***Suburb***, 2m/3km S of Glasgow city centre in Govanhill district. NS5962.
Polmont *Falk.* Population: 18,041. ***Town***, 3m/5km E of Falkirk. **24 D2** NS9378.
Polnoon *E.Renf.* ***Settlement***, 1m/2km SE of Eaglesham. **23 G4** NS5851.
Poltalloch *Arg. & B.* ***Locality***, in Argyll, 1m/2km NE of Crinan Loch. Many prehistoric remains in vicinity. **30 A5** NR8196.
Poltalloch Monuments *Arg. & B. Alternative name for Kilmartin Glen Monuments, qv.*
Poltalloch Stones *Arg. & B. See Kilmartin Sculptured Stones.*
Polton *Midloth.* ***Village***, on River North Esk, 1km SE of Loanhead. **25 G3** NT2864.
Polwarth *Edin.* ***Suburb***, 1m/2km SW of Edinburgh city centre. NT2372.
Polwarth *Sc.Bord.* ***Village***, 4m/6km SW of Duns. **27 E4** NT7450.
Pomona *Ork. Former name of Mainland, qv.*
Pond of Drummond *P. & K.* ***Lake/loch***, small lake NE of Drummond Castle and 2m/3km S of Crieff. NN8518.
Ponesk Burn *E.Ayr.* ***River***, rising on SW slopes of Hare Craig and flowing S down steep valleys to join River Ayr, 2m/3km E of Muirkirk. **15 F2** NS7130.
Pool of Muckhart *Clack.* ***Village***, 3m/5km NE of Dollar. **33 F4** NO0000.
Pool of Virkie *Shet.* ***Sea feature***, on N side of Sumburgh Airport, in S part of Mainland. HU3911.
Poolewe *High.* ***Village***, at head of Loch Ewe, Ross and Cromarty district, 4m/7km NE of Gairloch. National Trust for Scotland property N & E, including Inverewe gardens to N. **59 E1** NG8580.
Pools of Dee *Aber.* ***Lake/loch***, group of three pools in Cairngorm Mountains at source of River Dee, to NW of Ben Macdui. **52 B4** NH9700.
Porin *High.* ***Locality***, in Strathconon, Ross and Cromarty district, 2m/3km above head of Loch Meig. **60 C4** NH3155.
Port a' Ghàraidh *High.* ***Bay***, small bay on E shore of Sound of Sleat, on coast of Skye and Lochalsh district, 1m/2km SW of Glenelg. **49 D3** NG7917.
Port a' Mhurain *Arg. & B.* ***Sea feature***, inlet on S coast of Coll, to S of Crossapol Bay. **36 A4** NM1251.
Port a' Stoth (Anglicised form: Port Sto.) *W.Isles* ***Sea feature***, small inlet 1km SE of Butt of Lewis. **69 G1** NB5265.
Port Alasdair *W.Isles* ***Sea feature***, small inlet on E coast of Isle of Lewis, 3m/4km N of Cellar Head. **69 G1** NB5560.
Port Allen *D. & G.* ***Bay***, on W side of Wigtown Bay, 2m/3km E of Whithorn. **3 E2** NX4841.
Port Allen *P. & K.* ***Settlement***, on small inlet on N bank of Firth of Tay, 1m/2km S of Errol. **34 A2** NO2521.
Port Allt a' Mhuilinn *High.* ***Sea feature***, small inlet, 1m/2km SW of Strathy Point, Caithness district. **75 G2** NC8068.
Port an Aird Fhada *Arg. & B.* ***Bay***, small bay on S shore of Loch Scridain, Mull, to E of Aird Fada headland. **28 D2** NM4524.
Port an Duine Mhairbh *Arg. & B.* ***Sea feature***, inlet on W coast of Iona, 1m/2km W of Baile Mòr. **28 B2** NM2624.
Port Ann *Arg. & B.* ***Sea feature***, natural harbour on NW shore of Loch Fyne, 3m/4km SE of Lochgilphead. **22 A1** NR9086.
Port Appin *Arg. & B.* ***Village***, in Argyll, on E shore of Loch Linnhe, opposite N end of Lismore. Ferry to Port Ramsay on Lismore. **38 B5** NM9045.
Port Arnol *W.Isles* ***Bay***, on NW coast of Isle of Lewis, 1km NW of Arnol village. **69 D2** NB2949.
Port Askaig *Arg. & B.* ***Village***, and small port on E coast of Islay. Ferry to Feolin Ferry, Jura, on opposite side of Sound of Islay; car ferry service to West Loch Tarbert on mainland. **20 C3** NR4369.
Port Bàn *Arg. & B.* ***Sea feature***, small inlet on NE coast of Tiree. **36 A5** NM0947.
Port Bannatyne *Arg. & B.* Population: 1385. ***Village***, resort on S side of Kames Bay on E coast of Bute, 2m/3km N of Rothesay. **22 B3** NS0767.
Port Bun a' Ghlinne *W.Isles* ***Sea feature***, small inlet on E coast of Isle of Lewis, 3m/5km SW of Tolsta Head. **69 G3** NB5244.
Port Burg *Arg. & B.* ***Bay***, small bay on Loch Tuath, Mull, to S of Burg. **36 C5** NM3845.
Port Castle Bay *D. & G.* ***Bay***, 2m/4km W of Burrow Head. **3 E3** NX4235.
Port Ceann a' Gharraidh *Arg. & B.* ***Sea feature***, narrow inlet at NE end of Colonsay. **28 D5** NR4298.
Port Charlotte *Arg. & B.* ***Village***, on W side of Loch Indaal, Islay, 7m/11km NE of Rinns Point. **20 A4** NR2558.
Port Chubaird *Arg. & B.* ***Sea feature***, on W coast of The Oa, Islay, 2m/3km SW of Port Ellen. **20 B5** NR3342.
Port Donain *Arg. & B.* ***Bay***, small bay on E coast of Mull, 1m/2km NE of Rubha na Faoilinn. **29 G2** NM7329.
Port Driseach *Arg. & B.* ***Hamlet***, in Argyll, on W shore of Kyles of Bute, 1m/2km NE of Tighnabruaich. **22 A2** NR9873.
Port Dundas *Glas.* ***Suburb***, 1m/2km N of Glasgow city centre. NS5966.
Port Ellen *Arg. & B.* ***Small town***, and chief port of Islay, on S coast. Ruined Dunyvaig Castle is 14c. Several distilleries, including the well-known Lagavulin and Laphroaig. Airport at Glenegedale, 4m/7km NW. **20 B5** NR3645.
Port Elphinstone *Aber.* ***Hamlet***, 1km S of Inverurie across River Don. **54 C3** NJ7720.
Port Erroll *Aber.* ***Village***, on E coast, adjoining to SE of Cruden Bay, at N end of Bay of Cruden. **55 F1** NK0936.
Port Fada *Arg. & B.* ***Sea feature***, on E coast of Kintyre, 2m/3km SW of Claonaig. **21 G4** NR8554.
Port Geiraha *W.Isles* ***Bay***, small bay on E coast of Isle of Lewis, 3m/4km NW of Tolsta Head. **69 G2** NB5350.
Port Glasgow *Inclyde* Population: 19,693. ***Town***, old port and industrial town on Firth of Clyde, 3m/5km E of Greenock. 16c-17c Newark Castle (Historic Scotland) to E. **23 E2** NS3274.
Port Henderson *High.* ***Village***, on W coast of Ross and Cromarty district, 4m/6km SW of Gairloch across Gair Loch. **59 D2** NG7573.
Port Kilcheran *Arg. & B. See Kilcheran Loch.*
Port Laing *Fife* ***Bay***, small bay on Inverkeithing Bay, to N of North Queensferry. NT1381.
Port Leathan *Arg. & B.* ***Bay***, on W coast of Cowal peninsula, 5m/7km NW of Tighnabruaich. **22 A2** NR9176.
Port Leathan *Arg. & B.* ***Bay***, natural harbour at SW tip of Cowal peninsula, 5m/7km SW of Tighnabruaich. NR9267.
Port Logan *D. & G.* ***Village***, on W coast of Rinns of Galloway, 4m/6km NW of Drummore. **2 A2** NX0940.
Port Logan Bay (Also known as Port Nessock.) *D. & G.* ***Bay***, extending N to headland of Mull of Logan. NX0940.
Port Lotha *Arg. & B.* ***Sea feature***, narrow inlet on W coast of Colonsay, 3m/4km W of Scalasaig. **28 C5** NR3492.
Port Mary *D. & G.* ***Bay***, small bay, 1m/2km S of Dundrennan. **4 A2** NX7545.
Port Mholair *W.Isles Gaelic form of Portvoller, qv.*
Port Mhòr Bragar *W.Isles* ***Bay***, on NW coast of Isle of Lewis, 1m/2km N of Bragar. NB2849.
Port Min *High.* ***Sea feature***, small inlet on W coast of Ardnamurchan peninsula, 4m/7km NW of Kilchoan. **36 D3** NM4166.
Port Mine *Arg. & B.* ***Sea feature***, small inlet on W coast of Coll, to W of Feall Bay. **36 A4** NM1254.
Port Mòr *Arg. & B.* ***Bay***, with jetty, at N end of Gigha. **21 E4** NR6654.
Port Mòr *Arg. & B.* ***Sea feature***, inlet on S coast of Ross of Mull, 1m/2km NE of Rubh' Ardalanish. **28 C3** NM3617.
Port Mòr *Arg. & B.* ***Sea feature***, inlet on W coast of Colonsay. **28 C5** NR3594.
Port Mòr *High.* ***Coastal feature***, small inlet 2m/3km NE of Portmahomack. **62 B1** NH9287.
Port Mòr *High.* ***Hamlet***, with small harbour, near SE end of Muck, in Inner Hebrides. **36 D2** NM4279.
Port na Bà *Arg. & B.* ***Sea feature***, small inlet on N coast of Mull, 3m/4km E of Caliach Point. **36 C4** NM3854.
Port-na-Con *High.* ***Settlement***, on W shore of Loch Eriboll, Sutherland district, 5m/8km S of Durness. Ancient earth-house to N. **74 D2** NC4260.
Port na Craig *P. & K.* ***Settlement***, adjoining to S of Pitlochry across River Tummel. **41 E4** NN9358.
Port na Croise *Arg. & B.* ***Bay***, small bay on N shore of Loch Scridain, Mull, 1km SE of Bearraich. **28 D2** NM4326.
Port na Curaich *Arg. & B.* ***Bay***, small bay at S end of Iona. Supposed landing place of St. Columba in AD 563. NM2621.
Port na h-Eithar *Arg. & B.* ***Bay***, on SE coast of Coll, 3m/4km SW of Arinagour. NM2053.
Port na Long *High.* ***Settlement***, on Skye, between Loch Harport and Fiskavaig Bay, 3m/4km NW of Carbost. NG3434.
Port na Muice Duibhe *Arg. & B.* ***Bay***, small bay on SE coast of Mull, 3m/4km SW of entrance to Loch Spelve. NM6924.
Port nam Bothag *W.Isles* ***Sea feature***, small inlet, 1km S of Tolastadh bho Thuath, Isle of Lewis. **69 G3** NB5446.
Port nan Giùran *W.Isles Gaelic form of Portnaguran, qv.*
Port nan Long (Anglicised form: Newtonferry.) *W.Isles* ***Settlement***, on N coast of North Uist, 1m/2km N of Beinn Mhòr. **45 G2** NF8978.
Port Nessock *D. & G. Alternative name for Port Logan Bay, qv.*
Port Nis (Anglicised form: Port of Ness.) *W.Isles* ***Village***, on NE coast of Isle of Lewis, 2m/3km SE of Butt of Lewis. **69 G1** NB5363.
Port o' Warren *D. & G.* ***Settlement***, 6m/9km SE of Dalbeattie. **8 C5** NX8853.
Port of Brims *High.* ***Sea feature***, small inlet to S of Brims Ness on N coast. ND0471.
Port of Menteith *Stir.* ***Village***, at NE corner of Lake of Menteith, 5m/8km SW of Callander. **32 A4** NN5801.
Port of Ness *W.Isles Anglicised form of Port Nis, qv.*
Port of Spittal Bay *D. & G.* ***Bay***, 2m/3km SE of Portpatrick. **6 B5** NX0252.
Port Ohirnie *Arg. & B.* ***Bay***, small bay on SE coast of Mull, 2m/4km E of entrance to Loch Buie. **29 F3** NM6320.
Port Ramsay *Arg. & B.* ***Settlement***, at N end of Lismore, on Loch Linnhe. Ferry to Port Appin on mainland to E. **38 A5** NM8845.
Port Skigersta *W.Isles* ***Bay***, small bay near N end of Isle of Lewis, to NE of Sgiogarstaigh. **69 G1** NB5462.
Port Sonachan *Arg. & B. Alternative spelling of Portsonachan, qv.*
Port Sto *W.Isles Anglicised form of Port a' Stoth, qv.*
Port Vasgo *High.* ***Sea feature***, small inlet near mouth of Tongue Bay. **75 E2** NC5865.
Port Wemyss *Arg. & B.* ***Village***, at S end of Rinns of Islay, opposite Orsay. **20 A4** NR1651.
Port William *D. & G.* ***Town***, small resort with quay, on E shore of Luce Bay, 9m/15km SW of Wigtown. Sandy beaches. Remains of 11c chapel nearby. **2 D2** NX3343.
Portachoillan *Arg. & B.* ***Settlement***, on SE of seaward end of West Loch Tarbert, Kintyre, 1m/2km N of Clachan. **21 F4** NR7657.
Portankill *D. & G.* ***Bay***, small bay 2m/3km S of Cailiness Point. **2 B3** NX1432.
Portavadie *Arg. & B.* ***Village***, on E side of Loch Fyne, opposite Tarbert, 4m/6km SW across peninsula from Tighnabruaich. **22 A3** NR9269.
Portclair Forest *High.* ***Forest/woodland***, in Inverness district 4m/6km N of Fort Augustus. **50 C3** NH3815.

P

Portencross *N.Ayr.* ***Settlement***, on Firth of Clyde, 5m/9km NW of Ardrossan. Remains of medieval castle. **22 C5** NS1748.
Portencross Castle *N.Ayr.* ***Castle***, on coast at Portencross. Norman castle built on Roman fort and used as a prison in 18c for French prisoners of war. **22 C5** NS1748.
Portessie *Moray* ***Suburb***, E district of Buckie on N coast. **63 G3** NJ4466.
Portfield *Arg. & B.* ***Settlement***, on SE coast of Mull, 1km SW of entrance to Loch Spelve. **29 G2** NM7126.
Portgordon *Moray* ***Village***, on Spey Bay, 2m/3km SW of Buckie. **63 F3** NJ3964.
Portgower *High.* ***Settlement***, on E coast of Sutherland district, 2m/3km SW of Helmsdale. **73 F3** ND0013.
Portincaple *Arg. & B.* ***Settlement***, on Loch Long, 1m/2km N of Garelochhead. **31 E5** NS2393.
Portinnisherrich *Arg. & B.* ***Locality***, on E shore of Loch Awe, in Argyll, 8m/13km SW of Portsonachan. **30 B3** NM9711.
Portkil Bay *Arg. & B.* ***Bay***, on Firth of Clyde, 1m/2km E of Kilcreggan. NS2580.
Portknockie *Moray* Population: 1296. ***Village***, and resort on N coast, 4m/7km NE of Buckie. **63 G3** NJ4868.
Portlethen *Aber.* Population: 6224. ***Village***, on E coast, 6m/10km S of Aberdeen. **55 E5** NO9396.
Portmahomack *High.* ***Village***, on S shore of Dornoch Firth, 3m/5km SW of Tarbat Ness, Ross and Cromarty district. **62 B1** NH9184.
Portmore Loch *Sc.Bord.* ***Lake/loch***, small loch 2m/3km NE of Eddleston. **25 G4** NT2650.
Portnacroish *Arg. & B.* ***Village***, on Loch Laich, Argyll, on E side of Loch Linnhe. **38 B5** NM9247.
Portnaguiran New Lands *W.Isles* ***Settlement***, on Eye Peninsula, Isle of Lewis, 1km SW of Portnaguran. NB5536.
Portnaguran (Gaelic form: Port nan Giùran.) *W.Isles* ***Village***, at N end of Eye Peninsula, Isle of Lewis, 1m/2km W of Tiumpan Head. **69 G4** NB5537.
Portnahaven *Arg. & B.* ***Village***, at S end of Rinns of Islay, 1m/2km SE of Rubha na Faing. **20 A4** NR1652.
Portnalong *High.* ***Settlement***, 1m/2km SE of Ardtreck Point, Skye. **47 G1** NG3434.
Portnaluchaig *High.* ***Locality***, on W coast of Lochaber district, 2m/3km N of Arisaig. **37 F1** NM6589.
Portobello *D. & G.* ***Bay***, small inlet 8m/13km N of Portpatrick. **6 A4** NW9666.
Portobello *Edin.* ***Suburb***, on Firth of Forth, 3m/5km E of Edinburgh city centre. Extensive sands. **26 A2** NT3073.
Portpatrick *D. & G.* ***Small town***, resort with harbour on coast of Rinns of Galloway, 6m/9km SW of Stranraer. Originally developed as port for Ireland, but superseded by Stranraer from mid-19c. **6 B5** NX0054.
Portree *High.* Population: 2126. ***Small town***, port and chief town of Skye, situated on Loch Portree on E coast, about midway between Rubha Hunish in N and Strathaird Point in S. **58 A5** NG4843.
Portskerra *High.* ***Village***, near N coast of Caithness district, adjoining to NW of Melvich. **76 A2** NC8765.
Portslogan *D. & G.* ***Settlement***, 3m/5km N of Portpatrick. **6 A5** NW9858.
Portsonachan (Also spelled Port Sonachan.) *Arg. & B.* ***Village***, in Argyll, on E shore of Loch Awe, 8m/13km SW of Dalmally. **30 C2** NN0520.
Portsoy *Aber.* Population: 1822. ***Village***, on N coast, 6m/10km W of Banff. **64 A3** NJ5865.
Portuairk *High.* ***Settlement***, near W end of Ardnamurchan peninsula, in Lochaber district, 2m/3km E of Point of Ardnamurchan. **36 D3** NM4368.
Portvoller (Gaelic form: Port Mholair.) *W.Isles* ***Settlement***, on Eye Peninsula, Isle of Lewis, 1km S of Tiumpan Head. NB5636.
Portvoller Bay (Gaelic form: Bagh Phort Bholair.) *W.Isles* ***Bay***, on NE coast of Eye Peninsula, Isle of Lewis, to S of Portvoller. NB5636.
Portyerrock *D. & G.* ***Settlement***, on Portyerrock Bay, 2m/4km SE of Whithorn. **3 E3** NX4738.
Portyerrock Bay *D. & G.* ***Bay***, 1m/2km N of Isle of Whithorn. NX4838.
Possil Loch *Glas.* ***Lake/loch***, small loch and nature reserve on N side of Forth and Clyde Canal, 3m/4km N of Glasgow city centre. NS5869.
Possil Park *Glas.* ***Suburb***, 2m/3km N of Glasgow city centre. NS5868.
Potarch *Aber.* ***Settlement***, 2m/3km SE of Kincardine O'Neil. **54 B5** NO6097.
Potrail Water *S.Lan.* ***River***, rising on NW slopes between Ballencleugh Law and Scaw'd Law and running NE to join Daer Water and form River Clyde 2m/3km S of Elvanfoot. **16 A5** NS9513.
Potterton *Aber.* Population: 1144. ***Village***, 2m/3km SW of Balmedie. **55 E3** NJ9415.
Poundland *S.Ayr.* ***Settlement***, in Stinchar valley, 7m/11km NE of Ballantrae. **6 C2** NX1787.
Pow Burn *Fife* ***River***, rising E of Cowie and flowing SE, then NE into River Forth, 1km NW of Kincardine Bridge. **24 C1** NS9187.
Powfoot *D. & G.* ***Village***, on Solway Firth, 3m/5km W of Annan. **9 F4** NY1465.
Powmill *P. & K.* ***Village***, 4m/6km E of Dollar. **33 F5** NT0198.
Poyntzfield *High.* ***Settlement***, on Black Isle, 5m/8km SW of Cromarty. **61 G3** NH7164.
Pratis *Fife* ***Settlement***, 3m/5km NW of Kennoway. **34 B4** NO3806.
Presley *Moray* ***Settlement***, 5m/8km S of Forres. **62 C4** NJ0151.
Press Castle *Sc.Bord.* ***Historic house***, 17c mansion house, 2m/3km W of Coldingham. **27 F3** NT8765.
Pressendye *Aber.* ***Mountain***, 3m/4km N of Tarland. Height 2030 feet or 619 metres. **53 G4** NJ4908.
Pressmennan Lake *E.Loth.* ***Lake/loch***, 1m/2km SE of Stenton. **26 D2** NT6373.
Preston *E.Loth.* ***Village***, adjoining to N of East Linton. Mill (National Trust for Scotland) on banks of River Tyne dates from 18c; still in working order. Phantassie Doocot (National Trust for Scotland) dates from 16c. **26 C2** NT5977.
Preston *Sc.Bord.* ***Village***, 2m/4km N of Duns. **27 E4** NT7957.
Preston Law *Sc.Bord.* ***Mountain***, 3m/5km S of Peebles. Height 1863 feet or 568 metres. **16 D2** NT2535.
Preston Market Cross *E.Loth.* ***Historic/prehistoric site***, excellent example of early 17c Scottish market cross (Historic Scotland), 1km S of Prestonpans and 3m/5km NE of Musselburgh. Cylindrical base is surmounted by cross-shaft headed by a unicorn; only surviving example of market cross of its type in situ. **26 A2** NT3874.
Preston Merse *D. & G.* ***Coastal feature***, lowland coastal strip adjacent to Mersehead Sands to W of Southerness. **8 D5** NX9455.
Preston Mill and Phantassie Dovecot *E.Loth.* ***Historic house***, National Trust for Scotland property to NE of East Linton. 16c mill, one of oldest working watermills in Scotland. Dovecote or Doocot of beehive type, once having 544 pigeon nests. **26 C2** NT5977.
Preston Tower and Hamilton House *E.Loth.* ***Other feature of interest***, part-ruined 15c tower with 16c additions and 17c house (National Trust for Scotland) on S side of Prestonpans. **26 A2** NT3974.
Prestonfield *Edin.* ***Suburb***, of Edinburgh 2m/3km SE of city centre. NT2771.
Prestonpans *E.Loth.* Population: 7014. ***Small town***, on Firth of Forth, 3m/5km NE of Musselburgh. Hamilton House (National Trust for Scotland), built 1628. On E side of town is site of battle of 1745 in which Prince Charles Edward Stuart defeated government forces under Sir John Cope. Preston Market Cross (Historic Scotland) 1km S. **26 A2** NT3874.
Prestwick *S.Ayr.* Population: 13,705. ***Town***, and resort on Firth of Clyde, adjoining to N of Ayr. International airport. Golf's first Open Championship held here in 1860. Ruins of 12c Church of St. Nicholas. **14 B3** NS3525.
Prestwick International Airport *S.Ayr.* ***Airport/airfield***, international airport to NE of Prestwick. **14 B3** NS3626.
Priest Island (Also known as Eilean a' Chleirich.) *High.* ***Island***, uninhabited island, outlier of Summer Isles group, 4m/7km NE of Greenstone Point on W coast of Ross and Cromarty district. Area about 500 acres or 200 hectares. **70 B4** NB9202.
Priesthill Height ***Mountain***, on border of East Ayrshire and South Lanarkshire, 4m/6km NE of Muirkirk. Height 1614 feet or 492 metres. **15 F2** NS7232.
Priesthope Hill *Sc.Bord.* ***Mountain***, 3m/4km NE of Innerleithen. Height 1801 feet or 549 metres. **17 E2** NT3539.
Priestland *E.Ayr.* ***Settlement***, 1km E of Darvel. **15 D2** NS5737.
Prince Charles's Cave *High.* ***Cave***, 1m/2km S of Elgol, Skye. Reputed to be one of many hiding places of Charles Edward Stuart (Bonnie Prince Charlie) while evading English pursuers following Battle of Culloden. **48 B3** NG5112.
Prince Charles's Cave *High.* ***Cave***, on E coast of Skye, 4m/6km NE of Portree. Reputed to be one of many hiding places of Charles Edward Stuart (Bonnie Prince Charlie) while evading English pursuers following Battle of Culloden. **58 B5** NG5148.
Prince Charlie's Cave *High.* ***Cave***, on E side of Loch Ericht, 8m/12km N of Bridge of Gaur. Reputed to be one of many hiding places of Charles Edward Stuart (Bonnie Prince Charlie) while evading English pursuers following Battle of Culloden. **39 G3** NN4968.
Prior Muir *Fife* ***Settlement***, 3m/4km SE of St. Andrews. **34 D3** NO5313.
Priorwood Garden *Sc.Bord.* ***Garden***, National Trust for Scotland property in Melrose, adjacent to 15c ruins of abbey. Grows flowers specifically for drying. **17 G2** NT5433.
Proaig *Arg. & B.* ***Settlement***, on E coast of Islay, 10m/15km NE of Port Ellen. **20 C4** NR4557.
Prosen Water *Angus* ***River***, flowing SE down Glen Prosen to join River South Esk 3m/5km NE of Kirriemuir. **42 B3** NO4058.
Prospect Hill *Fife* ***Hill***, rising to over 180 metres, 5m/8km NW of Cupar and S of Firth of Tay. **34 B3** NO3118.
Protsonhill *Aber.* ***Settlement***, 1m/2km E of Gardenstown. **64 D3** NJ8164.
Provan Hall *Glas.* ***Historic house***, 15c mansion (National Trust for Scotland), 5m/8km E of Glasgow city centre. **24 A3** NS6666.
Provanmill *Glas.* ***Suburb***, 3m/4km NE of Glasgow city centre. NS6367.
Provost Ross's House *Aberdeen See Aberdeen Maritime Museum.*
Provost Skene's House *Aberdeen* ***Other feature of interest***, example of early burgh architecture in Guestrow, Aberdeen. This 16c house contains period rooms, museum and painted gallery. **55 E4** NJ9306.
Ptarmigan *Stir.* ***Mountain***, 1km SW of Ben Lomond. Height 2398 feet or 731 metres. NN3502.
Pubil *P. & K.* ***Settlement***, at W end of Glen Lyon, 9m/14km NW of Killin. **39 G5** NN4642.
Puldagon *High.* ***Settlement***, 3m/4km SW of Wick. **77 F4** ND3248.
Pulniskie Burn *D. & G.* ***River***, flowing generally W, to join Water of Minnoch near Larg, 7m/11km NW of Newton Stewart. **7 E3** NX3674.
Pulrossie *High.* ***Settlement***, 5m/7km W of Dornoch. **61 G1** NH7288.
Pulteneytown *High. Alternative name for Old Wick, qv.*
Pumpherston *W.Loth.* ***Village***, adjoining to NE of Livingston. **25 E3** NT0669.
Purdomstone Reservoir *D. & G.* ***Reservoir***, small reservoir, 2m/3km NE of Ecclefechan. NY2177.
Purves Hall *Sc.Bord.* ***Settlement***, 3m/5km SE of Greenlaw. **27 E5** NT7644.
Pykestone Hill *Sc.Bord.* ***Mountain***, 3m/5km SE of Drumelzier. Height 2417 feet or 737 metres. **16 C2** NT1731.

Q

Quaich *P. & K.* ***River***, running SE down Glen Quaich through Loch Freuchie, then E by Amulree to join Cochill Burn and form River Braan. **32 C1** NN9238.
Quair Water *Sc.Bord.* ***River***, rising in Ettrick Forest and flowing NE into River Tweed, 1m/2km S of Innerleithen. **17 E2** NT3335.
Quarrelton *Renf.* ***Suburb***, S district of Johnstone. NS4262.
Quarrier's Village *Inclyde* ***Village***, 2m/3km NW of Bridge of Weir. **23 E3** NS3666.
Quarry Head *Aber.* ***Coastal feature***, headland on N coast, 2m/3km SW of Rosehearty. **65 E3** NJ9066.
Quarry Hill *Aber.* ***Mountain***, surrounded by woodland, 4m/6km W of Gartly. Height 1443 feet or 440 metres. **53 G1** NJ4631.
Quarrywood *Moray* ***Locality***, 2m/4km W of Elgin. **63 D3** NJ1864.
Quartalehouse *Aber.* ***Settlement***, adjoining Stuartfield to N, 10m/16km W of Peterhead. NJ9746.
Quarter *S.Lan.* ***Village***, 3m/4km S of Hamilton. **24 B4** NS7251.
Queen Elizabeth Forest Park *Stir.* ***Forest/woodland***, area of forest, moor and mountainside extending from Aberfoyle to Loch Lomond and including Achray and Loch Ard Forests, Ben Lomond and part of The Trossachs. Total area about 70 square miles or 180 square km. **31 G5** NS4798.
Queen's Cairn *High.* ***Mountain***, in Wyvis Forest, 8m/12km NE of Gorstan. Height 2116 feet or 645 metres. **61 D2** NH4672.
Queen's View *P. & K.* ***Viewpoint***, at E end of Loch Tummel with magnificent views along loch to Schiehallion. Visited by Queen Victoria in 1866. Exhibition on Tay Forest Park at Visitor Centre, together with information on local walks and wildlife. **41 D4** NN8558.
Queen's View *Stir.* ***Viewpoint***, 1m/2km NW of Carbeth, overlooking Strathblane, and Campsie Fells to E. **23 G1** NS5180.
Queensberry *D. & G.* ***Mountain***, in Lowther Hills, 6m/10km W of Beattock. Height 2286 feet or 697 metres. **9 D1** NX9899.
Queensferry Museum *Edin.* ***Other feature of interest***, in South Queensferry, Edinburgh, with local history exhibitions. **25 F2** NT1378.
Queenside Muir *Renf.* ***Open space***, moorland area 5m/8km NE of Largs. **23 D3** NS2764.
Queenslie Industrial Estate *Glas.* ***Locality***, 4m/7km E of Glasgow city centre. NS6665.
Queensway *Fife* ***Locality***, industrial estate on NE side of Glenrothes. NO2701.
Queenzieburn *N.Lan.* ***Village***, 2m/3km W of Kilsyth. **24 A2** NS6977.
Quendale *Shet.* ***Settlement***, on Bay of Quendale, on S coast of Mainland, 4m/6km NW of Sumburgh Head. **83 F4** HU3713.
Quey Firth *Shet.* ***Sea feature***, inlet on NE coast of Mainland to S of Colla Firth. **84 C4** HU3682.
Quholm *Ork.* ***Settlement***, 1m/2km to W of Loch of Stenness, Mainland. **80 A5** HY2412.

Quidnish *W.Isles Anglicised form of Cuidhtinis, qv.*
Quilquox *Aber.* ***Locality***, comprising settlements of North Quilquox and South Quilquox, 3m/5km E of Methlick. **55 E1** NJ9038.
Quilva Taing *Shet.* ***Coastal feature***, small promontory on W coast of Mainland, 1m/2km SW of Melby. **82 A2** HU1657.
Quinag *High.* ***Mountain***, in Sutherland district 2m/3km N of Loch Assynt. Height 2650 feet or 808 metres. **71 E2** NC2029.
Quindry *Ork.* ***Settlement***, on NE side of Widewall Bay, South Ronaldsay, 2m/3km SW of St. Margaret's Hope. **78 D3** ND4392.
Quinhill *Arg. & B.* ***Settlement***, on Kintyre, adjoining to N of Clachan. **21 F4** NR7656.
Quinish *Arg. & B.* ***Locality***, on Mull, 5m/8km W of Tobermory. **36 D4** NM4254.
Quinish *W.Isles* ***Coastal feature***, rocks off SW coast of Pabbay. **45 G1** NF8886.
Quinish Point *Arg. & B.* ***Coastal feature***, headland at NW end of Quinish locality on Mull, 6m/10km NW of Tobermory. **36 D4** NM4057.
Quiraing *High.* ***Locality***, area of boulders, screes and rock pinnacles created by largest and most spectacular landslipping in Britain, 6m/9km SE of Rubha Hunish, Skye. **58 A3** NG4569.
Quoich *High.* ***River***, in Lochaber district, running S down Glen Quoich to Loch Quoich, 5m/7km NW of dam. NH0106.
Quoich Water *Aber.* ***River***, in Cairngorm Mountains, running S to River Dee 2m/3km W of Braemar. **52 C5** NO1290.
Quoig *P. & K.* ***Settlement***, 3m/4km W of Crieff. **32 D2** NN8222.
Quoigs *P. & K.* ***Locality***, 1km SW of Greenloaning. **32 D4** NN8305.
Quothquan *S.Lan.* ***Settlement***, 3m/5km NW of Biggar. **16 A2** NS9939.
Quoy Ness *Ork.* ***Coastal feature***, rocky cliff on E side of Els Ness peninsula on S coast of Sanday. Quoyness Chambered Cairn. **81 E3** HY6738.
Quoyloo *Ork.* ***Settlement***, on Mainland, 3m/5km W of Dounby. **80 A4** HY2420.
Quoynalonga Ness *Ork.* ***Coastal feature***, headland at W end of Rousay. HY3632.
Quoyness Chambered Cairn *Ork.* ***Historic/prehistoric site***, large chambered cairn (Historic Scotland) at Quoy Ness on Els Ness, Sanday. **81 E3** HY6737.
Quoys *Shet.* ***Settlement***, on Unst, to E of Loch of Cliff, 3m/4km N of Baltasound. **85 F1** HP6112.
Quoys of Reiss *High.* ***Settlement***, 1km E of Killimster. **77 F3** ND3357.

R

Raasay (Island of Raasay). *High.* ***Island***, sparsely inhabited island, 13m/21km N to S and up to 3m/5km wide, lying off E coast of Skye opposite Portree. **58 B5** NG5640.
Rabbit Islands *High.* ***Island***, group of islands in Tongue Bay off N coast of Caithness district. Inhabited by rabbits. **75 E2** NC6063.
Rachan *Sc.Bord.* ***Settlement***, 1m/2km S of Broughton. **16 C2** NT1134.
Rack Wick *Ork.* ***Bay***, on Westray, to W of Rackwick. HY4450.
Rack Wick *Ork.* ***Bay***, on W coast of Hoy, 2m/3km E of Rora Head. Settlement of Rackwick on the bay. **78 A3** ND2099.
Racks *D. & G.* ***Village***, on Lochar Moss, 4m/6km E of Dumfries. **9 E3** NY0374.
Rackwick *Ork.* ***Settlement***, on Westray, 1m/2km N of Pierowall. **80 C1** HY4449.
Rackwick *Ork.* ***Settlement***, on bay of Rack Wick, on W coast of Hoy, 2m/3km E of Rora Head. **78 B3** ND2099.
Radernie *Fife* ***Settlement***, 5m/8km SE of St. Andrews. NO4609.
Radnor Park *Renf.* ***Suburb***, 1m/2km NW of Clydebank town centre. NS4971.
Rae Burn *D. & G.* ***River***, flowing SW from Raeburnhead to join River White Esk 1km N of Eskdalemuir. **17 E5** NY2598.
Raeburnfoot *D. & G. See Eskdalemuir.*
Raemoir House *Aber.* ***Settlement***, 3m/4km N of Banchory. **54 B5** NO6999.
Raerinish Point *W.Isles* ***Coastal feature***, headland on E coast of Isle of Lewis, 2m/3km E of Crosbost. **69 F5** NB3924.
Raes Knowes *D. & G.* ***Mountain***, on S side of Glentenmont Burn, 4m/7km W of Langholm. Height 997 feet or 304 metres. **9 G2** NY2983.
RAF Memorial *Fife* ***Other feature of interest***, memorial at entrance to RAF Leuchars, 5m/8km N of St. Andrews, commemorating Norwegian squadron who were based here during World War II. **34 C2** NO4521.
Raffin *High.* ***Settlement***, 2m/3km S of Point of Stoer, Sutherland district. **70 C1** NC0132.
Rafford *Moray* ***Village***, 2m/3km SE of Forres. **62 C4** NJ0656.
Raggra *High.* ***Locality***, in Caithness district, 5m/8km SW of Wick. ND3144.
Rahoy *High.* ***Settlement***, on NE shore of Loch Teacuis, 1m/2km from head of loch. **37 F4** NM6356.
Rainberg Mòr *Arg. & B.* ***Mountain***, in N part of Jura, 4m/7km W of Lussagiven. Height 1486 feet or 453 metres. **21 D1** NR5687.
Rainigadale *W.Isles Anglicised form of Reinigeadal, qv.*
Rainigadale Island *W.Isles* ***Island***, islet in Loch Trollamarig to S of Reinigeadal. NB2201.
Rait *P. & K.* ***Village***, 7m/12km E of Perth. **34 A2** NO2226.
Rait Castle *High.* ***Castle***, ruined medieval castle in Nairn district, 3m/4km S of Nairn. NH8952.
Raitts Burn *High.* ***River***, flowing from E slopes of Beinn Bhreac and SE into River Spey, 2m/3km NE of Kingussie. **51 G4** NH7901.
Ramasaig *High.* ***Locality***, near W coast of Skye, 8m/13km S of Dunvegan Head. **57 E5** NG1644.
Ramasaig Bay *High.* ***Bay***, on Skye, to W of Ramasaig. **57 E5** NG1644.
Ramasaig Cliff *High.* ***Coastal feature***, on W coast of Skye to NW of Ramasaig. NG1544.
Rammerscales *D. & G.* ***Garden***, with wooded walks at Palladian house built in 1760, 1m/2km SW of Hightae. **9 E3** NY0877.
Ramna Stacks *Shet.* ***Island***, group of island rocks some 1m/2km N of Point of Fethaland. Nature reserve. **84 C3** HU3797.
Rams Ness *Shet.* ***Coastal feature***, headland at SW end of Fetlar. **85 F4** HU6087.
Ramscraigs *High.* ***Settlement***, near E coast of Caithness, 2m/3km SW of Dunbeath. **73 G2** ND1427.
Ranachan *High.* ***Settlement***, 2m/3km W of Strontian, Lochaber district. **37 G3** NM7961.
Randolph's Leap *Moray* ***Other feature of interest***, gorge in valley of River Findhorn, 8m/13km SE of Nairn. **62 B5** NH9949.
Ranfurly *Renf.* ***Settlement***, adjoining to S of Bridge of Weir. NS3964.
Rangely Kip *E.Loth.* ***Mountain***, 3m/4km E of Danskine. Height 1312 feet or 400 metres. **26 D3** NT6067.
Rankinston *E.Ayr.* ***Village***, 3m/5km NE of Patna. **14 C4** NS4514.
Rankle Burn *Sc.Bord.* ***River***, rising in mountains of Craik Forest, flowing N to Buccleuch and into Ettrick Water 2m/4km NE of Ettrick. **17 E4** NT3017.
Rannoch ***Large natural feature***, mountainous area between Loch Rannoch and Glen Lyon, spanning Highland and Perth & Kinross. Rannoch railway station on Glasgow to Fort William line is near NE end of Loch Laidon. **39 G4** NN5055.
Rannoch *High.* ***River***, in Lochaber district, running W to head of Loch Aline. **37 G5** NM7047.
Rannoch Forest *P. & K.* ***Large natural feature***, mountainous area to N of Rannoch, on W side of foot of Loch Ericht; also forests to S and SW of Loch Rannoch. **39 G3** NN4565.
Rannoch Moor ***Large natural feature***, upland tract to W of Rannoch spanning Highland and Perth & Kinross. Includes Loch Laidon, Loch Bà, and many small lochs or tarns, as well as a nature reserve. **39 F4** NN4050.
Rannoch School *P. & K.* ***Settlement***, on S side of Loch Rannoch, 4m/7km SW of Kinloch Rannoch. **40 A4** NN5956.
Rannoch Station *P. & K.* ***Other building***, station on West Highland line to Fort William, 15m/24km W of Kinloch Rannoch. **39 G4** NN4257.
Ranochan *High.* ***Settlement***, on N shore of Loch Eilt, 3m/5km E of Lochailort. **38 A1** NM8282.
Rapaire *W.Isles* ***Mountain***, on North Harris, 1m/2km W of head of Loch Langavat. Height 1486 feet or 453 metres. **66 D2** NB1313.
Raploch *Stir.* ***Suburb***, NW district of Stirling. NS7894.
Rapness *Ork.* ***Settlement***, on Westray, 6m/10km SE of Pierowall. **80 D2** HY5141.
Rapness Sound *Ork.* ***Sea feature***, stretch of sea dividing Faray from S end of Westray. **80 D3** HY5138.
Rappach *High.* ***Locality***, to N of Strath nan Lòn and containing many tributaries of Allt nan Luibean Molach. **71 E4** NC2302.
Rappach Water *High.* ***River***, formed from several streams in Rhidorroch Forest and flowing E into River Einig at W end of Glen Einig. **71 E5** NH3397.
Rascarrel *D. & G.* ***Settlement***, at Rascarrell Bay, 3m/5km E of Dundrennan. **4 B2** NX7948.
Rascarrel Bay *D. & G.* ***Bay***, 4m/6km E of Dundrennan. **4 B2** NX8048.
Rashy Height *D. & G.* ***Mountain***, 4m/6km NE of Thornhill. Height 1246 feet or 380 metres. **8 D1** NX9398.
Ratagan *High.* ***Settlement***, in Skye and Lochalsh district, on SW shore of Loch Duich, 1m/2km NW of Shiel Bridge, at head of loch. NG9119.
Ratagan Forest *High.* ***Forest/woodland***, to W of Ratagan. NG9020.
Rathen *Aber.* ***Village***, 4m/6km S of Fraserburgh. **65 F3** NK0060.
Rathillet *Fife* ***Settlement***, 4m/7km N of Cupar. **34 B2** NO3620.
Rathliesbeag *High.* ***Settlement***, 3m/4km NW of Spean Bridge. **39 E1** NN2185.
Ratho *Edin.* Population: 1620. ***Village***, 8m/12km W of Edinburgh. **25 F2** NT1370.
Ratho Station *Edin.* Population: 1159. ***Hamlet***, 1m/2km N of Ratho. **25 F2** NT1372.
Rathven *Moray* ***Village***, near N coast 1m/2km E of Buckie. **63 G3** NJ4465.
Rattar *High.* ***Settlement***, near N coast of Caithness district, 4m/6km SE of Dunnet Head. **77 E1** ND2673.
Rattray *P. & K.* ***Town***, on River Ericht opposite Blairgowrie. **41 G5** NO1845.
Rattray Bay *Aber.* ***Bay***, extends S from Rattray Head to Scotstown Head, 6m/9km N of Peterhead. **65 G4** NK1057.
Rattray Head *Aber.* ***Coastal feature***, headland with lighthouse on NE coast, 7m/12km N of Peterhead. **65 G4** NK1057.
Ravelston *Edin.* ***Suburb***, 2m/3km W of Edinburgh city centre. NT2274.
Ravenscraig Castle *Fife* ***Castle***, ruined 15c castle beside sea, in N part of Kirkcaldy. **34 A5** NT2992.
Ravenshall Point *D. & G.* ***Coastal feature***, headland on Wigtown Bay, 5m/8km SE of Creetown. NX5252.
Ravenstruther *S.Lan.* ***Locality***, 3m/5km E of Lanark. **24 D5** NS9245.
Rawyards *N.Lan.* ***Settlement***, adjoining to NE of Airdrie. **24 B3** NS7766.
Raxton *Aber.* ***Settlement***, 1m/2km NE of Tarves. **55 D1** NJ8732.
Rayne *Aber. Alternative name for Kirkton of Rayne, qv.*
Rea Wick *Shet.* ***Bay***, 2m/3km S of Garderhouse, Mainland. Reawick village is on the bay. HU3244.
Rearquhar *High.* ***Locality***, in Sutherland district, 4m/7km NW of Dornoch. **72 C5** NH7492.
Reaster *High.* ***Locality***, in Caithness district, 4m/7km SE of Castletown. **77 E2** ND2565.
Reawick *Shet.* ***Village***, on Mainland, on small bay of Rea Wick, 2m/3km S of Garderhouse. **82 C3** HU3244.
Reay *High.* ***Village***, near N coast of Caithness district, 10m/15km W of Thurso. Cnoc Freiceadain (Historic Scotland), prehistoric chambered cairn 3m/5km E. **76 B2** NC9664.
Reay Burn *High.* ***River***, flowing N into centre of Sandside Bay, on N coast of Caithness district. **76 B2** NC9665.
Reay Forest *High.* ***Large natural feature***, mountain area and deer forest in Sutherland district, extending from Foinaven SE to Ben Hee, and from Loch More NE to Glen Golly. Clan country of the Mackays. **74 B5** NC3039.
Red Castle *Angus* ***Castle***, 2m/3km NE of Inverkeilor, on S bank of Lunan Water estuary. Also known as Ederdover, ruins of 16c L-plan tower house. **43 E4** NO6850.
Red Craig *Aber.* ***Mountain***, 5m/8km SE of Ballater. Height 1965 feet or 599 metres. **53 G5** NO4290.
Red Deer Range *D. & G.* ***Leisure/recreation***, red deer viewing point on Brockloch Hill within Galloway Forest Park, 8m/13km NE of Newton Stewart. **7 G3** NX5173.
Red Head *Angus* ***Coastal feature***, small rock headland below hillfort, 3m/4km SE of Inverkeilor. **43 F5** NO7047.
Red Head *High.* ***Coastal feature***, headland on W coast of Island of Stroma. **77 F1** ND3477.
Red Head *Ork.* ***Coastal feature***, headland at N end of Eday. **81 D2** HY5640.
Red Holm *Ork.* ***Island***, islet between Eday and Westray at N end of Sound of Faray. HY5439.
Red Point *High. Alternative name for Rubha Ruadh, qv.*
Red Point *High.* ***Coastal feature***, headland on N coast of Caithness district, 3m/4km W of Reay. **76 B2** NC9366.
Red Point *High.* ***Coastal feature***, headland on W coast of Ross and Cromarty district, on N side of entrance to Loch Torridon. **58 D3** NG7267.
Redburn *High.* ***Settlement***, 2m/3km W of Evanton. **61 E3** NH5767.
Redburn *High.* ***Settlement***, in Nairn district, 7m/11km SE of Nairn. **62 B5** NH9447.
Redcastle *Angus* ***Hamlet***, to S of Red Castle, 2m/3km NE of Inverkeilor. **43 E4** NO6850.
Redcastle *High.* ***Settlement***, in Ross and Cromarty, district on N shore of Beauly Firth, 4m/6km E of Muir of Ord. **61 E5** NH5849.
Redcleuch Edge *Sc.Bord.* ***Mountain***, in Craik Forest, 2m/3km N of Craik. Height 1279 feet or 390 metres. **17 E4** NT3410.
Redcloak *Aber.* ***Settlement***, 1m/2km NW of Stonehaven. **43 G1** NO8586.
Redding *Falk.* ***Suburb***, 2m/4km SE of Falkirk. NS9278.
Reddingmuirhead *Falk.* ***Village***, 2m/4km SE of Falkirk. NS9177.
Redford *Aber.* ***Settlement***, 3m/4km E of Laurencekirk. **43 F3** NO7570.
Redford *Angus* ***Village***, 6m/9km NW of Arbroath. **43 D5** NO5644.
Redford *Edin.* ***Suburb***, 4m/6km S of Edinburgh city centre. NT2268.

Redheugh *Angus* ***Settlement***, 4m/7km NE of Dykehead, to N of Glenogil, in valley of Noran Water. **42 C3** NO4463.
Redhill *Aber.* ***Locality***, 2m/3km S of Loch of Skene and 4m/7km NW of Peterculter. **54 C4** NJ7704.
Redhill *Aber.* ***Settlement***, 3m/4km W of Rothienorman. **54 B1** NJ6836.
Redhill *Moray* ***Settlement***, on NW side of Fourman Hill, 1m/2km SE of Milltown of Rothiemay. **64 A5** NJ5646.
Redhouse *Aber.* ***Settlement***, 3m/4km N of Alford. **54 A2** NJ5820.
Redhouse *Arg. & B.* ***Settlement***, 5m/8km SW of Tarbert. **21 G3** NR8261.
Redhouses *Arg. & B.* ***Settlement***, on Islay, 1m/2km E of Bridgend. **20 B3** NR3562.
Redhythe Point *Aber.* ***Coastal feature***, headland on N coast, 1m/2km NW of Portsoy. **64 A3** NJ5767.
Redland *Ork.* ***Settlement***, on Mainland, 1m/2km NW of Woodwick. **80 B4** HY3725.
Redpath *Sc.Bord.* ***Settlement***, 3m/5km E of Melrose. **17 G2** NT5835.
Redpoint *High.* ***Settlement***, on W coast of Ross and Cromarty district, 3m/5km SW of Port Henderson. **58 D3** NG7369.
Redscarhead *Sc.Bord.* ***Settlement***, 2m/4km N of Peebles. **25 G5** NT2444.
Redshaw *S.Lan.* ***Settlement***, 2m/4km SE of Douglas. **15 G3** NS8628.
Reed Point *Sc.Bord.* ***Coastal feature***, small rocky headland on North Sea coast, 1m/2km NE of Cockburnspath. **27 E2** NT7872.
Reekie Linn *Angus* ***Waterfall***, in River Isla below Bridge of Craigisla, 4m/6km N of Alyth. **42 A4** NO2553.
Regoul *High.* ***Settlement***, 3m/5km S of Nairn. **62 A4** NH8851.
Réidh Eilean *Arg. & B.* ***Island***, islet 2m/3km off NW coast of Iona. **28 B2** NM2426.
Reiff *High.* ***Settlement***, on NW coast of Ross and Cromarty district, 3m/4km S of Rubha Coigeach. **70 B3** NB9614.
Reinigeadal (Anglicised form: Rainigadale.) *W.Isles* ***Settlement***, with youth hostel, in North Harris, on W side of entrance to Loch Seaforth. **67 E3** NB2201.
Rèisa an t-Sruith *Arg. & B.* ***Island***, small island midway between Craignish Point on mainland of Argyll and Aird of Kinuachdrach on NE coast of Jura. **29 G5** NR7399.
Rèisa Mhic Phaidean *Arg. & B.* ***Island***, small island 1m/2km W of Craignish Castle on mainland of Argyll. **29 G4** NM7500.
Reisgill *High.* ***Settlement***, 1km NW of Lybster. **77 E5** ND2336.
Reisgill Burn *High.* ***River***, stream in Caithness district, running S into Lybster Bay on E coast. **77 E5** ND2434.
Reiss *High.* ***Village***, in Caithness district, 3m/5km NW of Wick. **77 F3** ND3354.
Relugas *Moray* ***Settlement***, in Darnaway Forest, 7m/11km S of Forres. **62 B5** NH9948.
Remony *P. & K.* ***Settlement***, on SE shore of Loch Tay, 1m/2km SW of Kenmore. **40 C5** NN7644.
Renfrew *Renf.* Population: 20,764. ***Town***, old port and former ship-building town on S side of River Clyde, 5m/9km W of Glasgow. Car ferry across river to Yoker. Glasgow Airport to W. **23 G3** NS5067.
Renish Point *W.Isles* ***Coastal feature***, headland at S end of Harris, 7m/11km NE of North Uist across Sound of Harris. **66 C5** NG0482.
Rennibister Earth House *Ork.* ***Historic/prehistoric site***, prehistoric earth house (Historic Scotland) on S side of Bay of Firth, Mainland, 4m/6km W of Kirkwall. **80 B5** HY3912.
Renton *W.Dun.* Population: 2072. ***Small town***, on W bank of River Leven, 2m/3km N of Dumbarton. Industrial estate across river. **23 E2** NS3878.
Rerwick Head *Ork.* ***Coastal feature***, headland on N coast of Mainland, 6m/9km E of Kirkwall. **80 D5** HY5411.
Rescobie *Angus* ***Settlement***, 3m/5km E of Forfar. **42 D4** NO5052.
Rescobie Loch *Angus* ***Lake/loch***, small loch 4m/6km E of Forfar. **42 D4** NO5151.
Resipole *High.* ***Settlement***, on N shore of Loch Sunart, 2m/3km E of Salen. **37 G3** NM7264.
Resolis *High.* ***Settlement***, on S side of Cromarty Firth, Ross and Cromarty district, 2m/3km W of Balblair. **61 F3** NH6765.
Resourie *High.* ***Settlement***, 2m/3km SE of Scamodale, Lochaber district. **38 A2** NM8670.
Rest and be thankful *Arg. & B.* ***Locality***, in Argyll, at head of Glen Croe, 4m/6km NW of Ardgartan. **31 E4** NN2207.
Restalrig *Edin.* ***Suburb***, 2m/3km E of Edinburgh city centre. NT2874.
Restalrig Church *Edin.* ***Ecclesiastical building***, church restored during 19c and 20c, in suburb of Restalrig, 2m/3km E of Edinburgh city centre. Built on site of St. Triduana's Well, a site of pilgrimage from Middle Ages to Reformation. Churchyard includes lower part of St. Triduana's Chapel (Historic Scotland), unique hexagonal vaulted chamber built in 15c by James III to house shrine to St. Triduana. **25 G2** NT2874.
Restenneth Priory *Angus* ***Ecclesiastical building***, ruined chancel and tower of Augustinian priory church (Historic Scotland), 2m/3km E of Forfar. Lower part of tower is very early Romanesque. **42 C4** NO4851.
Reston *Sc.Bord.* ***Village***, on Eye Water, 4m/6km W of Eyemouth. **27 F3** NT8862.
Reswallie *Angus* ***Settlement***, 3m/5km E of Forfar. **42 D4** NO5051.
Rha *High.* ***River***, on Skye, running SW into Uig Bay. **58 A3** NG3963.
Rhaoine *High.* ***Settlement***, in Strath Fleet, 4m/7km E of Lairg. **72 B4** NC6405.
Rhegreanoch *High.* ***Settlement***, 1km NW of Loch Sionascaig. **70 C3** NC0916.
Rheindown *High.* ***Settlement***, in Ross and Cromarty district, 2m/3km S of Muir of Ord. **61 E5** NH5247.
Rhelonie *High.* ***Settlement***, 5m/8km NW of Bonar Bridge. **72 A5** NH5597.
Rhemore *High.* ***Settlement***, in Lochaber district, 3m/5km SE of Drimnin. **37 E4** NM5750.
Rhian *High.* ***Settlement***, 7m/11km N of Lairg. **72 A3** NC5616.
Rhicarn *High.* ***Locality***, in Sutherland district, 2m/3km NW of Lochinver. **70 C2** NC0825.
Rhiconich *High.* ***River***, rising on Reay Forest and running NW into Loch Inchard. NC2552.
Rhiconich *High.* ***Settlement***, at head of Loch Inchard, W coast of Sutherland district. **74 B3** NC2552.
Rhicullen *High.* ***Settlement***, in Ross and Cromarty district, 2m/3km N of Invergordon. **61 F2** NH6971.
Rhidorroch *High.* ***River***, running W into Loch Achall, Ross and Cromarty district, E of Ullapool, through Rhidorroch Forest. **71 E5** NH1994.
Rhidorroch *High.* ***Settlement***, on N side of Loch Achall, 3m/5km E of Ullapool. **71 D5** NH1795.
Rhidorroch Forest *High.* ***Open space***, deer forest in Ross and Cromarty district, E of Ullapool. **71 E5** NH1994.
Rhifail *High.* ***Settlement***, in Strathnaver, overlooking River Naver, Caithness district. **75 G4** NC7249.
Rhilean Burn *High.* ***River***, rising on N slopes of Carn an t-Sean-liathanaich and flowing NE into Leonach Burn, then into River Findhorn, 4m/6km SW of Ferness. Waterfalls in lower course. **52 B1** NH9139.
Rhilochan *High.* ***Locality***, in Sutherland district, 7m/11km NW of Golspie. **72 C4** NC7407.
Rhinduie *High.* ***Settlement***, 4m/6km E of Beauly. **61 E5** NH5845.
Rhinns of Galloway *D. & G.* *Alternative spelling of Rinns of Galloway, qv.*
Rhinns of Islay *Arg. & B.* *Alternative spelling of Rinns of Islay, qv.*
Rhinns of Kells (Also spelled Rinns of Kells.) *D. & G.* ***Large natural feature***, mountain range running N and S between Loch Doon and Clatteringshaws Loch. Summit is Corserine, 2670 feet or 814 metres. **7 F2** NX5083.
Rhireavach *High.* ***Settlement***, near E shore of Little Loch Broom, Ross and Cromarty district, 1m/2km SE of Scoraig. **70 C5** NH0295.
Rhiroy *High.* ***Settlement***, 1m/2km W of Leckmelm across Loch Broom. **60 A1** NH1489.
Rhonadale *Arg. & B.* ***Settlement***, on Kintyre, 2m/3km W of Carradale. **12 C2** NR7838.
Rhonehouse (Also known as Kelton Hill.) *D. & G.* ***Village***, 2m/3km SW of Castle Douglas. **8 B5** NX7459.
Rhu *Arg. & B.* Population: 1282. ***Village***, and resort on E side of Gare Loch, 2m/3km NW of Helensburgh. **23 D1** NS2683.
Rhubodach *Arg. & B.* ***Locality***, on NE coast of Bute, opposite Colintraive, Argyll, across Kyles of Bute. Car and pedestrian ferry service to Colintraive. **22 B2** NS0273.
Rhue *High.* ***Settlement***, on N shore of Loch Broom, 2m/4km NW of Ullapool. **70 C5** NH0997.
Rhum *High.* *Former spelling of Rum, qv.*
Rhumach *High.* ***Settlement***, 2m/3km SW of Arisaig, Lochaber district. **37 F1** NM6385.
Rhunahaorine *Arg. & B.* ***Settlement***, on W side of Kintyre, 2m/3km NE of Tayinloan. **21 F5** NR7048.
Rhunahaorine Point *Arg. & B.* ***Coastal feature***, headland on W coast of Kintyre, Argyll, opposite Gigha. **21 E5** NR6849.
Rhynd *P. & K.* ***Village***, 3m/5km SE of Perth. **33 G2** NO1520.
Rhynie *Aber.* ***Village***, 8m/13km S of Huntly. **53 G2** NJ4927.
Rhynie *High.* ***Settlement***, near E coast of Ross and Cromarty district, 1m/2km NE of Hill of Fearn. **62 A2** NH8479.
Ri Cruin Cairn *Arg. & B.* ***Historic/prehistoric site***, flat, circular cairn (Historic Scotland) of large water-washed stones at Slockavullin, 6m/10km NW of Lochgilphead. One of several cairns and ancient monuments in vicinity. **30 A5** NR8297.
Ribigill *High.* ***Settlement***, 2m/3km SW of Tongue, Caithness district. **75 E3** NC5854.
Riccarton *E.Ayr.* ***Suburb***, on S side of Kilmarnock. **14 C2** NS4236.
Riccarton Hills *W.Loth.* ***Large natural feature***, small range of hills rising to 833 feet or 254 metres, SE of Linlithgow. **25 E2** NT0173.
Rickarton *Aber.* ***Settlement***, 4m/7km NW of Stonehaven. **43 G1** NO8189.
Riddell *Sc.Bord.* ***Hamlet***, 4m/6km SE of Selkirk. **17 G3** NT5124.
Riddrie *Glas.* ***Suburb***, 3m/4km E of Glasgow city centre. Contains HM prison (Barlinnie). NS6366.
Riechip *P. & K.* ***Settlement***, 1m/2km N of Butterstone. **41 F5** NO0647.
Rienachait *High.* ***Settlement***, near W coast of Sutherland district, 1m/2km N of Stoer village. NC0429.
Riereach Burn *High.* ***River***, rising as Allt Creag a' Chait on Carn nan Tri-tighearnan and flowing N past Creag an Daimh, then into Allt Dearg just S of Cawdor. **62 A5** NH8449.
Rifail Loch *High.* ***Lake/loch***, small loch 2m/3km SE of Syre, Caithness district. **75 G4** NC7142.
Rigg *D. & G.* ***Village***, 2m/3km SW of Gretna Green. **9 G4** NY2966.
Rigg *High.* ***Settlement***, 3m/4km NE of The Storr, Skye. **58 B4** NG5156.
Rigg Bay *D. & G.* *Alternative name for Cruggleton Bay, qv.*
Riggend *N.Lan.* ***Settlement***, 3m/5km N of Airdrie. **24 B3** NS7670.
Righoul *High.* ***Settlement***, in Nairn district, 3m/5km S of Nairn. NH8851.
Rigifa *High.* ***Settlement***, near N coast of Caithness district, 2m/3km S of St. John's Point. ND3072.
Rigside *S.Lan.* ***Hamlet***, 1m/2km S of Douglas Water. **15 G2** NS8734.
Rimbleton *Fife* ***Suburb***, central district of Glenrothes. NO2600.
Rimsdale Burn *High.* ***River***, rising N of Lochan Sgeireach and flowing S into Loch Rimsdale, Caithness district. **75 G4** NC7339.
Ring of Brodgar *Ork.* ***Historic/prehistoric site***, ancient stone circle (Historic Scotland) on tongue of land between Loch of Harray and Loch of Stenness 4m/7km W of Finstown, Mainland. Twenty-seven stones are still standing out of an estimated original number of sixty. **80 A5** HY2913.
Ringdoo Point *D. & G.* ***Coastal feature***, point on E side of Wigtown Bay, 6m/9km SW of Kirkcudbright. **3 F2** NX6045.
Ringford *D. & G.* ***Village***, 4m/7km N of Kirkcudbright. **8 A5** NX6857.
Ringorm *Moray* ***Locality***, comprises Upper Ringorm and Nether Ringorm, 1m/2km NW of Charlestown of Aberlour. **63 E5** NJ2644.
Rinloan *Aber.* ***Settlement***, 6m/9km NW of Ballater. **53 E4** NJ2900.
Rinmore *Aber.* ***Settlement***, 5m/8km NE of Strathdon. **53 G3** NJ4117.
Rinn Druim Tallig *W.Isles* ***Coastal feature***, headland on NW coast of Isle of Lewis, 2m/3km NE of Bragar. **69 D2** NB3150.
Rinn Thorbhais *Arg. & B.* ***Coastal feature***, headland at SW end of Tiree. **36 A3** NL9340.
Rinnigill *Ork.* ***Settlement***, on E coast of Hoy, 1m/2km SW of Fara across strait. **78 C3** ND3193.
Rinns of Galloway (Also spelled Rhinns of Galloway.) *D. & G.* ***Coastal feature***, anvil-shaped peninsula at SW extremity of Scotland, running some 28m/45km N to S. Isthmus 6m/10km wide, from Loch Ryan to Luce Bay, connects peninsula to rest of mainland. **6 A4** NX0552.
Rinns of Islay (Also spelled Rhinns of Islay.) *Arg. & B.* ***Coastal feature***, peninsula on W side of Islay, with headland Rinns Point at its S end. **20 A4** NR2157.
Rinns of Kells *D. & G.* *Alternative spelling of Rhinns of Kells, qv.*
Rinns Point *Arg. & B.* ***Coastal feature***, headland at S end of Rinns of Islay. **20 A4** NR2157.
Risabus *Arg. & B.* ***Settlement***, on The Oa, Islay, 3m/5km NE of Mull of Oa. **20 B5** NR3143.
Risay *W.Isles* ***Island***, islet at entrance to Loch Leurbost, E coast of Isle of Lewis. NB3923.
Risga *High.* ***Island***, islet in Loch Sunart in Lochaber district, between islands of Carna and Oronsay. **37 F4** NM6160.
Rispain *D. & G.* ***Historic/prehistoric site***, earthworks of ancient rectangular camp (Historic Scotland), 1m/2km W of Whithorn. **3 E3** NX4239.
Rispond *High.* ***Settlement***, on Rispond Bay, W side of mouth of Loch Eriboll, N coast of Sutherland district. **74 D2** NC4565.
Rispond Bay *High.* ***Bay***, small bay on W side of mouth of Loch Eriboll, N coast of Sutherland district. NC4565.
Ristol *High.* *See Isle Ristol.*
Riverside *Stir.* ***Suburb***, to E of Stirling town centre and bordering S bank of River Forth. NS8094.
Roadside *High.* ***Settlement***, in Caithness district, 5m/9km SE of Thurso. **77 D2** ND1560.
Roadside *Ork.* ***Settlement***, on Sanday, 6m/10km SW of Tafts Ness. **81 E2** HY6841.
Roadside of Garlogie *Aber.* ***Locality***, strung out along road leading E from Garlogie, 3m/5km E of Echt. NJ7805.
Roadside of Kinneff *Aber.* ***Village***, near E coast, 3m/5km N of Inverbervie. **43 G2** NO8476.

Roag *High.* ***Settlement***, on Skye, 3m/4km SE of Dunvegan. **57 F5** NG2744.
Roan Fell ***Mountain***, straddling border of Dumfries & Galloway and Scottish Borders, 4m/7km NW of Newcastleton. Height 1863 feet or 568 metres. **10 C2** NY4593.
Roan Head *Ork.* ***Coastal feature***, headland on NE coast of Flotta. **78 C3** ND3896.
Roan Island *High. Alternative name for Eilean nan Ròn, qv.*
Roana Bay *Ork.* ***Bay***, 1m/2km N of Point of Ayre, Mainland. **79 E2** HY5805.
Roanheads *Aber.* ***Suburb***, coastal district of Peterhead. NK1346.
Roareim *W.Isles* ***Island***, one of Flannan Isles group, lying 2m/3km W of main island, Eilean Mòr, and on N side of Eilean a' Ghobha. NA6946.
Rob Roy and Trossachs Visitor Centre *Stir.* ***Other feature of interest***, in centre of Callander, 12m/20km NW of Stirling, with museum about Rob Roy's life. **32 B4** NN6207.
Rob Roy's Cave *Stir.* ***Cave***, crevices in rock on E shore of Loch Lomond 1km N of Inversnaid. NN3310.
Rob Roy's Grave *Stir.* ***Other feature of interest***, grave of Rob Roy who died in 1734 in Balquhidder, 4m/6km SW of Lochearnhead. **32 A2** NN5321.
Rob Roy's Prison *Stir.* ***Cave***, cavern formed by rocks on E shore of Loch Lomond 2m/3km W of Ben Lomond. NN3302.
Robert Burns Centre *D. & G.* ***Other feature of interest***, life and times of Robert Burns, set in old water mill in Dumfries. **9 D3** NX9775.
Robert Law *S.Lan.* ***Mountain***, 3m/5km NE of Douglas. Height 1332 feet or 406 metres. **15 G2** NS8732.
Roberton *Sc.Bord.* ***Village***, on Borthwick Water, 5m/7km W of Hawick. **17 F4** NT4314.
Roberton *S.Lan.* ***Village***, in Upper Clydedale, 4m/6km N of Abington. **16 A3** NS9428.
Roberton Burn *S.Lan.* ***River***, rising as Standing Burn between Scaur Hill and Wildshaw Hill, and flowing E to join River Clyde to E of Roberton. **15 G3** NS9528.
Robertstown *Moray* ***Settlement***, 3m/5km W of Craigellachie. **63 E5** NJ2444.
Robroyston *Glas.* ***Suburb***, 3m/5km NE of Glasgow city centre. NS6368.
Rochallie *P. & K.* ***Settlement***, 1km E of Bridge of Cally. **41 G4** NO1551.
Rockall *W.Isles* ***Island***, small uninhabited island lying 186m/300km W of St. Kilda. Height is about 63 feet or 19 metres, summit being surmounted by a navigation light installed in 1972.
Rockcliffe *D. & G.* ***Village***, on E side of Rough Firth, 5m/8km S of Dalbeattie. National Trust for Scotland properties in vicinity include Mote of Mark, site of ancient hillfort, and Rough Island, bird sanctuary in Rough Firth to S of village. **8 C5** NX8453.
Rockfield *Arg. & B.* ***Settlement***, on Kintyre, 1km SW of Claonaig. **21 G4** NR8655.
Rockfield *High.* ***Settlement***, on E coast of Ross and Cromarty district, 4m/6km SW of Tarbat Ness. **62 B1** NH9282.
Rockside *Arg. & B.* ***Settlement***, on Rinns of Islay, 1m/2km S of Loch Gorm. **20 A3** NR2263.
Rockvilla *Glas.* ***Suburb***, 1m/2km N of Glasgow city centre. NS5867.
Rodel (Gaelic form: Roghadal.) *W.Isles* ***Settlement***, at S end of South Harris, 1m/2km N of Renish Point across inlet of Loch Rodel. 16c St. Clement's Church (Historic Scotland). **66 C5** NG0483.
Roderick Mackenzie's Memorial *High.* ***Other feature of interest***, in valley of River Moriston, 13m/21km W of Invermoriston. Commemorates Roderick Mackenzie who, in 1746, pretended to be Prince Charles Edward Stuart, and was killed by soldiers searching for the Prince after Culloden. **50 B3** NH2311.
Rodger Law *S.Ayr.* ***Mountain***, in Lowther Hills, 7m/11km S of Elvanfoot. Height 2257 feet or 688 metres. NS9405.
Roe Ness *Shet.* ***Coastal feature***, headland 2m/3km SE of Easter Skeld, Mainland. **82 C3** HU3242.
Roer Water *Shet.* ***Lake/loch***, in N part of Mainland, 2m/3km NW of North Collafirth. **84 C4** HU3386.
Roesound *Shet.* ***Settlement***, on NE of Muckle Roe, at its connection to Mainland. **82 C1** HU3465.
Rogart *High.* ***Locality***, in Sutherland district, 4m/7km NW of head of Loch Fleet, on E coast. **72 C4** NC7303.
Rogart Station *High.* ***Other building***, railway station in Strath Fleet, 1m/2km SW of Rogart, Sutherland district. **72 C4** NC7202.
Roghadal *W.Isles Gaelic form of Rodel, qv.*
Rogie Burn *High.* ***River***, flowing from S of Carn Gorm, then SW into Black Water, 3m/4km W of Strathpeffer. **60 D3** NH4459.
Rogie Falls *High.* ***Waterfall***, salmon leap in course of Black Water, Ross and Cromarty district, 2m/4km W of Strathpeffer. **60 D4** NH4458.
Rohallion *P. & K.* ***Locality***, and castle 3m/4km SE of Dunkeld. NO0439.
Roineabhal *W.Isles Gaelic form of Roneval, qv.*
Roineval *High.* ***Mountain***, 3m/4km N of head of Loch Harport. Height 1440 feet or 439 metres. **48 A1** NG4135.
Roineval *W.Isles* ***Hill***, 3m/4km W of Baile Ailein, Isle of Lewis. Height 922 feet or 281 metres. **68 D5** NB2321.
Roinn a' Bhogha Shàmhaich *High.* ***Coastal feature***, headland in Lochaber district on Sound of Sleat and 4m/6km N of Mallaig across entrance to Loch Nevis. NG7002.
Roinn a' Bhuic *W.Isles* ***Coastal feature***, headland on NW coast of Isle of Lewis, 1km N of Cóig Peighinnean Bhuirgh. **69 E2** NB4057.
Roinn na Beinne *High.* ***Mountain***, in Knoydart, Lochaber district, 3m/4km NW of Inverie. Height 1446 feet or 441 metres. **48 D4** NG7302.
Rois-bheinn *High.* ***Mountain***, in Moidart, Lochaber district, 3m/5km S of Lochailort. Height 2893 feet or 882 metres. **37 G2** NM7577.
Roishal Mòr *W.Isles* ***Hill***, 8m/13km E of Carloway, Isle of Lewis. Height 571 feet or 174 metres. **69 E3** NB3341.
Roisnis an Ear *W.Isles Gaelic form of East Roisnish, qv.*
Romach Hill *Moray* ***Mountain***, 5m/8km SE of Forres. Height 1027 feet or 313 metres. **62 C4** NJ0650.
Romannobridge *Sc.Bord.* ***Village***, on Lyne Water, 3m/4km S of West Linton. **25 F5** NT1648.
Rome Hill *S.Lan.* ***Mountain***, 3m/5km E of Abington. Height 1853 feet or 565 metres. **16 A3** NS9724.
Romesdal *High.* ***Settlement***, on E side of Loch Snizort Beag, Skye, 6m/10km S of Uig. River Romesdal runs W into loch here. NG4053.
Rona (Also known as Island of Rona or South Rona.) *High.* ***Island***, uninhabited island of about 1600 acres or 650 hectares lying N of Raasay between W coast of Ross and Cromarty district and Trotternish on mainland of Skye. Lighthouse at N end. Island is nearly 5m/8km long N to S. **58 C4** NG6258.
Rona (Gaelic form: Rònaidh. Also known as North Rona.) *W.Isles* ***Island***, uninhabited island of about 300 acres or 120 hectares lying 44m/70km NNE of Butt of Lewis and NW of Cape Wrath. Nature reserve; breeding-ground of grey seals. HW8132.
Ronachan *Arg. & B.* ***Settlement***, on Kintyre, 1m/2km SW of Clachan. **21 F4** NR7454.
Ronachan Bay *Arg. & B.* ***Bay***, small bay to S of Ronachan Point, on Kintyre, 11m/18km SW of Tarbert. NR7455.
Ronachan Point *Arg. & B.* ***Coastal feature***, headland on W coast of Kintyre, Argyll, on S side of entrance to West Loch Tarbert. **21 F4** NR7455.
Rònaidh *W.Isles Gaelic form of Rona, qv.*
Rònaigh *W.Isles Gaelic form of Ronay, qv.*
Ronaldsvoe *Ork.* ***Settlement***, at N end of South Ronaldsay, adjoining to W of St. Margaret's Hope. ND4493.
Ronas Hill *Shet.* ***Mountain***, summit of Shetland Islands on Mainland between Ronas Voe and Colla Firth. Height 1476 feet or 450 metres. **84 C4** HU3083.
Ronas Voe *Shet.* ***Sea feature***, long inlet on NW coast of Mainland, on S side of Ronas Hill. **84 B4** HU2882.
Ronay (Gaelic form: Rònaigh.) *W.Isles* ***Island***, sparsely populated island of about 2 square miles or 5 square km off SE coast of North Uist, on E side of Grimsay. **56 C4** NF8956.
Roneval *W.Isles* ***Hill***, near S coast of South Uist, 4m/6km SE of Lochboisdale. Height 659 feet or 201 metres. **46 B3** NF8114.
Roneval (Gaelic form: Roineabhal.) *W.Isles* ***Mountain***, on South Harris, 2m/3km E of Leverburgh. Height 1509 feet or 460 metres. **66 C5** NG0486.
Ronnachmore *Arg. & B.* ***Settlement***, on Islay, 1m/2km SW of Bowmore. **20 B4** NR3058.
Rootpark *S.Lan.* ***Settlement***, 1m/2km NE of Forth. **25 D4** NS9554.
Rora *Aber.* ***Village***, on E side of Rora Moss, 5m/8km NW of Peterhead. **65 F4** NK0650.
Rora Head *Ork.* ***Coastal feature***, headland on W coast of Hoy. **78 A3** ND1799.
Rora Moss *Aber.* ***Open space***, moorland 6m/10km NE of Mintlaw. **65 F4** NK0351.
Rorandle *Aber.* ***Settlement***, to N of Cairn William, 5m/8km W of Kemnay. **54 B3** NJ6518.
Rosarie *Moray* ***Settlement***, 3m/5km W of Keith. **63 F4** NJ3850.
Rosarie Forest *Moray* ***Forest/woodland***, 5m/8km N of Dufftown. **63 F5** NJ3548.
Rosay (Gaelic form: Eilean Rosaidh.) *W.Isles* ***Island***, small uninhabited island on S side of entrance to Loch Erisort, E coast of Isle of Lewis. NB4220.
Roscoble Reservoir *Fife* ***Reservoir***, small reservoir 3m/5km W of Kelty. NT0993.
Rose Ness *Ork.* ***Coastal feature***, headland at SE end of Mainland, 9m/14km SE of Kirkwall. Lighthouse. **79 E3** ND5298.
Rosebank *S.Lan.* ***Locality***, on River Clyde, 3m/5km E of Larkhall. **24 C5** NS8049.
Rosebery *Midloth.* ***Locality***, 4m/6km SW of Gorebridge. NT3057.
Rosebery Reservoir *Midloth.* ***Reservoir***, 1km SE of Rosebery. **26 A4** NT3057.
Roseburn *Edin.* ***Suburb***, 2m/3km W of Edinburgh city centre. NT2273.
Rosehall *Aber.* ***Locality***, 1m/2km W of Turriff. NJ7149.
Rosehall *High.* ***Settlement***, at foot of Glen Cassley, in Sutherland district, 8m/12km W of Lairg. **71 G4** NC4702.
Rosehearty *Aber.* Population: 1202. ***Village***, fishing village on N coast, 4m/7km W of Fraserburgh. **65 E3** NJ9367.
Rosehill *Aber.* ***Settlement***, 1m/2km NE of Aboyne, on E side of Loch of Aboyne. **54 A5** NO5399.
Roseisle *Moray* ***Locality***, 2m/3km SE of Burghead. **62 D3** NJ1367.
Roseisle Forest *Moray* ***Forest/woodland***, bordering Burghead Bay to W of Roseisle. **62 D3** NJ1367.
Rosemarkie *High.* Population: 757. ***Village***, and resort on W side of Moray Firth, in Ross and Cromarty district, opposite Fort George. **61 G4** NH7357.
Rosemarkie Bay *High.* ***Bay***, extends to Chanonry Point on S coast of Black Isle. Masts above bay. **61 G4** NH7357.
Rosemount *P. & K.* ***Locality***, 1m/2km SE of Blairgowrie. **41 G5** NO1843.
Rosemount *S.Ayr.* ***Settlement***, 3m/4km NE of Prestwick. **14 B3** NS3728.
Roseneath *Arg. & B. Alternative spelling of Rosneath, qv.*
Rosewell *Midloth.* Population: 1063. ***Village***, 4m/6km SW of Dalkeith. **25 G3** NT2862.
Roshven *High.* ***Locality***, in Lochaber district, on S side of entrance to Loch Ailort. **37 G2** NM7078.
Roskhill *High.* ***Settlement***, on Skye, 2m/4km SE of Dunvegan. **57 F5** NG2745.
Roslin *Midloth.* Population: 1761. ***Village***, 2m/3km S of Loanhead. **25 G3** NT2763.
Roslin Castle *Midloth. Alternative spelling of Rosslyn Castle, qv.*
Roslin Chapel (Also spelled Rosslyn Chapel.) *Midloth.* ***Ecclesiastical building***, restored 15c church, 5m/8km SW of Dalkeith. **25 G3** NT2763.
Roslin Glen Country Park *Midloth.* ***Leisure/recreation***, adjacent to River North Esk, 1km SW of Roslin and 3m/4km NE of Penicuik. Over 40 acres of woodland in steep-sided valley. **25 G3** NT2662.
Rosneath (Also spelled Roseneath.) *Arg. & B.* Population: 1393. ***Village***, on W side of Gare Loch, 2m/3km NE of Kilcreggan. **23 D1** NS2583.
Rosneath Bay *Arg. & B.* ***Bay***, to SE of Rosneath, 2m/3km W of Helensburgh across Gare Loch. **23 D1** NS2682.
Rosneath Point *Arg. & B.* ***Coastal feature***, headland on Firth of Clyde, 2m/3km SE of Rosneath. **23 D1** NS2583.
Ross *D. & G.* ***Settlement***, on Ross Bay, on W side of Kirkcudbright Bay, 4m/7km S of Kirkcudbright. **3 G2** NX6444.
Ross *P. & K.* ***Settlement***, adjacent to S of Comrie across River Earn. **32 C2** NN7621.
Ross of Mull *Arg. & B.* ***Coastal feature***, long granite peninsula at SW end of Mull, running out to Sound of Iona. **28 C2** NM3920.
Ross Point *Stir.* ***Inland physical feature***, wooded headland on E side of Loch Lomond, 2m/3km S of Rowardennan. **31 F5** NS3695.
Ross Priory *W.Dun.* ***Settlement***, on S shore of Loch Lomond, 1m/2km NW of Gartocharn. **23 F1** NS4187.
Rossay *W.Isles* ***Island***, small uninhabited island off South Harris in East Loch Tarbert to W of Scalpay. NG2095.
Rossdhu House *Arg. & B.* ***Castle***, seat of the Colquhouns on W shore of Loch Lomond, 2m/3km S of Luss. **23 E1** NS3689.
Rossend Castle *Fife* ***Historic house***, ruined 17c house overlooking harbour at Burntisland. Former visitors to castle include Oliver Cromwell and Mary, Queen of Scots. Castle renovated during 1970s. NT2385.
Rossie Farm School *Angus* ***Settlement***, 3m/4km N of Inverkeilor. **43 E4** NO6653.
Rossie Island *Angus Alternative name for Inchbraoch, qv.*
Rossie Moor *Angus* ***Open space***, includes small areas of woodland and several small lochs, above 100 metres high, 4m/7km SW of Montrose. **43 E4** NO6554.
Rossie Ochill *P. & K.* ***Settlement***, 1m/2km NE of Path of Condie. **33 F3** NO0813.
Rossie Priory *P. & K.* ***Settlement***, at foot of Rossie Hill, 2m/3km NW of Longforgan. **34 A1** NO2830.
Rosskeen *High.* ***Settlement***, in Ross and Cromarty district, 2m/3km W of Invergordon. **61 F3** NH6869.
Rossland *Renf.* ***Hamlet***, adjoining to SE of Bishopton, 5m/8km NW of Paisley. NS4470.
Rosslyn Castle (Also spelled Roslin Castle). *Midloth.* ***Castle***, faint remains of 14c castle, rebuilt 16c-17c, above loop of River North Esk to SE of Roslin. **25 G3** NT2763.
Rosslyn Chapel *Midloth. Alternative spelling of Roslin Chapel, qv.*
Roster *High.* ***Settlement***, 3m/4km N of Lybster. **77 E5** ND2539.
Rosyth *Fife* ***Town***, adjoining to NW of Inverkeithing. Naval base on Firth of Forth to S. **25 F1** NT1183.
Rosyth Castle *Fife* ***Castle***, 15c tower (Historic Scotland) with later additions, 2m/4km SE of Dunfermline. NT1182.

R

Rothes *Moray* Population: 1345. ***Small town***, near left bank of River Spey 9m/15km SE of Elgin. Ruined medieval castle of the Leslies. **63 E5** NJ2749.
Rothesay *Arg. & B.* Population: 5264. ***Small town***, chief town and port of Bute, situated on Rothesay Bay on E coast, 7m/11km W of Wemyss Bay across Firth of Clyde. Ruins of St. Mary's Chapel (Historic Scotland) 1km S. **22 B3** NS0864.
Rothesay Bay *Arg. & B.* ***Bay***, on E coast of Bute, extending from Bogany Point in E to Ardbeg Point in N. **22 B3** NS0864.
Rothesay Castle *Arg. & B.* ***Castle***, mainly 14c castle (Historic Scotland), though parts are earlier, near Rothesay town centre. **22 B3** NS0864.
Rothiebrisbane *Aber.* ***Settlement***, 1m/2km W of Fyvie. **54 C1** NJ7437.
Rothiemay Castle *Moray* ***Castle***, on E side of Milltown of Rothiemay, 5m/8km N of Huntly. NJ5548.
Rothiemurchus *High.* ***Locality***, in Badenoch and Strathspey district, 2m/3km S of Aviemore. Rothiemurchus Forest is deer forest to S. **52 B4** NH9308.
Rothienorman *Aber.* ***Village***, 9m/14km S of Turriff. **54 C1** NJ7235.
Rothiesholm *Ork.* ***Settlement***, in S of Stronsay, between Bay of Bomasty and Bight of Doonatown. **81 E4** HY6223.
Rothiesholm Head *Ork.* ***Coastal feature***, headland at SW end of Stronsay. **81 D4** HY6121.
Rothney *Aber.* ***Hamlet***, adjoining to S of Insch. NJ6227.
Rottal *Angus* ***Settlement***, in Glen Clova, 6m/10km N of Dykehead. **42 B3** NO3769.
Rotten Calder *Alternative name for Calder Water, qv.*
Rough Castle *Falk.* ***Historic/prehistoric site***, earthworks of Roman fort (Historic Scotland) on best preserved length of Antonine Wall, 1m/2km E of Bonnybridge. **24 C2** NS8479.
Rough Firth *D. & G.* ***Sea feature***, estuary of Urr Water, 5m/8km S of Dalbeattie. Bird sanctuary on Rough Island (National Trust for Scotland), to S of Rockcliffe. **8 C5** NX8353.
Rough Island *D. & G. See Rockcliffe.*
Roughburn *High.* ***Settlement***, at W end of Loch Laggan, 10m/15km E of Spean Bridge. **39 F1** NN3781.
Roughrigg Reservoir *N.Lan.* ***Reservoir***, 3m/5km E of Airdrie. **24 C3** NS8164.
Round Church of Kilarrow *Arg. & B.* ***Ecclesiastical building***, built by Campbells of Shawfield as part of a planned village, and thought to be a copy of an Italian design. At Bowmore, 11m/18km NW of Port Ellen, Islay. **20 B4** NR3159.
Round Fell *D. & G.* ***Mountain***, 2m/3km S of Clatteringshaws Loch. Height 1319 feet or 402 metres. **7 G3** NX5372.
Round Hill *Moray* ***Mountain***, 6m/9km SW of Cabrach. Height 2188 feet or 667 metres. **53 F2** NJ3022.
Round Hill *Moray* ***Mountain***, to E of Black Water valley, 3m/4km W of Cabrach. Height 1873 feet or 571 metres. **53 F2** NJ3427.
Roundyhill *Angus* ***Settlement***, 2m/4km S of Kirriemuir. NO3750.
Rousay *Ork.* ***Island***, hilly island of about 16 square miles or 41 square km, lying 1m/2km off N coast of Mainland across Eynhallow Sound. **80 B3** HY4130.
Rousay Sound *Ork.* ***Sea feature***, sea passage between E coast of Rousay and Egilsay. **80 C3** HY4529.
Routenburn *N.Ayr.* ***Settlement***, adjoining to N of Netherhall, 1m/2km N of Largs. **22 D3** NS1961.
Row Head *Ork.* ***Coastal feature***, headland on W coast of Mainland to N of Bay of Skaill. **80 A5** HY2218.
Rowallan Castle *E.Ayr.* ***Castle***, mainly 16c castle (Historic Scotland), 3m/5km N of Kilmarnock. **23 F5** NS4342.
Rowanburn *D. & G.* ***Village***, 1m/2km E of Canonbie. **10 C4** NY4077.
Rowantree Hill *N.Ayr.* ***Mountain***, 3m/5km NE of Largs. Height 1404 feet or 428 metres. **22 D3** NS2362.
Rowardennan *Stir.* ***Locality***, including Rowardennan Lodge to N and Rowardennan Forest to SE, on E shore of Loch Lomond opposite Inverbeg. Ferry for pedestrians. NS3698.
Rowardennan Forest *Stir.* ***Forest/woodland***, on E shore of Loch Lomond to SE of Rowardennan Lodge. NS3896.
Rowardennan Lodge *Stir.* ***Settlement***, with youth hostel, on E shore of Loch Lomond, 1m/2km NE of Inverbeg across loch. **31 F5** NS3699.
Rowbank Reservoir *Renf.* ***Reservoir***, eastern part of reservoir 2m/3km S of Howwood. Western part known as Barcraigs Reservoir. NS3956.
Rowchoish *Stir.* ***Settlement***, on E side of Loch Lomond, 1m/2km E of Tarbet across loch. **31 F4** NN3304.
Roxburgh *Sc.Bord.* ***Village***, 3m/5km SW of Kelso. **18 A3** NT7030.
Roxburghe Castle *Sc.Bord.* ***Castle***, remains of castle between Rivers Teviot and Tweed, 1m/2km SW of Kelso. NT7133.
Roy *High.* ***River***, in Lochaber district, rising on N side of Creag Meagaidh and running down to Loch Roy, then continuing N for 3m/5km before turning SW and running down Glen Roy to River Spean, on S side of Roybridge. **50 C5** NN2780.
Royal Botanic Gardens *Edin.* ***Garden***, 1m/2km NW of Edinburgh city centre. Rock garden, Pringle Chinese Collection and glasshouses in 70 acres of landscaped gardens. **25 G2** NT2475.
Royal Burgh of Stirling Visitor Centre *Stir.* ***Other feature of interest***, in Stirling, giving history of Stirling castle. **32 C5** NS7992.
Royal Forest *High.* ***Large natural feature***, mountain area (National Trust for Scotland) N of Glen Etive, Lochaber district. Includes Buachaille Etive Mòr. **39 D4** NN2053.
Royal Museum of Scotland *Edin.* ***Other feature of interest***, in Chambers Street, Edinburgh, with exhibitions including natural history, technology and geology. **25 G2** NT2572.
Royal Observatory Visitor Centre *Edin.* ***Other feature of interest***, on Blackford Hill, 2m/3km S of Edinburgh city centre. Contains exhibitions on work of Observatory, tour of space and time, and collection of telescopes. **25 G2** NT2570.
Roybridge *High.* ***Village***, in Glen Spean, at foot of Glen Roy, in Lochaber district, 3m/5km E of Spean Bridge. **39 E1** NN2781.
Royl Field *Shet.* ***Hill***, 2m/3km W of Mail, Mainland. Height 961 feet or 293 metres. **82 C5** HU3928.
Roy's Hill *Moray* ***Mountain***, 3m/4km SW of Upper Knockando. Height 1692 feet or 516 metres. **62 D5** NJ1440.
Ru Bornaskitaig *High.* ***Coastal feature***, headland on N coast of Skye, 6m/9km N of Uig. **57 G2** NG3771.
Ru Stafnish *Arg. & B.* ***Coastal feature***, headland on E coast of Kintyre, 6m/9km SE of Campbeltown. **12 C4** NR7713.
Ruadh Mheall ***Mountain***, on border of Perth & Kinross and Stirling, 1m/2km NW of head of Loch Lednoch. Height 2237 feet or 682 metres. **32 B1** NN6731.
Ruadh-phort Mòr *Arg. & B.* ***Village***, on E coast of Islay, just N of Port Askaig. NR4269.
Ruadh Sgeir *Arg. & B.* ***Island***, 2m/3km SW of Ross of Mull. **28 C3** NM3014.
Ruadh-stac Mòr *High.* ***Mountain***, summit of Beinn Eighe, 5m/8km W of Kinlochewe in Ross and Cromarty district. Munro: height 3313 feet or 1010 metres. **59 F3** NG9561.
Ruadh Stac Mòr *High.* ***Mountain***, in Ross and Cromarty district, 8m/13km N of Kinlochewe. Munro: height 3011 feet or 918 metres. **59 G2** NH0175.
Ruaig *Arg. & B.* ***Settlement***, near E end of Tiree, 2m/3km W of Rubha Dubh. **36 B2** NM0647.
Ruanaich *Arg. & B.* ***Settlement***, on Iona, 1km SW of Baile Mòr. **28 B2** NM2723.
Rubers Law *Sc.Bord.* ***Mountain***, 2m/3km SE of Denholm. Height 1391 feet or 424 metres. **17 G4** NT5815.
Rubh' a' Bhaid Bheithe *Arg. & B.* ***Coastal feature***, headland at N end of Appin, on S side of mouth of Loch Leven. **38 C4** NN0259.
Rubh' a' Bhàigh Uaine *W.Isles* ***Coastal feature***, headland on E coast of Isle of Lewis, 3m/4km S of Stornoway. **69 F5** NB4229.
Rubh a' Bhaird *W.Isles* ***Coastal feature***, headland on S coast of Isle of Lewis, at W entrance to Loch Bhrollum. **67 F3** NB3101.
Rubh' a' Bhearnaig *Arg. & B.* ***Coastal feature***, headland at N end of Kerrera, 1m/2km NW of Oban, Argyll, across Sound of Kerrera. **30 A1** NM8431.
Rubh' a' Bhinnein *Arg. & B.* ***Coastal feature***, headland on NW coast of Coll, 4m/6km N of Arinagour. **36 B3** NM2263.
Rubh' a' Bhrocaire *High.* ***Island***, small uninhabited island (a headland at low tide) off NW coast of Ross and Cromarty district in Enard bay, to E of Eilean Mòr. NC0717.
Rubh' a Bhuachaille *High.* ***Coastal feature***, headland on NW coast of Sutherland district, 7m/11km SW of Cape Wrath. NC2065.
Rubh' a' Chairn Bhàin *Arg. & B.* ***Coastal feature***, headland on E coast of Gigha, near N end of island. NR6654.
Rubh' a' Chairn Mhòir *High.* ***Coastal feature***, headland in Lochaber district on S side of Sound of Arisaig, 2m/3km W of Roshven. NM6778.
Rubh' a' Chamais *Arg. & B.* ***Coastal feature***, headland on S side of Lagg Bay, on E side of Jura. **21 E2** NR5978.
Rubh' a' Chaoil *Arg. & B.* ***Coastal feature***, headland on W coast of Mull, on N side of entrance to Loch Tuath. **36 C5** NM3346.
Rubh' a' Choin *High.* ***Coastal feature***, headland on S side of Enard Bay. **70 C3** NC0314.
Rubh' a' Chrois-aoinidh *Arg. & B.* ***Coastal feature***, headland on W coast of Jura on S side of entrance to Loch Tarbert. **20 C1** NR5080.
Rubh' a' Geodha *Arg. & B.* ***Coastal feature***, headland on NE coast of Colonsay. **28 D5** NR4399.
Rubh' a' Mhàil *Arg. & B.* ***Coastal feature***, headland with lighthouse at N extremity of Islay. **20 C2** NR4279.
Rubh' a' Mharaiche *Arg. & B.* ***Coastal feature***, headland on W coast of Kintyre, 4m/6km N of Mull of Kintyre. NR5812.
Rubh' a' Mhill Dheirg *High.* ***Coastal feature***, promontory 4m/7km S of Point of Stoer, Sutherland district. **70 C2** NC0229.
Rubh' a' Mhucard *High.* ***Coastal feature***, headland at N end of Eddrachillis Bay, Sutherland district. **74 A5** NC1538.
Rubh' Aird an t-Sionnaich *High.* ***Coastal feature***, headland on W coast of Sutherland district, 1m/2km SW of Scourie. **74 A4** NC1443.
Rubh' an Aird Dhuirche *High.* ***Coastal feature***, headland on Skye at intersection of Loch Ainort and Loch na Cairidh. NG5729.
Rubh' an Dùnain *High.* ***Coastal feature***, headland on SW coast of Skye, on S side of entrance to Loch Brittle. Ancient galleried chamber 1km E, on Soay Sound. **47 G3** NG3816.
Rubh' an Dùnain *W.Isles* ***Coastal feature***, headland on NW coast of Isle of Lewis, 1km N of South Shawbost. **68 D3** NB2448.
Rubh' an Eun *Arg. & B.* ***Coastal feature***, headland with lighthouse on S coast of Bute, on E side of Glencallum Bay and 1m/2km NE of Garroch Head. NS1152.
Rubh' an Fheurain *Arg. & B.* ***Coastal feature***, headland on Sound of Kerrera, 3m/5km SW of Oban in Argyll. NM8226.
Rubh' an Fhir Leithe *High.* ***Coastal feature***, headland on W coast of Sutherland district, 5m/8km NW of Kinlochbervie. **74 A2** NC1863.
Rubh' an Iasgaich *High.* ***Coastal feature***, headland on SW coast of Sleat peninsula, Skye, 2m/3km N of Point of Sleat. NG5502.
Rubh' an Leanachais *Arg. & B.* ***Coastal feature***, headland on E coast of Jura, 1m/2km S of Lowlandman's Bay. **21 D2** NR5570.
Rubh 'an Leim *Arg. & B.* ***Coastal feature***, narrow rocky promontory forming E side of Lowlandman's Bay, Jura, 1km NE of Ardfernal across bay. **21 D2** NR5772.
Rubh' an Lochain *High.* ***Coastal feature***, headland on N coast of Scalpay, Skye and Lochalsh district. **48 C1** NG6132.
Rubh' an t-Sàilein *Arg. & B.* ***Coastal feature***, headland on W coast of Jura on N side of entrance to Loch Tarbert. **20 C1** NR5082.
Rubh' an t-Socaich Ghlais *High.* ***Coastal feature***, headland on NW coast of Sutherland district, 4m/7km S of Cape Wrath. NC2368.
Rubh' an t-Suibhein *Arg. & B.* ***Coastal feature***, headland on Mull, on N side of entrance to Loch Tuath. **36 C5** NM3645.
Rubh' Ard Eirnish *Arg. & B.* ***Coastal feature***, headland on N coast of Lismore, to E of Bernera. NM8039.
Rubh Ard Slisneach *High.* ***Coastal feature***, headland at NW point of Knoydart, Lochaber district, on S side of entrance to Loch Hourn. **48 D4** NG7409.
Rubh' Ardalanish (Anglicised form: Ardalanish Point.) *Arg. & B.* ***Coastal feature***, headland 1m/2km S of Ardalanish Bay. **28 C3** NM3719.
Rubh' Arisaig *High.* ***Coastal feature***, headland on coast of Lochaber district 3m/5km W of Arisaig. **37 F1** NM6184.
Rubh' Leam na Làraich *High.* ***Coastal feature***, headland on westernmost point of Muck. **36 C2** NM3979.
Rubha Aird Druimnich *High.* ***Coastal feature***, headland on N side of Ardnamurchan peninsula in Lochaber district, 9m/14km NW of Salen. **37 E2** NM5772.
Rubha Aird-mhicheil *W.Isles* ***Coastal feature***, headland on W coast of South Uist, 3m/4km N of Rubha Ardvule. **46 A1** NF7233.
Rubha Aird Shlignich *High.* ***Coastal feature***, headland on S side of Ardnamurchan peninsula in Lochaber district, 2m/3km NE of Auliston Point across Loch Sunart. NM5660.
Rubha Airigh Bheirg *N.Ayr.* ***Coastal feature***, on NW coast of Arran, 3m/4km NE of Pirnmill. **21 G5** NR8847.
Rubha an Dùin Bhàin *High.* ***Coastal feature***, headland in Lochaber district, 3m/5km NE of Point of Ardnamurchan. NM4470.
Rubha an Dùine *W.Isles Gaelic form of Scarts Rock, qv.*
Rubha an Fhasaidh *High.* ***Coastal feature***, headland on W coast of Eigg, 4m/6km NE of Galmisdale. **36 D1** NM4387.
Rubha an Ridire *High.* ***Coastal feature***, headland at S end of Morvern, Lochaber district. **29 G1** NM7340.
Rubha an t-Seileir *W.Isles Gaelic form of Cellar Head, qv.*
Rubha an t-Siùmpain *W.Isles Gaelic form of Tiumpan Head, qv.*
Rubha Ard Ealasaid *Arg. & B.* ***Coastal feature***, headland with pier on Sound of Mull, 1km N of mouth of Aros River, Mull. NM5645.
Rubha Ardvule *W.Isles* ***Coastal feature***, headland on W coast of South Uist, 10m/16km S of Ardivachar Point. **44 B1** NF7030.
Rubha Bàn *Arg. & B.* ***Coastal feature***, headland on NE corner of Oronsay. **20 B1** NR3889.
Rubha Bàn *High.* ***Coastal feature***, headland on W coast of Ross and Cromarty district, on N side of entrance to Gair Loch. NG7379.

R

Rubha Beag *Arg. & B.* ***Coastal feature***, headland on W coast of Cowal, 5m/8km NW of Tighnabruaich. **22 A2** NR9179.
Rubha Beag *High.* ***Coastal feature***, headland 2m/3km E of Greenstone Point, Ross and Cromarty district. **70 A5** NG8997.
Rubha Bhataisgeir (Anglicised form: Vatisker Point.) *W.Isles* ***Coastal feature***, headland on coast 1km E of Vatisker, Isle of Lewis. **69 F4** NB4839.
Rubha Bhilidh *W.Isles* ***Coastal feature***, headland on E coast of South Uist, 2m/4km E of Ben Corodale. **46 B1** NF8632.
Rubha Bholsa *Arg. & B.* ***Coastal feature***, headland on N coast of Islay, 3m/5km W of Rubh' a' Mhàil. **20 B2** NR3778.
Rubha Bhrollum *W.Isles* ***Coastal feature***, headland on S coast of Isle of Lewis, at E of entrance to Loch Bhrollum. **67 F3** NB3202.
Rubha Bhuic *W.Isles* ***Coastal feature***, headland on W coast of North Harris, 3m/4km SE of Huisinis. **66 C3** NB0108.
Rubha Bocaig *W.Isles* ***Coastal feature***, headland on E coast of South Harris, 3m/4km E of Greosabhagh. **67 D4** NG1891.
Rubha Bodach *Arg. & B.* ***Coastal feature***, headland on N coast of Bute, 1m/2km E of Buttock Point. NS0274.
Rubha Bolum *W.Isles* ***Coastal feature***, headland on E coast of South Uist, 4m/6km SE of Beinn Mhòr. **46 B2** NF8328.
Rubha Buidhe *High.* ***Coastal feature***, headland in Lochaber district, on N side of entrance to Loch Hourn from Sound of Sleat. NG7811.
Rubha Cam nan Gall *W.Isles* ***Coastal feature***, headland at northernmost point of Wiay. **45 G5** NF8847.
Rubha Carrach *High.* ***Coastal feature***, headland on N side of Ardnamurchan peninsula in Lochaber district, 4m/6km NE of Point of Ardnamurchan. NM4670.
Rubha Chaolais *High.* ***Coastal feature***, headland at W end of peninsula of Ardnish, Sound of Arisaig, on coast of Lochaber district. **37 F1** NM6980.
Rubha Chàrn nan Ceare *High.* ***Coastal feature***, headland on W coast of Sleat peninsula, Skye, 3m/4km N of Point of Sleat. NG5503.
Rubha Chorachan *High.* ***Coastal feature***, headland at S end of Uig Bay, Skye. **57 G3** NG3761.
Rubha Chràiginis *Arg. & B.* ***Coastal feature***, headland at extreme W end of Tiree. NL9245.
Rubha Chuaig *High.* ***Coastal feature***, headland on W coast of Ross and Cromarty district, on S side of entrance to Òb Chuaig. NG7059.
Rubha Chulinish *Arg. & B.* ***Coastal feature***, headland on N coast of Ulva. **36 C5** NM3942.
Rubha Cluer *W.Isles* ***Coastal feature***, headland on E coast of South Harris, 2m/3km S of Greosabhagh. **67 D5** NG1589.
Rubha Coigeach *High.* ***Coastal feature***, headland on NW coast of Ross and Cromarty district at NW point of Coigach and W point of Enard Bay. **70 B3** NB9818.
Rubha Cruitiridh *Arg. & B.* ***Coastal feature***, headland on S coast of Knapdale, Argyll, on W side of Loch Stornoway. **21 F3** NR7160.
Rubha Cuilcheanna *High.* ***Coastal feature***, headland on E side of Loch Linnhe in Lochaber district, opposite Sallachan Point. NN0161.
Rubha Deas *W.Isles* ***Coastal feature***, headland on E coast of Eye Peninsula, Isle of Lewis, 1m/2km S of Tiumpan Head. **69 G4** NB5735.
Rubha Dubh *Arg. & B.* ***Coastal feature***, headland at E end of Tiree. **36 A5** NM0948.
Rubha Dubh *Arg. & B.* ***Coastal feature***, headland on S coast of Mull, on W side of entrance to Loch Buie. **29 E2** NM5621.
Rubha Dubh *Arg. & B.* ***Coastal feature***, headland on E coast of Colonsay nearly 2m/3km S of Scalasaig. Another headland with lighthouse at Scalasaig itself has same name. NR3991.
Rubha Dubh *Arg. & B.* ***Coastal feature***, headland on NW coast of Bute opposite Tighnabruaich, Argyll, across Kyles of Bute. NR9872.
Rubha Dubh Ard *High.* ***Coastal feature***, headland on S shore of Loch Eishort, Skye, 4m/6km NE of Tarskavaig. NG6214.
Rubha Dùin Bhàin *Arg. & B.* ***Coastal feature***, headland on W coast of Kintyre, 5m/8km N of Mull of Kintyre. **12 A4** NR5914.
Rubha Fasachd *Arg. & B.* ***Coastal feature***, headland on E side of Loch Breachacha, Coll. **36 A4** NM1652.
Rubha Fiart *Arg. & B.* ***Coastal feature***, headland at SW end of Lismore, in Loch Linnhe. NM7835.
Rubha Fiola *Arg. & B.* ***Island***, small island N of Lunga and 1km E of Eilean Dubh Mòr. NM7110.
Rubha Fion-àird *Arg. & B.* ***Coastal feature***, headland in Argyll, at W extremity of Benderloch. NM8637.
Rubha Garbh-àird *Arg. & B.* ***Coastal feature***, headland at W end of Ardmucknish Bay, Benderloch, Argyll. **30 A1** NM8736.
Rubha Garbh Airde *Arg. & B.* ***Coastal feature***, headland on N coast of Seil, 2m/3km N of Balvicar. **29 G2** NM7620.
Rubha Garbh-ard *Arg. & B.* ***Coastal feature***, headland on N side of mouth of Loch Crinan. **29 G5** NR7895.
Rubha Garbhaig *High.* ***Coastal feature***, headland on NE coast of Skye, 4m/6km NW of Rubha nam Brathairean. **58 B3** NG4968.
Rubha Hallagro *W.Isles* ***Coastal feature***, headland on E coast of South Uist, 2m/3km S of entrance to Loch Sgioport. Lighthouse 1km S. NF8735.
Rubha Hellisdale *W.Isles* ***Coastal feature***, headland on E coast of South Uist, 2m/3km E of Beinn Mhòr. **46 B1** NF8430.
Rubha Hunish *High.* ***Coastal feature***, headland at N end of Skye, 9m/14km N of Uig. **57 G2** NG4077.
Rubha Idrigil *High.* ***Coastal feature***, headland to N of Uig Bay, Skye. **57 G3** NG3763.
Rubha Iosal *W.Isles* ***Coastal feature***, headland on E coast of Isle of Lewis, 1m/2km N of Kebock Head. **67 G2** NB4216.
Rubha Lagganroaig *Arg. & B.* ***Coastal feature***, headland on NE coast of Kintyre, 4m/6km SE of Tarbert. **22 A3** NR9163.
Rubha Lamanais *Arg. & B.* ***Coastal feature***, headland on W coast of Islay, 2m/3km NW of Loch Gorm. **20 A3** NR2068.
Rubha Leathann *W.Isles* ***Coastal feature***, headland on NW coast of Isle of Lewis, 1m/2km W of Siadar Uarach. **69 E2** NB3654.
Rubha Leumair *High.* ***Coastal feature***, headland 3m/4km N of Loch Inver, Sutherland district. **70 C2** NC0326.
Rubha Liath *Arg. & B.* ***Coastal feature***, stack off S coast of NE Tiree. **36 B2** NM0846.
Rubha Liath *Arg. & B.* ***Coastal feature***, on E coast of Islay, 9m/14km NE of Port Ellen. **20 C4** NR4755.
Rubha Liath *W.Isles* ***Coastal feature***, headland on SE coast of Eriskay, 2m/3km SE of Haunn. **46 B4** NF8009.
Rubha Maol *High.* ***Coastal feature***, headland on NW coast of Skye, on W side of entrance to Loch Bay. **57 F4** NG2456.
Rubha Maol na Mine *Arg. & B.* ***Coastal feature***, headland on SW coast of Gometra. **36 C5** NM3440.
Rubha Màs a' Chnuic *W.Isles* ***Coastal feature***, headland on South Harris, 1m/2km E of Toe Head. **66 B4** NF9794.
Rubha Meall na Hoe *W.Isles* ***Coastal feature***, headland on E coast of South Uist, 2m/4km SE of Lochboisdale. **46 B3** NF8217.
Rubha Mhic Gille-mhìcheil *W.Isles* ***Coastal feature***, headland on E coast of North Uist, 2m/3km N of Eigneig Bheag. **56 C3** NF9366.
Rubha Mòr *Arg. & B.* ***Coastal feature***, headland on N coast of Coll, 1m/2km W of NE end of island. **36 B3** NM2464.
Rubha Mòr *Arg. & B.* ***Coastal feature***, headland with pier on Sound of Mull, 1km NE of Salen, Mull. NM5743.
Rubha Mòr *Arg. & B.* ***Coastal feature***, headland on W coast of Islay at S end of Laggan Bay. **20 A5** NR2948.
Rubha Mòr *High.* ***Coastal feature***, peninsula on W coast of Ross and Cromarty district, to W of Enard Bay. **70 B3** NB9814.
Rubha Mòr *High.* ***Coastal feature***, large peninsula in Ross and Cromarty district separating Loch Ewe from Gruinard Bay. **70 A5** NG8696.
Rubha Mòr *High.* ***Coastal feature***, headland on E side of Loch Linnhe in Lochaber district, at NW end of Cuil Bay. **38 B4** NM9655.
Rubha Mòr *W.Isles* ***Coastal feature***, headland on SE coast of Barra, 2m/3km E of Castlebay. **44 C4** NL6997.
Rubha na Bearnaich *W.Isles* ***Coastal feature***, headland on SE coast of Eye Peninsula, Isle of Lewis. **69 G4** NB5531.
Rubha na Brèige *High.* ***Coastal feature***, headland to N of Enard Bay. **70 C3** NC0519.
Rubha na Caillich *Arg. & B.* ***Coastal feature***, headland on E coast of Jura, 1km S of Craighouse. **20 D3** NR5366.
Rubha na Caillich *High.* ***Coastal feature***, headland at easternmost point of Skye at N end of Kyle Rhea. NG8024.
Rubha na Carraig-géire *Arg. & B.* ***Coastal feature***, headland at S end of Iona. **28 B2** NM2621.
Rubha na Cille *Arg. & B.* ***Coastal feature***, headland in Argyll to W of Loch na Cille, at S end of peninsula on W side of Loch Sween. NR6879.
Rubha na Cloiche *High.* ***Coastal feature***, headland at S point of Raasay. NG5633.
Rubha na Creige Mòire *W.Isles* ***Coastal feature***, headland on E coast of South Uist, 2m/4km E of Lochboisdale. **46 B3** NF8320.
Rubha na Cruibe *W.Isles* ***Coastal feature***, headland on E coast of South Uist, 2m/3km E of Lochboisdale. **46 B3** NF8219.
Rubha na Faing *Arg. & B.* ***Coastal feature***, headland at SW point of Rinns of Islay. **20 A4** NR1553.
Rubha na Faoilinn *Arg. & B.* ***Coastal feature***, headland on S coast of Mull, on E side of entrance to Loch Buie. NM5921.
Rubha na Faoilinn *Arg. & B.* ***Coastal feature***, headland on SE coast of Mull, on NE side of entrance to Loch Spelve. **29 G2** NM7227.
Rubha na Fearn *High.* ***Coastal feature***, headland on W coast of Ross and Cromarty district, on S side of entrance to Loch Torridon. **58 D3** NG7261.
Rubha na Feola *High.* ***Coastal feature***, small bay on S shore of Upper Loch Torridon, 4m/6km SW of Torridon. **59 E4** NG8354.
Rubha na Feundain *Arg. & B.* ***Coastal feature***, headland at SW end of Kerrera. NM7826.
Rubha na Gainmhich *Arg. & B.* ***Coastal feature***, headland on promontory of Ard Imersay, S coast of Islay, 4m/7km E of Port Ellen. **20 C5** NR4346.
Rubha na Gibhte *W.Isles* ***Coastal feature***, headland on E coast of South Uist, 4m/7km NE of Lochboisdale. **46 B2** NF8225.
Rubha na Greine *W.Isles* ***Coastal feature***, headland on E coast of Eye Peninsula, Isle of Lewis, 3m/5km S of Tiumpan Head. **69 G4** NB5633.
Rubha na h-Airde Mòire *Arg. & B.* ***Coastal feature***, headland on W coast of Rinns of Islay at S end of Machir Bay. NR1960.
Rubha na h-Airde Uinnsinn *High.* ***Coastal feature***, headland on W side of Loch Linnhe in Lochaber district, 1m/2km W of entrance to Loch a' Choire. NM8752.
Rubha na h-Aiseig *High.* ***Coastal feature***, headland at northern point of Skye, 9m/14km N of Uig. **58 A2** NG4476.
Rubha na h-Earba *High.* ***Coastal feature***, headland on W shore of Loch Linnhe in Lochaber district, 3m/5km SW of Inversanda Bay. NM9155.
Rubha na h-Easgainne (Anglicised form: Strathaird Point.) *High.* ***Coastal feature***, headland on S coast of Skye at S end of Strathaird peninsula. **48 B3** NG5211.
Rubha na h-Ordaig *W.Isles* ***Coastal feature***, headland at SE end of South Uist, 3m/5km SE of entrance to Loch Baghasdail. **46 B3** NF8414.
Rubha na h-Uamha *Arg. & B.* ***Coastal feature***, headland (National Trust for Scotland) on Mull at W end of Ardmeanach. NM4027.
Rubha na' Leac *High.* ***Coastal feature***, headland on Raasay, 3m/5km N of Eyre Point. **48 C1** NG6038.
Rubha na Leacaig *High.* ***Coastal feature***, headland 1km W of Kinlochbervie, Sutherland district. **74 A3** NC2056.
Rubha na Lice *Arg. & B.* ***Coastal feature***, headland on NW coast of Kerrera. **29 G2** NM8029.
Rubha na Lice Uaine *High.* *Alternative name for Greenstone Point, qv.*
Rubha na Rodagrich *W.Isles* ***Coastal feature***, headland at southernmost point of Ronay. **56 C4** NF8953.
Rubha na Roinne *High.* ***Coastal feature***, headland on E coast of Rum, N of entrance to Loch Scresort. **48 A4** NG4200.
Rubha na Tràille *Arg. & B.* ***Coastal feature***, headland near southernmost point of Jura, 3m/5km S of Craighouse. **20 D3** NR5162.
Rubha nam Barr *Arg. & B.* ***Coastal feature***, on SE side of Sound of Jura, 3m/4km SW of Crinan. **29 G5** NR7591.
Rubha nam Bràithrean *Arg. & B.* ***Coastal feature***, headland on S coast of Ross of Mull, 4m/7km SW of Bunesssan. **28 D3** NM4317.
Rubha nam Brathairean *High.* ***Coastal feature***, headland on NE coast of Skye, 8m/13km E of Uig. **58 B3** NG5262.
Rubha nam Meirleach *High.* ***Coastal feature***, headland on Rum, near southernmost point of island. **47 G5** NM3691.
Rubha nan Cearc *Arg. & B.* ***Coastal feature***, headland at NW end of Ross of Mull. **28 C2** NM3125.
Rubha nan Clach *High.* ***Coastal feature***, headland on W coast of Skye, on SE side of entrance to Loch Bracadale. **47 F1** NG3033.
Rubha nan Còsan *High.* ***Coastal feature***, headland on W coast of Oldany Island, Sutherland district. **70 C1** NC0734.
Rubha nan Cùl Gheodhachan *High.* ***Coastal feature***, headland on W coast of Sutherland district, 5m/8km NW of Kinlochbervie. NC1964.
Rubha nan Gall *Arg. & B.* ***Coastal feature***, headland on N coast of Ulva, 1m/2km E of Rubha Chulinish. **36 D5** NM4141.
Rubha nan Gall *Arg. & B.* ***Coastal feature***, headland with lighthouse on N coast of Mull, 1m/2km N of Tobermory. NM5057.
Rubha nan Goirteanan *Arg. & B.* ***Coastal feature***, headland on W coast of Ardmeanach district of Mull, 4m/6km SW of Balnahard. NM4030.
Rubha nan Leacan *Arg. & B.* ***Coastal feature***, headland at S end of The Oa, Islay. Most southerly point of island. **20 B5** NR3140.
Rubha nan Oirean *Arg. & B.* ***Coastal feature***, headland on W coast of Mull, 2m/3km W of Calgary. **36 C4** NM3551.
Rubha nan Sailthean *Arg. & B.* ***Coastal feature***, headland on SE coast of Mull, on SW side of entrance to Loch Spelve. NM7227.

Rubha nan Uan *Arg. & B.* ***Coastal feature***, headland on NW coast of Coll, 4m/7km W of Arinagour. NM1657.
Rubha Port Scolpaig *W.Isles* ***Coastal feature***, headland on North Uist, 1km S of Aird an Rùnair. **45 E3** NF6868.
Rubha Quidnish *W.Isles* ***Coastal feature***, headland on SE coast of South Harris, 2m/3km S of Manais. **66 D5** NG1086.
Rubha Raonuill *High.* ***Coastal feature***, headland on N side of entrance to Loch Nevis, on coast of Knoydart, Lochaber district. **48 D5** NM7399.
Rubha Raouill *W.Isles* ***Coastal feature***, rock off SW coast of North Uist, 3m/5km SE of Aird an Rùnair. **45 E3** NF7166.
Rubha Réidh *High.* ***Coastal feature***, headland with lighthouse on W coast of Ross and Cromarty district 10m/16km NW of Poolewe. **58 D1** NG7391.
Rubha Righinn *Arg. & B.* ***Coastal feature***, headland at S point of Scarba. **29 G4** NM7002.
Rubha Robhanais *W.Isles Gaelic form of Butt of Lewis, qv.*
Rubha Rodha *High.* ***Coastal feature***, headland 3m/4km W of Lochinver. **70 C2** NC0523.
Rubha Romagi *W.Isles* ***Coastal feature***, headland on W coast of South Harris, 6m/10km N of Leverburgh. **66 C4** NG0396.
Rubha Rossel *W.Isles* ***Coastal feature***, headland on E coast of South Uist, 2m/4km NE of Hecla. **46 B1** NF8536.
Rubha Ruadh (Also known as Red Point.) *High.* ***Coastal feature***, headland on W coast of Sutherland district, on W side of entrance to Loch Laxford. **74 A3** NC1651.
Rubha Seanach *Arg. & B.* ***Coastal feature***, headland at S end of Kerrera. **29 G2** NM8025.
Rubha Sgeirigin *W.Isles* ***Coastal feature***, headland at southernmost point of Taransay. **66 B4** NF9998.
Rubha Sgor an t-Snidhe *High.* ***Coastal feature***, headland on SW coast of Rum, 2m/3km NW of Rubha nam Meirleach. **47 G5** NM3493.
Rubha Sgor-Innis *Arg. & B.* ***Coastal feature***, headland on NE coast of Coll, looking NE towards Eilean Mòr. **36 B3** NM2763.
Rubha Shamhnan Insir *High.* ***Coastal feature***, headland at northernmost point of Rum. **47 G4** NG3704.
Rubha Suisnish *High.* ***Coastal feature***, headland on S coast of Skye between Loch Eishort and Loch Slapin. **48 B3** NG5815.
Rubha Thearna Sgurr *High.* ***Coastal feature***, headland on SW coast of Skye, 1m/2km NW of entrance to Loch Brittle. **47 G3** NG3619.
Rubha Thormaid *High.* ***Coastal feature***, headland on N coast, 3m/5km NW of mouth of Tongue Bay. **75 E2** NC5468.
Rubha Vallarip *W.Isles* ***Coastal feature***, headland on S coast of South Harris, 1km E of Rodel. **66 C5** NG0682.
Rubislaw Quarry *Aberdeen See Hill of Rubislaw.*
Ruchazie *Glas.* ***Suburb***, 4m/6km E of Glasgow city centre. NS6566.
Ruchill *Glas.* ***Suburb***, 2m/3km N of Glasgow city centre. NS5768.
Ruchill Water *P. & K. See Water of Ruchill.*
Ruddons Point *Fife* ***Coastal feature***, headland on E side of Largo Bay. **34 C4** NO4500.
Ruel *Arg. & B.* ***River***, in Argyll, running S down Glendaruel to head of Loch Riddon. NS0078.
Rueval *W.Isles* ***Hill***, highest point on Benbecula, 3m/5km SE of Benbecula (Baile a' Mhanaich) Aerodrome. Height 407 feet or 124 metres. **45 G4** NF8253.
Ruilick *High.* ***Settlement***, 1m/2km NW of Beauly. **61 E5** NH5046.
Ruinsival *High.* ***Mountain***, on Rum, 4m/7km SW of Kinloch. Height 1732 feet or 528 metres. **47 G5** NM3593.
Ruisgarry *W.Isles Anglicised form of Ruisigearraidh, qv.*
Ruisigearraidh (Anglicised form: Ruisgarry.) *W.Isles* ***Settlement***, on Berneray, 1m/2km NE of Borve. **66 B5** NF9282.
Rule Water *Sc.Bord.* ***River***, running N by Bonchester Bridge and Bedrule to confluence with River Teviot, 4m/6km W of Jedburgh. NT5920.
Ruleos *W.Isles* ***Open space***, on Barra 3m/5km NE of Castlebay. **44 B3** NF7000.
Rum (Formerly spelled Rhum.) *High.* ***Island***, mountainous island of 42 square miles or 109 square km, roughly diamond-shaped, lying 7m/11km S of Rubh' an Dùnain on SW coast of Skye. Island is a National Nature Reserve and is owned by the Nature Conservancy Council, providing opportunities for geological and biological research. **47 G5** NM3798.
Rumble *Shet.* ***Island***, rock island off E coast of Whalsay, 3m/5km E of Clett Head. HU6060.
Rumbling Bridge *P. & K.* ***Village***, on River Devon, 4m/6km E of Dollar. **33 F5** NT0199.
Rumsdale Water *High.* ***River***, in Caithness district, flowing E and joining Glutt Water to form River Thurso, 4m/6km S of Altnabreac. **76 B4** ND0039.
Rumster Forest *High.* ***Forest/woodland***, large coniferous forest on E coast, 2m/3km NW of Lybster. **77 E5** ND2037.
Runacraig *Stir.* ***Settlement***, on NE side of Loch Lubnaig, 2m/3km SE of Strathyre. **32 A3** NN5714.
Runie *High.* ***River***, in Ross and Cromarty district, flowing SW to join River Kanaird 5m/7km N of Ullapool. **70 D4** NC1301.
Runtaleave *Angus* ***Settlement***, in Glen Prosen, 2m/3km NW of Balnaboth. **42 A3** NO2867.
Rusk Holm *Ork.* ***Island***, islet lying midway between Fers Ness, Eday and Point of Huro, Westray. **80 C3** HY5136.
Ruskie *Stir.* ***Settlement***, 3m/4km W of Thornhill. **32 B4** NN6200.
Rusko *D. & G.* ***Settlement***, 2m/3km N of Gatehouse of Fleet. **7 G5** NX5858.
Rusko Castle *D. & G. See Rusko Tower.*
Rusko Tower (Rusko Castle). *D. & G.* ***Castle***, restored Gordon stronghold, 3m/5km N of Gatehouse of Fleet. NX5860.
Russa Ness *Shet.* ***Coastal feature***, steep headland on Mainland on W side of entrance to Weisdale Voe. HU3646.
Russel *High.* ***Settlement***, on N shore of Loch Kishorn, Ross and Cromarty district. **59 E5** NG8240.
Russland *Ork.* ***Locality***, on E side of Loch of Harray, Mainland, 2m/3km S of Dounby. HY3017.
Rutherend *S.Lan.* ***Settlement***, 3m/5km SE of East Kilbride. **24 A4** NS6649.
Rutherford *Sc.Bord.* ***Village***, 6m/9km SW of Kelso. **18 A4** NT6430.
Rutherglen *S.Lan.* ***Town***, on S bank of River Clyde adjoining to SE of Glasgow. **24 A3** NS6161.
Ruthers of Howe *High.* ***Settlement***, in Caithness district, 8m/13km NW of Wick. ND3063.
Ruthrieston *Aberdeen* ***Suburb***, 1m/2km SW of Aberdeen city centre. **55 E4** NJ9204.
Ruthven *Aber.* ***Village***, 5m/7km N of Huntly. **64 A5** NJ5046.
Ruthven *Angus* ***Village***, on River Isla, 3m/5km E of Alyth. **42 A5** NO2848.
Ruthven *High.* ***Settlement***, 3m/5km SE of Moy. **52 A1** NH8133.
Ruthven *High.* ***Settlement***, 1km S of Kingussie across River Spey. **51 G5** NN7699.
Ruthven Barracks *High.* ***Other feature of interest***, remains of 18c military installations (Historic Scotland) built to keep Highlanders in check, 1m/2km S of Kingussie. **51 G4** NN7699.
Ruthven Water *P. & K.* ***River***, running NE to River Earn 4m/6km NE of Auchterarder. **33 E3** NN9717.
Ruthwell *D. & G.* ***Village***, near shore of Solway Firth, 6m/10km W of Annan. Cross (Historic Scotland) probably dating from late 7c, preserved in church. **9 F4** NY1067.
Ruthwell Cross *D. & G.* ***Historic/prehistoric site***, 7c Anglian cross (Historic Scotland) in Ruthwell Church, 2m/4km S of Carrutherstown. 18 feet high and carved with Runic characters. Considered to be one of the major monuments of Dark Age Europe. **9 F4** NY1068.
Rye Water *N.Ayr.* ***River***, issuing from Camphill Reservoir W of Kilbirnie and flowing S to River Garnock on E side of Dalry. NS2949.
Ryhill *Aber.* ***Settlement***, 1km SW of Oyne and 6m/10km NW of Inverurie. NJ6625.
Rysa Little *Ork.* ***Island***, small uninhabited island off E coast of Hoy and 1km NW of Fara. **78 C3** ND3197.

S

'S Airdhe Beinn *Arg. & B.* ***Hill***, 2m/3km W of Tobermory, Mull. Height 958 feet or 292 metres. **37 D4** NM4753.
Saasaig *High.* ***Settlement***, to S of Teangue, on E side of Sleat peninsula, Skye. NG6608.
Sabhal Beag *High.* ***Mountain***, 4m/7km E of Loch Stack and 3m/5km S of Loch Dionard. Height 2391 feet or 729 metres. **74 C4** NC3742.
Sabhal Mòr *High.* ***Mountain***, 4m/6km NE of Loch Stack, Sutherland district. Height 2306 feet or 703 metres. **74 C4** NC3544.
Sacquoy Head *Ork.* ***Coastal feature***, headland at NW end of Rousay. **80 B3** HY3835.
Saddell *Arg. & B.* ***Village***, near E coast of Kintyre, 8m/13km N of Campbeltown. **12 C2** NR7832.
Saddell Abbey *Arg. & B.* ***Ecclesiastical building***, in hamlet of Saddall, 5m/7km SW of Carradale. Built in 12c by one of the Lords of the Isles. Only the walls now remain. **12 C2** NR7832.
Saddell Bay *Arg. & B.* ***Bay***, to E of Saddell village, on E side of Kintyre peninsula. **12 C2** NR7832.
Saddell Forest *Arg. & B.* ***Forest/woodland***, astride Saddell Glen to W of Saddell, Kintyre. **12 C2** NR7733.
Saddell Water *Arg. & B.* ***River***, running SE past Saddell village to Saddell Bay, on Kintyre peninsula. NR7831.
Saddle Hill *High.* ***Mountain***, in Nairn district, 4m/6km S of Croy. Height 1233 feet or 376 metres. **61 G5** NH7843.
Saddle Yoke *D. & G.* ***Mountain***, to E of Blackhope Burn, 5m/8km NE of Moffat. Height 2411 feet or 735 metres. **16 C4** NT1312.
Saighdinis (Anglicised form: Sidinish.) *W.Isles* ***Settlement***, 1m/2km E of Locheport, North Uist. **45 G3** NF8763.
Sàil Chaorainn *High.* ***Mountain***, on Glenaffric Forest, Inverness district, 4m/6km S of head of Loch Affric. Munro: height 3287 feet or 1002 metres. **50 A3** NH1315.
Sàil Gorm *High.* ***Mountain***, situated between Loch a' Chàirn Bhàin and Loch Assynt. Height 2545 feet or 776 metres. **74 A5** NC1930.
Sàil Mhòr *High.* ***Mountain***, one of the peaks of Beinn Eighe, Ross and Cromarty district. Height 3218 feet or 981 metres. **59 F3** NG9360.
Sàil Mhòr *High.* ***Mountain***, in Ross and Cromarty district 4m/6km W of Auchtascailt at head of Little Loch Broom. Height 2516 feet or 767 metres. **59 G1** NH0388.
Saileag *High.* ***Mountain***, in Ross and Cromarty district, on N side of Glen Shiel. Munro: height 3146 feet or 959 metres. **49 G3** NH0114.
St. Abbs *Sc.Bord.* ***Village***, coastal village with small harbour, 3m/4km NW of Eyemouth. **27 G3** NT9167.
St. Abb's Head *Sc.Bord.* ***Coastal feature***, rocky headland with lighthouse, 1m/2km N of St. Abbs. Spectacular walks above 300 foot or 91 metre cliffs. National Nature Reserve (National Trust for Scotland) is most important location in SE Scotland for cliff-nesting birds. **27 G2** NT9167.
St. Adrian's Chapel *Fife* ***Ecclesiastical building***, remains of 12c chapel situated on Isle of May, at mouth of Firth of Forth. **35 E5** NT6598.
St. Aethans *Moray* ***Locality***, on N coast adjoining to E of Burghead. Site of St. Aethan's Well. NJ1168.
St. Andrews *Fife* Population: 11,136. ***Town***, historic town standing on rocky promontory on St. Andrews Bay, 11m/17km SE of Dundee across Firth of Tay and 9m/14km E of Cupar. University, founded 1411, is Scotland's oldest and third oldest in Britain. Royal and Ancient Golf Club based here, and is ruling authority on game of golf. Several golf courses, including famous Old Course. Remains of cathedral, priory and castle (Historic Scotland). Blackfriars Chapel (Historic Scotland) in South Street is vaulted side apse of church of Dominican friars, rebuilt in 1516. Scant foundations of St. Mary's Church (Historic Scotland), earliest collegiate church in Scotland. West Port (Historic Scotland), one of the few surviving city gates in Scotland, was built in 1589 and renovated in 1843. **34 D3** NO5016.
St. Andrews Bay *Fife* ***Bay***, 11m/17km SE of Dundee across Firth of Tay, and 9m/14km E of Cupar. St. Andrews historic town stands on rocky promontory on bay. **34 D3** NO1516.
St. Andrews Castle *Fife* ***Castle***, ruins of 13c castle (Historic Scotland) on rocky promontory overlooking sea at St. Andrews. Most of ruins date from later periods, including bottle-shaped dungeon in Sea Tower. Visitor Centre. **34 D3** NO5116.
St. Andrews Cathedral *Fife* ***Ecclesiastical building***, once largest church in Scotland (Historic Scotland), dating from 12c-13c, in St. Andrews. Remains include well-preserved precinct walls. **34 D3** NO5116.
St. Andrews Sea Life Centre *Fife* ***Other feature of interest***, at St. Andrews, includes displays and observation pools, with marine life. **34 D3** NO5116.
St. Ann's *D. & G.* ***Locality***, 6m/10km S of Beattock. **9 E1** NY0793.
St. Baldred's Boat *E.Loth.* ***Coastal feature***, rock on North Sea coast, 3m/4km NE of Whitekirk. **26 D1** NT6085.
St. Baldred's Cradle *E.Loth.* ***Coastal feature***, rock formation on North Sea coast, 3m/5km NW of Dunbar. **26 D1** NT6381.
St. Bean's Church *P. & K.* ***Ecclesiastical building***, 13c church with fine example of Pictish stone cross. In Fowlis Wester, 4m/7km E of Crieff. **33 E2** NN9224.
St. Blane's Church *Arg. & B.* ***Ecclesiastical building***, ruins of 12c Romanesque chapel (Historic Scotland) built on site of Celtic monastery on Bute, 1m/2km N of Garroch Head. **22 B4** NS0953.
St. Boniface Church *Ork.* ***Ecclesiastical building***, ruined 12c church on Papa Westray, 1km N of Holland. **80 C1** HY4852.
St. Boswells *Sc.Bord.* Population: 1128. ***Village***, 4m/6km SE of Melrose. **17 G2** NT5931.
St. Bride's Church *S.Lan.* ***Ecclesiastical building***, ancient church with restored 12c chancel (Historic Scotland), to N of Douglas by Douglas Water. **15 G2** NS8331.
St. Bridget's Church *Fife* ***Ecclesiastical building***, shell of 13c church (Historic Scotland) in Dalgety Bay, 2m/4km E of Inverkeithing. Much altered in 17c for Protestant worship. At W end is buried vault built for Earl of Dunfermline. **25 F1** NT1683.
St. Catherines *Arg. & B.* ***Settlement***, on E shore of Loch Fyne, in Argyll, opposite Inveraray (ferry for pedestrians). **30 D4** NN1207.
St. Catherine's Bay *Ork.* ***Bay***, wide bay on W coast of Stronsay. Linga Holm is at entrance to bay. **81 E4** HY6326.

St. Catherine's Dub *Aber.* ***Coastal feature***, headland at Collieston with views along the rocky coastline. **55 F2** NK0327.

St. Clement's Church *W.Isles* ***Ecclesiastical building***, cruciform church dating from c. 1500 (Historic Scotland) situated in settlement of Rodel, South Harris. Sculptured slabs and highly decorated. **66 C5** NG0483.

St. Colmac *Arg. & B.* ***Settlement***, on Bute, 2m/3km W of Port Bannatyne. Celtic cross, standing stone and stone circles in vicinity. NS0467.

St. Colm's Abbey *Fife* ***Ecclesiastical building***, well preserved monastic building, including 13c octagonal chapter house, on Inchcolm, 1km offshore from N bank of Firth of Forth. **25 F1** NT1882.

St. Columba's Cave *Arg. & B.* ***Other feature of interest***, cave 1m/2km NW of Ellary, containing rock-shelf with an altar, above which are carved crosses. Occupied from Middle Stone Age. **21 F2** NR7576.

St. Columba's Church *W.Isles* ***Ecclesiastical building***, medieval chapel at Aignis, at W end of Eye Peninsula, Isle of Lewis. **69 F4** NB4832.

St. Columb's Church *W.Isles* *See Eilean Chaluim Chille.*

St. Combs *Aber.* ***Village***, on NE coast, 4m/7km SE of Fraserburgh. **65 F3** NK0563.

St. Cormac's Chapel *Arg. & B.* *See Eilean Mòr.*

St. Cuthbert's Kirk *Edin.* ***Ecclesiastical building***, 1m/2km SE of Dalmeny Station. Rebuilt in 18c. Monument to Napier, inventor of logarithms. Thomas de Quincey buried in churchyard. **25 F2** NT1477.

St. Cyrus *Aber.* ***Village***, near coast, 5m/8km NE of Montrose. **43 F3** NO7464.

St. Davids *Fife* ***Settlement***, on St. David's Harbour, 1km SE of Inverkeithing. **25 F1** NT1482.

St. David's *P. & K.* ***Settlement***, 5m/8km N of Auchterarder. **33 E2** NN9420.

St. Duthus Chapel *High.* ***Ecclesiastical building***, built between 1065 and 1256 in Tain and containing remains of St. Duthus, transferred there 200 years after his death in 1065. Heritage Centre in grounds. **61 G1** NH7882.

St. Fergus *Aber.* ***Village***, near NE coast, 4m/7km N of Peterhead. **65 G4** NK0952.

St. Fergus Moss *Aber.* ***Open space***, moorland 2m/3km S of Crimond. **65 F4** NK0553.

St. Fillans *P. & K.* ***Village***, at foot, or E end, of Loch Earn, 5m/8km W of Comrie. **32 B2** NN6924.

St. Giles High Kirk *Edin.* ***Ecclesiastical building***, on Royal Mile, in Edinburgh. Dating from c. 1120 and almost destroyed by English Army in 1385. After rebuilding, became centre of Reformation in Scotland. **25 G2** NT2573.

St. Johns Church *P. & K.* ***Ecclesiastical building***, good example of cruciform church, in centre of Perth, dating largely from 15c. **33 G2** NO1123.

St. John's Head *Ork.* ***Coastal feature***, lofty headland on NW coast of Hoy, rising to 1140 feet or 347 metres, 3m/5km N of Rora Head. **78 A2** HY1803.

St. John's Kirk *S.Lan.* ***Settlement***, 1m/2km NW of Symington. **16 A2** NS9835.

St. John's Loch *High.* ***Lake/loch***, loch on NE side of Dunnet village, S of Dunnet Head on N coast of Caithness district. **77 E1** ND2272.

St. John's Point *High.* ***Coastal feature***, headland on N coast of Caithness district 6m/10km W of Duncansby Head. **77 F1** ND3175.

St. John's Town of Dalry (Also known as Dalry). *D. & G.* ***Village***, on Water of Ken, 2m/4km N of New Galloway. Its name comes from a former church of the Knights Templars. **8 A2** NX6281.

St. Katherines *Aber.* ***Settlement***, 5m/8km NW of Oldmeldrum. **54 C1** NJ7834.

St. Kilda (Also known as Hirta.) *W.Isles* ***Island***, steep rocky island, lying some 54m/86km W of South Harris and 35m/56km W of North Uist. Area about 3 square miles or 8 square km. Uninhabited since 1930, except for Army personnel manning radar stations. Ruined village on Village Bay at SE end. Cliffs below Conachair are highest sea cliffs in Great Britain. Island is chief island of St. Kilda group (all National Trust for Scotland, and collectively forming a nature reserve). See also Boreray, Dun and Soay. NF0999.

St. Leonards *Edin.* ***Suburb***, 1m/2km SE of Edinburgh city centre. NT2672.

St. Leonards *S.Lan.* ***Suburb***, to E of East Kilbride town centre. NS6554.

St. Machar's Cathedral *Aberdeen* ***Ecclesiastical building***, twin-towered 14c granite building on ancient site of worship in Aberdeen. Features include 16c oak ceiling and notable stained glass. The nave, dated 1520, still used as parish church. Ruined transepts (Historic Scotland) contain tomb of Bishop Dunbar. **55 E4** NJ9308.

St. Magnus Bay *Shet.* ***Bay***, large bay on W of coast of Mainland, extending S from Esha Ness to Ness of Melby and Papa Stour, and penetrating E, through Swarbacks Minn and Olna Firth, as far as Voe. **82 B1** HU2568.

St. Magnus Cathedral *Ork.* ***Ecclesiastical building***, at Kirkwall, on Mainland. Built between 1137 and 1200, though additional work went on over the next 300 years. Contains some fine examples of Norman architecture. **80 C5** HY4410.

St. Magnus Church *Ork.* ***Ecclesiastical building***, remains of church (Historic Scotland), probably of 12c, towards W side of Egilsay. Dedicated to Christian Norse ruler murdered on island in 1116. **80 C3** HY4630.

St. Margaret's Hope *Fife* ***Sea feature***, anchorage for Rosyth naval base on Firth of Forth. **25 E1** NT1882.

St. Margaret's Hope *Ork.* ***Village***, chief settlement on N coast of South Ronaldsay, at head of bay of same name. **78 D3** ND4493.

St. Martins *P. & K.* ***Settlement***, 5m/7km NE of Perth. **33 G1** NO1530.

St. Mary's *Ork.* ***Village***, on S coast of Mainland, 6m/10km S of Kirkwall. **79 D2** HY4701.

St. Mary's Chapel *Arg. & B.* ***Ecclesiastical building***, ruins of chancel of late medieval church (Historic Scotland), on Bute, S of Rothesay and at N end of Loch Fad. Includes two distinctive tombs. **22 B3** NS0863.

St. Mary's Chapel *High.* ***Ecclesiastical building***, in Crosskirk on N coast, 6m/9km W of Thurso. Irish style dry-stone chapel (Historic Scotland) with low doors, probably dating from 12c. **76 C1** ND0270.

St. Mary's Chapel *Ork.* ***Ecclesiastical building***, late 12c ruin on Wyre, with walls built of local whinstone. **80 C4** HY4426.

St. Mary's Collegiate Church *E.Loth.* *Alternative name for Church of St. Mary, qv.*

St. Mary's Croft *D. & G.* ***Settlement***, on W side of Loch Ryan, 4m/6km NW of Stranraer. Site of medieval chapel and well. **6 B4** NX0365.

St. Mary's Episcopal Cathedral *Edin.* ***Ecclesiastical building***, 1m/2km W of Edinburgh city centre. Built in 1879, with W towers added in 1917. Interesting interior and 276 foot or 84 metre high spire. **25 G2** NT2373.

St. Mary's Isle *D. & G.* ***Coastal feature***, peninsula running out from head of Kirkcudbright Bay. **3 G2** NX6749.

St. Mary's Kirk *Aber.* ***Ecclesiastical building***, roofless medieval parish church (Historic Scotland) at Auchindoir, 2m/3km N of Lumsden. Features carved early Romanesque doorway and early 14c sacrament house. **53 G2** NJ4724.

St. Mary's Loch *Sc.Bord.* ***Lake/loch***, loch in Ettrick Forest 13m/21km W of Selkirk. 3m/5km long SW to NE; maximum depth over 150 feet or 45 metres. **16 D3** NT2422.

St. Mary's Pleasance *E.Loth.* ***Garden***, restored 17c garden on SE side of Haddington next to River Tyne. **26 C2** NT5173.

St. Monance *Fife* *Alternative spelling of St. Monans, qv.*

St. Monans (Also spelled St. Monance.) *Fife* Population: 1373. ***Small town***, fishing town on Firth of Forth, 3m/5km W of Anstruther. Many old houses. **34 D4** NO5201.

St. Mungo *D. & G.* ***Locality***, 3m/5km S of Lockerbie. NY1476.

St. Mungo's Chapel *Fife* ***Ecclesiastical building***, National Trust for Scotland property in Culross, built in 1503 to commemorate the birthplace of St. Mungo. It is now in ruins. **25 D1** NS9986.

St. Ninians *Stir.* ***Locality***, S district of Stirling. **32 C5** NS7991.

St. Ninian's Bay *Arg. & B.* ***Bay***, S facing bay on W coast of Bute, 4m/6km SW of Rothesay. Remains of ancient chapel on headland. NS0361.

St. Ninian's Bay *Shet.* ***Bay***, forming S side of narrow isthmus between St. Ninian's Isle and W coast of Mainland. HU3620.

St. Ninian's Cave *D. & G.* ***Cave***, said to have been used as oratory by St. Ninian in 5c (Historic Scotland), at Port Castle Bay, 4m/6km W of Isle of Whithorn. **3 E3** NX4236.

St. Ninian's Chapel *D. & G.* ***Ecclesiastical building***, ruins of 13c chapel (Historic Scotland) at Isle of Whithorn, 3m/5km SE of Whithorn. **3 E3** NX4836.

St. Ninian's Chapel *Moray* ***Ecclesiastical building***, restored chapel built in 1755 at Tynet, 3m/5km NE of Fochabers. Oldest Scottish post-Reformation Catholic church still in use. **63 F3** NJ3761.

St. Ninian's Isle *Shet.* ***Coastal feature***, peninsula on W coast of Mainland, 9m/14km N of Sumburgh Head, joined to rest of Mainland by narrow spit of land at head. **82 C5** HU3620.

St. Ninian's Isle Church *Shet.* ***Ecclesiastical building***, remains of church on W side of Bigton Wick, 1km W of Bigton. **82 C5** HU3620.

St. Ninian's Point *Arg. & B.* ***Coastal feature***, headland on W side of St. Ninian's Bay. **22 B3** NS0361.

St. Olaf's Church *Shet.* ***Ecclesiastical building***, in Lund, overlooking Lunda Wick on W coast of Unst. Ruined 12c church, in use until 1785. **85 E2** HP5604.

St. Orland's Stone *Angus* ***Other feature of interest***, symbol stone (Historic Scotland) depicting hunting and boating scenes, 4m/6km W of Forfar. **42 C5** NO4050.

St. Palladius' Chapel *Aber.* *See Fordoun.*

St. Peter's Church *High.* ***Ecclesiastical building***, situated in Thurso on N coast. Ruins of medieval origin. Present church dates from 17c. **76 D2** ND1168.

St. Peter's Church *Moray* ***Ecclesiastical building***, roofless remains of 13c church with 14c parish cross (Historic Scotland), to E of Duffus on approach to Gordonstoun School. Includes base of 14c tower and 16c vaulted porch. Formerly centre of village until new Duffus planned in 19c. **63 D3** NJ1768.

St. Quivox *S.Ayr.* ***Hamlet***, 3m/5km NE of Ayr. **14 B3** NS3724.

St. Ronan's Bay *Arg. & B.* ***Bay***, small bay at Baile Mòr, E coast of Iona. NM2824.

St. Ronan's Church *W.Isles* ***Ecclesiastical building***, remains of church, thought to be 14c, situated in SW Rona. HW8032.

St. Serf's Island *P. & K.* ***Island***, in Loch Leven, towards SE corner. Ruins of medieval priory. **33 G4** NO1600.

St. Serf's Kirk *Fife* ***Historic/prehistoric site***, scant remains of 13c church dedicated to St. Serf at Dysart, to N of Kirkcaldy. Only 16c tower with dovecote (or doocot) survive. **34 B5** NT3093.

St. Serf's Priory *P. & K.* ***Ecclesiastical building***, on SE of St. Serf's Island in Loch Leven, 3m/5km SE of Kinross. Ruins of priory founded on site of earlier Culdee settlement. **33 G4** NO1600.

St. Tredwell's Chapel *Ork.* ***Ecclesiastical building***, on E bank of Loch of St. Tredwell, Papa Westray. Ruined chapel of unknown age where Christianity is supposed to be have been initiated in Orkney. **80 C1** HY4950.

St. Vigeans *Angus* ***Village***, 1m/2km N of Arbroath. St. Vigeans Sculptured Stones (Historic Scotland) are 32 Early Christian and Pictish stones set into cottages in village. Airfield to NW. **43 E5** NO6342.

Salachail *Arg. & B.* ***Settlement***, in Glen Creran, 5m/8km S of Ballachulish. **38 C4** NN0551.

Salachan Burn *High.* ***River***, stream in Lochaber district, running NW down Salachan Glen into Loch Linnhe opposite Eilean Balnagowan. NM9653.

Salachan Glen *High.* ***Valley***, carries Salachan Burn into Loch Linnhe opposite Eilean Balnagowan. **38 B4** NM9653.

Salen *Arg. & B.* ***Village***, on bay of same name on Sound of Mull, 9m/14km SE of Tobermory, Mull. **37 E5** NM5743.

Salen *High.* ***Village***, on bay of same name, on N shore of Loch Sunart, in Lochaber district. **37 F3** NM6864.

Salen Bay *Arg. & B.* ***Bay***, small bay at Salen, on coast of Mull. **37 E5** NM5744.

Salen Forest *Arg. & B.* ***Forest/woodland***, stretching SE from head of Loch Frisa, along its NE shore and towards coast and Sound of Mull, 2m/3km NW of Salen, Mull. **37 E5** NM5047.

Saligo Bay *Arg. & B.* ***Bay***, on W coast of Islay, 1m/2km W of Loch Gorm. **20 A3** NR2066.

Saline *Fife* Population: 1235. ***Village***, 5m/8km NW of Dunfermline. **33 F5** NT0292.

Saline Hill *Fife* ***Mountain***, 1m/2km NE of Saline. Height 1178 feet or 359 metres. **33 F5** NT0393.

Salisbury *Edin.* ***Suburb***, 1m/2km SE of Edinburgh city centre. NT2672.

Sallachan *High.* ***Settlement***, near mouth of River Gour, 1m/2km NW of Sallachan Point, Lochaber district. **38 B3** NM9863.

Sallachan Point *High.* ***Coastal feature***, low-lying promontory with beacon on W shore of Loch Linnhe in Lochaber district. **38 B3** NM9861.

Sallachry *Arg. & B.* ***Settlement***, 3m/4km NW of Inveraray. **30 C3** NN0712.

Sallachy *High.* ***Locality***, in Skye and Lochalsh district, on N shore of Loch Long, 3m/5km NE of Dornie. **49 F1** NG9130.

Sallachy *High.* ***Settlement***, on SW shore of Loch Shin, 3m/5km NW of Lairg. **72 A4** NC5508.

Salmond's Muir *Angus* ***Settlement***, 2m/3km NE of Carnoustie. **35 D1** NO5737.

Salsburgh *N.Lan.* Population: 1398. ***Village***, 5m/7km E of Airdrie. **24 C3** NS8262.

Salt Ness *Ork.* ***Coastal feature***, headland on W coast of Shapinsay 2m/4km N of Balfour. HY4719.

Saltburn *High.* ***Village***, on N shore of Cromarty Firth, Ross and Cromarty district, 1m/2km NE of Invergordon. Development in connection with North Sea oil. **61 G2** NH7269.

Saltcoats *N.Ayr.* Population: 11,865. ***Town***, salt town and resort on Firth of Clyde, adjoining to SE of Ardrossan. Harbour, with 19c Martello tower. **22 D5** NS2441.

Salterhill *Moray* ***Settlement***, 3m/4km N of Elgin. **63 E3** NJ2067.

Salthouse Head *Aber.* ***Coastal feature***, headland at S end of Peterhead Bay. NK1344.

Saltinish *W.Isles* ***Locality***, on Barra, 1m/2km SE of Scurrival Point. NF7007.

Saltness *Ork.* ***Settlement***, at S end of Hoy, 1km N of Melsetter. ND2790.

Salum *Arg. & B.* ***Settlement***, on Tiree, on E side of Salum Bay, on N coast, 2m/3km W of Rubha Dubh. NM0648.

Salum Bay *Arg. & B.* ***Bay***, on N coast of Tiree. **36 B2** NM0648.

Samala *W.Isles Anglicised form of Samhla, qv.*
Samalaman Island *High.* ***Island***, low-lying islet on S side of Sound of Arisaig, 3m/5km W of Roshven, Lochaber district. **37 F2** NM6678.
Samalan Island *Arg. & B.* ***Island***, islet at entrance to Loch na Keal, W coast of Mull, lying 1km NE of Inch Kenneth. **28 D1** NM4536.
Samhla (Anglicised form: Samala.) *W.Isles* ***Settlement***, on E side of Baleshare. **45 F3** NF7962.
Samphrey *Shet.* ***Island***, uninhabited island of about 200 acres or 80 hectares lying between SW end of Yell and NE coast of Mainland. **85 D5** HU4676.
Samson's Lane *Ork.* ***Settlement***, at centre of Stronsay. HY6525.
Samuelston *E.Loth.* ***Settlement***, on River Tyne, 3m/4km SW of Haddington. **26 B2** NT4870.
Sanaigmore *Arg. & B.* ***Settlement***, on N coast of Islay, 8m/12km NW of Bridgend. **20 A3** NR2370.
Sanaigmore Bay *Arg. & B.* ***Bay***, small bay on N coast of Islay, 1km SE of Tòn Mhòr. NR2371.
Sand *Shet.* ***Settlement***, at head of Sand Voe, Mainland. **82 C3** HU3447.
Sand Hill *Moray* ***Mountain***, 3m/5km S of Cabrach. Height 1797 feet or 548 metres. **53 F2** NJ3821.
Sand Water *Shet.* ***Lake/loch***, on Mainland in course of Burn of Sandwater, which rises as Burn of Pettawater above small lake of Petta Water, 2m/4km S of Voe. Stream flows S through Petta Water, Sand Water and Loch of Strom into Stromness Voe to E of Weisdale Voe. **82 D2** HU4154.
Sand Wick *Shet.* ***Bay***, wide sandy bay off E coast of Unst. **85 F2** HP6202.
Sand Wick *Shet.* ***Bay***, on N shore of St. Magnus Bay, on W side of Hillswick. HU2777.
Sand Wick *Shet.* ***Bay***, S facing bay on E coast of Mainland, 11m/18km S of Lerwick. At head lies Sandwick. HU4323.
Sanda Island *Arg. & B.* ***Island***, lying nearly 2m/3km off S coast of Kintyre across Sanda Sound. Measures 1m/2km E to W and 1km N to S. Lighthouse at S point. **12 C5** NR7204.
Sanda Sound *Arg. & B.* ***Sea feature***, divides Sanda Island from S coast of Kintyre. Nearly 2m/3km wide. **12 C5** NR7204.
Sandaig *Arg. & B.* ***Settlement***, adjoining to W of Middleton, near W coast of Tiree. **36 A2** NL9443.
Sandaig *High.* ***Locality***, at W end of Knoydart, Lochaber district, on Sandaig Bay, on N side of entrance to Loch Nevis. **48 D4** NG7101.
Sandaig *High.* ***Settlement***, on coast of Skye and Lochalsh district, 4m/6km SW of Glenelg. **49 D3** NG7714.
Sandaig Bay *High.* ***Bay***, on N side of entrance to Loch Nevis. Locality of Sandaig lies on bay. **48 D4** NG7101.
Sandaig Islands *High.* ***Island***, group of islets in Sound of Sleat off N side of entrance to Loch Hourn in Lochaber district. Lighthouse on Eilean Mòr, the islet farthest from mainland shore. **49 D3** NG7614.
Sanday *High.* ***Island***, in Inner Hebrides at SE end of Canna, to which it is connected at low tide. Sanday is 2m/3km E to W and has a maximum width N to S of 1km. Its N coast forms S shore of Canna Harbour. **47 F4** NG2704.
Sanday *Ork.* ***Island***, low-lying island some 14m/23km NE to SW and of varying width, in places less than 1km, lying 3m/4km S of North Ronaldsay and N of Stronsay at nearest points. Spur Ness at extreme SW of island is 17m/28km NE of Kirkwall, Mainland. Airfield near centre of island. **81 F2** HY6840.
Sanday Airfield *Ork.* ***Airport/airfield***, 1km W of Overbister, Sanday. **81 E2** HY6740.
Sanday Sound *Ork.* ***Sea feature***, sea area between islands of Sanday and Stronsay. **81 E3** HY6734.
Sandbank *Arg. & B.* Population: 1543. ***Village***, on S side of Holy Loch, Argyll, 2m/4km N of Dunoon. **22 C1** NS1680.
Sandend *Aber.* ***Village***, on Sandend Bay, N coast, which is 3m/4km E of Cullen. **64 A3** NJ5566.
Sandend Bay *Aber.* ***Bay***, 3m/4km E of Cullen. Sandend village lies on the bay. **64 A3** NJ5566.
Sandford *S.Lan.* ***Hamlet***, 1m/2km SE of Strathaven. **24 B5** NS7143.
Sandford Bay *Aber.* ***Bay***, on E coast S of Peterhead, between Burnhaven and Boddam. **65 G5** NK1243.
Sandfordhill *Aber.* ***Settlement***, near E coast, 3m/5km S of Peterhead. **65 G5** NK1142.
Sandgarth *Ork.* ***Settlement***, on SE end of Shapinsay, 6m/9km NE of Kirkwall across Shapinsay Sound. **80 D5** HY5215.
Sandgreen *D. & G.* ***Settlement***, on E shore of Fleet Bay, 3m/5km SW of Gatehouse of Fleet. **7 G5** NX5752.
Sandhaven *Aber.* ***Village***, on N coast, 2m/3km W of Fraserburgh. **65 E3** NJ9667.
Sandhead *D. & G.* ***Village***, coastal village on Sandhead Bay, on W side of Luce Bay, 7m/11km S of Stranraer. **6 B5** NX0949.
Sandhead Bay *D. & G.* ***Bay***, on W side of Luce Bay, 7m/11km S of Stranraer. Coastal village of Sandhead on the bay. NX0949.
Sandness *Shet.* ***Village***, near W coast of Mainland, adjoining to E of Melby. **82 A2** HU1957.
Sandness Hill *Shet.* ***Hill***, to S of Sandness. Height 817 feet or 249 metres. **82 A2** HU1957.
Sandquoy *Ork.* ***Settlement***, on Bay of Sandquoy, on N coast of Sanday, 2m/3km SW of Tafts Ness. **81 F2** HY7445.
Sandray (Gaelic form: Sanndraigh.) *W.Isles* ***Island***, uninhabited island of about 4 square km, 1km S of Vatersay and 3m/5km S of Barra. **44 B4** NL6491.
Sands of Forvie *Aber.* ***Coastal feature***, sandy waste on E coast between Collieston and Newburgh. Forvie Ness Nature Reserve located here. **55 F2** NK0227.
Sands of Luce *D. & G.* ***Coastal feature***, extensive sands along NW coast of Luce Bay, 1m/2km S of Glenluce. **6 C5** NX1654.
Sands of Nigg *High.* ***Coastal feature***, extensive sands in Nigg Bay, 3m/4km N of Cromarty across Cromarty Firth. Sands stretch for up to 3m/4km from N coast of Nigg Bay. **61 G2** NH7872.
Sandside Bay *High.* ***Bay***, 1m/2km N of Reay, on N coast of Caithness district, with Sandside Head on W side of entrance to bay. **76 B2** NC9665.
Sandside Burn *High.* ***River***, flowing N into W side of Sandside Bay, on N coast of Caithness district. **76 B3** NC9665.
Sandside Head *High.* ***Coastal feature***, headland on N coast of Caithness district on W side of entrance to Sandside Bay, 1m/2km NW of Reay. NC9566.
Sandside House *High.* ***Settlement***, 1km NW of Reay, Caithness district. **76 B2** NC9565.
Sandsound *Shet.* ***Settlement***, on E shore of Sandsound Voe. **82 C3** HU3548.
Sandsound Voe *Shet.* ***Sea feature***, narrow inlet between steep hills to W of Weisdale Voe, Mainland. HU3549.
Sandwick *Shet.* ***Settlement***, at head of Sand Wick, S facing bay on E coast of Mainland, 11m/18km S of Lerwick. **82 D5** HU4323.
Sandwick (Gaelic form: Sanndabhaig.) *W.Isles* ***Village***, on Isle of Lewis, 1m/2km E of Stornoway. Mast to N. **69 F4** NB4432.
Sandwood Bay *High.* ***Bay***, on NW coast of Sutherland district, between headlands of Rubh' an t-Socaich Ghlais and Rubh' a Bhuachaille. **74 B2** NC2266.
Sandwood Loch *High.* ***Lake/loch***, near NW coast of Sutherland district at foot of Strath Shinary, draining into Sandwood Bay. **74 B2** NC2264.
Sandy Edge *Sc.Bord.* ***Inland physical feature***, wooded ridge, 1312 feet or 400 metres high, to E of Leap Hill, 9m/14km S of Hawick. **17 G5** NT5201.
Sandyhills *D. & G.* ***Locality***, on Sandyhills Bay, small bay 5m/9km SE of Dalbeattie. NX8855.
Sandyhills *Glas.* ***Suburb***, 4m/7km E of Glasgow. NS6563.
Sandyhills Bay *D. & G.* ***Bay***, small bay, 5m/9km SE of Dalbeattie. NX8955.
Sangamore *High.* ***Settlement***, adjoining to SE of Durness, N coast of Sutherland district. NC4067.
Sango Bay *High.* ***Bay***, 3m/4km SE of Faraid Head, adjacent to Durness. **74 D2** NC4068.
Sangobeg *High.* ***Locality***, in Sutherland district, 2m/3km SE of Durness. **74 D2** NC4266.
Sanna *High.* ***Settlement***, on Ardnamurchan peninsula, 4m/6km NW of Kilchoan. **37 D3** NM4469.
Sanna Bay *High.* ***Bay***, in Lochaber district, with Sanna Point headland at its N end. **36 D3** NM4370.
Sanna Point *High.* ***Coastal feature***, headland in Lochaber district, at N end of Sanna Bay and 2m/4km NE of Point of Ardnamurchan. **36 D3** NM4370.
Sannaig *Arg. & B.* ***Settlement***, on Jura, 2m/3km S of Craighouse. **20 D3** NR5164.
Sanndabhaig *W.Isles Gaelic form of Sandwick, qv.*
Sanndraigh *W.Isles Gaelic form of Sandray, qv.*
Sannox Bay *N.Ayr.* ***Bay***, on NE coast of Arran, to E of Mid Sannox. **22 B5** NS0145.
Sanquhar *D. & G.* Population: 2095. ***Small town***, former mining and cotton town on River Nith, 10m/16km NW of Thornhill and same distance E of New Cumnock. Remains of castle to S. Tolbooth dating from 1735. World's oldest post office, in use since 1738. **15 F5** NS7809.
Sarclet *High.* ***Settlement***, on E coast of Caithness district, 5m/8km S of Wick. **77 F4** ND3443.
Sarclet Head *High.* ***Coastal feature***, headland to SE of Sarclet. **77 F4** ND3443.
Sark ***River***, rising on Leaheads Hill and flowing S along border of England and Scotland to head of Solway Firth, 1km SE of Gretna. **10 B4** NY3266.
Sarsgrum *High.* ***Settlement***, on E side of Kyle of Durness, 1m/2km S of Keoldale. **74 C2** NC3764.
Sauchar Point *Fife* ***Coastal feature***, headland on E side of Elie Ness and 1km SE of Elie town. **34 C5** NT4999.
Sauchen *Aber.* ***Village***, 4m/6km SW of Kemnay. **54 B3** NJ6911.
Saucher *P. & K.* ***Hamlet***, 3m/4km S of Burrelton. **33 G1** NO1933.
Sauchie Law *Sc.Bord.* ***Mountain***, in Craik Forest, 3m/5km SE of Ettrick. Height 1450 feet or 442 metres. **17 D4** NT2910.
Sauchieburn *Aber.* ***Settlement***, 3m/4km S of Fettercairn. **43 E3** NO6669.
Sauchrie *S.Ayr.* ***Settlement***, 3m/4km N of Maybole. **14 B4** NS3014.
Saugh Hill *S.Ayr.* ***Hill***, 2m/3km E of Girvan. Height 971 feet or 296 metres. **6 D1** NX2197.
Saughton *Edin.* ***Suburb***, 3m/5km SW of Edinburgh city centre. NT2071.
Saughtonhall *Edin.* ***Suburb***, to N of Saughton across railway. NT2172.
Saughtree *Sc.Bord.* ***Settlement***, 8m/12km NE of Newcastleton. **11 D2** NY5696.
Saughtree Fell *Sc.Bord.* ***Mountain***, with steep sides, to W of Dawston Burn, 5m/8km NW of Kielder. Height 1424 feet or 434 metres. **10 D2** NY5498.
Savalbeg *High.* ***Locality***, to SE of Savalmore. Numerous ancient cairns in vicinity. **72 A4** NC5907.
Savalmore *High.* ***Settlement***, in Sutherland district, 1m/2km N of Lairg. **72 A4** NC5808.
Saviskaill *Ork.* ***Locality***, on N coast of Rousay, 1m/2km S of headland of Saviskaill Head on shore of Saviskaill Bay. HY4033.
Saviskaill Bay *Ork.* ***Bay***, wide bay on Rousay, extending E from Saviskaill Head. On shore of the bay is locality of Saviskaill. **80 C3** HY4133.
Saviskaill Head *Ork.* ***Coastal feature***, headland on N coast of Rousay, 1m/2km N of Saviskaill and to W of Saviskaill Bay. **80 C3** HY4034.
Saxa Vord *Shet.* ***Hill***, to E of Burra Firth in N part of Unst. Height 935 feet or 285 metres. **85 F1** HP6316.
Scad Head *Ork.* ***Coastal feature***, headland on N coast of Hoy, 4m/6km E of Ward Hill. HY2900.
Scad Hill *P. & K.* ***Mountain***, in Ochil Hills, 3m/5km NW of Dollar. Height 1922 feet or 586 metres. **33 E4** NN9302.
Scadabay *W.Isles Anglicised form of Scadabhagh, qv.*
Scadabhagh (Anglicised form: Scadabay.) *W.Isles* ***Settlement***, at head of Loch Scadabay, off SE coast of South Harris, 5m/8km S of Tarbert. **67 D4** NG1792.
Scaddle *High.* ***River***, in Ardgour, Lochaber district, running E down Glen Scaddle to Inverscaddle Bay on W shore of Loch Linnhe. NN0268.
Scaladale *W.Isles Anglicised form of Sgaladal, qv.*
Scalasaig *Arg. & B.* ***Settlement***, on E coast of Colonsay, and chief settlement on island. Pier and lighthouse. **28 C5** NR3994.
Scalaval *W.Isles* ***Hill***, 3m/4km S of head of Little Loch Roag, Isle of Lewis. Height 853 feet or 260 metres. **67 D2** NB1419.
Scald Law *Midloth.* ***Mountain***, summit of Pentland Hills, 3m/5km W of Penicuik. Height 1899 feet or 579 metres. **25 F3** NT1961.
Scaliscro *W.Isles Anglicised form of Scealascro, qv.*
Scalla Field *Shet.* ***Hill***, 1m/2km E of East Burrafirth, Mainland. Height 922 feet or 281 metres. **82 C2** HU3857.
Scallasaig *High.* ***Settlement***, 3m/5km E of Glenelg, Skye and Lochalsh district. **49 E3** NG8619.
Scallastle *Arg. & B.* ***River***, on Mull, flowing NE to SE end of Scallastle Bay. NM7038.
Scallastle *Arg. & B.* ***Settlement***, on N bank of Scallastle River, 2m/3km NW of Craignure. Standing stone to NE. **29 G1** NM6938.
Scallastle Bay *Arg. & B.* ***Bay***, on Sound of Mull, extending SE from Garmony Point, Mull. **29 F1** NM6939.
Scalloway *Shet.* Population: 1056. ***Small town***, with harbour on W coast of Mainland, 5m/7km W of Lerwick. Remains of early 17c castle (Historic Scotland). **82 C4** HU4039.
Scalloway Castle *Shet.* ***Castle***, in Scalloway, Mainland, overlooking East Voe of Scalloway. Castellated mansion (Historic Scotland) built by Patrick Stewart, Earl of Orkney, in 1600 and abandoned fifteen years later. Garret and roof now missing. **82 D4** HU4039.
Scalpay *High.* ***Island***, of about 9 square miles or 23 square km and roughly circular in shape, lying off E coast of Skye mainland opposite Loch Ainort. Sparsely inhabited. Rises to height of 1298 feet or 396 metres. **48 C1** NG6030.
Scalpay (Gaelic form: Eilean Scalpaigh.) *W.Isles* ***Island***, 3m/4km by 1m/2km, at entrance to East Loch Tarbert, off North Harris, separated from main island by the narrow Sound of Scalpay. Village with N and S harbours at NW end; lighthouse at SE end. **67 E4** NG2395.
Scalpsie Bay *Arg. & B.* ***Bay***, S facing bay on W coast of Bute, 3m/4km NW of Kingarth. **22 B4** NS0557.
Scamadale *Arg. & B.* ***Settlement***, on N shore of Loch Scammadale. **30 A2** NM8820.
Scamodale *High.* ***Locality***, in Lochaber district, halfway along SE shore of Loch Shiel. **38 A2** NM8373.
Scanport *High.* ***Settlement***, in Inverness district, 4m/6km SW of Inverness. **51 F1** NH6339.
Scapa *Ork.* ***Settlement***, 1km S of Kirkwall, Mainland. **78 D2** HY4408.
Scapa Bay *Ork.* ***Bay***, with sheltered anchorage on S coast of Mainland, at NE corner of Scapa Flow. Bay extends inland to within less than 2m/3km of Bay of Kirkwall to N, on which Kirkwall town is situated. Pier on E side of bay provides landing facilities. **78 D2** HY4308.
Scapa Flow *Ork.* ***Sea feature***, large natural anchorage surrounded by islands of Hoy, Mainland, Burra, South Ronaldsay and Flotta, some 10m/16km E to W and 8m/13km N to S. Eastern approaches blocked by Churchill Barrier. **78 C2** HY4000.

Scapa Flow Visitor Centre *Ork.* ***Other feature of interest***, on E coast of Hoy, in old pump station. Local history and World War II museum. **78 C3** ND3094.
Scar *Ork.* ***Settlement***, on N coast of Sanday, with Roos Wick 1km to W. **81 E2** HY6645.
Scar Hill *Aber.* ***Hill***, 2m/3km S of Tarland. Height 981 feet or 299 metres. **53 G4** NJ4801.
Scar Hill *Aber.* ***Mountain***, 4m/7km N of Tarland. Height 1722 feet or 525 metres. **53 G3** NJ4811.
Scar Nose *Moray* ***Coastal feature***, headland on N coast on NE side of Portknockie. **64 A3** NJ4968.
Scaraben *High.* ***Mountain***, on Langwell Forest, Caithness, 4m/7km NW of Berriedale. Height 2053 feet or 626 metres. **73 F2** ND0626.
Scarastavore *W.Isles Anglicised form of Sgarasta Mhòr, qv.*
Scaravay *W.Isles* ***Island***, small uninhabited island at SE end of Sound of Harris, 4m/6km off E coast of North Uist. **56 D2** NG0177.
Scarba *Arg. & B.* ***Island***, uninhabited moorland island measuring about 5 square miles or 13 square km, lying 1km N of Jura across Strait of Corryvreckan. **29 F4** NM7004.
Scardroy *High.* ***Settlement***, at W end of Loch Beannacharain, 3m/5km NW of Inverchoran. **60 B4** NH2151.
Scares *D. & G.* ***Coastal feature***, group of rocks at entrance to Luce Bay, including Big Scare and Little Scares, about 7m/11km E of Mull of Galloway. NX2533.
Scarff *Shet.* ***Settlement***, 1km SE of Hamnavoe, Mainland. **84 B4** HU2480.
Scarfskerry *High.* ***Settlement***, on N coast of Caithness district, 7m/11km W of John o' Groats. **77 E1** ND2674.
Scarfskerry Point *High.* ***Coastal feature***, headland on N coast of Caithness district to NW of Scarfskerry. ND2674.
Scarinish *Arg. & B.* ***Village***, principal village and port of Tiree, situated on S coast between Hynish and Gott Bays. Lighthouse. Landing stage on Gott Bay. **36 B2** NM0444.
Scarp *W.Isles* ***Island***, rugged island, 3m/4km by 2m/3km, lying off W coast of North Harris across narrow strait of Caolas an Scarp. Small village at SE end of island. Scarp rises to height of 1012 feet or 308 metres. **66 B2** NA9615.
Scarts Rock (Gaelic form: Rubha an Dùine.) *W.Isles* ***Coastal feature***, on E coast of North Uist, 2m/3km E of Lochportain. **56 C2** NF9771.
Scarva Taing *Ork.* ***Coastal feature***, headland 1m/2km SW of Mull Head, Mainland. **79 E2** HY5708.
Scarwell *Ork.* ***Settlement***, near W coast of Mainland, 3m/5km W of Dounby. HY2420.
Scatraig *High.* ***Settlement***, 1m/2km SW of Daviot. **51 G1** NH7137.
Scatsta *Shet.* ***Locality***, on Mainland on E side of Sullom Voe, adjacent to Scatsta Airfield. HU3972.
Scatsta Ness *Shet.* ***Coastal feature***, headland on Sullom Voe to N of Scatsta, Mainland. HU3873.
Scaur *D. & G. Alternative name for Kippford, qv.*
Scaur Farm *D. & G.* ***Settlement***, 1km E of Glenkiln Reservoir, 7m/11km W of Dumfries. **8 C3** NX8677.
Scaur Hill *S.Lan.* ***Mountain***, rising to over 380 metres, 3m/4km E of Douglas. **15 G2** NS8830.
Scaur Water *D. & G.* ***River***, rising to N of Ox Hill and flowing E, then running SE to River Nith, 2m/3km S of Thornhill. **8 C1** NX8792.
Scaw'd Law *D. & G.* ***Mountain***, in Lowther Hills on border with South Lanarkshire, 2m/3km E of Durisdeer. Height 2168 feet or 661 metres. NS9203.
Scealascro (Anglicised form: Scaliscro.) *W.Isles* ***Settlement***, on E shore of Little Loch Roag, 2m/3km N of head of loch. **68 C5** NB1327.
Schaw *E.Ayr.* ***Settlement***, 1m/2km N of Drongan. **14 C3** NS4420.
Schiehallion *P. & K.* ***Mountain***, conical mountain of quartzite, 4m/7km SE of Kinloch Rannoch. Munro: height 3552 feet or 1083 metres. **40 C4** NN7154.
Sciberscross *High.* ***Settlement***, to N of River Brora, 4m/7km W of Gordonbush, Sutherland district. **72 C3** NC7710.
Scolpaig *W.Isles* ***Settlement***, on North Uist, 1km S of Griminis Point. **45 F2** NF7275.
Scolty *Aber.* ***Hill***, 1m/2km SW of Banchory. Height 981 feet or 299 metres. **54 B5** NO6793.
Scone Palace *P. & K.* ***Historic house***, castellated early 19c mansion on site of medieval abbey and palace, 2m/3km N of Perth across River Tay. Site has historical associations dating from 8c. Locality of Old Scone to E; village of New Scone 2m/3km to E, beyond Old Scone. Scone Airfield 2m/3km NE of New Scone. **33 G2** NO1126.
Sconser *High.* ***Settlement***, on Skye, on S side of Loch Sligachan. **48 B1** NG5131.
Scoonie *Fife* ***Suburb***, NW district of Leven. NO3801.
Scoor *Arg. & B.* ***Settlement***, near S coast of Ross of Mull, 3m/4km SE of Bunessan. **28 D3** NM4119.
Scootmore Forest *Moray* ***Forest/woodland***, afforested area astride Allt a' Gheallaidh immediately above its confluence with River Spey 11m/17km NE of Grantown-on-Spey. **53 D1** NJ1638.
Scoraig *High.* ***Settlement***, on NE side of Little Loch Broom, 2m/3km SE of Cailleach Head, on W coast of Ross and Cromarty district. **70 C5** NH0096.
Score Bay (Also known as Lùb Score.) *High.* ***Bay***, between Rubha Hunish and Ru Bornaskitaig, N coast of Skye. **57 G2** NG3973.
Score Head *Shet.* ***Coastal feature***, headland at E end of Outer Score, off N end of Bressay. **83 E3** HU5145.
Scotasay *W.Isles Anglicised form of Sgeotasaigh, qv.*
Scotland's Lighthouse Museum *Aber.* ***Other feature of interest***, museum at Kinnaird Head, Fraserburgh, commemorating Scottish lighthouses. Housed in a former castle which became a lighthouse in 1787. **65 E3** NJ9967.
Scotlandwell *P. & K.* ***Village***, 4m/6km W of Leslie. **33 G4** NO1801.
Scotnish *Arg. & B.* ***Settlement***, 4m/6km SW of Crinan. **21 F1** NR7588.
Scotsburn *High.* ***Locality***, 4m/6km N of Invergordon. **61 G2** NH7275.
Scotsburn *Moray* ***Settlement***, 3m/5km E of Forres. NJ0860.
Scotscalder *High.* ***Locality***, with railway station, in Caithness district, 8m/13km S of Thurso. **76 C3** ND0956.
Scotstarvit Tower *Fife* ***Historic house***, 15c tower house (Historic Scotland), 1km SW of Hill of Tarvit Mansion House and 1km NW of Gauldry. Remodelled in mid 16c and home of Sir John Scot, author of Scot of Scotstarvit's Staggering State of the Scots Statesmen. **34 B3** NO3711.
Scotston *Aber.* ***Hamlet***, 2m/3km NE of Laurencekirk. **43 F2** NO7373.
Scotston *P. & K.* ***Settlement***, in Glen Cochill, 5m/8km SE of Aberfeldy. **41 E5** NN9042.
Scotstoun *Glas.* ***Suburb***, on N bank of River Clyde, 3m/5km NW of Glasgow city centre. NS5368.
Scotstounhill *Glas.* ***Suburb***, to N of Scotstoun, 3m/5km NW of Glasgow city centre. NS5367.
Scotstown *High.* ***Village***, in Sunart, Lochaber district, 1m/2km N of Strontian. **38 A3** NM8263.
Scotstown Head *Aber.* ***Coastal feature***, headland at S end of Rattray Bay, 4m/6km N of Peterhead. **65 G4** NK1151.
Scottarie Burn *High.* ***River***, flowing NE into River Brora at NW end of Loch Brora, Sutherland district. **72 C4** NC8209.
Scottish Agricultural Museum *Edin.* ***Other feature of interest***, at Ingliston, 1m/2km W of Gogar, with exhibitions on history of Scottish agriculture. **25 F2** NT1472.
Scottish Deer Centre *Fife* ***Other feature of interest***, 3m/5km W of Cupar, 5m/8km SW of St. Andrews, with guided tours and falconry displays. **34 B3** NO3212.
Scottish Fisheries Museum *Fife* ***Other feature of interest***, at Anstruther, displaying boats and a fisherman's cottage. **35 D4** NO5603.
Scottish Marine Biological Station *N.Ayr. See Keppel Pier.*
Scottish Maritime Museum *N.Ayr.* ***Other feature of interest***, in Irvine town centre. Exhibits include vessels in harbour and early 20c shipworker's house. **14 B2** NS3138.
Scottish National Portrait Gallery *Edin.* ***Other feature of interest***, part of Royal Museum of Scotland in Queen Street, Edinburgh. Exhibits history of Scotland from 16c to present, with paintings of famous people involved in major events, including Mary, Queen of Scots and Robert Burns. Also contains National Collection of Photography. **25 G2** NT2574.
Scottish Tartans Museum *P. & K.* ***Other feature of interest***, in Comrie. A large collection concerned with material relating to Highland dress, tartans and their manufacture. NN7822.
Scott's View *Sc.Bord.* ***Viewpoint***, looking W over River Tweed and towards Melrose, 2m/3km NE of Newton St. Boswells. **17 G2** NT5934.
Scoughall *E.Loth.* ***Hamlet***, on rocky coast, 4m/7km SE of North Berwick. NT6183.
Scour Ouran *High. Anglicised form of Sgurr Fhuaran, qv.*
Scoured Rig *Sc.Bord.* ***Mountain***, 4m/7km NE of Lauder. Height 1191 feet or 363 metres. **26 C4** NT5851.
Scourie *High.* ***Village***, on W coast of Sutherland district, at head of Scourie Bay, 5m/8km W of Laxford Bridge. **74 A4** NC1544.
Scourie Bay *High.* ***Bay***, 5m/8km W of Laxford Bridge. Scourie village on W coast of Sutherland district at head. **74 A4** NC1544.
Scourie More *High.* ***Settlement***, 1km W of Scourie, on W coast of Sutherland district. **74 A4** NC1444.
Scousburgh *Shet.* ***Village***, near W coast of Mainland, 6m/10km N of Sumburgh Head. **83 F4** HU3717.
Scrabster *High.* ***Village***, and small port on W side of Thurso Bay, 2m/3km NW of Thurso, Caithness district. **76 C1** ND1070.
Screel Hill *D. & G.* ***Mountain***, 4m/7km S of Castle Douglas. Height 1125 feet or 343 metres. **8 B5** NX7755.
Scrinadle *Arg. & B.* ***Mountain***, on Jura, 7m/11km N of Craighouse. Height 1660 feet or 506 metres. **20 C2** NR5077.
Scrot Mòr *W.Isles* ***Island***, islet at S end of Heisker Islands group, to W of North Uist. **45 E3** NF6360.
Scuir of Eigg *High. Alternative name for An Sgurr, qv.*
Scuir Vullin *High. Anglicised form of Sgurr a' Mhuilinn, qv.*
Sculptor's Cave *Moray* ***Cave***, on N coast, 3m/5km W of Lossiemouth. NJ1770.
Scurdie Ness *Angus* ***Coastal feature***, headland with lighthouse on S side of mouth of River South Esk, 1m/2km E of Montrose. **43 F4** NO7356.
Scurrival Point *W.Isles* ***Coastal feature***, headland at N extremity of Barra. **44 B3** NF6909.
Scuthvie Bay *Ork.* ***Bay***, large wide bay on NE coast of Sanday, to NW of Start Point. **81 F2** HY7644.
Sea of the Hebrides ***Sea feature***, stretch of sea between Outer Hebrides and Inner Hebrides groups of islands. **36 A1** NM1287.
Seabank *Arg. & B.* ***Settlement***, 1m/2km N of Benderloch. **38 B5** NM9041.
Seafar *N.Lan.* ***Suburb***, central area of Cumbernauld. NS7574.
Seafield *Arg. & B.* ***Settlement***, at head of Loch Sween, 5m/8km W of Lochgilphead. **21 F1** NR7787.
Seafield *S.Ayr.* ***Suburb***, S district of Ayr. **14 B3** NS3320.
Seafield *W.Loth.* ***Hamlet***, 1m/2km E of Blackburn. **25 E3** NT0066.
Seaforth Head *W.Isles Anglicised form of Ceann Loch Shiphoirt, qv.*
Seaforth Island *W.Isles* ***Island***, uninhabited island, over 1m/2km by over 1km, rising sheer out of Loch Seaforth, Isle of Lewis, to a height of 712 feet or 217 metres. **67 E2** NB2010.
Seamill *N.Ayr.* ***Town***, summer resort on Firth of Clyde, adjoining to S of West Kilbride. **22 D5** NS2047.
Seana Bhraigh *High.* ***Mountain***, in Sutherland district, 4m/6km S of head of Loch an Daimh. Munro: height 3041 feet or 927 metres. **60 B1** NH2887.
Seana Mheallan *High.* ***Mountain***, in Ross and Cromarty district, 2m/3km E of Torridon. Height 1430 feet or 436 metres. **59 F4** NG9255.
Seater *High.* ***Locality***, near N coast of Caithness district, 3m/5km W of Duncansby Head. ND3572.
Seathope Law *Sc.Bord.* ***Mountain***, 4m/7km NE of Innerleithen. Height 1778 feet or 542 metres. **26 A5** NT3740.
Seatown *Aber.* ***Settlement***, near E coast, W of Rattray Head. **65 G4** NK1057.
Seatown *Moray* ***Locality***, harbour district of Lossiemouth. NJ2370.
Seatown *Moray* ***Settlement***, on coast, adjoining to W of Cullen. **64 A3** NJ5067.
Seatown *Moray* ***Suburb***, to E of Buckie town centre, on coast between Buckpool and Gordonsburgh. **63 G3** NJ4266.
Second Coast *High.* ***Settlement***, on S shore of Gruinard Bay, 6m/10km SE of Greenstone Point. **70 B5** NG9290.
Seenes Law *Sc.Bord.* ***Mountain***, in Lammermuir Hills, 2m/3km SE of Hopes Reservoir. Height 1683 feet or 513 metres. **26 C3** NT5560.
Seil *Arg. & B.* ***Island***, on E side of Firth of Lorn connected with mainland of Argyll by Clachan Bridge. Island is 5m/7km long N to S and 2m/3km wide. **29 G3** NM7617.
Seil Sound *Arg. & B.* ***Sea feature***, strait between Seil and mainland. **29 G3** NM7617.
Seilebost *W.Isles* ***Locality***, on South Harris, 1m/2km NE of Buirgh. **66 C4** NG0696.
Seisiadar (Anglicised form: Sheshader.) *W.Isles* ***Village***, on Eye Peninsula, Isle of Lewis, 3m/4km SW of Tiumpan Head. **69 G4** NB5534.
Selkirk *Sc.Bord.* Population: 5922. ***Small town***, royal burgh on hill above Ettrick Water, 9m/15km N of Hawick. Town has associations with Sir Walter Scott, and with Mungo Park, African explorer. Centre for touring Borders. **17 F3** NT4728.
Selkirk Glass *Sc.Bord.* ***Other feature of interest***, glass-blowing and crafts, 1km N of Selkirk. **17 F2** NT4630.
Sellafirth *Shet.* ***Settlement***, on Yell, 3m/5km NW of Burra Ness. **85 E3** HU5198.
Semblister *Shet.* ***Settlement***, overlooking The Firth, 1m/2km N of Garderhouse, Mainland. **82 C2** HU3350.
Senwick Hotel *D. & G.* ***Other building***, 3m/5km S of Kirkcudbright. **3 G2** NX6446.
Serpent's Mound *Arg. & B.* ***Historic/prehistoric site***, heap of large stones, supposedly a relic of pagan worship, about 300 feet or 90 metres long, near foot of Loch Nell in Argyll, 2m/4km SE of Oban. NM8726.
Seton Collegiate Church *E.Loth.* ***Ecclesiastical building***, late 15c church (Historic Scotland) with vaulted chancel and apse, 2m/3km E of Prestonpans. **26 B2** NT4175.
Seton Mains *E.Loth.* ***Hamlet***, 3m/4km E of Prestonpans. NT4275.
Setter *Shet.* ***Settlement***, at head of Weisdale, Mainland. **82 C2** HU3954.
Setter *Shet.* ***Settlement***, on E coast of Bressay, overlooking Voe of Cullingsburgh. **83 E3** HU5141.
Settiscarth *Ork.* ***Settlement***, on Mainland, 3m/5km N of Finstown and 2m/3km W of Bay of Isbister. **80 B5** HY3618.

Seumas Cleite *W.Isles* ***Island***, islet at entrance to Loch Leurbost, E coast of Isle of Lewis. NB4123.
Sgairneach Mhòr *P. & K.* ***Mountain***, 3m/5km W of Dalnaspidal Lodge. Munro: height 3250 feet or 991 metres. **40 A2** NN5973.
Sgaith Chùil *Stir.* ***Mountain***, on N side of Glen Dochart, 6m/10km W of Killin. Munro: height 3014 feet or 919 metres. **31 G1** NN4631.
Sgaladal (Anglicised form: Scaladale.) *W.Isles* ***River***, on North Harris, flowing E into Loch Seaforth at Ardvourlie Castle. NB1910.
Sgaorishal *High.* ***Hill***, 3m/4km SW of northernmost point of Rum. Height 912 feet or 278 metres. **47 G4** NG3501.
Sgaoth Aird *W.Isles* ***Mountain***, 3m/4km N of Tarbert, North Harris. Height 1834 feet or 559 metres. **67 D3** NB1604.
Sgaraman nam Fiadh *High.* ***Mountain***, in Monadhliath range in Inverness district 8m/12km NW of Newtonmore. Height 2814 feet or 858 metres. **51 F4** NH6106.
Sgarasta Mhòr (Anglicised form: Scarastavore.) *W.Isles* ***Locality***, on W coast of South Harris, 4m/6km N of Leverburgh. **66 C4** NG0092.
Sgarbh Breac *Arg. & B.* ***Mountain***, on NE corner of Islay, 6m/9km N of Port Askaig. Height 1194 feet or 364 metres. **20 C2** NR4076.
Sgeir a' Bhuic *High.* ***Island***, rock island at mouth of Loch Eriboll, N coast of Sutherland district, 2m/3km SE of Rispond. NC4763.
Sgeir a' Chaisteil *Arg. & B.* ***Island***, one of the Treshnish Isles group, lying immediately N of Lunga. **36 B5** NM2742.
Sgeir an Eirionnaich *Arg. & B.* ***Island***, one of the Treshnish Isles group, lying 1km NE of Lunga and 1km W of Fladda. NM2843.
Sgeir an Fheòir *Arg. & B.* ***Island***, small island of the Treshnish Isles group, lying between Fladda and Lunga. NM2843.
Sgeir Bharrach *Arg. & B.* ***Coastal feature***, headland on W side of Vaul Bay, on N coast of Tiree. **36 B2** NM0449.
Sgeir Eirin *High.* ***Island***, rock island off NE coast of Skye, 4m/6km SE of Rubha na h-Aiseig. **58 A2** NG4872.
Sgeir Fhada *High.* ***Island***, islet in Loch Carron, 1m/2km E of Lochcarron. **49 E1** NG9139.
Sgeir Ghobhlach *Arg. & B.* ***Island***, one of Torran Rocks group, 4m/6km SW of Mull. **28 B3** NM2712.
Sgeir Mhòr a' Bhrein-phuirt *Arg. & B.* ***Coastal feature***, rock off W coast of Jura, 1km N of Rubh' an t-Sàilein. **20 C1** NR5084.
Sgeir Moil Duinn *W.Isles* ***Coastal feature***, rock on NW coast of Scarp, 4m/6km NW of Huisinis, North Harris. **66 B2** NA9516.
Sgeir na Capaill *High.* ***Island***, one of Ascrib Islands group in Loch Snizort, 5m/8km E of Vaternish Point, Skye. NG3064.
Sgeir na h-Eigheach *W.Isles* ***Coastal feature***, on E side of entrance to Loch Claidh, Isle of Lewis, 8m/13km E of Tarbert. **67 E3** NB2800.
Sgeir na h-Iolaire *Arg. & B.* ***Island***, small island of the Treshnish Isles group, to W of Fladda. NM2843.
Sgeir nan Gall *High.* ***Island***, small island just off N coast of Oldany Island. **70 C1** NC0835.
Sgeir nan Gillean *High.* ***Island***, rock near W shore of Loch Linnhe off Rubha na h-Earba, 3m/5km NE of Rubha na h-Airde Uinnsinn, Lochaber district. NM9054.
Sgeir Shuas *High.* ***Coastal feature***, rock lying off N end of Rona. NG6261.
Sgeir Toman *W.Isles* ***Island***, one of Flannan Isles group, lying 1m/2km S of main island, Eilean Mòr. NA7245.
Sgeirean nan Torran *High.* ***Island***, group of island rocks near W shore of Loch Linnhe, nearly 2m/3km SW of Inversanda Bay, Lochaber district. NM9356.
Sgeotasaigh (Anglicised form: Scotasay.) *W.Isles* ***Island***, off North Harris in East Loch Tarbert, 3m/4km SE of Tarbert. **67 D4** NG1897.
Sgianait *W.Isles* ***Mountain***, near W coast of North Harris, 3m/4km NE of Huisinis. Height 1394 feet or 425 metres. **66 C2** NB0313.
Sgiath Bhuidhe ***Mountain***, on border of Stirling and Perth & Kinross, 8m/12km NW of Killin. Height 2526 feet or 770 metres. **31 G1** NN4638.
Sgiogarstaigh (Anglicised form: Skigersta.) *W.Isles* ***Village***, near N end of Isle of Lewis, 1m/2km S of Port Nis. Port Skigersta is small bay to NE. **69 G1** NB5461.
Sgitheach (Anglicised form: Skiack.) *High.* ***River***, in Ross and Cromarty district, flowing E into Cromarty Firth just S of Evanton. **61 E3** NH6165.
Sgodachail *High.* ***Settlement***, in Strathcarron, 7m/11km W of Bonar Bridge. **71 G5** NH4892.
Sgor an Lochain Uaine *Aber.* ***Mountain***, to NW of Cairn Toul summit within Cairngorms National Nature Reserve, 13m/21km NW of Braemar. Munro: height 4126 feet or 1258 metres. NN9597.
Sgòr Gaibhre ***Mountain***, on border of Highland and Perth & Kinross, 4m/7km SW of Ben Alder. Munro: height 3123 feet or 952 metres. **39 G3** NN4467.
Sgor Gaoith *High.* ***Mountain***, at W end of Cairngorm Mountains in Badenoch and Strathspey district, 6m/10km SE of Kincraig. Munro: height 3667 feet or 1118 metres. **52 B5** NN9098.
Sgòr Gaoithe *High.* ***Mountain***, at S end of Hills of Cromdale, and 3m/4km W of Bridge of Brown. Height 2060 feet or 628 metres. **52 C2** NJ0721.
Sgòr Mòr *Aber.* ***Mountain***, 5m/8km NW of Inverey, in Grampian Mountains. Height 2667 feet or 813 metres. **52 C5** NO0091.
Sgòr Mòr *Aber.* ***Mountain***, 6m/10km S of Braemar. Height 2909 feet or 887 metres. **41 G1** NO1182.
Sgor na Diollaid *High.* ***Mountain***, in Inverness district on S side of Glen Strathfarrar, 5m/7km NW of Cannich. Height 2683 feet or 818 metres. **50 B1** NH2836.
Sgor na h-Ulaidh *High.* ***Mountain***, in Lochaber district near border with Argyll & Bute, 5m/7km S of foot of Glen Coe. Munro: height 3260 feet or 994 metres. **38 D4** NN1151.
Sgor Reidh *High.* ***Coastal feature***, area of steep slopes, screes and rock outcrops near SW coast of Rum. **47 G5** NM3198.
Sgòrach Breac *High.* ***Hill***, on Sleat peninsula, 6m/10km NE of Tokavaig. Height 981 feet or 299 metres. **48 C3** NG6513.
Sgorach Mòr *Arg. & B.* ***Mountain***, with rounded summit, rising above E shore of Loch Tarsan. Height 1971 feet or 601 metres. **22 C1** NS0984.
Sgòran Dubh Mòr *High.* ***Mountain***, at W end of Cairngorm Mountains in Badenoch and Strathspey district, 6m/9km SE of Kincraig. Height 3644 feet or 1111 metres. **52 B4** NH9000.
Sgorr a' Choise *High.* ***Mountain***, in Lochaber district, 2m/3km S of Ballachulish. Height 2175 feet or 663 metres. **38 C4** NN0854.
Sgorr an Iubhair *High.* ***Mountain***, one of The Mamores, 2m/4km NW of Kinlochmore. Height 3283 feet or 1001 metres. **39 D3** NN1665.
Sgorr Bhogachain *Arg. & B.* ***Hill***, rocky hilltop on Islay, 4m/7km NE of Port Ellen. Height 918 feet or 280 metres. **20 B4** NR3951.
Sgorr Choinnich *P. & K.* ***Mountain***, peak 2m/4km E of Loch Ossian. Height 3047 feet or 929 metres. NN4468.
Sgorr Craobh a' Chaorainn *High.* ***Mountain***, 3m/5km S of Glenfinnan, Lochaber district. Height 2542 feet or 775 metres. **38 A2** NM8975.
Sgorr Dhearg *High.* ***Mountain***, peak of Beinn a' Bheithir in Lochaber district, 2m/4km S of Ballachulish. Munro: height 3359 feet or 1024 metres. **38 C4** NN0555.
Sgorr Dhonuill *High.* ***Mountain***, central peak of Beinn a' Bheithir, 3m/5km SW of Ballachulish. Munro: height 3283 feet or 1001 metres. **38 C4** NN0455.
Sgorr na Ciche *High.* *Alternative name for Pap of Glencoe, qv.*
Sgorr nam Faoileann *Arg. & B.* ***Mountain***, on E coast of Islay, 6m/9km S of Port Askaig. Height 1407 feet or 429 metres. **20 C3** NR4260.
Sgorr nam Fiannaidh *High.* ***Mountain***, summit of Aonach Eagach in Lochaber district, at W end of ridge. Munro: height 3172 feet or 967 metres. **38 D4** NN1458.
Sgorr Ruadh *High.* ***Mountain***, in Ross and Cromarty district 3m/5km NW of Achnashellach Lodge. Munro: height 3149 feet or 960 metres. **59 F4** NG9550.
Sgreadan Hill *Arg. & B.* ***Mountain***, on Kintyre, 6m/9km N of Campbeltown. Height 1302 feet or 397 metres. **12 C3** NR7429.
Sgribhis-bheinn *High.* ***Mountain***, 4m/7km SE of Cape Wrath, Sutherland district. Height 1217 feet or 371 metres. **74 C1** NC3171.
Sguide an Leanna *Arg. & B.* ***Sea feature***, narrow inlet on SW coast of Colonsay, 4m/6km SW of Scalasaig. NR3391.
Sgùman Coinntich *High.* ***Mountain***, in Killilan Forest, Skye and Lochalsh district. Height 2883 feet or 879 metres. **49 F1** NG9730.
Sgurr a' Bhac *High.* ***Mountain***, peak on border of Lochaber and Skye and Lochalsh districts 3m/5km N of Kinloch Hourn and 1m/2km E of Sgurr na Sgine. Height 2801 feet or 854 metres. NG9511.
Sgurr a' Bhealaich Dheirg *High.* ***Mountain***, on Kintail Forest (National Trust for Scotland) on border of Skye and Lochalsh and Inverness districts, 3m/4km NW of head of Loch Cluanie. Munro: height 3405 feet or 1038 metres. **49 G3** NH0314.
Sgurr a' Bhuic *High.* ***Mountain***, 3m/4km SW of Rhuba na h-Airde Uinnsinn, Lochaber district. Height 1866 feet or 569 metres. **38 A5** NM8350.
Sgurr a' Chaorachain *High.* ***Inland physical feature***, mountain ridge in Ross and Cromarty district, 3m/5km W of head of Loch Kishorn, rising to 776 metres. Radio mast. **59 D5** NG7842.
Sgurr a' Chaorachain *High.* ***Mountain***, peak on West Monar Forest, Ross and Cromarty district. Munro: height 3454 feet or 1053 metres. **59 G5** NH0844.
Sgurr a' Chaorainn *High.* ***Mountain***, 6m/9km NE of Strontian, Lochaber district. Height 2496 feet or 761 metres. NM8966.
Sgurr a' Chlaidheimh *High.* ***Mountain***, 3m/4km S of Kinloch Hourn, Lochaber district. Height 2758 feet or 841 metres. **49 F4** NG9403.
Sgurr a' Choinnich *Arg. & B.* ***Mountain***, above E shore of Loch Eck and 3m/5km SE of Glenbranter. Height 2168 feet or 661 metres. **31 D5** NS1595.
Sgurr a' Choire-bheithe *High.* ***Mountain***, peak at W end of Druim Chòsaidh, in Lochaber district. Height 2995 feet or 913 metres. **49 E4** NG8901.
Sgurr a' Choire Ghlais *High.* ***Mountain***, peak on border of Inverness and Ross and Cromarty districts, 4m/7km NE of dam of Loch Monar. Munro: height 3552 feet or 1083 metres. **60 B5** NH2543.
Sgurr a' Gharaidh *High.* ***Mountain***, 3m/5km N of Lochcarron, Ross and Cromarty district. Height 2394 feet or 730 metres. **59 E5** NG8844.
Sgurr a' Gharg Gharaidh *High.* ***Mountain***, mass in Glenshiel Forest, 3m/4km SW of Shiel Bridge. Height 2234 feet or 681 metres. **49 F3** NG9115.
Sgurr a' Ghlas Leathaid *High.* ***Mountain***, on Strathconon Forest, Ross and Cromarty district. Height 2768 feet or 844 metres. **60 B4** NH2456.
Sgurr a' Ghreadaidh *High.* ***Mountain***, peak of Cuillin Hills on Skye, to N of Sgurr Alasdair. Munro: height 3191 feet or 973 metres. **48 A2** NG4423.
Sgurr a' Mhadaidh *High.* ***Mountain***, in Cuillin Hills, Skye, 2m/3km NW of head of Loch Coruisk. Munro: height 3011 feet or 918 metres. **48 A2** NG4523.
Sgurr a' Mhaim *High.* ***Mountain***, in Lochaber district, on Mamore Forest S of Glen Nevis. Munro: height 3601 feet or 1098 metres. **39 D3** NN1666.
Sgurr a' Mhaoraich *High.* ***Mountain***, peak in Lochaber district 2m/3km E of Kinloch Hourn. Munro: height 3369 feet or 1027 metres. **49 F4** NG9806.
Sgurr a' Mhuidhe *High.* ***Mountain***, rising to over 480 metres, 1km NE of head of Loch Eilt, Lochaber district. **38 A1** NM8582.
Sgurr a' Mhuilinn (Anglicised form: Scuir Vuillin.) *High.* ***Mountain***, on Strathconon Forest, Ross and Cromarty district. Height 2883 feet or 879 metres. **60 B4** NH2655.
Sgurr a' Phollain *High.* ***Mountain***, on border of Ross and Cromarty and Inverness districts, 4m/6km NW of Erchless Castle. Height 2801 feet or 854 metres. **60 C5** NH3644.
Sgurr Alasdair *High.* ***Mountain***, on Skye, highest peak of the Cuillin Hills, due E of mountain rescue post at foot of Glen Brittle. Munro: height 3257 feet or 993 metres. **48 A2** NG4520.
Sgurr an Airgid *High.* ***Mountain***, in Skye and Lochalsh district, 1m/2km N of head of Loch Duich. Height 2758 feet or 841 metres. **49 F2** NG9422.
Sgurr an Doire Leathain *High.* ***Mountain***, on border of Inverness and Skye and Lochalsh districts, on S side of Glen Shiel. Munro: height 3313 feet or 1010 metres. **49 G4** NH0109.
Sgurr an Eilein Ghiubhais *High.* ***Mountain***, 3m/5km E of Mallaig. Height 1712 feet or 522 metres. **48 D5** NM7297.
Sgurr an Fhuarail *High.* ***Mountain***, on border of Inverness and Skye and Lochalsh districts, 2m/3km NW of head of Loch Cluanie. Height 3241 feet or 988 metres. NH0513.
Sgurr an Fhuarain *High.* ***Mountain***, in Lochaber district between Loch Quoich and head of Glen Kingie. Height 2962 feet or 903 metres. **49 F5** NM9897.
Sgurr an Gharaidh *High.* ***Mountain***, peak in Ross and Cromarty district 3m/5km N of Lochcarron. Height 2394 feet or 730 metres. NG8844.
Sgurr an Iubhair *High.* ***Mountain***, 7m/11km N of Sallachan Point, Lochaber district, 6m/10km W of Fort William. Height 2368 feet or 722 metres. **38 B2** NN0072.
Sgurr an Lochain *High.* ***Mountain***, peak on border of Lochaber and Skye and Lochalsh districts, 4m/7km N of Loch Quoich at foot of Glen Quoich. Munro: height 3293 feet or 1004 metres. **49 G3** NH0010.
Sgurr an Mhadaidh *High.* ***Mountain***, on Skye, peak of the Cuillin Hills. Height 3014 feet or 919 metres. NG4523.
Sgurr an Tarmachain *High.* ***Mountain***, 3m/5km NE of Pollock, Lochaber district. Height 2480 feet or 756 metres. **38 A2** NM8470.
Sgurr an Ursainn *High.* ***Mountain***, 2m/3km NE of head of Loch Beoraid, Lochaber district. Height 2680 feet or 817 metres. **38 A1** NM8887.
Sgurr an Utha *High.* ***Mountain***, peak in Lochaber district 2m/4km NW of Glenfinnan. Height 2611 feet or 796 metres. **38 A1** NM8883.
Sgurr Bàn *High.* ***Mountain***, one of the peaks of Beinn Eighe, Ross and Cromarty district. Height 3188 feet or 972 metres. NG9759.
Sgurr Ban *High.* ***Mountain***, in W part of Ross and Cromarty district, 3m/4km NE of Lochan Fada. Munro: height 3244 feet or 989 metres. **59 G2** NH0574.
Sgurr Beag *High.* ***Mountain***, peak on border of Lochaber and Skye and Lochalsh districts, 4m/7km NE of Kinloch Hourn. Height 2939 feet or 896 metres. NG9910.
Sgurr Beag *High.* ***Mountain***, peak in Lochaber district 2m/3km SE of head of Loch Quoich and 1km SW of Sgurr Mòr. Height 2919 feet or 890 metres. NM9597.

Sgurr Bhuidhe *High.* ***Mountain***, 3m/5km SE of Mallaig. Height 1443 feet or 440 metres. **48 D5** NM7294.
Sgurr Breac *High.* ***Hill***, 1m/2km N of Loch a' Ghlinne. Height 817 feet or 249 metres. **48 B4** NG5907.
Sgurr Breac *High.* ***Mountain***, in Ross and Cromarty district, 10m/15km NE of Kinlochewe. Munro: height 3280 feet or 1000 metres. **60 A2** NH1571.
Sgurr Breac *High.* ***Mountain***, in North Morar, Lochaber district, 3m/5km E of Tarbet. Height 2388 feet or 728 metres. **49 E5** NM8492.
Sgurr Chòinich *High.* ***Mountain***, in Lochaber district, 5m/8km NW of foot of Loch Arkaig. Height 2450 feet or 747 metres. **50 A5** NN1295.
Sgurr Choinnich *High.* ***Mountain***, peak on West Monar Forest, Ross and Cromarty district. Munro: height 3277 feet or 999 metres. **59 G5** NH0744.
Sgurr Chòinnich Mòr *High.* ***Mountain***, in Lochaber district 4m/6km E of Ben Nevis. Munro: height 3592 feet or 1095 metres. **39 E2** NN2271.
Sgurr Coire Choinnichean *High.* ***Mountain***, in Knoydart, Lochaber district, 2m/3km NE of Inverie. Height 2611 feet or 796 metres. **49 D4** NG7901.
Sgurr Coire nan Eun *High.* ***Mountain***, in Ross and Cromarty district 5m/8km N of lower end of Loch Monar. Height 2588 feet or 789 metres. **60 A5** NH1946.
Sgurr Coire nan Gobhar *High.* ***Mountain***, 3m/4km SE of Inverie, Lochaber district. Height 2424 feet or 739 metres. **49 E5** NM7997.
Sgurr Dearg *Arg. & B.* ***Mountain***, 4m/6km SW of Craignure, Mull. Height 2430 feet or 741 metres. **29 F1** NM6633.
Sgurr Dearg *High.* ***Mountain***, on Skye, peak of the Cuillin Hills. Munro: height 3234 feet or 986 metres. **48 A2** NG4421.
Sgurr Dhomhnuill *High.* ***Mountain***, in Ardgour, Lochaber district, 6m/10km NE of Strontian. Height 2913 feet or 888 metres. **38 A3** NM8867.
Sgurr Dhomhuill Mòr *High.* ***Mountain***, 3m/5km NE of Ardmolich, Lochaber district. Height 2339 feet or 713 metres. **37 G2** NM7475.
Sgurr Dubh *High.* ***Mountain***, peak in Coulin Forest, Ross and Cromarty district, 5m/8km SW of Kinlochewe. Height 2565 feet or 782 metres. **59 F4** NG9755.
Sgurr Dubh Mòr *High.* ***Mountain***, peak of Cuillin Hills on Skye. Munro: height 3096 feet or 944 metres. **48 A2** NG4520.
Sgurr Eilde Mòr *High.* ***Mountain***, on Mamore Forest in Lochaber district, 4m/6km NE of Kinlochleven. Munro: height 3306 feet or 1008 metres. **39 E3** NN2365.
Sgurr Eireagoraidh *High.* ***Mountain***, 3m/4km E of Mallaig. Height 1797 feet or 548 metres. NM7196.
Sgurr Fhuar-thuill *High.* ***Mountain***, on border of Inverness and Ross and Cromarty districts, 4m/6km NE of dam of Loch Monar. Munro: height 3441 feet or 1049 metres. **60 B5** NH2343.
Sgurr Fhuaran (Anglicised form: Scour Ouran.) *High.* ***Mountain***, peak on Kintail Forest (National Trust for Scotland) in Skye and Lochalsh district, 3m/5km SE of Shiel Bridge. One of the Five Sisters. Munro: height 3503 feet or 1068 metres. **49 F3** NG9716.
Sgurr Finnisg-aig *High.* ***Mountain***, in Leanachan Forest, 4m/6km SW of Spean Bridge. Height 2175 feet or 663 metres. **39 D2** NN1876.
Sgurr Fiona *High.* ***Mountain***, one of the peaks of An Teallach, in Ross and Cromarty district. Munro: height 3474 feet or 1059 metres. **59 G1** NH0683.
Sgurr Ghiubhsachain *High.* ***Mountain***, in Lochaber district, 4m/6km S of Glenfinnan. Height 2785 feet or 849 metres. **38 A2** NM8775.
Sgurr Leac nan Each *High.* ***Mountain***, in Skye and Lochalsh district, 4m/6km S of Shiel Bridge and 1m/2km W of The Saddle. Height 3014 feet or 919 metres. NG9113.
Sgurr Marcasaidh *High.* ***Mountain***, in Ross and Cromarty district, 6m/10km NW of Contin. Height 1902 feet or 580 metres. **60 C3** NH3559.
Sgurr Mhic Bharraich *High.* ***Mountain***, on border of Lochaber and Skye and Lochalsh districts, 2m/3km SW of Shiel Bridge. Height 2562 feet or 781 metres. **49 F3** NG9117.
Sgurr Mhic Choinnich *High.* ***Mountain***, in Cuillin Hills, Skye, 1m/2km W of head of Loch Coruisk. Munro: height 3109 feet or 948 metres. **48 A2** NG4521.
Sgurr Mhòr *High.* ***Mountain***, a peak of Beinn Alligin. Munro: height 3231 feet or 985 metres. **59 E3** NG8661.
Sgurr Mhurlagain *High.* ***Mountain***, in Lochaber district, 3m/4km NE of head of Loch Arkaig. Height 2886 feet or 880 metres. **49 G5** NN0194.
Sgurr Mòr *High.* ***Mountain***, in Ross and Cromarty district 4m/6km NE of head of Loch Fannich. Munro: height 3641 feet or 1110 metres. **60 B2** NH2071.
Sgurr Mòr *High.* ***Mountain***, peak in Lochaber district between Loch Quoich and head of Glen Kingie. Munro: height 3290 feet or 1003 metres. **49 F5** NM9698.
Sgurr na Ba Glaise *High.* ***Mountain***, rising to over 870 metres, in Moidart, Lochaber district, 3m/5km S of Lochailort. NM7777.
Sgurr na Banachdich *High.* ***Mountain***, peak of Cuillin Hills on Skye. Munro: height 3165 feet or 965 metres. **48 A2** NG4422.
Sgurr na Cairbe *High.* ***Mountain***, in Inverness district, 2m/3km W of W end of Orrin Reservoir. Height 2394 feet or 730 metres. **60 B5** NH3046.
Sgurr na Carnach *High.* ***Mountain***, peak on Kintail Forest (National Trust for Scotland) in Skye and Lochalsh district, 3m/5km SE of Shiel Bridge. One of the Five Sisters. Munro: height 3287 feet or 1002 metres. NG9715.
Sgurr na Ciche *High.* ***Mountain***, in Lochaber district 3m/4km SW of head of Loch Quoich. Munro: height 3411 feet or 1040 metres. **49 F5** NM9096.
Sgurr na Ciste Duibhe *High.* ***Mountain***, peak on Kintail Forest (National Trust for Scotland) in Skye and Lochalsh district, 4m/6km SE of Shiel Bridge. One of the Five Sisters. Munro: height 3369 feet or 1027 metres. **49 F3** NG9814.
Sgurr na Coinnich *High.* ***Mountain***, 3m/4km S of Kyleakin near E end of Skye. Height 2424 feet or 739 metres. **49 D2** NG7622.
Sgurr na Fearstaig *High.* ***Mountain***, peak on border of Inverness and Ross and Cromarty districts, 3m/5km NE of dam of Loch Monar. Height 3329 feet or 1015 metres. NH2243.
Sgurr na Feartaig *High.* ***Inland physical feature***, mountain ridge rising to 2827 feet or 862 metres on Achnashellach Forest, Ross and Cromarty district. **59 G5** NH0545.
Sgurr na Greine *High.* ***Mountain***, 2m/3km N of head of Loch Doilet, Lochaber district. Height 1630 feet or 497 metres. **38 A3** NM8170.
Sgurr na h-Aide *High.* ***Mountain***, in Lochaber district 2m/3km NE of head of Loch Morar. Height 2818 feet or 859 metres. **49 E5** NM8893.
Sgurr na h-Eanchainne *High.* ***Mountain***, 3m/5km N of Sallachan Point, Lochaber district. Height 2394 feet or 730 metres. **38 B3** NM9965.
Sgurr na h-Iolaire *High.* ***Hill***, on Sleat peninsula, Skye, 2m/3km E of Tarskavaig. Height 958 feet or 292 metres. **48 C4** NG6109.
Sgurr na Lapaich *High.* ***Mountain***, peak in Inverness district, 1m/2km N of Loch Affric. Height 3398 feet or 1036 metres. **50 A2** NH1524.
Sgurr na Lapaich *High.* ***Mountain***, on border of Inverness and Ross and Cromarty districts, 5m/7km NW of dam of Loch Mullardoch. Munro: height 3772 feet or 1150 metres. **50 A1** NH1635.
Sgurr na Moraich *High.* ***Mountain***, peak on Kintail Forest (National Trust for Scotland) in Skye and Lochalsh district, 2m/3km E of Shiel Bridge. One of the Five Sisters. Height 2873 feet or 876 metres. **49 F3** NG9619.
Sgurr na Muice *High.* ***Mountain***, on border of Inverness and Ross and Cromarty districts 2m/4km NE of dam of Loch Monar. Height 2922 feet or 891 metres. **60 B5** NH2241.
Sgurr na Paite *High.* ***Mountain***, 4m/6km E of Lochailort, to S of Loch Eilt. Height 1059 feet or 323 metres. **38 A1** NM8281.
Sgurr na Ruaidhe (Also known as Sgurr Ruadh.) *High.* ***Mountain***, on border of Inverness and Ross and Cromarty districts, 4m/7km SW of head of Orrin Reservoir. Munro: height 3257 feet or 993 metres. **60 B5** NH2842.
Sgurr na Sgine *High.* ***Mountain***, peak on border of Lochaber and Skye and Lochalsh districts, 3m/5km N of Kinloch Hourn. Munro: height 3100 feet or 945 metres. **49 F3** NG9411.
Sgurr na Stri *High.* ***Mountain***, 4m/6km N of Elgol, and 1km E of Loch na Cuilce, Skye. Height 1630 feet or 497 metres. **48 B3** NG5019.
Sgurr nan Caorach *High.* ***Hill***, 1m/2km N of Aird of Sleat, Skye. Height 918 feet or 280 metres. **48 B4** NG5802.
Sgurr nan Ceannaichean *High.* ***Mountain***, peak on Glencarron and Glenuig Forest, Ross and Cromarty district. Munro: height 3001 feet or 915 metres. **59 G5** NH0848.
Sgurr nan Ceathreamhnan *High.* ***Mountain***, on border of Inverness and Ross and Cromarty districts, 6m/9km W of W end of Loch Affric. Munro: height 3775 feet or 1151 metres. **49 G2** NH0522.
Sgurr nan Clach Geala *High.* ***Mountain***, in Ross and Cromarty district 3m/5km NE of head of Loch Fannich. Munro: height 3585 feet or 1093 metres. **60 A2** NH1871.
Sgurr nan Cnamh *High.* ***Mountain***, 5m/8km NE of Strontian, Lochaber district. Height 2299 feet or 701 metres. **38 A3** NM8864.
Sgurr nan Coireachan *High.* ***Mountain***, in Lochaber district 3m/4km SE of head of Loch Morar. Munro: height 3136 feet or 956 metres. **38 B1** NM9088.
Sgurr nan Coireachan *High.* ***Mountain***, peak in Lochaber district 2m/4km S of head of Loch Quoich. Munro: height 3126 feet or 953 metres. **49 F5** NM9395.
Sgurr nan Conbhairean *High.* ***Mountain***, peak on border of Inverness and Skye and Lochalsh districts, 4m/7km NW of dam of Loch Cluanie. Munro: height 3641 feet or 1110 metres. **50 A3** NH1213.
Sgurr nan Each *High.* ***Mountain***, in Ross and Cromarty district, 2m/3km NE of head of Loch Fannich. Munro: height 3027 feet or 923 metres. **60 A3** NH1869.
Sgurr nan Eag *High.* ***Mountain***, S peak of Cuillin Hills on Skye. Munro: height 3031 feet or 924 metres. **48 A3** NG4519.
Sgurr nan Eugallt *High.* ***Mountain***, 2m/3km SW of Kinloch Hourn. Height 2932 feet or 894 metres. NG9304.
Sgurr nan Gillean *High.* ***Mountain***, peak of Cuillin Hills on Skye. Munro: height 3165 feet or 965 metres. **48 A2** NG4725.
Sgurr nan Gillean *High.* ***Mountain***, 1m/2km NE of Rubha nam Meirleach, Rum. Height 2506 feet or 764 metres. **47 G5** NM3893.
Sgurr nan Gobhar *High.* ***Mountain***, W peak of Cuillin Hills on Skye. Height 2070 feet or 631 metres. NG4222.
Sgurr nan Saighead *High.* ***Mountain***, peak on Kintail Forest (National Trust for Scotland) in Skye and Lochalsh district, 2m/4km SE of Shiel Bridge. One of the Five Sisters. Height 3047 feet or 929 metres. NG9717.
Sgurr of Eigg *High.* *Alternative name for An Sgurr, qv.*
Sgurr Ruadh *High.* *Alternative name for Sgurr na Ruaidhe, qv.*
Sgurr Sgiath Airigh *High.* ***Mountain***, peak in Lochaber district 2m/3km SW of Kinloch Hourn. Height 2890 feet or 881 metres. **49 F4** NG9205.
Sgurr Sgumain *High.* ***Mountain***, on Skye, peak of the Cuillin Hills. Height 3106 feet or 947 metres. NG4420.
Sgurr Shalachain *High.* ***Mountain***, 2m/3km NE of Beinn Mheadhoin, Lochaber district. Height 1742 feet or 531 metres. **38 A4** NM8052.
Sgurr Thuilm *High.* ***Mountain***, on Skye, peak of the Cuillin Hills. Height 2883 feet or 879 metres. **48 A2** NG4324.
Sgurr Thuilm *High.* ***Mountain***, in Lochaber district 4m/6km SW of head of Loch Arkaig. Munro: height 3159 feet or 963 metres. **38 B1** NM9387.
Shader *W.Isles* ***River***, in N part of Isle of Lewis, running NW into Atlantic Ocean 1km W of Siadar Iarach, between Rivers Barvas and Borve. NB3754.
Shaggie Burn *P. & K.* ***River***, flowing SE, then SW near Falls of Monzie, into Turret Burn, 1km NW of Crieff. **33 D2** NN8523.
Shalloch *S.Ayr.* ***Mountain***, 4m/6km W of Loch Macaterick. Height 1778 feet or 542 metres. **7 E1** NX3792.
Shalloch on Minnoch *S.Ayr.* ***Mountain***, 9m/14km S of Straiton. Height 2522 feet or 769 metres. **7 E1** NX4090.
Shalmstry *High.* ***Settlement***, 2m/3km SE of Thurso. **76 D2** ND1264.
Shalunt *Arg. & B.* ***Settlement***, on Bute, 5m/8km NW of Rothesay. **22 B2** NS0471.
Shambellie Grange *D. & G.* ***Settlement***, 1km N of New Abbey. **9 D4** NX9667.
Shandon *Arg. & B.* Population: 1282. ***Hamlet***, on E shore of Gare Loch, 3m/5km S of Garelochhead. **23 D1** NS2586.
Shandwick *High.* ***Locality***, on Shandwick Bay, E coast of Ross and Cromarty district, 1km S of Balintore. **62 A2** NH8575.
Shandwick Bay *High.* ***Bay***, on E coast of Ross and Cromarty district, 1km S of Balintore. Locality of Shandwick on the bay. NH8675.
Shankend *Sc.Bord.* ***Settlement***, on Lang Burn, at foot of N end of Shankend Hill, 6m/10km S of Hawick. **17 G5** NT5205.
Shannochie *N.Ayr.* ***Settlement***, at S end of Arran, 6m/10km SW of Lamlash. **13 E3** NR9721.
Shantron *Arg. & B.* ***Settlement***, by Finlas Water, 5m/7km NE of Helensburgh. **23 E1** NS3487.
Shantullich *High.* ***Settlement***, on Black Isle, 1km NW of Munlochy. **61 F4** NH6353.
Shanzie *P. & K.* ***Settlement***, 2m/3km NE of Alyth. **42 A4** NO2750.
Shapinsay *Ork.* ***Island***, low-lying island of 10 square miles or 26 square km lying to N and E of Mainland, its SW corner being 1m/2km N of Car Ness across strait, The String, at W end of Shapinsay Sound. **80 D5** HY5017.
Shapinsay Sound *Ork.* ***Sea feature***, strait dividing Shapinsay from S of Mainland. **80 D5** HY5113.
Shaw Hill *D. & G.* ***Mountain***, on S side of Black Water of Dee, 5m/7km SW of New Galloway. Height 1263 feet or 385 metres. **7 G3** NX5872.
Shawbost *W.Isles* *Anglicised form of Siabost, qv.*
Shawhead *D. & G.* ***Village***, 6m/10km W of Dumfries. **8 C3** NX8775.
Shawlands *Glas.* ***Suburb***, 3m/4km SW of Glasgow city centre. NS5661.
Shaw's Hill *Sc.Bord.* ***Mountain***, 2m/3km S of Ettrickbridge. Height 1289 feet or 393 metres. **17 E3** NT3721.

Shaws Under Loch *Sc.Bord.* ***Lake/loch***, small loch 7m/12km NW of Hawick. **17 E4** NT3919.
Shaws Upper Loch *Sc.Bord.* ***Lake/loch***, small loch nearly 1km SW of Shaws Under Loch. NT3819.
Shawtonhill *S.Lan.* ***Settlement***, 4m/6km SE of East Kilbride. **24 A5** NS6749.
Shawwood *E.Ayr.* ***Locality***, adjoining to SE of Catrine. NS5325.
Sheanachie *Arg. & B.* ***Settlement***, at S end of Kintyre, 5m/7km NE of Southend. **12 C4** NR7512.
Sheandow *Moray* ***Settlement***, 3m/5km W of Dufftown. **53 E1** NJ2739.
Shearington *D. & G.* ***Locality***, 7m/11km SE of Dumfries. **9 E4** NY0366.
Sheaval *W.Isles* ***Hill***, 1m/2km E of Mingearraidh, South Uist. Height 731 feet or 223 metres. **44 C1** NF7627.
Shebster *High.* ***Settlement***, in Caithness district, 7m/11km SW of Thurso. **76 C2** ND0164.
Shee Water *P. & K.* ***River***, rising from numerous streams flowing S from Grampian Mountains and flowing S from Spittal of Glenshee through Glen Shee to become Black Water about 5m/7km SE of Kirkmichael. **41 G3** NO1169.
Sheep Island *Arg. & B.* ***Island***, small island off S coast of Kintyre across Sanda Sound, to N of Sanda Island. **12 C5** NR7305.
Sheep Rock *Shet.* ***Coastal feature***, rocky promontory on E coast of Fair Isle, connected to Mainland by narrow neck of land. **82 A5** HZ2270.
Sheigra *High.* ***Settlement***, near W coast of Sutherland district, 4m/6km NW of Kinlochbervie. **74 A2** NC1860.
Shell Bay *Fife* ***Bay***, small bay on E side of Largo Bay, between Ruddons Point and Kincraig Point. NO4500.
Shellachan *Arg. & B.* ***Settlement***, on S shore of River Euchar, 3m/5km S of Kilmore. **30 A3** NM8720.
Shellachan *Arg. & B.* ***Settlement***, 3m/5km SE of Taynuilt. **30 C2** NN0326.
Shelter Stone (Gaelic form: Clach Dhian.) *Moray* ***Inland physical feature***, large block of granite at head of Loch Avon, which broke away from crags above and is estimated to weigh over 1300 tons. **52 C4** NJ0001.
Shennanton *D. & G.* ***Settlement***, on River Bladnoch, 2m/3km NE of Kirkcowan. **7 E4** NX3463.
Shenval *Moray* ***Settlement***, 2m/3km N of Tomnavoulin. **53 E2** NJ2129.
Sheppardstown *High.* ***Settlement***, 4m/6km NW of Lybster. **77 E5** ND2039.
Sheriff Muir (Also spelled Sheriffmuir.) *Stir.* ***Open space***, moor to E of Dunblane. Scene of indecisive battle in 1715 between government troops and those of Old Pretender. **32 D4** NN8303.
Sheriffmuir *Stir. Alternative spelling of Sheriff Muir, qv.*
Sherramore *High.* ***Settlement***, in valley of River Spey, 4m/6km W of Laggan. **51 E5** NN5593.
Sheshader *W.Isles Anglicised form of Seisiadar, qv.*
Sheshader Bay *W.Isles Anglicised form of Bàgh Sheisiadar, qv.*
Shetland Museum *Shet.* ***Other feature of interest***, museum in Lerwick town centre, Mainland, with local history artefacts. **83 D3** HU4741.
Shettleston *Glas.* ***Suburb***, 3m/5km E of Glasgow city centre. **24 A3** NS6464.
Shewalton *N.Ayr.* ***Locality***, 3m/5km SE of Irvine. NS3436.
Shian Bay *Arg. & B.* ***Bay***, on NW coast of Jura, 3m/5km NW of entrance to Loch Tarbert. **20 D1** NR5287.
Shian Island *Arg. & B.* ***Island***, islet to N of Shian Bay on Jura. NR5288.
Shiant Islands *W.Isles* ***Island***, uninhabited group of islands and islets, 4m/6km off SE coast of Isle of Lewis. Garbh Eilean and Eilean an Tighe form one island as they are connected by a narrow neck of land. Eilean Mhuire lies 1km E. There are several islets to W. **67 F4** NG4198.
Shiaram Mòr *W.Isles* ***Island***, islet near W shore of West Loch Roag, W coast of Isle of Lewis. NB1036.
Shibden Hill *Sc.Bord.* ***Mountain***, 3m/5km W of Hownam. Height 1007 feet or 307 metres. **18 B5** NT7319.
Shiel *High.* ***River***, in Skye and Lochalsh district running NW down Glen Shiel to Shiel Bridge and head of Loch Duich. Kintail Forest (National Trust for Scotland) rises steeply from right bank. **49 F3** NG9319.
Shiel Bridge *High.* ***Village***, in Skye and Lochalsh district, at foot of Glen Shiel and at head of Loch Duich where A87 road crosses River Shiel. **49 F3** NG9318.
Shiel Burn ***River***, rising to S of Knock Hill and flowing SW to join River Isla, 3m/4km NW of Milltown of Rothiemay. **64 A4** NJ5149.
Shiel Dod *S.Lan.* ***Mountain***, in Lowther Hills, 4m/6km E of Durisdeer. Height 2191 feet or 668 metres. NS9403.
Shiel Hill *S.Ayr.* ***Hill***, on N side of Arecleoch Forest, 3m/4km W of Barrhill. Height 754 feet or 230 metres. **6 C2** NX1981.
Shiel Hill *S.Ayr.* ***Mountain***, 2m/3km S of Loch Bradan. Height 1666 feet or 508 metres. **7 F1** NX4194.
Shiel Muir *Moray* ***Open space***, moorland 4m/6km SE of Buckie. **63 G3** NJ4760.
Shieldaig *High.* ***Settlement***, in Ross and Cromarty district, 3m/4km S of Gairloch. **59 E2** NG8072.
Shieldaig *High.* ***Village***, on E shore of Loch Shieldaig, Ross and Cromarty district. **59 E4** NG8153.
Shieldaig Forest *High.* ***Open space***, deer forest in W part of Ross and Cromarty district to N of Upper Loch Torridon. **59 E3** NG8564.
Shieldaig Island *High.* ***Island***, small island (National Trust for Scotland) in Loch Shieldaig, Ross and Cromarty district, almost entirely covered in Scots pine. **59 D4** NG8154.
Shieldhall *Glas.* ***Suburb***, on S side of River Clyde, 4m/6km W of Glasgow city centre. NS5365.
Shieldhill *Falk.* Population: 2071. ***Village***, 2m/3km S of Falkirk. **24 C2** NS8976.
Shieldmuir *N.Lan.* ***Suburb***, 2m/3km SE of Motherwell. NS7755.
Shieldmuir Station *N.Lan.* ***Other building***, commuter railway station between Motherwell and Wishaw. **24 B4** NS7755.
Shielfoot *High.* ***Settlement***, on W bank of River Shiel, 1m/2km NW of Acharacle. **37 F2** NM6670.
Shielhill *Angus* ***Hamlet***, 3m/5km NE of Kirriemuir. **42 C4** NO4257.
Shiels *Aber.* ***Locality***, comprises Mains of Shiels and Nether Shiels, 3m/4km SW of Sauchen. **54 B4** NJ6509.
Shillay *W.Isles* ***Island***, westernmost of Heisker Islands group. Lighthouse has been disused since World War II. **45 D3** NF5962.
Shillay *W.Isles* ***Island***, small uninhabited island 5m/8km SW of Toe Head, W coast of South Harris. **66 A4** NF8891.
Shillay Mòr *W.Isles* ***Island***, uninhabited island in Loch Sgioport, E coast of South Uist. NF8438.
Shin *High.* ***River***, in Sutherland district running S from foot of Loch Shin to Invershin, 4m/6km NW of Bonar Bridge. NH5796.
Shin Forest *High.* ***Forest/woodland***, 3m/5km S of Lairg in Sutherland district. **72 A4** NC5701.
Shinnel Water *D. & G.* ***River***, rising on Trostan Hill and running SE past Tynron, then NE to Scaur Water on SW side of Penpont. **8 B1** NX8494.
Shinness *High.* ***Locality***, on E shore of Loch Shin, Sutherland district, 6m/10km NW of Lairg. NC5314.
Shinness Lodge *High.* ***Settlement***, in Shinness locality, on NE shore of Loch Shin, Sutherland district. **72 A3** NC5314.
Shira *Arg. & B.* ***Locality***, near head of Glen Shira, 7m/11km NE of Inveraray. **31 D3** NN1518.
Shira *Arg. & B.* ***River***, flowing SW from Loch Shira into Loch Fyne 1m/2km NE of Inveraray. **30 D3** NN1110.
Shirmers Burn *D. & G.* ***River***, flowing S into Loch Ken at Ringbane 3m/5km SW of New Galloway. **8 A3** NX6573.
Shiskine *N.Ayr.* ***Village***, on Arran, 1m/2km NE of Blackwaterfoot. **13 E3** NR9129.
Shiskine Fort *N.Ayr.* ***Historic/prehistoric site***, Iron Age hillfort 2m/3km E of Blackwaterfoot, Arran. **13 E3** NR9229.
Shochie Burn *P. & K.* ***River***, flowing SE to join Ordie Burn nearly 1km from confluence with River Tay, 4m/6km N of Perth. **33 F1** NO0930.
Shona Beag *High.* ***Island***, E part of Eilean Shona, and joined to it by narrow neck of land. **37 F2** NM6673.
Shoremill *High.* ***Settlement***, on S shore of Cromarty Bay, 3m/4km SW of Cromarty. **61 G3** NH7466.
Shoretown *High.* ***Settlement***, 6m/10km NE of Conon Bridge. **61 F3** NH6162.
Shortroads *Renf.* ***Suburb***, N district of Paisley. NS4765.
Shotts *N.Lan.* Population: 8756. ***Locality***, 6m/9km NE of Wishaw. **24 C3** NS8760.
Shulishader *W.Isles Anglicised form of Siulaisiadar, qv.*
Shuna *Arg. & B.* ***Island***, sparsely inhabited island of about 2 square miles or 5 square km, lying 1m/2km SW of entrance to Loch Melfort on coast of Argyll and 1km E of Luing across Shuna Sound. **29 G4** NM7608.
Shuna Island *Arg. & B.* ***Island***, sparsely populated island of about 300 acres or 120 hectares in Loch Linnhe, near E shore to NW of Portnacroish. Ruined castle at S end. **38 B4** NM9149.
Shuna Point *Arg. & B.* ***Coastal feature***, headland at S end of Shuna. **29 G4** NM7606.
Shuna Sound *Arg. & B.* ***Sea feature***, sea passage dividing Shuna from Luing. **29 G4** NM7608.
Shurrery *High.* ***Locality***, in Caithness district, 8m/12km SW of Thurso. **76 C3** ND0357.
Shurrery Lodge *High.* ***Settlement***, on W bank of Loch Shurrery. **76 C3** ND0356.
Siabost (Anglicised form: Shawbost.) *W.Isles* ***Locality***, comprises settlements of New, South and North Shawbost, 4m/6km NE of Carloway, Isle of Lewis. **69 D3** NB2546.
Siadar Iarach (Anglicised form: Lower Shader.) *W.Isles* ***Village***, adjacent to Siadar Uarach, near NW coast of Isle of Lewis, between Barvas and Borve. **69 E2** NB3854.
Siadar Uarach (Anglicised form: Upper Shader). *W.Isles* ***Village***, adjacent to Siadar Iarach, near NW coast of Isle of Lewis, between Barvas and Borve. **69 E2** NB3854.
Sibbaldbie *D. & G.* ***Settlement***, on Dryfe Water, 4m/6km N of Lockerbie. **9 F2** NY1487.
Sibster *High.* ***Settlement***, in Caithness district, 3m/4km NW of Wick. **77 F3** ND3252.
Siccar Point *Sc.Bord.* ***Coastal feature***, small rocky headland on North Sea coast, 3m/4km E of Cockburnspath. **27 F2** NT8171.
Sidhean an Airgid *W.Isles* ***Mountain***, to E of Loch Seaforth, 6m/10km SW of Cearsiadar. Height 1250 feet or 381 metres. **67 E2** NB2513.
Sìdhean Mòr *High.* ***Mountain***, 4m/7km E of Arisaig, Lochaber district. Height 1971 feet or 601 metres. **37 G1** NM7286.
Sìdhean na Raplaich *High.* ***Mountain***, in Morvern, Lochaber district, 2m/3km W of head of Loch Arienas. Height 1804 feet or 550 metres. **37 F4** NM6351.
Sidinish *W.Isles Anglicised form of Saighdinis, qv.*
Sidlaw Hills *P. & K.* ***Large natural feature***, range of hills on SE side of Strathmore, extending from Perth to vicinity of Forfar. Summit is Craigowl Hill, 1492 feet or 455 metres. **33 G2** NO2735.
Siggar Ness *Shet.* ***Coastal feature***, headland on SW coast of Mainland. **83 F5** HU3411.
Sighthill *Edin.* ***Suburb***, of Edinburgh, 4m/7km SW of city centre. College of Commerce. NT1971.
Sighthill Industrial Estate *Edin.* ***Locality***, in Edinburgh, to W of Sighthill. NT1970.
Sillyearn *Moray* ***Settlement***, to SW of Knock Hill, 4m/7km SW of Cornhill. Sillyearn Wood on hill adjacent to SW. **64 A4** NJ5254.
Silverbank *Aber.* ***Suburb***, E district of Banchory, on N bank of River Dee. NO7196.
Silverburn *Midloth.* ***Hamlet***, 2m/3km W of Penicuik. **25 G3** NT2060.
Silvercraigs *Arg. & B.* ***Settlement***, 3m/4km SE of Lochgilphead. **21 G1** NR8984.
Silverknowes *Edin.* ***Suburb***, 3m/5km NW of Edinburgh city centre. NT2076.
Silvermoss *Aber.* ***Settlement***, 5m/8km SE of Fyvie. **54 D1** NJ8333.
Silversands Bay *Fife* ***Bay***, on Firth of Forth, on E side of Aberdour. NT2085.
Silverton *W.Dun.* ***Suburb***, E district of Dumbarton. NS4075.
Silwick *Shet.* ***Settlement***, 1km SE of Westerwick, Mainland. **82 B3** HU2942.
Simprim *Sc.Bord.* ***Settlement***, 4m/6km N of Coldstream. **27 F5** NT8545.
Sim's Hill *P. & K.* ***Mountain***, 6m/10km NE of Dollar, in Ochil Hills. Height 1581 feet or 482 metres. **33 E4** NN9907.
Sinclair Castle *High.* ***Castle***, early 17c castle, twin of adjacent Girnigoe Castle and residence of Earls of Caithness, on S coast of Sinclair's Bay, 1km W of Noss Head. **77 F3** ND3754.
Sinclair's Bay *High.* ***Bay***, on E coast of Caithness district, extending N from Noss Head to Brough Head. **77 F3** ND3658.
Sinclair's Hill *Sc.Bord.* ***Settlement***, 3m/4km SE of Duns. **27 F4** NT8150.
Sinclairston *E.Ayr.* ***Settlement***, 2m/3km SE of Drongan. **14 C4** NS4716.
Sinclairtown *Fife* ***Suburb***, 2m/3km NE of Kirkcaldy town centre. NT2993.
Singdean *Sc.Bord.* ***Settlement***, in Wauchope Forest area of Cheviot Hills, 4m/6km N of Saughtree. **17 G5** NT5801.
Sinnahard *Aber.* ***Locality***, 5m/9km S of Lumsden. **53 G3** NJ4713.
Sior Loch *Arg. & B.* ***Lake/loch***, small loch in Argyll 8m/13km SE of Oban. **30 B2** NM9623.
Sir Walter Scott's Courtroom *Sc.Bord.* ***Other feature of interest***, early 19c Sheriff Court in Selkirk, where novelist Sir Walter Scott worked; displays and exhibitions about his life. **17 F3** NT4828.
Sithean Achadh nan Eun *High.* ***Mountain***, 2m/3km S of Dalnessie, Sutherland district. Height 1040 feet or 317 metres. **72 B3** NC6311.
Sithean Bhealaich Chumhaing *High.* ***Mountain***, 3m/4km NE of Portree, Skye. Height 1286 feet or 392 metres. **58 B5** NG5046.
Sithean Freiceadain *High.* ***Mountain***, 3m/4km SE of W end of Loch Craggie. Height 1594 feet or 486 metres. **72 B2** NC6323.
Siulaisiadar (Anglicised form: Shulishader.) *W.Isles* ***Village***, on Eye Peninsula, Isle of Lewis, 1m/2km NE of Garrabost. **69 G4** NB5335.
Skail *High.* ***Settlement***, in Caithness district, 9m/15km S of Bettyhill. Chambered cairn and broch nearby. **75 G4** NC7146.
Skaill *Ork.* ***Locality***, on W coast of Mainland, between Bay of Skaill and Loch of Skaill, 4m/6km W of Dounby. **80 A5** HY2318.
Skaill *Ork.* ***Settlement***, on W side of Egilsay. HY4630.
Skaill *Ork.* ***Settlement***, on coast at E end of Mainland, 2m/3km S of Mull Head. **79 E2** HY5806.
Skaill Taing *Ork.* ***Coastal feature***, headland with landing stage on Egilsay. HY4630.
Skara Brae *Ork.* ***Historic/prehistoric site***, remains of Neolithic settlement (Historic Scotland) on W coast of Mainland 4m/7km W of Dounby. **80 A5** HY2218.

S

Skares *Aber.* ***Settlement***, on NW side of Hill of Skares, 1m/2km NW of Kirkton of Culsalmond. **54 B1** NJ6334.
Skares *E.Ayr.* ***Village***, 3m/5km SW of Cumnock. **14 D4** NS5217.
Skarfskerry Point *High.* ***Coastal feature***, headland on N coast, 4m/6km SE of Dunnet Head. **77 E1** ND2574.
Skarpigarth *Shet.* ***Settlement***, to N of Voe of Footabrough, on W coast of Mainland. **82 A2** HU1950.
Skate Point *W.Isles* ***Coastal feature***, headland at W tip of Bearnaraigh. **44 A5** NL5480.
Skateraw *E.Loth.* ***Settlement***, 4m/7km SE of Dunbar. **27 E2** NT7375.
Skateraw Harbour *E.Loth.* ***Sea feature***, on rocky coast to NE of Skateraw. **27 E2** NT7375.
Skaw *Shet.* ***Settlement***, at head of small bay of Skaw Voe, on N coast of Whalsay, 1m/2km W of Skaw Taing. **83 E1** HU5966.
Skaw Taing *Shet.* ***Coastal feature***, headland at NE end of Whalsay. **83 F1** HU6066.
Skaw Voe *Shet.* ***Bay***, on N coast of Whalsay, with Skaw at its head. HU5866.
Skea *Ork.* ***Coastal feature***, headland on N coast of Mainland. **80 A3** HY2930.
Skea Skerries *Ork.* ***Island***, rocks 1km off S coast of Bakie Skerry, Westray. **80 C2** HY4440.
Skeabost *High.* ***Locality***, on Skye, 5m/8km NW of Portree. **58 A5** NG4148.
Skeabrae *Ork.* ***Settlement***, 1m/2km NW of Dounby. Disused airfield to W. **80 A4** HY2720.
Skel Wick *Ork.* ***Bay***, on E coast of Westray, to NE of Skelwick. HY4945.
Skelberry *Shet.* ***Settlement***, on Mainland, 1m/2km SE of Scousburgh. **83 G4** HU3916.
Skelberry *Shet.* ***Settlement***, on N shore of Dury Voe, 2m/3km E of Laxo, Mainland. HU4763.
Skelbo *High.* ***Settlement***, on S side of Loch Fleet, near E coast of Sutherland district, 4m/6km N of Dornoch. **72 C5** NH7995.
Skelbo Castle *High.* ***Castle***, ancient seat of the Sutherlands, to N of Skelbo on S side of Loch Fleet. **72 C5** NH7995.
Skelbo Street *High.* ***Settlement***, to SE of Skelbo. NH7994.
Skelda Ness *Shet.* ***Coastal feature***, headland on Mainland, 6m/10km W of Scalloway across The Deeps. **82 C3** HU3041.
Skelda Voe *Shet.* ***Sea feature***, inlet to N of Skelda Ness, on Mainland. HU3041.
Skeldon *E.Ayr.* ***Locality***, on N bank of River Doon, comprising Skeldon Hills, Skeldon House and Skeldon Mains, 1m/2km E of Dalrymple. **14 B4** NS3813.
Skelfhill Pen *Sc.Bord.* ***Mountain***, 3m/4km SE of Teviothead. Height 1745 feet or 532 metres. **17 F5** NT4403.
Skellister *Shet.* ***Settlement***, near E coast of Mainland, at head of South Nesting Bay. **83 D2** HU4654.
Skelly Rock *Aber.* ***Coastal feature***, rock on sands 2m/3km S of Balmedie. **55 E3** NJ9614.
Skelmonae *Aber.* ***Settlement***, 2m/3km NE of Methlick. **55 D1** NJ8839.
Skelmorlie *N.Ayr.* Population: 1736. ***Small town***, resort on Firth of Clyde, adjoining to S of Wemyss Bay, and 5m/9km N of Largs. **22 C3** NS1967.
Skelmorlie Aisle *N.Ayr.* ***Historic/prehistoric site***, 1km SE of Largs. Fine mausoleum of 1636 with painted roof and interesting tombs and monuments. **22 D4** NS2158.
Skelmorlie Castle *N.Ayr.* ***Castle***, restored castle dating from early 16c, 1m/2km S of Skelmorlie. NS1965.
Skelmuir *Aber.* ***Settlement***, 2m/3km S of Stuartfield. **65 E5** NJ9842.
Skelmuir Hill *Aber.* ***Hill***, 3m/5km E of Auchnagatt. Height 489 feet or 149 metres. **65 E5** NJ9841.
Skelpick *High.* ***Hamlet***, in Caithness district, 4m/6km S of Bettyhill. NC7255.
Skelpick Burn *High.* ***River***, flowing NW to join River Naver 3m/4km S of Bettyhill, Caithness district. **75 G3** NC7157.
Skelwick *Ork.* ***Locality***, on Westray, 4m/6km SE of Pirowall. **80 C2** HY4844.
Skeoch Hill *D. & G.* ***Hill***, rising to over 270 metres, 1m/2km E of Glenkiln Reservoir and 7m/11km W of Dumfries. **8 C3** NX8678.
Skeroblin Loch *Arg. & B.* ***Lake/loch***, small loch or tarn in Kintyre 4m/6km N of Campbeltown. NR7026.
Skeroblingarry *Arg. & B.* ***Settlement***, on Kintyre, 3m/5km N of Campbeltown. **12 C3** NR7026.
Skerray *High.* ***Settlement***, near N coast of Caithness district, 6m/10km NE of Tongue. **75 F2** NC6563.
Skerry of Eshaness *Shet.* ***Island***, rocky island off S end of Esha Ness on NW coast of Mainland. HU2076.
Skerryvore Museum *Arg. & B.* ***Other feature of interest***, museum in lighthouse at Hynish, 1m/2km S of Balemartin, Tiree. Exhibition on history of how lighthouse was built. **36 A3** NL9939.
Skervuile *Arg. & B.* ***Island***, rock with lighthouse, lying 2m/4km off E coast of Jura opposite Lowlandman's Bay. NR6071.
Skeun *W.Isles* ***Hill***, 2m/3km W of head of Little Loch Roag, Isle of Lewis. Height 869 feet or 265 metres. **68 C5** NB1024.
Skiack *High.* *Anglicised form of Sgitheach, qv.*
Skiag Bridge *High.* ***Bridge***, at road junction on NE side of Loch Assynt, Sutherland district, 2m/3km NW of Inchnadamph. NC2324.
Skibo Castle *High.* ***Castle***, built in 1898 by Andrew Carnegie on site of former castle, 4m/6km W of Dornoch. **61 G1** NH7389.
Skigersta *W.Isles* *Anglicised form of Sgiogarstaigh, qv.*
Skinidin *High.* ***Settlement***, on Skye, 2m/3km W of Dunvegan across head of Loch Dunvegan. **57 F5** NG2247.
Skinnet *High.* ***Settlement***, 1m/2km N of Halkirk. **76 D2** ND1261.
Skinsdale *High.* ***River***, in Sutherland district, running S from Borrobol Forest to Black Water, 11m/18km NW of Brora. **72 C2** NC7615.
Skipness *Arg. & B.* ***Village***, on Skipness Bay, on E coast of Kintyre, Argyll. **22 A4** NR9057.
Skipness Bay *Arg. & B.* ***Bay***, on E coast of Kintyre, Argyll. Skipness village is situated on bay. 13c castle (Historic Scotland). NR9057.
Skipness Castle *Arg. & B.* ***Castle***, ruins of fine 13c castle with 16c tower house in one corner (Historic Scotland), 15m/24km SE of Tarbert on E coast of Kintyre. Early 14c chapel nearby. **22 A4** NR9057.
Skipness Point *Arg. & B.* ***Coastal feature***, headland at entrance to Loch Fyne, 1m/2km E of Skipness. **22 A4** NR9057.
Skirling *Sc.Bord.* ***Village***, 2m/4km E of Biggar. **16 B2** NT0739.
Skirts of Foudland *Aber.* *See Hill of Foudland.*
Skirza *High.* ***Settlement***, near E coast of Caithness district, 3m/5km S of Duncansby Head. **77 F2** ND3868.
Skirza Head *High.* ***Coastal feature***, headland 1km E of Skirza. **77 F2** ND3868.
Skroo *Shet.* ***Coastal feature***, indentation on NE coast of Fair Isle. **82 A5** HZ2274.
Skuda Sound *Shet.* ***Sea feature***, sea passage between Uyea and S coast of Unst, to E of Clivocast. **85 E2** HP6000.
Skulamus *High.* ***Settlement***, on Skye, 1m/2km E of Broadford. **48 C2** NG6622.
Skullomie *High.* ***Settlement***, on Tongue Bay, Caithness district, 3m/5km NE of Tongue. **75 F2** NC6161.
Skye *High.* ***Island***, largest of Hebridean islands, 535 square miles or 1386 square km, separated from Scottish mainland by Sound of Sleat between Kyleakin and Kyle of Lochalsh, here less than 1km in width. The coastline is much indented. The island is mountainous, with Cuillin Hills rising to 3257 feet or 993 metres, and climate is moist. **47 G1** NG4532.
Skye Cottage Museum *High.* ***Other feature of interest***, housed in group of cottages at Kilmuir, near NW coast of Skye, 3m/5km S of Rubha Hunish. Displays include old documents and photographs. **57 G2** NG3971.
Skye of Curr *High.* ***Settlement***, in Badenoch and Strathspey district, 1km SW of Dulnain Bridge. **52 B2** NH9924.
Skyre Burn *D. & G.* ***River***, rising on W slopes of Meikle Bennan and flowing S to Fleet Bay via Skyreburn Bay, 3m/4km SW of Gatehouse of Fleet. **7 G5** NX5754.
Skyreburn Bay *D. & G.* ***Bay***, 2m/4km SW of Gatehouse of Fleet. NX5754.
Slack *Aber.* ***Settlement***, 4m/6km E of Gartly. **54 A1** NJ5730.
Slackhead *Moray* ***Settlement***, 2m/3km SW of Buckie. **63 G3** NJ4063.
Slaggan Bay *High.* ***Bay***, W facing bay at entrance to Loch Ewe, Ross and Cromarty district, 4m/6km NW of Aultbea. To E, ruined village of Slaggan. **70 A5** NG8394.
Slains Castle *Aber.* ***Other feature of interest***, site of 19c castle, now demolished, on granite headland above Port Erroll, on E coast 7m/11km S of Peterhead. See also Old Castle of Slains. **55 G1** NK1036.
Slains Park *Aber.* ***Hamlet***, 3m/4km NE of Inverbervie. **43 G2** NO8575.
Slamannan *Falk.* Population: 1430. ***Village***, 5m/8km SW of Falkirk. **24 C2** NS8573.
Slat Bheinn *High.* ***Mountain***, in Barrisdale Forest, 3m/4km NW of W end of Loch Quoich. Height 2299 feet or 701 metres. **49 F4** NG9102.
Slate Haugh *Moray* ***Settlement***, 3m/5km SE of Buckie. **63 G3** NJ4662.
Slatrach Bay *Arg. & B.* ***Bay***, on N coast of Kerrera, 3m/5km W of Oban across Sound of Kerrera. NM8129.
Slattadale *High.* ***Settlement***, on SW shore of Loch Maree, 6m/10km SE of Gairloch. **59 E2** NG8871.
Slaty Law *N.Ayr.* ***Mountain***, 4m/6km E of Largs. Height 1584 feet or 483 metres. **23 D3** NS2661.
Sleach Water *High.* ***River***, in Caithness district, flowing into Loch More 4m/7km E of Altnabreac. **76 C4** ND0746.
Sleat *High.* ***Locality***, parish and peninsula in SE Skye. Peninsula is connected to rest of island by isthmus between Loch Eishort and Loch na Dal and extends 14m/22km south-westwards to Point of Sleat, most southerly point of Skye. **48 C4** NG6309.
Sléiteachal Mhòr *W.Isles* ***Hill***, 4m/6km W of head of Loch Erisort, Isle of Lewis. Height 813 feet or 248 metres. **67 E2** NB2118.
Sletill Hill *High.* ***Hill***, in Sutherland district, 3m/5km NE of Forsinard. Height 918 feet or 280 metres. **76 B4** NC9246.
Sliabh Bainneach *Moray* ***Mountain***, 5m/8km NE of Dava. Height 1584 feet or 483 metres. **62 C5** NJ0741.
Slickly *High.* ***Settlement***, in Caithness district, 7m/11km SW of John o' Groats. **77 E2** ND2966.
Sliddery *N.Ayr.* ***Settlement***, near SW coast of Arran, 4m/6km SE of Blackwaterfoot. **13 E3** NR9322.
Sliddery Water *N.Ayr.* ***River***, rising on slopes of Cnoc na Dail and running SW out to sea, 1km S of Sliddery. NR9322.
Sliemore *High.* ***Settlement***, 2m/3km E of Nethy Bridge. **52 C2** NJ0320.
Sligachan *High.* ***Locality***, at head of Loch Sligachan, Skye, 8m/13km S of Portree. **48 A2** NG4829.
Sligachan *High.* ***River***, on Skye, running N from Cuillin Hills to head of Loch Sligachan. NG4829.
Sligga Skerry *Shet.* ***Island***, rock group lying off NW coast of Bigga, at S end of Yell Sound. HU4380.
Sligrachan Hill *Arg. & B.* ***Mountain***, in Argyll Forest Park, rising above E shore of Loch Eck. Height 1804 feet or 550 metres. **30 D5** NS1590.
Slioch *Aber.* ***Settlement***, 3m/4km SE of Huntly. **54 A1** NJ5638.
Slioch *High.* ***Mountain***, in Ross and Cromarty district 3m/5km N of head of Loch Maree. Munro: height 3214 feet or 980 metres. **59 G3** NH0068.
Slitrig Water *Sc.Bord.* ***River***, a continuation of Lang Burn, flowing N to join River Teviot at Hawick. **17 G5** NT5014.
Sloc Caol *W.Isles* ***Sea feature***, small inlet on E coast of Eriskay, 1m/2km E of Haunn. **46 B3** NF8012.
Slochd *High.* ***Locality***, in Badenoch and Strathspey district, 4m/6km W of Carrbridge. **52 A2** NH8424.
Slochd Mòr *High.* ***Other feature of interest***, mountain pass on A9 between Aviemore and Inverness, 9m/13km NW of Aviemore. **52 A2** NH8325.
Slockavullin *Arg. & B.* ***Settlement***, in Argyll, 1m/2km SW of Kilmartin. Many prehistoric remains in vicinity. **30 A5** NR8297.
Slogarie Farm *D. & G.* ***Settlement***, 3m/4km NW of Laurieston. **8 A4** NX6567.
Slongaber *D. & G.* ***Settlement***, 4m/6km NE of Corsock. **8 C3** NX8079.
Slug of Auchrannie *Angus* ***Waterfall***, in River Isla, to N of Auchrannie. NO2752.
Sluggan *High.* ***Settlement***, 6m/10km N of Aviemore. **52 A2** NH8721.
Sluggan Pass *High.* ***Other feature of interest***, mountain pass following course of Milton Burn past W slopes of Craigowrie, connecting Glenmore Forest Park with Strathspey. **52 B3** NH9414.
Slumbay *High.* ***Locality***, two adjoining localities, Easter and Wester Slumbay, on NW shore of Loch Carron to SW of Lochcarron, Ross and Cromarty district. NG8939.
Slungie Hill *P. & K.* ***Mountain***, in Ochil Hills, 3m/5km N of Carnbo. Height 1355 feet or 413 metres. **33 F4** NO0507.
Slymaback ***Open space***, hillslope on border of Perth & Kinross and Stirling, 6m/9km NE of Doune. **32 C3** NN7510.
Sma' Glen *P. & K.* ***Other feature of interest***, stony defile in Glen Almond, at SE edge of Highlands, 6m/9km N of Crieff. Traditional burial place of Ossian. **33 E1** NN9029.
Smailholm *Sc.Bord.* ***Village***, 5m/8km W of Kelso. 16c tower (Historic Scotland). **18 A3** NT6436.
Smailholm Tower *Sc.Bord.* ***Historic/prehistoric site***, well-preserved 16c Border peel tower (Historic Scotland) on isolated hillock beside small loch, 1m/2km SW of Smailholm. Contains tapestries and costume figures. Associations with Sir Walter Scott who spent some of his childhood at nearby Sandyknowe Farm. **18 A3** NT6436.
Small Isles *Arg. & B.* ***Island***, group of small uninhabited islands off E coast of Jura between Rubha na Caillich and Rubh' an Leanachais. From S to N they are: Eilean nan Gabhar, Eilean nan Coinein, Eilean Dìomhain, Pladda and Eilean Bhrìde. **21 D3** NR5468.
Smallburn *Aber.* ***Settlement***, 3m/5km NW of Hatton. **65 F5** NK0141.
Smallburn *E.Ayr.* ***Village***, 1km SW of Muirkirk. **15 E3** NS6826.
Smaull *Arg. & B.* ***Settlement***, on NW coast of Islay, 9m/13km NW of Bridgend. **20 A3** NR2168.
Smeaton *Fife* ***Suburb***, 1m/2km N of Kirkcaldy town centre. NT2893.
Smerclett *W.Isles* ***Locality***, near S end of South Uist, 2m/3km NW of Ludag. NF7415.

Smerral *High.* ***Settlement***, near E coast of Caithness district, 1m/2km NW of Latheronwheel. **77 D5** ND1733.
Smigel Burn *High.* ***River***, in Sutherland district, flowing W into Halladale River, 2m/3km N of Dalhalvaig. **76 B3** NC8957.
Smirisary *High.* ***Settlement***, near coast of Lochaber district, 5m/8km NW of Kinlochmoidart. **37 F2** NM6477.
Smith Art Gallery and Museum *Stir.* ***Other feature of interest***, founded in 1874 at Stirling, displaying paintings by Scottish artists, including Sir William Allan and John Duncan. Museum has botanical, geological and natural history collections. **32 C5** NS7894.
Smithstone *N.Lan.* ***Settlement***, 2m/3km W of Cumbernauld town centre. NS7275.
Smithstown *High.* ***Settlement***, on W coast of Ross and Cromarty district, 1km NW of Gairloch. NG7977.
Smithtown *High.* Population: 1530. ***Village***, in Inverness district, 3m/5km E of Inverness. **61 G5** NH7145.
Smoo Cave *High.* ***Cave***, large limestone cavern near N coast of Sutherland district, 1m/2km SE of Durness, containing waterfall from Allt Smoo. **74 D2** NC4167.
Smyrton *S.Ayr.* ***Settlement***, 2m/3km SE of Ballantrae. **6 C2** NX1080.
Snaip Hill *S.Lan.* ***Mountain***, 3m/5km S of Biggar. Height 1187 feet or 362 metres. **16 B2** NT0232.
Snar Water *S.Lan.* ***River***, rising on N slopes of Wanlock Dod, 1km N of Wanlockhead, and flowing N to join Duneaton Water 1m/2km SW of Crawfordjohn. **15 G4** NS8622.
Snarra Ness *Shet.* ***Coastal feature***, headland on Mainland with Voe of Snarraness to W and West Burra Firth to E, 3m/5km E of Melby. HU2357.
Sneuk Head *Ork.* ***Coastal feature***, headland on W coast of Hoy, 3m/5km SE of Rora Head. **78 A3** ND2095.
Snishival *W.Isles* ***Settlement***, on South Uist, 4m/7km NE of Rubha Ardvule. **46 A1** NF7634.
Snizort *High.* ***River***, on Skye, running N into head of Loch Snizort Beag 6m/9km NW of Portree. NG4148.
Soa *Arg. & B.* ***Island***, lying off E end of Gott Bay on S coast of Tiree. **36 B2** NM0746.
Soa *Arg. & B.* ***Island***, small island lying off S coast of Coll, opposite entrance to Loch Breachacha. **36 A4** NM1551.
Soa Island *Arg. & B.* ***Island***, small island, 2m/3km SW of Rubha na Carraig-géire, at S end of Iona. **28 B3** NM2419.
Soaidh Beag *W.Isles Gaelic form of Soay Beg, qv.*
Soaidh Mòr *W.Isles Gaelic form of Soay Mòr, qv.*
Soay *High.* ***Island***, of about 4 square miles or 10 square km lying off S coast of Skye across Soay Sound. Island is mainly flat, but rises to 455 feet or 108 metres in Beinn Bhreac. Literary associations with Gavin Maxwell, Ted Geddes and Lilian Beckwith. **48 A3** NG4514.
Soay *W.Isles* ***Island***, steep, rocky, uninhabited island (National Trust for Scotland) in St. Kilda group about 56m/89km W of North Harris and 37m/59km NW of North Uist, lying off NW end of St. Kilda itself. Area about 240 acres or 97 hectares. Haunt of sea birds. NA0601.
Soay Beg (Gaelic form: Soaidh Beag.) *W.Isles* ***Island***, small uninhabited island in West Loch Tarbert off coast of North Harris, to NW of, and adjacent to, Soay Mòr. **66 C3** NB0605.
Soay Mòr (Gaelic form: Soaidh Mòr.) *W.Isles* ***Island***, small uninhabited island in West Loch Tarbert, off W coast of North Harris. **66 C3** NB0605.
Soay Sound *High.* ***Sea feature***, stretch of sea separating Soay and Skye. **48 A3** NG4416.
Soay Sound *W.Isles* ***Sea feature***, stretch of sea separating North Harris from Soag Beag and Soay Mòr. **66 C3** NB0606.
Soay Stac *W.Isles* ***Island***, islet (National Trust for Scotland) situated between Soay and St. Kilda. NA0701.
Society *W.Loth.* ***Settlement***, on S side of Firth of Forth, 2m/3km W of Forth Road Bridge. NT0979.
Solas (Anglicised form: Sollas.) *W.Isles* ***Village***, near N end of North Uist, 5m/8km E of Griminis Point. **45 G2** NF8074.
Sole Burn *D. & G.* ***River***, rising in hills 3m/4km W of Kirkcolm and flowing S, then E, into Loch Ryan at Soleburn. **6 B4** NX0364.
Soleburn Bridge *D. & G.* ***Locality***, on W side of Loch Ryan, 3m/4km NW of Stranraer. Road crosses Sole Burn where it enters Loch Ryan. **6 B4** NX0364.
Sollas *W.Isles Anglicised form of Solas, qv.*
Solsgirth *P. & K.* ***Settlement***, 2m/4km SE of Dollar. **33 E5** NS9895.
Solway Firth ***Sea feature***, arm of Irish Sea between coasts of Cumbria (England) and Dumfries & Galloway (Scotland). Receives waters of Rivers Nith, Annan, Esk, Eden, Wampool, Waver and Derwent. Largely occupied by broad sands and notorious for dangerous tides. **4 B3** NY0050.
Solwaybank *D. & G.* ***Settlement***, 5m/8km W of Canonbie, on S side of Allfornought Hill. **10 B4** NY3077.
Soonhope Burn *Sc.Bord.* ***River***, small stream rising in Lammermuir Hills and flowing S to join Cleekhimin Burn 1m/2km E of Carfraemill. **26 C4** NT5253.
Soray *W.Isles* ***Island***, one of Flannan Isles group, lying nearly 1m/2km S of main island, Eilean Mòr. NA7245.
Sorbie *D. & G.* ***Village***, 4m/7km N of Whithorn. **3 E2** NX4346.
Sordale *High.* ***Settlement***, in Caithness district, 4m/7km SE of Thurso. **76 D2** ND1462.
Sorisdale *Arg. & B.* ***Locality***, on bay of same name, 1km S of NE end of Coll. **36 B3** NM2763.
Sorn *E.Ayr.* ***Village***, on River Ayr, 4m/6km E of Mauchline. **15 D3** NS5526.
Sorn Castle *E.Ayr.* ***Castle***, dates in part from 15c, 4m/6km E of Mauchline. NS5526.
Sorne Point *Arg. & B.* ***Coastal feature***, headland on N coast of Mull, 3m/5km W of Ardmore Point. **36 D4** NM4257.
Sornhill *E.Ayr.* ***Settlement***, 1m/2km S of Galston. **14 D2** NS5134.
Soroba *Arg. & B.* ***Settlement***, adjoining to S of Oban. **30 A2** NM8628.
Sortat *High.* ***Settlement***, in Caithness district, 6m/10km SE of Castletown. **77 E2** ND2863.
Soulseat Abbey *D. & G.* ***Ecclesiastical building***, founded in 12c and situated on peninsula on S shore of Soulseat Loch, 3m/4km SE of Stranraer. NX1058.
Soulseat Loch *D. & G.* ***Lake/loch***, 3m/4km SE of Stranraer. **6 C5** NX1058.
Sound *Shet.* ***Settlement***, on Mainland, on W side of Weisdale Voe, 1m/2km E of Tresta. **82 C2** HU3850.
Sound *Shet.* ***Village***, on Mainland, 1m/2km SW of Lerwick, near head of large inlet, Voe of Sound. **83 D3** HU4640.
Sound Gruney *Shet.* ***Island***, small island 1m/2km E of Burra Ness, Yell. **85 E3** HU5796.
Sound of Arisaig *High.* ***Sea feature***, large inlet on coast of Lochaber district, with two arms, Loch nan Uamh and Loch Ailort, passing to N and S respectively of peninsula of Ardnish. **37 F1** NM6580.
Sound of Barra *W.Isles* ***Sea feature***, sea passage between South Uist and Barra. **44 C2** NF7509.
Sound of Berneray *W.Isles* ***Sea feature***, strait separating Berneray and North Uist. **45 G2** NF9079.
Sound of Berneray *W.Isles* ***Sea feature***, stretch of sea separating Bearnaraigh and Mingulay. **44 A5** NL5681.
Sound of Bute *Arg. & B.* ***Sea feature***, sea area between Bute and N end of Arran. **22 A4** NS0155.
Sound of Canna *High.* ***Sea feature***, stretch of sea separating Sanday and Canna from Rum. **47 G4** NG3002.
Sound of Eigg *High.* ***Sea feature***, sea passage between islands of Eigg and Muck, in Inner Hebrides. **36 D1** NM4382.
Sound of Eriskay *W.Isles* ***Sea feature***, strait, about 1m/2km wide, between South Uist and Eriskay. **44 C2** NF7913.
Sound of Faray *Ork.* ***Sea feature***, channel between islands of Faray and Eday. **80 D3** HY5336.
Sound of Gigha *Arg. & B.* ***Sea feature***, sea passage between Gigha and Kintyre. **21 E5** NR6749.
Sound of Handa *High.* ***Sea feature***, narrow sea channel separating Handa Island from W coast of Sutherland district. **74 A4** NC1547.
Sound of Harris *W.Isles* ***Sea feature***, sea passage between South Harris and North Uist containing innumerable small islands and rocks. The four larger islands are Berneray, Ensay, Killegray and Pabbay. **66 B5** NF9681.
Sound of Hellisay *W.Isles* ***Sea feature***, strait separating numerous islets off NE coast of Barra from Hellisay, 1m/2km S of Balivanich. **44 C3** NF7403.
Sound of Hoxa *Ork.* ***Sea feature***, sea passage between Flotta and South Ronaldsay. **78 C3** ND3893.
Sound of Insh *Arg. & B.* ***Sea feature***, passage in Firth of Lorn between Insh Island and Seil. **29 G3** NM7419.
Sound of Iona *Arg. & B.* ***Sea feature***, sea strait between Iona and Ross of Mull. **28 B2** NM2822.
Sound of Islay *Arg. & B.* ***Sea feature***, narrow strait between Islay and Jura. **20 C2** NR3875.
Sound of Jura *Arg. & B.* ***Sea feature***, sea passage between Jura and Scottish mainland. **21 E2** NR6480.
Sound of Kerrera *Arg. & B.* ***Sea feature***, stretch of sea separating Kerrera from Scottish mainland. **30 A2** NM8227.
Sound of Luing *Arg. & B.* ***Sea feature***, sea passage to W of Luing, separating it from Scarba, Lunga, and neighbouring islands. **29 G4** NM7208.
Sound of Mingulay *W.Isles* ***Sea feature***, stretch of sea separating Mingulay and Pabbay. **44 A5** NL5986.
Sound of Monach *W.Isles* ***Sea feature***, sea passage between Heisker Islands group and W coast of North Uist. **45 E3** NF7063.
Sound of Mull ***Sea feature***, narrow sea passage between Mull and Morven on Scottish mainland. Width varies from 1m/2km to 3m/5km. **37 E4** NM5945.
Sound of Orfasay *Shet.* ***Sea feature***, separates S coast of Yell from Orfasay. HU4977.
Sound of Pabbay *W.Isles* ***Sea feature***, sea channel separating Pabbay and Berneray. **45 G1** NF9085.
Sound of Pabbay *W.Isles* ***Sea feature***, sea channel separating Pabbay and Sandray. **44 B5** NL6289.
Sound of Papa *Shet.* ***Sea feature***, strait 1m/2km wide separating Papa Stour island from Mainland. **82 A2** HU1758.
Sound of Pladda *N.Ayr.* ***Sea feature***, strait between Pladda and SE tip of Arran. **13 F4** NS0220.
Sound of Raasay *High.* ***Sea feature***, sea channel between Raasay and Skye. **58 B5** NG5654.
Sound of Rum *High.* ***Sea feature***, sea passage between Rum and Eigg, in Inner Hebrides. **36 C1** NM4390.
Sound of Sandray *W.Isles* ***Sea feature***, stretch of sea separating Sandray and Vatersay. **44 B4** NL6393.
Sound of Scalpay *W.Isles* ***Sea feature***, narrow strait between Scalpay and SE coast of North Harris. **67 E4** NG2297.
Sound of Shiant *W.Isles* ***Sea feature***, sea passage between Shiant Islands and SE coast of Isle of Lewis. **67 F4** NB3701.
Sound of Shillay *W.Isles* ***Sea feature***, sea channel separating Pabbay and Shillay. **45 G1** NF8890.
Sound of Shuna *Arg. & B.* ***Sea feature***, strait in Loch Linnhe between Shuna Island and mainland to E. **38 B5** NM9249.
Sound of Sleat *High.* ***Sea feature***, stretch of sea separating Scottish mainland from Sleat peninsula, Skye. **48 C4** NG6602.
Sound of Taransay *W.Isles* ***Sea feature***, stretch of sea separating Tarasaigh from South Harris. **66 C4** NG0498.
Sound of the Green Holms *Ork.* ***Sea feature***, narrow channel between Muckle Green Holm and Little Green Holm. HY5226.
Sound of Ulva *Arg. & B.* ***Sea feature***, narrow strait between Ulva and Mull. **29 D1** NM3640.
Sound of Vatersay *W.Isles* ***Coastal feature***, narrow strait between Barra and Vatersay. NL6397.
Sourhope *Sc.Bord.* ***Hamlet***, 2m/3km SE of Mowhaugh. **18 C4** NT8420.
Sourin *Ork.* ***Locality***, at E end of Rousay, 2m/3km N of Brinyan. **80 C3** HY4330.
Souter Head *Aberdeen* ***Coastal feature***, headland on E coast, 3m/5km SE of Aberdeen city centre. **55 E4** NJ9601.
Souter Johnnie's Cottage *S.Ayr.* ***Historic house***, National Trust for Scotland property in Kirkoswald. Home of original Souter (cobbler), John Davidson, as described in Burns' poem, Tam o' Shanter. Contains Burns relics, a restored workshop and a reconstructed ale-house with life-size stone figures from poem. **14 A5** NS2406.
South Alloa *Falk.* ***Settlement***, on S bank of River Forth, 1km SW of Alloa across river. **33 D5** NS8791.
South Ascrib *High.* ***Island***, most southerly of Ascrib Islands group in Loch Snizort. **57 G3** NG3064.
South Ballachulish *High.* ***Settlement***, on S side of mouth of Loch Leven, 3m/5km W of Glencoe village. **38 C4** NN0459.
South Balloch *S.Ayr.* ***Settlement***, on S side of River Strinchar, 3m/5km E of Barr. **7 E1** NX3295.
South Bay *Ork.* ***Bay***, wide bay on S coast of North Ronaldsay. **81 F1** HY7452.
South Bay of Eswick *Shet.* ***Bay***, to S of Eswick, Mainland. HU4853.
South Blackbog *Aber.* ***Settlement***, 4m/6km SE of Fyvie. **54 C1** NJ7932.
South Boisdale *W.Isles Anglicised form of Leth Meadhanach, qv.*
South Broomage *Falk.* ***Suburb***, on S side of Larbert. NS8681.
South Cairn *D. & G.* ***Settlement***, 4m/6km W of Kirkcolm. **6 A4** NW9769.
South Calder Water *N.Lan.* ***River***, rising on hills to E of Shotts and flowing W, passing Motherwell to N and flowing through Strathclyde Loch and into River Clyde. NS7257.
South Carbrain *N.Lan.* ***Locality***, industrial area in Cumbernauld to S of Carbrain. NS7674.
South Cardonald *Glas.* ***Suburb***, adjoining to S of Cardonald, 4m/6km SW of Glasgow city centre. NS5264.
South Collafirth *Shet.* ***Settlement***, at head of Colla Firth inlet, 6m/10km N of Sullom, Mainland. HU3482.
South Corrygills *N.Ayr.* ***Settlement***, on Arran, 2m/3km SE of Brodick. **13 F2** NS0334.
South Creagan *Arg. & B.* ***Settlement***, 1km S of Creagan across Loch Creran. **38 B5** NM9743.
South Crossaig *Arg. & B.* ***Locality***, one of two adjoining localities S of Crossaig Glen, on road running beside E coast of Kintyre, Argyll, 4m/7km SW of Claonaig. NR8351.
South Deep *Fife* ***Sea feature***, channel in River Tay estuary, between Mugdrum Island and S bank. **34 A3** NO2218.
South Dell *W.Isles Anglicised form of Dail Bho Dheas, qv.*

S

South Erradale *High.* ***Settlement***, on W coast of Ross and Cromarty district, 3m/4km N of Red Point. **58 D2** NG7471.
South Esk ***River***, rising SE of Braemar and running SE down Glen Clova, then E to Brechin and into North Sea at Montrose. **42 B3** NO7356.
South Esk *Midloth.* ***River***, rising on Moorfoot Hills and flowing N through Gladhouse and Rosebery Reservoirs to confluence with North Esk River, 1m/2km N of Dalkeith. **26 A3** NT3369.
South Flobbets *Aber.* ***Settlement***, 3m/5km SE of Fyvie. **54 C1** NJ7934.
South Galson *W.Isles* *Anglicised form of Gabhsunn Bho Dheas, qv.*
South Galson *W.Isles* ***River***, on Isle of Lewis, passing between Gabhsunn Bho Thuath and Gabhsunn Bho Dheas and flowing out to sea to N. **69 F2** NB4358.
South Garth *Shet.* ***Settlement***, just N of Gutcher, Yell. **85 E3** HU5499.
South Hall *Arg. & B.* ***Settlement***, to W of Inverneil Burn, 1m/2km W of Strone Point. **22 B2** NS0672.
South Harbour *Shet.* ***Bay***, on S coast of Fair Isle. **82 A5** HZ2069.
South Harris (Gaelic form: Ceann a Deas na Hearadh.) *W.Isles* ***Large natural feature***, S part of Isle of Lewis, joined to North Harris by narrow neck of land to SW of Tarbert, with West and East Loch Tarbert on either side. South Harris is dominated by craggy mountains, especially surrounding Beinn Dhubh in N part at 1660 feet or 506 metres, and the central An Coileach at 1266 feet or 386 metres, with cnoc and lochan terrain to E. **66 C4** NG0792.
South Harris Forest *W.Isles* ***Open space***, upland area on South Harris, to SW of Tarbert. **66 C4** NG1098.
South Havra *Shet.* ***Island***, uninhabited island of about 150 acres or 60 hectares lying 1m/2km W of coast of Mainland and about 1m/2km S of East and West Burra. **82 C5** HU3627.
South Head *High.* ***Coastal feature***, headland to S of Wick Bay. **77 F4** ND3749.
South Holms *Shet.* ***Island***, small island 1m/2km S of North Holms. **85 E1** HP5711.
South Hourat *N.Ayr.* ***Settlement***, 2m/3km W of Kilbirnie. **23 D4** NS2853.
South Inch *Aber.* ***Coastal feature***, beach with large pools, 1km SE of St. Combs. **65 F3** NK0662.
South Isle of Gletness *Shet.* ***Island***, one of two small islands to S of Glet Ness headland on E coast of Mainland. **83 D2** HU4751.
South Kessock *High.* ***Suburb***, of Inverness on S bank of Beauly Firth. **61 F5** NH6547.
South Kirkton *Aber.* ***Settlement***, adjacent to S of Echt. **54 C4** NJ7305.
South Kiscadale *N.Ayr.* ***Settlement***, forms locality of Kiscadale, along with North Kiscadale, and adjoins to W of Whiting Bay. NS0425.
South Laggan Forest *High.* ***Forest/woodland***, extending along both sides of Loch Lochy at its NE end. NN2894.
South Ledaig *Arg. & B.* ***Settlement***, 1km N of North Connel. **30 B1** NM9035.
South Lee *W.Isles* ***Hill***, on North Uist, 2m/4km S of Lochmaddy. Height 922 feet or 281 metres. **56 C3** NF9165.
South Lochboisdale *W.Isles* *Anglicised form of Taobh a' Deas Loch Baghasdail, qv.*
South Medwin *S.Lan.* ***River***, rising from streams flowing off Pentland Hills, flowing SW through a wide valley and joining North Medwin River to become Medwin Water before flowing into River Clyde, 1m/2km S of Carnwath. **25 E5** NS9844.
South Morar *High.* ***Locality***, mountainous coastal area of Lochaber district between Loch Morar to N and Loch nan Uamh to S. **37 G1** NM7587.
South Ness *Fife* ***Coastal feature***, headland on SE coast of Isle of May. **35 E5** NT6698.
South Ness *Ork.* ***Coastal feature***, headland and settlement with pier on peninsula of South Walls, on S side of entrance to North Bay. ND3091.
South Ness *Shet.* ***Coastal feature***, headland and southernmost point of Foula. **82 B5** HT9636.
South Nesting *Shet.* ***Locality***, forms locality of Nesting on Mainland, along with North Nesting. **83 D2** HU4554.
South Nesting Bay *Shet.* ***Bay***, enclosed by Nesting on E coast. The bay extends S from Hill of Neap to N end of Moul of Eswick. **83 D2** HU4956.
South Nevi *Ork.* ***Coastal feature***, on S coast of small island of Copinsay, off SE coast of Mainland. **79 E2** HY6000.
South Newton *N.Ayr.* ***Locality***, one of two adjoining localities at N end of Arran, opposite Lochranza across Loch Ranza. NR9351.
South Parks *Fife* ***Suburb***, in centre of Glenrothes. NO2601.
South Point *Arg. & B.* ***Coastal feature***, rocky headland on W side of S tip of Kintyre peninsula, 6m/10km W of Southend. **12 A5** NR5807.
South Queensferry *Edin.* ***Locality***, with harbour and lighthouse, at S end of Forth bridges. **25 F2** NT1278.
South Queich *P. & K.* ***River***, stream rising in Ochil Hills and flowing E to enter Loch Leven to S of Kinross. **33 F4** NO0112.
South Redbriggs *Aber.* ***Settlement***, to E of Wood of Hatton, 4m/7km SE of Turriff. **64 C5** NJ7945.
South Rona *High.* *Alternative name for Rona, qv.*
South Ronaldsay *Ork.* ***Island***, most southerly of main islands of Orkney group, measuring about 8m/12km N to S and 2m/4km E to W. Linked by Churchill Barrier to Burray, Glimps Holm, Lamb Holm and Mainland. **79 D4** ND4590.
South Shawbost *W.Isles* ***Settlement***, near NW coast of Isle of Lewis, forms locality of Siabost along with North and New Shawbost, 3m/5km W of Bragar. NB2546.
South Shian *Arg. & B.* ***Locality***, on S shore of Loch Creran, in Argyll. **38 B5** NM9041.
South Sound *Shet.* ***Sea feature***, sea passage between Hascosay and Ness of Vatsetter, Yell. **85 E3** HU5490.
South Tarbet Bay *High.* ***Bay***, small inlet on Loch Morar, 1km SE of Tarbet. NM7991.
South Tarbrax *S.Lan.* ***Locality***, 1m/2km S of Tarbrax. NT0254.
South Thundergay *N.Ayr.* *Alternative name for Auchamore, qv.*
South Top *Aber.* ***Mountain***, S summit of Beinn a' Bhùird mass in Grampian Mountains, 6m/9km NW of Braemar. Height 3861 feet or 1177 metres. **52 C5** NO0997.
South Ugie Water *Aber.* ***River***, rising to W of Maud and flowing E through Old Deer to join River North Ugie 1m/2km NE of Longside, forming River Ugie. **65 E5** NK0548.
South Uist (Gaelic form: Uibhist a Deas.) *W.Isles* ***Island***, of about 140 square miles or 365 square km between Benbecula (causeway connection) and Barra. Contains numerous lochs, especially on W side; mountains on E side rise to 2034 feet or 620 metres. **46 A1** NF7932.
South Upper Barrack *Aber.* ***Settlement***, 2m/3km W of Auchnagatt and 3m/5km SE of New Deer. **65 E5** NJ9042.
South View *Shet.* ***Settlement***, on White Ness, Mainland, 2m/4km NW of Scalloway across Whiteness Voe. **82 C3** HU3842.
South Voe of Gletness *Shet.* ***Sea feature***, small inlet to SW of Glet Ness headland, on E coast of Mainland. HU4651.
South Walls *Ork.* ***Coastal feature***, peninsula at SE end of Hoy, over 3m/5km E to W and nearly 2m/3km N to S, and joined to the rest of Hoy by narrow neck of land, The Ayre, carrying a road. **78 C4** ND3189.
South Wick *Shet.* ***Bay***, on NW coast of Mainland, bounded by Fugla Ness to N. **84 C3** HU3190.
Southbar *Renf.* ***Settlement***, 1km S of Erskine. **23 F3** NS4669.
Southdean *Sc.Bord.* ***Locality***, 5m/7km NW of Carter Bar. **11 E1** NT6309.
Southend *Aber.* ***Settlement***, 1m/2km SW of Turriff. **64 C5** NJ7148.
Southend *Arg. & B.* ***Village***, in Kintyre, 8m/13km S of Campbeltown. **12 B5** NR6908.
Southerness *D. & G.* ***Village***, small village and resort with disused lighthouse at Southerness Point, headland on Solway Firth, 3m/5km S of Kirkbean. **9 D5** NX9754.
Southerness Point *D. & G.* ***Coastal feature***, headland on Solway Firth, 3m/5km S of Kirkbean. **9 D5** NX9754.
Southfield *Edin.* ***Suburb***, of Edinburgh, 1m/2km S of Portobello. NT3072.
Southfield *Fife* ***Suburb***, on S side of Glenrothes. NT2699.
Southhouse *Edin.* ***Suburb***, 4m/7km S of Edinburgh city centre. NT2767.
Southmuir *Angus* ***Locality***, adjoining to S of Kirriemuir. **42 B4** NO3853.
Southpunds *Shet.* ***Locality***, on Mainland, 8m/13km N of Sumburgh Head. HU4020.
Southtown *Ork.* ***Settlement***, in S of Burray, 1km E of Burray village. **79 D3** ND4895.
Southwick *D. & G.* ***Settlement***, to NE of Caulkerbush, 7m/11km SE of Dalbeattie. NX9357.
Southwick Burn *D. & G.* ***River***, rising on W slopes of Maidenpap, flowing SE and joining with numerous other streams to flow through Caulkerbush and into Solway Firth on Mersehead Sands. **8 C4** NX9059.
Soutra Hill *Sc.Bord.* ***Mountain***, 2m/3km SE of Fala. Height 1207 feet or 368 metres. **26 B4** NT4559.
Soyal *High.* ***Locality***, 3m/4km W of Bonar Bridge. **72 A5** NH5791.
Soyea Island *High.* ***Island***, small uninhabited island off W coast of Sutherland district opposite mouth of Loch Inver. **70 C2** NC0422.
Spalefield *Fife* ***Settlement***, 2m/3km N of Anstruther. **35 D4** NO5506.
Spango Bridge *D. & G.* ***Bridge***, road bridge at confluence of Spango Water and Crawick Water, 6m/9km NE of Sanquhar. NS8217.
Spango Water ***River***, running E to Crawick Water at Spango Bridge, 6m/9km NE of Sanquhar. **15 F4** NS8217.
Spar Cave (Also known as Uamh Altrumain.) *High.* ***Cave***, on Skye, on W shore of Loch Slapin, 1m/2km N of Strathaird Point. **48 B3** NG5312.
Spartleton Edge *E.Loth.* ***Inland physical feature***, ridge running NW to SE in Lammermuir Hills 6m/10km S of Stenton. **27 D3** NT6565.
Spean *High.* ***River***, in Lochaber district, running W down Glen Spean to River Lochy, below Loch Lochy. **39 E1** NN1783.
Spean Bridge *High.* ***Village***, on River Spean in Lochaber district, 3m/5km E of foot of Loch Lochy at Gairlochy. Bridge built by Telford. Commandos trained hereabouts in World War II; Commando Memorial 1m/2km W. **39 E1** NN2281.
Spear Head *High.* ***Coastal feature***, headland on N coast of Caithness district, 2m/4km NW of Thurso. ND0971.
Speddoch *D. & G.* ***Settlement***, 2m/3km SW of Dunscore. **8 C2** NX8582.
Speinne Mòr *Arg. & B.* ***Mountain***, rising from NE shore of Loch Frisa, 3m/5km S of Tobermory, Mull. Height 1456 feet or 444 metres. **37 E5** NM5049.
Spey ***River***, major river of NE Scotland rising in Loch Spey on Corrieyairack Forest, 10m/16km S of Fort Augustus, and fed by many tributaries before flowing E past Laggan, then NE through Newtonmore and Kingussie through to Strathspey and into Loch Insh. It continues NE, following a winding course by Aviemore and Grantown-on-Spey, before turning N at Charlestown of Aberlour and continuing past Rothes to Spey Bay on Moray Firth at Kingston. Length 107m/172km. Lower course is noted for its profusion of distilleries, forming heart of Highland whisky industry. **63 F4** NJ3465.
Spey Bay *Moray* ***Village***, on bay of same name, on N coast, on E side of mouth of River Spey. **63 F3** NJ3565.
Spey Mouth *Moray* ***Sea feature***, River Spey mouth emptying into Spey Bay, 1km N of Garmouth, with Kingston on its E side. **63 F3** NJ3465.
Speybridge *High.* ***Settlement***, in Badenoch and Strathspey district, 1m/2km S of Grantown-on-Spey. **52 C2** NJ0326.
Speymouth Forest *Moray* ***Forest/woodland***, to S of Fochabers. **63 F4** NJ3657.
Speyside Heather Centre *High.* ***Other feature of interest***, ornamental garden, 2m/3km SW of Dulnain Bridge, with approximately 300 varieties of heather, together with an exhibition of historical uses of heather. Includes famous Clootie Dumpling Restaurant. **52 B2** NH9722.
Speyview *Moray* ***Settlement***, to SW of Charlestown of Aberlour across Burn of Aberlour. **63 E5** NJ2642.
Spidean a' Choire Leith *High.* ***Mountain***, summit of Liathach, Ross and Cromarty district. Munro: height 3457 feet or 1054 metres. **59 F4** NG9257.
Spidean Còinich *High.* ***Mountain***, with summit 1m/2km N of Loch Assynt. Height 2506 feet or 764 metres. **71 E2** NC2027.
Spidean Coire nan Clach *High.* ***Mountain***, summit of Beinn Eighe, 4m/7km SW of Kinlochewe in Ross and Cromarty district. Munro: height 3188 feet or 972 metres. NG9659.
Spidean Dhomhuill Bhric *High.* ***Mountain***, peak on border of Lochaber and Skye and Lochalsh districts, 4m/6km S of Shiel Bridge and nearly 1m/2km W of The Saddle. Height 3083 feet or 940 metres. **49 F3** NG9212.
Spidean Mialach *High.* ***Mountain***, peak on Glenquoich Forest, Lochaber district, 1m/2km N of dam of Loch Quoich. Munro: height 3267 feet or 996 metres. **49 G4** NH0604.
Spinningdale *High.* ***Village***, on N shore of Dornoch Firth, Sutherland district, 8m/12km W of Dornoch. **72 B5** NH6789.
Spital *High.* ***Settlement***, in Caithness district, 5m/8km W of Wattern. **77 D3** ND1654.
Spittal *D. & G.* ***Settlement***, 4m/7km W of Wigtown. **7 E5** NX3557.
Spittal *D. & G.* ***Settlement***, on E side of River Cree, 1m/2km N of Creetown. **7 F4** NX4760.
Spittal *E.Loth.* ***Settlement***, 2m/3km NE of Longniddry. **26 B2** NT4677.
Spittal Hill *High.* ***Hill***, 1km N of Spittal. Height 577 feet or 176 metres. **77 D3** ND1655.
Spittal of Glenmuick *Aber.* ***Hamlet***, 1km N of Loch Muick. Mountain Rescue Post. **42 B1** NO3085.
Spittal of Glenshee *P. & K.* ***Settlement***, on Shee Water, 13m/21km S of Braemar. **41 G3** NO1169.
Spittalfield *P. & K.* ***Village***, 5m/8km SW of Blairgowrie. Remains of Roman fortress at Inchtuthill, 1m/2km SE. **41 G5** NO1040.
Spo Ness *Ork.* ***Coastal feature***, rocky headland on W coast of Westray. **80 C2** HY4846.
Spoo Ness *Shet.* ***Coastal feature***, rocky headland on W coast of Unst, 1m/2km NW of Newgord. **85 E2** HP5607.
Spott *E.Loth.* ***Village***, 2m/3km S of Dunbar. **27 D2** NT6775.
Spott Burn *E.Loth.* ***River***, rising 1m/2km E of Stenton and flowing NE via Spott to North Sea, 1m/2km E of Dunbar. NT6978.

S

Spout of Ballagan *Stir.* ***Waterfall***, series of cascades in course of Ballagan Burn, 1m/2km NE of Strathblane. NS5780.
Spout Rolla *P. & K.* ***Waterfall***, in River Lednock to S of Loch Lednock Reservoir and 4m/6km NE of St. Fillans. **32 C2** NN7328.
Springboig *Glas.* ***Suburb***, 3m/5km E of Glasgow city centre. NS6564.
Springburn *Glas.* ***Suburb***, 2m/3km N of Glasgow city centre. **24 A3** NS6068.
Springfield *Arg. & B.* ***Settlement***, on E coast of Loch Riddon, 2m/3km S of Auchenbreck. **22 B2** NS0179.
Springfield *D. & G.* ***Village***, adjoining to E of Gretna Green. **10 B5** NY3268.
Springfield *Fife* ***Village***, 3m/4km SW of Cupar. **34 B3** NO3411.
Springfield *Moray* ***Settlement***, adjoining to N of Forres. **62 C4** NJ0460.
Springfield *P. & K.* ***Settlement***, 1m/2km S of Burrelton. **33 G1** NO1935.
Springfield Reservoir *S.Lan.* ***Reservoir***, small reservoir 4m/6km E of Carluke. **24 D4** NS9052.
Springholm *D. & G.* ***Village***, 6m/9km NE of Castle Douglas. **8 C4** NX8070.
Springkell *D. & G.* ***Settlement***, on E side of Kirtle Water, 4m/6km E of Ecclefechan. **9 G3** NY2575.
Springleys *Aber.* ***Settlement***, 2m/3km E of Rothienorman. **54 C1** NJ7437.
Springside *N.Ayr.* Population: 1364. ***Hamlet***, 3m/5km E of Irvine. **14 B2** NS3738.
Sprouston *Sc.Bord.* ***Village***, on S side of River Tweed, 2m/3km NE of Kelso. **18 B3** NT7535.
Spur Ness *Ork.* ***Coastal feature***, headland at SW end of Sanday. **81 E3** HY6033.
Spynie *Moray* ***Locality***, 2m/3km NE of Elgin. To N are ruins of Palace of Spynie (Historic Scotland). NJ2265.
Spynie Canal *Moray* ***Canal***, extension of Terchick Burn cut to serve as a transport link for merchants in Elgin. Canal flows E from near Gilston to NW side of Loch Spynie, then N into sea at Lossiemouth. **63 E3** NJ2370.
Spynie Palace *Moray* *Alternative name for Palace of Spynie, qv.*
Square Point *D. & G.* ***Locality***, 1km NE of Walton Park. **8 B3** NX7771.
Srath a' Chràisg *High.* ***Valley***, to S of Strath Vagastie in Sutherland district and carrying Allt Domhain. **72 A2** NC5325.
Srath na Seilge *High.* ***Valley***, carrying Black Water river and running SE in Ben Armine Forest. **72 B3** NC6820.
Srath nan Caran *High.* ***Valley***, running W into Loch na Creige Duibhe. NC2836.
Srianach *W.Isles* ***Coastal feature***, promontory on N side of entrance to Loch Shell. **67 G2** NB4010.
Sròn a' Chlaonaidh *P. & K.* ***Mountain***, on E side of S end of Loch Ericht, 4m/7km N of Bridge of Ericht. Height 2050 feet or 625 metres. **40 A3** NN5065.
Sròn a' Chleirich *P. & K.* ***Mountain***, on Dail-na-mine Forest, Forest of Atholl, 9m/14km NW of Blair Atholl. Height 2676 feet or 816 metres. **40 C2** NN7876.
Sròn a' Choire Ghairbh *High.* ***Mountain***, in Lochaber district, 9m/13km N of Spean Bridge across Loch Lochy. Munro: height 3067 feet or 935 metres. **50 B5** NN2294.
Sròn Ach' a' Bhacaidh *High.* ***Hill***, in Sutherland district, 4m/6km N of Bonar Bridge. Height 928 feet or 283 metres. **72 A5** NH6198.
Sròn an Dùin *W.Isles* ***Coastal feature***, headland on W coast of Mingulay. **44 A5** NL5480.
Sròn an t-Sluichd *High.* ***Mountain***, 3m/4km S of head of Loch Eil, Lochaber district. Height 1204 feet or 367 metres. **38 B2** NM9674.
Sròn Bheag *High.* ***Coastal feature***, headland on S coast of Ardnamurchan peninsula, 2m/3km SW of Kilchoan. **37 D3** NM4662.
Sròn Bheag *P. & K.* ***Mountain***, rounded summit in Rannoch district, 3m/4km N of Bridge of Ericht. Height 1689 feet or 515 metres. **40 A3** NN5262.
Sròn Choin *P. & K.* ***Mountain***, to N of Loch Errochty, 3m/4km NW of Trinafour. Height 1856 feet or 566 metres. **40 B3** NN6866.
Sròn Coire na h-Iolaire *High.* ***Mountain***, in Badenoch and Strathspey district 1km SE of S end of Loch a' Bhealaich Bheithe. Height 3132 feet or 955 metres. NN5170.
Sròn Doire *Arg. & B.* ***Settlement***, in Knapdale, 7m/11km N of Tarbert. **21 G2** NR8478.
Sròn Garbh *Arg. & B.* ***Coastal feature***, rocky headland to E of Ardfernal, Jura. **21 D2** NR5670.
Sròn Gharbh *Stir.* ***Mountain***, on SE side of Glen Falloch, 3m/4km S of Crianlarich. Height 2322 feet or 708 metres. **31 F2** NN3721.
Sròn Gun Aran *High.* ***Inland physical feature***, rounded ridge between the steep-sided valleys of Gleann Mòr and Alladale River. **60 D1** NH4088.
Sròn Mhòr *Arg. & B.* ***Mountain***, rising above River Massan, 1m/2km SW of Beinn Mhòr. Height 1670 feet or 509 metres. **22 B1** NS0989.
Sròn Mòr *P. & K.* ***Inland physical feature***, mountain ridge on W side of Glen Tarken rising to 2204 feet or 672 metres, 3m/4km NW of St. Fillans. **32 B2** NN6525.
Sròn na h-Airde Baine *High.* ***Coastal feature***, headland on W coast of Ross and Cromarty district, 1m/2km NW of Toscaig. **58 C5** NG6939.
Sròn na Lairig *High.* ***Mountain***, NE peak of Braeriach, in Cairngorm Mountains, on border with Aberdeenshire. Height 3884 feet or 1184 metres. NH9601.
Sròn nan Saobhaidh *High.* ***Mountain***, in Ross and Cromarty district, at NE end of Orrin Reservoir, 9m/13km W of Muir of Ord. Height 1338 feet or 408 metres. **60 D4** NH3951.
Sròn Ocrhulan *High.* ***Hill***, 3m/4km SE of Vaternish Point, Skye. Height 823 feet or 251 metres. **57 F3** NG2463.
Sròn Raineach *High.* ***Coastal feature***, headland on N coast of North Morar, 2m/3km E of Mallaig. **48 D5** NM7098.
Sròn Romul *W.Isles* ***Mountain***, highest point of Scarp, 3m/4km NW of Huisinis, North Harris. Height 1010 feet or 308 metres. **66 B2** NA9615.
Sròn Ruadh *W.Isles* ***Coastal feature***, headland on E coast of Isle of Lewis, 3m/5km NE of Stornoway. **69 F4** NB4636.
Sròn Ruail *High.* ***Coastal feature***, headland on Canna, to S of Garrisdale Point. **47 F4** NG2104.
Sròn Thoraraidh *High.* ***Mountain***, 3m/4km NE of Lochailort to N of Loch Eilt. Height 1256 feet or 383 metres. **38 A1** NM8083.
Sronphadruig Lodge *P. & K.* ***Settlement***, 6m/10km SE of Dalwhinnie. **40 C2** NN7178.
Stac a' Bhothain *High.* ***Coastal feature***, headland on E coast of Vaternish peninsula, 6m/10km SE of Vaternish Point, Skye. **57 F4** NG2859.
Stac an Aoineidh *Arg. & B.* ***Island***, islet off SW coast of Iona. **28 B2** NM2522.
Stac an Armin *W.Isles* ***Island***, islet (National Trust for Scotland) lying off N end of Boreray, about 52m/83km W of North Harris. Attains height of 643 feet or 196 metres. Haunt of sea birds. NA1506.
Stac Lee *W.Isles* ***Island***, islet (National Trust for Scotland) lying off W side of Boreray, about 52m/83km W of North Harris. Attains height of 1259 feet or 384 metres. Haunt of sea birds. NA1404.
Stac Mhic Mhurchaidh *Arg. & B.* ***Island***, islet on W side of Réidh Eilean, off NW coast of Iona. NM2426.
Stac na Cathaig *High.* ***Mountain***, in Inverness district, 9m/14km S of Inverness. Height 1463 feet or 446 metres. **51 F1** NH6330.
Stac Pollaidh (Anglicised form: Stac Polly.) *High.* ***Mountain***, well-known landmark in Ross and Cromarty district to N of Loch Lurgainn. Height 2011 feet or 613 metres. **70 D3** NC1010.
Stac Polly *High.* *Anglicised form of Stac Pollaidh, qv.*
Stacashal *W.Isles* ***Hill***, 6m/9km E of Breascleit, Isle of Lewis. Height 708 feet or 216 metres. **69 E4** NB3037.
Stack Clo Kearvaig *High.* ***Coastal feature***, stack just off N coast of Sutherland district, 3m/4km SE of Cape Wrath. **74 B1** NC2973.
Stack Islands *W.Isles* ***Island***, group of islets off S coast of Eriskay in Sound of Barra. **44 C3** NF7807.
Stack of Skudiburgh *High.* ***Coastal feature***, headland on W coast of Trotternish peninsula, Skye, 1m/2km NW of Uig. **57 G3** NG3465.
Stack of the Horse *Shet.* ***Coastal feature***, rocky promontory with natural arches on E coast of Yell, 1m/2km SE of Gassabrough. **85 E4** HU5381.
Stack of Ulbster *High.* ***Coastal feature***, stack on E coast, 2m/3km S of Thrumster. **77 F4** ND3341.
Stacks of Duncansby *High.* ***Coastal feature***, group of offshore rocks 1m/2km S of Duncansby Head. **77 G1** ND3971.
Stadhlaigearraidh (Anglicised form: Stilligarry.) *W.Isles* ***Village***, on South Uist, on W side of Loch Druidibeg. **46 A1** NF7638.
Staffa *Arg. & B.* ***Island***, uninhabited island of basaltic rock in Inner Hebrides, lying 5m/7km SE of Lunga in the Treshnish Isles group and 6m/9km N of Iona. Area 70 acres or 28 hectares. Island is owned by National Trust for Scotland. Among several notable caves the best known is Fingal's Cave. Various sea birds are to be seen. **28 C1** NM3235.
Staffin *High.* ***Village***, near NE coast, 6m/10km E of Uig. **58 A3** NG4867.
Staffin Bay *High.* ***Bay***, on NE coast of Skye, 6m/10km SE of Rubha Hunish. **58 A3** NG4868.
Staffin Island *High.* ***Island***, small uninhabited island to E of Staffin Bay, Skye. **58 A3** NG4969.
Stain *High.* ***Settlement***, on E coast, 1km S of Keiss. **77 F2** ND3460.
Stair *E.Ayr.* ***Village***, on River Ayr, 7m/11km E of Ayr. **14 C3** NS4323.
Stand *N.Lan.* ***Settlement***, 2m/4km N of Airdrie. **24 B3** NS7668.
Standburn *Falk.* ***Village***, 4m/7km SE of Falkirk. **24 D2** NS9274.
Standing Stones of Lubas *Arg. & B.* ***Historic/prehistoric site***, group of ancient standing stones on Bute, 1m/2km W of Kilchattan. NS0855.
Stane *N.Lan.* ***Village***, 1m/2km SE of Shotts. **24 C4** NS8859.
Stanecastle *N.Ayr.* ***Suburb***, adjoining Irvine to E. NS3340.
Stanely Castle *Renf.* ***Castle***, early 15c castle now standing in Stanely Reservoir, 2m/3km SW of Paisley. NS4661.
Stanely Reservoir *Renf.* ***Reservoir***, small reservoir 2m/3km SW of Paisley. NS4661.
Stanerandy Standing Stones *Ork.* ***Historic/prehistoric site***, two standing stones on top of prehistoric burial mound at Stanerandy in N part of Mainland. **80 A4** HY2627.
Staneydale Temple *Shet.* ***Historic/prehistoric site***, heel-shaped Stone Age temple (Historic Scotland) enclosed by stone circle, 1km S of Stanydale, Mainland. Provided central point of previously sizeable Stone Age community. **82 B2** HU2850.
Stanger Head *Ork.* ***Coastal feature***, headland on E coast of Westray, N of Rapness. **80 D2** HY5142.
Stanhope *Sc.Bord.* ***Settlement***, situated where Stanhope Burn enters River Tweed valley, 3m/5km S of Drumelzier. **16 C3** NT1229.
Stanhope Burn *Sc.Bord.* ***River***, rising on slopes of Dollar Law and flowing NW to River Tweed, 3m/4km SW of Drumelzier. **16 C3** NT1130.
Stanley *P. & K.* Population: 1274. ***Village***, on River Tay, 8m/12km SE of Dunkeld and 6m/9km N of Perth. **33 G1** NO1033.
Stanley Hill *P. & K.* *See Dunkeld.*
Stannergate *Dundee* ***Suburb***, 2m/3km E of Dundee city centre, adjacent to Firth of Tay. NO4330.
Stannery Knowe *E.Ayr.* ***Mountain***, with forested summit, 5m/8km NE of Patna. Height 1191 feet or 363 metres. **14 C4** NS4813.
Stantling Craig Reservoir *Sc.Bord.* ***Reservoir***, small reservoir in course of Caddon Water, 4m/7km NW of Galashiels. NT4339.
Stanydale *Shet.* ***Settlement***, on Mainland, 1m/2km N of Gruting. Neolithic remains (Historic Scotland). **82 B2** HU2850.
Staoinebrig (Anglicised form: Stoneybridge.) *W.Isles* ***Village***, near W coast of South Uist, 3m/5km NE of Rubha Ardvule. **46 A1** NF7433.
Star *Fife* ***Village***, 2m/3km NE of Markinch. **34 B4** NO3103.
Starkigarth *Shet.* ***Settlement***, 2m/3km S of Fladdabister, Mainland. **82 D5** HU4229.
Starr *E.Ayr.* ***Settlement***, at S end of Loch Doon, just S of mouth of Carrick Lane. **7 F1** NX4893.
Start Point *Ork.* ***Coastal feature***, headland with lighthouse at E end of Sanday. **81 F2** HY7843.
Stattic Point *High.* ***Coastal feature***, headland on SW side of entrance to Little Loch Broom, W coast of Ross and Cromarty district. **70 B5** NG9796.
Stava Ness *Shet.* ***Coastal feature***, headland on E coast of Mainland, on S side of entrance to Dury Voe. **83 E1** HU5060.
Staxigoe *High.* ***Village***, on E coast of Caithness district, 2m/3km NE of Wick. **77 F3** ND3852.
Steall Fall *High.* ***Waterfall***, in Glen Nevis, Lochaber district, 2m/3km SE of Ben Nevis. NN1768.
Steele Road *Sc.Bord.* ***Settlement***, on S side of Arnton Hill, 4m/6km NW of Newcastleton. **10 D2** NY5293.
Steele's Knowe *P. & K.* ***Mountain***, in Ochil Hills, 6m/10km N of Dollar. Height 1591 feet or 485 metres. **33 E4** NN9607.
Stein *High.* ***Settlement***, on W coast of Vaternish peninsula, Skye, 4m/6km SE of Ardmore Point. **57 F4** NG2656.
Steinacleit *W.Isles* ***Historic/prehistoric site***, burial cairn and stone circle (Historic Scotland) near NW coast of Isle of Lewis, 4m/6km NE of Barvas. **69 E2** NB3954.
Steinmanhill *Aber.* ***Settlement***, on S side of Steinman Hill, 3m/4km N of Fyvie. **64 C5** NJ7642.
Stell Hill *D. & G.* ***Mountain***, 3m/5km NE of Davington. Height 1263 feet or 385 metres. **17 D5** NT2705.
Stemster *High.* ***Settlement***, 3m/5km NE of Halkirk. **77 D2** ND1762.
Stemster *High.* ***Settlement***, 1m/2km N of Loch Stemster. **77 D4** ND1844.
Stemster Hill *High.* ***Hill***, 1km E of Loch Stemster. Height 813 feet or 248 metres. **77 D4** ND1941.
Stemster House *High.* ***Settlement***, 1km N of Loch Scarmclate. **77 D2** ND1860.
Stenhouse *Edin.* ***Suburb***, 3m/5km SW of Edinburgh city centre. NT2171.
Stenhouse Reservoir *Fife* ***Reservoir***, small reservoir 2m/3km NW of Burntisland. NT2187.
Stenhousemuir *Falk.* Population: 16,711. ***Town***, 2m/3km NW of Falkirk. Site of the Tryst, Scotland's largest livestock market, in 19c. **24 C1** NS8682.
Stenness *Ork.* ***Locality***, on Mainland at SE end of Loch of Stenness, 4m/6km SW of Finstown. HY3010.
Stenness *Shet.* ***Settlement***, on Mainland, at S end of Esha Ness, 2m/4km SW of Braehoulland. **84 B5** HU2177.

Stenscholl *High.* ***Settlement***, on Skye, 1m/2km NW of Staffin. **58 A3** NG4767.
Stenton *E.Loth.* ***Village***, 5m/7km SW of Dunbar. Ruins of Old Parish Church. **26 D2** NT6274.
Stenton *P. & K.* ***Settlement***, 3m/5km SE of Dunkeld. **41 F5** NO0640.
Stenton Old Parish Church *E.Loth.* ***Ecclesiastical building***, ruins of 16c church in grounds of 19c Stenton Church, 4m/7km SW of Dunbar. **26 D2** NT6274.
Steornabhagh *W.Isles* *Gaelic form of Stornoway, qv.*
Stepps *N.Lan.* Population: 4336. ***Suburb***, 5m/8km NE of Glasgow. **24 A3** NS6568.
Stevenston *N.Ayr.* Population: 10,153. ***Town***, industrial and former mining town, 2m/4km E of Ardrossan. **23 D5** NS2642.
Stewarton *D. & G.* ***Settlement***, 4m/6km S of Wigtown. **3 E2** NX4449.
Stewarton *E.Ayr.* Population: 6481. ***Small town***, 5m/8km N of Kilmarnock. Town once famous for hat-making. **23 F5** NS4145.
Stewartry Museum *D. & G.* ***Other feature of interest***, in Kirkcudbright, with local, historical and natural history exhibits. **8 A5** NX6851.
Stichill *Sc.Bord.* ***Village***, 3m/5km N of Kelso. **18 B3** NT7138.
Stilamair *W.Isles* ***Island***, islet off South Harris, to SW of Scalpay at entrance to East Loch Tarbert. NG2194.
Stilligarry *W.Isles* *Anglicised form of Stadhlaigearraidh, qv.*
Stinchar *S.Ayr.* ***River***, rising in Glentrool Forest Park and flowing N then W through Carrick Forest, then turning SW and running by Barr, Pinwherry and Colmonell to Ballantrae Bay on S side of Ballantrae. **6 C2** NX0781.
Stirkoke House *High.* ***Settlement***, 3m/4km W of Wick. **77 F3** ND3150.
Stirling *Aber.* ***Locality***, adjoining to W of Boddam, 3m/4km S of Peterhead. Quarry to S. **65 G5** NK1242.
Stirling *Stir.* Population: 30,515. ***Town***, historic town on slope of rocky eminence above S bank of River Forth, 21m/34km NE of Glasgow. Now a commercial and tourist centre. Medieval castle (Historic Scotland). Cambuskenneth Abbey (Historic Scotland), 1km NE. Some important battles during Wars of Independence fought here. Argyll's Lodging (Historic Scotland) in Castle Wynd is impressive 17c town house with principal rooms fully restored. Earthworks of formal garden of King's Knot (Historic Scotland), probably made for Charles I in 1628. Mar's Wark (Historic Scotland) is Renaissance mansion built by the Regent Mar in 1570; façade is main survivor. 15c-16c Stirling Old Bridge (Historic Scotland) was partly rebuilt in 1749. University at Airthrey, 2m/3km N. **32 C5** NS7993.
Stirling Castle *Stir.* ***Castle***, impressive medieval and later castle (Historic Scotland) in Stirling's historic centre, built on site of earlier castle. Mary, Queen of Scots was crowned here in 1543. **32 C5** NS7994.
Stirling Services *Stir.* ***Other building***, motorway service station at interchange of M9 and M80. **24 C1** NS8088.
Stittenham *High.* ***Settlement***, 3m/5km N of Alness. **61 F2** NH6574.
Stiughay *W.Isles* ***Island***, islet off North Harris in East Loch Tarbert, to W of Scalpay. NG2096.
Stiughay na Leum *W.Isles* ***Island***, islet off South Harris in East Loch Tarbert, on S side of Stiughay. NG2095.
Stix *P. & K.* ***Settlement***, 2m/3km NE of Kenmore. **40 C5** NN7947.
Stob a' Bhruaich Léith *High.* ***Mountain***, on border of Argyll and Lochaber districts, 3m/5km SW of Clach Leathad. Height 3086 feet or 941 metres. NN2045.
Stob a' Choin *Stir.* ***Mountain***, 3m/4km NE of head of Loch Katrine. Height 2837 feet or 865 metres. **31 G3** NN4116.
Stob a' Choire Mheadhoin *High.* ***Mountain***, in Lochaber district, 1km NE of Stob Coire Easain and 1m/2km W of Loch Treig. Munro: height 3628 feet or 1106 metres. **39 F2** NN3173.
Stob a' Choire Odhair *High.* ***Mountain***, on border of Argyll and Lochaber districts on NW side of Beinn Toaig and 2m/3km E of Stob Ghabhar. Munro: height 3106 feet or 947 metres. **39 E5** NN2546.
Stob a' Ghrianain *High.* ***Mountain***, summit of Druim Fada, 5m/8km N of Fort William. Height 2440 feet or 744 metres. **38 C1** NN0882.
Stob an Aonaich Mhòir *P. & K.* ***Mountain***, on SE side of Loch Ericht, 11m/18km SW of Dalwhinnie. Height 2804 feet or 855 metres. **40 A3** NN5369.
Stob an Duine Ruaidh *Arg. & B.* ***Mountain***, 1m/2km SW of Ben Starav, Argyll, on E side of Loch Etive. Height 2696 feet or 822 metres. **38 D5** NN1140.
Stob an Eas *Arg. & B.* ***Mountain***, in Argyll 4m/6km N of Lochgoilhead. Height 2401 feet or 732 metres. **31 D4** NN1807.
Stob an Fhàinne *Stir.* ***Mountain***, to N of Loch Arklet, 5m/8km NE of Tarbet across Loch Lomond. Height 2148 feet or 655 metres. **31 F3** NN3511.
Stob an t-Sluichd *Moray* ***Mountain***, 6m/9km E of Loch Avon. Height 3628 feet or 1106 metres. **52 D4** NJ1003.
Stob Aonaich Mhòir *P. & K.* ***Mountain***, on E side of Loch Ericht. Height 2804 feet or 855 metres. NN5369.
Stob Bac an Fhurain *Moray* ***Mountain***, one of the peaks of Ben Avon, N of Braemar. Height 3529 feet or 1076 metres. NJ1303.
Stob Bàn *High.* ***Mountain***, in Lochaber district, 3m/5km NW of Kinlochleven. Munro: height 3277 feet or 999 metres. **38 D3** NN1465.
Stob Bàn *High.* ***Mountain***, in Lochaber district, 4m/6km NW of head of Loch Treig. Munro: height 3205 feet or 977 metres. **39 E2** NN2672.
Stob Binnein (Also known as Stobinian and Ben A'an.) *Stir.* ***Mountain***, 1m/2km S of Ben More and 4m/6km SE of Crianlarich. Munro: height 3821 feet or 1165 metres. **31 G2** NN4322.
Stob Breac *Stir.* ***Mountain***, 7m/11km SE of Crianlarich. Height 2250 feet or 686 metres. **31 G3** NN4416.
Stob Choire Claurigh *High.* ***Mountain***, in Lochaber district 4m/7km NW of head of Loch Treig. Munro: height 3861 feet or 1177 metres. **39 E2** NN2673.
Stob Coir' an Albannaich ***Mountain***, on border of Argyll & Bute and Highland, 4m/6km E of head of Loch Etive. Munro: height 3424 feet or 1044 metres. **39 D5** NN1644.
Stob Coire a' Chairn *High.* ***Mountain***, in Mamore Forest, 3m/4km N of Kinlochleven. Munro: height 3218 feet or 981 metres. **39 D3** NN1866.
Stob Coire a' Chearcaill *High.* ***Mountain***, on Ardgour, 5m/8km W of Fort William across Loch Linnhe. Height 2526 feet or 770 metres. **38 C2** NN0172.
Stob Coire an Laoigh *High.* ***Mountain***, 6m/9km S of Spean Bridge. Munro: height 3660 feet or 1116 metres. **39 E2** NN2472.
Stob Coire an Lochain *Stir.* ***Mountain***, peak on SE side of summit of Stob Binneinn. Height 3496 feet or 1066 metres. NN4322.
Stob Coire Bhuidhe *Stir.* ***Mountain***, peak 1m/2km N of summit of Cruach Ardrain. Height 2804 feet or 855 metres. NN4022.
Stob Coire Easain *High.* ***Mountain***, in Lochaber district 4m/7km E of Ben Nevis. Height 3542 feet or 1080 metres. NN2372.
Stob Coire Easain *High.* ***Mountain***, in Lochaber district 3m/4km N of head of Loch Treig. Munro: height 3660 feet or 1116 metres. **39 F2** NN3073.
Stob Coire nan Cearc *High.* ***Mountain***, in Lochaber district 3m/5km NE of Glenfinnan. Height 2909 feet or 887 metres. **38 B1** NM9385.
Stob Coire nan Lochan *High.* ***Mountain***, in Lochaber district, 1m/2km S of Loch Triochatan in Glen Coe. Height 3657 feet or 1115 metres. NN1454.
Stob Coire Raineach *High.* ***Mountain***, summit at NE end of Buachaille Etive Beag, 1m/2km SE of Pass of Glencoe. Munro: height 3031 feet or 924 metres. NN1954.
Stob Coire Sgreamhach *High.* ***Mountain***, 2m/4km SW of Pass of Glencoe. Munro: height 3510 feet or 1070 metres. NN1553.
Stob Coire Sgriodain *High.* ***Mountain***, in Lochaber district between Loch Treig and Chno Dearg. Munro: height 3201 feet or 976 metres. **39 F2** NN3574.
Stob Creagach *Stir.* ***Mountain***, 5m/8km W of Balquhidder. Height 2965 feet or 904 metres. NN4523.
Stob Dearg *High.* ***Mountain***, summit at NE end of Buachaille Etive Mòr, 3m/5km SE of Pass of Glencoe. Munro: height 3352 feet or 1022 metres. **39 E4** NN2254.
Stob Diamh *Arg. & B.* ***Mountain***, in Ben Cruachan massif, 4m/7km NW of Dalmally. Munro: height 3273 feet or 998 metres. **30 C1** NN0930.
Stob Dubh *High.* ***Mountain***, in Lochaber district on E side of Glen Etive, 4m/6km NE of head of Loch Etive. Height 2896 feet or 883 metres. **39 D5** NN1648.
Stob Dubh *High.* ***Mountain***, summit at SW end of Buachaille Etive Beag in Lochaber district, 2m/3km S of Pass of Glencoe. Munro: height 3142 feet or 958 metres. **39 D4** NN1753.
Stob Garbh *Stir.* ***Mountain***, peak 1km N of summit of Cruach Ardrain. Height 3149 feet or 960 metres. **31 G2** NN4122.
Stob Ghabhar *High.* ***Mountain***, in Argyll 6m/9km NW of Bridge of Orchy. Munro: height 3565 feet or 1087 metres. **39 E5** NN2345.
Stob Glas *Stir.* ***Mountain***, peak 1km S of summit of Cruach Ardrain. Height 2732 feet or 833 metres. NN4020.
Stob Law *Sc.Bord.* ***Mountain***, 5m/8km SW of Peebles. Height 2050 feet or 625 metres. **16 D2** NT2233.
Stob Mhic Bheathain *High.* ***Mountain***, 6m/9km S of Glenfinnan, Lochaber district. Height 2365 feet or 721 metres. **38 B2** NM9170.
Stob na Broige *High.* ***Mountain***, summit at SW end of Buachaille Etive Mòr, 3m/4km SE of Pass of Glencoe. Munro: height 3132 feet or 955 metres. NN1952.
Stob na Cruaiche ***Mountain***, summit of A' Chruach on border of Highland and Perth & Kinross, between Blackwater Reservoir and Loch Laidon. Height 2424 feet or 739 metres. **39 F4** NN3657.
Stob Odham *Arg. & B.* ***Mountain***, on Knapdale, 5m/8km NW of Tarbert. Height 1843 feet or 562 metres. **21 G2** NR8174.
Stob Poite Coire Ardair *High.* ***Mountain***, rising to NW above Lochan a' Choire, 1m/2km NE of Creag Meagaidh. Steep, craggy SE slopes. Munro: height 3454 feet or 1053 metres. **39 G1** NN4288.
Stobinian *Stir.* *Alternative name for Stob Binnein, qv.*
Stobo *Sc.Bord.* ***Village***, on River Tweed, 5m/8km SW of Peebles. **16 C2** NT1837.
Stobo Castle *Sc.Bord.* ***Castle***, early 19c, 1m/2km SW of Stobo. NT1837.
Stobs *Sc.Bord.* ***Settlement***, 4m/6km S of Hawick. NT5009.
Stobwood *S.Lan.* ***Settlement***, 1m/2km SE of Forth. **25 D4** NS9552.
Stock Hill *Sc.Bord.* ***Mountain***, 4m/6km SW of Craik. Height 1565 feet or 477 metres. **17 E5** NT3203.
Stockay *W.Isles* ***Island***, easternmost of Heisker Islands group. **45 E3** NF6663.
Stockbridge *Edin.* ***Suburb***, 1km NW of Edinburgh city centre. NT2474.
Stockbridge *Stir.* ***Settlement***, adjoining to W of Dunblane. **32 C4** NN7601.
Stockinish Island *W.Isles* ***Island***, uninhabited island at entrance to Loch Stockinish, SE coast of South Harris, 6m/10km S of Tarbert. NG1390.
Stockval *High.* ***Mountain***, 1m/2km E of Talisker, Skye. Height 1364 feet or 416 metres. **47 G2** NG3529.
Stoer *High.* ***Village***, on W coast of Sutherland district, 5m/8km NW of Lochinver. To N is peninsula of Stoer, culminating in the headland Point of Stoer. Lighthouse on W point of peninsula nearly 4m/6km NW of village. **70 C2** NC0328.
Stone Hill *S.Lan.* ***Mountain***, 2m/3km NE of Rigside. Height 1030 feet or 314 metres. **15 G2** NS8936.
Stone of Setter *Ork.* ***Historic/prehistoric site***, Bronze Age standing stone in N of Eday, just N of Mill Loch. **81 D3** HY5637.
Stonefield *Arg. & B.* ***Settlement***, in Knapdale, 2m/3km N of Tarbert. **21 G2** NR8671.
Stonefield *S.Lan.* ***Locality***, 2m/4km NW of Hamilton. **24 A4** NS6957.
Stonehaven *Aber.* Population: 9445. ***Small town***, port on Stonehaven Bay, on E coast, 13m/21km S of Aberdeen. **43 G1** NO8785.
Stonehaven Bay *Aber.* ***Bay***, on E coast 13m/21km S of Aberdeen. Stonehaven port lies on bay. NO8786.
Stonehouse *D. & G.* ***Settlement***, 2m/3km NE of Haugh of Urr. **8 C4** NX8268.
Stonehouse *S.Lan.* Population: 5328. ***Village***, 3m/5km S of Larkhall. **24 B5** NS7546.
Stones of Stenness *Ork.* ***Historic/prehistoric site***, 1km N of Stenness, four standing stones (Historic Scotland) remain out of an estimated original twelve erected in Neolithic times. **80 B5** HY3011.
Stoney Byres Linn *S.Lan.* ***Waterfall***, with hydro-electric power station on River Clyde, 2m/3km W of Lanark. NS8544.
Stoneybridge *W.Isles* *Anglicised form of Staoinebrig, qv.*
Stoneyburn *W.Loth.* ***Village***, 4m/6km S of Bathgate. **25 D3** NS9762.
Stoneykirk *D. & G.* ***Village***, 5m/8km S of Stranraer. **6 B5** NX0853.
Stoneywood *Aberdeen* ***Village***, on NW outskirts of Aberdeen. **55 D3** NJ8911.
Stonganess *Shet.* ***Settlement***, on E coast of Yell, adjacent to Culli Voe. **85 E2** HP5402.
Stony Hill *E.Ayr.* ***Mountain***, 4m/7km SE of Muirkirk. Height 1843 feet or 562 metres. **15 F3** NS7221.
Stonybreck *Shet.* ***Settlement***, 1km SW of Fair Isle Airstrip. **82 A5** HZ2071.
Stormont Loch (Also known as Loch Bog.) *P. & K.* ***Lake/loch***, small loch 2m/3km S of Blairgowrie. **41 G5** NO1942.
Stornoway (Gaelic form: Steornabhagh.) *W.Isles* Population: 5975. ***Small town***, port and chief town of Isle of Lewis, situated on E coast, 22m/35km S of Butt of Lewis and 13m/22km E of Breascleit on W coast. Airport 2m/3km E towards Melbost. **69 F4** NB4232.
Stornoway Airport *W.Isles* ***Airport/airfield***, local airport, 2m/3km E of Stornoway, Isle of Lewis. **69 F4** NB4533.
Stornoway Harbour *W.Isles* ***Sea feature***, large natural harbour on S side of Stornoway, Isle of Lewis. **69 F4** NB4232.
Storybook Glen *Aber.* ***Leisure/recreation***, leisure park to E of Kirkton of Maryculter, 4m/6km NW of Portlethen. Nursery and fairytale fantasyland for children. **55 D5** NO8699.
Stotfield *Moray* ***Suburb***, W district of Lossiemouth. **63 E2** NJ2270.
Stoul *High.* ***Settlement***, on SW shore of Loch Nevis, 5m/8km E of Mallaig. **49 D5** NM7594.
Stourbrough Hill *Shet.* ***Hill***, 3m/4km NW of Walls, Mainland. Height 567 feet or 173 metres. **82 B2** HU2152.
Stove *Ork.* ***Settlement***, on Bay of Stove, in SW of Sanday. **81 E3** HY6135.
Stow *Sc.Bord.* ***Village***, on Gala Water, 5m/8km W of Lauder. **26 B5** NT4544.

Straad *Arg. & B.* ***Settlement***, near W coast of Bute, 3m/5km SW of Rothesay. NS0462.
Stracathro *Angus* ***Locality***, 2m/4km SE of Edzell. Site of Roman fort. **43 E3** NO6265.
Strachan *Aber.* ***Village***, on Water of Feugh, 3m/4km SW of Banchory. **54 B5** NO6792.
Strachur *Arg. & B.* ***Village***, 1km E of Strachur Bay, on E shore of Loch Fyne, in Argyll. **30 D4** NN0901.
Strachur Bay *Arg. & B.* ***Bay***, on E shore of Loch Fyne in Argyll. 1km E is village of Strachur. **30 C4** NN0801.
Strae *Arg. & B.* ***River***, in Argyll, running SW down Glen Strae to River Orchy 2m/3km W of Dalmally. **31 D1** NN1328.
Strahangles Point *Aber.* ***Coastal feature***, headland on W side of Aberdour Bay, 8m/12km W of Fraserburgh. NJ8765.
Straiaval *W.Isles* ***Mountain***, 1km NE of Laxadale Lochs, North Harris. Height 1276 feet or 389 metres. **67 D3** NB1904.
Strait of Corryvreckan (Also known as Gulf of Corryvreckan.) *Arg. & B.* ***Sea feature***, sea passage between Scarba and Jura. Notorious for tidal races and whirlpools. **29 F4** NM6902.
Straiton *Edin.* ***Suburb***, 5m/8km S of Edinburgh city centre. **25 G3** NT2766.
Straiton *S.Ayr.* ***Village***, on Water of Girvan, 6m/10km SE of Maybole. **14 B5** NS3804.
Straloch *Aber.* ***Settlement***, 2m/3km NW of Newmachar. **55 D2** NJ8521.
Straloch *P. & K.* ***Settlement***, in Glen Brerachan, 3m/5km NW of Kirkmichael. **41 F3** NO0463.
Strandburgh Ness *Shet.* ***Coastal feature***, headland at NE point of Fetlar. **85 F3** HU6793.
Strannda (Anglicised form: Strond.) *W.Isles* ***Settlement***, on South Harris, 2m/3km SE of Leverburgh. **66 C5** NG0384.
Stranraer *D. & G.* Population: 11,348. ***Town***, port and resort at head of Loch Ryan, 23m/37km W of Wigtown. Passenger and car ferry service to Larne in Northern Ireland, and also from Cairnryan on E side of loch. Castle House was home of Arctic explorer, John Ross. 16c Stranraer Castle. **6 B4** NX0660.
Strath *High.* ***Settlement***, 2m/3km SE of Watten. **77 E3** ND2552.
Strath an Lòin *High.* ***Valley***, carrying Allt Car and running W to E into Loch Shin. **71 G3** NC4117.
Strath Ascaig *High.* ***Valley***, carrying Allt Cadh an Eas, 1km S of Stromeferry, Skye and Lochalsh district. **49 E1** NG8633.
Strath Avon *Moray* ***Valley***, on SE side of Hills of Cromdale, 3m/5km N of Bridge of Brown. **52 D2** NJ1424.
Strath Bay *High.* ***Bay***, small bay to NE of Gairloch, Ross and Cromarty district. **59 D2** NG7977.
Strath Beag *High.* ***Valley***, running N to S from the head of Loch Eriboll. **74 C3** NC3854.
Strath Beag *High.* ***Valley***, in W part of Ross and Cromarty district, carrying Dundonell River N into head of Little Loch Broom. **59 G1** NH0988.
Strath Bogie *Aber.* ***Valley***, below E slopes of Clashmach Hill, carrying River Bogie N towards Huntly. **54 A1** NJ5138.
Strath Braan *P. & K.* ***Valley***, carrying River Braan NE to Strath Tay at Dunkeld. **33 E1** NN9840.
Strath Bran *High.* ***Valley***, carrying River Bran E from Achnasheen to Loch Luichart. **60 B4** NH2461.
Strath Brora *High.* ***Valley***, carrying River Brora, in Sutherland district, to Brora on E coast. **72 C4** NC7609.
Strath Burn *High.* ***River***, rising as Camster Burn and becoming Rowens Burn, then Strath Burn to N of Scorridet. It flows N and joins with Burn of Acharole, where it becomes Wick River 1km S of Watten. **77 E3** ND2350.
Strath Chrombuill *High.* ***Valley***, running E to W from N slopes of Fionn Bheinn and converging with Gleann Tanagaidh, 4m/6km NE of Kinlochewe. **60 A3** NH1164.
Strath Cuileannaich *High.* ***Valley***, carrying Abhainn an t-Srath Chuileannaich, in Sutherland district, SE into Strathcarron 8m/13km W of Bonar Bridge. NH4393.
Strath Dionard *High.* ***Valley***, in Sutherland district to E of Foinaven, carrying River Dionard N from Loch Dionard. **74 C3** NC3661.
Strath Dores *High.* ***Valley***, on SE side of N end of Loch Ness. **51 E1** NH5935.
Strath Earn *P. & K.* ***Valley***, carrying River Earn E from Loch Earn to head of Firth of Tay below Perth. **32 C2** NN9517.
Strath Fillan *Stir.* ***Valley***, carrying River Fillan SE towards Crianlarich. **31 F2** NN3428.
Strath Finella *Aber.* ***Valley***, to N of Strathfinella Hill, cutting through mountains of Drumtochty Forest in a W to E direction, 4m/7km NE of Fettercairn. **43 E2** NO6879.
Strath Fleet *High.* ***Valley***, in Sutherland district, carrying River Fleet to E coast, N of Dornoch. **72 B4** NC6702.
Strath Gairloch *High.* ***Settlement***, in Ross and Cromarty district, 1km NW of Gairloch. NG7977.
Strath Gartney *Stir.* ***Locality***, land on N shore of Loch Katrine. **31 G3** NN4610.
Strath Garve *High.* ***Valley***, in Ross and Cromarty district, 3m/4km N of Garve and carrying Black Water S to Loch Garve. NH4064.
Strath Gryfe *Inclyde* ***Valley***, carrying River Gryfe, or Gryfe Water, between Gryfe Reservoir and Bridge of Weir. **23 E2** NS3370.
Strath Halladale *High.* ***Valley***, carrying Halladale River in Caithness district, 6m/10km S of Melvich. **76 A4** NC8953.
Strath Isla *Moray* ***Valley***, carrying River Isla from Towiemore, through Keith, to Nethermills. **63 G5** NJ4250.
Strath Kanaird *High.* ***Valley***, running NE to SW and carrying River Kanaird, which flows into sea just S of Camas Mòr. **70 D4** NC1200.
Strath Lungard *High.* ***Valley***, carrying Allt Strath Lungard, 4m/6km S of Talladale. **59 F3** NG9164.
Strath Melness Burn *High.* ***River***, flowing NE into sea, 1m/2km W of mouth of Tongue Bay. **75 E2** NC5764.
Strath Mòr *High.* ***Valley***, carrying Abhainn an t-Stratha Mhòir N from head of Loch Slapin, Skye, and containing Loch na Sguabaidh and Lochain Stratha Mhòir. **48 B2** NG5624.
Strath More *High.* ***Valley***, in Sutherland district, carrying Strathmore river into Loch Hope. **74 D4** NC4550.
Strath More *High.* ***Valley***, carrying River Broom above Loch Broom, about 2m/3km S of head of loch, Ross and Cromarty district. Lael Forest runs down E side of valley. **60 A1** NH1882.
Strath Mulzie *High.* ***Valley***, in Sutherland district, carrying Corriemulzie River NE to confluence with River Einig. **71 E5** NH3192.
Strath na Sealga *High.* ***Valley***, carrying Abhainn Srath na Sealga NW into head of Loch na Sealga, in W part of Ross and Cromarty district. **59 G1** NH0680.
Strath nan Lòn *High.* ***Valley***, running SE to NW, carrying Allt nan Luibean Molach and containing several small lochs. **71 E4** NC2102.
Strath of Appin *Arg. & B.* ***Valley***, in Argyll, running across SW part of Appin from Loch Linnhe to Loch Creran. **38 B5** NM9445.
Strath of Appin (Also known as Appin of Dull.) *P. & K.* ***Valley***, broad valley carrying River Tay from its confluence with River Lyon E towards Aberfeldy. Upper section is narrow valley carrying lower course of Keltney Burn S to its confluence with River Lyon. **40 C4** NN7948.
Strath of Kildonan *High.* ***Valley***, in Sutherland district, carrying River Helmsdale between Kinbrace and Helmsdale. **73 D2** NC8923.
Strath of Orchy *Arg. & B.* ***Valley***, carrying River Orchy W to Loch Awe in vicinity of Dalmally, Argyll. **31 E2** NN1627.
Strath Ossian *High.* ***Valley***, carrying River Ossian between Loch Ghuilbinn and Loch Ossian. **39 G2** NN4172.
Strath Oykel *High.* ***Valley***, carrying River Oykel, Sutherland district, between Oykel Bridge and Invershin. **71 G4** NC4300.
Strath Peffer *High.* ***Valley***, carrying River Peffery E from Strathpeffer to Dingwall on Cromarty Firth. **61 D4** NH4958.
Strath Rannoch *High.* ***Valley***, in Ross and Cromarty district, carrying Allt Coire a' Chùndrain S to Black Water at Inchbae Lodge, at S end of Inchbae Forest. **60 C2** NH3972.
Strath Rory *High.* ***Valley***, carrying Strathrory River, Ross and Cromarty district and runs E into Balnagown River, 5m/7km N of Invergordon. **61 F2** NH6776.
Strath Rusdale *High.* ***Valley***, carrying Black Water in Ross and Cromarty district and running SE to River Averon, 5m/8km NW of Alness. **61 E2** NH5775.
Strath Sgitheach *High.* ***Valley***, carrying Abhainn Sgitheach E from W slopes of Cnoc na Gearraisich to Cromarty Firth at Evanton. **61 E3** NH5262.
Strath Shinary *High.* ***Valley***, carrying Lón Mòr NW into Sandwood Loch, 4m/6km NE of Oldshoremore, Sutherland district. **74 B2** NC2362.
Strath Skinsdale *High.* ***Valley***, carrying River Skinsdale in Sutherland district, 14m/22km NW of Brora. **72 C3** NC7518.
Strath Stack *High.* ***Valley***, running from NW to SE in Sutherland district below S slopes of Ben Stack and carrying Allt Achadh Fairidh. **74 B4** NC2540.
Strath Suardal *High.* ***Valley***, carrying Broadford River, 2m/3km SW of Broadford. **48 C2** NG6120.
Strath Tay *P. & K.* ***Valley***, broad valley below Loch Tay, carrying River Tay E past Aberfeldy. Valley turns S towards Dunkeld below confluence of Rivers Tay and Tummel. **41 D4** NO0043.
Strath Tirry *High.* ***Valley***, carrying River Tirry and running SE parallel with Loch Shin, in Sutherland district. **72 A2** NC4922.
Strath Tollaidh *High.* ***Valley***, 4m/6km SW of Rogart, running SE from Cregan Glas, Sutherland district. **72 B4** NC6800.
Strath Vagastie *High.* ***Valley***, carrying Allt a' Chràisg, in Caithness district, NE to head of Loch Naver. **72 A2** NC5430.
Strath Vaich *High.* ***Valley***, in Ross and Cromarty district carrying Abhainn Strath a' Bhàthaich and running S from Loch Vaich to join River Glascarnoch at Black Bridge, 2m/3km W of Inchbae Lodge. **60 C2** NH3573.
Strathaird *High.* ***Coastal feature***, peninsula on S coast of Skye between Loch Scavaig and Loch Slapin. **48 B2** NG5319.
Strathaird Point *High. Anglicised form of Rubha na h-Easgainne, qv.*
Strathallan ***Valley***, carrying Allan Water, NE of Dunblane, marking southern limit of Scottish Highlands in this area. **32 C4** NN8005.
Strathan *High.* ***Settlement***, near W coast of Sutherland district, 1m/2km SW of Lochinver. **70 C2** NC0821.
Strathan *High.* ***Settlement***, in Lochaber district, at head of Loch Arkaig. **49 F5** NM9791.
Strathardle *P. & K.* ***Valley***, carrying River Ardle SE to foot of Glen Shee, below Bridge of Cally. **41 F4** NO1054.
Strathaven *S.Lan.* Population: 6384. ***Small town***, former weaving centre 7m/11km S of Hamilton. **24 B5** NS7044.
Strathbeg Bay *Aber.* ***Bay***, wide bay on NE coast, extending NW from Rattray Head to Inzie Head and to N and E of Loch of Strathbeg. **65 F3** NK0760.
Strathblane *Stir.* ***Valley***, carries Blane Water NW from Strathblane, between NE edge of Kilpatrick Hills and SW edge of Campsie Fells. **23 G1** NS5182.
Strathblane *Stir.* Population: 1981. ***Village***, at head of Strathblane, 9m/14km N of Glasgow. **23 G2** NS5679.
Strathblane Hills *Stir.* ***Mountain***, massif with craggy S and SW slopes, on SW slopes of Campsie Fells to N of Strathblane. Summit is named Slackdhu. Height 1624 feet or 495 metres. **23 G1** NS5581.
Strathbogie *Aber.* ***Locality***, large area to S of Huntly, extending E and W of River Bogie and including its valley, Strath Bogie. **53 G1** NJ5237.
Strathbungo *Glas.* ***Suburb***, 2m/3km S of Glasgow city centre. NS5762.
Strathcarron *High.* ***Locality***, with railway station, at foot of Glen Carron, Ross and Cromarty district. **59 F5** NG9442.
Strathcarron *High.* ***Valley***, carrying River Carron E to Kyle of Sutherland at Bonar Bridge in Sutherland district. **72 A5** NH5192.
Strathclyde Country Park *N.Lan.* ***Leisure/recreation***, country park on E shore of Strathclyde Loch, 1m/2km W of Motherwell. 1000 acres of mixed woodland and parkland with artificial lakes, sandy beaches, accommodation, Scotland's first theme park and remains of Roman bathhouse. **24 B4** NS7357.
Strathconon *High.* ***Valley***, in Ross and Cromarty district, carrying River Conon E to Conon Bridge at head of Cromarty Firth. **60 D4** NH4055.
Strathconon Forest *High.* ***Open space***, deer forest astride River Meig. **60 B5** NH4055.
Strathdearn *High.* ***Valley***, carrying River Findhorn NE through NE section of Monadhliath Mountains towards lowlands SW of Forres. Upper section of valley typically has a broad valley floor, while middle and lower sections are gorge-like; this is most apparent at Streens section. Valley containing Funtack Burn and Loch Moy, to NW of Tomatin, is also referred to as Strathdearn. **51 G2** NH7724.
Strathdearn Forest *High.* ***Forest/woodland***, 10m/16km SE of Inverness. NH7724.
Strathdon *Aber.* ***Village***, on River Don, 12m/19km E of Tomintoul. **53 F3** NJ3512.
Strathenry Castle *Fife* ***Castle***, 1m/2km W of Leslie; 17c dovecote. NO2201.
Stratherrick *High.* ***Valley***, carrying Loch Mhòr, E of Loch Ness, in Inverness district. **51 D3** NH5017.
Strathfinella Hill *Aber.* ***Mountain***, rising steeply to E of Glensaugh and Loch Saugh, 3m/5km NE of Fettercairn. Height 1246 feet or 380 metres. **43 F2** NO6777.
Strathgarve Forest *High.* ***Open space***, with forested lower slopes, to N of Loch Garve. **60 D3** NH4063.
Strathgirnock *Aber.* ***Settlement***, 2m/3km W of Ballater. **53 F5** NO3395.
Strathglass *High.* ***Valley***, carrying River Glass, Inverness district, to its confluence with River Farrar near Struy Bridge. **50 C1** NH3835.
Strathisla Distillery *Moray* ***Other feature of interest***, distillery located in Keith, originally known as Milton distillery. Thought to be the oldest working distillery in Scotland, it has been producing malt whisky since 1786, possibly earlier. **63 G4** NJ4250.
Strathkanaird *High.* ***Village***, in Ross and Cromarty district on N side of Strath Kanaird, valley of River Kanaird, 5m/8km N of Ullapool. **70 D4** NC1501.
Strathkinness *Fife* ***Village***, 3m/5km W of St. Andrews. **34 C3** NO4516.
Strathlachlan *Arg. & B.* ***Locality***, in Argyll including Strathlachan Forest, Lachlan Bay and Castle Lachlan, and surrounding Strathlachlan River 6m/9km SW of Strachur. River flows SW to Loch Fyne via Lachlan Bay. NS0295.

Strathlachlan Forest *Arg. & B.* ***Forest/woodland***, on uplands S of Strathlachlan River. NS0194.
Strathlethan Bay *Aber.* ***Bay***, on E coast, 1km S of Stonehaven. **43 G1** NO8884.
Strathmarchin Bay *Aber.* ***Bay***, small bay on N coast of Buchan district, 1m/2km E of Portsoy. NJ6066.
Strathmiglo *Fife* ***Small town***, founded in 15c, 2m/3km SW of Auchtermuchty. **34 A4** NO2110.
Strathmore ***Valley***, great fertile valley separating highlands of Scotland from central lowlands and extending from foot of Loch Lomond to Stonehaven, although term is more generally applied to part between Methven and Brechin. **33 F2** NO4050.
Strathmore *High.* ***River***, in Sutherland district, rising on Reay Forest and running N down Strath More into Loch Hope, where it emerges as River Hope. **74 D4** NC4550.
Strathnairn *High.* ***Valley***, carrying River Nairn NE from Aberarder House to Daviot. **51 F1** NH6733.
Strathnairn Forest *High.* ***Forest/woodland***, in Inverness district 9m/14km S of Inverness. NH6930.
Strathnasheallag Forest *High.* ***Open space***, deer forest to E of Loch na Sealga in Ross and Cromarty district. **59 G1** NH0483.
Strathnaver *High.* ***Valley***, carrying River Naver, 10m/16km SE of Tongue, Caithness district. **75 G4** NC7045.
Strathnaver Museum *High.* ***Other feature of interest***, set in 18c church with 9c Pictish carved stone, in Bettyhill on N coast of Caithness district. Exhibits include Strathnaver Clearances, furniture and agriculture tools. **75 G2** NC7062.
Strathord Forest *P. & K.* ***Forest/woodland***, 2m/3km S of Bankfoot. **33 F1** NO0632.
Strathpeffer *High.* ***Village***, in Ross and Cromarty district, 4m/7km W of Dingwall. Resort, with mineral springs. **61 D4** NH4858.
Strathrannoch *High.* ***Settlement***, in Strath Rannoch, 8m/12km N of Gorstan. **60 C2** NH3874.
Strathrory *High.* ***River***, in Strath Rory, flowing E into Balnagown River 5m/7km N of Invergordon. NH6776.
Strathspey *High.* ***Valley***, central area of River Spey valley from Kingussie, past Grantown-on-Spey, to Charlestown of Aberlour. Separates Monadhliath Mountains from Cairngorm Mountains and provides a natural transport conduit through the Highlands. Popular tourist destination, providing outdoor activities, water and winter sports, with wilderness areas of surrounding estates and forest parks. Area noted for its wildlife, especially salmon and ospreys. **52 B3** NJ0025.
Strathspey Railway *High.* ***Other feature of interest***, tourist railway running 5m/8km from Aviemore to Boat of Garten, where there is a small railway museum. **52 B3** NH9115.
Strathtay *P. & K.* ***Settlement***, in upper valley of River Tay, 4m/6km SW of Pitlochry. **41 E4** NN9153.
Strathvaich Forest *High.* ***Open space***, deer forest in Ross and Cromarty district to S and W of Loch Vaich. **60 C2** NH3474.
Strathwhillan *N.Ayr.* ***Settlement***, on Arran, adjoining to SE of Brodick. **13 F2** NS0235.
Strathy *High.* ***River***, rising in mountains to S of Loch Strathy and flowing N through Strathy Forest. It then follows E side of forest and flows past Strathy village to N coast and into Strathy Bay. NC8465.
Strathy *High.* ***Village***, near N coast of Caithness district and mouth of River Strathy, 17m/28km W of Thurso. **76 A2** NC8465.
Strathy Bay *High.* ***Bay***, on N coast, 1km N of Strathy. **76 A2** NC8465.
Strathy Forest *High.* ***Forest/woodland***, afforested area astride River Strathy, 6m/9km S of Strathy village. **76 A2** NC8465.
Strathy Point *High.* ***Coastal feature***, headland with lighthouse, 3m/5km N of Strathy. **76 A1** NC8465.
Strathyre *Stir.* ***Valley***, carrying River Balvag from Loch Voil to Loch Lubnaig, past village of Strathyre. Set in middle of Strathyre Forest. NN5617.
Strathyre *Stir.* ***Village***, in middle of Strathyre Forest, 7m/11km NW of Callander. **32 A3** NN5617.
Strathyre Forest *Stir.* ***Forest/woodland***, in valley of River Balvag. Strathyre Forest Information centre and picnic area to S of Strathyre village. **32 A3** NN5617.
Stravanan *Arg. & B.* ***Settlement***, on Bute, 1km N of Stravanan Bay. **22 B4** NS0857.
Stravanan Bay *Arg. & B.* ***Bay***, on SW coast of Bute, 1m/2km W of Kingarth. **22 B4** NS0756.
Stravithie *Fife* ***Settlement***, 4m/6km SE of St. Andrews. **34 D3** NO5311.
Streap *High.* ***Mountain***, in Lochaber district 4m/7km NE of Glenfinnan. Height 2982 feet or 909 metres. **38 B1** NM9486.
Streap Comhlaidh *High.* ***Mountain***, peak to SE of Streap, forming part of a sinuous ridge. Height 2945 feet or 898 metres. NM9586.
Streens *High.* ***Valley***, gorge-like section of River Findhorn valley, part of larger Strathdearn, below E slopes of Carn nan Tri-tighearnan. Valley is deeply entrenched with River Findhorn meandering across narrow valley floor, creating spurs and steep valley sides. **52 A1** NH8637.
Strem Ness *Shet.* ***Coastal feature***, headland on NE coast of Foula. **82 B5** HT9741.
Strichen *Aber.* Population: 1112. ***Village***, 8m/13km S of Fraserburgh. Situated on northern branch of River Ugie known as North Ugie Water. **65 E4** NJ9455.
Stroan Loch *D. & G.* ***Lake/loch***, small loch in course of River Dee, 5m/8km S of New Galloway. **8 A4** NX6470.
Stròc-bheinn *High.* ***Mountain***, 3m/5km SW of Portree, Skye. Height 1312 feet or 400 metres. **48 A1** NG4539.
Strom Ness *Ork.* ***Coastal feature***, southernmost headland on North Ronaldsay. **81 F1** HY7651.
Strom Ness *Shet.* ***Coastal feature***, headland on S coast of Vaila, off Mainland. **82 B3** HU2245.
Strom Ness *Shet.* ***Coastal feature***, headland on W coast of Muckle Roe. **82 B1** HU2965.
Strom Ness *Shet.* ***Coastal feature***, long narrow peninsula 3m/5km NW of Scalloway. To E is parallel peninsula of White Ness, separated from Strom Ness by long narrow inlet of Stromness Voe. HU3743.
Stroma *High.* *See Island of Stroma.*
Stromay *W.Isles* ***Island***, small uninhabited island off NE coast of North Uist, 4m/6km N of Lochmaddy. **56 C2** NF9374.
Strome Castle *High.* ***Castle***, ruins of ancient castle (National Trust for Scotland), destroyed 1602, on N shore of Loch Carron, Ross and Cromarty district, opposite Stromeferry. **49 E1** NG8635.
Stromeferry *High.* ***Village***, on S side of Loch Carron, Skye and Lochalsh district, 8m/13km NE of Kyle of Lochalsh. Vehicle ferry to N shore. **49 E1** NG8634.
Stromemore *High.* ***Settlement***, on N shore of Loch Carron, 1km N of Stromeferry across loch. **49 E1** NG8635.
Stromness *Ork.* Population: 1890. ***Small town***, fishing port with ferry terminal, on inlet of Hoy Sound, 12m/20km W of Kirkwall, Mainland. **78 B2** HY2509.
Stromness Museum *Ork.* ***Other feature of interest***, in Stromness, Mainland, with local maritime and natural history exhibits. **78 B2** HY2508.
Stromness Voe *Shet.* ***Sea feature***, long narrow inlet separating Strom Ness from White Ness, Mainland. HU3743.
Stronachlachar *Stir.* ***Settlement***, on S shore of Loch Katrine, 2m/4km SE of head of loch. **31 G4** NN4010.
Stronchullin Hill *Arg. & B.* ***Mountain***, in Argyll Forest Park, 3m/4km NE of Orchard. Height 1797 feet or 548 metres. **22 C1** NS1786.
Strond *W.Isles* *Anglicised form of Strannda, qv.*
Strondeval *W.Isles* ***Hill***, near SW coast of South Harris, 1m/2km SE of Leverburgh. Height 692 feet or 211 metres. **66 C5** NG0384.
Strone *Arg. & B.* ***Village***, resort at Strone Point, Argyll, on W side of entrance to Loch Long. **22 C1** NS1980.
Strone *High.* ***Settlement***, on Urquhart Bay, on NW shore of Loch Ness, Inverness district. **51 E2** NH5228.
Strone *High.* ***Settlement***, in valley of River Lochy, 6m/9km NW of Fort William. **38 D1** NN1481.
Strone *Stir.* ***Settlement***, on N shore of Loch Katrine, 6m/9km NW of Brig o' Turk. **31 G3** NN4510.
Strone Glen *Arg. & B.* ***Valley***, in Kintyre, carrying Strone Water SE to Carskey Bay. **12 B5** NR6507.
Strone Point *Arg. & B.* ***Coastal feature***, headland at N end of Loch Fyne, 1m/2km NE of Inveraray. **30 D4** NN1108.
Strone Point *Arg. & B.* ***Coastal feature***, headland on Kyles of Bute on W side of entrance to Loch Striven, Argyll. **22 B2** NS0671.
Strone Point *Arg. & B.* ***Coastal feature***, headland on W side of entrance to Loch Long. **22 D1** NS1980.
Strone Point *High.* ***Coastal feature***, headland on Loch Ness, to SE of Strone, with ruins of Urquhart Castle (Historic Scotland). NH5328.
Strone Water *Arg. & B.* ***River***, in Kintyre, running SE down Strone Glen to join Breackerie Water as it enters Carskey Bay on S coast of peninsula. NR6507.
Stronechrubie *High.* ***Settlement***, on River Loanan, 2m/3km S of S end of Loch Assynt. **71 E3** NC2419.
Stronenaba *High.* ***Settlement***, in Lochaber district, 2m/3km NW of Spean Bridge. **39 E1** NN2084.
Stronlonag *Arg. & B.* ***Settlement***, above S bank of River Massan, 2m/4km NW of Benmore. **22 C1** NS1186.
Stronmilchan *Arg. & B.* ***Village***, in Argyll, 1m/2km NW of Dalmally. **31 D2** NN1528.
Stronsay *Ork.* ***Island***, irregularly shaped island, 7m/11km in length from NW to SE, and 12m/20km NE of Kirkwall on Mainland. **81 E4** HY6525.
Stronsay Airfield *Ork.* ***Airport/airfield***, close to N coast of Stronsay. **81 E4** HY6329.
Stronsay Firth *Ork.* ***Sea feature***, sea area between Stronsay and Shapinsay. **80 D4** HY5720.
Strontian *High.* ***River***, rising on W side of Sgurr Dhomhnuill and flowing NW, then SW to enter Loch Sunart at Strontian near head of loch. **38 A3** NM8161.
Strontian *High.* ***Village***, on N shore of Loch Sunart, Lochaber district, at mouth of Strontian River, which rises on W side of Sgurr Dhomhnuill. **38 A3** NM8161.
Strontoiller *Arg. & B.* ***Settlement***, 3m/5km E of Oban. **30 B2** NM9028.
Stronuich Reservoir *P. & K.* ***Reservoir***, small reservoir in course of River Lyon, 3m/5km E of Loch Lyon. **40 A5** NN5041.
Stronvar *Stir.* ***Settlement***, at head of Loch Voil, adjoining to SW of Balquhidder. **32 A3** NN5319.
Stroquhan *D. & G.* ***Settlement***, 2m/3km W of Dunscore. **8 C2** NX8483.
Stroul *Arg. & B.* ***Hamlet***, on W shore of Gare Loch, adjoining to NW of Rosneath. **23 D1** NS2483.
Struan *High.* ***Settlement***, 1km W of Bracadale, Skye. **47 G1** NG3438.
Struan *P. & K.* ***Village***, at confluence of Errochty Water and River Garry, 4m/6km W of Blair Atholl. Small museum of items of historical interest associated with the Clan Donnachaidh. **40 D3** NN8165.
Struie *High.* ***Mountain***, in Ross and Cromarty district, 5m/8km SE of Bonar Bridge. Height 1217 feet or 371 metres. **61 F1** NH6685.
Struie Hill *High.* ***Mountain***, rocky summit rising to over 380 metres, in Ross and Cromarty district, 5m/8km SE of Bonar Bridge. **61 F1** NH6786.
Strutherhill *S.Lan.* ***Suburb***, adjoining to S of Larkshall. NS7649.
Struthers *Fife* ***Hamlet***, 3m/5km S of Cupar. **34 B4** NO3709.
Struy *High.* ***Settlement***, at N end of Strathglass, 9m/14km SW of Beauly. **60 D5** NH4040.
Struy Bridge *High.* ***Bridge***, road bridge over River Farrar nearly 1km above its confluence with River Glass, Inverness district, and 1km SW of Erchless Castle. NH4040.
Struy Forest *High.* ***Open space***, deer forest to SW of Struy Bridge. **50 C1** NH4040.
Stuabhal *W.Isles* *Gaelic form of Stulaval, qv.*
Stuartfield *Aber.* ***Village***, 10m/16km W of Peterhead. **65 E5** NJ9745.
Stuarton *High.* ***Locality***, in Inverness district adjoining to S of Ardersier, on E shore of Inner Moray Firth or Inverness Firth. NH7854.
Stùc a' Chroin ***Mountain***, on border of Perth & Kinross and Stirling, 1m/2km SW of Ben Vorlich. Munro: height 3198 feet or 975 metres. **32 B3** NN6117.
Stuc Scardan *Arg. & B.* ***Mountain***, in Argyll, 4m/6km NE of Inveraray. Height 1597 feet or 487 metres. **30 D3** NN1114.
Stuchd an Lochain *P. & K.* ***Mountain***, 2m/3km SW of dam of Loch an Daimh. Munro: height 3149 feet or 960 metres. **39 G5** NN4844.
Stuck *Arg. & B.* ***Settlement***, above NE coast of Bute, 4m/6km NW of Rothesay. **22 B3** NS0670.
Stuck *Arg. & B.* ***Settlement***, 3m/5km SE of Glenbranter. **30 D5** NS1393.
Stuckbeg *Arg. & B.* ***Settlement***, on E shore of Loch Goil, 2m/4km S of Lochgoilhead. **31 E5** NS2197.
Stuckgowan *Arg. & B.* ***Settlement***, on W shore of Loch Lomond, 1m/2km S of Tarbet. **31 F4** NN3202.
Stuckindroin *Arg. & B.* ***Settlement***, at N end of Loch Lomond, 1km SE of Ardlui. **31 F3** NN3214.
Stuckreoch *Arg. & B.* ***Settlement***, on S shore of Loch Fyne, 3m/5km SW of Strachur. **30 C5** NS0599.
Stulaval (Gaelic form: Stuabhal.) *W.Isles* ***Mountain***, in North Harris, 1m/2km W of S end of Loch Langavat. Height 1899 feet or 579 metres. **66 D2** NB1312.
Stulaval *W.Isles* ***Mountain***, on South Uist 4m/6km N of Lochboisdale. Height 1227 feet or 374 metres. **46 B2** NF8024.
Stuley *W.Isles* ***Island***, uninhabited island off E coast of South Uist, 4m/6km NE of Lochboisdale. Island separated from coast by narrow Stuley Sound. **46 B2** NF8323.
Stuley Sound *W.Isles* ***Sea feature***, narrow sound separating Stuley from E coast of South Uist. NF8223.
Sturdy Hill *Aber.* ***Mountain***, 6m/9km N of Edzell. Height 1784 feet or 544 metres. **43 D2** NO5977.
Sty Wick *Ork.* ***Bay***, large wide bay on S coast of Sanday, bounded by Els Ness to W and Lang Taing to E. **81 E3** HY6839.
Suainaval *W.Isles* ***Mountain***, 6m/9km S of Gallan Head, and E of northernmost point of Loch Suainaval. Height 1407 feet or 429 metres. **68 B4** NB0730.
Suainebost (Anglicised form: Swanibost.) *W.Isles* ***Village***, near N end of Isle of Lewis, 2m/3km SW of Port Nis. **69 G1** NB5162.
Suardail (Anglicised form: Swordale.) *W.Isles* ***Village***, on Eye Peninsula, Isle of Lewis, 2m/3km SW of Garrabost. **69 F4** NB4930.
Succoth *Aber.* ***Settlement***, on lower slopes of Red Hill, 3m/4km S of Haugh of Glass. **53 G1** NJ4235.
Succoth *Arg. & B.* ***Hamlet***, at head of Loch Long, 1km N of Arrochar. **31 E4** NN2905.
Succothmore *Arg. & B.* ***Settlement***, 1m/2km E of Strachur. **30 D4** NN1201.

S

Sueno's Stone *Moray* ***Historic/prehistoric site***, remarkable glass-encased ancient sandstone obelisk (Historic Scotland), 23 feet or 7 metres high and bearing Celtic symbols, on NE side of Forres. Probably a cenotaph dating from end of first millennium AD. **62 C4** NJ0459.
Suidh' a' Mhinn *High.* ***Mountain***, 3m/5km N of Uig, Skye. Height 1148 feet or 350 metres. **58 A3** NG4068.
Suidhe Ghuirmain *High.* ***Mountain***, in Inverness district, 4m/7km SE of Cannich. Height 1896 feet or 578 metres. **50 C2** NH3827.
Suie Hill *Aber.* ***Mountain***, surrounded by woodland, 4m/7km N of Alford. Height 1361 feet or 415 metres. **54 A2** NJ5523.
Suie Lodge Hotel *Stir.* ***Other building***, hotel set in 6 acres of grounds in Glen Dochart, 6m/10km SW of Killin. **31 G2** NN4827.
Sùil Ghorm *Arg. & B.* ***Island***, islet with lighthouse, lying 1m/2km off NE end of Coll. NM2865.
Suilven *High.* ***Mountain***, near W coast of Sutherland district 5m/7km SE of Lochinver. Height 2398 feet or 731 metres. **71 D3** NC1518.
Suisgill Burn *High.* ***River***, in Sutherland district, flowing S and joining River Helmsdale 2m/3km N of Kildonan Lodge. **73 E2** NC8924.
Suisnish *High.* ***Settlement***, on Skye, near S coast between Loch Eishort and Loch Slapin. NG5916.
Suisnish Point *High.* ***Coastal feature***, headland at SW corner of Raasay, opposite Balmeanach Bay on Skye. **48 B1** NG5534.
Sula Sgeir *W.Isles* ***Island***, uninhabited island, nearly 1km long NE to SW, and nowhere more than 200 metres wide, situated about 41m/65km N of Butt of Lewis. Nature reserve. Several islets and rocks in vicinity. HW6230.
Sule Skerry *Ork.* ***Island***, islet with lighthouse, some 37m/60km W of Mainland. HX6224.
Sule Stack *Ork.* ***Island***, islet some 41m/66km W of Mainland. HX5617.
Sullom *Shet.* ***Settlement***, in N part of Mainland, on W shore of Sullom Voe. **84 C5** HU3573.
Sullom Voe *Shet.* ***Sea feature***, inlet some 8m/12km long and almost separating N part of Mainland from the rest. The voe, which runs N into Yell Sound, provides shelter for shipping. **84 C5** HU3573.
Sullom Voe Oil Terminal *Shet.* ***Other feature of interest***, 3m/5km NW of Firth, Mainland. **84 C5** HU3975.
Sulma Water *Shet.* ***Lake/loch***, 3m/4km N of Bridge of Walls, Mainland. Approximately 1m/2km long, N to S. **82 B2** HU2554.
Sumburgh *Shet.* ***Settlement***, on Mainland, 1m/2km N of headland of Sumburgh Head (lighthouse), at S extremity of island. **83 G5** HU4009.
Sumburgh Airport *Shet.* ***Airport/airfield***, airport for Shetland, to N of Sumburgh, at S end of Mainland. **83 G5** HU4009.
Sumburgh Head *Shet.* ***Coastal feature***, headland at S extremity of Mainland. Sumburgh settlement 1m/2km N. Lighthouse. **83 G5** HU4009.
Sumburgh Roost *Shet.* ***Sea feature***, area of sea to S of Sumburgh Head, off S coast of Mainland. **83 F5** HU3906.
Summer Isles *High.* ***Island***, group of uninhabited islands off NW coast of Ross and Cromarty district between Rubha Coigeach and Greenstone Point. **70 B4** NB9607.
Summerhill *Aberdeen* ***Suburb***, 2m/4km W of Aberdeen city centre. NJ9006.
Summerhill *D. & G.* ***Suburb***, W district of Dumfries. Location of Young Offenders' Institution. NX9576.
Summerlee Heritage Trust *N.Lan.* ***Other feature of interest***, museum to N of Coatbridge town centre. Exhibits include a 19c coal mine and a tramway, as well as social history displays. **24 B3** NS7265.
Summerville *D. & G.* ***Suburb***, NW district of Dumfries. NX9676.
Sunadale *Arg. & B.* ***Settlement***, on W coast of Kintyre, 1km N of Grogport. **21 G5** NR8144.
Sunart *High.* ***Locality***, in Lochaber district, between Loch Shiel and Loch Sunart. **37 F3** NM7966.
Sundaywell *D. & G.* ***Settlement***, 3m/5km W of Dunscore. **8 C2** NX8184.
Sundhope *Sc.Bord.* ***Hamlet***, 2m/3km SW of Yarrow. **17 E3** NT3325.
Sundhope Height *Sc.Bord.* ***Mountain***, 3m/5km W of Ettrickbridge. Height 1683 feet or 513 metres. **17 E3** NT3423.
Sundrum *S.Ayr.* ***Settlement***, 1km N of Joppa, with Sundrum Castle to N by Water of Coyle. **14 C3** NS4120.
Sunipol *Arg. & B.* ***Settlement***, near N coast of Mull, 1m/2km E of Caliach Point. **36 C4** NM3753.
Sunnylaw *Stir.* ***Hamlet***, 3m/5km N of Stirling. **32 C5** NS7998.
Sunnyside *Aber.* ***Settlement***, 2m/3km NW of Portlethen. **55 D5** NO8998.
Suntrap *Edin.* ***Garden***, 1km NW of Hermiston. Gardening advice centre catering particularly for owners of small gardens. **25 F2** NT1771.
Sunwick *Sc.Bord.* ***Settlement***, 3m/4km W of Paxton. **27 F4** NT8952.
Sursay *W.Isles* ***Island***, small uninhabited island in Sound of Harris, 2m/3km off NE coast of North Uist. NF9576.
Suther Ness *Shet.* ***Coastal feature***, promontory with lighthouse on N coast of Whalsay, NW of Brough village. HU5565.
Sutor Stacks *High.* ***Coastal feature***, headland on NE tip of Black Isle, 1m/2km E of Cromarty. **62 A3** NH8167.
Sutors of Cromarty *High.* ***Settlement***, 1km E of Cromarty. **62 A3** NH8066.
Swanbister *Ork.* ***Locality***, on Mainland, 1m/2km SW of Kirkbister. HY3405.
Swanbister Bay *Ork.* ***Bay***, to SE of Swanbister, with landing stage on W side. **78 C2** HY3505.
Swanibost *W.Isles Anglicised form of Suainebost, qv.*
Swanlaws *Sc.Bord.* ***Settlement***, 2m/3km S of Hownam. **18 B5** NT7716.
Swannay *Ork.* ***Locality***, at N end of Mainland, 4m/6km E of Brough Head. Loch of Swannay is large loch to E. HY2929.
Swannies Point *Ork.* ***Coastal feature***, headland on N coast of W part of Burray. ND4597.
Swanston *Edin.* ***Suburb***, 4m/7km S of Edinburgh city centre. Swanston Cottage was once a summer home of R.L. Stevenson. NT2367.
Swarbacks Minn *Shet.* ***Sea feature***, strait between Muckle Roe and islands of Vementry and Papa Little, off W coast of Mainland. **82 B1** HU3161.
Swartz Geo *Shet.* ***Coastal feature***, small indentation on SE coast of Fair Isle. **82 A5** HZ2170.
Swatte Fell *D. & G.* ***Mountain***, 4m/6km NE of Moffat. Height 2388 feet or 728 metres. **16 C4** NT1111.
Sweetheart Abbey (Also known as New Abbey.) *D. & G.* ***Ecclesiastical building***, ruin of 13c abbey dating from Early English to Decorated period (Historic Scotland), at New Abbey. Lady Devorgilla and embalmed heart of husband John de Baliol are buried here. **9 D4** NX9666.
Sweethope Hill *Sc.Bord.* ***Hill***, 1m/2km NW of Stichill. Height 731 feet or 223 metres. **18 A3** NT6939.
Sweyn Holm *Ork.* ***Island***, small uninhabited island off NE coast of Gairsay. **80 C4** HY4522.
Swiney *High.* ***Settlement***, in Caithness district, 1m/2km W of Lybster. **77 E5** ND2335.
Swinhill *S.Lan.* ***Settlement***, 2m/3km S of Larkhall. NS7748.
Swining *Shet.* ***Settlement***, overlooking Swining Voe, Mainland. **83 D1** HU4566.
Swining Voe *Shet.* ***Sea feature***, northward-facing inlet on E coast of Mainland, 2m/3km N of Dury Voe. HU4667.
Swinside Hall *Sc.Bord.* ***Settlement***, 2m/3km SE of Oxnam. **18 B5** NT7216.
Swinton *Sc.Bord.* ***Village***, 5m/8km N of Coldstream. **27 F5** NT8347.
Swinton Quarter *Sc.Bord.* ***Settlement***, 1km NE of Swinton. NT8447.
Swintonmill *Sc.Bord.* ***Hamlet***, 2m/3km SW of Swinton. **27 F5** NT8146.
Switha *Ork.* ***Island***, small uninhabited island 1m/2km E of South Walls peninsula at SE end of Hoy. Traces of Bronze Age settlements. **78 C3** ND3690.
Swona *Ork.* ***Island***, of about 60 acres or 25 hectares, 3m/5km W of Burwick, near S end of South Ronaldsay. Beacon at SW end. **78 C4** ND3884.
Swordale *High.* ***Settlement***, 2m/3km W of Evanton. **61 E3** NH5765.
Swordale *W.Isles Anglicised form of Suardail, qv.*
Swordland *High.* ***Settlement***, on N shore of Loch Morar, 1km S of Tarbert, Lochaber district. **49 D5** NM7891.
Swordle *High.* ***Locality***, near N coast of Ardnamurchan peninsula, 1km S of Ockle Point. **37 E3** NM5470.
Swordly *High.* ***Settlement***, near N coast of Caithness district, 2m/3km E of Bettyhill. **75 G2** NC7363.
Sworland *High.* ***Settlement***, in North Morar, on N shore of Loch Morar in Lochaber district, 1km S of Tarbet. NM7891.
Symbister *Shet.* ***Village***, chief harbour of Whalsay, near SW end of island. **83 E1** HU5362.
Symbister Ness *Shet.* ***Coastal feature***, headland with lighthouse on Whalsay to W of Symbister. HU5362.
Symington *S.Ayr.* Population: 1145. ***Village***, 4m/7km NE of Prestwick. **14 B2** NS3831.
Symington *S.Lan.* ***Village***, 3m/5km SW of Biggar. **16 A2** NS9935.
Symington Church *S.Ayr.* ***Ecclesiastical building***, small church in Symington with three 12c Norman windows. **14 B2** NS3831.
Syre *High.* ***Settlement***, in Strathnaver, 11m/18km S of Bettyhill, Caithness district. **75 F4** NC6943.

T

Taagan *High.* ***Settlement***, 1m/2km NW of Kinlochewe, at SE end of Loch Maree. **59 G3** NH0163.
Taberon Law *Sc.Bord.* ***Mountain***, 2m/3km SE of Stanhope. Height 2057 feet or 627 metres. **16 C3** NT1428.
Tabhaidh Bheag *W.Isles Gaelic form of Tavay Beag, qv.*
Tabhaigh Mhòr (Anglicised form: Tavay Mòr.) *W.Isles* ***Island***, small uninhabited island opposite entrance to Loch Erisort, E coast of Isle of Lewis. **69 F5** NB4222.
Tabost (Anglicised form: Habost.) *W.Isles* ***Settlement***, on Isle of Lewis, on S side of Loch Erisort, opposite Lacasaigh. **67 F2** NB3219.
Tabost (Anglicised form: Habost.) *W.Isles* ***Village***, near N end of Isle of Lewis, 1m/2km W of Port Nis. **69 G1** NB5263.
Tacher *High.* ***Settlement***, situated on Little River, 3m/5km N of Loch Rangag. **77 D4** ND1746.
Tacleit (Anglicised form: Hacklete.) *W.Isles* ***Settlement***, at S end of Great Bernera, W coast of Isle of Lewis, to W of road bridge connecting Great Bernera to main island. **68 C4** NB1534.
Tafts Ness *Ork.* ***Coastal feature***, headland at NE end of Sanday. **81 F2** HY7647.
Tahaval *W.Isles* ***Mountain***, near W coast of Isle of Lewis, 1m/2km E of Mealisval. Height 1689 feet or 515 metres. **68 B5** NB0426.
Tahay *W.Isles* ***Island***, small uninhabited island in Sound of Harris less than 1km off NE coast of North Uist. NF9675.
Tailor's Leap *Arg. & B.* ***Other feature of interest***, in Glen Nant, 2m/3km S of Taynuilt, where a tailor, who kept an illegal still, is reputed to have leapt across the stream above a waterfall to escape pursuing excisemen. **30 C2** NN0128.
Tain *High.* ***Settlement***, in Caithness district, 2m/3km SE of Castletown. **77 E2** ND2166.
Tain *High.* Population: 3715. ***Small town***, attractive town and royal burgh in Ross and Cromarty district on S shore of Dornoch Firth, 10m/15km NE of Invergordon. 14c church and interesting 17c tollbooth. **61 G1** NH7782.
Tain District Museum *High.* ***Other feature of interest***, exhibitions on history and culture of Tain area. **61 G1** NH7883.
Taing of Kelswick *Shet.* ***Coastal feature***, headland to S of larger headland of Lunna Ness on Mainland's E coast. **83 E1** HU4969.
Taing of Maywick *Shet.* ***Coastal feature***, headland on W coast of Mainland on W side of May Wick. HU3724.
Tairlaw *S.Ayr.* ***Settlement***, 3m/5km SE of Straiton. **14 C5** NS4000.
Talisker *High.* ***River***, flowing W past settlement of Talisker into Talisker Bay on W coast of Skye. NG3130.
Talisker *High.* ***Settlement***, near W coast of Skye, 4m/6km W of Carbost and 3m/4km SE of Rubha nan Clach. **47 G1** NG3230.
Talisker Bay *High.* ***Bay***, on W coast of Skye, to W of Talisker. **47 G1** NG3130.
Talisker Distillery *High.* ***Other building***, sole distillery on Skye established in 1830 at NW end of Carbost, on SW side of Loch Harport. Produces single malt whisky known as 'Lava of the Highlands'. NG3731.
Talisker Point *High.* ***Coastal feature***, headland on W coast of Skye at S end of Talisker Bay. NG3129.
Talla Bheith *P. & K.* ***Settlement***, on N shore of Loch Rannoch, 6m/10km W of Kinloch Rannoch. **40 A4** NN5658.
Talla Bheith Forest *P. & K.* ***Large natural feature***, upland area and game forest in Atholl, to E of Loch Ericht and N of Loch Rannoch. **40 A3** NN5567.
Talla Linnfoots *Sc.Bord.* ***Settlement***, at E end of Talla Reservoir, 3m/5km SE of Tweedsmuir. **16 C3** NT1320.
Talla Reservoir *Sc.Bord.* ***Reservoir***, 2km SE of Tweedsmuir. Length about 2m/4km SE to NW. **16 C3** NT1121.
Talladale *High.* ***Village***, on SW shore of Loch Maree, Ross and Cromarty district, 8m/13km SE of Gairloch. **59 F2** NG9170.
Talmine *High.* ***Village***, in Caithness district, on W shore of Tongue Bay. **75 E2** NC5863.
Tam o' Shanter Experience *S.Ayr.* ***Other feature of interest***, museum in Alloway detailing story of Robert Burns and Tam o' Shanter. **14 B4** NS3318.
Tamanaisval *W.Isles* ***Mountain***, near W coast of Isle of Lewis 2m/4km SE of Mealisval. Height 1532 feet or 467 metres. **68 B5** NB0423.
Tamanavay *W.Isles* ***River***, on Isle of Lewis, flowing W into Loch Tamanavay. NB0320.
Tamavoid *Stir.* ***Settlement***, 2m/3km S of Port of Menteith. **32 A5** NS5999.
Tandlehill *Renf.* ***Suburb***, adjoining to SE of Kilbarchan. NS4062.
Tanera Beg *High.* ***Island***, one of Summer Isles group. Lies 3m/5km W of NW coast of Ross and Cromarty district near Polglass. Area about 270 acres or 110 hectares. **70 B4** NB9607.
Tanera Mòr *High.* ***Island***, largest of Summer Isles group, being over 1 square mile or about 3 square km in area. Lies 1m/2km W of NW coast of Ross and Cromarty district across Badentarbert Bay. NB9807.
Tang Head *High.* ***Coastal feature***, headland on N coast, 5m/8km SE of Dunnet Head. **77 E1** ND2774.
Tang Head *High.* ***Coastal feature***, headland on E coast on N side of Sinclair's Bay. **77 F2** ND3560.

Tang Wick *Shet.* ***Bay***, on Esha Ness, Mainland, on N shore of the larger St. Magnus Bay. HU2377.
Tanglandford *Aber.* ***Settlement***, to S of Bridge over River Ythan, 3m/5km N of Tarves. **55 D1** NJ8835.
Tangwick *Shet.* ***Settlement***, on Esha Ness, Mainland, inland of bay of Tang Wick on N shore of larger St. Magnus Bay. **84 B5** HU2377.
Tangy *Arg. & B.* ***Settlement***, on Kintyre, 5m/8km NW of Campbeltown. **12 B3** NR6727.
Tangy Loch *Arg. & B.* ***Lake/loch***, small loch in Kintyre 5m/8km N of Campbeltown. **12 B3** NR6928.
Tankerness *Ork.* ***Locality***, and loch on Mainland, 2m/3km SW of Rerwick Head. **79 E2** HY5009.
Tankerness House Museum *Ork.* ***Other feature of interest***, in Kirkwall, Mainland. 16c house with exhibitions on Orkney archaeology and history. **80 C5** HY4510.
Tannach *High.* ***Settlement***, in Caithness district, 3m/5km SW of Wick. **77 F4** ND3247.
Tannachie *Aber.* ***Hamlet***, 3m/4km NE of Glenbervie. **43 F1** NO7883.
Tannachy *High.* ***Settlement***, adjoining to NE of Rhilochan, Sutherland district. **72 C4** NC7507.
Tannadice *Angus* ***Village***, on River South Esk, 8m/12km W of Brechin. **42 C4** NO4758.
Tannaraidh *W.Isles Gaelic form of Tannray, qv.*
Tannochside *N.Lan.* ***Suburb***, 1m/2km N of Uddingston. **24 B3** NS7061.
Tannray (Gaelic form: Tannaraidh.) *W.Isles* ***Island***, small uninhabited island at entrance to Loch Leurbost, E coast of Isle of Lewis. NB4023.
Tanshall *Fife* ***Suburb***, W district of Glenrothes. NO2500.
Tantallon Castle *E.Loth.* ***Castle***, ruined 14c castle (Historic Scotland) of red stone on rocky headland, 3m/5km E of North Berwick. **26 C1** NT5985.
Taobh a' Deas Loch Baghasdail (Anglicised form: South Lochboisdale.) *W.Isles* ***Settlement***, on S side of Loch Baghasdail, South Uist, 1m/2km SW of Lochboisdale. **44 C2** NF7717.
Taobh Dubh *High.* ***Mountain***, 1m/2km NW of Loch Uisge. Small tarn at summit. Height 1155 feet or 352 metres. **37 G4** NM7856.
Taobh Siar (Anglicised form: West Tarbert.) *W.Isles* ***Settlement***, 1km NW of Tarbert, North Harris. **66 D3** NB1400.
Taobh Tuath *W.Isles Gaelic form of Northton, qv.*
Tap o' Noth *Aber.* ***Mountain***, surmounted by ancient fort, 2m/3km NW of Rhynie. Height 1847 feet or 563 metres. **53 G2** NJ4829.
Taransay *W.Isles Anglicised form of Tarasaigh, qv.*
Taransay Glorigs *W.Isles* ***Island***, group of rocks about 3m/5km NW of Tarasaigh. **66 B3** NB0200.
Tarasaigh (Anglicised form: Taransay). *W.Isles* ***Island***, barely populated island, 4m/7km NE to SW and of varying width, lying 1m/2km off W coast of South Harris across Sound of Taransay. **66 C3** NB0200.
Taravocan *Arg. & B.* ***Settlement***, in valley of River Creran, 1m/2km NE of head of Loch Creran. **38 C5** NN0146.
Tarbat House *High.* ***Settlement***, on shore of Nigg Bay, 1km S of Milton. **61 G2** NH7773.
Tarbat Ness *High.* ***Coastal feature***, headland on E coast of Ross and Cromarty district, on S side of entrance to Dornoch Firth. Lighthouse. **62 B1** NH9487.
Tarbert *Arg. & B.* ***Settlement***, on Tarbert Bay, on E coast of Jura, 5m/7km SW of Ardlussa. **21 E1** NR6181.
Tarbert *Arg. & B.* ***Settlement***, on N part of Gigha, 2m/3km N of Ardminish. **21 E4** NR6551.
Tarbert *Arg. & B.* Population: 1347. ***Village***, at head of East Loch Tarbert at N end of Kintyre, Argyll. Main port for Loch Fyne fishing industry. Passenger boat services to Gourock. Remains of 14c castle on S side of loch. **21 G3** NR8668.
Tarbert *High.* ***River***, in Lochaber district rising on S slopes of Garbh Bheinn and flowing E along Glen Tarbert to Loch Linnhe at Inversanda Bay. NM9459.
Tarbert *High.* ***Settlement***, on W side of Salen Bay, 1km S of Salen, Lochaber district. **37 F3** NM6863.
Tarbert (Gaelic form: An Tairbeart.) *W.Isles* ***Village***, port of North Harris, situated on isthmus between East and West Loch Tarbert. **67 D3** NB1500.
Tarbert Bay *Arg. & B.* ***Bay***, on E coast of Jura. **21 E1** NR6082.
Tarbert Bay *High.* ***Bay***, small bay on S coast of Canna, 3m/4km E of Garrisdale Point. **47 F4** NG2405.
Tarbet *Arg. & B.* ***Village***, and resort on W shore of Loch Lomond, 7m/11km S of head of loch and 1m/2km E of Arrochar at head of Loch Long. **31 F4** NN3104.
Tarbet *High.* ***Settlement***, on W coast of Sutherland district, opposite Handa Island. **74 A4** NC1648.
Tarbet *High.* ***Settlement***, in North Morar, on S shore of Loch Nevis, Lochaber district, at head of small inlet. **49 D5** NM7992.
Tarbet Bay *High.* ***Bay***, on S shore of Loch Nevis, Lochaber district, 8m/12km SE of Mallaig. NM7992.
Tarbolton *S.Ayr.* Population: 1854. ***Village***, 5m/8km E of Prestwick. Bachelor's Club (National Trust for Scotland), 17c thatched house where Burns and friends formed club in 1780. **14 C3** NS4327.
Tarbrax *S.Lan.* ***Settlement***, 6m/10km NE of Carnwath. **25 E4** NT0255.
Tarf Bridge *D. & G.* ***Bridge***, crossing Tarf Water 1km E of Loch Ronald, 6m/10km NE of Glenluce. **6 D4** NX2564.
Tarf Water *D. & G.* ***River***, rising S of Barrhill on W slopes of Benbrake Hill and running SE to River Bladnoch, 1m/2km E of Kirkcowan. NX3460.
Tarf Water *P. & K.* ***River***, running E to head of Glen Tilt, 11m/17km NE of Blair Atholl. **41 E2** NN9879.
Tarff *High.* ***River***, in Inverness district, rising between Glendoe and Corrieyairack Forests and running W, then N down Glen Tarff to head of Loch Ness. NH3809.
Tarff Water *D. & G.* ***River***, flowing S to join River Dee 1km S of Tongland, 1m/2km N of Kirkcudbright. **8 A4** NX6853.
Tarfside *Angus* ***Village***, on Water of Tarf near its junction with River North Esk, 11m/17km NW of Fettercairn. **42 C1** NO4979.
Tarland *Aber.* ***Village***, 9m/14km NE of Ballater. On rocky knoll 1km SE is Tomnaverie Stone Circle (Historic Scotland). 2m/3km E is site of prehistoric Culsh Earth House (Historic Scotland). **53 G4** NJ4804.
Tarland Burn *Aber.* ***River***, rising to NW of Tarland and flowing SE to Aboyne, joining River Dee 2m/3km E of Aboyne. **54 A4** NO5597.
Tarner Island *High.* ***Island***, small uninhabited island in Loch Bracadale, nearly 1m/2km N of Wiay. **47 F1** NG2938.
Tarras Water *D. & G.* ***River***, running S to River Esk, 3m/4km S of Langholm. **10 B3** NY3780.
Tarrel *High.* ***Settlement***, 2m/3km SW of Portmahomack. **62 A1** NH8981.
Tarrnacraig *N.Ayr.* ***Settlement***, on Arran, 5m/8km W of Brodick. **13 E2** NR9334.
Tarsappie *P. & K.* ***Hamlet***, 2m/3km N of Bridge of Earn. **33 G2** NO1221.
Tarskavaig *High.* ***Village***, on Tarskavaig Bay, Skye, on W side of Sleat peninsula, 7m/11km N of Point of Sleat. **48 B4** NG5809.
Tarskavaig Bay *High.* ***Bay***, on W side of Sleat peninsula, 7m/11km N of Point of Sleat, Skye. **48 B4** NG5809.
Tarskavaig Point *High.* ***Coastal feature***, headland on N side of entrance to Tarskavaig Bay, Skye. NG5709.
Tarty Burn *Aber.* ***River***, rising to N of Newmachar and flowing N, then E into River Ythan estuary 1m/2km N of Newburgh. **55 E2** NJ9927.
Tarves *Aber.* ***Village***, 4m/7km NE of Oldmeldrum. Remarkable carvings on medieval altar tomb of William Forbes (Historic Scotland) in churchyard. **55 D1** NJ8631.
Tarvie *High.* ***Locality***, in Ross and Cromarty district, 3m/4km NW of Contin. **60 D4** NH4258.
Tarvie *P. & K.* ***Settlement***, on S facing hillside of Glen Brerachan, 6m/10km NE of Pitlochrie. **41 F3** NO0164.
Tathas Mhòr *W.Isles* ***Hill***, rising to over 300 metres to NW of Loch Claidh, 4m/6km S of head of Loch Shell, Isle of Lewis. **67 E3** NB2804.
Tauchers *Moray* ***Locality***, 4m/6km W of Keith. **63 F4** NJ3749.
Tavay Beag (Gaelic form: Tabhaidh Bheag.) *W.Isles* ***Island***, small island on W side of Tabhaigh Mhòr. NB4122.
Tavelty *Aber.* ***Settlement***, astride railway line, 1km N of Kintore. **54 C3** NJ7817.
Taversoe Tuick *Ork.* ***Historic/prehistoric site***, prehistoric two-storeyed cairn (Historic Scotland) on Rousay, 1km W of Brinyan. HY4227.
Tay ***River***, longest river in Scotland, rising on N side of Ben Lui and flowing generally E down Strath Fillan and Glen Dochart to Loch Tay, from where it issues as River Tay and flows past Aberfeldy, Dunkeld and Perth to Firth of Tay and E coast at Buddon Ness, E of Dundee. Total length 120m/193km. **33 G1** NO5429.
Tay Bridge ***Bridge***, 2m/3km rail bridge across Firth of Tay, between Dundee on N bank and Wormit on S. **34 B2** NO3927.
Tay Forest Park *P. & K.* ***Leisure/recreation***, large area containing several forests and encompassing towns of Kinloch Rannoch, Pitlochry, Dunkeld, Aberfeldy and Kenmore. Queen's View Centre on N shore of Loch Tummel is main interpretive centre of forest park. **40 C3** NN7762.
Tay Road Bridge ***Bridge***, 1m/2km road bridge across Firth of Tay, between Dundee and Newport-on-Tay, 2m/3km E of rail bridge. **34 C2** NO4129.
Tayburn *E.Ayr.* ***Settlement***, 4m/7km N of Galston. **23 G5** NS5143.
Taychreggan *Arg. & B.* ***Settlement***, 1km SE of Kilchrenan. **30 C2** NN0421.
Tayinloan *Arg. & B.* ***Village***, on W side of Kintyre, Argyll, 2m/4km S of Rhunahaorine Point. Ferry to Gigha. **21 E5** NR6946.
Taymouth Castle *P. & K.* ***Historic house***, early 19c mansion on S bank of River Tay, 1m/2km NE of Kenmore. **40 C5** NN7846.
Taynafead *Arg. & B.* ***Settlement***, 2m/3km S of Cladich. **30 C3** NN0918.
Taynish *Arg. & B.* ***Locality***, in Argyll, on W side of Loch Sween, just N of entrance to Linne Mhuirich. **21 F1** NR7283.
Taynish Island *Arg. & B.* ***Island***, off shore to SE of Taynish, 9m/14km W of Lochgilphead. NR7283.
Taynuilt *Arg. & B.* ***Village***, in Argyll, 1km SW of Bonawe. **30 C1** NN0031.
Tayock *Angus* ***Settlement***, 2m/3km NW of Montrose. **43 E4** NO6959.
Tayovullin *Arg. & B.* ***Settlement***, on W side of Loch Gruinart, Islay. **20 A2** NR2872.
Tayport *Fife* Population: 3346. ***Small town***, with harbour on S side of Firth of Tay, opposite Broughty Ferry. **34 C2** NO4528.
Tayvallich *Arg. & B.* ***Village***, in Knapdale, Argyll, on Loch a' Bhealaich, an inlet on W side of Loch Sween. **21 F1** NR7487.
Tealing *Angus Alternative name for Kirkton of Tealing, qv.*
Tealing Dovecot and Earth House *Angus* ***Historic/prehistoric site***, fine example of dovecot (Historic Scotland) built in 1595, 5m/8km N of Dundee. Nearby is a well-preserved Iron Age earth house or souterrain. **34 C1** NO4138.
Teampull Mholuidh *W.Isles* ***Ecclesiastical building***, 1km S of Butt of Lewis. Church dating from 12c and on site of much earlier church. **69 G1** NB5165.
Teampull na Trionaid *W.Isles* ***Ecclesiastical building***, ruined medieval church 1km NW of Cairinis, North Uist. **45 G3** NF8160.
Teanamachar *W.Isles* ***Settlement***, on W coast of Baleshare, SW of North Uist. **45 F3** NF7761.
Teanga Thunga *W.Isles* ***Coastal feature***, narrow spit of land protruding into River Laxdale estuary from N, 2m/3km NE of Stornoway, Isle of Lewis. NB4435.
Teangue *High.* ***Village***, on E coast of Sleat peninsula, Skye, 4m/7km NE of Ardvasar. **48 C4** NG6608.
Teaninich *High.* ***Locality***, on S side of Alness in Sutherland district. NH6569.
Teasses *Fife* ***Settlement***, 3m/5km N of Lower Largo. **34 C4** NO4008.
Teatle Water *Arg. & B.* ***River***, flowing W into Loch Awe, 3m/4km SW of Dalmally. **31 D2** NN1225.
Teindland *Moray* ***Open space***, upland tract 5m/9km SE of Elgin. NJ2655.
Teindland Forest *Moray* ***Forest/woodland***, on E side of Teindland. **63 E4** NJ2655.
Teinnasval *W.Isles* ***Mountain***, near W coast of Isle of Lewis 2m/3km SE of Mealisval. Height 1630 feet or 497 metres. NB0425.
Teith *Stir.* ***River***, formed by confluence of Garbh Uisge from Loch Lubnaig and Eas Gobhain from Loch Venachar at Callander, then running SE past Doune to River Forth 3m/4km NW of Stirling. **32 C4** NS7696.
Telegraph Hill *Sc.Bord.* ***Hill***, above North Sea coast, 4m/6km NW of St. Abb's Head. Height 571 feet or 174 metres. **27 F2** NT8570.
Telford Bridge *Moray* ***Bridge***, cast iron bridge built in 1815 by Thomas Telford, spanning River Spey to W of Craigellachie. **63 E5** NJ2845.
Telford Memorial *D. & G.* ***Other feature of interest***, 1km SW of Bentpath, memorial to Thomas Telford who worked, when an apprentice, on bridge at Langholm. **10 B3** NY3089.
Tempar *P. & K.* ***Settlement***, 1m/2km SE of Kinloch Rannoch. **40 B4** NN6857.
Templand *D. & G.* ***Village***, 2m/4km N of Lochmaben. **9 E2** NY0886.
Temple *Glas.* ***Suburb***, 4m/6km NW of Glasgow city centre. NS5469.
Temple *Midloth.* ***Village***, 3m/4km SW of Gorebridge. **26 A4** NT3158.
Temple Wood Stone Circle *Arg. & B.* ***Historic/prehistoric site***, adjoining to E of Slockavullin, 6m/10km N of Lochgilphead. Thirteen stones from original twenty forming a circle of 25 feet across. A stone burial cist is at centre. Bronze Age. **30 A5** NR8297.
Templehall *Fife* ***Suburb***, NW district of Kirkcaldy. NT2693.
Templewood *Angus* ***Settlement***, 2m/3km N of Brechin. **43 E3** NO6162.
Tenga *Arg. & B.* ***Settlement***, 4m/6km NW of Salen, at head of Glen Aros, Mull. **37 E5** NM5145.
Tents Muirs *Fife* ***Forest/woodland***, afforested area between Leuchars and Firth of Tay at Tentsmuir Point, 3m/4km E of Tayport. **34 C2** NO4825.
Tentsmuir Point *Fife* ***Coastal feature***, 3m/4km E of Tayport. Nature reserve S of point, behind Tentsmuir Sands. **34 D2** NO4825.
Tentsmuir Sands *Fife* ***Coastal feature***, 4m/6km SE of Tayport. NO5024.
Terally *D. & G.* ***Settlement***, adjacent to Terally Point, 3m/4km N of Drummore, on W side of Luce Bay. **2 B2** NX1240.
Terpersie Castle *Aber.* ***Castle***, small ruined castle 3m/5km NW of Alford. **54 A2** NJ5420.
Terregles *D. & G.* ***Hamlet***, 3m/4km W of Dumfries. **8 D3** NX9277.

Tervieside *Moray* ***Settlement***, 3m/5km NE of Tomnavoulin. **53 E1** NJ2330.
Teuchan *Aber.* ***Settlement***, 2m/3km N of Cruden Bay. **55 F1** NK0839.
Teviot *Sc.Bord.* ***River***, rising 6m/9km E of Eskdalemuir. River flows NE by Teviothead, Hawick and Roxburgh to River Tweed, SW of Kelso. **18 B3** NT7233.
Teviotdale *Sc.Bord.* ***Valley***, carrying River Teviot, running NE from Teviothead, through Hawick, to Ancrum Bridge, 1km SE of Ancrum. **17 F5** NT5317.
Teviothead *Sc.Bord.* ***Village***, in Teviotdale, 8m/13km SW of Hawick. **17 F5** NT4005.
Tewel *Aber.* ***Settlement***, 3m/5km W of Stonehaven. **43 G1** NO8285.
Tewsgill Hill *S.Lan.* ***Mountain***, 2m/3km E of Abington. Height 1866 feet or 569 metres. NS9623.
Texa *Arg. & B.* ***Island***, off S coast of Islay opposite Laphroaig. **20 B5** NR3943.
Thainston *Aber.* ***Locality***, comprises Upper Thainston and Nether Thainston, 1m/2km NW of Fettercairn. **43 E2** NO6375.
Thainstone *Aber.* ***Settlement***, with hotel on W side of River Don, 2m/3km S of Inverurie. **54 C3** NJ7618.
Thankerton *S.Lan.* ***Village***, 4m/7km W of Biggar. **16 A2** NS9738.
The Aird *High.* ***Coastal feature***, small peninsula separating Loch Treaslane from Loch Snizort Beag, 4m/6km SE of Lyndale Point, Skye. **58 A4** NG3952.
The Aird *High.* ***Coastal feature***, promontory on Skye, 2m/3km E of Rubha Hunish. **58 A2** NG4275.
The Aird *High.* ***Locality***, fertile district in Inverness district, S of Beauly. **61 E5** NH5642.
The Airde *High.* ***Inland physical feature***, large headland on E side of Loch Shin opposite Arscraig. **72 A3** NC5213.
The Ard *Arg. & B.* ***Coastal feature***, headland on S side of Port Ellen harbour, Islay. **20 B5** NR3644.
The Atlantic Bridge *Arg. & B. Familiar form of Clachan Bridge, qv.*
The Ayre *Ork.* ***Coastal feature***, narrow neck of land carrying a road, linking peninsula of South Walls with S end of Hoy. ND2889.
The Balloch *Moray* ***Open space***, hilly tract 3m/5km SE of Keith. **63 G5** NJ4748.
The Banking *Aber.* ***Settlement***, 3m/5km SE of Fyvie. **54 C1** NJ7833.
The Bar *High.* ***Coastal feature***, sandy spit extending 2m/3km from W end of Culbin Forest. **62 B3** NH9159.
The Barracks *P. & K.* ***Historic house***, mansion on S bank of River Gaur 1km above Loch Rannoch. Erected to accommodate government soldiers after the 1745 rising. NN4956.
The Bin *Aber.* ***Mountain***, surrounded by The Bin Forest, 3m/5km NW of Huntly. Height 1027 feet or 313 metres. **64 A5** NJ5043.
The Bin Forest *Aber.* ***Forest/woodland***, 2m/3km NW of Huntly, surrounding two rounded summits, The Bin at 1027 feet or 313 metres and Ordiquhill at 817 feet or 249 metres. **64 A5** NJ5143.
The Binn *Fife* ***Locality***, flat-topped hill area above steep escarpment, overlooking Burntisland and Firth of Forth. **25 G1** NT2387.
The Binns (Also known as House of the Binns.) *W.Loth.* ***Historic house***, spacious mansion (National Trust for Scotland) reflecting early 17c transition from fortified stronghold, 3m/5km E of Linlithgow. Home of Dalyell family since 1612. General Tam Dalyell raised Royal Scots Greys here in 1681. Famous for snowdrops and daffodils in spring. Woodland walk to panoramic view over Firth of Forth. **25 E2** NT0578.
The Birks *Aber.* ***Settlement***, 2m/3km S of Echt. **54 C4** NJ7402.
The Bore *Ork.* ***Sea feature***, channel to N of Mull Head, Papa Westray. **80 C1** HY4956.
The Brack *Arg. & B.* ***Mountain***, in Argyll 2m/3km W of Ardgartan on W shore of Loch Long. Height 2578 feet or 786 metres. **31 E4** NN2403.
The Braes *High.* ***Open space***, hillslope below E slopes of Ben Lee, 1km N of Peinchorran, Skye. **48 B1** NG5234.
The Bruach *Moray* ***Mountain***, on S side of Glen Avon, 6m/10km E of Loch Avon. Height 2342 feet or 714 metres. **52 D4** NJ1105.
The Buck ***Mountain***, on border of Aberdeenshire and Moray, 3m/4km SE of Cabrach. Height 2365 feet or 721 metres. **53 G2** NJ4123.
The Burn *Aber.* ***Settlement***, 2m/3km N of Edzell. **43 D2** NO5971.
The Cairnwell ***Mountain***, on border of Aberdeenshire and Perth & Kinross, 5m/8km N of Spittal of Glenshee. Munro: height 3060 feet or 933 metres. **41 G2** NO1377.
The Castle *Shet.* ***Coastal feature***, stack on E coast of Mainland, 1m/2km SE of North Roe. **84 C4** HU3787.
The Chancellor *High.* ***Inland physical feature***, mountain ridge rising to over 970 metres, on N side of Glen Coe, 3m/4km SW of Kinlochleven. **39 D4** NN1658.
The Clifts *Shet.* ***Coastal feature***, steep cliffs on N side of Ronas Voe, Mainland. **84 C4** HU3281.
The Cobbler *Arg. & B. Alternative name for Ben Arthur, qv.*
The Colonel's Bed *Aber.* ***Inland physical feature***, rock cut through by Ey Burn, 1m/2km S of Inverey. **41 F1** NO0887.
The Coyles of Muick *Aber.* ***Mountain***, with rock outcrops on E side, 4m/6km SW of Ballater. Height 1971 feet or 601 metres. **53 F5** NO3291.
The Craggan *High.* ***Mountain***, with rock outcrops to SE, 3m/5km S of Kildonan Lodge. Height 1581 feet or 482 metres. **73 E3** NC9016.
The Craigs *High.* ***Locality***, in Sutherland district, at foot of Strath Chuilionaich, 8m/13km W of Bonar Bridge. **71 G5** NH4791.
The Curr *Sc.Bord.* ***Mountain***, in Cheviot Hills, 4m/6km SE of Kirk Yetholm. Height 1850 feet or 564 metres. **18 C4** NT8523.
The Deeps *Shet.* ***Sea feature***, sea area to E of Skelda Ness, Mainland. **82 C3** HU3241.
The Deil's Heid *Angus* ***Coastal feature***, rocky headland 2m/3km NE of Arbroath. **43 E5** NO6741.
The Den *High.* ***Valley***, carrying Allt Dubhach on Black Isle NE to valley of Newhall Burn, 1m/2km W of Udale Bay. **61 F3** NH6863.
The Den *N.Ayr.* ***Settlement***, 2m/4km NE of Dalry and 2m/4km SW of Beith. **23 E4** NS3251.
The Devil's Point *Aber.* ***Mountain***, peak at SE end of Cairn Toul, in Cairngorm Mountains. Munro: height 3293 feet or 1004 metres. **52 B5** NN9795.
The Drums *Angus* ***Settlement***, in Glen Clova, 3m/5km SE of Clova. **42 B3** NO3569.
The Eileans *N.Ayr.* ***Island***, islets in Millport Bay at S end of Great Cumbrae. NS1654.
The Ell Shop and Little Houses *P. & K.* ***Other feature of interest***, restored 17c houses (National Trust for Scotland) in Dunkeld. Ell House contains National Trust for Scotland shop. **41 F5** NO0242.
The Faither *Shet.* ***Coastal feature***, headland on NW coast of Mainland on W side of entrance to Ronas Voe. **84 B4** HU2585.
The Fara *High.* ***Mountain***, in Badenoch and Strathspey district 2m/4km W of Dalwhinnie. Height 2988 feet or 911 metres. NN5984.
The Firth *Shet.* ***Sea feature***, wide part of inlet SE of Bixter, Mainland. Here Bixter Voe and Tresta Voe join before narrowing again at head of Sandsound Voe. HU3450.
The Foot *Ork.* ***Coastal feature***, rocky promontory on SE coast of Shapinsay. **80 D5** HY5315.
The Fungle Road *Aber.* ***Other feature of interest***, track across mountains of Forest of Birse, N from Birse Castle near Ballochan, to Birsemore, S of River Dee from Aboyne. **54 A5** NO5192.
The Galt *Ork.* ***Coastal feature***, point at NW extremity of Shapinsay, on W side of Veantrow Bay. **80 C4** HY4821.
The Giants Stones *Shet.* ***Historic/prehistoric site***, situated on Grind Hill just E of Hamnavoe, Mainland. Two stones, 6 feet and 8 feet tall, remains of former three stone alignment. **84 B4** HU2480.
The Glenkens *D. & G.* ***Locality***, N part of Stewartry district, comprising parishes of Balmaclellan, Carsphairn, Dalry, and Kells. NX5887.
The Glenlivet Distillery and Visitor Centre *Moray* ***Other feature of interest***, distillery 3m/4km NW of Tomintoul, with guided tours and displays of ancient equipment used in making whisky. **53 D2** NJ1929.
The Gloup *Ork.* ***Other feature of interest***, collapsed sea cave famous for strange gurgling noises made by movement of tide, 1m/2km S of Mull Head, Mainland. **79 E2** HY5907.
The Green *Arg. & B.* ***Settlement***, on N coast Tiree, 3m/5km NE of Rubha Chràiginis. **36 A2** NL9648.
The Hermitage *P. & K.* ***Forest/woodland***, area of forest (National Trust for Scotland) between River Tay and Ballinloan Burn, near to Falls of the Braan, 1m/2km SW of Dunkeld. Interesting walks and a delightful folly, Ossian's Hall, in gorge of River Braan. **41 F5** NO0042.
The Hirsel *Sc.Bord.* ***Historic house***, seat of Douglas-Home family, 1m/2km NW of Coldstream. **27 F5** NT8240.
The Hirsel Homestead Museum *Sc.Bord.* ***Other feature of interest***, 1m/2km NW of Coldstream, with local history of Hirsel House estate. **27 F5** NT8240.
The Hoe *High.* ***Hill***, near W coast of Skye, 6m/10km NW of Idrigill Point. Height 764 feet or 233 metres. **57 E5** NG1641.
The Hoe *W.Isles* ***Hill***, highest point on Pabbay. Height 561 feet or 171 metres. **44 A5** NL5987.
The Holehouse *D. & G. See Hollows Tower.*
The Hydroponicum *High.* ***Other feature of interest***, indoor garden at Achiltibuie, Ross and Cromarty district. Modern soil-less techniques enable growth of tropical plants, exotic fruit, vegetables, herbs and flowers. **70 C4** NC0109.
The Kame (Also known as Kame of Foula.) *Shet.* ***Coastal feature***, steep cliff on W coast of Foula, rising to 1220 feet or 372 metres. **82 B5** HT9340.
The Keen *Shet.* ***Coastal feature***, headland 1km SE of Housabister, Mainland. **83 E2** HU5057.
The Kettles *Moray* ***Open space***, marshy moorland between Green Hill and Bracken Noits, 3m/5km W of Rothes. **63 E4** NJ2350.
The King's Stone *D. & G. Alternative name for Bruce's Stone, qv.*
The Knock *D. & G.* ***Hill***, in S of Castle O'er Forest, 3m/5km E of Boreland. Height 935 feet or 285 metres. **9 G1** NY2291.
The Lodge *Arg. & B.* ***Settlement***, on W shore of Loch Goil, 2m/3km S of Lochgoilhead. **31 D5** NS1999.
The Machars *D. & G.* ***Locality***, between Luce Bay and Wigtown Bay. **3 E2** NX3752.
The Maiden *High. Anglicised form of A' Mhaighdean, qv.*
The Merse *Sc.Bord.* ***Open space***, fertile lowland area of rich farmland between River Tweed and Blackadder Water. It is bounded by Pentland, Moorfoot and Lammermuir Hills in N and Cheviot Hills in S. NT8246.
The Minch ***Sea feature***, sea passage between Isle of Lewis and Scottish mainland. **70 A3** NB7010.
The Mount *D. & G.* ***Other feature of interest***, 12c motte near ruins of Lochwood Tower, 4m/6km S of Beattock. **9 E1** NY0896.
The Mount *Sc.Bord.* ***Mountain***, in Pentland Hills, 4m/6km N of West Linton. Height 1761 feet or 537 metres. **25 F4** NT1457.
The Murray *S.Lan.* ***Suburb***, to S of East Kilbride town centre. NS6353.
The Needle *High.* ***Inland physical feature***, 120 feet or 36 metre high pinnacle of weathered volcanic basalt in Quiraing locality, inland from Staffin Bay, Skye, and 1km SE of Meall na Suiramach. **58 A3** NG4569.
The Neuk *Aber.* ***Settlement***, 3m/4km NE of Banchory. **54 C5** NO7397.
The Nev *Shet.* ***Coastal feature***, headland 1m/2km SE of Clibberswick, E coast of Unst. **85 F1** HP6611.
The North Head *Ork.* ***Coastal feature***, northernmost headland on Swona. **78 C4** ND3985.
The North Sound *Ork.* ***Sea feature***, sea area between islands of Sanday and Westray. **80 D2** HY5745.
The Noup *Shet.* ***Coastal feature***, rocky headland on N coast of Unst. **85 F1** HP6318.
The Oa *Arg. & B.* ***Coastal feature***, peninsula at S end of Islay, W of Port Ellen. Bold cliffs, especially to S and W. **20 A5** NR3044.
The Pennine Way ***Other feature of interest***, long distance footpath completed 1965, from Edale in Derbyshire to Kirk Yetholm in Scottish Borders; length about 250m/400km. NT8228.
The Pike *Sc.Bord.* ***Mountain***, in Craik Forest, 4m/6km SE of Ettrick. Height 1453 feet or 443 metres. **17 D5** NT2908.
The Pike *Sc.Bord.* ***Mountain***, 3m/4km SW of Shankend. Height 1515 feet or 462 metres. **17 F5** NT4904.
The Pineapple *Falk.* ***Historic house***, 18c pineapple-shaped building (National Trust for Scotland) set in 16 acres, 1m/2km NW of Airth. Building now used as a holiday home. **24 C1** NS8888.
The Pole of Itlaw *Aber.* ***Hill***, 4m/7km S of Banff. Height 443 feet or 135 metres. **64 B4** NJ6757.
The Prince's Cairn *High.* ***Other feature of interest***, reputed hiding place of Charles Edward Stuart (Bonnie Prince Charlie) whilst on run from English troops, 3m/4km SE of Arisaig in Druimindarroch. **37 F1** NM6984.
The Queen's Forest *High.* ***Forest/woodland***, coniferous forest in Badenoch and Strathspey district and mainly within the Glenmore Forest Park, N of Cairn Gorm. **52 B3** NH9709.
The Robbers' Waterfall *High. Alternative name for Eas nam Meirleach, qv.*
The Ron *Aber.* ***Coastal feature***, offshore rock on which lighthouse at Rattray Head is situated, 7m/11km N of Peterhead. NK1157.
The Rona *Shet.* ***Sea feature***, stretch of water dividing Papa Little from Mainland. **82 C1** HU3260.
The Rumble *Shet.* ***Island***, rock marked by beacon off S coast of Yell about 1km SW of Orfasay. HU4876.
The Saddle *High.* ***Mountain***, on border of Lochaber and Skye and Lochalsh districts, 4m/6km S of Shiel Bridge. Munro: height 3313 feet or 1010 metres. **49 F3** NG9313.
The Scalp *Moray* ***Mountain***, 3m/5km SE of Dufftown. Height 1597 feet or 487 metres. **53 F1** NJ3636.
The Scaurs *Aber. Occasional name for The Skares, qv.*
The Schil ***Mountain***, in Cheviot Hills, on border of Northumberland and Scottish Borders, 4m/7km SE of Kirk Yetholm. Height 1984 feet or 605 metres. **18 C4** NT8622.
The Shevock *Aber.* ***River***, rising on S side of Gartly Moor and flowing generally SE through Insch to join River Urie on NW side of Old Rayne. **54 B2** NJ6628.
The Shin *D. & G.* ***Mountain***, 2m/3km SW of Bentpath. Height 1174 feet or 358 metres. **9 G2** NY2889.
The Skares (Sometimes known as The Scaurs.) *Aber.* ***Coastal feature***, reef of almost submerged rocks at S end of Bay of Cruden, 9m/14km S of Peterhead. **55 F1** NK0833.
The Skerries *Shet. Alternative name for Out Skerries, qv.*

T

The Slate *Arg. & B.* ***Mountain***, in S part of Kintyre, 6m/9km SW of Campbeltown. Height 1263 feet or 385 metres. **12 B4** NR6316.
The Small Isles *High.* ***Island***, collective name for group of islands in Inner Hebrides comprising Rum, Eigg, Canna and Muck. NM3795.
The Snap *Shet.* ***Coastal feature***, headland at SE end of Fetlar, 1m/2km S of Funzie. **85 F4** HU6587.
The Sneug *Shet.* ***Mountain***, peak on Foula. Height 1371 feet or 418 metres. **82 B5** HT9439.
The Snub *Aber.* ***Coastal feature***, spit of land on W side of River Ythan estuary, 2m/3km N of Newburgh. NK0028.
The Socach *Aber.* ***Mountain***, 4m/7km W of Strathdon. Height 2355 feet or 718 metres. **53 E3** NJ2714.
The Soldier's Leap *P. & K.* ***Inland physical feature***, narrowest part of chasm in Pass of Killiecrankie. See Killiecrankie. **41 D3** NN9162.
The Sow *Ork.* ***Coastal feature***, rocky cliff on NW coast of Hoy. **78 A2** HY1802.
The Sow of Atholl (Also known as Atholl Sow.) *P. & K.* ***Mountain***, on Dalnaspidal Forest, Atholl, 1m/2km NW of Dalnaspidal Lodge. Height 2499 feet or 762 metres. **40 B2** NN6274.
The Spur *High.* ***Coastal feature***, rocky outcrop to N of Muckle Bay. **77 D1** ND1769.
The Storr *High.* ***Mountain***, in Trotternish, 7m/11km N of Portree, Skye. Height 2358 feet or 719 metres. Old Man of Storr, 160 foot or 49 metre stack, to E. **58 A4** NG4954.
The String *Ork.* ***Sea feature***, strait between Shapinsay and Car Ness on Mainland. HY4714.
The Study *High.* ***Inland physical feature***, natural terrace 3m/5km S of Kinlochleven, in Lochaber district, on N side of road running down Glen Coe. Commands view of glen. **39 D4** NN1756.
The Tails of the Tarf *Ork.* ***Coastal feature***, headland to S of Swona. **78 C4** ND3783.
The Thirl *High.* ***Coastal feature***, headland on N side of Dunnet Bay. **77 D1** ND1872.
The Three Sisters (Also known as The Three Sisters of Glen Coe.) *High.* ***Large natural feature***, three gaunt peaks overlooking Glen Coe in Lochaber district, on S side of glen. From E to W, Beinn Fhada, Gearr Aonach and Aonach Dubh. **38 D4** NN1655.
The Three Sisters of Glen Coe *High. Alternative name for The Three Sisters, qv.*
The Tind *Shet.* ***Coastal feature***, headland on E coast of Fetlar nearly 1m/2km E of Funzie. HU6790.
The Trossachs *Stir.* ***Large natural feature***, area surrounding wooded gorge, between Loch Achray and Loch Katrine, 13m/20km NW of Stirling. Extremely broken terrain and very attractive, comprising mountains, woods and lochs. Literary associations with Scott and Ruskin. **31 G4** NN4907.
The Vere *Shet.* ***Island***, isolated rock 2m/3km off E coast of Unst. **85 F2** HP6403.
The Veshels *Aber.* ***Coastal feature***, rocks off E coast, 3m/5km S of Cruden Bay. **55 F1** NK0731.
The Wig *D. & G.* ***Bay***, SW-facing bay on W side of Loch Ryan, 4m/7km N of Stranraer. NX0367.
The Wiss *Sc.Bord.* ***Mountain***, 4m/6km SE of St. Mary's Loch. Height 1932 feet or 589 metres. **17 D3** NT2620.
Thief's Hill *Moray* ***Hill***, in Wood of Ordiequish, 3m/5km S of Fochabers. Height 820 feet or 250 metres. **63 F4** NJ3654.
Thieves Holm *Ork.* ***Island***, islet off Car Ness, Mainland, 3m/4km NE of Kirkwall. HY4614.
Thirlestane *Sc.Bord.* ***Village***, 2m/3km E of Lauder. **26 C5** NT5647.
Thirlestane Castle *Sc.Bord.* ***Castle***, begun 1595, with later additions, on NE side of Lauder, next to Leader Water. **26 C5** NT5347.
Thomaston Castle *S.Ayr.* ***Castle***, 16c keep, 4m/6km W of Maybole. NS2309.
Thomastown *Aber.* ***Village***, 3m/6km SE of Huntly. **54 A1** NJ5736.
Thomshill *Moray* ***Locality***, 4m/6km S of Elgin. **63 E4** NJ2157.
Thornhill *D. & G.* Population: 1633. ***Small town***, on River Nith 13m/21km NW of Dumfries. Site of Roman signal station to S. **8 C1** NX8795.
Thornhill *Stir.* ***Village***, 7m/12km W of Dunblane. **32 B4** NS6699.
Thornliebank *E.Renf.* ***Suburb***, 4m/7km SW of Glasgow city centre. **23 G4** NS5559.
Thornly Park *Renf.* ***Suburb***, 1m/2km S of Paisley town centre. NS4861.
Thornroan *Aber.* ***Settlement***, 1m/2km N of Tarves. NJ8632.
Thornton *Angus* ***Settlement***, 1km E of Glamis. **42 B5** NO3946.
Thornton *Fife* Population: 1899. ***Village***, 4m/7km N of Kirkcaldy. **34 A5** NT2897.
Thornton *P. & K.* ***Settlement***, 3m/5km SE of Dunkeld. **41 F5** NO0740.
Thornton Castle *Aber.* ***Castle***, medieval fortress 2m/3km W of Laurencekirk, former seat of Strachan family. Grounds contain two ancient yew trees reputedly over 600 years old. NO6871.
Thorntonhall *S.Lan.* ***Suburb***, 3m/5km W of East Kilbride town centre. **23 G4** NS5955.
Thorntonloch *E.Loth.* ***Settlement***, on coast, 5m/8km SE of Dunbar. **27 E2** NT7574.
Thornyhill *Aber.* ***Settlement***, 1m/2km SW of Fettercairn. **43 E2** NO6372.
Thornyhive Bay *Aber.* ***Bay***, small rocky bay, 2m/3km S of Stonehaven. **43 G1** NO8882.
Thornylee *Sc.Bord.* ***Settlement***, in Tweed valley, 3m/4km NW of Caddonfoot. **17 F2** NT4136.
Threave *D. & G.* ***Settlement***, 2m/3km W of Castle Douglas. NX7362.
Threave Castle *D. & G.* ***Castle***, 14c tower of the Douglas family (Historic Scotland), on Threave Island on River Dee, 2m/3km W of Castle Douglas. **8 B4** NX7362.
Threave Gardens *D. & G.* ***Garden***, National Trust for Scotland property and School of Practical Gardening, 1m/2km SE of Threave. Gardens include woodland garden, peat plants, summer flowers, borders and heather. **8 B4** NX7362.
Threave Island *D. & G.* ***Island***, in River Dee, 2m/3km W of Castle Douglas. Threave Castle is on island. NX7362.
Threipmuir Reservoir *Edin.* ***Reservoir***, on Pentland Hills, 2m/3km SE of Balerno. **25 F3** NT1763.
Thriepley *Dundee* ***Settlement***, 2m/3km S of Newtyle. **34 B1** NO3038.
Thrumster *High.* ***Village***, in Caithness, 4m/6km S of Wick. **77 F4** ND3345.
Thundergay (Also known as Mid Thundergay.) *N.Ayr.* ***Locality***, on NW coast of Arran, 2m/3km NE of Pirnmill. **21 G5** NR8846.
Thunderton *Aber.* ***Settlement***, 3m/5km W of Peterhead. **65 F5** NK0646.
Thurdistoft *High.* ***Settlement***, on N coast, 1km E of Castletown. **77 E2** ND2067.
Thurso *High.* ***River***, rising in hills SE of Forsinard railway station and flowing N through Loch More and past Halkirk before continuing N to Thurso and into Thurso Bay. **76 D3** ND1168.
Thurso *High.* Population: 8488. ***Small town***, port on Thurso Bay, N coast of Caithness district, at mouth of River Thurso, 18m/30km NW of Wick. Most northerly town on British mainland. Cnoc Freiceadain Long Cairns (Historic Scotland) are two unexcavated Neolithic long-horned burial cairns 6m/9km SW. **76 D2** ND1168.
Thurso Bay *High.* ***Bay***, on N coast of Caithness district, with Thurso at centre of bay. **76 D1** ND1168.
Thuster *High.* ***Settlement***, 4m/7km W of Wick. **77 E3** ND2851.
Tianavaig Bay *High.* ***Bay***, on E coast of Skye, 3m/5km SE of Loch Portree. **48 B1** NG5138.
Tibbermore (Also known as Tippermuir.) *P. & K.* ***Village***, 4m/7km W of Perth. To SE is site of battle of 1644 in which Montrose defeated army of Covenanters and gained control of Perth. **33 F2** NO0523.
Tibbers Castle *D. & G.* ***Castle***, remains of late 13c castle beside River Nith, 2m/3km N of Thornhill. NX8698.
Tibbie Shiels Inn *Sc.Bord.* ***Settlement***, at E side of bridge which crosses St. Mary's Loch. Loch is known as Loch of the Lowes to S of bridge. **16 D3** NT2420.
Tibertich *Arg. & B.* ***Settlement***, 2m/3km SW of Ford. **30 A4** NM8402.
Tiel Burn *Fife* ***River***, rising 3m/4km N of Aberdour and flowing E to enter Firth of Forth on S side of Kirkcaldy. **34 A5** NT2790.
Tifty *Aber.* ***Settlement***, 7m/11km SE of Turriff. **64 C5** NJ7740.
Tigerton *Angus* ***Village***, 5m/7km NW of Brechin. **42 D3** NO5464.
Tigh a' Gearraidh (Anglicised form: Tigharry.) *W.Isles* ***Village***, on NW coast of North Uist, 3m/5km S of Griminis Point. **45 F2** NF7171.
Tigh Mòr na Seilge *High.* ***Mountain***, on Glenaffric Forest, Inverness district, 3m/5km S of head of Loch Affric. Height 3047 feet or 929 metres. NH1416.
Tighachnoic *High.* ***Settlement***, in Morvern, Lochaber district, 1km N of Lochaline. **37 F5** NM6745.
Tigharry *W.Isles Anglicised form of Tigh a' Gearraidh, qv.*
Tighnablair *P. & K.* ***Settlement***, 3m/5km S of Comrie. **32 C3** NN7716.
Tighnabruaich *Arg. & B.* ***Village***, resort in Argyll on W shore of Kyles of Bute, 3m/4km SW of entrance to Loch Riddon. Forest to N and S. Viewpoint (National Trust for Scotland) to NE with spectacular views of Kyles of Bute and islands in Firth of Clyde. **22 A2** NR9772.
Tighnacomaire *High.* ***Settlement***, in Glen Scaddle, Lochaber district, 6m/9km NW of Sallachan Point. **38 B3** NM9468.
Tighvein *N.Ayr.* ***Mountain***, in S part of Arran, 3m/4km SW of Lamlash. Height 1502 feet or 458 metres. **13 E3** NR9927.
Tillathrowie *Aber.* ***Settlement***, 4m/6km SE of Haugh of Glass. **53 G1** NJ4735.
Tillery *Aber.* ***Settlement***, 3m/4km NE of Newmachar. **55 E2** NJ9122.
Tillicoultry *Clack.* Population: 5269. ***Small town***, 3m/5km NE of Alloa. Tradition of milling and weaving based on water power. **33 E5** NS9197.
Tillyarblet *Angus* ***Hamlet***, 2m/3km NW of Kirkton of Menmuir. **42 D3** NO5167.
Tillybirloch *Aber.* ***Settlement***, 4m/6km W of Echt. **54 B4** NJ6707.
Tillycairn Castle *Aber.* ***Castle***, 5m/8km SW of Kemnay. **54 B3** NJ6611.
Tillycorthie *Aber.* ***Locality***, 3m/5km SE of Pitmedden. Includes Tillycorthie Mansion House and Tillycorthie Farm. **55 E2** NJ9023.
Tillydrine *Aber.* ***Hamlet***, 1km SE of Kincardine O'Neil. **54 B5** NO6098.
Tillyfar *Aber.* ***Settlement***, 3m/4km SW of New Deer. **65 D5** NJ8545.
Tillyfour *Aber.* ***Settlement***, 4m/6km S of Alford. **54 A3** NJ5910.
Tillyfourie *Aber.* ***Village***, 5m/8km SE of Alford. **54 B3** NJ6412.
Tillygreig *Aber.* ***Settlement***, 3m/4km N of Newmachar. **55 D2** NJ8822.
Tillypronie *Aber.* ***Settlement***, 4m/6km NW of Tarland. Symbol Stone nearby. **53 G4** NJ4307.
Tilt *P. & K.* ***River***, running SW down Glen Tilt to River Garry at Blair Atholl. **41 E2** NN8764.
Tima Water *Sc.Bord.* ***River***, flowing N to join Ettrick Water at Ettrick. **17 D5** NT2714.
Timsgarry *W.Isles Anglicised form of Timsgearraidh, qv.*
Timsgearraidh (Anglicised form: Timsgarry.) *W.Isles* ***Village***, near W coast of Isle of Lewis, 3m/5km S of Gallan Head. **68 B4** NB0534.
Tinga Skerry *Shet.* ***Island***, group of rocks in Yell Sound lying between islands of Brother Isle and Little Roe. HU4180.
Tingwall *Ork.* ***Settlement***, on NE coast of Mainland, 1m/2km N of Hackland. **80 C4** HY4022.
Tingwall *Shet.* ***Locality***, on Mainland, lying between Whiteness Voe and Dales Voe, to NW of Lerwick. HU4144.
Tingwall Airport *Shet.* ***Airport/airfield***, 1km NW of Veensgarth, Mainland. **82 D3** HU4145.
Tinnis Castle and Fort *Sc.Bord.* ***Castle***, to NE of Drumelzier. Early 16c ruin of stronghold of Tweedie family. **16 C2** NT1434.
Tinnisburn Forest *D. & G.* ***Forest/woodland***, partly in Scottish Borders, 4m/6km SW of Newcastleton. NY4382.
Tinto *S.Lan.* ***Mountain***, 3m/4km S of Thankerton. Height 2319 feet or 707 metres. **16 A2** NS9534.
Tinwald *D. & G.* ***Village***, 4m/6km NE of Dumfries. **9 E2** NY0081.
Tioram Castle (Sometimes known as Tirrim Castle.) *High.* ***Castle***, ruined stronghold of the Macdonalds on tidal islet in Loch Moidart in Lochaber district, opposite Dorlin. **37 F2** NM6672.
Tippermuir *P. & K. Alternative name for Tibbermore, qv.*
Tipperty *Aber.* ***Hamlet***, 3m/5km NW of Glenbervie. **43 F1** NO7282.
Tipperty *Aber.* ***Settlement***, on Tarty Burn, 3m/4km SE of Ellon. **55 E2** NJ9626.
Tipperweir *Aber.* ***Mountain***, 2m/3km E of Bridge of Dye. Height 1437 feet or 438 metres. **43 E1** NO6885.
Tiree *Arg. & B.* ***Island***, of the Inner Hebrides lying 2m/3km SW of Coll. Measures 11m/18km E to W and is of irregular shape, the total area being 29 square miles or 75 square km. The island is low-lying and windswept, but the climate is mild. Airfield 3m/4km W of Scarinish. **36 A2** NL9945.
Tiree Airport *Arg. & B.* ***Airport/airfield***, to N of Hynish Bay, Tiree. **36 B2** NM0044.
Tirga Mòr *W.Isles* ***Mountain***, in Forest of Harris 5m/8km SW of head of Loch Resort. Height 2227 feet or 679 metres. **66 C2** NB0511.
Tirindrish *High.* ***Settlement***, 1km E of Spean Bridge. **39 E1** NN2382.
Tirrim Castle *High. Occasional name for Tioram Castle, qv.*
Tirry *High.* ***River***, in Sutherland district, running S into Loch Shin 2m/3km N of Lairg. **72 A3** NC5609.
Tirryside *High.* ***Settlement***, in Sutherland district, on E side of Loch Shin near mouth of River Tirry. NC5610.
Tister *High.* ***Settlement***, 4m/6km S of Castletown. **77 D2** ND1961.
Tiumpan Head (Gaelic form: Rubha an t-Siùmpain.) *W.Isles* ***Coastal feature***, headland with lighthouse at NE end of Eye Peninsula, Isle of Lewis. **69 G4** NB5737.
Toa Galson *W.Isles* ***Coastal feature***, headland on NW coast of Isle of Lewis, 6m/9km SW of Butt of Lewis. **69 F1** NB4560.
Toab *Ork.* ***Settlement***, on mainland, on W side of Deer Sound, 5m/8km SE of Kirkwall. **79 E2** HY5006.
Toab *Shet.* ***Settlement***, on Mainland, to N of Sumburgh Airport. **83 G5** HU3811.
Tobermory *Arg. & B.* ***Town***, resort and chief town of Mull, situated on Tobermory Bay near N end of Sound of Mull. Former fishing village. **37 E4** NM5055.
Tobermory Bay *Arg. & B.* ***Bay***, on Mull, near N end of Sound of Mull. Wreck of Spanish galleon, blown up in 1588, lies at the bottom of the bay. **37 E4** NM5055.

Toberonochy *Arg. & B.* ***Village***, small village on Shuna Sound, on E coast of Luing. **29 G4** NM7408.
Tobha Mòr (Anglicised form: Howmore.) *W.Isles* ***Village***, near W coast of South Uist, 5m/7km NW of Beinn Mhòr. **46 A1** NF7536.
Tobson *W.Isles* ***Settlement***, on W coast of Great Bernera, 2m/3km NW of Breacleit. **68 C4** NB1338.
Tocher *Aber.* ***Settlement***, 3m/5km E of Kirkton of Culsalmond. **54 B1** NJ6932.
Todden Hill *D. & G.* ***Mountain***, in Carsphairn Forest, on border with East Ayrshire, 4m/6km SE of Dalmellington. Height 1565 feet or 477 metres. **14 D5** NS5303.
Toddun *W.Isles* ***Mountain***, 1m/2km SW of entrance to Loch Seaforth. Height 1732 feet or 528 metres. **67 E3** NB2102.
Todhead Point *Aber.* ***Coastal feature***, headland with lighthouse on E coast, 4m/6km NE of Inverbervie. **43 G2** NO8776.
Todhills *Angus* ***Settlement***, 1km N of Tealing. **34 C1** NO4239.
Todlachie *Aber.* ***Settlement***, 2m/3km SW of Monymusk. **54 B3** NJ6513.
Toe Head *W.Isles* ***Coastal feature***, headland on W coast of South Harris, 6m/10km NW of Leverburgh. **66 B4** NF9594.
Toft (Also known as Boath of Toft.) *Shet.* ***Settlement***, on NE coast of Mainland, 1m/2km NW of Mossbank across Tofts Voe. Vehicle ferry to Ulsta on Yell. **84 D5** HU4376.
Toftcarl *High.* ***Settlement***, 1km NE of Thrumster. **77 F4** ND3446.
Tofts *High.* ***Settlement***, in NE corner of Caithness district, 4m/6km S of John o' Groats. **77 F2** ND3668.
Tofts Voe *Shet.* ***Bay***, on E coast of Mainland, bounded by Toft Ness and Grunna Taing. HU4376.
Tokavaig *High.* ***Locality***, on Skye, near W coast of Sleat peninsula, 2m/3km NE of Tarskavaig. **48 C3** NG6011.
Tolastadh a' Chaolais (Anglicised form: Tolstachaolais.) *W.Isles* ***Village***, on Isle of Lewis, near E shore of East Loch Roag, 2m/3km NW of Breascleit. **68 C4** NB1937.
Tolastadh Bho Thuath (Anglicised form: North Tolsta.) *W.Isles* ***Village***, near E coast of Isle of Lewis, 2m/3km W of Tolsta Head. **69 G3** NB5347.
Tolastadh Úr (Anglicised form: New Tolsta.) *W.Isles* ***Village***, near E coast of Isle of Lewis, 2m/4km NW of Tolsta Head and 1km N of Tolastadh Bho Thuath. **69 G3** NB5348.
Toll Creagach *High.* ***Mountain***, in Inverness district 3m/4km SW of dam of Loch Mullardoch. Munro: height 3454 feet or 1053 metres. **50 A2** NH1928.
Toll of Birness *Aber.* ***Settlement***, at road junction, 4m/6km NE of Ellon. **55 F1** NK0034.
Tollcross *Glas.* ***Suburb***, 3m/5km E of Glasgow city centre. **24 A3** NS6363.
Tollomuick Forest *High.* ***Open space***, deer forest at head of Loch Vaich. **60 C1** NH3280.
Tolmachan *W.Isles* ***Settlement***, on E side of Loch Meavaig, North Harris. NB0905.
Tolmount (Also spelled Tolmounth.) *Angus* ***Mountain***, at head of Glen Callater in Kincardine and Deeside district, 8m/12km SE of Braemar. Munro: height 3142 feet or 958 metres. **42 A1** NO2080.
Tolmounth *Angus Alternative spelling of Tolmount, qv.*
Tolquhon Castle *Aber.* ***Castle***, remains of pink sandstone medieval castle (Historic Scotland), in wooded glen 1m/2km NW of Pitmedden. Built for Forbes family, includes 15c tower enlarged in 16c and ornamented gatehouse. **55 D2** NJ8728.
Tolsta Head *W.Isles* ***Coastal feature***, headland on E coast of Isle of Lewis, 12m/20km NE of Stornoway. **69 G3** NB5646.
Tolstachaolais *W.Isles Anglicised form of Tolastadh a' Chaolais, qv.*
Tolvah *High.* ***Settlement***, in Glen Feshie, 4m/6km S of Kincraig. **52 A5** NN8499.
Tom a' Chòinich *High.* ***Mountain***, on border of Inverness and Ross and Cromarty districts between Loch Affric and Loch Mullardoch. Munro: height 3644 feet or 1111 metres. **50 A2** NH1627.
Tom an Fhuadain *W.Isles* ***Settlement***, on S shore of Loch Odhairn, 2m/3km W of Kebock Head, Isle of Lewis. **67 F2** NB3914.
Tom an t-suidhe Mhòr *High.* ***Mountain***, 1m/2km SW of Bridge of Brown. Height 1742 feet or 531 metres. **52 C3** NJ1118.
Tom an Teine *High.* ***Hill***, 1m/2km SW of Spean Bridge. Height 613 feet or 187 metres. **39 E1** NN2179.
Tom Bailgeann *High.* ***Mountain***, in Inverness district, 5m/8km E of Drumnadrochit. Height 1522 feet or 464 metres. **51 E2** NH5829.
Tom Bàn Mòr *High.* ***Mountain***, in Ross and Cromarty district on NE side of Loch Glascarnoch. Height 2434 feet or 742 metres. **60 C2** NH3175.
Tom Buidhe *Angus* ***Mountain***, 4m/7km NW of Glendoll Lodge. Munro: height 3139 feet or 957 metres. **42 A2** NO2178.
Tom na Gruagaich *High.* ***Mountain***, summit of Beinn Alligin, 4m/6km NW of Torridon in Ross and Cromarty district. Munro: height 3024 feet or 922 metres. NG8560.
Tom Soilleir *Arg. & B.* ***Mountain***, 3m/4km E of Arduaine. Height 1197 feet or 365 metres. **30 A4** NM8409.
Tomatin *High.* ***Village***, in Inverness district, 8m/12km NW of Carrbridge. **52 A2** NH8029.
Tomatin Distillery *High.* ***Other feature of interest***, Scotland's largest single malt distillery, to NW of Tomatin. Situated on, and drawing its water from Alt-na-Frith, it is also one of Scotland's highest distilleries at 1028 feet or 313 metres. **51 G2** NH7929.
Tomb of the Eagles *Ork.* ***Historic/prehistoric site***, in SE corner of South Ronaldsay. Fine stalled chambered tomb dating from Stone Age. Name derives from sea eagles' claws found in tomb. **79 D4** ND4684.
Tombane Burn *P. & K.* ***River***, rising in Loch Creagh and flowing SE into River Braan, 1m/2km W of Trochry. **41 E5** NN9539.
Tombreck *High.* ***Settlement***, 8m/12km S of Inverness. **51 F1** NH6834.
Tomchrasky *High.* ***Settlement***, in Glen Moriston, 2m/3km W of Dalchreichart. **50 B3** NH2512.
Tomdoun *High.* ***Locality***, in Glen Garry, Lochaber district, 9m/14km W of Invergarry. **50 A4** NH1501.
Tomdow *Moray* ***Settlement***, 4m/6km N of Dava. **62 C5** NJ0044.
Tomich *High.* ***Locality***, on border of Ross and Cromarty and Inverness districts, 1m/2km NE of Beauly. NH5347.
Tomich *High.* ***Settlement***, 2m/3km SE of Lairg, Sutherland district. **72 B4** NC6004.
Tomich *High.* ***Settlement***, in Inverness district, 4m/6km SW of Cannich. **50 C2** NH3027.
Tomich *High.* ***Settlement***, 1m/2km N of Invergordon. **61 F2** NH7071.
Tomintoul *Moray* ***Village***, and resort in elevated position between River Avon and Conglass Water, 10m/16km SE of Grantown-on-Spey. **53 D3** NJ1618.
Tomintoul Museum *Moray* ***Other feature of interest***, museum in Tomintoul with reconstructed farm kitchen and smithy. **53 D3** NJ1618.
Tomlachlan Burn *High.* ***River***, rising on W slope of Carn nan Clach Garbha and flowing N into River Findhorn, 1km E of Dulsie. **52 B1** NH9342.
Tomnacross *High.* ***Settlement***, in Inverness district, 3m/5km S of Beauly. **61 E5** NH5141.
Tomnamoon *Moray* ***Settlement***, 5m/8km S of Forres. **62 C4** NJ0450.
Tomnaven *Moray* ***Settlement***, on E side of River Deveron, 6m/10km SE of Dufftown. **53 G1** NJ4033.
Tomnaverie Stone Circle *Aber.* ***Historic/prehistoric site***, stones dating from 1800-1600 BC (Historic Scotland) on rocky knoll 1km SE of Tarland. **53 G4** NJ4803.
Tomnavoulin *Moray* ***Village***, in Glen Livet, 5m/8km NE of Tomintoul. **53 E2** NJ2126.
Tomnavoulin Distillery *Moray* ***Other feature of interest***, distillery by River Livet at Tomintoul, with visitor centre in converted carding mill. **53 E2** NJ2125.
Tomnun *Angus* ***Mountain***, in Harran Plantation, 3m/5km SW of Balnaboth. Height 1551 feet or 473 metres. **42 A3** NO2764.
Tomont End *N.Ayr.* ***Coastal feature***, headland to E of White Bay at N end of Great Cumbrae. **22 C4** NS1759.
Tomont Hill *S.Lan.* ***Mountain***, in Lowther Hills, 3m/5km SE of Elvanfoot. Height 1653 feet or 504 metres. **16 A4** NS9812.
Tom's Cairn *Aber.* ***Mountain***, 3m/4km SE of Marywell. Height 1017 feet or 310 metres. **54 B5** NO6194.
Tomtain *N.Lan.* ***Mountain***, 2m/4km N of Kilsyth. Height 1486 feet or 453 metres. **24 B1** NS7281.
Tomvaich *High.* ***Settlement***, on E side of Upper Tomvaich Wood, 3m/4km N of Grantown-on-Spey. **52 C1** NJ0630.
Ton Burn *Aber.* ***River***, rising on E side of Corrennie Forest and flowing NE to join River Don, 1m/2km SW of Kemnay. **54 B4** NJ7115.
Tòn Mhòr *Arg. & B.* ***Coastal feature***, headland on N coast of Islay, 4m/7km SW of Ardnave Point. **20 A2** NR2371.
Tong *W.Isles Anglicised form of Tunga, qv.*
Tongland *D. & G.* ***Village***, 2m/3km NE of Kirkcudbright. Hydro-electric power station below reservoir. Early 19c road bridge by Telford spans River Dee to SW. **8 B5** NX6953.
Tongland Dam and Power Station *D. & G.* ***Other feature of interest***, largest of six Galloway hydro-electric power stations built in 1930s, 2m/4km N of Kirkcudbright. Visitor centre and tours. **8 B5** NX7054.
Tongland Loch *D. & G.* ***Lake/loch***, with islands and dam at S end, part of River Dee, 1km N of Tongland. **8 B5** NX7056.
Tongue *High.* ***Village***, near N coast of Caithness district on E side of Kyle of Tongue, 1m/2km S of road bridge across kyle. **75 E3** NC5956.
Tongue Bay *High.* ***Bay***, 3m/5km N of Tongue. **75 F2** NC5956.
Tongue House *High.* ***Settlement***, near causeway, on E side of Kyle of Tongue. **75 E3** NC5958.
Tor Castle *Moray* ***Castle***, ruins of castle N of Dallas, 9m/14km SW of Elgin. NJ1252.
Tor Ness *Ork.* ***Coastal feature***, headland on E coast of Mainland, to N of Broad Taing. **80 C5** HY4219.
Tor Ness *Ork.* ***Coastal feature***, headland on S coast of Stronsay on E side of entrance to Bay of Holland. **81 E4** HY6520.
Tor Ness *Ork.* ***Coastal feature***, rocky headland on N coast of North Ronaldsay. **81 F1** HY7555.
Tor Ness *Ork.* ***Coastal feature***, headland at S end of Hoy. Lighthouse to NW. **78 B4** ND2588.
Tor Point *High.* ***Inland physical feature***, promontory on E shore of Loch Ness, Inverness district, 1km NW of Dores. **51 E1** NH5935.
Torastan *Arg. & B.* ***Settlement***, in N part of Coll, 3m/5km N of Arinagour. **36 B3** NM2261.
Torbain *Moray* ***Settlement***, on E bank of River Avon, 3m/4km S of Tomintoul. **53 D3** NJ1613.
Torbeckhill Reservoir *D. & G.* ***Reservoir***, small reservoir 4m/6km NE of Ecclefechan. NY2379.
Torbeg *Aber.* ***Settlement***, on S side of River Gairn, 4m/6km NW of Ballater. **53 F4** NJ3200.
Torbeg *N.Ayr.* ***Village***, on Arran, 1m/2km N of Blackwaterfoot. **13 E3** NR8929.
Torbeg Hut Circles *N.Ayr.* ***Historic/prehistoric site***, hut circles, thought to date from Bronze Age, on Arran, 1km N of Blackwaterfoot. **13 D3** NR8929.
Torbothie *N.Lan.* ***Hamlet***, 1km NE of Stane. NS8859.
Torbraehead *D. & G.* ***Mountain***, 4m/6km N of Moniaive. Height 1312 feet or 400 metres. **8 B1** NX7896.
Torbreck Burn *High.* ***River***, flowing S and joining River Fleet 1km NW of Pittentrail. **72 C4** NC7103.
Torbrex *Stir.* ***Suburb***, 1m/2km SW of Stirling town centre. NS7892.
Torcastle *High.* ***Settlement***, in valley of River Lochy, 3m/5km N of Fort William. **38 D2** NN1378.
Tordarroch *High.* ***Settlement***, in Strathnairn, 8m/11km S of Inverness. **51 F1** NH6733.
Torduff Point *D. & G.* ***Coastal feature***, headland on Solway Firth, 2m/3km SE of Eastriggs. **9 G4** NY2663.
Torduff Reservoir *Edin.* ***Reservoir***, small reservoir 5m/8km SW of Edinburgh city centre. NT2067.
Tore *High.* ***Hamlet***, in Ross and Cromarty district, 5m/8km E of Muir of Ord. **61 F4** NH6052.
Tore Burn *Aber.* ***River***, rising to S of Tore of Troup valley and flowing N into sea at Cullykhan Bay, 3m/4km E of Gardenstown. **64 D3** NJ8365.
Tore Hill *High.* ***Mountain***, in Abernethy Forest, 8m/11km SE of Carrbridge. Height 1109 feet or 338 metres. **52 B3** NH9817.
Toreduff *Moray* ***Settlement***, 6m/10km W of Elgin. **62 D3** NJ1260.
Toremore *High.* ***Settlement***, 1km NE of Dunbeath, on E coast. **77 D5** ND1730.
Toremore *High.* ***Settlement***, 5m/8km S of Upper Knockando. **52 D1** NJ1535.
Torfichen Hill *Midloth.* ***Mountain***, in Moorfoot Hills, 2m/3km E of Gladhouse Reservoir. Height 1509 feet or 460 metres. **26 A4** NT3353.
Torgyle *High.* ***Settlement***, in Glen Moriston, 1m/2km E of Dalchreichart. **50 C3** NH3013.
Torhouse Stone Circle *D. & G.* ***Historic/prehistoric site***, Bronze Age recumbent circle of nineteen stones roughly sixty feet in diameter (Historic Scotland), 1km W of Little Torhouse and 4m/6km W of Wigtown. **7 E5** NX3856.
Torhousemuir *D. & G.* ***Locality***, 3m/5km NW of Wigtown. Ancient stone circle (Historic Scotland). NX3957.
Torloisk *Arg. & B.* ***Locality***, on Mull, on N side of Loch Tuath and 4m/7km S of Dervaig. NM4145.
Torlum *P. & K.* ***Mountain***, rounded summit, 3m/5km SE of Comrie. Height 1289 feet or 393 metres. **32 D3** NN8119.
Torlum *W.Isles* ***Settlement***, on Benbecula, 3m/5km S of Balivanich. **45 F4** NF7850.
Torlum Wood *P. & K.* ***Forest/woodland***, 4m/6km SE of Comrie. **32 D3** NN8218.
Torlundy *High.* ***Settlement***, 3m/5km NE of Fort William. **38 D2** NN1477.
Tormisdale *Arg. & B.* ***Settlement***, 4m/7km N of Portnahaven, on Rinns of Islay. **20 A4** NR1958.
Tormore *N.Ayr.* ***Settlement***, on W coast of Arran, 3m/4km N of Blackwaterfoot. Ancient standing stones to E. **13 D2** NR8932.
Tormsdale *High.* ***Settlement***, 1m/2km SE of Westerdale. **76 D3** ND1350.
Tornachean Forest *Aber.* ***Forest/woodland***, partly afforested area, to SE of Strathdon. NJ3710.
Tornagrain *High.* ***Settlement***, in Inverness district, 7m/11km NE of Inverness. **61 G4** NH7649.
Tornahaish *Aber.* ***Settlement***, on S side of River Don, 5m/8km SW of Strathdon. **53 E4** NJ2908.
Tornashean Forest *Aber.* ***Forest/woodland***, discontinuous forest surrounding Forbridge Hill above S bank of River Don, 3m/5km SE of Strathdon. **53 F3** NJ3810.

T

Tornaveen *Aber.* ***Settlement***, 3m/4km N of Torphins. **54 B4** NJ6106.
Torness *High.* ***Settlement***, in Inverness district, 5m/8km S of Dores. **51 E2** NH5827.
Torogay *W.Isles* ***Island***, small uninhabited island off NE coast of North Uist, 1km S of Berneray. NF9178.
Torosay Castle *Arg. & B.* ***Castle***, 19c castle near E coast of Mull, 1m/2km N of Lochdon. **29 G1** NM7235.
Torphichen *W.Loth.* ***Village***, 2m/4km N of Bathgate. Torphichen Preceptory (Historic Scotland). **25 D2** NS9672.
Torphichen Preceptory *W.Loth.* ***Ecclesiastical building***, at Torphichen, 5m/8km SSW of Linlithgow. Tower and transepts of former Scottish seat of Knights Hospitallers of St. John (Historic Scotland). 13c remains incorporated into present church. **25 D2** NS9672.
Torphins *Aber.* ***Village***, 6m/10km NW of Banchory. **54 B4** NJ6201.
Torquhan *Sc.Bord.* ***Hamlet***, 2m/3km NW of Stow. **26 B5** NT4447.
Torr a' Chaisteil *N.Ayr.* ***Historic/prehistoric site***, remains of Iron Age fort (Historic Scotland) at Corriecravie, Arran, 4m/6km SE of Blackwaterfoot. **13 E3** NR9223.
Torr Dubh *P. & K.* ***Open sp ce***, mountain slope on S side of Glen Errochty, 3m/5km NW of Tummel Bridge. **40 C3** NN7462.
Torr Fada *Arg. & B.* ***Hill***, 4m/6km S of Rubha nan Cearc, Ross of Mull. Height 279 feet or 85 metres. **28 C3** NM3219.
Torr Mòr *Arg. & B.* ***Hill***, above S coast of Bute, 1m/2km NE of Garroch Head. Height 479 feet or 146 metres. **22 C4** NS1052.
Torrachilty Wood *High.* ***Forest/woodland***, in Ross and Cromarty district around Loch Achilty, 4m/6km W of Strathpeffer. **60 D4** NH4356.
Torraigh (Anglicised form: Torray.) *W.Isles* ***Island***, small uninhabited island off E coast of Isle of Lewis 4m/6km N of Kebock Head. **69 F5** NB4220.
Torran *Arg. & B.* ***Settlement***, 1m/2km NE of Ford. **30 A4** NM8704.
Torran *High.* ***Locality***, on N shore of Loch Arnish, Raasay. **58 B5** NG5949.
Torran *High.* ***Settlement***, 4m/6km N of Invergordon. **61 G2** NH7175.
Torran Rocks *Arg. & B.* ***Island***, scattered group of rocks off SW end of Ross of Mull, 5m/8km S of Iona. **28 B3** NM2713.
Torran Sgoilte *Arg. & B.* ***Island***, one of Torran Rocks group, 4m/6km SW of Mull. **28 B3** NM2812.
Torrance *E.Dun.* Population: 2387. ***Village***, 6m/9km N of Glasgow. **24 A2** NS6274.
Torrance *S.Lan.* ***Settlement***, 1m/2km SE of East Kilbride, by Calder Water. Remains of Motte to W. **24 A4** NS6552.
Torrancroy *Aber.* ***Settlement***, at E end of Glen Nochty, 3m/4km NW of Strathdon. **53 F3** NJ3315.
Torray *W.Isles Anglicised form of Torraigh, qv.*
Torray *W.Isles* ***River***, flowing NW into River Barvas, 1km W of Barvas, Isle of Lewis. **69 E2** NB3549.
Torrich *High.* ***Settlement***, 3m/5km S of Nairn. **62 A4** NH8751.
Torridon *High.* ***River***, runs W into head of Loch Torridon, S of village of Torridon, Ross and Cromarty district. NG8955.
Torridon *High.* ***Village***, at head of Upper Loch Torridon, Ross and Cromarty district. **59 F4** NG8956.
Torridon Forest *High.* ***Large natural feature***, mountainous area (National Trust for Scotland) to N of Torridon. NG8958.
Torrie Forest *Stir.* ***Forest/woodland***, 3m/4km S of Callander. **32 A4** NN6303.
Torrin *High.* ***Village***, on Skye, 5m/7km W of Broadford. **48 B2** NG5720.
Torrinch *W.Dun.* ***Island***, in Loch Lomond 1m/2km SW of Balmaha. Part of nature reserve comprising also Inchcailloch and Clairinch. **23 F1** NS4089.
Torrisdale *Arg. & B.* ***Locality***, on Torrisdale Bay, on E coast of Kintyre, 1m/2km S of Dippen. **12 C2** NR7936.
Torrisdale *High.* ***Settlement***, on Torrisdale Bay, 2m/3km W of Bettyhill, Caithness district. **75 F2** NC6761.
Torrisdale Bay *Arg. & B.* ***Bay***, on E coast of Kintyre, 1m/2km S of Dippen. NR7936.
Torrisdale Bay *High.* ***Bay***, on N coast of Caithness district, W of Bettyhill. **75 F2** NC6962.
Torrisdale Castle *Arg. & B.* ***Castle***, 19c castle on Torrisdale Water, E coast of Kintyre, 2m/3km SW of Carradale. NR7936.
Torrisdale Water *Arg. & B.* ***River***, stream running E into Torrisdale Bay on E coast of Kintyre, 2m/3km SW of Carradale. NR7936.
Torrish *High.* ***Settlement***, to N of River Helmsdale, 4m/6km NW of Helmsdale, Sutherland district. **73 E3** NC9718.
Torrish Burn *High.* ***River***, in Sutherland district, flowing S and joining River Helmsdale 1km W of Torrish. **73 E2** NC9618.
Torroble *High.* ***Settlement***, 1m/2km S of Lairg, Sutherland district. **72 A4** NC5904.
Torry *Aberdeen* ***Suburb***, 1m/2km SE of Aberdeen city centre across River Dee. **55 E4** NJ9505.
Torry *Aber.* ***Settlement***, on N side of River Deveron, 1km NE of Haugh of Glass. **63 G5** NJ4340.
Torry *Fife* ***Locality***, on Torry Bay on N side of River Forth, 5m/8km W of Dunfermline. NT0186.
Torry Bay *Fife* ***Bay***, on N side of River Forth, 5m/8km W of Dunfermline. **25 E1** NT0186.
Torryburn *Fife* ***Village***, adjoins to E of Torry, 2m/4km E of Culross across Torry Bay. **25 E1** NT0186.
Torrylin Chambered Cairn *N.Ayr.* ***Historic/prehistoric site***, Neolithic chambered cairn (Historic Scotland) with visible compartments, on S coast of Arran, to S of Kilmory. **13 E3** NR9521.
Torsay *Arg. & B.* ***Island***, composed of slate, off Luing at entrance to Seil Sound. **29 G3** NM7613.
Torsonce *Sc.Bord.* ***Hamlet***, 1km S of Stow. **26 B5** NT4543.
Torterston *Aber.* ***Locality***, 3m/5km W of Peterhead. **65 F5** NK0747.
Torthorwald *D. & G.* ***Village***, 4m/6km E of Dumfries. Tower house dating from 14c. **9 E3** NY0378.
Torvaig *High.* ***Settlement***, 1m/2km NE of Portree, Skye. **58 A5** NG4944.
Torwood *Falk.* ***Hamlet***, 4m/7km NW of Falkirk. **24 C1** NS8484.
Torwoodlee House *Sc.Bord.* ***Historic house***, small Georgian mansion built in 1783 and subsequently modified in 19c, 2m/3km NW of Galashiels. **17 F2** NT4637.
Toryglen *Glas.* ***Suburb***, 2m/4km S of Glasgow city centre. NS6061.
Toscaig *High.* ***Settlement***, at head of Loch Toscaig, near W coast of Ross and Cromarty district, 4m/6km S of Applecross. **48 D1** NG7138.
Tostarie *Arg. & B.* ***Settlement***, on Mull, 1km W of Kilninian. **36 C5** NM3845.
Totaig *High.* ***Locality***, at entrance to Loch Duich, Skye and Lochalsh district, opposite Eilean Donan. NG8725.
Totaig *High.* ***Village***, on Skye, on W side of Loch Dunvegan, 4m/6km SE of Dunvegan Head. **57 F4** NG2050.
Totamore *Arg. & B.* ***Settlement***, 3m/5km W of Arinagour, Coll. **36 A4** NM1756.
Tote *High.* ***Village***, 6m/10km NW of Portree, Skye. **58 A5** NG4149.
Totegan *High.* ***Settlement***, 1km S of Strathy Point, Caithness district. **76 A2** NC8268.
Totronald *Arg. & B.* ***Settlement***, 4m/6km SW of Arinagour, Coll. **36 A4** NM1656.
Totscore *High.* ***Settlement***, on Skye, 2m/3km N of Uig. NG3866.
Totto Hill *Sc.Bord.* ***Mountain***, 5m/8km S of Gladhouse Reservoir. Height 1971 feet or 601 metres. **26 A5** NT3045.
Touch Burn *Stir.* ***River***, stream rising on Touch Hills and flowing NE through small reservoir to join River Forth, 2m/4km W of Stirling. NS7593.
Touch Hills *Stir.* ***Large natural feature***, range of low hills, 4m/6km W of Stirling. There are some small reservoirs. **32 C5** NS7291.
Toux *Aber.* ***Settlement***, 2m/3km N of Old Deer. **65 E4** NJ9850.
Toward *Arg. & B.* ***Settlement***, on Firth of Clyde, 6m/10km SW of Dunoon. **22 C3** NS1367.
Toward Castle *Arg. & B.* ***Castle***, medieval stronghold 1m/2km W of Toward Point. **22 C3** NS1167.
Toward Point *Arg. & B.* ***Coastal feature***, headland in Argyll on W side of Firth of Clyde, 6m/10km S of Dunoon. **22 C3** NS1367.
Toward Quay *Arg. & B.* ***Locality***, just W of Toward Castle. NS1167.
Towie *Aber.* ***Locality***, comprising Mains of Towie, Towie Barclay Castle and Towie Turner, 4m/6km S of Turriff. NJ7444.
Towie *Aber.* ***Settlement***, 2m/3km E of Rhynie. **54 A2** NJ5327.
Towie *Aber.* ***Settlement***, 1km W of New Aberdour. **65 D3** NJ8763.
Towie *Aber.* ***Village***, on River Don, 6m/10km SW of Lumsden. Remains of castle. **53 G3** NJ4412.
Towie Barclay Castle *Aber.* ***Castle***, remains of ruined castle dating from 16c, to S of Mains of Towie. **64 C5** NJ7444.
Towiemore *Moray* ***Settlement***, at confluence of Burn of Towie and River Isla, 4m/6km SW of Keith. **63 F5** NJ3945.
Town Yetholm *Sc.Bord.* ***Village***, on W side of Bowmont Water, 7m/11km SE of Kelso. **18 C4** NT8228.
Townend *W.Dun.* ***Suburb***, N district of Dumbarton. **23 F2** NS4076.
Townhead *D. & G.* ***Settlement***, 3m/5km S of Kirkcudbright. **3 G2** NX6946.
Townhead of Greenlaw *D. & G.* ***Village***, 2m/4km NW of Castle Douglas. **8 B4** NX7464.
Townhead Reservoir *N.Lan.* ***Reservoir***, 1m/2km E of Kilsyth, on site of battle in 1645. **24 B2** NS7378.
Townhill *Fife* ***Village***, 1m/2km NE of Dunfermline. **25 F1** NT1089.
Toy Ness *Ork.* ***Coastal feature***, headland on Mainland on N shore of Scapa Flow, 2m/3km SW of Kirbister. Landing stage on Swanbister Bay to NE. HY3504.
Trabboch *E.Ayr.* ***Locality***, 7m/11km E of Ayr. **14 C3** NS4321.
Tradespark *High.* ***Locality***, in Nairn district, 1m/2km W of Nairn. **62 A4** NH8656.
Tradespark *Ork.* ***Settlement***, 1km S of Kirkwall, Mainland. **79 D2** HY4508.
Trahenna Hill *Sc.Bord.* ***Mountain***, 2m/3km NE of Broughton. Height 1791 feet or 546 metres. **16 C2** NT1337.
Tràigh Chuil *W.Isles Gaelic form of Col Sands, qv.*
Tràigh Eais *W.Isles* ***Coastal feature***, beach on NW coast on Barra, 2m/3km NW of Ardmhòr. **44 B3** NF6906.
Tràigh Mhòr *Arg. & B.* ***Coastal feature***, strand of Gott Bay, Tiree. NM0547.
Tràigh na Cleavag *W.Isles* ***Coastal feature***, beach on South Harris, 3m/4km SE of Toe Head. **66 B4** NF9891.
Traligill *High.* ***River***, flowing W into S end of Loch Assynt at Inchnadamph. **71 E2** NC2421.
Tramiag Bay *Arg. & B.* ***Bay***, on E coast of Jura, 1km NE of Ardlussa. **21 E1** NR6688.
Tranent *E.Loth.* Population: 8313. ***Small town***, former mining town 4m/6km E of Musselburgh. **26 B2** NT4072.
Trantlebeg *High.* ***Settlement***, across river to E of Trantlemore. **76 A3** NC8853.
Trantlemore *High.* ***Settlement***, in Strath Halladale, in Caithness district, 7m/11km S of Melvich. **76 A3** NC8853.
Traprain *E.Loth.* ***Hamlet***, 1m/2km S of East Linton. **26 C2** NT5975.
Traprain Law Fort *E.Loth.* ***Historic/prehistoric site***, hillfort 2m/3km SW of East Linton. Site is thought to have been occupied until 11c. **26 C2** NT5874.
Traquair *Sc.Bord.* ***Village***, 1m/2km S of Innerleithen across River Tweed. **17 E2** NT3334.
Traquair House *Sc.Bord.* ***Historic house***, 17c mansion, with tower of earlier date, to N of Traquair on W side of Elibank and Traquair Forest. **17 E2** NT3334.
Treaslane *High.* ***River***, running N into head of Loch Treaslane on Skye. NG3951.
Treaslane *High.* ***Settlement***, on Skye, on W side of Loch Snizort Beag at entrance to Loch Treaslane. **57 G4** NG3953.
Trebister *Shet.* ***Settlement***, on Mainland, 2m/4km SW of Lerwick. HU4438.
Treig *High.* ***River***, in Lochaber district, running N from Loch Treig to River Spean 1m/2km below Loch Moy. **39 F2** NN3579.
Trelung Ness *Aber.* ***Coastal feature***, headland on E coast, 3m/4km S of Stonehaven. **43 G1** NO8881.
Tres Ness *Ork.* ***Coastal feature***, headland at SE point of Sanday. **81 F3** HY7137.
Treshnish *Arg. & B.* ***Locality***, near W coast of Mull, 2m/4km SW of Calgary and 1m/2km E of headland of Treshnish Point. **36 C5** NM3548.
Treshnish Isles *Arg. & B.* ***Island***, group of islands and rocks of Inner Hebrides, W of Mull and SE of Coll, comprising Bac Mòr (Dutchman's Cap) and Bac Beag, Cairn na Burgh More and Cairn na Burgh Beg, Fladda, Lunga, Sgeir a' Chaisteil, Sgeir an Eirionnaich, Sgeir an Fheòir and Sgeir na h-Iolaire. Although uninhabited by people, islands have a large population of seals, sea birds and rabbits. **36 B5** NM2741.
Treshnish Point *Arg. & B.* ***Coastal feature***, headland on W coast of Mull, 1m/2km W of Treshnish. **36 C5** NM3548.
Tressa Ness *Shet.* ***Coastal feature***, headland on N coast of Fetlar almost due N of Houbie. HU6294.
Tressait *P. & K.* ***Village***, on N side of Loch Tummel, 5m/8km SW of Blair Atholl. **40 D3** NN8160.
Tresta *Shet.* ***Settlement***, on S coast of Fetlar, at head of large bay called Wick of Tresta. **85 F3** HU6190.
Tresta *Shet.* ***Village***, on Mainland, at head of Tresta Voe. **82 C2** HU3651.
Tresta Voe *Shet.* ***Sea feature***, inlet on Mainland, 2m/3km E of Bixter. HU3651.
Trevine *Arg. & B.* ***Settlement***, on shore of NW arm of Loch Awe, 5m/8km SE of Taynuilt. **30 C2** NN0825.
Trimontium *Sc.Bord. See Newstead.*
Trinafour *P. & K.* ***Settlement***, in Glen Errochty, 1m/2km SE of dam of Loch Errochty. **40 C3** NN7264.
Trinity *Angus* ***Village***, 1m/2km N of Brechin. **43 E3** NO6062.
Trinity *Edin.* ***Suburb***, 2m/3km N of Edinburgh city centre. NT2476.
Trinity College (Also known as Glenalmond College.) *P. & K.* ***Educational establishment***, boys' public school in Glen Almond on S bank of River Almond, 9m/15km NW of Perth. NN9728.
Trislaig *High.* ***Settlement***, on W shore of Loch Linnhe, opposite Fort William. **38 C2** NN0874.
Triuirebheinn *W.Isles* ***Mountain***, on South Uist 2m/3km NE of Lochboisdale. Height 1171 feet or 357 metres. **46 B2** NF8121.

Trochry *P. & K.* ***Village***, in Strath Braan, 4m/6km SW of Dunkeld. **41 E5** NN9740.
Troisgeach *Stir.* ***Mountain***, to NW of head of Loch Lomond, 2m/3km W of Inverarnan. Height 2408 feet or 734 metres. **31 E3** NN2919.
Tromie *High.* ***River***, in Badenoch and Strathspey district running N from Loch an t-Seilich down Glen Tromie to River Spey, 1m/2km E of Kingussie. **51 G5** NH7701.
Tronach Head *Moray* ***Coastal feature***, headland on N coast between Findochty and Portknockie. NJ4768.
Trondavoe *Shet.* ***Settlement***, 2m/3km NE of Brae, Mainland. **84 C5** HU3770.
Trondra *Shet.* ***Island***, lying S of Scalloway, Mainland. Measures 3m/4km N to S and nowhere more than 1km wide. Road bridge link with Mainland across narrow strait at N end and with West Burra near S end. Sparsely inhabited. **82 C4** HU3937.
Troon *S.Ayr.* Population: 15,231. ***Town***, port and resort on Firth of Clyde, at N end of Ayr Bay, 6m/9km N of Ayr. Former coal and boat-building town. Several golf courses, one of which, Royal Troon, is a championship course. **14 B2** NS3230.
Trosaraidh *W.Isles* ***Settlement***, on South Uist, 3m/5km S of Dalabrog. **44 C2** NF7516.
Troswick Ness *Shet.* ***Coastal feature***, headland on E coast of Mainland, 1m/2km NE of Boddam. **83 G4** HU4117.
Trotternish *High.* ***Locality***, district and peninsula on Skye, N of isthmus between Portree and head of Loch Snizort Beag. **58 A3** NG4264.
Trottick *Dundee* ***Suburb***, 2m/3km N of Dundee city centre. NO4033.
Troup Head *Aber.* ***Coastal feature***, headland on N coast, 9m/14km E of Banff and 11m/17km W of Fraserburgh. **64 D3** NJ8267.
Troustan *Arg. & B.* ***Settlement***, on W coast of Loch Striven, 3m/5km N of Strone Point. **22 B2** NS0776.
Trows *Sc.Bord.* ***Settlement***, 3m/5km SW of Kelso. **18 A3** NT6932.
Trudernish *Arg. & B.* ***Settlement***, 8m/12km NE of Port Ellen, Islay. **20 C4** NR4652.
Truim *High.* ***River***, in Badenoch and Strathspey district, running N from Pass of Drumochter down Glen Truim through Dalwhinnie to River Spey, 5m/8km SW of Kingussie. NN6896.
Trumaisge Arraidh (Anglicised form: Trumisgarry.) *W.Isles* ***Settlement***, on N coast of North Uist, 5m/8km NW of Lochmaddy. **45 G2** NF8674.
Trumisgarry *W.Isles Anglicised form of Trumaisge Arraidh, qv.*
Trumpan *High.* ***Settlement***, on Skye, 4m/6km S of Vaternish Point. **57 F3** NG2261.
Tuarie Burn *High.* ***River***, in Sutherland district, flowing E to form Craggie Water, 1km W of Craggie. **72 D2** NC8620.
Tubhailt Mhic 'ic Eoghain *High. Alternative name for Maclean's Towel, qv.*
Tudhope Hill ***Mountain***, astride border of Dumfries & Galloway and Scottish Borders, 4m/7km SE of Teviothead. Height 1965 feet or 599 metres. **10 C2** NY4399.
Tugnet Icehouse Exhibition *Moray* ***Other feature of interest***, museum at Scotland's largest ice house, showing former salmon industry of Tugnet, 1km N of Garmouth. **63 F3** NJ3465.
Tuirnaig *High.* ***Settlement***, 2m/3km NE of Poolewe, Ross and Cromarty district. **59 E1** NG8783.
Tulach Hill *P. & K.* ***Mountain***, 1m/2km SW of Blair Atholl. Height 1542 feet or 470 metres. **41 D3** NN8564.
Tulchan *High. Alternative name for Burn of Tulchan, qv.*
Tulchan *P. & K.* ***Settlement***, in Glen Almond, 6m/10km NE of Crieff. **33 E2** NN9528.
Tullibardine *P. & K.* ***Locality***, 2m/4km W of Auchterarder. 15c chapel (Historic Scotland). NN9113.
Tullibardine Chapel *P. & K.* ***Historic/prehistoric site***, small church (Historic Scotland) 2m/3km NW of Auchterarder. Founded in 1446 and largely rebuilt c. 1500, it remains unaltered since that date. **33 E3** NN9013.
Tullibody *Clack.* Population: 6872. ***Small town***, 2m/3km NW of Alloa. Small pre-Reformation church. **33 D5** NS8695.
Tullibody Inch *Clack.* ***Island***, in River Forth, to S of Tullibody. NS8692.
Tullibole Castle *P. & K.* ***Castle***, tower bearing date 1608, 4m/7km W of Kinross. NO0500.
Tullich *Arg. & B.* ***Settlement***, 1m/2km SW of Kilmelford. **30 A3** NM8312.
Tullich *Arg. & B.* ***Settlement***, in Glen Aray, 5m/8km N of Inveraray. **30 C3** NN0815.
Tullich *High.* ***Locality***, 4m/6km NE of Invergordon, Ross and Cromarty district. NH7373.
Tullich *High.* ***Locality***, 1m/2km NW of Balintore. **62 A2** NH8577.
Tullich *High.* ***Settlement***, 10m/16km S of Inverness. **51 F2** NH6328.
Tullich *Moray* ***Settlement***, 2m/3km N of Dufftown. **63 F5** NJ3242.
Tullich *Stir.* ***Settlement***, in Glen Lochay, 4m/7km NW of Killin. **32 A1** NN5136.
Tullich Burn *Aber.* ***River***, stream running S into River Dee 2m/3km below Ballater. NO3997.
Tullich Hill *Arg. & B.* ***Mountain***, on E side of Loch Long, 2m/3km S of Arrochar. Height 2073 feet or 632 metres. **31 E4** NN2900.
Tullich Hill *P. & K.* ***Mountain***, on SE side of Loch Tay, 8m/12km N of St. Fillans. Height 2237 feet or 682 metres. **32 C1** NN7036.
Tullich Muir *High.* ***Settlement***, 4m/6km NE of Invergordon. **61 G2** NH7373.
Tulliemet *P. & K.* ***Settlement***, 1m/2km E of Ballinluig. **41 E4** NN9952.
Tullo Hill *Angus* ***Mountain***, 2m/3km W of Kirkton of Menmuir. Height 1036 feet or 316 metres. **42 C3** NO4964.
Tulloch *Aber.* ***Settlement***, to SE of Greenspot, 4m/7km SE of Fyvie. **54 D1** NJ8031.
Tulloch *High.* ***Locality***, on upland, 5m/8km NE of Aviemore. **52 B3** NH9816.
Tulloch *High.* ***Settlement***, 1km N of Bonar Bridge, Sutherland district. **72 B5** NH6192.
Tulloch *Moray* ***Settlement***, on hillside, 3m/5km SE of Forres, with historic settlement and field system to N. **62 C4** NJ0855.
Tulloch Hill *Angus* ***Mountain***, forested peak surmounted by Airlie Memorial Tower, 1m/2km NW of Dykehead. Height 1269 feet or 387 metres. **42 B3** NO3761.
Tulloch Station *High.* ***Other building***, station on West Highland line to Fort William, 9m/14km E of Spean Bridge. **39 F1** NN3580.
Tullochgorm *Arg. & B.* ***Settlement***, 1m/2km SW of Minard. **30 B5** NR9695.
Tullochgribban High *High.* ***Settlement***, 4m/6km NE of Carrbridge. **52 B2** NH9425.
Tullochvenus *Aber.* ***Settlement***, 2m/3km N of Lumphanan. **54 A4** NJ5807.
Tulloes *Angus* ***Settlement***, 3m/5km SW of Letham. **42 D5** NO5045.
Tullybannocher *P. & K.* ***Settlement***, in valley of River Earn, 1km W of Comrie. **32 C2** NN7621.
Tullybelton *P. & K.* ***Settlement***, 3m/4km SW of Bankfoot. **33 F1** NO0333.
Tullybothy Craigs *Fife* ***Coastal feature***, offshore rocks 1km N of Fife Ness. **35 E3** NO6310.
Tullyfergus *P. & K.* ***Locality***, comprises settlements of East and West Tullyfergus, 2m/3km W of Alyth. **42 A5** NO2148.
Tullymurdoch *P. & K.* ***Settlement***, 4m/6km NW of Alyth. **41 G4** NO1952.
Tullynessle *Aber.* ***Village***, 3m/4km NW of Alford. **54 A3** NJ5519.
Tulm Island *High.* ***Island***, long narrow islet in Duntulm Bay near N end of Skye, 7m/11km N of Uig. **57 G2** NG4074.
Tummel *P. & K.* ***River***, issuing from Loch Rannoch and running E through Dunalastair Water and Loch Tummel, turning SE through Linn of Tummel to its confluence with River Garry in Loch Faskally, then on past Pitlochry to River Tay S of Ballinluig. **41 E4** NN9751.
Tummel Bridge *P. & K.* ***Settlement***, on River Tummel, 1m/2km W of Loch Tummel; hydro-electricity power station. **40 C4** NN7659.
Tundergarth Mains *D. & G.* ***Settlement***, on E side of Water of Milk, 3m/5km E of Lockerbie. **9 F2** NY1780.
Tunga (Anglicised form: Tong.) *W.Isles* ***Village***, near E coast of Isle of Lewis, 3m/5km NE of Stornoway across River Laxdale estuary. **69 F4** NB4536.
Turbiskill *Arg. & B.* ***Settlement***, at head of Linne Mhuirich, 1km SW of Tayvallich. **21 F1** NR7385.
Turclossie *Aber.* ***Settlement***, 1m/2km N of New Pitsligo. **65 D4** NJ8857.
Turf Law *Sc.Bord.* ***Mountain***, rising to over 380 metres, 3m/5km NW of Carfraemill. **26 B4** NT4756.
Turin *Angus* ***Locality***, 3m/4km N of Letham. **42 D4** NO5352.
Turin Hill *Angus* ***Hill***, 4m/6km NE of Forfar. Hillfort of Kemp's Castle at summit. Height 827 feet or 252 metres. **42 D4** NO5153.
Turls Head *Shet.* ***Coastal feature***, headland on NW coast of Mainland, on E side of entrance to Ronas Voe. HU2886.
Turnberry *S.Ayr.* ***Village***, on Turnberry Bay, 5m/8km N of Girvan. Championship golf course. **14 A5** NS2005.
Turnberry Bay *S.Ayr.* ***Bay***, 5m/8km N of Girvan. Turnberry village is on bay. **13 G5** NS2005.
Turnberry Castle *S.Ayr.* ***Castle***, scant remains of castle, adjoining lighthouse, 1m/2km N of Turnberry. **13 G5** NS2005.
Turret *High.* ***River***, flowing S through Glen Turret into River Roy at Turret Bridge, 8m/12km NE of Roybridge. **50 C5** NN3391.
Turret Bridge *High.* ***Settlement***, at NE end of Glen Roy, 8m/12km NE of Roybridge. **50 C5** NN3391.
Turriff *Aber.* Population: 3948. ***Small town***, at confluence of River Deveron and Idoch Water, 9m/14km S of Banff. Centre of agricultural district. **64 C4** NJ7249.
Turvalds Head *Shet.* ***Coastal feature***, headland on W coast of Mainland, 2m/3km W of Brae. HU3268.
Tutim Burn *High.* ***River***, rising on W slopes of Beinn Rosail and flowing SE into River Oykel at Tuiteam Tarbhach. **71 G4** NC4301.
Twatt *Ork.* ***Settlement***, on Mainland, 3m/4km NW of Dounby. **80 A4** HY2724.
Twatt *Shet.* ***Village***, on Mainland, 1km N of Bixter. **82 C2** HU3253.
Twechar *E.Dun.* Population: 1499. ***Village***, 2m/3km SW of Kilsyth. Bar Hill Fort (Historic Scotland), 1km E, is highest fort on line of Antonine Wall. **24 A2** NS7075.
Tweed ***River***, rising at Tweed's Well, 6m/10km N of Moffat, and flowing by Peebles, Melrose, Kelso and Coldstream to North Sea at Berwick-upon-Tweed. Long section of lower course forms border of England and Scotland. **18 C2** NU0052.
Tweedbank *Sc.Bord.* ***Locality***, 2m/3km W of Melrose. NT5135.
Tweeddale *Sc.Bord.* ***Valley***, carrying River Tweed and running generally SW to NE from Glenbreck to confluence with Lyne Water, 3m/4km W of Peebles. **16 B3** NT1125.
Tweed's Well *Sc.Bord.* ***Other feature of interest***, source of River Tweed, 6m/10km N of Moffat. **16 B4** NT0514.
Tweedsmuir *Sc.Bord.* ***Settlement***, in Upper Tweeddale, 8m/12km S of Broughton. **16 B3** NT0924.
Twiness *Ork.* ***Coastal feature***, headland to W of Bay of Tafts, Westray. **80 C2** HY4941.
Twynholm *D. & G.* ***Village***, 3m/4km NW of Kirkcudbright. **8 A5** NX6654.
Tyndrum *Stir.* ***Village***, 4m/7km NW of Crianlarich. Has two railway stations, one on the Glasgow to Oban and one on the Glasgow to Fort William line. **31 F1** NN3330.
Tyne *E.Loth.* ***River***, rising on N slopes of Moorfoot Hills as Tyne Water, and becoming River Tyne below confluence with Birns Water 1m/2km E of Pencaitland. It then runs NE through Haddington and East Linton to North Sea, 3m/5km W of Dunbar. **26 C2** NT6480.
Tyne Mouth *E.Loth.* ***Sea feature***, where River Tyne enters North Sea, 3m/5km NW of Dunbar. **26 D1** NT6480.
Tyne Water ***River***, upper reaches of River Tyne rising on S slopes of Moorfoot Hills, just S of Tynehead and 7m/11km SE of Bonnyrigg. It flows N and then E to join with Birns Water, 1m/2km E of Pencaitland, becoming River Tyne. **26 A4** NT6480.
Tynehead *Midloth.* ***Settlement***, 3m/5km SE of Gorebridge. **26 A4** NT3959.
Tyninghame *E.Loth.* ***Village***, 2m/3km NE of East Linton. **26 D2** NT6179.
Tyninghame House *E.Loth.* ***Garden***, surrounding house, 4m/6km W of Dunbar. Herbaceous borders and terraces, and ruin of 12c St. Baldred's Chapel. **26 D2** NT6179.
Tynribbie *Arg. & B.* ***Village***, in Argyll, 1m/2km SE of Portnacroish. **38 B5** NM9346.
Tynron *D. & G.* ***Village***, on Shinnel Water, 2m/3km NE of Tynron. **8 C1** NX8093.
Tyrebagger Hill *Aberdeen* ***Hill***, in Kirkhill Forest, 1m/2km E of Blackburn. Height 820 feet or 250 metres. **54 D3** NJ8412.
Tyrie *Aber.* ***Settlement***, near N coast, 5m/8km SW of Fraserburgh. NJ9262.

U

Uachdar *W.Isles* ***Settlement***, at N end of Benbecula, 1km E of Benbecula (Baile a' Mhanaich) Aerodrome. **45 G4** NF7955.
Uags *High.* ***Settlement***, on SW coast of Ross and Cromarty district, opposite Crowlin Islands. **48 D1** NG7234.
Uamh Altrumain *High. See Spar Cave.*
Uamh Bheag ***Mountain***, on border of Stirling and Perth & Kinross, 4m/7km NE of Callander. Height 2181 feet or 665 metres. **32 B3** NN6911.
Udale Bay *High.* ***Bay***, on S side of Cromarty Firth, Ross and Cromarty district, to SE of Balblair, on N coast of Black Isle. **61 G3** NH7166.
Uddingston *S.Lan.* Population: 5367. ***Small town***, 4m/6km SW of Coatbridge. Ruins of 13c Bothwell Castle (Historic Scotland) stand among woods above River Clyde 1m/2km SW. **24 A3** NS6960.
Uddington *S.Lan.* ***Settlement***, 2m/4km NE of Douglas. **15 G2** NS8633.
Udny Castle *Aber.* ***Castle***, to N of Udny Green. Tower house dates from 14c and is crowned by ornamental turrets. NJ8826.
Udny Green *Aber.* ***Village***, 5m/7km E of Oldmeldrum. **55 D2** NJ8826.
Udny Station *Aber.* ***Village***, 6m/10km SE of Oldmeldrum. **55 E2** NJ9024.

T U

Udraynian Point *Arg. & B.* ***Coastal feature***, headland on E coast of Bute, at N end of Kames Bay. NS0768.
Udston *S.Lan.* ***Suburb***, adjoining to W of Hamilton. NS6955.
Udstonhead *S.Lan.* ***Settlement***, 2m/3km N of Strathaven. **24 B5** NS7046.
Ugadale Point *Arg. & B.* ***Coastal feature***, headland on E coast of Kintyre, 2m/4km S of Saddell. **12 C3** NR7828.
Ugie *Aber.* ***River***, rising as North and South Ugie Water, two branches which join 1m/2km NE of Longside. Combined river then flows E to North Sea on N side of Peterhead. **65 F5** NK1247.
Uibhist a Deas *W.Isles Gaelic form of South Uist, qv.*
Uibhist a Tuath *W.Isles Gaelic form of North Uist, qv.*
Uidh *W.Isles* ***Settlement***, with landing stage, on NE side of Vatersay. NL6596.
Uieseval *W.Isles* ***Mountain***, 4m/7km E of Tarbert, North Harris. Height 1096 feet or 334 metres. **67 E4** NG2298.
Uig *Arg. & B.* ***Settlement***, 1km NE of head of Loch Breachacha, Coll. **36 A4** NM1754.
Uig *Arg. & B.* ***Settlement***, 2m/3km N of Orchard. **22 C1** NS1484.
Uig *High.* ***Settlement***, on W side of Loch Dunvegan, Skye, 3m/4km S of Dunvegan Head. **57 E4** NG1952.
Uig *High.* ***Village***, on Uig Bay, Skye, on E shore of Loch Snizort, at foot of Glen Uig. **57 G3** NG3963.
Uig *W.Isles* ***Settlement***, near W coast of Isle of Lewis, 1km S of Timsgearraidh. NB0533.
Uig Bay *High.* ***Bay***, at foot of Glen Uig, on E shore of Loch Snizort, Skye. **57 G3** NG3963.
Uig Sands *W.Isles* ***Coastal feature***, beach to SW of Timsgearraidh, in estuary formed by various streams emptying into Camus Uig bay. NB0433.
Uigen *W.Isles* ***Settlement***, on coast of Isle of Lewis by Loch Roag, 4m/7km SE of Gallan Head. **68 B4** NB0934.
Uiginish *High.* ***Settlement***, 1m/2km NW of Dunvegan across Loch Dunvegan, Skye. **57 F5** NG2448.
Uiginish Point *High.* ***Coastal feature***, headland with beacon on Skye near head of Loch Dunvegan, 1m/2km NW of Dunvegan. NG2349.
Uigshader *High.* ***Settlement***, on Skye, 4m/6km NW of Portree. **58 A5** NG4246.
Uinessan *W.Isles* ***Island***, islet off easternmost point of Vatersay. NL6695.
Uisenis *W.Isles* ***Mountain***, 4m/6km SE of head of Loch Shell, Isle of Lewis. Height 1217 feet or 371 metres. **67 F3** NB3306.
Uisge Dubh (Anglicised form: Black Water.) *High.* ***River***, issuing from S of Loch an Laoigh and flowing S through Attadale Forest to confluence with River Ling below Beinn Dronaig, 3m/4km SW of summit. **49 G1** NH0240.
Uisge Dubh *High.* ***River***, flowing W from slopes of Carn na h-Easgainn into River Farnach, 10m/15km S of Inverness. **51 G1** NH6931.
Uisge Labhair *High.* ***River***, rising to E of Aonach Beag in Badenoch and Strathspey district and running SW into River Ossian in Lochaber district, near foot of Loch Ossian. **39 G2** NN4170.
Uisge Misgeach *High.* ***River***, rising to S of Meallan Odhar and flowing E to confluence with Garbh-uisge, near SE dam of Loch Monar, to form River Farrar. **50 A1** NH1837.
Uisgebhagh (Anglicised form: Uiskevagh.) *W.Isles* ***Settlement***, 7m/11km SE of Balivanich. **45 G5** NF8650.
Uisgnaval Mòr (Anglicised form: Uisnaval More.) *W.Isles* ***Mountain***, in North Harris 2m/4km W of Clisham. Height 2391 feet or 729 metres. **66 D3** NB1208.
Uisken *Arg. & B.* ***Settlement***, on Mull, 2m/3km S of Bunessan. **28 C3** NM3819.
Uiskevagh *W.Isles Anglicised form of Uisgebhagh, qv.*
Uisnaval More *W.Isles Anglicised form of Uisgnaval Mòr, qv.*
Ukna Skerry *Shet.* ***Coastal feature***, headland on W coast of West Burra. **82 C4** HU3531.
Ulbster *High.* ***Village***, on E coast of Caithness district, 7m/11km S of Wick. **77 F4** ND3240.
Ulfhart Point *High.* ***Coastal feature***, headland on Soay Sound, Skye, on W side of entrance to Loch Scavaig. NG4716.
Ulladale *W.Isles* ***River***, on Harris, rising in Forest of Harris and flowing NE to become River Housay and discharge its waters into head of Loch Resort. **66 C2** NB1017.
Ullapool *High.* ***River***, runs from Loch Acholl into Loch Broom on N side of Ullapool. **70 D5** NH1294.
Ullapool *High.* Population: 1231. ***Small town***, small fishing port and resort on E shore of Loch Broom, W coast of Ross and Cromarty district. Ferry for pedestrians across loch to Allt na h-Airbhe. Vehicle ferry to Stornoway. **70 D5** NH1294.
Ullaval *W.Isles* ***Mountain***, 2m/3km N of Cleiseval in Forest of Harris. Height 2162 feet or 659 metres. **66 C2** NB0811.
Ullinish *High.* ***Settlement***, on Skye, on E side of Loch Bracadale, 1m/2km W of Bracadale village. **47 G1** NG3238.
Ullinish Point *High.* ***Coastal feature***, headland 1m/2km S of Ullinish, Skye. NG3136.
Ulsta *Shet.* ***Settlement***, at SW end of Yell, on small bay of same name. Vehicle ferry to Toft on Mainland. **85 D4** HU4680.
Uluvalt *Arg. & B.* ***Locality***, on Mull near head of Loch Scridain, 3m/4km SE of Ben More. **29 E2** NM5429.
Ulva *Arg. & B.* ***Island***, sparsely inhabited island off W coast of Mull on S side of Loch Tuath. Measures 4m/7km E to W and 2m/4km N to S. High basalt cliffs at W end. Road bridge connection with neighbouring Gometra to W. **28 D1** NM3640.
Ulva Islands *Arg. & B.* ***Island***, pair of islands at entrance to Linne Mhuirich, Argyll. **21 F1** NR7182.
Ulzieside *D. & G.* ***Settlement***, 1m/2km S of Sanquhar, across River Nith and Euchan Water. **15 F5** NS7708.
Unapool *High.* ***Settlement***, on W side of mouth of Loch Glencoul, Sutherland district, 1km SE of Kylesku Ferry. **74 B5** NC2333.
Underhoull *Shet.* ***Settlement***, overlooking Lunda Wick, on W coast of Unst. **85 E2** HP5704.
Unifirth *Shet.* ***Settlement***, to W of Brindister Voe, Mainland. **82 B2** HU2856.
Union Croft *Aber.* ***Settlement***, 4m/6km NW of Stonehaven. **54 D5** NO8290.
Unst *Shet.* ***Island***, northernmost of main islands of Shetland Islands, with much indented coastline. Measures 12m/19km N to S and from 3m/4km to 5m/8km E to W. Crofting, fishing. Airfield at Baltasound. **85 E1** HP6110.
Unst Airport *Shet.* ***Airport/airfield***, to S of Baltasound, Unst. **85 F2** HP6207.
Uphall *W.Loth.* ***Locality***, and parish, on W side of Broxburn. **25 E2** NT0671.
Uphall Station *W.Loth.* ***Hamlet***, 1m/2km S of Uphall. **25 E2** NT0670.
Uplawmoor *E.Renf.* ***Village***, 3m/5km SW of Neilston. **23 F4** NS4355.
Upper Ardchronie *High.* ***Locality***, on S shore of Dornoch Firth, 1m/2km SE of Ardgay, Sutherland district. NH6188.
Upper Ardroscadale *Arg. & B.* ***Settlement***, on W coast of Bute, 3m/5km W of Rothesay. Burial mound to W on Watch Hill. **22 B3** NS0364.
Upper Barvas *W.Isles* ***Settlement***, on Isle of Lewis, 1km N of Barvas. NB3650.
Upper Bayble *W.Isles Anglicised form of Pabail Uarach, qv.*
Upper Bighouse *High.* ***Settlement***, on W side of Halladale River, 4m/7km S of Melvich. **76 A3** NC8857.
Upper Boddam *Aber.* ***Settlement***, 2m/3km N of Insch. NJ6230.
Upper Boyndlie *Aber.* ***Settlement***, forms locality of Boyndlie with Nether Boyndlie, near N coast, 5m/9km SW of Fraserburgh. **65 E3** NJ9162.
Upper Breakish *High. Alternative name for Breakish, qv.*
Upper Burnhaugh *Aber.* ***Settlement***, 1m/2km NW of Netherley. **54 D5** NO8394.
Upper Camster *High.* ***Settlement***, in Caithness district, 4m/6km N of Lybster. Grey Cairns of Camster (Historic Scotland), 1m/2km N. **77 E4** ND2641.
Upper Carloway *W.Isles Anglicised form of Mullach Charlabhaigh, qv.*
Upper Clyth *High.* ***Locality***, on E coast of Caithness district, 2m/3km E of Lybster. ND2737.
Upper Coll *W.Isles Anglicised form of Col Uarach, qv.*
Upper Dallachy *Moray* ***Village***, 1m/2km S of Nether Dallachy, on S side of disused airfield. **63 F3** NJ3663.
Upper Derraid *High.* ***Settlement***, 3m/5km N of Grantown-on-Spey. **52 C1** NJ0233.
Upper Diabaig *High.* ***Settlement***, 1m/2km E of Lower Diabaig, on N shore of Loch Diabaigas Airde, Ross and Cromarty district. **59 E3** NG8160.
Upper Eathie *High.* ***Settlement***, 3m/5km SW of Cromarty. **61 G3** NH7663.
Upper Gills *High.* ***Settlement***, 1km S of Gills. **77 F1** ND3272.
Upper Glendessarry *High.* ***Settlement***, in Glen Dessary, 3m/4km NW of head of Loch Arkaig, Lochaber district. **49 F5** NM9593.
Upper Glendevon Reservoir *P. & K.* ***Reservoir***, near head of Glen Devon to W of Glendevon. NN9104.
Upper Gylen *Arg. & B.* ***Settlement***, on Kerrera, 1m/2km NE of Rubha Seanach. **30 A2** NM8126.
Upper Halistra *High.* ***Settlement***, adjoins Lower Halistra, 5m/8km S of Vaternish Point, Skye. NG2459.
Upper Hawkhillock *Aber.* ***Settlement***, 6m/10km NE of Ellon. **55 F1** NK0039.
Upper Kilchattan *Arg. & B.* ***Settlement***, on Colonsay, 2m/3km NW of Scalasaig. **28 C5** NR3795.
Upper Kinchrackine *Arg. & B.* ***Locality***, in Strath of Orchy in Argyll. Adjoins to W of Dalmally. NN1527.
Upper Kirkhill *Aberdeen* ***Locality***, 2m/3km S of Aberdeen city centre across River Dee. NJ9402.
Upper Knockando *Moray* ***Settlement***, 1m/2km N of Knockando. **63 D5** NJ1941.
Upper Largo (Also known as Kirkton of Largo.) *Fife* ***Village***, forms locality of Largo with adjacent village of Lower Largo 1m/2km to SW. **34 C4** NO4203.
Upper Loch Torridon *High.* ***Lake/loch***, upper part of Loch Torridon, E of Shieldaig. **59 E4** NG7560.
Upper Lochton *Aber.* ***Locality***, 1m/2km N of Banchory. **54 B5** NO6997.
Upper Lybster *High.* ***Village***, 1m/2km N of Lybster. **77 E5** ND2435.
Upper Milovaig *High.* ***Settlement***, on Skye, forms locality of Milovaig, along with Lower Milovaig, 6m/10km W of Dunvegan. NG1549.
Upper Obney *P. & K.* ***Settlement***, 3m/4km NW of Bankfoot. **33 F1** NO0336.
Upper Ollach *High.* ***Locality***, on E coast of Skye, 5m/7km SE of Loch Portree. **48 B1** NG5136.
Upper Ridinghill *Aber.* ***Settlement***, 2m/3km SW of Crimond and 4m/6km SW of Loch of Strathbeg. **65 F4** NK0254.
Upper Sanday *Ork.* ***Locality***, on Mainland, 8m/12km SE of Kirkwall. **79 E2** HY5403.
Upper Shader *W.Isles Anglicised form of Siadar Uarach, qv.*
Upper Skelmorlie *N.Ayr.* ***Locality***, adjoining to NE of Skelmorlie. **22 D3** NS1967.
Upper Sonachan *Arg. & B.* ***Settlement***, on S shore of Loch Awe, 1km E of Portsonachan. **30 C2** NN0621.
Upper Sound *Shet.* ***Settlement***, on Mainland, to W of Sound. HU4640.
Upper Tillyrie *P. & K.* ***Hamlet***, 1m/2km NW of Milnathort. **33 G4** NO1106.
Upper Uphall *W.Loth.* ***Locality***, adjoining to N of Uphall. NT0672.
Upper Victoria *Angus* ***Settlement***, 2m/3km NW of Carnoustie. **34 D1** NO5336.
Upperton *Aber. See Peterhead.*
Uppertown *High.* ***Settlement***, at S end of Island of Stroma, in Pentland Firth. **77 F1** ND3576.
Uppertown *Ork.* ***Settlement***, at NW end of South Ronaldsay, 2m/3km W of St. Margaret's Hope. ND4193.
Upsettlington *Sc.Bord.* ***Settlement***, surrounded by parkland, on W side of River Tweed, 1m/2km SW of Norham. **27 F5** NT8846.
Ura Firth *Shet.* ***Sea feature***, large inlet of St. Magnus Bay on W coast of Mainland, separated from Ronas Voe to N by neck of land 1m/2km wide. **84 B5** HU2977.
Uradale *Shet.* ***Settlement***, 1m/2km SE of Scalloway, Mainland. **82 D4** HU4038.
Urafirth *Shet.* ***Settlement***, at head of inlet of Ura, with small Loch of Urafirth to N. **84 C5** HU3078.
Urchany *High.* ***Locality***, 5m/7km S of Nairn. **62 A5** NH8849.
Urchany and Farley Forest *High.* ***Open space***, plateau 4m/6km W of Beauly. **61 D5** NH4647.
Ure *Arg. & B.* ***River***, in Argyll, with head waters to N and W of Beinn Trilleachan, running W down Glen Ure to River Creran. **38 C5** NN0348.
Ure *Shet.* ***Settlement***, near N coast of Esha Ness, Mainland. **84 B5** HU2279.
Urgha *W.Isles* ***Locality***, on North Harris, 1m/2km E of Tarbert. **67 D4** NG1799.
Urie *Aber.* ***River***, running SE by Old Rayne and Pitcaple to River Don, 1m/2km SE of Inverurie. **54 B1** NJ7820.
Urie Lingey *Shet.* ***Island***, off N coast of Fetlar 1km N of Urie Ness. **85 F3** HU5995.
Urie Loch *N.Ayr.* ***Lake/loch***, small loch or tarn on Arran, 3m/5km NW of Whiting Bay. NS0028.
Urie Ness *Shet.* ***Coastal feature***, headland on N coast of Fetlar, 3m/5km NW of Houbie. HU5994.
Urlar Burn *P. & K.* ***River***, running NE into River Tay at Aberfeldy. Falls of Moness along course, 1m/2km S of Aberfeldy. **40 D5** NN8549.
Urquhart *High.* ***Settlement***, 1m/2km SW of Culbokie. **61 E4** NH5858.
Urquhart *Moray* ***Village***, 4m/7km E of Elgin. **63 E3** NJ2862.
Urquhart Bay *High.* ***Bay***, on NW shore of Loch Ness, 1m/2km E of Drumnadrochit. Rivers Coiltie and Enrick run into bay. NH5229.
Urquhart Castle *High.* ***Castle***, ruins of castle (Historic Scotland) on Strone Point, on Loch Ness. **51 E2** NH5228.
Urr Water *D. & G.* ***River***, issuing from Loch Urr and running S past Dalbeattie to Rough Firth and Solway Firth at Urr Waterfoot. **8 B4** NX8551.
Urrall Fell *D. & G.* ***Hill***, 3m/4km S of Loch Maberry and 8m/13km SE of Barrhill. Height 604 feet or 184 metres. **7 D3** NX2870.
Urray *High.* ***Locality***, containing settlements of Wester, Old and Easter Urray, 2m/3km NW of Muir of Ord. **61 E4** NH5052.
Urray Forest *High.* ***Forest/woodland***, in Ross and Cromarty district 5m/8km SW of Conon Bridge. NH4850.
Urvaig *Arg. & B.* ***Coastal feature***, headland at N point of Tiree, 1m/2km NW of Rubha Dubh. **36 B1** NM0850.
Usan *Angus Alternative name for Fishtown of Usan, qv.*
Ushat Head *High.* ***Coastal feature***, headland on N coast of Caithness district, 6m/9km W of Thurso. ND0371.

Uyea *Shet.* ***Island***, off N coast of Mainland. **84 C3** HU3192.
Uyea *Shet.* ***Island***, of about 600 acres or 240 hectares off S coast of Unst opposite Uyeasound. **85 E3** HU6099.
Uyea Sound *Shet.* ***Sea feature***, strait running between Unst and Uyea. Uyeasound village on S coast of Unst at head of the sound. **85 E3** HP5901.
Uyeasound *Shet.* ***Village***, on S coast of Unst, at head of Uyea Sound. **85 E2** HP5901.
Uynarey *Shet.* ***Island***, uninhabited island off SW coast of Yell, 1m/2km NW of Ulsta and 3m/5km W of Hamna Voe. **84 D4** HU4480.

V

Vacasay Island *W.Isles* ***Island***, small uninhabited island in East Loch Roag close to shore of Great Bernera. NB1836.
Vaccasay *W.Isles* ***Island***, small uninhabited island in Sound of Harris 1km off NE coast of North Uist. NF9774.
Vacsay *W.Isles* ***Island***, small uninhabited island in West Loch Roag, W coast of Isle of Lewis, 1m/2km W of Great Bernera. **68 C4** NB1137.
Vai Voe *Shet.* ***Bay***, small bay on N coast of Whalsay, 2m/3km NE of Brough. HU5766.
Vaila *Shet.* ***Island***, of about 1 square mile or 3 square km off Mainland at entrance to Vaila Sound. **82 B3** HU2346.
Vaila Sound *Shet.* ***Sea feature***, inlet between Mainland and Vaila, containing smaller island of Linga. At head of sound is village of Walls. **82 B3** HU2346.
Vaivoe *Shet.* ***Settlement***, at head of small bay of Vai Voe, on N coast of Whalsay, 2m/3km NE of Brough. HU5766.
Valla Field *Shet.* ***Inland physical feature***, hill ridge on Unst, extending N between Lunda Wick and Loch of Watlee. **85 E2** HP5807.
Vallay *W.Isles* ***Island***, off N coast of North Uist 2m/3km E of Griminis Point. Island measures 3m/4km E to W and about 1km N to S. **45 F2** NF7776.
Vallay Strand *W.Isles* ***Coastal feature***, mudflats separating Vallay from North Uist; fordable at low tide. **45 F2** NF7776.
Valleyfield *D. & G.* ***Settlement***, 3m/5km N of Kirkcudbright. **8 A5** NX6756.
Valleyfield *Fife* Population: 3162. ***Locality***, comprises High and Low Valleyfield, 1m/2km E of Culross. **25 E1** NT0086.
Valsgarth *Shet.* ***Locality***, on Unst, 1km N of Haroldswick. **85 F1** HP6413.
Valtos *W.Isles Anglicised form of Bhaltos, qv.*
Varragill *High.* ***River***, on Skye, running N into Loch Portree. NG4741.
Vat Burn *Aber.* ***River***, rising on Culblean Hill and flowing E to Loch Kinord. **53 G5** NO4399.
Vatarsay (Gaelic form: Bhatarsaidh.) *W.Isles* ***Island***, islet at entrance to Loch Leurbost, E coast of Isle of Lewis. NB4023.
Vaternish *High.* ***Coastal feature***, peninsula on Skye, on W side of Loch Snizort, culminating in headland of Vaternish Point. **57 F4** NG2658.
Vaternish Point *High.* ***Coastal feature***, headland on peninsula of Vaternish, Skye. **57 F3** NG2658.
Vatersay (Gaelic form: Bhatarsaigh.) *W.Isles* ***Island***, irregularly shaped island of about 3 square miles or 8 square km, off SW end of Barra across narrow Sound of Vatersay. **44 B4** NL6395.
Vatersay (Gaelic form: Bhatarsaigh.) *W.Isles* ***Settlement***, on S part of Vatersay. **44 B4** NL6394.
Vatersay Bay (Gaelic form: Bhatarsaigh Bay.) *W.Isles* ***Bay***, on E coast of Vatersay. **44 B4** NL6495.
Vatisker (Gaelic form: Bhatasgeir.) *W.Isles* ***Settlement***, near E coast of Isle of Lewis, 1km S of Bac. NB4839.
Vatisker Point *W.Isles Anglicised form of Rubha Bhataisgeir, qv.*
Vatsetter *Shet.* ***Settlement***, near E coast of Yell, 2m/3km SE of Mid Yell. HU5389.
Vatten *High.* ***Settlement***, on Skye, on E side of Loch Vatten at head of Loch Bracadale, 3m/5km SE of Dunvegan. **57 F5** NG2843.
Vaul *Arg. & B.* ***Settlement***, on W side of Vaul Bay, on N coast of Tiree, 2m/4km N of Scarinish. 1c-3c Dùn Mòr Vaul to NW. **36 B2** NM0448.
Ve Ness *Ork.* ***Coastal feature***, headland on S coast of Mainland. **78 C2** HY3705.
Ve Skerries *Shet.* ***Island***, group of rocks 3m/5km NW of Papa Stour. **82 A1** HU1065.
Veantrow Bay *Ork.* ***Bay***, wide bay on N coast of Shapinsay. **80 C4** HY5020.
Veensgarth *Shet.* ***Village***, on Mainland, 4m/6km NW of Lerwick. **82 D3** HU4244.
Veilish Point *W.Isles* ***Coastal feature***, headland on North Uist, 2m/3km N of Solas. **45 F2** NF8178.
Vementry *Shet.* ***Island***, uninhabited island of about 1000 acres or 400 hectares off W coast of Mainland, on S side of strait of Swarbacks Minn. Largest of the uninhabited islands of Shetland. Varied landscape with much bird life. **82 B1** HU2960.
Venchen Hill *Sc.Bord.* ***Hill***, 1m/2km N of Town Yetholm. Height 882 feet or 269 metres. **18 C4** NT8129.
Veness *Ork.* ***Settlement***, near to SE coast of Eday. **81 D4** HY5729.
Victoria Falls *High.* ***Waterfall***, in Slattadale Forest near S shore of Loch Maree, 1m/2km NW of Talladale. **59 E2** NG8971.
Vidlin *Shet.* ***Village***, on E coast of Mainland, at head of Vidlin Voe, 1m/2km N of Dury Voe. **83 D1** HU4765.
Vidlin Voe *Shet.* ***Sea feature***, inlet on E coast of Mainland, with village of Vidlin at its head, 1m/2km N of Dury Voe. **83 D1** HU4765.
Viewfield *Fife* ***Suburb***, in SW part of Glenrothes. NT2599.
Viewfield *High.* ***Settlement***, 2m/3km W of Thurso. **76 C2** ND0767.
Viewpark *N.Lan.* Population: 14,872. ***Suburb***, large suburban development, 2m/3km NW of Bellshill. **24 B3** NS7161.
Village Bay *W.Isles Alternative name for Loch Hirta, qv.*
Village of Ae *D. & G. See Ae Village.*
Vinegar Hill *High.* ***Open space***, hillside 5m/8km SE of Dalwhinnie. NN7080.
Vinny Burn *Angus* ***River***, rising 3m/5km SW of Forfar and flowing by Letham to Lunan Water at Friockheim. **42 D5** NO5949.
Vinquoy Chambered Cairn *Ork.* ***Historic/prehistoric site***, Neolithic chambered cairn in N of Eday, just N of Mill Loch. **81 D3** HY5637.
Virkie *Shet.* ***Locality***, on Mainland, at head of inlet called Pool of Virkie. HU3911.
Voe *Shet.* ***Sea feature***, inlet on SE coast of Mainland, adjacent to Boddam. **83 G4** HU4014.
Voe *Shet.* ***Settlement***, at head of Ronas Voe, Mainland. **84 C4** HU3381.
Voe *Shet.* ***Village***, on Mainland, at head of Olna Firth. **82 D1** HU4063.
Voe of Browland *Shet.* ***Sea feature***, inlet at head of main inlet of Gruting Voe, Mainland. HU2650.
Voe of Clousta *Shet.* ***Sea feature***, inlet on Mainland, to S of Vementry. HU3057.
Voe of Cullingsburgh *Shet.* ***Sea feature***, large inlet on NE coast of Bressay. HU5142.
Voe of Dale *Shet.* ***Bay***, on W coast of Mainland, with Mu Ness to N and Ness of Bakka to S. **82 A2** HU1751.
Voe of Scatsta *Shet.* ***Sea feature***, small inlet to NE of Scatsta, Mainland. HU3972.
Voe of Snarraness *Shet.* ***Sea feature***, inlet on W side of Snarra Ness, Mainland. HU2357.
Voe of Sound *Shet.* ***Sea feature***, large S facing inlet on Mainland, 1m/2km SW of Lerwick. HU4640.
Vogrie Country Park *Midloth.* ***Leisure/recreation***, country park 3m/4km NE of Gorebridge. Vogrie Burn flows through park which offers nature trails, walled garden, streams, ponds, golf course and a model railway. **26 A3** NT3763.
Vord Hill *Shet.* ***Hill***, in N part of Fetlar. Height 518 feet or 158 metres. **85 F3** HU6293.
Votersay *W.Isles* ***Island***, small uninhabited island off NE coast of North Uist, 3m/5km SE of Berneray. NF9476.
Voy *Ork.* ***Settlement***, on Mainland, to NW of Loch of Stenness. **80 A5** HY2515.
Vuia Beag *W.Isles* ***Island***, small uninhabited island in Loch Roag on W coast of Isle of Lewis, 2m/4km E of Miabhig. **68 C4** NB1233.
Vuia Mòr *W.Isles* ***Island***, uninhabited island in Loch Roag, W coast of Isle of Lewis, close to W shore of Great Bernera. **68 C4** NB1334.

W

Waas *High.* ***Locality***, in Caithness district, 2m/3km SW of Thurso. ND0766.
Wadbister *Shet.* ***Settlement***, near E coast of Mainland, on S side of Wadbister Voe, 1km W of Lambgarth Head, headland at end of promontory of Wadbister Ness. HU4349.
Wadbister Ness *Shet.* ***Coastal feature***, promontory on E coast of Mainland, culminating in Lambgarth Head. HU4449.
Wadbister Voe *Shet.* ***Sea feature***, on E coast of Mainland, to S of Girlsta. **82 D2** HU4350.
Wade's Bridge *P. & K.* ***Other feature of interest***, bridge across River Tay, started by General Wade in 1733 and considered finest of his bridges. On NW side of Aberfeldy. **41 D5** NN8549.
Wag *High.* ***Settlement***, in Langwell Forest, on N bank of Langwell Water, 2m/3km S of Morven. **73 F2** ND0126.
Waggle Hill *Aber.* ***Hill***, 3m/4km S of Cuminestown. Height 584 feet or 178 metres. **64 D5** NJ8046.
Walkerburn *Sc.Bord.* ***Village***, on River Tweed, 2m/3km E of Innerleithen. **17 E2** NT3637.
Walkerton *Fife* ***Settlement***, on N bank of River Leven, just W of Leslie. **34 A4** NO2301.
Wallace Monument *Stir.* ***Other feature of interest***, monument on hill 2m/3km NE of Stirling, to William Wallace, Scottish knight who raised army which routed English at Battle of Stirling Bridge (1297). As a result he became Protector of the Kingdom. Defeated at Battle of Falkirk (1298) he organized further Scottish resistance against English until he was captured in 1305 and executed by Edward I. **32 D5** NS8195.
Wallace Tower *S.Ayr.* ***Other feature of interest***, original 14c building of Sundrum Castle in Ayr, built for Sir Duncan Wallace, Sheriff of Ayr c. 1373. Now provides holiday accommodation. **14 B3** NS3420.
Wallacehall *D. & G.* ***Settlement***, 4m/6km NE of Eaglesfield. **9 G3** NY2877.
Wallace's Hill *Sc.Bord.* ***Mountain***, in Cardrona Forest, 2m/3km W of Innerleithen. Height 1506 feet or 459 metres. **17 D2** NT3036.
Wallacetown *Shet.* ***Settlement***, on Mainland, 2m/3km W of Bixter. HU3052.
Wallacetown *S.Ayr.* ***Settlement***, 1m/2km N of Dailly across Water of Girvan. **14 A5** NS2702.
Wallacetown *S.Ayr.* ***Suburb***, N district of Ayr. NS3422.
Walls *Shet.* ***Village***, in W district of Mainland known as Walls and Sandness. District also includes village of Sandness. **82 B3** HU2449.
Walls and Sandness *Shet.* ***Locality***, W district of Mainland. District includes villages of Walls and Sandness. HU2449.
Wallyford *E.Loth.* ***Village***, 1m/2km E of Musselburgh. **26 A2** NT3672.
Walston *S.Lan.* ***Village***, 5m/8km E of Carnwath. **25 E5** NT0545.
Walton Park *D. & G.* ***Settlement***, 5m/8km N of Castle Douglas. **8 B3** NX7670.
Wamphray Water *D. & G.* ***River***, running S from Croft Head to River Annan, 7m/11km S of Moffat. **9 F1** NY1095.
Wandel *S.Lan.* ***Settlement***, 3m/5km NE of Abington. **16 A3** NS9427.
Wandel Burn *S.Lan.* ***River***, rising to N of Duncangill Head and flowing NW to join River Clyde to N of Wandel. **16 A3** NS9427.
Wanlock Dod *D. & G.* ***Mountain***, 1km N of Wanlockhead. Height 1807 feet or 551 metres. **15 G4** NS8614.
Wanlock Water *D. & G.* ***River***, rising at Wanlockhead and flowing NE to join Crawick Water just NE of Spango Bridge. **15 G4** NS8217.
Wanlockhead *D. & G.* ***Village***, in former lead-mining area, 6m/10km E of Sanquhar. 19c beam engine (Historic Scotland). Nearby is Museum of Scottish Lead Mining. **15 G4** NS8712.
Wanlockhead Beam Engine *D. & G.* ***Other feature of interest***, rare early 19c wooden water-balance pump used to drain lead mines (Historic Scotland), along with track of horse engine and industrial artefacts, at Wanlockhead. **15 G4** NS8712.
War Ness *Ork.* ***Coastal feature***, headland at S end of Eday. **81 D4** HY5528.
Ward Burn *Stir.* ***River***, stream running NE to join Kelty Water 2m/3km E of Dalmary. **32 A5** NS5496.
Ward Hill *Ork.* ***Hill***, 3m/4km N of Orphir Bay, Mainland. Height 879 feet or 268 metres. **78 C2** HY3308.
Ward Hill *Ork.* ***Hill***, 1km S of Lythes. Height 387 feet or 118 metres. **79 D4** ND4588.
Ward Hill *Ork.* ***Mountain***, at N end of Hoy. Height 1571 feet or 479 metres. **78 B2** HY2202.
Ward Hill *Shet.* ***Hill***, situated in NW part of Fair Isle. Height 712 feet or 217 metres. **82 A5** HZ2073.
Ward Holm *Ork.* ***Island***, small islet 1m/2km W of Copinsay. HY5901.
Ward of Bressay *Shet.* ***Hill***, conical hill forming highest point on Bressay, 2m/3km N of Bard Head. Height 741 feet or 226 metres. **83 D4** HU4453.
Ward of Otterswick *Shet.* ***Hill***, 1km NE of Hill of Arisdale and to W of Otters Wick. Height 672 feet or 205 metres. HU5085.
Ward of Scousburgh *Shet.* ***Hill***, to NE of Scousburgh. Height 863 feet or 263 metres. HU3818.
Ward of Veester *Shet.* ***Hill***, 2m/3km N of Hoswick, Mainland. Height 843 feet or 257 metres. **82 D5** HU4126.
Wardhouse *Aber.* ***Settlement***, 2m/3km NE of Kennethmont. **54 A1** NJ5630.
Wardie *Edin.* ***Suburb***, 2m/3km N of Edinburgh city centre. NT2476.
Wardlaw Hill *E.Ayr.* ***Mountain***, with cairn and memorial at summit, 3m/5km S of Muirkirk. Height 1630 feet or 497 metres. **15 E3** NS6822.
Wardpark *N.Lan.* ***Locality***, industrial area, 2m/3km NE of Cumbernauld town centre. Site of Roman camp. NS7777.
Warriston *Edin.* ***Suburb***, 1m/2km N of Edinburgh city centre. NT2575.
Warroch *P. & K.* ***Settlement***, 1m/2km NE of Carnbo. **33 F4** NO0604.
Warse *High.* ***Locality***, near N coast of Caithness district, 2m/4km SE of St. John's Point. ND3372.

U
V
W

Wart Holm *Ork.* ***Island***, rock 1km W of Point of Huro at S end of Westray. HY4838.
Warth Hill *High.* ***Hill***, 2m/3km SW of John o' Groats. Height 407 feet or 124 metres. **77 F1** ND3769.
Wartle *Aber.* ***Settlement***, 4m/6km E of Tarland. **54 A4** NJ5404.
Wasbister *Ork.* ***Settlement***, on Rousay, 1m/2km S of Sacquoy Head. **80 B3** HY3932.
Watch Hill ***Mountain***, astride border of Dumfries & Galloway and Scottish Borders, 4m/6km NW of Newcastleton. Height 1647 feet or 502 metres. **10 C2** NY4390.
Watch Water *Sc.Bord.* ***River***, rising in Lammermuir Hills and flowing E to Dye Water, 1km W of Longformacus. Course includes Watch Water Reservoir. NT6857.
Watch Water Reservoir *Sc.Bord.* ***Reservoir***, in course of Watch Water, 2m/3km W of Longformacus. **27 D4** NT6656.
Watchman Hill *S.Lan.* ***Mountain***, in Lowther Hills, 1m/2km SW of Elvanfoot. Height 1489 feet or 454 metres. **16 A4** NS9415.
Water of Ae *D. & G.* ***River***, rising on E side of Queensberry and flowing S through Forest of Ae and Ae Village, then SE to Kinnel Water 2m/4km N of Lochmaben. **9 E2** NY0786.
Water of Ailnack (Ailnack Water). ***River***, running NE into River Avon, 1m/2km S of Tomintoul. Upper reaches known as Water of Caiplich or Caiplich Water. NJ1617.
Water of Allachy *Aber.* ***River***, flowing N to join with Water of Tanar in Forest of Glen Tanar, and then to River Dee, SW of Aboyne. **53 G5** NO4694.
Water of App *S.Ayr.* ***River***, running SW down Glenn App to Finnarts Bay, near N end of Loch Ryan. NX0572.
Water of Aven *Aber.* ***River***, running NE to Water of Feugh, 4m/7km SW of Banchory. **43 D1** NO6392.
Water of Bogie *Aber. See (River) Bogie.*
Water of Buchat *Aber.* ***River***, rising on Ladder Hills and running SE to River Don at Bridge of Buchat. **53 F3** NJ4014.
Water of Caiplich *See Water of Ailnack.*
Water of Charr ***River***, rising to NE of Sturdy Hill and running N to Water of Dye, 6m/10km N of Fettercairn. **43 E1** NO6182.
Water of Coyle ***River***, rising about 3m/5km N of Dalmellington and flowing NW to River Ayr, 4m/6km E of Ayr. Meanders in lower reaches. **14 C4** NS3921.
Water of Cruden *Aber.* ***River***, rising to W of Ardallie and flowing E to North Sea at N end of Cruden Bay. NK0935.
Water of Deugh ***River***, rising to N of Windy Standard on E side of Carsphairn Forest and flowing W, then S past Carsphairn to Kendoon Loch, 4m/6km N of St. John's Town of Dalry. **7 G1** NX6090.
Water of Dye *Aber.* ***River***, running N down Glen Dye to Water of Feugh on W side of Strachan. **43 E1** NO6691.
Water of Effock *Angus* ***River***, running NE down Glen Effock to River North Esk, 2m/3km W of Tarfside. NO4578.
Water of Feugh *Aber.* ***River***, rising in mountains of Forest of Birse and flowing E, by Strachan, to join River Dee opposite Banchory. **54 A5** NO7095.
Water of Fleet *D. & G.* ***River***, rising on E side of Cairnsmore of Fleet and running S past Gatehouse of Fleet into Fleet Bay and Wigtown Bay. NX5550.
Water of Gairney *Aber.* ***River***, flowing N to join with Water of Allachy, 1km S of Water of Tanar. **53 G5** NO4693.
Water of Girvan *S.Ayr.* ***River***, running N from Loch Girvan Eye, in Glentrool Forest Park, and flowing N through Loch Bradan Reservoir before turning NW past Straiton and then SW, 1m/2km W of Kirkmichael. It continues to flow SW past Dailly into Firth of Clyde to N of Girvan. **14 B5** NX1898.
Water of Glencalvie *High. See Glen Calvie.*
Water of Ken *D. & G.* ***River***, rising on Fortypenny Hill NW of Carsphairn and flowing S through Carsfad and Earlstoun Lochs, then past St. John's Town of Dalry and New Galloway to Loch Ken. **8 A1** NX6475.
Water of Lee *Angus* ***River***, running E down Glen Lee to join Water of Mark at head of Glen Esk, 3m/4km W of Tarfside. **42 B1** NO4480.
Water of Leith ***River***, rising on Pentland Hills and running N through Harperrig Reservoir, then NE through Edinburgh to Leith Harbour and Firth of Forth. **25 F3** NT2678.
Water of Luce *D. & G.* ***River***, formed by confluence of Cross Water of Luce and Main Water of Luce at New Luce, and flowing S, to W of Glenluce, into Luce Bay. NX1954.
Water of Malzie *D. & G.* ***River***, flowing generally E to join River Bladnoch 1km NE of Malzie and 4m/6km W of Wigtown. **7 E5** NX3754.
Water of Mark ***River***, running first NE, then SE to join Water of Lee at head of Glen Esk, 3m/4km W of Tarfside. **42 C1** NO4480.
Water of May *P. & K.* ***River***, running N into River Earn, 5m/8km SW of Perth. **33 F4** NO0418.
Water of Milk *D. & G.* ***River***, rising on S side of Castle O'er Forest and flowing SW, then S to River Annan 3m/5km W of Ecclefechan. **9 F2** NY1473.
Water of Minnoch ***River***, rising on S slopes of Eldrick Hill and running S through Glentrool Forest to join Water of Trool, 2m/3km SW of Loch Trool. **7 E3** NX3778.
Water of Nevis *High.* ***River***, in Lochaber district rising on Mamore Forest and running first NE, then W along S side of Ben Nevis, then NW to head of Loch Linnhe at Fort William. **39 E3** NN1074.
Water of Nochty ***River***, rising on Ladder Hills and flowing SE to River Don at Strathdon. **53 E3** NJ3512.
Water of Philorth *Aber. See Philorth.*
Water of Ruchill (Ruchill Water). *P. & K.* ***River***, running NE down Glen Artney to River Earn at Comrie. **32 C3** NN7721.
Water of Saughs *Angus* ***River***, flowing SE in mountains to NE of Glen Clova and SW of Glen Esk, and becoming West Water. **42 C2** NO4274.
Water of Tanar *Aber.* ***River***, running NE through Forest of Glentanar to River Dee, 1m/2km SW of Aboyne. **53 G5** NO5197.
Water of Tarf *Angus* ***River***, running S into River North Esk, just S of Tarfside. **42 C1** NO4979.
Water of Tig *S.Ayr.* ***River***, rising in Arecleoch Forest and running N, then W, to River Stinchar 2m/3km E of Ballantrae. **6 C2** NX1183.
Water of Trool *D. & G.* ***River***, issuing from Loch Trool and flowing SW down Glen of Trool to join River Cree, 6m/10km NW of Newton Stewart. **7 E3** NX3778.
Water of Tulla *Arg. & B.* ***River***, in Argyll, running SW to Loch Tulla. **39 F5** NN3044.
Water of Unich *Angus* ***River***, running E to Water of Lee, 6m/10km W of Tarfside. Falls of Unich, waterfall in course of stream, near its junction with Water of Lee. **42 B2** NO3980.
Water Sound *Ork.* ***Sea feature***, strait dividing N coast of South Ronaldsay from S coast of Burray. **78 D3** ND4395.
Waterbeck *D. & G.* ***Village***, 4m/6km NE of Ecclefechan. **9 G3** NY2477.
Waterfoot *E.Renf.* Population: 1300. ***Hamlet***, on W bank of White Cart Water, 2m/3km E of Newton Mearns. **23 G4** NS5655.
Waterhead *D. & G.* ***Settlement***, 8m/12km E of St. John's Town Dalry. **8 B2** NX7483.
Waterhead *S.Ayr.* ***Mountain***, in Carrick Forest, 1m/2km SE of Loch Bradan. Height 1548 feet or 472 metres. **7 F1** NX4495.
Waterhill of Bruxie *Aber.* ***Settlement***, 1m/2km E of Maud and 2m/3km W of Old Deer. **65 E5** NJ9447.
Waterloo *Aber.* ***Settlement***, 3m/4km SW of Hatton. **55 F1** NK0135.
Waterloo *High.* ***Settlement***, on coast of Skye, 1m/2km E of Broadford. NG6623.
Waterloo *N.Lan.* ***Village***, 1m/2km SE of Wishaw. **24 C4** NS8053.
Waterloo *P. & K.* ***Village***, 4m/7km SE of Dunkeld. **33 F1** NO0536.
Waterloo Monument *Sc.Bord.* ***Other feature of interest***, on Peniel Heugh Hill, 2m/3km NE of Ancrum. Erected by Marquis of Lothian after victory at Battle of Waterloo. **18 A4** NT6526.
Watermeetings *S.Lan.* ***Settlement***, 1km S of confluence of Portrail Water and Daer Water. **16 A4** NS9512.
Waterside *Aber.* ***Settlement***, on S bank of River Don, 1m/2km E of Strathdon. **53 F3** NJ3611.
Waterside *Aber.* ***Settlement***, on E side of River Ythan estuary. **55 F2** NK0027.
Waterside *E.Ayr.* ***Village***, in valley of River Doon, 3m/5km NW of Dalmellington. **14 C5** NS4308.
Waterside *E.Ayr.* ***Village***, 5m/8km NE of Kilmarnock. **23 F5** NS4843.
Waterside *E.Dun.* ***Locality***, 1m/2km E of Kirkintilloch. **24 A2** NS6773.
Waterstein Head *High.* ***Hill***, 1m/2km E of Neist Point, Skye. Height 971 feet or 296 metres. **57 E5** NG1447.
Wats Ness *Shet.* ***Coastal feature***, headland on W coast of Mainland, 5m/7km W of Walls. **82 A2** HU1750.
Watten *High.* ***Village***, in Caithness district, 8m/12km W of Wick. To N is Loch Watten, nearly 3m/5km NW to SE and up to 1km wide. **77 E3** ND2454.
Wattston *N.Lan.* ***Village***, 3m/5km N of Airdrie. **24 B3** NS7769.
Wauchope Burn *Sc.Bord.* ***River***, one of headwaters of Rule Water, flowing N through W part of Wauchope Forest. NT5809.
Wauchope Forest *Sc.Bord.* ***Forest/woodland***, forming part of Border Forest Park, 8m/13km SE of Hawick. **11 E1** NT6104.
Wauchope Water *D. & G.* ***River***, running SE, then NE to River Esk at Langholm. **10 B3** NY3684.
Waughton Hill *Aber.* ***Hill***, to W of Mormond Hill, 2m/3km NE of Strichen. Height 768 feet or 234 metres. **65 E4** NJ9657.
Waughtonhill *Aber.* ***Settlement***, below N side of Waughton Hill, 3m/4km NE of Strichen. NJ9758.
Waulkmill Bay *Ork.* ***Bay***, large sandy bay, bounded by Ve Ness to SW. **78 C2** HY3706.
Weachyburn *Aber.* ***Settlement***, 3m/4km N of Aberchirder. **64 B4** NJ6356.
Weather Ness *Ork.* ***Coastal feature***, headland at SE end of Westray, nearly 2m/3km SE of Stanger Head. HY5240.
Weaver's Cottage *Renf.* ***Historic house***, 18c handloom weaver's cottage (National Trust for Scotland), in Kilbarchan. Contains working loom and period furniture. **23 F3** NS4063.
Weaver's Point *W.Isles* ***Coastal feature***, headland with lighthouse on N side of entrance to Loch na Madadh, E coast of North Uist. NF9569.
Weddell Sound *Ork.* ***Sea feature***, channel between Fara and Flotta. ND3394.
Wedder Hill *S.Lan.* ***Mountain***, summit of Blackside ridge to NE of Sorn. Height 1424 feet or 434 metres. **15 D2** NS5930.
Wedder Holm *Shet.* ***Island***, off SE coast of Uyea. HU6197.
Wedder Law *D. & G.* ***Mountain***, in Lowther Hills, on border with South Lanarkshire, 3m/5km E of Durisdeer. Height 2184 feet or 666 metres. **16 A5** NS9302.
Wedderlairs *Aber.* ***Settlement***, 1m/2km NW of Tarves. **55 D1** NJ8532.
Wedderlie Burn *Sc.Bord.* ***River***, small stream rising in Lammermuir Hills and flowing S into Blackadder Water. **26 D4** NT6451.
Wee Queensberry *D. & G.* ***Mountain***, 1m/2km S of Queensbury and 6m/10km W of Thornhill. Height 1679 feet or 512 metres. **9 D1** NX9897.
Weem *P. & K.* ***Village***, 1m/2km NW of Aberfeldy across River Tay. **40 D5** NN8449.
Weem Hill *P. & K.* ***Mountain***, 3m/4km NW of Aberfeldy. Height 1607 feet or 490 metres. **40 D4** NN8251.
Weisdale *Shet.* ***Locality***, surrounding Burn of Weisdale valley on Mainland, to N of Weisdale Voe. **82 C2** HU3953.
Weisdale Voe *Shet.* ***Sea feature***, long inlet on Mainland, with Heglibister near head of voe on W shore. Burn of Weisdale drains into voe. **82 C3** HU3848.
Wellbank *Angus* ***Hamlet***, 4m/7km N of Broughty Ferry. **34 C1** NO4637.
Wellgrain Dod *S.Lan.* ***Mountain***, in Lowther Hills, 3m/5km W of Elvanfoot. Height 1814 feet or 553 metres. **16 A4** NS9017.
Wellhill *Moray* ***Settlement***, 3m/4km NW of Forres. **62 B3** NJ0061.
Wellwood *Fife* ***Hamlet***, 1m/2km N of Dunfermline. **25 E1** NT0988.
Wemyss Bay *Inclyde* Population: 1635. ***Village***, and bay on Firth of Clyde, 7m/11km SW of Greenock. Passenger boat terminus. **22 C3** NS1969.
Wemyss Castle *Fife* ***Castle***, restored 15c-17c building on rocky eminence to NE of West Wemyss, towards East Wemyss. NT3295.
Wemyss Point *Inclyde* ***Coastal feature***, headland to N of Wemyss Bay. **22 C2** NS1870.
West Affric *High.* ***Open space***, area of wild and rugged landscape covering over 9000 acres (National Trust for Scotland), adjoining to E of Kintail Forest and forming part of Glenaffric Forest. Lying 22m/35km E of Kyle of Lochalsh, it includes one of the most popular east-west Highland paths which was once old drove road taking cattle across Scotland from Skye to market at Dingwall. NH1015.
West Barns *E.Loth.* ***Hamlet***, 1m/2km W of Dunbar. **27 D2** NT6578.
West Benhar *N.Lan.* ***Settlement***, 1m/2km SW of Harthill. **24 C3** NS8863.
West Burra *Shet.* ***Island***, one of two long, narrow, adjacent islands S of Scalloway, Mainland, to W of Trondra. Road bridges at either end of Trondra give connection to Mainland. East Burra lies to E and is also connected by a road bridge. **82 C4** HU3632.
West Burra Firth *Shet.* ***Sea feature***, inlet on Mainland on S shore of St. Magnus Bay, 4m/6km E of Melby. HU2557.
West Burrafirth *Shet.* ***Settlement***, on Mainland, to W of head of West Burra Firth. **82 B2** HU2557.
West Cairn Hill *Sc.Bord.* ***Mountain***, on border of Scottish Borders and West Lothian in Pentland Hills, 5m/8km NW of West Linton. Height 1843 feet or 562 metres. **25 F4** NT1058.
West Cairncake *Aber.* ***Settlement***, 1m/2km E of Cuminestown. **64 D5** NJ8249.
West Calder *W.Loth.* Population: 2888. ***Village***, 4m/7km SE of Bathgate. **25 E3** NT0163.
West Canisbay *High.* ***Settlement***, to W of Canisbay, near N coast of Caithness district. ND3471.
West Carbeth *Stir.* ***Settlement***, 2m/4km W of Strathblane. NS5279.
West Cauldcoats *S.Lan.* ***Settlement***, 3m/5km S of Strathaven. **24 A5** NS6840.
West Clyne *High.* ***Settlement***, on E coast of Sutherland district, 2m/3km NW of Brora. **73 D4** NC8805.

West Croachy *High.* ***Settlement***, part of Croachy locality, in Inverness district, 5m/9km SE of Dores. NH6427.
West Dullater *Stir.* ***Settlement***, on S side of Loch Venachar, 3m/5km SW of Callander. **32 A4** NN5805.
West Dunnet *High.* ***Settlement***, 1km NW of Dunnet. **77 E1** ND2271.
West End *S.Lan.* ***Settlement***, 1m/2km W of Carnwath. **25 D5** NS9646.
West Ferry *Dundee* ***Suburb***, 3m/5km E of Dundee city centre. NO4431.
West Geirinish *W.Isles* *Anglicised form of Geirninis, qv.*
West Glen *Arg. & B.* ***Settlement***, 2m/3km NE of Tighnabruaich. **22 B2** NR9974.
West Helmsdale *High.* ***Settlement***, to W of Helmsdale. **73 F3** ND0115.
West Heogaland (Also spelled West Hogaland.) *Shet.* ***Settlement***, on Esha Ness, on NW part of Mainland. HU2278.
West Highland Museum *High.* ***Other feature of interest***, in centre of Fort William. Exhibits on local and natural history, tartan and Jacobite relics. **38 D2** NN1073.
West Hill *Sc.Bord.* ***Mountain***, at W end of Lammermuir Hills, 4m/6km SE of Fala. Height 1479 feet or 451 metres. **26 B4** NT4959.
West Hogaland *Shet.* *Alternative spelling of West Heogaland, qv.*
West Kame *Shet.* ***Large natural feature***, ridge of hills, running N to S, to SW of Voe, Mainland. **82 C1** HU3961.
West Kilbride *N.Ayr.* Population: 4488. ***Small town***, 4m/7km NW of Ardrossan. Law Castle, to NE of town, has late 15c tower. **22 D5** NS2048.
West Kip *Midloth.* ***Mountain***, in Pentland Hills Regional Park, 3m/5km NE of Carlops. Height 1804 feet or 550 metres. **25 F3** NT1760.
West Knock *Angus* ***Mountain***, 3m/5km SW of Tarfside. Height 2266 feet or 691 metres. **42 C2** NO4775.
West Langwell *High.* ***Settlement***, 2m/3km NW of East Langwell, Sutherland district. **72 B4** NC6909.
West Laroch *High.* *Former name of Ballachulish, qv.*
West Linga *Shet.* ***Island***, uninhabited island of 315 acres or 127 hectares lying off W coast of Whalsay and separated from it by Linga Sound. **83 E1** HU5364.
West Lingo *Fife* ***Settlement***, 5m/8km S of St. Andrews. **34 C4** NO4808.
West Linton *Sc.Bord.* Population: 1157. ***Village***, on E side of Pentland Hills, 7m/12km SW of Penicuik. **25 F4** NT1551.
West Loch Ollay *W.Isles* *See Ollay Lochs.*
West Loch Roag *W.Isles* ***Sea feature***, large inlet on W coast of Isle of Lewis, on W side of Great Bernera. **68 B4** NB1138.
West Loch Tarbert *Arg. & B.* ***Sea feature***, sea-loch in Argyll running NE from Ardpatrick Point, between Knapdale and Kintyre. Isthmus of only 1m/2km separates head of loch from East Loch Tarbert on Loch Fyne. Quay near West Tarbert at head of loch, with passenger services to Islay. **21 F3** NR8062.
West Loch Tarbert *W.Isles* ***Sea feature***, large inlet between W coast of North and South Harris. Village and port of Tarbert on isthmus between this inlet and East Loch Tarbert. **66 C3** NB0903.
West Lomond *Fife* ***Mountain***, summit of Lomond Hills 3m/4km S of Strathmiglo. Height 1712 feet or 522 metres. **33 G4** NO1906.
West Lunna Voe *Shet.* ***Bay***, on Mainland, W of Lunna and 4m/6km SW of Lunna Ness. HU4869.
West Mey *High.* ***Settlement***, to NW of Mey, near N coast of Caithness district. ND2873.
West Monar Forest *High.* ***Open space***, deer forest about head of Loch Monar, Ross and Cromarty district. **59 G5** NH0742.
West Morriston *Sc.Bord.* ***Hamlet***, 3m/5km SW of Gordon. NT6041.
West Muir *Angus* ***Settlement***, 3m/4km NW of Brechin. **43 D3** NO5661.
West Ness *Fife* ***Coastal feature***, rocky headland on S side of Crail Harbour. **35 E4** NO6106.
West Park *Aber.* ***Hamlet***, 1m/2km E of Crathes. **54 C5** NO7697.
West Reef *Arg. & B.* ***Island***, group of rocks to W of Torran Rocks group and 4m/7km SW of Mull. **28 B3** NM2313.
West Saltoun *E.Loth.* ***Village***, 5m/8km SE of Tranent and 1m/2km W of East Saltoun. **26 B3** NT4667.
West Sand Wick *Shet.* ***Bay***, small bay on W coast of Yell. HU4489.
West Sandwick *Shet.* ***Village***, 1km SE of West Sand Wick. **85 D4** HU4489.
West Shinness Lodge *High.* ***Settlement***, forms locality of Shinness along with Shinness Lodge, on E side of Loch Shin, 6m/10km NW of Lairg. **72 A3** NC5314.
West Tarbert *Arg. & B.* ***Settlement***, 1m/2km SW of Tarbert, at head of West Loch Tarbert. **21 G3** NR8467.
West Tarbert *W.Isles* *Anglicised form of Taobh Siar, qv.*
West Tarbert Bay *Arg. & B.* ***Bay***, one of two bays on either side of Gigha, near N end of island. **21 E4** NR6552.
West Tarbet *D. & G.* ***Locality***, 3m/5km S of Cailiness Point, on W side of Mull of Galloway. **2 B3** NX1430.
West Tofts *P. & K.* ***Locality***, 1km N of Stanley. **33 G1** NO1034.
West Voe *Shet.* ***Sea feature***, stretch of sea separating S sections of West and East Burra. **82 C5** HU3629.
West Voe of Quarff *Shet.* ***Bay***, on Clift Sound, on W of Mainland. HU4035.
West Voe of Sumburgh *Shet.* ***Bay***, to W of Sumburgh, on S of Mainland. HU4009.
West Water *Angus* ***River***, running SE to River North Esk, 2m/4km SE of Edzell. NO6266.
West Water Reservoir *Sc.Bord.* ***Reservoir***, on Pentland Hills, 2m/3km W of West Linton. **25 F4** NT1152.
West Wemyss *Fife* ***Village***, on Firth of Forth, 4m/6km NE of Kirkcaldy. **34 B5** NT3294.
West Yell *Shet.* ***Settlement***, on W coast of Yell, overlooking Ness of Sound. **85 D4** HU4583.
Wester Aberchalder *High.* ***Settlement***, on E shore of Loch Mhòr, 4m/6km E of Foyers. **51 E2** NH5520.
Wester Badentyre *Aber.* ***Settlement***, at head of valley, on S side of Hill of Brackans, 3m/5km NE of Turriff. **64 C4** NJ7652.
Wester Balgedie *P. & K.* ***Village***, 3m/5km E of Milnathort. NO1604.
Wester Culbeuchly *Aber.* ***Settlement***, 3m/4km SW of Banff. **64 B3** NJ6462.
Wester Dechmont *W.Loth.* ***Locality***, 3m/5km E of Bathgate. **25 E2** NT0270.
Wester Elchies *Moray* ***Historic house***, mansion above N bank of River Spey, 1km W of Charlestown of Aberlour across river. NJ2542.
Wester Fearn Burn *High.* ***River***, running E into Dornoch Firth at Wester Fearn Point, Ross and Cromarty district. **61 E1** NH6387.
Wester Fearn Point *High.* ***Coastal feature***, low-lying promontory protruding into Dornoch Firth, 3m/4km SE of Ardgay, Ross and Cromarty district. NH6388.
Wester Fintray *Aber.* ***Settlement***, on N side of River Don, 1m/2km E of Kintore. **54 D3** NJ8116.
Wester Gruinards *High.* ***Locality***, in Strathcarron, 7m/11km W of Bonar Bridge, Sutherland district. **72 A5** NH5192.
Wester Hailes *Edin.* ***Suburb***, 4m/7km SW of Edinburgh city centre. NT2069.
Wester Hoevdi *Shet.* ***Coastal feature***, headland on W coast of Foula. **82 B5** HT9338.
Wester Lealty *High.* ***Settlement***, 3m/5km NW of Alness. **61 F2** NH6073.
Wester Lonvine *High.* ***Locality***, 2m/3km N of Invergordon. **61 G2** NH7172.
Wester Newburn *Fife* ***Settlement***, 3m/4km NE of Lower Largo. **34 C4** NO4405.
Wester Ord *Aber.* ***Settlement***, 1m/2km S of Westhill. **54 D4** NJ8204.
Wester Pencaitland *E.Loth.* ***Village***, forms locality of Pencaitland, along with Easter Pencaitland, 4m/6km SE of Tranent. NT4468.
Wester Quarff *Shet.* ***Settlement***, 1m/2km W of Easter Quarff, at head of West Voe of Quarff, Mainland. **82 D4** HU4035.
Wester Ross *High.* ***Locality***, rugged highland area, roughly comprising W part of Ross and Cromarty district. Most easterly part is 9m/15km NW of Dingwall. Includes Beinn Eighe National Nature Reserve, Kinlochewe Forest, Lochrosque Forest and Strathbran Forest. **59 F3** NH1364.
Wester Skeld *Shet.* ***Hamlet***, on W part of Mainland, 2m/3km W of Reawick across Skelda Voe. **82 B3** HU2943.
Wester Slumbay *High.* ***Locality***, forms Slumbay, along with adjoining locality Easter Slumbay, on NW shore to Loch Carron to SW of Lochcarron, Ross and Cromarty district. NG8939.
Wester Wick *Shet.* ***Sea feature***, inlet on coast of Mainland, 5m/7km SW of Garderhouse. **82 B3** HU2842.
Wester Wick of Copister *Shet.* ***Bay***, small bay to SW of Copister, Yell. HU4778.
Westerdale *High.* ***Settlement***, on River Thurso, 5m/8km S of Halkirk, Caithness district. **76 D3** ND1251.
Westerfield *Shet.* ***Settlement***, on NE side of Tresta Voe, Mainland. **82 C2** HU3551.
Westerloch *High.* ***Settlement***, in Caithness district, 5m/8km N of Wick. ND3258.
Westerton *Aber.* ***Settlement***, 4m/6km SE of Banchory. **54 C5** NO7391.
Westerton *Angus* ***Settlement***, 1km N of Rossie School. **43 E4** NO6654.
Westerton *P. & K.* ***Settlement***, 4m/7km NW of Auchterarder. **33 D3** NN8714.
Westerwick *Shet.* ***Settlement***, on Mainland, at head of inlet of Wester Wick. **82 B3** HU2842.
Westfield *High.* ***Settlement***, in Caithness district, 5m/7km SW of Thurso. **76 C2** ND0564.
Westfield *N.Lan.* ***Suburb***, 2m/4km W of Cumbernauld town centre. NS7273.
Westfield *W.Loth.* ***Hamlet***, 3m/5km NW of Bathgate. **24 D2** NS9372.
Westfields of Rattray *P. & K.* ***Locality***, 1km N of Rattray. NO1746.
Westhall *Aber.* ***Settlement***, 1km N of Oyne. **54 B2** NJ6726.
Westhill *Aber.* Population: 8449. ***Small town***, 6m/10km W of Aberdeen. **54 D4** NJ8306.
Westhill *High.* Population: 1962. ***Hamlet***, 5m/8km E of Inverness. **61 G5** NH7244.
Westing *Shet.* ***Settlement***, just S of Newgord, on W coast of Unst. **85 E2** HP5705.
Westloch *Sc.Bord.* ***Hamlet***, 3m/5km SE of Leadburn. **25 G4** NT2551.
Westmuir *Angus* ***Village***, 1m/2km SW of Kirriemuir. **42 B4** NO3652.
Westness *Ork.* ***Settlement***, on SW coast of Rousay. **80 B4** HY3829.
Weston *Moray* ***Settlement***, 4m/6km S of Portknockie. **63 G3** NJ4962.
Westport *Arg. & B.* ***Settlement***, at N end of Machrihanish Bay, Kintyre, 5m/8km NW of Campbeltown. **12 B3** NR6525.
Westquarter *Falk.* ***Suburb***, 2m/3km SE of Falkirk. Dovecot (Historic Scotland) with heraldic panel dated 1647. NS9178.
Westray *Ork.* ***Island***, with area of 18 square miles or 47 square km, lying 6m/9km N of Rousay and 18m/28km N of Kirkwall, Mainland. The W part is hilly culminating in high coastal cliffs; E part is low-lying. **80 B2** HY4546.
Westray Airfield *Ork.* ***Airport/airfield***, to NE of Westray, just S of Bow Head. **80 C1** HY4551.
Westray Firth *Ork.* ***Sea feature***, sea area bounded by Westray to N, Eday to E, Egilsay and Rousay to S, with open sea to W. **80 C3** HY4537.
Westrigg *W.Loth.* ***Settlement***, adjoining to E of Blackridge. **24 D3** NS9067.
Westruther *Sc.Bord.* ***Village***, 7m/11km E of Lauder. **26 D4** NT6350.
Westside *Aber.* ***Settlement***, 2m/3km N of Netherley. **55 D5** NO8596.
Westside Church *Ork.* ***Ecclesiastical building***, roofless 12c Romanesque church (Historic Scotland) on Ness of Tuquoy, on S coast of Westray. Nave lengthened in later medieval times. **80 C2** HY4543.
Westwood *S.Lan.* ***Suburb***, 1m/2km W of East Kilbride town centre. NS6253.
Wether Hill *Aber.* ***Hill***, 3m/4km SW of Cornhill. Height 889 feet or 271 metres. **64 A4** NJ5654.
Wether Hill *D. & G.* ***Mountain***, 4m/6km S of Sanquhar. Height 1568 feet or 478 metres. **15 F5** NS7703.
Wether Hill *D. & G.* ***Mountain***, 6m/10km NE of St. John's Town of Dalry. Height 1263 feet or 385 metres. **8 B2** NX7087.
Wether Hill *D. & G.* ***Mountain***, rising to over 500 metres, 6m/9km W of Moniaive. **8 A1** NX7094.
Wether Hill *Fife* ***Mountain***, in Cleish Hills, 3m/4km NE of Saline. Height 1099 feet or 335 metres. **33 F5** NT0395.
Wether Holm *Shet.* ***Island***, off E coast of Mainland, 2m/3km SE of Firth. HU4672.
Wether Law *Sc.Bord.* ***Mountain***, 2m/3km E of Romannobridge. Height 1571 feet or 479 metres. **25 F5** NT1948.
Wethersta *Shet.* ***Settlement***, on Mainland, on tongue of land between Busta Voe and Olna Firth, 1m/2km S of Brae. **82 C1** HU3665.
Weydale *High.* ***Locality***, in Caithness district, 3m/5km SE of Thurso. **76 D2** ND1464.
Whale Firth *Shet.* ***Sea feature***, inlet on W coast of Yell, the head of which is 1km W of that of Mid Yell Voe on E coast. **85 D3** HU4891.
Whale Geo *Shet.* ***Coastal feature***, indentation on W coast of Yell, 3m/5km N of West Sandwick. **84 D3** HU4493.
Whale Point *Ork.* ***Coastal feature***, headland at NW end of Sanday. HY6545.
Whaligoe *High.* ***Settlement***, on E coast of Caithness district, 6m/9km NE of Lybster. **77 F4** ND3240.
Whalsay *Shet.* ***Island***, of some 8 square miles or 21 square km, off E coast of Mainland, opposite entrance to Dury Voe. **83 E1** HU5663.
Wharry Burn *Stir.* ***River***, flowing SW into Allan Water 1m/2km S of Dunblane. **32 D4** NN8201.
Whauphill *D. & G.* ***Village***, 4m/6km SW of Wigtown. **3 E2** NX4049.
Wheat Stack *Sc.Bord.* ***Coastal feature***, rock headland 4m/6km NW of St. Abb's Head. **27 F2** NT8671.
Wheedlemont *Aber.* ***Settlement***, 1m/2km SW of Rhynie. **53 G2** NJ4726.
Wheen *Angus* ***Settlement***, 3m/4km SE of Clova. **42 B2** NO3670.
Whifflet *N.Lan.* ***Suburb***, 1m/2km S of Coatbridge town centre. **24 B3** NS7364.
Whigstreet *Angus* ***Hamlet***, 4m/7km S of Forfar. Site of Roman camp 1km to E. **42 C5** NO4844.
Whim *Sc.Bord.* ***Settlement***, 2m/3km SW of Leadburn. **25 G4** NT2153.
Whinhill Reservoir *Inclyde* ***Reservoir***, 1m/2km S of Greenock. NS2774.
Whinny Hill *D. & G.* ***Hill***, rising to over 100 metres, 2m/3km N of New Abbey. **8 D4** NX9569.

Whinnyfold *Aber.* ***Settlement***, on E coast, opposite The Skares, 2m/3km S of village of Cruden Bay. **55 F1** NK0833.
Whitburn *W.Loth.* Population: 11,511. ***Town***, former iron and coal town, 3m/5km SW of Bathgate. **24 D3** NS9465.
White Cart Water ***River***, rising S of East Kilbride and running N to Cathcart, Glasgow, then NW through Paisley to join Black Cart Water 3m/4km N, flowing into River Clyde 1km further N. NS4968.
White Castle *E.Loth.* ***Historic/prehistoric site***, hillfort 3m/4km SE of Garvald. **26 D3** NT6168.
White Caterthun *Angus* ***Historic/prehistoric site***, well-preserved Iron Age fort (Historic Scotland) with massive stone rampart, nearly 1m/2km SW of Brown Caterthun and 5m/8km NW of Brechin. **42 D3** NO5566.
White Coomb *D. & G.* ***Mountain***, partly National Trust for Scotland property, 8m/12km NE of Moffat. Height 2696 feet or 822 metres. **16 C4** NT1615.
White Corries *High.* ***Locality***, skiing area in Lochaber district on N slope of Meall a' Bhùiridh. NN2652.
White Craig *S.Lan.* ***Mountain***, in Pentland Hills, 5m/8km NW of West Linton. Height 1424 feet or 434 metres. **25 E4** NT0753.
White Esk *D. & G.* ***River***, running S through Eskdalemuir and Castle O'er Forest to join River Black Esk and form River Esk, 8m/13km NW of Langholm. NY2590.
White Hill *Aber.* ***Mountain***, 1m/2km SE of Ballochan. Height 1870 feet or 570 metres. **42 D1** NO5388.
White Hill *Angus* ***Mountain***, 3m/5km NE of Rottal. Height 2552 feet or 778 metres. **42 B2** NO4073.
White Hill *Sc.Bord.* ***Mountain***, 2m/3km SE of Hawick. Height 987 feet or 301 metres. **17 G4** NT5211.
White Hill of Vatsetter *Shet.* ***Hill***, on headland of Gamla, E coast of Yell, 1km SE of Vatsetter. Height 105 feet or 32 metres. HU5489.
White Hope Edge *D. & G.* ***Mountain***, on edge of woodland, 5m/8km N of Benthpath. Height 1558 feet or 475 metres. **10 B2** NY3397.
White Loch *D. & G.* ***Lake/loch***, within grounds of Lochinch Castle, to W of Black Loch and 3m/5km E of Stranraer. Castle Kennedy is on isthmus which separates the lochs. **6 C4** NX1060.
White Loch *D. & G.* ***Lake/loch***, 5m/8km SE of Dalbeattie. **8 C5** NX8654.
White Loch of Myrton *D. & G.* ***Lake/loch***, 2m/3km E of Port William. **3 D2** NX3543.
White Meldon *Sc.Bord.* ***Mountain***, with hillfort, 2m/4km NW of Peebles. Height 1401 feet or 427 metres. **25 G5** NT2142.
White Mounth *Aber.* ***Mountain***, to SW of Lochnagar. Height 3447 feet or 1051 metres. **42 A1** NO2383.
White Ness *Shet.* ***Coastal feature***, long narrow peninsula on Mainland on W side of Whiteness Voe, 3m/4km NW of Scalloway. **82 C3** HU3843.
White Top of Culreoch *D. & G.* ***Mountain***, 4m/7km N of Gatehouse of Fleet. Height 1125 feet or 343 metres. **7 G4** NX6063.
White Water *Angus* ***River***, running SE into River South Esk, 3m/5km NW of Clova. **42 A2** NO2875.
Whiteacen *Moray* ***Settlement***, 2m/3km SW of Rothes. **63 E5** NJ2546.
Whiteadder Reservoir *E.Loth.* ***Reservoir***, in course of Whiteadder Water, about 3m/5km from source and 2m/4km NW of Cranshaws. **26 D3** NT6563.
Whiteadder Water ***River***, rising in Lammermuir Hills on Scottish Borders, 6m/10km NW of Cranshaws, and flowing through Whiteadder Reservoir, then SE into River Tweed 2m/3km W of Berwick-upon-Tweed. **27 F4** NT9751.
Whiteash Hill *Moray* ***Hill***, in wooded area 3m/4km E of Fochabers. Height 866 feet or 264 metres. **63 F4** NJ3857.
Whitebog *Aber.* ***Settlement***, 3m/5km N of Strichen. **65 E4** NJ9359.
Whitebridge *High.* ***Hamlet***, in Inverness district, at confluence of River Feehlin and Allt Breinag, 3m/5km S of Foyers. **51 D3** NH4815.
Whitebridge *High.* ***Settlement***, 1m/2km S of Scarfskerry. **77 E1** ND2672.
Whiteburn *Sc.Bord.* ***Settlement***, 4m/6km E of Lauder. **26 C5** NT5947.
Whitecairn *D. & G.* ***Settlement***, 1m/2km N of Glenluce. **6 D5** NX2059.
Whitecairns *Aber.* ***Settlement***, 7m/12km N of Aberdeen. **55 E3** NJ9218.
Whitecastle *S.Lan.* ***Settlement***, 3m/5km NW of Biggar. **25 E5** NT0141.
Whitecraig *E.Loth.* Population: 1209. ***Village***, 2m/3km S of Musselburgh. **26 A2** NT3570.
Whitecrook *D. & G.* ***Settlement***, adjacent to N of Sands of Luce, 2m/3km W of Glenluce. **6 C5** NX1656.
Whitecrook *Renf.* ***Suburb***, to E of Clydebank town centre. NS5069.
Whitecross *Falk.* ***Village***, 3m/4km W of Linlithgow. NS9676.
Whiteface *High.* ***Locality***, on N side of Dornoch Firth, 6m/9km W of Dornoch, Sutherland district. **61 G1** NH7089.
Whitefarland Bay *Arg. & B.* ***Bay***, on W coast of Jura, between Feolin Ferry and Carrugh an t-Sruith to N. NR4471.
Whitefarland Point *N.Ayr.* ***Coastal feature***, headland on W coast of Arran, 1m/2km S of Pirnmill. **21 G5** NR8642.
Whitefauld Hill *D. & G.* ***Mountain***, rising to over 360 metres on Forest of Ae, 8m/12km NW of Lochmaben. **9 E1** NY0293.
Whitefaulds *S.Ayr.* ***Suburb***, W district of Maybole. NS2909.
Whitefield *Aber.* ***Settlement***, 1km W of Oldmeldrum. **54 C2** NJ7927.
Whitefield *High.* ***Settlement***, 2m/3km SE of Watten. **77 E3** ND2753.
Whitefield *High.* ***Settlement***, on E shore of Loch Ness, 3m/5km across loch from Drumnadrochit. **51 E2** NH5528.
Whitefield *P. & K.* ***Locality***, comprises settlements of East Whitefield and Meikle Whitefield, 2m/3km SW of Burrelton. **33 G1** NO1734.
Whitefield Loch *D. & G.* ***Lake/loch***, 3m/5km SE of Glenluce. **6 D5** NX2355.
Whiteford *Aber.* ***Hamlet***, 5m/7km NW of Inverurie. **54 C2** NJ7126.
Whitehall *Ork.* ***Village***, on N coast of Stronsay, opposite Papa Stronsay harbour. **81 E4** HY6528.
Whitehaugh Forest *Aber.* ***Forest/woodland***, of conifers surrounding hill of Knock Saul, 5m/7km N of Alford. **54 A2** NJ5723.
Whitehill *Aber.* ***Settlement***, 3m/4km S of New Pitsligo. NJ8952.
Whitehill *Fife* ***Locality***, industrial estate in SW part of Glenrothes. NT2599.
Whitehill *Midloth.* ***Hamlet***, 2m/3km E of Dalkeith. NT3566.
Whitehill *Moray* ***Settlement***, 2m/4km SW of Gordonstown. NJ5354.
Whitehill *N.Ayr.* ***Settlement***, 3m/5km W of Kilbirnie, between Muirhead and Camphill Reservoirs. **23 D4** NS2656.
Whitehills *Aber.* ***Village***, 2m/4km NW of Banff. **64 B3** NJ6565.
Whitehills *Angus* ***Suburb***, adjoining to NE of Forfar. NO4651.
Whitehope Law *Sc.Bord.* ***Mountain***, 5m/8km N of Innerleithen. Height 2037 feet or 621 metres. **26 A5** NT3344.
Whitehouse *Aber.* ***Village***, 3m/5km E of Alford. **54 B3** NJ6214.
Whitehouse *Arg. & B.* ***Village***, in Kintyre, Argyll, 6m/9km SW of Tarbert. **21 G3** NR8161.
Whiteinch *Glas.* ***Suburb***, on N bank of River Clyde in Scotstoun district of Glasgow. NS5367.
Whitekirk *E.Loth.* ***Village***, 4m/6km SE of North Berwick. **26 C1** NT5981.
Whitelaw *Sc.Bord.* ***Hamlet***, 3m/5km SE of Duns. **27 F4** NT8352.
Whitelaw Hill *E.Loth.* ***Hill***, 4m/6km SW of East Linton. Height 584 feet or 178 metres. **26 C2** NT5771.
Whitelaw Hill *Sc.Bord.* ***Mountain***, 1m/2km SE of Stobo. Height 1561 feet or 476 metres. **16 C2** NT1935.
Whiteleen *High.* ***Settlement***, 2m/3km SW of Thrumster. **77 F4** ND3242.
Whitelees *S.Ayr.* ***Settlement***, 1m/2km E of Symington. **14 B2** NS3931.
Whiteleys *D. & G.* ***Settlement***, 2m/3km S of Stranraer. **6 B5** NX0657.
Whitelinks Bay *Aber.* ***Bay***, on NE coast, 1km SE of Inverallochy. **65 F3** NK0564.
Whitemill Point *Ork.* ***Coastal feature***, headland on N coast of Sanday, on W side of entrance to Otters Wick. **81 F2** HY7046.
Whitemire *Moray* ***Settlement***, 5m/8km SW of Forres. **62 B4** NH9754.
Whiten Head *High.* ***Coastal feature***, headland on N coast of Sutherland district, on E side of entrance to Loch Eriboll. **75 D2** NC5068.
Whiteness *Shet.* ***Locality***, on Mainland, at head of Whiteness Voe, 4m/7km N of Scalloway. **82 D3** HU4047.
Whiteness Head *High.* ***Coastal feature***, spit of land on Moray Firth 3m/5km E of Fort George, Inverness district. **61 G4** NH8058.
Whiteness Sands *High.* ***Coastal feature***, beach on S side of mouth of Dornoch Firth, 5m/7km NE of Tain. **62 A1** NH8386.
Whiteness Voe *Shet.* ***Sea feature***, long inlet on W coast of Mainland, S of Whiteness locality and 3m/4km W of Veensgarth. **82 C3** HU3944.
Whiterashes *Aber.* ***Village***, 4m/6km SE of Oldmeldrum. **55 D2** NJ8523.
Whiterow *High.* ***Settlement***, in Caithness district, 1m/2km S of Wick. **77 F4** ND3548.
Whiteside *W.Loth.* ***Hamlet***, 1km SW of Bathgate. **25 D3** NS9668.
Whiteside Hill *S.Lan.* ***Mountain***, in Lowther Hills, on border with Dumfries & Galloway, 3m/5km E of Ballencleuch Law. Height 1817 feet or 554 metres. **16 A5** NS9704.
Whitespout Lane *E.Ayr.* ***River***, running E from Loch Riecawr to join Eglin Lane and form Carrick Lane. NX4693.
Whitestone *Aber.* ***Hamlet***, 2m/3km W of Strachan. **54 B5** NO6492.
Whitestone *Arg. & B.* ***Settlement***, on Kintyre, 3m/5km SW of Carradale. **12 C2** NR7933.
Whitestripe *Aber.* ***Settlement***, on W side of Waughton Hill, 1km N of Strichen. **65 E4** NJ9456.
Whitewell *Aber.* ***Settlement***, 4m/6km N of Strichen. **65 E3** NJ9461.
Whitewreath *Moray* ***Settlement***, 3m/5km S of Elgin. **63 E4** NJ2357.
Whithorn *D. & G.* ***Small town***, historic town 9m/15km S of Wigtown. St. Ninian settled here in 5c, making it Scotland's first Christian settlement. Remains of 12c priory church (Historic Scotland), with museum. **3 E2** NX4440.
Whithorn Priory *D. & G.* ***Ecclesiastical building***, ruins of 12c priory church (Historic Scotland) on site of St. Ninian's 5c church at Whithorn, 10m/16km S of Wigtown. Includes museum. **3 E2** NX4440.
Whiting Bay *N.Ayr.* ***Bay***, wide E facing bay on SE coast of Arran, to S of Kingscross Point. **13 F3** NS0526.
Whiting Bay *N.Ayr.* ***Village***, and bay on E coast of Arran, 3m/5km S of Lamlash. **13 F3** NS0426.
Whitlam *Aber.* ***Settlement***, 2m/3km N of Newmachar. **55 D2** NJ8821.
Whitletts *S.Ayr.* ***Suburb***, E district of Ayr. **14 B3** NS3622.
Whitsome *Sc.Bord.* ***Village***, 4m/6km S of Chirnside. **27 F4** NT8650.
Whittliemuir Midton Loch *Renf.* ***Reservoir***, 1m/2km SE of Howwood. **23 F4** NS4158.
Wiay *High.* ***Island***, uninhabited island of about 500 acres or 200 hectares at entrance to Loch Bracadale, SW coast. Lies 2m/3km E of Idrigill Point, Skye. **47 F1** NG2936.
Wiay *W.Isles* ***Island***, uninhabited island of about 2 square miles or 5 square km off SE coast of Benbecula on N side of entrance to Bagh nam Faoileann. **45 G5** NF8746.
Wick *High.* ***River***, flowing SE from Loch Watten. At mouth is fishing port of Wick on Wick bay. **77 E3** ND3551.
Wick *High.* Population: 7681. ***Small town***, fishing port on Wick Bay, E coast of Caithness district, at mouth of Wick River. Airport 1m/2km N. Largest herring port in Europe in 19c, with fleet of over 1000 boats. **77 F3** ND3650.
Wick Airport *High.* ***Airport/airfield***, local airport to N of Wick. **77 F3** ND3652.
Wick Bay *High.* ***Bay***, off E coast of Caithness district, at mouth of Wick River. Fishing port of Wick is on the bay. ND3750.
Wick of Aith *Shet.* ***Bay***, small bay on Fetlar, to E of Aith. HU6389.
Wick of Belmont *Shet.* ***Bay***, at SW end of Unst. Vehicle ferry plies from here across Bluemull Sound to Gutcher on Yell. HP5600.
Wick of Breakon *Shet.* ***Bay***, on N coast of Yell, to E of Gloup Voe. HP5205.
Wick of Copister *Shet.* ***Bay***, small bay to S of Copister, Yell. HU4878.
Wick of Gossabrough *Shet.* ***Bay***, on E coast of Yell, to N of Gossabrough. HU5383.
Wick of Gruting *Shet.* ***Bay***, on N coast of Fetlar, 2m/3km NE of Houbie. **85 F3** HU6592.
Wick of Gutcher *Shet.* ***Bay***, on E coast of Yell, at S end of Bluemull Sound. HU5499.
Wick of Houbie *Shet.* ***Bay***, an arm of the much larger Wick of Tresta, on S coast of Fetlar. HU6290.
Wick of Mucklabrek *Shet.* ***Bay***, wide bay on SW coast of Foula. **82 B5** HT9437.
Wick of Shunni *Shet.* ***Bay***, on W coast of Mainland, on N side of Fitful Head. **83 F4** HU3515.
Wick of Skaw *Shet.* ***Bay***, on NE coast of Unst, 1m/2km NE of Norwick. HP6616.
Wick of Tresta *Shet.* ***Bay***, large bay on S coast of Fetlar. **85 F4** HU6190.
Wick of Vatsetter *Shet.* ***Bay***, small bay on E coast of Yell, to NW of Vatsetter. HU5389.
Wide Firth *Ork.* ***Sea feature***, sea channel between islands of Mainland and Shapinsay. **80 C5** HY4315.
Wideford Hill *Ork.* ***Hill***, 3m/4km W of Kirkwall, Mainland. Prehistoric chambered cairn (Historic Scotland) on NW side of hill. Height 738 feet or 225 metres. **80 C5** HY4111.
Wideford Hill Chambered Cairn *Ork.* ***Historic/prehistoric site***, on Wideford Hill, 3m/4km W of Kirkwall, Mainland. Neolithic chambered cairn (Historic Scotland) with central chamber and unusually small entrance passage. **80 C5** HY4112.
Widewall *Ork.* ***Locality***, on W coast of South Ronaldsay, 2m/3km S of St. Margaret's Hope. To NW is large bay of same name. **78 D3** ND4391.
Widewall Bay *Ork.* ***Bay***, large bay on W coast of South Ronaldsay. **78 D3** ND4292.
Wife Geo *High.* ***Coastal feature***, small indentation 3m/4km S of Duncansby Head. **77 F1** ND3969.

Wigtown *D. & G.* Population: 1117. *Small town*, on hill above River Cree estuary, at head of Wigtown Bay and on N side of River Bladnoch. Torhouskie Stone Circle, dating from around 2000BC, nearby. **7 F5** NX4355.

Wigtown Bay *D. & G. Bay*, extends E from Burrow Head to Little Ross, with Wigtown on NE side of bay. **3 F2** NX5148.

Wigtown Sands *D. & G. Coastal feature*, mud and sand flats to N of River Bladnoch, 2m/3km NE of Wigtown. **7 F5** NX4556.

Wildmanbridge *S.Lan. Settlement*, 2m/3km NW of Carluke. NS8353.

Wildshaw Hill *S.Lan. Mountain*, 4m/7km SE of Douglas. Height 1227 feet or 374 metres. **15 G3** NS9028.

Wilkieston *High. Settlement*, in Ross and Cromarty district, 1km SW of Tarbat Ness on E coast. **62 B1** NH9486.

Wilkieston *W.Loth. Village*, 2m/3km SW of Ratho. **25 F3** NT1268.

William Law *Sc.Bord. Mountain*, 3m/4km NW of Galashiels. Height 1315 feet or 401 metres. **17 F2** NT4739.

Williamsburgh *Renf. Suburb*, E district of Paisley. NS4964.

Williamston *W.Loth. Locality*, industrial estate, 2m/3km SE of Livingston town centre. NT0866.

Willowbrae *Edin. Suburb*, of Edinburgh, 1m/2km W of Portobello. NT2873.

Willowgrain Hill *D. & G. Mountain*, 2m/3km SW of Wanlockhead. Height 1686 feet or 514 metres. **15 G4** NS8412.

Wilson's Pike *Sc.Bord. Mountain*, 5m/8km SW of Kielder. Height 1361 feet or 415 metres. **10 D3** NY5589.

Wilton *Sc.Bord. Suburb*, W district of Hawick. **17 F4** NT4914.

Winchburgh *W.Loth.* Population: 2535. *Village*, 6m/10km E of Linlithgow. Niddry Castle, 1km SE, is ruined 15c tower. **25 E2** NT0974.

Wind Fell *Mountain*, on border of Dumfries & Galloway and Scottish Borders, 6m/9km E of Moffat. Height 2178 feet or 664 metres. **16 C5** NT1706.

Windhill *High. Settlement*, in Ross and Cromarty district, 1m/2km S of Muir of Ord. **61 E5** NH5348.

Windlestraw Law *Sc.Bord. Mountain*, 4m/7km NE of Innerleithen. Height 2162 feet or 659 metres. **26 A5** NT3743.

Winds Eye *Aber. Mountain*, to N of Gartly Moor, 3m/5km SE of Huntly. Height 1030 feet or 314 metres. **54 A1** NJ5534.

Windy Gyle *Mountain*, on border of Northumberland and Scottish Borders, 4m/7km SW of The Cheviot. Height 2030 feet or 619 metres. **18 C5** NT8515.

Windy Hill *Arg. & B. Hill*, highest point on Bute, 2m/3km NW of Kames Bay. Height 912 feet or 278 metres. NS0469.

Windy Standard *D. & G. Mountain*, 6m/10km NE of Carsphairn. Height 2289 feet or 698 metres. **15 E5** NS6201.

Windy Standard *E.Ayr. Mountain*, partly forested summit 3m/5km SE of Dalmellington. Height 1761 feet or 537 metres. **14 D5** NS5204.

Windy Yet *E.Ayr. Settlement*, 4m/7km NE of Stewarton. **23 F4** NS4750.

Windygates *Fife* Population: 1645. *Village*, 2m/3km NW of Methil. **34 B4** NO3400.

Windyheads Hill *Aber. Hill*, 3m/4km S of Pennan Head and 2m/3km W of New Aberdour. Height 758 feet or 231 metres. **65 D3** NJ8561.

Winless *High. Settlement*, in Caithness district, 4m/7km NW of Wick. **77 E3** ND3053.

Wintercleuch Fell *S.Lan. Mountain*, in Lowther Hills, 4m/7km SE of Elvanfoot. Height 1804 feet or 550 metres. **16 A4** NS9711.

Wintercleugh *S.Lan. Settlement*, 4m/7km S of Elvanfoot. **16 A4** NS9610.

Winterhope Reservoir *D. & G. Reservoir*, 6m/10km W of Langholm. NY2782.

Winton House *E.Loth. Historic house*, early 17c mansion 1km N of Pencaitland across Tyne Water, 3m/5km SE of Tranent. Formerly seat of Earls of Winton. **26 B3** NT4369.

Wishach Hill *Aber. Mountain*, on Gartly Moor, surrounded by woodland, 5m/8km SE of Huntly. Height 1374 feet or 419 metres. **54 A1** NJ5733.

Wishaw *N.Lan.* Population: 29,791. *Town*, 3m/5km SE of Motherwell. **24 B4** NS7954.

Wisp Hill *Mountain*, astride border of Dumfries & Galloway and Scottish Borders, 4m/6km S of Teviothead. Height 1952 feet or 595 metres. **10 B2** NY3899.

Wiston *S.Lan. Village*, 7m/11km SW of Biggar. **16 A2** NS9531.

Witchburn *Arg. & B. Settlement*, on Kintyre, adjoining to W of Campbeltown. **12 C4** NR7019.

Witton *Angus Settlement*, 2m/3km NE of Bridgend. **43 D3** NO5670.

Woden Law *Sc.Bord. Mountain*, in Cheviot Hills, 3m/5km SW of Chatto. Hillfort at summit. Height 1387 feet or 423 metres. **18 B5** NT7612.

Wolfelee *Sc.Bord. Settlement*, 1m/2km S of Hobkirk. **17 G5** NT5809.

Wolfelee Hill *Sc.Bord. Mountain*, 1km SE of Wolfelee. Height 1289 feet or 393 metres. **17 G5** NT5908.

Wolfhill *P. & K. Village*, 6m/10km N of Perth. **33 G1** NO1533.

Woll *Sc.Bord. Hamlet*, 4m/6km S of Selkirk. **17 F3** NT4621.

Wood of Dundurcas *Moray Forest/woodland*, wooded hillside 2m/3km NE of Rothes. **63 E4** NJ2951.

Wood of Ordiequish *Moray Forest/woodland*, on E side of River Spey, 2m/3km S of Fochabers. **63 F4** NJ3555.

Wood Wick *Ork. Bay*, to E of Woodwick. **80 B4** HY3823.

Wooden Loch *Sc.Bord. Lake/loch*, just S of Eckford. NT7025.

Woodend *Aber. Locality*, comprises Upper and Lower Woodend on N bank of River Don, 3m/4km N of Monymusk. **54 B3** NJ6718.

Woodend *High. Settlement*, in Strathdearn, 2m/3km SE of Tomatin. **51 G2** NH7926.

Woodend *High. Settlement*, 2m/4km W of Strontian, Lochaber district. **37 G3** NM7860.

Woodend *P. & K. Settlement*, in valley of River Lyon, 1m/2km W of Fortingall. **40 C5** NN7147.

Woodend Loch *N.Lan. Lake/loch*, 2m/3km NW of Coatbridge. **24 B3** NS7066.

Woodfield *S.Ayr. Suburb*, N district of Ayr. NS3424.

Woodhall *Inclyde Suburb*, 1m/2km E of Port Glasgow. NS3473.

Woodhall Loch *D. & G. Lake/loch*, narrow loch 1m/2km N of Laurieston. NX6667.

Woodhaven *Fife Suburb*, in central area of Newport-on-Tay. **34 C2** NO4126.

Woodhead *Aber. Locality*, 1m/2km SE of New Aberdour. **65 D3** NJ8962.

Woodhead *Aber. Village*, 8m/13km SE of Turriff and 2m/3km E of Fyvie. **54 C1** NJ7938.

Woodland Bay *S.Ayr. Bay*, 2m/3km S of Girvan. NX1795.

Woodside *Aberdeen Suburb*, 2m/3km NW of Aberdeen city centre. **55 E4** NJ9109.

Woodside *D. & G. Settlement*, 4m/7km E of Dumfries. **9 E3** NY0475.

Woodside *Fife Suburb*, SE district of Glenrothes. **34 A4** NO2800.

Woodside *N.Ayr. Settlement*, 1km N of Beith. **23 E4** NS3455.

Woodside *P. & K. Village*, adjoining to N of Burrelton, 2m/3km SW of Coupar Angus. **33 G1** NO2037.

Woodtown *Aber. Settlement*, 2m/3km N of Edzell. **43 E2** NO6072.

Woodwick *Ork. Settlement*, on Mainland, 6m/10km N of Finstown. HY3823.

Woolfords Cottages *S.Lan. Settlement*, 7m/11km N of Carnwath. **25 E4** NT0057.

Work *Ork. Settlement*, 2m/3km NE of Kirkwall, Mainland. **80 C5** HY4713.

Worm Hill *Sc.Bord. Mountain*, overlooking Tweed valley, 1m/2km NW of Stanhope. Height 1774 feet or 541 metres. **16 C2** NT1130.

Worm Law *S.Lan. Mountain*, partly wooded mass, 3m/4km NE of Forth. Height 1122 feet or 342 metres. **25 D4** NS9756.

Wormiehills *Angus Locality*, 2m/3km SW of Arbroath. **35 E1** NO6138.

Wormistone *Fife Hamlet*, 1m/2km N of Crail. **35 E4** NO6109.

Wormit *Fife Locality*, on S side of Firth of Tay, 2m/3km SW of Newport-on-Tay. **34 B2** NO3926.

Wormit Bay *Fife Bay*, to W of Wormit, on S side of the Firth of Tay. NO3825.

Wrae *Aber. Settlement*, on NW side of Wood of Wrae, 2m/3km N of Turriff. **64 C4** NJ7252.

Wrangham *Aber. Settlement*, 2m/3km N of Insch. **54 B1** NJ6331.

Wren's Egg *D. & G. Historic/prehistoric site*, remains of Bronze Age stone circle (Historic Scotland), 2m/3km SE of Port William. NX3642.

Wrightpark *Stir. Settlement*, 2m/3km S of Kippen. **32 B5** NS6492.

Wrunk Law *Sc.Bord. Mountain*, 2m/3km NW of Longformacus. Height 1194 feet or 364 metres. **27 D4** NT6759.

Wuddy Law *Angus Hill*, 3m/5km NE of Friockheim. Height 433 feet or 132 metres. **43 E4** NO6252.

Wyndburgh Hill *Sc.Bord. Mountain*, 3m/4km NW of Note o' the Gate. Height 1647 feet or 502 metres. **17 G5** NT5503.

Wyre *Ork. Island*, small inhabited island, 2m/3km E to W and 1m/2km N to S but tapering to a point at W end, lying off SE coast of Rousay across Wyre Sound. Remains of 12c Cubbie Roo's Castle. Ruined chapel (Historic Scotland), probably late 12c. **80 C4** HY4426.

Wyre Sound *Ork. Sea feature*, strait separating Wyre and Rousay. **80 C4** HY4327.

Wyvis Forest *High. Open space*, deer forest in Ross and Cromarty district to W of Loch Glass. **61 D2** NH4671.

Wyvis Lodge *High. Settlement*, 9m/15km NE of Garve, at W end of Loch Glass. **61 D2** NH4873.

Y

Yair Hill Forest *Sc.Bord. Forest/woodland*, 3m/5km NW of Selkirk. **17 F2** NT4333.

Yardstone Knowe *Sc.Bord. Mountain*, 3m/5km SW of Stow. Height 1683 feet or 513 metres. **26 B5** NT4042.

Yarrow *Sc.Bord. Settlement*, on Yarrow Water, 7m/11km W of Selkirk. **17 E3** NT3527.

Yarrow Feus *Sc.Bord. Settlement*, 1m/2km SW of Yarrow. **17 E3** NT3425.

Yarrow Kirk *Sc.Bord. Ecclesiastical building*, at Yarrow, 4m/6km SW of Yarrowford. Church dating from 1640. **17 E3** NT3527.

Yarrow Water *Sc.Bord. River*, issuing from St. Mary's Loch and running E through Ettrick Forest to Ettrick Water, 2m/3km SW of Selkirk. **17 E3** NT3527.

Yarrowford *Sc.Bord. Hamlet*, 4m/6km NW of Selkirk. **17 F3** NT4030.

Yell *Shet. Island*, one of the main islands of Shetland Islands, situated between Mainland and Unst, and separated from the former by Yell Sound. **85 D3** HU4990.

Yell Sound *Shet. Sea feature*, separates Yell Island from Mainland. **84 D3** HU4086.

Yellowcraig *E.Loth. Nature reserve*, on rocky shore 2m/3km W of North Berwick, where rock pools and shells provide varied interest. Nature trail. **26 C1** NT5185.

Yesnaby *Ork. Settlement*, near W coast of Mainland, to S of Bor Wick. **80 A5** HY2216.

Yester Castle *E.Loth.* See Gifford.

Yester House *E.Loth.* See Gifford.

Yetholm Loch *Sc.Bord. Lake/loch*, small loch 1m/2km W of Town Yetholm. NT8027.

Yetholm Mains *Sc.Bord. Hamlet*, 1m/2km NE of Kirk Yetholm. NT8329.

Yett *N.Lan. Village*, adjoining to W of Newarthill, 3m/4km NE of Motherwell. NS7759.

Yetts o'Muckhart *Clack. Village*, 4m/6km NE of Dollar. **33 F4** NO0001.

Yieldshields *S.Lan. Hamlet*, 2m/3km E of Carluke. NS8750.

Yinstay Head *Ork. Coastal feature*, headland on N coast of Mainland, 2m/3km W of Rerwick Head. HY5110.

Yoker *Glas. Suburb*, 5m/8km NW of Glasgow city centre. Car ferry to Renfrew across River Clyde. **23 G3** NS5169.

Yonder Bognie *Aber. Settlement*, 4m/7km SW of Aberchirder. **64 A5** NJ5946.

Younger Botanic Gardens *Arg. & B. Garden*, 1km N of Benmore, includes formal gardens, woodlands and collections of rhododendrons and conifers. Viewpoints of Holy Loch and Eachaig valley. **22 C1** NS1485.

Ythan *Aber. River*, rising at Ythanwells and flowing E to Bruckhills, NE to Mains of Towie, and S to Fyvie. It then meanders before turning SE to Methlick and Ellon, where it widens and turns S again, to flow into North Sea at Newburgh Bar, 12m/19km N of Aberdeen. River is noted for fishing. **55 E1** NK0023.

Ythanwells *Aber. Village*, 7m/11km E of Huntly. Here is source of River Ythan. Site of Roman camp 1m/2km E. **54 B1** NJ6338.

Ythsie *Aber. Locality*, comprises North Ythsie, South Ythsie, Little Ythsie and Milltown of Ythsie, 1m/2km E of Tarves. **55 D1** NJ8830.

W
X
Y
Z